MORE OPENING NIGHTS ON
BROADWAY

MORE OPENING NIGHTS ON

BROADWAY

A CRITICAL QUOTEBOOK

OF THE MUSICAL THEATRE

1965 THROUGH 1981

STEVEN SUSKIN

FOREWORD BY LARRY GELBART

Schirmer Books

An Imprint of Simon & Schuster Macmillan
New York

Prentice Hall International
London   Mexico City   New Delhi   Singapore   Sydney   Toronto

Schirmer Books
An Imprint of Simon & Schuster Macmillan
1633 Broadway
New York, New York 10019

Library of Congress Catalog Card Number: 96-20226

Printed in the United States of America

Printing Number
2 3 4 5 6 7 8 9 10

Library of Congress Cataloging-in-Publication Data

More opening nights on Broadway : a critical quotebook of the musical theatre
   from 1965 through 1981 / Steven Suskin : foreword by Larry Gelbart.
      p.   cm.
   Includes bibliographical references and index.
   ISBN 0-02-864571-5 (alk. paper)
   1. Musicals—First performances—New York (State)—New York
2. Revues—First performances—New York (State)—New York
3. Musical theater—New York (State)—New York—Reviews
I. Suskin, Steven.
ML1711.8.N3M8 1997
792.6'09747'109045—dc20   96-20226
                                                                 CIP
                                                                 MN

This paper meets the requirements of ANSI/NISO Z39.28-1992 (Permanence
of Paper).

for
Helen

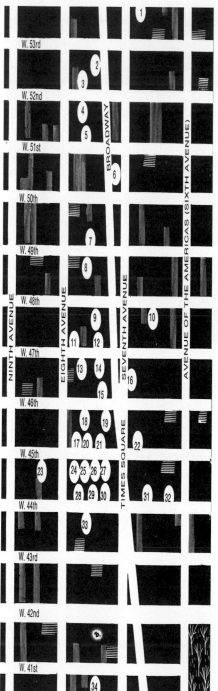

THE THEATRES

1. **George Abbott**
   152 West 54th Street

2. **Broadway**
   Broadway at 53rd Street

3. **Anta**
   245 West 52nd Street

4. **Alvin**
   250 West 52nd Street

5. **Mark Hellinger**
   Broadway at 51st Street

6. **Winter Garden**
   1634 Broadway

7. **Ambassador**
   215 West 49th Street

8. **Eugene O'Neill**
   230 West 49th Street

9. **Longacre**
   220 West 48th Street

10. **Cort**
    138 West 48th Street

11. **Biltmore**
    261 West 47th Street

12. **Barrymore**
    243 West 47th Street

13. **Brooks Atkinson**
    256 West 47th Street

14. **Edison**
    240 West 47th Street

15. **Lunt-Fontanne**
    205 West 46th Street

16. **Palace**
    Broadway at 47th Street

17. **Imperial**
    249 West 45th Street

18. **46th Street**
    226 West 46th Street

19. **Helen Hayes**
    210 West 46th Street

20. **Music Box**
    239 West 45th Street

21. **Morosco**
    217 West 45th Street

22. **Lyceum**
    149 West 45th Street

23. **Martin Beck**
    302 West 45th Street

24. **Golden**
    252 West 45th Street

25. **Royale**
    242 West 45th Street

26. **Plymouth**
    236 West 45th Street

27. **Booth**
    222 West 45th Street

28. **Majestic**
    245 West 44th Street

29. **Broadhurst**
    235 West 44th Street

30. **Shubert**
    225 West 44th Street

31. **Hudson**
    141 West 44th Street

32. **Belasco**
    111 West 44th Street

33. **St. James**
    246 West 44th Street

34. **Billy Rose**
    208 West 41st Street

CONTENTS

Foreword by Larry Gelbart xv

OVERTURE

THE MUSICALS

CONTENTS XII

CURTAIN CALLS

FOREWORD

Before you move on to enter this book so lovingly devoted to the theatre, I thought we might spend a moment or two together out here in the lobby. I know I can never step into one without triggering a rush of Broadway memories. If you're short of your own, try a few of mine.

1. I am out of town, trying to whip a new musical into shape for Broadway. The show hasn't got a prayer. Or, rather, that's all it has. It is terminally ill. Nothing is working. Except the audiences' feet toward the exits. In Washington, DC, the producers decide to replace the director/choreographer. Before going, he assembles the cast onstage. His pride wounded, but his ego still intact, he tells them: "Everything in this show is mine. The concept. The design. The costumes, the characters, the plot, most of the dialogue, a lot of the lyrics, most of the ideas for the songs and each and every dance step. Now that it's all gone wrong, I guess they have to blame *somebody*."

2. A borrowed memory from my late friend, smart-as-a-whip Cy Howard. Cy was once called in to doctor an ailing musical, to hopefully revive it with artificial inspiration by the show's producer, Alfred Bloomingdale, a gentleman who had dreams of transcending the mundane world of retail. Cy

caught one performance of the pathetic production out of town, then offered this advice to Bloomingdale: "Close the show and keep the store open nights."

3. Lunch with a highly important, very powerful entrepreneur. He has read the first draft of a new play I have written. He loves the work. He praises it lavishly. He is very keen on producing it and presenting it in one of his theatres. He has only one question: "Can it be about something else?" He goes on to assure me that changing the script's central idea won't take a lot of work. I assure him the lunch is over.

4. Broadway economics being what they are (a vodka at intermission can now cost more than a ticket once did—and be far more entertaining), I am in previews in New York with a musical too costly to try out out of town. Coming up the aisle after the final curtain one night is a theatre hero of mine, a walking legend, Garson Kanin. The very first play I ever saw on Broadway, the theatrical gem which I adopted as my standard, was his *Born Yesterday*. He grasps my arm firmly, and fixes me with a stern look. "I've got just one suggestion for you," he says. Everything stops. My breathing, my heart, the world. And then he gives me his suggestion. "Don't change a single word of it," he says. "Not one word." Now, there's a man I could lunch with forever.

5. I am invited to the opening night on Broadway. It's a play which every bone in my body tells me I am not going to enjoy. But the writer/director is an old friend. I dread how socially awkward it is going to be if the show proves to be as awful as I feel it will be. I am in for a big surprise. It is even worse than I had expected. It is excruciating. I head for the men's room after the first act, hoping to avoid seeing my friend and having to lie about what a wonderful evening I'm having. He is, of course, standing at the head of the aisle, waiting for me. My lying tongue freezes in my mouth. I am speechless. I can't tell him the truth, nor can I lie to him. As it turns out, he can't lie to me either. "Isn't it fabulous?" he says. "Isn't it great?" he gushes. Now, that's a real friend.

6. I know the show must go on. Then there are the ones that go on and on and on. *Camelot*, for instance. I warned Milton Berle that it was a very long show. More like endless. He went anyway. He decided to leave at the end of the first act, which was endless enough for him. As he was being helped into his overcoat by the hatcheck girl, Frederick Loewe, the show's composer, appeared at his side, disappointment written all over his face. "You're not leaving, Milton? You're not staying for the second act?" "Of course I'm staying," Milton replied. "It's just that it's freezing in there." With that, the hatcheck girl handed Milton his hat. Milton snapped, "Why the hell're you giving me my hat? I'm not going anywhere!" He stood talking with Loewe, telling him how much he loved the show, for the balance of the intermission. And then he watched the just-as-endless second act, all the while melting in his overcoat.

7. My wife, singer/actress Pat Marshall, played "Babe" for a year in the original production of *The Pajama Game* at the St. James Theatre. One night, cast members waiting to go on for the opening number heard what they thought were snores coming from a stagehand who appeared to be snoozing on a couch in the living room set. The snore, it turned out, was a death rattle. The snooze was the Big Sleep. As he expired, the unfortunate fellow fell forward, his body coming to rest in the wings. Told by the police not to move the corpse, the valiant actors, singers, and dancers stepped gingerly over the fallen stagehand on their entrances and exits, until an ambulance took him away at the intermission. The corpse can only be grateful that this didn't happen at *Camelot*, or it would still be lying there. (I hesitated telling this story, fearing that the unions might demand two dead stagehands in all future Broadway productions!)

So much for Memory Lane. Now, why don't we put on our overcoats, go inside, and catch the shows?

Larry Gelbart

OVERTURE

"The other day I saw my two-and-a-half-year-old on the kitchen table singing a Jerry Herman song," remarked one Dianna Shively, from Orange, California. "I've never been so happy." This rather terrifying quote was found in the paper of record, the *New York* ("All the News That's Fit to Print") *Times*. What is to become of that poor (off-) Broadway baby?

He must learn some decorum, some sense of control. At least I assume it's a boy; a damsel of like vintage'd be chirping "Tomorrow," no doubt. But our young have got to be carefully taught that you can't go through life sittin' on the kitchen table with Jerry. Picture this misguided tyke at nursery school, advising his playpals to "Open a New Window" as he's pelted with kicks and missiles from red and white Power Rangers. See him, now, at summer camp, pelted with stale marshmallows by the campfire as he exhorts the boys to "Put on Your Sunday Clothes." Imagine the poor lad in the college cafeteria surrounded by cool dudes, beer-swilling coeds, and steroid-laced varsity men, imploring one and all to "Tap Your Troubles Away." That is, if he makes it out of kindergarten alive.

We must stop this musical comedy menace, this canker that randomly infiltrates the most innocent of babes and marks them, one way or other, for life. Or at least find some way at an early age to mask this proclivity, to tone the tinsel down.

After all, musical comedy is no longer an acceptable affectation in today's modernized, digitized world. The fall from grace can be seen, clear as clear, all around us. Go to the record store: Broadway cast album CDs—haphazardly thrown in with movie soundtracks, for heaven's sake—take up but a rack or so; less than jazz or new age or budget classical, even. Go to the bookstore: one measly shelf hidden away behind all those rows of cookbooks. Go to the TV news: clip after clip of brawling football players, brawling hockey players, brawling political players, and even brawling figure skaters, with only the biggest of Broadway openings meriting a brief encapsulated mention. Go to the information highway—website after website after website on just about anything, but nary a cybersytic byte for Jerry Herman.

The Broadway musical was the cream of American popular culture for more than sixty glorious years. Its Al Jolsons and Flo Ziegfelds, George Gershwins and Cole Porters, Gertie Lawrences and Mary Martins set styles, tastes, and fashions across the land. The man in the street danced to its songs, courted to its songs, wed to its songs, and—in times of war—marched to its songs. The theatre was the epitome of sophistication; even the movies glamorized the Broadway musical. And now look at us. Broadway's lucky to get an occasional two-page spread in *People* magazine.

The theatre is dying, of course, as they've been telling us since the fall of '92 (1892, that is). Musical comedy prospects have grown especially dire, with new practitioners of the craft few and far between. The whole street could dry up and the production pace shrivel to nothing, the public at large wouldn't even blink as they loaded up the van for another trip to the shopping mall. They'd miss *Cats*, though.

But . . . but . . . there still appears to be *some* life in Broadway, some business left in show business. During the 1995–1996 season, Broadway reaped some $436,107,774. And Broadway, of course, is a nongeographical realm; add in touring productions of Broadway-based shows and you come up to $1.2 billion, which represents a lot of spare greenbacks any way you look at it. And that figure doesn't include those pesky service charges tacked onto phone orders, inordinate sums that go into *some*body's pocket but not to the actors, writers, producers, investors, or other otherwise deserving recipients.

The folks who actuarize such things tell us that in a given season more people attend the Broadway theatre than all the New York City-based sports teams combined, and I'm inclined to believe 'em. And while things ain't what they used to be, an isolated hit—a *Chorus Line*, a *Les Misèrables*, or a *Phantom of the Opera*, say—can be just as much of a must-see, worldwide phenomenon as *My Fair Lady*, *Oklahoma!*, or even *H.M.S. Pinafore*. The musical theatre can still generate a dynamo of interest, publicity, and stardust, even under the meagre conditions of the present day.

I guess if the great unwashed populace can be addicted to talk shows, net surfing, *Star Trek*, Monday night football, professional wrestling, professional mud wrestling, political mud wrestling, television soap opera, or the royal soap opera of the day—the Windsors, the Rainiers, the Onassises, or Charles and Di, take your pick—there's no reason they shouldn't spend a considerable amount of their time and energies, and a sizable chunk of their personal exchequer, on musical comedy. Which has, rightly or wrongly, been deemed "the most glorious words in the English language." (This quote came from someone who was producing a musical comedy within a musical comedy about a musical comedy—*42nd Street*—and was written by a couple of fellows who mined millions out of the field in the process. But that doesn't make it an overexaggeration, d'you think?)

So maybe it's all right to be nuts about the musical theatre. But please, Mrs. Shively, buy that boy some Frank Loesser or Rodgers and Hart. Before it's too late.

o   o   o

It is not uncommon, in the course of researching some old musical or other, to find yourself stumbling upon the credits or reviews of some *other* old musical (or other). With a show you remember, you might want to see what the critics—who saw it when it was new and, presumably, fresh—had to say. With one you're only vaguely familiar with, you might want to delve in and slake your curiosity. And you sometimes turn up one of those unknown, brief-lived enterprises that makes you sit up and say, "Huh?" These oft-forgotten shows make for especially fascinating browsing. Common sense tells us that the authors, producers, and presumably investors felt certain that the item in question was destined to be a surefire hit. So much for common sense.

I remember some years ago looking up the unhappy Richard Rodgers/Stephen Sondheim opus *Do I Hear a Waltz?* There I was, suddenly faced with five pages-worth of reviews of a brief-lived tuner titled *Flora, the Red Menace.* Now, I'm not especially pro-Liza or anti-Liza (or Judy or Barbra, either); like a blue plate meatloaf, when she is good she is very good, but mix in too much of this 'n' that and she'll end up repeating on you. With *Flora's* notices at my fingertips, I briefly considered what I already knew about this 1965 musical:

a. Liza was a relatively unknown nineteen-year-old. As relatively as possible with relatives like Vincente Minnelli and Judy Garland.
b. The star sounds pretty good on the cast recording.
c. The show was a failure.
d. Young Liza nevertheless managed to cop the best actress Tony Award (though not until after *Flora* slipped into the Red and shuttered).

With *Flora's* clippings at my fingertips, I wondered:

a. Did the critics judge Liza on her own merits?
b. Just how bad was *Flora?*
c. Did everyone realize that they were watching a distinctive superstar-to-be?

Walter Kerr of the *Herald Tribune* took care of the first question right off the bat, introducing her as "Liza Minnelli, who no longer needs to be identified as Judy Garland's daughter and I apologize for just having done so," while informing us that her profile seemed to be made of Silly Putty. John Chapman of the *Daily News* opined that she "looks rather like an underprivileged Jackie Kennedy and can put zing into a song even when the song doesn't have zing." Well, that certainly sounds like the Liza we've come to know. John McClain of the *Journal-American* told us that the new star "looks like a charming little rabbit designed by Walt Disney to look like Judy Garland, her mother." Not bad. He went on to report that "she fractured with charm a resplendent audience. There seems no possible way it can be less than a shattering success." So much for John McClain. Norman Nadel of the *World-Telegram & Sun*, too, was taken by the neophyte's distinctive appearance, with "the face of a startled rabbit—wide, watchful eyes and an apprehensive upper lip." But he went on to state precisely what I wanted to know: that Minnelli "established, beyond the shadow of a doubt, that she is herself and no second-edition Judy. A man who described her as 'this year's Barbra Streisand' also was missing the point. Liza is this year's Liza—individual, unduplicated and electrifying—and she will be a star on her own terms for as many years as she can and will give so generously of her talent, spirit and love." These were even better personal reviews than Streisand herself received for *Funny Girl*. Overall, the critics were pretty much in agreement on *Flora*: a bright new performer with limitless possibilities; a somewhat entertaining score from a novice pair of songwriters worth watching (they came back a year later with *Cabaret*), but an enterprise scuttled by a troubled, inconclusive book and an unfocused point of view. These opening night reports, some twenty years old when I stumbled on them, were still interesting, illuminating, and to the point. But I was writing about *Do I Hear a Waltz?* at the time—or was it *On a Clear Day?*—so I turned back to what I was doing (after taking a detour to read about an intriguing failure called *Drat! The Cat!* and the scathing reception afforded the legendary *Kelly*).

This was an isolated incident, and the negligible *Flora* hardly merits such scrutiny. But after numerous such wanderings through the musical theatre storehouse I became convinced that there was material worth mining in the old and yellowing reports of the first-night critics, and thus it was that *Opening Night on Broadway: A Critical Quotebook of the Golden Era of the Musical Theatre* came to be. The infinite amount of potential material needed winnowing down to fit one volume; it seemed logical to start in 1943 with *Oklahoma!* and continue through 1964, when the twin hits *Hello, Dolly!* and *Fiddler on the Roof* signaled the end of an era. A Golden Era, in fact. Which, as it happened, knocked the following year's Liza and *Flora* out of the lineup. Oh, well.

Opening Night on Broadway seems to have contained an effective and entertaining combination of fact, opinion, and information; so much so that people, and my publishers, kept asking for a post–1964 volume. And I kept hesitating. The Golden Era was just that, with shows like *Carousel, South Pacific, Guys and Dolls, My Fair Lady, West Side Story*, and *Gypsy*. I knew all too well that the best show list of the

subsequent period was sure to prove relatively depressing. How interesting would such a book be to read, let alone write? But I finally
decided to at least take a look at what a second *Opening Night on
Broadway* would entail.

The first book encompassed a twenty-two-year span; thirty years,
taking us through 1994, would surely prove too hefty to handle.
(*Opening Night* clocked in at 810 pages.) So I started to examine the
shows, year by year, knowing of no clear-cut climax—as *Dolly!* and
Fiddler provided the first book—but hoping to find some logical stop-
date.

What were the major developments of the latter-day musical theatre, anyway? An increase in expenses and ticket prices, balanced by a
decrease in both quantity and quality, certainly. And there was the obvious adjustment as rock and other youth-oriented music forms nudged
theatre music—a mainstay of the pop world since the invention of the
victrola—off the charts, nary to return. But what developed within the
field of musical theatre since the turn of the Golden Era?

a. the arrival of the concept musical, typified by the collaboration of Stephen Sondheim and Hal Prince. Moody, highly
theatrical, not necessarily popular, and mostly financial busts;
but always forward-moving and intriguing. On the other
hand, there was

b. the faltering of the old-fashioned book musical, typified
by the persistent failures of Golden Era greats Richard
Rodgers, Alan Jay Lerner, Jule Styne, and Gower Champion.
They—and other survivors—kept reformulating the tired old
formulas until their "new" shows—formerly a cause for theatre parties, advance sales, and assorted hoopla—met merely
with apathy and snickers, and I don't mean the kind with nuts
in 'em. And the not-so-old-timers—Jerry Herman, Charles
Strouse, John Kander, Cy Coleman—didn't fare much better.
This was counterbalanced by

c. the increasing prominence of the choreographer/director,
typified by the work of Michael Bennett. Bennett, a key
member of the early Sondheim/Prince team, seemed to build

his musicals out of the physical bricks of the theatre—
scenery, costumes, lighting, and the actors' bodies themselves—with a seeming indifference to song and story.
Which, given the quality of latter-day song and story, might
have been a good idea. The overall dearth of product set the
(empty) stage for

d. the emergence of the (mostly British) supermusicals with
"pop" topics, massive physical productions, and expert marketing overcoming (often) indifferent material. Their
unprecedented long runs began to tie up prime Broadway
musical houses for decades at a shot. Not so good for the production pace and the critical development of new talent, but
very good for the theatre owners.

Now, the far-reaching Sondheim/Prince team had eventually
"gone about as fur as they could go (yes, sir!)," to borrow words from
Mr. Hammerstein; the pair parted Company after a particularly torturous misadventure in 1981. A year that, similarly, saw Michael Bennett's
final offering. And Gower Champion's swan song had arrived just
before, in 1980, under spectacular circumstances as he ended his
post–Golden Era famine—six, count 'em, megaflops—with a song-
and-dance smash just hours after shrugging off this mortal coil. Not so
for the great Richard Rodgers, who kept composing long after age and
illness had dimmed his muse. Rodgers's final musical died shortly
before he himself did, on the penultimate day of 1979.

As for the invasion of the spectacular spectacles, *Cats* pattered into
town   in   1982—just   after   Bennett,   Champion,   and   the
Sondheim/Prince team all left the not-so-level playing field. The end
of an era: not a golden one, perhaps, but a seventeen-year span that
brought forth the complete Sondheim/Prince output; the entire career
of Michael Bennett (whose *Dreamgirls* was the final musical of 1981);
virtually all of the razzle-dazzle method-over-material masterworks of
Bob Fosse; and Gower Champion's free fall followed by his final,
phoenix-like *42nd Street*. Setting the stage, figuratively, for the massive
mass-marketed triumphs that have increasingly dominated Broadway
since 1982. And thus it is that I've settled on the period from the end

of the Golden Era through 1981—with *Man of La Mancha* and *Dreamgirls* as markers—for *More Opening Nights*.

•   •   •

As I began to examine the era, I found—to my surprise—a wealth of interesting entertainments. Not great, certainly, but certainly interesting. As musical theatre developed, the attainments and aspirations of forward-minded creators grew more complex. This, correspondingly, affected the reviewers and their reviews; it is difficult to give an in-depth analysis of an unconventional, groundbreaking musical like *Cabaret* or *Company*, say, in the same breezy manner as one might handle the relatively simplistic *Sound of Music* or *Dolly!* A constructive critic is not necessarily one you agree with, but one who supports and explains his opinions. The more complex the show's aspirations, the more complex the criticism. Therefore, while *More Opening Nights* covers four fewer years and far fewer productions (206, against 275), the excerpts are necessarily fuller and the discussions correspondingly longer. The individual entries run to about five pages each, compared with fewer than three in the earlier volume. What with longer initial runs, reissued cast albums, and all-too-frequent revivals, these 1965–1981 musicals are more familiar to readers than those of the earlier volume (which go back before many of us were born). The reviews excerpted herein can jog our memory on the elements we remember; moreover, they reintroduce and recover elements we might *not* remember. Especially when the opinion expressed is contrary to one's own recollection—and when that opinion is, further, reasonably validated.

Virtually all of the book musicals of the period have been included, as even the most inconsequential of them tend to have a fascination all their own. Revues of minimal interest—to me, at least—have been excluded; so have ethnic-oriented entertainments, be they gospel or Yiddish, which seem to have little bearing on the discussion. Neither have we included all the many revivals of the era, which began sprouting up with alarming frequency back around 1973. Thirty-four are discussed herein—a full sixth of the shows in this book. (About half a dozen more revivals have been excluded.) Some of these easily deserve discussion as new, reconceived productions, like *No, No, Nanette* and Hal Prince's *Candide*, but all too many were mere retreads mounted for the sole purpose of filling roadhouses. Not only did 1965–1981 Broadway see two revivals each of Golden Era hits *My Fair Lady* and *Camelot*, it also saw twin carbons of both *Hello, Dolly!* and *Fiddler on the Roof*, whose original runs ran into the 1970s. (There were also two Richard Kiley-headed returns of *Man of La Mancha*—which didn't even open until 1965 in the first place!)

Taking note of the interest promulgated by the inclusion of hidden credits and "ghost" billing in the earlier book, I've tried to uncover as much of this information as possible, always remembering that a mere mention in a gossip column does not signify fact. The rarer illustrations in the first book also proved extremely popular. Accordingly, I have gone for the most intriguing illustrative material possible and avoided the all-too-familiar record-album covers and production photos reproduced elsewhere.

Numerous reference books are available that detail what the shows were about; *Opening Night* and *More Opening Nights* aim to tell us, rather, what the shows were *like*—and why. The first-night reviews help us re-create not just the plot but the *thrill* of the Broadway musical.

DOLLARS AND SENSE

The schedule of top ticket prices in *Opening Night on Broadway* provided considerable bemusement, so let's repeat it as we bring the ducat dollars up to date.

Oklahoma!	1943	$4.40
Bloomer Girl	1944	$5.40
Carousel	1945	$6.00
Annie Get Your Gun	1946	$6.60
As the Girls Go	1948	$7.20
South Pacific	1949	$6.00
Call Me Madam	1950	$7.20
Guys and Dolls	1950	$6.00
Wonderful Town	1953	$6.60
Damn Yankees	1955	$8.05
Seventh Heaven	1955	$8.30
My Fair Lady	1956	$7.50
New Girl in Town	1957	$9.20

West Side Story	1957	$7.50
The Music Man	1957	$8.05
Goldilocks	1958	$9.90
Gypsy	1959	$9.40
The Sound of Music	1959	$9.90
Carnival	1961	$8.60
Hello, Dolly!	1964	$9.40
Funny Girl	1964	$9.60
On a Clear Day	1965	$11.90
Zorbá	1968	$15.00
Annie	1977	$20.00
The Act	1977	$25.00
Evita	1979	$30.00
42nd Street	1980	$40.00
Cats	1982	$45.00
La Cage aux Folles	1983	$47.50
Cabaret (revival)	1987	$50.00
Jerome Robbins' Broadway	1989	$55.00
Jerome Robbins' Broadway (post–opening)	1989	$60.00
Miss Saigon	1991	$65.00
Grease (revival)	1994	$67.50
Kiss of the Spider Woman	1994	$70.00
Show Boat (revival)	1994	$75.00

Jerome Robbins' Broadway established an all-time high $55 top when it opened in February 1989, and closed out the decade by establishing an all-time high $60 in November. By January 1990 it was on twofers, and by Labor Day it was gone, but the price prevailed. *Miss Saigon* opened in the fall of 1991 at the same $60, but with a $100 tab for the "best" seats. (Author's Note: the best seats for *Miss Saigon* were in the outer lobby.) This special (?) offer was withdrawn in March 1992, with producer Cameron Mackintosh compensating by raising the "regular" top to $65 at both *Saigon* and *Phantom*. (He simultaneously lowered the bottom price for the uppermost pews to $15; charge more for 1,200 choice seats, less for 200 no-choice seats, that sort of thing.) No harm done, because—unlike at *Robbins*—audiences eagerly *wanted* to see *Saigon* and *Phantom*. By the end of 1993 every musical on Broadway was getting 65 bucks. Or at least *trying* to get it. The revival of *Grease* raised the lid to $67.50 in June 1994—this is getting ridiculous—

topped two months later with a $70 tariff at *Kiss of the Spider Woman*. Expensive musical playing in Broadway's smallest musical house, producer Garth Drabinsky explained. (Also, cast replacement Vanessa Williams had just opened to especially strong reviews.) Another two months later Ol' Man River rolled on in—*Show Boat*'s sixth full-scale local mounting—with a *$75* tariff. Expensive musical playing in Broadway's *largest* musical house, producer Garth Drabinsky explained. Ticket buyers concurred, indicating once again that no price is too high for a show people want to see. As for shows that people *don't* want to see . . . . The higher the price, the higher the half-price.

Yes, costs keep going up and inflation keeps inflating, but you don't have to be an economist to realize that there is something seriously wrong with this scale of scales. Broadway broke the $10 barrier in 1965, just as the Golden Era ended and the decline began. *The Music Man*, which opened with an $8.05 top, netted a profit of about $23,000 a week at capacity (circa 1958); costs six years later were such that *Dolly!*—even with a 15 percent higher $9.40 top, was able to net only $14,500 a week. *Dolly!* did all right, though. From 1964 to 1977 the ticket tariff had doubled, and within only three years *doubled again*. These increased prices affected long-running musicals, too, which need to keep up with increased costs (and keep up with the competition). A perhaps unparalleled example: *A Chorus Line*, which opened in 1975 at $15, closed in 1990 at $50! *Cats*, meanwhile, has gone from $40 to $70 (so far)—although much of their business is done at cut rates. The higher the price, the higher the half-price. And now we're looking at a big-ticket tab of $75. Today's shows, though, are correspondingly more entertaining. (Just kidding.)

And while it has absolutely no relevance, it is interesting to note in passing that *As the Girls Go*, *Seventh Heaven*, *Goldilocks*, *On a Clear Day*, *Zorbá*, *The Act*, *Jerome Robbins' Broadway*, and *Kiss of the Spider Woman*—each of which saw fit to raise the prevailing price plateau—all floundered and flopped. That's show biz.

Ticket prices, of course, are symptomatic of costs, and costs are ever-rising. *Kelly*, the very first musical of the post–1964 years, broke all records with a deficit of $650,000. The show was capitalized at $450,000, but tryout losses and out-of-town fixings come high. Costs on the ultra-lavish, ultra-troubled 1960 musical *Camelot* ballooned from the budgeted $480,000 to an astounding $675,000, causing it to be redubbed *Costalot*; they recovered their deficit and accumulated a nice profit, though. The more modest *Fiddler on the Roof*, which opened four months before *Kelly*, was budgeted at $375,000 and cost $450,000 to open. (Sometimes it does make sense for the producer to go out of pocket for improvements. It helps if you've got someone like Jerry Robbins doing the improving, though.) The year 1967 was especially dismal for musicals: only six opened—all dreary flops—with a seventh, the fabled *Mata Hari*, shuttering en route. Actors Equity closed down Broadway with a three-day strike in June 1968, and—what a coincidence—within months the ticket top hit $15, an increase of more than 50 percent within just four years. Production costs were up, too, with that year's not-so-happy *Happy Time* closing with an unprecedented million-dollar loss (on an $800,000 investment). Ten years later both *King of Hearts* and *Ballroom* broke the $2-million plateau while the concurrent *Platinum* lost $1.75 million, *Grand Tour* dropped $1.5 million, and *A Broadway Musical* proved a bargain at a cool million—all five opening within a grisly twelve weeks. The end of the decade also saw a quick escalation in ticket prices, with the top doubling from $20 (1977) to $40 (1980). Ticket prices, costs, and losses have continued to march onward, but then you didn't expect them to get lower, did you?

We also find an escalation in the length of run necessary to show a profit—which is to say that higher ticket revenues were more than offset by increasing production and operating costs. Theoretically, a show can afford to run indefinitely so long as it covers its weekly operating costs. Theoretically. In order to *recoup*, though, it must generate not only enough to cover these costs, but also weekly operating profits in amounts that—over the course of the run—exceed the original production cost. This is oversimplified, surely, and doesn't take into account potentially sizable income from additional productions, movie sales, stock and amateur rights, and logo-emblazoned coffee mugs and baseball caps, but it can be seen that the length of run itself doesn't signify success.

Through the Golden Era it was an accepted truth that a new book musical that ran a year—roughly 416 performances—was certain to make back its investment. There were a handful of exceptions to the one-year-profit rule, the first being *As the Girls Go*, Mike Todd's 1948 girl-and-leg show that failed despite 412 performances and an outlandishly high $7.20 top. (*South Pacific*, which opened five months later, charged a mere six bucks.) Other long-run failures included *Happy Hunting*, a 1956 tuner that made it through 418 showings on Ethel Merman's star power; *Destry Rides Again*, David Merrick's 1959 cowboy musical with Andy Griffith valiantly laboring to fill Jimmy Stewart's boots 472 times; and *Do Re Mi*, the 1960 Phil Silvers laugh fest loved by the critics but caviar to the general public for 400 sessions. The erstwhile theatrical community was shocked, though, in 1961 when Jerry Herman's maiden effort, the soppy *Milk and Honey*, became the first show to pass the 500-performance mark and *still* lose money (543 performances). The year 1964 saw two additions to the 500-plus flop club: *What Makes Sammy Run?*, which ran until Steve Lawrence ran out of his contract after 540; and—speaking of running Sammy—Mr. Davis's own *Golden Boy*, which tipped the scales at 569. Five hundred performances clearly no longer guaranteed anything. The 1973 Debbie Reynolds vehicle, *Irene*, slogged through 594 showings, breaking all box office records along the way (thanks in part to the new Minskoff Theatre, with 1,039 top-priced orchestra seats; the St. James, with a similar 1,600-odd overall seating capacity, has only 676 on the floor and 326 hard-to-sell ducats up in the lofty second balcony). But *Irene* also set records with outlandishly higher running costs and royalties, garnering front-page coverage with an investigation by the attorney general's office. *Purlie* (1970, 689 perfs) neared the 700-mark while *Candide* (1974, 740 perfs) surpassed it, with both Broadway Theatre tenants succumbing to real estate-related obstacles. Black sheep *Purlie* was forced out of not one but two theatres, the additional moving costs sealing its fate; *Candide*'s scaled-down seating capacity subjected it to onerous labor demands, with investors forced to face the music (and the musicians' union). *Woman of the Year* (1981) had no such obstacles: just outlandishly high royalties, a bad book and score, and Lauren Bacall/Raquel Welch/Debbie Reynolds in the lead for 770 performances. The longest-running failure through the 1965–1981 period was 1973's poorly managed *Raisin*, for which 847 performances were not enough. It took eighteen years, but *The Will Rogers Follies* finally managed to trump *Raisin* with 983 showings—that's two years, three months—although subsidiary rights might eventually push it into the black. In which case the record holder becomes the 1993 *Kiss of the Spider Woman*, kissing off after 906 chuckle-filled perfs—proving that you can run anything indefinitely if you have grit, perseverance, and five or six million bucks (U.S.$) to burn.

There's no need for a schedule of profitable shows with the *briefest* lives, but let's stop to point out that the two most impressive book musicals in this light—the leastes' with the mostes', as Irving Berlin might have said—were David Merrick's twin 1965 imports *Roar of the Greasepaint* (232 perfs) and *Pickwick* (with an astoundingly low 56). The producer recouped costs on both during extensive pre-Broadway tours, a trick he learned with his 1963 *Oliver!* Unlike *Oliver!*, though, these two tuners met stony New York receptions. Merrick kept them running only as long as presold theatre parties allowed him to break even, which proves that there's more than one way to skin a critic. The showman also got profits out of the low-octane *110 in the Shade* (1963, 333 perfs) and *Sugar* (1972, 505 perfs). Hal Prince's longer-running *Follies* (1971, 522 perfs), *Sweeney Todd* (1979, 558 perfs), and *Candide*—unquestionably superior shows—all lost money, which says something about quality, commerce, and David Merrick. Two other low-performance, subpar musicals that barely managed to turn a profit (thanks to supplemental income from post–Broadway activity) were Alan Jay Lerner's 1969 Kate Hepburn vehicle, *Coco* (332 perfs), and Richard Rodgers's 1970 Danny Kaye vehicle, *Two by Two* (with 343). Why d'you suppose these two ended in the black?

While we're at it, we might as well state that fourteen of the shows included in this book ran but one performance. (A couple might as well have closed during intermission.) Taking our statistics one drastic step further, let us first deduct revues and revivals from the 206 productions included in this book. This leaves us with 157 new book musicals that opened from 1965 through 1981. Of these, *36 closed within the week.* That is 23 percent, one out of four. While this might not surprise a perpetual theatregoer of the period with a good memory for the bad, it does give one cause to pause.

◦   ◦   ◦

The Golden Era contained some golden periods, indeed. In the spring of 1947, for example, you could take in the original productions of *Oklahoma!*, *Carousel*, *Annie Get Your Gun* (with Ethel Merman), *Finian's Rainbow*, and *Brigadoon*. In the spring of 1951 you could try for *Kiss*

Me, Kate, South Pacific, Call Me Madam (with Ethel Merman), *Guys and Dolls*, and *The King and I*. Things were still somewhat tolerable in the spring of 1960, with *My Fair Lady*, *The Music Man*, *Gypsy* (with Ethel Merman), *The Sound of Music*, *Fiorello!*, and *Bye Bye Birdie* on tap.

Once you approach the mid-1960s—and leave the Golden Era— the list starts to thin out. The long-running trio of *Hello, Dolly!*, *Fiddler*, and *Man of La Mancha* made the latter half of the decade fairly tolerable; you could still get in a decent week of theatregoing in the fall of 1966, when they were joined by *Sweet Charity*, *Mame*, and *Cabaret*, or in the spring of 1970 when the trio—including ol' Ethel, again, as Dolly Levi— had *Hair*, *Promises, Promises*, *1776*, *Applause*, and *Company* for company. But I wouldn't recommend taking this particular exercise much further.

The only knockdown, can't-get-a-house-seat, ultra-smash hits of the 1965–1981 period were *Man of La Mancha* (which, like *Annie Get Your Gun*, precipitated its own ticket scandal), *Hair*, *A Chorus Line*, and *Annie*. Compare this list with the Golden Era's *Oklahoma!*, *Annie* (the other one), *South Pacific*, *Guys and Dolls*, *Fair Lady*, *The Music Man*, *The Sound of Music*, *Dolly!*, and *Fiddler*. On second thought, let's not make that comparison.

Coming off the Golden Era, one might suspect that 1965 arrived with gold still in the air. This was not quite the case. There had already been a falling off in quality in the early 1960s, the exceptions being the impeccable Pulitzer Prize-winner *How to Succeed in Business without Really Trying* (1961) and 1964's expertly staged *Dolly!* and *Fiddler*. As the calendar turned to 1965, in fact, Broadway had a mere *three* attractions that had passed their first anniversary mark—the lowest number since 1942 and one that in this new era of "now and forever" long runs we're unlikely to see again. Furthermore, only one of the three, the aforementioned *How to Succeed*, was a musical. (The other two: comedy hits *Never Too Late* and *Barefoot in the Park*.) The 1964 musicals continuing into the new year consisted of *Dolly!*, *Funny Girl*, and—from the fall season—*Fiddler*, as well as ultimate failures *Oh, What a Lovely War*, *Golden Boy*, *Ben Franklin in Paris*, *Bajour*, and *I Had a Ball*.

◦   ◦   ◦

The encroaching inroads of the rock era knocked Broadway's traditional composers off the field and into retirement, we are told.

Nonsense. Well, partial nonsense. Rodgers, Lane, Bernstein, and Styne *all* wrote musicals after the dawning of the Age of Aquarius, stuff like *Two by Two, Rex, I Remember Mama, Carmelina, 1600 Pennsylvania Avenue, Look to the Lilies, One Night Stand,* and *The Red Shoes.* The trouble with these shows was decidedly *not* in the ears of the beholders. The composers of the "younger" generation—Bock, Merrill, Adler, Strouse, Coleman, Herman, Kander, and Schmidt—similarly had plenty of trouble. No need to list titles here, let's not get depressing. Only one important composer, in fact, escapes this group, but then it is pointless to compare any of these gents to Stephen Sondheim.

And what of the newer, post–Golden Era era composers? First let's consider the year of arrival of composers active after 1964 (with three or more Broadway scores to their credit), by year of their first complete score. The second date indicates the year of their most recent (or final) score, including shows that closed on the road. Composers in italics are deceased; an asterisk (*) indicates those who are still active and reasonably likely to reappear along the Rialto.

Pre–Golden Era

Richard Rodgers (1925/1979)	*Harold Rome* (1937/1973)
Frederick Loewe (1938/1973)	Burton Lane (1940/1979)
Hugh Martin (1941/1989)	

Early Golden Era

Robert Wright/George Forrest (1944/1989)	*Leonard Bernstein* (1944/1976)
Jule Styne (1947/1993)	*Frank Loesser* (1948/1965)

Late Golden Era

Richard Adler (1954/1976)	Albert Hague (1955/1974)
Jerry Bock (1956/1970)	Bob Merrill (1957/1990)
Meredith Willson (1957/1969)	*Moose Charlap* (1958/1972)

*Charles Strouse (1960/1993)	*Cy Coleman (1960/1991)
Jerry Herman (1961/1983)	*Stephen Sondheim (1962/1994)
*John Kander (1962/1993)	*Harvey Schmidt (1963/1996)

1965–1975

Mitch Leigh (1965/1993)	Galt MacDermot (1968/1984)
Gary Geld (1970/1978)	*Larry Grossman (1970/1985)
*Andrew Lloyd Webber (1971/1994)	*Stephen Schwartz (1972/1991)
*Marvin Hamlisch (1975/1993)	

1976–1986 (make that 1996)

Absolutely Nobody

Which is to say, no one has made the list in the last twenty years. Not one. There are some talents around and about, certainly, led by William Finn (who has only been represented on Broadway once, alas). Maury Yeston and Stephen Flaherty (with two each) and perhaps Alan Menken are likely to break the barrier; the late Jonathan Larson, of course, will not. David Shire and Robert Waldman, both of whom have been writing for Broadway since the late 1960s, have precious little to show for it. And Claude-Michel Schönberg, with *Les Misérables* and *Miss Saigon* to his credit, has shown a certain vogue. But it has been more than twenty years without even a Marvin Hamlisch, for cripe's sake.

Enough said?

NOTES ON THE EXCERPTS

The excerpts have been selected from more than 1,500 reviews of musicals that opened on Broadway from January 1, 1965, through December 31, 1981. Calendar years have been used rather than "seasons," as the latter can be confusing. (Some say the season begins on Labor Day, others pick the first Monday in June. Award deadline dates, meanwhile, have fluctuated through the years.) No effort has been made to include every musical produced during this period; productions of minimal interest have been ignored unless the critics told us something worth noting. Critical comments have been edited for clarity and concision. Redundant reportorial information—"the new musical comedy, which opened last night at the Shubert Theatre"—has been deleted, except where it adversely affects the writing style. Other unnecessarily repeated phrases have been condensed: "Sondheim and Prince" for example, might be used in place of "composer/lyricist Stephen Sondheim and director Harold Prince." Contemporary references that might be obscure to today's reader have been clarified in brackets. "Theatre" has been used over "theater" throughout, except where "Theater" was part of a title or producing organization. I've taken the liberty of condensing and juxtaposing critical thoughts, always careful to preserve the critic's personal style. Errors in identification, spelling, and song titles have been corrected. The aim has been to make the excerpts readable, concise, and informative while still reflecting the general tone of the entire original review.

THE CREDITS

Discussion of each show is preceded by credits for the production. Headings have been standardized: people with "production staged by" and "dance and ensembles by" billing are listed as, respectively, director and choreographer. Sometimes multiple and/or conflicting credits were listed; these have been clarified as necessary. Similarly, the phrase "in association with" has been used for all associate and "by arrangement with" producers. Star performers have been listed, as per the official billing. Featured performers are for the most part listed; alterations have been made in some cases, such as instances where the entire cast—leads and chorus—was listed in alphabetical order. We have tried to approximate the prominence of billing, as opposed to the actual order; billing on a line by itself has been moved ahead of other performers in a clump. A show's billing occasionally changed, as when Joel Grey was moved above the title after the opening of *Cabaret*. We have generally used the official opening night billing. Married couples working on the same show have been so indicated, as this is rarely an incidental occurrence. The date of the official Broadway opening is given, as well as the name of the theatre. Many long-running shows moved from theatre to theatre; this information is included only when a nonprofit or Off-

Broadway production engagement transferred to a commercial run. Information has been given on Pulitzer Prizes, New York Drama Critics' Circle Awards, and Tony Awards won by the productions. Awards categories, rules, and seasonal cutoff dates changed over the years, leading to seeming inconsistencies.

The official billing, though, does not always tell the full story. Musical theatre, as we've been told on innumerable occasions, is a collaboration. The success of a musical is not determined by the quality of the material the writers wrote, but by what it all looked like from orchestra center, months or years later, on Opening Night. On any number of occasions, people whose names don't appear in the "official" billing were instrumental to a show's failure or success. Blame for a poorly assembled musical often goes to the director, but does a director who has been called in at the last minute to try to salvage a disaster deserve all the abuse? How about the guy who guided the writers, chose the designers, approved the designs, cast the cast, rehearsed the actors, and remained in charge through two or three tryout towns? Sudden cast changes can also make an enormous difference: a show written to order around a specific star can be severely weakened (or enhanced) when said star is suddenly fired or quits (or dies). If the reader gets the idea that proceedings don't always proceed as planned, the reader will be getting the right idea. One of the things we discover is that some of our best musicals actually benefited from unplanned detours. Inside squabbles, ghosts, skeletons—sometimes alluded to by the critics, though the names were rarely named—can be crucial to an explanation of what made these musicals work. Or not work.

THE ILLUSTRATIONS

More than half of the entries are accompanied by the original artwork, or logo, created to attract ticket buyers. Artwork has been reproduced from heralds (program inserts used to encourage advance sales), window cards, souvenir programs, sheet music, and record album covers. Many such materials credit people who departed before the Broadway opening, as indicated. Logos were sometimes changed along the way to stimulate sales; at least, that's what the producers intended. Rather than simply reproduce the overly familiar artwork of Broadway's biggest hits—which most readers can find on their CD shelves—we've eschewed the familiar for the unique. Broadway's most active poster artists of the period include Hilary Knight, Tom Morrow, Fay Gage, Tony Walton, and Frederick Marvin. Also represented are Al Hirschfeld, Jack Davis, Clyde Smith, Joe Eula, David Byrd, James McMullan, Nick Nappi, Doug Johnson, Bob Gill, and the composer Harvey Schmidt. The illustrations included are dedicated to those theatre enthusiasts who on Sunday mornings do not first grab for the sports section or crossword puzzle, but eagerly turn to the amusement pages for that first glance at the new announcement ads. Sometimes the ad proves more amusing than the show, alas.

THE BROADWAY SCORECARD

The quoted excerpts usually reflect the critic's opinion of the show in question. But what was the consensus of the reviews? Were they in agreement, or sharply divided as to a show's merits (or flaws)? And how did their opinions ultimately affect the box office? The Broadway Scorecard offers a capsulized summary of each show's critical and commercial reception. The reviews fall into five categories:

RAVE: A rave is a rave is a rave, no question about it. The critic is saying, simply and strongly, go! Sometimes there's a little incidental carping, but the critic's overall enthusiasm is clear.

FAVORABLE: The very fact that a good review is not a rave is a qualification. Favorable reviews usually indicate one of two things. The show might be good, pleasant, entertaining, well-crafted, intelligent—but it's simply not earthshaking. Other favorable reviews tell us that the show is not so good but more than redeemed by a performance or two, or the dances, or even the sets. The critic is clearly recommending that you attend, you should like it. Probably.

MIXED: Some elements of the show work, others don't. The critic doesn't exactly tell you to buy a ticket, but he refrains from advising against it. Constructive critics sometimes rewarded adventurous failures with mixed reviews, suggesting you'll want to see it if you're really interested in musical theatre (but go quickly). Mixed reviews also occur when critics like a show they think their readers won't. Other mixed reviews are simply inconclusive or poorly written; you can't tell whether the critic liked it or not.

UNFAVORABLE: The polite category for shows that aren't good

enough or just don't work. The review might be matter of fact or regret-
ful, but the conclusion is always the same: don't bother to go. A favorable review might say that the brilliant so-and-so makes mediocre
material shine; an unfavorable review says that even the brilliant so-
and-so can't make up for the mediocrity.

PAN: There are shows that don't work, and then there are shows that
can't—and shouldn't—work. It's not merely that the critic didn't enjoy
the show; there's a distinct tone of annoyance. Pans are the most entertaining reviews to read and the easiest to write: since the perpetrators
are unquestionably guilty, no holds are barred. Respectable failures usually get unfavorable reviews, as the critics tend to give the creators the
benefit of a doubt—unless they *really* don't deserve it. Then no holds
are barred, especially when the creators have a megahit or two on their
résumés.

This scoring system is not perfect, as two people reading the same
review will not necessarily agree on the rating, but it gives us an idea.
Remember, too, that all critics are not created equal, at least insofar as
the weight of their opinion. One pan from the right reviewer—or the
wrong reviewer, as it were—can overpower multiple raves. (*Follies*
received four good reviews, including three raves. But Clive Barnes in
the *Times* was mixed, Walter Kerr in the Sunday *Times* was unfavorable,
and *Follies* gave up the ghost.) There can be little question about a show
that received unanimous reviews, good, bad, or indifferent. If the ratings range across the scorecard, though, things, are not so clear-cut. For
a variety of reasons, some shows were not covered by all of the newspapers generally polled to tabulate the scorecard. We have in these cases
added ratings from television or magazine critics to give us a uniform
six opinions per show. It should be remembered that the scorecards can
only reflect the opinions of the critics included; other reviewers might
well have loved a show that none of our discerning aisle-sitters smiled
upon. Further discussion of the scorecards can be found in the
Broadway Scorecard Summary in the back of the book.

The show's financial success or failure is indicated by the "$" entry,
which tells whether it ultimately made money ("+") or lost money ("–").
These records are not always available; furthermore, figures reported in
the press are not necessarily accurate. (Showmen have a tendency to exaggerate, especially when not under oath.) Where exact figures have been

impossible to find or verify, we offer well-educated guesses. We have similarly graded profit/loss on productions from nonprofit organizations.

The number of performances—beginning with the official opening, not including previews—is also included in the scorecard. Various reference books sometimes differ on this statistic; researchers tend to accept these figures unquestioningly, so mistakes and even typos can be carried over into newer reference books. (For several seasons the invaluable *Theatre World* series, widely used as the prime reference source for such matters, unaccountably included previews in their performance totals.) Where discrepancies exist, I've used the earliest, authentic-seeming source—and in several cases have actually gone back to the calendar and counted.

THE THEATRES

The particular theatre in which a show played sometimes had a definite (if subtle) influence on the results. This had to do not only with the location, physical layout, and condition of the house, but with past experiences there. *Follies* seemed to fit, physically, psychologically, and historically, at the Winter Garden. Gwen Verdon and Bob Fosse's *Chicago* played the 46th Street, home of their consecutive 1950s hits *Damn Yankees*, *New Girl in Town*, and *Redhead*. *Sweeney Todd* was conceived, physically, to fill the Uris—which perhaps dictated that show's ultimate failure.

Several theatres that housed shows discussed in this book have been demolished, while others have undergone name changes. To avoid confusion, departed and/or renamed theatres are identified below.

> The **George Abbott** was located at 152 West 54th Street, on the south side of the street between 6th and 7th Avenues. Originally the **Craig**, it was also called the **54th Street** and the **Adelphi**. It was demolished in 1970.

> The **Alvin**, built by the Gershwins' producers Al(ex) Aarons and Vin(ton) Freedley, is the present **Neil Simon**.

> The **ANTA** (American National Theatre & Academy), originally the **Guild** (built by the Theatre Guild), is the present **Virginia**.

The **Eden/Entermedia**, at 189 Second Avenue, was originally the **Yiddish Art Theatre** and later served as home of the **Phoenix Theatre**. It is now a multiplex cinema.

The **46th Street** is the present **Richard Rodgers**.

The **Harkness** was located at 1887 Broadway, between 62nd and 63rd Streets. Originally the **Colonial** and briefly the **Walter Hampden**, it was demolished in 1977.

The **Helen Hayes** was located at 210 West 46th Street, just across from the **Lunt-Fontanne**. Originally the *Folies-Bergère* (a theatre restaurant), it was also called the **Fulton**. It backed up to the **Oliver Morosco**, at 217 West 45th Street across from Shubert Alley. Both were demolished in 1982 (along with the **Bijou**, **Astor**, and **Gaiety/Victoria**) despite vehement protests from members of the theatrical community. The **Marquis** now stands in their place, which doesn't seem an especially equitable trade-off. (The **Little Theatre**, at 238 West 44th Street, was renamed the **Helen Hayes** in 1983.)

The **Hudson**, located at 141 West 44th Street, has been incorporated into the Millenium Broadway Hotel.

The **Billy Rose**, originally the **National** and briefly the **Trafalgar**, is the present **Nederlander**.

The **Uris** is the present **Gershwin**.

ACKNOWLEDGMENTS

My very first day on Broadway—as a teenaged "gofer"—I was fairly awestruck, what with a hundred glorious window cards on the office walls and six Tony Awards gathering theatre dust on the bookshelf behind Mr. Merrick's desk high atop the St. James Theatre. On the *second* day, though, as I was happily typing *Hello, Dolly!* royalty checks, I noticed that while composer/lyricist Jerry Herman was putting away a pretty penny, songwriters Bob Merrill, Lee Adams, and Charles Strouse were all getting checks as well. None of whom, officially, had anything to do with *Hello, Dolly!* Either Merrick was mistakenly spreading out extra checks ("Money is like manure," per the future Mrs. Vandergelder) or there was some hidden explanation that didn't appear on the title page of the program. I marched right into Jack Schlissel's office—with its extra deep armchairs placed low opposite the diminutive general manager's high throne, and a dartboard emblazoned with Gower Champion's smiling countenance (left over from their *Happy Time* battles) hidden on the wall behind the door—and got myself an answer. I've been asking questions ever since.

More *Opening Nights on Broadway* couldn't exist, needless to say, without the critics (or the producers and writers and directors and actors, for that matter). I hereby offer them—the critics—my deepest appreciation. Most are no longer actively on the aisle, others no longer with us, but their (usually) apt and informative comments remain. *Opening Night on Broadway* rescued the words of these gentlemen (mostly) from yellowing pages of old newsprint and celluloid coils of microfilm, accessible primarily in library collections, and put them on the shelf with our CD collections, where they are ever so much more handy. The reviews excerpted in *More Opening Nights on Broadway* are more current—both chronologically and in many readers' memories—but every bit as ephemeral, and will hopefully prove as valuable and intriguing as the material from the earlier period. Especially well represented in and integral to this volume are Clive Barnes, Frank Rich, Richard Watts, Doug Watt, Martin Gottfried, Howard Kissel, and the great Walter Kerr.

Many (though far from all) of the newspaper reviews excerpted in this book are reprinted, in full, in the *New York Theatre Critics' Reviews* series. A sizable amount of the information was gathered from articles, interviews, press releases, and column items that appeared in various New York and tryout town newspapers, as well as from the infinitely helpful *Variety*. (Everything you read in papers is not necessarily accurate: part of the job of the hapless press agent is to get certain things *into* print and keep other things *out*!) Information has also been gathered from souvenir programs, record album liner notes, the revised and highly informative liner notes accompanying many compact disc reissues, and private letters and contracts.

Extensive accounts exist of the creation of a number of these shows. Especially helpful and recommended to the reader are books and articles by Christopher Davis, Don Dunn, Lewis H. Lapham, Ken Mandelbaum, and Hal Prince. (See bibliography for details.) Two books examining a full season's worth of shows are highly informative, highly entertaining, and highly recommended: William Goldman's classic *The Season* (1968–69) and Jack Gaver's lesser-known *Season In Season Out* (1965–66).

This book was researched mostly at the Billy Rose Theatre Collection of the Performing Arts Research Center at Lincoln Center, whose knowledgable and accommodating staff was extremely helpful. And patient. Kevin Winkler and Richard Buck are due special thanks. I was also fortunate to stumble on the collection of the newly established Goodspeed Opera House Library of the American Musical Theatre (Kristin Johnson, Librarian), which is already becoming an invaluable repository for researchers.

The best way to uncover accurate information, of course, is to ask the right questions of someone who (a) was there at the time, (b) is relatively unbiased, and (c) is willing to talk to you. Especially helpful in finding answers has been a core group of friends and coworkers I've had the pleasure of associating with over the years: Mitchell Erickson, the late Leo Herbert, Mark Bramble, Samuel "Biff" Liff, Gene Wolsk, the late Charles Blackwell, Alan Hall, Kim Sellon, Mary Jo Slater, the late Arlene Grayson, Janice Herbert, Richard Kidwell, Frank Marino, Jon Handy, Janet Beroza, John Bonanni, Manny Kladitis, Leonard Soloway, and Max A. Woodward. These folks worked on/produced/ wrote or were in other ways connected with a good (and sometimes not-so-good) 80 percent of the shows discussed in this book. Together, they provided informed access to a multitude of firsthand information. I myself was involved with a chunk of these musicals, which has decidedly *not* given them preferential treatment. Don't cry for me, *Shenandoah*.

Another group of theatrical associates has kindly fielded specific questions, namely Shirley Herz, Michael P. Price, Gary Gunas, William Rosenfield, Manny Azenberg, Nina Skriloff, Bert Fink, Peter Howard, Morty Halpern, Matt Farrell, George Wachtel, Adrian Bryan-Brown, Harriet Slaughter, Keith Sherman, Norman Rothstein, and Jay Kingwill. Jon Wilner and Peter LeDonne's special assistance was of immense help. As before, Max Woodward, Richard Kidwell, and

Paul Newman graciously allowed use of their extensive collections of theatrical artwork. (Imagine unearthing the closing notice for *Mata Hari!*) Finally, I'd like to thank the following for general assistance and other accommodations: William C. Appleton, Tiki Davies, Kate Glasner, Dorothy Nichols, Skipp Porteous, Mark D. Sendroff, Barbara Ann Simon, Molly Smith, and Jane Tamlyn.

THE MUSICALS

THE ACT

"A New Musical," previously entitled *In Person* and *Shine It On*

music by John Kander

lyrics by Fred Ebb

book by George Furth

directed by Martin Scorsese (replaced by Gower Champion)

choreographed by Ron Lewis (with Gower Champion)

produced by Cy Feuer and Ernest H. Martin, presented by The Shubert Organization

starring Liza Minnelli and Barry Nelson

with Arnold Soboloff (replacing Lorry Goldman, who replaced Leonard Gaines), Gayle Crofoot, Roger Minami, Christopher Barrett, and Mark Goddard

opened October 29, 1977   *Majestic Theatre*

WALTER KERR, *TIMES*

Liza, Liza, skies are gray. I don't mind so much that the various people who've put together *The Act* have been opportunistic enough to keep Liza Minnelli on stage, singing and singing and dancing and dancing, throwing back her head and crooking her knee in that chanticleer stance we all know so well. If she must perform so uninterruptedly that she hasn't time for a sip of water, a nibble on a sandwich, or an unflustered costume change (some are made on stage by ripping her apart or basting her together in more or less full view), she can still get something out of that. She can get at least two show stoppers and an occasional "bravo" from left field (at which she grins, conspiratorially), though that's not exactly a monumental reward for the monumental work she's been doing (12 numbers by my count, not including reprises). And she can belt till her voice goes broke. Coming straight on at us, snapping the brim of her white fedora much as mother Judy used to snap the brim of her black one, she attacks with a bold and regular and don't-say-no-to-me beat. She is skilled, she is indefatigable, she is able at every angular twist and turn, and she is wasting her best talents. That's what I mind. With all the proficiency she's acquired, with all the power she can bring to a downbeat (heavily miked), with all the magnetism she exerts in the thrust of an elbow or the lift of an ankle, singing and dancing aren't really her truest gifts, which is probably why all the dances in *The Act* come to seem the same dance, all the songs the same song. Down deep, she's an actress. The star is left, then, going through the motions of emotion before she's been able to create any, and we're relieved, finally, when she gets into one or another of her sequined red, blue and purple gowns to show off her legs again and earn her living on high-kicks. But that's backwards for Miss Minnelli, and *The Act* can be regarded as a betrayal. Continuing in mere floor shows, she'll turn into a mechanical doll. There's got to be a film script or a play lying fallow somewhere, one that would tease into life once more the actress's finest natural equipment. Liza, please look for it.

HOWARD KISSEL, *WOMEN'S WEAR DAILY*

If, out of sheer perversity, you wanted to make a case for *The Act*, you might say its creators were ahead of their time—they assumed that by the time *The Act* reached New York we would already have legalized gambling and there would be a need for this kind of entertainment as a respite from the crap tables. Both the book and the songs are totally synthetic, utterly devoid of honest emotions. From all we've read about this show over the last few months, the book has probably been trimmed drastically, so we have been spared much—but the result is something that looks like an outline for a book rather than the real thing. Kander and Ebb have been writing for Liza Minnelli for a dozen years now, so they tend to write vehicles for her—carefully designed to take advantage of everything she can do, but devoid of content, musical or emotional. The combination of book and score adds up to the hollowest material for Broadway in memory. What makes all these sins cardinal rather than venal is the arrogance of the whole conception—the idea of doing a musical in which all the songs but one are sung by the star (the exception is sung by the dancers, who complain that they

SAN FRANCISCO

Civic Light Opera

40TH ANNIVERSARY SEASON

A FEUER & MARTIN PRODUCTION

LIZA MINNELLI

in the New Musical Play

"SHINE IT ON"

also starring

BARRY NELSON

with
LEONARD GAINES · GAYLE CROFOOT
and
MARK GODDARD

Book by
GEORGE FURTH

Music by   Lyrics by
JOHN KANDER   FRED EBB

Scenery Designed by   Costumes Designed by   Lighting Designed by   Sound Designed by
TONY WALTON   THEA VAN RUNKLE   THARON MUSSER   ABE JACOB

Musical Direction   Orchestrations   Dance Arrangements   Vocal & Choral Arrangements
STANLEY LEBOWSKY   RALPH BURNS   RONALD MELROSE   EARL BROWN

Miss Minnelli's Hairstyle   Production Stage Manager
SYDNEY GUILAROFF   PHIL FRIEDMAN

Choreography by
RON LEWIS
·
Directed by
MARTIN SCORSESE

JULY 19 through AUGUST 27

Now at the Newly Refurbished

ORPHEUM THEATRE

at the Civic Center (8th & Market)

1192 MARKET STREET · SAN FRANCISCO 94102

FOR TICKET INFORMATION (415) 552-4002

RIDE BART TO THE CIVIC LIGHT OPERA

The Act, a.k.a. *Shine It On*, a.k.a. *In Person*, a.k.a. *Liza with a Zero*. Among the many departees was the costume designer; no wonder, if this sketch is an indication. Preliminary credits. (artwork by Thea Van Runkle)

do all the work and she gets the applause ["Little Do They Know"], a clever idea but not an accurate one, since Minnelli works as hard and dances as well as most of them, and they are the best gypsies in town, except for the ones down the block at the Shubert [in *A Chorus Line* (1975)]). Even Ethel Merman's shows have duets and trios (but then she is just a star—the press invariably refers to Minnelli as a superstar). Here she doesn't make you aware of how hard she's working—she knocks herself out but it seems effortless. She sings beautifully, her dancing is dazzling—but all the material is empty, so the effect is nil. (We will overlook her wooden acting since the book is so primitive.) For those of us who take musical theatre seriously, *The Act* is a disturbing throwback; for tourists, it's perfect, though they will be more aware than locals that when you pay these prices for a show in Vegas, at least they throw in a couple of drinks.

DOUGLAS WATT, *DAILY NEWS*

It's not Liza Minnelli IN *The Act* that you catch at the Majestic, where the vibrant, long-legged song-and-dance star was introduced Saturday night in a big-band stage show with a sunburst opening effect. Liza Minnelli IS *The Act*, a performer out to kill an audience with everything except bodily contact, and it almost goes without saying that on her own terms she emerges triumphant. Evidently because of a touching desire on the part of all concerned to make this a Broadway "musical" rather than just another in-person show, there is a thread of a story. What is one to say of such cold perfection? Yes, cold, for this show, and especially the glacial love-story interludes with their corny smart talk ("book" by George Furth), is all technique and expertise "as cold as a stripper's behind," to quote [co-star Barry] Nelson. Whatever else the star radiates, it's not warmth, though I'm aware that those balcony devotees who got so caught up in Michelle's adventures that they hollered "We love you, Liza!" would kill to refute this. And after awhile, I got tired of the constant assault on the senses. Although Gower Champion, in charge during recent weeks, receives no program mention ("directed by Martin Scorsese" and "choreography by Ron Lewis"), I thought I could detect his light hand everywhere.

०   ०   ०

"If I can make it there, I'll make it anywhere. . . ." So goes the song. The star, director, songwriters, supporting players (2), arrangers, and even the costume designer of the 1977 movie *New York, New York* took their *Act* to Chicago. It was called, originally, *In Person* (although it was greeted as *Liza with a Zero*). Throwing out Thea Van Runkle's costumes ("Hello, Halston?") and supporting comic Leonard Gaines (from *N.Y., N.Y.*), *In Person* moved to the coast. They had already settled on *The Act* as the new title, but San Francisco was home of the American Conservatory Theatre (the A.C.T.) so they temporarily used *Shine It On* (a song title). After warning local ticket subscribers that the show was "adult-oriented"—refunds available—Los Angeles finally greeted *The Act* ("looked more like the rehearsal," said the local *Times*.) Next morning director Scorsese's wife filed for divorce. Nothing to do with Ms. Minnelli, of course, whose hubby, Jack Haley Jr., gave her a gold "Valium" as an opening night present (before they got *their* divorce). The star finally assented to dumping the director—due to an attack of asthma, they said, or maybe the affair was over? Gower Champion came in as Scorsese's replacement (in more ways than one) and proceeded to fix the show. As if it were that simple. "Scorsese's a terrific little guy," commented producer Cy Feuer (who's a terrific little guy himself), "a film genius, but, um, this is theatre." *The Act* cost about $900,000 to open in Chicago, but overtime fixings do not come cheap; the producers spent another $320,000 along the road to Broadway. (On the bright side, they were able to amass an impressive $450,000 in operating profits during the fifteen-week, record-breaking tryout tour.) And so *The Act* finally came to town. "Don't blame us for the shape the show is in," asserted librettist Furth, "it's all Scorsese's fault." There could be some truth to this; while the director was very much in attendance during the tryout, he apparently spent performance time not in the auditorium with a notepad but backstage in the star's dressing room. "Gower has had only three weeks to repair the damage Scorsese did," Furth continued, although he later sued the producers for a cool mill for reducing *his* royalties to help pay for Gower. Hollywood producer-director Stanley Donen, meanwhile, sued Furth, Kander, Ebb, and Minnelli for *two* mill, claiming he brought them all together in the first place and was frozen out of *The Act*. Feuer had foreseen the show's Broadway reception ("I'm going to go there and get the hell kicked out of me by all of the newspapers and then do great business anyway"). But the great business wasn't quite as great as expected, despite a record-high $25-top. *The Act* was dealt a severe blow when the star started missing performances—twenty-six in all, a full ten percent of the New York run. As there was no show without Liza, there was no understudy. The work week was cut down to seven performances, then it dwindled down to six. And then there were none. "This is one the Shubert Organization is not going to get rich from," to quote Gerry Schoenfeld. Oh, and Liza did get remarried—not to the director, or to the director's replacement (who stepped in to play Minnelli's husband during his vacation, her *on*stage husband that is)—but to the assistant stage manager, whose father had been the assistant stage manager of her 1965 debut-musical *Flora, the Red Menace*. Whatever that may mean. (You think I make this stuff up?)

A Tony Award was won by Liza Minnelli (actress).

BROADWAY SCORECARD
/ PERFS: 233 / $: –

RAVE	FAVORABLE	MIXED	UNFAVORABLE	PAN
	2	1	1	2

AIN'T MISBEHAVIN'

"The New Fats Waller Musical Show"

music mostly by Thomas "Fats" Waller (1904–1943)

based on an idea by Murray Horwitz and Richard Maltby, Jr.

conceived and directed by Richard Maltby

choreographed by Arthur Faria

produced by Emanuel Azenberg, Dasha Epstein, The Shubert Organization, Jane Gaynor, and Ron Dante

starring Nell Carter, Andre De Shields, Armelia McQueen, Ken Page, and Charlaine Woodard (replacing Irene Cara)

opened May 8, 1978   *Longacre Theatre*

CLIVE BARNES, *POST*

A joyous celebration. Fats Waller was one of the great jazz pianists of our time—he mastered the style of the stride piano and made it into a special musical form of fun and fantasy. He lived well and died young. Like his friend, Louis Armstrong, he was a comedian as well as musician. A comedian with a black soul and a black heart. You will find giggles galore at the show, which struts and parades with glee. It could however have, just perhaps, been called the last of the great black minstrel shows, for Waller, with his indisputable greatness, always seemed slightly more conscious than most jazzmen of his potential white audience. *Ain't Misbehavin'*, which I loved, accurately reflects this. It started at the Manhattan Theatre Club earlier in the season, and it is going to cross the world. The production has been changed slightly, but it is basically the same. And basically gorgeous. This really is Fats Waller on Broadway. It is a memorial that breathes. It is a testament to a curious genius—one of the very few people you seem to know from the memories of their recorded voice. It has been conceived and directed by Richard Maltby, Jr. It involves a fine veteran jazzman on piano, Luther Henderson, a good orchestra, and five performers who will sweep your heart away. Maltby's staging has taken Waller's musical voice and transfixed it for our present time. The music—not just Waller's but the essence of Waller's recordings—is at one level. The performance is attitudinized. It takes a slightly objective, slightly satirical, slightly—if you like—camp point of view. In all this it seems that Luther Henderson, credited as pianist, a bearded figure in a derby, and also for musical supervision, orchestrations and arrangements, has been essential. Maltby has put the show together with great finesse. But what really makes Waller live again out there on that Broadway stage are five lovely, loving, fantastic, fantasticated people. The cast. All of them work together to make *Ain't Misbehavin'* quite simply a Broadway show that you will never forget. And it is really Waller. It really is.

RICHARD EDER, *TIMES*

What whistles, hoots, throws off sparks and moves at about 180 miles an hour, even though it is continually stopped? *Ain't Misbehavin'*. This musical recreation of Fats Waller is a whole cluster of marvels. No self-respecting audience could let it go on without interrupting it continually, and if the audience last night was self-respecting to start off, it ended up in a state of agitated delight. A whole series of the jazz worlds of the time, uptown and downtown, raffish and posh—the posh had an edge of mockery to it—funny and startlingly beautiful, came to life. We are conducted through it by five singers, a gentle-fingered, garter-sleeved pianist named Luther Henderson, and a small band in the background. When Henderson got into his most vigorous stride—a two-beat rhythm: bass-note, chord, bass-note, chord—the piano sidled sideways as if being pumped. At the end of the first act, when the cast cake-walked off-stage, the piano bobbed along after them. The company warms up with the show's title song, engagingly performed. This is ground-level, relatively speaking; pleasant as it is, it leads up to one of the half-dozen totally charged, hair-raising numbers that lift the show from merely delightful to electrifying. This first peak is "Honeysuckle Rose." Rather, it is Ken Page, portly, loose-jointed and gravel-voiced, holding his stomach so it won't get away and belting out one note that he holds past resuscitation. Having held it, he tastes it, wrinkles his mouth, and looks rueful. And into his arms, like a large parcel mailing itself, sidles Nell Carter. Round-faced and rounder-bodied, she establishes beyond doubt and with lyric conviction that she is unquestionably the honeysuckle rose that all the fuss is about. Miss Carter can blare like a trumpet, moan like a muted trumpet, and do 100 variations on breathiness. Her "Mean to Me" is sung quietly, but with a silvery, delicate pungency—her round face suddenly becomes a prism of shifting expressions—that could lead an army.

WALTER KERR, *TIMES*
[Headline: "A Rousing *Ain't Misbehavin'*"]
To put it as judiciously as possible, *Ain't Misbehavin'* has a first act that will knock your ears off and a second that will come back for the rest of you. This sung, spoken, squealed, whispered, growled and windswept tribute to Fats Waller originated as a cabaret entertainment at the Manhattan Theatre Club, where it seems to have blown the roof away. Noticing the draft, and the demand for seats, its five performers have now tapped, slithered and swivel-hipped their way from the East 70's to the West 40's. Let's pass over the evening's first half, which is merely rousing. Suffice it to say that "Honeysuckle Rose" is given a partly sweet and partly burst-steampipe manhandling, womanhandling, and whatever other kind of handling there is by Ken Page and Nell Carter (Miss

Carter can provide as simple a word as "you" with enough syllables to put "antidisestablishmentarianism" to shame); that "Squeeze Me" is done in a shy libidinous hush by a slightly oversize kewpie-doll named Armelia McQueen; and that a piano solo called "Handful of Keys" turns out not to be a solo at all because everybody in the company becomes part of the piano, with the hefty Mr. Page taking care of the bass on his own. Perhaps I should mention that there is also an actual piano onstage beneath the purplish art-deco arches, a dusty chocolate-colored upright whose ivories are—mercifully—well moored to their wires; otherwise they'd likely be landing in our laps. But on to Act Two, which contains four or possibly five of the most explosively satisfying numbers I've ever come across in one of these revue-style rundowns. . . . Directed ever so precisely by Richard Maltby, Jr., with Luther Henderson hovering over the beautifully varied arrangements, the whole thing is exhilirating. Go and exhilirate yourself.

DOUGLAS WATT, DAILY NEWS
[Headline: "Joy Reigns Supreme"]
Jump for joy! *Ain't Misbehavin'* has moved downtown from its inspired beginnings at the Manhattan Theatre Club and transformed the Longacre into the warmest, most convivial spot in town. *Ain't Misbehavin'* is a rhapsodic treatment of songs and piano solos (newly equipped with words) either wholly composed by, collaborated on or else simply played or recorded by the late great Thomas (Fats) Waller. In spirit it evokes the late days of the Prohibition era when "vipers" smoked "reefers" and bootleg booze could be the worst or best, depending on your source of supply. Though the songs—especially such famous Waller numbers as "Honeysuckle Rose," "Keepin' Out of Mischief Now" and the title piece—often became international favorites transcending color lines, their interpretations by blacks (Waller and others) is and always has been matchless. And so it is here. When chunky Nell Carter, a black Mae West with a voice that could sound reveille for an entire regiment or croon it to sleep, lights into "Cash for Your Trash" or, with the pleasingly plump Armelia McQueen, lines out some advice for young ladies with "Find Out What They Like," your hat's in the air along with your head and the rest of you. And dig Miss Nell's "Mean to Me." Or when large Ken Page, nursing a drink at a nightclub table, uproariously insists

"Your Feet's Too Big"; or Andre De Shields, a Sportin' Life who's all snake hips in slow motion, inhales and exhales "The Viper's Drag"; or the slender Charlaine Woodard declares she's "Keepin' out of Mischief Now"; or Miss McQueen, practically embroidered to the back of the piano, sweetly implores "Squeeze Me"—well, you'll be enthralled. And as if all the struttin', sashayin' and dancin'—and, sweet Lord, do they dance!—weren't enough to transport you along with those voices, consider the quiet moment when, all five on stools, they tear your heart out, individually and collectively, with that unique "(What Did I Do to Get So) Black and Blue." Since this is Broadway, the land of bristling microphones and loudspeakers by the carload, there is a tape deck and a pair of sound consoles at the rear of the theatre that look elaborate and complicated enough to send the show into space. But that's just what the cast of *Ain't Misbehavin'* does all by itself. Wow!

◦ ◦ ◦

Songwriter anthology revues can be treacherously difficult to pull off. One song after another after another after another can lead to monotony, no matter how entertaining the songs might be individually. *Ain't Misbehavin'*—compiled from songs identified with, though not necessarily written by, Thomas Waller—handily managed to skirt the hazards by capturing the personality of the bigger-than-life "Fats" and presenting it onstage. A strong and stellar cast certainly helped: Nell Carter sang herself to stardom, Armelia McQueen countered Carter, and Ken Page more or less stood in for the songwriter. (Orchestrator/arranger Luther Henderson, at the keys, was also of inestimable help in keeping the joint jumpin'.) Waller had never been especially visible along Broadway. The 1929 revue *Hot Chocolates* is memorable solely for one immortal song fashioned by Waller and lyricist Andy Razaf, namely "Ain't Misbehavin'." *Early to Bed*, a 1943 romp about college athletes who mistake a bordello for a girls' seminary, was his second and final visit; Waller died at the age of thirty-nine, during the show's 380-performance run. *Ain't Misbehavin'* was a smash from its very inception, when it was mounted in a cabaret space at the Manhattan Theatre Club. With a full-scale set by John Lee Beatty (and Charlaine Woodard replacing Irene Cara) the show triumphantly transferred to Broadway, where it frolicked for almost four years. A tenth anniversary original cast revival fizzled, though, despite—or perhaps because of?—the presence of Nell Carter, who was now a "big star" and threw the ensemble piece off kilter.

Winner of the New York Drama Critics' Circle Award. In addition to winning the Tony Award for Best Musical, Tonys were won by Richard Maltby Jr. (director) and Nell Carter (supporting actress).

BROADWAY SCORECARD
/ PERFS: 1,604 / $: +

RAVE	FAVORABLE	MIXED	UNFAVORABLE	PAN
5	1			

AMBASSADOR

"A New Musical," initially produced in 1971 in London

music by Don Gohman

lyrics by Hal Hackady

book by Don Ettlinger and Anna Marie Barlow (replacing Robert Upton)

based on the 1903 novel *The Ambassadors* by Henry James

directed by Stone Widney

choreographed by Joyce Trisler

produced by Gene Dingenary, Miranda D'Ancona, and Nancy Levering

starring Howard Keel and Danielle Darrieux

with David Sabin, Carmen Matthews, M'el Dowd, and Andrea Marcovicci

opened November 19, 1972   Lunt-Fontanne Theatre

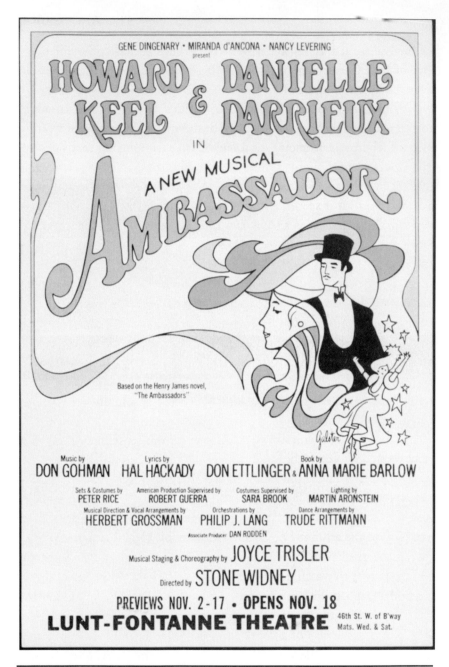

GENE DINGENARY • MIRANDA d'ANCONA • NANCY LEVERING
present

HOWARD & DANIELLE
KEEL DARRIEUX

IN

A NEW MUSICAL

AMBASSADOR

Based on the Henry James novel,
"The Ambassadors"

Galster

Music by   Lyrics by   Book by
DON GOHMAN   HAL HACKADY   DON ETTLINGER & ANNA MARIE BARLOW

Sets & Costumes by   American Production Supervised by   Costumes Supervised by   Lighting by
PETER RICE   ROBERT GUERRA   SARA BROOK   MARTIN ARONSTEIN

Musical Direction & Vocal Arrangements by   Orchestrations by   Dance Arrangements by
HERBERT GROSSMAN   PHILIP J. LANG   TRUDE RITTMANN

Associate Producer DAN RODDEN

Musical Staging & Choreography by   JOYCE TRISLER

Directed by STONE WIDNEY

PREVIEWS NOV. 2-17 • OPENS NOV. 18
LUNT-FONTANNE THEATRE   46th St. W. of B'way
                                                Mats. Wed. & Sat.

"An *Ambassador* with no diplomatic immunity," said Clive Barnes, with Doug Watt noting "each number seems calculated to stop the show, only by slowing it up." (artwork by Galster)

CLIVE BARNES, *TIMES*

The vulgarity of trying to make a Broadway musical out of what is defensibly Henry James's finest novel would be almost appealing had it succeeded. Unfortunately, *Ambassador* is effete and pallid, and not even the considerable efforts of its lively stars can make its anemia seem anything other than pernicious. The show is not a disgrace, merely a pity. One would have thought that its lack of success when it was staged in London more than a year ago would not have encouraged its Broadway presentation. But it seems that London's loss was never intended to be New York's gain. This is an *Ambassador* with no diplomatic immunity. Poor James's skeleton must be whirling around in its Cambridge graveyard.

JOSEPH H. MAZO, *WOMEN'S WEAR DAILY*

Ambassador is purportedly set in the Paris of 1906. Actually, it takes place on the Broadway of the '50s. The production is yet another bit of proof that the New York theatre is the second institution in the country to be 20 years behind the needs of the populace. (The first, of course, is the government.) *Ambassador* is not absolutely awful; it is merely awfully banal. The music, by Don Gohman, is totally unmemorable, yet it evokes memories of a lot of other music, such as the songs from *My Fair Lady* [1956]. The lyrics, by Hal Hackady, are indeed hack-a-day. The entire production seems designed to soothe the sensibilities of that theatrical pet, the tired businessman, but if he is really tired, the clichés will probably soothe him so much he'll fall asleep. It is possible, of course, that Danielle Darrieux will wake him up now and again. Darrieux has so much charm and such command of her craft that she is a delight to watch even when the authors have given her nothing worthwhile to do. She is the only excuse for happiness in the entire affair. The production apparently was conceived in the belief that 1950s Broadway was the best of all possible worlds, and it proceeds to become the best of all possible arguments against its own viewpoint. It will probably be a dandy tax loss for somebody.

DOUGLAS WATT, *DAILY NEWS*

While there is nothing grievously wrong with last night's new musical, there is nothing very right about it, either. It is so conventional and downright corny that it winds up looking and sounding like a pale imitation of other period musicals, several of which came to mind as the evening drifted along in its inoffensive and uneventful way. Each number seems calculated to stop the show, as the late Prof. Alexander Drummond once observed in a backstage note to a hopeful actress, only by slowing it up. And Peter Rice's scenery and costumes for the ensemble have a seedy look that suggest that the *Belle Époque* might have been centered in old Coney Island. The songs, though lacking in any true invention, are at least literate, and it so happened that two of the most affecting of them, "Love Finds the Lonely" and a maiden's breathless cry called "Mama," fall to a lovely ingénue named Andrea Marcovicci, whose singing of them raised my spirits. But she was given little else to occupy her, alas.

○   ○   ○

Unable to raise the necessary financing for Broadway, the American producers decided to first mount their *Ambassador* in London (in 1971), where it was indeed somewhat cheaper (only $240,000). Excuse me, less expensive. Having lost *that* money, they added bookwriter Barlow to the package; replaced choreographer Gillian Lynne with Joyce Trisler; and then went ahead and did it on Broadway (another $360,000 down the tubes). Some savings. *Ambassador*'s mannered atmosphere was evident in the very opening moment of the show, when the curtain rose and the chorus sang "Stop the clock/The *Belle Époque!*"

BROADWAY SCORECARD
/ PERFS: 9 / $: –

RAVE	FAVORABLE	MIXED	UNFAVORABLE	PAN
			1	5

ANGEL

"A New Musical," previously entitled *All the Comforts of Home*

music by Gary Geld

lyrics by Peter Udell

book by Ketti Frings and Peter Udell

based on the Pulitzer Prize-winning 1957 play *Look Homeward, Angel* by Ketti Frings, from the 1929 autobiographical novel by Thomas Wolfe

directed by Philip Rose

choreographed by Robert Tucker

produced by Philip Rose and Ellen Madison

starring Frances Sternhagen and Fred Gwynne

with Don Scardino, Joel Higgins, Leslie Ann Ray, Patricia Englund, and Patti Allison

opened May 10, 1978   Minskoff Theatre

CLIVE BARNES, *POST*

[Headline: "Wingless *Angel*"]

To be honest I never quite knew what I thought of Thomas Wolfe's novel *Look Homeward, Angel*, which I struggled with as a youth. I was entranced by its romanticism, its image, to use Wolfe's later phrase, as life between a web and a rock. I was also appalled by its fustian rhetoric. However, I had no doubts whatsoever about Ketti Frings' 1957 Pulitzer Prize-winning adaptation of the novel as a play. This was a poor, diluted thing, owing as much to William Inge, I should have imagined, as to Wolfe. Last night Miss Frings—helped by the team that a few seasons back gave us the successful but culturally uneventful *Shenandoah* [1975]—devised a musical version of her play. The songs hardly helped, although probably they hardly hurt either. It was a vulgarization to begin with, so why not go the whole hog and make it into an old-fashioned musical with a new-style lachrymosity to it? Why not a musical version of *A Portrait of the Artist as a Young Man* [James Joyce's 1916 work], replete with Irish jigs? Peter Udell has produced the lyrics— "People are like petals put upon a pond, drifting, drifting, drifting," etc., etc., etc. They are not all that awful, but they are worse than Miss Frings. The music by Gary Geld seems to be a pastiche of Jerome Kern. I love Kern. But I doubt whether Kern would compose like Kern were he alive today. And even should he be so foolish, he would not escape the results of such folly. The music sounds faintly like agreeably tuneful music in someone else's elevator. Philip Rose, who is also the producer, has directed the show as if it were a fifties' melodrama—watch the way all those people eye one another and react to the message. The scenery by Ming Cho Lee is a knockout. The original play was designed by Jo Mielziner. Lee was Mielziner's apprentice. He has learned decorative sorcery of infinite value. This design is perhaps a homage to Jo—it takes his concept of interplanes of reality, and yet uses it with a different flair. It was just the show that didn't work.

RICHARD EDER, *TIMES*

Throughout *Angel*, the tall frame house that serves as its principal set turns first this way, then that way, and finally shudders around in a complete circle. It is like an insomniac tossing in a clammy bed. Its writhings are understandable. *Angel* is a damp and oppressive amalgam of bathos. It has lyrics of the consistency of cornbread soaked in milk, a whole collection of indifferent performances and a score of sufficient banality to furnish a number or two for the piped music on airplanes waiting to take off. *Angel* is based on Ketti Frings's adaptation of *Look Homeward, Angel*, and without having seen it I cannot say whether this *Angel* is a travesty of it, or simply a travesty of Thomas Wolfe's torrential novel. Frings collaborated on the book, but the main responsibility seems to lie with Gary Geld and Peter Udell, the composer-lyricist team that did *Shenandoah*. That was fairly bland, but *Angel* takes its empty candy-box quality to monumental lengths: it is famine in a candy factory. The authors have made pastel-colored postcards out of Wolfe's Gants. *Angel* has no feeling to it, only slickness, and the oddities are flattened out into marshmallows, and these are hooked together in awkward and absurd transitions. Eliza Gant's boarding house is a rest home for musical clichés. Each step of the way has its forgettable song. The performances have no shine to them, at best they are losing battles. Don Scardino is likable as Eugene, and has a boyish springiness that wears out quickly. Joel Higgins, as Ben, manages to make our chests hurt when he coughs, but doesn't get much else to do. Frances Sternhagen has some proficiency as Eliza Gant, but she wavers continually between feeling and folksiness, and becomes as improbable as everyone else. Fred Gwynne is plain bad as old Gant. He caricatures the role of eccentric drunk and wastrel artist by waggling his hands, screwing up his mouth and rolling or contorting his remaining features. Somebody should disconnect his eyebrows. Geld's score is so thin and trite as to make us notice Don Walker's orchestration. It's vulgarity is unfailing. Philip Rose's contribution as director seems negligible. It is putting things too strongly to call *Angel* a disaster. It is a desert.

CHRISTOPHER SHARP, *WOMEN'S WEAR DAILY*

Angel fails on two counts. It contains so many arcane references to *Look Homeward, Angel* that those who aren't familiar with the subject will probably feel left out. It is likely, however, that those who have read Wolfe's book or seen Frings' play will be even more confused. There is nothing about this production that is like anything Thomas Wolfe would have done. The Wolfe prototype resembles the novelist about as much as Stan Laurel resembled Oliver Hardy. The music and lyrics by Gary Geld and Peter Udell have ignored the wealth of folk music that has come out of Wolfe's North Carolina and opted instead for a sound that is as unimposing as Muzak. This production is also handicapped in that it doesn't have a strong lead singer to push these cumbersome songs along. Frances Sternhagen, who plays Wolfe's mother, is a fine actress in the Julie Harris style, but she doesn't sing well at all here. She tries to sing in character, cracking her voice as she maneuvers around the music, but the songs—which are corny enough without her—turn into cracked corn with her. Fred Gwynne is also very entertaining as the father, but as a singer he's pathetic. Don Scardino's Eugene would remind us of Thomas Wolfe if Wolfe had been a foot shorter and had lost 100 points from his I.Q. The only outstanding aspect of this production is Joel Higgins' depiction of Eugene's sickly brother, Ben. Higgins is one of the few performers who can tie all the loose strings of his character together when he sings. His voice is outstanding. But even with the superb voice of Higgins and the fine acting by Sternhagen, this *Angel* falls far short of being seraphic.

0   0   0

This third and final offering from the *Purlie* (1970) boys had been skedded for production by Circle in the Square, simultaneously with their second musical, *Shenandoah*. But things didn't work out, and *Angel*—the weakest of the three—floundered until it was finally taste-tested at a dinner theatre (Northstage Theatre Restaurant, in the wilds of Glen Cove, Long Island). The entrée proved overdone, bland, and tough, obviously ill-suited to further exposure. So naturally they transferred it to Broadway. Five sittings only, no reservation necessary.

BROADWAY SCORECARD
/ PERFS: 5 / $: –

RAVE	FAVORABLE	MIXED	UNFAVORABLE	PAN
	1		2	3

ANNIE

"A New Broadway Musical"

music by Charles Strouse

lyrics by Martin Charnin

book by Thomas Meehan

based on the comic strip *Little Orphan Annie* (since 1924) by Harold Gray

directed by Martin Charnin

choreographed by Peter Gennaro

presented by Mike Nichols; "Produced by Irwin Meyer, Stephen R. Freidman, Lewis Allen"; "Produced by Alvin Nederlander Associates Inc. [James M. Nederlander], The John F. Kennedy Center for the Performing Arts [Roger L. Stevens], Icarus Productions [Mike Nichols]"; "Produced in association with Peter Crane" [all accorded title page billing]

starring Andrea McArdle, Reid Shelton, Dorothy Loudon, Sandy Faison, and Robert Fitch

with Raymond Thorne, Laurie Beechman, and Barbara Erwin

opened April 21, 1977   *Alvin Theatre*

CLIVE BARNES, *TIMES*

To dislike *Annie* would be tantamount to disliking motherhood, peanut butter, friendly mongrel dogs and nostalgia. It also would be unnecessary, for *Annie* is an intensely likable musical. You might even call it lovable, it seduces one, and should settle down to being a sizable hit. Because I usually have a healthy, normal, W. C. Fields attitude toward performing children and performing dogs, this means more from me than it would coming from someone who customarily swoons at the theatrical glint of a little girl's petticoat, or the canine grin of a histrionically inclined pooch. The show, which originated, like so many other Broadway musicals, at Michael Price's Goodspeed Opera, has a rare kind of gutsy charm. It takes what could be the pure dross of sentimentality and turns it into a musical of sensibility. The music by Charles Strouse is tuneful and supportive. It is neither unduly inventive nor memorable, but the overall impression is distinctly pleasing. It is amiable music that washes over one in a manner both comforting and comfortable. The worst aspect of the show is Martin Charnin's lyrics, which are bland to the point of banality; but even this could have been intentional, for obviously nothing is intended to disturb the show's air of amiable nostalgia. It is meant to be a show to experience, not a show to think about. Where Charnin, in his capacity as director or, possibly, Mike Nichols in, for him, the unusual capacity of producer, have been superbly effective is in giving the show a style of its own. Here the collaborators are provided with a jet-propelled lift from the settings by David Mitchell. If ever that old joke about leaving the theatre humming the scenery was justified, this could be the occasion. The neatly stylized costumes by Theoni V. Aldredge add considerably to the spectacular visual brilliance of the show, which is one of the best-looking Broadway musicals we have had in years. The Broadway musical was once celebrated all over the world for its sheer efficiency. In recent years this reputation has been somewhat tarnished, despite occasional inspirations. *Annie* really works on all levels. It is that now rare animal—the properly built, handsomely groomed Broadway musical. And leapin' lizards (sorry, I had to say it somewhere!), you're welcome.

MARTIN GOTTFRIED, POST
[Headline: "Leapin' Lizards! *Annie* Has Hit the Big Bucks"]
Annie is at the heart of musical comedy, big, warmhearted, funny and overflowing with spirit. Innovative? It's practically reactionary—a book show thoroughly, even brazenly conventional, from structure to style. Yet the damned thing works, God knows it works, and working is the theatre's absolute excuse. *Annie* is a delightful new old-fashioned show and on a Broadway that's gone so long without musicals till this week, it couldn't be more welcome. *Annie*, bless its show business heart, deals in out-and-out greasepaint sentiment. It has no qualms about arbitrarily dressing its chorus as the impoverished unemployed and setting them to song and dance. It cheerfully makes Franklin D. Roosevelt a

musical comedy figure, vocal limitation and all. Hell, this is a show with
an orphan girl, a chorus of children, a dog and Christmas Eve. Indeed,
for all its unabashed corniness and disregard of theatrical progress,
Annie presents the kind of show we've missed. It hardly advances musical theatre but theory must step aside for any production that simply
works and *Annie* works. It has hit stamped all over it.

WALTER KERR, *TIMES*

I know you'll go to *Annie* without any nudging from me, and I'd be the
last to say you nay. I was in fact a naysayer when I first saw the entertainment at the Goodspeed Opera House last summer. Thought it did-
n't have a chance. But two things have happened since, one to it, one to
me. The most important thing that's happened to it is that the authors
have made up their minds about what they're doing: to Harold Gray's
popular, aggressively reactionary comic strip, and to Daddy Warbucks,
ruthless apostle of rugged individualism and champion F.D.R.-hater of
all time. What they've done to the script is drop it (not even a credit for
Mr. Gray on the program): gone are the derisive snorts, from Annie and
others, as Roosevelt routs fear on the radio. And Warbucks, once baffling-
gly ambiguous as he sanctified private enterprise while virtually forcing
the New Deal upon the President, is now a staunch but common-sensical Republican who concedes that Roosevelt is a "human being" after all.
Fair enough. If you're going to adapt materials for another medium,
you're free to take liberties; they just have to be consistent liberties, that's
all. What's happened to me is that I've acquired a new respect for Mike
Nichols's prescience. I've always known about his other talents, but I
hadn't fancied him as mythmaker, prophet, seer. Nichols, pretty much
single-handedly, decided to take over the property and mount it on
Broadway, and what I want to know is how he knew that this was the
very moment in history when audiences had decided to forswear sophistication, forswear sanity even, and go for a revel in the lovely preposterous. The show isn't kidding. It *means* to be unbelievable. That, I would
now guess, is its whole appeal. Though Nichols himself is a man who
finds it extraordinarily difficult to get his tongue out of his cheek, he has
done nothing to push his creative people toward parity. Except for the
blowsily maniacal tarantula that Dorothy Loudon makes of her orphanage head-mistress (she seems to have come from *Mad* magazine rather
than the Chicago *Tribune* syndicate), *Annie* doesn't care much about

building jokes. It doesn't even push for a calculated charm, which probably spares it coyness. At heart it's straight, bland as those blank eyes that Annie's always had, open, expansive, opulent, innocent.

DOUGLAS WATT, *DAILY NEWS*
If there is such a thing as a kiddie show for adults, then I suppose *Annie* must be it. The big, splashy, sentimental, old-fashioned musical had the audience applauding vociferously when it wasn't rapt in the tale of the 11-year-old orphan, or, as in the case of a lone female voice breaking the silence, gasping with pleasure when Daddy Warbucks tells Annie, "I love you." For Charles Strouse's score, while mirroring the '30s, is dismayingly commonplace, substituting energy for worth in such pieces as "N.Y.C.," a Times Square paean to the city; "Easy Street," in which the conspirators sing and dance about their rosy future, and a few other instances in which sound and movement are used to disguise the thin musical material, whose usually commonplace lyrics with their often predictable rhymes are the work of director Martin Charnin. Peter Gennaro is responsible for the breezy dance routines. *Annie* goes down as easily as an Orange Julius and would, indeed, make an ideal Christmas show (especially Miss Loudon as a Wicked Witch of the East Side) for children, say, from 7 to 11. But as I have remarked, Wednesday's audience ate it up, so perhaps it's for kiddies of all ages, who may very well keep it humming for months to come.

o　o　o

Annie began trodding her long road to Broadway in 1971, when Martin Charnin chanced upon an anthology of strips about the little orphan. He brought in Tom Meehan (with whom he'd worked on TV) and Broadway veteran Charles Strouse, just then flush with *Applause* (1970). The trio finished the piece in mid-1973—but funds with which to mount it were impossible to raise. A stock tryout was finally arranged for the summer of '76 at the Goodspeed Opera House, which had sent its '74 *Shenandoah* and '75 *Very Good Eddie* successfully to Broadway. *Annie* at Goodspeed was merely a fair-to-middlin' kids' show with mediocre songs, but Mike Nichols happened upon it and more or less adopted little *Annie*. The presence of golden-boy Nichols pried open enough checkbooks to buy her a new red dress, though it took a lot of checkbooks (as evidenced by the half-dozen producer credits). The curly wigged waif came out from behind her silver-lined cloud and found, bet your bottom dollar, that her cloud was indeed lined with sterling. Nichols, of course, was a director—and one with a magic touch. (He had never produced before; neither had any of the principal partners except Lewis Allen, whose credits included the 1965 *Half a Sixpence*.) The Goodspeed *Annie* needed a magic touch, certainly, and was indeed transformed on its way to the Big Time, leading some to assume the logically assumable. But Mike Nichols, in fact, did not direct *Annie*; he was omnisciently present through the tryout and in constant attendance, but it was Marty Charnin in the rehearsal halls and Marty Charnin giving the actors notes. Nichols and the authors had morning meetings, though, at which point the director—Nichols, I mean—no doubt contributed ideas, suggestions, and one would guess a few jokes. Most crucially, Nichols seems responsible for *Annie*'s secret weapon—a germ of reality, a grain of truth—without which the musical would have remained merely a fair-to-middlin' kids' show with mediocre songs. The show also benefited greatly from the post–Goodspeed presence of Dorothy Loudon, who stepped in to turn a subsidiary role into a star turn. (Nichols's first musical attempt, a Lewis Allen-produced 1962 summer stock tryout called *The World of Jules Feiffer*, featured Loudon as *Passionella* with songs by Sondheim.) *Annie*'s two Nichols-less sequels were undernourished, certainly. *Annie 2 (Miss Hannigan's Revenge)* was pronounced dead on arrival at its 1990 Kennedy Center tryout, even with Dorothy Loudon kicking up a storm. (To those who say we should be less critical of "family shows" and heed audience reaction instead, I offer this eyewitness report: a sweet little ribboned-and-bowed miss, sitting in the sixth row off the aisle, threw up late in the first act—'round about the time the lyricist rhymed "squash" with "galoshes." Everybody's a critic!) *Annie 3*, officially known as *Annie Warbucks* (1993), followed the original's Goodspeed path but ignominiously dead-ended Off-Broadway. Charnin's theatre work is typically facile and clever, but he was never accused of being tasteful. Hence his musical theatre record of one Nichols-produced smash hit, eleven non-Nichols errors. <u>Just Cause Dept.</u>: Charnin returned to the Alvin from one of his absences, took a look at the cast, and fired a bunch of 'em. Which directly resulted in a new Actors' Equity rule forbidding the firing of actors simply because you don't like 'em anymore.

Winner of the New York Drama Critics' Circle Award. In addition to winning the Tony Award for Best Musical, Tonys were won by Charles Strouse and Martin Charnin (score), Tom Meehan (book), Peter Gennaro (choreographer), Dorothy Loudon (actress), David Mitchell (scenic design), and Theoni V. Aldredge (costume design, tied with Santo Loquasto for *The Cherry Orchard*).

BROADWAY SCORECARD

/ PERFS: 2,377 / $: +

RAVE	FAVORABLE	MIXED	UNFAVORABLE	PAN
4	I	I		

ANYA

"The Musical Musical!"

music and lyrics by Robert Wright and George Forrest (based on themes of Sergei Rachmaninoff [1873-1943])

book by George Abbott and Guy Bolton

based on the 1953 drama *Anastasia*, Guy Bolton's adaptation of the 1948 French play *La Tsarina* by Marcelle Maurette

directed by George Abbott

choreographed by Hanya Holm

produced by Fred R. Fehlhaber

starring Constance Towers, Michael Kermoyan (replacing George London), Lillian Gish, and Irra Petina

with George S. Irving, Boris Aplon, Ed Steffe, John Michael King, Karen Shepard, and Margaret Mullen

opened November 29, 1965   Ziegfeld Theatre

FRED R. FEHLHABER

presents

CONSTANCE MICHAEL LILLIAN
TOWERS KERMOYAN GISH

ANYA

A New Musical

also starring **IRRA PETINA**

with **GEORGE S. IRVING   BORIS APLON   ED STEFFE**
JOHN MICHAEL KING   KAREN SHEPARD   MARGARET MULLEN

Book by **GEORGE ABBOTT** and **GUY BOLTON**
(Based upon "ANASTASIA" by MARCELLE MAURETTE and GUY BOLTON)

Music and Lyrics by **ROBERT WRIGHT** and **GEORGE FORREST**
(Based on themes of S. RACHMANINOFF)

Musical Numbers and
Choreography by **HANYA HOLM**

Scenery by   Costumes by   Lighting by
ROBERT RANDOLPH   PATRICIA ZIPPRODT   RICHARD CASLER

Musical Direction by   Orchestrations by
HAROLD HASTINGS   **DON WALKER**
Original cast album by UNITED ARTISTS RECORDS

Production
Directed by **GEORGE ABBOTT**

ZIEGFELD THEATRE 6th AVE. at 54th STREET
MATS. WED. & SAT.

Citing some dialogue about Ivan the Terrible, Walter Kerr advised "If I were *Anya*, I'd watch out who I called terrible." (artwork by Tom Morrow)

WALTER KERR, *HERALD TRIBUNE*

In spite of the fact that *Anya* is an old-fashioned musical, it isn't any good. I put the case mildly. *Anya* opens with a full chorus of voices, dimly lighted behind a crest of all the Russias, calling out "Anya!" more or less in the manner of those sturdy baritones who used to call out "Chloe!" in that celebrated song of the swamplands. To the best of my knowledge no one ever found Chloe, but they do find Anya. They find the poor thing in an insane asylum after a thwarted suicide attempt. The child has leaped into a river only to be rescued—such is her luck—just in time to appear in this musical. "What is that song?" she says to herself, trying hard to remember a theme from Rachmaninoff, which shouldn't be as difficult as she makes it because all of the songs in the show are themes from Rachmaninoff. Failing to remember it, she sings another song, now that the orchestra is warmed up, and sings it prettily, too, much too prettily for what happens while she is singing it. While she is singing it another asylum inmate enters, listens a moment to the song, and then has a fit of hysterics. Criticism comes early these nights. Eventually Anya—Constance Towers plays the role, wide-eyed and at first in a green sweater—is spirited away to a chateau where she is offered for inspection by peasants. Blind Russian peasants can always tell a princess by feeling her finger-tips, even if they have obviously just been brought in from Eighth Avenue, and quite a few babushkas bob low—the balalaikas are silenced for the moment—and all the kneeling extras keep their hands clasped until they have finished saying their lines. When they have finished saying their lines they get to their feet again so as to be able to sway slightly while singing a ditty called "Snowflakes and Sweethearts." According to the lyrics, "Where there's a snowbird, there's a change of scene to come." The musical is now at the Ziegfeld, but I think I see a snowbird. . . . It seems Anya has fallen in love with Bounin, apparently because he shares billing with her above the title. [When angry, he yells:] "Get me the lash, the whip! Maybe Ivan the Terrible had the right idea after all!" If I were *Anya*, I'd watch out who I called terrible. No matter who the real Anastasia was I am going to cling to my blind conviction that the George Abbott who is listed as co-librettist and director is not the real George Abbott.

JOHN MCCLAIN, *JOURNAL-AMERICAN*

The whole thing is large and lavish, and they have fine voices going for them, but it seemed to me extremely dated. There was the other fact that the heroine is revealed as a hopeless mental case during most of the early episodes. Constance Towers has, in my opinion, the most unrewarding role seen around here in many a moon. She is actually quite decorative and she has a capable set of pipes, but for a large part of the evening she remains as unattractive as possible, which is somewhat. In the final analysis it is a sort of out-dated musical about someone you don't have too much interest in. I don't care if she was Anastasia or not.

NORMAN NADEL, *WORLD-TELEGRAM & SUN*

The initials S. R. stand for Sergei Rachmaninoff and Sigmund Romberg—a thought which had never occurred to me until the opening of *Anya* last night. Publicized as a "musical musical," it actually is nothing more, or frequently much less, than an old-fashioned operetta. I do not mean to slight the memory of Romberg, who was a dear man, a good friend, and a grand melodist. But when Rachmaninoff themes sound like Romberg ballads, something is very wrong. It isn't only the music. The staging, by Abbott, either obscures or ignores the depths and values of *Anastasia*, just as the Wright-Forrest score cheapens the Rachmaninoff themes. Except for two of three performances, it is an insensitive and tasteless treatment. Drab, predictable lyrics are the rule. The enormous gulf between *Anya* as it is and *Anya* as it might have been is revealed in the radiance which Constance Towers bestows on the role of the princess. She stands like a queen above the surrounding shambles. Lillian Gish adds some vitality to the second act. George Abbott does some musicals notably well. However, both the writing and direction of *Anya* indicate that he had the wrong concept from the very beginning. If you merely reread *Anastasia* and listen to some good recordings of Rachmaninoff's music, you'll be years ahead.

◦   ◦   ◦

"Song-tinkers" Wright and Forrest enjoyed stupendous success de-composing songs by Grieg (*Song of Norway* [1944]) and Borodin

(*Kismet* [1953]), but their raids on Victor Herbert (*Gypsy Lady* [1946]), Villa-Lobos (*Magdalena* [1948]), and Rachmaninoff were not so happy. These adapted scores were tuneful, at least, which was not necessarily the case with their "original" scores for *Spring in Brazil* (1945), *The Carefree Heart* (1957), *Kean* (1961), and *A Song for Cyrano* (1973). Also in the latter group was the 1958 Paul Muni–starrer *At the Grand*, which was revised and recycled somewhat successfully thirty-one years later as *Grand Hotel. Anya* herself received a twenty-four-year facelift with a 1989 stock production called *The Anastasia Game*, but she proved not to have legs. The 1965 *Anastasia* musical, by the way, *was* successful in closing down the Ziegfeld—which opened in 1927 with another mish-mash Guy Bolton operetta, *Rio Rita.*

BROADWAY SCORECARD
/ PERFS: 16 / $: –

RAVE	FAVORABLE	MIXED	UNFAVORABLE	PAN
			2	4

APPLAUSE

"A New Musical"

music by Charles Strouse

lyrics by Lee Adams

book by Betty Comden and Adolph Green (replacing Sidney Michaels)

based on the 1950 screenplay *All About Eve* by Joseph L. Mankiewicz, from the 1946 short story *The Wisdom of Eve* by Mary Orr

directed and choreographed by Ron Field

produced by Joseph Kipness and Lawrence Kasha, in association with Nederlander Productions and George M. Steinbrenner III

starring Lauren Bacall

with Penny Fuller (replacing Diane McAfee), Len Cariou, Robert Mandan, Ann Williams, Brandon Maggart, Lee Roy Reams, and Bonnie Franklin

opened March 30, 1970   *Palace Theatre*

CLIVE BARNES, *TIMES*

Whatever it is Miss Bacall possesses, she throws it around most beautifully, most exquisitely and most excitingly in a musical called *Applause* (it's really all about someone called Eve) which last night reclaimed the Palace Theater once more from the always invidious threat of moving pictures. Miss Bacall is a honey, and the book is among the best in years—so who is going to care too much about the second-rate music? Not, I am sure, the public. We have little enough—why should we now be choosy? Seriously, Miss Bacall is a sensation. She sings with all the misty beauty of an on-tune foghorn. She never misses a note—she is not one of your all-talking musical dramatics—and although her voice is not pretty, it does have the true beauty of unforgettability. Her danc-

JOSEPH KIPNESS & LAWRENCE KASHA
IN ASSOCIATION WITH
NEDERLANDER PRODUCTIONS & GEORGE M. STEINBRENNER III
PRESENT

LAUREN BACALL

IN

"APPLAUSE"

A NEW MUSICAL

BOOK BY

BETTY ADOLPH
COMDEN AND GREEN

MUSIC BY

CHARLES STROUSE

LYRICS BY

LEE ADAMS

BASED ON THE FILM "ALL ABOUT EVE"
AND THE ORIGINAL STORY BY MARY ORR

WITH

LEN ROBERT
CARIOU MANDAN

ANN BRANDON
WILLIAMS MAGGART

LEE ROY REAMS · BONNIE FRANKLIN

AND

PENNY FULLER

SCENERY BY   COSTUMES BY   LIGHTING BY
ROBERT RANDOLPH   RAY AGHAYAN   THARON MUSSER

MUSICAL DIRECTION & VOCAL ARRANGEMENTS BY   ORCHESTRATIONS BY   DANCE & INCIDENTAL MUSIC ARRANGED BY
DONALD PIPPIN   PHILIP J. LANG   MEL MARVIN

DIRECTED & CHOREOGRAPHED BY

RON FIELD

ORIGINAL CAST ALBUM BY abc

The gracious star takes a bow against a spotlight. Doesn't look much like Bacall, does it? (artwork by Clyde Smith)

ing is more conventional—she is averagely, if beautifully, groovy. Her acting is her own thing. Miss Bacall is probably going to be the Marlene Dietrich of the 1980's—she has that same enchantingly cool asexual sexuality. She has that same well-bred air of experience hard-won and the sensibility of well-trimmed honesty. She is the kind of girl everyone would be proud to have as a sister; but she is also a bright, bright star, fascinating but unmenacing. Even potential hit shows are entitled to a few weaknesses and with *Applause* it is the music, which while never unpleasant, has a kind of "here-we-go-round-again" sound to it that is more soothing than stimulating. I got the impression that the Lee Adams lyrics were a lot more lively than was the score by Charles Strouse. Even so Mr. Strouse never actually does anything wrong. But then he never does such a great amount that is actually right. Len Cariou as the wonderboy director, straight as an arrow and as fast as Mike Nichols, is a bluff, tough delight: just the kind of person that no one in the audience would mind carrying off Miss Bacall. I always knew Mr. Cariou could act very well indeed, yet I was surprised he could sing. (Yet I was not surprised about Miss Bacall being able to sing; I would even expect her to be great at chess.) The cast as a whole was superior but it was Miss Bacall's night. She is a good lady, and New York is going to love her and love her—we take her to our brittle hearts.

JOHN CHAPMAN, *DAILY NEWS*
If Lauren Bacall put her mind and her other bountiful equipment to it, she could make a hit out of *Coco* [1969]. She and all her playmates have brought a smashing hit to the Palace—and the Palace Theatre is just the right place for this show, which is all about show biz.

MARTIN GOTTFRIED, *WOMEN'S WEAR DAILY*
Applause came coasting into the Palace Theatre with all the drive that confidence inspires, and though a lot of that confidence was rooted in a false belief in its own publicity, the show still has it. The new musical overrode its flaws with a fake security that was a lot like the very show business it meant to criticize. Though its genuine assets are limited to a great star performance, excellent music and glittering polish, they are adequate enough, especially these days, when the traditional polish of Broadway musicals has become not so traditional. The show follows

Joseph Mankiewicz's screenplay roughly, as musicals are forced to do while sandwiching musical numbers between plot sketches. Adolph Green and Betty Comden have hardly the sophistication of Mankiewicz and their book is the weakest part of the show (their out-dated style of satire having long since become self-satirical), but at least they have been kept from writing lyrics. Still, the story elements remain and they are good ones. Perhaps it comes on too foolishly as a hymn to tough old show business, but it does include a well written role and Lauren Bacall has capitalized on it sensationally. Miss Bacall has all the material an actress could possibly want, and all the talent and drive to capitalize on it. She works her ass off. She is seldom off-stage and when she is on she is either singing, dancing or acting. It is the acting that is most impressive because Miss Bacall creates a real and special character, turning the most important acting trick of actually becoming somebody else (you truly forget it is Bacall). Her Margo Charming is selfish and generous, tough and touchy, paranoid and perceptive. As a singer, Miss Bacall has a slightly more than serviceable, well, baritone, but she is thoroughly musical and senses the music, the rhythm, of everything she sings: she performs the music. She also dances—throwing everything into it, as she does with whatever she is called upon to do. She is marvelous and sensational. Robert Randolph's sets, aside from being handsome and hugely expensive, were as technically elaborate as anything I've yet seen. So, the show is good looking. It is by no means funny or perceptive and is never as thrilling as it thinks it is. Still, it is a glittering, super-professional splash of musical theatre and Broadway hasn't seen that in a long time.

WALTER KERR, *TIMES*
[Headline: "Bacall Takes Your Breath Away"]
Miss Bacall, with this thundering appearance, ceases being a former movie star and becomes a star of the stage, thank you. Miss Bacall side-steps nothing. Narrowing her eyes until they glitter as dirtily as a sharp piece of glass on a lawn you're roaming barefoot, roaring out her rage with the impassioned hurt of a spoiled child, springing into abandoned dance to express everything from foolish benevolence to fasten-your-seat-belts fury, she is Medea, Medusa, and Theda Bara combined and dyed blond. Though she gives over whole scenes and numbers to other people (some very good other people), she seems at all times to stand astride the show, her hair flying straight up, a genie emerging from a

tree trunk with arms stretching like branches to embrace and over-shadow and shelter everything within sight. Take your breath away? Indeed. What's more, she never gives it back. You may have wondered why I called her a cheetah a few paragraphs ago, considering that she has no spots. Let the dictionary persuade you: "The legs are long and adapted for swift dashes, and the claws are slightly if at all retractable." . . . Bonnie Franklin turns up whenever the principals turn Villageward, and she really has nothing to do with the show but to stop it. Shaggily red-headed, with a smile like the one they sometimes paint on lollipops, slapping her chaps and tossing her neckerchief to the apparently high winds, she needs only to be turned loose to take over. Larceny is the word for it, and that's an irony, in a show that is about a coming-up youngster stealing a march on the stars; do the authors and director really mean to say it's beginning to happen all over again, right here?

o   o   o

The widow Bogart, with offers few and far between, tried her hand at musical comedy—and found herself a bona fide sensation in a big bouncing manufactured-to-a-tee hit. *Applause* was not an especially good show—Charles Strouse's attempts at contemporary sound were weak and grating, the lyrics weren't up to Lee Adams's prior *Golden Boy* (1964) and *It's Superman* (1966), and the libretto trivialized the durable *All About Eve*—but it was frisky, at least. Glitzy, too. Ron Field, of *Cabaret* (1966) fame, had his game leading lady/icon tossed about the stage by the chorus boys, some of whom incidentally pranced about bare bottomed; it was that kind of show. *Applause* underwent typical birthing troubles, the producers tossing Sidney Michaels's libretto and their Eve Harrington (Diane McAfee) out en route; but a professional package was duly assembled. The show's prospects were not harmed by being the tenth musical of a long and dismal season, the year of the one-word titles (*Coco* and *Jimmy* and *Purlie* and *Georgy* and *Gantry*); it looked especially good at the end of a dreary week that brought both *Minnie's Boys* and *Look to the Lilies*. So a combination of the time, the place, and the gal made *Applause* seem pretty exciting, indeed. *Company* was just around the corner—already in Boston, actually—but the bulk of the Broadway audience preferred Bacall and company better than the Sondheim/Prince opus, anyway. For the record, the Margo Channing story went back to an experience that Viennese-born emigré actress

Elisabeth Bergner and her husband, producer Paul Czinner, had with an unscrupulous young actress they befriended during the war. Mary Orr—actress, playwright, and prolific writer, wife of director Reginald Denham—named her Eve Harrington in her short story *The Wisdom of Eve.* The stage star in the original story, for what it's worth, was named Margola Cranston.

In addition to winning the Tony Award for Best Musical, Tonys were won by Ron Field (director and choreographer) and Lauren Bacall (actress).

BROADWAY SCORECARD
/ PERFS: 896 / $: +

RAVE	FAVORABLE	MIXED	UNFAVORABLE	PAN
3	3			

THE APPLE TREE

"A New Musical," previously entitled *Come Back! Go Away! I Love You!*

music by Jerry Bock

lyrics by Sheldon Harnick

"book by Messrs. Harnick and Bock"; additional book material by Jerome Coopersmith

based on the 1904 journal *Extracts from Adam's Diary (translated from the original Ms.)* by Mark Twain; the 1882 short story *The Lady or the Tiger?* by Frank R. Stockton; and the 1953 cartoon-story *Passionella* by Jules Feiffer

directed by Mike Nichols

choreographed by Lee (Becker) Theodore (replaced by Herbert Ross); "additional musical staging" by Herbert Ross (in size double that of Lee Theodore)

produced by Stuart Ostrow

starring Barbara Harris, Larry Blyden, and Alan Alda

with Carmen Alvarez, Jackie Cronin, Michael Davis, Neil F. Jones, Marc Jordan, Robert Klein, Barbara Lang, Mary Louise, Jay Norman, and Jaclynn Villamil

opened October 18, 1966   *Shubert Theatre*

MARTIN GOTTFRIED, *WOMEN'S WEAR DAILY*

The Apple Tree is a musical that is divided into three parts and never gets back together again. But its divided parts are not just the separate stories that make its three mini-musicals. They are the components of musical theatre that were too separately contributed by some of the finest Broadway talents (in Broadway's best, most capable sense). The music, the story, the dance, the movement, the shape and basis and manner of *The Apple Tree* hang, like so many apples, never forming a tree and, even separately, never amounting to much. Polished neatly, they fell upon the Shubert Theatre stage last night. The problem lay with the conception. Bock and Harnick chose stories related in terms of Adam, Eve and The Devil. A reasonably original idea. But of these stories, only the middle one was basically musical and the others demanded the artificial interception of dance and song. This is not musical theatre but story with song, the former not justifying the latter's fraudulent sentimentality. This can be well done, as it has been in all the old-fashioned musicals that still noise up Broadway. But Bock and Harnick, writing the first book in their successful career, had no experience in even the old-style mixing of music, dance and story. As a result, they wound up copying old schemes in spite of their obvious determination to be "new." Nor did they have much help from their director, Mike Nichols, whose lack of musical theatre experience made him unsure, forgetful of rhythmic needs, and prone to rely on irrelevant interests that had served him well in comedies but were all wrong for the special needs of the musical. Not only is there little dancing in this production, but the movement, musical or otherwise, is minimal. Nichols is an extremely talented director but the musical theatre is no longer (if it ever was) just another variation on the Broadway theme. This production is a reasonable example of the error in forgetting that. It looks good but it is unknowing.

WALTER KERR, *TIMES*

As an evening's entertainment, *The Apple Tree* starts high and then scoots downward on a pretty steep slope, but first we must pause, men, and say it for Barbara Harris. Exquisite, appetizing, alarming, seductive, out of her mind, irresistible and from now on unavoidable. Would you believe just plain nice? "Whatever I am, I'm certainly a beautiful one" is practically the first remark out of her face in the opening musical playlet, and whoever you are, you're going to agree. The actress is now back in the strict sense. She wasn't really back—not quite—in last season's *On a Clear Day* [1965]. There she was a shade furtive, edging upstage away from us, holding a bit of her heart in hiding. But at the Shubert the lights are on, the voice is big, the composed liquid smile is as open and confiding as a bank vault blown apart by the best dynamite. This is the Barbara Harris of *From the Second City* [1961], returned to demand tribute from the First [City]. Director Mike

Nichols has surrounded himself with first, second and third assistants to puff the proceedings out—the program lists additional help on the musical staging, the underscoring, and even the libretto—but the puffing is just so much high pressure pretending to be meat and potatoes. Nichols has polished the proceedings until they shine with professional confidence, and it may be partly thanks to him that Miss Harris is once more a 1,000-kilowatt glow worm. But, as Genesis has hinted, things are tougher outside Eden.

NORMAN NADEL, *WORLD JOURNAL TRIBUNE*
[Headline: "Three Hits in One! *Tree* Flourishes"]
The three liveliest, loveliest musicals of the year. Each exhilarating on its own terms, they coexist contentedly under the collective title of *The Apple Tree*, and rarely has theatre entertainment been more fruitful. Let's face it: three musicals—and such musicals—for the price of one is the greatest innovation in the musical theatre since plots, not to mention one of the best bargains. Each has its own author, its own story, its own style, its own overture and its own everything else. They do share the talents of Barbara Harris, Alan Alda and Larry Blyden, plus Jerry Bock and Sheldon Harnick, Mike Nichols and quite a few others, backstage and onstage. All of these remarkable people, however, can and do go Jekyll and Hyde one better, and I cannot imagine *The Apple Tree* being any more fresh and unique in each of its parts if it were to be done with a trio of entirely separate creators and performers. Furthermore, as each segment deals with a fair amount of story and characterization within a relatively short time, they all move swiftly, with something comic, satirical, tender or pleasantly musical happening every minute. You've seldom seen evidence of so much and so varied talent in one theatre. Eddie Sauter's orchestral arrangements, Elliot Lawrence's shaping of the musical score, and Tony Walton's sets and costumes are just some of the elements which work so well. The greatest achievement of director Nichols, the three stars, Bock, and Harnick is their collective ability to transform themselves to fit each of their three stories. Magic.

RICHARD WATTS, JR., *POST*
The most gratifying revelation made by *The Apple Tree* is that Eve, the mother of us all, was Barbara Harris. It is also a little chastening,

because with such a head start the human race should have done better with itself. There are many high triumphs of the imagination in the vastly original musical comedy by Jerry Bock and Sheldon Harnick, but it is Miss Harris who provides it with the extra touch of stage magic. The imagination is not confined to the conception and the humor in the writing. It is likewise to be found in every element of the physical production. It has been staged by Mike Nichols with the inventive skill we have come to expect from him. The setting and costumes by Tony Walton are handsome and colorful, and there is an effective use of movies in *Passionella*. Miss Harris is so delicious in everything she does, charming, touching, satirical and fascinating, that the two male stars are hard put to it to keep up with her but they are excellent. *The Apple Tree* has the freshness of genuine inventiveness.

०   ०   ०

While certain properties naturally call for an expansive musical handling (like Frank Loesser's *The Most Happy Fella* [1956] and Bock and Harnick's *She Loves Me* [1963]), many Broadway musicals tend to be filled out with extraneous songs and production numbers. Is there another way to handle these not-quite-full evenings? Is it possible to reduce the plot to essentials—told in song—rather than expand the material to fill two and a half hours? A well-written short story works better than an overblown novel; is there a musical theatre equivalent? With *Fiddler on the Roof* (1964) under their belt, and the resulting security of knowing they never again need lift pencil and rhyming dictionary unless they felt like it, Bock and Harnick joined librettist Jerome Coopersmith—with whom they'd worked while doctoring the score of *Baker Street* (1965)—for an evening of musical one-acts. "We regard it as an adventure," said the composer in June 1965. "We really don't know how it will come out." The three bites of this apple began as Guy de Maupassant's *Boule de Suif*, Bernard Malamud's *Angel Levine*, and Marcel Ayme's *Martin, the Novelist*. By the time the authors got down to serious work, the entries were Bruce Jay Friedman's *Show Biz Connections*, Nathaniel Hawthorne's *Young Goodman Brown*, and Mark Twain's take on the Garden of Eden. The three, in tandem, demonstrated "the progress of man's relationship to woman in the only way that progress can be traced—backwards." Work progressed (backwards?), with Hawthorne giving way to *Lady or the Tiger*. The lineup underwent a final alteration when director Mike Nichols replaced Jerry Robbins, three months before rehearsals began. While *The Apple Tree* was Nichols's first Broadway musical, a summer stock tryout he staged in 1962—*The World of Jules Feiffer*—included a one-act version of *Passionella* with songs by Stephen Sondheim and Dorothy Loudon as the sniveling chimney sweep. Nichols excised *Show Biz Connections* and set Bock and Harnick to writing their own version of the Feiffer. (Nichols also suggested casting Al Freeman Jr. as Adam and his brethren, which Ostrow rejected as "too gimmicky.") Librettist Coopersmith departed at this time, because most of the narrative was carried in the songs (or so it was explained). But freedom from conventional restraints tends to create newer, unconventional restraints. The decision to link the musicalettes with a common man-woman-temptation theme, with corresponding centuries-apart-but-identical roles for the stars, provided a special set of problems. And three musicals are harder to sustain than one. If the first is strong, the others necessarily look weaker; if you lose your audience with the first, you're lost. *The Apple Tree*'s second, medieval bite appears always to have been a problem (hence the change from Hawthorne to Stockton). The closing act in the original "backward progress" scheme was so strong that it was moved upfront to start the evening. And *Passionella*, while delightful in its own way, seems very much like a written-to-order star vehicle designed to punch up a faltering evening. An intricate monthly order-of-billing rotation was worked out for Harris, Alda, and Blyden, but there was no question who was giving the star performance. The final result: almost, but not quite. Loaded with class and quality, though.

A Tony Award was won by Barbara Harris (actress).

BROADWAY SCORECARD
/ PERFS: 463 / $: –

RAVE	FAVORABLE	MIXED	UNFAVORABLE	PAN
3	1	1	1	

LEON URIS' ARI

"A New Musical based on his novel *Exodus*"

music by Walt Smith (additional music by Peter Howard and Bob Bernstein)

book and lyrics by Leon Uris

based on his 1957 novel *Exodus*

directed by Lucia Victor

choreographed by Talley Beatty

produced by Ken Gaston and Leonard Goldberg in association with Henry Stern

starring David Cryer and Constance Towers

with John Savage, Jacqueline Mayro, Martin Ross, C. K. Alexander, Norwood Smith, Mark Zeller, Jack Gwillim, and Jamie Ross

opened January 15, 1971   Mark Hellinger Theatre

CLIVE BARNES, *TIMES*
[Headline: "Uris' Lighthearted *Ari*"]
No novel that has sold 20 million copies can be said to be devoid of popular interest, and although I have never read Leon Uris's novel or even seen the film made from it, it was clearly within its own terms of reference highly successful. The musical *Ari* just as clearly is not. Uris is trying to write a serious musical, and, indeed, it must be one of the least lighthearted musicals in Broadway history, which is a kind of record. But seriousness is not always a substitute for art, and in adapting his novel he has not only exposed his inexperience in the theatre, but also suggests that his writing skills while obviously of the very worthy kind that can contrive best sellers, may not be especially remarkable assets for the writing of serious literature, even serious dramatic literature. Apart from the initial situation of the story itself and a couple of the songs, almost everything else about *Ari* is faulty. Uris made two serious mis-

KEN GASTON and LEONARD GOLDBERG
in association with HENRY STERN
present

LEON URIS'

A New Musical Based on his Novel
EXODUS

Book and Lyrics by   Music by
LEON URIS   WALT SMITH

Starring
DAVID CRYER · CONSTANCE TOWERS
Also Starring
MARTIN ROSS · C. K. ALEXANDER
NORWOOD SMITH · MARK ZELLER · JACK GWILLIM
JAMIE ROSS · JOSEPH DELLA SORTE
and
JOHN SAVAGE · JACQUELINE MAYRO
        as Dov   as Karen

Scenery Designed by   Costumes by   Lighting by
ROBERT RANDOLPH   SARA BROOK   NANANNE PORCHER

Vocal Arrangements &   Dance & Incidental Music
Musical Direction by   Orchestrations by   Arranged by
STANLEY LEBOWSKY   PHILIP J. LANG   PETER HOWARD

Production Stage Manager: WADE MILLER

Associate Producers: RONALD RECKSEIT, LISA LIPSKY

Choreography by
TALLEY BEATTY

Production Directed by   Original Cast Recording by
LUCIA VICTOR

NATIONAL THEATRE, Washington
Tues., December 22 thru Sat., January 2
Evenings at 7:30   Matinees Wed. and Sat. at 2:00

"Despite the fact that *Exodus* still sells more than 20,000 copies a month and was made into a popular film, Mr. Uris has always felt that the addition of music and lyrics would give the story an added dimension." And it did, indeed.

takes—the first in electing to write his own musical book, and the second to write his own lyrics. The dialogue is about as bright as a grimy window pane, and as lively as a slow corpse. A further aide to the show's soporific nature is provided by his lyrics, which are banal and clumsy. David Cryer, as Ari, once again pushes forward his claims to be regarded as the most interesting young leading man in Broadway musicals, the best find since Richard Kiley. He sings magnificently and acts with engaging simplicity.

MARTIN GOTTFRIED, *WOMEN'S WEAR DAILY*
Ari represents several of the reasons why Broadway theatre has collapsed, and for that it is to be despised. Perhaps there have been other productions nearly as incompetent, this may simply be the last straw. What is most upsetting about *Ari* is the spectacle of professional theatre people—and I'm talking about directors, orchestrators, set designers, to an extent even actors—fleecing naive producers and incompetent creators merely to get work, aware from the start that the project is sub-professional. Hustling is one of the theatre's less admirable traditions, but in a situation like this it is sordid. Nearly as disgusting is the effect that such a show has on the last of the faithful—those audiences still commited to the theatre despite the staggering disappointments of the recent past. Why should they ever come back again? Can they believe that a theatre capable of presenting grade school work as professional will ever do much better? The production is primitive in all ways. Robert Randolph's sets are abysmally designed and shabbily executed. Lucia Victor's staging is, by turns, sluggish and ragged. Walt Smith's songs would be rejected by a summer resort for a weekend show. Talley Beatty actually choreographed a concentration camp ballet, nearly matched by a rifle dance later in the first act, which was all I could bear and I couldn't bear that. As for Uris's book, it is the equal of his lyrics. David Cryer is the male lead, singing every line of dialog as though he were John Raitt and it was still 1955. Constance Towers plays his romance, a girl the show describes as a Gentile nurse with a tragic past, and I leave it at that.

DOUGLAS WATT, *DAILY NEWS*
It couldn't have been easy but the makers of last night's *Ari* have managed to take one of modern history's most stirring achievements, the

formation of the state of Israel, and convert it into a humorless and numbingly dull musical. As if Uris's book with its soap-opera romance thrown in wasn't bad enough, he has also contributed the show's pedestrian song lyrics. And the composer, Walt Smith, has been of absolutely no help, having provided a score that would have sounded tired and even dated in the days of *The Desert Song* [1926]. It is all rather infuriating when you consider the thrilling source material and the cheap use that has been made of it.

⸭   ⸭   ⸭

A musical version of *Exodus*! Now there's a surefire idea, huh? Surefire enough to guarantee enough angels to fund it, at least, and sell a few theatre parties. The show did not include Ernest (*I'm Solomon* [1968]) Gold's theme song from the popular 1960 filmization; nor did it include the movie's Paul Newman and Eva Marie Saint. (It did have Broadway's first concentration camp ballet, though.) Now, if this had been an Alex Cohen production, *Ari* would have had *real* stars, Gower in place of his assistant Lucia, and maybe Jerry or Jule as tunesmiths. The result—if not the size of the budget and the loss—would undoubtedly have been the same. Tyro producers Gaston and Goldberg, incidentally, were twenty-eight and twenty-four, respectively; they bounced right back with *Heathen!* (1972), and "bounce" is the operative word. It will be noted that the so-called Jewish musical (and the Jewish theatre party business) sustained a mortal, though not fatal, blow in 1970-1971, with *The Rothschilds*, *Two by Two*, and *Ari* in quick succession. And then came *Follies*, which theatre party audiences liked even *less*.

BROADWAY SCORECARD
/ PERFS: 19 / $: –

RAVE	FAVORABLE	MIXED	UNFAVORABLE	PAN
			1	5

BAKER STREET

"A Musical Adventure of Sherlock Holmes"

music and lyrics by Marian Grudeff and Raymond Jessel (additional music and lyrics by Jerry Bock and Sheldon Harnick)

book by Jerome Coopersmith

based on the 1891 story *A Scandal in Bohemia* and other adventures of Sherlock Holmes (written 1887-1927) by Sir Arthur Conan Doyle

directed by Harold Prince

choreographed by Lee Becker Theodore

produced by Alexander H. Cohen

starring Fritz Weaver, Inga Swenson, and Martin Gabel

with Peter Sallis, Patrick Horgan, Teddy Green, Paddy Edwards, Martin Wolfson, Daniel Keyes, and Jay Norman

opened February 16, 1965   Broadway Theatre

JOHN CHAPMAN, *DAILY NEWS*

After one of the most prolonged and intensive ballyhoo campaigns since Billy Rose and Richard Maney opened *Jumbo* at the Hippodrome, Alexander H. Cohen opened *Baker Street* last evening. Now he can take it easy and so can all those people who bought tickets without waiting for permission from the critics. *Baker Street* is an absolutely captivating entertainment. Without seeming to push the show, Harold Prince, the director, has kept it in steady motion. It starts with a bang when a marksman takes a shot at Holmes thought the window of his Baker Street flat and ends with a triumph when the superhuman Holmes returns from certain death and recovers all of Queen Victoria's jewels. There is a wonderful chase through designer Oliver Smith's byways and cellars of foggy London. There is a miraculous escape from a devilish

ALEXANDER H. COHEN
presents

FRITZ WEAVER   INGA SWENSON

MARTIN GABEL

BAKER STREET

A MUSICAL ADVENTURE OF SHERLOCK HOLMES

Book by
JEROME COOPERSMITH

Music and Lyrics by
MARIAN GRUDEFF & RAYMOND JESSEL

Adapted from the Stories by
SIR ARTHUR CONAN DOYLE

Choreography by
LEE BECKER THEODORE

Production Designed by
OLIVER SMITH

Lighting by
JEAN ROSENTHAL

Costumes Designed by
MOTLEY

Musical Direction by
HAROLD HASTINGS

Orchestrations by
DON WALKER

Dance Arrangements by
JOHN MORRIS

Production Directed by
HAROLD PRINCE

"It is the scenery that counts most," opined Walter Kerr, "a passion to ransack the theatrical warehouse—an extravaganza that looks like three World's Fairs rolled into one." (artwork by John Fehnie)

bomb. Holmes gets some extraordinary help from some urchins called the Baker Street Irregulars, who are headed by an extraordinary young man named Teddy Green. The music and lyrics by Marian Grudeff and Raymond Jessel, a pair of Canadians, are just right for what they are trying to do—particularly the lyrics. Anybody who can write "When the stately Holmes of England is no more" is just right for *Baker Street* [lyric by Sheldon Harnick]. Better see it yourself. As Weaver, Miss Swenson, Sallis, and Virginia Vestoff sing it, "What a night this is going to be."

WALTER KERR, *HERALD TRIBUNE*

So often I hate myself in the morning. *This* morning it's because *Baker Street* has opened and I like its attitude. I only wish it knew how to keep its attitude up. The conception is nice and somehow it just doesn't grow on you. Everything is too patiently overextended, to begin with, [and] there's a certain fuzziness about the staging that fails to say exactly *when* a particular joke is being made. The tongue-in-cheek point is there [Weaver's Sherlock "believes it all with one eye and has a handsome wink in the other"], somehow, but in a very generalized, lazy, unfocused way. We sort of have to pick it out of the air as the plot toddles along, and frequently the toddling is more evident than the underlying jest. And there is a musical risk about toying with songs that are jocularly intended as irrelevant: the irrelevance tends to outlast the conceit. . . . Mr. Smith's sewers and stairways and overpasses are marvelously swift and seamy. But in the end it is the scenery that counts most, and that's always dangerous. A visit to Madame Tussaud's isn't quite the same thing as a musical comedy with a *joi de vivre* of its own. The attitude is fundamentaly promising, and the special effects are more than that, they deliver. But in due time there are too many tricks. The eye that winks grows tired, and such devices [eventually] call attention to what we are really watching: not so much a love affair with the ghost of Holmes as a passion to ransack the theatrical warehouse—an extravaganza that looks like three World's Fairs rolled into one.

NORMAN NADEL, *WORLD-TELEGRAM & SUN*

"Thank God for the Baker Street Irregulars!" The words must have crossed Sherlock Holmes' mind, if not his lips, during several criminal cases which the ingenious little "street arabs" of Victorian London helped to solve. The same thought occured to me, and possibly to producer Alexander Cohen as well, about 20 minutes after the opening of the opulent new musical *Baker Street* last night. Up to that point, more than ordinary competence was evident in several aspects of the show. But—except for a brief burst of action in the first scene as Holmes outwits an assassin—nothing exciting had happened. Then just in time, there were the Baker Street Irregulars, with an exuberant young Englishman named Teddy Green as Wiggins, their leader. "Leave It to Us, Guv," they sang, as they swung into the first of two life-giving dance numbers by choreographer Lee Theodore. Only then did *Baker Street* begin to glow with something more than the electric lighting which Jean Rosenthal has deployed ingeniously in all its scenes. Thereafter it sagged for a while, picked up enormously toward the end of act one, and held strong almost to the end. I cannot believe that last night's performance was the best this company can do. Director Harold Prince isn't the man who will settle for halting action, uncomfortable pauses and scenes which go flat when they should sparkle. Sound effects were so loud that they shattered the very mood they are designed to create. For all Miss Swenson's personal charm, and the lyric loveliness of her singing voice, her scenes simply didn't go well. Perhaps this was the toughest writing problem-injecting romance into a story about that resolute misogynist, Sherlock Holmes.

HOWARD TAUBMAN, *TIMES*

Faced by several of the gravest dangers in a perilous career, Sherlock Holmes naturally surmounts them in *Baker Street*. The new musical that celebrates his masterly intellect and his feats of detection must also contend with difficulties—a slow beginning, some forced humor and some production numbers that are imposed rather than organic—but it overcomes them. Before the end of the first half it has caught the master detective's mood and style, and the second half is capital fun. In its swiftly changing sets, its fogs, its clanging Big Ben, in a sequence wherein Holmes and Irene wander through the haunts of the underworld, *Baker Street* has atmosphere and illusion. There is a charming moment, managed with the help of Bil Baird's Marionettes, which creates a scene of delightful magic as the Diamond Jubilee Parade and the

Queen in her royal coach pass by. If you'll relax, like Holmes with his fiddle, you'll enjoy more than half of this musical.

*   *   *

Baker Street was chock-full of thrills, chills, and London fog. Everything, in fact, except a decent score and a charismatic star capable of pulling off the caper. Alexander H. Cohen assembled quite an extravaganza, although he curiously assigned the songs to the untried Marian Grudeff and Raymond Jessel. (One can't fault the showman here; he later produced even poorer musicals written by top composers Jerry Herman, Jule Styne, and Richard Rodgers.) When director Josh Logan left the project, Hal Prince readily accepted. He had grave misgivings about the score, but wasn't about to pass up his first opportunity to direct a full-scale, big-budget musical: *Baker Street* cost a walloping $630,000. (Prince's *Fiddler on the Roof* [1964], which opened earlier that season, came in way over budget at only $450,000.) Following a lackluster tryout reception, Cohen finally acceded to Prince's demands and brought in *Fiddler*'s Bock and Harnick to write four songs (at $5,000 per, plus a 1 percent royalty) but this was too little too late. It did allow the ghost-lyricist to concoct a deliciously Harnickian pun about "the stately Holmes of England"—which critic John Chapman, logically, attributed to Grudeff and Jessel. The grandiose producer also provided a $30,000 animated sign covering the facade above the Broadway Theatre marquee, featuring a burglar on a ladder being pushed away from a window by a blonde while being shot at by another bloke with a flashing revolver, captioned "Sherlock Holmes of *Baker Street* taught James Bond everything he knows." The show outside *on* Broadway proved more exciting than the show *in* the Broadway, and Conan Doyle's detective eventually packed up his deerstalker and vanished in a cloud of smoke and red ink.

A Tony Award was won by Oliver Smith (scenic designer).

BROADWAY SCORECARD

/ PERFS: 3 I 3 / $: –

RAVE	FAVORABLE	MIXED	UNFAVORABLE	PAN
1	1	1	2	1

BALLROOM

"A New Musical"

music by Billy Goldenberg

lyrics by Alan and Marilyn Bergman

book by Jerome Kass (replaced by Larry Gelbart)

based on the 1975 teleplay *The Queen of the Stardust Ballroom* (uncredited) by Jerome Kass

directed and choreographed by Michael Bennett; co-choreographed by Bob Avian

produced by Michael Bennett; coproduced by Bob Avian, Bernard Gersten, and Susan MacNair

starring Dorothy Loudon and Vincent Gardenia

with Marilyn Cooper, Patricia Drylie, Victor Griffin, Sally-Jane Heit, Bernie Knee, Mary Ann Niles, Howard Parker, Lynn Roberts, and Rudy Tronto

opened December 14, 1978   Majestic Theatre

CLIVE BARNES, *POST*

[Headline: "Bennett's Musical Sprinkled with that Special Stardust"] Naturally the expectations of the piece have been tremendous. Could he, would he, repeat the success, or even the innovative originality of *Chorus Line* [1975]? In my opinion he hasn't—but he has come up with a show that deserves to be a sizeable hit. It is exquisitely contrived, super-sharp and calculated to hit Broadway right in its pocket book. It combines the Broadway audience's current preoccupation with dancing, and its traditional concern with life beyond the middle years. And the show is built like a Swiss watch. It ticks. There is a certain form of musical—becoming increasingly common—where you talk about the staging and the choreography first, and then throw in a few remarks about the music and all that jazz as an afterthought. This is one of those musicals, and Bennett has done a remarkable job with it. The scenes beautifully phase into one another like cinematic dissolves. The ball-room episodes are the specialty of the evening. But where Bennett scores is as a director, and the way he can adroitly place dances in their dramatic context. The performances from top to toe are bewitching. Dorothy Loudon has always been one of my very favorite musical stars, and I have never seen her give a performance less than fantastic. Here she has the role of her career, and she gives it with a chipper, transcen-dental gutsiness, and that lovely raspy voice, that should make her the queen of Broadway, let alone the Stardust Ballroom. Her co-star Vincent Gardenia glitters just as brightly and just as softly. He is utterly charming and completely convincing—like Miss Loudon he tremu-lously yet firmly avoids sentimentality, and achieves a naturalness that is art's last reward. The fault of the show is obvious—the story is trivial enough scarcely to be worth an answer by Dear Abby; [it is] an agony column set to the waltz, the foxtrot, the cha-cha-cha and the tango. The virtues are equally obvious. Heart. These people are oddly real. Second. Style. Robin Wagner's setting, all flash with subtle taste, and the deli-cately evocative costumes by Theoni V. Aldredge, and the suggestive lighting by Tharon Musser, all provide Bennett with a working envi-ronment of taste. And he comes through with a show that from start to finsh has the ephemeral but great grace of style. It brings class to Broadway.

RICHARD EDER, *TIMES*

For a while, as *Ballroom* introduces its characters, its situation, an initial pair of songs and a few dances, it keeps to an oddly subdued tempo, interesting in its unexpectedness. Nothing very exciting or witty or beautiful happens in the first half hour of this musical about old people finding love at a golden-age ballroom; but it is tasteful and unforced. With someone of the caliber of Michael Bennett in charge, the natural assumption is that he and his authors are keeping their powder dry. The assumption holds for a while. But around the halfway mark [with no intermission] the suspicion begins to grow that the powder is never going to be lit at all. And finally it becomes evident that it is not pow-der, but dust. *Ballroom* has remarkably little going for it. As producer,

Bennett has chosen to assign his directorial and choreographic talents to a book that manages to be both smarmy and perfunctory, like a radio serial under threat of cancellation. This book, mainly by Jerome Kass, is joined to music of no perceptible character by Billy Goldenberg—at its best it can be lively but a very lived-in lively—and lyrics by Alan and Marilyn Bergman. These lyrics set out prosy footnotes to tell us what the characters are feeling. They so totally lack any wit or grace that it is some kind of high point when Miss Loudon guys the pleasure she has found in her first trip to the ballroom with a deprecatory chant of "cha-cha-cha." Loudon is almost invariably winning; so much so that her truly awful speeches about living her own life arouse sympathy as much as dismay. Gardenia manages to get some charm and dignity out of a totally passive role. He does not sing; he is sung at and about. It is stretching things to say that he dances; rather, he is danced with. The effect is of Miss Loudon wheeling around a large pet owl. *Ballroom*, apart from the moments of strength I have mentioned, is not merely a very weak show. It is a condescending one; the authors have given their old characters not a spark of wit or originality or life. The contempt for the material may not be conscious or willed, but it is there all the same; and we, who are asked to enter into the life of the show are its victims.

WALTER KERR, *TIMES*
[Headline: "*Ballroom* Glides but Doesn't Grow"]
I must confess to one surprise. I hadn't expected the special quality of Miss Loudon's performance. The actress normally works very broadly. When she played the orphanage-mistress in *Annie*, she was out for comic blood, and she got it; in the process, though, she came close to devouring all the other little cartoons. Here, suddenly, she is quite moving as we meet her, running a junk-shop that's been stocked with the debris of her life. She remains so as she ventures her first footwork at the Stardust, as fearfully tentative as a kid summarily called on the carpet. And after she's struck up a promising acquaintance with Vincent Gardenia ("I'm with the government, I'm a mailman"), the simultaneous yearning and self-mockery she's able to work into a song called "Somebody Did Alright for Herself Tonight" is fetching indeed. A real advance for a bona-fide actress. I must also confess to a surprise I wanted but didn't get. As the evening glided on, reflected in a melange

of mirrors beneath one of those crystal balls that seems to produce a snowstorm-in-reverse, I wanted something else to happen. Loudon, the dancers and *Ballroom* as a whole are unmistakably appealing for—let's pick an arbitrary point—half the evening. After that, they don't get any less appealing. But they don't get any more appealing, either, and they should. That's to say, we want something to grow a little, some emotional change to realert us, some unexpected curve in the narrative to catch us quite off guard. The entertainment continues to flow smoothly toward the waltz in black-and-white that will cap it, but we're aware that we're really on hold. The difficulty, I think, is that librettist Jerome Kass has closed out all of his possibilities too soon. Mr. Gardenia is married, and unable to leave his wife. That door is shut. As a result, the later scenes are pretty plainly composed of retread, though I can't say I lost my fondness for any of the folk involved or my admiration for what Mr. Bennett has achieved. Call it a somewhat incomplete musical adventure that is winning nonetheless.

DOUGLAS WATT, *DAILY NEWS*
[Headline: "A Pretty *Ballroom* Lacks Excitement"]
Give Michael Bennett a floor full of dancers to work with and he can create visual enchantment. And he does time and again in *Ballroom*. But neither the book nor the songs properly support the director-choreographer, this time also functioning as producer, and the evening lacks bite and excitement. The Stardust Ballroom, looking much too magical for its Bronx setting in Robin Wagner's eye-catching design with its revolving and retractable mirrored globe and even revolving mirrored walls, is a sort of senior citizen's refuge. Though the folk who gather here are learning the hustle, their hearts and limbs responds most enthusiastically to the samba, fox-trot, waltz, tango and cha-cha. Interestingly, however, and perhaps because Jonathan Tunick's superlative orchestrations reach a crescendo here, a climactic dance with a disco beat provides the most stimulation. The book being negligible, that leaves the songs, and they're negligible, too. They are, in fact, so commonplace that they seem almost a parody of the swing-band era and Tin Pan Alley. They could give the '40s a bad name. . . . Theoni V. Aldredge's costumes and Tharon Musser's lighting are all that could be desired, and the Stardust band, with its white-haired male crooner

[Bernie Knee] and cutesy-pie girl singer [Lynn Roberts], are perfect. But like the spectral figures dancing to past sounds into a silent future, *Ballroom* seems to evaporate before our eyes.

◦ ◦ ◦

Michael Bennett conceived his *Ballroom* as a memorial to dancers—not the still-hopeful gypsies of *A Chorus Line*, but the former gypsies who have been forced out into the civilian world, who've "kissed the day goodbye," if you will. Which is ironic, in that it was the dancers that killed *Ballroom*. Not the dancers so much as the dance, for the dance in *Ballroom*—the ballroom itself—was separate and apart from the drama. The show had a skeleton of an involving, dramatic story, and at least two satisfyingly sympathetic characters, but a good half of the evening was spent at a dance exhibition of faceless noncharacters we didn't know. Even more dangerous, less than half of the score was lavished on the principals. One solitary principal, that is, the widow Bea. The rest of the songs were given to two band singers at—you guessed it—the ballroom, and served merely as dance accompaniment. It is possible to express drama through lyric-less music—look at vast stretches of *On the Town* (1944) and *West Side Story* (1957), or ballet itself, for that matter; but when the songwords bear no relation to the story or the characters, we just stop listening. Thus we're left with a great deal of concept grafted onto a not especially congruent story. The song spotting process was severely restricted by the selection of a nonsinging leading man, and the whole of *Ballroom* was hamstrung by writers unfamiliar with the demands of the theatre. Librettist Jerome Kass had written the original teleplay, drawn from the life of his mother; William Goldenberg (dance music arranger of Bennett's early *Henry, Sweet Henry* [1967]) and the Bergmans (whose only show had been the 1964 flop *Something More!*) had provided the incidental songs for TV. But their *Ballroom* songs, with the exception of Bea's five numbers, were all too incidental, and *The Queen of the Stardust Ballroom* was lost in the shuffle (and the tango and the lindy). Bennett called in Larry Gelbart to polish the script, which he did ably, but he couldn't doctor the dance sections. All the contributing flaws of *Ballroom* were specific choices of Bennett, of course. He was trying to come up with something different, as he had on *A Chorus Line*. But no matter how arresting the dancers and the dancing were, you eventually found your attention wandering away from the stage to the playful reflections of the mirror ball darting across the Majestic auditorium.

A Tony Award was won by Michael Bennett and Bob Avian (choreographers).

BROADWAY SCORECARD
/ PERFS: 116 / $: –

RAVE	FAVORABLE	MIXED	UNFAVORABLE	PAN
1	2	1		2

BARNUM

"The New Musical"

music by Cy Coleman

lyrics by Michael Stewart

book by Mark Bramble

suggested by events in the life of Phineas Taylor Barnum (1810-1891)

directed and choreographed by Joe Layton

produced by Judy Gordon, Cy Coleman, and Maurice and Lois F. Rosenfield, in association with Irvin Feld and Kenneth Feld

starring Jim Dale

with Glenn Close, Marianne Tatum, Terri White, Leonard John Crofoot, and William C. Witter

opened April 30, 1980   *St. James Theatre*

JIM DALE

in

BARNUM

A New Musical

Music by
Cy Coleman

Lyrics by
Michael Stewart

Book by
Mark Bramble

Directed and Staged by
Joe Layton

Call CHARGIT: (212) 239-7177 and charge your tickets on all major credit cards.

TICKETRON: (212) 977-9020 • GROUP SALES BOX OFFICE: (212) 398-8383

ST. JAMES THEATRE
44th St. W. of B'way 398-0280

A jubilant Barnum doffs his top hat, looking a whole lot more like Jim Dale than the real-life P.T. (artwork by Tony Walton)

CLIVE BARNES, *POST*

[Headline: "Jim Dale: The Greatest Show on Earth"]

Jim Dale is a one-man, three-ring, four-star circus in *Barnum*. *Barnum* is boisterous, brash and bright, it has a catchy, clever and occasionally very beautiful score by Cy Coleman and some tongue-twistingly adroit lyrics by Michael Stewart. And a fantastic cast led by the aforementioned Dale, who is individually one of the greatest shows on earth. I loved *Barnum*, but even its fondest lover can see the story is flawed. Mark Bramble has struggled hard to inject life into Barnum's life, but Bramble's book emerges as a library of good intentions. However, this said and faced, it scarcely matters. What makes Dale a great performer is his nerveless, yet still nervy, skills, the ability to take unlikely risks. Many comedians pratfall, but Dale freefalls. One minute he will be metaphorically jumping through a blazing hoop, and the next he will be sitting alone on stage caressing a spotlight with an outrageously sentimental grin combined with cynical eyebrows. As Barnum he is a knockout. He sings, he dances, he juggles, he jumps, he tells jokes, he makes discreet love to the audience, not to mention the cast, and walks across the stage on a high-wire singing a happy song. He sometimes displays his technique with the pride of a matador and his red cloak. Yet what also makes *Barnum* such fun is the whole concept of life as a circus. Not a rare concept, but here actually carried out by actors with genuine, or at least handsomely simulated, circus skills. This makes a dramatic cliché real. The cast is lovely. Glenn Close, as the wife, has the ungrateful task of playing lilac to Dale's vermillion, and succeeds. But the final impression of *Barnum* is Barnum and Dale themselves, alone, and then a coruscation of circus curtain calls. Grab this one.

HOWARD KISSEL, *WOMEN'S WEAR DAILY*

You want to like *Barnum* as soon as you enter the St. James Theatre and see David Mitchell's stunning 19th-century circus set, painted in nostalgically soft hues, and hear your nervous usherette warn you to keep your legs and elbows out of the aisles. You expect a musical about America's master showman to be something of a three-ring circus, and *Barnum*, which uses its aisles as auxiliary rings, certainly lives up to expectations. Dancing in the aisles, however, even in a circus show, is generally a diversionary action, a way of camouflaging the absence of substance on the stage. Mark Bramble has written an ambitious book, trying to give us the main points of Barnum's career at the same time they suggest that, as a proponent of humbug, he was, even if ironically, a major American visionary. This is an interesting idea but it is never attacked with sustained wit or imagination. Though the key moments of Barnum's career have been staged like circus acts—a confrontation with his wife, for example, is done like a lion tamer's act—one senses the images are forced, however clever. The show flirts with a concept it never quite realizes. The climactic number in the second act has Barnum singing that he is the prince of humbug—which is what he sang when the show opened. Few, of course, will worry about the show's inability to fulfill its own ideas because director-choreographer Joe Layton has created such a dazzling display of theatrical ingenuity. He uses his 17 extremely talented performers so adroitly they seem like a cast of thousands. Which brings us to Cy Coleman's score. At its best, a few pieces of Americana based on rags and march music, it is quite beguiling. But one senses that Coleman is straining to do Something Big. His best work always had an effortless quality to it. Here, as in *Twentieth Century*, he is aiming for more impressive effects without enough emotional substance in the lyrics and book to back him up. Nevertheless *Barnum* is great fun.

FRANK RICH, *TIMES*

Is there anything that Jim Dale can't do? Dale, who roared into town last night in *Barnum*, is not your everyday song-and-dance man. Oh, he sings just fine—in the bright style of the old British music hall—and he can kick up his legs until his feet nearly collide with his forehead. But, for this fellow, such gifts are merely a point of departure. During the course of a busy evening, Dale shows off enough tricks to make all but a Houdini dizzy. He leaps from a trampoline, he rides a unicycle, he walks a tightrope, he conducts a marching band, he dons a carrot-colored wig and plays the clown. Yet his best stunt may be the simplest of them all. When the curly-haired Dale comes forward to address the audience, his arms spread wide as if to embrace the St. James Theatre's entire second balcony, he immediately transforms a gargantuan circus of a show into his own joyous playpen. This man can create magic—the magic of infectious charm—even on those rare occasions when he's standing still. With a human wonder like Dale all about, it would be ungracious to belabor the shortcomings of the musical that tries (not too hard) to contain him. *Barnum* has plenty of other virtues besides its star, but, to get the bad news out of the way fast, it doesn't have a book. If there is anyone who deserves to share Dale's star billing it is the designer, David Mitchell. His circus-ring set extends above the St. James's proscenium, into the boxes, and then adds a few boxes of its own. There is a candy-striped curtain, yards of red-white-and-blue bunting and, way back upstage, the glimmer of a mammoth tent. When circumstances require it, Mitchell is not averse to sending scenery flying from all directions, including the floor. Yet the set is more than a collection of pretty gimcracks. Its roseate, gaslight glow and golden crown of letters spelling out "America" suggest another, deeper entertainment: one that really explores the life and times of P. T. Barnum. *Barnum* is not that musical. It is, in its hero's vernacular, "a humbug": a relentless flow of acts that provides the illusion of miracles rather than the miracles themselves. But if it is not the greatest show on earth—or even the greatest musical on 44th Street—*Barnum* and its crack ringleader nonetheless deliver an evening of pure, exhilarating fun.

DOUGLAS WATT, *DAILY NEWS*
[Headline: "*Barnum* Humdinger Story of a Humbug"]
Barnum may not be the greatest show on earth, but last night's circusy new musical is colorful, eye-catching and abundantly high-spirited. Set to a buoyant, tuneful score by Cy Coleman, and with the agile Jim Dale in the title role, it radiates good cheer. Joyously staged by Joe Layton, and resplendently designed, costumed and lighted [by David Mitchell, Theoni V. Aldredge, and Craig Miller], *Barnum* skims the career and private life of the flamboyant 19th-century American impresario and master of flimflam Phineas Taylor Barnum in terms more affectionate, sentimental and patriotic than we could stomach were it not for the fact that Dale is playing himself at all times. Even so, the salutes to life, liberty and Thomas Jefferson get a bit thick at times coming from this humbug artist. Though various encounters are meant to take place in towns and cities throughout this country and Europe, the permanent setting is a circus with a Ringmaster announcing the high spots of Barnum's career as feats, which P. T. then pro-

ceeds to enact. The method is somewhat akin to that used in the musical *Chicago*, but lighthearted rather than acrid. The stage is almost always alive with circusy trappings. There are no animals, though there are amusing representations of tigers and an elephant, but there are jugglers, clowns, a terrific baton-wielder, an aerialist, a one-man-band, and other features of the tanbark. And arrayed along the back is the full orchestra, playing excellent Hershy Kay arrangements, with twin pianists in boxes on opposite sides of the house filling in with honky-tonk choruses. Whether bouncing from a small trampoline up to a tiny balcony where Chairy sits watching, or else actually walking a tightrope at the end of the first half, Dale is nimble and engaging. He and Glenn Close, who makes a charmingly firm-minded Chairy, have a lovely duet in "The Colors of My Life." *Barnum* is a lively, fun-filled evening of theatre, and one with style. If nothing else, it's likely to make your kids, or even you, run away from home to "Join the Circus," as the finale stimulatingly beckons.

◦　　◦　　◦

In April of 1974 Bramble and I headed to Madison Square Garden (with comp tickets) to take in Barnum & Bailey; a college classmate had thrown up her hands to join the circus, and was making her debut in clown white. Next morning the phone rings. "What do you think about a P. T. Barnum musical, with acrobats and circus acts and everything?" Sounded a bit unwieldy and not too promising, but what do I know? Two producers, five songwriters (including Harry Nillson), and four years later, Bramble took it to David Merrick, for whom he had managed *Sugar* (1972) and *Mack & Mabel* (1974) after starting his career in 1970 answering the showman's phones. "Get Jim Dale to commit and I'll do it," said Merrick, so he did. "Good," said the producer. "Get Cy Coleman and I'll do it." Okay, done. "Good, now get Mike Stewart and I'll do it." Mike had just written his first set of lyrics, for *I Love My Wife* (1977). "Now, let me have the rights to *42nd Street*, too." And so Merrick optioned *Barnum*, announced it, and the songwriters wrote the score. And then Merrick dropped it. (All of which, mind you, was business as usual for Merrick.) New producers were duly found, including Coleman himself; director Joe Layton was hired; and Jim Dale and the P. T. Barnum musical finally glided into the St. James, six years after that first visit to Madison Square Garden, to high acclaim for everybody—except, of course, the long-suffering bookwriter.

Tony Awards were won by Jim Dale (actor), David Mitchell (set designer, tied with John Lee Beatty for *Talley's Folly*), and Theoni V. Aldredge (costume designer).

BROADWAY SCORECARD
/ PERFS: 854 / .$: +

RAVE	FAVORABLE	MIXED	UNFAVORABLE	PAN
1	5			

THE BEST LITTLE WHOREHOUSE IN ·TEXAS

"A New Musical Comedy"

music and lyrics by Carol Hall

book by Larry L. King and Peter Masterson

based on a 1974 *Playboy* magazine article by Larry L. King

directed by Peter Masterson and Tommy Tune

choreographed by Tommy Tune

produced by Universal Pictures (Stevie Phillips)

starring Henderson Forsythe, Carlin Glynn (Masterson), and Delores Hall

with Pamela Blair, Clint Allmon, Jay Garner, J. Frank Lucas, Don Crabtree, Joan Ellis, Susan Mansur, and "The Rio Grande Band"

opened April 17, 1978   *Entermedia Theatre*
transferred June 19, 1978   *46th Street Theatre*

(Note: the first-night reviewers covered the show at its Entermedia Theatre première)

CLIVE BARNES, *POST*

If all the tarts with hearts of gold currently at the Entermedia Theatre banded together they could buy out Fort Knox. *The Best Little Whorehouse in Texas* is a fun new musical. Its pleasures are surprisingly innocent, and despite a certain amount of raunchy language and semi-graphic situations that might bring a blush to sheltered cheeks—should there nowadays be any sheltered cheeks still around—the humor and good nature of the piece make it cheerfully inoffensive. Indeed it is, depending perhaps on your family, just good family entertainment. The story happens to be rather too predictable, which leads to a weak ending. However it is told with a good deal of gusto and a wealth of comic detail, chiefly concerned with Texas politics, both small-time and big-time. Considering the subject matter, the show is beautifully clear-eyed and totally free of the gooey sentimentality you might have feared. It calls a spade a spade with a frankness that is exhilaratingly delicate. Although the girls are perhaps unusually good-natured, and seemingly as healthy in mind and body as cheer-leaders, there is still a refreshing tough honesty about their portrayal. There are no rose-colored illusions here. What we have here is rumbustious genre musical, full of flavor, charmingly accurate in its tonality of place and time, and, best of all, consistently amusing. Carol Hall's music, vigorously played by the Rio Grande Band, has about it the rustic air of a country fair, all ribbons and chickens, and her ballad-like lyrics are most attractive. The book has as many turns in it as a Texas dirt-track but gets there in the end—and certainly the story it has to tell has the distinct advantage of being different. The show already looks pleasingly slick—a Busby Berkeley production number for six girls and twelve dummies is a riot—and if it were to move to Broadway, where it is presumably aimed, it could be made even smoother with time and experience. A strange, old-fashioned, new-fashioned musical, full of simple sentiments, dirty words, political chicanery and social hypocrisy, decent jokes, indecent jokes, bubbling performances and music with a bustle.

RICHARD EDER, *TIMES*

A musical on a milk diet. It takes a small, bright, wry idea and expands and dilutes it at the same time. *Whorehouse* is based on a magazine article by Larry King. It told of the mushrooming political and media furor that ended up in the closing of a brothel that had gone along for years with the general toleration if not satisfaction of the community. There is some fun in the idea, some sharply written dialogue that catches a local Texas flavor, and some agreeable songs. It is all put together too loosely and blandly, though; it has good humor but not the manic ferocity that makes good humor infectious. Some of the situation's possibilities are nicely caught. The governor appears oozing his way through a press conference with a song and soft-shoe routine aptly called "The Sidestep." Jay Garner acts and dances the hard-pressed governor like a bowl of jello trying to flee through a keyhole. There is one brilliant number, a dance routine in which the football team's cheerleaders come on. Each of the six is a blue-eyed, vacant-faced blonde. Each carries two life-sized, blue-eyed, vacant-faced blonde dolls attached, one to each arm. The 18-member line is hilarious; the dolls—thanks to some ingenious springy legs—bouncing even more idiotically than the dancers. The other dance numbers are less interesting, and are carried out with no great skill. The book is not really strong enough to carry a full musical: the figure of Mona, and the possibilities of irony in the notion of a polite and home-like brothel are soon used up. The best scenes are those involving the sheriff, played with a fine, frustrated fieriness by Henderson Forsythe. There are some fine lines—a number of them unprintable here—that convey beautifully the sinewy bite of Texas speech. Hall's songs are frequently pleasant, and several have some real character. The small adjectives that come to mind with *Whorehouse*—"pleasant," "agreeable"—are like school gold stars given for things that have turned out well. There is a great deal that, if it does not come out badly, does not really come out at all. It is a show that marks a lot of time; one fitted for compliments rather than for enthusiasm.

CHRISTOPHER SHARP, *WOMEN'S WEAR DAILY*
The Best Little Whorehouse in Texas is actually located in that vast desert between respectability and profanity. The show has come to us in time to help fill that great void. There is more than enough respectable entertainment playing in New York, and a surplus of profane entertainment, but this new musical is something we haven't seen for awhile: a delightful evening that is respectably profane. It is more fun than a beer-toting hayride at a Mardi Gras. Based on the historic last days of one of the oldest whorehouses in Texas, a place where college students

celebrate football victories with hookers who are elaborately costumed as prom queens, the show is galvanized by the heelkicking choreography of Tommy Tune. This musical is also supplied with some villainous heels who deserve to be kicked. The plot is based on the efforts of a crusading TV newsman-watchdog to close the place down. He finally succeeds, but it is clear that the "victory" only backfires. But if the denouement is bittersweet, the entertainment is not. This show, in fact, could help make ungarnished heterosexuality fashionable again.

DOUGLAS WATT, *DAILY NEWS*
[Headline: "*Best Little Whorehouse* This Side of Heaven"]
If you can allow yourself to think for a couple of hours that whores are angels in disguise and that a town brothel is heaven on earth, then there's no reason why you shouldn't have a whale of a good time. Carol Hall's songs, mostly countrywestern, are as lively and engaging as the 27 performers (not counting the dandy six-piece band on stage). This happy-go-lucky view of small-town vice and statewide corruption, 100% American and both utterly and charmingly free of Brecht-Weill mannerisms, has been delightfully staged by Tommy Tune, who also devised the bright dance routines, and co-librettist Masterson. Though there are references to the big, bad world outside, *The Best Little Whorehouse* is very much on the sunny side of the street. The talk is racy and unrestrained, but all in fun. Henderson Forsythe is a delight as the town sheriff who must, against his will, close the Chicken Ranch. Carlin Glynn is cool, sleek and amusing as the firm but tolerant madam. Aside from a musical nod to Stephen Sondheim in a number called "Hard Candy Christmas," and a fetching ballad of a waitress's lost dreams ("Doatsey Mae," beautifully delivered by Susan Mansur), Hall's pieces run to the spirited and uncomplicated, and rightfully so. The matchless Delores Hall, cast as the house servant, almost walks off with the show with her one solo, "Twenty-Four Hours of Lovin'," and undoubtedly would have sewn up the whole evening had she been handed a near-closing piece. The musical theatre has been notoriously inhospitable to whorehouses in the past. But *The Best Little Whorehouse in Texas*, being both sunny enough and funny enough, may change things with its cheerful disregard for reality. I'm only surprised they don't sell Girl Scout cookies in the lobby.

○   ○   ○

They came from Texas. Texan Larry L. King (no relation to the Larry without the L.) wrote a *Playboy* magazine article about the closing of the Lone Star State's favorite Chicken Ranch, and he didn't mean Colonel Sanders. Texan Pete Masterson, a respected but little-known dramatic actor (*The Trial of Lee Harvey Oswald* [1967], *The Poison Tree* [1976]), lassoed Texan Carol Hall (of TV's *Free to Be . . . You and Me* [1974]) into writing a score, and steered King himself into collaborating on the book. They then corralled Texan Tommy Tune into choreographing and codirecting, and the best little Chicken Ranch moved on up to the second-best state of the nation. Universal Pictures bought the land out from under 'em; that is to say, they made an upfront deal for all rights. Rather than spending millions on the movie rights to a hit Broadway musical—Universal paid $5.5 million for *A Chorus Line* (1975), *Annie* (1977) went for almost $10 million—the studio owned them outright, with the Entermedia version costing them considerably less than one half of one of those millions. Yes, the authors were paid for the use of their work in the movie version; not as much as the authors of *Annie*, certainly, but far more than the authors of *The Act*, *On the Twentieth Century*, or *Timbuktu!*, to name three other 1977–1978 musicals without upfront movie guarantees. Thus, Universal not only got to make the (pretty bad) 1982 Dolly Parton/Burt Reynolds filmization, they also reaped a Texas-size stake from the stage show. The plan was to open downtown at the larger-than-Off-Broadway Entermedia—the old Yiddish Art Theatre, spawning ground of *Oh! Calcutta!* (1969), *Grease* (1972), and, in its days as the Phoenix, *The Golden Apple* (1954) and *Once Upon a Mattress* (1959)—and move triumphantly to Broadway. *Whorehouse* did just that, although the show was not without the usual turmoil, including a last-minute postponement of the opening for fine tuning. Fine tuning in the course of which the heart of the show was bypassed, with Pamela Blair's material whittled right out from under her. (Her solos were cut, too, with one of 'em—"Bus from Amarillo"—mysteriously turning up a couple of previews later in the mouth of Carlin Glynn, also known as Miss Mona, also known as Missus Masterson.) *Whorehouse*, with one of the best little show titles in history, was a big hit indeed, providing Universal with a gusher of crude. Sixteen years later the same group of Texans cantered into town with *The Best Little Whorehouse Goes Public* (1994)—Cavetis Sequellus, which is to say Beware of Sequels—and the folks back at the ol' studio dropped 7 mill in less time than it takes to fire up the mesquite.

Tony Awards were won by Henderson Forsythe (supporting actor) and Carlin Glynn (supporting actress).

BROADWAY SCORECARD
/ PERFS: 1,584 / $: +

RAVE	FAVORABLE	MIXED	UNFAVORABLE	PAN
3	2	1		

BILLY

"A Now Musical," previously entitled *Billy Be Damned*

music and lyrics by Ron Dante and Gene Allan

book by Stephen Glassman (replacing Robert Upton)

based on the novella *Billy Budd*, posthumously published in 1924, by Herman Melville (1819-1891)

directed by Arthur A. Seidelman

choreographed by Grover Dale

produced by Bruce W. Stark in association with Joseph Shoctor

starring Laurence Naismith, John Beal, Jon Devlin, and Robert Salvio

with Dolph Sweet, Barbara Monte, Alan Weeks, George Marcy, William Countryman, and Igors Gavon

opened March 22, 1969   *Billy Rose Theatre*

CLIVE BARNES, *TIMES*

The failure of some little fly-by-night farce is of no particular account to anyone but the actors and other people left unemployed by the producers' irresponsibility. Yet in writing of the failure of *Billy* I find myself

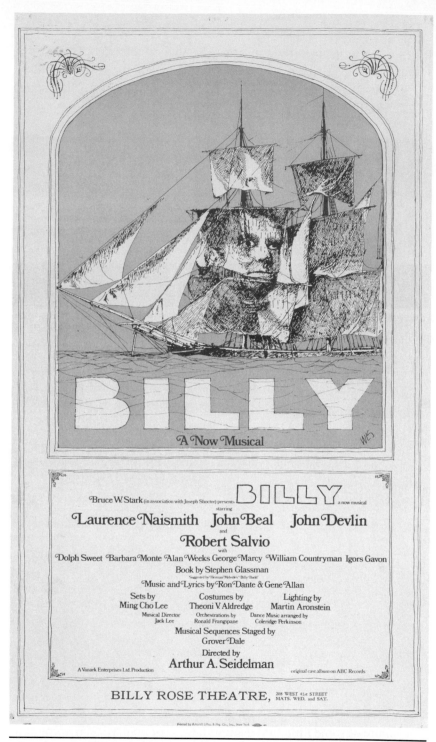

BILLY
A Now Musical

Bruce W. Stark (in association with Joseph Shoctor) presents **BILLY** a now musical
starring
Laurence Naismith   John Beal   John Devlin
and
Robert Salvio
with
Dolph Sweet   Barbara Monte   Alan Weeks   George Marcy   William Countryman   Igors Gavon
Book by Stephen Glassman
"Suggested by Herman Melville's 'Billy Budd'"
Music and Lyrics by Ron Dante & Gene Allan
Sets by   Costumes by   Lighting by
Ming Cho Lee   Theoni V Aldredge   Martin Aronstein
Musical Director   Orchestrations by   Dance Music arranged by
Jack Lee   Ronald Frangipane   Coleridge Perkinson
Musical Sequences Staged by
Grover Dale
Directed by
Arthur A. Seidelman
A Vanark Enterprises Ltd. Production   original cast album on ABC Records

BILLY ROSE THEATRE, 208 WEST 41st STREET
MATS. WED. and SAT.

Billy, "A Now Musical" at the Billy Rose. Who's playing Fannie Brice?
(artwork by "WLS")

approaching the musical with a hushed and cemetery walk. It had honest aspirations. But although it tried hard it sank with all hands. In almost every department—except notably one, the designing—*Billy* was a victim of under-intelligence and subachievement. The musical suffers from a book that reduces the Melville story to the level of pulp adventure. The essence of *Billy Budd*, the confrontation of good and evil, is completely lost. There are times when it seems that librettist Glassman has not even read Melville—only been told about him by an overambitious producer. This is a shoddy job, but in a class apart from and above the music and lyrics. If the book is unfair to Melville, the music and lyrics positively insult his genius. They are like graffiti on the wall of literature. I feel pity for the perpetrators, Ron Dante and Gene Allan, for I presume they can have no conception of what they have done. They imagined they were creating a "rock" musical. They show about as much understanding of rock as did Bing Crosby in his earlier days, and the lyrics can charitably be called only infantile and banal. I hope they will not take it too personally when I say that *Billy* is a perfect example of the axiom that nothing kills a show so effectively as lack of talent. Arthur A. Seidelman's direction is as effective as it could be. It moves fast—but it is difficult just by bailing to stop a sinking ship from fulfilling its destiny. The musical sequences directed by Grover Dale were, luckily, brilliant. Mr. Dale, in his first assignment as a Broadway choreographer, shows real talent. The dance ensembles, every one of them, displayed a vigor and gutsyness the rest of the show woefully lacked. But the only really worthwhile thing about *Billy* was the superb setting by Ming Cho Lee, which showed how style can be given even to naturalism. Mr. Lee was responsible—Tony award nominations not to the contrary—for the best designing of last season, in *Here's Where I Belong* at this same Billy Rose Theatre. Like *Billy*, the show opened and closed on the same night.

MARTIN GOTTFRIED, *WOMEN'S WEAR DAILY*
Like some New England Lorelei, Herman Melville's *Billy Budd* has long attracted would-be adaptors to their dooms. Saturday night's victim was called *Billy*, and I must say it is the clumsiest and most childish grasp of Melville that I have yet seen, a crude, teeny-bopper attempt to reduce the novel's strange sense of good-and-evil to a comment on conscientious objectors and the war in Vietnam. The start is, well, startling: a burst of muscular, even electric dance that is to prove typical of

its choreographer, Grover Dale. Though *Billy* doesn't have a whole lot of dancing, there is more than enough to prove Dale an original. Considering the triteness of Broadway choreography, the bulk of it so chorus-boy, I think this newcomer has a freshness and technique that is exhilarating indeed. Mr. Seidelman tries very hard to transpose Dale's stark masculinity of dance into a poetic staging and this is very effective in the beginning, especially upon Ming Cho Lee's towering set of rigging and masts. (If nothing else, I am awed by Ming's suspension of a mast from the flies, especially since it is strong enough to carry a man.) But none of these efforts managed to camouflage Glassman's amateur book-writing. Robert Salvio, an extremely talented actor, goes a long way toward realizing the intangible holiness of *Billy*, and sings not only well but in a stylized way uncommon to Broadway. The company behind him is considerably less certain of itself and some of them (especially Laurence Naismith as the Captain, John Devlin as the Master-at-Arms) were played not just absurdly but with a very unprofessional sense of let's-get-it-over-with. Melville triumphs again over those who would use him. In this case, his competition was minor.

RICHARD WATTS, JR., POST
Laurence Naismith, who once was Santa Claus in a musical comedy [the 1963 *Here's Love*], appeared to be playing him again. . . . If they are going to have music on a British warship, let it be *Pinafore*.

●   ●   ●

The authors finally knuckled under and changed the title. Seemed that the Billy Rose Estate had a problem booking *Billy Be Damned* into the Billy Rose. Even so, the phone room at *Billy* got calls asking "Who's playing Fannie Brice?"—or could that just have been press agent Harvey Sabinson straining to get *anything* in the paper? One performance and out.

BROADWAY SCORECARD
/ PERFS: I / $: –

RAVE	FAVORABLE	MIXED	UNFAVORABLE	PAN
I				5

THE BOY FRIEND

a revival of the 1954 British "Musical Comedy of the Roaring 20s"

book, music, and lyrics by Sandy Wilson

directed by Gus Schirmer

choreographed by Buddy Schwab

produced by John Yorke, Don Saxon, and Michael Hellerman

starring Judy Carne

with Sandy Duncan, Ronald Young, Jeanne Beauvais, Leon Shaw, Harvey Evans, Barbara Andres, and Marie Paxton

opened April 14, 1970   *Ambassador Theatre*

MARTIN GOTTFRIED, *WOMEN'S WEAR DAILY*

The last time I saw *The Boy Friend* it was 15 years ago and I sneaked in during the first intermission. Things have changed a great deal since then. I don't have to sneak into the theatre anymore—as a matter of fact, I sometimes have to sneak out, which I think says something about both the theatre and me. Things have changed in other ways too: though there have been a lot of copies of *The Boy Friend* kind of show (from *Little Mary Sunshine* [1959] to the still-running *Dames at Sea* [1968, both off-Broadway]), none has ever been so consistent, so perfectly conceived. This kind of camp—replica rather than parody—has already become dated so that *The Boy Friend*, a nostalgic "Musical Comedy of the 1920s," is itself a nostalgic "Musical Comedy of the 1950s." That's sad, I guess. Even sadder is the way it was revived. Sandy Wilson's show is in its own way a classic but it hasn't been well reproduced. This new version tends to be heavy-handed. What hurts most is director Gus Schirmer's heavy-handed attack, over-emphasizing the gestures and pronunciations until the tone moves from camp to burlesque. This is just wrong, and the sloppiness of the company in both over-stylization and simple matters of English dialect only added weight to the heaviness. Still, Judy Carne was marvelous as Polly, the flapper heiress who finally gets a boy friend. This isn't a lead role in an ordinary sense (the character doesn't even sing one solo). But for some indefinable reason, the character is a talent-projecting one and of course it is the part that sprang Julie Andrews to stardom. Carne projects her talent with confidence and charm. Her voice is pure, true and clear, a soprano that doesn't scratch out the lyrics. Carne is one of the few Britishers in the company—she is billed as "the Sock-It-to-Me Girl from *Laugh-In*"—billing I'm sure she deplores and billing, I assume, designed to draw business from those who watch that program often enough to know who the "Sock-It-to-Me Girl" is. Miss Carne is entirely delightful. I'm afraid she has little support. . . . The lack of imagination is the key to this let-down by (or perhaps of) an old friend; a lack of imagination that extends to a producer looking to milk some more money out of a proven winner. And meanwhile, what ever happened to Sandy Wilson?

WALTER KERR, *TIMES*
[Headline: "Girl Watching Made Easy"]
A wench named Sandy Duncan, hitherto of *Canterbury Tales* [1969] and now flattened out into a dizzy, elbow-flapping, 1920-ish surf-board, comes on as a member of the four-girl chorus and almost instantly wipes the stage clean of any other presence. Bent backward, her red-headed bob bobbing to the ratchety clockwork of the beat, dancing cheek to belt-buckle with the white-shoed boy who brought her, she is the girl John Held, Jr. [the '20s wood-block cartoonist] had in mind holding. The rest of the revival works hard, breathes heavily, turns pale sometimes. There's too much white space around every-thing—unpainted portals, half-empty fringes where there ought to be more girls or more flower baskets or more something—and the pro-duction is altogether too conscious that camp has come into being, and been analyzed and devitalized, since *The Boy Friend* first plucked out its pleasant copycat tunes. Judy Carne is bland, but no more, in the role Julie Andrews once made meringue of, and no one ever leaves the stage without giggling directly into the amplifying system. The whole giddy pastiche needs to take itself much more seriously. But Miss Duncan is serious, very serious, about leaping up off Harvey Evan's knee because, as she says. "Someone's coming." This is a case of the effect producing

the cause, for someone does come. She is also marvelously in earnest about appearing for a number in toeshoes. The number isn't a toedance, the entire project is preposterous, and then, having shown us how delicately she can work, she proceeds to tap on the toes. I'm not sure the twenties were that truly inspired, and choreographer Buddy Schwab no doubt deserves a special nod. Gus Schirmer, over-all director, doesn't; if it weren't for Miss Duncan, the whole thing would be on the soggy side.

◦   ◦   ◦

Perhaps the producers were oblivious to the fact that they had a star right under their noses; or maybe they were simply so sure that the Sock-It-to-Me Girl was going to sell oh-so-many tickets that nothing (and I mean nothing) mattered. In any event, Sandy Duncan—fresh from her Tony-nominated debut in *Canterbury Tales* and replacing Leland Palmer in the Off-Broadway hit *Your Own Thing* (1968)—lit up the stage, with an energetic assist from Harvey Evans as her Charleston-ing boyfriend. Everything else about this revival of Sandy Wilson's 1954 spoof was pale and drab. It remains baffling that Duncan—despite finally attaining unquestioned Broadway stardom with the 1979 revival of *Peter Pan*—has to this date *still* never originated a role in a Broadway musical, more than twenty-five years since she first hit the street. Categorically Speaking Dept.: In one of the stranger bits of Tony Award category determination, Duncan (playing a subordinate role with below-the-title billing) was this time nominated for *best* actress—against Elaine Stritch and Susan Browning of *Company* and winner Helen Gallagher of *No, No, Nanette*. Patsy Kelly (starred *above* the title in *Nanette*) took the supporting actress award, against *Company*'s Barbara Barrie (with more prominent and larger billing than Browning) and Pamela Myers.

BROADWAY SCORECARD

/ PERFS: 111 / $: −

RAVE	FAVORABLE	MIXED	UNFAVORABLE	PAN
1		1	1	3

BRIGADOON

a touring revival of the 1947 romantic musical fantasy

music by Frederick Loewe

book and lyrics by Alan Jay Lerner

suggested by the 1862 German story *Germelshausen* by Friedrich Wilhelm Gerstäcker (uncredited)

directed by Vivian Matalon

choreographed by Agnes de Mille, recreated by James Jamieson

produced by Wolf Trap, presented by Zev Bufman and The Shubert Organization

starring Martin Vidnovic, Meg Bussert, and John Curry

with Frank Hamilton, Marina Eglevsky, Stephen Lehew, Elaine Hausman, Mark Zimmerman, Jack Dabdoub, Casper Roos, Mollie Smith, and Kenneth Kantor

opened October 16, 1980   *Majestic Theatre*

WALTER KERR, *TIMES*

I'm not sure that this revived *Brigadoon* proves anything about the vitamin-enriched dances that Agnes de Mille introduced and dozens of choreographers promptly adopted, but it does call attention to one problem they've left us with. Dances aren't like songs. You can't just pass out tenor and baritone parts among trained singers and have them hit the right notes at the right time right off. Dances are more like woodsmoke, curling away from you just when you want to get the essence of one in your fist. As they are subtler for being unwritten, they are also more supple, more elusive, more personal to the choreographer. Yes, there may be some kind of notation on paper to serve as a rough guide; but it's still a matter of interior impulse, a vital surge rising to inform old and generalized gestures with new and specific meaning—and that's got to be reborn each time. For *Brigadoon*, Miss de Mille is at hand, but she is working through an assistant, James Jamieson, and with new dancers governed by impulses of their own. The results are curious. We do get a real feel of what de Mille accomplished [until] we come to the evening's two most memorable numbers. "Come to Me, Bend to Me" still brings eight girls in night-before-the-wedding pastels forward to dip gently, retract gracefully, sweep in shoulder-to-shoulder unison, slide their feet sideways like mysteriously grounded birds. And the incredible "Funeral Dance," in which the woman whose lover has died rises from his body to wrap a shawl about her head and then express her mourning through the retarded gyrations of a reel is performed with impeccable technical expertise by Marina Eglevsky. But in both cases the accomplishment is technical. The intimate, directly sensual connection between motive and movement is not quite present. Miss de Mille still has it in her head, of course. But her assistant and her dancers are not as imaginative as she. And that represents a real difficulty for a show that depends as heavily upon dance as *Brigadoon* does. Over the years some dancers will intuit the connection, let it lift them up; others will not. Whenever it doesn't happen, *Brigadoon* is likely to be in trouble.

HOWARD KISSEL, *WOMEN'S WEAR DAILY*

Although Lerner and Loewe went on to make several major contributions to the American musical theatre, they never wrote a better show than *Brigadoon*, which has a wonderfully endearing book, an absolutely glorious score and unusually dramatic ideas for dance. The story of the little 18th-century Scottish town that comes to life once a century, and where a troubled American finds love and solace, is a latter-day fairy tale—but all you have to do to believe it is to believe in the power of music. No one who has heard "Heather on the Hill" and "Almost Like Being in Love" well sung can doubt that the world has isolated spots of magic on its crusty, worn surface. Currently the most magical spot on the crusty, worn surface of Broadway is the Majestic Theatre. Director Vivian Matalon has treated Lerner's charming book with earnestness and respect, making the story a compelling one, not just a chance to let the singers rest their voices. Because the dramatic tone is so strong, the singing and dancing are set off more strikingly. He has assembled a superlative cast. As the romantic leads, Martin Vidnovic and Meg

Bussert both sing with an emotional genuineness and a musicianship that is thrilling. We have not heard this kind of excitement in our musical theatre for a long time, since most of the recent shows have been either too embarrassed or too unskilled to deal with romance in so full-throated a way. The dancing honors of the evening go to Marina Eglevsky, who does the profoundly moving dance of mourning with great power. John Curry is expectedly elegant as the sullen Harry Beaton, dancing with particular grace in the chase scene. Agnes de Mille's original choreography still has tremendous honesty and strength. Unlike most of the revivals of the last few years, which have been cheap-looking road shows done with concern only for the bottom line, *Brigadoon* has been rethought, restructured with respect and intelligence. The show may be even more solid dramatically than it was 30 years ago. Musically it has never been better—I can't wait for the cast album. This *Brigadoon* is quite simply the best sung, best acted, best danced, best produced revival of a musical since the death of City Center.

FRANK RICH, *TIMES*

Brigadoon may be about a Scottish miracle, but its new revival offers a miracle that is pure Broadway. When the show's romantic leads, Meg Bussert and Martin Vidnovic, come together late in Act I to declare their love, they at once send the audience into the stratosphere of ecstasy and catapult themselves into the loftiest firmament of musical comedy performers. It's the kind of magic that can happen when young talent, a great song and plain old sexual chemistry all spring up in the same theatre at the same time. It happens when Vidnovic, playing a New York tourist, returns from picking some heather from one of the show's misty, idyllic hills. This actor, an exemplary Jud in last season's *Oklahoma!*, is now plainly a man in love. As he trots in with his basket of foliage, his feet have only a passing acquaintanceship with the ground. And it's a totally uncomplicated love, because no one has yet told him that his dream girl lives in a spectral, 18th-century village that wakes up only one day each century. So Vidnovic, a coltish figure in jeans and a turtleneck, just starts singing in a big, rich voice: "What a day this has been!/What a rare mood I'm in!/Why, it's almost like being in love!" Suddenly, he's dancing, too, with springy abandon. As he flies into his second chorus, a door opens in a cottage above him, and out steps Miss Bussert. This actress, the charming Marian the Librarian of last spring's ill-fated *Music Man*, is a demure young woman with wispy auburn hair, a hesitant grin and a voice that soars on a crystalline yet sugar-free sweetness. When she sings "Almost Like Being in Love," it's not almost like being in love. It's the real thing. One wonders if the Majestic has seen anything like her since Mary Martin and Barbara Cook held court in the 40's and 50's. Lest we get too dizzy here—and be warned that Vidnovic and Bussert may knock you senseless—it must be added that not all of *Brigadoon* is quite so airborne. Still, Bussert and Vidnovic convince us that anything is possible. This pair is so exciting that they really must have a modern romantic musical that's all their own. While they wait for someone to write them one, *Brigadoon* will amply serve as a delightful temporary haven.

·   ·   ·

Brigadoon returned to Broadway after thirty-three years with a new, full-scale production (incorporating the original Agnes de Mille choreography). While Lerner and Loewe's score might not be quite so sparkling as *My Fair Lady* (1956), *Brigadoon* has the heart and warmth that their Shavian musical lacks. Frederick Loewe's limited output includes some truly beautiful music, notably in parts of *Paint Your Wagon* (1951) and *Gigi* (the 1958 film), but *Brigadoon* is surely his most moving work. *Brigadoon* was remarkably effective when it first opened in 1947, its theme of love transcending death speaking directly to audiences who had just undergone a world war. By 1980 the story seemed old-fashioned and somewhat out of date. One wonders, though, if the message—"when you love someone deeply, anything is possible, even miracles"—might not be especially relevant today.

BROADWAY SCORECARD
/ PERFS: 134 / $: –

RAVE	FAVORABLE	MIXED	UNFAVORABLE	PAN
1	4	1		

BRING BACK BIRDIE

"A Brand New Musical Comedy"

music by Charles Strouse

lyrics by Lee Adams

book by Michael Stewart

a sequel to their 1960 musical satire *Bye Bye Birdie*

"conceived and directed" (and choreographed) by Joe Layton

produced by Lee Guber, Shelly Gross, Slade Brown, and Jim Milford

starring Donald O'Connor, Chita Rivera, and Maria Karnilova

with Maurice Hines, Marcel Forestieri, Robin Morse, Evan Seplow, Jeb Brown, Frank DeSal, and Lynda Ferguson

opened March 5, 1981   Martin Beck Theatre

CLIVE BARNES, *POST*

[Headline: "Send Back *Birdie!*"]

The kind of show that teaches one to be grateful for small mercies. Such as the final curtain. . . . There are at least two stunning, gilt-edged performances [by Chita Rivera and Maria Karnilova], a few decent numbers, and a frenetically energetic staging by Joe Layton that sometimes resoundingly hits the bell. And there is nothing much wrong with the rest that couldn't be put right by World War III. The new Michael Stewart story is about as engaging as a wet flounder on a dry night—stale, flat and unprofitable. Its human interest would hardly appeal to a dwarf pygmy, its jokes must have been left somewhere on the way to the theatre, and the very real spirit of the original show is here simply the specter at the famine. Only two chances have been taken for the new show to make an intelligent comment on its predecessor. The first is a telephone sequence for the kids. In the first show, in a highly original setting of Modular boxes, the kids telephoned one another that a beauty had been "pinned" by a hero. Ah, sweet innocence! In the new show the kids all have cordless, transistor telephones, and are eagerly discussing a 16-year-old's decision to set up house with her boyfriend. The only other sign of the shifting times is that Conrad Birdie, like Hamlet, is now fat and scant of breath. Joe Layton, as director/choreographer, runs round the show with the manic energy of a little Dutch boy with only one pair of hands faced with a dam burst like a showering faucet. He does well, but nothing could be well enough. And the scenery by David Mitchell, all be-decked with TV monitors, looks like ABC network news on a bad night. Chita Rivera, superwoman herself, tries, almost singlehandedly to get this heavier-than-lead dirigible off the ground. She is magnificent, she is commanding, and at least three times she shows her ability to stop a show that has never even started.

FRANK RICH, *TIMES*

[Headline: "*Birdie* After the Bye Bye"]

Perhaps *Bye Bye Birdie* was a less than classic musical, but it had a friskiness, a wise-guy sense of humor and a witty, tuneful score that linger brightly in the memory. A parody of the rock-and-roll craze, it was an explosion of youthful Broadway talent. It launched the careers of its then-obscure authors; it turned Miss Rivera and her leading man, Dick Van Dyke, into full-fledged stars; it made an ex-hoofer named Gower Champion the hottest choreographer in town. If the first *Birdie* was invigorating, the new one is depressing right up until the curtain call [in which the stars perform "Rosie," the "loose-limbed, moonlit finale" of *Bye Bye Birdie*]. Although its creators have done plenty of fine work since their first success, you'd never guess it from this mess. *Bring Back Birdie* is not only far inferior to its predecessor, but it is also woefully tired—as if everyone involved had abandoned hope. Instead of doing *Bring Back Birdie*, these people should have brought back *Bye Bye Birdie*. Or maybe they should have left their and our fond memories in peace. *Bring Back Birdie* begins as an amiable shambles and devolves into total chaos. Mr. Stewart unleashes a slew of confused, satirically toothless subplots that involve everything from an extramarital affair to a Hare Krishna cult to a fraudulent funeral. By the end, the show has run off in so many cryptic directions that you may think each member of the cast has been handed a different lousy script. The score that interrupts this book has a death wish. For some reason, Strouse and

Adams have taken many of the song ideas from the original *Birdie* and written updated versions that invite devastating comparisons. Joe Layton, the director and choreographer, hasn't given even the better songs any zip. In *Barnum*, Mr. Layton took up the reins of Mr. Champion's razzle-dazzle tradition, but here he's reverted to the lazy Joe Layton of *Platinum*. On those rare occasions when he has an idea for a dance routine—a roller-skating number, for instance—he loses interest before he gets around to executing it. The solo turns he's given his stars are so flavorlessly repetitive that they blur into one continuous banality. Though *Bring Back Birdie* aspires to bring back everyone's happy youth, it has sent its creators and audience alike crashing into a gloomy middle age.

DOUGLAS WATT, *DAILY NEWS*
[Headline: "Fogbound *Birdie* Lost in Flight"]
Chita Rivera's great legs are as limber as ever, and she gives off sparks from head to toe whenever she's on stage; but all on her own, for *Bring Back Birdie*, last night's stale musical, is like some prehistoric beast gasping for breath in an alien environment. With a plodding book (Michael Stewart's) for a body, and leaden music (Charles Strouse's) and commonplace lyrics (Lee Adams's) to propel it, the thing is unable to lift itself off the ground. Rarely have writers of this trio's attainments appeared less interested in their work. There were times when I felt I was watching a revival of one of those idiotic musicals of the '20s whose original score had been lost to be replaced with a patchwork of tunes by forgotten writers. When *Bring Back Birdie* isn't simply dragging itself across the stage in one dull musical number after another, and through a series of desperate plot developments, it is busy being tasteless. Although the discovery of Birdie in Arizona is a momentarily amusing scene, his transformation into a corpulent, bewigged imitation of the late Elvis Presley in the singer's last years as a performer, right down to the tight flashy costumes the overweight star wore, is shockingly repellent. One learns from the program's "Who's Who" that Marcel Forestieri, the actor playing this role, is a professional Presley impersonator known as "Little El." He is a sad sight. O'Connor, grown a bit thick around the middle himself, has little to do other than a couple of perfunctory tap and soft-shoe routines. Joe Layton has staged the entire show, rashly taking additional credit for "conceiving" the production. As

in those silly oldtime musical comedies, the writers have resorted to any means to keep the show going, including such outdated devices as a punk-rock group called "Filth" and a Moonies (here called "Sunnies") tribal meeting. If it weren't for designer David Mitchell's basic scenic scheme, a forest of active color TV sets calling to mind the late Gower Champion's charming network of phone-calling teenagers in the earlier show, we'd never for a moment believe all this was taking place in the present.

●   ●   ●

Bye Bye Birdie—after twenty happy years—remained a top money earner on the stock and amateur circuit for licensor Tams-Witmark. But how often can the same high school do *Bye Bye Birdie* before the local parents throw their hands over their ears in collective horror at that first caterwauling "We love you, Conrad"? So Tams's Louis Aborn called the authors for a sequel, just for amateurs. What's the harm, 'long as nobody sees it? Enter suburban tent producers Guber and Gross, who'd made a killing with their 1977 *King and I* revival. These were the same gentlemen who in 1967 produced *Sherry!*, and who in 1974 had the bright idea of transmogrifying the twenty-five-year-old Carol Channing vehicle *Gentlemen Prefer Blondes* (1949) into the Carol Channing vehicle *Lorelei*. They also produced the 1967 stock tryout of Michael Stewart's computer dating musical, *How Do You Do, I Love You*, a Phyllis Newman-starrer that would've marked Maltby and Shire's Broadway debut if it'd made it to Broadway. Hearing tell of the just-for-amateurs *Bring Back Birdie*, Guber and Gross snapped it up. Stewart, with 1980 hits *Barnum* and *42nd Street* running, was especially skeptical about exposing the half-baked sequel to the harsh glare of Broadway; but Lee Adams had been undergoing a dry spell since *Applause* in 1970 (a dry spell that continues to this day), and Charles Strouse—whose *Annie* (1977) was the town's reigning hit—never blanched from an opportunity for more Broadway exposure (seven consecutive flops since *Annie*, and counting). And so the gang proceeded, with grave misgivings. When they auditioned the material for Gower Champion, who'd guided the first *Birdie*, his response was simply "Why are you doing it?" Nobody had an answer, but they did it, and how. Everybody's a Critic Dept.: Midway through his solo "Middle Age Blues" at the final Saturday matinee, O'Connor forgot the words and got down on his hands and knees, looking to the pit for prompting. Then he lay down flat on the stage. "You sing it," he yelled to the conductor. "I always hated this song, anyway."

BROADWAY SCORECARD
/ PERFS: 4 / $: –

RAVE	FAVORABLE	MIXED	UNFAVORABLE	PAN
				6

A BROADWAY MUSICAL

"A Musical about a Broadway Musical"

music by Charles Strouse

lyrics by Lee Adams

book by William F. Brown

production supervised by Gower Champion

director/choreographer unbilled (George Faison replaced by Gower Champion)

co-choreographed by George Bunt

produced by Norman Kean and Garth H. Drabinsky

with Warren Berlinger (replacing Julius LaRosa), Gwdya DonHowe (Kean), Irving Allen Lee (replacing Ron Ferrell), Alan Weeks, Patti Karr (replacing second-billed Helen Gallagher), Larry Marshall, Larry Riley, Tiger Haynes, and Anne Francine

opened December 21, 1978   Lunt-Fontanne Theatre

CLIVE BARNES, *POST*

[Headline: "*A Broadway Musical* Just Dribbles Away"]

A sorry evening in the theatre. *A Broadway Musical* is—guess what?—about the making of a Broadway musical. It happens to be the making of a Broadway disaster. It is all to do with a pitiful show called *Sneakers.* This is intended to express black exploitation in the symbolic terms of basketball, and it very understandably flops—this is the musical within the musical, you understand—in Washington, D.C. Undaunted by failure, the producer of this fictitious *Sneakers* substitutes his Las Vegas cabaret star with the young black author of the book and decides to risk all on Broadway. Man, he should never have done that! If ever there was a show that should have stopped in Washington—or even Boston, Philadelphia or Peoria—that producer had it. *A Broadway Musical* is a grotesquely wrongheaded venture, and one can only feel a decent sympathy for the very talented people who have somehow gotten themselves involved in it. It is in essence a parody of a parody. The creation of a Broadway musical is, as we all know in show business, a kind of divine madness, at its best a craze of genius, at its worst a bay of pigs. You could create a marvelous film documentary on it. But *A Broadway Musical* is not a documentary. It is a musical that by its own definition has to pretend to be a flop—and succeeds only too effortlessly. We are being shown—very effectively—the anatomy of a Broadway failure. The musical team of Charles Strouse and Lee Adams is formidable indeed, but here sounds less than inspired. To some extent their task was self-destructive—they had to suggest songs that were the amusing echoes of songs that need to be devastatingly bad. They had to create camp, rather than comment on camp. A difficult task—and one idly wonders why they attempted it. Gower Champion came into the show during its workshop period, in an effort to pull it all together. He hasn't, but he obviously tried hard. Champion, who is a wonderfully resourceful director of musicals—the show is described as "supervised" by him rather than directed and choreographed—has done a very skilful job. But nothing can defeat conceptual banality. The cast, assisted all the way by Champion, does its best, like men and women singing songs while clinging onto a lifeboat.

MEL GUSSOW, *TIMES*

A Broadway Musical was designed as a Broadway musical about the making of a Broadway musical. The originator and the co-producer of

the show, Norman Kean, has apparently experienced many of the typical tribulations of the genre—false starts, hirings, firings, rewritings on
the road. As *A Broadway Musical* entered its own tryout, life began imitating art imitating life. Before the show opened last night, it had
changed its director and lost two of its stars. Gower Champion, who is
as much a musical surgeon as a play doctor, was called in for repairs. He
is now credited, tentatively, as production supervisor. Having seen the
show, one can understand the tentativeness. *A Broadway Musical* seems
not so much directed—or written—as glued together from spare parts.
The idea of course is to create a spoof, to make fun of all the Broadway
intrigue and duplicity. This may be amusing to read about in gossip
columns, but it is a thin thread for a musical comedy. The play's twist is
that the musical is black; blackness, we are told, "is the magic formula
of today." A cynical white producer grasps a drama called *The Final
Point* by a new black author—a locker-room basketball play "about the
exploitation of a human being," and decides to subvert it into an upbeat
musical entitled *Sneakers*. This is the framework for a string of slack
tunes and show business wisecracks about blacks on Broadway, Jewish
theatre party ladies (a song called "Yenta Power") and lawyers with steel
clauses. Probably the people who would be most offended by this enterprise are those who continue to be hopeful about the state of the
Broadway musicals. The music and words are by Charles Strouse and
Lee Adams, whose credits run from *Bye, Bye, Birdie* (staged by Mr.
Champion) to *Applause*. No applause this time around. The book by
William F. Brown, who wrote *The Wiz*, is beneath the score. Mr.
Champion has attempted to streamline this tired vehicle with bright
lights, spangled costumes and a high-stepping chorus line, with famil-
iar Champion touches. The cast performs with eagerness, even as the
show sinks. The lyrics of one of the songs run, "Nada, nothing, zero,
zip," which could suffice as a four-word description for *A Broadway
Musical*.

CHRISTOPHER SHARP, *WOMEN'S WEAR DAILY*

If songs are the sails that help move a musical to its destination, then *A
Broadway Musical* should be considered well equipped. The new show
has one song that's outstanding, one that has a beautifully haunting
sound and a catchy title number. The outstanding number, "The 1934

Hot Chocolate," is a show stopper, but composer Charles Strouse and lyricist Lee Adams prove they can stop the show with music as well as push it toward its goal again when they want to. Along the way, they have a great deal of fun with the words and music. But if the sails are in top condition, the boat itself isn't quite ready. The book about a white producer trying to exploit a serious young black playwright by musicalizing his drama has built-in difficulties. It offers a choice of staging the musical as a farce, or with a racial hard edge. Should it be an insider's look at Broadway? Or should it have less arcane and more general interest? Unfortunately, instead of making choices, this production tries to do it all. The racial hard edge is inevitably there but it is diminished by farcical razz-matazz. The inside look at Broadway alternates with caricature. While the show still doesn't have a unifying form, it has been polished almost to the point of sterility. The several funny rough edges this show had in workshop have been rinsed out with the result that everything is neater, cleaner and also slicker. But there are moments that are unforgettably rich. Anne Francine as a theatre party power is wonderfully comic, and Alan Weeks does a ticklish job in his role as a Broadway composer. The wistful beauty, "The 1934 Hot Chocolate," is Strouse and Adams at their "Once Upon a Time" best and it is beautifully realized by Tiger Haynes. Director Gower Champion and his choreography crew sensitively dressed that number up, but they did too much with another gem, "You Gotta Have Dancing." As it was delivered in somewhat different form by Helen Gallagher in workshop, the song's simplicity but clear angles left the effect of intimate communication. It's too much of a Broadway big deal in this rendition by Patti Karr, but it still has a delicious sound. It is tragic that this show's substantial parts do not add up to a more substantial whole.

o   o   o

The travails of black-themed musicals written (or produced) by middle-aged white men is not unknown. Strouse and Adams had scored the Sammy Davis vehicle *Golden Boy* (1964); William F. Brown had written *The Wiz* (1975); and George Faison had stepped into the racial minefield of *1600 Pennsylvania Avenue* (1976) as replacement director/choreographer. The 1976 all-black revival of *Guys and Dolls*—another case in point—used Off-Broadway's Edison Theatre for auditions. Proprietor Norman Kean (who had played landlord to the long-running Gospel-tuner *Don't Bother Me, I Can't Cope* [1972]) observed said auditions and thought, "Hmmm." And proceeded to expose himself to the travails of black-themed musicals written (or produced) by middle-aged white men. Kean regularly operated on a shoestring; hence, the furthest out-of-town he could manage for his tryout was Harlem. So *A Broadway Musical* tried out at the Riverside Church, with a five-piece band. In moving down to 46th Street, Kean lost his two stars (Julius LaRosa and Helen Gallagher) and—needless to say—canned his black director-choreographer. Gower Champion, at the nadir of his career, made a half hearted rehabilitory stab at the material, but the fate of *A Broadway Musical* was preordained. (The wife of the producer in *A Broadway Musical* was played by the wife of the producer of *A Broadway Musical*, Gwyda DonHowe. In 1988 Kean murdered her and then jumped to his death.)

BROADWAY SCORECARD
/ PERFS: 1 / $: −

RAVE	FAVORABLE	MIXED	UNFAVORABLE	PAN
			1	5

BUBBLING BROWN SUGAR

"A New Musical Revue"

existing music and lyrics by various writers; additional music by Danny Holgate, Emme Kemp, and Lillian Lopez

book by Loften Mitchell

based on a concept by Rosetta LeNoire

directed by Robert M. Cooper

choreographed by Billy Wilson

produced by J. Lloyd Grant, Richard Bell, Robert M. Cooper, and Ashton Springer, in association with Moe Septee, Inc.

starring Avon Long, Josephine Premice (replacing Thelma Carpenter), Vivian Reed, and Joseph Attles

with Ethel Beatty, Carolyn Byrd, Chip Garnett, Barry Preston, Barbara Rubenstein, and Vernon Washington

opened March 2, 1976   Anta Theatre

CLIVE BARNES, *TIMES*

[Headline: "*Bubbling Brown Sugar* Boils"]

This really is the musical season for the golden oldies. Last night *Bubbling Brown Sugar* came to the boil—after a little warming up—and although it purports to be a musical history of Harlem it is really a thin but acceptable excuse for a bundle of old Harlem tunes, interspersed with some evocative names and some rather bad jokes. It takes some time to get going—the time in fact it takes for the "concept" by Rosetta LeNoire of a nostalgic journey down Harlem's memory lane to be established by Loften Mitchell's somewhat rambling book. But what really gets it bubbling is some of the most likable and lovable music around—including music specially written for the show, dazzling choreography by Billy Wilson, and performances that take off with the noise, speed and dazzle of the Concorde. Here and there the book does attempt to make labored social comment about the changing stature of the black man, but it tends to be a little exploitive and even patronizing. However, the many blacks in the audience did not seem to think so. What would a honky know? The choreography is by Billy Wilson, who has made his career in Europe, including a long stint with the National Ballet of Holland. This was his Broadway debut and he got the show moving magnificently, the dancing being some of the best to be seen currently on Broadway. As Wilson is also credited with the musical staging and as the show is hardly anything but musical staging, it is difficult to see precisely what the director Robert M. Cooper did, but it all goes as smoothly as black velvet.

MARTIN GOTTFRIED, POST
[Headline: "*Sugar*: How Sweet It Is"]
Bubbling Brown Sugar didn't get a title like that for nothing. There is much that is technically wrong with the musical, but there's one thing that's technically perfect—it's terrific. Broadway's money is too smart to come up with ideas like this, which is why Broadway's smart money doesn't come up with shows like this. The idea was to have a couple of black youngsters run into a trio of black show business old timers on a Harlem street. The oldsters then rummage through "our old theatrical trunk" before taking the kids back "through time and space" to see the Harlem of old. A terrible idea for a book? It is a miserable one. But it is a pretext more quickly forgiven than a crazy tip on a winning horse. Because from the opening boogaloo through the closing, smashing tap dancing finale in top hats and tails, *Bubbling Brown Sugar* is gorgeous entertainment. But what makes the show work as a theatre force is its contagious effervesence, a highness of spirit that just about never lets down. Although Loften Mitchell's book is sometimes just plain awful (if it talked about Harlem being "a place that make things happen" once more you'd want to strangle it), it does string the musical numbers together, at least until Robert M. Cooper (the director) and Wilson finally say the hell with it. By that time, the songs and dancing are going so strong that nothing can stop the show.

WALTER KERR, *TIMES*

Since by definition revues lack narratives to push them, and since they're composed of bits and pieces supplied by many hands, revues need something to glue them together. The performers, ergo, must be used as cement, reappearing regularly enough to identify themselves and invite intimacy, establishing themselves boldly enough (alone or in shifting combinations) to make you forget what's missing in the glow of new, firm friendships. A revue is an artfully designed collage of personality or it's nothing. But I was endlessly frustrated waiting for people to come back so I could get to know them better, or wondering—for considerable spans of musical time—what they were doing there at all. Halfway through the first act a sizzling witch (well, she bewitched me) with a body capable of shimmying sideways and doing Charleston back-kicks at one and the same time, and with a habit of sucking her cheeks to a pucker as the pace grew faster, did a superlative job on "Sweet Georgia Brown," backed up by two agile dancers in blue tuxedos who could be twins but aren't. Naturally, I kept waiting for this dynamic creature—Vivian Reed, the program told me it was—to reappear. Approximately an hour and a half later she did reappear, identifiably, to change pace completely and hold stage with a still, intense solemnity as she lavished brilliant gospel lifts on "God Bless the Child." But where had she been in the meantime, and why had I been left biting my nails so long? I see now—the program again—that she hadn't really vanished, she'd been easing in and out of quartets and the like. But she'd vanished rhythmically during the long hiatus, vanished as a force, and that's no way to build a lasting relationship. The ragged placement of people and numbers hurts, because *Bubbling Brown Sugar* hasn't really anything else to go on. The format is close to simple-minded, taking forever to say what it's going to do and then, as often as not, doing it incoherently. A theatrical trunk is lugged on stage early, so that lanky, sassy Josephine Premice can snatch from it bits and pieces of costuming that once belonged to [Bert] Williams, [Ethel] Waters, [Florence] Mills. But, for all the incidental goodies it contains, that's a sloppily packed trunk.

•   •   •

"Black" revues had been a Broadway staple for years, with two mainstream hits—Eubie Blake's 1921 Musical Melange *Shuffle Along*, and *Blackbirds of 1928* (with a "white" score from the debuting team of Jimmy

McHugh and Dorothy Fields)—among the numerous offerings. The pace slackened in the racially conscious 1960s, but the success of the 1967 Pearl Bailey Company of *Hello, Dolly!*, *Purlie* (1970), and *Raisin* (1973) demonstrated that there was a black audience eager to spend money on theatre tickets. By the mid-1970s producers weren't afraid to return to the old-time ethnic tap dance show. *Bubbling Brown Sugar*—with black stars and white supporting players—brought the formula back to Broadway in a ragtag but successful package. It wasn't until *Ain't Misbehavin'* came along in 1978, though, that we had a color-blind first-class A-number-one hit, which was conceived, as it happened, for an all-black cast.

BROADWAY SCORECARD
/ PERFS: 766 / $: +

RAVE	FAVORABLE	MIXED	UNFAVORABLE	PAN
2	3		1	

BUCK WHITE

"A New Musical"

book adaptation, music and lyrics by Oscar Brown, Jr.

based on the 1968 play *Big Time Buck White* by Joseph Dolan Tuotti

directed by Oscar Brown, Jr. and Jean Pace

produced by Zev Bufman in association with High John Productions (Oscar Brown, Jr., Jean Pace, and Sivuca)

starring "Muhammad Ali a/k/a Cassius Clay"

with Herschell Burton, David Moody, Ron Rich, Ted Ross, Eugene Smith, and Charles Weldon

opened December 2, 1969   *George Abbott Theatre*

ZEV BUFMAN
in association with HIGH-JOHN PRODUCTIONS
presents
MUHAMMAD ALI (A/K/A)

CASSIUS CLAY in

A New Musical

BUCK WHITE

(in alphabetical order)

with HERSCHELL BURTON   DAVID MOODY   RON RICH
TED ROSS   EUGENE SMITH   CHARLES WELDON

Music and Lyrics by OSCAR BROWN, JR.

Book Adapted by OSCAR BROWN, JR.

From An Original Play by JOSEPH DOLAN TUOTTI

Musical Arrangements by MIKE TERRY & MERL SAUNDERS
Orchestrations by MIKE TERRY
Musical Direction by MERL SAUNDERS

| Scenery Designed by | Lighting designed by | Costumes Designed by | General Manager |
| EDWARD BURBRIDGE | MARTIN ARONSTEIN | JEAN PACE | ROBERT KAMLOT |

Staged by OSCAR BROWN, JR. & JEAN PACE

| Dramatic Play Originally Presented in N.Y. by ZEV BUFMAN In Association with RON RICH & LEONARD GRANT | Original Los Angeles Dramatic Production by RON RICH | Musical Version Originally Presented in San Francisco by MEL GOLDBLATT AND DIALOGUE BLACK/WHITE COMPANY |

Original Cast Album on BUDDAH RECORDS

GEORGE ABBOTT THEATRE
152 West 54th Street, N.Y.C.

Evgs. Tues. thru Fri. at 8:30: Sat. at 7 & 10
Mats. Wed. at 2, Sun. at 3

Printed by Artcraft Litho. & Ptg. Co., Inc., New York

Buck White, or *Who's Afraid of Cassius Clay?* Some producers will try anything for a buck (white). (artwork by Mozelle)

CLIVE BARNES, *TIMES*

Muhammad Ali, also known as Cassius Clay for stage purposes, is heavyweight champion of the world, by right and dignity if not by name, and he is beautiful. *Buck White* is not quite so beautiful, and this is a pity. Mr. Tuotti's play was both curious and audacious. It opened with a scene of pure black comedy—with energetically cartoonlike characters making cheerfully racist jokes about black and white alike. We await the arrival of the hero—a black militant leader, Big Time Buck White. The farce mounted upward, with wilder and wilder jokes until, suddenly, Buck White arrives. And instead of being yet another amiable zany, he is a real person. Buck White invites questions from the audience, and after a couple from plants, he actually gets serious questions and answers them in a witty, humane but entirely serious fashion. It was a most impressive stroke of theatre. And this has been lost in the musical. The first part is as funny as ever—if anything funnier. When Cassius Clay strides down the aisle, looking like a great African prince with his beard and Afro haircut, it seems as though, against earlier probabilities, the musical will work out. But then everyone connected with the show makes a mistake. Instead of having Buck White answer real questions and deal with serious problems, the producers have just a couple of plants in the audience, one serious-minded black and a deliberately stupid John Bircher of a white man. The whole dramatic power of the original play is washed over in a frothy sea of wellmeaning clichés, with Buck White crooning abrasively about slavery and the need for black militancy. Originally this was more of a confrontation than a play, and with that confrontation removed, the flimsy dramatic structure collapses. How is Mr. Clay? He emerges as a modest, naturally appealing man; he sings with a pleasant, slightly impersonal voice, acts without embarrassment and moves with innate dignity. You are aware that he is not a professional performer only when he is not performing; when left in the background, he disappears completely in a manner no experienced actor would. For all this, he does himself proud.

MARTIN GOTTFRIED, *WOMEN'S WEAR DAILY*

A warm-hearted but sloppy and amateur musical version of *Big Time Buck White*, brought to Broadway for the purely commercial reason of its star, Cassius Clay. In being "warmhearted," it is a slur to the original and to the cause. In selling Clay, it is treating him as merchandise, it is being crude and cruel. He is paraded onstage, not much differently from the way prize-fighters (or murderers, for that matter) were in Twenties vaudeville. His entrance has been staged so that Clay is led on stage from the rear of the audience, looking frightened and bewildered, treated for all the world like King Kong. It is awful. Clay does his best to recite the [scripted question-and-answer] responses, managing a reasonable high school performance. But though this is the most you can expect from him, why should you be paying professional theatre prices [$12.90 top] to listen to such a reading? Obviously, you are being asked to pay them for the privilege of staring at Clay (he is billed as "Muhammad Ali a/k/a Cassius Clay," the "a/k/a" standing for "as known as"). How different is such staring from a freak show? And even worse, is this what Clay is now reduced to? He has been stripped of his heavyweight title on the presumption of guilt for refusing to enter the army. That's presumption of guilt. It isn't the way our system is supposed to work. He has been deprived of his livelihood as well as, possibly, his rights. Now being paraded in a Broadway show, how different is it from "Jack Jefferson" in *The Great White Hope* [1968]? Jefferson, denied his title and legally hassled, finally sunk to playing *Uncle Tom's Cabin* in a circus. *Buck White*, in this version, and under these conditions, is not so far away from *Uncle Tom's Cabin* as it may seem. Even more unpleasant is the misguided, paid-for-at-the-box office adulation of black audiences, who think they are seeing their hero in a play of black militance, when they are actually watching a man who was stripped of his achievement and denied his convictions by white men and who is now, in effect, a slave to commercial purposes. Clay aside, there isn't much to the show and it obviously would never have come to Broadway without him.

WALTER KERR, *TIMES*
Buck White pretends to be furious, pretends to be arranging for black/white confrontation tonight. But *Buck White* is only saying "boo!" and saying it in such a plainly artificial way that not even the presence of the champion of the dispossessed, the sincere and urgent Cassius Clay, can breathe any felt fire into it. At this moment, and on the New York stage, it's a case of the fire last time. When *Big Time Buck White*

was done off-Broadway a year ago, the sense of eye-to-eye contact, with the white eye getting spat into, was entirely real. The evening never had anything else. It was nonexistent as drama, inept as comedy, inexplicable in its use of stage-Negro stereotypes everybody has been eager to get rid of, unorganized even as polemic. But as we sat in a tiny, crowded house while a sleepy black ambled down the aisle and smiled as he suggested we had come to get hurt, we did begin to feel we were in the presence of people capable of hurting us, and when Buck White finally arrived to stir the latent furies in some performers who'd merely been quarreling among themselves so that they would now come to us directly and carry the quarrel to our ankles and our coat lapels, we may have bridled but we burned. The event was immediate, abrasive, insulting, outrageous, worrying, unfair. But because we had been the first to be unfair, it was just. Bad for our egos and our nerves; bad even for the cause of reason; but necessary, penitentially, for our souls. *Big Time Buck White* put a fist into our faces, or as close to our faces as the laws governing public performance allow, and I doubt that many people ever tried to walk away from it. Mr. Clay himself, when he comes to the podium in Afro wig, chunky brown beads and prophet's gown, gentles the night. He does his chores well enough, but he happens to have the lightest and least dominant voice among the performers; he also has the most tranquil face. Beyond that, I would guess, he is an ardent man but not a mighty hater. He seems nice, not murderous. . . . Obviously Mr. Clay, who prefers to be known as Muhammad Ali but whose better-known name appears a good 10 times larger on the program, is in a position to be exploited.

●   ●   ●

The protest play *Big Time Buck White* originated in Watts before traveling Off-Broadway in 1968 (for 129 performances). The addition of songs, not surprisingly, removed the play's menacing roughness and improvisatory threat; redrafting the material for a title-stripped world champion boxer (shades of Jack Johnson, and the still-running Pulitzer Prize-winner *The Great White Hope*) also sanitized the danger. An unknown, raging-and-fuming revolutionary might petrify a 1969, middle-class audience, but nobody expected the gold-fisted Ali to leap down from the stage and start a fracas. The boxer changed his name upon conversion to the Black Muslim religion in 1964; producer

Bufman, a man of indiscriminate tastes, chose to hype "Cassius Clay" in type 250 percent the size of Ali. Precisely what market of ticket buyers, one wonders, was he trying to reach?

BROADWAY SCORECARD
/ PERFS: 7 / $: –

RAVE	FAVORABLE	MIXED	UNFAVORABLE	PAN
	1	3		2

CABARET

"The New Musical Comedy"

music by John Kander

lyrics by Fred Ebb

book by Joe Masteroff

based on the 1951 play *I Am a Camera* by John van Druten, from the novellas comprising *The Berlin Stories* [*The Last of Mr. Norris* (1935) and *Goodbye to Berlin* (1939)] by Christopher Isherwood

directed by Harold Prince

choreographed by Ronald Field

produced by Harold Prince (in association with Ruth Mitchell)

starring Jill Haworth, Jack Gilford, Bert Convy, and Lotte Lenya

with Joel Grey, Peg Murray, and Edward Winter

opened November 20, 1966   Broadhurst Theatre

MARTIN GOTTFRIED, *WOMEN'S WEAR DAILY*
Cabaret is two musicals and one of them is enormously striking and magnificently executed. However, that marvelous part of it is a style, a sense, an attitude, rather than a complete scheme of musical theatre,

First-rate artwork drawn directly from the lyric: "Come taste the wine, come hear the band. Come blow a horn, start celebrating; right this way your table's waiting." Note the snouted pig at the upper right table. (artwork by Tom Morrow)

and apparently at a loss to fulfill it, writer Joe Masteroff was forced into conventional Broadway musical plotting to fill out the evening. As a result, *Cabaret* is schizoid, and schizophrenic theatre will not do. Opening last night, it floundered in its own weaknesses. The difference between the cabaret and the plot halves of *Cabaret* could not be more striking. On the one hand there are unique ideas, striking uses of lighting and movement, a sense of the bizarre. And on the other the same old romance, secondary romance and sketched-in complications. Seldom do these parts blend and the cabaret sequences generally have nothing to do with the story. So the story is uninteresting, unamusing and time-consuming, and Harold Prince staged it according to the thoroughly ordinary demands of its genre. Occasionally it is interrupted by a Broadway-style ballad, staged in the stock manner of old-style musicals. The staging, however is quite another story in the cabaret sequences. And it is not Prince's but that of choreographer Ronald Field. The dances, the movement, the conception of the cabaret parts are marvelous. Field worked with the grotesque, the vulgar, the garish to create an expressionistic vision of the musical style as well as the hell-bound mood of this Berlin. John Kander's music was equally inspired by this end of the production, and while those few ballads on the story side of things were mundane, the cabaret music was superb—cheap, bitter, dissonantly melodic and long-lined. What is good in *Cabaret*— and there are things in it that are great—is what was done by Field and his fantastic visions, helped by a first-rate company and complemented by genuinely artistic sets and lighting [scenic design by Boris Aronson, lighting design by Jean Rosenthal]. How depressing that its originality was sacrificed to the needs of traditional plot schemes.

WALTER KERR, *TIMES*

Cabaret is a stunning musical with one wild wrong note. I think you'd be wise to go to it first and argue about that startling slip later. The first thing you see as you enter the Broadhurst is yourself. Designer Boris Aronson, whose scenery is so imaginative that even a gray green fruit store comes up like a warm summer dawn, has sent converging strings of frosted lamps swinging toward a vanishing point at upstage center. Occupying the vanishing point is a great geometric mirror, and in the mirror the gathering audience is reflected. We have come for the floor show, we are all at tables tonight, and anything we learn of life during the evening is going to be learned through the tipsy, tinkling, angular vision of sleek rouged-up clowns, who inhabit a world that rains silver. This marionette's eye view of a time and place in our lives that was brassy, wanton, carefree and doomed to crumble is brilliantly conceived. *Cabaret* has elected to wrap its arms around all that was troubling and all that was intolerable with a demonic grin, and insidious slink, and the painted-on charm that keeps revelers up until midnight making false faces at the hangman. Master of Ceremonies Joel Grey bursts from the darkness like a tracer bullet, singing us a welcome that has something of the old *Blue Angel* in it, something of Kurt Weill. Mr. Grey is cheerful, charming, soulless and conspiratorially wicked. In a pink vest, with sunburst eyes gleaming out of a cold-cream face, he is the silencer of bad dreams, the gleeful puppet of pretended joy, sin on a string. We are left now with the evening's single, and all too obvious, mistake. One of the cabaret tables is empty, the table reserved for Sally Bowles. Producer-director Prince, in a totally uncharacteristic lapse of judgement, has miscast a pretty but essentially flavorless ingénue, Jill Haworth, in the role. Given the difficult things *Cabaret* is trying to do, she is a damaging presence, worth no more to the show than her weight in mascara. With the kooky heroine canceled out, the emotional air [is] steadily drained from a show that takes its style and its subject matter seriously. The style is there, though, driven like glistening nails into the musical numbers, and I think you'll find they make up for what's missing.

NORMAN NADEL, *WORLD JOURNAL TRIBUNE*
Heavily rouged and with lips rendered kissable in the style of the time, Joel Grey is the emcee, effeminate in every twist, turn, utterance and gesture. Later he even appears "in drag," as one of the chorus girls. It's quite an impersonation. Jill Haworth's role as Sally Bowles requires a seasoning in musical theatre that she lacks. But the audience is not likely to mind, or even notice this, for several interesting reasons: first, Sally is really a naive, vulnerable sort, for all her sordid experience, making a great show of sinful sophistication. So Haworth's ungainliness on stage blends conveniently into Sally's naive awkward manner. It isn't a complete success, but it's a cover-up. Second, Sally is a poor singer, so even if Haworth pushes and strains her voice, it's in character. . . . Except that the vulgarity is laid on too heavily, *Cabaret* is a scintillat-

ingly unconventional musical play, in its best moments, and only mildly unsatisfying in its lapses. "Telephone Song," sung in the club, excited the audience in all areas—choreography, costumes, and music. "Tomorrow Belongs to Me" is a lovely ballad, and its metamorphosis into a Nazi marching song is one of the most ingenious musical turns of the evening. One thing that never lapses is director Prince's sense of theatre. Even to the final ensemble scene, which is anticlimatic and a trifle mawkish, he sets a commanding stage.

RICHARD WATTS, JR., POST
Cabaret is both brilliant and remarkable. The musical play is a bright, handsome and steadily entertaining show, and yet at the same time it manages to include in its scope a growingly horrifying depiction of the slow and ominous encroachment of the Hitler madness that was soon to dominate Germany and threaten to engulf the world. Everything about *Cabaret*, including the casting, works out. Joe Masteroff's book effectively combines the grave and the cheerful in the story, John Kander's score and Fred Ebb's lyrics capture the proper mood admirably, Boris Aronson's setting is imaginative and handsome, and Hal Prince, the producer, has staged his own show expertly. The dance and nightclub numbers have been excitingly and humorously directed by Ronald Field. Patricia Zipprodt's costumes have imagination and humor, too. It is the glory of *Cabaret* that it can upset you while it gives theatrical satisfaction.

0   0   0

Following protagonist Cliff Bradshaw's arrival in Berlin, the creators of the musical version of *I Am a Camera* wrote a musical "prologue," five song fragments showing various denizens of debauched 1930s Berlin. One about Herman the German, one featuring an exotic Chinese girl, and so forth. Inevitably, they decided to take the clumped fragments out of the prologue and space them throughout the book scenes, a thread to tie the show together. Inevitably, they decided to rewrite the fragments as vulgarized reflections, or illustrations, of the book scenes just seen. And, inevitably, they grew intrigued by one of the characters singing the fragments—no, not the Chinese girl but the macabre, Peter Lorre-like Master of Ceremonies. So intrigued that they chucked the others and came up with new, debauched slots for their strange little man. (One of the five original fragments, expanded to full length, remained as the opening number, "Wilkommen.") And thus the cabaret concept of *Cabaret* was formulated—this particular larger-than-life character could hardly exist outside the cabaret setting—and the part that made Joel Grey famous evolved. Which goes to show that there are only small parts, not small actors. Or is that short actors? As for director Prince, with four failures including the unsuccessful-yet-delightful *She Loves Me* (1963) to his credit, *Cabaret* suddenly established him as a musical theatre visionary with a strikingly novel sense of style. But his vision was somewhat unfocused, the entertainment ever so much more entertaining when they all left the musical comedy boarding house. What good is sitting alone in your room, anyway? *Cabaret* worked better in theory than in practice, the brilliant cabaret material offsetting the mundane romance (or the mundane romance sinking the brilliant cabaret material, take your pick). Either way, it sure was interesting, and Prince was no longer a producer-who-wanted-to-direct but a *director* (who produced his own shows). Producer Prince, meanwhile, tried to keep the potentially abrasive material palatable for middle-class audiences. Following the engagement party for Lotte Lenya and the Jewish grocer Jack Gilford, for example, the Master of Ceremonies sang of his love for a gorilla who "doesn't look Jewish at all." Director Prince kept the song; producer Prince, with regrets, self-censored the tag line to help keep *Cabaret* comfortable for its audience and, therefore, successful. "*West Side, Company*, and *Follies* didn't sell out; *Cabaret* did," said the producer. (Sell out tickets, or integrity? Or both?) "My shows don't do as well now at the box office as *Cabaret* did because now I do them exactly as I want to do them," he continued. "It has cost me something, and the price at the moment isn't too high." But this was back in 1974, before *Pacific Overtures* (1976), *Merrily We Roll Along* (1981), *A Doll's Life* (1982), and *Grind* (1985)—after which Mr. Prince ducked out of the high-price producing grind (with great relief, one suspects). "What Would You Do?" Dept.: In a climactic moment, Lenya sang a searing song of guilt over the abandoning of her Jewish fiancé. When her husband, Kurt Weill, fled Berlin in March 1933, Lenya fled, too—to Monte Carlo. (What would you do?) The pair soon reconciled and emigrated together to America in 1935. "A good Jew always forgives his wife," said Weill.

Winner of the New York Drama Critics' Circle Award. In addition to winning the Tony Award for Best Musical, Tonys were won by John Kander and Fred Ebb (composer and lyricist), Harold Prince (producer), Harold Prince (director), Ronald Field (choreographer), Joel Grey (supporting actor), Peg Murray (supporting actress), Boris Aronson (scenic designer), and Patricia Zipprodt (costume designer).

BROADWAY SCORECARD

/ PERFS: 1,166 / $: +

RAVE	FAVORABLE	MIXED	UNFAVORABLE	PAN
2	2	2		

CAMELOT

an "original star" revival of the 1960 musical play

music by Frederick Loewe

book and lyrics by Alan Jay Lerner

based on the 1958 chronicle *The Once and Future King* by T. H. White

directed by Frank Dunlop; original New York production staged by Moss Hart

choreographed by Buddy Schwab

produced by Mike Merrick and Don Gregory

starring Richard Burton, Christine Ebersole, Richard Muenz, and Paxton Whitehead

with Robert Fox, James Valentine, William Parry, and Thor Fields

opened July 8, 1980   New York State Theatre

MIKE MERRICK & DON GREGORY PRESENT

RICHARD BURTON

CHRISTINE EBERSOLE   RICHARD MUENZ

LERNER & LOEWE'S
CAMELOT

ALSO STARRING PAXTON WHITEHEAD
WITH ROBERT FOX AND JAMES VALENTINE
BOOK AND LYRICS BY ALAN JAY LERNER   MUSIC BY FREDERICK LOEWE
BASED ON "THE ONCE AND FUTURE KING" BY T.H. WHITE   ORIGINAL NEW YORK PRODUCTION STAGED BY MOSS HART
SETS AND COSTUMES BY DESMOND HEELEY   LIGHTING DESIGN BY THOMAS SKELTON
MUSICAL DIRECTOR FRANZ ALLERS
ORCHESTRA CONDUCTOR JAMES MARTIN   SOUND DESIGN JOHN McCLURE
ORCHESTRATION BY ROBERT RUSSELL BENNETT & PHIL LANG   PRODUCTION SUPERVISOR JERRY ADLER   PRODUCTION COORDINATOR STONE WIDNEY
CHOREOGRAPHY BY BUDDY SCHWAB
DIRECTED BY FRANK DUNLOP
A DOME/CUTLER — HERMAN PRODUCTION
JULY 2 – AUG. 23 ONLY! NEW YORK STATE THEATER, LINCOLN CENTER

An old and tired King returns as "little more than a burnt-out dummy," per Clive Barnes. "His face is leathery and unanimated, his arms droop to his side, and his hands are flaccid. A Knight to forget." (artwork by "Weller")

CLIVE BARNES, *POST*

[Headline: "A Knight to Forget"]

Twenty years ago *Camelot* was the necessary encore by Frederick Loewe and Alan Jay Lerner to their fabulously successful *My Fair Lady* [1956]. Everyone agrees that the original *Camelot* opened on Broadway half-baked, and had to be re-heated into success. This present version is simply half-baked. The real problem about *Camelot* is that it is not, never was, nor never will be, a particularly good musical. It was Loewe's last score and it has a tentativeness about it that one would hardly associate with the assertive composer of *My Fair Lady*, or even *Brigadoon* [1947]. The title song is sweet, as are some of the other numbers, but that special surge needed by all truly great musicals remains resolutely unsurged. Lerner, one of the few master craftsmen in our lyric theatre, has done what he can with this story based on T. H. White's novel, but it is still much more book than literature. The storytelling of this pseudo-Arthurian legend seems endless, even with such excisions that are the kindest cuts of all. Lerner's lyrics remain as nimble as unleashed whippets. Burton, however, looks wan. Four years ago he appeared on Broadway in *Equus* [the 1974 drama, following Anthony Hopkins and Anthony Perkins in the role] and I thought he was tremendous—it seemed like the happy resurgence of a once promising career. In *Camelot* he seems little more than a burnt-out dummy. His face is leathery and unanimated, his arms droop to his side, and his hands are flaccid. Yes, there are glints of greatness. The sonorous intonation has not entirely deserted him, and his final scene has a nobility and compassion that totally transcends everything that has gone before. But it is too little, too late. I see no reason for this revival but one. As I entered the theatre there was a line at the box office buying tickets for a once and future Burton. So why not? No one told you that the theatre was not out to make money. Perhaps the tragedy is that Burton could once have made magic.

FRANK RICH, *TIMES*

Who says that you can't go home again? Last night Richard Burton returned to the kingdom of *Camelot*, and it was as if he had never abdicated his throne. True, Burton is older now—as are we, as is *Camelot*—but he remains every inch the King Arthur of our most majestic storybook dreams. This actor doesn't merely command the stage; he seems to own it by divine right. Splendidly outfitted in a black-and-gold robe, his blue eyes awash in melancholy, he takes over the show from his first entrance and doesn't ever let go. By the time he sings for a final time of that "one brief shining moment that was known as Camelot," the audience is ready to weep for every noble ideal that ever has been smashed on the hard rocks of history. Burton's powerful yet vulnerable Welsh voice seems to slide a full, shattering octave on the word "moment" alone. At that instant, the theatre is so hushed that nothing short of a prayer could serve as an encore. Burton's feat is all the more amazing because *Camelot* never was and still is not a great Broadway musical: even in 1960, it received mixed reviews and was rightfully deemed a letdown. Nonetheless *Camelot*'s simple idealistic credo is now inextricably linked to the simpler America of another time. *Camelot* opened a month after the 1960 Presidential election and was still touring in November, 1963. When confronting the show today, it is all but impossible to forget that it was a favorite of John F. Kennedy's. [These] associations can give it an unearned, if still affecting, poignancy, but they don't quite cover up its flaws. Without Burton, it might well be a chore to sit through; [but] middle age suits him and King Arthur well. Though he is given every opportunity to ham up his familiar role, he shocks us by doing exactly the reverse. Burton performs on an intimate scale; he can do more with a downcast, faraway look or a deep-throated cry or a slight shift in posture than most actors can do with all their equipment operating at full throttle. One might debate Burton's decision to recreate this old theatrical conquest—is he retreating into a safe showbiz haven or simply regrouping his artistic forces?—but his performance tends to render such questions moot. In *Camelot*, he is our once, our present and—who knows?—maybe even our future king.

DOUGLAS WATT, *DAILY NEWS*

Twenty years later, *Camelot* is still in trouble; not just the place, but the whole big gorgeous whooping crane of a show—half lovely, half dopey and ultimately a bore. Not that the Lerner-Loewe revival will fail to pack them in wherever it goes. With Richard Burton an even more assured and engaging King Arthur than in 1960, and with a large, well-drilled cast and scads of scenery and costumes, it is bound to be the thing to see, something along the lines of the Radio City Music Hall

Easter show minus the Rockettes. *Camelot* was Loewe's swan song. And it isn't hard to see why. Though the score contains some characteristically lovely melodies admirably suited to the more conventional aspects of what is, at bottom, a very ordinary love triangle involving extraordinarily-named people, it is unable to rise to the higher aspirations of Lerner's book, which falls somewhere between *Parsifal* [1882] and *The Vagabond King* [1925], falling most of the way. Lerner's lyrics are something else again, smart and entertaining and touching most of the way, so that he can even be forgiven rhyming "pedestal" with "better still." And some of the songs are, as you know, enchanting. But *Camelot* is too long and, too often, too silly and pretentious. Eventually, Burton is the whole show, and I'd have gladly settled for a solo reading from Mallory or White by that distinctive, irresistible voice. But in a smaller, unmiked house in which so many of the words would not be garbled and lost. And, as you've probably been informed, he looks just great, hardly a day over 1960.

o   o   o

Why in the world would world-class celebrity Richard Burton, the once (if not future) king of the English-speaking stage, submit to this twilight return to his star-making role of twenty years hence? For about sixty thousand reasons a week. Producers Mike Merrick and Don Gregory made Richard Burton and Rex Harrison offers they couldn't refuse, sending them crisscrossing the land with recreations of their legendary roles in the two Lerner and Loewe biggies. *Camelot* did well, featuring a reeling performance from a reeling star (until he reeled once too often and withdrew, indisposed); *My Fair Lady*, with a healthier but underenthused 'enry 'iggins, proved somewhat more somnambulent. Burton returned to the stage once more, in an ill-advised 1983 airing of *Private Lives* opposite two-time former *frau* Elizabeth, and died at the age of fifty-eight on August 5, 1984.

BROADWAY SCORECARD				
/ PERFS: 56 / $: +				
RAVE	FAVORABLE	MIXED	UNFAVORABLE	PAN
	2			4

CAMELOT

a return engagement of the 1980 touring company of the 1960 musical play, with a replacement star

music by Frederick Loewe

book and lyrics by Alan Jay Lerner

based on the 1958 chronicle *The Once and Future King* by T. H. White

directed by Frank Dunlop; "original New York production staged by Moss Hart"

choreographed by Buddy Schwab

produced by Mike Merrick and Don Gregory

starring Richard Harris, Meg Bussert, Richard Muenz, and Barrie Ingham

with James Valentine, Richard Backus, William Parry, and Thor Fields

opened November 15, 1981   Winter Garden Theatre

HOWARD KISSEL, WOMEN'S WEAR DAILY

Despite its lush score, *Camelot* was a great bore when it opened 20 years ago because it was so talky and because the disparity between the witty, arch tone in which it began and the somber, mournful tone in which it ended was so great. Despite the return of its original star, *Camelot* was a great bore a year ago because the wit that lightened the piece had been largely jettisoned to make it more suitable for an aging, less ingenuous Richard Burton. Despite a sprightlier cast, the version of *Camelot* now at the Winter Garden is still a great bore, because the problems that were not solved when the show was new are still apparent. The production remains dreary, the choreography coy. If *Camelot* retains a hold on us it may be because of its close association with John F. Kennedy, who used to listen to the album, particularly the title song, before he went to bed, a fact revealed by his widow just after the assassination. All that seems like ancient history—an entire generation is now able to vote for whom such facts have no emotional meaning. For some of us the association is still strong—despite, rather than because of, revivals like this one.

FRANK RICH, *TIMES*

Maybe there can be *Camelot* without Richard Burton, but it didn't happen in the revival that opened last night. While this is, in broad outline, the same production that Burton brought to the New York State Theatre 17 months ago, it is now ruled by Richard Harris as King Arthur. Harris is by no means an abject pretender to the throne—in fact, he previously occupied it in the Hollywood version—but his performance is at odds with the very essence of the show's appeal. Its often gorgeous score notwithstanding, that appeal has little to do with the musical's actual text. *Camelot* endures for a very simple and potent reason: this 1960 show is forever tied to our most idealized and sentimental memories of John F. Kennedy's fallen Presidency. Whether by accident or design, Burton heightened this emotional link by creating a King Arthur who exemplified the witty, youthful and sexy Kennedy style. Harris's Arthur, while by no means bad, is far more dour. This performance is, heaven knows, a regal piece of showmanship—full of grand, arrogant gestures, royal pauses and vocal extravagances of the old school. Although the actor's effects sometimes have little to do with the meaning of his lines, they do command the stage. What's fatally missing from this King, however, are sexual passion and a sense of humor. These qualities are not only crucial because they're needed to give *Camelot* the Kennedy glow, but also because the material itself requires them. Lerner's libretto is, most of all, the story of a love triangle involving Arthur, his Queen and Lancelot—and sizzle it must. While Harris does show some affection for his Guenevere, it is that of a misty, doting father, not a red-hot lover. Humor is just as essential, for it is the enlivening ingredient of Arthur's character. Harris's somber, introspective renditions of such light songs as "I Wonder What the King Is Doing Tonight?" and "What Do the Simple Folk Do?" are certainly noble and novel, but they're also ill advised. No doubt some audiences—especially young ones new to *Camelot*—will still be captivated by this three-hour evening. They'll be able to discover the score afresh and to enjoy Harris's performance on its own terms. The rest of us, I'm afraid, must face the fact that the glories of *Camelot* now live best on the original cast album—and in our fond memories of round tables past.

DOUGLAS WATT, *DAILY NEWS*
[Headline: "*Camelot* Returns to a Less than Royal Welcome"]
The more I see it, the more it calls to mind a splendid coronation ceremony with the grandstand collapsing at the finish.

◦   ◦   ◦

With the sudden withdrawal of the ailing Richard Burton from their Big Money revival, producers Mike Merrick and Don Gregory scrambled for a suitable replacement (rather than canceling lucrative bookings). They stumbled on Richard Harris, a nonsinging movie star with no Broadway experience; he escaped service in the infamous *Kelly* (1965) when his contract expired before the fabled flop went into production. Harris played the cuckolded King in the rather dismal 1967 film version of the Lerner and Loewe musical. This happy circumstance, for some unexplainable reason, proved to sell tickets in admirable numbers and resulted in a rather quick Broadway return engagement. Harris returned to *Camelot* for another mid-1980s tour, which fortunately bypassed the mainstream. Despite its well-recognized flaws, *Camelot* continues to have hinterland appeal as a vehicle for long-in-tooth stars way too creaky to pull off the early portions of the evening. *Another* touring revival of *Camelot*—starring Robert Goulet, the original Lancelot—lumbered into the Gershwin in 1993, where it proved awfully wheezy.

BROADWAY SCORECARD
/ PERFS: 48 / $: +

RAVE	FAVORABLE	MIXED	UNFAVORABLE	PAN
	1		1	4

CAN-CAN

a revival of the 1953 musical comedy

music and lyrics by Cole Porter

book by Abe Burrows

directed by Abe Burrows; "entire production staged and choreo-graphed" by Roland Petit

produced by James M. Nederlander, Arthur Rubin, Jerome Minskoff, Stewart F. Lane, Carole J. Shorenstein, and Charles D. Kelman

starring Zizi Jeanmaire (Petit), Ron Husmann, and Avery Schreiber

with Swen Swenson, Pamela Sousa, David Brooks, Tommy Breslin, Michael Dantuono, and Mitchell Greenberg

opened April 30, 1981   Minskoff Theatre

HOWARD KISSEL, *WOMEN'S WEAR DAILY*

Unlike most of the musicals that have been revived in the last few years, *Can-Can* never was regarded as a Broadway landmark. Cole Porter's score has a few vintage songs ("I Love Paris," "*C'est Magnifique*" and "It's All Right with Me") that could easily be inserted into almost any other show; a few "clever" songs that no longer seem witty or special; and many bland songs, one of which sounds like a poor man's version of his own "Begin the Beguine." Abe Burrows' book was standard for its time, but now its contrived plot and stale gags seem particularly ram-shackle. Still a show set in Paris in 1893 has a certain appeal, and David Mitchell's smashing period sets are so evocative that for a while I thought *Can-Can* might be a pleasant if not exceptional evening. About 15 minutes into the first act, however, I found my blood starting to con-geal as the first can-can of the evening was done to tacky new disco arrangements by Donald York and with the dancers grinning smugly as if disco can-can were somehow daring or imaginative. Roland Petit, who choreographed the show, is at his best when he gives his dancers difficult athletic turns, at his worst when the dances, instead of building toward a climax, are simply full of fussy, precious bits. Though he has a striking apache dance and ultimately pulls all the stops out for the final can-can (the momentum of which he again breaks with disco), his work has a great deal to do with the joylessness of the production. With her hair done up in a tight bun, her face frozen into a hard smile almost as immobile as an Oriental mask, Zizi Jeanmaire reminds us of the tough *chanteuses* we see in turn-of-the-century posters. But she conveys little charm or warmth, making the love story at the heart of the show not very plausible. She can still dance, though her work sometimes seems effortful; also Petit relies on the same ploy the choreographer of *Woman of the Year* [1981] did to deal with an aging star—have the men toss her around. Like Mitchell's marvelous sets, Franca Squarciapino's costumes—particularly the fanciful ones for Jeanmaire—steal the show. Among other things, *Can-Can* may be the most ineptly stage-managed show I have ever seen—a curtain dropped in and slunk out of a scene early and a blackout hit before one of Avery Schreiber's sight gags was supposed to end a scene. *Hèlas!*

FRANK RICH, *TIMES*

A lot of energy and money has been poured into the revival of *Can-Can*. This is one of the most handsome shows of the season, and it is tireless in its attempts to please the audience. But mediocre material, no matter how it's sliced, is still mediocre material. *Can-Can* never was a first-rate musical, and now, almost three decades after its original production, it stands on even shakier legs. In a show that more often recalls the Broadway of 1953 than the Montmartre of 1893, one is also grateful for the presence of Zizi Jeanmaire [who] gives *Can-Can* its one authentic link to the world it wishes to celebrate. This pixie-ish performer, with her lacquered hair, gravelly voice and flat-out music-hall delivery, need but appear to transport us to the *Folies Bergère*. She also has the only French accent in the show—an asset she holds, almost hilariously, like a sledgehammer over the rest of the cast. Leaping into the midst of a bevy of Middle Western-sounding *boulevardiers* for her first entrance, she booms out *"What iz all ziz?"* As it happens, Miss Jeanmaire's entrance proves to be the biggest laugh in the whole show. Abe Burrows's windy book, which he has reworked for the occasion, is below his best efforts. If you're really going to use a book like this, there's only one way to play it—for keeps. Unfortunately, the two leading men at the Minskoff do not contribute greatly to that task. Avery Schreiber seems to feel he's playing a vulgarian, rather than a Bulgarian, sculptor; his mugging only reminds us how forced the book's fun is. As the judge, Ron Husmann has the show's best voice, but he's stiff even when his character ostensibly loosens up. Nor is there much chemistry (or, for that matter, eye contact) between him and Jeanmaire. Without convincing lovers, the show's central plot quickly petrifies into deadwood; at the same time, the songs attached to it lose their emotional life's blood. Watching that superb finale ["Can-Can"] or hearing Jeanmaire sing "I Love Paris" or contemplating Mr. Mitchell's scenery, one can plainly see that there are still some kicks to be had from *Can-Can*. Roughly 40 minutes' worth, I'd say, scattered like stardust across a longish night.

o   o   o

Can-Can was a highly mediocre musical in its day, redeemed by Michael Kidd's colorful choreography, the sparkling performance of red-headed dancing soubrette Gwen Verdon, and a large advance sale (with help from the considerable airplay of three Cole Porter tunes). None of the above were reproducible thirty years later, of course; and what remained—the material itself—was as drab as before. Coproducer Artie Rubin—general manager for the Nederlanders—had been a chorister in the original, indicating that this revival was fueled by a nostalgically hazy memory. This *Can-Can* seemed to exist, in fact, for the sole purpose of filling the Minskoff Theatre, although filling was not, perhaps, the appropriate term.

BROADWAY SCORECARD
/ PERFS: 5 / $: –

RAVE	FAVORABLE	MIXED	UNFAVORABLE	PAN
	1	1		4

CANDIDE

a revised version of the 1956 comic operetta

music by Leonard Bernstein

lyrics by Richard Wilbur; additional lyrics by Stephen Sondheim and John Latouche

book by Hugh Wheeler (replacing the 1956 libretto by Lillian Hellman)

based on the 1759 satire by François Marie Arouet de Voltaire

directed by Harold Prince

choreographed by Patricia Birch

produced by The Chelsea Theater Center of Brooklyn (Robert Kalfin, Michael David, and Burl Hash) in conjunction with Harold Prince and Ruth Mitchell

starring Lewis J. Stadlen

with Mark Baker, Maureen Brennan, Sam Freed, June Gable, and Deborah St. Darr

opened March 10, 1974   Broadway Theatre

CLIVE BARNES, *TIMES*

First things first. Bigger can be better. The Chelsea Theater's production of Leonard Bernstein's *Candide*, which has just moved from the Chelsea premises at the Brooklyn Academy of Music to the Broadway Theatre, proves this abundantly. *Candide* is even sharper, funnier, wittier and, if possible, more musically elegant than it was in Brooklyn. It had its official Broadway press opening Sunday afternoon, and it went like champagne. Conceivably this is the best score ever written for a Broadway musical. Well, perhaps, "best" is a controversial word—for who decides between giants such as Gershwin, Porter or Bernstein. But certainly the *Candide* score is the most sophisticated and ambitious.

This is a musical for people who like serious theatre, in addition to people who just like musicals. When *Candide* was first staged, everybody bought and loved the record—but many found the stage show disappointing. It was a show sunk by its book, and, just as much, by the conventional approach. Harold Prince the new director, has said to hell with the past. He has kept, of course, the music, and most of the lyrics by the poet and Molière translator, Richard Wilbur, but brought in a new book by Hugh Wheeler. He has also added a couple of lyrics by Stephen Sondheim, which can never be a bad idea. Then he has put the entire thing into a giant fun-house of an environmental theater. The production has been designed by those experts, Eugene and Franne Lee, and they have knocked the innards out of this respectable Broadway house and made it into an obstacle course of seats, musicians' areas, catwalks, drawbridges and playing platforms, with one conventional stage thrown in at the end of the space for good measure and convenience. Marvelous music—a mixture of Strauss, Offenbach and even Sullivan—remains forever and cheekily Bernstein. The liquidly witty lyrics and Wheeler's absurdist but delightful book all lend themselves willingly to Prince's alchemy. Prince has, in the past, given Broadway innumerable gifts, but nothing so gaudy, glittering and endearing as this. It is one of those shows that take off like a rocket and never come down. This is a doll of a show. I loved it and loved it. I think Voltaire would have loved it too.

MARTIN GOTTFRIED, *WOMEN'S WEAR DAILY*

Candide is definitely better at the Broadway than it was at Chelsea, even if it does have a corny, college Coney Island lobby (hot dogs, peanuts whose shells are to be thrown on the floor). Eugene and Franne Lee made the various stages bigger, not only for the sake of playing room, but also so that the much larger audience could see everything. This gives the company greater freedom to move, and, more than ever, Prince's ability to work unitedly with a choreographer—Patricia Birch—is unique and tremendous. While there is little dance as such in *Candide*, there is a great deal of dance movement and musical staging, both of which are far more consequential to a musical's musicality than a dance number. Ms. Birch's work is terrific. After all this I am sorry to say the show still doesn't work and it's that damned book again. Hugh

Wheeler's adaptation of the original Lillian Hellman libretto has solved the problem of too many scenes in too many settings but at the great theatrical price of using a narrator to tell the story more often than letting the actors do it. Since (an appreciably restrained) Lewis J. Stadlen plays not only the narrator but several other main characters as well, these problems combine instead of coexist, which is only worse. Then there is Leonard Bernstein's music, which is everybody's reason for trying to make *Candide* work in the first place. First written as operetta satire, it no longer seems so when the show is not produced as operetta satire. The score is so superb, though, that it always came through as great music, as well as great theatre music, as well as satirical music, and it still does. Considering all this excellent work, and admiring Prince's instinct to avoid "art" for the higher virtue of successful theater, it is too bad *Candide* never really gets anything going for itself, any excitement. The reason is obvious: it is a salvage job rather than something begun afresh. I can understand the attraction. I've always wanted someone to make the show work myself. But at its roots the shaggy-dog story of it all, the philosophy of it all, the foolishness of the innocent hero of it all, the reliance of it all on a single point (the senselessness of optimism)— *Candide* was and remains as heavy as all intellectual whimsy.

WALTER KERR, *TIMES*
[Headline: Is This the Best of All Possible *Candides*?"]
Candide may at last have stumbled into the best of all possible productions. I take back "stumbled," instantly. For there is nothing at all inadvertent about the magician's pass director Harold Prince has made at the song-and-dance celebration of Voltaire's calculated insult to "the best of all possible worlds." Prince has looked at the materials, long, hard, and lovingly, decided what kind and degree of theatrical impudence is called for, got himself a new and free-floating libretto by Hugh Wheeler, and then simply rebuilt a theatre to suit Leonard Bernstein's sweetly irreverent score. Ever since *Candide* was first attempted on Broadway in 1956—there was book trouble, production trouble, tone trouble—everybody and his brother has come up with ideas about salvaging the glittering, grinning Bernstein melodies and the muted ironies of certain of Richard Wilbur's lyrics. But no one—until now— had thought of making the entire event spin just as Voltaire's novel

spins, dizzily from rape to earthquake, restlessly from Lisbon to Constantinople, feverishly and foolishly from luscious dreams of "breast of pheasant, apple pie" to syphilis and pox and the poisoned darts of aborigines. The original is short, breathless, cantankerous, and cavalier. Prince has thrown words, notes, and players at us with the same windswept effrontery. Though the actors are working in and about us— a rifleman shot a brigand dead within inches of my nose—the design of the unending chase is so firm, the performers are so secure in their climbing and tumbling and round-the-earth footwork, that we are able to join the journey and still *see* it with the detachment that Voltaire prescribes. Which only proves, once again, that detachment is more nearly a psychological than a physical matter. Though there is obviously no great open space for dancing, choreographer Patricia Birch has discovered that by distributing her cavorting figures over bridge and ramp, hill and dale, she can give us the effect of being buoyantly borne aloft on steps that are, taken by themselves, quite simple. And the speed cuts the dross away so that we can arrive at another melody all the sooner (the present version runs for an hour and 45 minutes, without intermission, and seems very close to Bernstein uninterrupted). It does more than save time for music, it sets tone for music. I wouldn't wait, if I were you. It's an evening of enormous charm.

DOUGLAS WATT, *DAILY NEWS*

There's a barrel of free peanuts and there are soft drinks for sale in the lobby of the Broadway Theatre, where a circusy atmosphere has been created for Leonard Bernstein's *Candide*. It's as good a way as any to approach the century's wittiest operetta score. Enclosed and carpeted walkways lead the playgoer from the lobby to his particular section of environmental theatre. That theatre, patterned by designers Eugene and Franne Lee on a larger scale than before but at the same time cutting the Broadway Theatre capacity in half (to 900), consists of an intermingling of performing and spectator areas on various levels gained by means of ramps and steps. And there are times when the performers thread their way through those spectators seated on stools in a centrally located pit (the rest are on wooden benches). Just as there are performing areas of varying shapes and sizes, so there are musicians' areas dividing the orchestra into sections (winds, strings, percussion) spotted throughout the house. The book, even as revised by Hugh Wheeler, is still something of a drag and even confusing at times. But Prince's inventive staging, like an imaginatively prepared party with bright surprises scattered all over the place, helps compensate for the story's repetitiousness, as evidenced by all the smiling faces in the house. But the spirited and richly melodic score is the main thing. And though in choosing singers as much for their appearance and ability to move as their voices (the Candide and Cunegonde are short and comical-looking but fleet of foot), Prince has slighted the score to some extent. It is nevertheless a delight even in this cut version.

◦   ◦   ◦

If they asked me, I could write a book—a rather complex book, it'd turn out to be—about the different versions of Leonard Bernstein's *Candide*. Not to mention Lillian Hellman's *Candide*, Hal Prince's first Broadway version (under discussion here), Prince's subsequent 1982 and 1997 versions, and others. Bernstein wrote his glorious 1956 score as a grand spoof of costume operetta. ("The best light opera since Richard Strauss wrote *Der Rosenkavalier* in 1911," averred John Chapman in the *Daily News*.) Lillian Hellman's libretto was aimed at the McCarthy-era witch hunts, though, while director Tyrone Guthrie—like Hellman, a musical theatre novice—appeared to be working in a high classical style.

The combined genres did not combine, resulting in a seventy-three-performance shambles. Happily, the score by Bernstein and poet Richard Wilbur—with prior contributions from John Latouche and Dorothy Parker—was gloriously memorialized. *Candide* underwent several ill-fated productions over the years, including a sixty-performance 1959 London edition (with libretto revisions by Mike Stewart, directed by Robert Lewis) and a full-scale 1971 touring revival that wilted after only four months (mounted by Edwin Lester's Civic Light Opera, revised and directed by Sheldon Patinkin). When Hal Prince and the Chelsea Theater Center set about rescuing the tarnished jewel of a musical, they jettisoned Hellman's work altogether (with her concurrence) and went back to Voltaire. *Candide* turned into a freewheeling, street-theatre-of-a-lark, just right for the eighteenth-century wanderer—and the contemporary younger generation, who, having finally seen America extricate itself from the futile Vietnam mess, were now witnessing Nixon's futile attempts to extricate himself from the Watergate mess.

The environmental production—with playing areas placed amidst the audience—was heavily influenced by the *Teatro Libero di Roma*'s "Theatre in the Surround" production of *Orlando Furiouso*, which struck up a tent in Bryant Park for a twenty-nine-performance New York visit in 1970. Hugh Wheeler's libretto called for exchanges, additions, and emendations to the score, resulting in five contributions by Hal Prince's favorite lyricist, just then cooling his heels between *A Little Night Music* (1973) and *Pacific Overtures* (1976). Stephen Sondheim, as it happens, had been working with Bernstein on *West Side Story* (1957) back during the creation of *Candide*; the two were written simultaneously, in radically different musical styles. But there are overlaps, and some music was shifted from one to the other: "One Hand, One Heart" was a duet for the young lovers—Candide and Cunegonde—while "Oh Happy We" first belonged to the *West Side* couple. "Gee, Officer Krupke" came from the Venice scene, where it was replaced with "What's the Use?" Lyricist Latouche's tag line was "Where does it get you in the end?" (sung by a character with, you'll remember, only one buttock). The new *Candide* was an instant success at the Chelsea's 180-seat theatre, and even more of a success—artistically, that is—at the Broadway, with its 1,700 capacity reduced to 900. (It had been similarly reconfigured for its previous tenant, the 1972 *Dude*, which was also designed by Eugene Lee.) This reduction proved to be the footloose *Candide*'s Achilles' heel, as it were. The producers assumed that manpower rules for a 900-seat house applied, but the Musician's Union cited their contract—which listed the Broadway Theatre by name, not seating capacity. *Candide* was scored and budgeted (and could make space in the cluttered auditorium) for only thirteen players; the union, realizing that Prince and the Chelsea had already spent too much money on the reconstruction to change their plans, insisted on their prerogative. The show's payroll was stuck with thirteen "walkers"—nonplaying union-card holders who walk in once a week, pick up a paycheck, and waltz out. This drove the breakeven point to fatal heights, eventuating in the inevitable failure of what was unquestionably the best musical of the season. Despite its unhappy end, the 1974 *Candide* finally got the show off the legendary flop list and onto the world stage. It has remained prominently present, in various configurations, ever since—although it has never sounded as good, musically, as it did in Bernstein and Hershy Kay's original 1956 orchestration.

Winner of the New York Drama Critics' Circle Award. Tony

Awards were won by Hugh Wheeler (book), Harold Prince (director), Eugene and Franne Lee (scenic design), and Franne Lee (costume design). The production also received a special Tony Award, leading to the establishment of a Best Revival category in 1977.

BROADWAY SCORECARD
/ PERFS: 740 / $: –

RAVE	FAVORABLE	MIXED	UNFAVORABLE	PAN
5		1		

CANTERBURY TALES

an import of the 1968 British "Ribald Musical Comedy"

music by Richard Hill and John Hawkins

lyrics by Nevill Coghill

book by Martin Starkie and Nevill Coghill

based on Nevill Coghill's translation of the 1387–1400 work by Geoffrey Chaucer

directed by Martin Starkie ("after the original London production"—with original director Vlado Habunek uncredited)

choreographed by Sammy Bayes

produced by Management Three Productions, Ltd. (Jerry Weintraub and Martin Kummer) and Frank Productions, Inc. (Frank Loesser and Allen B. Whitehead), by arrangement with Classic Presentations, Ltd.

starring George Rose, Hermione Baddeley, and Martyn Green

with Roy Cooper, Ed Evanko, Sandy Duncan, Ann Gardner, Edwin Steffe, Reid Shelton, and Bert Michaels

opened February 3, 1969   Eugene O'Neill Theatre

CLIVE BARNES, *TIMES*

By and large I would say that the musical *Canterbury Tales* is worth seeing—at the Phoenix Theatre in London, England. It came to the Eugene O'Neill Theatre on Broadway last night, and the proposition seemed slightly more questionable. The idea for the show is a delightful one. Nevill Coghill, a theatrically inclined retired Oxford professor, has adapted some of Chaucer's 14th-century poems. Chaucer is still fresh, gay and innocent, as well as being the most English of poets. All this feeling for the English countryside in spring, and the boisterousness of an England emerging from the Middle Ages, to some extent communicated itself in the London production, making it a beguiling evening, if not a memorable one. At the time I found it "mildly enchanting." On Broadway the mildness seems to have the edge on the enchantment. Although I do not personally care for [the translation], it works well enough for the book of the musical. Professor Coghill's lyrics are another matter, being rather less than graceful, and the music by Richard Hill and John Hawkins, a kind of Chaucerian rock—grossly overblown and overamplified for Broadway—while merry enough, and sweet enough, does sound rather more incidental and accidental than transcendental. It is, however, loud. *Canterbury Tales*, then, still has Chaucer in its favor. But in London it also had remarkably stylish staging and performance. The staging is described as "directed by Martin Starkie after the original London production," and certainly the splendid scenery by Derek Cousins and the colorfully springlike costumes by Loudon Sainthill appear to be identical. Yet Starkie's direction seems much coarser, much more emphatic than it was in London. There Starkie was listed merely as the co-director, while the director was named Vlado Habunek, Yugoslavia's leading man of the theatre and a director of marked talent. Similarly the original dances were by David Drew, a choreographer from Britain's Royal Ballet, and while the new dances by Sammy Bayes aim closely at the same effects—sometimes remarkably closely—there is a difference in quality. Mr. Starkie has tried hard, but I have a hunch that Mr. Habunek might have done better. Also, with respect, it is a pity that the star of the London production, Wilfred Brambell, could not have been prevailed upon to play his original part of the Steward on Broadway [where it was played by George Rose]. He made an enormous difference.

MARTIN GOTTFRIED, *WOMEN'S WEAR DAILY*

Geoffrey Chaucer's *Canterbury Tales* has had a reputation for rollicking literary humor for so long (six centuries) we are prone to accept it at face value, all the more so because "bawdy" is almost synonymous with Chaucer. Chaucer, too, carries with him the sense of good gray scholars swilling down the ale, swirling their academic gowns and raising hell in the old quad. What then would seem more appropriate than a musical right out of the old man's tales? It opened last night at the Eugene O'Neill when it should have opened in the library stacks. *Canterbury Tales* is a graduate school show. Imported from England, it shows the British still struggling to be loose in the musical theatre form. There is so little attempt to do anything theatrical with the stories, you imagine these scholars blithely assuming that the Chaucer they love could not but entertain theatre audiences too. The humor is desperately Chaucerian, the renowned bawdiness running to lines like "I have a noble cock," and song titles like "Hymen, Hymen." With everyone on stage laughing at his own business, you'd think the humor might at least be contagious but the result, I fear, was quarantine, all the fun remaining on the actors' side of the curtain. Sammy Bayes was given a great deal of dance time and managed to make the least of his experience with Jerome Robbins [as assistant choreographer of *Fiddler on the Roof* (1964)]. Instead of learning from Robbins' approach to dance theatre, Bayes merely learned the *Fiddler on the Roof* steps. If you look even less than carefully, you can see the old *Fiddler* business right in the old medieval middle. The direction by Martin Starkie was derivative in another sense, looking very much like a Shakespearean comedy at some summer festival. Finally, the individual performances. Sandy Duncan is pretty as a button, with the constant guile of a willing young lady. Ed Evanko, unfortunately just as pretty, is her young man most of the time. George Rose stopped the show with a dumb wedding night number ["If She Has Never Loved Before"] that was as carefully devised to be a show-stopper as was the audience advised to let it happen—nobody really believing the number was that good. And Hermione Baddeley, too often sounding like Gingold, but wildly funny at the very end as the most haggard old bag I've seen on a stage. By then, though, it wasn't of much consolation. Otherwise, it is dusty fun from academe.

◦   ◦   ◦

This British hit lost something in the overseas translation and fell flat on Broadway. But then, *1776* (1969, from an olde American legend) went belly up on the West End. The light-rock ribaldry of *Canterbury Tales* was all very well for swinging London, but *Hair* (1968) was playing around the corner by the time the show reached the Colonies. *Canterbury Tales* did serve as the Broadway debut of Sandy Duncan, that Elizabethan lass from Texas, and garnered her a Tony nomination. The importing producers included the great Frank Loesser, whose corporation occasionally presented musicals (including *The Music Man* [1957] and *How to Succeed* [1961]). *Canterbury Tales* turned out to be Loesser's final effort; he died shortly after the closing, on July 28, 1969.

A Tony Award was won by Loudon Sainthill (costume design).

BROADWAY SCORECARD
/ PERFS: 121 / $: –

RAVE	FAVORABLE	MIXED	UNFAVORABLE	PAN
2			2	2

CARMELINA

"A New Musical"

music by Burton Lane

lyrics by Alan Jay Lerner

book by Alan Jay Lerner and Joseph Stein

directed by José Ferrer

choreographed by Peter Gennaro

produced by Roger L. Stevens, J. W. Fisher, Joan Cullman, and Jujamcyn Productions

starring Georgia Brown and Cesare Siepi

with John Michael King, Gordon Ramsey, Howard Ross, Virginia Martin, Grace Keagy, and Josie de Guzman

opened April 8, 1979   *St. James Theatre*

GEORGIA BROWN   CESARE SIEPI

in A New Musical

Carmelina

Lyrics by
ALAN JAY LERNER   Music by
BURTON LANE

Book by
ALAN JAY LERNER and JOSEPH STEIN

with
JOHN MICHAEL KING   GORDON RAMSEY   HOWARD ROSS
VIRGINIA MARTIN   GRACE KEAGY   JOSSIE DE GUZMAN

Sets Designed by
OLIVER SMITH   Costumes Designed by
DONALD BROOKS   Lighting by
FEDER

Musical Direction &
Vocal Arrangements by
MAURICE LEVINE   Orchestrations by
HERSHY KAY   Dance Music Arranged by
DAVID KRANE

Choreographed by
PETER GENNARO

Directed by
JOSE FERRER

Produced by WHITEHEAD-STEVENS PRODUCTIONS

OPERA HOUSE AT THE KENNEDY CENTER
MARCH 7-24 Only!

INSTANT-CHARGE (202) 857-0900   GROUP SALES (202) 634-7201

The wearily old-fashioned *Carmelina* "does all of the easiest things awkwardly and most of the difficult things with confidence and a considerable charm," per Walter Kerr.

CLIVE BARNES, *POST*

Carmelina is a resolute attempt to put back the clock on the Broadway musical. The story tries—quite successfully—to hold our interest, the music is unabashedly romantic, it is even set in Southern Italy, and the hero is played by an operatic bass baritone. Although it is unacknowledged on the program the story line has been loosely based on Melvin Frank's 1968 film *Buona Sera, Mrs. Campbell*. The dialogue is persuasive and witty, and Lane and Lerner have done wonders with a score as Neapolitan as a rich spaghetti sauce. This is Lane's best score since the great *Finian's Rainbow* [1947], and the Hershy Kay orchestrations are brilliant. Lerner's lyrics twist in the sunlight of his invention—fantastic. Nowadays only Stephen Sondheim has this gorgeous gift for lyric language. José Ferrer has directed with style, Peter Gennaro's dances are simple and effective, Oliver Smith's settings recreate every small Southern Italian town you ever knew, and Donald Brooks' costumes have elegance and authenticity, which is a difficult match to act. The cast is exceptionally good, particularly vocally. So what is wrong? Everything is according to formula—the pattern is perfect. Yet I am still giving *Carmelina* two cheers rather than three. Why? It is just too old-fashioned. It is not exactly a pastiche, it is certainly not a copy, and yet it never, for all its brownie points picked up on the way, has the imprint of an original. It could have been done 10 years ago—and should have been. *Carmelina* is a friendly musical that is not going anywhere it hasn't been, and not saying anything it hasn't seen, but it is awe-inspiringly professional, and with its lilt of romantic music and its honest sentiment, could work for the audience. I hope it does.

RICHARD EDER, *TIMES*

Cesare Siepi's voice, very big if no longer very supple, quite overmasters the frail *Carmelina*. It is a voice in search of something to sing. It is like a mastiff trying to make a meal out of popcorn. *Carmelina* is the work of two distinguished names in the history of the American musical. Alan Jay Lerner wrote the lyrics and collaborated on the book; Burton Lane wrote the music. Neither one is here near keeping up with himself. *Carmelina* has a few pleasant moments in it, and there is a certain game professionalism to some of the others; but it is a very undernourished piece of work. The book is as faded as something picked up at a

Goodwill sale. It is set in a tiny Neapolitan village sometime in the early 1960's. The inhabitants include a breadseller, a fruit-seller, a mustached mayor and a shovel-hatted priest; and they all bubble. Lerner's lyrics strain for freshness but don't often find it. When he has Carmelina rhyme "Jehovah" with "I'm starting over" and go on with "I demand the biggest share of all the clover" it sounds like something inspired by a 3 A.M. vigil in a hotel room. The show has two dance numbers, but neither one is more than conventional and their performance is routine. The Italian village square designed by Oliver Smith is also routine; it is invaded half a dozen times by Carmelina's living room that trundles on, towing behind it an unruly kitchen. When the living room stops, the kitchen bumps into it. *Carmelina* is at best an exercise in harmlessness, and I suppose it mostly succeeds at it.

WALTER KERR, *TIMES*

Some new musicals are strange because they mean to be. *Sweeney Todd* [1979], let's say. And other new musicals are strange because they're trying so hard not to be. Quite the strangest thing about *Carmelina* is the fact that it does all of the easiest things awkwardly and most of the difficult things with confidence and a considerable charm. I suppose you know the plot: having slept with three Yanks in a single busy month and having given birth to a daughter in consequence, Miss Brown has notified each that he is the proud father of a daughter and has, for 17 rather well-heeled years, received triple support in the parlay. Now the men are back in town for a regimental reunion and there's only one pretty, well-educated daughter to go 'round. Trapped, rather. Lerner and Lane might easily have run into a trap of their own right off the bat. How *do* you set up the exposition, which must account for a pretty rapid turnover in the heroine's generously bestowed affections, without making the poor girl a whore, and a remarkably mercenary one at that? Composer and lyricist have responded by handing Miss Brown the show's loveliest melody, a bit of prime Lerner/Lane that is infinitely adaptable to the comings and goings of transient but reasonably sincere lovers ("Someone in April/When he went out the door/Said thank you for April"). If the song's line is lyrical and the visitors are gentlemen, there's an undercurrent of humor that can surface on demand and can even grow quite caustic when Brown decides that, lovely as April was, the month left her with more than enough to remember it by. The song works in three ways: as something blessedly hummable, as irony and as plot. It may even work in a fourth. The audience with which I saw *Carmelina* seemed neither pleased nor displeased with the familiar setting, the insecure opening staging. (I do think it's a mistake to ask Mr. Siepi to put his still-noble voice to the work of singing a romantic ballad while standing on a table-top. He's obviously brave enough and sturdy enough to do it; but we get nervous.) Once "Someone in April" had become three someones in April, though, the theatregoers around me were hooked, hooked and ready for the next two hurdles the authors would genially overcome.

○   ○   ○

"It's Time for a Love Song" goes the opening number of *Carmelina*, and perhaps it was. But *Carmelina* itself was not only behind the times—which might have been forgiveable—but underwritten and poorly assembled. Since the retirement of composer Frederick Loewe in 1960, Alan Jay Lerner's search for a collaborator had taken him through Richard Rodgers (who threw up his hands in dismay) to Burton Lane for *On a Clear Day* (1965); André Previn for *Coco* (1969); John Barry for the 1971 road-flop *Lolita, My Love*; and Leonard Bernstein for *1600 Pennsylvania Avenue* (1976). With another opportunity in the offering, Lerner went back to Lane who—with misgivings—agreed to another try. (Lerner's final effort was set to music by Charles Strouse, the 1983 one-night-only *Dance a Little Closer*.) With work proceeding at Lerner's typically lethargic pace, Joe Stein came in to help with the libretto; the pair had collaborated on singer Hildegarde's radio show back in the old, pre-*Brigadoon* (1947) days. The plot—about three GIs who discover after twenty years that they've been paying child support for the same bambina—seemed remarkably similar to a 1968 Sophia Loren movie called *Buona Sera, Mrs. Campbell*. Lerner insisted that *his* work was original, based on a newspaper article that Melvin Frank, screenwriter of *Buona Sera*, also must have seen. (Was the real-life *signorina* named Campbell?, one wonders.) Lerner added that he and his collaborators had screened the film, and didn't like it. (His disavowal recalls a similar sensitivity on *Brigadoon*, which despite vehement protestations was clearly borrowed from Friedrich Wilhelm

Gerstäcker's *Germelshausen*. Lerner's denials in that case only served to publicize the truth, and unnecessarily so, as the true origins of the *Brigadoon* story do not in any way detract from the excellence of Lerner's work.) Be that as it may, the striking thing about *Carmelina* was that random portions of Lerner's lyrics—the sections he spent enough time on?—were so very good that you could recognize the imprint of the man from *My Fair Lady* (1956). This amidst the otherwise very ordinary rubble. Without any extraordinary spark, *Carmelina* came across as it was: old-fashioned, second-rate, and remarkably out of place. $1,062,500 down the drain, including a hundred thou from Claus von Bulow.

BROADWAY SCORECARD
/ PERFS: 17 / $: –

RAVE	FAVORABLE	MIXED	UNFAVORABLE	PAN
	1	1	1	3

CELEBRATION

"A New Musical"

music by Harvey Schmidt

book and lyrics by Tom Jones

directed by Tom Jones

choreographed by Vernon Lusby

produced by Cheryl Crawford and Richard Chandler; "a Portfolio Production" (Tom Jones and Harvey Schmidt)

with Susan Watson, Ted Thurston, Keith Charles, and Michael Glenn-Smith

opened January 22, 1969   *Ambassador Theatre*

CLIVE BARNES, *TIMES*
Once upon a time—for this is a fable—a man called Tom Jones and a man called Harvey Schmidt sat down and pondered. They pondered and they pondered. They pondered on what was wrong with the Broadway musical, and they decided (at least this would be my guess) that it lacked simplicity, magic and uplift. Last night the curtain rose on their *Celebration*, which might be thought of as an unpretentiously pretentious fairy tale for adults. At its worst it seemed like a Madison Avenue apology for art, and all the simplicity, magic and uplift that had been lavished on the show came out as chic and heartless. At its best, and it very definitely has a best, there is a campy style of originality here, some nice lines from Jones, some sweetly percussive melodies from Schmidt, some pretty performances, all adding up to a musical decently above the admittedly flagging average. The story is all rather fey, coy and cutesy. I think Jones must have realized the cutesy side of it, because every so often he injects a thundering great vulgarity into the text to keep on reminding the audience that it is in a theater rather than a nursery school. Yet undoubtedly they do want to introduce a new look into the Broadway musical, and *Celebration* is a musical with a certain style of its own. Sophisticated—even knowing—perhaps is the best inclusive term for Schmidt's music, which, while more gently pleasant than truly memorable, is scored for a nine-piece percussion ensemble that often pings up a storm. Jones also—adept at combining winsomeness with a naughty leer—often turns a good line with a deft wit. As director he has engineered a well-constructed experimental look, full of masks and symbols, but, regrettably, uses such props and devices rather more in the modish manner of a smart window decorator than that of the forward looking man of the theatre. To sum up then, if you like your musicals soft-centered in a slightly different way, full of affirmative statements about life, God, and youth and yet flavored with a sprinkling of mildly dirty jokes, *Celebration* may be for you. It does provide an undemanding evening that is altogether less adventurous than it might at first seem.

JOHN CHAPMAN, *DAILY NEWS*
A hapless, helpless, hopeless little musical charade. It tries to be cute and smart but it just isn't. It is sticky and icky.

MARTIN GOTTFRIED, *WOMEN'S WEAR DAILY*

I wish Tom Jones and Harvey Schmidt hadn't been working on *Celebration* for so long. The new musical has been the dream of this very talented team and they've worked at it, on and off, for close to eight years. But a lot has happened to the theatre—and us—during those years and *Celebration* has the look of its age. There are moments in it that reflect fairly recent theatre attitudes, but there are others that are the Off-Broadway of *The Fantasticks* [1960]. So though *Celebration* seems highly experimental when compared to other Broadway musicals, it's not because the show is so fresh but rather because Broadway's are so archaic that anything even eight years out of date will seem inventive. It is much too intimate for a big house and is lost on the Ambassador's wide stage. Everything about it, from the concept to the production to the sound of the orchestra is small scale. Finally, it has the kind of loose organization and cheerful inconsistency that you are sometimes willing to overlook when you're in a cozy house, but is unavoidably amateur under big-time conditions. Jones and Schmidt seem quite aware of the stickiness, but instead of solving the problem in the planning stage, they just let it lie on stage. Half the show is charm (and half of *that* is sticky), the other half is self-satirical. This is exactly what happened in *The Fantasticks* and it seems as if they, when on their own, are torn between the sentimental and a kind of show-biz sophistication. The tearing produces a torn work. Much of *Celebration* is delightful but other parts are embarrassing or boring. There are regular attempts at ritual (these using many wonderful masks designed by Schmidt himself) but they really don't have much to do with the show and seem as if the authors merely decided that a theatre celebration would have to use ritual. Still, I'm glad they got *Celebration* out of their system and it is by no means a disaster. Contrarily, it is regularly delightful and sometimes has the best kind of theatre effect—when you wish a scene or a song would go on forever you're enjoying it so much. But the key to any successful work is organization and confidence. Even the coyness of this leotard show is a flaw secondary to those lacks.

RICHARD WATTS, JR., *POST*

A musical play called *The Fantasticks* has been an off-Broadway triumph for almost a decade without notable help from this reviewer. Last night *Celebration*, another musical by the same authors reached

Broadway and there is, of course, the possibility that it will be a case of history's alleged tendency to repeat itself. But I thought it placed some handicaps in its own path. It is, to start with, one of those pseudo morality plays, and they are extremely difficult to do without letting the bogusness show. It is all right when they are being satirical, but when they are in dead earnest and the story is dealing seriously with youth, beauty and old age, and how the young and innocent inevitably win out over the old and corrupt, and riches are nothing, they may be telling you the truth, but they can bring out the skepticism in all brackets of play-goers. The trouble is, I think, that the story never comes to interesting life and the effort to invest it with allegorical overtones merely seems tiresomely pretentious while decreasing the charm.

o   o   o

Flush with funds from their hit *I Do! I Do!* (1966), Tom Jones and Harvey Schmidt bought a West 48th Street brownstone and converted it into the Portfolio Studio, the better to develop experimental musicals more *Fantastick*al than not. *Celebration* was born at Portfolio in 1968, although it evolved from an earlier contemporary-musical-in-progress called *Ratfink*—about one James J. Ratfink—which was first announced in 1961 by Cheryl Crawford. Crawford was a pioneering name in musical theatre and nonmusical theatre as well. A founding member of both the Group Theatre and the Actors Studio, Crawford produced the acclaimed 1942 revival of *Porgy and Bess*, which firmly established the piece as a masterwork. This was followed by such important "progressive" musicals as Kurt Weill's *One Touch of Venus* (1943), Lerner and Loewe's *Brigadoon* (1947) and *Paint Your Wagon* (1951), Weill and Lerner's *Love Life* (1948), and Marc Blitzstein's *Regina* (1949). Crawford and her author/partners decided, perhaps fatally, to eschew the Off-Broadway arena and move *Celebration* from the 100-seat Portfolio to the 1,100-seat Ambassador. They managed their experiment wisely, though, raising $250,000—double their anticipated production costs. Their original projections held, allowing them a $125,000 cushion (extraordinary at the time) to handle extra advertising and the expected operating losses until such time as the show caught on. *The Fantasticks* had run in the red for four months before turning the corner on Sullivan Street, but the Broadway corner was never turned. *Celebration* gradually used up the reserve and, inevitably, closed after fourteen weeks. The unquestionable charms and modest production requirements of *Celebration* allowed a strong nonprofessional afterlife, however, especially in the protest-prone 1970s. (David Merrick, producer of *110 in the Shade* [1963] and *I Do! I Do!*, had a lasting effect on the boys, serving as model for *Celebration*'s rapacious Edgar Allan Rich.)

BROADWAY SCORECARD
/ PERFS: 110 / $: –

RAVE	FAVORABLE	MIXED	UNFAVORABLE	PAN
		1	3	2

CHARLIE AND ALGERNON

"A Very Special Musical," originally produced (in Canada and London) as *Flowers for Algernon*

music by Charles Strouse

book and lyrics by David Rogers

based on the 1959 short story *Flowers for Algernon* by Daniel Keyes

directed by Louis W. Scheeder

choreographed by Virginia Freeman

produced by The Kennedy Center, Isobel Robins Konecky, Fisher Theatre Foundation and the Folger Theatre Group (Michael Sheehan and Louis W. Scheeder)

with P. J. Benjamin, Sandy Faison, Edward Earle, Robert Sevra, Nancy Franklin, Patrick Jude, and Julienne Marie

opened September 14, 1980   Helen Hayes Theatre

WALTER KERR, *TIMES*

[Headline: "Nothing to Sing About"]

There are romantic musicals and satirical musicals, grotesque musicals and family musicals, spectacular musicals and intimate musicals. You name it, and it'll turn up. But, I wonder, is there really such a thing as a worrywart musical? I mean one that's frowning all the time, raising its voice in song only to say what a sorry day this has been, dipping into its principals' pasts to show what really rotten childhoods they had and peering into their futures to see nothing but disaster ahead. Oh, the people in the cast of unhappy characters may take turns being morose, with one brightening up a bit just as another heads into profound depression. But overall they're troubled, troubled, troubled, from over-ture to exit-music. The question about so much gloom being this: will it dance? *Charlie and Algernon*, which opened ever so broodingly at the Helen Hayes last Sunday, won't dance. The one bit of footwork that does not go askew is the duet done by [the formerly retarded] Charlie, who is now a fully developed human being, and Algernon, who is a mouse. The two have become friends earlier, when they were compet-ing to see which could get through his respective maze fastest—with Algernon usually winning. Lately, with his I.Q. growing exponentially, Charlie's been doing the winning. But Algernon is not a proud mouse. No bitterness. He remains altogether happy to be doing rhythmic pat-terns across Charlie's twitching shoulders, joining him in a vaudeville sashay from portal to portal, crawling straight up his extended leg when invited. Algernon is not only of native talent; that mouse has been doing his homework. P. J. Benjamin, as Charlie, is good in the buck-and-wing duo, too, but I've given Algernon more credit here because discrimination will probably keep him from getting a Tony nomination, or even other parts. . . . I don't suppose there's any subject in the world that *can't* be turned into a musical, given a lot of inspiration and just a little luck. Some people once made a Broadway smash out of a labor union's demand for a seven-and-a-half-cent raise. But, just to be on the safe side, it might be wise to ask—before plunging into all that work—if there's anything in the material that will automatically bind a musi-cals' feet or tie its tongue. Or simply give everyone on stage too much to scowl about.

Charlie and Algernon is subtitled "a very special musical." Since it is about a man and a mouse who, in a laboratory experiment, have their brain power dramatically strengthened (the mouse becomes a whiz at problem solving, the man goes from being retarded to genius-level intelligence), *Charlie and Algernon* should indeed have been "a very special musical." The trouble is that *Charlie and Algernon* is a thoroughly ordinary musical. Throughout the evening one is conscious of how material that demanded especially sensitive treatment, situations that cried out for intimacy and warmth, were handled in a standardized manner. David Rogers' book oversimplifies complex psychological moments and tries to spruce things up with gags. His lyrics are equally simpleminded when they are not amateurish. ("You're somebody fine/But still you ain't mine.") Charles Strouse has set Rogers' short, rhythmically crude phrases straightforwardly, occasionally reaching for harmonic or contrapuntal sophistication, for unexpected intervals, but generally settling for a commercial idiom that only reminds us of the thoroughly uncommercial, unstandard nature of the story. The brightest moment in the intermission-less evening is a solo Charlie sings, ironically characterizing the experiment in which he and the mouse have participated, as a piece of exhibitionism, science going show biz in its hunger for grants and publicity. During the number Algernon, an actual white mouse, crawls up Benjamin's leg and fairly steals the show (which is not as difficult as it may sound). Benjamin's show biz gestures, though they fit the conceit, work against whatever sympathy one has developed for the character (as they do earlier in a song that tries to get laughs from the fact Charlie can read *Robinson Crusoe* and *War and Peace* in one sitting—the plot summaries he gives in snappy verses might have been amusing 30 years ago in the hands of Comden and Green, but they fall flat here). The only people who seem to have believed *Charlie and Algernon* was "a very special musical" were the advertising copywriters.

Charlie and Algernon bills itself as "a very special musical." That's probably as good a way as any to describe a show whose premise springs from science fiction and whose title characters are a retarded man and a sprightly white mouse. Then again, *Charlie and Algernon* is special only up to a point. Though this musical boasts unusual heroes and enough philosophical truisms to fill a dozen fortune cookies, it is a very ordinary and at times very irritating entertainment. The evening's source material is *Flowers for Algernon*, the Daniel Keyes novel that also served as the basis for the 1968 movie *Charly*. It's a fable about a pair of scientists who invent a psychosurgical technique for transforming idiots into geniuses. Having successfully upgraded the I.Q. of their laboratory mouse—that's Algernon—the ambitious doctors operate on Charlie, a brain-damaged bakery worker, to prove that their magic can also benefit humankind. But, needless to say, there are some things that man wasn't meant to tamper with. There's nothing wrong with this sentimental little tale, predictable though it may be, but there is much amiss with the way it is retold in *Charlie and Algernon*.

* * *

The 1959 short story *Flowers for Algernon* rose from an inauspicious beginning—in *The Magazine of Fantasy and Science Fiction*—to widespread anthologization and quick recognition as a classic of its type. Sterling Silliphant adapted it for *CBS Playhouse* in 1961 as *The Two Worlds of Charley Gordon*, later recycling his teleplay into the 1968 motion picture *Charly*. (Cliff Robertson copped an Oscar in the latter, but then he wasn't upstaged by a tap-dancing mouse.) David Rogers, a prolific amateur-play author, was commissioned by Dramatists Play Service to create a stage version for the high school market, and this in turn led to the musicalization. The Rogers-Strouse *Flowers for Algernon* received a Canadian tryout at the Citadel in Edmonton, Alberta, in December 1978, resulting in a June 14, 1979, London production starring Michael Crawford and directed by Peter (*Oliver!* [1963]) Coe. The West End *Flowers for Algernon* flopped after twenty-eight performances, and that was that. Until . . . until the folks at Dramatists Play Service were able to arrange a third professional production, by the Folger Theatre Group, as part of their two-play season at Kennedy Center's Terrace Theatre in March 1980. This revised version—now dubbed *Charlie and Algernon*—was remounted that fall at the Kennedy Center's larger Eisenhower Theatre and despite its obvious mediocrity brought in to Broadway. All that for universal jeers and a measly seventeen performances. You can build a better mousetrap. . . .

BROADWAY SCORECARD
/ PERFS: 17 / $: –

RAVE	FAVORABLE	MIXED	UNFAVORABLE	PAN
			2	4

CHICAGO

"A Musical Vaudeville"

music by John Kander

lyrics by Fred Ebb

book by Fred Ebb and Bob Fosse (with Herb Gardner)

based on the 1926 satire by Maurine Dallas Watkins

directed and choreographed by Bob Fosse; "associate director: Stuart Ostrow"

produced by Robert Fryer and James Cresson in association with Martin Richards, Joseph Harris, and Ira Bernstein

starring Gwen Verdon, Chita Rivera, and Jerry Orbach

with Barney Martin, Mary McCarty, and M. O'Haughey (third-featured David Rounds's role eliminated)

opened June 3, 1975   *46th Street Theatre*

Legs, thighs, and "All That Jazz" helped sell *Roxie Hart*. (artwork by Tony Walton)

CLIVE BARNES, *TIMES*

[Headline: "*Chicago* Disappoints"]

Form or content, shadow or substance—those classic alternatives of artistic endeavor had their day in court at the 46th Street Theatre last night. Well, not really. For neither content nor substance were truly represented, and the result was a foregone conclusion; Bob Fosse's new musical, *Chicago*, is one of those shows where a great deal has been done with very little. One might be tempted to say that never in the history of the Broadway theatre has so much been done by so many for so few final results—but then one remembers *Pippin* [1972]. Indeed, one remembers *Pippin* through quite a lot of *Chicago*, and when one is not remembering *Pippin* one is remembering *Cabaret* [1966] and when one is not remembering *Cabaret* one is remembering *Roxie Hart* [the 1942 film adaptation of the play *Chicago*]. There is a great deal of glossiness to admire in *Chicago*. We are given three superlative, knock-em-in-the-aisles performances by three stars who glitter like golddust all evening, Gwen Verdon, Chita Rivera and Jerry Orbach. Even more, there is the incredibly authoritative directorial voice of Fosse (stentorian, individual and precisely articulated), unfortunately shouting hoarsely over a desert of style. Style is everywhere; *Chicago* drips with it like a dowager with opals. Tony Walton's setting, dominated by an orchestra platform with translucent pillars at the side decorated with cut-out images of the period, and Patricia Zipprodt's atmospheric and imaginative costumes are similarly effective, and full of chic, but something more than chic. This is not merely the evocation of a period but a comment on it. This pervasive suggestion of commentary, of standing aside from a time and a place and hinting at it with a wry, at times even cynical objectivity, is both the show's salient virtue and also the aspect of it that links it, like an umbilical cord, to *Cabaret*. The slow-motion prowling choreography—that soft-shoe shuffle for chalk-faced ballerinas and mocking song-and-dance men, all given with a sharp-edged and macabre lilt—or those almost monumentally inventive production numbers (give Fosse a chair, lights and Miss Rivera and he will run you up a show-biz gem) have become the hallmarks of Fosse's work and style. But where does it all lead? A couple of years ago Fosse created a one-minute television commercial for *Pippin* that helped the other 119 minutes no end. He should start work on another commercial.

MARTIN GOTTFRIED, *POST*

Chicago is as dazzling a demonstration of the craft of musical theatre as you're ever going to see on a Broadway stage. But curiously, for all the virtuosity of its technique—the fantastic stage pictures, the integrity of style in movement, design and music—the show is seldom thrilling. More often, it is awesome. Yet I'm not sure whether or not "thrilling" is just something we've been taught to expect from musicals. Certainly, there is no question that *Chicago* is a tremendous accomplishment, a show as only the stage can provide, an example of the most advanced and professional in musical theatre, a sight to see. Though there have been many great contributions to the production, there is no question that it is Bob Fosse's show and that everything has been dictated by the style he chose to imprint on it. That style is an expressionistic, acid distortion of prohibition Chicago—a German style that, frankly, has less than the least connection with the show's subject matter. Fosse has subtitled the production "a musical vaudeville," and that is just what is. If, because of the tricky scheme, the story has taken second place to the vaudeville numbers, so have the stars been made subservient to the show itself. Fosse has obviously grown more interested in choreographing for groups than for soloists and the heart of this show is more with its amazing (and amazing-looking) dancers and dancing and mood and appearance than with its leading characters. But that doesn't leave room for a heart. The only moment of true feeling is struck by Barney Martin, who does the Ted Lewis number—"Mr. Cellophane"—with all the corny but real heartbreak of the vaudeville trouper. Otherwise, *Chicago* is in the hands of a Fosse at the peak of technical and conceptual strength; a Fosse positively reveling in his dexterity; but a Fosse without emotion. If it never quite grabs you by the seat of your pants, it is still striking indeed.

WALTER KERR, *TIMES*

[Headline: "*Chicago* Comes On Like Doomsday"]

Chicago's problem is one of atmospheric pressure. It's altogether too heavy to let the foolish story breathe. I am sure that Bob Fosse is sick to death of hearing about its resemblance to *Cabaret*. It's he, though, who has put so many of those garish, deliberately seedy, images back on the stage: the black stockings, one rolled beneath the knee, the other hiked above it to meet a blood-red garter; the perfect circles of rouge that make manipulable puppets of the wicked chorus girls; the virtual umbrellas of blue eye shadow that make lids hang heavy, heavy over bored, impertinent faces; the black netting, the black fringe, the tweaked fedora-brims, the spiked heels and the occasionally polka-dotted legs that seem to belong to underweight lady bugs. Round and about and above and below, the moodily darkened air is relieved mainly by coiling trails of cigar smoke, spider-web lines of scarlet neon. And the format is *Cabaret*'s format: the earlier enterprise introduced its narrative steps as reflections of a floorshow, with a decadently grinning *compère* masterminding the proceedings. *Chicago* calls itself a vaudeville bill, with an M.C. telling us that the evening is to be filled with murder, adultery, greed, treachery "and all those things near and dear to our hearts," while a 1920's band wails and thumps overhead on a filigreed gold balcony. But. *Cabaret* had a nasty, glowering, lowering weight hanging over it to account for its black-sick humors up front: the threat, and then the presence, of Nazi Germany. *Chicago* has no such evil genie in the wings to dictate its insistent darkness, its grotesquerie. Al Capone wasn't Hitler and Cicero wasn't Munich. It's *Front Page* [1928] territory, complete with sob-sisters, and all it wants is enough air, wit, and dimpled wickedness to make its light-minded lechery extravagantly jolly. In short, another time, another place, another—nonsensical rather than gloomy—world. Fosse, of course, is a man without peer when it comes to making navels undulate, hips quiver, toes stutter, white spats and white gloves create succulent patterns against the night sky. But his undue insistence on the tawdriness of it all crowds wit to the wall. I suspect that the greatest damage is done by the imposed "vaudeville" routining. Indeed, the story-line with its built-in satire has really been lost altogether, sacrificed to stunts and soft-shoe. *Chicago* is a very sleek show. It just seems to be the wrong one.

DOUGLAS WATT, *DAILY NEWS*
[Headline: "A Bold and Cynical *Chicago*"]
Bold, cynical and stylish as can be, *Chicago* is a musical out to kill. And if Tuesday's glittering new show somehow misses the mark, applaud it for its daring and moments of brilliance. This is a Bob Fosse show all the way from its cocked head to its pointed toes. The whole thing moves like a well-oiled machine. Taking a trivial melodrama of the '20s,

Fosse and his collaborators have constructed a corrosive cabaret show in which murder and its aftermath are presented as show turns, each one announced in Brecht-Weill fashion. Indeed, the show's esthetic is very similar to that of *Cabaret*, whose film version Fosse directed and whose songs were the work of Kander and Ebb. But this is jazzy old Chicago, not jazzy old Berlin. The two corrupt cultures are dissimilar, and the existential treatment accorded that breezy, raucous, wildly American city doesn't quite jibe. Perhaps more to the point, the grand conception and many striking details are bound to an utterly negligible story with an unsavory heroine. The ambience is sexy and sulphurous throughout. And it is small wonder that Roxie's patsy of a husband, nicely played by Barney Martin, wins the audience with a self-disparaging clown number titled "Mr. Cellophane." (Wasn't cellophane a '30s triumph, though?) In addition to the overall brilliance of his choreography, Fosse creates by far the sexiest dance routines imaginable. As in *Pippin*, he works here with a group of stunning girl dancers (accompanied by boys, of course) who frame the action in sinuous, provocative movement, usually in slow motion. The tension in his movement and his eye for groupings are richly effective. Patricia Zipprodt's costumes are eye-catching, so much so that one comes away with the impression that all that the girls, including Miss Verdon and Miss Rivera, wear are black bras, skimpy black panties, garter belts and high heels. Put *Chicago* down as a luridly effective spectacle, one too bountiful for words . . . at least for the words used here.

o   o   o

Gwen Verdon arrived on Broadway in 1948 as choreographer Jack Cole's assistant on *Magdalena*. Her big break came in 1953 with choreographer Michael Kidd, as the soubrette in *Can-Can*. (She stopped the show so cold in the "Garden of Eden" ballet on opening night that she was rushed back onstage for another bow—*en deshabille!*) When Verdon signed for her first starring role, as Lola in *Damn Yankees* (1955), she teamed with yet another distinctive choreographer: Bob Fosse. She remained a Fosse dancer—*the* Fosse dancer, perhaps—for the rest of her career. Verdon moved into the unlikely role of Anna Christie in *New Girl in Town* in 1957, followed by the 1959 *Redhead* (with which Fosse made his directorial debut). After a rather hectic decade in which she had become a ticket-selling star on par with Martin and Merman,

Verdon hung up her dance shoes, married Fosse, and had a child (her second). In 1966 she came back as *Sweet Charity*, with Fosse launching the second, remarkable half of his career. And then she rested again, until the mid-1970s, when she decided to do one last musical (at the age of 50). Verdon had long wanted to play Roxie Hart, the murderous murderess of Maurine Watkins's 1926 satire *Chicago*, but Watkins had refused to grant the rights. (Imagine, if you will, how different *Chicago* would have been if they'd done it when planned, back in 1966 instead of *Charity*.) With Watkins now gone and her heirs assenting, Fosse assigned the score to Kander and Ebb, with whom he'd worked on the film version of *Cabaret* and the TV special *Liza with a Z*. (Both projects appeared in 1972 along with *Pippin*–winning director Fosse an unprecedented and unimaginable Tony-Oscar-Emmy triple crown!) The *Chicago* plan was to present the musical numbers in the style of vaudeville acts, connected by sketch-like scenes to be coauthored by Ebb and Fosse (neither of whom had ever written a libretto). As had happened before—on the not-too-dissimilar Weill/Lerner/Kazan *Love Life* (1948) for example—and since—on the Yeston/Kopit/Tune *Nine* (1982)—an intriguing theoretical concept ultimately served to tie the hands of the creators. But *Chicago* had bigger problems, namely the heart attack(s) that the chimney-smoking, pill-popping, vodka-swilling director suffered the first week of rehearsals. (See the 1979 film *All That Jazz* for details, if you feel you need details.) Three months later the show was restarted, undergoing a typically turmoiled tryout before alighting, finally, at the 46th Street (home of *Yankees*, *New Girl*, and *Redhead*). The abrasive *Chicago* was not an easy show to like—one imagines Fosse *intended* it not to be an easy show to like—but it managed a decent run, boosted by an S.R.O. nine-week stretch when Liza (with a Z) subbed for the ailing Verdon. But a happy time was not had by all. (See *All That Jazz* for details, if you feel you need details.)

BROADWAY SCORECARD
/ PERFS: 923 / $: +

RAVE	FAVORABLE	MIXED	UNFAVORABLE	PAN
	2	2	2	

A CHORUS LINE

"A New Musical"

music by Marvin Hamlisch

lyrics by Edward Kleban

book by James Kirkwood and Nicholas Dante (with jokes by Neil Simon)

suggested by events in the lives of various participants in the show's development (uncredited but remunerated)

"conceived, choreographed and directed" by Michael Bennett; co-choreographed by Bob Avian

produced by the New York Shakespeare Festival (Joseph Papp) in association with Plum Productions (Michael Bennett)

with Carole (Kelly) Bishop, Pamela Blair, Wayne Cilento, Kay Cole, Ronald Dennis, Baayork Lee, Priscilla Lopez, Robert LuPone, Donna McKechnie, Don Percassi, Michel Stuart, Thomas (Thommie) J. Walsh, and Sammy Williams

opened May 21, 1975	*Newman Theatre, New York Shakespeare Festival*
transferred July 25, 1975	*Shubert Theatre*

(Note: the first-night reviewers covered the show at its Newman Theatre première, except for Walter Kerr who covered it at the Shubert)

CLIVE BARNES, *TIMES*

The conservative word for *A Chorus Line* might be tremendous, or perhaps terrific. Michael Bennett's new-style musical opened last night, and the reception was so shattering that it is surprising if, by the time you read this, the New York Shakespeare Festival has got a Newman Theatre still standing in its Public Theatre complex. It was that kind of reception, and it is that kind of a show. We have for years been hearing about innovative musicals; now Mr. Bennett has really innovated one.

It is easy to see from where *A Chorus Line* evolved. It is in direct succession to Harold Prince's *Company* [1970], and, to a lesser extent, *Cabaret* [1966] and *Follies* [1971]. The debt is unmistakable, but it has been paid in full. What makes *A Chorus Line* so devastatingly effective is its honesty of subject matter—so that even its faults can work for it. The music by Marvin Hamlisch is occasionally hummable and often quite cleverly drops into a useful buzz of dramatic recitative. Hamlisch is not such a good composer as he was in the movie *The Sting* [1973] when he was being helped out by Scott Joplin, but he can pass, and the lyrics by Edward Kleban do more than that, they pass with a certain distinction, while the look of the show (an explosion of mirrors that may owe something to the *Cabaret* set but is still food for reflection) and the cast is 105 per cent marvelous. Honesty is the policy of Bennett's show, and from opening to the stupendous closing chorus, it is stamped indelibly as Bennett's show. His choreography and direction burn up superlatives as if they were inflammable. In no way could it have been better done. Everything is made to work. While there will be some to find fault, perhaps with a certain reason, with the hard-edged glossiness of *A Chorus Line*, it is a show that must dance, jog and whirl its way into the history of the musical theatre. *Oklahoma!* [1943] it isn't, but no one with strength to get to the box office should willingly miss it. You will talk about it for weeks.

MARTIN GOTTFRIED, POST

At a time when producers are taking choruses out of their musicals for the sake of economy, director Michael Bennett has taken everything else out. For in the dance chorus he has found the very heart of the Broadway musical. *A Chorus Line* is a dazzling show: driving, compassionate and finally thrilling. It is a major event in the development of the American musical theatre. Bennett's work is simply awesome, doubtless helped by his assistant Bob Avian. The stage is bare except for designer Robin Wagner's series of tall, rotating mirrors. The dancers are merely in rehearsal costumes, until the finale. Yet, the stage pictures are magnificent, lighted fabulously by Tharon Musser, as patterns of dancers move into arrays and then separate. These aren't just chorus people. They are people. Marvin Hamlisch's music, as it had to be, is utterly subservient to the show's needs. If he has any composing personality, he denied it. The best thing about his music is that it is that rare animal, the theatre *score*. It isn't just a series of songs but an evening's worth of music designed to function as part of a stage work. Its consistency is in its dance rhythms. With no few thanks to the superb orchestrations of Bill Byers, Hershy Kay and Jonathan Tunick, Hamlisch's music—the underscoring, the continuity, the dance arrangements—captures the very spirit and essence of rehearsal music. That had to be its intention. *A Chorus Line* is meant as a chorus musical and its *cast* is the star, a company tremendously talented and brutally sincere. Certainly, the show owes something to *Cabaret* in its expressionistic style, as does the music in its cutting edge. Bennett's use of mirrors is also reminiscent of his work in *Follies*. He would doubtless admit to having learned from Harold Prince, the director of those innovative productions and a pioneer of such exciting concept musicals. The line of development is thoroughbred. But with this show, Bennett steps out on his own as a star director-choreographer—one of striking singularity—one whose staging wizardry and theatrical muscle are deepened by a swelling humanity. He is now a major creative force and *A Chorus Line* is purely and simply magnificent, capturing the very soul of our musical theatre.

WALTER KERR, *TIMES*
[Headline: "*A Chorus Line* Soars"]
Everything is even better at *A Chorus Line*. During the months of playing, first at the downtown Public, then during previews at the Shubert on Broadway, certain mysterious and possibly miraculous changes have taken place. Actually, nothing of Michael Bennett's brilliant surface— his godlike way with instantaneously shifting shafts of light, his powerhouse advances of the full company on an audience already mesmerized—has been altered. Yet this restlessly orchestrated mix of music, speech, song and sculptured movement has now acquired an absoluteness of line, a dynamic control over space, that is stunning in both its economy and its force. A simple falling into place took my breath away at the Shubert. Glossy, impertinent, ruefully aging and very funny Carole Bishop had begun a number explaining how everyone was beautiful at the ballet, wistful Nancy Lane had taken over for a second phrase, bouncing Kay Cole for a third. Suddenly the one, two, three of

it had arranged them into a downstage-upstage diagonal that is no more than ordinary geometry. Yet the effortlessness of the design, the minimum preparation for its arrival, the transfixed firmness of its completion all conspire to make the familiar unexpectedly beautiful, unchallengeable as taste. The people not only fill but possess the territory they occupy, without them it would not be there at all. I felt they would carry it away with them after the last glittering curtain-call had been high-kicked, leaving the Shubert a shell. And the people have matured, learned to know themselves in a way that lets *you* know them, smile at them, indulge them, root for them, earlier than before. Pamela Blair, complaining of having constantly lost jobs because her physical endowments weren't exactly a match for her dancing skills, always had a funny number in "Dance: Ten, Looks: Three." But it was funny-brash, trading somewhat on marketable vulgarisms. Now it is funny-brash-warm, not just a slick sales job but a report from a hapless, though philosophical, heart. The evening's occasional repetitions and easy pitches are still there; but they belong to somebody now, they've been absorbed into a relationship between performers and audience that is as intimate and friendly as it is commanding. Well, you've been trying to get in anyway, and you'll be seeing it sooner or later. Just rest assured that it's an absolute marvel.

DOUGLAS WATT, *DAILY NEWS*
[Headline: "Tell Me, Little Gypsy"]
Yes, indeed. *A Chorus Line*, which has been showering sparks on Lafayette St. for several weeks now during previews, finally burst into full flame last night. Thus, this daringly simple, brilliantly staged entertainment takes its place as the hottest new thing in town and firmly establishes itself as the most exciting Broadway musical in several seasons. Literally, it's Off-Broadway, but I don't see how anybody will be able to stop it from moving uptown. Bennett, who has already been responsible for the musical staging of the decade's two outstanding musicals to date, *Company* and *Follies*, has no equal in teasing a dance number into shape, building it from bits and pieces into a suddenly dazzling whole. He has effected this most notably here in a show-stopping turn ("The Music and the Mirror") by the striking Donna McKechnie, who plays a mature featured dancer trying to land a chorus job with a

director she once lived with, and in a totally unexpected curtain-call number after the play is over and the stage has been blacked out. The latter, a thrilling simplification of the "Loveland" sequence in *Follies*, all at once provides a resolution and a happy ending and is guaranteed to lift you right out of your seat after more than two hours of uninterrupted theatrical magic, most of it in dance form. Hamlisch has provided a supple and nicely varied score which, though notably lacking in the least melodic or harmonic originality, borrows tastefully and is, happily, the obvious work of a genuine musician, a fact resulting in some superb arrangements by Bill Byers, Hershy Kay and Jonathan Tunick that are played by a knockout 16-piece orchestra backstage. Kleban's lyrics are articulate, expressive, uncluttered and entertaining. Their big song, which must have been played 50 times and is used for that smashing finale, is a rhythmic, mildly sardonic love song bearing the title "One." Robin Wagner's stage design consists of a series of pivoting flats along the back wall, mirrors on one side and black surfaces on the other. But artless as the setting, Theoni V. Aldredge's costumes and Tharon Musser's expressive lighting appear to be up to then, wait and see what all three have in store for you at the finish. *A Chorus Line* is a splendid achievement.

·   ·   ·

Enough has been written about the birth and creation of *A Chorus Line* to obviate my adding to the tale—five volumes, so far, devoted to the show and its resident genius. Suffice it to say that the entertainment was at one and the same time new-fashioned and old-fashioned, wisely bitchy and softly gooey as a bar of Turkish Taffy that's been left out in the hot sun too long. More important, it gripped its audience by the proverbial seat of its pants and held theatregoers breathless on the edge of their cushions. Somewhat surprising when you consider that the characters were "show people" far removed from the dreams and desires of the everyday civilians who flocked to see the show on Broadway and across the country. Your typical, out-of-work musical-show gypsy— "God I'm a dancer, a dancer dances"—served as a metaphor for everyone in the audience who ever thought "I can do that," I guess. *A Chorus Line* was not especially well made; unlike the great musicals of the 1940s and 1950s, the show's sine qua non was not the score but the staging. *South Pacific* (1949) or *Guys and Dolls* (1950) or *Fair Lady* (1956) or even *West Side* (1957) will always work given an adequate production, but I wouldn't want to see a Bennett-less *Chorus Line*. The score, in places, tended to sound almost as if Bennett had first staged the musical numbers and then ordered Hamlisch to provide music by the bar. This paint-by-numbers approach is how show choreographers often work with dance arrangers. Bennett was, first and foremost, a show choreographer; Hamlisch arranged dance music for the choreographer's early *Henry Sweet Henry* (1967), and achieved fame and Oscars arranging Scott Joplin's rags into the score for *The Sting*. While the *Chorus Line* score contained some first-class musical theatre material— "At the Ballet," "Nothing," and "Dance: Ten; Looks: Three" stand out— much of it sounded like filler. Significantly, the most effective part of the eveningful of dancers baring their souls and psyches—the searing saga of a drag queen, which won Sammy Williams a Tony Award—was the one life story told *without* music.

Winner of the Pulitzer Prize for Drama. Winner of the New York Drama Critics' Circle Award. In addition to winning the Tony Award for Best Musical, Tonys were won by Marvin Hamlisch and Edward Kleban (score), James Kirkwood and Nicholas Dante (book), Michael Bennett (director), Michael Bennett and Bob Avian (choreographers), Donna McKechnie (actress), Sammy Williams (supporting actor), Carole Bishop (supporting actress), and Tharon Musser (lighting design).

BROADWAY SCORECARD

/ PERFS: 6,137 / $: +

RAVE	FAVORABLE	MIXED	UNFAVORABLE	PAN
6				

COCO

"The New Musical"

music by André Previn

book and lyrics by Alan Jay Lerner

based on the life of *couturière* Gabrièlle "Coco" Chanel (1883–1971)

directed by Michael Benthall (doctored by Michael Bennett)

choreographed by Michael Bennett

produced by Frederick Brisson and Montfort, Inc. (Alan Jay Lerner)

starring Katharine Hepburn

with George Rose, Gale Dixon, David Holliday, René Auberjonois, and Jeanne Arnold

opened December 18, 1969   Mark Hellinger Theatre

CLIVE BARNES, *TIMES*

I know so little about the celebrated names in the wild, gay world of women's fashion that I once suspected that Coco was the name of a low-calorie chocolate drink. In fact, it is the nickname of Gabrièlle Chanel, whose totally unexciting life has been contorted into the subject of a musical play, which opened last night with, most fortunately, the largest box-office advance in Broadway history. There is an advertisement in the current *Playbill* that says—rather cheekily—"Wouldn't you rather be in Vegas?" I had always imagined that, Devil's Island apart, there was no place I would rather *not* be in than Las Vegas. There were one or two moments in the first act when I began to wonder whether the verdict had been a little hasty. The story of *Coco* is simple to the point of disappearance. Michael Benthall, who staged the piece, has a charming way with a revolving stage. Indeed, at some times dur-

"A show in the marvelous Ziegfeld tradition" (per the advertising herald). Kate Hepburn smiles on the grand staircase, looking like "the chief usher at Radio City Music Hall" (per the *Women's Wear* critic). Post–Broadway tour credits. (costume design and artwork by Cecil Beaton)

ing the show everything seems to be on the move except the plot. Rather more striking than the direction were the dances devised by Michael Bennett. One exultant number, when Coco is deliriously celebrating her triumph with the American buyers ["Ohrbach's, Bloomingdale's, Best & Saks"], is quite definitely one of the best staged musical numbers I have ever seen. It has something the show as a whole somewhat lacks—class. Class and style. And this is where Hepburn comes in. She is a blithe spirit, a vital flame. Her voice is like vinegar on sandpaper; her presence is a blessing. She growls out the most ordinary lines as if they were pearls of great price, gems of wit, nuggets of wisdom. She grins and she is enchanting. She prowls gloweringly down to the footlights, mutters a word for ordure in an idiomatically terse fashion, and remains devastatingly charming. Her singing voice is unique— a neat mixture of faith, love and laryngitis, unforgettable, unbelievable and delightful. Dear Miss Hepburn—perhaps they should have made a musical of your life rather than the dress designer. However, with all that money in the bank, all those theatre parties in the offing, and Hepburn on the top of the world, even fiascos can have happy endings. Hepburn has a nice line to say in the play: "Commercial failure all by itself does not make you an artistic success." So true. But, then, neither does commercial success. Does it?

JOHN CHAPMAN, *DAILY NEWS*
[Headline: "*Coco* Belongs to Kate Hepburn, Leaving Not Much for the Rest of Us"]

MARTIN GOTTFRIED, *WOMEN'S WEAR DAILY*
Coco is a show that decided to build the whole lobby of the Radio City Music Hall on the stage of the Mark Hellinger Theatre and just about did it, with Katharine Hepburn as the chief usher. Now the Music Hall is a perfect example of '30s decor, Coco Chanel is a great designer and Katharine Hepburn is a magnificent lady. The Music Hall's lobby, however, is not a Broadway musical and though I don't know very much about Chanel's fabrics, I doubt that she got where she is with this kind of material. As for Hepburn, she had as much of a chance to be neat as a doily under a seven-tier wedding cake. *Coco* isn't terrible. It's just a lobby. The trappings are so grandiose and the costumes so elaborate

that if there was a human or theatrical element ever present, it could not possibly have survived the sheer onslaught of stuffed luxury. [Production design by Cecil Beaton.] Alan Jay Lerner's book isn't a story—it's an engraving on the side of a building. André Previn's music is orchestrated for the movies, so thick you have to eat it with a spoon. Directing it is like moving an elephant. Seeing it is like riding one. And the elephant is white. Hepburn talks her way through the songs, singing only when necessary and then just barely carrying the tunes. It isn't terribly important since the tunes can barely carry themselves. Lerner's book is so busy trying to put clever words in her mouth that it never gives her a chance to be either Chanel or Hepburn. Instead, she is an actress with too many costume changes and a bad makeup job, controlling a stage that is too big to drive. There is hardly any dancing at all in the first act, except one of the fashion shows that tries (and fails) to be choreographic. There is a bit more after the intermission, but only because at that point the show attempts to be something entirely different—a standard musical comedy. When the four department store buyers appear to rescue Chanel's collection, they look as if they are about to sing the businessman quartet from, say, *Promises, Promises* [1968], which they promptly do (more or less). *Coco* is [like a] big cake with two little people—Hepburn and Chanel—standing on top. They are there to be used as lures, but have nothing to do with the glop beneath.

WALTER KERR, *TIMES*

The new occasion purports to be about a dress designer named Chanel—Coco to intimates—but it is nothing of the sort. It is, as an evening, plainly and simply about a phenomenon called Katharine Hepburn. Not that the events dramatized, or undramatized if you want to know the truth, have anything to do with Miss Hepburn's past history. Her own life cannot conceivably have been so lifeless. But each time the actress comes down the up staircase—she comes down it scowling, comes down it serene, comes down it like a cavalry attack, comes down it drunk—she is coming down it to be Hepburn, to be present before all of us, to stand with her feet apart and her hands in her pockets and her chin tilted high as the balcony's eye because that is the image we have of her and she wants to assure us that it is absolutely real. It is. The character of the evening is personal, and the person is not Chanel. Composer André Previn opened up, or closed down, his songs so that Hepburn's indulgent cackle can manage them; there are marches to keep an obvious beat, there are spaces for hand-clapping, there are voices from the wings [Jon Cypher on tape] as supernatural controls. A dance has been arranged so that Miss Hepburn, in a black dress that looks like a licorice brownie, can do her finest quadrille since *Little Women* [the 1933 film version] at twice the speed. When she rises, she rises to stalk the curtain-line from left to right and back again so that she can look at us and confide in us and, though whipless, behave in general like a musical-tamer. The show has become a showcase, an open palm of respect. Hepburn will never be old enough or tired enough to undergo one of those official evenings of tribute; and so it's been arranged right now, with her doing all the work. If *Coco* is anything, it is Miss Hepburn's gala Benefit Performance, for our benefit. The feeble story is feebly told. Much of the comedy is bad fag comedy hung about the neck of a homosexual designer, the villain of the piece; at one point René Auberjonois squeals and snatches his hand away because he has inadvertently let it rest on the breast of a tailor's dummy (a designer?). The songs are soundtracked, the young love interest is sidetracked.

RICHARD WATTS, JR., *POST*

A surprisingly dull show, seriously handicapped by an inferior book and a very minor score. Hepburn is wonderful in the title role. She never convinces you that she is Coco Chanel, and I don't think she tries to very hard. The important matter is that she is one of the most fascinating and attractive women in the world. She can be humorous despite a paucity of amusing lines to speak, she is moving when the story calls for it, and while I suppose she hasn't much of a singing voice, she can put over a song. The splendid Hepburn is emphatically the heroine of *Coco* in more than name. She even tosses off a four-letter word with high style.

o   o   o

Casting about for a show of his own after coproducing *The Pajama Game* (1954), *Damn Yankees* (1955), and *New Girl in Town* (1957), Frederick Brisson began courting couturière Coco Chanel for the rights to her life story. (His three hits had been developed and actively produced by Bobby Griffith and Hal Prince, although Brisson—the one with the money—got first billing.) Chanel wasn't quite ready to sign, and it took eight years of dickering before the lady finally agreed. Brisson had in the meantime offered the project to the pre-*Camelot* (1960) Lerner and Loewe, but Lerner wasn't sure and Loewe *was* sure he didn't like it. Lerner and his brief partner Richard Rodgers also looked at Chanel before settling on their aborted *I Picked a Daisy* collaboration. In 1965, just after *On a Clear Day* opened, Brisson signed Lerner (without a composer) to do the adaptation. But first there was a screen adaptation of *Paint Your Wagon* (1951) to do. Unable to entice Loewe back to work, Lerner turned to conductor/composer André Previn to provide the necessary new songs, then invited him along on the *Coco* project. There had been talk of the producer's wife playing the title role, which would have been fine as she was Rosalind Russell; one gets the impression from a couple of veiled statements that she didn't much like the draft turned in by Lerner. Then Katharine Hepburn stepped into the picture, and who could ask for a bigger ticket-selling star? (Chanel was thrilled by the idea of Hepburn portraying her, as what woman wouldn't be? Then she learned that they'd gotten the *wrong* Hepburn; she thought they meant Audrey.) While Lerner's creative clear days were clearly past, his ties to Paramount Pictures—who had films of both *Paint Your Wagon* (1969) and *On a Clear Day* (1970) in production—resulted in the studio undertaking *Coco*'s entire $900,000 capitalization (which included $150,000 worth of Cecil Beaton costumes). The unwieldy turntable on which the set was set caused *Coco* to eschew the traditional out-of-town tryout for in-town previews, forty of them. The word of mouth was bad and loud, as was the show. *Coco* broke a ticket price threshold, becoming the first musical to charge fifteen bucks for all evening performances. (*Clear Day* had broken a previous plateau in 1965, moving to a then-unprecedented $11.90 top.) The sixty-year-old Kate's presence more or less atoned for *Coco*'s weaknesses, and the show did well enough until she left (as contracted) after nine months. French star Danielle Darrieux could not sustain it, business plummeting from $97,500 to $27,500 in one week, and *Coco* closed shortly thereafter at a loss.

Hepburn's post–Broadway tour allowed the show ultimately to move—marginally—into the profit column, but a good time was had by none.

Tony Awards were won by René Auberjonois (supporting actor) and Cecil Beaton (costume designer).

BROADWAY SCORECARD
/ PERFS: 332 / $: +

RAVE	FAVORABLE	MIXED	UNFAVORABLE	PAN
		1		5

COME SUMMER

"A New Musical"

music by David Baker

book and lyrics by Will Holt (book doctored by Burt Shevelove)

based on the 1954 novel *Rainbow on the Road* by Esther Forbes

directed by Agnes de Mille (doctored by Burt Shevelove)

choreographed by Agnes de Mille

produced by Albert W. Selden and Hal James

starring Ray Bolger

with David Cryer, Cathryn Damon, Barbara Sharma, Margaret Hamilton, William Cottrell, William LeMassena, and John Gerstad

opened March 18, 1969   *Lunt-Fontanne Theatre*

Lanky Ray Bolger kicks up his heel as he points to his billing. "*Come Summer* is so awful that I suspect it will not last until the spring," said Clive Barnes, giving it "about as much chance of success as half a million $1 bills in a bonfire." (artwork by Hilary Knight)

CLIVE BARNES, *TIMES*

Theodore Kalem, the wildly dramatic critic of *Time* magazine, flunked out last night. At the Lunt-Fontanne Theatre, where incidentally they were giving what I presume was the first public performance of a musical called, if memory serves, *Come Summer*, Mr. Kalem did not leave at the intermission. This, in my opinion, was a mistake. The show deserved no less. *Come Summer* is so awful that I suspect it will not last until the spring—and already it is getting suspiciously warm for this time of the year. The book by Will Holt, who also accepts responsibility for the lyrics, is so flimsy that it is almost unnoticeable. There is a peddler wandering aimlessly around New England—a kind of peddler on the hoof—who has a friend, who marries a girl, and leaves her and . . . am I boring you? I'm sorry. As for the music by David Baker, this was so unmemorable that you hopefully came out of the theatre humming "Oklahoma!" It sounded like the orchestrations for a virtually nonexistent score. The strange thing is that apart from the book, lyrics and music *Come Summer* is not all that bad. Agnes de Mille's staging is beautifully stylish; it has a class that the show does not even aspire to. It has the best dancers and the best dancing on Broadway—William Glassman in a solo is especially brilliant—and the entire staging is a delight. The trouble is that it has virtually nothing to be a delight about. Anything de Mille could do she did. It was a director's show from start to finish, and she accepted the challenge of trying to whip the thing into shape. But frankly, if you don't have a good book, if you don't have good lyrics, if—above all—you don't have good music, you stand about as much chance of success as half a million $1 bills in a bonfire. . . . David Cryer, gives a portrayal that deserves to be remembered far, far longer than the little show that occassioned it. Cryer—I suspected this seeing him off Broadway last season—is a major musical talent. This is his first big Broadway break, and a bad break at that. But no one who looks a little like Nureyev, sounds a little like Corelli, and has a personality all of his own, has much to worry about for the future.

MARTIN GOTTFRIED, *WOMEN'S WEAR DAILY*

Come Summer is so much like a Forties musical it almost passes for a plastic fantastic. A set out of *Oklahoma!* [1943] beside American-primitive flats, drops, scrims, trolleys, even a traveler curtain. Broadway-folksy music with all kinds of brass, Agnes de Mille doing

dream ballets with pony-tailed girls bobbing their heads, and Ray
Bolger tap-dancing and singing, both out of rhythm. The joke (I wish
it were one) begins with the romantic leads falling in love a solid five
seconds after they meet. She is your solid New England girl, lonely but
strong, right? He is a peddler-artist, traveling with a business hustler,
not sure he's got the old wanderlust out of his system. They become
engaged, which doesn't please the hustler, his meal-ticket being in danger. The girl doesn't please the kid either, being kind of pushy, and he
almost leaves her until it's time to end the show (which could have been
a whole lot sooner—like last Saturday). Between, or among, all of this
is a whole lot of dancing camouflaged as padding, or vice-versa, and a
secondary plot that just about makes the primary one *Ulysses*. In this
secondary plot a sort of old girl friend of the young man is not too
happy with her about 598-year-old husband. Small wonder, since he is
doing something like the classic old, old man in a turn of the century
melodrama, straight out of Sid Caesar. Miss de Mille has directed this
so that Ray Bolger can be a star—that is, she leaves him alone, and
directs around him, which may have been just as well. Bolger plays the
business hustler with the stage presence that always made me wonder
why he ever was a star. As singer and as dancer, I find him a man with
neither grace, style nor a musical sense. Aside from driving the conductor half crazy with wrong meters, he refused to have anything to do
with what was happening on stage. I felt a little sorry about Cathryn
Damon, who finally got away from playing pink-haired toughies to find
just about the dumbest role of the season (the girl friend). But I don't
think she will be stuck with it for very long.

RICHARD WATTS, JR., *POST*
Ray Bolger is a glorious dancer, who can light up a stage through his
seemingly easygoing magic. Not exactly a youth any longer, he can
make every step seem a marvel of grace, agility and humor. The only
trouble last night was that he was constantly being interrupted by a
musical comedy called *Come Summer*, which kept getting insistently in
his way. Then the tidings of the evening ceased to be exhilarating. I
think we would all have been happier if Bolger had suddenly gone into
"Once in Love with Amy" and danced to it for an hour or two.

◦   ◦   ◦

A late attempt at an *Oklahoma!*-style pastorale, *Come Summer* was old-fashioned and exceedingly drowsy. Agnes de Mille—choreographer of the Rodgers and Hammerstein landmark as well as *Bloomer Girl* (1944), *Carousel* (1945), *Brigadoon* (1947), and *Paint Your Wagon* (1951)—had directed two shows previously. Both *Allegro* (1947) and *Out of this World* (1950), though, were ill-formed and troubled. *Come Summer*'s meager offerings included the final appearance of Ray Bolger; a reunion of the lanky dancing star with Margaret Hamilton, better known as the Scarecrow without a brain and the Wicked Witch of the West; strong performances from David Cryer and Cathryn Damon, both of whom might have acheived stardom in a day of traditional musical comedies; and a rather memorable logging dance, with lumberjacks riding the river against a rollered Oliver Smith cyclorama.

BROADWAY SCORECARD
/ PERFS: 7 / $: –

RAVE	FAVORABLE	MIXED	UNFAVORABLE	PAN
		I	2	3

COMIN' UPTOWN

"A New Musical," originally entitled *Christmas Is Comin' Uptown*

music by Gary Sherman

lyrics by Peter Udell

book by Philip Rose and Peter Udell

based on the 1843 novel *A Christmas Carol* by Charles Dickens

directed by Philip Rose

choreographed by Michael Peters

produced by Ridgely Bullock and Albert W. Selden in association with Columbia Pictures

starring Gregory Hines

with Larry Marshall, Robert Jackson, Saundra McClain, Tiger Haynes, Deborah Burrell, Jennifer Lewis, Loretta Devine, and Esther Marrow

opened December 20, 1979   Winter Garden Theatre

CLIVE BARNES, POST

Gregory Hines, the star of *Comin' Uptown*, which opened in midtown last night, is an explosive force and should probably be patented. No one ever becomes a star overnight, but some nights the firmament is kind to you and you finally get noticed. Hines, who played Scrooge as if he were riding a motorcycle in a horse race, will never have to be discovered again. The guy's terrific, whether he is acting with woebegone grace, singing with a soul-like beat and a heart-like bleat, or simply dancing up Hurricane Gregory and suggesting he is the best tap dancer in the world since Bill Robinson. This new musical adaptation of Charles Dickens's *A Christmas Carol* is calculated to make Dickens shake rather more than Marley's ghost, but it has a most winning vigor, a spanking vitality, a gold garland of performances, and particularly in its design image, a very special and attractive style. There are difficulties. The book by Philip Rose and Peter Udell is as pedestrian as a tortoise, and Udell's lyrics prove scarcely more nifty. The music by Garry Sherman, ranging from disco to gospel, is brash, electric, loud, over-amplified, yet not unduly distinguished. So with a book as flat as Holland in the rainy season and music that has an insistently recycled air as if you had heard it before, you might well wonder what could be done. Oddly enough quite a lot—probably enough to make this the surprise musical sleeper of the season. Rose as director is a far different operator from Rose as author. He starts the show at steam-heat and never really lets the temperature fall. Robin Wagner has contributed some very beautiful and ingenious settings that give the show a perfect style of its own and offer the one truly Dickensian touch to the evening. Rose keeps the whole thing bubbling like brown sugar. The driving force of the show is, nevertheless, that dynamo called Hines. When he does his final tap number, taking out every stop in sight, throwing all caution to every wind he can scent, you get to see a great performer in almost shattering action. No, he is not an overnight sensation. Remember him stopping almost the entire street in *Eubie!* [1978]? But if you thought the man was good in *Eubie!*, my friends, you ain't seen nothin' yet.

WALTER KERR, *TIMES*
[Headline: "Scrooge Struts in *Comin' Uptown*"]
There's a body of opinion around town that dismisses the practice of reviving classic musicals on the grounds that we'd be better off with new musicals at any price. In the case of *Comin' Uptown*, the new musical at the Winter Garden, I'd say the price was too high. You can take that literally. There is more expensive, though not particularly attractive, scenery on the Winter Garden's stage than this updated, all-black version of Dickens's *A Christmas Carol* can possibly find any use for. Acres and acres of snow-laden brownstones glide by as miserly old Scrooge—not so very old as that remarkable dancer, Gregory Hines, plays him—starts out on his journey into Christmases Past. In any event, the talented Hines has much to awe him as he looks backward to his youth and then forward to his unmourned death. What Hines doesn't have, unfortunately, is a part to play or any real opposition to contend with. . . . The

crusher for me, finally, came with choreographer Michael Peter's decision to keep Hines's antic feet under wraps until we were practically ready to go home. The performer does do a bit of period strutting during that first backward trek to his youth, but he's so constantly surrounded by a stageful of pretty, prancing, jumping-jack girls that he's hard to pick out. You keep waiting for some solo work, and are denied it in the rush. At last, all too late, Scrooge is back in his dingy room and, a reformed fellow now, he leaps into uncontrollable jubilation. There's no one to obscure him, not even one more ghost, and he takes to his freedom like a riveter gone mad, spitting taps against the floor while his body slips dangerously sideways, staggering with unaccountable glee in the rhythms of a gangster being gunned down. He even keeps the delirium going while he's pretending to tap on his bed clothes, which is impossible. Perfectly splendid, and couldn't he have made us happier earlier? Despite the energy that's spent like money, the Show Won't Move, preferring to play pretty much the scenes over and over again. Scrooge is awakened in his room by so many spectral visitors that I thought he'd never get any sleep. *Comin' Uptown* is careless and costly, elaborate and enervating. God bless us all, Tiny Tim.

DOUGLAS WATT, *DAILY NEWS*
[Headline: "*Uptown* Is Real Downer"]
Comin' Uptown, last night's lavishly appointed new musical comedy, made me think of basketball. It's only the final minutes that really count. All evening long, you wait for Gregory Hines, who's been asked to carry far too much on his slight shoulders as a black Scrooge, to break loose and go into his dance, which he eventually does to joyous effect. But the rest of the evening is a ponderous bore. *Comin' Uptown*, which shouts its extravagance, looks as though its authors and sponsors were intent on creating another *Wiz*, and unfortunately for them, they have, but without the style that overcame the earlier black musical's shortcomings. Everybody tries hard, but it's a devil of a nuisance waiting all night for Hines to straighten up and fly right.

*   *   *

Philip Rose entered the Broadway arena in 1959 with a play that everybody said would obviously fail. The remarkable (and deserved) success of his first attempt—Lorraine Hansberry's *A Raisin in the Sun*—set a pattern. When everybody told him his *next* new project was headed for failure, he would just smile and—remembering *Raisin in the Sun*—plunge right on ahead. And almost invariably lose. (Rose, a poker-playing pal of "Doc" Simon, was apparently the model for Vinnie, the short, balding, thick-glassed poker-playing pal of Oscar and Felix.) If the Hansberry play and the 1964 Diana Sands/Alan Alda comedy, *Owl and the Pussycat*, made some money, and *Shenandoah* (1975) eked out a small profit, Rose's other gambles proved busts. The musical failures included *Bravo Giovanni!* (1962), *Cafe Crown* (1964), *Purlie* (1970), *Angel* (1978), and the opus in question. And there were a passel-ful of nonmusical failures, too. *Comin' Uptown*, Rose's fifth black-themed production, owed its existence to Sidney Poitier—star of *A Raisin in the Sun*—who had a development deal with Columbia Pictures and put in a good word. Noting 20th Century Fox's *Wiz* (1975) windfall, and feeling their own pockets tingling from investments in *Dancin'* (1978) and *Sugar Babies* (1979), Columbia came in on *Comin' Uptown*. (Universal also went looking for a black family musical, plunging on Mike Nichols's *Alice* [1978], which starred Debbie Allen in an alcoholic Wonderland and shuttered ignominiously in Philadelphia. Notice how one fluke hit always seems to spawn several big budget carbon bombs?) Anyway, another million four down the ol' Broadway moneyhole.

BROADWAY SCORECARD
/ PERFS: 45 / $: –

RAVE	FAVORABLE	MIXED	UNFAVORABLE	PAN
	1	1	2	2

COMPANY

a musical comedy, previously entitled *Threes*

music and lyrics by Stephen Sondheim

book by George Furth

directed by Harold Prince

choreographed by Michael Bennett

produced by Harold Prince in association with Ruth Mitchell

starring Dean Jones (replaced shortly after the opening by Larry Kert)

with Barbara Barrie, Elaine Stritch, George Coe, John Cunningham, Teri Ralston, Charles Kimbrough, Donna McKechnie, Charles Braswell, Susan Browning, Steve Elmore, Beth Howland, Pamela Myers, and Merle Louise

opened April 26, 1970   *Alvin Theatre*

CLIVE BARNES, *TIMES*

[Headline: "A Guide to New York's Marital Jungle"]

Company, a show that opened last night at the Alvin Theatre and about which I have some personal reservations, deserves to be a hit in a lean season. It is a very New York show and will be particularly popular with tourists—especially those from Vladivostok and Westchester—who will get the kind of insight into New York's jungle that you perceive in the survival-kit information provided by *New York* magazine. Indeed, if you like *New York* magazine you will probably love *Company*. Creatively Sondheim's lyrics are way above the rest of the show; they have a lyric suppleness, sparse elegant wit, and range from the virtuosity of a patter song to a kind of sweetly laconic cynicism in a modern love song. The music is academically very interesting. Sondheim must be one of the most sophisticated composers ever to write Broadway musicals, yet the result is slick, clever and eclectic rather than exciting. It is the kind of music that makes me say "Oh, yeah?" rather than "Gee whiz!" The conception has two difficulties. In the first place these people are just the kind of people you expend hours each day trying to escape from. They are, virtually without exception trivial, shallow, worthless and horrid. The second fault is a structural one. Here is a series of linked scenes, all basically similar to one another, and it is left to the director to find a variety of pace and character. This Mr. Prince has not done. It may not be his fault. The odds were against him. . . . The setting by Boris Aronson is admirable—a mixture between an East Side multiplex, Alcatraz and an exhibition display of some 20 years ago demonstrating the versatility of elevators. Michael Bennett is one of those artists who carry the past into the future, and stylizes his view of it into a signature. Of course you can see the influence of Gower Champion, and all the other champions, yet his choreography has genuine vitality, and it is one of the major joys of the show. I was antagonized by the slickness, the obviousness of *Company*. But I stress that I really believe a lot of people are going to love it. Don't let me put you off. Between ourselves, I had reservations about *West Side Story* [1957].

MARTIN GOTTFRIED, *WOMEN'S WEAR DAILY*

A tremendous piece of work, thrilling and chilling, glittering bright, really funny (and not so funny), exceedingly adult, gorgeous to look at and filled with brilliant music. It is an ensemble or chamber musical with words and music and musical movement and dance that flow, organically, from the same source. Yet, it hasn't the self-conscious look of an "experimental musical" because it is so sleekly professional. The production is staged on a Boris Aronson set that is as sleek, cold and bitter as these people—as the show itself, at least for the first act. *Company* is brutally unsentimental mostly because it is so grownup and frightfully honest. Aronson's gorgeous set looks like stainless steel scaffolding and has minimal changes except for giant projections of the New York street scene and a couple of elevators that make the place look like the technological age in which it exists. Harold Prince moves the cast through this environment as if it were all part of the same machine and his work is superb, the best he's ever done. Prince, for a long time, has been emulating Jerome Robbins to the point of transference and though the influence could not be better, his work has often been imitation. This time, he is not trying to do art things with rural Greece (*Zorbá* [1968]) or pre-war Germany (*Cabaret* [1966]), but working with New York and New York people—things personally familiar to him. Moreover, they modulate smoothly into Michael Bennett's dances, which aren't numbers but dance moments that sometimes grow into movements. Bennett's work is superlative and though his dancers are actors he hasn't faked it for them. It is dance all right and exciting. The general excitement, though, grows from Sondheim's music. It is at once intricate and simple, serious and theatrical. He is the most exciting, stimulating, theatre-minded composer at work today. His freedom from standard forms, his meters, harmonies, modulations, long-lined constructions (which braid in and out of the action), dissonances and plain music are so superior to what we hear in the theatre that comparisons are absurd. The lyrics he wrote for himself combine absolute craft with a content that matches the show's and, in patter songs, they are in a class with W. S. Gilbert himself. Jonathan Tunick's inventive, transparent orchestrations showed musical respect, appreciation and shared values. The show is magnificent.

WALTER KERR, *TIMES*
[Headline: "Original and Uncompromising"]
Company is brilliantly designed, beautifully staged, sizzlingly performed, inventively scored, and it gets right down to brass tacks and brass knuckles without a moment's hesitation, staring contemporary society straight in the eye before spitting in it. The mood is misanthropic, the view from the peephole jaundiced, the attitude middle-aged mean. That, of course, is a highly original stance for a Broadway musical to be taking, and just about everything else in *Company* is equally original, equally uncompromising. Boris Aronson's steel-gray structure (which at first looks like the prison setting for *The Last Mile* [a 1930 death-row melodrama], no doubt appropriately) becomes, as director Harold Prince sends his people skittering through space, a breath-taking mobile, an interlocked Tinker-Toy of rippling platforms, sighing elevators, spun-glass spindles for dancers to chin themselves on. Prince's own work is immaculate: jog-trotting waiters spin past tables without colliding, or without taking orders, like lagged metal figures on a children's game board; the entire company dissolves and reassembles at will in the heavens, malicious gods and goddesses changing shapes as cumulus clouds do. Stephen

Sondheim has never written a more sophisticated, more pertinent, or—this is the surprising thing in the circumstances—more melodious score; and the lyrics are every bit as good. To dress the songs, and to drive them in hiked-shoulder sidesteps straight across the stage, choreographer Michael Bennett has applied endlessly inventive high-pressure patterns; often he uses entirely traditional devices, say straw hats and canes, in provocative new ways, letting the hats slash the air and the canes slap the floor to stress the harshness of what is being stomped out ("Side by Side by Side"). Songs and dances pop up out of nowhere to assert themselves independently. All of this is exemplary. Now ask me if I liked the show. I didn't like the show. I admired it, or admired vast portions of it, but that is another matter. I left *Company* feeling rather cool and queasy, whatever splendors my head may have been reminding me of, and there is a plain reason for that. At root, I didn't take to Mr. Jones's married friends any more than he did. I agreed with him. They're not a bunch you'd care to save, or even spend a weekend with. The fact that the entertainment doesn't mean them to be doesn't help much; *it* has integrity, *I* had a slight case of aversion. Personally, I'm sorry-grateful.

RICHARD WATTS, JR., *POST*

Company is busily concerned with contemplating the pros and cons on the subject of matrimony, and I guess the cons come out slightly ahead. The new musical comedy is careful to avoid any charge of sentimentality and it is elaborate, at times witty, and occasionally tuneful. But I thought it was also surprisingly uningratiating. There is no doubt that the first-night audience disagreed with me strongly. I don't usually pay much attention to these specialized reactions, and some of the applause came from spectators whose hands were raised high in the air, a sign of exhibitionism I mistrust particularly. Yet I wouldn't think of questioning the genuineness of most of it from massed playgoers who even acclaimed the rise and descent of some on-stage elevators. *Company's* somewhat ironical salute to man's need for companionship undeniably includes some amusing interludes on the hazards of domesticity and the pleasant possibilities of bachelorhood, but there is little that seemed to me likeable. It isn't possible for me to deny that I found *Company* disappointing.

◦ ◦ ◦

"The next Harold Prince musical will be *Threes*, starring Tony Perkins," said the April 1969 press release, thus beginning Broadway's great adventure: the eleven-year, six-show collaboration of composer/lyricist Stephen Sondheim and director Hal Prince. Only two of the shows were financially successful, with a third being so artistically over-whelming—the one about the demon barber—that financial gradings are inapplicable. But all six, individually and en masse, were the most interesting, intriguing, and sometimes infuriating musicals of their time. The pair had worked together before, of course, when Prince pro-duced Sondheim's *West Side Story* and *A Funny Thing* (1962). But this new collaboration would be different. Audiences in 1970 were prepared for Prince's strikingly strong directorial vision, having seen *Cabaret* and the lesser *Zorbá*. Sondheim's musical emergence with *Company* was more of a surprise, to general audiences at least. He had clearly demon-strated his brilliance, technical proficiency, and freedom from form in the astounding *Anyone Can Whistle* (1964), but that was a quick flop known only, if at all, from the out-of-print cast album. *Company* broke all rules of musical dramaturgy as it forged a new type of musical. Gone—or should we say altered?—were plot, narrative, subplot, scenes and scene changes, and the usual method of storytelling. Now many things were happening at once, multiple characters in separate conver-sations in different locales crowding the stage simultaneously. Sondheim, meanwhile, demonstrated his amazing ability to meld voices into a contrapuntal mosaic—with as many as fourteen characters singing concurrently (but not together), along with four harmonizing pit singers. Thus the audience, accustomed to having their attention carefully focused on one thing at a time, was presented with a maze of choices. They weren't going to catch everything, they weren't going to get every word, but then that was the intent. Sondheim and Prince (with choreographer Bennett, orchestrator Tunick, and designer Aronson) used music and movement to weave an atmospheric tapestry with any number of intriguing, overlapping parts. Come see us again, you'll find something you missed the first time. Score and staging inno-vations abounded, but what of the script? Oh, yes, that script of sketch-like fragments. (The musical sprang, not surprisingly, from an unpro-duced George Furth evening of unconnected one-acts.) The free-form style of the book worked well, complementing the groundbreaking efforts in music and staging; if only Furth's contributions had matched the tone, taste, and wit of his collaborators. Sondheim's score made *Company* the most important musical in what seemed like forever, while Prince and associates made the stage uncommonly alive and theatrical. So did it matter, much, if you sometimes had to grit your teeth at the cheap dialogue? The show—and not just the book—had another hidden problem, a hollowness at the hero's core. *Company* is not antimarriage: the message, rather, is "two is difficult but one is impossible." But—and it's a big but—there's not a person on that stage (i.e., in Robert's world) that one could imagine the hero being happy or even moderately content with. All are unattractive, flawed, or weak. This cuts at the core of the message. Seeing as how the creative team was so inarguably expert, this was surely their specific choice. One can't help but think that their views on Robert ("Bobby baby, Bobby bubi, Bobby, Robert darling") and matrimony were flavored by their own firsthand outlooks: Tony Perkins and Leonard Bernstein, to name but two members of the creators' social circle, both enjoyed long and relatively successful—if unconventional—marriages. Choreographer Bennett also "tried" matrimony—with his lead dancer from *A Joyful Noise* (1966), *Promises, Promises* (1968), *Company*, and *A Chorus Line* (1975)—but not so happily ever after. If the creators *had* unconventional thoughts about Robert, they certainly wouldn't have said so at the time, but this might help explain why Robert was left with nobody to tap dance with. (Prince's *Cabaret* similarly placed its leading man in a not-very-convincing romance of convenience—musical comedy convenience, that is—which left an even bigger hole at that show's center.) That said, *Company* remains a groundbreaking, form-breaking milestone. While the show itself dated severely within the decade—and by the time of the 1995 Broadway revival positively creaked—Sondheim's brilliant score remains bright and vibrant after (heaven help us) more than a quarter century. And will no doubt remain so. Casting Dept.: Although originally announced as the lead, Tony Perkins—who starred in Frank Loesser's 1960 *Greenwillow* and the 1966 Sondheim/James Goldman TV minimusical *Evening Primrose*—opted out. Disneyesque leading man Dean Jones took the part, although it did not seem to suit him; he was gone within a fortnight of the opening, with a hepatitis diagnosis fabricated for the press. (Jones returned to Broadway and the Alvin in 1986 in a show perhaps more suited to his image, the Shroud of Turin musical *Into the Light*. Yes, I said the Shroud of Turin musical, which after six perfs was permanently pressed.) Jones's understudy, Larry Kert—juvenile of Prince's *West Side Story* and *A Family Affair* (1962), more recently languishing in *Breakfast at Tiffany's* (1966) and *La Strada* (1969)—stepped into the role and made it (ambiguously) his.

Winner of the New York Drama Critics' Circle Award. In addition to winning the Tony Award for Best Musical, Tonys were won by Stephen Sondheim (music), Stephen Sondheim (lyrics), George Furth (book), Harold Prince (director), Harold Prince (producer), and Boris Aronson (scenic design).

BROADWAY SCORECARD
/ PERFS: 706 / $: +

RAVE	FAVORABLE	MIXED	UNFAVORABLE	PAN
3	2		1	

COPPERFIELD

"A New Musical"

book, music, and lyrics by Al Kasha and Joel Hirschhorn

based on the 1850 novel *The Personal History of David Copperfield* by Charles Dickens

directed and choreographed by Rob Iscove

produced by Don Gregory and Mike Merrick

starring Brian Matthews, Leslie Denniston, Barrie Ingham, Carmen Mathews, Mary Mastrantonio, Michael Connolly, Evan Richards, and George S. Irving

with Beulah Garrick, Christian Slater, Mary Stout, and Lenny Wolpe

opened April 16, 1981   *ANTA Theatre*

FRANK RICH, *TIMES*

After sitting through *Copperfield*, you may seriously question whether its creators have ever actually read their ostensible source material. You may even question whether they've read the Classics Comics version. But there's one thing you won't question. Al Kasha and Joel Hirschhorn, who wrote this show's book, music and lyrics, have definitely, but definitely, seen lots of hit Broadway musicals. *Copperfield* seems an almost scientific attempt to recreate, by slavish imitation, some of those familiar shows. The experiment proves a total failure— there are still a few frontiers that even science can't conquer—but *Copperfield* is hard to beat for sheer *déjà vu*. This is the kind of musical that sends you out of the theatre humming every score other than the one you've just heard. Don't think that this kind of project is as simple as it looks: some real creative decisions are involved. Take, for instance, the matter of naming the show. *Oliver!* [1963] has an exclamation point at the end of its title, *Annie* [1977] does not, and so what is one to do? It takes more than a few sleepless nights to resolve esthetic questions like that. Of course, derivativeness is not new in Broadway musicals that aspire to be pure commercial entertainments. The real problem with *Copperfield* is that its authors are not good mimics. From the music to the scenery to the cast, everything about this show looks tacky in comparison to its prototypes. And when the writers actually attempt to come up with fresh ideas—well, look out! The cast is less than the best that money can buy. The title character seems an almost peripheral figure in the proceedings. He's played by two decent singers—one boy, one man—who are nothing if not chips off the same block. The block is made of wood. One expects better from the score, if only because the authors have won two Academy Awards—for their theme songs from *The Poseidon Adventure* [1972] and *The Towering Inferno* [1974]. (What? You don't remember them?) Some of the music is mildly tuneful, after its many fashions, but the lyrics are, at best, unintentionally funny. Rob Iscove's choreography departs from the show's norm, in that it seems to have been culled from flops rather than hits.

DOUGLAS WATT, *DAILY NEWS*

[Headline: "A Computerized *Copperfield*"]
Copperfield may just be the first fully-computerized musical. It is as if Dickens had been fed to a machine, buttons pressed, and out came

book, songs, scenic and costume designs, and a batch of mechanical performances. A false note is struck by the performance as a whole, as if the actors were mindlessly running through parts they'd been doing for a year or more and were sick and tired of by now. This is because the evening is relentlessly on the go, as though a moment's pause, with no shifting scenery or moving actors, would cause the entire flimsy edifice to collapse. Under the busy and undistinguished staging of Rob Iscove, who is also responsible for the commonplace dance routines, everything is done in broad strokes. Smiles, frowns, strides, "takes"—all are so much larger than life and so simplified as to make the actors resemble animated cartoon figures. And this, in turn, has obviously resulted from the puerile book-and-song reduction of *David Copperfield* by the team of Al Kasha and Joel Hirschhorn. Trying to crowd as much as possible into a couple of hours has resulted in a succession of flats and furniture sliding on and off. All of this busyness turns on the bland songs (a pretty but quickly forgettable "Circle Waltz," a love ballad called "I Wish He Knew," a bustling "Lights of London" routine, and so on) with rhymes that, when they are not discouragingly predictable, as in most instances, are merely silly ("Here's a book in Latin/It's the tongue to chat in"). The show is as harmless as a vanilla milk shake. *Copperfield* just barely qualifies as live theatre. Push another button.

o   o   o

With their high-priced 1980–1981 revivals of Burton in *Camelot* and Rex in *Fair Lady* storming the country, producers Mike Merrick and Don Gregory decided to create a classic musical of their own. Hence, *Copperfield*—which did not quite cause *Oliver!* to blush in shame. (*Annie*, for that matter, moved into the ANTA from the Alvin, across the street, once *Copperfield*'s dust had settled.) Typically, the producers hired untried writers for their own quasi-*Sound of Music* (1959), and placed the whole thing under the charge of Rob Iscove, director/choreographer of the 1979 revival of *Peter Pan*. Except Iscove had been tossed from *Peter Pan*, as everyone knew (except Gregory and Merrick?), with Ron Field publicly—but without billing—stepping in to "fix" the show for Broadway. Oh, well. Making their Broadway debuts were songwriters Al Kasha and Joel Hirschhorn, coming to town with back-to-back Oscars for "The Morning After" from *The Poseidon Adventure* and "We May Never Love Like This Again" from *The Towering Inferno*. Their success with disaster films proved them imminently suited for Broadway. Kasha and Hirschhorn had, in fact, also provided additional songs for Al's brother Larry's stage version of *Seven Brides for Seven Brothers*, which had already undergone *two* failed pre-Broadway try-outs. Perseverance pays off, we are told, so a third attempt finally made it to the Alvin in 1982 (for five, count 'em, performances). The boys have steered clear of 52nd Street since. So far.

BROADWAY SCORECARD

/ PERFS: 13 / $: –

RAVE	FAVORABLE	MIXED	UNFAVORABLE	PAN
		1	1	4

CRY FOR US ALL

"A New Musical," alternatively entitled *Who to Love*

music by Mitch Leigh

lyrics by William Alfred and Phyllis Robinson

book by William Alfred and Albert Marre

based on the 1965 drama *Hogan's Goat* by William Alfred

directed by Albert Marre

choreographed by Todd Bolender

produced by Mitch Leigh in association with C. Gerald Goldsmith

starring Joan Diener, Robert Weede, and Steve Arlen (replacing John Reardon)

with Tommy Rall, Helen Gallagher, Dolores Wilson, Edwin Steffe, and William Griffis

opened April 8, 1970   *Broadhurst Theatre*

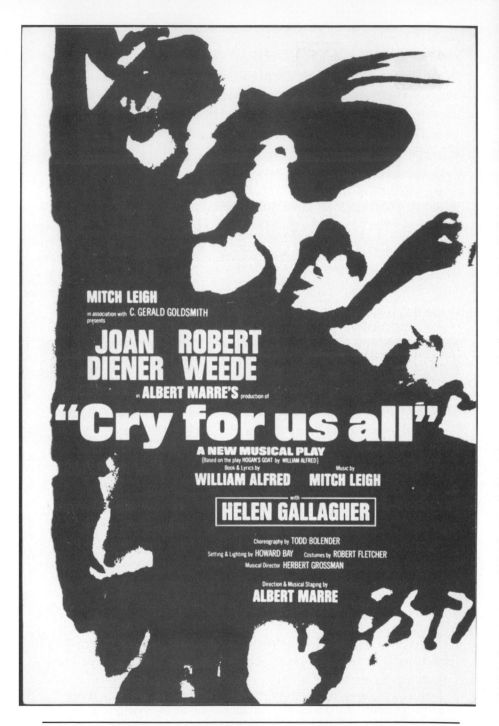

MITCH LEIGH
in association with C. GERALD GOLDSMITH
presents

JOAN   ROBERT
DIENER   WEEDE

in ALBERT MARRE'S production of

"Cry for us all"
A NEW MUSICAL PLAY
(Based on the play HOGAN'S GOAT by WILLIAM ALFRED)
Book & Lyrics by   Music by
WILLIAM ALFRED   MITCH LEIGH

with
HELEN GALLAGHER

Choreography by TODD BOLENDER
Setting & Lighting by HOWARD BAY   Costumes by ROBERT FLETCHER
Musical Director HERBERT GROSSMAN

Direction & Musical Staging by
ALBERT MARRE

This Rorschach-ian blot perfectly captures the nature of the show: something about a girl in a hat, real blurry. (artwork by Fay Gage)

CLIVE BARNES, *TIMES*

Whoever imagined that William Alfred's verse-drama *Hogan's Goat* could be made into a Broadway musical? It was called *Cry for Us All*. I found myself crying only for Mr. Alfred. This is the kind of musical for which one feels tempted to offer a diagnosis, rather than a criticism. Alfred's original play had almost everything going for it. There was a style, a feel for the period, an understated poetic line and imagery. As a musical it has become an inflated bore. Which is a special pity because there are good things in it. Yet, essentially, it fails because it is neither one thing nor another—not serious enough for a drama, not light-hearted enough for a musical. The music is by Mitch Leigh, composer of *Man of La Mancha* [1965], and it tries to strike the same declarative note, with melodic lines floating heroically above insistent drum-beats, and musical hearts on every musical sleeve. But the story does not sustain such emotional insistence. It is a drama of people rather than ideas, and a musical-comedy style perfectly suitable for a gentle pastiche around the theme of Don Quixote and his "impossible dream" has very little relevance to Brooklyn, the Irish, politics and 1890. The book—written by Alfred in collaboration with director Albert Marre—drifts most disconcertingly, trying to make some reasonable adjustment between the conventions of drama and the needs of musical comedy. It just doesn't work. It collapses in compromise. Not all is bad. There are numbers here that might climb a hit parade—we have heard many worse in many better musicals—and there is a dramatic atmosphere, a certain feeling for place and people. But almost everything that's good about the show eventually works to its own detriment, for the standards it needs for success are the dramatic standards of opera rather than operetta. Never in the history of the theater, with the possible exception of *West Side Story* [1957], has there been a successful musical comedy or operetta on a truly tragic theme. Think about it. If the producers and backers of *Cry for Us All* had thought about it they would have saved themselves a mound of money. Less ambitious musicals have proved far more successful in the deployment of far less talent. Unfortunately, this is only a cold comfort to carry away from a theatre.

MARTIN GOTTFRIED, *WOMEN'S WEAR DAILY*

When I first saw *Hogan's Goat* four years ago, it was so corny and melo-dramatic I suspected, halfway through, that it was supposed to be a satire. It turned out to be low tragedy. Now, Mitch Leigh has set it to music and it opened last night as low tragedy with songs. The new title is *Cry for Us All*, which is apt enough because (to paraphrase Jerry Lee Lewis) there's a whole lot of crying going on. There is a pity in all of this: Leigh is a fine composer who needs knowledgeable advice about what to do with his ability. There is a great deal of music in this show—more than 20 musical numbers—but one song has nothing to do with another, musically, and few of them (I think just one) have anything to do with turn-of-the-century Irish Brooklyn, where the story takes place. Considering the wealth of music in Irish culture—folk music, popular music, jigs and reels, and even operetta music—Leigh has remained remarkably aloof from it. His score exists in a hodgepodge of German, Spanish, Aaron Copland and American-vaudeville influences. Nevertheless, it contains a great deal of very substantial music—music that is inventive, rhythmically interesting and very singable. The score has little, however, to do with the theatre, and that is simply because *Cry for Us All* has no musical idea behind it. Leigh had the power over this show (he produced it) and was able to muscle in all his songs, which was a shame because he evidently hasn't any ideas about making those songs part of a production whole. The performances are weak though the voices are much better than usual on Broadway. The show has been tilted so that Stanton's wife is the central figure; she also has many costume changes; she is played by the director and co-author's wife, Joan Diener. Miss Diener has a range of expression that is best described as pancake make-up. Her singing is from the neck up. She looks exclusively at the audience. The lyrics by Mr. Alfred and Phyllis Robinson are dreadful. Leigh has had trouble finding good lyricists. He must find one, as he must find someone to open the possibilities of integrated musical theatre to him. He is much too fine a composer to indulge himself, on so simple a level, with limitless songs.

RICHARD WATTS, JR., POST

The musical version can be the graveyard of distinguished plays. I didn't believe William Alfred's *Hogan's Goat* was quite as fine a drama as its enthusiasts proclaimed it, but it was an interesting and powerful work of considerable impressiveness. Yet in *Cry for Us All* it turned out to be what I'm afraid is little short of disastrous. Since one of its adapters is

Mitch Leigh, who composed the splendid score for *Man of La Mancha*, it was to be hoped that the music would be freshly delightful. It is true that several of the songs are attractive, but they have a disturbing way of sounding like leftovers from the wonderful show about Don Quixote. Indeed, there is one other reminder of that sensational success. The production makes extensive use of long and ominous staircases. Howard Bay [designer of *La Mancha*] has designed a striking atmospheric setting that features those staircases and whirls around more vigorously than the plot does. Robert Weede brings his strong voice and forceful presence effectively to the role of the Brooklyn Mayor and Joan Diener, the memorable Dulcinea of *Man of La Mancha*, sings and plays attractively as the luckless wife of the opposition candidate. Helen Gallagher is as always engagingly charming as an unfortunately minor cog in the plot, and Steve Arlen sings agreeably as the young politician. But it's a shame about the ambitious *Cry for Us All*.

○   ○   ○

Important, groundbreaking musicals come not from obviously commercial ideas but from the long shots: cowboys fighting over who takes the gal to the box social, juvenile delinquent ballet dancers with switchblades, milkmen heroically enduring yenta-ish wives and pogroms, errant madmen jousting with windmills. You get the idea. *Hogan's Goat*, a Brooklyn turn-of-the-century love triangle soap opera, presented obvious adaptational difficulties. This did not deter Messrs. Leigh and Marre (and Missus Marre, too); did they not succeed beyond rational expectations with their first impossible dream of a musical? This one, though, proved simply impossible. *Cry for Us All* was troubled from the first, undergoing an especially arduous tryout. Leigh and Marre's second musical, *Chu-Chem*, "the first Chinese-Jewish musical," had mercifully shuttered in Philadelphia in 1966 (although it would rise again, like a moo shoo phoenix, for a brief Broadway gasp in 1989). *Cry for Us All*, their third, wept its way along the bitter New Haven/Boston/New York trail, with the director's wife's role growing bigger and bigger along the interstate. (Their fifth musical, *Home Sweet Homer* [1976], also thudded noisily on Broadway, while numbers four—*Halloween* [1972]—and six—the Glynis Johns-headed *April Song* [1980]—threw in the soggy towel after stock tryouts.) Among the *Cry for Us All* alterations was a name change to the perplexing *Who to Love*, after one of Ms. Diener's arias (imagine calling the ticket broker and saying "Gimme two to *Who to Love* Tuesday night"). After painting out the houseboards, they changed 'em once more, going back to the cheerier *Cry for Us All*. "I'm positive that the voices in this musical are the best ever put together in the history of all Broadway shows," attested Yale-bred Mitch Leigh (*né* Irwin Mitchnick from Brooklyn) during the break-in. "The musical has a sound never before heard on Broadway. You don't feel at all impressed by the music because you hardly know it's there. The climax of the score comes above the scene. The abstract becomes the realistic abstract." This from the guy who wrote "Nobody Doesn't Like Sara Lee." The pity of it is, the score is actually quite intriguing. There's a workable and possibly exciting musical buried within the overexcesses of *Cry for Us All*. Don't blame the composer for the hopeless shambles that lumbered its way to the Broadhurst stage. Blame the producer.

BROADWAY SCORECARD

/ PERFS: 9 / $: -

RAVE	FAVORABLE	MIXED	UNFAVORABLE	PAN
		1	2	3

CYRANO

"A Musical Adaption"

music by Michael J. Lewis

book and lyrics by Anthony Burgess

based on his 1971 adaptation of the 1897 French drama *Cyrano de Bergerac* by Edmond Rostand

directed by Michael Kidd (replacing Michael Langham)

choreographer uncredited (Michael Kidd)

produced by Richard Gregson and APJAC International

starring Christopher Plummer

with Leigh Beery, Mark Lamos, James Blendick, Patrick Hines, Louis Turenne, and Arnold Soboloff

opened May 13, 1973   Palace Theatre

CLIVE BARNES, *TIMES*

Cyrano, in which Christopher Plummer triumphed at the Palace Theatre last night, is altogether very good and partly excellent. Why the qualification? Well, simply because the music is the weakest part of this particular musical. Indeed, there are times when one wished the music would simply go away, and others when one could easily imagine that it had. This score imitates more than it conquers, reminds more than it enchants. However, in a somewhat stolid way it serves its purpose of providing a musical framework for Anthony Burgess's adroit and classic adaptation and a musical frame for Christopher Plummer's most touching and memorable portrayal. The part suits him the way a sheath suits a rapier. Plummer embraces the physicality of the part—his swordplay is beautifully deft (my compliments to his dueling mentors, Patrick Crean and Erik Frederiksen), his movements singularly apt, and his whole performance has a kind of kinetic grace. He is also unusually successful—helped here by Burgess and his director—in making Cyrano a man without sentimentality, which is very rare indeed. Even Ralph Richardson, perhaps the best postwar Cyrano in English, never quite evaded the suspicion of a milked tear. Plummer is most effective in his development of the role, making Cyrano a poetic hero rather than a roistering buffoon with a heart as big as his nose. His aging in the last scene, his eyes gummy with pain and his gallant but broken voice, is exquisitely done, but this is only the final plume in a great performance. Yes, the musical does lack that overwhelming surge of music, but its assets are sufficient enough. Particularly since Plummer is acting his heart out in one of the best performances of many a season.

MARTIN GOTTFRIED, WOMEN'S WEAR DAILY

It is easier to understand why *Cyrano de Bergerac* has been turned into a Broadway musical than why Christopher Plummer agreed to star in it. Edmond Rostand's ugly duckling romance is inherently musical in its swashbuckling, lavish, aristocratic set; its deeply romantic story; and its shameless poetry. In fact, musicalization has been tried before, evidently with no greater success than the production that just opened. The reason these adaptations never work is not because the play defies musicalization. It is, I think, because the story is so rich and familiar that the adaptors are fearful of editing it and as a result do a halfway *Cyrano* with the music superfluous rather than complementary. At least, this is what has happened with the current version. As for why Plummer accepted the role, one can surmise—without necessarily being cynical—that he did it for the money, the work, for the chance to work in a musical he could respect and for Michael Langham, a superb classical director who had helped him with one of his greatest personal successes, a straight *Cyrano* at Canada's Shakespearean Festival. Langham would surely treat the play with respect. But the vagaries and necessities of the commercial musical theatre being what they are, a classical director does not frequently work out and Langham was replaced by Michael Kidd, an experienced director-choreographer. Brought in, I am sure, to make the play more musical and choreographic, Kidd did not do it. He has provided neither choreography nor movement. The production is an average version of the play except for a brilliant actor in the main role; it is occasionally and unnoticeably stopped at arbitrary points for unneces-

sary songs; and there is little dancing except for here and there a decorative parade of court entertainers. The question remains about
Plummer's presence. Certainly, he is magnificent even though,
unchecked, he tends to ham. Like every Cyrano, he looks like a handsome actor wearing a funny, fake nose (someday there will be a really
ugly Cyrano), but his balcony scene is unforgettable. Still, seeing him
only reminds you of what else he might have been doing. In fact,
Christopher Plummer is one of the greatest actors alive and he has not
been seen on the New York stage since *The Royal Hunt of the Sun* in
1964. That is disgraceful.

WALTER KERR, *TIMES*
If you stop to think about it, it's odd that anyone should have wished to
make a musical of *Cyrano* because *Cyrano de Bergerac* is virtually a musical to begin with. The original Rostand melodies are, of course, all verbal melodies, rococo cadenzas that ripple from tongues that still seem
to be tasting bon-bons. But even if they are words, they are words
orchestrated for voices: arias without end, mocking duets, passages of
whispered counterpoint, the long lingering coda beneath fluttering fall
leaves in a convent garden. Which means (a) that you've got to take
something that is already one kind of music and turn it, a bit gratu-
itously, into another kind, and (b) that anything you add in the way of
incidental dance or other musical mountebankery is apt to be very incidental indeed. The latter is certainly the case in the handsomely autum-
nal red-brown mounting of the romantic melodrama at the Palace. As
for the tunes that supplant some of Rostand's elaborately phrased set-
pieces, most are a shade less exhilarating than sheer language might
have been. One, in particular, tends to give the game away. When
Cyrano foxily delays a rival so that Roxana and Christian can be hastily
married, he does so with a gloriously irrelevant apostrophe to the
patient moon (the moon being patient to stand for so much spur-of-
the-moment nonsense). But here it has become a trick piled upon a
trick, and thereby overtricked: Christopher Plummer must sing a
tongue-twister called "Thither, Thother, Thide of the" which places all
of the emphasis on his simple ability to get tough syllables out rather
than on what is imaginative in the moment. When you consider that
lyricist Anthony Burgess has interlarded the lisped and otherwise tan-

gled consonants with asides on the order of "Of course they only do it when it's dark" and "Not a stitch on, of course," adding, for less than good measure, a costume-ball variant of a burlesque-house grind, the suspicion that Rostand's own kind of playfulness has been reduced to something more commonplace increases. Between the substitutions and the window-dressing, the text finds itself gasping to get the good out of its scenes. We seem to be waving the play away in order to get on to production values, hurrying past the cause of it all—and the hurt of it all—for fear we may not catch up with the music.

○   ○   ○

Rather than simply remounting the 1971 Guthrie Theatre production of Anthony (*A Clockwork Orange*) Burgess's adaptation of the Rostand classic, Burgess and director Michael Langham decided to turn it into a full-scale Broadway musical. And they did. The old boy had been cobbled into at least three closed-out-of-town tuners: *Cyrano de Bergerac* (1932), a Shubert-produced costume operetta; Vernon Duke's *The Vagabond Hero* (1939), a revision of the former; and the 1973 Wright and Forrest summer stock tryout *A Song for Cyrano* with Joe Ferrer. The Plummer version made it to Broadway, at least, and the 1993 Netherland-bred *Cyrano: The Musical* proved that there are *no* limits if you don't mind how many millions of guilders you toss into the shredder. Burgess's nonmusical adaptation, on the other hand, proved highly successful when the Royal Shakespeare Company brought its acclaimed production—with Derek Jacobi in putty nose—to the Gershwin in 1984.

A Tony Award was won by Christopher Plummer (actor).

BROADWAY SCORECARD
/ PERFS: 49 / $: -

RAVE	FAVORABLE	MIXED	UNFAVORABLE	PAN
1	1	1	3

DANCIN'

"A New Musical Entertainment"

existing music and lyrics by various writers

conceived by Bob Fosse (uncredited)

directed and choreographed by Bob Fosse

produced by Jules Fisher, The Shubert Organization, and Columbia Pictures (and Bob Fosse)

with Gail Benedict, Sandahl Bergman, Rene Ceballos, Christopher Chadman, Wayne Cilento, Jill Cook, Vicki Frederick, Richard Korthaze, Edward Love, John Mineo, Ann Reinking, and Charles Ward

opened March 27, 1978   *Broadhurst Theatre*

CLIVE BARNES, *POST*

If I had just one word to describe Bob Fosse's new musical I would probably choose "tremendous." Given another I might have casually selected "fantastic." It is that kind of musical. It opened last night, and with any justice at all it should run for as near forever as forever can be. It is also something quite different. It is a musical without a book. The show is totally about *Dancin'*. And that, by the way, is its title. It is gorgeously, succinctly accurate. What Fosse has done is to create a new theatrical form—and his sheer originality could well be overlooked in the impact of the actual show. Fosse is to Balanchine or Robbins precisely what Johann Strauss was to Richard Strauss. Opera already has operetta—now, with Fosse, dance also has its new popular form. What happened at the Broadhurst last night was simply the birth of a new concept. The show has some of our best Broadway gypsies—and a few fellow-travelers from ballet—prancing and dancing through the air with love and experience. And it is a knockout. I happen to have a special fondness for dancers. But, believe me, they have never been used on Broadway so well. What the kids in *Dancin'* do is dance. And how

Music and Lyrics by Johann Sebastian Bach, Ralph Burns, George M. Cohan, Neil Diamond, Bob Haggart, Ray Bauduc, Gil Rodin & Bob Crosby, Jerry Leiber & Mike Stoller, Johnny Mercer & Harry Warren, Louis Prima, John Philip Sousa, Carole Bayer Sager & Melissa Manchester, Barry Mann & Cynthia Weil, Felix Powell & George Asaf, Sigmund Romberg & Oscar Hammerstein II, Cat Stevens, Edgard Varèse, Jerry Jeff Walker

Note how small Bob Fosse's billing is. No matter; the artwork—hats, hands, and lots of leg—has his name written all over it. (artwork by Bob Gill)

superlatively they dance. They are so alive, so brilliant, so up to the very moment of the beat. Fosse has created a pattern of dance, a web of movement, that is pure show business and then just a little bit more. He has taken popular dance and flown it like a kite. It floats, it soars and it makes images in the air. Fosse can capture a gesture, a moment, a split-second of dance. His dancer will be caught in a strobo-instant of reality. The dancer will somehow—in mid-dance—freeze for one conceptual image. It is always a pop image. Also it is always sexy. Fosse uses sexual imagery with an almost terrifying abandon. In its cool cynicism it comes close to the sexless—but the power and the force of the impression never fails. Every time you fear that Fosse might be cheap, he suddenly does something so marvelous, and so honest, that he practically wrenches your heart. Always Fosse's choreography is flying.

RICHARD EDER, *TIMES*

There must be hundreds of thousands of footsteps in *Dancin'*. They twinkle and flash, they have fire and sometimes force, but only occasionally do they make this gaudy production really move. *Dancin'* is designed to be a musical show purely and simply about dancing. There is no story uniting its dozen numbers, and each number itself has no more than a theme or a rudimentary skit to hang its dancing upon. Likewise the music exists purely to serve the dancers. After a career of threading his movement and dance through plots and songs, Fosse has declared his independence. With appealing audacity, the proclamation is made right at the start that this is to be "an almost plotless musical." But it is like the frosting declaring its independence from the cake. Fosse is one of the architects and craftsmen of the dance style of American musicals. It is a style that possesses many qualities, and many of them are evident in this show. The genre has wit, excitement, impudence and gaiety. But it lacks the intensity, the seriousness, to be its own bones. It can give color and flavor, but it needs words, music, a plot—even a silly plot—to carry it. It does not seem able—judging from this attempt, anyway—to be its own structure. At its strongest, *Dancin'* has the qualities of a spectacular recital rather than an integrated musical show. It has a few marvelous numbers, and a good many weak ones, but the strength remains in compartments and doesn't manage to spin over. If anything unifies the show, in fact, it is the performances rather than the concept. Above all, it is Miss Reinking. There are other first-rate performers, but she is clearly the star. Reinking possesses a number of striking attributes: her legs are very long and she is very beautiful, but mostly it is that everything she has dances—her hair, her teeth, her expression. Her face dances, and this sets her off from a lot of merely very good dancers in the show whose faces merely concentrate. Precision and style mark the evening at its best; but too frequently they are in the service of very little. The hollowness shows; it becomes a gaudy and elaborate mask covering nothing; a deification of emptiness.

WALTER KERR, *TIMES*
[Headline: "*Dancin'* Needs More"]
Almost as though he were mortally fearful of succumbing to alien temptations, warding off evil by putting a hex and a pox on all that might distract him from his best talents, he's banished the libretto entirely, banished numbers that are simply sung, banished everything but the rush and stomp and pat and piston-like thrust of hands and feet, the glide and spin and sinuous self-assertion of bodies. Dance can stand by itself when it aspires to—and achieves—the interior integrity of ballet. But this is mainly show dancing, these are the steps that have distinguished and/or set fire to *Sweet Charity* [1966] and *Cabaret* [Fosse's 1972 film version] and *Pippin* [1972]. But at their best they are not intended for independent statement; they are decorative, illustrative, meant for reinforcing something else. They want a book, if only a book to fight with. Some kind of challenge is needed here, to push the often brilliant Fosse to maximum freshness, to beginning-middle-end completeness. I think we all understand that musical-comedy books, feeble though they often are, accomplish something. They press the evening's characters toward crises, toward moments so urgent that some sort of detonation's in order. The situation's going to splinter and the splinters are going to fly off in the air. Which is what the dancers are for: to fly off into the air. The poor libretto's never going to manage anything quite that spectacular; so dance takes over. But in *Dancin'* there's nothing that *requires* the dancing, no stepping-off place, no trigger, no cry for immediate help. And that means that each of its numbers must start from the floor, must generate its own need and build to its own satisfaction of that need. Ingenious as Fosse is, he cannot overcome the

relative coolness. A degree of anxiety shows. He has felt it necessary to use spoken introductions; these are awkward and generally weak. Neon signs repeating the show's title drop in from the heavens now and then; smoke machines and luminous confetti are called upon for assistance; singers carrying mikes climb proscenium-arch ladders to no particular purpose; the incidental comedy gets right down to bosom-peeking (shades of Willie Howard!). And, most curiously, Willa Kim's costumes are so covered with curlicues, polka dots, outer-space antennae and whorls of contrasting color that very often the dancers' body-lines are seriously obscured. The gimmickry suggests a lack of confidence in the evening's premise: that dancing is enough.

DOUGLAS WATT, *DAILY NEWS*

If you're alive, see *Dancin'*. If you're not, get up and go anyway. Last night's new musical will make you feel like spring and make you wish you were born a dancer. At the very least, it'll make you spring to life. Broadway's peerless *Dancin'* man, Bob Fosse, has given over the entire evening to dancing, with snatches of singing and snippets of talk (some his own, recorded). Sixteen of the most vibrant and gifted young dancers to be found—including the shapeliest, sexiest, leggiest girls ever—spin, swirl, slither, tap, tumble and leap through a succession of musical numbers ranging from Bach to Cohan, from Cat Stevens to Edgard Varèse, and practically into your lap. Certainly into your heart. *Dancin'* is Bob Fosse at his lustrous and unstinting best and, perhaps, the most stylish musical you'll ever witness. Now, let's see: left foot, right foot, turn. . . .

◦   ◦   ◦

Director/choreographer Bob Fosse began the second, major part of his career with *Sweet Charity*—and a libretto he himself sculpted. (During rehearsals he asked Neil Simon—who had been backing him up—to take over, affording the latter full credit.) Fosse's fights with the authors of *Pippin* are well documented; during the tryout, the director himself decided what magic to do and went ahead, oblivious of the opinions of the writers. (And it's a good thing, of course, that he did.) Fosse developed *Chicago* (1975) from inception, battling and bullying Kander and Ebb and sharing book credit with the latter. All of this, mind you, with the best of intentions, trying to match the material itself to his own vision of it. ("Perhaps in the future all musical comedies should be written by choreographers," wrote Brooks Atkinson in appreciation of Fosse's directing debut, the 1959 Verdon vehicle *Redhead.*) Fosse's difficulty with collaborators led to the choreographic revue *Dancin'*, an evening's worth of musical comedy dance numbers without *any* inhibiting book. He also did away with songwriter collaborators; by selecting existing songs by writers who were not present in the rehearsal hall, Fosse was able to use the material any way he wished. (One of the myriad musical sketches in Frank Loesser's workbooks for the 1965 road failure *Pleasures and Palaces* is playfully entitled "What Does Bobby Want?") With his hands unfettered—or should we say feet unfettered?—Fosse came up with some brilliant numbers combined in a slightly uneven whole: it appears that story and characters *do* help give meaning to musical numbers. But *Dancin'*—Bob Fosse *Dancin'*, that is—was exuberant and stylish enough to be a major hit in New York and on the road. For his next—and final—experiment, Fosse again worked collaborator-less, using existing pop songs and writing his own libretto. But you just can't do it alone, to borrow a phrase from the acrobatic murderess in *Chicago.* The 1986 *Big Deal* was a big mess, and a highly unwieldy 5 million dollar one to boot. Fosse died in Washington, DC, on September 23, 1987, at the age of sixty. Backstage, rehearsing a touring revival of *Sweet Charity*, of a heart attack. Just like *All That Jazz.*

Tony Awards were won by Bob Fosse (choreographer) and Jules Fisher (lighting design).

BROADWAY SCORECARD
/ PERFS: 1,774 / $: +

RAVE	FAVORABLE	MIXED	UNFAVORABLE	PAN
2	2		1	1

DARLING OF THE DAY

"A New Musical," previously entitled *Alice Chalice*, *The Great Adventure*, and *Married Alive!*

music by Jule Styne

lyrics by E. Y. Harburg

book uncredited (Nunnally Johnson with revisions by Roger O. Hirson, replacing S. N. Behrman, who replaced Keith Waterhouse and Willis Hall)

based on the 1913 comedy *The Great Adventure* by Arnold Bennett, from his 1908 novel *Buried Alive*

directed by Noel Willman (replacing Albert Marre, who replaced Steven Vinaver, who replaced Peter Wood)

choreographed by Lee (Becker) Theodore (replacing Peter Gennaro)

produced by The Theatre Guild and Joel Schenker

starring Vincent Price and Patricia Routledge

with Brenda Forbes, Peter Woodthorpe, and Teddy Green

opened January 27, 1968   *George Abbott Theatre*

MARTIN GOTTFRIED, *WOMEN'S WEAR DAILY*

The structure is so mechanical, so amateur, and so Forties Broadway that it was lucky to keep its scenery from collapsing. The [novel's interesting] story is here played almost by some grade school class. The company is there, working up routines as if killing time around the Actors' Equity offices between chorus calls. The songs are elsewhere, astonishingly familiar, and conducted by a Buster Davis frantically following the wan-

THE THEATRE GUILD and JOEL SCHENKER
present

VINCENT   PATRICIA
PRICE ROUTLEDGE

In A New Musical

MARRIED
ALIVE!

also starring

PETER   BRENDA
WOODTHORPE FORBES

with

TEDDY GREEN

Music by   Lyrics by
JULE STYNE E. Y. HARBURG

Book by
NUNNALLY JOHNSON

(Based on Arnold Bennett's "Buried Alive")

Scenery Designed by   Costumes Designed by   Lighting Designed by
OLIVER   RAOUL PENE   PEGGY
SMITH   DUBOIS   CLARK

Dance Music   Orchestrations   Musical Direction and
by   by   Vocal Arrangements by
TRUDI   RALPH   BUSTER
RITTMAN   BURNS   DAVIS

Choreography by LEE THEODORE

Directed by
STEVEN
VINAVER

GEORGE ABBOTT THEATRE

152 WEST 54th STREET

OPENS SATURDAY EVENING
JANUARY 20th

Matinees Wednesdays & Saturdays

"A sunlit musical comedy bursting with melody," said the blurb, "brimming with an artful blend of hilarity and romance. It should be the top musical smash of the year." Nope. *Darling of the Day* opened without any librettist listed, always a bad sign. Preliminary credits.

dering pitch and rhythm of leading man Vincent Price. His sheer clum-siness, utter ignorance of key, and movie monster dance style almost overshadowed his unusual and remarkable impression of cardboard. Poor Mr. Davis, speeding up and slowing down his orchestra to follow the Price singing. No such problem with Patricia Routledge, who played the wife as if an apple on a string, rosy, bouncing and delicious.

WALTER KERR, *TIMES*
[Headline: "Patricia is My *Darling*"]
I understand there are some insane people going around this town say-ing that they didn't care all that much for *Darling of the Day*. I'd stay away from them if I were you. As a self-appointed friend, I ask you—ask you seriously—if you'd really want to miss the most spectacular, most scrumptious, most embraceable musical comedy debut since Beatrice Lillie and Gertrude Lawrence came to this country as a package [in *Charlot's Revue of 1924*]. The package in this case—and I don't think I've ever seen a *pinker* package—is named Patricia Routledge, and she is a fighter, a dirty fighter. She has the sweeping jaw of someone saying hello to mother after having won the Golden Gloves, she handles her elbows like someone who's got on and off a subway train at the stops she had in mind, and she comes in low. If *pow!* means anything at all anymore, it means what happens to you when the lady stops nuzzling her tipsy nose against a door frame (no reason whatever for her doing this, except that the dancing chorus isn't paying attention to her), turns her arctic-sunrise eyes in your direction, hikes one corner of her mouth high to the left so that it seems to be held in place by a clothes-pin, and then smiles with what is left to smile with. Coming across the ring, she seems to tiptoe on her heels. She brushes away a tear as though she still had the mitts on. And when she hiccups her way into a show-stopper called "Not on Your Nellie"—this is a real show-stopper, a natural show-stopper, not a clamoring bargain-basement job that has figured out all the pressure points—she hiccups like a woodwind stealing into the pit at dawn. Becoming a coloratura in her cups, she lets you know the cups are mint *Sèvres*. I warn you: if you don't catch her act now, you'll someday want to kill yourself. I'll help you. The score is one of the very best Jule Styne has ever composed for the theatre, E. Y. Harburg's lyrics are much more fun than the cloddish rhyming we're accustomed to, and the book—my God, even the book—is full of pleasant surprises.

DAN SULLIVAN, *TIMES*

The trouble with most Broadway musicals these days isn't that they're cream puffs; it's that they're soggy cream puffs. The latest was served to the apparently famished audience Saturday night. It is based on a crunchy little novel and it has a yummy female star in Patricia Routledge. Otherwise, it is about as intriguing a confection as those to be found on the bargain counter of your local bakery at the end of a very long day. Blandness and staleness are the problems, and since the show was concocted by such sharp people as Nunnally Johnson, Jule Styne and E. Y. Harburg, it is hard to understand why. Johnson's name no longer appears on the program, which suggests that he is not very happy about the book, which is good judgement on his part. *Darling of the Day* follows the novel with reasonable fidelity, but carefully irons out all the quirks in the hero's character—the timidity, the occassional (disastrous) stabs of courage, the ironic contrast between the painter's genius and the man's small-town soul. What is left is a zero-hero, played with friendly blandness by Vincent Price. Price, who used to be a movie bad-die, goes to special pains here to convince us that he is really a nice guy: lots of frank smiles and coy lecture-circuit twinkles. He sings, too, and not badly. But he is not a man to make bricks with straw, and straw is just what his part is made of. Routledge, who really can sing, has more to work with as the young widow slightly past her prime, and it is a joy to watch her. With those rosy cheeks and that comfortable bosom, she makes you think inevitably of buttered toast, crisp linen and good smells from the kitchen. Every artist's dream wife-mother, in short: all common sense and unselfish solicitude. But a lively wench with a couple of beers in her. Routledge's performance suffers a little from the lack of some effective male cantankerousness to set it off, and when she is not around we are stranded indeed. There is not much to be done about *Darling of the Day*, a show whose familiar trimmings cannot quite disguise the hole in the middle, where the hero ought to be.

RICHARD WATTS, JR., *POST*

The only complaint I have about *Darling of the Day* is against its rather aimless title. Otherwise the long-delayed musical comedy seems to me thoroughly delightful. It has charm, tunefulness, humor, imagination, a good book, impeccable taste and a handsome production. And above all it has a young woman from England named Patricia Routledge, who is a veritable host in herself and justifies that title. The pleasures· of the evening are vastly added to by Jule Styne's music and E. Y. Harburg's lyrics. Styne, who sometimes appears to be curiously neglected when the best popular show-tune composers of our time are being listed, has provided a fresh and winning succession of unashamedly melodious numbers, and Harburg's words are well suited to them. *Darling of the Day* is a superior musical comedy, and Miss Routledge is a treasure.

o   o   o

Four titles, five librettists, and four directors speak for themselves. (Steven Vinaver, the director who took the show through rehearsals and onto the road, came from Off-Broadway's *The Mad Show* [1966]. Just thought you'd want to know.) Where were the producers? The Theatre Guild, in the old days, originated *Porgy and Bess* (1935), *Oklahoma!* (1943), *Carousel* (1945), and *Bells Are Ringing* (1956), but those were the old days. The shame is that *Darling of the Day* had a truly sparkling score, easily Styne's best post–*Funny Girl* (1964) work and Harburg's finest since *Finian's Rainbow* (1947). But the rest was a misaligned mess. On opening night Clive Barnes decided to go to the ballet and sent the *Times*'s second stringer instead, who presented *Darling* with a devastating pan. Kerr, Chapman, and Watts all liked it, as did Barnes, who eventually mentioned the show in a later column, but audiences sure didn't, and *Darling of the Day* soon sputtered out—breaking *Kelly*'s $650,000 record deficit, nearing the $750,000 mark. (Little did everyone know that the month's big musical, *The Happy Time*, with heavyweights Merrick, Champion, and Goulet in attendance, would eventually wipe both of 'em off the books with a million-dollar wipeout.) It should be added—why not?—that *Buried Alive*, in an adaptation by Leonard Spigelgass, was initially announced by the Guild in the summer of 1963 as a nonmusical vehicle for the Lunts.

A Tony Award was won by Patricia Routledge (actress, tied with Leslie Uggams for *Hallelujah, Baby!*).

BROADWAY SCORECARD

/ PERFS: 32 / $: –

RAVE	FAVORABLE	MIXED	UNFAVORABLE	PAN
2	1		1	2

A DAY IN HOLLYWOOD—A NIGHT IN THE UKRAINE

"A Musical Double Feature" import of the 1979 British revue

music by Frank Lazarus

book and lyrics by Dick Vosburgh

additional music and lyrics by Jerry Herman

vintage songs featuring music by Richard Whiting

based, in part, on the 1888 playlet *The Bear* by Anton Chekhov

directed and choreographed by Tommy Tune; co-choreographed by Thommie Walsh

produced by Alexander H. Cohen and Hildy Parks (Cohen)

with Priscilla Lopez, David Garrison, Frank Lazarus, Stephen James, Peggy Hewett, Kate Draper, Niki Harris, and Albert Stephenson

opened May 1, 1980   *John Golden Theatre*

CLIVE BARNES, POST

What is one to say? *A Day in Hollywood—A Night in the Ukraine*, which opened last night, is worth a month in the country. It is crazy, zany magic—it is an extravaganza of the old time Hollywood of Grauman's Chinese Theatre, and the ever-new, ever-fresh Marx Brothers, updated, transformed and transmogrified into symbols of the comic spirit of their time. It all comes together as a smashing show, classy, sassy nostalgia combined with the zip and zap of the day after tomorrow. The meat of the evening is *A Night in the Ukraine*. Imagine Chekhov's one-act play *The Bear* as it might have been given by the Marx Brothers. It

Serge B. Samovar makes a frontal assault on the widow Pavlenko; Gino, the gardener, seems to be plucking away at a bicycle wheel. (artwork by James McMullan)

is simply pure madcap idiocy, with one liners and non-sequiturs cheerfully chasing one another down the corridors of infamy. This show is probably the funniest thing to hit New York since pastrami. The curious thing is that it was not always so fabulously ludicrous as it is now. I first saw this musical double feature last season in London. The second part was even there triumphant, and the show was one of the major hits of the London season, but the first part, that *Day in Hollywood*, struck me as about as entertaining as *Three Years in the Gulag Archipelago*. But what the producers, Alexander Cohen and Hildy Parks, and the director/choreographer, Tommy Tune, not to mention the designer, Tony Walton, have done, is sensational. They have taken gold and turned it into uranium, and made the retroactive radioactive. With this one show Tune goes to the top of the class with such choreographer/directors as Michael Bennett, Bob Fosse, Joe Layton and the incomparable Jerome Robbins. The staging is so breathtakingly original—for example, watch out for the cut-out of the famous dancing feet in the first act—that it simply zooms. Walton's scenery is style personified. Even his dropcurtain of the famous footprints in the concrete sands of time outside Grauman's Theatre is conceptually perfect, and his setting for the Chekhov, which with its unending perspectives of corridors is, I suspect, influenced by Wakhevitch's famous design for *Boris Godunov*, is pure enchantment. The cast play like the winners in a World Series. Please take in this Hollywood popcorn epic—they don't make films like that anymore.

MEL GUSSOW, *TIMES*

A double-barreled pastiche of the golden days of the silver screen. The show is of British origin, the creation of Dick Vosburgh (book and lyrics) and Frank Lazarus (music), who is also one of the more antic members of the cast. However, the evening's top billing unquestionably should go to Tommy Tune as director and choreographer. Tune is the toe-tapping Broadway heir to Busby Berkeley. What his predecessor did with 50 dancing girls and a sound stage, he can do, in cameo, with four feet. In several senses, the high spot of the evening is a number called "Famous Feet." Far above the footlights on a ribbon-thin catwalk of a stage we see only the dancing feet of Niki Harris and Albert Stephenson. Clattering their heels, the dancers merrily impersonate a cavalcade of stars: Judy, Charlie, Fred, Marlene, and even Mickey and Minnie. They all seem to dance on air; it is as if they are lightfooted puppets on strings. For Tune the idea is a small miracle of theatrical inventiveness, and it provides a perfect comic counterpoint to the reel life on the main stage below. In the second half we move to Russia to spend *A Night in the Ukraine*, which is the screenplay that Anton Chekhov did not write for the Marx Brothers. The source of the script is Chekhov's *The Bear*, that short vaudeville that made Tolstoy laugh. If he had seen *A Night in the Ukraine*, Tolstoy might have grinned all the way home to Yasnaya Polyana. As written by Vosburgh, this is a crackling compendium of Marx Brothers comedies, packed with all the obligatory gambits, routines and running gags. Instead of playing Captain Spaulding, the African explorer, this Groucho is Samovar the Lawyer, which also happens to be the title of a clever Gilbert and Sullivan-like patter song. Chico is a faithful footman who can be bought for any price and Harpo is a maid-chasing, horn-beeping gardener. In performance, the second act is not quite as amusing as it should be. . . . In his design for *A Night in the Ukraine*, Mr. Walton is an expert miniaturist, with a plush, long-corridored Russian estate that has the detail of a Pollock's toy theatre. The presiding maestro of the evening is Mr. Tune. For him, the show is a marvelous directorial feat.

WALTER KERR, *TIMES*

Mr. Tune is marked by his apt, mellifluous name—and also by his long legs and dancing feet. For most of us, our first vision of him as a performer was marching up and down a mini-staircase in the musical *Seesaw* [1973]. It was as if his limbs had sprouted into stilts. In his role as director and choreographer, he has also stressed feet; remember the boot-stomping football team in *The Best Little Whorehouse in Texas* [1978]? For his new show, Tune uses feet as a motif. Before the show begins, on the curtain we see a simulation of the pavement outside Grauman's Chinese Theatre, where celebrities became immortal by stepping into wet cement. The first half of the revue takes place inside Grauman's, where six actors dressed as ushers lead us on a nostalgic musical cavalcade. The centerpiece is a number called "Famous Feet." Above the actors in a narrow ribbon of space, which look like a kind of a recessed movie marquee, two dancers, Niki Harris and Albert Stephenson, are seen only from the waist down. In a fast-moving series of solos and duets—there is also one trick trio of the Marx Brothers—the two prance through impersonations of Charlie Chaplin, Fred Astaire and Ginger Rogers, Tom Mix (we know it is him rather than a generic cowboy because it says Tom on one boot and Mix on the other), Judy Garland being chased by Dracula, Marlene Dietrich, and Mickey and Minnie Mouse on spindly legs and bulbous feet. None of these vignettes goes on a moment too long and one follows the other in quicksilver succession. Because we do not see their arms and heads, the dancers seem disembodied, and in an additionally artful device, Tune has his figures floating on air. Obviously there is some unseen backstage—or in this case, upstage—contrivance that whisks them off the ground as if they were puppets on a string. When Mickey Mouse kicks, his leg appears to levitate—a case of suspended animation. At one point, feet are replaced by a vista of large white-gloved hands, and later the dancers tap-toe across an enlarged piano keyboard.

o   o   o

This intimate two-part musical revue gave Alexander Cohen a decent-sized hit, the only successful musical of his long career (going back to Of "V" We Sing in 1942). Tommy Tune, a *Baker Street* (1965) Irregular and a Michael Bennett dancer in both *A Joyful Noise* (1966) and *How Now, Dow Jones* (1967), had gone from associate choreographer of Bennett's *Seesaw*—in which he also appeared in the role of associate choreographer—to full choreographer and codirector of *The Best Little Whorehouse in Texas*. *Hollywood/Ukraine*, his first solo Broadway show, firmly established him as a top, original talent. The dazzling "Famous Feet" number was not so original, though; it was lifted from *Double Feature*, a November 1979 musical Tune choreographed (to Mike Nichols's direction) at New Haven's Long Wharf Theatre. *Double Feature*, coincidentally enough, was *also* set in a Tony Walton-designed movie-house lobby, with Michel Stuart costumes, with the feet of Niki Harris and Albert Stevenson dancing to a tune called "Just One Step at a Time." Written by Jeffrey Moss, *Double Feature* ultimately limped Off-Broadway in October 1981 for seven performances—without Tune, Nichols, or any of the others. That's show business.

Tony Awards were won by Tommy Tune and Thommie Walsh (choreographers) and Priscilla Lopez (supporting actress).

BROADWAY SCORECARD
/ PERFS: 588 / $: +

RAVE	FAVORABLE	MIXED	UNFAVORABLE	PAN
2	4			

DEAR WORLD

music and lyrics by Jerry Herman

book by Jerome Lawrence and Robert E. Lee (doctored by Joe Masteroff)

based on the 1948 play *The Madwoman of Chaillot*, Maurice Valency's adaptation of Jean Giraudoux's posthumously produced 1945 play *La Folle de Chaillôt*

directed by Joe Layton (replacing Peter Glenville, who replaced Lucia Victor)

choreographed by Joe Layton (replacing Donald Saddler)

"proudly" produced by Alexander H. Cohen

starring Angela Lansbury

with Milo O'Shea, Jane Connell, Carmen Mathews, Kurt Peterson, Pamela Hall, William Larsen (replacing Michael Kermoyan), and Miguel Godreau

opened February 6, 1969   Mark Hellinger Theatre

ALEXANDER H. COHEN

proudly presents

ANGELA LANSBURY
DEAR WORLD

Music and Lyrics by
JERRY HERMAN

Book by
JEROME LAWRENCE and **ROBERT E. LEE**

Based on a play by
JEAN GIRAUDOUX, as adapted by **MAURICE VALENCY**

with
JANE **CARMEN**
CONNELL **MATHEWS**

and
MILO O'SHEA

Scenic Production by · Costumes Designed by · Lighting by
OLIVER SMITH **FREDDY WITTOP** **JEAN ROSENTHAL**

Musical Direction & Vocal Arrangements by · Orchestrations by · Dance Arrangements by · Incidental Arrangements by
DONALD PIPPIN **PHILIP J. LANG** **JOHN MORRIS** **DOROTHEA FREITAG**

Associate Producer · Production Supervisor · Production Associate
HILDY PARKS **JERRY ADLER** **ROY A. SOMLYO**

Production Directed and Choreographed by
JOE LAYTON

ORIGINAL CAST ALBUM ON COLUMBIA RECORDS   MUSIC PUBLISHED BY EDWIN H. MORRIS & CO. INC.

The Countess Aurelia throws up her hands and shrugs as a parade of stagers and play-doctors try to "rip the stitches out, kill the infection and cut out the growth." (costume design by Freddy Wittop)

CLIVE BARNES, *TIMES*

Dear World—Dear Heavens!—Dear Tickets: that in telegraphese seems to be my message from the Mark Hellinger Theatre, where last night *Dear World* emerged, better late than never, for post-preview scrutiny. For most of the time it stubbornly refuses to get off the ground, except when it is gracefully flounced up airborne by a delicate kick from the adorable Miss Lansbury, who not only can make magic out of nothing but has to. The music by Jerry Herman is French in manner—which means a concertina is lurking behind every bar. Herman does not seem to have decided whether he wants to evoke Jean Sablon or Jacques Brel, and the indecision is not very helpful to him. Looking at all three of Herman's last scores I am beginning to harbor the suspicion that he has only written one musical—and it's getting worse! But for one minor miracle I suspect that *Dear World* would never have seen the gloom of day. The minor miracle is Miss Lansbury and whether or not the musical itself is worth seeing—for it is extraordinarily tenuous—no connoisseur of musical comedy can afford to miss Lansbury's performance. It is lovely. She comes on looking like a Bette Davis in silks. Her eyes are black caverns, her face all white and pink, her expression that of yesteryear. She could be a Beardsley *Salome* 40 years-on, there is wild poetry in every mincingly genteel gesture. Her dancing is exquisite, she moves like a camp vision of Bernhardt, and her acting and singing perfectly express a character seen in precise musical comedy terms. The other show-stopping performance is young Miguel Godreau as the Deaf Mute. For years it has been evident that Godreau was potentially a great performer, and, in a sense, it is sad to see him wasted in this kind of thing when he should be properly employed in a dance company. However he dominates every part of the show that is not dominated by Lansbury—not only with his dancing (which does enable the rather indifferent title song to be cheered) but with a silent presence that seems to burn like a flame. So there it is. Whether it is worth seeing will depend entirely on whether you want to treasure the memory of Miss Lansbury. It is a memory worth treasuring in an evening that seems destined to be forgotten.

MARTIN GOTTFRIED, *WOMEN'S WEAR DAILY*

Dear World might well have been called *Floorscraper, Can't-Can't* or *Queer World*. The Jerry Herman musical that opened last night has more patchwork than material, which might well be all right if the patches were matches. But you can have only so many irrelevant musical numbers killing time before it has to be called murder. After spending the first thirty minutes of a pretty short show marking time, *Dear World* settles down into the mud. The Jerome Lawrence–Robert E. Lee book is about a crazy lady in Paris whose underground home is about to be destroyed by some capitalists looking for oil deposits. Seeing this as a fight between old, elegant individualism and modern, sterile industrialism, she sets out to destroy the businessmen and save the world. Or, as Mr. Herman puts it in his lyric, "So we beg you/To take this solemn oath/Kill the infection/Cut out the growth." It's the kind of writing to set Yeats to worrying. As is "So be a dear world/And get well soon." The lines are from the title song, which—as you know—is as inevitable as a mother image in a Herman musical: chorus line music and the leading lady at the top of a flight of steps. Angela Lansbury is the leading lady—the mother hen of neo-Busby Berkeley—and she plays it looking like after it happened to Baby Jane. Eyes drenched in black, wig drenched in red dye and clothes drenched in bizarre Baroque. The shame—aside from the supermother into which Lansbury has been made—is that she had the kernel of a fabulous characterization. Though looking terribly tired and underweight, and sounding it, the lady projected—from moment to moment—a person of spooky intensity. But the show is a shambles and when it came round to a weird-indeed love scene with a very young and rather pretty young man, I'm afraid even she saw the light. Or the dark. Milo O'Shea, who plays The Sewerman, was pretty well ignored. A small piece of one song and about 27 lines. All one can say about O'Shea is that he was pretty brave to wear his strange costume. I suppose the light on his cap was helpful in looking for something to do. . . . A musical that belongs to the Broadway of 20 years ago, and would have been as great a disaster then as it was last night.

WALTER KERR, *TIMES*

Just listen to Angela Lansbury, looking like a wedding cake made of cobwebs, sing "I Don't Want to Know." Wickedness has taken over in high places, greed is about to raze Paris to the ground—but she won't be told. The actress, who is endearing throughout the evening and at her commanding best here, does push the truth away, reserving a little corner of fantasy to live and take her tea in. Moving to the footlights, eyes hurt with the years and angry with mascara, jaw tight and every feather aquiver, she pushes it away with nervous energy, a will of steel and a rhythm she has caught by the throat. The words say, sharply, "I will not have it!" But the melody doesn't say that at all. It is a gentle concertina wheeze, a sighing playground-in-the-park Parisian jingle, a pastiche of all those Before Piaf frosty-morning tunes that seem to have been born on carousels and fed regularly with roast chestnuts. Take it by itself and you could skip to school with it. Take it by the jugular, which is what Lansbury does, and you've used it against itself, provocatively, a song surprised by its own unexpected passion. The effect doesn't always work out for composer Jerry Herman. *Dear World* is attractive when it is staying close to its addled Good People, the ravaged frumps in feather boas who live in cellars and are willing to take one day off to save the town. It is in trouble whenever it turns to the Bad People, the connivers who have discovered oil in the waters of Paris. Even the Good People have to fight pretty hard to overcome a moralizing lyric ("Dear World") forced upon them by the depredations of those scoundrels. This last song tries the gambit again, you see: harsh images, snuggle-up tune. But we can really only listen to the tune of "Dear World" if we want to enjoy the song. The lyric phrases—"rip the bandages off, dear world," "take the stitches out, dear world . . . stand up on your crutches with pride, dear world"—grate on us and refuse to be toyed with, or pleasantly mismatched with melody, because they are no longer lyric at all, they are ordinary flat-footed sentences unprepared to dance with any tune. Clearly you can pit an emotion against the music; you just can't pit prose against the music.

RICHARD WATTS, JR., *POST*
[Headline: "Trapped in the Paris Sewers"]
So much hard work and so many weeks of industrious previews have gone into the making of *Dear World* that it would have been poetic justice if it could have turned out to be a brilliant show. But the melancholy truth, it seems to me, is that the musical comedy is, despite a picturesque performance by Angela Lansbury, disappointingly mediocre. *The Madwoman* was greatly admired when it was done as a straight

play, although it is only fair for me to add that I was not among its critical enthusiasts. I believe that the Giraudoux fantasy was a provocative
idea to begin with but had a very scanty narrative to keep it going. *Dear
World* is by no means a terrible show. It is actually quite pleasant.
Unfortunately, it never comes to stimulating life musically, dramatically
or humorously. The mad countess is so buried in grotesque makeup that
there is little of the handsome Miss Lansbury left, but her skill and
vitality are still there, and she is the evening's major blessing. *Dear World*
didn't prove the happy surprise of the season.

o   o   o

Having proved with *Mame* (1966) that he was no mere one-show tunesmith, the composer/lyricist of *Hello, Dolly!* (1964) turned to an old
favorite of his. Jerry Herman had appeared in a college production of
Giraudoux's *Madwoman of Chaillot* during his undergraduate days at
the University of Miami; over the years, in fact, he had unsuccessfully
tried to option the rights. With all doors now open to him, arrangements were made and Herman assembled his *Mame* librettists,
Lawrence and Lee; his *Mame* star Angela Lansbury, with sidekick
comedienne Jane Connell; his *Mame* music men, Phil Lang and Don
Pippin; his *Dolly!* design team; and Lucia Victor, Gower Champion's
longtime assistant, who had been responsible for "restaging" the Pearl
Bailey company of That Show. For producer, Herman turned to the one
man who would be sure to spend as much money as any author could
desire: Alexander H. Cohen, whose musicals cost more and lost more.
Cohen saw himself as another Merrick, although he had heretofore
been unable to attract so-called first-rate talent. (He was still smarting
from his *Hellzapoppin'!* fiasco. The 1967 Soupy Sales version, which
closed out of town, not the 1976 Jerry Lewis version, which closed out
of town. Don't ask.) The new musical was duly assembled and publicized, amassing an impressively strong advance sale and pushing the
Broadway ticket up to an astounding $12.50! But *Dear World*, at center,
was empty. Giraudoux was a man of words, and his posthumously produced protest play was a cobweb of idea, ideal, and principle—elements
not especially adaptable to the musical theatre. And Herman's score,
while pleasingly tuneful, was transparent, his mechanics of song manufacturing suddenly baldly visible. Herman has been critically trounced

over the years; the attacks seem to have been brought on, initially, by several of his impossibly banal *Dear World* songs. The title number provides a case in point, with Angela and the company imploring the ailing universe to "be a dear world, and get well soon." Herman's world was "wounded," "poisoned," "beaten," "blinded," and "on the critical list" (rhymed with "patient dismissed"). This is what we call a list song—Cole Porter was pretty good at it—and Herman importunes his D. W. to "rip the bandage off," "take the ambulance," "make the fever break," "have the surgery," "rip the stitches out," and, memorably, "kill the infection, cut out the growth." This is the *world* they're singing to, not somebody's mother. Herman's scores were, generally, a mixture of good and not-so-good, but the occasional inanity—"Stand on your crutches with pride, world!"—tended to overpower the rest, making him a plump and willing target for snipers. As was to be expected, *Dear World* underwent a rocky tryout. Lucia Victor was gone within a fortnight, not seeing eye to eye with the star. Lansbury had Cohen import British director Peter Glenville (who had been canned from Merrick's 1959 Jackie Gleason vehicle *Take Me Along*), with whom she'd worked on nonmusicals. As the Broadway opening was pushed back from December 26 to February 6, Glenville departed for "previous commitments." In came Joe Layton, who did his best to mop things up. *Dear World* went through an unprecedented fifty-seven previews—breaking the 1968 *Golden Rainbow*'s record—to accommodate fixin's and all those directors, but there was nothing at center, just cobwebs. Angela Lansbury's highly acclaimed performance wasn't enough to carry the show against audience apathy. Ailey-trained dancer Miguel Godreau, playing the Deaf-Mute—the role Jerry Herman essayed in college—came off best of the others, but then, he didn't have to sing any of those lyrics.

A Tony Award was won by Angela Lansbury (actress).

BROADWAY SCORECARD
/ PERFS: 132 / $: –

RAVE	FAVORABLE	MIXED	UNFAVORABLE	PAN
	1		3	2

THE DESERT SONG

a touring revival of the 1926 costume operetta

music by Sigmund Romberg

book and lyrics by Otto Harbach, Oscar Hammerstein 2nd, and Frank Mandel

additional lyrics by Edward Smith

suggested by the adventures of Abd-el-Krim and his band of Riffs in French Morocco

directed by Henry Butler

choreographed by David Nillo

"the Lehman Engel production," presented by Moe Septee in association with Jack L. Wolgin and Victor H. Potamkin

starring David Cryer, Michael Kermoyan, Jerry Dodge, Shepperd Strudwick, and Stanley Grover

with Chris Callan

opened September 5, 1973   Uris Theatre

MARTIN GOTTFRIED, *WOMEN'S WEAR DAILY*

The Broadway season has begun early, which would be a good sign, except that the show is *The Desert Song*, which is a bad sign. A new sort of producer has arisen—a producer operating on the basis of mass appeal and looking to make his money on cross-country tours of giant theatres in brief, pre-sold engagements. The actual value of the show is irrelevant and New York, with its critics and its demand for professionalism, is but an afterthought. There have been at least a half-dozen such shows touring the country this past summer, some planning to wind up on Broadway and others not caring. *The Desert Song* is but one of them and, for all I dread, it may be the best. What can be said for the material itself? Doubtless the book was typical for a 1926 operetta—

Morocco, the French Foreign Legion, a hero who is the governor's cowardly son and, secretly, the daring, masked, Robin Hood-like Red Shadow. It is Gilbert and Sullivan without the satire, the lyrics and book genuinely naive and embarrassing. Ironically, the music is wonderful. Sigmund Romberg may not have composed the kind of song any of us cares to hear anymore, but he sure could write a melody, which is more than I can say for most contemporary theatre composers. His songs do tend to sound alike, perhaps because there are so many reprises. The first scene has two songs, both repeated in the same scene, "One Alone" has two reprises and the title song three. They also sound alike because they are sung alike—by robust baritones and shrieky sopranos. Placed, as the songs and singers are, before the most cardboard of sets that also seem the same no matter where the scene, the entire show becomes an unbelievable experience, a cut-rate revival in a dated style of revivals being performed in a lavish and gigantic new Broadway theater. There is nothing to say about the company. They got work and they did it. It was probably embarrassing enough for them on the road but in New York it does require some courage for David Cryer to step out there in his Red Shadow costume out of an old movie serial and sing "The Desert Song" and "One Alone" three times each (always well).

WALTER KERR, *TIMES*
[Headline: "1975 Wrongs *Desert Song*"]
Of course *The Desert Song* is preposterous. But, I ask you, how can you not feel a twinge of regret at losing a form foolish enough, outrageous enough, trusting enough to arrive at *The Desert Song*'s first-act curtain? The Red Shadow, that damnedly elusive fellow who keeps helping Moroccan tribesmen give their colonial oppressors what-for, has finally been trapped in a doorway. At the Uris the Red Shadow is exceedingly red: he looks like Captain Marvel dyed lobster, and possibly, just possibly, played by Charlie Brown. Anyway, you can see him. You can also see the pistol that is trained smack on him, held firmly in the hand of Margot Bonvalet, the girl he loves who doesn't want to love him. (She is a loyal colonial, being so French.) But. Suddenly, from the wings, pop the Red Shadow's band of Riff warriors, swathed in their black whorls and with scimitars raised. Certainly they can take

care of little Margot, even if she does wear boots. It is not to be. While the underscoring from the pit keeps its Moorish curlicues doing staccato throbs, the Red Shadow utters a manly dictum. If Margot fires and drops him dead, she is not to be harmed. Then, turning to her with the musical rhythm intact, he half-speaks, half-sings a line I shall long cherish, especially when I am unable to sleep. It is: "You hold the pistol" (spoken), "and," with a suitable gesture, "here is my heart" (sung). The effect, in its upstanding idiocy, is sublime. If you think that's all there is to it, you're wrong. Now, while Margot keeps the pistol trained on that very exposed heart, he plunges directly into "Blue heaven, and you and I," which, in case no one has ever told you, is the beginning of the title song. Margot can have her will of him at any time. (In her place, I might have; a good Red Shadow should be able to reach the climactic E-note without closing down his vocal chords.) She does not avail herself of the option. She is unable to. As the song pounds on, caroling the praise and the promise of the desert's "starlit sky," Margot's arm trembles, raises, weakens. Slowly, ever so slowly, the pistol is lowered.

RICHARD WATTS, JR., POST
It happened that by some peculiar chance I reviewed *The Desert Song* when it was first presented in 1926 and said it was a pretty foolish show but had a good romantic score by Sigmund Romberg and would have a long, successful run [it did, with a then-impressive 471 performances]. Covering the affectionate revival that opened last night, I felt so unchanged about it that I was tempted to reprint my original notice. Quite wisely, I think, the production takes its nonsensical story seriously, realizing that to mock it would be painting the lily. On the other hand, there is some intended comedy which is less funny than the dramatic sections. *The Desert Song* is silly still but it has the virtue of knowing that it is.

∘   ∘   ∘

Philadelphia-based producer Moe Septee decided that it was time to go back to operetta, so he got together with veteran music man Lehman Engel and mounted not one but two full-scale Romberg chestnuts for road consumption. Neither did well and only one creaked into

Broadway. The other, for the record, was the 1924 old-Heidelberg-sudser *The Student Prince*, with a cast headed by such stars as Harry Danner (who?), Richard Torigi (who??), and George Rose-in-a-box, as they say.

BROADWAY SCORECARD

/ PERFS: 15 / $: —

RAVE	FAVORABLE	MIXED	UNFAVORABLE	PAN
	2	1		3

DO I HEAR A WALTZ?

"A New Musical"

music by Richard Rodgers

lyrics by Stephen Sondheim

book by Arthur Laurents

based on his 1952 play *The Time of the Cuckoo*

directed by John Dexter

choreographed by Herbert Ross (replacing Wakefield Poole, who retained billing as "choreographic associate")

produced by Richard Rodgers

starring Elizabeth Allen and Sergio Franchi

with Carol Bruce, Madeleine Sherwood, Julienne Marie, Stuart Damon, and Fleury D'Antonakis

opened March 18, 1965   46th Street Theatre

Do I Hear a Waltz?, or *Death in Venice* (*in New Haven*). The stars might as well have hung themselves from that gondola mooring pole. Preliminary credits.

WALTER KERR, *HERALD TRIBUNE*

Do I Hear a Waltz? is an entirely serious and very dry musical about an American tourist who goes to Venice and doesn't have any fun. What more can I tell you? I can tell you that it is careful, deliberate, and in a way quite honest about carrying out its earnest intentions. Indeed, the scenery will tell you that before very many panels have dropped into place. With a restraint that can only have been conscientious, Beni Montresor has washed all of the primary colors, and even a great many of the pastels, out of the cupcake-city that straddles so many islands and replaces them with a steady, quite severe, copper haze. [The sets] have been permanently bronzed, washed over with a delicate Arthur Rackham blur that sometimes seems peculiarly English—when a light dip of green is applied to a few leaves during a garden party we might very well be in Chichester—and when a traveling spinster holds up to the light one piece of deep-red Venetian glass the suddenness of the color in so much that is near beige is startling, as perhaps it was meant to be. Why was it meant to be, and what is the monochrome for? We have a straight play, played at straight-play pace, virtually unrelieved by either dancing or comedy, soberly acted, economically directed, and depending for its life on Richard Rodgers' thoughtful songs. I call them thoughtful because they, too, cling close—firmly, with some dignity—to the plainness in Leona's life. Sondheim seems a perfectly agreeable rhyming companion for Rodgers to be doing his work with, and if the excursions into animation never quite lift the roof off it is no doubt because they, like the narrative, are at heart mild complaints. The most effective music comes, significantly, when the corners of a bright tune are turned down. There is a chorus of "We're Gonna Be All Right" in which [the young married couple] hush their voices and rein in their spirits to suggest that it may *never* be all right. The contrast has an edge to it, and for a moment the overcast crackles. And a ballad for three women, "Moon in My Window," is rich with the bittersweet of broken promises and unexpectedly assuaged hearts. But there is—as the play is saying—an emotional drought in Venice, and while musical comedy asceticism is a rare and perhaps admirable thing it cannot, and does not, do much for the evening's pulse.

JOHN MCCLAIN, *JOURNAL-AMERICAN*

There are at least two spectacular things about the new musical. One of them is the scenery by Beni Montresor, a newcomer, and the other is the portrait of a slipshod Venetian maid by a young Greek lady named Fleury D'Antonakis. Miss D'Antonakis, the little maid who walks through the proceedings with her listless Venetian shuffle, is a blessing and a delight. And there are those absolutely magnificent beige and pastel etchings by Montresor which fall magically into place, with lighting by Jules Fisher, and they are occasionally almost breathtaking. Without lowering the curtain or stopping the action he gives us an atmospheric tour and a simple lesson in stage artistry. Otherwise, this is not by any means a bellringer. The score is agreeable but certainly short of world-shaking. They have some good and probably popular numbers, like the title song, but very little indigenous to the locale or highly exciting anywhere. When the leading lady started talking about hearing a waltz somebody said she ought to go to Austria, obviously a plausible remark even though it was not heeded, and there were others like "What Do We Do? We Fly!" which got part of the cast but not the story off the ground. It is not the kind of show for big numbers. In fact, it is not a big one on any basis: the boys should do better.

NORMAN NADEL, *WORLD-TELEGRAM & SUN*

A mellow, sunshine-yellow musical of considerably less than epic proportions, but generous in its ardor. It is, on the whole, a beguiling blend of softness and radiance, suggesting velvety Venetian gold. Its premiere was never less than artful, even when the material descended to the conventional level, which happened occasionally. Its story is both romantic and honest, a combination which goes wonderfully well when set to music—especially Richard Rodgers' music. Rodgers has managed to combine the airy consonance and gentle lyricism of Italian music with his own penchant for chromatics alternating with augmented intervals. It works quite well, producing songs which sound agreeably Venetian, but still fresh and at home in an American musical. Stephen Sondheim's lyrics are clever, ebullient and comfortably phrased. Elizabeth Allen seems a lot prettier and a stronger personality, and less apt to be lonely, than Shirley Booth, who created the stage role, or Katharine Hepburn, who did it on the screen. Laurents hasn't changed

Leona much, but among him, Miss Allen and director John Dexter, they have altered the shadings. . . . The scene changes are as lyric as gondolas on Venetian canals.

RICHARD WATTS, JR., *POST*

The Venice of the American tourist provides a colorful background of which Richard Rodgers takes expert advantage in *Do I Hear a Waltz?* It is so winning in its score, lyrics, setting, cast, production, spirit and general atmosphere that it offers an evening of charming and tasteful entertainment despite certain strong reservations I have concerning the libretto by Arthur Laurents. In a Richard Rodgers show, the music deserves first attention, and his latest score, while perhaps not one of his most spectacular, is tuneful and thoughtfully appealing. The lyrics contributed by Stephen Sondheim are deft and intelligent, and the attractive numbers are delightfully sung. And a most important virtue is the handsome and imaginative settings of Venice designed with distinction by Beni Montresor. Nevertheless, there is the libretto to be considered. Perhaps there is something to the view that American women are very guileless about love and Italian men very wise on the subject, but the topic as a plot basis appears to work out better in Henry James than in a musical play. As for the heroine, since she is played by the beautiful Elizabeth Allen, it seems odd that she is in a bit of difficulty acquiring a man and I can only attribute it to her loathesome habit of calling them "Cookie."

○   ○   ○

Award-winning playwright Arthur Laurents made his mark in the musical theatre with librettos for *West Side Story* (1957) and *Gypsy* (1959). But then he turned to directing, first with the unsuccessful *I Can Get It for You Wholesale* (1962) and then with the disastrous *Anyone Can Whistle* (1964), which he also wrote. This sent him back to his 1952 comedy hit *The Time of the Cuckoo*, which had been adapted for the screen as the 1955 Katharine Hepburn vehicle *Summertime*. Richard Rodgers, meanwhile, had written his own lyrics for the moderately successful *No Strings* (1962), but was actively looking for a partner to replace the recently deceased Oscar Hammerstein. A much-heralded collaboration with Alan Jay Lerner disintegrated when their

I Picked a Daisy was canceled (although Lerner rewrote it, with composer Burton Lane, as the 1965 *On a Clear Day You Can See Forever*). In his continuing search for a lyricist, Rodgers even tried a few songs with Lionel (*Oliver!* [1963]) Bart—compared to whom Lerner and Larry Hart were veritable models of even-tempered dependability. Hammerstein-protegé Stephen Sondheim, meanwhile, had written lyrics for the two aforementioned Arthur Laurents hits, but saw himself principally as a composer. His first Broadway attempt was *A Funny Thing Happened on the Way to the Forum* (1962), a hit, but one for which the songwriter received little respect. (The show won six Tonys, including Best Musical and Best Book, but Sondheim's score was not even nominated; *Stop the World*, *Little Me*, and even *Bravo Giovanni* were.) His next effort was the aforementioned *Whistle*, with which Broadway wrote him off as a composer for the rest of the decade. Sondheim was wary of *Cuckoo* and Rodgers, but he was chummy with Laurents (and Rodgers's daughter, Mary) and otherwise unoccupied. And thus it was that Rodgers, Laurents, and Sondheim—all highly talented, all with nothing else to do—joined for *Do I Hear a Waltz?* Adding to the mismatched assemblage was innovative British director John Dexter, who was grand for opera but not a musical theatre man. (He was also temperamental, shall we say, with a propensity to sadistically harangue female performers.) Determined to avoid the clichéd Venice of the American tourist, the authors conscientiously steered clear of singing gondoliers, overstuffed choruses, and the like. "We're not going to have the natives dancing with tambourines," promised Rodgers; they decided to have no dancing at all, in fact, which proved to be a miscalculation. (*South Pacific* [1949] was also conceived as a nonchoreographed show, with dance sequences patterned by director Josh Logan to approximate what servicemen and nurses might come up with themselves; on *Waltz* they had a dance assistant to help out with the nonmovement.) Once the New Haven reviews came out, Herb Ross came in (the very day after his *Kelly* [1965] opened and closed). The lack of choreography, though, only served to accentuate the overall somberness of the proceedings: "a sad little comedy with songs," per Rodgers. And an antiromantic one, too, though one man's notion of romance sometimes differs from another's. While not an especially tolerant man, Rodgers had worked closely with divergent types over the years. Larry Hart, Herbie

Fields, and Josh Logan, for example, always deferred to the domineering Rodgers; the *Waltz* group, though, didn't. (They called the sixty-two-year-old Great Man of the Theatre "Godzilla" behind his back.) Dexter and Laurents and Ross were anything but solicitous of Rodgers, but even more difficult for the composer was to find Sondheim—Oscar's protegé, who served as a teenaged gofer back in the days of *Allegro* (1947)—siding with the enemy. It was a clique, and Rodgers was the odd man out. He arrived at a rehearsal in Boston one day and discovered changes being made without his knowledge or permission. For Rodgers—not only the composer, but producer and owner of the whole enterprise—this was too much. Communication dwindled, civility ceased, collaboration died, and from that time on everybody simply wanted to finish his work and get as far away from *Do I Hear a Waltz?* as possible. "I watched him grow from an attractive little boy to a monster," said Rodgers of his collaborator in a much-quoted remark. This was meant as a compliment, in fact, given during a joint interview in which noncomposer Sondheim—no doubt holding his tongue, biting his cheek, and crossing his toes under the table—offered that he was "taking a back seat because the best man for this score is Dick." "I'd be the last one to dispute that," said the legendary Mr. Rodgers.

BROADWAY SCORECARD
/ PERFS: 220 / $: —

RAVE	FAVORABLE	MIXED	UNFAVORABLE	PAN
	2	1	3	

DOCTOR JAZZ

"A New Musical"

music and lyrics mostly by Buster Davis

book by Buster Davis (with Paul Carter Harrison, billing removed; doctored by Joseph Stein)

entire production supervised by John Berry

directed by Donald McKayle (replaced by John Berry)

choreographed by Donald McKayle

produced by Cyma Rubin

starring Bobby Van, Lola Falana (replacing Freda Payne), and Lillian Hayman

with Peggy Pope (replacing fourth-billed star Joan Copeland), Jack Landron (replacing Frank Owens), and Hector Jaime Mercado

opened March 19, 1975   Winter Garden Theatre

CLIVE BARNES, *TIMES*

Nothing happened at the Winter Garden Theatre on Wednesday night. Let me explain: a musical called *Doctor Jazz* opened, and it was often pretty to look at, and it employed, none too usefully, a fair assortment of talents, but as a musical it was a non-event, an unhappening. The credit on the playbill says "book, music and lyrics (mostly by) Buster Davis" and they are (mostly) disastrous. As a musical director and vocal arranger, it appears that Davis has worked on more than 25 Broadway musicals. Now he has put them all together into one big grab bag, and grabbed the wrong things. He has come up with unlimited tedium. The story line is more of a dash than a line. The music is at its best when it is not written by Davis, but there are a few unmemorably efficient numbers, and the arrangements by Luther Henderson and Davis himself are

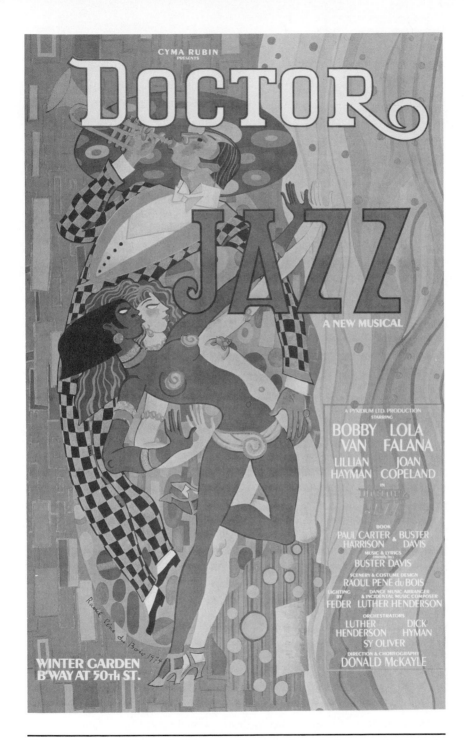

Doctor Jazz or *Nanette's Revenge.* Spectacular window card, though.
Preliminary credits. (artwork by Raoul Pène du Bois)

extremely expert, making everything sound a little better than it might, which is just as well. The musical starts out in 1917 and, presumably, ends up in the mid-nineteen-twenties but no attempt to define its period has been made by Donald McKayle, who directed and choreographed the show, or by John Berry, who supervised "the entire production." McKayle's dance numbers are a particular disappointment, particularly when one remembers that in his own ballet *District Storyville* at the beginning of the sixties, he made a witty and loving celebration of New Orleans, its jazz cats and its cat houses. What was there is what is precisely lacking in the atmosphere and tenor of *Doctor Jazz*. Raoul Pène du Bois has designed the show with a definite style, but not one that bears any particular relationship to his subject. The performers, poor dears, were rather like people running through a maze. The musical is beset with thickets and booby-traps. There were no real characters to portray, and the cast worked frantically hard trying to make bricks without even a last straw to cling to. What went wrong was everything.

MARTIN GOTTFRIED, *POST*

The usual reason for failed musicals is that their original ideas were unmusical to begin with. The idea behind *Doctor Jazz* is so good, with such theatrical potential, that the show's failure is all the more disheartening because of the might-have-been. The musical that might have been and the one that opened last night couldn't be more different. *Doctor Jazz* is about a black singer-dancer who goes from New Orleans to Harlem to Broadway under the guidance of a white man. She might also have symbolized the corruption of pure black jazz in its journey from ragtime and Dixieland to homogenization by the white swing bands of the Forties. She might also have symbolized America's parallel use and repression of black energies in the same period. I can only imagine that this was the show's original purpose. However, *Doctor Jazz* has been put through the pre-Broadway mill, patched up and pasted together by hired professionals who could not have had that original, emotional commitment to a show that makes for a soul (the raceless variety). It is now, astoundingly, a hackneyed backstage story of a girl who rises to stardom at the price of her happiness. Believe me, I am making it sound less trite than it is. Who is responsible for the show's structure—one number after another staged without plot excuse? Donald McKayle is credited as director, but the program calls the "entire production supervised by John Berry." Thanks to a distorting sound system, the lyrics are unintelligible, but they are credited "mostly" to Davis along with the book and music. Did Davis think up the shabby idea of having one scene after another set in a theatre for the sake of a number? Did McKayle? Did Berry? Did the last writer, Joseph Stein, think it up? Or the original one, Paul Carter Harrison? I wish programs could be honest. I doubt that it was Harrison. He is an extremely gifted playwright who has a real flair for musical theatre. I wonder what his original concept for *Doctor Jazz* was? This lavish, shallow, senseless product must seem the most absurd of jokes to him. It is the lacquered waste of a great idea.

DOUGLAS WATT, *DAILY NEWS*

A shapely, compact, cream brown bundle of talent and charm named Lola Falana, a sparkling young woman who sings and dances with authority, could almost certainly walk away with the Winter Garden, given a fair chance. But *Doctor Jazz*, a musical that opened there last night and that looks like something left over from the World's Fair, the 1939 one, is too much even for her. Though Donald McKayle has designed some energetic dance numbers (and a slithery one, too, for a seminude brothel scene), his staging of the book itself is deadly. But then, so is Buster Davis' flaccid book. Davis, a first-rate vocal arranger of long standing in the Broadway arena, is also responsible for the newly written songs, and I'm afraid they are pretty awful, though they and the oldies have been smartly arranged by Luther Henderson, Dick Hyman and Sy Oliver. *Doctor Jazz* is an insult to jazz and everybody in it, but numbingly dull and senseless though it is, it at least serves to introduce us to the adult and irrepressible Miss Falana, last seen here more than 10 years back as a teenage chorus girl in *Golden Boy* [1964]. She's a delight.

◦   ◦   ◦

Cyma Rubin confounded Broadway when her hopeless-sounding 1971 revival of *No, No, Nanette*—with Ruby Keeler, for gosh sake—was not only a hit but a highly entertaining one to boot. But *No, No, Nanette*, as everybody knew, was really Harry Rigby's show, even though Rubin fired him before it opened. Everybody also knew that Rubin—"the Black Witch," they called her—was universally deplored. What would she do without Harry?, they wondered. How bad would it be?, they hoped. Rubin followed Vincent Youmans's 1925 *Nanette* with a lavishly stylish 1978 production of George Gershwin's 1926 *Oh, Kay!*, with *Nanette*'s Donald Saddler, Buster Davis, and Raoul Pène du Bois in attendance. *Oh, Kay!* shuttered out of town, *Doctor Jazz* didn't—mainly because it opened cold (if you'll pardon the expression) in New York—and was carted off to the dump four days later. "It's like a healthy child that dies in your arms," Rubin commented—to the press—during the torturous preview period. (The producer's own healthy child, *Nanette* veteran Loni Zoe Ackerman, quit during rehearsals. Costar Joan Copeland also quit, while director Donald MacKayle and co-librettist Paul Carter Harrison were ousted along the way.) *Doctor Jazz* was the brainchild of *Nanette*'s Buster Davis, a show created, scripted, and scored by a vocal arranger who'd never before done any of the above. The show was blessed with a decent-sounding title and a stylish window card by Pène du Bois but everything else was a mess. Perhaps what *Nanette* would have looked like minus the ministrations of director/adapter Burt Shevelove?

BROADWAY SCORECARD
/ PERFS: 53 / $: +

RAVE	FAVORABLE	MIXED	UNFAVORABLE	PAN
5	1			

DRAT! THE CAT!

a musical spoof, previously entitled *Cat and Mouse*

music by Milton Schafer

book and lyrics by Ira Levin

directed and choreographed by Joe Layton

produced by Jerry Adler and Norman Rosemont, "a Rogo Production" (Norman Rosemont/Robert Goulet)

starring Lesley Ann Warren and Elliott Gould

with Jane Connell, Jack Fletcher (replacing third-billed star Eddie Foy, Jr.), Charles Durning, Lu Leonard, and Gene Varrone

opened October 10, 1965   Martin Beck Theatre

JOHN CHAPMAN, *DAILY NEWS*

Some of it is quite funny—and it should be, for the author is Ira Levin, who once wrote *No Time for Sergeants* (1955). Some of it is not so, for it is difficult to maintain a burlesque-fantasy through a long evening. But when things slow down somewhat or a gag or a joke wears thin, there is compensation in the shape—and what a shape!—of 19-year-old Lesley Ann Warren. She is an almost unbelievably beautiful and considerably talented singer and dancer who has the role of a cat thief. She doesn't steal cats; she steals diamonds. . . . Quite often David Hays' scenery is the funniest part of the show, for it has any number of tricks. It revolves, it sinks, it pops up and it flitters around town from a masquerade ball to a pier to a spooky woods near Yonkers. Often the scenery quiets down to give a song number its turn. I suggest that, now that the opening night is over, Layton get out a snickersnee and shorten several song numbers and scenes. *Drat! The Cat!* simply must move faster or the audience will catch up with it. And I just wish I could catch up with Lesley Ann Warren, but my wife probably wouldn't turn me loose.

"I am going to promise you, here and now, that Miss Warren looks exactly like the poster. Exactly," said Walter Kerr. "Makes you wonder what you ever had against cats."

WALTER KERR, *HERALD TRIBUNE*

Drat! The Cat! is a musical comedy about an exceedingly wicked girl—
the kind you wouldn't bring home to mother, but would keep for yourself—and she does any number of terrible things. She is a jewel thief
with very long legs and black laced boots and fur-trimmed hips, and as
soon as she has snatched anything she leaps into the air for glee, leaps
so high that she has to race across balconies and whip over suspension-
bridges before she can slip down slyly into her dark, diamond studded
lair. I don't know if you've noticed the posters for the entertainment—
I began studying them during intermission—but they feature a masked,
feline, witch of a wench who makes you wonder, on inspection, what
you ever had against cats. I am going to promise you, here and now, that
Miss Warren looks exactly like the poster. Exactly. She is entrancing
when she moves, entrancing when she hesitates, entrancing when she
smokes the fiercest cigarette since Scarface was a boy. Having great dark
eyes which really don't leave much room for the rest of her face, she goes
on to add a beatific pout and a come-hither snarl that ought to have
gentlemen lining up to join the police force tomorrow. I have a hunch
writers are going to be going out of their way to write shows for Miss
Warren before long. . . . *Drat! The Cat!* doesn't satirize anything in particular, or ar least not anything recent. It simply cuts itself free of meaning and goes on holiday, taking a terrible burden off the shoulders of
musical comedy and suggesting that idiot—even irreverent—improvisation may be the escape we've all been looking for. Admit that it's a bit
sloppy, and then pay attention to how much fun it is. Deep down inside,
as they say in the lyrics [actually "Deep in Your Heart"].

NORMAN NADEL, *WORLD-TELEGRAM & SUN*

As far as I'm concerned, it was Joe Layton night on 45th St., as *Drat!
The Cat!* opened at the Martin Beck Theatre. This inspired young
director and choreographer, with a tremendous assist from designer
David Hays, has lifted the new "musical spoof" out of what might otherwise have been a generally mediocre and sometimes forced effort at
hilarity. They don't make it great, but they do help to make it enjoyable.
Layton, like Gower Champion in *Hello, Dolly!*, believes in uninterrupted action, so that there always is plenty to watch. Designer Hays'
contribution includes such subtleties as the wealthy Lucius Van Guilder

home done in money green, adorned with currency protraits of presidents and inlaid with coins. His elevating bridge can be anything from a balcony at the Van Guilders' to a railway trestle. All sorts of ingenious little sets erupt out of the stage apron, which also houses a useful trapdoor for disposing of players swiftly. A basement cell where Elliott Gould is chained to a water pipe that leaks real water, is one of the niceties. . . . As the evening progressed, I found myself appreciating the orchestrations [by Hershy Kay and Clare Grundman] more than the melodies, which are not striking. Composer Milton Schafer actually sustains the show best with the continuity of agreeable music, rather than as a songsmith.

◦   ◦   ◦

Drat! The Cat! almost made it, not that almost has ever been enough. But with a little bit of luck—or better timing—or a stronger-handed, clout-wielding producer at the helm, it just might have worked. The project originated with *My Fair Lady* (1956) producer Herman Levin (no relation to author Ira Levin). Herman lost heart following the drubbing of his 1963 Noël Coward musical *The Girl Who Came to Supper* and dropped *Drat!*—which was immediately picked up by *MFL* stage manager Jerry Adler and Norman Rosemont, vice president of Alfred Productions (as in Al Lerner and Fred Loewe). The title role went to Joey Heatherton; when she tried to block the casting of Elliot Gould (of the 1962 *I Can Get It for You Wholesale*), though, she was told that casting was none of her business and sent packing. Lesley Ann Warren, who had attracted attention in *110 in the Shade* (1963) and the 1965 revision of Rodgers and Hammerstein's TV musical *Cinderella*, was signed in Heatherton's place. The third star was Eddie Foy, who played the stars' fathers—hers in Act I, his in Act II. He quit in Philadelphia. (Producer Rosemont's other musical, simultaneously trying out in Boston, simultaneously lost *its* star—Louis Jourdan of *On a Clear Day*. And you thought it was easy producing Broadway musicals?) Composer Milton Shafer had written another near-miss musical, the 1962 *Bravo Giovanni*. Shafer and Levin gave their leading man an especially pretty ballad, "She Touched Me," which the leading man's *Funny Girl*-of-a-wife recorded. (She also provided $50,000 of the $500,000 capitalization.) Levin, meanwhile, sat right down and wrote himself the 1967 novel *Rosemary's Baby*. *Drat!*'s demise also ended the musical comedy lives of costars Warren and Gould, both of whom Had What It Takes. Gould did fine enough on the big screen, of course, but at heart he was one of those up-from-the-chorus sort of guys, up from the chorus of *Say, Darling* (1958) and *Irma la Douce* (1960).

BROADWAY SCORECARD
/ PERFS: 8 / $: —

RAVE	FAVORABLE	MIXED	UNFAVORABLE	PAN
	3	1	2	

DREAMGIRLS

a new musical, previously entitled *One Night Only*, *Big Dreams*, and *Dream Girls*

music by Henry Krieger

book and lyrics by Tom Eyen

suggested by events in the career of the Supremes (uncredited)

directed and choreographed by Michael Bennett; co-choreographed by Michael Peters

produced by Michael Bennett, Bob Avian, Geffen Records (David Geffen), and the Shubert Organization

starring Obba Babatunde, Cleavant Derricks, Loretta Devine, Ben Harney, Jennifer Holliday, and Sheryl Lee Ralph

with Deborah Burrell, Vondie Curtis-Hall, Tony Franklin, and David Thomé

opened December 20, 1981   Imperial Theatre

CLIVE BARNES, POST

[Headline: "Rousing *Dreamgirls*, but the Story of a Women's Rock Group Does Have Some Flaws"]

Some shows are rather like prizefights. They seem to be sparring with the audience—when suddenly, wham-bang, from a somewhat muddy blue sky, comes a knockout punch that leaves the audience happily pulverized. It nearly happens in the new Michael Bennett musical *Dreamgirls*. The putative knockout comes just before the end of the first act. A woman has been fired from a risingly successful Motown singing group—fired by the manager, her former lover. She is dumpy and awkward and doesn't fit into the group's projected image. It's show business, but it is also the breakdown of her individual family. Tearfully, her voice breaking with a mixture of heart and soul, blood and tears, she announces to her lover and the audience/world: "And I Am Telling You I'm Not Going." The musical teeters in its tracks—like a bucket of ice water, reality has torn through the shabby, rather ordinary tinsel curtain. Then Bennett blows it. Instead of ending the act on a soul-shriek he suddenly brings on the dancing girls just for one fatal minute. Artistically the show is finished there and then. Well, not quite finished; Bennett still has Jennifer Holliday in there slugging away for him. Miss Holliday is just tremendous—something like a battle ship should be named after her. If the phrase "an overnight star" means anything at all it will surely be applied to this 21-year-old singing sensation. The voice runs from velvet to sandpaper, it breaks like a mountain stream, it giggles and cries like a baby, it moans in ecstasy and it sings the blues even when, musically, the blues are not there. This voice is a miracle ingredient. And one day it will find its music. That day was not last night. . . . Bennett's staging is dynamic enough—except the choreography bears an odd air of parody that is almost patronizing. Even the vigor of the dancing seems intentionally exaggerated—almost any black choreographer, Alvin Ailey, Billy Wilson or George Faison would almost certainly have done a better, even fairer, job. Will this show that wowed Boston be a hit in New York? Who knows? Many worse shows than this achieved just that. But somehow, at least to me, despite the passing merits, *Dreamgirls* seemed an idea muddled, a dream gone adrift.

WALTER KERR, *TIMES*
[Headline: "Rich Dessert without the Main Course"]

Dreamgirls may be the most restlessly impersonal musical I've ever come across. In charting the rise of a black singing group resembling The Supremes, Mr. Bennett has at his disposal a stageful of performers so technically accomplished that they can blast away on trumpets while twirling their knees counterclockwise until you're terrified they'll fly off. He has girls and to spare, each of them able not only to strip vocal gears somewhere between gospel and neo-pop but also to change costumes apparently by metamorphosis: you're looking at them in green and suddenly they're in white. He has 30 separate songs, if I counted correctly. He has plexiglass towers that can ice-skate about the stage floor doing geometric arabesques, he can lower walkways from the heavens that look as though he'd inherited everything left over from the George Washington Bridge. And he doesn't trust any of it. I conclude he doesn't trust it because he is strangely unwilling to zero in on any one dance, on any one song, on any one twist or turn of plot development and stay with it until it's explored the immediate territory thoroughly, until it's *finished*. This jitteriness is prophetically in evidence from the beginning: a finger-snapping bit of snake-hips is begun on a street corner, then sharply aborted; a failing vaudevillian begins to strip away his clothing to get down to the soul music he's lost, and we jump backstage—courtesy of all that animated scenery—to hear the reaction there. It's like being next door to the show going on and picking up half of it. Bennett spends his evening—and ours—ever so carefully ducking any invitation to go for broke. He does it sleekly, even delicately; he seems to be offering us rich desserts if we'll just forget about the meat and potatoes. But he's playing a cagey, evasive game, and after a time you see why. He has neither a score nor a book to work with. Henry Kreiger's melodies make the unthinkable mistake of sounding all alike: in a show based on a quarrel of sounds, the composer hasn't taken the trouble to underline the differences. Similarly, Tom Eyen's narrative suffers mightily from not being one. The kaleidoscope at the Imperial, everlastingly changing its patterns and its boldly splattered hues, is all very efficient. It is also, I regret to say, all very remote.

FRANK RICH, *TIMES*

When Broadway history is being made, you can feel it. What you feel is a seismic emotional jolt that sends the audience, as one, right out of its wits. While such moments are uncommonly rare these days, one popped up last night at the end of the first act of Michael Bennett's beautiful and heart-breaking new musical, *Dreamgirls*. Jennifer Holliday begs [her manager/lover] to let her stay in a song titled "And I Am Telling You I'm Not Going." Miss Holliday is a young woman with a broad face and an ample body. Somewhere in that body—or everywhere—is a voice that, like Effie herself, won't take no for an answer. As Holliday physically tries to restrain her lover from leaving, her heart pours out in a dark and gutsy blues; then, without pause, her voice rises into a strangled cry. Holliday just keeps riding wave after wave of painful music—clutching her stomach, keeling over, insisting that the scoundrel who has dumped her is "the best man I'll ever know." The song can end only when Bennett matches the performer's brilliance with a masterstroke of his own—and it's a good thing that Act I of *Dreamgirls* ends soon thereafter. If the curtain didn't fall, the audience would probably cheer Jennifer Holliday until dawn. If Holliday's solo is one of the most powerful theatrical coups to be found in a Broadway musical since Ethel Merman sang "Everything's Coming Up Roses" at the end of Act I of *Gypsy*, so *Dreamgirls* is the same kind of breakthrough for musical stagecraft that *Gypsy* was. In *Gypsy*, Jerome Robbins and his collaborators made the most persuasive case to date (1959) that a musical could be an organic entity. Bennett has long been Robbins's Broadway heir apparent. But last night the torch was passed, firmly, unquestionably, once and for all. Bennett has fashioned a show that strikes with the speed and heat of lightning. Is *Dreamgirls* a great musical? Well, one could quarrel with a few lapses of clarity, some minor sags, the overpat and frantic plot resolutions of Act II. But Mr. Bennett and Miss Holliday have staked *their* claim to greatness. And if the rest of *Dreamgirls* isn't always quite up to their incredible level, I'm willing to suspend judgment until I've sampled the evidence another four or five times.

DOUGLAS WATT, *DAILY NEWS*

[Headline: "Empty Dream"]

All style and no substance, as flashy as a shopgirl's dream and just as empty. Ever since *A Chorus Line* (1975), one must think of each of his new efforts as "the Michael Bennett musical" because, while the prestigious Broadway director-choreographer writes neither the words nor the music, the end result bears his unmistakable stamp. And so it is with *Dreamgirls*. Tom Eyen's cynical book about the rise to fame and eventual dissolution of a black female vocal trio, one clearly inspired by the Supremes, has sent stage patterns, movement and sound whirling about in Bennett's head. And what he has come up with is an example of razzle-dazzle dependent to an enormous extent on the glittery, extravagant, thoroughly professional work of scenic designer Robin Wagner, costumer Theoni V. Aldredge and lighting designer Tharon Musser. Thousands of lights on walls, on sliding and revolving towers, on rising and descending bridges, and along advancing and receding stairways and platforms wink at us or illuminate an endless array of showy costumes. *Dreamgirls* often resembles an outrageous fashion show set to music. The best part—in fact, the only good part—of Eyen's book touches on the scrungy aspects of the recording business. His lyrics are commonplace but worthy of Henry Krieger's musical pastiches of the '60s and early '70s. *Dreamgirls* represents an inordinate expenditure of talent and money on a musical that resembles a series of rehearsal periods for some slick TV commercial.

o   o   o

Like *A Chorus Line* and *Ballroom* (1978), *Dreamgirls* began with a series of workshops. Unlike Michael Bennett's two previous musicals, though, the show wasn't initially developed by Bennett. Author/director Tom Eyen had achieved some success with the Off-Broadway hit *The Dirtiest Show in Town* (1970), a frisky *Oh! Calcutta!* (1969) not for tourists; he achieved some Broadway notoriety with the closed-in-previews *Rachael Lily Rosenbloom—and don't you ever forget it!* (1973). Eyen and composer Henry Kreiger auditioned *One Night Only* for Bennett, who agreed to take it on as a producing project and brought in Michael Peters—whose work on the short-lived *Comin' Uptown* (1979) he had admired—to choreograph. Over the course of four workshops, Bennett took over the staging from Eyen, with Peters becoming co-choreographer. Because *Dreamgirls* evolved slowly—and because Bennett's design team of Robin Wagner (sets), Tharon Musser (lights), and Theoni V. Aldredge (costumes) was on hand and in attendance—the physical production concept became a key element in shaping the material. Wagner and Bennett came up with a scheme of five large, Plexiglas light towers, offset by four overhead lighting bridges, which could be lowered from the flies. With the verticals and horizontals fully mobile, Wagner could frame any area of the stage, add set dressing or props, and instantly create any scenic locale desired. This mobility allowed Bennett and Peters to move the actors and/or the scenery, simultaneously or apart. "Steppin' to the Bad Side," for example, built from an intimate quartet to a striking full-stage picture, with dancers snaking across the tops of the light bridges. But despite the overall staging brilliance, *Dreamgirls* seemed all dressing with no foundation underneath. The principal characters were well developed, and the roles extremely well performed, but the innumerable songs, with a couple of exceptions, seemed like continuous background music, the plot continually lost in the shuffling. The towers allowed Bennett to use striking cinematic techniques—cuts, fades, and such—which might well have blunted the impact of the script. Still, the not-wholly-satisfying *Dreamgirls* was a hit, and at $3.5 million the most expensive show Broadway had ever seen. It also proved to be Bennett's final offering. *Scandal*, a 1983 sex-driven piece, was dropped after extensive development and workshopping. Bennett also withdrew from the 1986 London rock musical *Chess* just prior to rehearsals. (They went ahead, though, with the ingeniously spare, chessboard-like set Bennett and Wagner had devised. Replacement director Trevor Nunn couldn't quite figure out how to use it, piling on heaps of realistic scenery to give an unwieldy look to an unwieldy show.) The reason for Bennett's aborted efforts, it turned out, was his failing health. The forty-four-year-old Bennett died on July 2, 1987—just four days after the international touring company of *Dreamgirls* opened a Broadway revival at the Ambassador. To better reviews but a disappointing 177-performance run.

Tony Awards were won by Tom Eyen (book), Michael Bennett and Michael Peters (choreographers), Ben Harney (actor), Jennifer Holliday (actress), Cleavant Derricks (supporting actor), and Tharon Musser (lighting design).

BROADWAY SCORECARD
/ PERFS: 1,522 / $: +

RAVE	FAVORABLE	MIXED	UNFAVORABLE	PAN
1	2		2	1

DUDE—THE HIGHWAY LIFE

"A New Musical"

music by Galt MacDermot

book and lyrics by Gerome Ragni

directed by Tom O'Horgan (replacing Rocco Bufano)

choreographer unbilled (Tom O'Horgan replacing Louis Falco)

produced by Adela and Peter Holzer

starring William Redfield and Rae Allen (with third-billed costar Michael Dunn written out)

with Salome Bey, Allan Nichols, Delores Hall, Ralph Carter (replacing Kevin Geer), Nat Morris, and Nell Carter

opened October 9, 1972   Broadway Theatre

MARTIN GOTTFRIED, *WOMEN'S WEAR DAILY*

Dude is the show with the subtitle "The Highway Life." It is the show that reunites the basic team that created *Hair* [1968]. It is not about a gay hustler. It is not about the highway life, whatever that may be. But it is very much like *Hair* in its disorganization and lack of concept. *Dude* is incoherent, childish and boring, and it is very noisy about it, but some very worthwhile things about it should be pointed out. In the first place, it changes the playing area of Broadway musical from the traditional proscenium house to a large (and yet intimate) arena with lots of ramps and a central stage. This was probably done at an impractical cost and, from another point of view, what did the Broadway Theatre do to *Dude* to deserve this? But the change in perspective is very refreshing and, with a director like O'Horgan who knows what to do with all that space, it becomes less of a gimmick and more of an exciting theatre place. Secondly, *Dude* has a musical score by Galt MacDermot, who could be one of our theatre's most effective, sophisticated and innova-

Kevin Geer was fired from the title role during rehearsals but left his image behind. Director, choreographer, and 3'6" third-billed star Michael Dunn all departed during previews, with *Dude* itself soon hitting the highway altogether. Preliminary credits.

tive composers. Unfortunately, he is too prolific and not disciplined enough for his own good. He writes a great deal of music—the two versions of *Hair* had almost completely different scores; *Two Gentlemen of Verona* [1971] has almost enough music for two versions, and besides *Dude* (which lists 35 numbers when the average show has about 15), he has still another show [*Via Galactica*] coming in this season. But MacDermot's problem seems to be a refusal to discard songs and an over-willingness to mix styles. Variety of musical style could be refreshing and useful in a show, but MacDermot's versatility seems purposeless. Dismissing the second-rate music in *Dude*, there is still an excellent score remaining. O'Horgan ends the show with the devil figure being crucified in a theatre seat and being hoisted into the air. Analogies with the audience might be drawn.

WALTER KERR, *TIMES*

Dude might have been waved away as just another failed musical if it hadn't been for two things: its pedigree and its challenge. We were entirely aware of both as we sat—in the foothills, in the mountains, in the valleys, among the trees [as the various seating areas were called on the tickets]—watching it on opening night. The pedigree? *Dude* was by the authors of *Hair*, that watershed rock festival that changed the minds of the country about what it wanted to look at and listen to. The challenge? The producers and authors of *Dude* made it plain by word and woodwind, by hammer and chisel, that they were out to restructure the contemporary theatre in every conceivable way. Let's take the restructuring first, since that is where the occasion's failure is most obvious and most immediate. The show had begun with the notion that the physical theatre itself must be reshaped if the audience we're going to have inside it are to take on a new and different life. To bring this about the Broadway Theatre was torn apart and rebuilt, the old orchestra floor was completely covered over with a green whirlpool of a stage, what had formerly been the stage became a steep bank of seats facing the old bank of seats that had constituted the balcony, small pockets of spectators were tucked into the spaces between so that the acting area should seem to be entirely surrounded by attentive eyes, a rock group was suspended from one theatre-box and a collection of country fiddles caged at some distance across the house, the ceiling became a tangle of baroque cupids, rigging and the vine-leaves of Tarzania. . . . Before drawing what conclusions we can, mention should be made of one young performer. Ralph Carter, as the boy-Dude, firmly occupied every inch of space he was allotted, back straight, head up, squared mouth quivering with breathtaking glissandos. Conclusions? Rock musicals, if they are to sustain themselves as genuine theatre pieces rather than arena concerts, are going to have to meet the obligations earlier musicals have accepted, always with difficulty, often with pain. Music *is* the ultimate making of any musical. But the music must have something to stand on, something other than its own beat to move it, something to demand one particular song rather than another at a particular moment, hopefully something in the way of wit to keep it company.

RICHARD WATTS, JR., *POST*

At the Broadway Theatre last night, where *Dude* was having its opening performance, those of us whose tickets were marked "foothill" had to do some climbing. There we found the playhouse interestingly transformed. In the center was a small round stage totally surrounded by members of the audience, some apparently located in the "valley" or on the "hill." Up and down the aisles the actors kept rushing while they clutched their microphones with the wires trailing behind. Everything started promisingly. The first of the players descended from the ceiling on a trapeze, actors representing such positive and negative forces as Mother Earth, the Moon, Bread and Zero arrived, and I thought the scene was, as some of the dialogue suggested, the Garden of Eden. Tom O'Horgan, the director, has employed a lot of ingenious ideas for staging and for a long time the ingenuity works. But eventually it becomes evident that in the process of production something has been overlooked. They forgot to include a play, and I felt it grew confusing on purpose. *Dude* has a subtitle, which is *The Highway Life*, and it was one of the many things about a disappointing evening that puzzled me. What is a "highway life"? I at least gathered that the narrative had to do with good, evil, the need for love, and the conflict between constructive and destructive urges in mankind. But the way in which it goes about making its points struck me as being more bewildering than illuminating. I'll cheerfully admit it may be my fault that, outside of knowing there is a young man named Dude, I found out little about him. Is he perhaps a kind of modern Christ? There are good things, like the moment when two of the players start to do a scene from Shakespeare, but not enough of them. The large cast includes such well-known players as William Redfield and Rae Allen. All of them are talented, particularly Ralph Carter in the title role. But my favorite member of the company was a perky little stout black girl whose name I was unable to discover [Nell Carter, presumably]. *Dude* has an attractive home and it was undeniably a novelty. But after the first half hour it made me unhappy.

o   o   o

"Go back to your seat," snapped Gerry Ragni at a patron trying to sneak out of the final performance of *Dude*. "Just go sit down and suffer with everybody else. Suffer!" The worldwide success of *Hair*, the American Tribal Love-Rock musical, naturally led producers to think that there was gold in them thar hills. Adela and Peter Holzer—whose sizable investments in *Hair* and *Sleuth* had already proved to be gold mines— figured they might as well mine their own. The Medusa-haired Ragni was the wilder of the two lyricist-librettists-leads of *Hair* (he played Berger). As best as anyone could figure, *Dude* dealt "with the struggle between man and nature, and the attempt to find universal love." So said the press release, anyway. (The cast list, incidentally, was broken down in *Playbill* as The Theatre Stars, The Shubert Angels, and The Theatre Wings.) Dude was a modern Everyman, although his course seemed to parallel Ragni's own; the dialogue contained angry veiled-but-personal references to *Hair* coauthor James Rado and producer Michael Butler. "I never knew who Dude was," admitted composer Galt MacDermot. "Early on I accepted *Dude* as a totally illogical musical." Illogical might well describe the casting of Kevin Geer, a friend of Ragni's, in the title role. It was discovered a couple of weeks into rehearsal that he simply could not sing. (It's usually better to find out stuff like this *before* you hire an actor. Ragni surely saw *some* talent in Geer; that's his posterior on the poster.) So the twenty-three-year-old Geer was fired, over Ragni's objections, and replaced by eleven-year-old Ralph Carter. Now Ralph, even at eleven, was highly professional, a fine performer, and far more mature than the thirty-three-year-old Ragni. But some of the material written for the character seemed unlikely coming from the mouth of a babe, so the role was split in two and Nat Morris undertook the older Dude. The show moved into the gutted Broadway, which had been transformed into an environmental theatre-in-the-round, the audience sectioned in valleys ($15 top), foothills, mountains, trees, and treetops. Ragni insisted that the stage be covered with dirt, which at the first preview permeated the first ten rows of valley. So they "wetted it down," which turned the second preview into a mudbath. Then felt strips, which lodged in the singers' throats. They ended up with brown plastic, but you've got to admire them for trying. (Set designer Eugene Lee, who had done a similar if less extensive job on the ANTA Theatre for the comparably wacky 1970 play *Wilson in the Promised Land*, would once again carve up the restored Broadway for its very next attraction, that eighteenth-century tale of the highway life *Candide* [1974].) Anyway, after five bedlamic previews director Rocco Bufano (another friend of Ragni's, who'd never directed on Broadway, before or since) and choreographer Louis Falco (ditto) were given the gate. Previews were halted and the show taken over by Tom (*Hair*) O'Horgan, who had similarly stepped in and shaken up the 1971 *Jesus Christ Superstar*. "I came in as an act of conservation," he said, "and because I think it's immoral to waste all that money." But there's only so much one can do. O'Horgan tried to pull the show into focus and made sundry changes, including the elimination of both the nudity and the character played by third-billed star Michael Dunn (the 3' 6" actor best remembered for his unique performance in Edward Albee's 1963 adaptation of Carson McCullers's *Ballad of the Sad Café*). The revised and revamped *Dude* opened, surprisingly enough, to universal jeers. The Holzers naturally blamed the critics, although the show was regularly booed in performance (and not only by members of the press). "I didn't want to make money," said Adela, who would later bunk with Scarsdale Diet doctor-murderess Jean Harris in the pen. "I just wanted to follow my career of helping the theatre." The director was reflective on the closing. "It's still better than *Follies* or *Hello, Dolly!*," said Tom. "It has one of the best scores. Who's to say it's not enough just as a concert?" "Go back to your seats and suffer with everybody else," said Gerry. "Suffer!"

BROADWAY SCORECARD
/PERFS: 16/$: —

RAVE	FAVORABLE	MIXED	UNFAVORABLE	PAN

6

THE EDUCATION OF H*Y*M*A*N K*A*P*L*A*N

"A New Musical"

music and lyrics by Paul Nassau and Oscar Brand

book by Benjamin Bernard Zavin

based on the 1937 *New Yorker* stories by Leonard Q. Ross (a.k.a. Leo Rosten)

directed by George Abbott

choreographed by Jaime Rogers

produced by André Galston, Jack Farren, and Stephen Mellow

starring Tom Bosley

with Barbara Minkus, Gary Krawford, Hal Linden, Honey Sanders, Dick Latessa, Beryl Towbin, and Donna McKechnie

opened April 4, 1968   *Alvin Theatre*

CLIVE BARNES, *TIMES*

Pleasant, often gently ingratiating, *The Education of H*Y*M*A*N K*A*P*L*A*N* is a modest musical. Of course, as Winston Churchill once said of Clement Attlee, it has quite a lot to be modest about. On the other hand, in this famine year for musicals it is better than most. Presumably, Paul Nassau and Oscar Brand envisaged *H*Y*M*A*N K*A*P*L*A*N* as a kind of sequel to *Fiddler on the Roof* [1964], but in this noble aspiration it fails. And the reason is the fault of Nassau and Brand themselves, for it is only when *H*Y*M*A*N* is at its very best that it can suggest *Fiddler* at its very worst. George Abbott, faced with a booky-book, nostalgic and dangerously familiar-sounding music, and

ANDRE GOULSTON, JACK FARREN
and STEPHEN MELLOW
present

TOM BOSLEY

in

THE EDUCATION OF

H*Y*M*A*N

K*A*P*L*A*N

a New Musical

Book by
BENJAMIN BERNARD ZAVIN
Music & Lyrics by
PAUL NASSAU & OSCAR BRAND
Based upon the stories by
LEO ROSTEN
Designed by
WILLIAM & JEAN ECKART

Lighting by
MARTIN ARONSTEIN

Costumes by
WINN MORTON

PRODUCTION DIRECTED BY
GEORGE ABBOTT

ERLANGER THEATRE
PHILADELPHIA

Special Public Previews Fri. Eve. March 1 and Sat. Mat. and Eve. March 2

Opens Mon. Eve. March 4 thru Sat. Eve. March 23

Opening night at 7:30; All other Eves. at 8:30; Mats. Wed. and Sat. at 2:00

Evenings Mon. thru Thurs. Orch. $7.50; Loges $7.00
1st Balc. $6.00, 5.00; 2nd Balc. $4.00, 3.50, 3.00
Evenings Fri. and Sat. Orch. $8.00; Loges $7.50
1st Balc. $6.50, 5.50; 2nd Balc. $5.00, 4.50, 3.50
Sat. Matinees Orch. $6.00; Loges $5.50; 1st Balc. $4.50; 2nd Balc. $3.50, 3.00
Wed. Matinees Orch. $5.00; Loges $4.50; 1st Balc. $4.00; 2nd Balc. $3.00, 2.50

Word filtered in during intermission that Martin Luther King had been assassinated. "I might have had the leisure to put in the asterisks between the letters in Hyman Kaplan's name," wrote Richard Watts. "Otherwise, I think my verdict would have been unchanged even if issued without a national tragedy hanging over it."

lyrics whose main claim to distinction is in being the first musical to use the word "paradigm," does wonders. He is helped especially by the dances and musical numbers, very vigorously staged by Jaime Rogers. It is no accident that the first-night audience's biggest cheer went to a mass dance number, "I Never Felt Better in My Life," given by the about-to-be-deported aliens on Ellis Island. This had real excitement. Unusually for a musical, *H*Y*M*A*N* seemed to get better as it went along, and one reason for this was the very likable performers. Tom Bosley as Hyman, roly-poly, argumentative, opinionated and yet curiously lovable if only for a streak of humility running like a backbone down his arrogance, has a good part, and does it easy justice. Never descending to caricature, Bosley, whether singing, dancing or just plain acting, was consistently admirable. He did, however, nearly have the show stolen from him by Hal Linden, a model of smug authority as the self-satisfied husband that Rose's mother has picked out for her in the old country. Linden, exuding complacency out of his very pores, has only one number, "Old Fashioned Husband," but this he did brilliantly, and he made this bridegroom-to-be so dazzlingly unpleasant that he was even able to win your sympathy. Just two things still puzzle me about *H*Y*M*A*N K*A*P*L*A*N*. First, remembering (or at least recalling) some of the numbers that were retained, I wonder what the ones were like that were dropped on the road. And, second, where did Mr. Kaplan get all those asterisks in his name?

MARTIN GOTTFRIED, *WOMEN'S WEAR DAILY*

If there is ever an original cast album of *The Education of H*Y*M*A*N K*A*P*L*A*N* (and I doubt it), it ought to be released on 78 rpm records. The musical that opened last night is a parade of Forties–early Fifties musical comedy clichés and virtually a parody of the kind of direction that George Abbott provided at that time. Mr. Abbott has also directed this production and his work includes a Jewish mother who sings like a Broadway belter and a second male lead who manages to combine the grinning baritone of a John Raitt with Ethel Merman's grace notes. The old time show-biz goes even beyond this—probably half the songs begin with drum rolls and the jokes run to things like "So it got quiet, like the garment center on Christmas Eve." This is a show that goes beyond the dreadful, beyond camp. Benjamin Bernard Zavin's book is based on Leo Rosten stories, spiced—a better word would be smothered—by the unmistakable contributions of Mr. Abbott. There is no sense carping on the inadequacies of its writing nor in putting down the hackneyed and even trashy music by Paul Nassau and Oscar Brand (though it is amusing that they once complained that Broadway was distorting their artistic inclinations [in connection with their 1966 *A Joyful Noise*]). Still, there were some good things, mostly the choreography of Jaime Rogers. Rogers has been cheated out of credit for some very fine dances in other Broadway musicals [notably *Golden Boy* (1964)] but this time his name is right on the program and his work, as usual, is splendid. Oh, on a couple of occasions he falls into Broadway clichés too, but then this show seems to have been financed with them. Most of the time, Rogers is stylish and energetic, and his Ellis Island immigrant dance is wonderfully dignified. It also almost entirely avoids being influenced by Jerome Robbins' *Fiddler on the Roof* work and considering the similarity of subject matter the avoidance was almost impossible. Tom Bosley played the title role with his usual geniality and was in very good voice. Barbara Minkus was almost okay—even often—until the old pizazz creeped in to reveal the tin fakery in her plain lady. But Hal Linden was absolutely swell as the villain of the piece (the man contracted to be her husband)—a natural comic with a fine voice. But what does any of this mean when the show ends—I swear it—with the pledge of allegiance?

RICHARD WATTS, JR., POST

*The Education of H*Y*M*A*N K*A*P*L*A*N* faced one of the most abominable ironies in the annals of senseless American violence in its first performance at the Alvin Theatre last night. It is a musical comedy celebrating the glories of the national dream as learned by an eager immigrant, and, as the audience was filing back for the second act, it heard of the assassination of Martin Luther King. The shock destroyed any possibility of appreciating the fun of cheerful make-believe. Unfortunately, too, it is not a very entertaining show to begin with. It makes for a flat and essentially unexhilarating evening. It is sometimes believed that, if newspaper play reviewers had more time to work on their notices, they might be more creditable examples of writing and criticism. With additional time at my typewriter, I might have had the leisure to put in the asterisks between the letters in Hyman Kaplan's name, which he thought of as stars to express his patriotism for a new land. Otherwise, I think my verdict would have been unchanged even if issued without a national tragedy hanging over it.

·   ·   ·

By late 1968 there was little place on Broadway for a "pleasant" musical. (It seemed like there was little place for any musical, in fact. There hadn't been a hit since *I Do! I Do!* in 1966.) Had it been considerably better, *H*Y*M*A*N K*A*P*L*A*N* would have *still* been a hard sell; even the theatre parties didn't want it. Opening night was dramatic, at least, with Mayor Lindsay rushing out of the theatre mid-performance to quell a potential riot in Harlem. Producers will do anything for publicity, it seems, so a week after the opening the *H*Y*M*A*N* men sent out a release heralding that they were donating that night's receipts (if any?) to King's Southern Christian Leadership Conference, with Sammy Davis making a speech during intermission. This swelled attendance, no doubt. If *H*Y*M*A*N* accomplished little else, it did get Hal Linden out of the shadows. His performance (in a small role) was universally praised, the prominence thus afforded leading directly to the lead in *The Rothschilds* (1970).

BROADWAY SCORECARD

/ PERFS: 28 / $: –

RAVE	FAVORABLE	MIXED	UNFAVORABLE	PAN
	3		2	1

EUBIE!

"A New Musical Revue"

music by Eubie Blake (1883–1983)

lyrics by Noble Sissle and others

"devised and directed" by Julianne Boyd

"choreographer and tap choreography" by Henry LeTang; "chore-ographer and musical staging" by Billy Wilson (replacing Dana Manno)

produced by Ashton Springer in association with Frank C. Pierson and Jay J. Cohen

with Ethel Beatty, Terry Burrell, Leslie Dockery, Lynnie Godfrey, Gregory Hines, Maurice Hines, Mel Johnson, Jr., Lonnie McNeil, Janet Powell, Marion Ramsey, Alaina Reed, and Jeffery V. Thompson

opened September 20, 1978   Ambassador Theatre

WALTER KERR, *TIMES*

If you don't know when to applaud at *Eubie!*, Gregory Hines will tell you. *Eubie!* is the new cabaret-style musical celebrating the tunes of composer Eubie Blake, who happens to have been the first man to move an all-black show from Harlem to Broadway and storm the town with it. (That was in 1921, and the show was called *Shuffle Along*). And Gregory Hines is a dancer, though that is rather understating the fact. Hines has a brother—Maurice is his name—with whom he mostly works, and when the two of them rattle their tap-shoes along the tops of barrels and crates to the beat of "Dixie Moon," you feel fairly certain that sooner or later they'll drill a hole through a barrel, a crate, or the stage floor itself and promply vanish into it. But toward the end of *Eubie!*'s second act, Gregory gets to do a solo stint called "Hot Feet." Hurtling through space at a speed only slightly faster than light, Hines senses that the audience is about to explode with enthusiasm. "Not yet,

not yet!" he cries, throwing himself onto a little circular bench and con-
centrating on nothing more than the remarkable sounds coming from
his heels and his toes. Approaching another crescendo, he forestalls
interruption: "I'll tell you when!" he calls out. And, a couple of cyclonic
spins later, he gives us fair warning: "Soon!" Finally, when it's perfectly
obvious that his shoes must go to the repair shop, he exults, "Now!"
And, of course, the pent-up house comes down. It takes a pro to do a
thing like that. If *Eubie!* doesn't have the powerhouse impact of a similar entertainment, the Fats Waller album called *Ain't Misbehavin'*
[1978], it's partly because its numbers are so distributed that we don't
get to know the performers as well and partly because Waller had, as a
composer, a more original mind. Blake is much more content to work
within the standard Tin Pan Alley phrasings of early jazz ("There's a
Million Little Cupids in the Sky," "Oriental Blues"). He's fine at that,
though, and the over-all styling places Blake in a special time and a special atmosphere, honorably.

CHRISTOPHER SHARP, *WOMEN'S WEAR DAILY*
Whether or not Eubie Blake's music has the powers of a fountain of
youth, it has the effect of turning a heterogeneous audience into a har-
monious crowd of youthful spirits. But Blake—who is still an active
music man at age 95—has something magical about him. He comes from
an age that included personalities like Leo Tolstoy, Henry James and
Queen Victoria, and from a world that was peopled with the likes of
Scott Joplin and Fats Waller. Blake is old black magic in the flesh, and the
revue of his songs at the Ambassador Theatre has the impact of a magical tapestry set into sound. *Eubie!* doesn't present the sophisticated,
many-things-happening-at-once sounds of *Ain't Misbehavin'*. Like the
lines in the Bible, Blake's songs give very simple ideas the echo of eter-
nity. His most famous song, "I'm Just Wild About Harry," doesn't explain
very much at all in words and it doesn't develop musically, but somehow
the song says everything. Obviously Blake never intended to be the kind
of composer who develops an idea in a song. Blake's ideas are immediate,
because he has a gift for finding a sound that captures a total experience.
His best songs have as many shades of color as the skin of a rainbow
trout, but it takes him only a couple of seconds to present that spectrum.
The production at the Ambassador is particularly apt because of the way
it matches the variety of color in Blake's music with sets and performers

who also present many facets. There is a lot of exciting tap dancing, too. My only reservation is that the show didn't really pull out all the stops to excite the audience. This is the kind of show where that is called for, and "I'm Just Simply Full of Jazz" simply wasn't big enough to get the audience buzzing at intermission. But the show ends with a finale that will possibly keep your toe tapping through the night.

○   ○   ○

When an unlikely show becomes a smash hit, the next seasons tend to bring a handful of carbons of said unlikely show. But said unlikely show must of necessity have contained *something* out of the ordinary—like the larger-than-life exuberance of Fats Waller, as magically recaptured in *Ain't Misbehavin'*—to account for its uniqueness. *Eubie* offered a modicum of entertainment, but none of the dynamite of the Waller show. But then, Eubie Blake himself had none of the larger-than-life qualities—physically, personality-wise, or musically—of the younger, sassier, piano-playing showman. If an outright, stand-'em-in-the-aisles, record-breaking smash like *Ain't Misbehavin'* comes along once every fifty years or so (the last one being Eubie Blake's own *Shuffle Along*), why should anyone expect the next black songwriter anthology to do the same? Especially if it has the misfortune to open during a newspaper strike. What *Eubie* did have was thirty-two-year-old tap dancer Gregory Hines, formerly of the family act Hines, Hines and Dad. (*Eubie* also featured tapping brother Maurice, but not Dad. The brothers had danced on Broadway before—Gregory was eight—in the 1954 Sigmund Romberg operetta *The Girl in Pink Tights*, choreographed by Agnes de Mille.) In less time than it takes to whistle "I'm Just Wild About Harry," Gregory displayed that he was not just another tap dancer, and that whatever the fate of *Eubie*, he would indeed be back.

BROADWAY SCORECARD
/ PERFS: 439 / $: –

RAVE	FAVORABLE	MIXED	UNFAVORABLE	PAN
1	4	1		

EVITA

an import of the 1978 British musical

music by Andrew Lloyd Webber

lyrics (and libretto) by Tim Rice

based on events in the life of Eva Duarte Perón (1919–1952)

directed by Harold Prince

choreographed by Larry Fuller

produced by Robert Stigwood in association with David Land

starring Patti LuPone, Mandy Patinkin, and Bob Gunton

with Mark Syers and Jane Ohringer

opened September 25, 1979   Broadway Theatre

CLIVE BARNES, *POST*

[Headline: "A Stunning *Evita* Seduces with its Gloss"]

When was the last time you came out of a musical humming the politics and then not being quite sure what those politics were meant to be? *Evita* is a stunning, exhilarating theatrical experience, especially if you don't think about it too much. I have rarely if ever seen a more excitingly staged Broadway musical. Its director Harold Prince has designed and developed a virtually faultless piece of Broadway fantasy that has shadow exultantly victorious over substance, and form virtually laughing at content. This pop-opera, by Andrew Lloyd Webber and Tim Rice, is wonderfully entertaining in everything but the aftertaste of its pretensions. But don't cry for them anyone—this deserves to be a sizeable hit. Seeing it in London I suggested that it could perhaps have been called *Springtime for Evita*. Such a point was obvious, and was taken by the authors and Prince in the preparation of this significantly changed Broadway version. It needed to be radicalized. Here the social criticism, embodied in the unlikely but dramatic presence of Che Guevara as occasional mock participant and bitterly ironic commentator, has been strengthened and emphasized. They have upped the Brechtian atmosphere—but unfortunately Brecht himself was not around. The fault of the whole construction is that it is hollow. We are expected to deplore Evita's morals but adore her circuses. We are asked to accept a serious person onstage, and yet the treatment of that person is essentially superficial, almost trivial. The gloss of the surface is meant to be impenetrable—and it is. But what a gloss! Everything Prince has ever learned from himself, Robbins, Fosse and Bennett is here practically etherealized. Not a chance is missed and every chance is taken. All the performances are far better than in the London version, but never more so than in the casting of Miss LuPone as the whore with a heart that has a Swiss bank account number. This Evita of urchin grandeur spits aspiration, she dissolves in her own glory, she keeps her head, her style, her pocketbook and a voice that can belt like Merman and melt like Piaf. You must see *Evita*. For all the disappointments of its undelivered promises and eroded aspirations, it is a definite marker-point in the ongoing story of the Broadway musical. The performances are etched in the blood of expertise, and the masterly ingenuity of the staging will deservedly become a classic Broadway memory.

WALTER KERR, *TIMES*
[Headline: "A Bold Step Backwards"]
There's an eerily prophetic line close to the very opening of *Evita* that chooses to sing about the brief, bizarre life of Eva Perón and her joint rule of Argentina with her dictator-husband, Juan. The evening opens with the announcement of her death at 33. Che Guevara—complete with stogie, tam, fatigues and flowing mane—provides a mocking obbligato to the cries of mourning, cries that have the staccato ring of nails being driven into a coffin. The lady's coffin is not yet closed, though. That will be done by Che himself, slapping the great lid shut and sending clouds of dust flying into the bleak, steelwork sky. He then sings the couplet that is going to prove both accurate and, to the entertainment, damaging: "As soon as the smoke from the funeral clears/We're all gonna see she did nothing for years." That is precisely the problem confronting director Harold Prince and the authors. As they have charted out the enterprise, we almost never see any of [the major plot events] happen dramatically onstage. We hear about them at second-hand, mainly from the omnipresent Che who slips in and out

among the dancers to tell us that dirty deeds are afoot. Whenever Che is briefly silent, we are getting the news from lyrics or recitative sung by top-hatted aristocrats, breathless messengers, almost anyone at hand. It is rather like reading endless footnotes from which the text has disappeared, and it puts us into the kind of emotional limbo we inhabit when we're just back from the dentist but the novocaine hasn't worn off yet. This keeps us permanently outside the action. Because vital scenes are simply absent, there are no conclusions, no judgments, we can arrive at on our own. The evening is not boring, though the Rice-Webber score sometimes sounds as though Max Steiner had arranged it for Carmen Miranda; the lyrics, however, lack the odd and very human perceptions that often distinguished *Jesus Christ Superstar* [1971]. If your curiousity stays alive at *Evita* in spite of all the undramatized hearsay that isn't going to satisfy it, it's due to the authoritative crackle of ringmaster Prince's whip. Listen, the whip says. You listen. And go home wondering why the authors chose to write a musical about materials they were then going to develop so remotely, so thinly.

HOWARD KISSEL, *WOMEN'S WEAR DAILY*

Like *Jesus Christ Superstar*, *Evita* is history seen as a form of show business. Since Eva Perón was more directly related to show biz than Jesus, one would expect the Rice/Lloyd-Webber material to be more pointed than their earlier show. Alas, it is only more banal. The best-known song in the score, "Don't Cry For Me, Argentina," starts with a paraphrase of the opening line of an old Latin standard, "Yours," veers off into the first line of "Rose Marie," then quotes a few consecutive phrases from Brahms' *Violin Concerto* before going off on its own. Another song blatantly recalls the Beatles' "Yesterday." Most of the music is characterless, often singsong—perhaps it was kept deliberately simple to guarantee we would be able to grasp Rice's banal lyrics. If the material is predictable, Harold Prince's staging is not. The permanent set, by Timothy O'Brien and Tazeena Firth, consists largely of girders and a moving bridge (rather like that in *Sweeney Todd*). [The London *Evita* predated *Sweeney*.] Flanks of spotlights in both wings make the acting space seem like a sports arena, a place for momentous contests. The starkness and austerity of the basic set are modified by an enormous, mobile movie screen, which, sometimes dominating the forestage, sometimes hovering almost subliminally at the back, projecting images of the real Eva, gives one the sense of watching an epic. The most exciting moments in the show are two stunningly staged political rallies, where Prince makes adroit use of every inch of stage space as well as the prodigious, specially designed technology. (All the stagecraft is enhanced by David Hersey's lighting, which gives everything an eerie, haunting glow.) There have been reports *Evita* has been modified since its London production, where there was concern the fascistic heroine was somehow being glorified. If she had been, it would at least have given *Evita* a perverse fascination—like the one that surrounds *Don Giovanni* or *Richard III*. As it is, Evita is an astringent character, too much an object of satire and moralistic comment ever to come to life, despite the admirable efforts of Patti LuPone. From its very title, *Evita* promises to be outrageous. It is as if a musical about Eva Braun were titled *Fraulein* or *Little Eva*. These days, however, we have outgrown outrage. The material takes us back to the Sixties, even while the stage craft propels us into the Eighties.

DOUGLAS WATT, *DAILY NEWS*
[Headline: "*Evita* Equals Empty and is Vulgar to Boot"]
There's a great big gap in the middle of *Evita*, and the name of the gap is Evita, the popular name for Eva Duarte Perón. For that matter, there's not much around the gap, either. This new work by the creators of *Jesus Christ Superstar* is as spectacularly vulgar, in its way, as its predecessor, but whereas the earlier piece was exhilarating, the new one is dispiriting and even pointless. Lloyd Webber's score, while melodic and musically literate, is rather staid, and in spite of its concessions to South American rhythms it is about as Latin as a steak-and-kidney pie. It consists entirely of set pieces (there is no spoken dialogue), and its stiffness is at least partly due to Rice's plodding lyrics ("although she's dressed to the nines, at sixes and sevens with us . . ." and "the people, they need to adore me, so Christian Dior me" or "I'm their Savior, that's what they call me, so Lauren Bacall me"). A great deal of fine talent and energy have been expended, but *Evita* is a dud. Maybe *Che*?

•   •   •

Like *Jesus Christ Superstar*, *Evita* began its stage odyssey as a highly successful concept record album. But while the Nazareth tuner was a collection of pop-rock songs given a glossily theatrical production, in

Evita the songs themselves were highly theatricalized. Much credit for this goes to Harold Prince, whose editing and focusing powers had been keenly developed in a decade of Sondheim collaborations. (*Evita* opened in London on June 21, 1978, just before Prince turned to *Sweeney Todd* [1979].) The person in the director's chair had become an increasingly key force in the musical theatre, at least in good musical theatre. Robbins, Fosse, and Bennett all ruled (and at times terrorized) their writers in an effort to get what *they* wanted on the stage. The two Georges—Abbott and Kaufman, of the old school—formed and molded their songwriters' contributions, too, but they were accomplished librettists as well as directors. Unlike the others, Prince was neither choreographer nor writer; his producing skills, though, proved an immense help in assembling and coordinating the work of the writers and the increasingly crucial design team. A strong directorial hand in itself doesn't guarantee success, as Prince himself demonstrated in his post–*Evita* string of ill-conceived ventures (*Merrily We Roll Along* [1981], *A Doll's Life* [1982], *Grind* [1985], and *Roza* [1987]). Prince didn't write these, of course, but when dealing with concept musicals, the "conceptor" must be held accountable. *Evita*, though, was all to Prince's credit, his guidance transforming Lloyd Webber and Rice's not-uninteresting song album into a dazzling stage entertainment. *Evita*'s libretto was more like a string of singing postcards than a traditional book, but this fit in with the show's pseudo-documentary aspect. It all proved highly workable, thanks in large part to the use of the highly powered narrator/character Che (who seems descended from the Master of Ceremonies of *Cabaret* [1966] and the Reciter from *Pacific Overtures* [1976]). The score itself is quite good, towering over Lloyd Webber's other efforts. Sure, there's a tendency toward musical repetition—which can easily happen when the evening is all music and the composer isn't Sondheim or Bernstein or Weill—and the overabundance of sung dialogue set to heavily percussive syncopation eventually becomes droning. But there are also more than a half dozen fine songs, certainly a rarity in musicals of the 1970s, and Hal Prince's supervision of the entire enterprise was instrumental in making *Evita* intriguing and exciting. And it did just fine, despite a grumpy reception by the gentlemen of the press. Sir Andrew and the Prince Dept.: It is no accident that Lloyd Webber's two most successfully crafted works are his Prince musicals, *Evita* and the 1986 *Phantom of the Opera*.

Winner of the New York Drama Critics' Circle Award. In addition to winning the Tony Award for Best Musical, Tonys were won by Andrew Lloyd Webber and Tim Rice (score), Tim Rice (book), Harold Prince (director), Patti LuPone (actress), Mandy Patinkin (supporting actor), and David Hersey (lighting design).

BROADWAY SCORECARD
/ PERFS: 1,566 / $: +

RAVE	FAVORABLE	MIXED	UNFAVORABLE	PAN
1		1	2	2

FIDDLER ON THE ROOF

an "original star" revival of the 1964 musical

music by Jerry Bock

lyrics by Sheldon Harnick

book by Joseph Stein

based on the 1894 short story collection *Tevye and His Daughters* by Sholem Aleichem

original direction and choreography by Jerome Robbins, reproduced by Ruth Mitchell (direction) and Tommy Abbott (choreography)

produced by Nederlander Productions, Inc., The Shubert Organization, and the John F. Kennedy Center for the Performing Arts, in association with Theatre Now, Inc.

starring Zero Mostel

with Thelma Lee, Ruth Jaroslow, and Paul Lipson

opened December 28, 1976   Winter Garden Theatre

CLIVE BARNES, *TIMES*

Everyone must be entitled to a favorite musical. Mine, apart from *Aida*, is *Fiddler on the Roof.* I have seen it about 15 times, and always with pleasure. I customarily cry in the same places and spend all of the finale surreptitiously dusting down tears. I shall always remember how I first heard of *Fiddler.* I was living in London. Jerome Robbins was passing through. He called from the airport, I think I was interviewing him. I asked him what he was doing. He said a musical based on Sholem Aleichem. I said: "Nice! Off-Broadway?" He said, no—it was a big show, big. I said: "Nice!" I always believe in humoring geniuses. But a *musical* based on Sholem Aleichem? On Tuesday night, that musical returned for a limited run. It was heaven. Come to think of it, the show should never have left New York. It should be a fixture, like the Empire State Building. I had [seen Mostel in the role], of course, but never wrote about him. Almost every other Tevye, from Luther Adler onward, became part of my critical territory. But never Zero. And now, I am speechless. *Fiddler* is a celebration of two people, Mr. Robbins and Mr. Mostel. Two people who are less than close. The book, music, lyrics were all superb. But the chemistry was Robbins and Mostel. Now that chemistry is back. Mostel does indeed bring something quite extraordinarily special to the show. Mostel is an outrageous actor and, quite probably—even perhaps quite definitely—should not be encouraged. He does go too far. In the present *Fiddler*, he is almost being paid to see how far he is willing to go and, like many of our greatest actors, he is self-indulgent. At times he seems to be adlibbing, his eyebrows pierce heavenward with a downright exaggeration, and his eyes boggle at the drop of a joke. Mostel never plays anything other than Mostel. This should be ghastly, but simply because Mostel happens to be so interesting, it works like a grand slam. Mostel gambles everything on being Mostel. It is a fascinating, daring spectacle. Mostel has no real right to be charming, but he could charm the birds off the trees in a deserted aviary. He is the kind of monster you would unavailingly search Loch Ness for, and, in passing, make into a legend.

WALTER KERR, *TIMES*

[Headline: "Zero Mostel is a Force of Nature"]

I am sorely tempted to pronounce Zero Mostel simply unreviewable and let it go at that. What is one to say of him? That he is a magnificent, wholly legitimate, actor capable of tearing your heart out as he bends himself double, brow pouring sweat, over the milkcart he must push on alone? No, you can't quite say that, indelible as the image is, because just a few minutes earlier he has been bringing down the house with a cross-eyed grimace—tongue lolling wildly—contorted enough to resurrect vaudeville, burlesque, and possibly the commedia dell'arte in one great swivel of his head. The swivel undercuts the sweat, the seriousness of the second image can't be taken at face value because of what the man has so recently been doing with his face. Do you treat him as a clown, almost as a king among clowns, because the manic impulse to which he so frequently surrenders is, for him, irresistibly real, a seizure rather than a posture, an inspiration from his *daimon* rather than a reflex acquired during long years of stand-up entertaining? The professional fool intercepts the great actor, the role the actor is playing inhibits the fool—somewhat. Zero Mostel is a mighty presence rather than a completely honest performer, so enormous in his nimble bulk and so violent in his willed impact that he doesn't invite judgment, he defies it, successfully. You can measure what he's doing, if you want to; but it's not going to get you anywhere, he's going to roll right on over you no matter what. . . . When *Fiddler* first opened in 1964, I was among the very, very few who felt that its promise and real achievement had been compromised in an effort to make deeply affecting but "downbeat" materials safely commercial. Naturally I went back hoping to see the error of my ways, not theirs. I'm still troubled. Of course there are heart-warming passages to be cherished, just so long as the entertainment sticks reasonably close to its ethnic roots. But some of the line-gagging is less than the occasion demands; the ballads written for three interchangeable pairs of young lovers are themselves interchangeable enough to go into almost any other show; and the danced nightmare, so important to the narrative, still seems to me the least well-defined of Mr. Robbins's contributions to the musical comedy stage. Call me stubborn. It won't hurt *Fiddler*.

* * *

Zero Mostel *was* Tevye. And after nine months in the original Broadway production, producer Hal Prince sent him out to pasture. For Mostel had stopped playing Bock-Harnick-Stein-Robbins-Aleichem's

Tevye as soon as the reviews were in; it became Tevye Mostel, with the immensely inventive actor "inventing" and changing what the creators had painstakingly wrought. Expecting a handsomely lucrative renewal contract, the star was no doubt stunned by the sudden loss of his role-of-a-lifetime, and his larger-than-life persona made it difficult for him to find suitable acting roles. Zero's only (brief) Broadway visit in the next decade was in Alex Cohen's bewildering and overblown 1974 version of James Joyce's *Ulysses in Nighttown*; a 1968 vehicle, the Robbins-Bernstein-Sondheim-Guare-Brecht *A Pray for Blecht*, never made it past the workshop stage. (We may remain forever grateful that Mel Brooks created Max Bialystock for Mostel in the 1968 film *The Producers*.) *Fiddler*, meanwhile, ended its record-breaking run in 1972 and a group of theatre owners, counting potential touring profits, were glad to invite Mostel back to Anatevka with a deal worth his weight in gold. So Zero hit the road, despite failing health. Within four months of his final *Fiddler* performance, the sixty-two-year-old Mostel died on September 8, 1977 (during the pre-Broadway tryout of *The Merchant*, Arnold Wesker's adaptation of Shakespeare's Venetian comedy).

BROADWAY SCORECARD

/ PERFS: 167 / $: +

RAVE	FAVORABLE	MIXED	UNFAVORABLE	PAN
3	3			

FIDDLER ON THE ROOF

another revival of the 1964 musical

music by Jerry Bock

lyrics by Sheldon Harnick

book by Joseph Stein

based on the 1894 short story collection *Tevye and His Daughters* by Sholem Aleichem

directed and choreographed by Jerome Robbins; Ruth Mitchell, associate director

produced by Eugune V. Wolsk and James M. Nederlander

starring Herschel Bernardi and Maria Karnilova

with Ruth Jaroslow and Paul Lipson

opened July 9, 1981   New York State Theatre

RICHARD F. SHEPARD, *TIMES*

If you were a rich man, you couldn't buy a better show than the joyous recreation of *Fiddler on the Roof*. You can't dismiss it as a rerun of the Broadway hit that ran for 3,242 performances from 1964 to 1972. It's more than that. Tradition. That's what it is. Mr. Bernardi has a wonderful way with the person of Tevye. With his sagging shoulders and weary walk that mask a strength of body and character, he is the very essence of the poor man who perseveres through family *tsuris*, through pogrom, through uprooting. Bernardi is so much at home as Tevye, you might, in momentary lapse of fancy, imagine that you are listening to Sholem Aleichem, in original Yiddish. Higher praise you won't get. *Fiddler* will run for seven weeks at Lincoln Center. If you have not seen it live, you will have the thrill of discovery. If you have seen it before, there is the thrill of rediscovery.

DOUGLAS WATT, *DAILY NEWS*

Anatevka isn't Shangri-la or even Brigadoon; it's better than both—real people live there. Vanishing into the countryside dust stirred by the gathering storms of early 20th Century Russia, the hamlet lingers in our hearts and minds. This is a classic musical, and as a summer attraction at Lincoln Center it's utterly captivating. Herschel Bernardi, who has been playing Tevye off and on since the village milkman didn't have songs (he was here and on the road in the early '50s in *The World of Sholem Aleichem* [1953]), is starred in the role he inherited from the late Zero Mostel during the Broadway run and which he held for two years to be succeeded by practically everybody except Barbra Streisand, and he is perhaps the most authentic Tevye of them all. Without the huge, commanding presence of Mostel in the lead (though it's unlikely that even he could have been so all-encompassing in this vast theatre) the excellence of the show as a whole is more evident, particularly the rare value and beauty of Jerome Robbins' choreography and overall direction. With its sense of the changes in the air in 1905 Russian society, at a time when the great Jewish emigration to America was reaching flood tide, *Fiddler* remains an unusually compelling musical play, and for the time being the State Theatre has been turned into a heartwarming shtetl.

◦　　◦　　◦

Zero Mostel at his best was the best Tevye. But Zero was at his best for only about two and a half weeks. Herschel Bernardi followed Luther Adler as the third Broadway Tevye and remained for two years, leaving to create Tevye's Mediterranean stepbrother *Zorbá*. By many accounts he was the finest Tevye—other than Zero Mostel (at his best).

BROADWAY SCORECARD
/ PERFS: 53 / $: +

RAVE	FAVORABLE	MIXED	UNFAVORABLE	PAN
5	1			

THE FIG LEAVES ARE FALLING

"A New Musical Comedy"

music by Albert Hague

book and lyrics by Allan Sherman

directed by George Abbott (replacing Jack Klugman)

choreographed by Eddie Gasper

produced by Joseph Harris, Lawrence Carr, and John Bowab

starring Barry Nelson and Dorothy Loudon

with Kenneth Kimmins (replacing third-starred Jules Munshin), Jenny O'Hara, Jay Barney, Louise Quick, David Cassidy, Helon Blount, and Alan Weeks

opened January 2, 1969   Broadhurst Theatre

CLIVE BARNES, *TIMES*

Into each life some fig leaves must fall, but too many have fallen in mine. In fact, there is nothing much wrong with *The Fig Leaves Are Falling*, which last night boldly arrived at the Broadhurst Theatre, that a new book, new music, new lyrics, new settings, new direction, new choreography and a partially new cast would not quite possibly put right. The costumes were adequate. No, let me be fair, more than adequate [designed by Robert Mackintosh]. There have been worse stories for musicals, *East of Eden* for one [ref. the previous winter's *Here's Where I Belong*]. But unfortunately the author, Allan Sherman, has made some grave mistakes. In the first place, he loses all touch with human reality (and inhuman reality for that matter) when he has his hero live in Larchmont. Now it just so happens that I know a man who lives in Larchmont—my distinguished colleague Mr. Walter Kerr—and I just know that people are not like that in Larchmont. Mind you, Mr.

"The fig leaves are falling, ain't it appalling," to quote the title song. It rhymes, anyway. (artwork by Raymond)

Sherman, not content with Larchmont, also makes jokes about ballet and modern dance. The man must have some kind of suicide wish. But the real trouble with Sherman is his writing. This lacks something in wit, charm and imagination. His rhyming lyrics are more predictable than a railway timetable, which brings me to the music by Albert Hague. It reaches its nadir with a raucous spoof of rock circa Presley, and rarely gets up. It is music constantly busy going somewhere else in the wrong direction, and it is not so much old-fashioned as unfashioned. I would have imagined that better shows than this have closed in New Haven—probably even in Larchmont. But the director George Abbott is a game one, and he works like a beaver to get this one alive and running. He tries raffling a chicken in the auditorium (it smelled like a turkey to me). So what is good? One tremendous thing called Dorothy Loudon. She stopped the show [with "All of My Laughter"]— at least would have stopped it had it ever been properly started. Loudon is lovely, adorable, beautiful, wonderful, superb and the kind of girl every man wants to call mother. She has a voice from way back when, and a gleam in her eye never fiercer than when facing deflation. The important thing about her is that she is both lovable and vulnerable, so much so that I feel personally affronted at the way this show wastes her.

MARTIN GOTTFRIED, *WOMEN'S WEAR DAILY*
The Fig Leaves Are Falling is so naive as musical theatre and as a point of view that I feel out of proportion attacking it as menace. Yet, the show that opened last night is a dirty old man's product, not only in terms of sex but in terms of the reigning (but tottering) values that have gotten this country into the fix it is presently in. A fix represented by such productions as this. Like so many people who have let themselves grow old, *The Fig Leaves Are Falling* is frightened by America's youth revolution. The whole business of young idealism, with its insistence on humanity and decency, has boggled these old minds, threatening to tear down the only world it knows—the world of motels and suburbs and marital cheating. But there is one part of this revolution that this mentality finds very appealing and that, of course, is sexual freedom. Now *there* is something that appeals to those old men—all those mini-skirts willing to be lifted. This new show is hot for a peek under those skirts and then a dash right home to wife, family and approval (once the fun has been had). In short, the have your cake and eat it school of

American animal husbandry. That is the implication of the production. The point of all this seems to be that there is no difference between hippies, Yippies, black revolutionaries and supple young girls with long hair; that all their interests, from art to music to literature and politics, are silly; and that a marriage's value is measured by its longevity, not by its satisfaction. But only so long as the guy can have a sex vacation with a 24-year-old once in a while to give him a sense of masculinity (in fact, as emasculated men will dream it, this girl does all the seducing). I guess this is what happens when the defenders of the official morality get their hands on the ideas of young America.

RICHARD WATTS, JR., POST
It's all about how a husband with a nice wife and two attractive teenage children suddenly decides to break loose from his matrimonial bonds and go off with a pretty girl rather alarmingly called Pookie. Since the young temptress is played by the appealing Jenny O'Hara, whose sister Jill is scoring a triumph next door in *Promises, Promises* [1968], you might expect that the wife had quite a problem on her hands in trying to hold her errant spouse, but you would be wrong. Indeed, the cards are so heavily stacked against poor little Pookie from the start that one begins to fell sorry for the girl. Once Miss Loudon has started putting over her songs, the final decision is beyond question. Meanwhile there is a lot about modern youth, protest parades and the fatuousness of the middle-aged trying to ape the young. I thought the one witty moment arrived when a black [Alan Weeks] popped out and announced that he was the compulsory Negro in the show. . . . In several numbers, the members of the chorus appear scantily clad, and I can't say I felt it added to their attractiveness.

●   ●   ●

"The *Fig Leaves* are wilting before they fall," came the word from the Philadelphia tryout. Not a good sign. Allan Sherman was famous for a series of novelty record albums featuring fractured lyrics to old tunes. (Best known was the 1962 chart-topper *My Son the Folk Singer*, which featured that classic summer camp saga "Hello Mudduh, Hello Fadduh" set to Ponchielli's "Dance of the Hours.") This in itself did not qualify him for writing a Broadway musical, but then, lack of qualifications never stopped anybody. Sherman selected composer Albert Hague as his partner. Hague debuted in 1955 with the pleasing *Plain and Fancy*, but this was followed by a mediocre-to-poor score for the Gwen Verdon/Bob Fosse hit *Redhead* (1959); a far poorer score for quick flop *Cafe Crown* (1964); and a similar effort for this similar *Fig Leaves*. Hague's final show was the 1974 Bette Davis vehicle *Miss Moffat*, which closed in Philadelphia through no fault of the music (which was nonetheless pretty glum). For director they went right to the top and got—Jack Klugman? That's what the press releases say. Three months before rehearsals, actor Klugman made the best move of his directing career and hightailed it to Hollywood. The call went out to old man Abbott, who by the late '60s seemed to accept any salvage job that came his way. The show struggled through its tryout, the highlight of which was the exit of costar comic Jules Munshin. He was replaced by his understudy, although word around the theatre was that Sherman himself was angling for the part. On a family note, *Fig Leaves* featured Jenny O'Hara, whose sister Jill was strummin' her guitar next door to the Broadhurst in *Promises, Promises*, and eighteen-year-old David Cassidy, whose father, Jack, was clowning around on 52nd Street in *Maggie Flynn* (1968). Two lessons for would-be authors: it can be inadvisable to raffle off a turkey (or was it a chicken?) to the audience, lest the audience get the wrong idea; and it is exceedingly unwise to rhyme the title phrase of your title song, "The Fig Leaves Are Falling," with "ain't it appalling?" Needless to say, they repeated that line ad nauseum, literally so. Booking Dept.: The Broadhurst had been vacated by the long-running 1966 hit *Cabaret* (which was exiled to the barn-of-a-Broadway) to make way for *A Pray for Blecht*. This featured a Bernstein-Sondheim score, a libretto by John Guare, from Eric Bentley's translation of Brecht's *The Exception and the Rule*, and Zero Mostel, under the direction of Jerry Robbins. When producer Stuart Ostrow was forced to postpone—*Blecht* "wasn't ready," and never would be—*Fig Leaves* fell into the desirable Broadhurst. But not for long.

BROADWAY SCORECARD

/ PERFS: 4 / $: —

RAVE	FAVORABLE	MIXED	UNFAVORABLE	PAN
	1		2	3

THE FIRST

"A New Musical"

music by Bob Brush

lyrics by Martin Charnin

book by Joel Siegel with Martin Charnin (the latter in extremely small type)

based on events in the career of Jackie Robinson (1919–1972)

directed by Martin Charnin

choreographed by Alan Johnson

produced by Zev Bufman and Neil Bogart, Michael Harvey, and Peter A. Bobley

with David Huddleston (replacing Darren McGavin), Lonette McKee, David Alan Grier, Clent Bowers, Court Miller, Trey Wilson, and the voice of Red Barber

opened November 17, 1981   Martin Beck Theatre

FRANK RICH, *TIMES*

If you're going to do a musical about how Jackie Robinson broke the color barrier in major league baseball, there are two very difficult tasks that must be done right: you must find a singing actor who can imper-sonate the charismatic Robinson of legend, and you must find a method for simulating baseball games on stage. The paradox of *The First* is that both these tough demands have been met well—and that the mere rou-tine tasks of creating a musical haven't been met at all. While this show offers about five minutes of baseball and a promising star in David Alan Grier, its back is broken by music, lyrics, book and direction that are the last word in dull. *The First* is remarkably successful in draining the pas-sion out of an exciting true-life story. Joel Siegel and Martin Charnin's book consists of windy, if sincere, scenes that are written with all the fla-vor of a civics-class chalk talk. The structure that connects them is almost brazenly undramatic. It takes most of Act I merely for Robinson to sign his contract; in the meantime, the authors repeat or overexplain information, give us second-hand descriptions of offstage events and wander down blind alleys to introduce incidental characters. For humor, we generally get the slapstick antics of obese chorus members. Worse still, the librettists distance us from their central conflict—between Robinson and his more racist teammates. Presumably for legal reasons, the real-life story's villains are fictionalized here—but they are also turned into typical musical-comedy clowns. That is not acceptable. By making Robinson's antagonists into wholly buffoonish sit-com red-necks, the authors have trivialized and muted the real hatred that their hero had to face. While the baseball sequences are superbly done, Charnin's waxworks staging of the book scenes makes it hard to believe he's the same man who directed *Annie* [1977]. Time after time, we must watch actors sit around a table or desk—chatting in place, as if poising for an official photograph. The evening's fullest accomplishments belong to the designers—David Chapman (sets), Carrie Robbins (costumes) and Mark B. Weiss (lighting). Unlike the authors, they give the musical a colorful, Brooklyn ambience, and they use daring, abstract effects to take us smack into Ebbets Field for the two innings of ballplaying that end the evening. Yet even their inventive finale can't disguise the fact that *The First* is otherwise one long seventh-inning stretch.

DOUGLAS WATT, *DAILY NEWS*
[Headline: "*The First* Strikes Out"]
I don't know how else to say it: *The First*, a musical about Jackie Robinson that opened last night, never gets to first base. It seems to dawdle forever (it's quite long), and really has nothing more to tell us than what is implicit in the title, that Robinson broke the racial barrier in major league baseball, where only the ball had been white up to then, when Branch Rickey signed him for the Brooklyn Dodgers' farm club, the Montreal Royals, in 1946, and brought him down to Ebbets Field the following year. It may be that with a score of any quality—Bob Brush's music lends fresh meaning to the term commonplace—or lyrics of the slightest distinction—Martin Charnin's are only a cut above the music they accompany—*The First* would show some signs of movement. Actually, the moments of greatest interest are of a balletic nature as they show that noble team in silhouette before the game, or in prac-

tice (the players handle the ball well, and there's at least one good fungo hitter), or, in a detail, Robinson stealing a base. Only a genuine game could truly save the show, and the Beck stage can't quite accommodate one in spite of David Chapman's clean and clever stage designs. For a first act curtain we have the figure of Robinson on the field in his Brooklyn debut amidst catcalls, boos and the hurling of a watermelon which splits open at his feet. Actually, according to a friend who was there at the time, he was greeted with warm applause. And had *The First* followed suit, we could all have been out of the theatre a good hour earlier.

o   o   o

Time: April 1980. Place: Tax Accountant's office. Characters: a TV Drama Critic and a Big Broadway Director. Dialogue: Nice to meet ya, hey I got an idea for a musical. Result: a big tax loss. Cross-fade to the Eleven O'Clock News, November 17, 1981. ABC-TV invites New York's three major newspaper critics to pinch-hit for rookie librettist Joel Siegel (who is on leave, but has wisely not given up his day—or, rather, night—job). Richard Eder can't, as he is contractually obligated to the *Times's* radio station. Clive Barnes sends regrets, saying "I like Joel Siegel more than I liked the show." Doug Watt, however, tapes a cut-down version of his review (as above)—which ABC pulls at the last minute, leaving a hole in the broadcast. "After all," said the news director, "Joel is one of our boys." As for Martin Charnin, consider the Broadway (or Broadway-bound) musicals written or directed by him: *Annie*, on the one hand, and *Hot Spot* (1963), *Zenda* (1963), *Mata Hari* (1967), *La Strada* (1969), *Nash at Nine* (1973), *Two By Two* (1970), *Music! Music!* (1974), *I Remember Mama* (1979), *The First*, *Annie 2* (1990), and *Annie Warbucks* (1993) on the other hand. The moral—all my stories have morals—is that if you are going to have one lucky hit, it might as well be *Annie*.

BROADWAY SCORECARD
/ PERFS: 37 / $: –

RAVE	FAVORABLE	MIXED	UNFAVORABLE	PAN
	1	1	1	3

FLORA, THE RED MENACE

"The New Musical Comedy"

music by John Kander

lyrics by Fred Ebb

book by George Abbott and Robert Russell

based on the 1963 novel *Love is Just Around the Corner* by Lester Atwell

directed by George Abbott

choreographed by Lee (Becker) Theodore

produced by Harold Prince

with Liza Minnelli, Bob Dishy, Mary Louise Wilson, Cathryn Damon, Robert Kaye, Stephanie Hill, James Cresson, Dortha Duckworth, Joe E. Marks, and Louis Guss

opened May 11, 1965   *Alvin Theatre*

JOHN CHAPMAN, *DAILY NEWS*

[Headline: "Liza Minnelli Puts Needed Zing in Songs of *Flora*"]

In the title role of *Flora, the Red Menace* is Liza Minnelli, who looks rather like an underprivileged Jackie Kennedy and can put zing into a song even when the song doesn't have zing. An affectionately demonstrative audience was on her side last evening at the opening of the show. When the musical cuts away from the book and allows itself some sprightly song, dance and comedy turns—staged by Lee Theodore—it is most entertaining. When it has to get on with the plot, which may be less satirical than all the authors hoped, it seems to be marking time. It concerns itself with the less than hellish doings of a communist cell

HAROLD PRINCE

presents

A NEW MUSICAL COMEDY

"FLORA, THE RED MENACE"

Based on the novel "Love is Just Around the Corner" by LESTER ATWELL

with

LIZA MINNELLI

MARY LOUISE WILSON   CATHRYN DAMON   ROBERT KAYE

STEPHANIE HILL   JAMES CRESSON   DORTHA DUCKWORTH

JOE E. MARKS   LOUIS GUSS

and **BOB DISHY**

Book by

GEORGE ABBOTT and **ROBERT RUSSELL**

Music by
JOHN KANDER

Lyrics by
FRED EBB

Dances and Musical Numbers staged by **LEE THEODORE**

Settings by
William and Jean Eckart

Costumes by
Donald Brooks

Lighting by
Tharon Musser

Musical Direction by
Hal Hastings

Orchestrations by
Don Walker

Dance Arrangements by
David Baker

Original Cast Album — RCA Victor

Production Directed by **GEORGE ABBOTT**

ALVIN THEATRE

52nd ST. WEST of BROADWAY

Opens Tues. Eve. May 11

Matinees Wednesday and Saturday

Previews Wednesday, May 5 thru Monday, May 10

Nineteen-year-old Liza looks bright and eager, but I'd question the wisdom of drawing a bomb into the logo. With lit fuse, no less.

which the innocent Liza has been flimflammed into joining. About the worst this group can do toward wrecking the nation is to stage an arty and absolutely horrible symbolic ballet. The songs are bouncy, and they seem best when the unusual Miss Minnelli is singing them. In this, her first Broadway show, she should have quite a vogue.

WALTER KERR, *HERALD TRIBUNE*

Liza Minnelli, who no longer needs to be identified as Judy Garland's daughter and I apologize for just having done so, has many a fetching way about her. Her smile, for instance, is marvelously unsteady, always eager to shoot for the moon, always on the verge of wrinkling down to half-mast. Her profile, which seems to be made of what the children call Funny Putty or something like that, rambles upward nobly, like a crocus asserting itself before the weather has quite turned. To get even with the slippery uncertainty of her nose, her lower lip plunges forward in profound challenge, especially on the second syllable of two-syllable words. When, in *Flora, the Red Menace*, she sings her own name, Flora, she belts that final "a" out as though she were mad at it, and the effect couldn't be less angry, more childlike, or more charming. She also acts lyrics extremely well. As she sings "When it all comes true, it's a funny thing but the bells don't ring," you believe in her problem, her perplexity, and in the general perversity of life, love and show business. I am going to have to mention here a perversity of show business. The bells don't ring much in *Flora, the Red Menace*, either. George Abbott's new musical has George Abbott's neat abhorrence of nonsense. Most everything is straight, tidy, pretty much on the level. But was there really so little bubble to those faraway days, wasn't there—even in the worrying—more heart and more fun? Perhaps nobody wanted to get our heroine in too deep [as a Communist]. Is that why *Flora, the Red Menace* pulls its punches?

NORMAN NADEL, *WORLD-TELEGRAM & SUN*

[Headline: "Liza Minnelli Sings Her Own Tune"]

"I am me!" sang Liza Minnelli in ungrammatical exuberance, as *Flora, the Red Menace* reached its inconclusive conclusion last night. Here and there in the opening night audience lurked the suspicion that the authors had a second meaning in mind. It could be Miss Minnelli's declaration of artistic independence from her famous parents, film director-producer Vincente Minnelli and singer Judy Garland. In any case, it wasn't needed, because much earlier in the evening Minnelli had established, beyond the shadow of a doubt, that she is herself and no second-edition Judy. A man who described her as "this year's Barbra Streisand" also was missing the point. Liza is this year's Liza—individual, unduplicated and electrifying—and she will be a star on her own terms for as many years as she can and will give so generously of her talent, spirit and love. The girl has the face of a startled rabbit—wide, watchful eyes and an apprehensive upper lip. There is something charmingly gauche about her toe-in stance, and the way she charges into situations as if her physical momentum would overcome her inner trepidation. The aspect of blended innocence and courage make her perfect. The new musical slumps dangerously after intermission, after a first act which is a delight almost all the way. The sole redeeming scene of the second half is the ideological ballet, "The Tree of Life," which features, of all things, a fat ballet dancer. He is Neil J. Schwartz, and a prize. The ending is so poorly done that you don't realize the show is over until the cast starts parading onto the stage.

HOWARD TAUBMAN, *TIMES*

The comrades and the period that begot them should be ideal material for spoofing in a musical today, now that we are enjoying our post-McCarthy sanity and our unparalleled affluence. *Flora, the Red Menace* is an attempt to take advantage of this material. But, alas, this new musical has caught little of the flavor of the nineteen-thirties. As for poking fun at the comrades, it is as mechanical as a joke book and as simple-minded as a fable for infants. Even if one is charitable and views the musical as a mild parody, it is primitive. A promising idea has not been enlivened by a creative spark. The songs provide a little first-aid, but not enough to keep the musical pulsing vigorously. And Liza Minnelli brings her youth and eagerness to bear on the role, but her freshly burgeoning talent is not yet overpowering enough to save a faltering production. If one didn't know that Miss Minnelli is Judy Garland's daughter, one would suspect it. With her big eyes, tilted nose, generous mouth and bangs that fall over her forehead, she looks a good deal like her mother. But she also has a quality of her own. She sings one of the show's ingratiating songs, "A Quiet Thing," with a delicacy that speaks well not only for her self-restraint but for the discipline imposed by her wise and experienced director, Mr. Abbott. Tempting lightning to strike again, Kander and Ebb have tried to supply Minnelli with her "Over the Rainbow." She breaks into "Sing Happy," a bluesy number with a desperately nonchalant rhythm and with outbursts of passionate, lamenting sound. Minnelli lets herself go. The voice is not yet distinctive, but she can keep the rhythm pounding and driving, and can belt out the climactic tones. She can convey a human emotion in song. She is going to be a popular singer, all right.

*   *   *

Budding director Harold Prince made his debut in 1962 as out-of-town replacement on the ill-fated *A Family Affair*. The music was distinctive, so Prince—who in his spare time was producing shows like *Fiddler on the Roof* (1964)—invited composer John Kander (and his new collaborator, Fred Ebb) to work on what would become *Flora*. When the book-in-progress proved more than librettist Bob (*Take Me Along* [1959]) Russell could rustle, Prince's mentor Abbott was called in for a fix. Abbott and Prince and everybody naturally assumed that the Great Old Man should direct, so Mr. A. not-so-naturally assumed the directorial reins. Not-so-naturally, in that subversive satire founded on the red scares of the 1930s—and addressing the red purges of the 1950s—was not the sort of nonsense Broadway's no-nonsense septuagenarian had much truck with. (When asked to confirm that *Flora* was his 105th show, Abbott commented "Who cares about statistics? The important thing is whether the show is good or not.") Prince's direction of *Flora* might not have made the difference, but it would have certainly made *a* difference. The producer, though, was inarguably busy at the time. *Flora* was his fourth show of the season, following *Fiddler*, *Baker Street*, and the play *Poor Bitos*. He thereafter cut his activity down to one at a time. The nineteen-year-old Liza (with a Z) received one of the more staggering sets of opening night bouquets ever, with the critics having the sense to point out that she wasn't merely somebody's daughter. Not enough to put *Flora* over, though. Over the decades Minnelli would return to the Rialto at high and low ebb, always with material from her favorite songsmiths.

A Tony Award was won by Liza Minnelli (actress).

BROADWAY SCORECARD
/ PERFS: 87 / $: –

RAVE	FAVORABLE	MIXED	UNFAVORABLE	PAN
2		1	3	

FOLLIES

"A New Musical," previously entitled *The Girls Upstairs*

music and lyrics by Stephen Sondheim

book by James Goldman

directed by Harold Prince and Michael Bennett

choreographed by Michael Bennett

produced by Harold Prince in association with Ruth Mitchell

starring Alexis Smith, Gene Nelson, Dorothy Collins, John McMartin (replacing Jon Cypher), and Yvonne De Carlo

with Fifi D'Orsay, Mary McCarty, Ethel Shutta, Arnold Moss, Ethel Barrymore Colt, Michael Bartlett, and Sheila Smith

opened April 4, 1971   *Winter Garden Theatre*

CLIVE BARNES, *TIMES*

Follies is the kind of musical that should have its original cast album out on 78's. It carries nostalgia to where sentiment finally engulfs it in its sickly maw. And yet—in part—it is stylish, innovative, it has some of

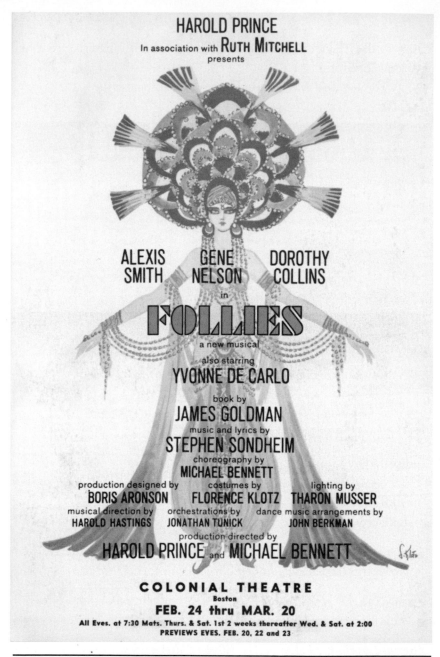

HAROLD PRINCE
In association with RUTH MITCHELL
presents

ALEXIS   GENE   DOROTHY
SMITH   NELSON   COLLINS
in

FOLLIES
a new musical

also starring
YVONNE DE CARLO

book by
JAMES GOLDMAN
music and lyrics by
STEPHEN SONDHEIM
choreography by
MICHAEL BENNETT

production designed by   costumes by   lighting by
BORIS ARONSON   FLORENCE KLOTZ   THARON MUSSER

musical direction by   orchestrations by   dance music arrangements by
HAROLD HASTINGS   JONATHAN TUNICK   JOHN BERKMAN

production directed by
HAROLD PRINCE and MICHAEL BENNETT

COLONIAL THEATRE
Boston
FEB. 24 thru MAR. 20
All Eves. at 7:30 Mats. Thurs. & Sat. 1st 2 weeks thereafter Wed. & Sat. at 2:00
PREVIEWS EVES. FEB. 20, 22 and 23

The pivotal role of Ben had not been cast when this herald for the Boston tryout was printed. The next-generation ad—with David Byrd's more familiar "cracked Statue of Liberty" design—listed Jon Cypher in the role ultimately created by John McMartin. Preliminary credits. (costume design by Florence Klotz)

the best lyrics I have ever encountered, and above all it is a serious attempt to deal with the musical form. A theatre [the home of the fictional *Weismann's Follies*] is being torn down. Weismann throws a reunion party, and all the Weismann girls out of the graveyard and the geriatric ward get together for one final bash. They sing a few of their old numbers and open up a few of their old sores. Among them are Buddy and Sally, and Ben and Phyllis. Years ago, in 1941, Buddy loved Sally, Sally loved Ben, Phyllis loved Ben, and Ben loved Ben. Buddy married Sally, Ben married Phyllis, but their marriages are not working out. (They rarely do in Stephen Sondheim musicals.) When, to give this all-too-eternal quadrilateral dramatic dimension, Goldman first has their lives intercut with the ghosts of their earlier selves, and finally puts all eight of them into an ironic Follies routine that is meant to comment on their personal and marital plights—by the faded beard of Pirandello he has gone too far. Sondheim's music comes in two flavors—nostalgic and cinematic. The nostalgic kind is for the pseudo-oldie numbers, and I must say that most of them sound like numbers that you have almost only just forgotten, but with good reason. This non-hit parade of pastiche trades on camp, but fundamentally gives little in return. It has all the twists and turns of yesteryear, but none of the heart. The lyrics are as fresh as a daisy. I know of no better lyricist than Sondheim—his words are a joy to listen to, even when his music is sending shivers of indifference up your spinet. The man is a Hart in search of a Rodgers, or even a Boito in search of a Verdi. There are many good things here—I think I enjoyed it better than the Sondheim/Prince last torn marriage manual *Company* [1970], and obviously everyone concerned here is determined to treat the musical seriously as an art form, and such aspiration must be encouraged. Yet perhaps too many little old ladies are passing by just lately.

MARTIN GOTTFRIED, *WOMEN'S WEAR DAILY*
[The mixed couples] story is the weakest part of the show, grasped by its makers as a device to hold it together despite their every impulse to throw it away. Sondheim and Prince finally did throw such stories away (with *Company* which, though produced last year, was conceived after *Follies*) because that is where their theatre has been leading. *Follies* was not quite ready to rely completely on concept as the organizational

replacement for a book, and so it falls back on the shaky support of a story. James Goldman was given short shrift by Prince and Sondheim, who were obviously more interested in the concept. Prince has made the show into a constant ballet—it is the most complete dance theatre since *Fiddler on the Roof* [1964]—and he has solved the problem of integrating choreography into his work by making Michael Bennett both choreographer and co-director. The music and movement are perpetual, the dances spectacular. As the showgirls take turns remembering and performing their old acts, the action blends seamlessly into spooky mirages from a show business carrousel. From solo turns to production numbers and finally into a miniversion of a full-fledged Follies show (turned expressionist), they have recreated the past with dazzling success. Nor is it ever camp, not ever, and that is important because the show is the antithesis of camp. *Follies* does not mock the past. Sondheim's work is stunning, though in choosing this show's theme he has willed himself into his most dangerous area as a composer. His score is a recreation of every song writer of the '20s and '30s. It is a brilliant trick, consummately pulled off—in the stunning lyrics as well as in the music—but it is a trick nevertheless and, anyhow, Sondheim has just got to stop his compulsive satirizing. He is much too good a composer for it. For all the mimicry of old show music, he has refreshed it with his own melodic invention, harmonic ingenuity, metric surprises and structural explorations. Moreover, Jonathan Tunick gave him what are surely the finest orchestrations in the history of the musical theatre (and that includes Weill and Bernstein). [The creators], and an orchestrated, enormous and fabulously talented company, achieve a structure of production that is quite nearly colossal, and for whatever the lapses and overlength of the show (no intermission and over two hours), *Follies* is utterly magnificent. Every other musical should have its faults.

WALTER KERR, *TIMES*
[Headline: "Yes, Yes, Alexis! No, No, *Follies!*"]
Follies is intermissionless and exhausting, an extravaganza that becomes tedious for two simple reasons: its extravagances have nothing to do with its pebble of a plot; and the plot, which could be wrapped up in approximately two songs, dawdles through 22 before it declares itself done. No one likes to dismiss the ingenuity that producer/director Harold Prince has splattered all over the Winter Garden stage—plat-

forms bearing jazz bands gliding in out of the dark, curtains made of candy-box lace raining down from the skies, the ghosts of showgirls past stalking in black-and-white butterfly wings through the ruins of a once-festive playhouse—but ingenuity without inspiration can quickly become wearing and we are not too long in our seats before we realize that no one on the creative staff has had an idea for the evening capable of sustaining its weight in silvered feathers. [Scenic design by Boris Aronson, costume design by Florence Klotz.] James Goldman has done the libretto; everyone else is rather grimly chained to it. It is trivial and unclear. The huge entertainment has nothing in mind but to introduce us to [the four fretting principals], let us watch them drift in and out among the other guests in groping search of one another, let us hear them state and restate in song the present temperatures of their lives, and then, in a burst of red top hats and tails, puts them through a remembered Follies performance ("Loveland") by way of exorcising their regrets. Why didn't Mr. McMartin marry Miss Collins in the first place?? No one really says. The fact that the musical pastiches do not have any real relationship to the marital squabbles at hand—the two marriages of the evening could be dropped into *Company* without fuss or loss or even anyone's noticing it—poses a serious problem for composer Stephen Sondheim, one I do not think he has solved: the need to fuse—in a cohesive score—these not-quite-remembered echoes with the contemporary cross-hatched love stories. He can't just split the score down the middle. He's caught half way, and the narrowness of the middle range grows monotonous. Mr. Prince is willing to make his musicals dark, or at least caustic, with liveliness worked in only where it is legitimate; and that is courageous. Unfortunately, the liveliness here is all left-field, and the legitimacy in the love-stories that ought to give the evening its solid foothold is skimpy and sadly routine.

DOUGLAS WATT, *DAILY NEWS*
[Headline: "A Stunning Musical About an Eerie Stage Reunion"]
A pastiche so brilliant as to be breathtaking at times. Indeed, it struck me as unlikely that the tools and resources of the Broadway musical theatre had ever been used to more cunning effect than in this richly imaginative work. Don't let the title mislead you. Nostalgia is not simply the undercurrent of the evening. It is the very subject of it. The follies are those committed by four people momentarily transported to the past.

For *Follies* is a ghost story taking place on the naked stage of a partially demolished theatre, to which a number of Follies performers, now either retired or in other walks of life, have been invited for a final reunion bash. The chilly place is inhabited by the shades of showgirls, pale-faced and gowned in black and white, who weave slowly about, striking poses on the iron stairs and platforms. They go unnoticed by the partygoers who file in wearing wide smiles as they come forward to peer into the once-familiar auditorium. It's going to be a fun night. . . . The scene is suddenly transformed, apotheosized, as lacy scenery envelops the stage and we are in "Loveland," a musical romance drenched with elaborate, costumed showgirls, painted and bewigged chorus people and strong echoes of the early Richard Rodgers and Kurt Weill. The four principals, first merely trapped in it, proceed to star in it each acting out his own folly. The scene is splintered and disappears as McMartin is doing his own grand turn. It is morning and, the Walpurgis Night over, the two couples are alone on stage as the daylight streams in through the gaping rear wall. They exit through it, separately, to resume their former lives.

◦   ◦   ◦

The Girls Upstairs began life as a mystery musical and transmuted into a ghost musical; it was ultimately overrun with ghosts of the past, ghosts of the present, and a ghost of a chance. The Stephen Sondheim/James Goldman piece was initially optioned by David Merrick and Leland Hayward, who let it languish. It was then undertaken by Stuart Ostrow, circa *1776* (1969), who was just then producing the (unproduced) Bernstein/Sondheim/Guare/Robbins/Mostel *A Pray by Blecht*. When Sondheim and Goldman parted with Ostrow, Hal Prince—who already had theatres booked for *Company*, which Sondheim wrote while waiting around for *The Girls Upstairs*—agreed to take on the piece, which was totally reconceived and rewritten and redubbed *Follies* (and came to be known, as things grew dire, as Hal Prince's *Follies*). As with *Company*, Sondheim's work was innovative, inventive, and stunningly theatrical. But while the script and production of the first Sondheim/Prince show supported the score, *Follies* was supremely overproduced, overscripted, and overghosted. Yes, the pallid black-and-white mannequins stalking the stage were stunning (although seemingly left over from Bennett's 1969 *Coco*). Yes, *Follies* was incredibly artistic, and there are many who consider it the most breathtakingly spectacular theatrical event ever (although I maintain that at least half of those who consider it the most breathtakingly spectacular theatrical event ever never actually saw it), but the artistic pretension itself caused *Follies* irremediable problem. (Did I say "pretension"? I meant "production." Really I did.) The opening moments of *Follies* seemed to be saying, "Look, folks, this is art." And the following sections added, "If you don't appreciate our art, that's your problem." At which point a sizable chunk of the audience was lost, and not going to be won back. No matter *what* the creators did, no matter how good the show was. Once they're gone, they're gone. All those people who considered it breathtakingly spectacular and went back repeatedly couldn't make up for the droves who were driven away (and spread the bad word to their friends). The score was ill-served by a truncated and notoriously sloppy cast recording, which, nevertheless, provided far more enjoyment than going and sitting through all those damn ghosts again. Yes, Sondheim could have written duets or quartets or octets for the leads battling with their former selves, and would surely have woven remarkable vocals in the process. He assiduously avoided doing this, though, save in two places: "Waiting for the Girls Upstairs," for the four leads and their counterparts, and the overstuffed soprano's Friml-ish "One More Kiss." Which were all the more stunning because they were his only such use of the device. Everybody else's work was "artistic" throughout, and boy, did they let us know it. *Follies*, with its exciting score and inarguably memorable trappings, was a show that merited repeat visits, with four being a pretty fair number. But it was awfully hard to get through the first time.

Winner of the New York Drama Critics' Circle Award. Tony Awards were won by Stephen Sondheim (score), Harold Prince and Michael Bennett (director), Michael Bennett (choreographer), Alexis Smith (actress), Boris Aronson (scenic design), Florence Klotz (costume design), and Tharon Musser (lighting design).

BROADWAY SCORECARD

/ PERFS: 522 / $: −

RAVE	FAVORABLE	MIXED	UNFAVORABLE	PAN
3	1	1	1	

42ND STREET

"The Song & Dance Extravaganza"

music by Harry Warren

lyrics by Al Dubin

book by Michael Stewart and Mark Bramble (briefly billed as "Lead-Ins and Crossovers by")

based on the 1932 novel by Bradford Ropes and the 1933 screenplay by James Seymour and Rian James

"Direction and Dances" by Gower Champion

produced by David Merrick

starring Tammy Grimes and Jerry Orbach

with Wanda Richert, Lee Roy Reams, Joseph Bova, Carole Cook, Danny Carroll, James Congdon, Don Crabtree, and Karen Prunzcik

opened August 25, 1980   Winter Garden Theatre

CLIVE BARNES, *POST*

[Headline: "Gower's Legacy"]

Life should never try to imitate art. It is too painful. Last night at the Winter Garden Theatre, Gower Champion had what was perhaps the biggest success of his considerable career with the David Merrick musical *42nd Street*. Champion was not around for the applause. He had died that afternoon, and a crumpled, virtually inaudible Merrick had to squelch the ovation with the announcement of his death. It all seemed more like show business than life, or, for that matter, death. For Merrick, this is a most formidable triumph—indeed, it may even be the first time an American show is actually better than its publicity. The idea of doing *42nd Street* originated with Michael Stewart, who saw the classic 1933 movie and felt that nearly 50 years later, Broadway was perhaps ready for it. He enlisted the help of Mark Bramble with the

A fairly pedestrian early ad for David Merrick's Song & Dance Extravaganza.

book—called here, oddly enough, "Lead-Ins and Crossovers"—got the rights and presented it to Merrick. The rest will probably be Broadway history, or at least a wildly tapping footnote to it. The result is a hit parade perfectly in period, perfectly adjusted to what there is of a story, and absolutely delightful. The huge heartbeat rhythms of Warren's music seem to call out for tap-dancing, and here the clicker-clack of 40 happy hoofers becomes, as it must, part of the musical fabric. The cast could scarcely be better. Tammy Grimes is superbly acidulated as the leading lady with a tongue so wicked that you suspect a jokewriter in the wings, a mordant wit and manner distant enough to offer a new dimension to hauteur. Jerry Orbach looked a little bit dour as the director (in retrospect, one cannot help wondering whether he knew something the rest of the cast did not) but his portrait of the celebrated Broadway toughie/softie, with his sad eyes and permanently ruffled attitude proved nicely done. The real triumph of *42nd Street*, which gets the new season off in a blaze of applause, belongs however to Merrick and Champion. It's great to have Merrick back—what was the man doing all those years away, gardening?—but here let us hear it for Gower for one last time. Not because the guy is dead, but because he is still, gloriously, gloriously, alive, somewhere between 42nd Street and the Winter Garden Theatre on Broadway. No one has to say: "Bye Bye Gower." He has left a permanent mark.

HOWARD KISSEL, *WOMEN'S WEAR DAILY*

It is hard to view *42nd Street* with objectivity. A week ago, from all reports, it seemed a musical geared for tourists and the expense account crowd. David Merrick's announcement that he would not open until he received word from On High added a bizarre note, though one suspected the God of Merrick, who took such an active interest in Show Business, might be a different deity from the God of Abraham, Isaac and Jacob. But the death of Gower Champion removed the frivolity, making it seem a Last Will and Testament. Even had the circumstances not been so sad, *42nd Street* would have been counted one of Champion's finest achievements, full of imagination, full of the old-fashioned showmanship for which he was justly celebrated. Under the cirumstances, however, what might have seemed glittering becomes unbearably poignant. Of the great choreographers of the last few decades, Champion was not a structural innovator. Nor did he weigh his steps down with much emotional freight. But he had other strengths—an almost infallible knowledge of how to make an audience's collective jaw drop (like a chorus streaming down a runway on the audience's side of the orchestra pit in *Hello, Dolly!* [1964]); and a film director's sense of composition, of how to make every inch of stage space count (the thrill of the telephone number in *Bye Bye Birdie* [1960] was that by filling the stage with cubicles, from the top down, he brought movement to space that generally remains dead). Both these gifts are used beautifully in *42nd Street*. Some of the numbers work simply because it has become rare to see so many dancers on a stage doing complicated steps with such precision and flair. Others like the "Shadow Waltz," which makes playful, witty use of shadows dancing across a large screen, and "Shuffle Off to Buffalo," an hommage to the coyer side of Busby Berkeley—have genuine cinematic sparkle. Moreover Champion had a marvelous gift for comic dance, here at its best in a dance where a new girl, wending her way through intricate steps for the first time, confuses everyone—though her mistakes are funny, the number miraculously never loses its flow and grace. Champion's musicals, at their best, had that ineffable magic, none more so than *42nd Street*.

FRANK RICH, *TIMES*

If anyone wonders why Gower Champion's death is a bitter loss for the American theatre, I suggest that he head immediately to the Winter Garden, where *42nd Street* opened last night. This brilliant showman's final musical is, if nothing else, a perfect monument to his glorious career. Indeed, *42nd Street* has more dancing—and, for that matter, more dancers—than Champion has ever given us before. As it fortunately happens, this show not only features his best choreography, but it also serves as a strangely ironic tribute to all the other musicals he has staged over the past two decades. See Champion's work in *42nd Street* and try not to weep. The excuse for the dances, of course, is the 1933 film that started Warner Brothers on its binge of backstage movie musicals during the Depression. In truth, the screen version of *42nd Street* did not have that many musical numbers, but David Merrick, the show's producer, has solved that problem by outfitting his stage extravaganza with a whole crop of other hits from the Harry Warren-Al Dubin song catalogue. With the aid of the best Robin Wagner sets, Tharon Musser lighting and Theoni V. Aldredge costumes that Merrick's money can buy, Champion has been given an unparalleled opportunity to let his considerable imagination go berserk. Unfortunately, as has frequently been the case for Champion in recent seasons, nothing else in his latest show comes close to matching the style and sheen of his handiwork. Part of the problem is the addition of all those numbers, which are so good and plentiful that they make the story seem an unwanted intrusion into the action. But an even greater difficulty has to do with the simple matter of tone. For the most part, we simply grin and bear the forced gaiety of the plot advancing scenes while waiting for Champion to get his dancers tapping once more. Given the show's uncertain attitude, the evening's stars are often left stranded. Then again, perhaps no performers can be expected to compete with this show's dance numbers or with the tragic real-life drama that surrounded the opening at the Winter Garden last night. The flaws of *42nd Street* are undeniably real and damaging. But, for now at least, they are nothing next to Gower Champion's final display of blazing theatrical fireworks.

*   *   *

Mike Stewart and Mark Bramble were sitting in the Carnegie Hall Cinema watching the 1933 movie musical *42nd Street* back during the production period of *The Grand Tour*, circa 1978 B.V. (Before Videocassette). "I wish we were working on *this* instead," said one to the other, and Broadway's grandest "Song & Dance Extravaganza" was born. Jerry Herman demurred, insisting they *had* to keep the original score—couldn't do it without "Shuffle Off to Buffalo," "You're Getting to be a Habit with Me," and the gaudy, bawdy title tune—so they dusted off the Harry Warren/Al Dubin catalogue to supplement the five songs used in the film. They gave the show to David Merrick—a mixed blessing, but they knew that if he said he would come up with thirty-six girls, he would indeed come up with thirty-six girls, amidst, as the early teaser ads said, "a cast of 54 (some younger)." When potential investors told Merrick the project was doomed, he decided to mount it out of his own pocket and began to run up $2.4 million worth of costs. (He bought out three small investors already in place, giving him complete control without any fiscal oversight whatsoever.) Things looked dire when *42nd Street*'s Kennedy Center tryout met a poor response. The show needed polishing, and Gower Champion was unable to do it. Champion had been ill for several years; a mysterious, lingering condition had first appeared during *Mack & Mabel* in 1974, postponing rehearsals, cutting short that show's tryout, and apparently contributing to its fatalistic outlook. When Champion appeared stuck for *42nd Street* improvements, Merrick "surreptitiously" imported director/choreographers Joe Layton and Ron Field for advice—and placed them in the audience, where the unsuspecting Gower haplessly stumbled upon them (a typical Merrick trick). What Merrick didn't know was just how ill Champion was—the director was undergoing constant blood transfusions in his Watergate Hotel room. *42nd Street* came to Broadway and mysteriously went back into rehearsal, as previews were postponed and the opening date was changed and changed and changed. The producer issued illogical statements, explaining that he was waiting for "the Great Man way up there" to send a courier telling him when to open. Merrick has finally gone nuts was the inference— and the press gleefully covered the story. (In fact, Merrick decided late in the Washington run that the two big pivoting towers on either side of the set *had* to be cleared totally off stage for the grand finale. It can't be done, he was told, because the pivoting mechanism was built into the onstage base of the towers. "Do it," he said. "We'll have to rebuild the whole thing," he was told. "Do it," he said. The show moved to New York without its set, causing the postponement. Other producers would have blamed the delay on technical problems; by issuing "crazy" pronouncements, Merrick kept the show in the news and interest mounting.) Merrick also decided to change the billing to reflect the style of old movie musicals; thus, the opening night program credited the librettists for "Lead-ins and Crossovers." The authors readily agreed, little knowing it would be interpreted as a nasty slam. Merrick quickly reinstated the "book" billing but the harm was done; at Tony time he apologized for costing the authors the award. *42nd Street* opened dramatically, with the curtain-call announcement of Champion's death earlier that day at the age of sixty. The combination of the show's ebullience and Champion's tragic but timely exit pushed *42nd Street* into quick sellout status and immense financial success throughout the English-speaking world.

In addition to winning the Tony Award for Best Musical, a Tony Award was won by Gower Champion (choreographer).

BROADWAY SCORECARD
/ PERFS: 3,486 / $: +

RAVE	FAVORABLE	MIXED	UNFAVORABLE	PAN
4	2			

FRANK MERRIWELL
(OR HONOR CHALLENGED)

"A New Musical"

music and lyrics by Skip Redwine and Larry Frank

book by Skip Redwine, Larry Frank, and Heywood Gould

based on the 1896 "dime novel" *Frank Merriwell, or First Days at Fardale* by Burt L. Standish [William Gilbert Patten]

directed and choreographed by Neal Kenyon

produced by Sandy Farber and Stanley Barnett in association with Nate Friedman

with Larry Ellis, Walter Bobbie, Bill Hinnant, Liz Sheridan, and Neva Small

opened April 24, 1971   *Longacre Theatre*

CLIVE BARNES, *TIMES*

George Jean Nathan—no mean critic, or at least no meaner than most—in the *American Mercury* for September, 1925, offered his opinion that Burt L. Standish, the pseudonymous author of *Frank*

Merriwell, was "one of America's most peculiarly eminent practitioners of the art of fiction. His curious song deserves to be sung." On Saturday night at the Longacre Theatre, Standish's "curious song" was sung. It needed to be sung better. *Frank Merriwell* is a musical even though the music is the least admirable aspect of a modestly deplorable venture. This is the kind of music that if you came out of the theater humming it, you would never notice. It is all too forgettable for description. The book was worse. It was too descriptive to be forgettable. The music and lyrics are distinctively undistinguished, and like the book, are more wrong-headed than any real head can comfortably accommodate. The performances suffer from everything else. However, I must make one exception. Bill Hinnant—who once made a Snoopy that even scared the Red Baron—is here cast as a Spanish spy, and on every entrance managed to interpolate a touch of insane sanity into the proceedings. Quite what Hinnant was meant to be doing I was never altogether sure, but when he was there he certainly raised my spirits, so that by the end I was breath-batedly waiting for his all too rare intrusions into a mood best described as morosement.

WALTER KERR, *TIMES*
[Headline: "Tonight We Open, Tonight We Close"]
Let me tell you about the new closings. I seem to have spent the entire week just past seeing plays that you will never see—do you feel jealous?—and I am sure that there is always a little something to be learned from the mishaps that hope for a thousand nights but wind up with only the one. *Frank Merriwell* was a very bad musical. You knew it was going to be a very bad musical in the first two minutes, before so much as a villain had slunk behind a tree. (The show did have a very good villain in Bill Hinnant, the erstwhile Snoopy of *You're a Good Man, Charlie Brown* [1967]; as Hinnant mangled a Spanish accent by multiplying sibilants, or imitated the sound his dynamite was shortly going to make in the heroine's ears, Snoopy would have been proud.) In the very first chorus number, while the students of Fardale College waited for Frank Merriwell to arrive by train, three girls marched in with picket placards proclaiming Fardale "Unfair to Women." With this incursion of Women's Lib into a spoof of turn-of-the-century college didoes, you knew that the authors had already lost their heads; no critic would be required to perform the

decapitation later. The evening was without wit or period feeling or panache, and it effectively disposed of the current notion that nostalgia works automatically, without help from men of talent and taste.

DOUGLAS WATT, *DAILY NEWS*
[Headline: "*Frank Merriwell* Gets Defeated By Broadway!"]
A dog. This is the first production to take advantage, if that's the word for it, of Broadway's new limited-gross agreement. This means that with the 14 actors working for scale ($164.50) and members of the other unions involved working below scale (at around $200 apiece), the show can get by with a $5 top provided the weekly gross does not exceed $25,000. (To meet this latter condition, the Longacre balcony is closed off.) Scenery and costume costs have been similarly cut. Now you might suppose that such limitations would fire the imaginations of all concerned. But there is no trace of imagination in *Frank Merriwell*. It simply has the pathetic appearance of a stunted little show trying to act and sound like its big brothers. It makes *It's Superman* seem, in retrospect, like a masterpiece.

◦   ◦   ◦

As had happened before, and as would happen again, rapacious producers and unyielding unions—faced with dire economic conditions and chronic unemployment along the Main Stem—cooperatively compromised on a formula designed to stimulate increased production of bad shows.

BROADWAY SCORECARD
/ PERFS: 1 / $: –

RAVE	FAVORABLE	MIXED	UNFAVORABLE	PAN
				6

A FUNNY THING HAPPENED ON THE WAY TO THE FORUM

a revival of the 1962 comedy musical

music and lyrics by Stephen Sondheim

book by Burt Shevelove and Larry Gelbart

based on plays of Plautus (254–184 B.C.)

directed by Burt Shevelove

choreographed by Ralph Beaumont

produced by Larry Blyden; presented by David Black in association with Seymour Vall and Henry Honeckman

starring Phil Silvers

with Larry Blyden, Lew Parker, Carl Ballantine, Reginald Owen, Lizabeth Pritchett (replacing Nancy Walker), Pamela Hall, John Hansen, Carl Lindstrom, Joe Ross, Bill Starr, and Chad Block

opened March 30, 1972   *Lunt-Fontanne Theatre*

CLIVE BARNES, *TIMES*

Everyone ought to have a favorite Broadway musical. Personally my favorite for 10 years has been *A Funny Thing Happened on the Way to the Forum*. Last night *A Funny Thing* happened once again, and I fell in love with it as desperately as ever. This is the funniest, bawdiest and most enchanting Broadway musical that Plautus, with a little help from Stephen Sondheim, Burt Shevelove and Larry Gelbart, ever wrote. Pseudolus rides again. I approached this new production with some trepidation, for not only did I adore the original Broadway show so much, but I also remember what became of it when, with a different

A Funny Thing with Pseudolus Silvers very much in charge. Those glasses provide a nice touch, don't you think? (costume design by Noel Taylor)

cast, it was roughly transplanted to London [in 1963, headed by comedian Frankie Howerd]. But on this occasion the new production can be taken on its own terms. The book has been slightly rewritten, Sondheim has added a couple of new songs and taken another couple out, and Shevelove has restaged the musical with a verve equal to the original. Few musicals have been so well-crafted as this. Sondheim's music is original and charming, with considerable musical subtlety but a regard for down-to-earth show-biz vigor that is precisely what is needed. And, as always, his lyrics are a joy to listen for. The American theatre has not had a lyricist like this since Hart or Porter. The book by Shevelove and Gelbart is, deep down where it matters, all farce, and I salute its cheap and stylish vulgarity. Phil Silvers, a newly restrained and histrionically elegant Phil Silvers, takes Pseudolus and makes the part his own. From his shabby Roman slave dress, to his jaunty horn-rims, Mr. Silvers is a total delight. His timing could win a tennis championship, his innuendoes are as insinuating as a snake, and his comic resource and naturalness are absolutely winning.

MARTIN GOTTFRIED, *WOMEN'S WEAR DAILY*

Since Broadway seems to have forgotten what the musical theatre is all about, not to mention how to make it, perhaps the only way to save the baby is to revive the father. As it is, though *Forum* was a respectable enough hit nine years ago, it never really was appreciated for the masterwork it is. The show is a true classic and there aren't many in our musical theatre, which is notorious for dating even the most significant of work. This is because *Forum* has a book that is not only marvelous but without period in respect to its style. The Burt Shevelove-Larry Gelbart script is tremendously funny—it is literary, consistent and impeccably structured. It may well be the best book in all our musical theatre. And since Shevelove himself has directed this revival, the tone of the production is wed to that of the libretto. Who could understand the humor better than the author, especially when the humor is as oddball as this? (To a eunuch: "Don't lower your voice to me.") Shevelove makes the revival a show of whole cloth and even funnier than it was the first time around. Moreover, with all due respect given Zero Mostel, it was Phil Silvers whom the creators had first wanted and it is easy to understand why. Silvers personifies the kind of burlesque comedy that *Forum* is all about and, unlike Mostel, will suppress his stage ego for the sake of a production. The final contribution that makes for the revival's success is Stephen Sondheim's score, which went unappreciated even when the show was winning its various prizes. Since this music cannot be separated from the book, you almost forget it is there—the composer suffers because of his very success. It is easier to notice Sondheim's lyrics—they are so clever they are a dazzling exercise on their own. But his music is superb: technically fresh, filled with melody, accurate in satire and, most of all, theatrically conceived. Two song changes have not been advantageous. The deletion of "Pretty Little Picture" is just unexplainable—the music was engaging and the lyric, as the stage show goes, furthered the plot, not to mention being funny, [though] nobody could terribly miss "That'll Show Him." The replacements ["Farewell" and "Echo Song"] are weaker. Watching them not work is a real lesson in the whys of retaining and deleting material.

WALTER KERR, *TIMES*

It is only 10 years old, and that's supposed to be too soon [for a revival]. But it isn't too soon, not a minute too soon. The theory, I suppose, is that everyone will feel he's seen either the original or the movie rather recently and already had his laugh. But who in heaven's name ever said a man couldn't laugh *twice*? I laughed twice and thrice and started in all over again, and I now figure that if future seasons are going to be as skimpy and as dull as this one, I may have to have *Funny Thing* to keep me going every year, doctor's orders. Besides, my memory is beginning to slip, and in 10 years I'd forgotten some of the jokes. (I had seen the [1966] movie in the meantime, but the movie had forgotten the jokes.) Actually, I don't know if I'd forgotten them. I think they may be new. They certainly sound new as Phil Silvers says them, though that of course may just be carelessness on his part. Silvers is a very mysterious man. His jokes aren't like other people's jokes. Other comedians carefully lay in a foundation and then wham you with a surprise. Silvers whams with no foundation, which may be illegal. There is no reason, for instance, why I should have tumbled half from my seat just because Larry Blyden, as one slave in pastel rags, asked, "How did we get into so much trouble?", and Silvers, as another though much loftier slave, replied, "A little here, a little there, it adds up." When someone asks him if a rumored plague is contagious, and he comes back with, "Did you ever hear of a plague that wasn't?", you know, by God, he is proud of that plague. He is a radiant fellow, particularly in ruin, and if a corpse should topple off a bier, he is ready with an explanation that makes you feel an idiot for not having thought of it. (He says, "Well, she sort of rolled over. *You* know.") Happiness, for Silvers, is the worst that can happen. For the audience it is watching him gloat over it. Well, enough of this trying to account for the man. We mustn't look a gift laugh in the teeth, certainly not when they are Mr. Silvers's teeth, bared in a ghastly smile.

∘   ∘   ∘

And a very funny *Funny Thing*, one of the most hysterical evenings in the theatre this viewer has ever experienced. Phil Silvers fit the material so well that it almost looked like the show had been written for him. And it was. He didn't much like the script, though, and turned thumbs down. Milton Berle was next in line, with the role ultimately passed to the pre-*Fiddler* Zero Mostel. This revival, with Pseudolus in Sgt. Bilko's horn-rims, originated at the Center Theatre Group's Ahmanson Theatre in Los Angeles. Nancy Walker played Domina, with Sondheim adding an additional song ("Farewell") for her; unavailable to make the East Coast transfer, her role was undertaken by Lizabeth Pritchett. Costar Larry Blyden determined to move it to Broadway and—with some trouble—arranged the necessary financing. Coauthor Burt Shevelove, by now an established director courtesy of *No, No, Nanette* across 46th Street, staged the show. *Forum* was extravagantly received by the critics, but did absolutely no business. Zilch. Zero (not as in Zero). Tom Poston stepped in when Silvers suffered a minor stroke, but the comedians soon folded up their togas. A 1996 revival fared much better, with Nathan Lane picking up Pseudolus's third Tony. But I remain a Phil Silvers man.

Tony Awards were won by Phil Silvers (actor) and Larry Blyden (supporting actor).

BROADWAY SCORECARD				
/ PERFS: 156 / $: –				
RAVE	FAVORABLE	MIXED	UNFAVORABLE	PAN
5	1			

GANTRY

"The New Musical"

music by Stanley Lebowsky

lyrics by Fred Tobias

book by Peter Bellwood

based on the 1927 novel *Elmer Gantry* by Sinclair Lewis

directed and choreographed by Onna White

produced by Joseph Cates and Jerry Schlossberg

starring Robert Shaw and Rita Moreno

with Wayne Tippit, Ted Thurston, Tom Batten, David Hooks, Bob Goren, Zale Kessler, and David Sabin

opened February 14, 1970   George Abbott Theatre

CLIVE BARNES, *TIMES*

Charisma is a quality hard to define but easy to recognize. Robert Shaw, the Gantry in *Gantry*, possesses charisma. His co-star Rita Moreno, Sister Sharon Falconer to his hell-fire preacher, has grace and a beauty you can never forget. The show makes them need every quality they can muster. This is an unusual, if musically commonplace, musical. It is not as good as it should have been yet it has enough pure theatrical electricity in its air to make it possibly worth seeing. This electricity comes primarily from the cast and the staging by Onna White. But come it does. The musical is a travesty of Sinclair Lewis' novel. The music I suppose might quite aptly be described as Bible-belt. It is full of sanctimonious harmonies and a watery fervor less than fervent. The book and lyrics suffer from a misunderstanding of Sinclair Lewis—a great writer who deserves better of posterity. Elmer Gantry is one of the enormous characters of American literature, a hypocrite, a poseur who finally takes everything—even exposure—in his stride to achieve clay-footed success. The Gantry of this musical is an amiable eccentric, a lit-

The cast album cover was ready, but the show wasn't. *Gantry* closed before reaching the recording studio. (costume design by Ann Roth)

tle ambivalent in his morality, a rabble-rousing demagogue, but fundamentally an appealing person. With respect, I think that Mr. Lewis would have puked at him. Mr. Shaw, superbly suggestive with the material he is given, is so evidently capable of a blazing performance, corrupt, evil and yet malignantly persuasive, that he could have shattered the theatre. [Even so,] Shaw gives as good a performance as you will find in this or many other a season. The good things in *Gantry* are exciting. Miss White treats a musical as a total movement style. Here she is recreating the concept of the hell-fire revival meeting, and her entire production moves toward that end. At times it is almost a wonder that the audience applauds rather than shouts out "Hallelujah!" Her timing is superb—White loves pauses and reactions. She also sees dance and movement as an integral part of her creation. What was done was well done. You will have seen many, many worse musicals. But with that cast, that director, even the nicely appropriate scenery of Robin Wagner and costumes by Ann Roth, it could have been so much better. I recommend it, albeit gently, to nearly everyone except, perhaps, admirers of Sinclair Lewis.

MARTIN GOTTFRIED, *WOMEN'S WEAR DAILY*

It has now become commonplace for Broadway musicals to be amateurishly produced and assembled—a vast irony considering that they once represented our theatre at its most professional. Ten years ago, *Gantry*, a sloppy, listless, but most of all, insecure new musical, would have been surprising for its sheer lack of polish. Today, its crudity is nothing unusual. It opened Saturday night with its cast practically reading the closing notice on stage. The show is a mess and the reason is that there was nobody around who knew how not to make a mess. Beginning with a good story that had essential ties with musical ideas (revivalism) and theatre appearances (the revival tent)—and a main character who was a performer himself (a revivalist) working in a theatrical situation (revival meetings)—neither the director-choreographer nor her associates knew what to do with it. There was no basic conception of how to musicalize this story, not even the simple decision of when to put a song into a scene or what kind of song to put there. It is frightened musical-making and the show trembles so much that had the audience but clapped its hands (which it had few reasons to do), I'm sure *Gantry* would have fled. In the light of [the material and production], Robert Shaw's performance as Gantry was almost miraculous. He is of course a good actor. He has a smile nice enough to warm a whole theatre (which is important for Gantry, who is simultaneously charming, phoney, stupid and instinctively crafty). Shaw isn't always sure where the notes are, but he acts as though he is, which is important, and his baritone is very agreeable. Rita Moreno was just like any musical movie actress (see Mitzi Gaynor, Ann-Margret) in being a little singing-dancing machine who needs engineers and photographers to enlarge her. She played Sister Sharon with what must be called stage absence and was sung right off the stage by Gloria Hodes' fabulous voice (Moreno would slit Onna White's throat if she knew how that duet made her look, even with Miss Hodes dressed down to look like a scrub-lady). As for the chorus, it should be sentenced to a year of bus-and-truck company work for unprofessional conduct—you don't give up on any stage even when the show is as naive as *Gantry*.

o　　o　　o

Joe Cates produced three musicals, adaptations of Budd Schulberg's novel *What Makes Sammy Run?*, Bernard Shaw's comedy *Caesar and Cleopatra*, and Sinclair Lewis's *Elmer Gantry*. The selection of such intriguing properties says something, presumably, about Cates's taste. He was less discerning in his selection of adaptors, though, entrusting the pieces to creators with little Broadway experience. This sometimes works out, like when some guy entrusted his 1960 rock 'n' roll lampoon to the unknown Charles Strouse, Lee Adams, Mike Stewart, and untried-as-director Gower Champion, but most of the time you come up all thumbs. *Sammy* (1964) had a score by uninspired pop-songwriter Ervin Drake, script by novelist Schulberg (whose work was doctored), and direction by musical novice Arthur Storch (who was fired). *Her First Roman* (1968) was written, songs as well as book, by Drake (whose score was heavily doctored) and staged by the *I'm Solomon* (1968) team of Michael Benthall and Donald McKayle (both of whom were fired). Nobody was fired from *Gantry*, but the three writers were new to Broadway, and choreographer Onna White—of *The Music Man* (1957), *Mame* (1966), and the 1968 film version of *Oliver!* (for which she nabbed an Oscar)—was untried as a director. While *Sammy* was a long-running flop and *Roman* was a calamitous flop, *Gantry* was merely an unheralded, negligible flop. Unable to afford an out-of-town tryout, the show played thirty-two underattended previews at the Abbott. Cates, in a not-uncreative move, attempted to import twelve Boston/ Washington/Philadelphia critics to catch an early performance and turn in (to him) the equivalent of out-of-town notices. The New York critics objected, for some reason feeling threatened, so Cates was forced to scrap the idea. There's little else to be said about the enterprise other than that it was the only score by the respected and immensely likable musical director Stanley Lebowsky, best known as the onstage band-leader in Bob Fosse's *Chicago* (1975), and that it was the final attraction at the George Abbott Theatre, also known as the Adelphi (hosting *On the Town* [1944] and *Billion Dollar Baby* [1945]) and the 54th Street (with *No Strings* [1962] and *What Makes Sammy Run?*). Yes, it was out of the way—on the south side of 54th, between Sixth and Seventh— but it was a nice, comfy, one-balcony 1,434-seater. It became a lovely little parking lot immediately following *Gantry*'s demise, and so remained for more than twenty years.

BROADWAY SCORECARD
/ PERFS: I / $: −

RAVE	FAVORABLE	MIXED	UNFAVORABLE	PAN
	I	I	I	3

GEORGE M!

"A New Musical"

music and lyrics by George M. Cohan (with revisions by Mary Cohan)

book by Michael Stewart and John and Fran Pascal

based on the life of George M. Cohan (1878–1942)

directed and choreographed by Joe Layton

produced by David Black, Konrad Matthaei, and Lorin E. Price

starring Joel Grey

with Betty Ann Grove, Jerry Dodge, Jill O'Hara, Bernadette Peters, Jamie Donnelly, and Harvey Evans

opened April 10, 1968   *Palace Theatre*

CLIVE BARNES, *TIMES*

I loved him when he was Cagney, I would obviously have loved him when he was Cohan himself, and, yes, at the Palace Theater last night I loved him when he was Joel Grey. I'm just a sucker for the style—it involves all that nostalgia for bright lights and Broadway that only a Hollywood-nurtured European can really savor to the full. *George M!*, in fact, has a lot going for it. With the book it is burdened by, it needs every bit of it. The musical is a scrappy, ill-prepared, mediocrely written account of George M. Cohan, his life, career, loves and songs. It does one very smart thing to begin with—it uses many, many of the old Cohan songs. Another smart thing was to cast Joel Grey as George M. Cohan. Sharp as a whiplash, either with his derby tilted down to his nose, or his eyes cast upward sightlessly searching the middistance of destiny, with his cane twirling, or his arms thrown out in that supremely egocentric empty embrace of show business, Mr. Grey operated. Mr. Grey operated, operated and operated. He screwed himself into one tight, taut bundle of nerves, threw himself at the show and came out on top and smiling like a tiger. He sang, lightly and beltingly, he danced, with a frenetic passion and a God-given sense of timing, and when all else failed, he even acted the script that they had been inconsiderate enough to give him. Indeed, once in a while, he even made sense of its show-biz platitudes, although nothing on earth could be done about the show's shapelessness. The authors have been so intent at getting as many of Cohan's songs in as possible that the story staggers along in fits and starts. When it is fitting rather than starting you virtually forget about it altogether. But here the producers have done another very smart thing—they have hired Joe Layton to stage it. Layton has put the whole thing together like a mechanical musical box. The audience went out, for the first time this season, humming the music, even if most of it was more than 50 years old. I notice that *George M!* has been declared ineligible for this season's Tony Awards. If it is any consolation it can have a personal Tony Award from me, and Mr. Grey can have a couple.

MARTIN GOTTFRIED, *WOMEN'S WEAR DAILY*

An entertainment in showbiz clichés, not really a musical about Cohan but a musical about musicals about Cohan, if you know what I mean. It was a risk that Layton took but I think it was the only chance he had, considering the material presented to him in the book and score. It opened last night and for all my sympathy with Layton's work, the production is pretty bad. There is only so much you can do with tap-dancing, with super-speed staging, with overamplified microphones, with cardboard-cutout sets and overstaging. And there is only so much kidding you can drape over a script that (I confidently suspect) was never meant for kidding. Joel Grey is the star of *George M!* and he is meant to have a real-star part rather than a mock star part. If everything else is being kidded, Grey's role isn't and Layton has staged him for big time stuff, baby. The business that they are trying to kid everywhere else in the show is laid on straight and juicy for Grey. In short, this is one of the weirdest musicals I've ever seen. And one of the noisiest. And one of the most confused.

WALTER KERR, *TIMES*

[Headline: Yankee Doodle's Out of Breath]
In telling the story of a brash, cocky, crowing, everlastingly pushy entertainer named George M. Cohan, the makers of *George M!* have come

up with a brash, cocky, crowing, everlastingly pushy show. It would seem to fit, but it's skipped a beat. A few nights ago I listened to a woman who'd known Cohan describe her astonished first meeting with him. "He was a tough man," she said, "tough as nails—but he spoke so *softly!*" (I knew him slightly myself, in his later years. He spoke very softly.) The softness of speech that caused him to drop most of his words out of one corner of his lower lip as though he could easily throw away everything he'd fought so hard to get, the undercut that put a slippery floor beneath all the braggadocio, the out-of-kilter smile that seemed to mock the demands he was making of an audience even while he went on making them, is the contradiction that's missing in *George M!* It's also what made the man winning—a short man straining upward on elevator shoes forever, winking at you to call attention to the shoes. He wasn't modest, but he was an okay kid. The show itself—on its very own terms—needs an undercut, a contradiction, a change of pace, a flash of charm inside the challenge if it is ever going to seem anything more than whizbang mechanical. Director-choreographer Joe Layton is prodigal with lively mechanics: headlong hoofers, hairbreadth tumblers, dogs flipping skyward over table tops, caterwauling maidservants, manic managers, race and stomp and furious rat-a-tat-tat. The whole show is a photo finish, except that the race never ends. Oh, how it needs a grace note, a quiet girl, a pause for breath, a stroll in the sun. Mr. Grey does not ask for a rest, though we do, and when he is bouncing backward on his toes, walking ecstatically on his heels, or ducking into a boxing stance for "Harrigan" we are bound to like and admire his energy, his animation, his crescent-moon smile. All he wants is what his director won't give him: the ease that turns a blast into a breeze. Well. The songs are hurryblurred, the lyrics vanish, the show becomes a memory of machine-gun feats. In a bad season for Broadway musicals, it's probably the best new one now available. But it could have been much, much nicer.

o   o   o

Louis Aborn of Tams-Witmark, the performing rights licensing firm, called Mike Stewart—whose *Bye Bye Birdie* (1960) was near the top of Tams's charts—and asked if he could figure out a way to package all those grand old George M. Cohan songs (and earn some money off of them). Stewart sketched out an idea, and since he wasn't interested in working just then—the *Dolly!* (1964) industry was churning out royalties from a handful of simultaneous productions—he invited his sister and brother-in-law to collaborate. Joel Grey was primed for stardom, as they say—Hal Prince had elevated him over the title during the run of *Cabaret* (1966), in fact—and the Man Who Owned Broadway was the perfect role for him at the perfect time. But the show had a relentless, pace and a lack of true feeling. *George M!* missed the Tony Award deadline, opening just after a season that included *The Happy Time*, *How Now, Dow Jones*, *Illya, Darling*, and Tony-winner *Hallelujah, Baby!*—all flops, and rightly so. Hence, Clive Barnes and his "personal Tonys." By the time the next awards deadline rolled around, *George M!* was long gone and forgotten; Jerry Orbach took the Tony for *Promises, Promises*, and Joel Grey was left with a yellowing set of accolades. Clive Barnes's rave review—his first for a musical, after eight months on the job—did give the patchwork *George M!* a longer run (and a smaller loss) than the other flops. <u>Sociological Note:</u> 1968 was not, perhaps, the time to attract great audiences with patriotic pablum from the guy who wrote "Over There" ("for the Yanks are coming," etc.). They even had trouble with some of the chorus kids, who chafed at waving flags during the "Yankee Doodle Dandy" number. Two weeks after *George M!* opened, they were wrapping chorus kids in the red, white, and blue (and yellow) in the new not-so-American Tribal Love-Rock Musical half-a-block west on 47th Street.

A Tony Award was won by Joe Layton (choreographer).

BROADWAY SCORECARD
/ PERFS: 427 / $: −

RAVE	FAVORABLE	MIXED	UNFAVORABLE	PAN
2	2		1	1

GEORGY

"A New Musical"

music by George Fischoff

lyrics by Carole Bayer (Sager)

book by Tom Mankiewicz

based on the 1966 screenplay *Georgy Girl* by Margaret Forster and Peter Nichols, from the 1966 novel *Georgy Girl* by Margaret Forster

directed by Peter Hunt

choreographed by Howard Jeffrey

produced by Fred Coe in association with Joseph P. Harris and Ira Bernstein

starring Dilys Watling, John Castle, Melissa Hart, and Stephen Elliott

with Louis Beachner, Helena Carroll, and Cynthia Latham (Myra Carter written out during tryout)

opened February 26, 1970   Winter Garden Theatre

CLIVE BARNES, *TIMES*

Whatever it is that is wrong with *Georgy*, the new musical, is wrong for too long. It has some good performances, a brightly literate book, a few characterizations of a depth unusual in a musical. But it never takes off, never flies, never whirls you in the air with that special happiness. Was the idea good or bad in the first place? A musical of the film *Georgy Girl* sounds terrible at first but gets better the more you think of it. That is its danger. Imagine then a mod and swinging London as a setting for two girls, one glamorous, one homely. The glamorous one gets married, has a baby and leaves it, and for a time, her husband, with her friend, the kooky, little ugly duckling, Georgy. It is literary, of course, but then so was *My Fair Lady* [1956]. It has sharply defined characters difficult

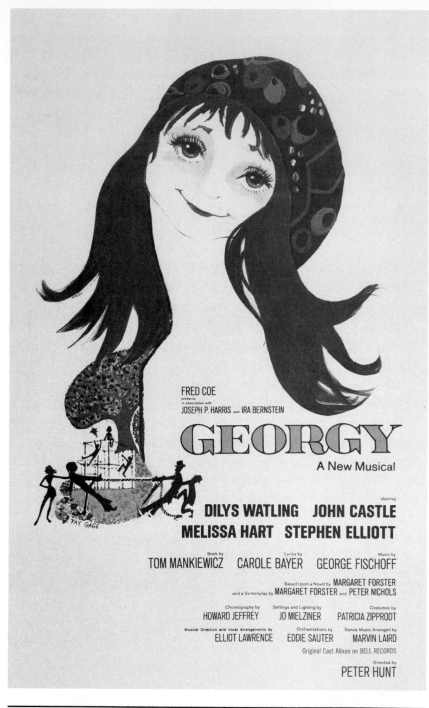

FRED COE
presents
in association with
JOSEPH P. HARRIS and IRA BERNSTEIN

GEORGY
A New Musical

starring

DILYS WATLING   JOHN CASTLE

MELISSA HART   STEPHEN ELLIOTT

Book by
TOM MANKIEWICZ

Lyrics by
CAROLE BAYER

Music by
GEORGE FISCHOFF

Based Upon a Novel by MARGARET FORSTER
and a Screenplay by MARGARET FORSTER and PETER NICHOLS

Choreography by
HOWARD JEFFREY

Settings and Lighting by
JO MIELZINER

Costumes by
PATRICIA ZIPPRODT

Musical Direction and Vocal Arrangements by
ELLIOT LAWRENCE

Orchestrations by
EDDIE SAUTER

Dance Music Arranged by
MARVIN LAIRD

Original Cast Album on BELL RECORDS

Directed by
PETER HUNT

FAY GAGE

A forlorn waif heralding a forlorn waif of a musical. People left
whistling the title song from the film version. (artwork by Fay Gage)

to place in a musical comedy context, but then so had *The King and I* [1951]. Yes, perhaps it could have worked. And, just perhaps, had it not been for the music and lyrics it might have worked. But George Fischoff's music and Carole Bayer's lyrics rarely rose above the hopefully anonymous. Do you remember the movie with Lynn Redgrave and Alan Bates? If you don't remember the movie I bet you will the theme song "Georgy Girl," which danced all over the hit parade. The tune isn't in the stage show, although all the time Fischoff's music and Eddie Sauter's orchestrations seem to be teetering on the brink of it. But the simple insistency of that one tune that somehow, at its time and in its place, seemed to sum up the chimes of old Bow Bells and the charms of new Carnaby Street, was worth all of this score put together. The waif-like Dilys Watling, all common-sensical radiance, was adorable—the kind of girl you would be glad to give your seat to in the underground. John Castle, as the irresponsible Jos, also had just the right flip air. Melissa Hart and Stephen Elliott, completing the quartet, also seemed absolutely right. I liked [the featured players]; I liked all the dancers; I liked—well, I liked the movie. And I liked it much more. When I left the theatre, swung through the swing doors onto a cold Broadway—I found I was softly humming. It was that theme music to the movie. Sorry.

MARTIN GOTTFRIED, *WOMEN'S WEAR DAILY*

Georgy is by no means successful, though neither is it a mess, and considering Broadway's musical theatre over the past few seasons that's something to be grateful for. There has been a dreadful lack of professionalism for so long a time I had been wondering whether we had run into an eternal amateur night. The musical that opened last night may have made any number of errors in judgment, but in terms of execution it is entirely competent and considering that, along with its several (if not many) qualities, you could do a lot worse in search of an entertainment. The problems in judgment I think started with the choice of *Georgy Girl* as the basis for a musical. It was a choice I suspect motivated by an eagerness to use rock music on the stage. Broadway's producers are suddenly awoken to a change in America's taste in popular music—awoken after a 15-year nap. Unaware of exactly what that change meant (and means) they are mere opportunists in search of an opportunity. Just guessing, I would think that the producer of *Georgy* read *Georgy Girl* as a movie about "mod, swinging London." The trouble with such thinking was that "mod, swinging London" was a fad concept, that it had little to do with rock music and that the story of *Georgy Girl*, though a good story, had even less to do with rock music. It is a real, a sad and an interesting story. Unhappily, it is not a story of which musical theatre is made. However, the work of Peter Hunt, the director, didn't suggest that he knew exactly how to make musical theatre. In fact, whatever is musical in *Georgy* looks to be the work of Howard Jeffrey, the choreographer. George Fischoff's music is mediocre, an easy-listening kind of rock crammed into the show-tune style, orchestrated with disinterest (and consequently ordinariness) by the extremely talented Eddie Sauter. There is one song, however—a duet called "Sweet Memory"—that was lovely and interesting. If Fischoff wrote it he should continue in that direction. He might also urge his lyricist, Carole Bayer to watch her prosody, her clichés and her content ("Love, it's written on their faces/You'll find it in the strangest places"). . . . Everything and everyone else was polished, leaving the show a high-shine pair of brown shoes worn with a blue suit.

o   o   o

Fred Coe was a producer from Alligator, Mississippi (that's what it says), with a reputation for quality. His credits included, in consecutive years, William Gibson's *The Miracle Worker* (1958) and *Two for the Seesaw* (1959), Tad Mosel's Pulitzer-winner *All the Way Home* (1960), Paddy Chayefsky's *Gideon* (1961), and Herb Gardner's *A Thousand Clowns* (1962). His musical experience was more limited, though. As the originating producer of *Fiddler on the Roof* (1964), he invited Hal Prince into the project when he had trouble raising the money; by the time the tryout began, Coe had withdrawn. (His name can be found on the original ads for the show, including the herald reproduced in *Opening Night on Broadway*.) *Georgy*, his other musical attempt, was no *Fiddler*. Based on the popular British film *Georgy Girl*—which starred Lynn Redgrave as a forlorn waif of a heroine—*Georgy* was a forlorn waif of a musical without any out-of-the-ordinary excitement to support it. The team Coe assembled, oddly enough, had almost no Broadway musical experience. The exception was lighting designer-turned-director Peter Hunt, with one musical—the previous season's *1776*—to his name; his only musical since has been the not-so-

Goodtime Charley (1975). *Georgy*'s negligible score by George Fischoff and Carole Bayer (who would return in 1979 with Marvin Hamlisch and *They're Playing Our Song*) didn't help. The absence of the film's title song, in fact, was clearly a liability and universally noted. A song with lyrics, incidentally, by actor Jim Dale (to music by Tom Springfield).

BROADWAY SCORECARD

/ PERFS: 4 / $: –

RAVE	FAVORABLE	MIXED	UNFAVORABLE	PAN
	1	1	4	

GIGI

a stage adaptation of the 1958 film musical

music by Frederick Loewe

book and lyrics by Alan Jay Lerner

based on his screenplay, from the 1944 novella by Colette and the 1951 dramatization by Anita Loos

directed by Joseph Hardy (replaced by Alan Jay Lerner)

choreographed by Onna White

produced by Edwin Lester (for The Los Angeles and San Francisco Civic Light Opera) and Saint-Subber

starring Alfred Drake, Agnes Moorehead, Maria Karnilova, and Daniel Massey

with Karin Wolfe (replacing Terese Stevens), George Gaynes, and Joe Ross

opened November 13, 1973   Uris Theatre

CLIVE BARNES, *TIMES*

Where are the snows of yesteryear? Can you re-invent champagne? A bold and brave attempt is being made at the Uris Theatre, where last night *Gigi* fluttered in. Some of the songs are new, but most of the songs are old. And this remains an enchanting score with dazzling lyrics. Four or five of the songs are standards, although, simply because of their close integration with the story, comparatively few of them are more than happily familiar and none of them are hackneyed. The outstanding new number is "The Contract," in which Gigi's great-aunt and grandmother settle the legal arrangements under which Gaston, Gigi's lover, should become her protector. It is this number that points up both the daring dexterity of Lerner as a lyricist—the man makes lyrics such fun—and the musical imagination of Loewe. Loewe is a composer who develops numbers rather than merely reprising them, and it gives his musicals an unusually rich texture.... So can you re-invent champagne? Yes, you can. But it may come out tasting just a little more like New York State than *Veuve Clicquot* the second time around. But as another Parisian might have said—champagne is champagne.

MARTIN GOTTFRIED, *WOMEN'S WEAR DAILY*

[Headline: "*Gigi*: As Big and Stylish As a Department Store"]

Gigi is indicative of the current depressing attitude toward the musical theater as a marketplace for packaged versions of established properties. Though our musical theatre needs nothing more than a good, successful show, and though I would naturally like to see that happen, the vulgar emptiness of the *Gigi* stage version does seem to be what its progenitors deserve. After having toured the country according to the latest technique of making hay before the New York sun doesn't shine, this bastard version of a new musical barely mustered the energy to open at the Uris Theatre. It is as big and as stylish as a discount store; it is burdened by a book paradoxically heavy and thin; the familiarity of most of its songs—which were familiar because of their imitativeness to begin with—makes the production seem a revival, and the shabby opulence of the set makes it seem a touring revival at that; finally, it has been badly miscast and heavily directed. This might be surprising considering the reputation for quality that its authors have developed over the years, though it is less surprising when you realize that the reputation is based,

really, on only *My Fair Lady*. In fact, Lerner's sophistication as a lyricist-librettist has always, I feel, been overrated, and in this his work is
obvious and sometimes gross. As for Loewe, though always a formidable melodist, he has been away from the theatre for 13 years and has,
frankly, grown rusty. I am very sorry to say this about Loewe, who I do
consider a wonderful composer, and am simply sorry that he has stayed
away so long and suffered the inevitable consequences of inactivity. I
have less sympathy for Lerner, an average lyricist who is technically
inconsistent, an obsessive rhymer and an ersatz Continental, in this case
also genuinely gross. Alfred Drake suppresses his usual ham to the
extent of limiting it to enough for Thanksgiving dinner, as opposed to
his usual supply for all major holidays plus sandwiches. Moreover, his
French pronunciations and dialect are self-conscious and supercilious.
Others in leading roles are no more appropriate. Maria Karnilova's left-
over Yiddish dialect from *Fiddler on the Roof* [1964] is, one might say,
mildly distracting for Gigi's grandmother.

WALTER KERR, *TIMES*
Of course, we've already heard the first song Alfred Drake sings,
"Thank Heaven for Little Girls," and we've heard it sung well, by
Maurice Chevalier. But we had one relationship with Chevalier on
screen: a long-distance love of the man, the kind of affection one can
feel for an icon hung up on a wall, a fondness that had to function—as
all movie fondnesses function—by remote control. And that's ok. It has
its ghostly, hence somewhat god-like, virtues. We have another sort
with Mr. Drake. It's not simply a matter of his being there in the flesh,
pearl-gray top hat and boutonniere and all. I'm not going to badger you
with the less than hot news that the stage offers "in person" what the
screen can only offer in sometimes preferable absentia. You see, it's not
just that he's up there, *now*. It's that he's been up there before, and when
he does stroll on from the portals to wish us good evening and to call
attention to a softly lighted Gigi blowing out the candles on her birthday cake, we are pleased by more than his voice, more than his suave
deportment, more than his barely suppressed wink. We are pleased, if
you will, by the fact that the man is still around, alive and grinning,
looking all the younger for the bright silver at his temples that is plainly
make-up—the very same man we watched emerge in *Oklahoma!* [1943]

and take off in *Kiss Me, Kate* [1948], prove his range as a fine Iago, suffer failures here and there [including *Sing Out, Sweet Land!*, a 1945 folk musical written and directed by Kerr], and go on going on. He grew while we were present, and if he is riper now, more lethal with a line and slyer with a modulation, the maturing process is something we were in on, something we had a hand in (by sitting on our hands, or not sitting on them, as occasion required). We are greeting a friend rather than an idol, and as the applause comes up it's not just for tonight but for all the nights we have spent together, trying to figure the theatre out. [At the end of the show] Mr. Drake picks up the "Little Girls" refrain lightly, then with more ardor, and happily carries the decorous carnival to its curtain. *Gigi* belongs not to little girls but to such of their unsorrowing elders as still have the high heart to sing about them.

o   o   o

Looking for a *My Fair Lady* follow-up, the creators of that 1956 landmark musical considered *Gigi*. Alan Jay Lerner was intrigued, but Fritz Loewe and director Moss Hart both disliked it. Not long thereafter Lerner got a call from film producer Arthur Freed, for whom he'd scripted the 1951 Oscar-winner *An American in Paris*. Lerner owed M-G-M another picture; would he take a look at a property they owned, *Gigi*? Lerner's first draft swayed Loewe, and history and ten Oscars were made. Two years later, during the *Camelot* tryout, Loewe turned to Lerner and said, "My boy, I can't do it anymore," and left for Palm Springs and Monte Carlo. Eleven years later, Lerner enticed Loewe back for the motion picture *The Little Prince* (which wasn't released until 1974). During the writing of which Civic Light Opera producer Ed Lester made one of his periodic requests for a stage version of *Gigi*. Loewe agreed, because "we were having such a good time working together." All the pieces fell in place, save two—critical pieces, which doomed the stage adaptation to failure. The first was the matter of Gigi herself. Extensive auditioning to fill the slippers of Leslie Caron resulted in . . . nobody. Then Kate Hepburn, Lerner's *Coco* (1969), called to say she'd found the perfect girl in a London rock production of *Carmen*. Thus twenty-year-old pop singer Terese Stevens was imported to play the little girl "whose sparkle turned to fire." But Stevens's contemporary style was sorely at odds with the ethereal material. "She was marvelous," explained Lerner, "but casting her as Gigi was like asking Ethel Merman to play Little Jo." Stevens was replaced by standby Karin Wolfe, who explained in a rather curious interview that Terry left "because she had to pay double income tax." Wolfe, at twenty-eight, was a bit seasoned for the part, having made her debut as a *Bye Bye Birdie* teenager back in 1960; she proved adequate, but *Gigi* called for a more-than-adequate title performance. The other problem, which Loewe and Hart recognized back in 1956, was that *Gigi* was basically an intimate, small-scale love story. It could be dressed up on the screen—with Paris locations and Beaton designs—but was unable to carry the weight of a full stage musical. A six-month pre-Broadway tour was arranged "to insure against losses," as the saying goes. The show underwent the usual patching on the road—songs added, songs replaced, and yet another director ditched in Detroit—but you can't make a silk purse out of a polyester cravat. Looking back on the stage *Gigi*, Lerner faulted the overblown production imposed on what was basically a charming, intimate story—"like putting a saddle on a Pekingese." When Loewe was asked during the tryout about future composing plans, he said, "I have a limited time to amuse myself, amuse my soul. And when I do, I'd rather play the *Appassionata*." The composer died on February 14, 1988—outlasting Lerner, who struggled through *1600 Pennsylvania Avenue* (1976), *Carmelina* (1979), and *Dance a Little Closer* (1983) before his death on June 14, 1986.

A Tony Award was won by Frederick Loewe and Alan Jay Lerner (score).

BROADWAY SCORECARD

/ PERFS: 103 / $: –

RAVE	FAVORABLE	MIXED	UNFAVORABLE	PAN
	2	1		3

GODSPELL

"A New Musical Based on *The Gospel According to St. Matthew*"

music and new lyrics by Stephen Schwartz; additional song by Jay Hamburger and Peggy Gordon

conceived and directed by John-Michael Tebelak

produced by Edgar Lansbury, Stuart Duncan, Joseph Beruh, and The Shubert Organization

with Don Scardino, Lamar Alford, Laurie Faso, Lois Foraker, Robin Lamont, Elizabeth Lathram, Bobby Lee, Tom Rolfing, Marley Sims, and Valerie Williams

opened May 17, 1971   Cherry Lane Theatre (Off-Broadway)
transferred June 22, 1976   Broadhurst Theatre

(Note: the following first-night reviews were based on the 1976 reopening at the Broadhurst Theatre)

RICHARD EDER, *TIMES*

Godspell has no bones, but it has many small sinews and darting reflexes. They serve beautifully to bear along its energy, its gaiety, its wit—all the qualities that are displayed through movement. They are not enough to sustain it when it stands still to be grave. This musical suits itself best in its first part; its inventive—and, after five years, still fresh—variations on the life and parables of Jesus. The second part, with betrayal and cruci-fixion, doesn't work as well. The sparkle becomes sentiment; the senti-ment becomes sententious. Piccolos can't do slow movements: you need a flute. So much said, all of *Godspell's* virtues are brilliantly exercised, and its weaknesses gracefully gotten past, in its Broadway premiere. . . . It is hard for Jesus not to be upstaged. Don Scardino succeeds by letting himself be upstaged. He looks radiant without looking fatuous, and acts as a quiet master of ceremonies who dominates when he must, some-times singing, sometimes with a surging leap or two.

MARTIN GOTTFRIED, *POST*

After a five-year off-Broadway run and phenomenal international success, *Godspell* moved to the Broadhurst Theatre last night, where it provided not a single clue to its popularity. It is *Hair* [1968] with a haircut; that is, it's not only amateurish and period experimental but accusably calculated to be inoffensive. No nudity, no dirty words, no suggestions of sex, no challenges to establishment anything, it is even conventionally religious. Come to think of it, perhaps that explains its popularity. A G-rated rock show. I had seen it originally at the Café La Mama and found its first act so obnoxiously precocious I left at the intermission. John-Michael Tebelak had conceived the show to fulfill his master's requirement at school and that was all too believable. The main difference between the La Mama version and this one is a different musical score, composed by Stephen Schwartz. Schwartz went on, if that is how it must be described, to do the songs for *Pippin* [1972] and *The Magic Show* [1974], both of which are still running. As he modestly points out in his biographical notes, that makes him "the first composer-lyricist in Broadway history to have three hits running concurrently in New York." It puts him ahead of Irving Berlin, Cole Porter, Frank Loesser and Stephen Sondheim. In the sheer luck category, anyhow. The shows may well be still running despite his scores, which are musical in the technical sense only, if that. "Day by Day," the hit song from *Godspell*, is but eight measures long and is repeated endlessly. Perhaps Schwartz wrote himself out with it. Tebelak has taken a company of ten actors and had them dressed in love child costumes whimsical enough for a hippie window at Macy's—Raggedy Ann to Superman sweatshirt. Their stage is flanked by mesh wire fencing with overhead lamps, looking like a schoolyard attic and created by an understandably uncredited designer. There the actors play. They shout and make living pictures and jump around on one leg, being terribly cute. They spread so much love they make one yearn for hatred. So the show has no thrust, no continuity, no musical sense. There are no dances and the musical staging is spent not on the songs, which could have used anything, but on the corps movements that were corny even when this show was new. Small wonder none of us want any part of brotherhood anymore.

DOUGLAS WATT, *DAILY NEWS*

A touch of the old nasty could have a bracing effect on *Godspell*, which last night began spilling its good will and guilelessness across the stage of the Broadhurst and into the aisles. But then, it's gone along very well without it for the past five years. This is the Our Gang musical version of *The Gospel According to St. Matthew* that opened at La Mama early in 1971 and was taken over by commercial managers for an off-Broadway run that ended only a week or so ago to make ready for the move to Broadway. A few of the original players remain, which only goes to prove that in show business nobody is ever unlucky enough to grow up. Ten raggedy kids (though, in costumer Susan Tsu's hands, the rags are very colorful) foregather at night in a dismal-looking city playground with a high wire fence. But instead of having a '50s rumble, they have a '60s love-in as they sing, clown, mug, mime, ventriloquize and do imitations of George Burns, Ed Wynn, Paul Lynde, Jimmy Durante and others in order to bring the New Testament to life. Stephen Schwartz' songs, which touch many bases from waltz to soft shoe to rock, have a pleasingly perky air about them and in at least one instance, the hit "Day by Day," the music rises above the merely functional. There's also an attractive choral plaint, "By My Side," with music by Peggy Gordon and lyrics by Jay Hamburger. Schwartz, incidentally, has evidently touched up his lyrics this time out, and the brief spoken portions of the entertainment contain references to such things as *A Chorus Line* [1975] and the Presidential campaign. [Jimmy Carter won.] But *Godspell* is too cute for my taste in the long run. (It lasts over two hours, by the way.) Still, speaking of long runs, there's no arguing the fact that it has had one, and doubtless thousands of children have responded to it over the years. It does seem a slightly dated form of theatre, however, and one in need of an occasional cutting edge to make all those smiles more acceptable.

◦　◦　◦

John-Michael Tebelak began his *Godspell* (archaic spelling of gospel) as a college project, while going for his master's at Carnegie-Mellon. After graduation he workshopped a freewheeling, improvisational version—with songs by the cast—at Café La Mama. Producers Edgar Lansbury (Angela's little brother) and Joseph Beruh picked up the piece, added songs by Stephen Schwartz, and opened downtown at the Cherry Lane on May 17, 1971. This was the heyday of the Off-Broadway musical revue. For kids: *You're a Good Man, Charlie Brown* (1967, four years). For hip adults: *Hair* (1967, from the Shakespeare Festival). For knowing adults: *Jacques Brel Is Alive and Well and Living in Paris* (1968, four-and-one-half years). For socially conscious adults: *The Me Nobody Knows* (1970, transferred to Broadway). For furtive adults: *Let My People Come* (1974, transferred to Broadway). For prurient adults: *Oh! Calcutta!* (1969, transferred to Broadway). All hits, all eventually reaching Broadway through transfer or revival. *Godspell*—for those too sophisticated for *Charlie Brown* but not enough for *Jacques Brel*—moved within three months to the larger Promenade (operated by Lansbury and Beruh, named for the 1969 Al Carmines musical with which the house opened). After an astounding 2,118 performances Off-Broadway, the producers decided to transfer to the Main Stem and ran fifteen months more. Stephen Schwartz followed *Godspell* with the hits *Pippin* and *The Magic Show*; John-Michael Tebelak, though, was never heard from again.

BROADWAY SCORECARD

/ PERFS: 527 / $: +

RAVE	FAVORABLE	MIXED	UNFAVORABLE	PAN
2	1	2		1

GOLDEN RAINBOW

"A New Musical"

music and lyrics by Walter Marks

book by Ernest Kinoy (replacing Arnold Schulman)

based on the 1957 comedy *A Hole in the Head* by Arnold Schulman, from his 1955 teleplay *The Heart's a Forgotten Hotel*

directed by Arthur Storch (replaced by Steve Lawrence)

choreographed by Tom Panko (with Onna White, replacing Ronald Field)

a Diplomat production (Steve Lawrence and Eydie Gorme), presented by Joseph P. Harris and Ira Bernstein

starring Steve Lawrence and Eydie Gorme (Lawrence)

with Joseph Sirola, Scott Jacoby, Sid Raymond, Will Hussung, and Marilyn Cooper

opened February 4, 1968   Shubert Theatre

CLIVE BARNES, *TIMES*

Golden Rainbow seems to have been having previews for so long [43, over 5 weeks] that I began to wonder if it ever was going to open, but last night open it did. To some extent what you think about *Golden Rainbow* will be conditioned by how highly you regard its extremely likable stars, Steve Lawrence and Eydie Gorme. But even if you adore them the other side of idolatry, you should be warned that as a vehicle for its stars *Golden Rainbow* is at best ramshackle. The musical is set in Las Vegas. I have often thought that with the possible exception of Devil's Island in the monsoon season, there is no place I would rather not go to more than Las Vegas. *Golden Rainbow* confirms my deepest suspicions. The character of Larry, it might be observed, has more than a little in common with Lawrence's earlier Broadway success, Sammy Glick in *What Makes Sammy Run?* [1964]. And to the no less pressing question now relevant—what makes Larry walk?—the answer must be the slow pace of a musical that seems to die a thousand deaths, although it is sporadically and efficiently shaken into spurts of life by the sweetly, glossily naturalistic expertise of Mr. Lawrence and Miss Gorme. The steel-tipped, bouncy rubber heel is an interesting character for a musical, but the book and songs rarely keep him in view. The insult wisecracks thrown between Lawrence and Gorme are tossed with a dazzling casualness. But there is no real bite—it is all rather like two comedians pretending to put each other down with a comic feud. As a result, Lawrence and Gorme, who positively gleam with so much talent that you start by feeling sorry for them and then end up almost proud of what they can do with their material, are left giving a series of slickly contrived cabaret acts while the show sinks around them. The fault, you see, is not in our stars, but in a musical that resolutely wants to be everything to everyone and ends up like an end-of-season television spectacular. A reliable source tells me that while the two of them were horsing around, ad-libbing at Saturday afternoon's show, they jocularly suggested putting a bomb under my seat for the opening. *Mes enfants*, if it's a bomb you've got, it doesn't matter whose seat you put it under.

MARTIN GOTTFRIED, *WOMEN'S WEAR DAILY*
Despite its structure as a vehicle for two, ignoring the structural needs of musical theatre for the sake of displaying its stars, *Golden Rainbow* gets through its first act as a genuine entertainment and that's more than I can say for any musical that's opened on Broadway over the last two years. Things don't hold up quite nearly so well after the intermission, in fact the whole business nearly collapsed last night at the Shubert Theatre. Still, for plain diversion and night club humor—which can be fun if it comes around only once a year—*Golden Rainbow* flashes good show biz razzle-dazzle for very much of its time. *Golden Rainbow* has not been approached as musical theatre as much as a showcase for its stars. Because of that, Ernest Kinoy and his songwriting partner Walter Marks had to gear all their work to spotlighting the couple. There are only two musical scenes—the production numbers—that do not have either Gorme or Lawrence or both singing, and except for a vague acknowledgement of secondary comedy characters they (and

the boy, charmingly played by Scott Jacoby) dominate all the book material. Moreover, their dialogue is as much special material as their songs and when I say "special material," I mean it in the specific, night club sense. Kinoy's book is really a series of floor show exchanges, a collection of wisecracks and patter, and most of them are funny in a Jewish-Vegas way. Because this seems to be the only kind of dialogue material that Gorme can handle I suppose it was a blessing for her, but Lawrence has a natural talent for the stage and it was a pity that he was given so small a chance to show it. His sheer stage strength, so obvious in *What Makes Sammy Run?*, could have been better used than this. With Marks providing a volley of custom-made songs, everything is very entertaining. Lawrence sings, Gorme sings, they both sing, they exchange jokes with Lawrence always keeping a wary, Broadway-veteran eye on his wife. But that's about the most one can say about it. This really is no way to make a musical and it gets away with as much as it does because of night club jazz rather than theatre excitement. But it does get away with something, and take that for what it's worth.

WALTER KERR, *TIMES*

Steve Lawrence needs a show that will keep out of his way, but they don't make musicals like that any more. Lawrence belongs to an all but vanished breed: the sort of entertainer who breezes past plot, glides along with the girls, hums to himself, notices the audience over his shoulder, stands hands on hips waiting for the pit to wake up, picks up the beat from some quiet throb in the basement, and doesn't fuss about anything because he knows he can always segue into three sock numbers he's been doing since kindergarten closed. Today we call it nightclub, but there was a time when it did nicely at the Winter Garden. I once saw Al Jolson finish off a show by clapping his hands, calling the company together, and explaining in that breathless milky baritone that it was close to 11 o'clock, the stagehands would soon have to be paid overtime, and whoever had stolen the pearls had better give them back right now because the plot was over. When the man in charge is good enough, you can put everything else on the cuff. Lawrence is quite good enough, shifty and easy and likable and quick, for this kind of thing—with Eydie Gorme to keep him comfortable company—but he's been born just a little too late to find a musical loose enough to fit him. *Golden Rainbow*, like all other musicals nowadays, is based on a play and keeps worrying about it, even insists on winding up its sentimental and not very interesting story line. (Exception: there's one tough straight sequence around a Las Vegas crap table that is neatly and fiercely staged by Arthur Storch, with much help from a real actor named Joseph Sirola—but what is it doing here when Mr. Lawrence only wants to be out on the desert sands dancing lazily around rocks and kidding Nelson Eddy?)

RICHARD WATTS, JR., POST
They have even put the Fall of Babylon into *Golden Rainbow*. The new musical comedy also has two pleasant performers in Steve Lawrence and Eydie Gorme, as well as an energetic production and several tuneful if reminiscent songs. Yet it seemed to me that the show offered at best only a moderately diverting evening's entertainment. Lawrence, who created the title role in *What Makes Sammy Run?*, still appears to be playing Sammy Glick, this time entangled in the hotel business in Las Vegas. Since *Golden Rainbow* is adapted from a play that I recall as interesting, it is surprising that it isn't more eventful as a libretto. It has to be eked out with production numbers, the most ambitious of which is that Fall of Babylon, and, while the episode has its amusing moments, it is disappointingly flat. Things are at their best when Lawrence and Gorme ignore the book and merely sing, which is something they do with skill and the appearance of enjoying themselves. The songs are at their most pleasant when they are cheerful. But even when the score composed by Walter Marks was being at its best, it had a way of bringing up disturbing memories. There was a song I enjoyed particularly [presumably "I've Gotta Be Me"], but it kept reminding me of one of the fine numbers in Leslie Bricusse's score for *Roar of the Greasepaint* [1965, presumably "Who Can I Turn To?"]. The stars receive valuable support from a boy actor named Scott Jacoby, who plays the dubious hero's devoted son with believable feeling and charm. When he and Lawrence were singing "We Got Us," all seemed momentarily well. The fact as I see it is that *Golden Rainbow* really isn't a bad musical comedy. It simply has the great misfortune to be not particularly interesting.

•   •   •

Steve Lawrence received nothing but accolades for his performance in *Golden Rainbow*, with critical slams leveled at just about everyone else. Of course, the key decisions (or, more likely, *all* decisions) were made by—you guessed it. So Mr. Lawrence (& the Missus) looked golden, in effect, by surrounding themselves with flax. Some rainbow. Arnold Schulman's 1957 comedy was about a ne'er-do-well—played by Paul Douglas, with Frank Sinatra essaying the part in the 1961 screen version—who is perennially bailed out by his conservative, stable, elder brother. The locale was switched from Miami Beach to the Miami Beach-of-the-Sixties, Las Vegas, which made some sort of sense; but casting Eydie Gorme in the Davey Burns/Edward G. Robinson role— well, you figure it out. Needless to say they added a romantic angle, which made hash (or shall we say craps?) of the whole mess. The project initiated with songwriter Walter Marks, who'd made a fairly reasonable debut—not especially good, but certainly not embarrassing—with the 1964 flop *Bajour*. Marks provided Lawrence with one hit song, "I've Gotta Be Me." (The *Hole in the Head* movie had an even better one, the Jimmy Van Heusen/Sammy Cahn Oscar-winner "High Hopes.") The stars brought in nominal producers, the respected general managers Joseph P. Harris and Ira Bernstein, who had known enough to bail out of their two previously optioned musicals, *Kelly* (1965) and *Hallelujah, Baby!* (1967). (Joe Harris should not be confused with the other Joseph Harris, coproducer of the 1966 *Sweet Charity* and *Mame*—although Joe was general manager of both.) Steve and Edyie's Diplomat Productions ruled *Golden Rainbow*, though, with an ironfisted glove. When Schulman suggested that the show be done like a musical, not a night-club, he was fired (from the adaptation of his own play). Mike Stewart stepped in, found he couldn't please the Lawrences, and stepped out quickly. Finally, TV-writer Ernest Kinoy, who had collaborated with Marks on *Bajour*, came in to finish off *Hole in the Head*. Director Arthur Storch—who had been dumped from Lawrence's earlier musical, *What Makes Sammy Run?*—was dumped, as was choreographer Ron Field (who was also fired from *his* prior show, *Sherry!* [1967]. What a way to follow up *Cabaret* [1966]). The advance sale, meanwhile, topped a million—the Lawrence-Gorme tandem was made to order for theatre parties—so the official opening was pushed off while the show was being, as they say, "fixed." After forty-three numbing previews *Golden Rainbow* finally rolled the dice. The highlight of the opening came when a pastie flew off one of the "Las Vegas showgirls" on the chorus line. (Carole Bishop, actually, who would later win a Tony on a different chorus line at the same Shubert.) "Millions for production," ad-libbed producer/star Lawrence, "but not one cent for glue."

BROADWAY SCORECARD

/ PERFS: 385 / $: –

RAVE	FAVORABLE	MIXED	UNFAVORABLE	PAN
	1		1	4

GOOD NEWS

"The 30's Musical," a revised version of the 1927 "Collegiate Musical"

music and lyrics by B. G. DeSylva, Lew Brown, and Ray Henderson

book by Laurence Schwab, B. G. DeSylva, and Frank Mandel; adaptation by Garry Marshall (replacing Abe Burrows)

directed by Michael Kidd (replacing Abe Burrows)

choreographer unbilled (Michael Kidd replacing Donald Saddler)

produced by Harry Rigby and Terry Allen Kramer

starring Alice Faye, Gene Nelson (replacing John Payne), and Stubby Kaye (replacing Eddie "Rochester" Anderson)

with Marti Rolph, Scott Stevensen, Jana Robbins, Barbara Lail, Wayne Bryan, Joseph Burke, and Tommy Breslin

opened December 23, 1974   St. James Theatre

"You'd be tired, too, if you'd been knocking about the country all year," said Doug Watt. "Keep your sunny side up," said DeSylva, Brown, & Henderson. Preliminary credits.

CLIVE BARNES, *TIMES*

[Headline: "*Good News* for Lovers of the Obvious"]

I took the precaution of seeing the production at last Saturday's matinee, wanting to see this particular show with a live, paying, unbiased
audience. That audience loved *Good News*. It applauded every oldie as
it came up, it gushed over Alice Faye, it laughed at jokes obvious
enough to give banana skins a bad name, and it just had a lovely experience. With certain reservations, I did not. The score is a mishmash.
What these new nostalgia musicals tend to be is a medley of hit songs
held together with a little campy dialogue preferably garnished with a
few formerly well-known film stars, in the present instance Miss Faye
and Gene Nelson, who has recently taken over from the formerly
better-known John Payne. *Good News* is certainly not badly delivered.
It is now directed and (presumably) partly choreographed by Michael
Kidd. On the road it had been directed by Abe Burrows and choreographed by Donald Saddler, who now both disown the work. In such
circumstances it is impossible to know who did what and to which, but
the complete staging, now bearing the Kidd signature, is very good. It
has a sense of style, a sense of period and a few bursts of energy that
really work. Faye, cast as an astronomy professor (she must be astronomy's biggest surprise since Einstein), is not the most animated leading
lady one has seen. She has a leathery, unbending way with her, but her
light baritone voice is pleasing, and she unquestionably dances with the
guts of a Ruby Keeler.

MARTIN GOTTFRIED, *POST*

The first show I've ever seen that was stolen by the vocal arranger. It is
a joyless, mechanical reproduction that misses the whole point of nostalgia shows, which is to look at a sweet and simple past entertainment
from an oblique but affectionate angle. The revival that opened last
night has no angle at all. The company is trained and scrubbed; the
scenery and traffic are efficiently managed; the familiar songs are sung;
and nothing happened. It seems to have been mounted for the sake of
reuniting Alice Faye with John Payne, the co-stars of the old 20th
Century Fox musicals. It toured so long Payne's contract expired a couple of weeks ago and [the show] may have been repaired so persistently
it expired as well. Gene Nelson is now co-starring with Miss Faye,

which probably made no difference since starred though they may be, they have only featured roles. Moreover, the director seems to have made every effort to keep them on stage as seldom as he can and apart whenever possible. Since Nelson and Faye are as compatible as oil and water, and since, combined, they have the stage presence of a balcony seat, there really should be a follow spot to let you know when one or the other is performing. I refer to "the director" because some programs at the Saturday night preview listed Abe Burrows as director and Donald Saddler as choreographer, while others credited their successor, Michael Kidd, with both. Since some of the staging and certainly some of the jokes bear the Burrows stamp, and some of the choreography is clearly the work of Saddler's it is difficult to assign their credit or blame to Kidd, whose hectic dancing style is also evident. If you get the impression that there is not exactly a consistency to the show, you are getting the idea. That was no joke, however, about the vocal arranger. The singers have been given dazzling harmonization and stylings, just off the nose, between accuracy and parody, which is how the whole show should have been done. It is hardly surprising that these arrangements were made by someone as talented as Hugh Martin.

DOUGLAS WATT, *DAILY NEWS*

Good News, which began its career a bit over a year ago in Boston, finally made it to New York last night. It wasn't a triumphant arrival; it was more like the end of the road. You'd be tired, too, it you'd been knocking about the country all year. Miss Faye, disconcertingly, doesn't look much like the Alice Faye we remember, but she's still slim and slinks on and off in a variety of gowns and dresses [designed by Donald Brooks], shakes a left leg from time to time, and sings a couple of songs. Miss Faye, so low-keyed in her approach that you forget her whenever she's off stage, doesn't add much to the show. Gene Nelson, cast as Tait's coach, genially tags along after her and gets to execute a few butterflies [dance steps]. Stubby Kaye, playing the trainer, does little except lead on several different animals (dog, goat, skunk, llama) as prospective mascots until late in the second half, when he's allowed to lead the male chorus in "Sunny Side Up" and to score at last. The only other time I saw *Good News* was many years ago when it was used, with altered lyrics, as the basis of an industrial show with a line of automobiles as the main attraction. I rather missed those cars last night.

○   ○   ○

No, No, Nanette (1971)—from which coproducer Harry Rigby was unceremoniously bounced—begat *Irene* (1973), which begat *Good News*. Or, Ruby Keeler to Debbie Reynolds to Alice Faye. Diminishing returns, wouldn't you say? *Good News* underwent one of those yearlong pre-Broadway tours, beginning December 7, 1973, in Philadelphia, designed to earn gobs of greenbacks en route, but the money somehow seems to go out faster than it comes in when you're fixing a broken-down show. Especially when you replace the book, direction, and choreography. The troupe finally reached New York and began an endlessly extended preview period—fifty-one in all—during which costar John Payne (of the 1947 movie *Miracle on 34th Street*) ankled. When John Payne is your big male lead—and *he* quits—things are rough indeed. Like in those old-fashioned musicals, Rigby and Co. finally pulled everything together and opened. *Good News* got bad news, and within a fortnight Alice and Gene and Stubby and the goat, skunk, and llama were back on the lam. Capitalized at half a million dollars, *Good News* went *way* over budget and closed with a loss of $1,250,000.

BROADWAY SCORECARD
/ PERFS: 16 / $: −

RAVE	FAVORABLE	MIXED	UNFAVORABLE	PAN
	1			5

GOODTIME CHARLEY

"A New Musical"

music by Larry Grossman

lyrics by Hal Hackady

book by Sidney Michaels

suggested by events in the lives of Charles VII of France (1403–1461) and Jeanne D'Arc (1412?–1431)

directed by Peter H. Hunt (doctored by Bob Fosse)

choreographed by Onna White (replacing Dennis Nahat)

produced by Max Brown and Byron Goldman in association with Robert Victor and Stone Widney

starring Joel Grey

with Ann Reinking, Susan Browning, Louis Zorich, Richard B. Schull, Jay Garner, and Grace Keagy

opened March 3, 1975   Palace Theatre

CLIVE BARNES, *TIMES*

Clearly no effort has been spared on *Goodtime Charley*. It has the well-scrubbed look so often betokening frantic days and sleepless nights. But was all the effort worthwhile? It does give us Mr. Grey, perky, exuberant and touching as a little king lost, and it does give us Ann Reinking glistening sweet as Joan of Arc. Joan of Arc? Yes, this musical happens to be the first in which the heroine goes up in smoke before the final curtain. Still, if Bernard Shaw could make Joan of Lorraine into a sort of comedy [the 1923 *Saint Joan*], why should not Sidney Michaels, Larry Grossman, and Hal Hackady make the story of Joan into a sort of a musical? Ask the producers. The tone of the book is uncertain. It tries to be both flippant and serious, but it really succeeds in being neither. The story of a little guy's being made into a king is not a bad idea at all—but although Grey is the star, the story rests on Joan. This is a conflict of narrative interest that Michaels never resolves. Whose story is this? We never find out. Grossman's music is agreeably lyrical without being memorably tuneful; it all sounds like one of those Hollywood background scores where emotion is unsuccessfully chasing an all too elusive melody. So far, not so good. With this book and this score, *Goodtime Charley* is not going to be one of the musicals that can light up Broadway's history books. There are one or two jokes (which I will refrain from quoting) but too much of the dialogue is on the level of Joan's casual remark, "Well, I sure don't want to burn," which is so dangerously close to banality that it isn't even funny. But the cast and the staging do everything that can be done for *Goodtime Charley* short of giving it a blood transfusion. So many good performances and so much effort have gone into *Goodtime Charley* that it seems almost unjust that the results are not more invigorating. But there is always Grey and Reinking to relish—and any evening with such relishment can hardly be called wasted.

HOWARD KISSEL, *WOMEN'S WEAR DAILY*

If you were doing a movie satirizing Broadway and needed a scene showing the campy mentality too often at work there, any scene from *Goodtime Charley* would do. The musical tells the oft-told story of Joan of Arc from the point of view of the ineffectual king she served. To succeed with this sort of wrong-end-of-the-telescope conception requires greater wit and outrageousness than Sidney Michaels, Hal Hackady and Larry Grossman seem capable of. The material never goes beyond facile cleverness, or worse, coyness, which makes the basic idea seem, in the lighthearted early scenes, absurd and sophomoric, and in the later, "serious" scenes, ludicrously overblown. Joel Grey is an actor capable of the most dazzling pyrotechnics, but *Goodtime Charley* never makes proper use of him. Ultimately, the show is as much an insult to his talent as it is to our intelligence. Joan of Arc seems largely a nag. Her desires and emotions never seem deeper than those of the average teenager who wants to be a cheerleader and wear the class ring of the football captain. The rest of the actors are really pawns for Peter Hunt to set in a series of cutesy poses. They mince across the stage, assume their children's-book-illustration poses or say lines such as "I'm-a the Pope" convincingly enough to reinforce one's impression that the only way *Goodtime Charley* can be taken seriously is as a sendup of pretentious musicals. The costumes by Willa Kim are perfect storybook creations, the pleasantest thing about the show. . . . From my seats (C-5 and C-7), I was able to see about a third of the stage. I saw most of the action, which takes place down front, but missed two-thirds of Rouben Ter-Arutunian's sets, most of which had a certain grandness of form but seemed to use bland or faded colors. I'm sure I was given these seats as an ingenious ploy by the press agent, who, knowing my generous instincts, thought I would assume that whatever I wasn't seeing must somehow be better than what I was. But it does seem outrageous that, in the unlikely event *Goodtime Charley* lasts beyond Saturday, unsuspecting patrons will have to pay $15 for such not-so-choice locations. The real hero of the evening is Jonathan Tunick, whose superb orchestrations make Grossman's thin, boring score sound more respectable than it deserves to.

DOUGLAS WATT, *DAILY NEWS*

It's hard to imagine what voices urged Joan of Arc to turn to a song-and-dance career on Broadway. That's not her style, as a bloodless musical called *Goodtime Charley*, in which Joan gets second billing, proved Monday night at the Palace, nor does it suit the Dauphin very well, either. Sidney Michaels, who provided the book, has taken his cue from Anouilh who was, in turn, indebted to Shaw in infusing the relationship between Joan and Charles with wit. But in Michaels' hands, the wit becomes crude humor, and the passion, not to mention the intellectual content, is sorely missing. Instead, a dreadful air of solemnity and, worse, lifelessness keeps creeping over the proceedings so that it continually threatens to come to a dead halt. As the Dauphin and star of the show, the cricket-like Joel Grey is given surprisingly little of interest to do and he understandably appears at a loss much of the time. And dancer Ann Reinking, though a striking-looking heroine, neither sings nor speaks with much thrust, and is allowed to exercise her shapely legs mostly by prancing her way through a production number devoted to Joan's battlefield conquests. Oddly, the only moment of real charm to overtake the evening arrives when Susan Browning, playing a voluptuous lady of the court and mistress to Charley, and Richard B. Shull, playing a humbling page, join in a duet ["Merci, Bon Dieu"]. The song is negligible, but the singers are disarming. Not much else about *Goodtime Charley* is. Jay Garner and Louis Zorich huff and puff to bring comic life to the roles of the Archbishop and General, but they are finally defeated for good in a heavyhanded "Confessional" duet. Larry Grossman's tunes are often provocative, but Hal Hackady's lyrics are of considerably less interest; so much so, that it becomes increasingly difficult to keep one's mind on them. Rouben Ter-Arutunian has designed a chaste basic setting, a white rotunda with curved steps against which a few Maxfield Parrish–like backdrops blend very nicely and in front of which hanging foliage is sometimes used to evoke pleasant memories of Joseph Urban's opera designs. Willa Kim's costumes are likewise attractive. Charley may have been out for a good time, but Joan decidedly wasn't, and any attempt to reduce her moving and endlessly reverberating story to Broadway musical terms is plain foolishness.

o   o   o

Another misguided musical from the *Minnie's Boys* boys, the songwriters and producers of the 1970 Marxical comedy. And once again they sabotaged themselves by casting a star in a subsidiary role and shifting focus away from the major character(s). The scenario goes like this: the leading role calls for a girl who can pass for a teenager; no such performer *with any ticket-selling potential* can be found; somebody notices that this or that star, who *is* available and looking for a Broadway musical comeback, could very well play one of the other roles; said star is contacted, interested, and raring to go; and the die is cast. Now this is not always such a very bad thing; the show I've just described—the one about the budding stripper and her Mama Rose—turned out pretty well. But in that case there were authors and a director/choreographer who had a definite tack to take, and a star more or less willing to go along with them. In Hackady, Grossman, and Michaels's hands, though, *Saint Joan* became *The Joel Grey Show*. (Imagine, if you will, rewriting the story of the Maid of Orléans and calling it *Goodtime*

Charley.) The producers seemed to have their eye on the success of that other medieval musical about an unmotivated French ruler, *Pippin* (1972). "Imagine what kind of hit *Pippin* would have been if they had a star," they no doubt reasoned, eagerly signing up Grey and subverting whatever vision their authors might have had. Here was a scamp-of-a-Charley given all sorts of songs and dances with which to entertain, while poor Joan turned on her spit. *Goodtime Charley*, in its final form, seemed to exist solely for the purpose of selling tickets on Joel Grey's name. The initial interest was not insubstantial, but after thirteen weeks the presold advance was used up and the show folded. With negligible material and a pronounced lack of star charisma, a *Goodtime* was had by none.

BROADWAY SCORECARD
/ PERFS: 104 / $: -

RAVE	FAVORABLE	MIXED	UNFAVORABLE	PAN
			1	5

GOT TU GO DISCO

"A New Musical"

music and lyrics by Kenny Lehman, John Davis, Ray Chew, Nat Adderly Jr., Thomas Jones, Wayne Morrison, Steve Boston, Eugene Narmoze, Betty Rowland, Jerry Powell, and Ashford and Simpson

book by John Zudrow

conceived and created by Joe Eula (billing removed, although retaining billing as costume designer); based on the fairy tale *Cinderella*

directed by Larry Forde (replacing Joe Eula, who replaced John Zudrow)

choreographed by Jo Jo Smith and Troy Garza; additional choreography by George Faison

produced by Jerry Brandt and Gotta Dance, Inc., in association with Roy Rifkind, Julie Rifkind, Bill Spitalsky, and WKTU-Radio 92

with Irene Cara, Patrick Jude (replacing Scott Holmes), Rhetta Hughes, Joe Masiell, Patti Karr, Lisa Raggio, and Jane Holzer

opened June 25, 1979   *Minskoff Theatre*

CLIVE BARNES, *POST*

[Headline: "*Disco* Turns Out To Be a Fast Hustle"]

Got Tu Go Disco is said to be the most expensive show ever staged on Broadway but then who is counting? Certainly it looks an odd mixture of the clearly lavish and obviously tacky. Which possibly ideally evokes the grand spirit of disco. The show is the brainchild of impresario Jerry Brandt, who years ago gave us that archetypal, semi-disco down in Greenwich Village, The Electric Circus. At times it seems to be the intention to recreate on stage the impression of a Studio 54, for people who could not buy their way into the real thing in a thunderstorm. Yet at other times *Got Tu Go Disco* appears to have far more serious aspirations. Indeed at times it even seems to be a musical, just like any other musical, with a story and songs, and people dancing and all having a swell time. Just like *Annie* (1977) or *Il Trovatore* (1853). John Zudrow, the man credited—should that be the word—with the book, has written two novels, and lived nine years in a monastery. He has based the theme on the story of *Cinderella*—a poor little girl working in the rag trade who wants to go to the disco and become queen of the ballroom. Pretty smart, huh? A sort of modernization perhaps of an eternal theme rendered madly relevant for contemporary consciousness—for Cinderellas never die, they just disco away. Now having got that, what else do we need but music? Twelve men and women labored heartily over the music. It must have been like being called for jury duty. They have pitted their talents together and emerged with a score that will surely prove memorably unmemorable. You don't have to listen to music. At the final preview which I attended I noticed some people had earplugs—and that could be a better concession bet than the orange drink. Yet the decor by James Hamilton proves magnificently tasteless in true disco style. It has lights, chrome, glitter, an orchestra in a cage like a three-tiered wedding cake, moving staircases and beads, bangles and baubles everywhere. Will it catch on? Well, German measles periodically does.

RICHARD EDER, *TIMES*
Like the boxes that give off a neutral hum for insomniacs to sleep by, disco's music and strobe-light spectacle exist not to be heard or seen but to shut out hearing and seeing; to provide a neutral region where the customers can dance their fantasies alone. Apart from the sheer mediocrity of most of the effort involved, this is perhaps the central fallacy of *Got Tu Go Disco*. The point of disco is to participate. The dancing, the music and the performances in *Got Tu Go Disco*, strung around an apathetic story, may well re-create what is to be found in discos. But that is just the trouble. Their lack of bite or character makes them as uninteresting to watch as a row of barflies drinking themselves silly. Apart from drawing customers—at $50-a-seat opening-night prices, the Minskoff seemed only about three-quarters filled—it is hard to fig-

ure out what is the purpose of *Got Tu.* For much of last night it seemed to be an extended commercial for New York's best-known discothèque; two of the performers, in fact, are Studio 54's barman and the man who keeps people out. At other times it was like a demonstration show for a record salesmen's convention. What it never was—except, perhaps, for a brief showing of flare and spirit by Rhetta Hughes—was theatre of any kind. The show is played out so perfunctorily that the principal performers never relinquish their hand mikes. Irene Cara and Patrick Jude emerge from a climactic embrace clutching their mikes as if they were ice-cream cones they were unwilling to putdown. Cara seems embarrassed in her droopy Cinderella phases; when she emerges triumphantly she is still droopy. This is probably deliberate; the show's thesis, such as it is, is that disco is not just for the beautiful few, but for the unspectacular many. Cara represents these, but it is a poor way to work up to a climax for a musical. Jude is bland; he should not wipe his mouth after kissing if he intends to play a lover. The message seems to be that disco has no particular character, requires no particular effort and therefore is good for everyone. Not for a theatre audience, though.

DOUGLAS WATT, *DAILY NEWS*
[Headline: "*Disco* Going Nowhere"]
Got Tu Go Disco is a big, flashy musical, an amateurish attempt to capture the hypnotic excitement of a disco palace on a theatre stage. The problem is one of esthetic distance: the audience can't dance (there's not even a center aisle at the Minskoff) and is thus reduced to a houseful of gradually wilting wallflowers. The scenery and costumes are the epitome of chic trash; the sound from the big band stage rear and from the performers, who all grasp hand-held mikes, pulsates through the house. But we are apart, seated and listening to the insistent and tedious disco beat without being able to move to it (I'm told being stoned is almost a prerequisite). And what *Got Tu Go Disco* finally amounts to is an overblown Radio City Music Hall production number from the old days. Even at that, it lacks the Rockettes. *Got Tu Go Disco* is pure trash, and as meaningless as its title. Discothèques are trashy, too, of course, but you can get caught up in their trash.

●   ◉   ◉

"I don't know enough about Broadway to stage a bad show, so it's got to be good," said producer Jerry Brandt to the *Daily News*. And there you have it. Brandt was a jeans-entrepreneur-turned-rock-promoter, owner of the East Village disco The Electric Circus, and discoverer of Patti LaBelle. His astrologer, he explained, advised him to put the "tu" in *Got Tu Go Disco* because it was a "money spelling." (Or was it because of his cross-promotion with WKTU-Radio 92?) Costume designer Joe Eula conceived and created this disco-*Cinderella*, directing it as well. (Who he, Geoffrey Holder?) As the show underwent tumultuous turmoil he was banned from the premises, although his costumes remained. Larry Forde, the stage manager, tried to make sense of things and succeeded in at least getting the curtain up. But not for long. The astrologer's money spelling turned out to be apropos: *Got Tu Go Disco* was Broadway's most expensive failure (at the time). Officially capitalized at two million, it is estimated that more than three went down the disco drain.

BROADWAY SCORECARD
/ PERFS: 8 / $: –

RAVE	FAVORABLE	MIXED	UNFAVORABLE	PAN
				6

THE GRAND TOUR

"The Musical," previously entitled *Jacobowsky and the Colonel*

music and lyrics by Jerry Herman

book by Michael Stewart and Mark Bramble

based on the 1944 comedy *Jacobowsky and the Colonel* by S. N. Behrman, adapted from the Austrian play *Jacobowsky und der Oberst* by Franz Werfel (unproduced in its original version until 1958)

directed by Gerald Freedman (doctored by Tommy Tune)

choreographed by Donald Saddler (doctored by Tommy Tune)

produced by James M. Nederlander, Diana Shumlin, and Jack Schlissel in association with Carole J. Shorenstein and Stewart F. Lane

starring Joel Grey and Ron Holgate

with Florence Lacey, Stephen Vinovich, George Reinholt, Gene Varrone, Chevi Colton, Grace Keagy, Travis Hudson, and Jay Stuart

opened January 11, 1979   Palace Theatre

RICHARD EDER, *TIMES*

The Grand Tour is a musical that is often amiable and sometimes more than that. But it is a patchwork, and an incomplete one. Its engaging moments run in different directions, pull different ways, and leave large areas looking decidedly thin. The effect is that of first-rate talents working at their occasional second-best, and having occasional third thoughts about it. *Jacobowsky* was a considerable success when it came out in 1944. The story of an unlikely partnership between an aristocratic Polish colonel and an ingenious Polish Jew who join forces to escape from occupied France, balanced irony and sentiment. At this remove, the sentiment has corroded some of the iron; still, there is some lively intelligence in it and a number of finely biting lines. But in making a musical out of a play, a good deal of nuance is lost; and much of the quality of *Jacobowsky* was nuance. In compensation there should be an infusion of energy, songs and dances and all the rest, establishing a new rhythm and bounce that make up for the simplifications. It is this guiding energy that is lacking. Herman's score is no masterpiece, nor is it his own best work but it is often agreeable. Grey is, of course, the center of the evening. Sometimes this is to the good. Under stress his portrait of a kind of shriveled angel works very well. He opens his eyes very wide and the pupils are like the points of two invisible exclamation points. But it is a performance that frequently crosses over into the self-indulgent. This Jacobowsky is too pleased with his own charm; Grey has things his own way just a bit too often. There are sections of *Tour*, in fact, that seem to be there just to give Grey more exposure. For example, there is a Jewish wedding interpolated to provide the occasion for a dance so long and so elaborate—at the same time it is neither particularly original nor very interesting—that it quite pulls the musical out of shape. This is part of the lack of conviction, the sense of tinkering, of putting in a bit of this and a bit of that because some of it is bound to work; that is the central weakness of *Tour*.

WALTER KERR, *TIMES*
[Headline: "A Detour for Joel Grey"]
Somebody's got to figure out what to do with Joel Grey. Ever since the diminutive performer burst upon us in *Cabaret* [1966], an apparition from one of the seamier suburbs of Hell, he's been—rightly enough—a nominal star. No one was going to forget the painted puppet's face that leapt at us out of the dark, voicing an evil welcome in three or four languages, a trim and tidy nightmare of rouge, lipstick, pomade. The presence was otherworldly, netherworldly. Its invitation was as sleek as the Berlin music-hall world it came from was sick, and we responded to the image with instant awe, fascinated by its bloodcurdling good will, its impeccably precise animation, the calculated lure of its very loathsomeness. Brilliantly complex, sinuous and diamond-hard; and more than deserving of the Tony it got. Since then, though, there's been a problem of following up. Just how is the undeniably talented Grey to be prop-

erly used? He wasn't really a proper George M. Cohan in the *George M!* [1968] of 10 years ago: he didn't quite command the stage space so constantly allotted him, didn't quite fill the shoes of the somehow more substantial song-and-dance-man he was impersonating. Now, in *The Grand Tour*, he comes a mite closer, especially when he is flinging himself through the jackknife turnabouts and stammering heel stomps of a dance that is all angular energy. But there's still a gap. Though there's a piercing light now and again in Grey's narrow, closely spaced eyes, it's once again not exactly starlight. Why not, and where can the glitter, the scale, and the shimmering authority of *Cabaret* be found another time? It's lurking there somewhere, waiting for the right lucky stroke to pluck it out of hiding. And so I kept watching Grey slave away—pretty literally. Watching, I remembered one thing. In *Cabaret*, Grey had—in effect—been masked, stylized from head to toe. That gleaming face that so transfixed us had been simplified as a clown's face is simplified, turned into a neutral white background with strong slashes of color for accent. And it was the accent, of course, that expanded to embrace stage and auditorium, the styling that made a trifle of a man seem a leering titan. Does Mr. Grey require some sort of stylization, some sort of boldly imposed accent, to give him the oversize we associate with a star? I think so.

HOWARD KISSEL, *WOMEN'S WEAR DAILY*

One of those musicals conceived with an eye less to the requirements of musical theatre than to those of Jewish theatre parties. Even the title sounds more like a package vacation deal than something about a hapless Jew and an anti-Semitic Polish colonel racing through France one step ahead of the Nazis. *The Grand Tour* follows the general pattern of Jerry Herman musicals—a perfectly respectable play is eviscerated to make room for music and lyrics of surpassing inanity. In Herman's hands everything is trivialized, reduced to a varsity show kind of cuteness. At the beginning of the show, for example, Jacobowsky has to persuade the stubborn arrogant Polish colonel by appealing to the colonel's patriotism. The plea is couched in terms like "so the sausage'll keep getting stuffed/and the sheep getting shorn/do it for P-O-L-A-N-D." Like Herman's other scores, the music for *Grand Tour* is simple and catchy—phrases are repeated often enough within a song, and the songs themselves are reprised often enough that you'd have to be a musical idiot not to go out humming some of the tunes. Philip J. Lang has done a marvelous camouflage orchestration, pulling every trick out of the orchestrator's hat—bells, accordions—to make it sound rich. Wally Harper conducts with great gusto, compensating for the score's lack of drama. . . . Gerald Freedman's direction lacks style, drive, or imagination. The most unforgivable of his sins is that he has given Joel Grey almost nothing to do. For the most part Grey stands quite still and delivers his lines in a high-pitched, plaintive voice. The tone is that of a martyr—whether the martyr is Jacobowsky the potential prey of the Nazis or Grey the victim of the material is not clear. Grey, the focal point of the show, spends so much time being winsome and pathetic one never really enjoys his presence. Donald Saddler has choreographed in his customarily clean manner—here, considering the nature of the subject, it is all a bit too clean, too spiffy, too standard. This is particularly true in a Jewish wedding scene (one of the show's many attempts to extort crude laughs from Hadassah ladies) in which the dancers perform authentic enough steps, but in an unusually stiff, unidiosyncratic way, like a bunch of Bronxville Jaycees doing *Fiddler on the Roof*.

◦   ◦   ◦

Producer Diana Shumlin first announced her musical *Jacobowsky and the Colonel* with a score by Stan Daniels, book by Leonard (*Destry Rides Again* [1959]) Gershe, and a cast headed by Alec McCowen and Richard Kiley. (Having heard Daniels's banal and tasteless *So Long, 174th Street* [1976], one can only imagine what he would have done to the sensitively themed *Jacobowsky*.) Unable to get the show mounted, Shumlin turned to her friend Mike Stewart, who agreed to undertake the project providing that his *Dolly!* (1964) and *Mack & Mabel* (1974) collaborator, Jerry Herman, be invited along, too. Herman concurred, Mark Bramble joined as colibrettist, and *Jacobowsky* was finally viable. Director Gerald Freedman and choreographer Donald Saddler were enlisted on the strength of their innovative work on *The Robber Bridegroom* (1976), Gower Champion having turned his old colleagues down. But *The Grand Tour* was derailed by a central error in casting. The character of Jacobowsky, as written by Werfel and Behrman, is warm, charming, and sympathetic; Viennese emigrant Oscar Karlweis created it, and Danny Kaye played the 1958 motion picture version, *Me and the Colonel*. Joel Grey, of course, is neither warm, charming, nor sympathetic. But Jacobowsky was also meant to be a tiny man, physically, and in this (at least) Joel Grey was perfect. Other, larger actors were under consideration—including Jerry Orbach and Jimmy Coco, either of whom would have made up in charisma what they lacked in diminuitivity. But the decision was made to go with the jockey-sized Grey (who, incidentally, was just about the same size as the composer). A winning Jacobowsky was the key to *The Grand Tour*, and without it everybody might just as well have stayed home. (The presence of Richard Kiley as the Colonel, needless to say, would also have helped enormously.) Tommy Tune came to the San Francisco tryout to try to help out, but there wasn't much to be done; he added some balloons. And so Joel Grey returned to the Palace, home of *George M!* and *Goodtime Charley* (1975), and monopolized the stage to the detriment of all else. Capitalized at $950,000, *The Grand Tour* lost money here and there and everywhere, accumulating a whopping deficit of $1,457,183.

BROADWAY SCORECARD

/ PERFS: 61 / $: –

RAVE	FAVORABLE	MIXED	UNFAVORABLE	PAN
	2			4

THE GRASS HARP

"A Delightful New Musical," previously entitled *Yellow Drum*

music by Claibe Richardson

book and lyrics by Kenward Elmslie

based on the 1952 play by Truman Capote, from his 1951 novella

directed by Ellis Rabb

choreographed by Rhoda Levine

"The University of Michigan Professional Theatre Program's Production," presented by Theatre 1972 (Richard Barr, Charles Woodward, and Michael Harvey)

starring Barbara Cook, Carol Brice, Karen Morrow (replacing Celeste Holm), Ruth Ford, Max Showalter, and Russ Thacker

opened November 2, 1971   Martin Beck Theatre

CLIVE BARNES, *TIMES*

The Grass Harp is unpretentious—understandably unpretentious. It is based on the novel and play by Truman Capote that were both folksy and fey. The musical is also folksy and fey, in so far as it has any real character at all, for it is the kind of a show that is almost as difficult to dislike as to like. The book and lyrics by Kenward Elmslie are concerned with all the verities of simplicity. Dolly Talbo was once good to some gypsies, and they gave her a miracle gypsy dropsy cure, which apparently cures a great deal more than dropsy and appears to promote sensations of alcoholism. The intention is doubtless to celebrate America's dream of homespun innocence, and the intention is probably a good one. But Capote's concept of pastoral innocence and goodness suffers from mawkish sentimentality and dies quietly with scarcely a murmured protest. The musical has little chance of recovering from the disadvantages imposed upon it by Capote's sensibility—but in all fairness it does not make very strenuous efforts to escape.

The music by Claibe Richardson, while not being memorable, is not entirely forgettable. At its best it has a country-and-banjo jauntiness to it, and at its worse it sounds like the background music to an agrarian documentary on educational television. The best aspect of the evening was in a few of the performances. Barbara Cook could do little more than radiate frustrated life-spirit as the frustrated and life-spirited Dolly, but Carol Brice was splendidly matter-of-fact and throatily expansive as Catherine, and Karen Morrow came in like a hot breath of show business as the heaven-fire revivalist preaching love and flowers. At one moment a judge says, "Oh, the energy I have spent in hiding from myself." That phrase not only offers a fair example of the quality and texture of the work's thought and expression, it could also perfectly well serve as a motto for the evening. But there is no hiding place.

MARTIN GOTTFRIED, *WOMEN'S WEAR DAILY*
I don't know what in the world the University of Michigan's Professional Theatre Program is doing involving itself (as a sponsor) with a Broadway musical like *The Grass Harp*, but I can only suggest that if it wants to get itself into the commercial theatre, it had better find itself some professionals. *The Grass Harp* is an hour and a half long, which is short for a musical but, in this case, nowhere near short enough. It is based on Truman Capote's novel of the same name, though there is hardly any comparison. Capote's writing, then as now, was exquisite. Kenward Elmslie's adaptation is clumsy, and since the story deals with eccentricity and the fey, the clumsiness makes it seem stupid. Ironically, the tree house [to which the characters retreat] is the only interesting thing about this production. James Tilton has designed a huge loop of swirling branches, very much in the style of Aubrey Beardsley, and it is marvelously striking. Otherwise, the production wouldn't move unless you struck it. Ellis Rabb, the director, has contributed virtually nothing to it except lethargy and uncertainty. Barbara Cook, now growing matronly, still has the most beautiful voice in all of theatre and shamed it in application to this tripe. But most shamed was the idea of non-commercial theatres. When Rabb was running the A.P.A. as an alternative to Broadway's commercialism, was *The Grass Harp* what he had in mind as better theatre, too?

DOUGLAS WATT, *DAILY NEWS*
[Headline: "Good Cast Climbs Goo-Goo Tree to Play Stringless *Grass Harp*"]
Cloying nonsense, a lopsided ball of cotton candy. There was, I gather, an appealing poetic quality about these misfits in the novel and the play Capote later extracted from it. Here, though, they seem little more than a small band of crazies.

•   •   •

The Grass Harp covered itself in weeds in its very opening moment, when the spinster star trotted down to the apron and announced to one and all that the sudden appearance of a "cat cloud" overhead signified that it was "dropsy-cure weather." (That is, the season in which you whip up batches of secret gypsy tonic to ease that dread affliction. What *is* dropsy, anyway?) There's something sublimely ridiculous about the sound of the word *dropsy*; from that moment it didn't much matter whether the show was good or bad. *The Grass Harp* lost the audience—the New York audience, anyway—right there, before the first word of the first refrain; everything that followed seemed just plain silly. *The Grass Harp* was first mounted in 1966 by the Trinity Square Rep in Providence, Rhode Island. Adrian Hall directed a cast including Barbara Baxley (in the Cook role), Elaine Stritch (as Baby Love), and both Carols Brice and Bruce (the latter between stints in *Do I Hear a Waltz?* [1965] and *Henry, Sweet Henry* [1967]). Kermit Bloomgarden optioned the property but eventually dropped it, after which Ellis Rabb's A.P.A. picked up the rights. The nonprofit Association of Producing Artists was founded in 1960 by Rabb, with its home base at the University of Michigan in Ann Arbor. The group joined forces with the similarly foundering Phoenix Theatre in 1964, but was defunct before the decade's end—and before it could mount *The Grass Harp*. Richard Barr and associates, producers of Edward Albee and other esoteric fare, stepped in, and a tryout was arranged at the University of Michigan's spanking new $3.5-million facility. (Detroit *Press* review: "The new house works. The new show doesn't, though.") *The Grass Harp* was the third Capote novella transformed for the musical stage, following *House of Flowers* (1954) and *Breakfast at Tiffany's* (1966). Perhaps musical theatre wasn't his medium? Capote's own dramatization of *The Grass Harp*—with an incidental score by Virgil Thomson—

managed thirty-six performances at the Martin Beck in 1952, a princely reign compared to the 7 the tuner was able to attain twenty years later at the same playhouse.

BROADWAY SCORECARD
/ PERFS: 7 / $: -

RAVE	FAVORABLE	MIXED	UNFAVORABLE	PAN
1	1		1	3

GREASE

"A New '50s Rock 'N Roll Musical"

book, music, and lyrics by Jim Jacobs and Warren Casey

directed by Tom Moore

choreographed by Patricia Birch

produced by Kenneth Waissman and Maxine Fox (Waissman) in association with Anthony D'Amato

with Adrienne Barbeau, Walter Bobbie, Barry Bostwick, Carole Demas, Ilene Kristen, Timothy Meyers, Kathi Moss, Marya Small, and Garn Stephens

opened February 14, 1972   Eden Theatre
transferred June 7, 1972   Broadhurst Theatre

(Note: the first-night reviewers covered the show at its Eden Theatre première)

CLIVE BARNES, TIMES
They are starting to be nostalgic about 1959 now—and almost all I can remember about it is that it was a great year for Burgundy. However, it was probably quite good for Coca-Cola as well. *Grease*, which origi-

nated in Chicago, is a parody of one of those old Elvis Presley movies—
and if that is what you think you are ready for, please don't let me stop
you. It is said to be set at a reunion of a high school class of 1959, but
very little is made of the reunion aspect. However, as most of the so-
designated teenagers look trustworthily over 30, perhaps they were
meant to be playing their past. The music is the loud and raucous noise
of its time. It is meant to be funnier than it is, but the authors are forever being frustrated by the nature of what they are satirizing and its
comparative nearness to contemporary pop music. Interestingly, the
score is usually at its best when we are being given comic versions of
tearjerking ballads—such as the heroine's plaintive lament "It's Raining
on Prom Night." There is a cosy aggressiveness to the show, a deliberately loud-mouthed and facetious tastelessness that some will find
attractive, especially, I imagine, those who were teenagers in Middle
America at the end of the 1950's. But the show is a thin joke. As with
almost all pastiches, once the initial joke has been established, it is
bound to wear thin. If there is a place in New York for a modern 1950's
rock parody musical from Chicago, then *Grease* might well slide into it.
If there is a place. The first-night audience seemed genuinely to enjoy
it, so perhaps there is.

MARTIN GOTTFRIED, *WOMEN'S WEAR DAILY*
It is in their music that Jacobs and Casey have been most successful
and most mistaken. They have been successful in duplicating the early
rock 'n' roll sound of Bill Haley and Buddy Holly and the early black
groups (like The Penguins) that brought rock 'n' roll across the racial
line—though there are no blacks in the show to sing them, since music
but not people had crossed the color barrier in the late '50s. But they
have used the corniest of the music and they have forgotten the energy
of Elvis Presley, the invention of Chuck Berry, the ingenuity of the
Everly Brothers. They have concentrated on laughing at their era, forgetting to appreciate it. Nostalgia musicals and warm camp work best,
I think, when there is essential quality within the gross taste that is
being ridiculed and *Grease* has not remembered that. Its only real
appreciation of its period is in terms of innocence, and that isn't
enough. Meanwhile, we are asked to feel warmly toward a vulgar mentality that finds amusement in exposing bare bottoms in public and

standing around with chains and zip-guns. I did not find much likable about hoods when I was in high school, and I do not find it now. Nevertheless, the production itself is superb. Tom Moore has uncannily duplicated the look and behavior of his period. Though the actors are slightly too old for their roles, their manners of speech, movement and looks are so accurate that one is easily transported to a New Jersey-style high school of 13 years ago. Given the rut and repetition of the songs, they have been composed and sung with an amazing fidelity to the originals. The performances are all energetic and straight-faced, and Moore's company discipline is very admirable. But finally, there is no respect for the originals being mocked, and that leaves an understandable but critical hole in the show's heart. The songs kidded were just too awful; the characters who populate it are too shallow and stupid. And everything, finally, becomes repetitious. It is material that such superior talents as Sid Caesar and Frank Zappa found too thin and ungrateful for extended satire—Caesar could (and did) take care of it in a 10-minute sketch.

WALTER KERR, *TIMES*
The show's state of mind is disarming, its sociology would seem to be accurate (I wasn't in high school at the time), its tunes by Jim Jacobs and Warren Casey are often attractive in themselves as well as wryly nostalgic, and its two principals are so personable and so skilled that I wish the composer-librettists had had the plain good sense to concentrate on them more. Barry Bostwick is the boy, an angular and eel-like sort of Tony Perkins cadaver, and he is not only funny when he is jerking his head into a rapid "square" in order to convey what he thinks of a chap in immaculate tan shorts and patterned socks, he is even more ingratiating when he's caught out in a fat lie. He's sung, in "Summer Heat," of the girl he so easily made out with during the profitable vacation months, only to come face to face with her, newly registered at Rydell. The boast in his bright face turns to egg on the instant, he suddenly not only doesn't know what to do with his animated hands, he doesn't know where those 20 or 30 fingers have come from. The show digs a little here, catching the awkward kid behind the cavalier, and it might have investigated this sort of possibility oftener. Carole Demas is the girl, stuck for a time with that appliquéd pink poodle [skirt] and not

quite in rhythm with the girls who slip out windows for the evening, pretty, appealing, believably innocent as she makes an amusing lament of "It's Raining on Prom Night" and believably liberated later. Whenever these two meet—at a drive-in movie for a film about were-wolves, at a hamburger palace—the show itself seems to come together, like pieces of scenery riding in from the wings to meet. If *Grease* becomes attenuated and rather wearing in the second half, it's because it keeps replaying its atmospheric effects instead of getting on with what probably ought to be the love story. It dawdles over jargon too much, as though just hearing the lunchroom, street-corner, school-gym inflections of the period would be enough to keep us content between numbers. And it starts up paths—one of the girls gets pregnant—it isn't going to bother to pursue. The book rambles, and has to keep picking up after itself, which is a chore.

DOUGLAS WATT, *DAILY NEWS*

The Eden Theatre is a-tingle. *Grease*, which opened there last night, is a lively and funny musical—as well as the dancingest one in town—that brings back the look and sound of the teenage world of the late 1950s with glee. It's a winner. Rydell High's class of '59 is a spirited one com-posed largely of delinquents. The boys wear ducktails and pompadors and leather jackets and behave like latterday Dead End Kids or, better yet, their *West Side Story* [1957] contemporaries. The girls wear curls, bobbysox, pedal-pushers and the like and are as immoral as the boys. And both groups revel in gutter language, I should caution you, some-times carrying it to extremes. But the main thing is, they're all great fun. The show moves swiftly and without a hitch from cafeteria to pajama party, prom, Burger Palace and drive-in movie, among other places. The boys are forever striking cool, sharp attitudes; the girls are full of wise-cracks. And how they sing and dance in this most stylishly staged and choreographed show! The songs that Jim Jacobs and Warren Casey have provided for the show are dandies, niftily arranged and wonder-fully evocative of the period. Not since *Bye Bye Birdie* [1960] has the inane world of the early rockers been presented with such zip and charm. But that work only touched on the music of the time. *Grease* is wholly immersed in it. Patricia Birch's dances are a constant delight, and Tom Moore has attended to the overall direction brightly. The sheer energy of *Grease* carries all before it. Rydell's class of '59 may have been mindless and uncouth but, boy, did it have rhythm. Dig.

º   º   º

A couple of out-of-work actors in Chicago started fooling around one day, and look at what they wrought. *Grease* didn't have much in the way of music, and the humor was sophomoric. What *Grease* did have—and what is more important, perhaps, than well-crafted songs and intelligent playcraft—is widespread appeal. This "New 50's Rock 'N Roll Musical" brought patrons into the theatre who had never been in the theatre before. And some of them, twenty-five years later, remain theatregoers. Who do you think's been going to *Cats* all these years? (Just kidding. Well, partially kidding.) The early 1970s were an especially deadly spell for the professional theatre, with poor-quality shows and a notably dwindling audience base. So please don't take *Grease* and its 3,388 performances for granted. . . . Wanna play producer? Imagine that your show has opened to poor reviews and no business. You're on the hook personally for a hundred thousand or so that you certainly don't have. The experts—managers and advertising men—advise you to cut your losses and just close the damn thing. And *no*body is buying tickets. Some guy comes along and offers to cover the deficit, all you gotta do is sign over your share of the profits. (*What* profits?) What do you do? Close the show and go into debt, or take the guy's money?? Waissman and Fox made the logical choice, selling out most of their interest to Windy City showman Tony D'Amato. Yes, they did manage to retain their weekly producers' royalty, which over the years—and the multiple companies— provided gobs and gobs of grease. And even 9 percent of the profits can be substantial on a show with substantial profits. But still, think of those lost millions. So, what would you have done?

BROADWAY SCORECARD
/ PERFS: 3,388 / $: +

RAVE	FAVORABLE	MIXED	UNFAVORABLE	PAN
1	2		1	2

GUYS AND DOLLS

a revival of the 1950 "Musical fable of Broadway"

music and lyrics by Frank Loesser

book by Jo Swerling and Abe Burrows (actually by Burrows, who replaced Swerling)

based on the 1931 story *The Idyll of Miss Sarah Brown* and other characters from the works of Damon Runyon

"entire production under the supervision of Abe Burrows"

directed and choreographed by Billy Wilson

produced by Moe Septee in association with Victor H. Potamkin

starring Norma Donaldson, Robert Guillaume, Ernestine Jackson, and James Randolph

with Edye Byrde, Clark Morgan, Ken Page, Christophe Pierre, and Emett "Babe" Wallace

opened July 21, 1976   *Broadway Theatre*

CLIVE BARNES, *TIMES*

Yes, it still works. *Guys and Dolls* remains as wry and as funny, as enchanting and as entrancing as ever. This musical based on Damon Runyon's never, never land of a mythic Broadway that never was still seems magical. That floating crap game just keeps on floating. The interesting thing about *Guys and Dolls* is how beautifully cohesive all its elements happen to be. This musical fable of gamblers, hustlers and Salvation Army saviors has a very special charm. The music and lyrics by Frank Loesser—on the revival it seems that almost every number is a hit, and on the first night many of them were welcomed with a recognitionary nod of applause—have enormous charm. There is a rough jazziness to the score, and a bitter dryness to the lyrics, that go together like gin, vermouth and the New York skyline. The present producers, possibly taking a leaf out of David Merrick's book for *Hello, Dolly!*

[1964], have made this *Guys and Dolls* entirely black. It doesn't seem to matter at all. The musical works as admirably black as it worked admirably white. More and more it seems obvious that the pickling factor in a musical—the element that keeps it alive—is the music. Loesser's score has a bounce that jumps off the stage. Song after song emerges with a sort of pungent charm, and the words and the music are beautifully matched. . . . The present production is described as being "under the supervision" of Burrows, but having been directed and choreographed by Billy Wilson. So who quite did which?

MARTIN GOTTFRIED, *POST*
[Headline: "*Guys and Dolls* Suffers in the Black Version"]
If thirty minutes of exhilarating entertainment cannot undo the ninety minutes of near-drudgery that came first, they can at least make them easier to forget. The revival of *Guys and Dolls* picks up on a second act that is happily long on music and short on story and kicks it right on home. Considering the implausibility of this show's idea, that's a triumph of know-how over know-little. For the idea behind this production is surely misguided. It is an all-black *Guys and Dolls*. It's become wearisome to keep pointing out the offensiveness of all-black versions of white shows. There is a basic racism to them: the blackness of the actor is being used as a theatrical motif. It is a condescending exotica attitude that was supposed to have passed with minstrel shows and *Carmen Jones* [Oscar Hammerstein's 1943 Deep South remolding of Bizet's opera]. However, the commercial value of today's all black shows, as with all commercial values, rides roughshod over that. All-black versions of white shows also make as much sense as all-white versions of black shows. Material that was written specifically for one milieu is recklessly stretched to fit another or, as is more commonly the case, is simply ignored. This couldn't be truer than it is with *Guys and Dolls*, a show very white and very Jewish. The show's book has some superficial elements that seem transferable to black urban life: streetfront churches and the gambling scene. But these are trivial similarities as inconsequential as the few outright Yiddishisms that have been deleted. The songs, the jokes and the dialogue that create the show's very nature are Jewish through and through. Frank Loesser's score, the only thing really classic about the show, has been made almost equally

invisible, in an aural way, by a new set of arrangements. Only Danny Holgate and Horace Ott knew what they were doing in resetting the famous songs to beguine, samba and two-step rhythms, fitted out with bland, big band voicings. If this was an attempt to fit Loesser's score with a soul sound, it was like putting mayonnaise on a corned beef sandwich and calling it all-American. The only song that took the soul conversion, of course, was "Sit Down You're Rockin' the Boat," being that it was a show stopping spiritual to begin with. It still is.

HOWARD KISSEL, WOMEN'S WEAR DAILY

Guys and Dolls remains a masterful show because its story, its dialog, its lyrics and its music all have a unique, unmistakable style—a giddy, whimsical eloquence that has no basis in standard grammar but draws its strength from something more solid, the New York pavement. When Big Jule says of his own pair of dice, "I had the spots removed, but I remember where they formerly were," he achieves, by his simple insertion of "formerly," what every good writer tries to—his style is the perfect expression of his logic. Even though Big Jule claims he is from Cicero, Ill., his syntax owes a great deal to 52nd St. in its heyday and Brooklyn (not the real Brooklyn, the mythical one). The dialog in *Guys and Dolls* is on such a stylized, bizarrely lyric level that the book and the lyrics flow effortlessly into each other. Frank Loesser's lyrics are marvelous because they use slang so unself-consciously. The score itself, of course, is magnificent, both in its musical range—it has everything from a formal fugue to a gospel hymn—and in its absolute sharpness in conveying milieu and mood (no one has ever written a New York mood song better than "My Time of Day"). The current all-black revival succeeds largely because the original material is so solid. The only point where the show really explodes, as it ought to all along, is when Ken Page jubilantly, superbly, sings "Sit Down You're Rocking the Boat." It is the one moment—possibly because its gospel style is black to begin with—where everything about the production seems comfortable, not forced. It is the first time during the evening when the revised orchestrations suit the music—elsewhere they awkwardly "update" it, or, in the case of "I've Never Been in Love Before," actively sabotage it. The physical production is thoroughly unimpressive—perhaps because no one made a firm decision about whether the show is still set in Times

Square or further uptown, the sets have absolutely no flavor. One wonders if the show might have had more energy, more vitality if it had been revised to reflect black reality; but who would have the nerve to revise such a wonderfully crafted book or so gorgeous a score? The show is still extremely enjoyable, but watching it is like examining Big Julc's dice—you tend to remember how things formerly were.

o   o   o

Blame it on *The Wiz* (1975). A new black ticket-buying market across the country created a demand (the producers thought) for black musicals. Poor *Guys and Dolls* got caught in the crossfire, and looked pretty uncomfortable when Sky Masterson started singing to a disco beat. Abe Burrows, the radio writer called in when Jo Swerling's original libretto was chucked out, was back on hand to provide authentication, but this was not the Burrows who'd gone on to conquer Broadway as author/director of *How to Succeed* (1961), *Cactus Flower* (1965), and other hits. Burrows ran into a wall with *Breakfast at Tiffany's* (1966); he was fired from that ill-fated fiasco, and nudged aside as well on his subsequent musicals—the 1974 Alice Faye version of *Good News*, the 1976 Jerry Lewis version of *Hellzapoppin!*, this *Guys and Dolls*, and the 1981 revival of his own *Can-Can* (1953). Loesser and Burrows's durable fable of Broadway survived the misguided outing nevertheless, returning to Broadway in full glory in 1992.

BROADWAY SCORECARD / PERFS: 239 / $: −				
RAVE	FAVORABLE	MIXED	UNFAVORABLE	PAN
1	1		4	

GYPSY

a revival of the 1959 "Musical fable"

music by Jule Styne

lyrics by Stephen Sondheim

book by Arthur Laurents

based on the 1957 memoirs by Gypsy Rose Lee (Rose Louise Hovick, 1914–1970)

directed by Arthur Laurents

original production directed and choreographed by Jerome Robbins

choreography reproduced by Robert Tucker

produced by Barry M. Brown, Fritz Holt, Edgar Lansbury, and Joseph Beruh

starring Angela Lansbury

with Rex Robbins, Zan Charisse, Mary Louise Wilson, Gloria Rossi, Maureen Moore, John Sheridan, Bonnie Langford, John C. Becher, Denny Dillon, Don Potter, Charles Rule, and Richard J. Sabellico

opened September 23, 1974   Winter Garden Theatre

CLIVE BARNES, *TIMES*

[Headline: "*Gypsy* Bounces Back with Zest and Lilt"]

Lightning never strikes twice! Right? Wrong! At the Winter Garden Theatre last night, Angela Lansbury shattered the town (theatrically speaking, of course) in *Gypsy*. And on May 21, 1959, at the Broadway Theatre just up the road, Ethel Merman did the same trick in the same show. But it was a different lightning. Broadway has opened its season with *Gypsy*, and although this is a sort of revival, it is the kind of revival

Angela, with her name in lights (like Mama Rose in the show's finale),
swings those pearls. (artwork by Hilary Knight)

we cannot have too much of. Everything about *Gypsy* is right. The Jule Styne score has a lilt and a surprise to it. The music bounces out of the pit, assertive, confident and cocky, and has a love affair with Stephen Sondheim's elegantly paced, daringly phrased lyrics. And then there is the book by Arthur Laurents. Most important of all, this new Broadway *Gypsy* has brought over Angela Lansbury as Rose. Her voice has not got the Merman-belt, but she is enchanting, tragic, bewildering and bewildered. Miss Lansbury not only has a personality as big as the Statue of Liberty, but also a small core of nervousness that can make the outrageous real. *Gypsy* is one of the best of musicals and it improves with keeping. We start the new season with a musical to think about, ponder and love.

MARTIN GOTTFRIED, *POST*

Gypsy is simply a powerhouse, and it came as a surprise to me. When this revival played London last winter, it looked done for the sake of Angela Lansbury, who was very good in what was otherwise a limp show. But opening a ten-week engagement at the Winter Garden last night, it showed its class—muscle, assurance, depth and sheer power. It is one of the landmarks in the American musical's growth to maturity, rising above the ephemera of entertainment to stake a genuine claim to greatness. The heart of *Gypsy* is Mama Rose, a woman utterly different from anyone we have ever seen in a musical. Disregarding Ethel Merman's once-acknowledged ownership of the role, Lansbury created it anew. It is she who takes the insensitive, cruelly ambitious Rose and makes her first pitiful and then gallant; she who grasps the running theme of Rose's dreams and goes beyond them into near madness and the lady's iron-clad heart. Lansbury spearheads the show's brutality and then overcomes it with devastating compassion. Similarly, Styne's music is a part of the overall tension. On recordings, it is a magnificent score, but on stage is where it shows its theatricality. It is probably the most consistent score in all of musical theatre, and as a whole may well be the best. Remember—"Everything's Coming Up Roses" isn't a cheerful song. It is blind optimism in the face of disaster. And as for "Rose's Turn," sung in the midst of Rose's breakdown, it is unparalleled. At last I understand the reason for not ending the show with it—what director could resist using the real audience's applause as Rose's hallucination? Lansbury sings it as if everything she did all evening was leading up to it, which it was.

WALTER KERR, *TIMES*
[Headline: "*Gypsy* is Still Mysteriously Perfect Theatre"]
The crucial sequence—the moment when we understand that *Gypsy* is capable of unexpected but apparently limitless dramatic expansion—probably comes in an alleyway, outside a stage door, while Louise sits with desperate eyes fixed on a male dancer. The dancer is in the process of building his own act ["All I Need Is the Girl"]. The girl who would like to be the girl is right there, her taut tomboy's face composed, her neglect entirely without self-pity. As the quite remarkable Zan Charisse plays (and refuses to primp) her, she seems to have had the braces removed from her teeth just yesterday, to be as sexless and as patiently pensive as a Rouault clown. Without the boy's noticing she is at last impulsively on her feet behind him and miming him exuberantly in a "flash finish." But, dancing perfectly, she doesn't look like his partner. For one thing, she is still wearing the brown felt trousers assigned to her in Baby June's act: she plays the hind legs of a cow. When we learn, a scene later, that the boy she has matched step for step has promptly run off with Baby June, we realize—through our quite germane dismay—how perfectly we've been set up for the fall. Playwright, composer, and librettist have, for us, glued two people in the number, then ripped them apart. After that, we can expect almost any degree of substance they care to give us in the second act. We get it. In Angela Lansbury's puritanical dismay at having the act booked into a burlesque house, quickly canceled by the matter-of-fact greed that overtakes her once Gypsy Rose is offered stardom. In Lansbury's edgy, despairing uselessness when the star is at last born and her own work done. In the terrible manic downbeat—in the pit and in her fist—of Lansbury's final thrust at nonexistent glory, "Rose's Turn." It's the weave, so securely leading us to an ultimate emotional haymaker rare in musicals, that is so astonishing. We must not forget, by the way, that the dances have been re-created from Jerome Robbins's originals, and that Laurents has this time directed as well. Many cooks made the superlative broth. The show, as entertainment and as craftsmanship, remains as dazzling as it was on the day it was so felicitously born.

HOWARD KISSEL, WOMEN'S WEAR DAILY

The major change, of course, is the star. The bluster, the boisterousness, the coarseness that seemed to come effortlessly to Merman go against Lansbury's natural elegance. But she is made up to look square-jawed and frowzy, and she has a monomaniacal gleam in her eye, like an aging prizefighter who makes up in swagger what he has lost in sinew. Merman's vocal prowess and physical presence suggest the Super Chief barreling along at full speed; Lansbury's voice, which ranges from a mousy upper register to a tough, gravelly quality deep in the larynx, and her emotional intensity are on a more human scale. The fact that she does not overpower every scene enhances the drama around her. This Rose seems more vulnerable, and in her moments of crisis, more affecting. In Merman, all Rose's triumphs and agonies came through that incredible voice; Lansbury's is a more encompassing physical performance—her whole body conveys Rose's determination, her jubilance and sorrows. When she learns that the daughter she has lavished all her love and attention on has struck off on her own, she sits for the longest time transfixed, her eyes glaring with astonishment, shock and rage. But it is not simply a passive reaction—it is as if her batteries are being recharged, and in a moment, all the energies that were running frantically through her are now being poured just as frantically on the other daughter in the tremendous first-act closing, "Everything's Coming Up Roses." Later in the show, when she hears the words "star spot," it is like a starving dog sniffing red meat—the desire, the lust could not be more tangible than Lansbury makes them; the ruthless decision to make Louise a stripper so she can be a star seems a logical, necessary, inevitable physical craving on the part of Mama Rose's whole being.

*   *   *

Fritz Holt—stage manager of Sondheim's *Company* (1970) and *Follies* (1971)—wanted to become a producer, and he determined that mounting *Gypsy* in London was just the way to go about it. The Styne-Sondheim-Laurents "musical fable" had never been seen in the West End, as Ethel Merman refused to go. (She never did take a show abroad.) Holt and partner Barry Brown contacted Merman, who refused to go. After Angela Lansbury (of Sondheim's 1964 *Anyone Can Whistle*) turned them down, the role was accepted by Elaine Stritch (of

Company). But the producers were unable to raise the money with Stritch as lure—at which point Lansbury decided that she would, after all, like to give it a try. The successful London run opened May 29, 1973, at the Piccadilly; when Lansbury departed to take *Gypsy* back to America, she was replaced by Dolores Gray (who had filled Merman's moccasins for the full 1,304-performance London run of the 1946 *Annie Get Your Gun*). Angela and company began a six-month pre-Broadway tour on March 25, 1974, winding up with fifteen weeks at the Winter Garden. People had always said *Gypsy* was good, but you need Merman. Once Angela had launched into her own portrayal, people said *Gypsy* was good, but you need Merman or Lansbury. When the piece was once again revived in 1989 with TV-star Tyne Daly in the lead, people finally realized that it's the material itself that makes *Gypsy* brilliant. The original production was certainly successful in its day, but the show was generally slighted. The 702-performance run was half as long as other hits; the creators and performers were totally overlooked in the awards races, losing out to *The Sound of Music* and *Fiorello!* And the misguided 1962 motion picture version (with Roz Russell and Natalie Wood as mother and child) didn't help matters. But some people recognized *Gypsy*'s worth from the first. Like Walter Kerr, who wrote back on that opening night in 1959: "I'm not sure whether *Gypsy* is new-fashioned, or old-fashioned, or integrated, or non-integrated. The only thing I'm sure of is that it's the best damn musical I've seen in years."

A Tony Award was won by Angela Lansbury (actress).

BROADWAY SCORECARD

/ PERFS: 120 / $: +

RAVE	FAVORABLE	MIXED	UNFAVORABLE	PAN
4	2			

HAIR

"The American Tribal Love-Rock Musical"

music by Galt MacDermot

book and lyrics by Gerome Ragni and James Rado

directed by Tom O'Horgan

choreographed by Julie Arenal

produced by Michael Butler

with Steve Curry, Ronald Dyson, Sally Eaton, Leata Galloway, Paul Jabara, Diane Keaton, Lynn Kellogg, Melba Moore, Shelley Plimpton, James Rado, Gerome Ragni, and Lamont Washington

opened April 29, 1968   *Biltmore Theatre*

CLIVE BARNES, *TIMES*

[Headline: "It's Funny and Frank"]

What is so likable about *Hair*, that tribal-rock musical that last night completed its trek from downtown, via a discothèque, and landed, positively panting with love and smelling of sweat and flowers, at the Biltmore Theatre? I think it is simply that it is so likable. So new, so fresh and so unassuming, even in its pretensions. Since I have had a number of letters from people who have seen previews asking me to warn readers, and, in the urbanely quaint words of one correspondent, "Spell out what is happening on stage," this I had better do. Well, almost, for spell it out I can not, for this remains a family newspaper. However, a great many four-letter words, such as "love," are used very freely. At one point—in what is later affectionately referred to as "the nude scene"—a number of men and women (I should have counted) are seen totally nude and full, as it were, face. Frequent approving references are made to the expanding benefits of drugs. Homosexuality is not frowned upon. The American flag is used in a manner that not everyone

A patriotic message for the Age of Aquarius.

would call respectful. Christian ritual also comes in for a bad time, the authors approve enthusiastically of miscegenation, and one enterprising lyric catalogues somewhat arcane sexual practices more familiar to the pages of the Kama Sutra than the *New York Times*. So there—you have been warned. Oh yes, they also hand out flowers. And then there is Tom O'Horgan's always irreverent, occasionally irrelevant staging—which is sheer fun. O'Horgan has worked wonders. He makes the show vibrate from the first slowburn opening—with half-naked hippies statuesquely slow-parading down the center aisle—to the all-hands together, anti-patriotic finale. Some of his more outlandish ideas were once in a while too much, but basically, after so many musicals that have been too little, too much makes a change for the good. The essential likability of the show is to be found in its attitudes and its cast. You probably don't have to be a supporter of Eugene McCarthy to love it, but I wouldn't give it much chance among the adherents of Governor [Ronald] Reagan. *Hair*'s attitudes will annoy many people, but as long as Thoreau is part of America's heritage, others will respond to this musical that marches to a different drummer. Incidentally, the cast washes.

JOHN CHAPMAN, *DAILY NEWS*
[Headline: "*Hair* Is Itchy, Twitchy & Dirty"]
After the season's weirdest publicity buildup, they gave *Hair* its official opening last evening. The show is subtitled "the American tribal love-rock musical," and I guess this fits it whatever it means. I guess the pro-ducer, Michael Butler, is waiting for me to damn this whatsit as cheap, vulgar, foul-mouthed and tasteless so he can make some of his money back. And so it is. But it has some other qualities which I liked—par-ticularly the zestful abandon of the young cast, the dances staged by Julie Arenal and some of the songs written by Gerome Ragni, James Rado and Galt MacDermot. The show on my side of the footlights was pretty funny, too. They had stunk up the theater with incense and dead flowers—early goldenrod, I think—and the audience included many elderly gentlemen wearing goiter-sweaters, chains and beads who must have thought they were helling around as if they had just come up from East Village, instead of down from Central Park West. "Tribal love-rock" is not my type of music, for I was brought up on "Traumerei," "Souvenir" and "Glow-Worm." It is just too damned loud, being insanely electronified like Eddie Fisher. I couldn't hear all the words for

the racket. Just as well, no doubt, for the sponsors of *Hair* have been promising to use lots of dirty words. I did manage to understand a few, but I didn't faint. They also promised a Big Nude Scene, with a few nekkid boys and girls aiming right at me. I didn't faint here, either, for the stage was dimly lit. Hardly anybody in this twitchy, itchy extravaganza wears shoes and they all kept running up and down the center aisle waving their calluses at me. . . . But *Hair* is no show to take a lady to. End of plug.

WALTER KERR, *TIMES*

Surely all of the people going to *Hair*—and all of the people seem to be going to *Hair*—imagine that they're exposing themselves to a very hard sell. They know that amplified guitars will press like thumbs against their eardrums, that backward-somersaulting hippies will keep them company down the aisles, that rigged scaffolding along the high walls will rock to the throb of rock, that when the last frock-coated freak-out has swung over their heads on a rope the writhing chorus on stage will disentangle itself long enough to offer up five or six full-front nudes. They go braced. And they dissolve in contentment, if not in something close to delight, because they needn't have braced themselves at all. The show isn't a hard sell. It isn't even a sell. And that, I think, is the secret of its success. Yes, the din is dynamic, the stomp is perpetual, the put-on is unflagging, the nudes are there. But there is no pressure to make you buy the bag, no fear in the performers. They aren't wooing you, anxiously. Neither are they walloping you, desperately. They are simply beside you, like bears coming into your cabin in Yellowstone Park, soliciting no love, causing no trouble, occupying a lot of space but effortlessly belonging. They float free—free of your pleasure (*take* pleasure, if you wish), free of design (or any designs upon you), free of all urgency except the inspiration of the beat. The performers themselves are content to do anything, say anything, be anything, just so long as nothing is *demanded*. And for the audience this relaxation of demand, of consciousness of position, of the need to behave in any one way is quickly soothing by association. It doesn't even feel its obligation *as an audience*: to applaud, to stay, to analyze. Freed of obligation by the uncommitted playfulness, it is freed of inhibition, too. The audience snuggles in. It isn't envious. It just feels accepted, which is for everyone, a rare sensation. . . . The show has lost something in innocence since its production at the Public Theater earlier this season. The occasion has subtly grown older, in some cases to the point of seeming dangerously over-30ish. (James Rado, one of the authors, is now doing the helplessly draft-resisting Claude, and he's quite a big boy.) Night-clubbery creeps in from time to time, compromising an original authenticity.

RICHARD WATTS, JR., POST

It may not please the young people in *Hair* to be told that the most winning quality of their show is its air of innocence. The so-called "American tribal love-rock musical," which had its Broadway opening last night, is strewn with those four-letter words and goes in for a few tentative forays into nudity, but, although they try pretty hard to be bold and outrageous, their rescuing virtue is their inescapable youthful naïveté. There is also to the evening's credit the rock score by Galt MacDermot. Music with a rock beat has a way of sounding the same to me, but MacDermot's songs have a pleasant lift to them. The book, if it may be called that, is no doubt trying to be shocking. It has its fling at sacrilege, it is scornful toward the flag, and it is particularly and childishly fond of the most familiar of the four-letter epithets. It isn't witty or particularly funny. But the boys and girls of the company, strive as they may to seem terribly sophisticated, are so guileless about it that it appears almost touching. The title is, I gather, symbolic. The shaggy locks of the boys stand for virility, and, when deprived of them, they are compared to shorn Samsons. This is what happens to one [James Rado] who is going to be sent despite his reluctance to Vietnam. But *Hair* isn't strong in its moments of propaganda. The young fellow, when he loses his flowing hirsute adornment, looks so much better than he did before the surgery that it becomes quite an argument in favor of the army. It has a surprising if perhaps unintentional charm, its high spirits are contagious, and its young zestfulness makes it difficult to resist.

o   o   o

"The American Tribal Love-Rock Musical" first opened at Joe Papp's New York Shakespeare Festival on October 29, 1967. In stepped one Michael Butler, Indian rights enthusiast and black sheep scion of the high-flying aviation family. Butler financed the transfer of the

Shakespeare Festival's production to Cheetah, a West-side dis-cothèque—not a theatre, as Papp and director Gerald Freedman were convinced the show could not work in a proscenium house. Clive Barnes, new man at the *Times*, served as cheerleader, leading off his cri-tique of *How Now, Dow Jones* with "Let me be positive. On Dec. 22 the first American Tribal Love-Rock Musical, *Hair*, moves to Cheetah on Broadway. The rest of the news of Broadway musicals is not so good. . . ." The uptown *Hair* frizzed, though, after only five weeks. But Butler did not give up. The initial production rights having expired after the Cheetah closing, he reoptioned the show (without Papp and company) and made some changes. Freedman was replaced by avant-garde director Tom O'Horgan—best known for his work at Café La Mama—who oversaw a complete make-over. The already sketchy book material was further whittled down, resulting in a string of songs with connective dialogue of comic-strip-caption-like complexity. The origi-nal design team (including Ming Cho Lee and Theoni Aldredge) was replaced by some talented newcomers (including Robin Wagner and Jules Fisher). The cast, which had been significantly altered for the Cheetah run, was once again recast, with authors Rado and Ragni drafted into the leads. (Ragni had appeared in the downtown NYSF production, along with other departees Jonelle [*Two Gentlemen of Verona*] Allen and Jill [*Promises, Promises*] O'Hara—the latter of whom had acted with the boys in the 1964 Off-Broadway one-performance flop *Hang Down Your Head and Die.*) Furthermore, a decidedly campy tone was added to the proceedings, somewhat diffusing the antiwar sentiments; the original production ended with toy tanks rolling across the stage shooting at each other, while the Broadway production ended with everybody celebrating "Let the Sunshine In." And oh, yes, there was that innocuous but nevertheless *outré* ticket-selling nude scene. People had watched naked women on stage for centuries, but scraggly-haired hippie boys without their clothes or even a guitar on raised eye-brows and packed 'em in. (The author/lyricist/stars did not appear nekkid, though; just as well, as Rado—playing the draft-age dropout—was a thirty-four-year-old whose own *Hair* had permanently receded, and you wouldn't want to wear a wig in a let-it-all-hang-out nude scene.) Most important, the American Tribal Love-Rock Musical was (a) refreshing, (b) tuneful, and (c) fun. So what's not to like? The fluffed-out new *Hair* proved a gold mine for Butler and his Natoma

Productions; the Shakespeare Festival retained a small interest, but a strand of *Hair* proved worth more than full ownership of that season's *Dow Jones, Henry, Sweet Henry, The Happy Time, Darling of the Day, Golden Rainbow, Here's Where I Belong, H*Y*M*A*N K*A*P*L*A*N,* and *I'm Solomon* combined. On the Job Training Dept.: In the year preceding the Shakespeare Festival production, James Rado served—improbably and briefly—as romantic "second-man" in both *A Joyful Noise* and *Hallelujah, Baby!* prior to their official openings.

BROADWAY SCORECARD

/ PERFS: 1,742 / $: +

RAVE	FAVORABLE	MIXED	UNFAVORABLE	PAN
1	5			

HAIR

a revival of the 1968 "American Tribal Love-Rock Musical"

music by Galt MacDermot

book and lyrics by Gerome Ragni and James Rado

directed by Tom O'Horgan

choreographed by Julie Arenal

produced by Michael Butler in association with K. H. Nezhad

with Perry Arthur, Cleavant Derricks, Loretta Devine, Randall Easterbrook (replacing B. G. Gibson, who replaced David Patrick Kelly), Ellen Foley, Michael Hoit (replacing Doug Katsaros), Alaina Reed (replacing Trudy Perkins), Iris Rosenkrantz (replacing Annie Golden), Scott Thornton, Deborah Van Valkenburgh, Kristen Vigard, and Charlaine Woodard

opened October 5, 1977   *Biltmore Theatre*

RICHARD EDER, *TIMES*

[Headline: "Revived *Hair* Shows its Gray"]

Nothing ages worse than graffiti. *Hair*, the hippie musical, was a raffish slogan scrawled in day-glo upon the institutional walls of the late 1960's. Its message—liberation, joy, pot and multiform sex, the vision of youth as a social class of its own and, in short, the notion that there can be flowers without stalks, roots or muck to grow in—has faded. It is too far gone to be timely; too recently gone to be history or even nostalgia. Its revival has no particular occasion to it, and so it must stand or fall quite baldly upon its merits. It falls, or rather, it sags. Its virtues remain, but 10 years after its first appearance they look much feebler than they must have seemed at the time. Its glow is forced; its warmth becomes sentimentality and worse, sententiousness. Even before it starts, it is clear that the audience is to be the object of a great deal of planned spontaneity. Robin Wagner's set, pyramided and festooned with laundry, a jukebox, carvings, love-signs, is on display, and so is the cast. The young actors, in beads and tie-dyed regalia, prowl the aisles calling out cheerfully to each other, standing on the seats and chatting with the spectators. Even after the show began the audience was never neglected: at one point Michael Hoit, the male lead, hurled himself with a cry of "Mother!" onto the lap of the critic from *The Wall Street Journal*. Other curious associations intrude. Some of the loving smiling done by the cast is not all that different from the classic teeth-baring of the old-fashioned chorus line. A rousing, stomping episode with placards bearing antiwar slogans and denouncing L. B. J. has something of the old-battles-refought quality of an American Legion reunion. Mr. Hoit is agile and goofily commanding as Berger. Cleavant Derricks is funny and explosive as the short but vigorous black lead. Randall Easterbrook is less satisfactory as Claude. He is bland and excessively soulful, but then of all the characters Claude by now seems the least sufferable. His part calls for saintly attitudes to the point where we wish somebody would drop a guitar upon him.

HOWARD KISSEL, *WOMEN'S WEAR DAILY*

I first saw *Hair* under duress in 1971, in the company of a friend's sister, who had spent the last 10 years in a convent and was dying to see it. Even then, *Hair* was already a period piece—it let her know where we had been in 1967. Apart from this quaintness, it was, as theatre, appalling—most of the cast could neither act nor sing. Virtually all that happened on the stage was incoherent, but the audience didn't seem to mind; they were theatrically innocent, alarmingly responsive to the cheapest tricks in director Tom O'Horgan's bag. In retrospect *Hair* was the beginning of an era of amateurism on Broadway. Now that Broadway is returning to professional standards, I greeted the revival of *Hair* with a certain dread—but I found my reactions more complex than I anticipated. To begin with, though only 10 years have passed since *Hair* opened, the mannerisms, the styles that gave it life are now evidently as passé as those of '50s greasers or '40s bobbysoxers—the current cast clearly has to make an effort to re-create the mindless freedom of the hippies. The other odd feeling you get watching professionals carry placards with the political slogans of the Johnson years is an awareness that the styles of other decades—'50s haircuts, the '40s makeup—had to do with externals; during the '60s everything was rooted in politics. Now that many of the issues vibrant then have been deliberately muted, the show seems to have had its guts removed. Ten years ago *Hair* was a way of confronting, possibly enlightening, "bourgeois" audiences. Now the very inclusion of politics seems to trivialize the issues. O'Horgan has restaged the show with fewer gimmicks. He no longer tries to manipulate the audience. But taking the dust off only makes it apparent that the show itself was really the first Broadway theatre aimed at the TV generation—*Hair* is composed of segments rarely lasting more than four minutes strung together no more tightly than the Johnny Carson Show. Only the commercials are missing.

DOUGLAS WATT, *DAILY NEWS*
Hair resumed last night after a five-year breather, and the long, loose-jointed "tribal rock" musical seemed little changed in the 10 years since it first appeared. The cast is totally new, but the show remains essentially a lively and tuneful staged rock concert that would have benefitted by being reduced to an hour. It is Galt MacDermot's score—the music of, at the time, a schooled middle-aged concert composer—that holds up. Mostly, anyway. At its best—and it has many high spots—it distinguishes the crude but pointed lyrics of Gerome Ragni and James Rado, who also provided the practically unnoticeable "book." And the band, in the stage-left jalopy, is first rate [musical direction by Kirk Nurock]. [But] *Hair*, like long, undisciplined hair for hair's sake, has gone out of style. It and the '60s seem, at least at the moment, as dated

as *Irene* [1919] and the First World War. The terms "be-ins" and "psychedelic" and others employed in *Hair* conjure up a far-distant past in which the "flower children" who throng the Biltmore stage sound like and appear to be garish echoes of the Dead End Kids. Add a touch of "love," or at least the repeated incantation to this mysterious god. But it's gone, kids, gone, lost in a marijuana cloud as we tiptoe uncertainly through the saintly '70s. Still, they are also the nostalgic '70s, and Lord knows! 10 year's time may have produced a whole new audience of thirtyish oldsters whom *Hair* can waft back to the days of the S.D.S., Weathermen, Chicago, the Steps of the Pentagon—to a gritty, lusty, aching, Nirvana whose true name is Youth.

o   o   o

The original *Hair* was snaggy, shaggy, ratty, matty, oily, and greasy, not to mention flaxen-waxen. But times change, tastes change; spangled and spaghettied hair was passé ten years later, and so—I'm afraid—was the show. Without the novelty of "the happening," as it were, it was revealed that nothing much happened; the skeletal structure of the material linking the songs was—well, skeletal. What did work, taken out of time, was Galt MacDermot's music. What in 1968 was progressive and up-to-the-minute—at least to audiences storming away from that season's *Henry, Sweet Henry, How Now, Dow Jones,* and *Golden Rainbow*—turned out to be highly melodic and quite durable. American Tribal Love-Rock or no, songs like "Aquarius," "Easy to Be Hard," "Let the Sunshine In," and "Where Do I Go?" need no disclaimers. There was trouble finding suitable leads—the thirty-five-year-old Gerry Ragni clearly wanted to re-create his expelled-from-high-school Berger, while James "Claude Hooper Bukowski" Rado—bald and forty-four—knew enough to stay away from the role of the young draftee. But that didn't keep the Medusa-haired Ragni from chomping away, and authorial prerogative resulted in the termination—to the show's detriment—of both Doug Katsaros (Berger) and David Patrick Kelly (Claude). What was most remarkable about this new-styled *Hair*, though, was the array of fresh acting talent on display (assembled by casting director Mary Jo Slater). The unknown, and in most cases new-to-Broadway, troupe included Cleavant "Hud" Derricks, Ellen "Sheila" Foley, tribe-member Peter Gallagher (who decamped during the endless preview period to replace Treat Williams in the long-running *Grease*), Annie "Jeannie" Golden (ditto, to appear in the concurrent *Hair* film), Kristen "Crissy" Vigard, and—in the joined-at-the-hip, pseudo-Supreme "White Boys" dress—Loretta Devine, Alaina Reed, and Charlaine Woodard. Also in the cast, for seven of the show's seventy-nine previews, was your humble servant, pressed into action due to a combination of untimely firings, illnesses, and slipped disks. And I was good, if decidedly non-hippielike.

BROADWAY SCORECARD
/ PERFS: 43 / $: –

RAVE	FAVORABLE	MIXED	UNFAVORABLE	PAN
				6

HALF A SIXPENCE

an import of the 1963 British musical

music and lyrics by David Heneker (with lyrics revised by Michael Brown)

book by Beverley Cross (revised by Hugh Wheeler)

based on the 1905 novel *Kipps* by H. G. Wells

directed by Gene Saks (replacing Word Baker)

choreographed by Onna White

produced by Allen-Hodgdon (Lewis Allen and Dana Hodgdon), Stevens Productions (Roger L. Stevens) and Harold Fielding (with Harry Rigby billed inconsistently)

starring Tommy Steele

with Ann Shoemaker (replacing Charlotte Rae), James Grout, Carrie Nye, Polly James, Grover Dale, Will Mackenzie, Norman Allen, and John Cleese

opened April 25, 1965   *Broadhurst Theatre*

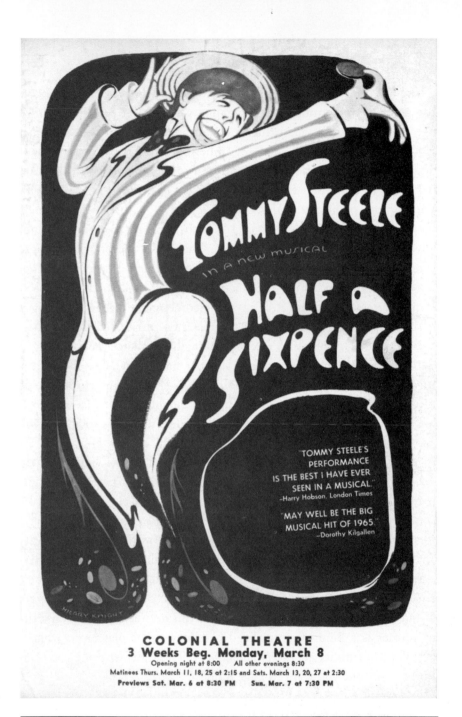

"Tommy Steele can do a bit of everything a bit better than most people," said Walter Kerr. "A tiptoe kick, a strut, a sudden spin about the floor when he should be behaving sedately. All attractive, all accomplished, all not quite exhilirating." (artwork by Hilary Knight)

WALTER KERR, *HERALD TRIBUNE*

There are no lapses of taste in *Half a Sixpence*, but one should be able
to say something more stirring about a musical than that. *Half a
Sixpence* is neat, but not stirring. It is deft on its feet, but not stirring. It
is warmly designed, with a bath of amber light spilling over the leaded-
glass curlicues that cover it from portal to portal, but not stirring. And
why not? I'm sure that H. G. Wells' libretto has something to do with
the evening's blandness. Wells, of course, was not a librettist, nor can he
ever have imagined himself one. In a way, I'm glad that Wells is not
alive to see how quaint he has become. The production staff, to be sure,
is not only alert to the fact that the message (Money—don't let this get
out—doesn't always bring happiness) is quaint, it is cheerfully determined to make capital of it. If anything comes close to being stirring it
is the dances that Onna White has apparently rearranged from Robert
Prince's British originals. [Prince was actually the dance music arranger,
with imprecise billing.] There is a dizzying spin to the business of mea-
suring ribbon by the unfurling spool, there is an engaging curtain made
of yard-goods to flick dancers in and out of sight, there is a fast number made of so many banjo strokes that you think the participants will
surely have one. All attractive, all accomplished, all not quite exhilirating. I think much the same thing must be said of the evening's star,
Tommy Steele. Steele can do a bit of everything a bit better than most
people: a tiptoe kick, a strut, a sudden spin about the floor when he
should be behaving sedately. He rattles a banjo smartly, too. What I
miss is a signature. Most performers who come to this sort of celebrity
write their names with one bold swipe that makes them easy to identify, easy to caricature, easier than easy to imitate. Steele seems to me a
collection of sound qualities in which no one quality makes a bigger
sound than the others. And I suppose it's this imprecise definition—the
performer is a kind of generalized Cockney—that plays into what is
tidy but too familiar about *Half a Sixpence*. The show isn't one you want
to fault. It's one you want to have more fun with.

JOHN McCLAIN, *JOURNAL-AMERICAN*

[Headline: "A Big Blooming Hit"]
It ran for something like two years in London, but I am told that it has
been vastly gussied-up for this U.S. showing with the kind of zingy

choreography that Onna White can deliver, and while I don't know where London left off and New York began the fact remains that it is a splendid evening of musical theatre. It should be around for many a moon. Mr. Steele, a sort of gorblimey Eddie Bracken, moves well and sings acceptably and projects a magnetic personality. As a musical comedy star he has all the ingredients—he can dance in the production numbers, score solidly in a single, persuasively act out a straight scene, and he can even play the banjo.

NORMAN NADEL, *WORLD-TELEGRAM & SUN*
[Headline: "Steele Glitters in *Half a Sixpence*"]
Half a Sixpence has come a long way—up—since I saw it in London two years ago. Then it was a typical, tapioca pudding English musical—pleasant but bland. Last night it appeared no less pleasant but a lot livelier. It still is mostly tapioca pudding, but in its dance numbers more like cherries jubilee. The new musical could establish Tommy Steele, one of England's top popular singers, as an American favorite. In so doing, it might attract a teen-age audience back to the Broadway musical theatre, which would be quite an achievement. Its beat is bouncy, its mood is merry, and its songs are readily and agreeably singable. What lifts *Half a Sixpence* above its original self are the dances and musical production numbers designed and directed by Onna White. White has reproduced in dance the sprightly sentiment, the youthful ebullience and the turn-of-the-century manners that motivate the songs and dialogue. Several times during the evening, these numbers move far, far ahead of the show as a whole, which is perfectly all right with the audience. A simple little tune will be developed into an ambitious dance production inspired by everything from the London music hall to *Swan Lake*. The fascinating thing is that it usually works. "Money to Burn (Buy Me a Banjo)" sets the pattern for most of the show's musical numbers. Steele sings it, after which it is set in motion by one of the season's most exuberant and talented dance companies. The star is a part of it all the way, tossing in a banjo solo as the number approaches its climax. Several numbers are embellished with *entrechats*, toe work, toeleaps and other ballet techniques which have a welcome, tongue-in-cheek effect here. Thus, a show which strolled in London is skipping merrily in its New York debut.

HOWARD TAUBMAN, *TIMES*

The bare bones of H. G. Wells's *Kipps* have been invoked to fashion a Victorian soap opera to music. Are you easily moved to tears and laughter? *Half a Sixpence* has enough to gratify the most sentimental tastes. Do you find sentimentality repellent? *Half a Sixpence* will give you a touch of indigestion. But it will also disarm you by its unabashed commitment to sweetness and light. And its company, led by the engaging young Briton Tommy Steele, sings and dances with so much spirit that the musical numbers compensate in some measure for the stickiness of the book. Onna White, the choreographer, has devised a series of dances that give the musical its principal excuse for being. If your standards in musicals are not rigorous, you will be entertained by the friendly, wholesome corn in *Half a Sixpence*. But the chances are that you will enjoy this musical most where it has freshness—in its production numbers.

◦   ◦   ◦

Seems like the choreographer helped make this one work, doesn't it? The "gorblimey" Tommy Steele and all those production numbers combined for an enjoyable, if not first-class package, and a fifteen-month run. Onna White didn't get a Tony Award—not against Jerry Robbins's *Fiddler on the Roof*—but *Sixpence* netted her assignments on both *Mame* (1966) and her Oscar-winning stint on the 1968 film version of *Oliver!* As for Word Baker, it seems that starting your career with an unconventional hit like *The Fantasticks* (1960) can work against you. His two Broadway musicals were the 1962 *A Family Affair*, on which he was replaced by first-time director Harold Prince, and *Half a Sixpence*, where he was axed for another musical comedy novice. (The original British *Sixpence* was directed by John Dexter.) Prince and Gene Saks both found future directing assignments over the years; as for Baker? well, *The Fantasticks* keeps on running. . . .

BROADWAY SCORECARD
/ PERFS: 512 / $: +

RAVE	FAVORABLE	MIXED	UNFAVORABLE	PAN
2	2	1	1	

HALLELUJAH, BABY!

"A New Musical"

music by Jule Styne

lyrics by Betty Comden and Adolph Green

book by Arthur Laurents

directed by Burt Shevelove (replacing Gene Saks)

choreographed by Kevin Carlisle (replacing Peter Gennaro)

produced by Albert W. Selden and Hal James, Jane C. Nusbaum and Harry Rigby

starring Leslie Uggams, Robert Hooks, and Allen Case (replacing James Rado)

with Lillian Hayman, Barbara Sharma, Marilyn Cooper, Winston DeWitt Hemsley, and Alan Weeks

opened April 26, 1967   Martin Beck Theatre

MARTIN GOTTFRIED, *WOMEN'S WEAR DAILY*

It is quite remarkable that despite the proven professionalism of nearly everyone involved with *Hallelujah, Baby!*, the musical seems the work of not amateurs but confused and uncertain people. The reason, though, is not nearly so perplexing. Although Jule Styne can be one of Broadway's most exciting composers. Although Betty Comden and Adolph Green are long-experienced lyricists. And although Arthur Laurents is by far the most knowing, most competent book writer for the musical theatre, they all have always needed a leader—somebody to work them together, bring out their best, and most of all, show the way. Burt Shevelove, the director, has a wonderfully clever theatre mind but he has had no experience in staging for the musical theatre and it shows badly. With everybody wandering off in separate directions, *Hallelujah, Baby!* was forced onto the Martin Beck stage while flying off into every corner. It is a misguided and unguided production that manages to ignore the endless musical possibilities in its subject matter. But then again, the subject

"When the weather's better, we'll get together, you and me." The song was cut during the tryout, but the umbrella logo remained. Billy Dee Williams replaced Robert Hooks after the opening. (artwork by Hilary Knight)

matter itself was hopelessly mistaken for the basis of a musical. *Hallelujah, Baby!* is supposed to trace the American Negro's 20th Century history in song and dance, and if that sounds like some television producer's silly idea for a silly program, it is just the way this production rings. How is one really supposed to make cohesive musical theatre out of two hours of snippets illustrating the tone and sounds of 60 years' worth of history? Leslie Uggams is a terrific singer with a rich, thrusting, marvelous voice, and while Styne did not give her super material she did well. She could not act her way out of a telephone booth. Robert Hooks was amiable and small-voiced in the ludicrous role of her young man (he goes from Pullman porter to Negro leader). And Allen Case is bland as a white liberal, finally being rejected to keep pace with the surface of today's racial situation. Styne's score was on-again, off-again, sometimes fresh, sometimes tired. The Comden-Green lyrics were competent at best, strained and clichéd at worst. Shevelove's direction was entirely unmusical and lax, overemphasizing the book and keeping movement and dance minimal. That is exactly how to create a drag.

WALTER KERR, *TIMES*

Leslie Uggams has a smile that suggests she knows something we don't know, and I imagine Broadway is going to keep her around long enough to find out what that gleeful, dark-eyed, warmly modest and slyly kept little confidence may be. I think I liked her best—and wondered what she was thinking most—last night when she sat all by her lonesome at one end of a bar decorated with upside-down hearts and tried turning her own heart upside down to a Jule Styne tune called "Talking to Yourself." The mood of the moment was that of the 1940's, and a very smoky wail came out of the girl and out of the past to wrap a memory of lost midnights around everyone in sight. I feel sure it did. But the show, the show seemed to be talking to itself, too. I can't imagine who else it might have had in mind. *Hallelujah, Baby!* can't really be talking to Negroes, who have long since ceased to think of themselves as perennial patsies who need to be escorted by loving, liberal white hands across streets to near-safety. And it can't very well be talking to white liberals, either, not at this late date, not when do-gooders have seen the folly of being patronizing to all God's chillun, not when the Invisible

Man has ceased being invisible and has become a face, a force, and even a fury to be reckoned with. The musical [which the authors] have put together with the best intentions in the world is a course in Civics One when everyone in the world has already got to Civics Six. Mr. Laurents, alas, simply puts down what we all know even more simply than we know it, practically on the level of those grade-school readers that announce "Jim is a man, Jim lives next door to us." There are no real tries for wit, in lyrics or libretto, and the wisdom, I'm afraid, is old-fashioned platitudinizing, in or out of tune. The tipoff may be that the evening's heartiest responses are handed to an out-and-out Aunt Jemima, played with apparent relish and magnificent abandon by a stove-shaped *chanteuse* named Lillian Hayman. Something about the show coils back in on itself, turning progress itself into a kind of naïveté. The editorial seems to be carried over from yesterday's editions.

NORMAN NADEL, *WORLD JOURNAL TRIBUNE*
[Headline: "Amen to *Hallelujah!*"]
There's a lovely little idea at the heart of *Hallelujah, Baby!* Though the musical spans two-thirds of a century, everybody in it remains the same age. As Leslie Uggams explains right at the start: "I stay 25; that's nice for a girl." It's nice for the audience, too, because Miss Uggams at 25, or whatever her actual age happens to be, makes the 67 years of the story and the two-plus hours of the show pass a great deal more swiftly than they might without her. What it amounts to as entertainment is one stereotype of the musical stage after another. It would be a tedious evening indeed except for the manner in which the show keeps its sense of humor on racial issues, and for the warmth, charm, energy and talent of the players and dancers. Miss Uggams opens the show stage center, which is where director Burt Shevelove places her repeatedly thereafter; it's his most prudent move all evening. We know perfectly well that she's going to sing like sunlight; Dear Heaven, what a glory abides in that girl's voice! What we're less prepared for is her assurance as an actress, which is evident all the time, even though she never tries any variations on a basic characterization. Her opening "My Own Morning" is pleasantly melodic, though just a warmup for what is to come. "I Wanted to Change Him" provides a more full-bodied Uggams, with "Being Good Isn't Good Enough" to display a different facet of

her musical personality. The stinger, midway through act two, is the title song, which all but brought the audience to its feet last night. Winston DeWitt Hemsley and Alan Weeks, two hoofers who brighten the show every time they appear, are the star's dancing companions in the title tune. The success of her numbers is all the more remarkable when you consider that musically the show is conventional.

∘   ∘   ∘

Arthur Laurents, author of *Gypsy* (1959) and director of *I Can Get It for You Wholesale* (1962), brought this Lena Horne vehicle to David Merrick (who had produced both musicals, as well as Horne's 1957 *Jamaica* and four Jule Styne shows). When Lena opted out, the producer knew enough to pull the plug. "Every producer along the line has turned down something that eventually becomes a big hit," Merrick— who also dropped *Happy Hunting* (1956), *Goldilocks* (1958), *It's Superman* (1966), and *Follies* (1971)—explained to the press. "I haven't made a big mistake like that yet. *Hallelujah, Baby* may very well be my first one." "I hope Mr. Merrick is right," Laurents commented tartly. "It happened to me before when about ten producers turned down *West Side Story* [1957]." (Columnists reported accusations—presumably from Laurents—that Merrick dropped the project due to racism; it appears, though, that the producer was less bothered by the politics than by Laurents's book revisions.) *Hallelujah, Baby!* was picked up by general managers Joe Harris and Ira Bernstein, who were hoping to move into the producing ranks. They signed director Burt Shevelove, replacing the departed Gene Saks; they signed choreographer Peter Gennaro; and they then dropped the whole thing, dissatisfied with Laurents's book revisions. (They had also bowed out of their first proposed production, the 1965 *Kelly*.) Helen Jacobson, of the Show of the Month club, next picked up the show. *She* didn't like Laurents's next set of revisions, and dropped the stillborn *Baby!* two months later. At which point Al Selden and Hal James, two men of *La Mancha* (1965), took on the show; Selden had been composer to lyricist Shevelove on *Small Wonder* (1948) and the 1951 Nancy Walker road-flop *Month of Sundays*. Despite the overwhelming success of *La Mancha*, the new producers were unable to raise the money—are you beginning to think *Hallelujah, Baby!* was ill-fated?—so they took on Jane Nusbaum and

Harry Rigby as partners, and the show finally went into rehearsal. And then the *real* problems began. As had happened before, and would happen again, a black-themed musical from well-meaning white liberals ended up in an interracial tangle. A black voice was added to the staff when choreographer Kevin Carlisle was brought in, but this made little difference other than picking up the dancing. It was a difficult era and a difficult problem, not one easily resolved in a musical comedy. (In January 1970 Betty-and-Adolph-and-Arthur's pal Lenny threw his infamous "radical chic" cocktail party to raise funds for the defense of the Black Panthers. Several years later Bernstein tried *his* hand at a race-relations musical, *1600 Pennsylvania Avenue* [1976], which made the earlier show look as smooth and successful as the 1969 musical pageant *1776*.) The resulting *Hallelujah, Baby!* was neither pro nor con, neither here nor there. Two first-rate performances from first-rate performers Leslie Uggams and Lillian Hayman gave the show a modicum of entertainment value, earning them both Tony Awards (with another going to the songwriters—the only such honor Styne ever received). But that was long after *Hallelujah, Baby!* had breathed its final "Amen."

In addition to winning the Tony Award for Best Musical, Tonys were won by Jule Styne, Betty Comden, and Adolph Green (score), Leslie Uggams (actress, tied with Patricia Routledge for *Darling of the Day*), and Lillian Hayman (supporting actress).

BROADWAY SCORECARD

/ PERFS: 293 / $: −

RAVE	FAVORABLE	MIXED	UNFAVORABLE	PAN
1	2		1	2

HAPPY END

a revised version of the 1972 Yale Repertory Theater adaptation of the 1929 musical play

music by Kurt Weill

lyrics by Bertolt Brecht

book and lyrics adapted by Michael Feingold; newly conceived by Robert Kalfin

based on the original German book by Elisabeth Hauptmann (originally credited to "Dorothy Lane")

directed by Robert Kalfin (replacing Michael Posnick) and Patricia Birch

choreographed by Patricia Birch

produced by Michael Harvey and Chelsea Theater Center (Robert Kalfin and Michael David)

starring Meryl Streep (replacing Shirley Knight), Bob Gunton (subbing for the injured Christopher Lloyd), and Grayson Hall

with Liz Sheridan, Benjamin Rayson, Tony Azito, Alexandra Borrie, Christopher Cara, Joe Grifasi, and Robert Weil

opened April 26, 1977	*Brooklyn Academy of Music*
transferred May 7, 1977	*Martin Beck Theatre*

(Note: the first-night reviewers covered the show at its Brooklyn Academy première)

CLIVE BARNES, *TIMES*

Lovers of Kurt Weill, arise. Get to see the Chelsea Theater Center production of the Weill/Brecht musical *Happy End*, which officially opened at the Brooklyn Academy of Music last night and is scheduled to end there this weekend. The company is confident of transferring the production to Manhattan—but please take no chances. Beseige Brooklyn, in case it is too late. *Happy End* has a curious history. It is described in the Chelsea program somewhat ingenuously as having lyrics by Bertolt Brecht (which is undoubtedly true), music by Kurt Weill (another plus for history) and an "original German play by Dorothy Lane." The last statement is false. The work was intended as a sequel to *The Threepenny Opera* [1928], and it was first stated that the book was based by Brecht on a short story by "Dorothy Lane." She and her story were apparently fictitious, and Brecht himself later disavowed the book, saying it was the work of his secretary and sometime collaborator, Elisabeth Hauptmann. The first performance in Berlin, on Sept. 2, 1929, proved to be a fiasco. And the work remained lost until the early 1960's, when it was revived in Germany. Brecht, it seems, never took any interest in the work. With Kurt Weill it was an altogether different matter. Although he was working on his masterpiece *Mahagonny* at the time, and as a result he almost threw off *Happy End*, he still knew what he had achieved. It was a breakthrough for the composer. As he later wrote: "Formally, instrumentally and melodically it is so clear an advance on the *Threepenny Opera* that only such helpless ignoramuses as the German critics could overlook it." Musically, it is a great advance on anything Weill had produced before, and "Bilbao Song," "*Matrosen* [Sailors'] Tango" and "Surabaya Johnny" have become classics in the Weill repertory. The performance of the show comes from Meryl Streep as Hallelujah Lil. She is a knockout. Making no attempt to imitate the Lenya growl, she sings and acts with uttermost sweetness and enormous style. She alone would make *Happy End* worth seeing, but in truth it is a musical that needs no recommendation other than itself. It charms, it giggles and it moves.

MARTIN GOTTFRIED, *POST*
Happy End may have the catchiest score that Kurt Weill ever wrote other than *The Threepenny Opera*, but it is a slapdash and unentertaining work with a history more interesting than it is. At its 1929 première, the show bombed in Berlin and was closed immediately, just like any other turkey. Although it has been produced by American regional theatres, it was given its New York première only last night, closing the current season of the Chelsea Theater Center in the Brooklyn Academy of Music. Why has Chelsea bothered with it? Well, this vigorous institution has always been fascinated by chamber musicals (*The Beggar's*

Opera, Candide, Polly). But perhaps a practical and historically repetitive reason was involved too: *The Threepenny Opera* was recently a great success and helpful moneymaker for The New York Shakespeare Festival, just as it was 8 years ago for the Schiffbauerdamm Theatre. Could Chelsea have been looking for a commercial sequel just as Brecht and Weill were? The one reason I can't believe is honest appreciation of the show. It is painfully uninteresting, a chore rather than a pleasure, an aimless and jerry-built work that makes the wonderful but awkward *Threepenny* look like a model of dramatic craftmanship. *Happy End* was intended as sheer entertainment, blatantly commercial and therefore inevitably uncommercial. It now is neither Brechtian, German nor American. Feingold's adaptation plays fast and loose with an uncredited translation and Kalfin tried to mask the show's defects with flashy staging. This basic distrust of the materials shows through and makes the production both insincere and unidentified. But the songs are indeed wonderful. As "Hallelujah Lil, the Saint of South Canal Street," Meryl Streep is given the chances by the script to show off her proven skill. I didn't know she could sing and still don't. Her soprano is thin and of uncertain acquaintance with pitch. Bob Gunton is hardly a Brechtian "toughest crook in Chicago." But in all fairness, he assumed the role over the weekend, taking over for an injured actor, just as Miss Streep came into the show late. Indeed, the whole production has been troubled, officially opening now even though the engagement ends this week. The show was plainly jinxed, not worth the pain and Chelsea deserves better luck.

DOUGLAS WATT, *DAILY NEWS*

Happy End is a treat: musical comedy with a wicked leer and some of Kurt Weill's most sinuously seductive songs. And yet this 1929 progenitor of *Cabaret* [1966] and the current *Chicago* [1975] is scheduled to close Saturday after an accident prone career of almost two months. The final blow fell on Thursday of last week when, after a change of directors and a replacement of the female lead, the leading man tore two ligaments and was forced to turn over his role to an understudy. The decision was made to "open" anyway, and I can't tell you how grateful I am to have seen this rarely performed work. *Happy End* was a sort of throwaway piece by Bertolt Brecht, who wrote the lyrics while occupied with his play *St. Joan of the Stockyards*, and Weill, who was at work on *Mahagonny*. The pair's initial collaboration, *The Threepenny Opera*, had gone over so well in Berlin the year before that the producer demanded a follow-up piece immediately. And it flopped, due to an emotional, ad-libbed speech thrown into the last act by Brecht's actress-wife, a political activist. The book, by the way, was attributed to a "Dorothy Lane," a friend of Brecht's who preferred anonymity. . . . Meryl Streep leads the parade as Lt. Lillian Johnson (Hallelujah Lil), acting with precisely the right touch of lightness and poignancy, and she polishes off that master-piece, "Surabaya Johnny," as well as "The Sailor's Tango" with splendid expressiveness, though I could have wished for a slightly throatier delivery than her lyric soprano treatment. Take heart, one and all. There are indications—though no hard evidence—that happy *Happy End* will happily find a Manhattan home ere long.

∘   ∘   ∘

The critics reviewed *Happy End* during the final week of its Brooklyn run, with a replacement director, a new leading lady, and understudy Bob Gunton subbing for the injured Christopher Lloyd. Which might explain why the reviews seem overenthusiastic. Neither Weill nor Brecht ever saw *Happy End* remounted after its disappointing 1929 première, and for good reason. Yes, it has some brilliant music, but a satisfyingly crafted theatre piece it's not. The ambitious Broadway transfer was underfinanced, sparsely attended, and pretty much incoherent. The latter-day American popularity of *The Threepenny Opera* also brought forth another baffling reconstruction of a Weill-Brecht rarity: the 1930 *Rise and Fall of the City of Mahagonny*, mounted Off-Broadway in 1970 as the memorably disastrous *Mahagonny*, with Frank Poretta (replacing Mort Shuman), Barbara Harris, and Estelle Parsons staggering through the leading roles.

BROADWAY SCORECARD
/ PERFS: 75 / $: –

RAVE	FAVORABLE	MIXED	UNFAVORABLE	PAN
2	2	1		1

HAPPY NEW YEAR

"A New Musical"

music and lyrics by Cole Porter; "songs edited" by Buster Davis

"made into a musical" by Burt Shevelove

based on the 1928 comedy *Holiday* by Philip Barry

directed by Burt Shevelove

choreographed by Donald Saddler

produced by Leonard Soloway, Allan Francis, and Hale Matthews, in association with Marble Arch Productions (Lord Lew Grade and Martin Starger)

with Leslie Denniston (replacing Victoria Snow), Kimberly Farr (replacing Leigh Beery), Michael Scott (replacing William Atherton), Edward Evanko, John McMartin (replacing Ted Follows), Richard Bekins, and William Roerick (replacing Eric Donkin)

opened April 27, 1980   *Morosco Theatre*

CLIVE BARNES, *POST*

Those great names Cole Porter and Phillip Barry ought to go together as ecstatically as Franklin and Roosevelt or Lincoln and Center. Burt Shevelove's idea of making a musical from a Barry play and throwing in Porter music ought to be an unalloyed delight. Last night at the Morosco Theatre the result was distinctly alloyed. It wasn't precisely Granada, as Porter put it, it was much more Asbury Park. The book could do with a few zingy one-liners—come to think of it two-liners, or even ocean-liners, would not have been entirely misplaced—and you won't come out humming any music you didn't go in remembering. Still, that's true of most of the new musicals these days. And it is a playful, tuneful, civilized musical. The real trouble with *Happy New Year* is that you have to create a musical. You cannot fabricate them over other people's cold genius. Shevelove is a smart cookie as a director, but he hasn't quite got the creative mystery that could awaken into life this almost possible dream. He has created awesome mayhem on *Holiday*, turning a stylish comedy of manners into a commonplace musical. Shevelove started his project at the Shakespeare Festival in Stratford, Ontario. He would have been well-advised to have left it right there. He has worked on it, made a few slight changes to the book, almost entirely replaced the score—it was originally unknown Porter—and changed the cast. It is now perhaps seven, even eight times as good as the bardic disaster in Stratford. And it still doesn't quite work. Yet because of the remnants of Barry's play hanging disconsolately around, the Porter tunes, always the real turtle soup and never the mock, and a handful of talented performances, the evening misses with some degree of distinction. Nothing truly comes together. But some of its hole is rather more than its parts. The play is strewn with pauses for artfully but artificially introduced songs that seem as strangely abrasive as boulders on sandpaper. The scenery by Michael Eagan looks rather like chunks of monumental masonry reduced to jumble-sale trivia, but the costumes by Pierre Balmain (supervised by John Falabella) are gems of period re-creation. These are absolutely stunning with all the class in the world, and also my compliments to the anonymous wig-makers, hairdressers and make-up artists. They make everyone look like passengers on the maiden voyage of the S.S. *Normandie*.

DOUGLAS WATT, *DAILY NEWS*
[Headline: "An Earthbound Party"]
Up in heaven, Cole Porter and Philip Barry, who never collaborated down here below, have probably been turning out dazzling musicals year after year. Would that one such effort, even the least, had floated down to the Morosco last evening where *Happy New Year*, a pale imitation of the genuine article, opened. This intimate musical has been concocted by Burt Shevelove from Barry's romantic comedy *Holiday* and from a sampling of Porter songs familiar and unfamiliar. Shevelove hasn't had sufficient faith in the story, which Barry's buoyant dialogue carried off, to leave it alone, or simply trim it to musical needs. He's invented a Narrator, played by a whitehaired John McMartin in a dinner jacket. The Narrator is an oldster living in the present and cueing us in on the events taking place in the Seton mansion. When he isn't

introducing scenes, McMartin leans against the proscenium looking on with a benign smile that almost certainly conceals utter boredom. The songs skip all over Porter's career, and I do mean skip, for such standards as "At Long Last Love," "Ridin' High" and "You Do Something to Me" make far less impression than they should. The entrancing "Easy to Love" is used only as a musical accompaniment, in various tempos, for a Saddler ballroom dance scene. Oddly, Porter's presence is often felt most strongly in the background music played by an offstage band. A zippy introductory chorus of "Just One of Those Things" raises our expectations; a haunting piano solo of "Looking at You" underscores a love scene; and band backgrounds of "Let's Do It" and "You've Got That Thing" lift our spirits temporarily [orchestrations by Luther Henderson]. But *Happy New Year* never takes off for long. Even Linda's private New Year's Eve party in the top-floor playroom is earthbound. Funny, though she never belonged in the same theatre with Barry, I kept longing for the young Ethel Merman's exultant, startlingly clear voice, particularly in those songs she introduced. And I kept wishing for something else: for Barry and Porter locked up right now in a New Haven or Boston hotel room, dashing off new scenes and new songs and, of course, a whole new show.

o   o   o

What an idea! Songs by Cole Porter, play by Philip Barry. Both wrote smart, sophisticated material, both were high society, both were silver-spoon millionaires. But—and it turned out to be a big but—they were not members of the same club, socially or professionally. (Porter and his pals belonged to a club, all right, but it wasn't one where you sat around reading the social register.) And their styles simply didn't mesh. If Porter and Barry had wanted to collaborate, they surely would have. (One of the ailing Porter's final projects was a poor 1956 film-musical-ization of Barry's *The Philadelphia Story*, redubbed *High Society*. But this came long after the playwright's death in 1949.) Burt Shevelove had been extremely successful patching together a new *No, No, Nanette* (1971), but the original material—an inconsequential old farce—was far more malleable. *Holiday* was a first-class high comedy of manners; improvements, Shevelove learned, came much more difficultly. The original plan was to use unknown Porter songs, but there was another problem: while the best of them might prove worth discovering, it's certainly certain that some of them *belonged* in the trunk. Replacing them with famous songs merely shifted the weakness, with "new" characters singing songs we've heard before, constantly interrupting the proceedings to remind us they're wearing borrowed clothes. And if Barry's characters speak like Katharine Hepburn (whom he wrote so well for), Porter's characters speak like Ethel Merman (whom he wrote so well for). And so went *Happy New Year*, a flat champagne cocktail served in a chilled dixie cup.

BROADWAY SCORECARD

/ PERFS: 17 / $: –

RAVE	FAVORABLE	MIXED	UNFAVORABLE	PAN
1	1	1		3

THE HAPPY TIME

"A New Musical"

music by John Kander

lyrics by Fred Ebb

book by N. Richard Nash

based on the 1950 play by Samuel A. Taylor, from the 1945 stories by Robert L. Fontaine

"directed, filmed and choreographed" by Gower Champion

produced by David Merrick

starring Robert Goulet and David Wayne

with Julie Gregg (replacing Willi Burke), George S. Irving, Jeanne Arnold, Charles Durning, and Mike (Michael) Rupert

opened January 18, 1968   Broadway Theatre

"*The Happy Time* certainly cheered me up" says the quote from the *Times*, without explaining why Clive needed a little cheering. The other quotes, mostly from secondary publications, are not exactly inspiring. (costume design by Freddy Wittop, photographs by Friedman-Abeles)

CLIVE BARNES, *TIMES*

It has a certain style, a certain charm, even a certain distinction that put it above the rest of this season's so far sadly sparse crop. Certainly it cheered me up, and for reasons that will be apparent I needed a little cheering. Returning from a lecture in Pittsburgh, I was scheduled to reach Kennedy Airport at 5:30 P.M. yesterday, but my flight arrived 100 minutes late. I dashed as fast as my cab could carry me to the Broadway Theatre. I arrived 40 minutes late, but the curtain had been held for me for 30 minutes. I gained my seat 10 minutes after the curtain, a sadder but wiser man. . . . It is good to have a story line of interest in a musical, but better if that story line is part of the whole concept. Here the moving force of the show is the director, Gower Champion. It is interesting that after a period of composer musicals (one used to refer to the "new Cole Porter musical" or the "new Rodgers and Hammerstein") we have definitely passed into a period of "director's musical." Today we have "Abbott musicals," "Robbins musicals," "Fosse musicals" and, as in this case, a "Champion musical." As befits a former dancer and choreographer, Champion uses beautifully free and open movement patterns, so that one scene all but swirls into the next. Also the movement is extraordinarily choreographic, based largely on those old, sweet and campy vaudeville routines. Of all Champion's successes, from *Bye Bye Birdie* [1960] on, this is the most remarkable simply from the directorial aspect, for the basic material is not as strong as that in, say, *Hello, Dolly!* [1964]. Champion uses what he has got with gossamer sweetness and zest. Most of the ensembles are brightly staged, and a song-and-dance trio for Goulet, Wayne and Mike Rupert ["A Certain Girl"] proved a pastiche delight. But when Champion attempted a proper ballet he came a sore cropper, for this quite lengthy ballet does nothing to advance the plot and merely shows the ironic poverty of Champion's actual choreographic abilities. Champion might do best to stick to staging at which he is a master and leave choreography to someone else. The show will certainly not offer you the happiest time of your life— but a happy time? Moderately—especially if you need cheering up.

MARTIN GOTTFRIED, *WOMEN'S WEAR DAILY*

So much of a musical's success depends on the simple musicality of its central idea that it is always a wonder how a group of otherwise talented people could have chosen a rhythmless, tuneless idea and then tried dancing to it. The central story of *The Happy Time* is so entirely unmusical that the composer, lyricist and choreographer were foredoomed not only to irrelevance but to a production that had no music-theatre identity at all. When it is musical, it is very musical, but then when it is musical it has very little to do with *The Happy Time*. The songs and the dances could be easily lifted and then dropped in to a dozen different stories and be just as relevant. We are left with an unmusical musical that has an instantly forgettable, old-fashioned score, an abundance of wonderful dances, a perfectly ridiculous book and an overall quality that can best be defined as duration. What is interesting, I think, is how Champion managed to add great and wonderful bunches of dance to it, considering that nobody was doing anything remotely musical. It is especially interesting because Champion has developed a remarkable method of finding a musical style for every show he directs and then setting everything to its rhythm. Unable to do this with *The Happy Time*, he was forced to direct the non-musical sequences as straight-play and he did it badly, even considering the material. So, great chunks of leaden dialogue weigh down this production until Champion can invent a dance cue, and then everything bursts into great charges of choreography. He keeps these going for as long as he can, as if he didn't know when the next opportunity would come along. Unfortunately, the songs of John Kander were not nearly so good, stock and very boring old-time Broadway. Kander is capable of better. As usual, his talented lyricist—Fred Ebb—turned in a metric, musical and sensible set of lyrics though again the thoughts could have been applying to almost any story. Robert Goulet played the hero in his well known hero way, a grinning, square-jawed, patent leather vocalist for some Forties swing band in a Betty Grable movie. Mr. Goulet, with the clenched fists ever eager to spread-eagle into a final note, manages to have a very true and yet musically insensitive voice.

WALTER KERR, *TIMES*
The Happy Time, a thoroughly expensive musical now at the Broadway, has no light bulb, and that is its cross. In the absence of any new thought, director Gower Champion has made use of projected slide-film, slapping snapshots of quaint villagers all over a cyclorama that

would have drowned *Blow-Up* [the 1966 film. Goulet's character was a photographer]. But here the technique creates a vast cavern, accenting the hole at the heart of things: it makes the stage inside it seem dark and gloomy. Because the ingenious Champion must improvise without inspiration, we catch him at his work piecing tactics together. Here are the balloons, here are the streamers, here are the mountainous stepladders that can be used to make a number called "The Life of the Party" all too obviously in the *Hello, Dolly!* tradition. But they are arbitrarily introduced and mechanically fused; not even David Wayne, doing dandy right and left kicks as he descends a staircase higher than Carol Channing or Pearl Bailey ever dreamed of, can make the first step seem necessary. (Mr. Wayne is incontestably delightful, however, as he teases us ever so drolly into a show-stopping trio called "A Certain Girl.") John Kander and Fred Ebb, lacking that first twist of mind that led them into composing the brittle, sneaky score for *Cabaret* [1966], are working at half-staff, too. . . . If I were a producer of large-scale musical comedies, with an eye out to rejuvenating the whole business so that in the long run the long run would come to life again, I think I'd reverse gears, rent the smallest house on Broadway, spend as little as possible, snatch up any youngsters who have real notions that aren't retreads, and see what I could grow out of it. The big Broadway show needs to surprise itself all over again; a pebble may start the landslide where massed boulders won't.

RICHARD WATTS, JR., POST

The Happy Time, to put it in a nutshell, is a struggle between a brilliant production and a mediocre book, and I'm afraid the book proved the dominating force. The new musical has the advantage of Gower Champion's characteristically imaginative staging, a pleasant score and several attractive performances, but the sentimental tale of a French-Canadian family is a difficult burden for it to carry. Champion, as if aware of the narrative deficiencies, has thrown all of his skill into keeping things moving with a succession of sparkling song and dance numbers and inventive stage devices. Champion is always industriously at work. Those enlarged color photographs pop up, the stage machinery is frequently in motion, and actors climb up and down ladders and ropes, but, above all, they dance. *The Happy Time* would have been better off it had been all production. Since the virtues of *The Happy Time* are under consideration, it should be noted without delay that David Wayne is up to his old trick of stealing the show. Playing a raffish grandfather, he makes the old fellow reminiscent of Cap'n Andy in *Show Boat* [which Wayne played in the 1966 Music Theater of Lincoln Center revival], but he is consistently delightful and, against odds, amusing.

。　　。　　。

Gower Champion's first four musicals—*Bye Bye Birdie* (1960), *Carnival* (1961), *Hello, Dolly!* (1964), and *I Do! I Do!* (1966)—placed him at the top of his field, the undisputed Broadway Man of the Decade, an unstoppable talent. Need I go on? Gower did—on to seven, count 'em, *really* bad shows (including such horrors as the out-of-town flop *Prettybelle* [1971], *Rockabye Hamlet* [1976], and *A Broadway Musical* [1978]) before drawing his career, and life, to a close on a high point in 1980 with *42nd Street*. *The Happy Time* (musical) wasn't even really *The Happy Time* (play). David Merrick, who held the musicalization rights, rejected the version turned in by original author Sam Taylor. But he liked the title and the French Canadien locale, so he took an altogether different property by Richard Nash—of *110 in the Shade* [1963]—and transplanted it. (Merrick had a longstanding feud with Richard Rodgers, coproducer of the play and longtime friend of Taylor, with whom he collaborated on the 1962 *No Strings*. Which could have had something to do with Merrick's treatment of Taylor and his play.) Superimposed on Taylor's and Nash's notions of *The Happy Time* were Gower's own, which focused on the protagonist's occupation as a photographer and developed into a slide show blown up to Broadway Theatre-sized proportions. John Kander and Fred Ebb, just coming in from the *Cabaret*, provided an intimate, charming score that was all-too-overwhelmed by the overproduction. All told, *The Happy Time* was misguided, misconceived, and—well, misdirected. Champion, naturally, received two Tony Awards for his trouble. Notwithstanding which *The Happy Time* went down in history as the first show to drop a million bucks, back in the days when a million bucks was still a lot of dough. Critical Preview Dept.: First-night critics had long been angling for a little extra time to digest what they saw, instead of having to rush out at final curtain (or before) to meet their deadlines. David Merrick went so far as to cancel the final preview of his 1966 import *Philadelphia, Here I Come!* when he spied then-*Times* critic Stanley Kauffmann taking his seat. "A large rat got in the generator," explained Mr. Merrick. (Kauffmann was thus forced to attend the show's opening—and, as it happens, gave the show its *only* unfavorable review. This was in his sixth week as *Times* drama critic—he lasted only five months in all.) Merrick got into another tangle with the *Times*'s aislesitter when Clive Barnes arrived late for the opening of *The Happy Time*. The curtain was held— enraging a testy audience (who had no recourse) and the other first-night critics (who *did*)—and finally started thirty minutes late. Barnes, who missed the opening scenes, gave the show a better review than his colleagues, a mixed notice amidst a sea of negatives. Clive again upset the opening night applecart two weeks later at Broadway's next musical première. He didn't show up *late* for *Darling of the Day*, which arrived in town with deadly word-of-mouth; he simply decided to cover a ballet opening instead, and without notifying the producers, sent second-stringer Dan Sullivan to fill his seats. The show received evenly mixed reviews—two raves, one favorable, one unfavorable, two pans—including a laudatory valentine (appearing two weeks later) from Walter Kerr in the Sunday *Times*. But Sullivan's pan in the all-important daily *Times* clearly did in *Darling of the Day*. (Barnes eventually caught the show as it ended its four-week, $750,000-down-the-drain run—and liked it.) Having learned some rather severe lessons, the Broadway establishment decided that perhaps it *was* okay for the first-night press to cover pre-view performances, and it soon became standard practice.

Tony Awards were won by Gower Champion (director and chore-ographer) and Robert Goulet (actor).

BROADWAY SCORECARD

/ PERFS: 286 / $: –

RAVE	FAVORABLE	MIXED	UNFAVORABLE	PAN
		1	1	4

HEATHEN!

"A New Musical"

music and lyrics by Eaton Magoon Jr.

book by Sir Robert Helpmann and Eaton Magoon Jr.

directed by Lucia Victor

choreographed by Sammy Bayes

produced by Leonard J. Goldberg and Ken Gaston, in association with R. Paul Woodville

with Yolande Bavan, Edward Rambeau, Russ Thacker, and Mokihana

opened May 21, 1972   *Billy Rose Theatre*

CLIVE BARNES, *TIMES*

Aloha, Aloha and still more Aloha. We were given for our sins a musical about Hawaii last night, and before it was halfway through I realized with a stab of pain that I would have rather have been in Las Vegas. *Heathen!* is a more powerful advocate for some kind of organized religion than Billy Graham. It takes place on two levels, just like Grand Central Terminal. The show had a terminal look to it. One level is 1819 and the other level is 1972. Times change, but the story is the same: woman needs man and man must have his mate. The show was produced by the wonderful people who last season gave us *Ari* [1971], Leonard J. Goldberg and Ken Gaston. *Heathen!* maintains their level of producing excellence, or at least falls little short of it. To say that it is the worst Broadway musical of the season would run the risk of overpraising its virtues. But believe me, this was no way to spend an evening.

DOUGLAS WATT, *DAILY NEWS*

[Headline: "*Heathen* Ends Broadway Season with a Thud"]
A shambles. It's so bad that it could put a blight on tourist trade

The set resembled "three pieces of a huge diaper hung out to dry above a couple of bleached dog bones on the ground." And that was *Heathen*'s high spot.

through the entire Pacific. Cheap to look at and even worse to listen to, the whole thing resembles a production number for a stripper who failed to appear that night in a tacky Las Vegas night club. The authors of the book, Sir Robert Helpmann (so help me) and Eaton Magoon, Jr., have tried to show us, the one superimposed on the other, the Hawaii of 1819 and the 1972 model. This must have been a rather sad experience for Helpmann, who was once a distinguished figure in the world of British ballet. Magoon alone must bear responsibility for the simply dreadful songs, words and music both, that keep interrupting this fascinating epic. Sammy Bayes' choreography seemed to consist mainly of native dances in which everybody jumped around or threatened each other with poles when they weren't trying to avoid bumping into one another. Jack Brown's setting resembled three pieces of a huge diaper hung out to dry above a couple of bleached dog bones on the ground that were pushed from place to place to serve as props. The costumes [designed by Bruce Harrow] looked as though they had been rented in Philadelphia. Thus ends another Broadway season.

◦   ◦   ◦

A vanity production showcasing the wealthy Hawaiian songwriter, whose other Broadway opus—the 1961 Don Ameche-starrer *13 Daughters*—was similarly received. *Heathen!* was also the second (and final) musical from the youthful producers of the *Exodus*-based *Ari*. And it was the *sixth* Broadway musical in less than a year and a half to shutter after only one performance. (All right, I'll name them: *La Strada, Gantry, Blood Red Roses, Frank Merriwell, Wild and Wonderful*, and *Heathen!*) As for the boy producers, in 1979 Goldberg was found murdered in his bedroom—handcuffed and shot in the head—the morning following his thirty-third birthday; Gaston died four years later, at the age of forty-one.

BROADWAY SCORECARD
/ PERFS: | / $: —

RAVE	FAVORABLE	MIXED	UNFAVORABLE	PAN
				6

HELLO, DOLLY!

an all-Negro replacement company of the long-running musical comedy

music and lyrics by Jerry Herman (additional music and lyrics by Bob Merrill, unbilled)

book by Michael Stewart

based on the 1954 farce *The Matchmaker* by Thornton Wilder, a revision of his 1938 comedy *The Merchant of Yonkers*, from the 1842 Austrian farce *Einen Jux Will er Sich Machen* by Johann Nestoy, and the 1835 English farce *A Day Well Spent* by John Oxenford

directed and choreographed by Gower Champion; restaged by Lucia Victor, dances restaged by Jack Craig

produced by David Merrick

starring Pearl Bailey and Cab Calloway

with Emily Yancy, Jack Crowder, Chris Calloway, Winston DeWitt Hemsley, Sherri Peaches Brewer, Mabel King, Morgan Freeman, and Roger Lawson

opened November 12, 1967   St. James Theatre
[continuing original run, which opened January 16, 1964]

CLIVE BARNES, *TIMES*

One thing is certain about Mr. Merrick: he has showmanship running out of his ears. Who else would have thought of bringing Pearl Bailey, Cab Calloway and a whole Negro cast to the St. James Theatre to revive the fortunes of the musical *Hello, Dolly!*, which has only been running 68 years or so and will now run for 168 years or so more? Before saying that I adored this new *Dolly!*, let me admit that I went prejudiced. I had not been bowled over by it earlier, and frankly, my sensitive white liberal conscience was offended at the idea of a non-integrated Negro show. It sounded too much like *Blackbirds of 1967*, and all too patronizing for words. But believe me, from the first to the last I was overwhelmed. Maybe Black Power is what some of the other musicals need. For Miss Bailey this was a Broadway triumph for the history books. She had no trouble at all in stopping the show—her problem was getting it started again. On her entrance the audience wouldn't even let her begin. After about a minute's applause, she cleared her throat, grinned amiably, and with those gargling gurgles murmured: "I've a few more words to say in this show." She took the whole musical in her hands and swung it around her neck as easily as if it were a feather boa. Her timing was exquisite, with asides tossed away as languidly as one might tap ash from a cigarette, and her singing had that deep throaty rumble that is—at least to me—always so oddly stirring. By the second act the audience was not merely eating out of Miss Bailey's hand, it had started to chew at her fingernails. When she came to the actual "Hello, Dolly!" number with that entrance into the Harmonia Gardens down the red carpet, the curtains at the top parted just slightly, she slipped in, paused and then, while the audience roared, came down the steps like a motherly debutante. Through this whole number, with a gesture here and a grind there, she kept the crowd roaring. As she pranced, hips wagging and eyes a'joy, around on the runway in front of the orchestra, waving cheerfully to the original Dolly, Carol Channing, sitting there center front in a blaze of platinum hair, the audience would have elected her Governor if she'd only named the state.

WALTER KERR, *TIMES*
[Headline: "Life with *Dolly* is Delovely"]
Eventually people are going to stop going back to see *Hello, Dolly!* They'll just settle down and live there. It's lovely living just now—high living, light living, let's-get-about-on-tiptoe living, and what's most remarkable about it is not that Pearl Bailey is remarkable (which she is) but that the whole show makes you feel as though you'd just stepped onto one of those old-fashioned garden swings that somebody had already set in motion and that was going to go on swooping and diving, soaring and dipping and soaring again, until it finally took off for the moon. Apollo rockets forsooth. The Government is working on the wrong project. Though I'd clearly remembered Gower Champion's manic management of his shoo-fly waiters, skewering dinners on the

run, as well as the runaway on the runway that constitutes the title number, I'd really forgotten how flute-happy and how carbonated a number of the other songs were. When the orchestra struck up "Dancing" during the second-act overture at a recent matinee, a child who will never see two again simply sailed out of her seat in the very first row and went winging up and down the aisle like a sea gull who'd been sipping brandy. She couldn't help it. Personally, I felt like bolting back to the lobby to buy myself a box of chocolates, an impulse I haven't had since I saw Louise Groody in *No, No, Nanette* [1925] but I am made of stronger stuff and I suppressed it. As for Miss Bailey, I know what she's found (the keys to the city, the hearts of the town), but I don't know what she's looking for. She's always bent slightly forward, elbows raised, fingers dripping from her wrists as though they'd been hung up for the night, surveying the floor, the pit, the auditorium at her feet, clearly expecting that in all that vast landscape she'll find someone or something to tell her a secret. When she seems to hear the secret she cocks her head reflectively, in the manner of someone who's checking her jaw to see if the novocaine has worn off, and decides that yes, she's got it and yes, she likes it. If she likes it a lot, she'll sing a song, holding the song clamped between her hands in mid-air: she appears to be juggling a horizontal stack of books there, pressing the melody tight so that nothing will fall. Nothing does.

RICHARD WATTS, JR., POST

You really haven't seen *Hello, Dolly!* unless you've seen it in the production headed by Pearl Bailey and Cab Calloway that has now taken over at the St. James. I've always had respect for the expertness of the phenomonally successful musical comedy, but I didn't fall in love with it until I saw it done with enormous zest, gaiety and charm by a wonderfully attractive and talented all-Negro cast. I attended it at a preview last Saturday afternoon, where the audience was otherwise devoid of the regular first-nighters. It was made up of paying customers, many of whom probably didn't know in advance that an entirely new cast was going in, and I have rarely been among so many unaffectedly enthusiastic spectators. In fact, at the end of the performance it appeared that they were determined to climb onto the stage *en masse* and embrace the splendid Miss Bailey. There has never been any doubt of Bailey's skill as a performer or her ability to project a song. There have been times, however, when faced by a book show, she had been tempted to thrust the book to one side and go ahead with her one-woman act. In *Dolly!* she resists the temptation and really acts the role, playing the part charmingly and humorously. It does seem a shame that the role of Horace Vandergelder, the Yonkers curmudgeon, is not more important, because Calloway plays it with the finest relish. But this is my only quibble. Pearl Bailey and the new *Hello, Dolly!* are a collective delight.

○   ○   ○

Having already passed its third anniversary—4th Smash Year!, in the parlance—the New York production of *Hello, Dolly!* still had legs, and Betty Grable, too. But the show's multiple-company success created a hunger for leading ladies, and at some point along the way someone came up with the redoubtable Pearlie Mae Bailey. (Gower and Mike Stewart had apparently toyed with a black-star replacement scheme for *Bye Bye Birdie* [1960]—Sammy Davis and, say, Diahann Carroll—but the plan never came to fruition. Stewart also put a black company into his long-running *I Love My Wife* [1977], and there was talk of doing the same for *42nd Street* [1980].) Not even Merrick quite knew what to expect when the Bailey company premièred at the National Theatre in Washington. The reaction—critically, economically, and publicity-wise—was so ecstatically phenomenal that the showman decided to bring Pearl & Co., en masse, into the St. James. "But what are we sup-posed to do with the New York cast? Fire them?" Merrick was asked. "Yes," said the Abominable Showman. . . . Bailey remained in the New York company for twenty-five months, after which she took to the road. Merrick's other Dollys included Ginger Rogers, Eve Arden, Martha Raye, Dorothy Lamour, and Phyllis Diller. Not to mention Mary, Ethel, and Carol herself. Enough Already About Who Wrote *Hello, Dolly!* Dept.: At the request of Jerry Herman, the clarification below was included in later printings of *Opening Night on Broadway*:

> During the Detroit tryout, Bob Merrill, Lee Adams and Charles Strouse were called in to help doctor the show. "Elegance" and "Motherhood March" were written by Merrill and Herman. Adams and Strouse sub-mitted a song entitled "Before the Parade Passes By"; this was not used,

however. Herman wrote the version performed in the show, retaining the title.

Both versions of "Before the Parade Passes By" were duly copyrighted, with the Adams and Strouse version receiving the earlier registration. ASCAP, the music rights organization, which licenses nontheatrical public performance of the *Dolly!* score (and remunerates the authors accordingly), lists only one version in their Index of Performed Compositions, with "Lee Adams, Jerry Herman, and Charles Strouse" credited as members "having an interest in" the song. Merrick at first refused Strouse and Adams a royalty—"*I* never asked you to work on the show," said the producer, whose song-doctor of choice had been Merrill (from *Carnival* [1961]). "Go to Gower. Maybe *he'll* pay you." Merrick eventually settled a $150-a-week royalty on the pair, roughly equivalent to one-quarter percent of the gross capacity at the show's initial $9.40 top. Merrill is the sole author listed by ASCAP for both "Motherhood" and "Elegance." The latter—quite a dandy song, in fact—appears to have been originally devised for Thelma Ritter and cronies in *New Girl in Town* (1957), although the lyric was clearly refitted by Herman for "all the guests of Mister Hackl." Merrill got a full three-quarter percent of the Dolly/Vandergelder purse—more than the designers, orchestrator, arrangers, and Adams and Strouse combined. Which, with multiple companies and large-capacity touring houses mounted up to a pretty penny.

Special Tony Awards were won by Pearl Bailey, David Merrick, and even Carol Channing.

BROADWAY SCORECARD
/ PERFS: 2,844 / $: +

RAVE	FAVORABLE	MIXED	UNFAVORABLE	PAN
6				

HENRY, SWEET HENRY

"A New Musical"

music and lyrics by Bob Merrill

book by Nunnally Johnson

based on the 1958 novel *The World of Henry Orient* by Nora Johnson and the 1964 screenplay by Nora Johnson and Nunnally Johnson

directed by George Roy Hill

choreographed by Michael Bennett

produced by Edward Specter Productions and Norman Twain

starring Don Ameche and Carol Bruce

with Robin Wilson, Neva Small, Louise Lasser, Alice Playten, and Milo Boulton

opened October 23, 1967   Palace Theatre

CLIVE BARNES, *TIMES*

Whatever it is that happened to the American musical is not likely to be put right by *Henry, Sweet Henry*. It opens with one of those bustling, little, hopeful overtures where, sickeningly, you feel that all the tunes are already old acquaintances if not precisely old friends. At once it seems that imagination is going to be at a premium, and it is. The main trouble is with the music and lyrics by Bob Merrill, which are feeble. They could have been written any time within the last 20 or 30 years and take no account of the enormous changes in popular music. Perhaps if the music and lyrics were better examples of their type it might still have managed to have been a sweet, old-fashioned thing, but even so, the story and book would have sunk it. And these are not so much bad as unsuitable. The show was virtually stopped a couple of times (mind you,

EDWARD SPECTER PRODUCTIONS, INC.
and
NORMAN TWAIN
present

HENRY, SWEET HENRY
A NEW MUSICAL

Starring
DON AMECHE

Co-Starring
CAROL BRUCE

with
NEVA SMALL · LOUISE LASSER · ALICE PLAYTEN

and introducing
ROBIN WILSON

Book by **NUNNALLY JOHNSON**
Music & Lyrics by **BOB MERRILL**
·Based upon the Novel "THE WORLD OF HENRY ORIENT" by NORA JOHNSON

Choreography by
MICHAEL BENNETT

Entire Production Directed by
GEORGE ROY HILL

ORIGINAL CAST ALBUM ON ABC RECORDS

PALACE THEATRE
Broadway at 47th Street, N. Y. 10036

The teenaged heroines hang onto Henry Orient's coattails, while the star of the show seems intent on getting the hell out of there.

it hadn't worked up a great deal of momentum) by Alice Playten, a poi-
sonous child with the heart of a *gauleiter* and the voice of a ship's siren.
With manic glares at the audience she puppet-strutted her way through
"Nobody Steps on Kaffritz," belting out her music like a toy Merman.
The briskly modest dances arranged by Michael Bennett proved the
most original aspect of the show, even though one of the set pieces
["Weary Near to Dyin'"] had to pillory hippies again. (I like hippies and
Broadway is making me like them more and more.)

MARTIN GOTTFRIED, *WOMEN'S WEAR DAILY*
Considering that musicals are the most exciting and the only truly modern American theatre on the Broadway stage, it is remarkable how so
many of them refuse to take advantage of the great strides of recent
years. They insist on hanging on to the old little-bit-of-plot schemes
with incidental songs and incidental dances in old brassy styles. You
would think that any Broadway composer, having heard what Bernstein
and Sondheim could do, would leap through those newly-opened musical doors into long-lined, deeply textured music. That any Broadway
director, who having seen Robbins' work, would demand continuous
musical-choreographic staging rather than stacked slices of story, song
and dance. You would think that, but Broadway continues to prove how
backward it can be when it sets its mind to it. The lastest example of
archaic musical theatre is *Henry, Sweet Henry*. Apparently stark raving
ignorant of recent developments, it is constructed as if nothing had happened to the musical theatre since 1945. And to make things worse, it is
not even good-1945. It is a smattering of story clipped to cliché songs,
cliché staging and worse-than cliché humor. Nunnally Johnson's book
would not be less interesting if it didn't exist at all, but with lines like
"Let's buzz for the fuzz" it is positively painful. And George Roy Hill
has managed, you almost have to admire him for it, to stage everything
with precisely the apt boring touch. A promising new choreographer
sneaked in with some nice dances but since nobody was around to help
blend them into the production as a whole, they had to hang limply from
the clothesline that such musicals use for structural schemes. They could
not help *Henry, Sweet Henry* from being the shiny hackwork it really is.
I can think of few things more annoying than a young girl belting songs
like Barbra Streisand, but one of those few things is having to pay atten-

tion, all night long, to a stageful of such young girls and their precocious little male counterparts. With Don Ameche as the adult contrast, I mean it doesn't leave you the world, now does it? To say that Mr. Ameche is no Peter Sellers [who created the role in the film version] is to say that The McGuire Sisters aren't exactly The Beatles.

WALTER KERR, *HERALD TRIBUNE*
Henry, Sweet Henry is an unpretentious musical that could probably have been fixed fairly easily if its creators hadn't been there before. Both librettist Nunnally Johnson and director George Roy Hill had worked on *The World of Henry Orient*, the charming film on which the current show is based, and, being so familiar with the materials, have this time skipped plot points. Because they know what's happening, they assume everyone else does, too. As a result, the proceedings at the Palace hop, skip and jump very much like a randomly cut film. But if you can tolerate the skipping, you may enjoy the hopping and jumping. The show is, in its own way, as courageous as *Cabaret* [1966]: it comes out foursquare for apple cheeks, adolescent daydreams, gawkiness and innocence just as though these things might still be real even when they are thoroughly out of fashion.

RICHARD WATTS, JR., *POST*
[Headline: "The Troubles of Henry Orient"]
There was audience enthusiasm last night for the singing of Alice Playten. Miss Playten, who emphatically doesn't need a microphone, would have gratified me more if I hadn't been under the impression that she was attempting an imitation of Sophie Tucker. The chorus of very young girls is always eager and lively, but the choreography isn't exactly electrifying. There is inevitably a number in which hippies frolic, and I thought the most amusing moment in the evening was achieved by the introduction of a protest sign, brandished about by one of them, that read "Hands off plucky little China."

○   ○   ○

Songwriter Bob Merrill displayed an unexpected level of taste and sensitivity in the 1961 *Carnival*, making his stab at the little girls' *World of Henry Orient* seem not all *that* impossible. The *Henry, Sweet Henry* score was not lacking in taste, but most of the taste was bad. On the positive side *Henry* was not so troubled as Merrill and Johnson's 1966 collaboration *Breakfast at Tiffany's*, which died during previews. So much for the positive side. *Henry, Sweet Henry* fleetly came and went, leaving budding choreographer Michael Bennett with a second Tony nomination his second time out for his second flop. (He kept tabs on *Henry's* dance music arrangers, William Goldenberg and Marvin Hamlisch, eventually enlisting them both to compose scores for him.) As for featured player Alice Playten, who monopolized the reviews and overshadowed the putative heroine, it should be reported that the twenty-year-old overnight sensation was already a veteran of three Merrick musicals, with *Oliver's* Bet (1963) and *Dolly's* Ermengarde (1964) following a 1961 touring stint as Merman's Baby Louise. On the Record Dept.: In the scramble by record companies to capture the next big hit, ABC-Paramount–On Stage plunked down one million bucks for half-interests in four big Broadway musicals. Alas, they turned out to be a trio of 1964 offerings from producer Lester Osterman—*High Spirits, Fade Out–Fade In*, and *Something More!*—and the specimen at hand. *Henry's* teenaged chorus girls pretty much described the proceedings in the very opening number, when wordsmith Merrill had them declaim "La bore, la nuts, la crap, la stink." This rhymed with "I'll drink some ink and die," and thus it was for the bitter*Sweet Henry*.

BROADWAY SCORECARD
/ PERFS: 80 / $: –

RAVE	FAVORABLE	MIXED	UNFAVORABLE	PAN
	1	1		4

HER FIRST ROMAN

"Ervin Drake's New Musical"

book, music, and lyrics by Ervin Drake (additional songs by Jerry Bock and Sheldon Harnick)

based on the 1907 comedy *Caesar and Cleopatra* by George Bernard Shaw

directed by Derek Goldby (replacing Michael Benthall)

choreographed by Dania Krupska (replacing Kevin Carlisle, who replaced Donald McKayle)

produced by Joseph Cates and Henry Fownes in association with Warner Bros.–7 Arts

starring Richard Kiley and Leslie Uggams

with Claudia McNeil, Bruce McKay, Cal Bellini, Earl Montgomery, Brooks Morton, Larry Douglas, and Barbara Sharma

opened October 20, 1968   Lunt-Fontanne Theatre

CLIVE BARNES, *TIMES*

Speaking frankly, I think you would be better advised to hang around until *Her Second Roman* turns up and give *Her First Roman* a discreet miss. Some highly talented people get doused in the Nile with the sinking barge. For Mr. Drake I feel less pity than for the rest. He has permitted his name to be put on the program about five times as large as Shaw's. The music and lyrics I presume he wrote himself, but the book is taken almost verbatim from Shaw's play. It is the music and lyrics that spoil the evening. Of course, to make room Drake has had to carve quite a chunk out of Shaw's play, and he is not an especially adept carver. But the basic mistake is to believe that you can take [the play] and hold up the action every so often for a feeble song or a little bit of *Aida*-like spectacle and imagine you have a musical on your hands. What you have on your hands is something quite different. Even if

RICHARD KILEY LESLIE UGGAMS

in

ERVIN DRAKE'S
New Musical

HER FIRST ROMAN

Based on Bernard Shaw's Caesar & Cleopatra

with

CLAUDIA McNEIL

| Earl Montgomery | Brooks Morton | Larry Douglas | Barbara Sharma |

| Diana Corto | Jack Dabdoub | Phillip Graves |

CAL BELLINI

and BRUCE MacKAY

| Sets and Costumes by
MICHAEL ANNALS | Lighting by
MARTIN ARONSTEIN | Orchestrations and
Vocal Arrangements by
DON WALKER | Musical Direction
and Dance Arrangements by
PETER HOWARD |

Original Cast Album by Atlantic Records

Production Associate Irwin T. Denberg   Production Manager Tom Porter

Hair styles designed by Ernest Adler   Costumes executed by Ray Diffen Stage Clothes

Production Supervised by ROBERT WEINER and GEORGE THORN

Dances and Musical Numbers staged by

KEVIN CARLISLE

Directed by

MICHAEL BENTHALL

THE PLAY TAKES PLACE IN EGYPT FROM OCTOBER 48 THROUGH MARCH 47 B.C.

Cleopatra grabs a grape (or is it an olive?) while she is grabbed by
Caesar (or is it Marc Antony?). No matter, *Her First Roman* might as
well have been her last. Preliminary credits. (artwork by John Fehnie)

music and lyrics had been three times as good, I doubt whether the musical could have worked satisfactorily. There is an enormous difference in speed, timing and even basic nature between a serious play and a musical. This must have presented the directors (Derek Goldby is the only one cited on the program, so his predecessor can be permitted to exit with anonymity, if not with grace) with an extraordinarily difficult problem. Half the cast automatically played as if it were a book for a musical, while the other half played as if it were the play, with only Richard Kiley, as Caesar, comfortably bestriding both worlds. Of the performances, my condolences—and very genuine condolences they are—must go first to Kiley and to his co-star, Leslie Uggams. Kiley's singing always has a certain heroic tone to it that gives an almost moral dimension. It is an extraordinarily interesting voice, inimitable and attractive. If you were going to cast the play itself, you could do a lot worse than to cast Kiley. Miss Uggams is a great musical performer, but you would not at this stage of her career cast her as Shaw's child-queen. So there it is. A sad story. There were times in there when a man could almost have withered away in pity for all concerned.

MARTIN GOTTFRIED, *WOMEN'S WEAR DAILY*

Broadway lives in its own world—a world where time doesn't pass and where lessons aren't learned. *Her First Roman* is based on *Caesar and Cleopatra*. And naturally, the scene is Egypt. It begins with a male chorus and an opening number called "What Are We Doing in Egypt?" The next song is called "Hail to the Sphinx." I know you think I'm kidding. I know it sounds like a parody. I'm not kidding and it *looks* like a parody. I wish it were a parody. It isn't fun to think that a musical based on *Caesar and Cleopatra* opened with "What Are We Doing in Egypt?" and continued with "Hail to the Sphinx." And meant it seriously. Mr. Drake, I'm afraid, is not yet up to Broadway hackwork. Like his previous show, *What Makes Sammy Run?* [1964], this one has not mastered the clichés, the formulas, the structural gimmicks that comprise true Broadway junk. It is but a pale imitation of trash. So, the book is silly in an un-Broadway way, the music is old-time pop (rather than old-time showtune) and the lyrics follow the romance and sentimentality of what once was juke box thinking rather than your Shubert Alley line. We are left with a silly romance in silly costumes, a lot of bare-chested men, endless jokes about the name of Cleopatra's maid (Ftatateeta) and a series of sets that look like room dividers from a super-motel [scenery and costumes designed by Michael Annals]. Drake's lyrics are on a similar level ("He pursues her and besieges/Through the haystacks and the beaches"). The melodies are their match despite Don Walker's understated orchestrations. In fact, between the understated orchestrations and the understated tunes, you are barely aware of the music. A problem, however, is this: everybody in the New York theatre knows that Drake did not compose all the music for the show, yet the program credits him with it. So he must be officially blamed for what he didn't write as well as what he did. This kind of misrepresentation is part of the same old-time mentality that fertilizes such shows in the first place. In short, your usual Nile musical, chorus boys with too much body make-up and an overdose of flat scenery. In this version, with its comic combination of Broadway innocence in the conception and Broadway grind in the execution, Egypt would have been better off at the hands of the Israelis.

WALTER KERR, *TIMES*

Her First Roman made such obvious mistakes that a good half of the audience could have stood up, said where and when, and pointed out to the management the rearranged road to happiness. The mistakes were the songs. They were the wrong songs in the wrong places. It isn't enough to dump whole pages of Shaw's dialogue onto a stage full of tip-tilted sphinxes, barrages of Roman shields, and Claudia McNeil. (When Claudia McNeil comes onto a stage, it's pretty full whether you've got all that other stuff or not.) What you've got to do—the one thing you *must* do—is establish a magnetic field into which an aging Caesar and a schoolgirl Cleopatra can be drawn against their wills, their intelligences, their intentions. They can't stand, Egypt-wigged and Roman-nosed, at opposite sides of the stage, or the world, forever, thinking their own thoughts. They've got to merge, spiritually, yearningly, perhaps insanely, but done against all resistance, and the merging must be done in the music. Melody will make the heat that Caesar thinks he can no longer generate, rhythm will describe the Cleopatra who ought to be a kitten on the keys. Let Shaw do the talking. What did composer Ervin Drake do, even though he had a singer-actor as skillful as Kiley and a bug-in-a-rug as cute as Uggams (Cleopatra is wrapped in a rug, you know, and it was where Miss Uggams was cutest, stretched out on that magic carpet just before it made a tamale of her) ready to hand? He forced Cleopatra, together with her Equity chorus of handmaidens, to sing a song about Ptolemy. *Ptolemy.* Who's he to waste our whistling on? He was, of course, Cleopatra's kid brother; we'd met him, he was rather a pest, he wasn't musical, if you know what I mean. The fact that you could incorporate into the lyrics the notion that no one could "tolerate Ptolemy," though it is both alliterative and true, just wasn't enough [lyric by Sheldon Harnick]. There was more important work to be done. But did Caesar do it? No, he sang about "Rome," where we hadn't been and where we weren't even planning to go until next summer. . . . The costumer who clamped upon Miss Uggams a wig that carefully erased every line of her fetching face should be shot at sunrise, Egyptian-time.

o   o   o

Once upon a time there was a fellow named 'enry 'iggins, and you know the rest. So it seemed natural that somebody would talk the Shaw Estate into another dip into the master's work. (G. B. S. himself authorized a musicalization of one of his plays, *Arms and the Man*, in 1908— and after seeing *The Chocolate Soldier* Oscar Straus wrought, placed all his plays off limits until his death in 1950.) *Caesar and Cleopatra* offered legendary characters and a couple of obvious star parts, but like *Pygmalion* it called for literate, witty treatment. Instead it got Ervin Drake, whose theatre experience consisted of the music and lyrics for the not-so-good *What Makes Sammy Run?* Whereas Drake had never written a libretto, it was only natural for the producers to allow him to hack away at the book as well. So what did they expect? As if to compound their problems before they started, British director Michael Benthall was assigned to stage the production. Benthall was championed by the Shaw Estate, who well remembered his triumphant Laurence Olivier–Viven Leigh double bill of *Antony and Cleopatra* and *Caesar and Cleopatra*. But that was in 1950, now it was 1968, and Benthall had never directed a musical; his first opened just before *Roman* went into production, namely *I'm Solomon*. Benthall brought *Solomon*'s Donny McKayle along with him, but he was gone before rehearsals began and replaced by Kevin Carlisle (who had also been replacement choreographer on the 1967 Leslie Uggams-starrer *Hallelujah, Baby!*). Things went as expected, which is to say they opened in Boston and fired the director and new choreographer. Benthall was replaced by bright-haired-boy Derek Goldby, who had just wowed 'em with the 1968 Tom Stoppard import *Rosencrantz and Guildenstern Are Dead. He* had never done a musical, either. Goldby was just then developing the upcoming Bock and Harnick tuner *The Rothschilds* (from which he, too, would be fired), which resulted in a house call by the *Fiddler* (1964) boys. They wrote three songs—and doctored the book?—for twenty-five thousand bucks, to be paid after the opening. At which point the producers evaded the bill, pleading poverty due to poor business (and poorer producing). *Her First Roman* needed more than a few new songs, though; the score and play were barely integrated, and Drake was clearly no Alan Jay Lerner. To combat what he himself considered "a down, dark, anti-public show," Drake changed the ending and sent Cleo happily back to Roma with Julius. So much for Marc Antony. (Dramatist Drake, on the original ending: "I find it of utmost significance that Shaw himself failed with it.") *Her First Roman* eventually lumbered into town, gave everybody a chance to shake their heads at such a senseless waste, folded its voluminous tents, and barged down the Hudson to the scenery dump.

BROADWAY SCORECARD				
/ PERFS: 17 / $: –				
RAVE	FAVORABLE	MIXED	UNFAVORABLE	PAN
	1			5

HERE'S WHERE I BELONG

"A New Musical," previously entitled *East of Eden*

music by Robert Waldman

lyrics by Alfred Uhry

book by "Alex Gordon" (a.k.a. Gordon Cottler, replacing Terrence McNally)

based on the 1952 novel *East of Eden* by John Steinbeck

directed by Michael Kahn

choreographed by Tony Mordente (replacing Hanya Holm)

produced by Mitch Miller in association with United Artists

starring Paul Rogers and Nancy Wickwire

with Walter McGinn, James Coco, Ken Kercheval, Heather MacRae, Bette Henritze, Dena Dietrich, Patricia Kelly, and Casper Roos

opened March 3, 1968   Billy Rose Theatre

CLIVE BARNES, *TIMES*

The most distinguished aspect of *Here's Where I Belong* is the scenery by Ming Cho Lee. But no one ever walked out of a theatre humming the scenery. One wonders whether this study of two brothers and their father could ever have been made into a satisfactory musical. It is too serious—and yet in a musical, lightness is always breaking in. As a result, the climax of the play, the big moment between the unloved son and his unbending father, comes strangely after a jolly family song-and-dance number. The mind cannot adjust so easily. The story is unusually somber for a musical, and the attempts to introduce a little light relief every so often are merely painful. The bland joint efforts of Messrs.

Here's Where I Belong at the Billy Rose, home of one-performance flops. "Sing Along with Mitch" Miller's battle with librettist Terrence McNally garnered more interest than the show. Preliminary credits.

Gordon, Waldman and Uhry should probably have ended up not only *East of Eden* but West of Philadelphia. Which brings me back to Ming Cho Lee. Lee's scenery was beautiful and convincing, it had the atmosphere of the novel and the feel for the period. Before the show started, Oriental members of Actors' Equity picketed outside the theatre, protesting, with some justice, at the selection of a non-Oriental [James Coco] to play the role of the Chinese houseboy in the show. The way Mr. Lee is going—he also designed the Shakespeare Festival's *Ergo*, which also opened last night—he will soon have Occidental designers picketing him, on the grounds of unfair competition.

JOHN CHAPMAN, *DAILY NEWS*

The highlight of the evening is a rousing music-and-dance number about a lettuce harvest.

MARTIN GOTTFRIED, *WOMEN'S WEAR DAILY*

Amateur theatre, pathetically financed to be big-time but frightened, impotent and novice at the core. *Here's Where I Belong* is roughly based on John Steinbeck's *East of Eden*, and when I say "rough" I'm talking about sandpaper. Probably, if you didn't remember the story you'd never get it from Alex Gordon's book. Robert Waldman composed a musical score that is more than pleasant if you're willing to overlook its being 15 years behind the times and its obvious influence by Copland, Bernstein and Sondheim. This was far more acceptable than Alfred Uhry's lyrics, often too embarrassing for quotation. The pity is that so many talented and experienced people—Rogers, Wickwire, Lee, Kahn—are dependent upon any producer who has the money to hire them, however naive he and his material may be. Beginner producers with beginner products should hire beginner casts for beginner audiences.

o　　o　　o

Sing Along with Mitch Miller's sole Broadway offering offered not much to sing along with. The record producer/television personality had set up a development deal with MCA (the parent company of Universal). When he brought in the "developed" Steinbeck musical, MCA bowed out. Fortunately (?), United Artists stepped in and came to the rescue with $500,000. "The hottest thing about *Here's Where I Belong*," came the word from the Philadelphia première, "was a fire among some spotlights in a balcony box." Not an auspicious beginning. Producer Miller demanded rewrites; librettist McNally refused; Miller brought in novelist Gordon Cottler to do the rewrites; McNally demanded his name be removed; Miller refused, stating, "85–90% is his and he has retained royalties, so his name stays on." All of this happened in the papers, just about the only press coverage the barely visible *Here's Where I Belong* got. "Alex Gordon" went into the opening night programs, as several reviewers had quipped only weeks earlier that *Darling of the Day* was so bad that the author had taken his name off of it. "I request you leave me out of it," McNally wrote to the man from the *Times*. "The critics have given me raps before but the work was mine. And when they give me praise I want that work to be mine, too. It's my name, the only one I have, and I worry about it." In his review Barnes simply referred to Alex Gordon as "a name new to me, and one not elaborated upon in the customary biographical note in the Playbill." *Here's Where I Belong* was gone by the time the reviews hit the street, anyway.

BROADWAY SCORECARD
/ PERFS: 1 / $: –

RAVE	FAVORABLE	MIXED	UNFAVORABLE	PAN
		1		5

HOME SWEET HOMER

"A Musical Romantic Comedy," previously entitled *Odyssey*

music by Mitch Leigh

lyrics by Charles Burr and Forman Brown (replacing Erich Segal)

book by Roland Kibbee and Albert Marre (replacing Erich Segal)

based on the ninth-century B.C. epic poem *The Odyssey* by Homer

"book and musical staging" by Albert Marre

choreographer unbilled (Billy Wilson, name removed)

produced by The John F. Kennedy Center for the Performing Arts (Roger L. Stevens, Martin Feinstein, and Alex Morr)

starring Yul Brynner, "co-starring" Joan Diener (Marre), and "also starring" Russ Thacker

with Diana Davila, Martin Vidnovic, Shev Rodgers, P. J. Mann, Ian Sullivan, and Darel Glaser

opened January 4, 1976   Palace Theatre

CLIVE BARNES, *TIMES*

It took Odysseus 20 years to get back to his wife, Penelope. It did not take as long for the musical based on Odysseus and called, a little cutely perhaps, *Home Sweet Homer*, to get to the Palace Theatre, where it docked yesterday. Yet it does seem to have been quite a time. The word of mouth on the show was bad out of town, and bad in town. Well, luckily *Home Sweet Homer* is not as bad as people said it was. Unluckily it is not all that much better. Still, it does have Yul Brynner as the wandering, homecoming Odysseus, it has a score that, for apparent reasons, will remind many of *Man of La Mancha* [1965], it is attractively and quite originally set, and while it may well be more of a myth than a hit, it might please audiences from out of town. That is, always assuming there are any out-of-town audiences who have not actually seen it on its earlier peregrinations. The music is by Mitch Leigh, who wrote *La*

THE JOHN F. KENNEDY CENTER FOR THE PERFORMING ARTS presents

YUL BRYNNER
in
ODYSSEY
A musical play
co-starring
JOAN DIENER
Book and Lyrics by
ERICH SEGAL
Music by
MITCH LEIGH
with
DIANA DAVILA · CATHERINE LEE SMITH · MARTIN VIDNOVIC
also starring
RUSS THACKER
Choreography by
BILLY WILSON
Scenery and Lighting by   Costumes by
HOWARD BAY   HOWARD BAY and RAY DIFFEN
Musical Direction   Orchestrations   Dance Arrangements
ROSS REIMUELLER   BURYL RED   DANNY HOLGATE
Produced for Kennedy Center Productions Inc. by
ROGER L. STEVENS, MARTIN FEINSTEIN, ALEXANDER MORR
Production and Musical Staging Conceived by
ALBERT MARRE

OPERA HOUSE
KENNEDY CENTER
DEC. 19 - JAN. 25 ONLY
INSTANT CHARGE™ 254-3050 • THEATER PARTY/GROUP SALES 254-3626
INFORMATION 254-3770 • (Box Office & Instant Charge open Sunday, Dec. 1)

Home Sweet Homer began it's yearlong *Odyssey* to Broadway with wind in its sails but no one manning the rudder. What is the John F. Kennedy name doing on this, anyway? Preliminary credits.

Mancha, but while the stylistic link between the two musicals is therefore neither fraudulent nor unexpected, it is not to the advantage of the newcomer. The truth is that *Home Sweet Homer* sounds either too much like its distinguished predecessor, or too little. It teases with a similarity it never lives up to. It makes all the right noises, but has few of the right tunes—it is as though that old "Impossible Dream" had this time proved really impossible. A pity, because a lot of talent has gone into shaping *Home Sweet Homer* and one would have liked it to have been a Homer run. . . . At times you could imagine yourself watching a parody called *Kung Fu Comes to Athens.*

MARTIN GOTTFRIED, POST

[Headline: "The Ill-Equipped Pursuit of the Misconceived"]
Home Sweet Homer is so bad it must have been trying. I doubt that Erich Segal, of *Love Story* [the best-selling 1970 novella] fame, intended to desecrate Homer, of *The Iliad* fame, when he set out to adapt its sequel, *The Odyssey,* to the musical stage. History will have to survive without knowing what Segal intended since in-production changes prompted him to remove his name from the program. One can hardly blame him. I'm surprised there were any names on the program at all. Joan Diener, playing Penelope, informs the audience of her loyalty despite an abundance of suitors. Loyalty would not seem her problem since the suitors look and act like competitors in a moron's beefcake contest. Some examples of her experiences are also acted out. I say "acted out" because the overall performance, as directed by Albert Marre, would not reflect well on a school pageant. Diener does seem the silliest of all onstage, but it is only because the most attention was paid to her part. Howard Bay's scenery, aside from a few props, consists of a couple of giant pendants hung before a glittering curtain, making the show look as if it were set in the lounge of a Las Vegas hotel. There is no choreography, unsurprising since there is no choreographer. Mitch Leigh's songs are of his "Impossible Dream" variety, a variety of one, the throb song that pretends it has a melody. Even were there melody, however, only the orchestra could have hinted at it since Diener and Brynner always manage to be on either side of the right tone. Brynner does have stage presence and an occasional charm, though it never quite compensates for a lack of appreciable acting or singing talent. His accent may be untraceable

but it is thick enough to make his lines and lyrics sound as if he were reading them backwards, which may have been just as well. *Home Sweet Homer* demonstrates the monstrous capacities of the musical theatre when its forces are placed in the hands of the ill-equipped in the pursuit of the misconceived.

DOUGLAS WATT, *DAILY NEWS*
[Headline: "A Buried, Harried Brynner"]
What is there to say of a musical whose songs, diligently hammered out of lead, are just so many stage waits and whose book is so lame that a mock boulder-lifting contest seems to offer promise? Such is the discouragingly named *Home Sweet Homer*, a hopelessly arch treatment of *The Odyssey* that came to rest at the Palace Sunday afternoon after its own long odyssey on land. For close to two interminable hours (there is no intermission, evidently a precaution against losing the entire audience at half-time), the book and the songs keep pushing one another aside listlessly. Leigh, best known for his *Man of La Mancha* score, favors broad melodies that always seem to be climbing with measured tread-steps leading to nowhere in particular. With these carefully sculpted, mostly slow-moving and uninteresting tunes equipped with equally uninteresting words, the songs drift by practically unnoticed. None of them, by the way, is suitable for dancing and there is, in fact, no dancing in *Home Sweet Homer*. No dancing and no ensemble singing either in this strange musical. Brynner is really all the show has to offer. As Penelope, a svelte Joan Diener sports a fetching succession of costumes, both loose and clinging, and sings in that shaky, semi-legit voice of hers. Her speech and carriage are something else again. Playing the grande dame, she manages to create the impression of an imperious hostess in a surburban restaurant and I wouldn't have been the least surprised at seeing her walk on at some point carting an armload of menus. Others in the cast include Russ Thacker, who plays and sings the juvenile role of Telemachus as though he were warming up for *Good News*. All in all, a deadly afternoon.

◦   ◦   ◦

Having an enormous worldwide success one's first time out doesn't necessarily destroy a person's talent. But it can sure inflate an ego to epic— and creatively fatal—proportions. *Man of La Mancha* (1965) and "The

Impossible Dream" made Mitch Leigh a name to be reckoned with, and Woe to the Wicked (as the Knight Errant used to say). While *Cry for Us All* (1970) was an overblown failure, the score was not insubstantial, seeming to imply that the composer—with a little discipline and some stimulating collaborators—might indeed live up to his promise. But *Home Sweet Homer* marked a turning point; every bar of music seemed to sing that Mitch Leigh was not to be taken seriously. His subsequent Broadway scores have proved musically barren, namely *Saravá* (1979), *Chu-Chem* (1989), and *Ain't Broadway Grand* (1993). Earlier incantations of the last two folded in Philadelphia in 1966 and 1988, respectively, and two more efforts—*Halloween* (1972) and the Glynis Johns-starrer *April Song* (1980)—never made it to Broadway. Not an impressive lineup, as even Mr. Leigh might admit. *Home Sweet Homer* found Yul Brynner in limbo, awaiting his final return to huzzahs in the 1977 and 1984 revivals of *The King and I* (the latter produced by Leigh). *Odyssey*, as it was originally called, seemed created solely for the purpose of selling tickets on Brynner's name, which it did in some of the many ports visited during its twelve-and-one-half-month pre-Broadway tour. Yale classicist Erich Segal—also the Erich Segal of *I'm Solomon* (1968) and *Love Story*—jumped ship along the way, and was replaced by Nobody Much; Mitch Leigh, as usual, called the shots. The battered vehicle that finally foundered into the Palace was incomprehensibly poor. Albee Marre and his wife were themselves no strangers to the classics; back in 1962 Joan played Helen—the one from Troy—opposite Menasha Skulnik's Menelaus (and George Segal's Paris) in *La Belle*, which never made it out of Philly. The librettist, for the record, was Brendan Gill. <u>All in the Name Dept.</u>: The powers that be, we are told, decided that the title *Odyssey* gave the show a scholarly, stuffy connotation; they changed it to the more "fun" *Home Sweet Homer* lest anyone think the show classical. Perish the thought.

BROADWAY SCORECARD

/ PERFS: 1 / $: –

RAVE	FAVORABLE	MIXED	UNFAVORABLE	PAN

6

HOW NOW, DOW JONES

"A New Musical Comedy"

music by Elmer Bernstein

lyrics by Carolyn Leigh

book by Max Shulman (doctored by George Abbott)

based on an original idea by Carolyn Leigh

directed by George Abbott (replacing Arthur Penn)

choreographed by Gillian Lynne (replaced by Michael Bennett)

produced by David Merrick by arrangement with Edwin H. Morris & Co., Inc.

starring Anthony Roberts, Marlyn Mason, and Brenda Vaccaro

with Hiram Sherman, Barnard Hughes, James Congdon (replacing George Coe), Sammy Smith, Charlotte Jones, and Rex Everhart

opened December 7, 1967   Lunt-Fontanne Theatre

CLIVE BARNES, *TIMES*

Let me be positive. On Dec. 22 the first American Tribal Love-Rock Musical, *Hair*, moves to Cheetah on Broadway. The rest of the news of Broadway musicals is not so good. Last night, for example, *How Now, Dow Jones* opened. One of the more interesting aspects of this is that its title is devoid of a question mark. Not *How Now, Dow Jones?* but simply *How Now, Dow Jones*. Perhaps they did not wish to risk an answer. Personally, I feel that a more suitable title might be *How to Try in Business Without Really Succeeding*—but certainly they try. Rarely before have I seen so much energy confused with invention, or noise confused with music. But if you have not got either a strong book or a strong score, any musical is in trouble. In my opinion *How Now, Dow Jones* has a score as enlivening as an endless chain of ticker tape and a story as likely as a Lonely Hearts column in *The Wall Street Journal*. First to explain the story—but no, that I cannot do. The story is inexplicable.

DAVID MERRICK

by arrangement with EDWIN H. MORRIS & CO., INC.

presents

A NEW MUSICAL COMEDY

HOW NOW, DOW JONES

starring

ANTHONY   MARLYN   BRENDA
ROBERTS   MASON   VACCARO

with

GEORGE COE   SAMMY SMITH   MADELINE KAHN   CHARLOTTE JONES
ED STEFFE   JENNIFER DARLING   ARTHUR HUGHES

and

HIRAM **SHERMAN**

Book by   Lyrics by   Music by
MAX SHULMAN   CAROLYN LEIGH   ELMER BERNSTEIN

Based on an original idea by Carolyn Leigh

Scenic Production by   Costumes Designed by
OLIVER SMITH   ROBERT MACKINTOSH

Dance and Incidental Music
Arranged and Conducted by   Orchestrations by
PETER HOWARD   PHILIP J. LANG

Directed by
ARTHUR PENN

Dances and Musical Numbers Staged by
GILLIAN LYNNE

Associate Producer
SAMUEL LIFF

Original Cast Album by
RCA VICTOR

SHUBERT THEATRE
PHILADELPHIA

Tues. Eve. Oct. 10 thru Sat. Eve. Oct. 28

Opening Night 7:30; Other Evenings 8:30   Matinees at 2:00

Matinees 1st Two Weeks Thurs. & Sat.; 3rd Week Wed. & Sat.

A Theatre Guild-American Theatre Society Subscription Play

"Wall Street is now a playground for adults, with eye-filling, shapely lasses garbed in miniskirts, dancing all along the thoroughfare. Get your tickets now!," said Mr. Merrick's copywriter. "It's an investment that's safe, sure and solid, and you'll watch those laugh-coated, rhythm-spiced dividends roll in." Preliminary credits.

The lyrics, by Carolyn Leigh, are a huge cut above the music they are droned to, although I am bound to add that as the whole idea of the show was Miss Leigh's to begin with, she perhaps ought to take her luck where she finds it. There is also George Abbott's direction—a positive powerhouse that has forgotten what it is doing with the power but keeps on pounding anyway. To be frank, I couldn't help feeling that the best joke came in the *Playbill*. David Merrick, who has more pizzazz than anyone else on Broadway, has had his formerly eulogistic biographical note replaced with the stark simplicity of "Mr. Merrick is best known as the distinguished producer of the musical *Breakfast at Tiffany's*" [1966].

MARTIN GOTTFRIED, *WOMEN'S WEAR DAILY*

How Now, Dow Jones is still another example of the musical that begins with talented and original people who have only the vaguest idea of exactly what they want to do. With the need to actually put something on that stage and have it last for two hours, frenzy moves in where conception fails to tread. Noise replaces sound, panic replaces movement and they cover over the whole business—usually assisted by specialists-in-emergency—relying on facility rather than organized inspiration. The result is always confusion laid over with Formica, splitting through that slippery veneer. If Max Shulman, Carolyn Leigh and Elmer Bernstein had any idea for musical theater when they began work on *How Now, Dow Jones*, that idea is nowhere apparent. From the look of things, it was conceived, in doomed vague terms, as a musical about the stock market. That is exactly what it is. And that is exactly not enough. Sliding in a romantic story that might as well have been set in a Broadway-anywhere, they proceeded to sacrifice their talents to an originality-eating theatre machine. Most of their work came up anonymous, as most work does when spit out of that dreadful gadget. The only trouble is, Leigh and Shulman and Bernstein are not hacks. She is one of the most intelligent and musical lyricists in the theatre and her work for this production shows it. Abbott staged the whole business without a trace of interest in content, seeking the speed and the flash that once passed for entertainment. It passes no more.

WALTER KERR, *TIMES*

How Now, Dow Jones is well put together by a man who has never had an identity crisis, George Abbott. Unfortunately, Mr. Abbott has only directed, and the show is shy a few things, such as an amusing book, melodic songs, lyrics with life to them, and dancing. The dancing is marching, if that. . . . Anthony Roberts, whose face is a running battle between slumped eyebrows and happy teeth, is engaging.

o   o   o

Here's a show that ran six months-plus solely on a catchy title (and the resulting half-million-dollar advance). And it would have lasted longer if not for the June 1968, Actors' Equity strike, which closed Merrick's longer-running *I Do! I Do!* (1966) as well. George Abbott—a decidedly non-Merrick type, from the opposing Hal Prince camp—accepted an emergency call, stepping in and whipping the show into professional shape. Abbott followed Arthur Penn, whom he had also replaced (as director/colibrettist) on *Fiorello!* (1959), in that case receiving a Pulitzer for his efforts. No Pulitzer here. British choreographer Gillian Lynne, represented by Merrick's 1965 imports *Roar of the Greasepaint* and *Pickwick*, was also sent home; she retained her billing, thus keeping Michael (*Henry, Sweet Henry* [1967]) Bennett's name out of the credits. The assignment paid off for the young choreographer, though; Merrick rewarded him with his first first-class opportunity, *Promises, Promises* (1968). Also cut in Boston were the role of Miss Whipple, played by young Madeline Kahn, and the question mark after the title. The pesky punctuation gave the teaser ad "*How Now, Dow Jones?* A new musical comedy hit" an unwanted line reading. That's the Way the Record Spins Dept.: Having made a pretty penny on *Hello, Dolly!*, RCA-Victor handed Merrick two million bucks to invest in his upcoming productions (the label providing 75 percent of the capitalization of each show). The initial offering, Woody Allen's first comedy, *Don't Drink the Water*, turned a healthy profit; the rest of the money went down with *Breakfast at Tiffany's, How Now, Dow Jones, Mata Hari*, and *The Happy Time*. So much for investing in show business.

A Tony Award was won by Hiram Sherman (supporting actor).

BROADWAY SCORECARD
/ PERFS: 221 / $: −

RAVE	FAVORABLE	MIXED	UNFAVORABLE	PAN
3				3

HOW TO BE A JEWISH MOTHER

"A New Comedy with Music"

music by Michael Leonard

lyrics by Herbert Martin

conceived by Seymour Vall; sketches uncredited (Seymour Vall, replaced by Renee Taylor and Joseph Bologna)

based on the 1965 book by Dan Greenburg

directed by Avery Schreiber (replacing Frederick Rolf)

choreographed by Doug Rogers

produced by Jon-Lee and Seymour Vall

starring Molly Picon and Godfrey Cambridge

opened December 28, 1967   Hudson Theatre

CLIVE BARNES, *TIMES*

Normally I do not steal writers' jokes. With *How to Be a Jewish Mother*, which limped haltingly (but not haltingly enough) into the Hudson Theatre last night, I intend to indulge myself. The scene is a Bronx kitchen. A lovable Jewish mother is sending her lovable Jewish son to school by himself for the first time. She is giving him lovable Jewish sandwiches. He says (lovably): "They sell good sandwiches at the cafeteria." The mother looks at him, with one eye clouded with pity and the other blurred with skepticism. She gives him a lovable smile, and ripostes: "I ask you, Marvin, if the sandwiches were any good would they sell them?" I thought the play's backers were going to die of laughter at that. *How to Be a Jewish Mother* looks and sounds like a small comic gift book expanded to unendurable proportions. Its jokes are old and mild and if, physically speaking, one can creak with palsy, this play with its

JON-LEE *presents*

MOLLY PICON AND GODFREY CAMBRIDGE IN

HOW TO BE A JEWISH MOTHER

A NEW COMEDY WITH MUSIC

MORRIS A. MECHANIC THEATRE
CHARLES CENTER, BALTIMORE   685-2624
1 WEEK ONLY BEG. MON. DEC. 11
Evenings at 8:30   Matinees Wed. and Sat. at 2:00
Prices: Mon. thru Thurs. Evenings Orch. and Mezz. $7.00; Balc. $5.00, 4.00, 3.00
Fri. and Sat. Evenings Orch. and Mezz. $7.50; Balc. $5.50, 4.00, 3.00
Wed. and Sat. Matinees Orch. and Mezz. $5.00; Balc. $4.00, 3.00

"Mr. Cambridge portrays a whole gallery of roles," promised the herald, "including those of a Catskill Mountains social director, an international spy, a butcher, and King Lear." Enough said. (artwork by Galster)

abominable music (by Michael Leonard, with lyrics by Herbert Martin) creaks with palsy. And sometimes it struck me as frankly racist. There were jokes about Negroes that lacked taste, and much of the humorously defensive anti-Semitism was, to me at least, rather unpleasant and singularly unfunny. Although I was surprised to find that excellent Negro comedian Godfrey Cambridge lending himself to such a farrago, his anarchic presence was always welcome. There were times when he had a leer of honesty and when he looked at the audience with a sweet contempt. No man managing that can be all bad. I have long been a fan of Miss Picon and she still smiles like an angel with heartburn. Here she gallantly tries to inject life and vigor into the wilting script. Once in a while—no thanks to the authors—Picon and Cambridge achieve a few moments of simple fun. Miss Picon, cooingly incisive, clashing with a Mr. Cambridge thrashing gently around the stage like a black panther with white backlash, more than once offer the possibility of a dramatic encounter. But the authors' susceptibility for the obvious effectively prevents it. The funniest thing on view all evening was a poster of the late Lenny Bruce. I don't know about the Greeks, but Lenny would have had a word for *How to Be a Jewish Mother*.

MARTIN GOTTFRIED, *WOMEN'S WEAR DAILY*

Dan Greenburg's *How to Be a Jewish Mother* managed to be both humorous and intelligent about the whole Jewish mother thing. Seymour Vall has "conceived" a theatre piece from it, and since no program credit is given for the actual writing I assume he did that as well. Rather, he did it as badly. The stage version is a rag-tag Catskill entertainment, amateurishly written and directed as a Saturday night in the social hall. It isn't even worth being irritated by its chintzy hustling of Jewish business. As it happens, Vall uses little of Greenburg's original material. His version is a series of sketches which illustrate some of the more obvious Jewish mother characteristics—all very tired business: domination of husbands and sons, food obsessions, husband-shopping for the daughter and so on. It is all very tired. There are two actors in the production—Molly Picon, you might say type-cast, as the Jewish mother and Godfrey Cambridge as, variously, her husband, her son and the mother of her son-in-law. Cambridge, as you know, is Negro and I'd rather not speculate on the motives for casting him—it should be obvious enough that he was hired just because he was Negro (with the implied attitude—"wouldn't it be funny to have a colored son for a Jewish mother?"). But Cambridge's color is used beyond this—it is used to drag in a host of just-as-tired white liberal routines. As for the material itself, it is dreadful. The performances seem entirely uncoordinated and undirected. Both Picon and Cambridge are shameless muggers and director Avery Schreiber seemed unable to curb their bad habits or provide any substitute. Picon even does a somersault for a cheap laugh. Cambridge himself spent the evening waggling his eyebrows, grinning broadly, and pitifully reading dated liberal jokes (for example, as he dances, "Some of that famous rhythm, folks"). There was also some music—five songs accompanied by a Bar Mitzvah band (piano, drums, accordion) in a balcony box. No doubt Michael Leonard—a talented composer—purposely wrote the music that way in hope of matching the style of a show that had none. However, his assignment was hopeless and he was forced to grind out junk-type songs. Nevertheless, he wrote an exquisite ballad ["Since That Time We Met"] and it was a shame that he had such inadequate voices to sing his songs.

o   o   o

"Someone left the chicken out of the soup" was the word from Glenna Syse, covering the tryout for the *Chicago Sun-Times*. Dan Greenburg's 1965 best-seller, *How to Be a Jewish Mother*, was one of those "impulse" novelty books. A natural for Jewish theatre parties, no? Seymour Vall optioned the rights and hired Jess Korman and Stefan Kanfer to dramatize it for Gertrude Berg. But Berg died in the fall of 1966, and *How to Be a Jewish Mother* died in the winter of 1967. Vall ran a company called First Theatre Investing Service, which pooled small investors and bought big shares in big shows (like *Fiddler on the Roof* [1964] and *Sweet Charity* [1966], for example). *How to Be a Jewish Mother* he produced himself; Jon and Lee, the names above the title, were his kids. (Thanks, Dad, putting my name on a Broadway bomb.) It should be noted that the score came from Michael Leonard and Herbert Martin, the pair who wrote three especially good recorded-by-Streisand songs (including "I'm All Smiles") for the especially poor 1965 musical *The Yearling*. *Jewish Mother* was their second and final faltering shot at the mainstem. For the record, a second piece of Jewish Mother literature, Bruce Jay Friedman's *A Mother's Kisses*, was in 1968 turned into an even bigger full-scale musical comedy (and an even bigger full-scale flop).

"What I Did Between Shows" Dept.: On Wednesday, January 12, at 5:25 P.M., Godfrey Cambridge took a fire ax and smashed part of the backstage sprinkler system. "I'm accident prone," he apologized to police. At 7:10 P.M., he took the ax and smashed *another* part of the sprinkler system. (It seems that his dressing room was rundown, filthy, and freezing.) The Hudson, which was rescued from nudie films by *How to Be a Jewish Mother*, went quickly back to the way of all flesh.

BROADWAY SCORECARD
/ PERFS: 21 / $: −

RAVE	FAVORABLE	MIXED	UNFAVORABLE	PAN
			2	4

HURRY, HARRY

"A New Musical Comedy"

music by Bill Weeden

lyrics by David Finkle

book by Jeremiah Morris, Lee Kalcheim, and Susan Perkis

directed by Jeremiah Morris

choreographed by Gerald Teijelo

produced by Peter Grad (and David Seltzer, name removed during previews)

with Samuel D. Ratcliffe (replacing Bill Hinnant), Mary Bracken Phillips, Phil Leeds, Liz Sheridan, and Louis Criscuolo

opened October 12, 1972   *Ritz Theatre*

CLIVE BARNES, *TIMES*

The story is about a poor little rich boy who wants to be happy, and its best aspect is that it ends unexpectedly soon and its worst is that even that is far too late. The rich boy tries Greece, Africa, Broadway, sex and fortune-telling as a therapy for his misery. Personally, I could only concentrate on my own misery—before the show had been on 10 minutes, I found myself thinking: "*Hurry, Harry*, hurry, hurry, hurry!"

MARTIN GOTTFRIED, *WOMEN'S WEAR DAILY*

Hurry, Harry is one of the most peculiar disasters I have ever seen, going through several distinct stages of trouble before settling into catastrophe. With the first act just past the midway point, all hope is lost—all regrets relinquished—and one is left with the last advantage at the musical disaster over the dramatic disaster: a program that lists the songs so that you can tell exactly how much more you're going to have to sit through.

*   *   *

Back in the early 1970s you could still finance a Broadway musical with five-hundred-dollar scraps from relatives, retainers, and suburban dentists. Gone are the days. *Hurry, Harry*'s Weeden and Finkle were best known for their song "That Guilty Feeling," an interpolation in *I'm Solomon* (1968). So much for that.

BROADWAY SCORECARD
/ PERFS: 2 / $: –

RAVE	FAVORABLE	MIXED	UNFAVORABLE	PAN
				6

I DO! I DO!

"A New Musical"

music by Harvey Schmidt

book and lyrics by Tom Jones

based on the 1951 comedy *The Fourposter* by Jan de Hartog

directed and choreographed by Gower Champion

produced by David Merrick

starring Mary Martin and Robert Preston

opened December 5, 1966   *46th Street Theatre*

MARTIN GOTTFRIED, *WOMEN'S WEAR DAILY*

A warm and very original musical that has the handsome, if glossy, looks of an expensive greeting card and occasionally the sentiments of a cheaper one. They have thrown out the sliding, dropping, rolling scenery, the dancing choruses and the blasting brasses of the ordinary, old-time Broadway musical and have settled for a cast of two and a quiet, extremely musical play. This is not quite the direction in which the musical theatre has been moving, but directions are never as consequential as individual works. Jones and Schmidt decided to try things this way and well they should have. Their work is lovely and strong, capitalizing on the special exhiliration of the very best kind of performers. *I Do! I Do!* avoids its story's natural inclination toward the mawkish and does many fine theatre things. It is the result of a splendid teamwork between authors and director. Schmidt designed his Americana, dance-rooted score to be almost endlessly musical, which fit exactly into the kind of choreographic directing that Gower Champion handles so well. The movement was casually dance-like, breaking out regularly into informal choreography that never once had the look of a "number." The rich, mellow style was consistent. The finest thing about this production is exactly that—its style. From the very start, when the two appear onstage looking like photographs before a rich cyclorama, and as Oliver Smith's handsome, simple, single set slides in with a fourposter and some striking designs, the production keeps its antique polish. The consequence is a work of remarkable consistency, fine musicality, warm rhythms and superb performances.

WALTER KERR, *TIMES*

For the purposes of *I Do! I Do!*, a Santa Claus who shall here be known as David Merrick has hitched a very high-powered Donner and a very high-powered Blitzen to a very low-powered One Horse Shay. The show that comes out of the teamwork will still do for Christmas, though your passion for it is going to depend heavily upon the depth of your devotion to two of the fastest-starting sprinters the contemporary stage knows. . . . Then, courtesy of director Gower Champion, there are all those engaging things the two do together when their hearts are high. One of them is literally the soft-shoe to end all soft-shoes, because it is done with no shoes at all. Barefoot, you see, in nightgowns, hand in hand about the alarm-clock, happy as only newlyweds can be ("I Love My Wife," it's called). Of course, they're cutting up didoes pretty constantly together, because there are only the two of them in the whole show and I supposed their New Year's Eve dido, in which they try their itching fingers at ukuleles, fiddles and saxophones, may prove as memorable—if carefully rigged—as any. The stars, they're great. What about the material? It's on the whole barely passable, a sort of carefully condensed time capsule of all the clichés that have ever been spawned by people married and/or single. Not that the familiarity would matter so much if the lines were fresh from the mint and the lyrics gleaming with new wit. Though the lines and lyrics serve as bridges that the principals can manage to get across, they're never anything much more than that, with the result that the weather is sometimes seasonably mild. Generally you can do the rhyming right along with the folks on stage. But, of course, there are those folks on stage to reckon with. They make a handsome couple. I even see what he sees in her.

NORMAN NADEL, *WORLD JOURNAL TRIBUNE*

First, praise must go to Jan de Hartog. About 80 per cent of the success of *I Do! I Do!* is his, and the sentimental marital comedy which was a hit some years ago simply has become a hit all over again. De Hartog described 50 years of a marriage, from the wedding night through all the joys and adversities that such a union can include. I've watched and reviewed it many times; the lines, the situations and the two personalities never have shown the slightest wear. In fact, they were as fresh as new last night, and in the hands of such as Preston and Martin, beautifully realized. Everything that has been added, in the way of music, lyrics and scenic devices, is bonus, but the source and substance are de Hartog's. Last night the critics were seated further from the stage than usual, which could have been to make the stars look younger (producer David Merrick might think of something like that), but there was no need. Neither evokes the vulnerable innocence of youth as Hume Cronyn and Jessica Tandy did in *The Fourposter*, but they substitute a becoming eagerness. Mary Martin will have the gift of youthfulness as long as she lives. The music doesn't begin to enhance things until the two of them sing "My Cup Runneth Over." During "Love Isn't Everything," they are first cluttering then clearing the stage of children's toys and clothes. This pleasantly rhythmic blending of action, properties, music and story is director Champion's best touch. Preston has his moment with "A Well Known Fact," but she follows with "Flaming Agnes," in the flippant style of her "Honey Bun" number in *South Pacific* [1949]. What makes *I Do! I Do!* unique is the fact that you are always watching two of the most talented and entertaining performers in the American musical theatre. There is no distraction; the stage is theirs all evening. It is a happy show, generous, with charm and lavish with love.

○   ○   ○

I Do! I Do! was written to order for Mary Martin, and therein lie both its strengths and weaknesses. The characters age fifty years during the course of the evening. Jessica Tandy, who created the role in *The Fourposter*, was a youthful forty-two at the time, somewhere on the younger side of Agnes's middle age. Mary, though, was fifty-three. Now, Mary Martin at fifty-three need offer no apologies as a performer, certainly. But she brought to the role a certain dignified tone, due not only to age but also to an apparent change in personality. Mary seemed to have undergone a transformation in 1959 upon donning the habit and wimple of Maria von Trapp. The kittenish hoyden ceased to be kittenish, the cornily vivacious Nellie Forbush stopped turning cartwheels, and a demure prudity overtook the exuberant Lost Boy of only a few years earlier. Jones and Schmidt, to keep their star happy, had to provide material suitable to a grandmother; the raciest this "Flaming Agnes" gets is donning a pigeon-feathered hat topped with peacock plume. Preston, at any age, had talent, energy, and onstage charisma to spare, but Martin set the sugarcoated, geriatric tone of the material. (This didn't abate even when played by "younger" performers, such as Carol Lawrence and Gordon MacRae—the matinee cast, who ultimately replaced Mary and Bob—or Carol Burnett and Rock Hudson, who mated for two road tours in the 1970s.) *I Do!* underwent the typical rocky tryout, with the producer flying in doctors as he had on his previous Gower musical, *Hello, Dolly!* (1964). But Schmidt and Jones—unlike novice Jerry Herman—were able to withstand Merrick. When he arrived at the stage door of the Colonial bearing Comden, Green, and Styne interpolations in his fist, they just said no. (Merrick usually got his way by threatening to close the show, but with *I Do!*'s stars and tremendous advance sale, Schmidt and Jones were able to outbluff the master bluffer.) The final package worked well enough, but it was simply a nice show with lovable ticket-selling stars and an ingeniously devised staging. If *I Do!* proved to be Jones and Schmidt's biggest moneymaker (other than *The Fantasticks* [1960]), it is also their least distinctive work by far. The fiftieth anniversary of Agnes and Michael called for a champagne toast, but Mary changed the order to warm Ovaltine and a milk biscuit.

A Tony Award was won by Robert Preston (actor).

BROADWAY SCORECARD

/ PERFS: 561 / $: +

RAVE	FAVORABLE	MIXED	UNFAVORABLE	PAN
3	2	1		

I LOVE MY WIFE

"A New Musical"

music by Cy Coleman

book and lyrics by Michael Stewart

based on the 1975 French comedy with songs *Viens Chez Moi, J'Habite Chez une Copine* (*Come to My House, I Live at a Girlfriend's*) by Luis Rego and Didier Kaminka

directed by Gene Saks (replacing Joe Layton)

choreographed by Onna White (replacing Joe Layton)

produced by Terry Allen Kramer and Harry Rigby, by arrangement with Joseph Kipness

with Lenny Baker, Joanna Gleason, Ilene Graff, and James Naughton

opened April 17, 1977   Ethel Barrymore Theatre

CLIVE BARNES, *TIMES*

[Headline: "A Deft, Diverting Musical Delight"]

I Love My Wife is bright, inventive, amusing and breezy. And it even takes place in Trenton, N.J. But it is a different kind of a musical. It is something of a musical play. Now the theme is cigarette-paper thin: two couples, observers at the barricades of the sexual revolution, are deciding whether to become combatants. It is a little more complicated than that, but not much. It wins no brownie points for profundity, yet it is lighthearted, light-fingered and original. What Coleman and Stewart have done is breathtakingly simple, but no one—so far as this aging memory can recall—has ever done it before. They have taken the band and put it up on stage. Ah, how about *Cabaret* [1966] you say, or how about *Chicago*? [1975]. Right you are, but this is different. The musicians are welded into the play, as a kind of Greek chorus. They play, they sing, they dress up in fancy clothes, and they keep commenting on the action. At times they are the action. It is a beautifully amusing idea and it gives the musical a different dimension. This is all the more marked in that, generally, the numbers sung by the official acting cast—just the two couples—are more in the nature of commentary rather than action. The result is like a play with musical subtitles. Where Stewart scores almost more than in his book is with his lyrics, which are neat, nifty and very literate. Cy Coleman's music runs the gamut from blues to barrel house, from country and western to marching band. But it is always tuneful, infectious and slightly impish. This makes it sound like a singing leprechaun with mumps, but in fact it is a great deal funnier and much more versatile.

MARTIN GOTTFRIED, *POST*

A thoroughly disarming entertainment. I can't see the harm in a healthy, well-adjusted, sentimental and cheerful musical about sex and marriage. *I Love My Wife* may owe more to the movie *Bob and Carol and Ted and Alice* [1969] than it does to the unidentified Luis Rego play it credits in its program, but it is still friendly and charming, beautifully directed and engagingly performed. It will do just nicely, thank you. The musical that opened last night is not one of your grab you by the throat and smother you with noise shows. I don't mind those either. What I do mind are small shows that try to pretend they're big. This one is just right for what it tries to be, at least once it gets going. A patently commercial Broadway musical with a warm amiable spirit is not about to challenge our morals; we know these are nice people in the orthodox sense and that no wife-swapping is going to occur with them around. That's why we can sit back and enjoy the impossible possibility. What makes it especially enjoyable is the easy, whimsical humor with which Saks has directed the show and the inventive way that Cy Coleman's good time score has been set into it. Most of the songs are set with lovely arbitrariness. The two wives break into a country and western number; the musicians arrive in Santa Claus outfits, or marching band uniforms, or pajamas; a husband lifts his wife atop a white piano that slides on as she goes up. Coleman's score is not of a piece. *I Love My Wife* does not have an inherently musical book to provide the basis for such a score. But Coleman has provided a series of singable, performable songs that with but few exceptions match this easy-going, light-headed and unreal style.

WALTER KERR, *TIMES*

I Love My Wife has decided that if you're going to have musicians around there's no sense in hiding them in the pit. Why not toss them into the plot, where they can help the sexual revolution along by slipping right into bedrooms with their ever-ready bass viols or, if relief from the plot is needed, they can put on striped blazers to go with their banjos and help a couple of chaps get through a dandy buck-and-wing? Librettist-lyricist Michael Stewart has left loopholes everywhere for guitarists in woolen pajamas to slip through, and director Gene Saks has manipulated the slipperiness so deftly that you wouldn't be able to tell a clarinettist from a character if the members of the combo didn't all wear beards (and sometimes Santa Claus costumes). Here they've been so insinuated into the central goings-on that they can serve as inner voices, sometimes seraphic, more often Mephisthophelean. And, being so ready to hand, they can do another thing. If a Cy Coleman song is wanted—and they're all cheerful enough to be wanted—there's no fussing about how to work it in. You just have the mingling principals join hands with the impish interlopers. Then there's another good excuse for liking *I Love My Wife*, and even for thinking of it as a fairly daring departure: it's funny. There's a zany on the prowl who will in future (and right now) have to be reckoned with. His name is Lenny Baker and he looks like Marcel Marceau might look if Marceau's mother ever called him into the house and scrubbed that white stuff off his face. He even behaves like Marceau, once in a while: watch him seem to be walking slowly against the wind, for no good reason whatever, as he reluctantly unbuttons a shirt. He is more nervous than Marceau, to be sure: his idea of relaxing is to hike his shoulders into the air six times, twitchily, and then skip a beat before starting all over again, and he is able to parlay the alarm in his eyes as he takes a drag of a joint into something like three minutes of laughter without help from the librettist, those sneaky musicians, or anybody. The presence of a clown in a contemporary musical is an innovation all by itself; the occasion should be marked. Do go, and do mark it.

◦　◦　◦

Francophile Mike Stewart, who'd enjoyed much of his post–*Dolly!* (1964) time on the Continent, stumbled on Luis Rego's sex-comedy-with-songs in Paris. Determining that it was adaptable into an intimate, contemporary musical, he enlisted his *Seesaw* (1973) collaborator, Cy Coleman. Coleman was without a lyricist—Dorothy Fields died in 1974—so Stewart decided to write his own, brought in *Seesaw* producer Joe Kipness (to whom he owed a musical), and everything fell into place. *Until* just before rehearsals were set to begin, at which point Kipness lost two-thirds of his capitalization and canceled the production. Quick scrambling brought forth replacement producers Harry Rigby and Terry Allen Kramer. (Kippy, who under similar circumstances was maneuvered out of credit on Stewart's *Mack & Mabel* [1974], held out for outlandish "by arrangement with" billing (listed *above* the names of the actual producers.) With that settled and the money in place, *I Love My Wife* began rehearsals. Ten days in, director Joe Layton became incapacitated, breaking an arm, a leg, a pelvis, and pretty much crushing one side of his body. (As best as one can determine, Layton fell out of somebody's loft bed.) His creative influence on the show remained, the innovative use of onstage musicians recalling his work on Richard Rodgers's *No Strings* (1962). After a few director-less days, Gene Saks—who had initially turned down the project —and choreographer Onna White rushed in and readied the show for Philadelphia, where it met with awful reviews and horrendous business. A pre-Broadway closing was contemplated, debated, and overruled. *I Love My Wife* previewed to ghastly word of mouth; things were so dire that coproducer Rigby sold off his share of the show. (Weary of Harry's moaning, Terry Allen Kramer's wealthy husband bought him out under the marquee just before the curtain rose on opening night.) In the meanwhile, though, general manager Jack Schlissel—who had spent twenty years with David Merrick—craftily suggested they move the opening just ahead of that week's already-scheduled *Annie* and *Side by Side by Sondheim*. The critics were starved for entertainment: Broadway's most recent musicals, going back almost two years, included such spectacularly depressing offerings as *Home Sweet Homer*, *Pacific Overtures*, *Rockabye Hamlet*, *Rex*, *So Long, 174th Street*, *1600 Pennsylvania Avenue*, *Something's Afoot*, and *Music Is*. Which Jack figured could translate into a shot in the arm for the first decent musical to come along. (He also assumed *Wife* would get slammed if it followed *Annie* and *Sondheim*.) For whatever reason, *I Love My Wife* received especially kindly reviews. The show enjoyed a long and profitable run, buoyed as business ebbed by the importation of a somewhat older cast—headed by 1960s counterculture heroes Tom and Dick Smothers—followed by (shades of *Dolly!*) an all-black cast.

Tony Awards were won by Gene Saks (director) and Lenny Baker (supporting actor).

BROADWAY SCORECARD
/ PERFS: 872 / $: +

RAVE	FAVORABLE	MIXED	UNFAVORABLE	PAN
2	2	1		1

I REMEMBER MAMA

"The Musical"

music by Richard Rodgers

lyrics by Martin Charnin; additional lyrics by Raymond Jessel

book by Thomas Meehan

based on the 1944 comedy by John van Druten, from the stories comprising the 1943 collection *Mama's Bank Account*, by Kathryn Forbes

directed by Cy Feuer (replacing Martin Charnin)

choreographed by Danny Daniels (replacing Graciela Daniele)

produced by Alexander H. Cohen and Hildy Parks

starring Liv Ullman

with George S. Irving, George Hearn, Elizabeth Hubbard, Dolores Wilson, Betty Ann Grove, Maureen Silliman (replacing Kate Dezina), Armin Shimerman, Myvanwy Jenn, Kristen Vigard, and Tara Kennedy

opened May 31, 1979   Majestic Theatre

"Let me put it this way, Ethel Merman is not running for cover," said the producer. "A tedious failure," said the *Times*. (artwork by James McMullan)

RICHARD EDER, *TIMES*

Despite all the large and estimable names that are or have been associated with *I Remember Mama*, the result is not a marriage but a divorce of talents. At the end of its much-postponed and choppy progress to the Majestic Theatre, this big and expensive musical has buried most of the strengths it possesses under a mass of clichés and a pervading, forced cuteness. And the two principal elements in its performance— Liv Ullmann as Mama, and five young actors as her children—are badly chosen in the first instance, and badly employed in the second. Whatever the original notion behind turning the venerable play about a Norwegian immigrant family into a musical—and after the extensive revolving-door process that substituted or supplemented the original director, lyricist, choreographer and a performer or two—the clear emphasis by the time it opened was upon whatever strength Miss Ullmann could bring to her role. She is unsuited to it. It is not so much that her singing is hoarse and lacking suppleness, and that her dancing is so constrained that she almost seems to be counting the steps as she moves. The overwhelming difficulty is that this actress, who can perform with such force and subtlety that she conveys the pain and nuance of pure thought, is hopelessly lost in the sugary simplicity of this musical's Mama. Martin Charnin and Thomas Meehan, whose collaboration on *Annie* [1977] managed to find genuine wit and originality amid the sentiment, have found very little beside stale wit and mobilized sentiment in *Mama*. The book and, generally speaking, the lyrics are flat when they are not painful. Richard Rodgers's score includes several nice pieces. Most of the score is fairly bland, though; and several times Rodgers brings up heavy violins or chimes to butt in on some particularly sticky dramatic scene. Ullmann apart, the adult performers are pleasant enough. The children are appealing enough in themselves but they are poorly served. They are required to stand about beaming while Mama and Papa sentimentalize. They are like carefully placed spotlights. The children sing a horrendous piece entitled "Mama Always Makes It Better" at Miss Ullmann, posturing and smirking as if she were a box of cornflakes in a television commercial. All in all, *Mama* is a tedious failure. Following *Carmelina* by not many months, it begins to seem that Broadway's nostalgia boom is becoming a nostalgia bust.

WALTER KERR, *TIMES*

Normally, when an incoming musical is plainly in need of a thoroughgo-
ing overhaul out of town, the overhaul takes the form of a massive hype:
the dances get faster, longer and louder, the principals find themselves
belting tunes oftener at much brighter tempos, the gags grow broader and
the sharply reduced libretto scurries out of the way at a sometimes dizzying pace. The results can be incoherent or, if coherent, vulgar. But that
isn't what's happened to *I Remember Mama*, which never made any secret
of its pre-opening difficulties. The reshaping—on the evidence of the
show presently set before us—was done with a needle rather than a blow-
torch. Scenes are neatly sewn, the piecework flows with the rectitude of
those overlapping lace curtains that grace the evening's 1910 doorways.
The repair work would seem to have been done not in panic but carefully
and conscientiously. All to what effect? Blandness, placidity, for the most
part inconsequence. The entertainment really is like the sampler it resembles: no matter what the figures in the foreground happen to be doing at
the moment, they are essentially as formal and as still as the people
behind them. If virtue is its own reward, in this case it is its only reward.
In spite of the affectionate tumble of turrets and scalloped porch-fronts
that designer David Mitchell has provided, in spite of the Rodgers
imprint on at least three freshly melodic songs, in spite of the sturdy,
energetic, ever-so-willing comings and goings of Miss Ullmann, there's a
dullness about the evening that just can't be shooed away. And it's lodged,
I'm sorry to say, right at the heart of the matter, in the fact that the mama
whose memory is reported as so indelible is nowhere very clearly—or at
all emphatically—defined. It so happens that I'd never been exposed to *I
Remember Mama* in any of its many earlier incarnations. Not knowing
Mama, I expected to make her acquaintance now. I never did. Perhaps
authors and director, for all their earnestness in trying to make the musical-comedy quick-fix a simple and decent one, have overlooked one vital
challenge. Have they tended to *assume* mama's character, mama's authority, mama's charm, instead of facing up to the fact that these things had
to be established anew? The lapse may be understandable in the ready-
made circumstances. But it's fatal.

DOUGLAS WATT, *DAILY NEWS*

I Remember Mama is like a faded picture postcard: the outlines are
inviting, but the color's missing. The charm of the John van Druten

play and the Kathryn Forbes stories trails as thinly through the occasion as the wisps of smoke from Uncle Chris' ever-present cigar. This evanescent quality extends to Richard Rodgers' score. The attractive tunes are unmistakably his, and better on the whole than those from either of his last two shows, but they are teasing echoes of the grand years with Oscar Hammerstein. *I Remember Mama* is a tasteful period musical in the R&H idiom, but almost totally lacking in the R&H energy. It is like a musical they might have considered writing together but didn't, and probably with good reason. For in common with *Life With Father* [the long-running 1939 family comedy], which they once had in mind, *Mama* has been through so many transformations that it must be played out by now. In any event, the present adapters haven't been able to make the story fresh again. With the passing years, *Mama* seems to have receded ever further into the dimmer recesses of memory.

๏   ๏   ๏

Is their a fjord in your future? How about a new family musical, from the authors of *Annie* and the composer of *The Sound of Music* [1959]. Based on a long-running play, popular film, and seven-year sitcom hit. Sounds pretty snappy, doesn't it? Well, maybe not. At least, it didn't sound so good to investors. Despite his habit of lacing his prospecti with topflight creators and—in this case—a major international movie star, Alex Cohen needed a record 323 investors to cough up the $1,250,000 capitalization; he even ran classified newpaper ads in nine cities to entrap new investors. And if you take into account the fact that half of the show's backing came from one source, Universal Pictures, Cohen needed 322 foolhardy folk to cough up the other $625,000. (Cohen's musicals had an extremely low investor's return rate, resulting in a correspondingly low rate of return investors—especially after they took a gander at the lavish self-promoter's eyebrow-raising financial statements.) What they got for their money was a typical Alex Cohen musical—ill-conceived, misguided, and rife with squabbling creators, with lots of publicity marking the birth and documenting the downfall. (Like his two Angela Lansbury vehicles, for instance, Jerry Herman's *Dear World* [1969] and the 1971 *Prettybelle*, which closed out of town despite—or because of—the efforts of Jule Styne, Bob Merrill, and Gower Champion.) The musicalization of *Mama* sprang from the mind

of director/lyricist Martin Charnin; the selling point was the presence
of Richard Rodgers, with whom Charnin had written *Two by Two*
(1970). ("That doesn't discourage me," said Rodgers of his lyricist.
"Everybody has failures.") Rodgers and Hammerstein, in fact, had followed *Oklahoma!* (1943) by producing the nonmusical *I Remember
Mama*, for an impressive 714 performances. But this was an old, tired,
and ailing Rodgers; while he came up with the requisite tunes, they
were—well, tired. Rodgers barely outlasted the show, dying as the year
came to an end. And there was Liv Ullmann, who'd starred for Cohen
in the acclaimed 1977 revival of *Anna Christie*. "Let me put it this way,"
said the producer when asked early on if Liv could sing. "Ethel Merman
is not running for cover." Cohen complimented her, though, with a
$26,000 weekly guarantee against 10 percent of the gross. The
Philadelphia opening was not so hot (*Variety* sez "I Dismember
Mama"). Charnin was axed the next morn. Cy Feuer, the *Guys and Dolls*
(1950)/*How to Succeed* (1961) producer whose directing credits were
more pedestrian—*Whoop-up* (1958), *Skyscraper* (1965), *Walking Happy*
(1966)—was brought in, announced Cohen, because his ideas "were so
collateral to my own." Given Cohen's record of musical show ideas, that
should have disqualified him right there. But no. Charnin's departing
remarks: "Ms. Ullman and I do note see 'I to I' about how musicals are
made. To make a long and ugly story short, there's no longer a fjord in
my future." This made Charnin feel better, except he went off and had
a minor heart attack. The star expressed her condolence: "I hope that
Martin Charnin will start doing something more constructive than
blaming his failures and illnesses on other people. It's starting to be too
tempting to answer him back." But these recriminations came later.
Along with Feuer, Cohen brought in lyricist Ray Jessel—from Cohen's
1965 *Baker Street*, which should have disqualified him right there—and
simultaneously replaced choreographer Graciela Daniele with Danny
Daniels (from Feuer's *Walking Happy*). *Mama* loped into the Majestic—
home of Rodgers's *Carousel* (1945) and *South Pacific* (1949)—and set up
house, postponing the opening three weeks for fixing time. Cohen had
the forethought and the clout to clear the delay with the *Times*; he did-
n't want Richard Eder barging in "before the show was ready," as he had
on the recent *Saravá*. The extra time and all forty previews didn't help,
with The Man from the *Times* labeling *Mama* "a tedious failure."

Cohen responded with a statement to the press, complaining that Eder "has provoked outrage in the theatrical community, particularly because he continues the savage nature of his attack on great artists who work in our theatre." Which, of course, only went to publicize the fact that *Mama* was—well, a tedious failure. At the same time, Cohen aired intriguing radio commercials ("*I Remember Mama* opened to great critical and public acclaim"). The show limped on four months as the parties ran out, at which point the Shuberts pulled the plug to free the Majestic for a lackluster Michigan Opera Company revival of *The Most Happy Fella*. "I still see my *Mama*," said Charnin on the eve of the Broadway opening. "My *Mama* goes on in my head every night and they stand up and cheer it every night." Yeah, and your *Hot Spot* and *Mata Hari* and *Annie 2*, too.

BROADWAY SCORECARD

/ PERFS: 108 / $: –

RAVE	FAVORABLE	MIXED	UNFAVORABLE	PAN
	1			5

I'M SOLOMON

"A Musical Fable," previously entitled *In Someone Else's Sandals, Solomon/Solomon* and *King Solomon and the Cobbler*

music by Ernest Gold (replacing Alexander Argov)

lyrics by Anne Croswell

"special material" by David Finkle and Bill Weeden

book by Anne Croswell and Dan Almagor (replacing Erich Segal, Anne Croswell, and Zvi Kolitz); "American adaptation in collaboration with Zvi Kolitz"

based on the 1938 Israeli comedy *King Solomon and the Cobbler* by Sammy Gronemann

directed by Michael Benthall

choreographed by Donald McKayle

produced by Zvi Kolitz, Solomon Sagall, and Abe Margolies

starring Dick Shawn, Carmen Mathews, and Karen Morrow

with Salome Jens, Fred Pinkard, Paul Reed, Barbara Webb, and Mary Barnett "with a cast of 60"

opened April 23, 1968   *Mark Hellinger Theatre*

CLIVE BARNES, *TIMES*

King Solomon, wise, rich and yet restless, is counterposed with his physical double, Yoni, a cobbler, the perfect fool, innocent and feckless. Solomon decides to change places with the cobbler, and soon finds that what is taken for wisdom in the palace may be mere foolishness in the marketplace. The background of *I'm Solomon* is interesting and perhaps revealing. It started life as a play, written in German, by a Zionist lawyer, Sammy Gronemann, who emigrated to Palestine in the 1930's. This play, *King Solomon and the Cobbler*, won wide popularity in

DICK SHAWN
IN
I'M SOLOMON
A NEW MUSICAL

also starring
CARMEN MATHEWS KAREN MORROW
and
SALOME JENS
WITH A CAST OF 60

Book by
ANNE CROSWELL and **DAN ALMAGOR**

Lyrics by
ANNE CROSWELL

Music by
ERNEST GOLD

Based On An Original Play
"KING SOLOMON AND THE COBBLER" by **SAMMY GRONEMANN**
American Adaptation in Collaboration with **ZVI KOLITZ**

Settings by
ROUBEN TER-ARUTUNIAN

Costumes by
JANE GREENWOOD

Lighting by
MARTIN ARONSTEIN

Orchestrations by
HERSHY KAY

Musical Direction &
Vocal Arrangements by
GERSHON KINGSLEY

Dance Arrangements by
DOROTHEA FREITAG

Associate Producers: **PHILIP TURK** and **KALMAN GINZBURG**

Dances & Musical Numbers Staged by
DONALD McKAYLE

Entire Production Directed & Supervised by
MICHAEL BENTHALL

MARK HELLINGER THEATRE
51st Street, West of Broadway

Printed by Artcraft Litho. & Ptg. Co., Inc., New York

I'm Solomon, "with a cast of 60" and designer Rouben Ter-Arutunian in a box. The artwork is left over from the preliminary title, *In Someone Else's Sandals*.

Palestine, and, much later, was produced in New York in Yiddish. Most recently the Cameri Theatre in Tel Aviv, apparently exponents of what is known as "modern native realism" in the contemporary Israeli theatre, used this as the basis for a folk musical, which won international acclaim in London, Paris and at Montreal's Expo '67. However, this new musical is not a translation of this. The original music by Alexander Argov has been discarded, to be replaced by a score by the Hollywood composer Ernest Gold; a new book and lyrics have also been provided. In its basic story line it is still *King Solomon and the Cobbler*, but the show, to use the title of one of its better numbers, is "In Someone Else's Sandals." At times the sandals fit a little loosely. When it was all finished, and even the Queen of Sheba had arrived, I found myself wondering what the Israeli original was like, and what this one might have achieved before being flattened by the show-business mangle.

MARTIN GOTTFRIED, *WOMEN'S WEAR DAILY*

The splendor that was Jerusalem. It is difficult to say which is more ridiculous, a Broadway parody of a Hollywood spectacle or the original itself. *I'm Solomon*, however, is something else—a Broadway attempt at actually being a Hollywood spectacular. I would say you'd have to see it to believe it, only seeing it really isn't worth the trouble. The musical opened last night at the Mark Hellinger, complete with belly dancers, veils, courtesans and pounding drums. Even a score by Ernest Gold (who wrote the score for *Exodus* and managed to paraphrase its incredible theme for the Broadway show-tune vernacular). I swear to you, the opening line is, "My newest entertainment for the tavern—imported from Syria," and we move right into a belly dancer production number. There is no sense trying to be even minimally serious about this production, nor is there any point in spending a great deal of time trying to be amusing about its extraordinary ineptitude. It is, of course, vulgar and silly, absurdly staged by Michael Benthall. What is striking, though, is the amateurism in producing and in creation to which the Broadway musical theatre has fallen. There was a time, and not very long ago, when musicals—however misconceived they might be—were certain to be professionally executed. Today it has become commonplace for a bad musical to be bad where musicals had never been bad before: in matters of scenic layout, orchestration, costume execution. That is, in matters of craft. The large company sloshed around in crazy costumes [designed by Jane Greenwood] in front of Rouben Ter-Arutunian's crazy carved-ivory scenery. Finally, the wonderful Salome Jens walked on as the Queen of Sheba and against all odds (and clothes) was exquisite. A very weird evening, that's all to be said. The only thing missing wasn't missing at all—one character really asked, "First time in Jerusalem?" Grant it innocence.

o   o   o

The 1938 comedy *King Solomon and the Cobbler* gained new life in the summer of 1964 with a musical version at Tel Aviv's Cameri Theatre. The production was also presented elsewhere, including a May 1967 stint as part of the World Theatre Season at London's Aldwych Theatre. Determining that the fairy tale-like aspects of the show were too childlike for Broadway, producer Zvi Kolitz went in for full-scale improvements. He presumably figured that the substitution of Ernest Gold—composer of the soundtrack for the 1960 film *Exodus*—couldn't hurt the potential theatre party business. (What potential theatre party business?) Anne Croswell, lyricist of the 1963 Vivien Leigh vehicle *Tovarich*, was chosen as collaborator; and Yale Classics professor Erich Segal provided—and withdrew—a libretto, as he would on the 1976 *Odyssey*-based *Home Sweet Homer*. (In between he wrote a slender tear-jerker of a 1970 novella called *Love Story*.) *I'm Solomon* is remembered chiefly as the show in which the set designer was billed in a box. Which does, indeed, tell us something.

BROADWAY SCORECARD

/ PERFS: 7/ $: –

RAVE	FAVORABLE	MIXED	UNFAVORABLE	PAN
			2	4

ILLYA DARLING

"A New Musical," previously entitled *Never on Sunday*

music by Manos Hadjidakis

lyrics by Joe Darion (doctored by Stephen Sondheim)

book by Jules Dassin (replacing John Patrick)

based on the 1960 screenplay *Never on Sunday* by Jules Dassin

directed by Jules Dassin (doctored by Joseph Anthony)

choreographed by Onna White

produced by Kermit Bloomgarden (for Jules Dassin and Melina Mercouri) in association with United Artists

starring Melina Mercouri (Dassin) and Orson Bean

with Titos Vandis, Nikos Kourkoulos, Despo, Hal Linden, Harold Gary, Rudy Bond, and Joe E. Marks

opened April 11, 1967   *Mark Hellinger Theatre*

JOHN CHAPMAN, *DAILY NEWS*

Miss Mercouri is All Girl. She isn't on stage more than a minute before she strips down to a bikini, and from here on she has a costume change with every scene. Nothing she wears serves as much of a disguise. It's *Never on Sunday* in three dimensions—maybe four—with colorful costuming by Theoni V. Aldredge.

MARTIN GOTTFRIED, *WOMEN'S WEAR DAILY*

While it has what can be reasonably described as music and lyrics, it is in practically no way musical theatre. This might imply book trouble, but the trouble with *Illya* goes deeper than its book (which, as it happens, is perfectly dreadful). To write music for the theatre, a composer must have a sense of stage needs and while Manos Hadjidakis is well away from Shubert Alley musical clichés, he has no awareness of the-

"She's a creature you'd be happy to take home to mother if mother was out," per Walter Kerr. But "*Illya Darling* makes movies seem better than ever."

atre demands. For all its Greek sound, his score is repetitious and strapped into the same "song" habit as most any local tunesmiths. Now this is not entirely to Hadjidakis' blame. While a musical is a blend of many contributions, there must be one person running it and that person—usually the director—should be able to lead. Dassin apparently was too unaware of musical theatre to provide much leadership, having trouble enough writing a plausible book. *Illya Darling* tells a story that is almost impressively idiotic. Miss Mercouri has a deep and weak voice, but it is a true one and she sings nicely enough although it is difficult to understand her lyrics (perhaps just as well since Joe Darion's, when understandable, are pretty foolish).

WALTER KERR, *TIMES*

I think they've made a slight mistake. They've left the show in Detroit, or wherever it was last warming up, and brought in the publicity stills. There they all are, glossy and frozen, staring at us like billboards from the stage of the Mark Hellinger. Melina Mercouri, leggy and luscious as before, clasping a shy sailor to her very warm breast. Melina Mercouri stripped down to a minibikini, ready to plunge off the piers of Piraeus. Melina Mercouri locked in the muscular embrace of a handsome dock worker without a shirt. Melina Mercouri propped up in bed on her elbows, crying a little through cigarette smoke over three weeks' love lost because of overindulgence in virtue. Melina Mercouri is, of course, something to contemplate in these and other postures as the camera seems to snap. Making a swash-buckling—or earring-swishing—entrance from amid the tiny matchstick masts with which designer Oliver Smith has dotted his harbor, she seems to have stepped right off the half-shell. The lady's smile is as broad as the blaze of noon, her eyes are curiously fierce behind the indefatigable grin, and when she throws her arms wide apart to suggest that the whole world is welcome to them, she must throw them wider apart than anyone since Jolson, once the champ. Measurements might be taken, here and elsewhere. She's a creature you'd be happy to take home to mother if mother was out. But it's all in the nature of a Personal Appearance, which is not quite the same thing as a musical comedy. Choreographer Onna White, who can dance an idea as economically and precisely as anyone about, is given no ideas. She fills as best she can, with a virile male chorus linking arms and stomping out scissors-steps vigorous enough to bring the tavern down—if you care about the tavern, which isn't housing much plot at the moment. *Illya Darling*, inadvertently and unluckily, makes movies seem better than ever.

HERBERT KUPFERBERG, *WORLD JOURNAL TRIBUNE*
[Headline: "Melina's Movie Better"]
Illya Darling has two things going for it, and both of them are blonde. One is Melina Mercouri, as decorative a Greek as has existed since Venus de Milo. The second is an energetic lady orchestra leader named Karen Gustafson [replacing Lehman Engel], who keeps the atmosphere rippling and throbbing with the bouzouki and non-bouzouki music of Manos Hadjidakis. Between the two of them they sometimes make the show live up to a description wryly applied by Mercouri to one of the songs: "It's very charming but has a low intellectual level." But more often mere words take over—trite words from the book by Jules Dassin, and even triter words from the lyrics of Joe Darion—and the soggy side of *Illya* dispels the occasional glimpses of Mediterranean sunshine. The little, low-budget movie has been made over into a big, expensive Broadway show, with music and dances added, but with other elements, including its original charm, missing. Mercouri herself is not the kind of girl who gets lost in translation. With her shapely figure, charming accent, throaty voice, and swinging blonde hair she's enough to begin a new Greek revival. Considering her calling, no one expects to find her clad in sackcloth, but designer Theoni V. Aldredge has nevertheless managed to dress—or rather undress—her in a dazzling variety of attire, including a Greek tunic, a mini-bikini, a set of black-lace unmentionables, and a split-front working dress. Voyeurs of the world, unite. So charming is Mercouri that you almost believe her. . . . For all the enthusiasm with which Miss Gustafson whips the orchestra along, the music eventually becomes repetitive, not to say interminable. Movies are better than ever.

*   *   *

"*Illya Darling* rests on the premise that Melina Mercouri is irresistible. Even if one accepts this highly unlikely premise, this is a tasteless, heavy-handed show beyond anyone's capacity to bring to life," said Edwin Newman of WNBC-TV. The producers, as is their habit, reduced this in their quote ads to "Melina Mercouri is irresistible."

Newman complained and the producers apologized, claiming there was "no intent to deceive." Perish the thought. Jules Dassin—author, director, producer, and costar of the 1960 movie *Never on Sunday*—ran *Illya Darling*. And never bothering to have it properly musicalized, ran it aground. The expatriate Dassin, who started in the Yiddish theatre, had one Broadway musical to his credit (the ill-fated 1952 Bette Davis revue *Two's Company*) before fleeing the blacklist. Producer Kermit Bloomgarden, a supportive friend of many blacklist victims, originally announced *Never on Sunday* for the fall of 1962 (with lyrics most probably by E. Y. Harburg). The international success of the 1964 Dassin-Mercouri film *Topkapi* moved *Illya* back into high gear, with full funding from United Artists. Award-winning playwright John Patrick (of *Teahouse of the August Moon* [1953], *The World of Suzie Wong* [1958], etc.) came aboard, along with *Man of La Mancha* (1965) lyricist Joe ("You can barbecue my nose/Make a giblet of my toes") Darion. Patrick didn't make it to rehearsals, though, withdrawing "to avoid a conflict with the author of the original story." During the stormy tryout Bloomgarden brought in director Joe Anthony (of his 1956 production *The Most Happy Fella*) and lyricist Stephen Sondheim (of his 1964 *Anyone Can Whistle*) to help out, but Dassin—and his lovely wife, Melina—didn't seem to need help. When musical director Lehman Engel was fired in Toronto, his assistant, Karen Gustafson, was promoted—becoming, apparently, the first female conductor to originate a full-scale musical on Broadway. And still one of not so very many. As was to be expected, *Melina, Darling*—oops, *Illya*, I mean—drifted into the Hellinger and treaded water for eight months, leaving passels of disgruntled theatre partygoers in her considerable wake. Oh, and composer Manos Hadjidakis refused his Tony nomination, complaining that he had little control over his work. Seems he had trouble with the director.

BROADWAY SCORECARD

/ PERFS: 320 / $: –

Rave	Favorable	Mixed	Unfavorable	Pan
	1	1	1	3

IRENE

a revised version of the 1919 musical comedy

music by Harry Tierney

lyrics by Joseph McCarthy

additional music and lyrics by Charles Gaynor, Jack Lloyd, Wally Harper, and Otis Clements

book by Hugh Wheeler and Joseph Stein, from an adaptation by Hugh Wheeler, Harry Rigby, and David Rogers

directed by Gower Champion (replacing Sir John Gielgud)

choreographed by Peter Gennaro (replaced by Gower Champion)

produced by Harry Rigby, Albert W. Selden, and Jerome Minskoff

starring Debbie Reynolds, Patsy Kelly, Monte Markham, George S. Irving (replacing Billy de Wolfe), and Ruth Warrick (replacing Natalie Shafer)

with Ted Pugh, Carmen Alvarez, and Janie Sell

opened March 13, 1973   Minskoff Theatre

CLIVE BARNES, *TIMES*

[Headline: "*Irene* Bustles Merrily and Relentlessly"]

There is probably a market for *Irene*, the almost-new musical comedy that opened the completely new Minskoff Theatre last night, and I sincerely hope it finds it. One can only admire so much energy and effort. Doubtless, many people will enjoy it. The elegant lady sitting next to me remarked to her husband halfway through the first act: "It is all so refreshing, and they don't take their clothes off.". . . For some, doubtless, the performances will carry all. Debbie Reynolds has already made theatrical history by receiving a Tony Award nomination the day before her Broadway debut. She proved a game trouper who worked

Theater

RICHARD M. NIXON

Old Musical Draws
Raves From New Critic

President Nixon saw the revival of the 1919 musical "Irene" at a pre-Broadway tryout in Washington last night. His "review," based on wire service reports, follows:

"Irene" was a great show. I think this will be a big hit in New York, perhaps not with New Yorkers, but with the out-of-towners. I don't want to get into the business of criticizing some of the new art, but these days it is very difficult to find a movie or play you really want to take your family to.

People are getting tired of all that way-out stuff.

"Irene" has a lot of fun in it. This is one the whole family can enjoy.

Debbie Reynolds is just a superstar. In the movies she was rather tight, but this time she showed real range. She's a fine actress and a fine dancer.

I've never seen a show before with three dance num-

'Irene'

A musical comedy by Hugh Wheeler with music by Harry Tierney and lyrics by Joseph McCarthy. Cast headed by Debbie Reynolds, Patsy Kelly, Monte Markham, George S. Irving and, Ruth Warwick. Directed by Gower Champion. Choreography by Peter Gennaro. Sets and costumes by Raoul Pene DuBois.

bers that were real show-stoppers.

I should say I've seen "Irene" before, but I'm not really quite that old.

Everybody's a Critic Dept.: Would *you* buy a used car from this smiling fellow?

with a ferocious friendliness. Her face is a little bland and her voice a little characterless, but she is clearly willing to do anything for the sake of the show—even baton-twirling, which she does awfully well. By far the most professional and polished performance comes from George S. Irving, who long has been one of the funniest and smoothest performers around Broadway and here takes another chance to show it. His Madame Lucy stole a show that was never guarded as closely as it might have been. Patsy Kelly, for example, got some laughs but did have to travel quite a distance for them. Indeed she left few stones unturned and quite often having turned them, threw them. *Irene* is undemanding, raucous, frequently cheerful, and the best 1919 musical in town.

MARTIN GOTTFRIED, *WOMEN'S WEAR DAILY*
The World's Fair mentality has come, as perhaps the final and ugliest of the vultures, to replace Broadway's living flesh with a mechanical replica. *Irene* is to the idea of theatre what processed cheese is to the idea of food, what Disneyland is to the idea of amusement parks, what Muzak is to the idea of music, what Richard M. Nixon is to the idea of presidency, and it is hardly surprising that (a) he liked it and (b) made a point of publicizing the fact. The show belongs at the new, comfortable, acoustically perfect, characterless and very temporary-looking Minskoff Theatre. I wouldn't be surprised if, at the end of every performance, the actors were plugged out, disassembled and put into little boxes for storage until the next day. *Irene* is a period motel, pridelessly made, bought and paid for with devalued currency. There is no style to it, no purpose, no human energy. It is simply manufactured. . . . Gower Champion is a tremendously gifted choreographer-director who has no peer in staging a show with continuous musicality; who can devise a production motif, create every move and gesture, and drill a company into flawless precision. Though the choreography for *Irene* is credited to Peter Gennaro, the look of the dances is Champion's. The problem is it is the look he created for *Hello, Dolly!* [1964]. With a show that has no indigenous style, one could well understand his problem in setting it to movement, but it is saddening that he fell back on an artificial solution. The nature of this artificiality is personified by the star. Debbie Reynolds has as true a singing voice as I have yet heard on stage; she

dances with easy competence; unsurprisingly, she is an accomplished baton twirler. (I am sure she can roller skate, tap dance, juggle and do contortions.) But she is utterly unmusical—her songs are generated frequencies, her dances are mechanical movements. She is the original living doll, a performer in the sense that a vending machine is a restaurant. Perhaps, as Nixon has said—with his traditional disinterest, objectivity and trustworthiness—*Irene* is a show for "tourists" rather than "New Yorkers." A "tourist," of course, is not one who travels but one who is a manufactured customer for manufactured entertainment. All you tourists out there, plug in your battery packs, get on the escalators and obey the "applause" sign.

WALTER KERR, *TIMES*

If you are going to revive a 1919 musical, you can, decently, do one of two things: (a) you can revive a 1919 musical; or (b) you can create something that looks like, sounds like, moves like, feels like everybody's idea of a 1919 musical. The real thing or consistent pastiche. But not a stylistic botch that embraces everything from a new book that is exactly as unfunny as the old one would probably have been, a melange of songs that includes a few from *Irene* and quite a few from later or even entirely contemporary sources, orchestrations that are steadfastly of the late twenties or early thirties if they are steadfastly anything at all, and a great deal of paint slapped on portals and backdrops that do not so much suggest the stage decor of a period as they do the remains of a sidewalk art show in the Village after all of the best primitives have gone. Debbie Reynolds, God knows, is game, shaking her pretty reddish locks as she takes tomboy flops onto a sofa, crawling under pianos, doing kickstep rideouts about as well as any Rockette possibly could, letting herself be flipped head over heels in a jig, taking a flying leap into the boys' arms from the tops of a battery of player pianos. The girl is accomplished. I think she can do *anything*—except face us and hold us by contact. But the show is virtually without real contact, it is so determined to keep going—past what is dubious about it, no doubt. The going is slick, breathless, firm. Gower Champion, who inherited the entertainment out of town, has seen to it that there are no gaps in the staging, no frayed edges to the sheet-music. But the ultimate effect of so much efficiency applied to so cavalier a grab-bag is one of sheer heartlessness. And the one thing you should not be, if you are going to bother doing *Irene*, is heartless.

◦   ◦   ◦

Producer Harry Rigby, having been forced out of the 1971 revival of *No, No, Nanette,* came up with an even better idea: *Irene,* the "Alice Blue" 1919 musical, with Debbie Reynolds herself. Ruby Keeler was a kind of dumpy old grandmother, still able to handle a tap dance or two, but Debbie was a *real* entertainer, capable of kicking up a storm. And she sure did. *Nanette* had demonstrated the folly of hiring a director with a great name (Busby Berkeley) but no experience directing musicals; so Rigby did it again, paging John Gielgud of all people. ("Why *Irene?*" a reporter questioned. "Why not?" retorted Sir John.) On *Nanette* they were canny enough to supplement their septuagenarian figurehead early on with the canny Burt Shevelove, who not only directed but reshaped the adaptation; *Irene,* though, forged ahead obliviously. The production that took the stage for the Toronto première was ill-formed and poorly reviewed, with the "Debbie Reynolds" show receiving further international (bad) publicity when the star developed laryngitis. Rather than send on understudy Janie Sell, the star decided to "act" the performance with her lines read by the golden-voiced Gielgud. The audience, feeling shammed, responded with boos and catcalls. Debbie turned on the throng. "I don't have to be here," she rasped. "I could be home with my seven maids." Her voice soon returned, while Gielgud soon departed. Gower Champion, an old M-G-M stablemate of the stars, came in to help out while expressing no great enthusiasm. (His billing suggestion: "Why don't we say 'Salvaged by Gower Champion?'") But *Irene* was first and foremost a misconceived, mediocre show with only one mitigating factor. An important factor, though: Debbie Reynolds—in 1973, in *Irene*—sold tickets. She had a lot of especially loyal fans, and they were the sort of fans who would gladly pay to see their darling. (Poor Debbie captured the hearts of America when Eddie Fisher dumped her and her babies for that home-wrecker Liz Taylor, front-page news back in 1959. One of those babies, Carrie, accompanied Mom to Broadway as an *Irene* chorus girl.) *Irene* was a sellout smash, setting box office records in the new, large-capacity Minskoff Theatre and enjoying the best week in

Broadway history, breaking Kate Hepburn's 1969 *Coco* mark with $144,689. But one year—and six million dollars—after the opening the investors had still to receive any return on their investment. Not a nickel. An attorney general's investigation illuminated just how and why this could happen. Yes, business during the tryout and in New York was land-office. But, alas, overtime changes and replacements and rehearsals don't come cheap, driving the production costs up from the budgeted $800,000 to a staggering $1,492,000. (That number has a certain ring to it, doesn't it?) The extra $700,000 was covered by first-priority loans from coproducers Al Selden and Jerry Minskoff—which meant that *Irene* had to earn $700,000 of operating profit to cover the loans *before* the show could begin to pay back the investors. And while your typical big musical is saddled with outsized costs, *Irene*'s weekly royalty base swelled to a staggering 24.75 percent of the gross—making it difficult, indeed, to accumulate much in the way of running profit. (A normal total for authors, stagers, rights holders, and producers might be 16 percent; *Irene* was paying two directors, and—reportedly—thirteen writers and songwriters. I can only track down eleven of 'em; sorry.) The show paid back most of the overcall by the end of the New York run, with profits from the post–Broadway tour ultimately reducing the investors' loss to a half mill or so. "Fortunately, *Irene* was a hit," said coproducer/theatre-owner Minskoff. "Unfortunately, it cost too much."

A Tony Award was won by George S. Irving (supporting actor).

BROADWAY SCORECARD

/ PERFS: 594/ $: –

RAVE	FAVORABLE	MIXED	UNFAVORABLE	PAN
		1	2	3

"IT'S A BIRD, IT'S A PLANE, IT'S SUPERMAN"

"The New Musical Comedy," previously entitled *It's Superman!*

music by Charles Strouse

lyrics by Lee Adams

book by David Newman and Robert Benton

based on the comic strip *Superman* (which first appeared in 1938)

directed by Harold Prince

choreographed by Ernest Flatt

produced by Harold Prince in association with Ruth Mitchell

starring Jack Cassidy

with Bob Holiday, Michael O'Sullivan, Patricia Marand (replacing Joan Hotchkis), Don Chastain, Linda Lavin, and "The Flying Lings"

opened March 29, 1966   Alvin Theatre

STANLEY KAUFFMANN, *TIMES*

Superman is fun. It opened last night, and the sum of everything to be said about it is: it's fun. It is easily the best musical so far this season, but, because that is so damp a compliment, I add at once that it would be enjoyable in any season. It has some tunes that are at least recognizable as tunes, brisk lyrics, some clever staging and some very engaging performers. What's best, the whole show has been based on a witty point of view. Superman is Big, Strong, Noble. But he is also something else that has been true all along and that we may not have noticed. He is a bit of a boob. All the Superman attributes are treated with such ultra fidelity that the inevitable result is satire. The general tone can be shown in a typical line. Someone asks Superman scornfully: "Where did you get that name?" Soberly and thoughtfully he replies, "It seemed to fit." Flying in by wire, Bob Holiday as Superman comes on dull. But we soon see that this is the point. He is consciously modest, incessantly good-doing and dull. The production of this show is considered by some to be part of the Pop Art boom, but its approach is far from the usual view of Pop as grim glorification of the banal. Mr. Prince, his authors and cast have not merely reproduced *Superman*, large and up close, as a Pop painter would do. They have made a show about a super-boob from outer space who lives by pasteurized milk and pasteurized standards, on whom a whole city depends for its moral force and ethical practice. The show's attitude is, I think, gently horrified at the implications, as well as being amused. And amusing. How nice it is to go to a purported entertainment and actually be entertained. What a novelty!

WALTER KERR, *HERALD TRIBUNE*

Whenever the new musical gets its tongue far enough into its cheek, it's cornball-cozy. Trouble is, it runs out of cheek. The show is lame where it daren't be—in the wink that's supposed to come along with all the whizzing through the air. Items to admire include the overture, very nattily arranged by Eddie Sauter from Charles Strouse's generally skipping score, bits of *Batman*-type dialogue scattered blandly here and there ("Great Scot! Did I hear right?" exclaims Clark Kent as an orange spotlight flips down over him and freezes him off from his listening fellows), and, above all, a telephone booth that bows. Clark Kent turns into Superman by slipping inside a telephone booth, of course, and it is one of director Hal Prince's more fetching conceits that when the quick-change is done the booth itself can dance away, nodding farewell to mark the parting. I've held off on Jack Cassidy because it is he who makes the greatest use of the available vacancies. When the story-line isn't doing much, and the song he's singing doesn't really matter to it, Mr. Cassidy takes off on his own, with variations. During a song called "You're the Woman for the Man," he tries dancing with his teeth (I think that's what he was doing last night), he slides on his knees to a finish that must give the wardrobe-woman horrors, he tiptoes and spins and behaves like a lavender-shirted sneak, wearing the expression of a dirty-minded angel as he purloins the show. It's all invention, it is of no conceivable significance, and it's nifty. But *Superman* is on the whole only half-sly vaudeville, yelling for help whenever it starts to wind down and finding it in fairish acrobats, medium-grade slugfests, and random though energetic choreography. It looks slick, we must say that; but its wit is on the lazy side.

NORMAN NADEL, *WORLD-TELEGRAM & SUN*

The title pretty well sums up the show; whatever else happens, *It's Superman* who makes the evening airily, nonsensically satirical. I don't just mean Bob Holiday's performance as the comic strip hero, though heaven knows, he has the Superman instinct like no other actor who comes to mind. But a lot of people connected with this merry adventure into the ridiculous have the Superman instinct, and know just what to do. As gleefully wicked as Superman is wholesome, Jack Cassidy blends oily smoothness, unshatterable conceit, staunch singing and all the vaudeville razzamatazz in the book into his part as a *Daily Planet* columnist. Note—and enjoy—his "The Woman for the Man," in a style reminiscent of the stage and screen musicals a generation ago. Slick. The show has trouble sustaining its comic level when Superman (or Clark Kent) isn't around and busy. It seems that producer Harold Prince usually has the right idea, but director Harold Prince can't quite put it into effect. Also, ensemble scenes tend to look routine, with some exceptions. The reprise of "It's Superman," with the cast cuddled in comic strip boxes, works the way you'd like everything to work [scenic design by Robert Randolph]. I got a kick out of the way Strouse's music sounds in the pit, notably the first and second act overtures as orchestrated by Eddie Sauter. This must be said for *Superman*: you leave the theatre smiling, and the smile lasts all the way home.

DOUGLAS WATT, *DAILY NEWS*

[Headline: "*Superman* Shows Early Hardening of Arteries"]
It's not a bird, it's not a plane and it's not even a salami. It's *Baker Street* [Prince's 1965 musical] in drag. In place of the invincible Holmes, we have the unconquerable spirit of [Superman]. And replacing Prof.

Moriarty in the Doyle canon is a mad scientist named Dr. Sedgewick. He's a 10-time loser of the Nobel prize, which is the closest thing to a joke I remember hearing all evening long.

◦   ◦   ◦

All right, how *do* you get young audiences into the theatre? With a pop musical, perhaps. *Batman* had hit the airwaves—twice a week—in January 1966, and suddenly "op" was pop. For a while, anyway. (*Superman* had been in development, in fact, since 1964, under the aegis of David Merrick—who over the years dropped more than a dozen musicals subsequently produced unsuccessfully.) Songwriters Strouse and Adams set out to do to 1960s pop what they had done to Elvis in *Bye Bye Birdie* (1960). Strouse was far more successful on the earlier show, where he had a richer target; Adams, meanwhile, provided *Superman* with a sterling set of comedy lyrics. The show's lack of center—or perhaps its determined centering on a delicious, subsidiary character played to the hilt, or maybe *past* the hilt, by Jack Cassidy—proved its particular hunk of kryptonite, though. In an attempt to find the "youth" market, producer Prince tried creative pricing, with the orchestra split into three different sections ($12 for the best, $10 for the most, and $9 for the fringes). During the run, he even switched to a four-matinee week (Wed., Thurs., Sat., and Sun.). But neither the youths—nor the adults—bothered with *Superman*. Librettists David Newman and Robert Benton came out best of all, parlaying their contact (and contract) with the Man of Steel into the 1978 motion picture blockbuster.

BROADWAY SCORECARD
/ PERFS: 129 / $: –

RAVE	FAVORABLE	MIXED	UNFAVORABLE	PAN
	4		1	1

JESUS CHRIST SUPERSTAR

"A New Musical"

music by Andrew Lloyd Webber

lyrics by Tim Rice

based on "the last seven days in the life of Jesus of Nazareth"

"conceived for the stage and directed by Tom O'Horgan" (replacing Tito Capobianco)

produced by Robert Stigwood in association with MCA, Inc., by arrangement with David Land

with Jeff Fenholt, Yvonne Elliman, Ben Vereen, Barry Dennen, Paul Ainsley, Bob Bingham, and "Randall's Island"

opened October 12, 1971   Mark Hellinger Theatre

CLIVE BARNES, *TIMES*

Nothing could convince me that any show that has sold two-and-one-half million copies of its album before the opening night is anything like all bad. But I must also confess to experiencing some disappointment when *Jesus Christ Superstar* opened last night. It all rather resembled one's first sight of the Empire State Building. Not at all uninteresting, but somewhat unsurprising and of minimal artistic value. Rice and Lloyd Webber are young Englishmen of obvious talent. Rice's intention was clearly to place Christ's betrayal and death into a vernacular more immediate perhaps to our times. His record sales would presumably indicate his success in this aim, but he does not have a very happy ear for the English language. There is a certain air of dogged doggerel about his phrases that too often sounds as limp as a deflated priest. It is surely unfortunate, even bathetic, to have Christ at his moment of death remark solemnly: "God forgive them! They don't

Robert Stigwood
in association with MCA, Inc.
by arrangement with David Land
presents

JESUS CHRIST SUPERSTAR

Lyrics by
TIM RICE

Music by
ANDREW LLOYD WEBBER

JEFF FENHOLT   YVONNE ELLIMAN   BEN VEREEN
BARRY DENNEN   PAUL AINSLEY   BOB BINGHAM
                    RANDALL'S ISLAND

Associate Producers
GATCHELL and NEUFELD

Scenic Design by   Lighting Designed by   Costumes Designed by   Stereo Sound Designed by
ROBIN WAGNER   JULES FISHER   RANDY BARCELO   TAPLIN PRODUCTIONS

Musical Direction by   Orchestrations by   Production Supervisor
MARC PRESSELL   ANDREW LLOYD WEBBER   CHARLES GRAY

Conceived for the Stage and Directed by
TOM O'HORGAN

Original Broadway Cast Album On Decca Records

MARK HELLINGER THEATRE
51st STREET at BROADWAY   MATS. WED. & SAT.

Mr. Lloyd Webber comes to town. Who knew??

know what they are doing." The sentiments are unassailable, but the language is unforgivably pedestrian. The music itself is extraordinarily eclectic. It runs so many gamuts it almost becomes a musical cartel. Lloyd Webber is an accomplished musician and he has emerged with some engaging numbers. The music does have the bustling merit of vitality, which is what has made its records sell, and what Tom O'Horgan has seized upon in his monumentally ingenious staging. Ever since his beginning at La Mama, O'Horgan has tried to startle us. Once he startled us with small things, now he startles us with big things. This time, the things got too big. For me, the real disappointment came not in the music—which is better than run-of-the-mill Broadway and the best score for an English musical in years—but in the conception. There is a coyness in its contemporaneity, a sneaky pleasure in the boldness of its anachronisms, a special, undefined air of smugness in its daring. Christ is updated, but hardly, I felt, renewed. For all this, *Superstar* seemed to me less than super.

MARTIN GOTTFRIED, *WOMEN'S WEAR DAILY*

Jesus Christ Superstar is an enormously successful record album, called a "rock opera" in one of pop music's pathetic and pointless efforts to gain respectability by imitating orthodox forms. It is also an awful album, overproduced and over-orchestrated in vain compensation for underinspiration and a complete lack of the qualities that make for rock music—vitality, rhythm, state of mind, musicality. But no matter. It required no imagination to envision as a commercially viable stage production. Nor did it require any imagination to hire Tom O'Horgan to conceive and create this stage version, O'Horgan being Broadway's Mister Rock and Roll, thanks to *Hair* [1968]. The only trouble is, to capitalize on the record's sales, Andrew Lloyd Webber's music had to be used; the mood of this music in no way resembles the mood of "the last seven days in the life of Jesus of Nazareth" (as the program describes the action); and O'Horgan does not particularly like rock and roll, as he would be the first to tell you. Otherwise, the show was in great shape. *Jesus Christ Superstar* is, at its worst, a production that leaves you with a so-what feeling. For all its physical beauty, extravagance, enormity of orchestration and complexity of audio production, it provides no feeling—no sense of anything happening in a theatre. It is simply there, a superexpensive juke box playing the entire (87-minute and 16-second) score of the record album, note for note and lyric for miserable lyric. You could as well be listening to the record—if you could stand it all the way through. I tried twice as preparation and never made it. Visually, it is something else. Although O'Horgan can well be charged with selling out for accepting this assignment, he is still a director who is bringing many of the newer theatre techniques to a Broadway that needs them desperately. The surrealistic and awesome sets, costumes and objects, very much the color and texture and look of melted bones, were gorgeously devised by Robin Wagner (scenic design) and Randy Barcelo (costumes), but every once in a while they would be insulted by a Jesus rising on a stage elevator in a white sequin gown, for all the world as if in an Easter show at the Radio City Music Hall. Which, ultimately, is what *Jesus Christ Superstar* really is.

WALTER KERR, *TIMES*
[Headline: "A Critic Likes the Opera, Loathes the Production"]
The title page of the program for *Jesus Christ Superstar* stresses that Tom O'Horgan has not only directed the production but has "conceived" it. It is not an immaculate conception. All that had to be done with it was to put it on a stage baldly—baldness is very much of its essence—and, after establishing a few simple traffic directions, let it sing for itself. Instead, O'Horgan has adorned it. Oh, my God, how he has adorned it. Christ first appears, flaxen-haired and willowy, rising from a huge goblet or chalice, draped in a silver sequined gown that can be spread to circus-tent proportions. He looks like Dolores [the mannequin-like model] in the *Ziegfeld Follies of 1924*. Judas is easier to look at, if he were ever alone. He is never alone. He has as restless companions four purple creatures who strongly resemble those Fisk Tire men made of rubber rings that appeared in billboard advertisements when I was a boy, and their main function seems that of intercepting Judas and tossing him about madly whenever he is in danger of getting a lyric across to an audience. If Mary Magdalene is finishing her charming "I Don't Know How to Love Him," she is not permitted to finish it in peace, hers or ours; Jesus must be dragged away from her, by four to six stalwart intruders, on what seems a large slice of eggplant so that the song's ending is blurred. What at first seems a front-curtain turns out to be

more nearly a drawbridge; as it is lowered away from us a gaggle of loin-clothed creepy-crawlers, virtually the O'Horgan trademark, come scrambling over the top of it like lice on the loose. They serve no function. They are simply there to let us know that O'Horgan is there, inventive fellow that he is. I have not seen any of the concert versions that have been touring the country, but I suspect that—having less money to spend and perhaps no O'Horgan of their own—they may be, in their enforced austerity, much better. There are still two conceivable reasons for going to the Hellinger. If you haven't listened to the album and don't intend to, the materials are—on their chosen level—worth knowing. And of course you may want to attend simply to see how long a way a lot of bad taste can go. The results are spectacular.

DOUGLAS WATT, *DAILY NEWS*
[Headline: "*Jesus Christ Superstar* is Full of Life, Vibrant with Reverence"]
Jesus Christ Superstar, which as everybody knows opened last night, is so stunningly effective a theatrical experience that I am still finding it difficult to compose my thoughts about it. It is, in short, a triumph. Tom O'Horgan, who conceived the production and directed it, has brought the work to brilliant life. It's by far the best thing he has ever done. Andrew Lloyd Webber's score is vibrant, richly varied and always dramatically right and much the same things can be said of Tim Rice's lyrics. The songs are, indeed, marvelous and although they rock a good deal of the time there are other interesting influences in it—nicely handled references to Prokofiev and Weill, to name two, and some lovely string and choral writing. Starting with what is basically a bare, raked stage, O'Horgan has set it ablaze with action (it is probably the most energetic show I've ever seen) and special effects. By use of a dazzling assortment of set pieces (most of them descending from the flies), props and costumes, he has filled the stage with color and movement. I suppose you'd have to call Judas the star role, since it is psychologically the most arresting one, and here a baritone named Ben Vereen is simply magnificent, singing and acting with a vitality that is almost unbelievable and yet with nuance, as well. The story in itself, is, of course, unbearably moving, but the great accomplishment of Webber and Rice has been to make it so strikingly immediate.

o　　o　　o

Innovative staging, spectacular scenery, and innocuous song after song after song, often derivative and set to inexpert lyrics: this would come to be the pattern for many (but not all) of Andrew Lloyd Webber's musical entertainments. Curious, in that Lloyd Webber's music itself is far less memorable than the overall effect. The scores of *South Pacific* (1949) or *My Fair Lady* (1956), say, contain more song hits than Lloyd Webber has come up with in all his work to date. Yet his name is as highly bankable as the Rodgers and Hammerstein banner, so the man is doing something right besides selecting properties cannily and marketing them across the world. *Superstar* marked a smash Broadway debut for the twenty-three-year-old composer Lloyd Webber (Tim Rice, his collaborator, was already all of twenty-six). And unlike Lloyd Webber's future super-smashes, the stage version of *Superstar* originated not in the West End but right here on old Broadway, at the longtime home of *My Fair Lady* (and at present writing a church).

BROADWAY SCORECARD
/ PERFS: 7 1 1 / $: +

RAVE	FAVORABLE	MIXED	UNFAVORABLE	PAN
2			3	1

JIMMY

"A Musical Play of the Life and Good Times of Jimmy Walker," previously entitled *Beau James*

music and lyrics by Bill and Patti Jacob

book by Melville Shavelson

based on the 1957 screenplay *Beau James* by Jack Rose and Melville Shavelson, from the 1949 biographical novel by Gene Fowler

directed by Joseph Anthony

choreographed by Peter Gennaro

produced by Jack L. Warner in association with Don Saxon and Harry Mayer

starring Frank Gorshin, Anita Gillette, and Julie Wilson

with Jack Collins, Larry Douglas, William Griffis, Sybil Bowan, Dorothy Claire, and Evan Thompson

opened October 23, 1969   Winter Garden Theatre

CLIVE BARNES, *TIMES*

If they were able to base a musical on La Guardia you would have thought a musical based on Jimmy Walker might well have sent you doing a wild Charleston all down Broadway. One day some one may carve a great musical out of Walker's life, times, booze and girls, but it was not sad, brave *Jimmy*, which subsided gamely into the Winter Garden last night. What is there salvageable? First there is Frank Gorshin making his Broadway debut as Jimmy, the Tammany tap dancer. He has a certain Cagney-like, pugnacious charm, and a nervy, driven vitality. Helping Gorshin every unavailing inch of the way were Anita Gillette and Julie Wilson. This was not the kind of show that could be stopped, but every so often both of these girls threatened to

FRANK GORSHIN
ANITA GILLETTE   JULIE WILSON
in

"Jimmy"

A Musical Play of the Life and Good Times of Jimmy Walker

with

JACK COLLINS

DOROTHY CLAIRE   LARRY DOUGLAS   WILLIAM GRIFFIS   SIBYL BOWAN   EVAN THOMPSON

Book by MEL SHAVELSON
(Based on the novel "Beau James" by GENE FOWLER)
and the screenplay by JACK ROSE and MELVILLE SHAVELSON

Music and Lyrics by
BILL and PATTI JACOB

Scenic Production by
OLIVER SMITH

Directed by
JOSEPH ANTHONY

Costumes Designed by
W. ROBERT LAVINE

Projections Designed by
CHARLES E. HOEFLER and
JAMES HAMILTON

Lighting by
PEGGY CLARK

Musical Numbers Staged by
PETER GENNARO

Musical Direction and Vocal Arrangements by
MILTON ROSENSTOCK

Musical Arrangements by
JACK ANDREWS

Assistant Choreographer
BILL GUSKE

Production Stage Manager
WILLIAM ROSS

Dance Arrangements by
JOHN BERKMAN

Hair Styling & Make Up
JIM SULLIVAN

"I know it is sometimes said that Hollywood is killing Broadway," reported Clive Barnes, "but I didn't know that people were allowed to send guerrilla parties over to speed up the job." (artwork by A. Weymar)

start it. Gillette, pretty and vulnerable, with a voice that was just made for Broadway, fought the show like a delicate tigress refusing to be caught in a net. But she had nothing to fight with but her very considerable talents. Almost precisely the same could be said of Julie Wilson, back on Broadway after too long an absence. As the gutsy, embittered but determined wife, she gave every number, every scene and every joke much more than it could reasonably have hoped for. But every number, every scene and almost every joke, remained ungrateful. What else was good? Well, at no time did anyone in the cast cry out for assistance or even for new material, and the conductor, the experienced and highly professional Milton Rosenstock, and so far as I could tell the orchestra remained awake from beginning to end. Although this is a musical with only three flaws—the book, the music and the lyrics—they proved fatal. The score was at its best, I thought, when it reminded me, ever so faintly, of "Mad About the Boy." Bill and Patti Jacob, according to the program, worked in Hollywood, "where their magic touch was felt on the Motorola Christmas Special." Whatever it was they did to Motorola did not work very well on *Jimmy*. A final thought: the producer was J. L. Warner, one of the great men in American movies. Give us a break Mr. Warner. I know it is sometimes said that Hollywood is killing Broadway, but I didn't know that people were allowed to send guerrilla parties over to speed up the job.

WALTER KERR, *TIMES*
It means to be rough and tough and talk out of the side of its mouth (with a Tammany brogue and a sneer and a leer), and that wouldn't be a bad attitude for a musical to take provided a groatsworth of wit could be slipped into each wallop. Frank Gorshin, who is simply too narrow a man for the part, plays Jimmy Walker as though he had a microphone tucked directly behind his teeth, and an assortment of elderly Hibernian character men march stoutly through what seems an endless series of St. Patrick's Day parades pretending to be overweight Al Smiths and the like. Between the Pats and the mikes, we are confronted with a continuous roar in honor of a very slight figure with vanishing blue eyes whom we never get to know very well and whom we don't much like. The text spends ten-tenths of its time telling us what a bum Walker was, what a boozer, what a chaser, what a dupe and what a

dunce. I should think it would inspire a thousand librettists to rush right out to their typewriters to write musicals in the man's defense. The best of them could then rehire Julie Wilson, who is mellow and handsome and something for a drowning audience to cling to as the anti-hero's inexplicably neglected wife.

RICHARD WATTS, JR., *POST*
The only remarkable thing about it is that it has no exclamation mark after the title.

o   o   o

Mr. Warner, producer of the 1927 talking picture *The Jazz Singer*, (starring Al Jolson), came to town with all the money in the world—a million point three, anyway, which was a fortune back in those days—and proceeded to produce up a storm. For that sort of money he could have hired celebrated, knowledgeable Broadway types, which of course wouldn't have guaranteed success either. Guess he figured that if a high school teacher could sit down and write himself *1776* (1969), and if a small-town music man could concoct a yarn about a small-town *Music Man* (1957), why not gamble on Bill and Patti Jacob, who, after all, were blessed with the Motorola "magic touch"?

BROADWAY SCORECARD
/ PERFS: 84 / $: –

RAVE	FAVORABLE	MIXED	UNFAVORABLE	PAN
				6

JOSEPH AND THE AMAZING TECHNICOLOR DREAMCOAT

the Manhattan premiere of the 1968 children's oratorio

music by Andrew Lloyd Webber

lyrics by Tim Rice

based on a story from the Old Testament

directed and choreographed by Tony Tanner

produced by Zev Bufman, Susan R. Rose, Melvyn J. Estrin, and Sidney Shlenker, by arrangement with the Robert Stigwood Organization and David Land

with Bill Hutton, Laurie Beechman, David Ardao, Tom Carder, Philip Carrubba, Robert P. Hyman, Randon Lo, Steve McNaughton, Charlie Serrano, and Gordon Stanley

opened November 18, 1981   *Entermedia Theatre*
transferred January 24, 1982   *Royale Theatre*

(Note: the first-night reviewers covered the show at its Entermedia Theatre première)

CLIVE BARNES, *POST*

[Headline: "*Technicolor Dreamcoat* Has Faded"]

A group of parents gathered together at St. Paul's School in London one winter afternoon in 1968 could scarcely have been aware that they were sitting in the shadow of history. They were. They were hearing the first public performance of a work by Andrew Lloyd Webber and Tim

Rice. It was a brief 25-minute cantata called *Joseph and the Amazing Technicolor Dreamcoat*. Webber and Rice's later collaborations, *Jesus Christ Superstar* [1971] and *Evita* [1979] were only just around the corner, the corner with the bank on it. *Joseph* itself, always intended to be performed by schools and colleges, was eventually expanded and went commercial. A production by Frank Dunlop for his Young Vic Company was successful at the Edinburgh Festival and later became a hit in London's West End. Dunlop later gave the work its first American professional staging at the Brooklyn Academy of Music. Last night *Joseph*, rainbow-hued dreamcoat at the ready, made its Manhattan debut. One would like to say sadly delayed debut, but on that I have doubts. Lloyd Webber as a composer has a useful knack of combining various pop forms, chiefly rock oriented, with the otiose religiosity of liturgical music. Yet Lloyd Webber can write tunes—notably so—and his music has a brash, swinging, self-congratulatory style of its own. In *Joseph*, as in the later works, they use an operatic formula, with no book, everything being conveyed by songs. This, I think, was a first in the popular musical theatre. Lloyd Webber seems to be at his best when he is backed up with an extremely fancy staging—Tom O'Horgan's Broadway presentation of *Superstar*, Harold Prince's lovingly elaborate simplicities in *Evita*, or most spectacular of all Trevor Nunn's fantastic production of Lloyd Webber's latest London hit, *Cats* [which reached Broadway in 1982]. In this new *Joseph*, directed by Tony Tanner, a somewhat shabby element emerges. It looks as though it was done on the cheap. This is the kind of show some people might find likeable. I don't think I could actually like anyone who found it lovable.

CHRISTOPHER SHARP, *WOMEN'S WEAR DAILY*
All the noise and razzle-dazzle cannot disguise the fact that the work is essentially children's theatre. It doesn't make for bad children's theatre, since all the scenes are overproduced in a way only children can really appreciate. For the same reason, the current revival makes for terrible adults' theatre. The score sounds like an English musical fantasy of overpowering American rhythm. It is the kind of music played in London bars that advertise authentic American hamburgers.

o   o   o

With *Evita* selling out, memories of the spectacular *Jesus Christ Superstar* still fresh, and the not-yet-imported *Cats* already a major West End hit, it seemed a worthwhile bet to brush off Andrew Lloyd Webber and Tim Rice's slight, campy collection of song pastiches on a biblical theme. And there proved to be quite an audience for it, too. *Joseph* had originally been seen Stateside when British director Frank Dunlop restaged the Young Vic production as part of the inaugural (and final) season of his brief-lived BAM Theatre Company. If you *had* to see the Lloyd Webber oratorio once, you might as well've caught Dunlop's version, which opened December 30, 1976, for a limited engagement of twenty-two performances. Choreographed by Graciela Daniele, it featured David-James Carroll, Cleavon Little, and Virginia Martin.

BROADWAY SCORECARD

/ PERFS: 757 / $: +

RAVE	FAVORABLE	MIXED	UNFAVORABLE	PAN
I	3			2

A JOYFUL NOISE

"A New Musical," previously entitled *The Insolent Breed*

music and lyrics by Oscar Brand and Paul Nassau

book by Edward Padula (and Dore Schary, billing removed)

based on the 1959 novel *The Insolent Breed* by Borden Deal

directed by Edward Padula (with Michael Bennett, uncredited; replacing Dore Schary, who replaced Ben Shaktman)

choreographed by Michael Bennett

produced by Edward Padula and Slade Brown in association with Sid Bernstein

starring John Raitt and Swen Swenson

with Susan Watson (replacing Teresa Rinaldi, who replaced Donna McKechnie), Karen Morrow (replacing Gay Edmond, who replaced Mitzi Welch), Clifford David (replacing James Rado), George Mathews (replacing Allan Louw), Leland Palmer, Art Wallace, and The Motley Crew (including Tommy Tune)

opened December 15, 1966   Mark Hellinger Theatre

MARTIN GOTTFRIED, *WOMEN'S WEAR DAILY*

There was a fine idea for a musical at the root of *A Joyful Noise*—an idea based on folk music and the Nashville Sound of the record industry. Oscar Brand was just the kind of guy to write its music, but Brand and his collaborator, Paul Nassau, got mixed up with people who demanded a "Broadway" look, a "Broadway" sound. As a result, still another chance for a fresh musical went down the drain, dragged most of the way by an interfering, irrelevant injection of brassy nonsense, put together cheaply and ignorantly. Another reflection of the demand for "Broadway" values was the choice of John Raitt for the singer. Raitt is a fine performer with an excellent and remarkably true baritone. But he is a romantic

EDWARD PADULA and SLADE BROWN
in association with SID BERNSTEIN
present

JOHN RAITT

in

A JOYFUL NOISE

A New Musical

by EDWARD PADULA
Music & Lyrics by OSCAR BRAND & PAUL NASSAU
Based on Borden Deal's "The Insolent Breed"

Also Starring SWEN SWENSON

Featuring

GEORGE   LELAND   ART
MATHEWS   PALMER   WALLACE

JORDAN REED   THE MOTLEY CREW
and

KAREN   CLIFFORD
MORROW   DAVID

with

SUSAN WATSON

Settings & Lighting by
PETER WEXLER

Costumes by
PETER JOSEPH

Musical Director RENE WIEGERT

Orchestrations & Vocal Arrangements   Dance Music by
WILLIAM STEGMEYER   LEE HOLDRIDGE

Dances & Musical Numbers Staged by
MICHAEL BENNETT

14
LOW PRICE
PREVIEWS
NOV. 28 thru DEC. 9
OPENS DEC. 10

"A DANDY DELIGHT" —GLOVER, AP

MARK HELLINGER THEATRE
237 W. 51st St.   ·   Mats. Wed. & Sat.

What do you do when your director insists his name be removed from the show but you can't afford new window cards? You print up a 1" x 9" strip with a quote from the tryout ("A Dandy Delight") and glue it all over Dore Schary. Preliminary credits. (artwork by Joe Eula)

leading man and a mature one. This part called for an electric performer—a young Presley. Similarly, Swen Swenson made no sense as
his ambitious manager-agent, always spreading limp wrists to move
into a Forties Gene Kelly dance. Edward Padula's direction was almost
as awkward as his book, keeping the performers motionless despite the
music's itch to move. As for Michael Bennett's musical staging and
choreography, it moved from pseudo-de Mille to pseudo-Robbins to
even pseudo-Gennaro, depending on whether the music was folksy,
gutsy or finger-snapping.

WALTER KERR, *TIMES*

In *A Joyful Noise* every time a song is over the lights go out immediately.
This, I believe, is to prevent dialogue. But dialogue, like some other dis-
eases, is not so easily warded off. It can always sneak back in just *before*
a song, or even right in the middle of one, and at the Mark Hellinger
this sheer persistence, this peculiar adhesiveness, finally presents us with
a double difficulty. One is to know in what century the musical takes
place. The other is to know in what century it was written. Once we
have satisfied ourselves that Mr. Raitt's voice is as sturdy and sunny as
we choose to remember it, we notice something else, something faintly
disturbing. Beneath that guitar there are some pretty tight blue jeans,
and, what with the curly hair and all, our eyes cross. Are we looking at
Elvis (Presley) or Johnny (Appleseed)? What time is it? The girls are
pretty and pink and starchily ruffled, and they squeal. They stand over
in a corner and squeal at the sight of this footloose, manly, ever-so-
fetching stranger. When you see five of them bunched together with
their petticoats perked high as they peek coyly and whisper, you know
they at least go back to Lynn Riggs [author of the 1931 folk play *Green
Grow the Lilacs*, source material for the 1943 *Oklahoma!*]. And when
they roll their eyes toward the moonlight, scrape their feet and whistle
innocently (just so the elders won't know what they're thinking about),
it's pretty plainly *Floradora* [1899] time. Librettist Edward Padula
seems to have put his people together out of pieces of hotel stationery.
It's all rather like the Dick Powell–Ruby Keeler musical version of *The
Scarlet Letter*. Well, the girl gets married and the baby comes and Mr.
Raitt gets rich—he's accompanied by a lively, trumpet-voiced blonde
named Karen Morrow—and through it all we alternate dizzily between
clap-your-hands square dances and Big Town frenzies in which every-

one wears gold on gold and spangles on spangles. In the end, Mr. Raitt gets religion and we get vertigo and that's how clambakes are born. Peter Wexler's settings are at least simple, although they do leave a lot of empty space around the actors, suggesting that something, somewhere, has been cut out of the show. Not enough.

NORMAN NADEL, *WORLD JOURNAL TRIBUNE*
[Headline: "*Joyful Noise* a Thud"]
"Make a joyful noise unto the lord!" commands the 101st Psalm in words that ring with the exhiliration of faith. Everlasting innocent that I am, I expect the same surge of glory from a musical titled *A Joyful Noise* and I am bitterly disappointed when nothing like that comes forth. Joy is conspicuously absent, except in the singing of John Raitt and the exuberance of the ensemble dancing. In scripting and the handling of the story, *A Joyful Noise* is painfully mawkish. "You're the star but I call the shots." "But you got the whole world in your string-pickin' hands." "All the fun went out of it—the joy of singin' the way I feel." "With him you're something, without him you're nothing." All four of these wholly predictable lines occur within one minute. We welcome production numbers and songs if for no other reason than they interrupt the dialogue. Edward Padula, who coproduced, has no one to blame but himself. He wrote the playbook and directed, botching both jobs. Karen Morrow appears at the start of Act Two. Miss Morrow's is a real talent, and she deserves better songs, better makeup, better costuming and better direction than she gets here. I might add that Susan Watson also is a victim of her role; she has no recourse but to be relentlessly, maddeningly sweet—there is no relief. The dancing ensemble is always true to the title. Whatever the choreography of the moment, they step, skip and prance with joy. But so much else is banal, cumbersome and just badly done that *A Joyful Noise* winds up as a whimper.

◦   ◦   ◦

The Insolent Breed began as a Kermit Bloomgarden project, with a book by John Gerstad. After Bloomgarden dropped the property, Ed (*Bye Bye Birdie* [1960]) Padula picked it up: "I wanted to do a show exploring the folk-song phenomenon, just as *Bye Bye Birdie* explored the teenage, rock 'n' roll phenomenon." The only good idea Ed Padula had was to hire one of his gypsies from the 1964 flop *Bajour* to choreograph. Michael

Bennett had been working in television, dancing on—and providing choreography for—the teen dance show *Hullabaloo*. He brought along a few of his pals: *Hullabaloo* dance partner Donna McKechnie, who got fired on the road ("appealing but terribly monotonous," per Kevin Kelly in the Boston *Globe*); pint-sized veteran Baayork Lee, who'd been kicking around since playing the littlest Siamese princess in Jerry Robbins's *The King and I* (1951); and tall Texan Tom Tune, who changed his billing during the tryout to the more mellifluous Tommy. Padula employed a novel financing scheme for *Joyful Noise*, arranging a guaranteed-against-loss summer stock tryout that would cut his production budget down to only $350,000. (Theoretically, that is; when all was said and sung and done, *Noise* lost $540,000.) Director Ben Shaktman, of Boston's Charles Playhouse, was fired early along the stock trail, with Padula himself taking over the reins. When Broadway appeared to be not a pipe dream but a realistic possibility, star John Raitt—understandably uncomfortable in the enterprise—pushed for a major overhaul and Padula finally enlisted Dore Schary as director and colibrettist. Schary brought with him $100,000 from RKO; he also effected the last of the many cast changes by hiring Karen Morrow, who began her career playing *The Unsinkable Molly Brown* (1960) for him on the road. As *A Joyful Noise* neared the end of its tryout, Schary quit—leaving Padula and the twenty-three-year-old Bennett to mop up. (The latter eschewed codirector billing, figuring it was bad enough that his first choreography credit was a surefire flop.) *Noise* came and went, leaving Bennett with a Tony nomination his first time out. "It began as a lovely, bucolic enterprise," said composer Oscar Brand. "But the record companies and the moneychangers were afraid that it didn't have enough 'contemporary music.' In order to be produced, Paul Nassau and I composed an entirely new score. The financial interests then nodded sagely and comfortably and let us go on. We died."

BROADWAY SCORECARD

/ PERFS: 12 / $: –

RAVE	FAVORABLE	MIXED	UNFAVORABLE	PAN
	1		2	3

KELLY

"A New Musical"

previously titled *Never Go There Anymore*

music by Moose Charlap

book and lyrics by Eddie Lawrence (book doctored by David Goodman, Leonard Stern, and Mel Brooks; additional music and lyrics by Jack Segal)

suggested by Steve Brodie's purported jump off the Brooklyn Bridge on July 23, 1886

directed by Herbert Ross (replacing Peter Coe, who replaced Lindsay Anderson)

choreographed by Herbert Ross

produced by David Susskind and Daniel Melnick in association with Joseph E. Levine

starring Wilfrid Brambell, Jesse White, Mickey Shaughnessy, Leon Janney, and Eileen Rodgers (top-billed Ella Logan's role eliminated)

with Don Francks (replacing Roy Castle, who replaced Richard Harris), Anita Gillette, Steve Elmore, Hamilton Camp, and Brandon Maggart (the roles played by Jack Creley and Avery Schreiber eliminated)

opened February 6, 1965   Broadhurst Theatre

WALTER KERR, *HERALD TRIBUNE*

Kelly is a bad idea gone wrong. To put the idea into as few words as possible, *Kelly* is a musical about a young man who wants to go jump in the river and everybody except his girl tries to stop him. His girl loves him, you see. Or perhaps you don't see, which makes two of us. "Oh, you great big bridge, connecting Brooklyn and New York," Kelly sings, tak-

David Susskind and Daniel Melnick in association with Joseph E. Levine present
a new musical
KELLY

Book and Lyrics by EDDIE LAWRENCE   Music by MOOSE CHARLAP

starring

ELLA LOGAN   WILFRID BRAMBELL

JESSE WHITE   MICKEY SHAUGHNESSY   LEON JANNEY

with

ANITA GILLETTE

EILEEN RODGERS   JACK CRELEY

and

DON FRANCKS

Scenic Production by OLIVER SMITH
Costumes by FREDDY WITTOP   Lighting by THARON MUSSER
Musical Director, SAMUEL MATLOVSKY   Orchestrations by HERSHY KAY   Dance Music by BETTY WALBERG

Directed and Choreographed by HERBERT ROSS

Associate Producer, ROBERT L. LIVINGSTON   Original Cast Album by COLUMBIA RECORDS

SHUBERT THEATRE   BOSTON
Wed. Eve., Jan. 20 thru Sat. Eve., Feb. 6
Matinees Wednesday and Saturday

"A genuine fun show replete with whistleable tunes and high hilarious interludes," said the blurb. Poor Hop Kelly seems to hide his head in the East River. No wonder. Preliminary credits.

ing care of the exposition and expressing his admiration in a double-play that might have had old Walt Whitman chewing his whiskers in envy. A structure which stands so tall and strong and steady and sturdy simply has to be jumped off of. Any fool can see that. The catch is that we're not going to see it and we know it. I mean we're not going to see the actual full jump, at least not until they sell the movie rights. And any musical which spends its entire evening getting us breathlessly ready for an event which nobody is going to get a decent look at is a musical that's kidding. Occasionally they rhyme the spoken dialogue, though considering the state the lyrics are in they might have thought twice about that. Mr. Charlap, who can write a perfectly good tune when he isn't trying too hard, tries very hard on a couple of occasions and comes out sounding like a Mott Street Menotti. The effort to be different is different, all right, but not better. Handsome, black-haired Eileen Rodgers flounces by in scarlet, smoking a cigar, and stops long enough to wish, musically, that she were one of the boys; having seen the boys you wonder why. You never do get to know why this particular song comes in this particular place, or why a whole neighborhood of sailors, tarts, drunks and schoolgirls-with-lollipops stop everything to go into a vigorous Herbert Ross dance, or why Pop Kelly is locked in a broom closet and then vanishes from the aforesaid without a trace. Some people have it made.

NORMAN NADEL, *WORLD-TELEGRAM & SUN*

There is some virtuoso tuba playing in the otherwise commonplace overture to *Kelly*. Mark it well, because nothing else that entertaining happens during the next 55 minutes. *Kelly* has precious little to offer except to tuba afficionados willing to blow $9.90 on three minutes of basso embellishments, and for that money you could hire the tuba player yourself [orchestrations by Hershy Kay]. Somehow, almost everything about the show seems to have turned out wrong. The play does appear to have been tampered with unmercifully, which might be a point in [librettist] Lawrence's defense. It's hard to believe his original book could have been this disjointed and empty. Francks is a competent performer, though hardly able to hold his own in scenes with a polished young star such as Miss Gillette. Her role doesn't amount to much, but she does pack it with personality, in appearance, demeanor and voice. There is a good musical in the colorful story of the Brooklyn Bridge. *Kelly* certainly isn't it.

HOWARD TAUBMAN, *TIMES*

Ella Logan was written out of *Kelly* before it reached the Broadhurst Theatre Saturday night. Congratulations, Miss Logan. Eddie Lawrence and Moose Charlap, the authors, were so upset about excisions and changes that they asked the court to enjoin the opening. I don't know about the merits of what has been eliminated from *Kelly*. But to judge by what is left, there are ample criticial, if not legal, grounds for an injunction. For *Kelly* is without freshness and imagination. It's book is as wooden and hollow as the musicals that were in fashion decades ago when Steve Brodie, the prototype of its hero, took his famous plunge from the Brooklyn Bridge. Kelly himself is a one-dimensional character, and the events that precede his dive at the end of the musical could be condensed into a song or two. One can put up with contrived plots if there are compensations of spirit and charm. What *Kelly* offers is energy and perspiration by a well-meant, hard-working troupe. Herbert Ross's staging is as uninspired as his material. Even his choreography, with its lively angularities, begins to look monotonous before the evening is over. One can imagine what *Kelly* hoped to be, but the milieu and its people, resisting the effort and expense poured into them, refuse to come to life. Don Francks is bouncy and athletic enough as Kelly, but he cannot overcome the sad fact that Kelly as daredevil and lover is a blustering fathead. The burden of comedy is entrusted to Jesse White as a gambler and Mickey Shaughnessy as a world's heavyweight champ. They are honest performers, but this is the kind of exchange they must cope with: "You can't welsh on an Englishman." "Why don't you English on a Welshman?" If you were the judge, wouldn't you pronounce a severe sentence?

◦   ◦   ◦

"Our aim is for an entertainment closer to *The Threepenny Opera* than *Do Re Mi*." So said Moose Charlap, composer of the hapless *Whoop-Up* (1958) and *The Conquering Hero* (1961). Lyricist/librettist Eddie Lawrence had never served in either capacity; he was best known locally as the featured comic—the bookie with the "Simple Little System"—in

Bells Are Ringing (1956). *Kelly* was first optioned by Herbert Greene (of *The Music Man* [1957]), and then by Joe Harris and Ira Bernstein. Edward Padula (of *Bye Bye Birdie* [1960]) came next, signing Richard Harris to play the title role and Lindsay Anderson to direct. Padula switched directors, bringing in Peter Coe (of *Oliver!* [1963]), but then called the whole thing off. When three sets of producers drop out, citing "extreme differences" with the authors, beware of the authors. *Kelly* was scooped up by TV producers David Susskind and Daniel Melnick, with backing from Hollywood's Joseph E. Levine. "The other producers wanted to change the kid into some kind of knight in shining armor, like a crummy love story," complained Lawrence. (Historical note: Steve Brodie—on whom Hop Kelly was patterned—himself appeared on Broadway in an 1891 melodrama entitled *Money Mad*, in which he did, indeed, jump off the painted-on-canvas Brooklyn Bridge.) *Kelly* went into production and duly hopped on down to Philly, where reaction was bad. Real bad. The mean and petulant Mack the Knife-type title character proved universally unlovable, and recriminations quickly took over. The producers blamed the writers for the story's harshness. ("If they wrote *My Fair Lady*," complained Susskind, "Eliza Doolittle would have a cleft palate and a limp.") The writers blamed the producers for the elegant musical comedy trappings. ("Suddenly you're competing with *My Fair Lady*," complained Charlap. "In East Germany they would understand how to do this play." "Well, if it's a stiff," offered Lawrence, "we can always charge admission to let the people see the sets and costumes.") And the actors just fretted. ("If we go to Boston with this stuff, the critics will kill us," complained comedian Jesse White.) They did (go to Boston) and they did (kill us), despite attempts by comedy writer David Goodman to place the title character in a more sympathetic light. The authors stormed off to their lawyers, seeking an injunction to prevent violation of their artistic vision. "It's not our show anymore," complained Charlap, "it's tenth-rate television jazz. These men are not human beings, they're beasts." "Those slobs ought to be down on their hands and knees for all the creative collaboration they're getting," complained Susskind. Costar Eileen Rodgers, of *Fiorello!* (1959) and *Tenderloin* (1960), sent a postcard to her agent saying, in full, "Heeeeeeeeeeeeeeeeeeelp!" The Boston reviews were even worse than Philly's, causing the producers to cut short the engagement after only five performances. In rushed comedy writers Leonard Stern and

Mel Brooks, who'd just finished the pilot for their sitcom *Get Smart*. First order of business was to write out the role of top-billed Ella Logan, who had wowed 'em back in 1947 as the lass from Glocca Morra in *Finian's Rainbow*. "You get a lot of laughs with the mother," complained Lawrence. "Two laughs, Eddie," said Mel. "Nobody understands my jokes," complained Lawrence. "She softens the show," explained the voice of reason, whose past included two musical comedy nightmares—*Shinbone Alley* (1957) and *All American* (1962)—and whose future included the 1968 film *The Producers*. (Talk about hands-on research.) "She's out there selling torn rubber raincoats." (What???) With the litigious Moose and Eddie refusing to do rewrites, another additional writer—Jack Segal—was brought in for a song. And so *Kelly* geared up for New York. Coproducer Melnick hypothesized that the small-sized Broadhurst might help the show. "It's an intimate house, not much bigger than our living room." "We should have done it in our living room," countered Linda Rodgers Melnick. "It would have been cheaper." (Her sister, Mary, composed the 1963 Judy Holliday vehicle *Hot Spot*, the biggest flop of the 1960s—until *Kelly*. Herb Ross did that one, too.) Susskind contributed to the pre-opening ballyhoo by putting a group of fortune tellers on his television interview show. All five, remarkably enough, forecast that *Kelly* would be a smash hit. The New York reviews were so bad—and the show was so overbudget—that it never saw the light of another day. One-performance flops have become commonplace, but the actuality of $650,000 thrown away in one night put the undistinguished *Kelly* in the spotlight. That record was soon broken—and how! Overheard at the Box Office Dept.: A foursome came to the box office opening night with tickets for *Oh What a Lovely War*, which had been forced out of the Broadhurst when *Kelly* fled Boston. "We want our money back," they complained. "So do I," said coproducer Joseph E. Levine, passing by the window.

BROADWAY SCORECARD
/ PERFS: 1 / $: –

RAVE	FAVORABLE	MIXED	UNFAVORABLE	PAN

6

THE KING AND I

an "original star" revival of the 1951 musical play

music by Richard Rodgers

book and lyrics by Oscar Hammerstein 2nd

based on the 1943 biographical novel *Anna and the King of Siam* by Margaret Landon

"entire production directed by Yuriko"

"originally choreographed by Jerome Robbins"

produced by Lee Guber and Shelly Gross

starring Yul Brynner and Constance Towers

with Michael Kermoyan, Hye-Young Choi, Martin Vidnovic, June Angela, Susan Kikuchi, John Michael King, Larry Swansen, Gene Profanato, and Alan Amick

opened May 2, 1977   Uris Theatre

CLIVE BARNES, *TIMES*

Yul Brynner is a great actor—or at the very least a great acting presence—not because of what he does but because of what he is. He strides on a stage caught in the invisible spotlight of his personality. He gestures, gesticulates, and moves with the certainty of an automaton and the grace of a dancer. Often he is very still, his body seemingly carved out of time, and his voice—both speaking and singing—while musical, and pleasing enough, has a comparatively small compass. His facial expressions are limited, but intensely alive, and interestingly they show few transitions. One moment he will be serious, then in a flash grinning, with apparently no facial change in between. He dominates but also charms. He is Ghengis Khan in a Savile Row suit and a Maserati. . . . Richard Rodgers had that knack of being able to write a musical score where every number seemed worth numbering, and one left the theatre with one's head in a happy swirl of melody. Hammerstein's lyrics were usually more apt than clever, more humorous than witty, but they always worked. Always worked—that was the secret of those old Broadway musicals. They were efficient: they worked. But, of course, nowadays we forget the clinkers and only remember the jewels. The production is described as being directed by Yuriko, who danced Eliza in the original version, and it follows along traditional lines most effectively. One of the particular joys of the original was the ballet *The Small House of Uncle Thomas*, choreographed by Jerome Robbins. It was one of the most imaginative dance episodes ever devised for Broadway, and luckily Mr. Robbins has been brought in for this revival to ensure its accuracy and pristine freshness. Incidentally, the good dancing is led by the lovely Susan Kikuchi—who happens to be Yuriko's daughter. But this is not nepotism, merely tradition.

WALTER KERR, *TIMES*

One of the reasons we can settle down so comfortably with *The King and I* is that we are not, at the moment, in such very desperate need of it. Luckily, just before Yul Brynner and company decided to stop their profitable touring and bring the celebrated Rodgers-Hammerstein operetta into New York, Broadway turned up at least two new entertainments, *I Love My Wife* and *Annie* [both 1977], with original books and original scores that proved us capable of creating a little (or a lot of) fun of our own. With our pride at least moderately restored, we were able to drop into seats, stare at the facing gold lions that decorate the front curtain, and feel altogether relaxed, ready to take the show on its own terms. It is a warming presence there, obviously born of a tradition that is gradually being replaced, just as obviously studded with matched melodies and lyrics so irresistible that we're going to cling to them for dear life no matter what turns our sluggishly changing theatre may take. Let "Hello, Young Lovers" come along at its own sweet pace, let "The March of the Siamese Children" perform its dramatically vital—not merely cute—function, squander "Getting to Know You" anytime you like because there's always "We Kiss in a Shadow," "Something Wonderful," "I Have Dreamed," and "Shall We Dance?" in reserve. Good God! Did Rodgers never sleep? While we are being literally enveloped by sounds rich enough to surprise us even when we are remembering them, aren't we bothered by what is dated in the book, in the styling? Very, very rarely. . . . Mr. Brynner's speech has become a bit careless after such long familiarity with the role but his fiery physical command of the stage hasn't abated a bit. When he halts abruptly during the Western dance he is being taught, stands dynamically erect for a moment, and then, eyes blazing fire, strides toward the baffled Anna of Constance Towers to firmly clap his hand to her waist in a European embrace, the effect is menacing, funny, and exhilarating all at once. Miss Towers is lovely in a gown that may be copper or may be peach or may be both, and the exuberance with which she sheds her primness and soars away across the floor promptly and properly brings down the house. And what is music for, if not to sweep us off our feet?

DOUGLAS WATT, *DAILY NEWS*

It is far and away the most beautiful show in town, musically and in all other respects. This 1951 musical is one of the masterpieces of the Rodgers and Hammerstein canon, equipped with one of Rodgers' most masterly scores and perhaps Hammerstein's most secure and appealing libretto. It moves like silk and has what is probably the best group of singers heard in any of its many revivals hereabouts. The particular reason for its return is the presence of Yul Brynner, after a quarter-century of moviemaking, in the role he created, the King of Siam. Though he gives the same striking performance that made him a star in the first place, he seems even better, if anything, because he has in a sense grown into the role of the mature monarch who, having spawned close to 100 children by his numerous wives and issued countless proclamations, dies at the end. But it must be remembered that though Brynner came close to stealing the original, *The King and I* was really designed for the late Gertrude Lawrence, who died during its run. And it was she, as Anna Leonowens, who got the largest share of the songs. Given half a chance, the nonsinging Brynner made the most of his one solo, "A Puzzlement." Though Miss Lawrence's mere presence could charm an entire theatre, she wasn't much of a singer, being inclined to stray from pitch time and again. On the other hand, the lovely and accomplished Constance Towers sings the many gems thrown her way beautifully and acts the role with grace and conviction. The music flows by like a dream. But, then, so does the entire show.

o   o   o

After Yul Brynner's *Home Sweet Homer* (1976) debacle—one performance and out—it was back to the Role That Made Him Famous. When *The King and I* first appeared in 1951, the star was clearly Gertrude Lawrence; she initiated the project and enlisted Rodgers and Hammerstein to write and produce it. The virtually unknown Brynner was at the time directing the early TV talk show *The Stork Club* (Abe Burrows, writer/producer; Yul Brynner, director; Sidney Lumet, assistant director). Brynner's one Broadway appearance had been as Mary Martin's husband in the 1946 Chinese folk fable *Lute Song*. ("Kidnap him if you have to, but get him," Mary told Oscar.) *The King and I* brought Brynner instant fame and a best supporting actor Tony Award (and ultimately a best actor Oscar for the 1956 film version). When Gertie Lawrence succumbed to cancer midway through the run, she requested—on her deathbed—that Brynner's name be moved above the title. It was, and remained there for the rest of his life. Seven years after the close of this revival, Brynner made a third Broadway visit as the King. Suffering from cancer himself, he was forced to quit after performance number 4,635—per the press release—and died three months later on October 10, 1985, at the age of sixty-five.

BROADWAY SCORECARD

/ PERFS: 719 / $: +

RAVE	FAVORABLE	MIXED	UNFAVORABLE	PAN
2	2	1	1	

KING OF HEARTS

"A New Musical"

music by Peter Link

lyrics by Jacob Brackman

book by Joseph Stein (replacing Steve Tesich)

based on the 1966 screenplay *Le Roi de Couer* by Philippe de Broca, Maurice Bessy, and Daniel Boulanger

directed by Ron Field (replacing A. J. Antoon)

choreographed by Ron Field (replacing Miguel Godreau)

produced by Joseph Kipness and Patty Grubman in association with Jerome Minskoff

with Donald Scardino (replacing Robby Benson), Pamela Blair, Millicent Martin, Gary Morgan, Bob Gunton, Gordon J. Weiss, Jay Devlin, Mitzi Hamilton, and Michael McCarty

opened October 22, 1978   Minskoff Theatre

CLIVE BARNES, *POST*

[Headline: *"King of Hearts* is a Wild Card"]

King of Hearts will doubtless please some people very much. Others, I suspect will be irritated. Few I imagine will find themselves on middle ground. I do. It is a musical of whimsy, without quite enough poetry. Of fantasy without quite enough magic. . . . Santo Loquasto—at what cost I shudder to contemplate—has built a town square that in Baedeker's famous guide-book would be termed as "worth a detour." Its architecture is a mixture of gothic, French provincial and pure wit, and it adds up to a toytown of the spirit. Moreover it moves round on a revolve to reveal not only different perspectives, but also, at the back, a handsome seedy bordello complete with a ramshackle bedroom which shows just the lift of poetry that the show generally lacks. Moreover at every step of the way Loquasto is backed by the fiery imagination of the costume

A pixillated Don Scardino dances on dynamite while the diminutive Millicent Martin swings on a trapeze descended from a birdcage. That's what it looks like, anyway. "What did I know?" alibied Ron Field. (artwork by Frederic Marvin)

designer, Patricia Zipprodt, who has taken the show as a visa to fairy-land, and has emerged with some of the most delicately imagined costumes even she has ever created. The staging is exemplary. The cohesive energy that Ron Field gives it, as director and choreographer, is extraordinary. It is an achievement something on the same level as that gusto Bob Fosse gave to *Pippin* [1972], a musical with similarly faulty material. Field rushes the show on, but always with finesse. He has a special triumph in a big circus scene, where he has his stars actually performing genuine trapeze acts, and he gives a nice atmospheric touch to that scene—so haunting in the movie—where the inmates of the asylum find themselves wandering through the battlefield, as bizarre spectators to a game called war. What is good about *King of Hearts* is perfectly good, and often in its way, elegant. Yet the show is definitely no Royal Flush. It is going to be something like the film—it will have hot detractors and fiery adherents. And just a few luke-warm analysts. Certainly it is not a waste of time or money to find out where you stand.

WALTER KERR, *TIMES*

King of Hearts spends most of its time high up in air when what it should be doing is getting its feet on the ground. Everything is geared to spectacular scenic effects, with the most important things happening at the tips of towering pyramids while the story-line, poor thing, is left to limp along below somewhere, gasping for breath. Our first glimpse of the village of DuTemps is dazzlingly comprehensive: dozens of toothpick balconies and matchstick stairways seem to converge upon one another to form a town that resembles an ominous birdcage hung from a mountain-top. Above it all rises an illuminated clock-face, alongside a bell waiting to be struck by a mechanical man with a mallet. Eventually, along about 10:30, something important is going to happen up there. In the meantime, villagers are running screeching in all directions, some on bicycles, some towing sluggish pigs, while lyrics meant to keep us in touch with the situation are filtered through microphones that seem to be suffering from metal fatigue. I know that one of the early songs was 16 to 18 lines underway before I caught a single word, and the single word—I'm not making this up—just happened to be "incomprehensible." But, courtesy of the magic of designer Santo Loquasto, the stage has turned inside out and we are now with the inmates of the local lunatic asylum, whose beds are piled like a light-ning-struck jungle gym atop one another. A lookout peering through the great oval barred window at the peak of the back wall reports the fact that the town seems to be emptying out, while the remaining inmates sing a song listed on the program as "A Stain on the Name" and bounce about on their teetering trundle beds. By this time, snatching at a line here and a straw there, we've begun to put together the rudiments of a narrative (I imagine it would help a lot if you'd seen the Philippe de Broca film of the same name on which the libretto is based; I hadn't). . . . No one ever seems to take a *necessary* step, sing a necessary song; everything is geared to the necessary splash of spectacle while the narrative nods. Which is really no way to put together a cohesive, or even coherent, musical. Everybody's overwhelmed by it, and the result is handsome, expensive and a serious muddle.

HOWARD KISSEL, *WOMEN'S WEAR DAILY*

In Philippe de Broca's film *King of Hearts*, set at the close of World War I, the inmates of a French insane asylum take over a provincial town when the "sane" inhabitants evacuate it, fearing a German attack. In the empty streets and houses, the patients act out their fantasies and, in their dotty, charming way, assure us their insanity is as nothing com-pared to the armed insanity around them, a notion that appealed greatly to college students during the Vietnam years, when *King of Hearts* became a cult film. This sort of thinking is easy to accept if you assume sanitariums are filled with people more sinned against than sinning, rather than cases like "Son of Sam." In the musical version, the differ-ences between the sane and the insane are summarized all too neatly by one of the characters: "Those who care about people are put away; those who care about nothing but themselves roam about freely." If the show itself had a simple, unaffected directness we might be able to accept such fey wisdom, but the musical has a brash theatricality that works against its would be innocent highmindedness. One of the inmates, for example, imagines he is a circus ringmaster, a pretext that allows us to have a full-blown circus number to open Act II, partly in choreographic conceits like a tightrope walker pantomiming her way along an imagi-nary rope drawn on stage by her partner, partly in actual circus feats on trapezes, ropes and a bicycle suspended in the air. The stage is full of energy and color but the "Let's wow 'em" attitude seems out of synch with the basic earnestness of the material. At other times, the staging by Ron Field, though lively and full of high spirits, seems rather ordinary, as in a big splashy number in a brothel which includes, quite predictably, a can-can—if these inmates are disturbed their can-can should not be so conventional; nor should it be so professional if they are as altruistic as the premise insists. Santo Loquasto's sets (particularly the interior of the asylum, with beds arrayed in an almost Chagallian defiance of gravity) and Patricia Zipprodt's costumes have the feeling for period, the wit and richness the material lacks. Ron Field's direction and choreography are vigorous and entertaining, but lack an overall perception of the material that might have made it more than a conventional musical.

●   ●   ●

The pacifistic French film *King of Hearts* was a box-office failure that became a revival-house "cult hit" among college-age Vietnam War protestors. The big-budget Broadway musical *King of Hearts* was geared to mass audiences—the majority of whom were decidedly noncollegiate nonpacifists. To bridge this not-insubstantial gap, the creators of the musical made the following adjustments: none. Actually, the whole thing was magnified to gargantuan dimensions. An initial production was mounted at the Westport Country Playhouse in the summer of 1977 with book by Steve Tesich (screenwriter of the upcoming 1979 *Breaking Away*), direction by A. J. Antoon (of *That Championship Season* [1972]), and movie star Robby Benson—who started out as a singing scion of *The Rothschilds* (1970)—in the lead. *King of Hearts* was totally revamped for Broadway, with Joe Stein (of *Fiddler on the Roof* [1964]) and Ron Field (of *Applause* [1970]) taking over the reins. Here's a quote from Field, in what would be his only credited full-scale Broadway assignment following the 1971 revival of *On the Town*: "Santo Loquasto's sets got rave reviews just about everywhere. But I think they destroyed the show. I'm not blaming Santo. Genius he is, sweet he is, but I got his drawings late. They looked okay, what did I know?" This was the guy in charge, the man who made all the decisions. I got the drawings late? What did I know?? Capitalized at $1,100,000, *King of Hearts* was bathed in red ink. The show went over budget—*way* over budget—with the loss listed at $1.8 million. The producers poured in additional out-of-pocket monies, reportedly taking the figure to the far side of $2 million. (*King of Hearts* was Broadway's most expensive failure for all of two months, when Michael Bennett's glittering *Ballroom* nudged it aside.) Most of the loss came from the family of coproducer Patty Grubman, who ended up with happy memories and some old fish—which is to say that Joe Kipness reportedly signed over equity in his seafood emporium as the musical floundered.

BROADWAY SCORECARD
/ PERFS: 48 / $: –

RAVE	FAVORABLE	MIXED	UNFAVORABLE	PAN
		1	1	4

LA STRADA

"The New Musical"

music and lyrics by Lionel Bart; "additional music and lyrics" by Martin Charnin (lyrics) and Elliot Lawrence (music)

book by Charles K. Peck, Jr.

based on the 1954 screenplay by Federico Fellini, Tullio Pinelli, and Ennio Flaiano

directed by Alan Schneider

choreographed by Alvin Ailey (replacing Joyce Trisler)

produced by Charles K. Peck, Jr., and Canyon Productions, Inc. (B. G. Cantor)

starring Bernadette Peters, Larry Kert, and Stephen Pearlman (replacing Vincent Beck)

with Anne Hegira (replacing Miriam Phillips), Lucille Patton, Peggy Cooper, and John Coe (fourth-billed Patricia Marand written out during tryout)

opened December 4, 1969   Lunt-Fontanne Theatre

CLIVE BARNES, *TIMES*

It is a long *La Strada* that has no turning. Unfortunately, the book is weak, and the music and lyrics by Lionel Bart are undistinguished to the point of Muzak-like oblivion. This really is music to forget to. Incidentally, from a slip in the program—a kind of last-minute admission, I suppose—I note that "at this performance additional music and lyrics by Martin Charnin and Elliot Lawrence." You couldn't tell where one part ended and the other part began. Indeed, Messrs. Charnin and Lawrence may well be the first lyricist and composer to succeed in actually copying Lionel Bart. Now for the good—and the irony is that the good is often so very good. Perhaps good enough for a visit. The choreography by Alvin Ailey has something of the style of Fellini fantasy and at the end does give the whole show a much-needed shot in the arm.

Gelsomina's trumpet lies shattered on the cobblestones, much as Lionel Bart's score was shattered on *la strada*. The logo, not coincidentally, points downhill. (artwork by Emil Marin)

Then there are the settings by Ming Cho Lee, which are atmospheric, dusty, brilliantly conveying the sense of Fellini's Italy and theatrically adroit in the way various components turn inside out on one another always maintaining a sense of movement in the show. Finally and most important there is the cast. In a different show the birdlike and croaky Bernadette Peters would have become a star overnight. This refugee dame from *Dames at Sea* [1968] has everything going for her as Gelsomina. She looks right, she sounds right, and Alan Schneider uses her kooky mannerisms, breathily corny modulations of voice and show-biz inflections with great skill. Even at the end, after her lover has murdered a man once interested in her, she maintains the role intact, crawling around making mouse-like noises of misery like a broken animal. I hope that Peters stays around a bit with this—in any case I think she'll soon be back. In such circumstances, the superficiality of the book and the sheer bland triteness of the music seem all the more annoying. So if you go, go for the staging and the acting, forget the music and more or less ignore the book. You will enjoy Miss Peters against a landscape by Mr. Lee that really does justify Fellini and the memory of a fine movie.

JOHN CHAPMAN, *DAILY NEWS*

[Headline: "Musical *La Strada* on the Wrong Road"]
A generally lugubrious show. Once in a while its leading lady, Bernadette Peters, who seems to be playing the heroine of *Dames at Sea* all over again, gives the show a lift, but not for long. I don't think anybody could lift a musical like *La Strada* more than a couple of inches. *La Strada* has been most beautifully staged with bewitching sets by Ming Cho Lee, fine costumes by Nancy Potts and effective incidental dances by Alvin Ailey. But I'd rather see a good revival of *Carnival* [1961].

MARTIN GOTTFRIED, *WOMEN'S WEAR DAILY*

Alan Schneider obviously had little control over his actors, who roamed the stage spreading show-biz mannerisms like cream cheese on a bagel. The over-all result was bound to be sloppy and out of control. Indeed it was. The production began with Schneider's hopes pinned on a mood of quiet music and dance. For the first five minutes you could almost see what he was trying to do. You could sense, in fact, that it might work. Alvin Ailey's choreography was soft and sad (and was to be excellent throughout). But with Bernadette Peters' first attempts to mimic the inspired clowning of Giulietta Masina in the movie, catastrophe was imminent. Peters is a neat performer despite her tendency to speak like a squeezed balloon. Her cutey-poo, pigeon-toed, Groucho Marx crouch and belter mannerisms knew no restraint, though, especially when egged on by Larry Kert, playing the Fool as if it were a chorus boy's dream. Between these two, the worst of show business destroyed any hope for softness, and Schneider could no more control them than he could do anything with Stephen Pearlman's sluggish playing of Zampano. Lionel Bart's music was sweet and simple, enormously improved by Eddie Sauter's orchestrations. It was also interrupted, on occasion, by some stock Broadway brass added to the score by Elliot Lawrence. Neither of the two composers seemed aware that the show was supposed to be Italian.

• • •

Charles K. Peck—whose one contribution to the art of Broadway had been as co-librettist (with Pearl S. Buck, no less) of the dismal 1960 Maureen O'Hara vehicle *Christine*—rode back to town producing as well as writing and generally destroying *La Strada*. It would be difficult successfully to translate Fellini's brilliant, atmospheric masterpiece to the stage, certainly, but not necessarily impossible. This *La Strada* didn't have a chance, especially since poor Lionel Bart was indisposed, as they used to say. Bart's *La Strada* began with a studio cast recording, like *Jesus Christ Superstar* (1971) would shortly thereafter. Unlike Lloyd Webber and Rice, though, Bart had no brilliant career manager pushing him from behind; the only one pushing Lionel Bart was Lionel Bart. Anyway, the original *La Strada* score is rather effective, but with the composer oceans away from the Detroit tryout, all but three of his songs were chucked out on *la strada*.

BROADWAY SCORECARD
/ PERFS: 1 / $: –

RAVE	FAVORABLE	MIXED	UNFAVORABLE	PAN
	1			5

LENA HORNE:
THE LADY AND HER
MUSIC

a new revue

concept by Lena Horne and Sherman Sneed

directed by Arthur Faria

produced by James M. Nederlander, Michael Frazier, and Fred Walker, in association with Sherman Sneed and Jack Lawrence

starring Lena Horne

opened May 12, 1981   *Nederlander Theatre*

CLIVE BARNES, *POST*

[Headline: "Lena Takes Broadway By Storm"]

Sorry, this has to be a love letter. The sexiest woman on Broadway is a 63-year-old grandmother. The name is Lena Horne. She opened last night in her own show and she was bewitching, making stormy weather into blue skies. Her talent is cyclonic—on this viewing she is quite simply, here and now, one of the greatest entertainers of our time. Her appearance is said to mark a comeback, but if the woman can come back like this one wonders why on earth she ever went away. The title, in a sense, tells it all, *The Lady and Her Music.* And both are exquisitely surprising. The character she chooses for herself is that of a survivor. She is game and plucky and above all delightful. She is not ashamed to show her scars, nor is she ashamed to be willfully playful. In fact—the lady is not ashamed. Because the lady is quintessentially a lady. She can smile and she can snarl. She can be gracious and she can be unexpectedly and deliciously dirty. She grins naughtily and she has the entire audience in the same land of rapture that she is in herself. So much for the lady—how about the music? It is strange. Before this show I would not have remotely described myself as a Lena Horne fan—although in just a little more than two hours, two grueling, tough, sweating, hours,

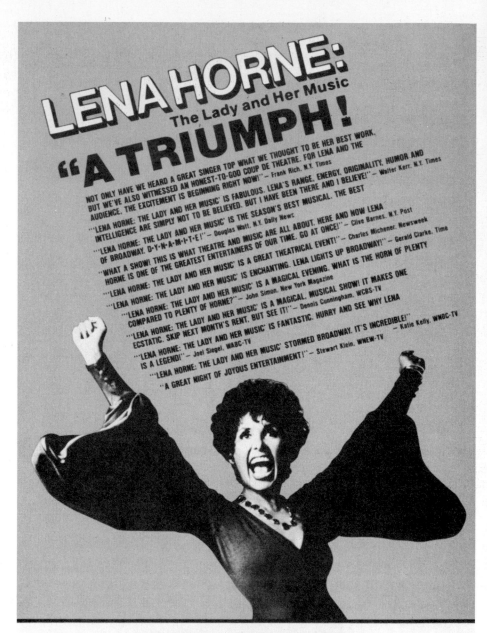

The lady is triumphant, all right—with ecstatic raves to prove it.

she turned me into a Lena Horne freak. Previously—and I was clearly wrong—I had never thought much of her singing. I regarded her as a run of the mill pop singer, but not a classic singer in the way of say, an Ella Fitzgerald or Mel Tormé. Here she astounded me. First she commands with a special vocal presence, that odd dramatic individuality of a Maria Callas, but also she has that incredible jazz sensibility that can transform the simply ordinary into the simply extraordinary. What a show! This is what theatre and music are all about. The lady may be a tramp, but she is irresistible. Go at once.

WALTER KERR, *TIMES*
[Headline: "Hail to a Horne of Plenty"]
One of the 6,000 things I like about Lena Horne is that she didn't rush her new entertainment onto Broadway in time to qualify for a Tony nomination. The deadline for Tony nominations came along just before mid-month, and, as you may remember, half a dozen enterprises began an unseemly push and shove to see which could get themselves booked into theatres before midnight struck and this season's fancy-dress ball was declared over. Meantime, Lena Horne waited until the whole untidy nonsense was ended and, two days later, swept onto the stage of the Nederlander in a blazing white gown, extended one elegant arm to the audience (palm up) as though inviting it to rise and take a bow (how does she manage to suggest that the drumroll of applause is really for the rest of us and not for her?), and then proceeded to whisper, blast, babytalk, kid, wail, gyrate, laugh through a lyric, wrestle a melody until it'd taken all the falls there are—and then do "Stormy Weather." Twice. The lady's range, energy, originality, humor, anger and intelligence are simply not to be believed. But I have been there and I believe. On the night I attended, I might mention, the people out front were giving her a standing ovation during the *first* act and plainly wondering what kind of adequate tribute they could possibly cook up for later on. Moral: if you've got Lena Horne, what on earth would you do with a Tony? But notice that I'm speaking of Lena Horne as though we knew all about her, as though we'd long since become accustomed to her entire rainbow of styles, as though she'd been here before—pretty much on these terms. She hasn't. I'm not sure she's been *anywhere* before now displaying the imagination and discharging the voltage that's crackling all the way from the backstage wall to the far end of the foyer. We all recog-

nize Miss Horne, of course. From a few films, perhaps; possibly from her only other Broadway musical show appearance in *Jamaica* [1957]. But all at once, sustained for more than two hours, gentling and/or exploding 25 or more songs in a row? With virtually no help? Certainly I'd never been exposed to this experience. And that means I didn't *know* the performer at all. An enormously complex woman and—at this late date—a freshly exciting one.

FRANK RICH, *TIMES*

About midway through the first act, Lena Horne does the one thing we know she's going to do before we even arrive at the theatre. Sliding into her best Metro-Goldwyn-Mayer stance, she looks up into a spotlight and proceeds to sing the hell out of "Stormy Weather." The moment doesn't disappoint. As Miss Horne has already demonstrated in the evening's warm-up numbers she's in transcendent voice and, at age 63, as beautiful and elegant as ever. You can be sure that she sings "Stormy Weather" so it will stay sung. Still, there's something disconcerting about her decision to give us this treat so early in the evening. It's an unspoken rule of recitals like this that a singer saves her trademark number for the evening's ultimate, or at least penultimate, spot. The star still has a good hour of singing to go after "Stormy Weather," and we begin to wonder how in the world she can possibly top her most famous show-stopper. But Lena Horne—as we should have learned by now—is nobody's fool. Late in her show's second half, she announces her next number by saying "I had to grow into this song." And then what does she do? Why, she sings "Stormy Weather" all over again. Only this time she sings it as if she *had* just grown into it, as if she had never sung it before. Before she even hits the first lyric, she lets loose with a gospel cry that erupts from her gut with almost primeval force. Then she bobs gently up and down, staring into her hand mike, letting the words pour out. By the time she tells us that "it's raining all the time"—packing about a dozen torrential notes into the word "raining"—she is blind with sweat and tears. And so is the audience. Not only have we heard a great singer top what we thought to be her best work, but we've also witnessed an honest-to-God *coup de théâtre*. Miss Horne is out to prove something in this revue, and it's not merely that her talents and looks are unbruised by the years. She doesn't simply present herself as a sur-vivor—a favorite device of older stars who come back to Broadway—

but as an artist who is still growing, who is only now reaching the peak of her powers.

DOUGLAS WATT, *DAILY NEWS*
[Headline: "Spell Her D*Y*N*A*M*I*T*E"]
Lena Horne is the season's best musical, Tonys or no Tonys. As a matter of fact, they should invent a whole new category for her: something like Best of Broadway, period. The lady, one of the two or three most beautiful women of our time, is at the peak of her artistry in this two-hour show, which includes a few dancers and, spread across the stage behind her, a terrific band with a superb trio nestled within it. Looking like several millions dollars in a white gown in the first half (Good Lord! she was wearing white the first time I saw her, as a young thing called Helena Horne, a small but stunning part of a Carnegie Hall concert featuring the Basie band and others) and a scarlet one wrapped in a silvery robe held with a fashion model's exquisite poise in the second, she stalks the stage exulting in every minute. Her voice and body are a catalogue of all superior means of expression in popular music; now crooning and almost motionless, now growling and grinding her hips, and now scaling the heights with a flick of the finger or a wicked glance. (I'm thinking of running away from home.) Only two popular singers of our time have come on like champs, ready to kill and confident of doing so: Sinatra and Horne, and Lena is the one with a whole voice left. So she kills; feinting, jabbing, always on the mark. She kills now with a difference. Time was, when the bitterness at Hollywood's neglect (her scenes would be cut out of films for showings in the South, as she tells us) was still strong, the killing instinct and the hostility that went with it created a powerful tension. She was great then, but now she's greater still and can discuss that past. Now, there's vast humor, excitement and, yes, love in her performance. The lady is the most.

o   o   o

Broadway had seen nightclub-style star concerts before, but Lena Horne was not just some song stylist singing her greatest hits. Horne started out in 1933 as a fifteen-year-old dancer in Harold Arlen revues at the Cotton Club. Full stardom came ten years later, when she recreated Arlen's "Stormy Weather" in the motion picture of the same name. Horne mesmerized Broadway in 1957 in Arlen and Harburg's *Jamaica*, a Caribbean holiday fashioned around her. (It was actually intended for Harry Belafonte; when he withdrew, it was refitted for Horne.) *Jamaica* was a hit, but only by virtue of the star's performance. Two other Broadway musicals were written for her, Arlen and Mercer's *St. Louis Woman* (1946) and Styne, Comden, and Green's *Hallelujah, Baby!* (1967). Horne withdrew from both, objecting to the stereotypical types of the former and the outdated liberal slant of the latter. But here, at sixty-three, came *The Lady and Her Music*, a grand triumph, and fashioned solely in the Lady's own terms.

Winner of a special citation from the New York Drama Critics' Circle. A special Tony Award was won by Lena Horne.

BROADWAY SCORECARD
/ PERFS: 333 / $: +

RAVE	FAVORABLE	MIXED	UNFAVORABLE	PAN
6				

THE·LIEUTENANT

"A New Rock Opera"

book, music, and lyrics by Gene Curty, Nitra Scharfman, and Chuck Strand

based on events surrounding the March 16, 1968, massacre at My Lai, South Vietnam

directed by William Martin

choreographed by Dennis Dennehy

produced by Joseph S. Kutzreba and Spofford J. Beadle

with Eddie Mekka

opened March 9, 1975   *Lyceum Theatre*

CLIVE BARNES, *TIMES*

[Headline: "*The Lieutenant*: Musical with Something Worth Singing"]
The massacre at My Lai was one of the saddest, indeed one of the most horrendous episodes in American history, not only for what happened but also for the implications of those happenings. It is not, one would have imagined, a very viable subject for a Broadway musical. Yet *The Lieutenant* has a passion and vitality not often found in musicals these days. It is also, and this may be even rarer, a musical with something to say worth saying. *The Lieutenant* is accurately described as a "rock opera." It is entirely operatic in form—there is no linking dialogue whatsoever, and music and dance carry the entire burden of the story. It works very well, indeed, for the tension is never broken by the emotional shifting of gears that spoken dialogue inevitably brings with it. The music is attractive and supportive. Although described as "rock," it in fact covers a lot of territory, including old-fashioned vaudeville and even a touch of a comic barbershop quartet sung by a trio. There is satire here as well as drama, and the lyrics, while a few of the rhymes are occasionally agonized, tell the opera's story with clarity and punch. You can also understand every word that is being sung, which is a distinct credit for the cast. Ironically enough, the major virtues of the show, its pace and slickness, are also the source of its chief shortcoming. The three authors, the director and the choreographer have concentrated on a style that has something of the relentless show-biz pressure of a TV dance routine or an industrial show. This presentation is unusual on Broadway, and although it is in its own loud way impressive, it also carries with it a hint of superficiality. The result is a show that, oddly enough, is slightly more serious than it seems. This rock-opera is unusual entertainment, sharp in its aspiration, modest in its resources and silkily assertive in its achievement. It deserves to do well.

MARTIN GOTTFRIED, *POST*

Unfortunately, relevance does not equal stage value. This production is as theatrical a disaster as the war is a moral and political one. Perhaps "disaster" is too substantial a description for *The Lieutenant*. Were this self-styled rock opera skimpier, it wouldn't be there at all and theatrical castastrophe requires a certain ambition, monumentally ill-conceived.

This show is on a summer camp level, without the vaguest notion of professional standards. To charge $9.00 a ticket for such an amateur night is only consistent with its naïveté. The rock music is embarassingly derivative of The Who's *Tommy*. The painful volume of amplification cannot disguise the small-time rock group quality of the music. The lyrics are what the score deserves. "Public knowledge would bring disgrace/The U.S. Army would lose its face." The large company was willing to work but William Martin seemed less than able to direct it. The choreographer, Dennis Dennehy, was apparently under the impression that he was auditioning for industrial shows.

DOUGLAS WATT, *DAILY NEWS*
[Headline: "*The Lieutenant* is Shattering"]
A shattering anti-recruitment poster. In sharp, telling strokes punctuated by lively dance numbers, it boldly reenacts for us—in stylized terms, of course—the My Lai massacre and its aftermath. The central character, though not named, is obviously William Calley, and he is presented as a victim of the dehumanizing war machine. The 90-minute show opens and closes with a catchy recruiting song, "Join the Army." At the end, it attracts another jobless innocent, as the spotlighted figure of the lieutenant stands at attention in the background. The unexplainable heart of the matter remains unexplained. The lieutenant's sudden decision to slaughter the villagers—men, women and children—is glossed over with the unsatisfactory suggestion that it was prompted by his captain's phoned command to stop dawdling and get out of there. But though the lieutenant's final impulse can probably never be isolated, the show is a very graphic presentation of the external facts from a viewpoint that is only occasionally sardonic. More often, because the events are so recent, *The Lieutenant* is simply a harrowing distillation of the most infamous of the Vietnam atrocities. The atmosphere of *The Lieutenant* is akin to a brash pop version of Berg's *Wozzeck* [1925]. This lieutenant, like that earlier German soldier, is a damned man. But, of course, *The Lieutenant*, perhaps piping hot last year, couldn't foresee a "happy" ending and new beginning in the form of a potential and enormously lucrative lecture career for the anti-hero.

0   0   0

The 1968 My Lai incident—in which American soldiers, in search of Viet Cong guerrillas, killed 347 civilians—fueled the anti-Vietnam War protest movement. In 1971 Lt. William L. Calley was court-martialed and sentenced to life imprisonment; in September 1974 his conviction was overturned and he was released. All of which resulted in this rather unusual rock opera, which originated at Joseph S. Kutzreba's Queens Playhouse. Despite impressively strong reviews from the *Times* and the *News*, there was no audience for *The Lieutenant* and it shuttered after a week. Eddie Mekka—in the title role—received a Best Actor Tony nomination, though.

BROADWAY SCORECARD

/ PERFS: 9 / $: —

RAVE	FAVORABLE	MIXED	UNFAVORABLE	PAN
1	2	1		2

A LITTLE NIGHT MUSIC

"A New Musical"

music and lyrics by Stephen Sondheim

book by Hugh Wheeler

based on the 1956 screenplay *Sommarnattens leende* (*Smiles of a Summer Night*) by Ingmar Bergman

directed by Harold Prince

choreographed by Patricia Birch

produced by Harold Prince in association with Ruth Mitchell

starring Glynis Johns, Len Cariou, and Hermione Gingold

with Victoria Mallory, Laurence Guittard, Patricia Elliott, Mark Lambert, Judy Kahan, D'Jamin Bartlett, George Lee Andrews, Despo, Barbara Lang, Benjamin Rayson, Teri Ralston, Beth Fowler, and Gene Varrone

opened February 25, 1973   Shubert Theatre

CLIVE BARNES, *TIMES*

At last a new operetta! At last resonances and elegances in a Broadway musical. *A Little Night Music* is heady, civilized, sophisticated and enchanting. It is Dom Perignon. It is supper at Laserre. It is a mixture of Cole Porter, Gustav Mahler, Antony Tudor and just a little of Ingmar Bergman. And it is more fun than any tango in a Parisian suburb [ref. Marlon Brando's 1972 film *Last Tango in Paris*]. The real triumph belongs to Stephen Sondheim, who wrote the music and lyrics. The music is a celebration of 3/4 time, an orgy of plaintively memorable waltzes, all talking of past loves and lost worlds. Despite the idea of a waltz-musical, which somehow suggests one of Strauss's, or the title, so redolent of Mozart, it seems that Sondheim is aiming at the lilt of Mahler. There is a peasant touch here, a sense of country values. For all its sophistication it is a story in which the stables are more important than the chandeliers. Then, of course, there are Sondheim's breathtaking lyrics. They have the kind of sassy, effortless poetry that Cole Porter mastered. The mother announces grandly: "I acquired some position/Plus a tiny Titian," and this is coming from a lyricist who only seconds before has dazzlingly made "raisins" rhyme with "liaisons." Grace is abounding—who but Sondheim would dare: "The hip-bath, the hip-bath, how can you trip and slip into a hip-bath?" You have to be very hip, and Sondheim is. It is also a particular triumph for Harold Prince. For years he has been attempting to bring—or so it has seemed to me—something of the sensibility of the serious lyric theatre, specifically perhaps the ballet, into American musicals. Here he has pulled it off in a way he didn't in *Follies* [1971] or *Company* [1970]. People have long been talking about Prince's conceptual musicals; now I feel I have actually seen one of the actual concepts. *A Little Night Music* is soft on the ears, easy on the eyes, and pleasant on the mind. It is less than brash, but more than brassy, and it should give a lot of pleasure. It is the remembrance of a few things past, and all to the sound of a waltz and the understanding smile of a memory. Good God!—an adult musical!

MARTIN GOTTFRIED, *WOMEN'S WEAR DAILY*

A Little Night Music is exquisite to look at; it has a wonderful score; its lyrics are a model of the craft. I saw it twice, liked it better the second time, and find that what it is trying to do is more interesting than what it did, for the show has little life, little musical theatricality and little reason for its own existence. Coming as it does after their adventurous and inspired *Company* and *Follies*, the new Sondheim-Prince musical is a deep disappointment for me. This enormously talented team has been solitarily evolving the Broadway musical theatre. Though a show of theirs that does not work is still beyond the talent and imagination of most everyone else who does musicals, it is depressing to find them stepping backwards and the main problem, I think, was a conceit. The conceit was to create a musical of classical elegance. [Bergman's] screenplay had a complex story line, as opposed to the fluid scripts that Prince has developed in replacement of the book of the old fashioned musical. *A Little Night Music* has a script—a play with song cues—that goes back to his days before *Cabaret* [1966] in terms of dramatic structure. And worse, this script dominated the show despite its flaccid and undynamic tone. The story simply goes along, developing plot without much humor or charm, and certainly no dramatic peaks. Nevertheless, Sondheim's score is enchanting, without question his finest yet, a true progress and development for him as a composer. His melodies are strong and lyrical; his harmonies, as usual, are disarmingly grateful to Ravel; his dissonances are refreshing and effective; his varied applications of three-four time keep the songs interesting and different; the structures are nearly all of inventive length and style; his music is always singable and theatrical, doubtless due to a familiarity with the operas of Janáček. And once more it has been dazzlingly orchestrated by Jonathan Tunick. Sondheim is also the only lyricist, probably, who could have done such a score justice, and though one could quibble with a word choice here or a syllable accent there, it would be ridiculous in the face of his formidable craftsmanship, invention and poetry. . . . For all of Florence Klotz' magnificent costumes and Boris Aronson's beautiful, picture-book set, the show does not find the classicism it seeks. Given Prince's tremendous, proved and important talent, it is a letdown.

WALTER KERR, *TIMES*

I have my reservations about *A Little Night Music*, but they are the kind of reservations you like to tuck in your pocket for later reference so as not to interfere with your pleasure in what is going on. The show itself, adapted from an Ingmar Bergman film and set to talkative tunes by the restlessly inventive Stephen Sondheim, is a thing of considerable grace—sometimes a bit self-consciously so—with the courage of its quaintness, a love of the half-light, and open arms for the talents of three irresistible women [Glynis Johns, Patricia Elliott, and D'Jamin Bartlett]. . . . What with the period and the mood, Sondheim is able to indulge a surprising bent for near-operetta melody. He remains his own man, though, seeing to it that even light waltzes have a barely suppressed cry to them, working out double soliloquies and then trios with cool crosstalk that snaps like icicles, playing with lyrics as though a keyboard could spell (I won't tell you how he rhymes "indiscriminate" with "women it," but he does, handsomely). The score is as friendly as it is musically rich. To my reservations. I haven't seen the Bergman film, but I think I might have guessed from the curious structure of the entertainment that it was motion-picture born and bred. There is an omnipresent quintet hovering about in Boris Aronson's fetchingly painted wings, ready at any time to blot out the principals and do a mannered, half-danced crossover. In effect, the quintet functions as a cutter, clipping off scenes before they have really been played out, obliging us with dissolves as we leap from discontented pair to discontented pair. The device seems to me intrusive and fundamentally false to the theatre (the theatre is a place in which scenes *are* played out, its sophistication comes from pursued substance rather than from quick ellisions) and I found myself resisting the fragmentations. And curiously, the unraveling of the passage at hearts is quite tamely routine. The right virgins get the right young men, the old flames find a hearth to return to. We have come a highly complicated way to a thoroughly uncomplicated point, and, somehow, we expected the quirky freshness of the styling to produce conclusions odder and more interesting than that. Even so, the score is a gift, the ladies are delightful, and Harold Prince has staged the moody meetings with easy skill.

DOUGLAS WATT, *DAILY NEWS*
[Headline: "*Little Night Music*: Operetta That's Exquisite But Fragile"]
Exquisiteness is so much the concern of *A Little Night Music*, a beautifully designed and staged operetta of intimate proportions that opened last night, that there is little room for the breath of life. Light mockery and occasional laughter float on the sweetly-scented night air, but the atmosphere is sterile. Though much of the talk and activity are given over to sex, there seems to be little of it around. Stephen Sondheim's carefully wrought score, which never opens itself to an actual love song, is entirely in waltz time or variations on it. It is delicate in nature and creates, with its excellently shaped lyrics, something of the effect of Ravel's *Valses Nobles et Sentimentales* equipped with superior Broadway rhymes. The effect of Hugh Wheeler's book, on the other hand, is that of a cross between Shakespeare and Chekhov humors with strong overtones of Broadway brashness. Everywhere, *A Little Night Music* reveals the work of superior theatrical craftsmanship. But stunning as it is to

gaze upon and as clever as its score is, with its use of trio and ensemble singing, it remains too literary and precious a work to stir the emotions.

●   ●   ●

Following the nervous hit *Company* and the total loss of *Follies*, the Prince-Sondheim team turned to a more traditional and less experimental piece. A costume operetta, in fact. Of course, their idea of a costume operetta was a far cry from *Naughty Marietta* (1910). *A Little Night Music*—or *Naughty Desirée?*—was dark, somber, and at times positively Chekovian. (Sweden, after all, is way up on the world suicide chart.) Prince and Sondheim had been trying to get the rights to Jean Anouilh's 1950 comedy *Ring Round the Moon* since *West Side Story* (1957) days. When that proved continually unavailable, they switched their focus to Jean Renoir's 1939 film *Rules of the Game*, finally settling on the Bergman *Smiles of a Summer Night*. Hugh Wheeler was a respected if unsuccessful playwright, with *Big Fish, Little Fish* (1961) prominent among his credits; he had doctored the American version of *Half a Sixpence* (1965) and prepared the initial adaptation of Harry Rigby's *Irene* (1973), and as Patrick Quentin (among other aliases) penned dozens of mystery novels. Wheeler scripted Prince's first film, the 1970 Angela Lansbury-starrer *Something for Everyone*, after which he was brought in as librettist of *Night Music* (and Prince's next three projects). If producer Prince was looking for an audience-friendly crowd-pleaser, Sondheim provided his most advanced work to date. *Company* and *Follies* had been collections of songs: plot-related songs, dazzling songs, but individual songs. The *Night Music* songs, though, were parts of an interwoven *score!* Much has been made of the fact that all are in variations of three-quarter time. This was a neat trick for an inveterate puzzle-man to pull off, but relatively inconsequential; the score's the thing, and I contend the meter don't matter. Sondheim's songs are all of a piece, yet each is unique in content and form. Item: an opening scene with three separate, moody solos—which ultimately weave into one grand-and-glorious trio. Item: a singing quintet serving as Greek chorus (or is that Swedish chorus?) in a series of interlaced concerted numbers. Item: an octet composed of three generations of women reading letters, with emendations from that Swedish chorus. Item: three remarkable duets for strangely paired characters—a man rhapsodizing to his ex-mistress about his child bride; the man and his ex-mistress's current lover jealously comparing notes; and the mistress's ex-lover's child bride commiserating with the mistress's current lover's long-suffering wife. And most remarkably of all the first act finale, which interweaves six characters and seven "scenes" into a grand, eleven-voice "Weekend in the Country." *A Little Night Music* was indeed successful, although not a blockbuster. While consciously catering to the audience, it was still a bit of a rough go. (So how cheery could it be, with Bergman, Chekhov, and Sondheim on hand?) The seventeen-month run was about the same length as the concurrent *Irene*, less than *No, No, Nanette* (1971), *Two Gentlemen of Verona* (1971), and *Raisin* (1973), and far shorter than superhits *Pippin* (1972) and *Grease* (1972). And if you want some really frightening statistics, the number of Sondheim musicals since *Night Music* (at this writing): seven. The number of financially successful Sondheim musicals since *Night Music* (at this writing): zero. The number of important scores, though, is seven-for-seven.

Winner of the New York Drama Critics' Circle Award. In addition to winning the Tony Award for Best Musical, Tonys were won by Stephen Sondheim (score), Hugh Wheeler (book), Glynis Johns (actress), Patricia Elliott (supporting actress), and Florence Klotz (costume designer).

BROADWAY SCORECARD

/ PERFS: 601 / $: +

RAVE	FAVORABLE	MIXED	UNFAVORABLE	PAN
1	2	1	1	

LOOK TO THE LILIES

"A New Musical," previously entitled *Some Kind of Man*

music by Jule Styne

lyrics by Sammy Cahn

book by Leonard Spigelgass

based on the 1962 novel *Lilies of the Field* by William E. Barrett

directed by Joshua Logan

choreographer unbilled (Peter Gennaro, replaced by Joyce Trisler)

produced by Edgar Lansbury, Max J. Brown, Richard Lewine, and Ralph Nelson

starring Shirley Booth and Al Freeman, Jr.

with Titos Vandis, Taina Elg, Carmen Alvarez, and Patti Karr

opened March 29, 1970   Lunt–Fontanne Theatre

CLIVE BARNES, *TIMES*

There are three kinds of musicals in this world—great musicals, bad musicals and professional musicals. *Look to the Lilies* is a professional musical, capable of giving a decent amount of pleasure to a lot of people. You will not, I think, go home waltzing down the sidewalk—which is just as well, as the play came in with a blizzard—but at least you shouldn't be cussing. It has strong music by Jule Styne and effective lyrics by Sammy Cahn, and that is where the quality of the musical lies. To be sure, Styne has given us better music. But this music works pleasantly enough. It has some memorable moments and is particularly welcome in a season where so many Broadway producers seem to have gone tone deaf, stone deaf, or both. The story is all heart, so much so that it may give the sensitive heartburn. The performances are a lot better than the staging, which is poor. It is essentially a static story—the little dancing there is is attributed to no one on the program and the

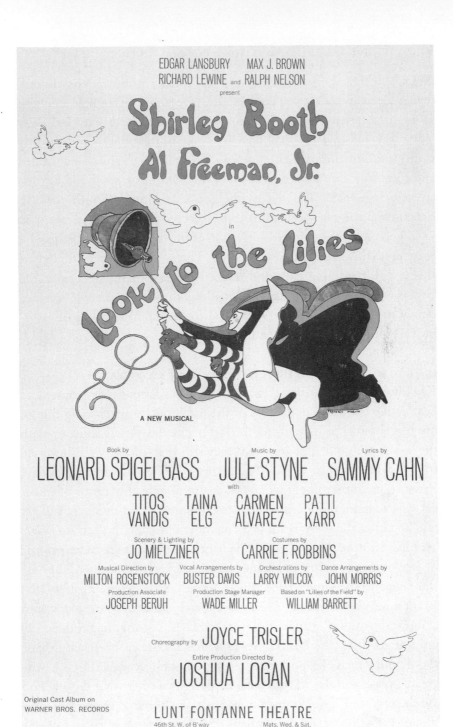

EDGAR LANSBURY   MAX J. BROWN
RICHARD LEWINE and RALPH NELSON
present

Shirley Booth
Al Freeman, Jr.

in

Look to the Lilies

A NEW MUSICAL

Book by   Music by   Lyrics by
LEONARD SPIGELGASS   JULE STYNE   SAMMY CAHN

with

TITOS   TAINA   CARMEN   PATTI
VANDIS   ELG   ALVAREZ   KARR

Scenery & Lighting by   Costumes by
JO MIELZINER   CARRIE F. ROBBINS

Musical Direction by   Vocal Arrangements by   Orchestrations by   Dance Arrangements by
MILTON ROSENSTOCK   BUSTER DAVIS   LARRY WILCOX   JOHN MORRIS

Production Associate   Production Stage Manager   Based on "Lilies of the Field" by
JOSEPH BERUH   WADE MILLER   WILLIAM BARRETT

Choreography by   JOYCE TRISLER

Entire Production Directed by
JOSHUA LOGAN

Original Cast Album on
WARNER BROS. RECORDS

LUNT FONTANNE THEATRE
46th St. W. of B'way   Mats. Wed. & Sat.

Looks more like the Flying Nun to me. Or are they wrestling?
Pre–opening credits. (artwork by Frederic Marvin)

director, Joshua Logan, has done little to make it move. Miss Booth, with a German accent you could strain sauerkraut through, is a delight as the totalitarian Mother Superior who is determined that God's way is her way and that He shall have it. There is great depth and shading to this performance, which is never exaggerated but always controlled and comically emphasized. Mr. Freeman, who has a good and aggressive singing voice, also makes the most of Homer Smith (or Mr. Schmidt as the nuns call him), even succeeding to a large extent in making credible the strange motivation of this handyman and bum who is suddenly inspired to build a church. The scenes between the two of them, with mounting trust and respect between them, are among the best-played scenes in the current Broadway theatre. So there it is, a nice family musical. It would be very good for diamond wedding anniversaries, especially Catholic weddings.

MARTIN GOTTFRIED, WOMEN'S WEAR DAILY

Broadway's old guard, in its hopeless, headstrong, desperate and destructive last stand in defense of the traditional way of doing things, has just about shot its wad. As the last of the old-timers show up with the last of their old-time musicals, they still keep doing what they used to do—what used to work, hoping that somehow it can work again. Perhaps one more time it will work again, despite silly forms of musical construction, the songs and dances and production numbers will get it all together the old way for just one more nostalgic thrill. But *Look to the Lilies* isn't the show to do it. The names of the past are there—music by Jule Styne, direction by Joshua Logan, sets by Jo Mielziner. They are still dialed to the same station: they choose a well-known property (the Academy Award–winning *Lilies of the Field*) and decide to make it into a musical without wondering whether there is anything inherently musical about it (there isn't). Styne writes a score in his usual urbane show-tune style, never bothering to think that music should fit the people, the place and the story. Mielziner designs settings that drop in and out the way they have dropped in and out of a hundred shows, not even stopping to think that the climax of this particular story is a scenic effect (a completed chapel), and that it should be built on stage. And finally, Logan patches together a song, a piece of story and some chorus work. It just can't automatically work anymore. I don't mean that

Look to the Lilies is a disaster; the evening is only occasionally annoying. But that is the most that can be said for it. The humor is heavy and the story's central quality—the maternal relationship between a Mother Superior and a black criminal—has been ruined by a combination of insensitive direction and actor problems. Shirley Booth returned to Broadway with this show after too many years of waste—if financial security—in television [winning multiple Emmy awards as *Hazel* (1961–66)]. She is still a wonderful actress and plays the Mother Superior with vast sensitivity. Al Freeman, Jr., was [also] very good. Unfortunately, he was unable to establish any kind of on-stage rapport with Miss Booth and they spent the evening as strangers. Whatever the reason, personalities or direction, the invisible gap between the two took the life out of the show, whatever there might have been.

○   ○   ○

The late 1960s were an especially difficult time for musical theatre veterans. In a two-and-a-half-year stretch—just following the 1968 opening, coincidentally, of *Hair*—Rodgers, Lerner, Bock, Harnick, Kander, Ebb, Jones, Schmidt, and even Jerry Herman all suffered failure along the Rialto. It is no wonder that Jule Styne, in his mid-sixties, was experiencing trouble. His talent was still alive—*Hallelujah, Baby!* (1967) and especially *Darling of the Day* (1968) displayed him in fine form—but both musicals had been beset by overwhelming birthing difficulties. *Look to the Lilies* addressed racial themes, as had *Hallelujah, Baby!*, but for all of the troubles the earlier musical underwent, Styne had Comden, Green, and Laurents by his side. (For better *and* for worse.) Driven by compulsion and financial necessity to keep working, the composer aligned with lesser lights Sammy Cahn and Leonard Spigelgass for *Lilies*, and the results were exceedingly drab. Styne provided his poorest score (unless his 1993 opus *The Red Shoes* deserves the crown); while the man had his share of failures, his work was always at least tuneful. Usually, that is. Sammy Cahn's lyrics, on the other hand, were painfully bad. ("The price is eight to seven, that there is or ain't a heaven," the hero exclaims; or even better, the title song advises: "You are vexed, annoyed, perplexed/Wond'ring what is coming next/A problem, like smoke, goes up and down the chimney/Be smart, take heart, from the anemone.") It is harder to dismiss Joshua Logan arbitrarily.

An unquestionable giant of the musical theatre, his career underwent a breakdown in the early 1950s after he underwent a breakdown. While Logan partially rebounded, his musicals following the earnest-but-overstuffed *Fanny* in 1954 were unenduringly dismal: Irving Berlin's *Mr. President* (1960); *All American* (1962); *Mame* (1966), not dismal but from which he was bounced long before rehearsals began; the *Picnic*-musicalization *Hot September* (which opened and closed in Boston in hot September 1965); *Look to the Lilies*; and the Bette Davis–headed *Miss Moffat* (which opened and closed in cold Philadelphia in 1974). These from the director—and in some cases coauthor/coproducer as well—of *Annie Get Your Gun* (1946), *Mister Roberts* (1948), *South Pacific* (1949), *Picnic* (1953), and others. *Look to the Lilies*, incidentally, was intended as a Merman vehicle. One can only imagine the outspoken Ethel's assessment of those anemones in the chimney.

BROADWAY SCORECARD
/ PERFS: 25 / $: –

RAVE	FAVORABLE	MIXED	UNFAVORABLE	PAN
1		1	1	3

LORELEI; OR, GENTLEMEN *STILL* PREFER BLONDES

"The Season's Biggest and Best Musical Comedy," a revised version of the 1949 musical *Gentlemen Prefer Blondes*

music by Jule Styne

lyrics by Leo Robin; "new" lyrics by Betty Comden and Adolph Green

book by Anita Loos and Joseph Fields; "new" book by Kenny Solms and Gail Parent

based on the 1926 novel *Gentlemen Prefer Blondes* by Anita Loos

directed by Robert Moore (replacing Betty Comden and Adolph Green, who replaced Joe Layton)

choreographed by Ernest Flatt (replacing Joe Layton)

produced by Lee Guber and Shelly Gross

starring Carol Channing

with Dody Goodman, Tamara Long, Peter Palmer, Lee Roy Reams, Brandon Maggart, Jack Fletcher, Jean Bruno, Bob Fitch, and Ian Tucker

opened January 27, 1974   Palace Theatre

CLIVE BARNES, *TIMES*

[Headline: "'49 Musical Comedy is Now Heavier Going"]

I never saw Miss Channing in the original Broadway version, but I suspect, from seeing a later London production [in 1962, starring Dora Bryan], that she must have carried it. She still carries it—but it is heavier going. Robert Moore has staged the show with a raised eyebrow showing, and Ernest O. Flatt has come up with the kind of choreogra-

Lee Guber & Shelly Gross present

CAROL CHANNING
as
LORELEI

A Musical Comedy

New Music by	New Lyrics by		New Book by	
JULE STYNE	BETTY COMDEN	& ADOLPH GREEN	KENNY SOLMS	& GAIL PARENT

Based Upon the Musical Comedy
GENTLEMEN PREFER BLONDES

Book by	Music by	Lyrics by
ANITA LOOS & JOSEPH FIELDS	JULE STYNE	LEO ROBIN

with

DODY GOODMAN TAMARA LONG PETER PALMER LEE ROY REAMS

BRANDON MAGGART BROOKS MORTON JEAN BRUNO

Original Cast Album on MGM-VERVE Records

Entire Production Staged by
JOE LAYTON

3 WEEKS ONLY!
TUES. MAY 15 — SAT. JUNE 2
NATIONAL THEATRE
1321 E Street N.W.
Washington, D.C. 20004

All Evenings 7:30 Matinees 2 p.m. on Wed. May 16 & 23
Monday May 28 (Memorial Day) and All Saturdays; and
3 p.m. on Sunday May 20.
Monday thru Saturday Evenings: Orch. $12.00; 1st. Balc.
$12.00, 10.00, 8.00; Upper Balc. $4.50
All 6 Matinees: Orch. $8.50; 1st Balc. $8.50, 7.50, 6.00
Upper Balc. $4.00

FOR GROUP SALES TELEPHONE 387-7502

"The only entertainer left who can carry a whole show by herself, portal to portal," wrote Walter Kerr. "Shinier than her own anklets, bigger than her moist heart, maybe the only creature extant who can live up to a Hirschfeld." Preliminary credits.

phy that went out of fashion before it ever came in. Television killed it stillborn in the forties, or, to be charitable, the fifties. The cast, with one exception, is unexceptionable—which brings me, at last, to Miss Channing, and the producers have only themselves to blame for its taking me so long. Miss Channing is two saucer eyes under an unkempt mop, two great legs and a voice range that goes from a purr to a gurgle, from a gurgle to a sigh, from a sigh to a growl and from a growl to a screech. Her timing is such that if she were a railroad system, even Mussolini would have eaten his heart out. She plays with lines so beautifully that one longs for her to have been given better lines to play with. Watch her when she has just been given what she thinks is yet another diamond bracelet from her lover. She tries to clasp it on her wrist but he takes it away, and to her amazement puts it around her ankle. Her piteously beaming eyes look up to God in supplication and admiration. In a tiny voice, coming out of the contemplative side of her larynx, she murmurs: "Another place . . . I never even thought of!" Carol Channing is *Lorelei*'s best friend.

MARTIN GOTTFRIED, *WOMEN'S WEAR DAILY*
It is fair, I think, to assume that this version is more revival than sequel, but the main thing is that it doesn't have the look or feel of a revival. It has energy, polish and style, though its technique is sorely dated and its jokes are often flat; it is the first genuinely professional musical of the season; it has million dollar looks; it has the wonderful main character of Lorelei Lee, played as only she can be played by Carol Channing; and so on balance it is a good enough old fashioned musical, worth the price of admission, which is more than you can say for most musicals these days. Let me say this for Channing: I am in love with her. She has the easy magnetism that fairly announces: here is a star. She has brains and she knows it, she can be superior without snickering, she loves to entertain and she does it. Every one of today's manufactured superstars should be dragged to the Palace to take a look at her and see what work, talent, showmanship, clout and class really are. That said, there is a rest-of-the-show to contend with. Nothing worse can be said of its humor than to quote it: "As the French say, tushy!" *Lorelei* is evenly professional, never great and never terrible, never exciting and never boring. It is diverting, certainly, and beautiful and it has Carol Channing. That should be enough for one night.

WALTER KERR, *TIMES*
[Headline: "Carol Is a Show's Best Friend"]
Carol Channing and *Lorelei* are exactly where they belong, at the Palace. If the new/old entertainment that has been shaken down by a dozen or so successive hands resembles anything at all, it resembles one of those peacock-fan, aerodrome-portaled "tab" musicals that used to roam the better vaudeville circuits with at least a rhinestone of a star set dead center in a spotlight. In this case, no rhinestone. The real Carol Channing, golden girl, tiger, tiger, burning bright, shinier than her own anklets, bigger than her moist heart, maybe the only creature extant who can live up to a Hirschfeld. Do you know what I mean by living up to a Hirschfeld? Hirschfeld always lives up to the people he draws, but the people he draws don't always live up to him. Don't explode in the same way, like new constellations doing *tour jetés* in the heavens. Here's the exception: mascara to swim in, nobly tragic mouth, the face of a great mystic about to make a terrible mistake. To get right down to it, do you realize—I seem to be asking a lot of questions today—that C. C. may be the only entertainer left who can carry a whole show by herself, portal to portal? Or even compete with her own lobby photos? Or stand there with her hands clasped and make you believe she's surprised you like her? No doubt I think she and her show belong at the Palace because of something the lady does as the first act curtain is coming down. She won't quit. Here's this curtain descending, right on top of her, as though some stagehand had been told to lower it exactly at 9 no matter what was going on, and she fights it. Tries to hold back the fringe that is engulfing her, battles the batten with her strong right elbow, gets to her knees and keeps on singing, winds up with no more than a finger keeping in touch with us. I haven't seen anybody do anything like that since the days when Rosetta Duncan used to ride up with the asbestos. It's a nice kind of thing to see. People playing with the very stage that cradles them, and keeping contact long after more reasonable souls have gone to their dressing rooms.

* * *

Lucky indeed is the actor who finds a legendary role-of-a-lifetime, as Carol Channing did at the age of twenty-nine when she transformed Anita Loos's Roaring Twenties gold digger into a Hirschfeld cartoon of a diamond-digging vamp. As gratifying as this identification can be, it has its downside; no matter what Channing did, she couldn't get out from under the shadow of Lorelei Lee for fourteen years. Then suddenly she stumbled into a *second* role-of-a-lifetime, that damned exasperating *Dolly!*, and Ms. Channing lived happily ever after. But if Lorelei had somewhat typed her, the Lorelei/Dolly combination took over her life, her persona, and even her offstage makeup. This is somewhat unfortunate, as the true Channing—a smart woman and a fine actress, an artist *capable* of turning Lorelei and Dolly's songs and lines into larger-than-life legends—has been in hiding behind her platinum wig for so many years now that only the shell is publicly visible. As the mid-1970s rolled around, Dolly had gone about as far as she could go, at least for a while. What's a gal to do? Audiences did not want to see Carol Channing, the actress; they wanted Carol/Lorelei/Dolly, the *attraction*. Thus it was that the Carol Channing Show, or two characters in search of a spotlight, was nudged back to that "Little Girl from Little Rock." Of course, *Gentlemen Prefer Blondes* needed considerable revision to allow for a fifty-three-year-old gold digger. And imagine the producers' surprise when they got around to actually reading *Gentlemen Prefer Blondes* and found that it was old-fashioned, clumsy, and clunky. (It was, in truth, old-fashioned, clumsy, and clunky back in 1949, but welcomed as a nostalgic throwback by audiences surfeited with dramatic musicals like *Brigadoon*, *Street Scene*, *Allegro*, *Love Life*, *South Pacific*, and *Lost in the Stars*.) Convinced that the reconstituted Ms. Channing/Lee would sell tickets like hotcakes—at least on the road—suburban tent entrepreneurs Guber and Gross decided to make the money first, before braving the severe Broadway critics. *Lorelei* was at the beginning of a trend, opening *way* out of town—Oklahoma City, on February 24, 1973—and inching its way (slowly) to Broadway. You make a lot of money on the road, goes the theory; but it somehow doesn't work out that way. Especially when you keep *changing* things, like directors and songs. (Lyricists Comden and Green themselves were drafted as directors-of-record for a couple of months, until Robert Moore—of *Promises, Promises* [1968]—stepped in to fine-tune the show for the Palace.) The Broadway critics handled the ravaged *Lorelei* with kid gloves, giving it the benefit of many doubts. But audiences weren't fooled, and the old gal whimpered away. And a 1995 Broadway revival of *Gentlemen Prefer Blondes*—without Carol or the *Lorelei* "improvements"—fared even worse. <u>Lost on the Road Dept.</u>: How did that extended tryout scheme work, anyway? *Lorelei* was capitalized at $500,000; with all the changes, it cost about $700,000 to get to Broadway. They recovered about $350,000 during the tryout (on ticket receipts of $5 million), another hundred in town, and closed with a loss of around $250,000.

BROADWAY SCORECARD
/ PERFS: 320 / $: –

RAVE	FAVORABLE	MIXED	UNFAVORABLE	PAN
1	3	1	1	

LOST IN THE STARS

a revival of the 1949 "Musical Tragedy"

music by Kurt Weill

book and lyrics by Maxwell Anderson

based on the 1948 novel *Cry the Beloved Country* by Alan Paton

directed by Gene Frankel

choreographed by Louis Johnson

produced by Roger L. Stevens and Diana Shumlin for The John F. Kennedy Center for the Performing Arts

starring Brock Peters

with Jack Gwillim, Rod Perry, Gilbert Price, Leonard Jackson, Rosetta LeNoire, Margaret Cowie, Staats Cotsworth, Damon Evans, and Giancarlo Esposito

opened April 18, 1972   Imperial Theatre

CLIVE BARNES, *TIMES*

Kurt Weill was the greatest composer ever to write for Broadway, and his genius shone brightly last night when his last musical, *Lost in the Stars*, was restaged with resource and imagination. We will hear no better music on Broadway this season, nor I suspect next, nor the seasons after that. Weill was unique, a major composer who wanted to write for the popular theatre, and not only wanted to, but could. Because of Weill's contribution, *Lost in the Stars* is a considerable piece of musical theatre. The adaptation of the novel has been made by Maxwell Anderson, and the book and the lyrics are stiff, stilted and ponderous. There is no way that any production can avoid this. In most of his greatest works Weill collaborated with Bertolt Brecht, and Maxwell Anderson was no Brecht. Indeed, looking back he hardly seems to have been a Maxwell Anderson, for few dramatists' careers could have been based so successfully on such slender talent. Here the shape of the drama is awkward, the dialogue largely uninteresting and the lyrics frequently clumsy. Yet the story of this South African pastor and his son and his conscience is still on its own terms very moving. Apart from music, what finally makes the evening a success is the superb performance by Brock Peters as the pastor. Peters is a model of gnarled and tortured integrity, unbending in his moral courage, terrible in his grief. He takes the music and sings it with courage, and in the scene when he is waiting for his son to be hanged, a scene that could easily be maudlin, his moral force and conviction are tremendous. Here Peters seems in his agony to brush aside the playwright's liberal hopes of black and white children playing together in the South African veldt and in the painstruck glare of his tears to summon up a tragic realization of a race enslaved. It is a riveting performance. It is a pity, however, that the performance of the orchestra was not as good as the performance of the cast. The faults with *Lost in the Stars* are easily enough enumerated, and I think just about as easily forgiven. People talk about innovative musicals—this is a tragic musical that extended the range of the musical theatre. It brings dignity, passion and grand music to Broadway.

MARTIN GOTTFRIED, *WOMEN'S WEAR DAILY*

You don't have to be black to dislike *Lost in the Stars*. The Maxwell Anderson–Kurt Weill musical seems to have studied at the Albert Schweitzer school of racial relations, which taught a benevolence of parent to child. That should offend a modern white man as much as a black. But, on the other hand, this operetta was, after all, written in 1949, and were we to discard worthy works of the past on the basis of their outdated thinking, we would be left with neither literature nor history. The question is whether *Lost in the Stars* is a worthy work and the answer is, partly. The worthy part, unsurprisingly, is Kurt Weill's music. Weill's adjustment to Broadway was not altogether happy, and his music for *Lost in the Stars* is sometimes cynical with its sentimentally stirring anthems and catchy, quasi-show tunes, but for the most part it demonstrates how superior a trained musician is to the ordinary tunesmith. Weill's technique, coupled with his theatrical and melodic instinct, produced a score that had musical appeal without being simpleminded, a score that was not restricted to formula, a score that could have longer songs, weaving and developing. Weill also proved that it is definitely possible for a composer to find the time to do his own orchestrations. The advantages are tremendous—the full production of the *Lost in the Stars* music has the same musical tone of voice as the melodies themselves; the underscoring and connecting music are not merely rehashes of other songs in the show. In all these musical respects, the score for this show is exciting and absorbing, infinitely more satisfying than a set of simple show tunes. There is little more to go on. My only complaint about the musical side of things is the corny choral arrangements [by Weill]. My only complaint about the rest is that it is a sluggish, clumsy, blackfolks show.

RIGHARD WATTS, JR., POST
A brilliant new production, with Brock Peters giving a magnificent performance in the leading role. It retains all of its power, and certainly all of its timeliness. Although it is the tragic story that moved me most, the Kurt Weill score is an outstanding achievement of one of the greatest modern popular composers for the theater. It is virtually of an operatic nature, and is therefore not of the sort I feel most confident in writing about. But there is no denying its beauty and distinction. It may even possess a hit song in a number called "Big Mole," as charmingly put over by a boy named Giancarlo Esposito. The narrative faithfully follows the distinguished novelist's unforgettable story, and the emotional power is all there. The songs and the vivid dances are skillfully incor-

porated in it, and it is a case of integration that works out admirably. Gene Frankel's direction, Louis Johnson's choreography, and the setting by Oliver Smith combine to bring out a splendid production that is worthy of one of the most striking and original of American musical dramas. Peters, who has a fine voice to begin with, is at once heroic and warmly human as the tragic Stephen Kumalo, while Gilbert Price is appealingly moving as the son. When I saw *Lost in the Stars* for the first time 23 years ago I had reservations about it, but I must have improved in taste during the interval because now I like and admire it unreservedly.

o   o   o

While Kurt Weill achieved a moderate amount of success during his fourteen years in America—including two hit shows (*Lady in the Dark* [1941] and *One Touch of Venus* [1943]) and two immortal songs ("September Song" and "Speak Low")—his work was vastly underrated until after his death. With Marc Blitzstein's 1954 Off-Broadway adaptation of *The Threepenny Opera*—and the jukebox success of the "*Moritat*" ("Mack the Knife")—Weill's reputation began a steady upswing. This well-received Kennedy Center mounting of his final work came to Broadway with high hopes, but in 1972 audiences just weren't interested in its uncompromising message of racial tolerance. (Hadn't been in 1949, either.) And if they were, Max Anderson's sledgehammer approach to Alan Paton's first-rate novel would've scared 'em off anyway. The composer, ironically, received his strongest Broadway reviews ever. Not that they helped attract audiences. Weill died during the musical's original run on April 3, 1950, at the age of fifty. That production of *Lost in the Stars* ran for 281 performances, not the 28 mistakenly printed in *Opening Night on Broadway*. Sorry about that, please correct your copy, page 403.

BROADWAY SCORECARD

/ PERFS: 39 / $: −

RAVE	FAVORABLE	MIXED	UNFAVORABLE	PAN
4			2	

LOVELY LADIES, KIND GENTLEMEN

"A New Musical Comedy"

music and lyrics by Stan Freeman and Franklin Underwood

book by John Patrick

based on his Pulitzer/Drama Critics/Tony Award-winning 1953 comedy *Teahouse of the August Moon*, from the 1951 novel by Vern J. Sneider

directed by Lawrence Kasha

choreographed by Marc Breaux

produced by Herman Levin

starring Kenneth Nelson, Ron Husmann, David Burns (replacing Bernie West), and Eleanor Calbes

with Remak Ramsay and Lou Wills

opened December 28, 1970   Majestic Theatre

CLIVE BARNES, *TIMES*

Oh, dear! I come to bury *Lovely Ladies, Kind Gentlemen*, not to praise it, but there were one or two decent things, and three or four half-decent things, about this strangely dated musical that modestly opened last night. It was based on a 1953 play, *The Teahouse of the August Moon*. This story of East and West adjustment during the American Army's 1946 occupation of Okinawa had a great deal of slightly humorous charm in its day. As a consequence, I think two basic questions need to be asked. The first is whether the play itself would today be worth reviving? I think the answer is no: it is a little too cute, a little too coy, a little too patronizing to the defeated Asians. Precisely geared for its time, it is now out of joint. The second question is whether it might be

"I come to bury *Lovely Ladies, Kind Gentlemen*, not to praise it," said Clive Barnes. The poor geisha girl does seem to be wearing a shroud. Preliminary credits. (artwork by Tom Morrow)

improved by a little happy music and a few gay lyrics? As the music and lyrics provided by Stan Freeman and Franklin Underwood sound like chop-suey of almost compelling unoriginality, this I feel is a more open question. But no: I don't think anything could really have helped except second thoughts about the first idea. The play had originally a freshness and deftness about it that the musical completely lacks. The music is as expressionless as an egg, and the lyrics positively chug where they should only flow. I can, however, put in a kind word for the orchestrator, Philip J. Lang, who sometimes gave the score a pleasantly embalming touch of professionalism. The direction by Lawrence Kasha and the choreography by Marc Breaux seemed almost intent on making the worst of a bad job. (It is amazing how, generally speaking, bad Broadway choreography is.) Of course there isn't much you can do with a musical where the best music is a fractured quotation from "Deep in the Heart of Texas" and the best line comes from *Hamlet*.

MARTIN GOTTFRIED, *WOMEN'S WEAR DAILY*

There isn't enough going on in *Lovely Ladies, Kind Gentlemen* to call it a catastrophe. The musical version of *Teahouse of the August Moon* has a sluggish first act and slows down after intermission. It is slow because its creators pinned up the blueprint of a basic 40's–50's Broadway musical and then tried to overlay John Patrick's 1953 play, not having any idea of their own for a singular personality nor even, it seemed, the desire or energy to create something worthwhile. They had the further disadvantage, though at this point they were already demonstrating a disadvantage fetish, of having Patrick do his own adaptation. Apparently, the makers of *Lovely Ladies, Kind Gentlemen* never thought about creation—what this thing was they were making or why they wanted to make it—but instead concentrated on commercial matters: what would be its ticket-selling factor? Since none of the creative staff was well known, nor any of the actors, the draw would have to be the source, Patrick's original play. This, I think, is the key to this show's mentality. Who, after all, remembers *Teahouse of the August Moon*, and what was it other than a passing Broadway hit of 17 years ago? To those whose theatre minds are chained to the succession of transient commercial successes of the past, "hits" like *Teahouse* equal "theatre." And so, in foolishly thinking that *Teahouse* was their key to success, the makers of *Lovely Ladies, Kind Gentlemen* threw the balance of creative power to Patrick, who naturally kept as much of his play in the production as he possibly could. Stan Freeman's songs were then inserted in artificial gaps of the story and, as I recall, just one dance and one production number, were spliced into the thing. Lawrence Kasha proceeded to stage it as if it were a straight play and the result, predictably, was a summer stock revival of *Teahouse* with non-denominational Broadway tunes here and there. Aside from David Burns, a professional among novices, the performers are without personality or show sense of their own. Exactly like the production. That is precisely the problem of today's Broadway.

WALTER KERR, *TIMES*

Something chilling is happening to us. I noticed it on the opening night of *Lovely Ladies, Kind Gentlemen*. For a long time we've known that performers were growing increasingly dependent upon microphones, and a good many scolding words have been devoted to the subject. But lo! Now *we* are growing dependent upon them. At one point early in the evening, David Burns, an admirable man who approaches a gag or a song with the stance of a wrestler (he always throws it, be it song or gag), happened to turn his head in such a way that his body mike was temporarily disconnected. At least I think that's what happened. And do you know what? Instantly we wanted that mike back on, full up. We've grown accustomed to that big, blatant, tinhorn sound in the theatre and we don't want its decibels or its dehumanization reduced. That's terrible. We've been earwashed. . . . When making a musical of an earlier, charming play, one must first be certain that the addition of music doesn't wipe out the charm automatically. How automatically? In the case of *Lovely Ladies* it worked this way. Sakini, that ingratiating native who seems all grinning compliance but is actually mastering the Americans sent over to master him, was, in the original *Teahouse*, a fellow who crept up on you [played by David Wayne]. First, you believed in his obeisances; gradually, you caught onto the sunny, sneaky secret of his total command. That was fun. In the musical, though, the evening opened with Sakini (Kenneth Nelson with his palms up) before the front curtain, singing out the plot for us, already an irrevocable master of ceremonies. The beans, soy or whatever, had now been spilled.

Following the song, there was really nothing to do but watch him do what we knew he was going to do. The song was called "With a Snap of My Finger," and that said it all, right there. Through the evening the songs tended to function either as giveaway or afterthought, with the noble exception of a bit of barroom pastiche ("You've Broken a Fine Woman's Heart") bellowed through quivering wattles by the faultless Mr. Burns.

• • •

"I come to bury *Lovely Ladies, Kind Gentlemen*, not to praise it." In an open letter to the editor of the *Times*, producer Herman (*My Fair Lady* [1956]) Levin lashed out at the theatre's most powerful aislesitter, asserting that not only those connected with the show but also other critics and the public were "outraged and sickened" by the first line of the Barnes review. (The cast picketed the *Times* Building, with four-legged featured player Lady Astor wrapped in a sandwich board proclaiming "Clive gets my goat.") The Shakespearian quote, Levin wrote, "is an expression of animosity so repellent, so insulting, so obnoxious, so unnecessary, so cruel and so unprofessional that we would be caitiff dogs if we did not express our resentment and rejection of it in every possible way." Levin paused to attack Barnes's xenophobic tendencies, then went on to promise, "We refuse to be buried! We will fight to the limit of our financial ability to keep *Lovely Ladies, Kind Gentlemen* alive." The letter had little effect, naturally, especially since it appeared the day after Levin closed down his *chaya* and packed it in. (That's teahouse, to you.)

BROADWAY SCORECARD

/ PERFS: 19 / $: —

RAVE	FAVORABLE	MIXED	UNFAVORABLE	PAN
	2			4

MACK & MABEL

"The Musical Romance of Mack Sennett's Funny and Fabulous Hollywood"

music and lyrics by Jerry Herman

book by Michael Stewart (replacing Leonard Spigelgass)

based on an idea by Leonard Spigelgass, suggested by events in the lives of Mack Sennett (1880–1960) and Mabel Normand (1898–1930)

directed and choreographed by Gower Champion

produced by David Merrick

starring Robert Preston and Bernadette Peters (replacing Kelly Garrett, who replaced Marcia Rodd)

with Lisa Kirk, James Mitchell, Jerry Dodge, Christopher Murney, Tom Batten, Bert Michaels, Nancy Evers, Robert Fitch, and Stanley Simmonds

opened October 6, 1974   Majestic Theatre

CLIVE BARNES, *TIMES*

First for the good news. With the splashy *Mack & Mabel*, which splashed, at times rather damply, into the Majestic Theatre Sunday night, wide-eyed, diminutive and contralto Bernadette Peters found herself a major Broadway star. Also Gower Champion's staging of this overly talkative saga of the silent screen is the most elaborate bag of tricks we have been offered since Bob Fosse's *Pippin* [1972]. Then there are Robert Preston and one or two very catchy and one or two lushly attractive songs by Jerry Herman. For that matter it's nice to have the producer David Merrick back where he belongs. *Mack & Mabel* is subtitled "a musical love story," and as someone pertinently remarks in the

The John F. Kennedy Center for the Performing Arts
presents The DAVID MERRICK Production of

ROBERT   BERNADETTE
PRESTON PETERS

in

MACK & MABEL

Book by   Music and Lyrics by
MICHAEL STEWART JERRY HERMAN

Also Starring
LISA
KIRK

with
JERRY DODGE   CHRISTOPHER MURNEY   TOM BATTEN
BERT MICHAELS   NANCY EVERS   ROBERT FITCH   STANLEY SIMMONDS
and
JAMES MITCHELL

Musical Director and
Vocal Arrangements   Orchestrations by   Dance Music by
DONALD PIPPIN **PHILIP J. LANG** **JOHN MORRIS**
Scenic Design by   Costume Designs by   Lighting Designed by
ROBIN WAGNER **PATRICIA ZIPPRODT** **THARON MUSSER**
Associate Choreographer   Production Supervisor
BUDDY SCHWAB   **LUCIA VICTOR**
Associate Producer   Based on an idea by   In Association with
JACK SCHLISSEL **LEONARD SPIGELGASS** **EDWIN H. MORRIS**

Original Cast Album by ABC Records

Directed and Choreographed by
GOWER CHAMPION

"I thought, oh, goddam it, here comes that whole thing about if the star comes back let's sing her song," said Gower. "I'm going to keep writing this kind of song until I'm 85," said Jerry. "Loaded with all the zip of a dead flounder," said Dick Coe in the *Washington Post*.

course of the musical, "love stories are not traditionally told with dynamite." That might be some of the trouble. The musical tries to be too
explosive. We have all seen a musical with book trouble before, but this
one has book trouble so bad that it is practically library trouble. The
story was in any case meant as merely a prop for a musical that intended
to be a homage to the silent comedy, rather as *Follies* [1971] was a
homage to the Ziegfeld revue. Unhappily, it seems to have been forgotten that it is impossible to re-create, or even to affectionately suggest,
those silent comedies on the stage. This is cruelly, and perhaps mistakenly, established right at the beginning when a broken Mack demands
"What do they know about making moo-vies?" and, on a huge screen,
shows us a brilliantly composed montage of silent movies. This is the
musical's best moment. Champion has peaked too early. Champion
throws everything at the audience, including even a bathtub, in which
Mack briefly ponders. Never have so many props propped up so much
show. We have Mabel coming down a rope; a shower of bathing beau-
ties swizzling down a multicolored corkscrew slide; Mack suspended
over the audience on a giant camera dolly; and dozens of special effects,
some of which would have been worthy of Busby Berkeley—and many
of which were.

MARTIN GOTTFRIED, *POST*
It would have been so great for *Mack & Mabel* to be a success. New
York is in the mood for a hit Broadway musical, the theatre could use
the boost and why not this one, stocked with the team that made *Hello,
Dolly!* [1964] and a legitimate star in Robert Preston. Why then no
show? Because in the graduation of a musical from idea to production—in this case, from thinking of a Mack Sennett musical to opening last night—more is involved than hard work. In fact, *Mack &
Mabel* shows a lot of hard work (that's one of the things that's wrong
with it) but that is all it shows. Champion and Herman and Stewart
never made the musical about Sennett and Normand and silent movies
and slapstick comedy and Keystone Kops that they had to have had in
mind when they began. Somewhere, they lost track of the look and
rhythm and spirit of that idea, so obviously a natural for musicalization. For a choreographer-director, especially one as talented and
stage-wise as Champion, there is a depressing lack of musical staging.

The show just isn't musical. In fact, there is little dancing in the first act, and while there is a great deal more in the second, an appalling amount of it is in the cakewalk style that was so fresh in *Dolly!* Champion seems to fall back on this whenever he feels the need for a sure-fire number and the more he does it, the less sure the fire. Herman's music is as frustrating as usual. Without seriously comparing him to Irving Berlin, he has a similar instinct for strong, simple melodies and straight-forward (if not particularly clean) lyric writing. But Herman seems irresistibly drawn to other songs and much of this score keeps you wondering what it is reminding you of. He also included a number shamelessly like "Hello, Dolly!" ["When Mabel Comes in the Room"] and Champion was just as shameless in repeating the staging of it. Unfortunately, the total musical staging that made *Dolly!* a model of choreography-direction is nowhere to be seen. The show's feel is basically noise trying to pass for enthusiasm and is exemplified by an amplification imbalance that drowns out the singing with the knowledgeable but harsh, Broadway-cliché orchestrations of Philip J. Lang. The show's look is expense without point. The show's quality is professionalism without identity.

WALTER KERR, *TIMES*
[Headline: "*Mack & Mabel* Makes Gloomy Musical Comedy"]
I have rarely seen so much talent so dispirited as the creative souls peering through the gloom at the Majestic. There it all is. Robert Preston to play Mack Sennett, the "dumb Irishman" who was so busy inventing Keystone Kops that he forgot to tell Mabel Normand he loved her, ready to put his restless buzz saw of a voice behind the whole lumbering business and push. Bernadette Peters, pale as a silent film but topped with massed curls that half-suggest she has a nest of ravens in her hair, perfectly prepared to leap from a catwalk and ride down a scaffolding-pipe if that will help any to get things going. Gower Champion, master of the production number that builds and builds and builds, watching sequence after sequence come apart in his hands as though the world was made of matchboxes with nothing inside. And all of them turning to composer-lyricist Jerry Herman as if to say "You tell the story, we'll just sit here." Telling the story through the songs, and

the songs alone, is a profitless business for a musical comedy. In point of fact, *Mack & Mabel* hasn't got a story to begin with. Nobody knows if Mack Sennett loved Mabel Normand as much as she may have loved him, nobody knows why the two broke up, and nobody knows precisely what she had to do with the untimely-murdered director, William Desmond Taylor. (Nobody knows who killed William Desmond Taylor, either. I now think he died of inertia.) But, of course, history is unimportant where sheer entertainment is to be had, and librettist Michael Stewart could have made up a story if he'd had a mind to. Instead, he has chosen to lean on the myth of *Mack & Mabel*, let the mysteries stand, invented no emotional line of his own, and simply asked Herman to intercept things whenever anyone got near a possible scene. The evening's one solid laugh comes from that most primitive of silent clowns' discoveries: that if you're going to push a pie into a man's face it's better to have the man duck and the pie land in the face of the woman standing just beyond. A rather elementary success.

DOUGLAS WATT, *DAILY NEWS*

An amiable fool of a musical so desperately anxious to tickle our funnybones and touch our hearts that it succeeds in doing neither. I spent the evening feeling sorry for it. It's really a shame, because everything about *Mack & Mabel* is designed to please, with the unfortunate exception of the book and songs. The admirable Robert Preston is as vigorous and winning a leading man as ever, and the equally prognathic Bernadette Peters is a cute and appealing leading lady. Furthermore, Gower Champion, who has staged the entire show, has pulled out all the stops in what is, in addition, an excellently designed production [scenic design by Robin Wagner, costume design by Patricia Zipprodt]. Jerry Herman's songs, in spite of excellent orchestrations by Philip J. Lang, have a way of all sounding pretty much alike, brisk and empty. A love song, "I Won't Send Roses," isn't bad, but the welcome-back number called "When Mabel Comes in the Room" that opens the second half is embarrassingly reminiscent in design and execution of "Hello, Dolly!," this time with the honored lady riding a boom instead of descending a long flight of stairs. The truth probably is that Sennett and Miss Normand were not especially interesting people in themselves, and the emerging movie business had, as we all know, a great deal more to offer than a pie in the face.

•   •   •

The idea of a musical about Mack Sennett originated with Leonard Spigelgass and West Coast producer Ed Lester in 1971. Lester brought in Jerry Herman, who toiled a year with Spigelgass before determining the collaboration wasn't going to work. The composer then turned to Mike Stewart, who undertook the task of structuring a new book around the existing songs. Stewart brought the project to producer Joe Kipness, with whom he had a three-show deal, but their unpleasant rupture on *Seesaw* (1973) caused another change in producers. (Merrick bought out the colorful Kippy for 10% of the profits—i.e., $0—but not until a squad of underworld goons stormed into Merrick's St. James Theatre headquarters one Saturday morning, terrorized the elevator man, and slashed the furnishings. Of the *wrong* office, as it happened; they got general manager Jack Schlissel's door instead of Merrick's. Kipness was also bought out of Stewart's *I Love My Wife* [1977], the only profitable show of the trio.) With the addition of Gower Champion, the original *Dolly!* team was complete. And then the fun began. Two days into rehearsal Gower fired leading lady Marcia Rodd (from *Your Own Thing* [1968] and Neil Simon's 1969 comedy *Last of the Red Hot Lovers*). A new girl with a great voice had turned up in the just-opened Sammy Cahn song revue, *Words and Music* (1974), and Gower decided that Kelly Garrett *must* be his Mabel. It took Garrett a week and a half to get out of her show and out to Los Angeles, where the Mabel-less *Mack* was rehearsing, at which point they discovered that this girl-with-the-marvelous-voice *couldn't act*. At all. After a week of work, they threw in the towel, again. Scrounging through the list of callback rejects, they stumbled on a diamond. Bernadette Peters, Joel Grey's sister in Stewart's *George M!* (1967) and the Ruby Keeler-ish ingénue in the Off-Broadway *Dames at Sea* (1968), had already starred in not one but three musical flops: Lionel Bart's *La Strada* (1969); the 1971 revival of *On the Town*; and as Carlotta Monti, opposite Mickey Rooney's Bill Fields, in the 1971 tryout of Al Carmines's *W.C.* Whatever the ultimate fate of *Mack & Mabel*, it finally established Peters as a star. (The other title role, for that matter, had originally been cast with Merrick-veteran Jerry Orbach, from the Champion/Stewart *Carnival* [1961] and *Promises, Promises* [1968]. The actor was nudged aside before contracts were signed when Bob Preston expressed interest in the role, although Orbach got the lead in the next and final Merrick/Champion/Stewart offering, *42nd Street* [1980].) The San Diego premiére indicated that the show's rough going was going to continue. Champion, Herman, Stewart, and Merrick—Broadway kings of 1964—were each suffering through a string of failures, and as conditions worsened, panic set in. While other shows—including *Dolly!* itself—had been fixed on the road, this one wasn't going to be, for *Mack & Mabel* was intrinsically flawed in conception. What made Sennett's films work, Gower told a reporter covering the tryout, "were incredible mechanical gags—buildings falling down, horses riding through living rooms, cars going off piers. What do I have? One adorable fire engine." Gower also took an uncharacteristic swipe at his songwriter, fighting "tooth and nail" over the pesky, *Dolly!*-like "When Mabel Comes in the Room" number. ("The elevator runs a little quicker," they sing, "just as if it didn't wanna stop at another floor." This in 1923 Hollywood.) "I thought, oh, goddam it, here comes that whole thing about if the star comes back let's sing her song," said Gower. "I'll never do it again, and I've already told Jerry that." "I'm proud of it," countered the composer, "and I'm going to keep writing this kind of song until I'm 85, because that's what's missing in musical theatre." Okay, Jerry. The number stayed, and like Herman's title song for the 1969 *Dear World* was roundly slammed. Merrick did not exude confidence in the show, sensing that Gower and Jerry and Mike wouldn't be able to turn *M & M* around. Not only did he sense it, he told the press. "Sure, they did it with *Dolly!*, but I can think of other shows where they did not." Fixed up (?) and polished, *Mack* moved into the Kennedy Center for its final pre-Broadway stop. "Loaded with all the zip of a dead flounder," said Dick Coe in the *Post*. At which point Merrick, deeply immersed in the production of his big-budget 1974 film version of *The Great Gatsby*— and simultaneously undergoing an especially contentious period in his on-again, off-again war with the third Mrs. Merrick—seems to have simply lost interest in the show. *Mack & Mabel* limped into New York with abnormally minimal advertising and almost no promotion. Merrick left word to pull the plug once the advance ran out and—like

Mabel & Mack before him—headed to Hollywood. His Broadway operations slowed down to a crawl until decade's end, when he rebounded—with Gower and Mike—and returned to Broadway and *42nd Street*.

BROADWAY SCORECARD

/ PERFS: 65 / $: -

RAVE	FAVORABLE	MIXED	UNFAVORABLE	PAN
			1	5

MAGGIE FLYNN

"A New Musical"

previously titled *Beautiful Mrs. Flynn*

music and lyrics by Hugo Peretti & Luigi Creatore and George David Weiss

book by Hugo Peretti & Luigi Creatore, George David Weiss, and Morton Da Costa

based on an idea by John Flaxman, suggested by the 1863 New York Draft Riots

directed by Morton Da Costa

choreographed by Brian MacDonald

produced by John Bowab

starring Shirley Jones (Cassidy) and Jack Cassidy

with Robert Kaye, Sibyl Bowan, William James, Jennifer Darling, Peter Norman, Robert Roman, Robert Mandan, Austin Colyer, and Stanley Simmonds

opened October 23, 1968   ANTA Theatre

JOHN BOWAB
presents

SHIRLEY JACK
JONES CASSIDY

in
A New Musical
MAGGIE
FLYNN

Book, Music and Lyrics by   and
HUGO LUIGI GEORGE
PERETTI CREATORE DAVID WEISS

Book in collaboration with
MORTON DA COSTA
(Based on an idea by John Flaxman)
with
ROBERT KAYE

Settings Designed by
WILLIAM and **JEAN ECKART**

Costumes by
ROBERT LaVINE

Lighting by
THARON MUSSER

Musical Direction and Vocal Arrangements by
JOHN LESKO

Orchestrations by
PHILIP J. LANG

Dance Music Arranged by
TRUDE RITTMANN

Dances and Musical Numbers Staged by
BRIAN MACDONALD

Entire Production Directed by
MORTON DA COSTA

Original Cast Album by RCA VICTOR
Produced in association with
HARRIS ASSOCIATES, INC. & LEVIN-TOWNSEND, INC.

ANTA THEATRE
52nd Street West of Broadway
Evgs. 8:30. Mats. Wed. 2:00 & Sat. 2:30

Printed by Artcraft Litho. & Ptg. Co., Inc., New York

This cornucopious artwork contains just about everything but the race riots central to the story. Two of the eight orphans are depicted on the lower left, with (naturally) tambourines. (artwork by Jack Woolhiser)

CLIVE BARNES, *TIMES*

Whatever it is that has happened to the musical is not likely to be put right by *Maggie Flynn*, which bravely opened at the ANTA Theatre last night. It is the best musical in town since *Her First Roman* [which opened three days earlier]. Morton Da Costa directed the "entire production," and collaborated on the book, which, in turn, was based upon an idea by John Flaxman. Mr. Flaxman's idea, as I see it, was to set *The Sound of Music* [1959] played blackface against the background of the New York Draft Riots of 1863. It was a strange idea. I am very square about musicals and feel that the most important thing about them is the music. Now Mr. Peretti and Mr. Creatore, direct from their joint triumph of writing a song for Elvis Presley that not only was featured in the film *Blue Hawaii* [1961] but also sold three and a half million copies (only one of their 18 golden record hits!) even with the assistance of Mr. Weiss, who also apparently has had more hits than most of us have had hot dinners, have blooped. The music—to nearly steal a joke from Walter Kerr that I have long lusted after—is of the kind of dullness that gave ditchwater a bad name. There are a few funny lines—seven if I counted correctly. The stars of the show were likable enough—I only wish I had been seeing them in *Oklahoma!* [1943].

MARTIN GOTTFRIED, *WOMEN'S WEAR DAILY*

It's been almost two years since anything approaching a good musical opened on Broadway and right now I'd settle for an obituary set to a couple of choruses of "That's Amore." *Maggie Flynn* is a good deal more than that, though it's hardly any breakthrough in the musical theatre. But it is entertainment, it is musical, it has strong pushy performances and it sings out. There is hardly anything in it that is surprising, but its endless show-business gimmicks are grand and I think the key to that is Jack Cassidy. Cassidy is the king of show-biz—his egotism can never wilt, his brass never tarnish, and he knows it. He has never been ashamed to flaunt it, and camp be damned. He is, in the oldest and truest sense, a performer. Everything he does he struts, and so what if it is cornball? That is how this show is built, from the formula songs with their juicy, obvious harmonies to the nightmare ballet and the shameless use of cute children (they even do a chorus line)—black children, yet. *Maggie Flynn* has absolutely no sense of time, of change, of new theatre patterns. And yet it all works because the songs are singable, the music never stops, the guts never burst and, most intangibly, the thing just works. All of this is written in impossible musical theatre clichés, straight out of the early Fifties Broadway—rich ladies called "Mrs. Updike," a sliding trombone for a drunk scene, prostitutes sprawling around jail cells, tons of period costumes and scenery, and lilting, soft-shoe, irrelevant tunes. The lyrics run from "Why can't I ring the curtain down?" to "And by the way we love the whole world too." The dialogue is hardly brighter ("Don't go out any more than you have to, there's unrest in the streets"). And yet, the whole business has the confidence of Cassidy opening the show by tossing a hat fifteen feet to hook a hat rack. It is the fake, fake confidence of Broadway—I'm dead sure everyone in the show thought it was going to be a disaster—and that brass is swell with me.

WALTER KERR, *TIMES*
Everything was in perfect sync, slick as a penny whistle, colorful as the cover of a dime novel, tooled, trimmed, orderly, planned. Can you really go wrong with a number called "Mr. Clown," in which the jolly Mr. Cassidy plucks from a trunk ruffs and cuffs and ziggurat-shaped caps to plant on the heads of whores and children as they leap to a hurdy-gurdy tune? And in jail, besides? The mixture is not only exotic, it is suggested for mature and immature audiences as well. *The Sound of Music* may have done it before, but not really all that much better, or let's say all that much more proficiently. The songs are all in the right places, calculated to let you in on the repressed yearning Jones and Cassidy feel for each other (and for the whole wide lovable world), and they have the further peculiarity of sounding rather like songs, which sets them apart a bit in today's musical theatre. They're not exactly mint fresh or original, [but] they do have the virtue of setting you humming at intermission. You don't hum them, exactly; but I did find myself humming something (never could quite figure out what it was), and that's a gain. The composers are at least on the right track, whatever the caboose may look like. . . . The show makes *no* mistakes. Except that we never smile free. A free smile is the smile that happens when nobody has made a joke, when no one has asked you to smile, when the smile just comes up quietly of its own accord because you are so in accord with the caper

onstage. It's the smile that's left over when the house lights go up. Here we applaud, acknowledge, grant a kind of expert put-togetherness. And we only observe; we don't surrender. Why? Because Jones is too sleekly accomplished? Because Cassidy hasn't a glint in his eye, only power in his voice? Or because director Morton Da Costa has edited the whole business with such finesse that he has finessed the one trick he needed, the charm that melts? It feels as if it's been made by, and run through, a machine. We'd have taken a little looseness in exchange for the feeling that someone was home, really at home, tonight. That's musicals. You can't lick 'em. You've just got to pray.

◦   ◦   ◦

One day back in the summer of '63 more than a thousand New Yorkers were killed during a riot protesting the draft. No, not the Vietnam War; the Civil War, 1863. Angry White Men were enraged that they were being drafted and sent to fight, while the free blacks of the Union states were allowed to stay home. (They had many privileges, those Northern blacks, let me tell you.) The mobs, typically, saw fit to begin their attack at the colored orphanage on 5th Avenue, just below 44th Street. The kids were spirited away to safety, no doubt by some kindly schoolmarm or other. Now, there's an idea for a musical comedy! Shirley Jones and a bunch of cute kids! (including pint-sized Irene Cara and Giancarlo Esposito). Think of the theatre parties! And so, yet another hopeless *Sound of Music* spinoff. First-time producer John Bowab, who was simultaneously assembling that masterwork *The Fig Leaves Are Falling*, trotted out and signed up a trio of pop songwriters. Hugo & Luigi, as they were popularly called, were best known in the trade as record producers (including the 1962 *Little Me* cast album). George David Weiss previously served as veteran-called-in-to-supplement-novices on two other patchwork flops, the 1956 Sammy Davis-starrer *Mr. Wonderful* (where the novice was Jerry Bock) and *First Impressions*, Abe Burrows's 1959 mangle of *Pride and Prejudice*. Hugo & Luigi and Weiss were not unknown to one another, having collaborated on the not-insubstantial 1961 jukeboxer "The Lion Sleeps Tonight." *Maggie Flynn* was guided, though, by Morton Da Costa, who enjoyed four consecutive hits in the late 1950s (including *Auntie Mame* [1956] and *The Music Man* [1957], both of which he also guided to the screen). But he had more recently undergone a precipitous fall, with three massive disasters (*Saratoga*

[1959], *Hot Spot* [1963], and *Sherry!* [1967]). Da Costa was to receive only one Broadway musical assignment from 1967 until his death in 1989, and *Maggie Flynn* was it. Of course, the notion of violently fatal draft riots was ridiculously far-fetched when *Maggie Flynn* opened. But then, this was a year before Kent State.

BROADWAY SCORECARD
/ PERFS: 82 / $: -

RAVE	FAVORABLE	MIXED	UNFAVORABLE	PAN
	3		2	1

THE MAGIC SHOW

"A New Musical"

music and lyrics by Stephen Schwartz

book by Bob Randall

magic by Doug Henning

directed and choreographed by Grover Dale

produced by Edgar Lansbury, Joseph Beruh, and Ivan Reitman

with Doug Henning, Anita Morris (Dale), Dale Soules, David Ogden Stiers, Cheryl Barnes, Annie McGreevey, and Robert LuPone

opened May 28, 1974   *Cort Theatre*

CLIVE BARNES, *TIMES*

Let me point out one thing first. This review of *The Magic Show* is written under severe duress. I have a nasty feeling that if I do not give it an unadulterated rave, the star, a young magician called Doug

Henning, might turn me into a lizard, a frog or a pumpkin. If we have fewer critics around next season than we had this season, you will know why. They, poor fools, underestimated young Mr. Henning. However, honesty prevails. I cannot give it an unadulterated rave, so I will have to take my chance with an adulterated rave. Henning is terrific. He is the greatest illusionist I have ever seen and, particularly as a child, I have seen plenty. He is amazing. On the other hand the show is awful. This is a *Magic Show* where they should keep the magic and abandon the show. Do you recall those rather awful movie musicals that were based on Sonja Henie's ability to skate or Esther William's ability to swim? *The Magic Show* is like that, only immeasurably more feeble. The songs by Stephen Schwartz sounded much alike, and Bob Randall's book was not clever enough to be camp and not smart enough to be silly. Personally, I think Henning would do better as a nightclub act or heading a vaudeville bill. I would also love to see him brought in as a consultant to opera and ballet companies—let's have a few highbrow stage illusions that actually work. And there is no doubt whatsoever about his talent. I just know my children are going to love him—and even on a second time round, I still won't know how the tricks work.

MARTIN GOTTFRIED, *WOMEN'S WEAR DAILY*

Its star is not only the most terrific magician I have ever seen, but he also wears no white tie and tails and he doesn't do patter while he works. In fact, Doug Henning has long hair, wears T-shirts and jeans and looks as if he is 14 (pounds and years). The show that director-choreographer Grover Dale built around him is equally distant from vaudeville—a skeletal stage, a garish, German Expressionist look and a mainly rock score by Stephen Schwartz (who wrote *Godspell* [1971] and *Pippin* [1972]). But the main thing in the show is its tricks, and they are fantastic and incredible. Henning's floating women, his sawed-in-half women, his women rearranged in a stack of boxes so the head is in the middle and the knees beneath the feet—I just couldn't believe my eyes. The problem is that, for all the Expressionist costumes and rock music—and despite Henning's hippy look—the show is still him doing an act. The magic has not been incorporated into the show but, rather, the show is an excuse for him to do the act. Despite Henning's avoidance of the corny in his own looks; despite the artistic look that Dale tried to give the show; despite Schwartz's sometimes ambitious music, the structure of *The Magic Show* is still corny. That is because Bob Randall's book is clumsy and unimaginative, probably the worst story you could imagine for a magic show. As a result, whatever Dale tried to lay on top of it as production concept neither lies there nor is even clear. As for Schwartz's music, it is almost as disorganized—some songs rocking, some show tunes, some folky, some Andrews Sisters' camp—and the lyrics are self-consciously tricky. It is also amplified to death because, when you can listen beneath the noise, some quality is there. But the show tries too hard to make up in noise what it lacks in physical size and personnel. And still it has magic so fabulous I could watch the tricks all night.

WALTER KERR, *TIMES*

It is exactly what it says it is: an evening devoted to making levitating girls disappear, a woman tied up in a sack into a man tied up in a sack, a circus-y chorine in a cage becomes a prowling cougar in the twinkling of an unwary eye. To tell the truth, my own eye was only half unwary; I saw the chorine's legs skip away from the cage while, beneath its great red drape, two or three masked harlequins gave it a swift, distracting spin. But I didn't see the cougar get into it, and I am still lost in admiration for the beast's dexterity. In fact, I am lost in admiration for the beast. The show is the kind that parents will take children to on the pretext that they are doing the children a favor. But they go for their own fun, really, for the fun [they] remember from youthful Aprils when Sells Floto came to town, for the fun that was in them when their own bones might break but would rapidly, magically mend. And they come to have a lost promise renewed, the promise that anyone could become anything he chose provided someone would just tell him the trick. *The Magic Show* is not entirely unsullied. In an effort to gloss over what should not be glossed over—its charming and quite desirable naïveté—it has been provided with a feeble story of sorts, with gratuitous and even monotonous songs by Stephen Schwartz and with jokes about rabbits that should not be permitted to multiply (the jokes, that is to say; I don't care about the rabbits). If the star of the occasion, magician Doug Henning, were entirely serious about his business, he would promptly make the rest of the show disappear.

•   •   •

The great magic feat here was pulling a long-run hit out of a very empty hat. The diminuitive, scraggly mustachioed, bell-bottomed Doug Henning was so likable and so unpretentious that he managed to pull it off. Sawing Barbara Walters in half on the *Today Show* helped turn *The Magic Show* into an early sellout (although Henning'd have surely gotten more publicity if he hadn't put her back together again). The enterprise was also helped by the fact that producers Lansbury and Beruh also had *Godspell* in their stable. The earlier Stephen Schwartz musical, which had been running Off-Broadway since 1971, had an enormous following of happily satisfied group sales buyers—the perfect market for *The Magic Show*. In 1976 *Godspell* finally moved to Broadway, at which point *it* was peddled to *Magic Show* buyers. Quite a racket, while it lasted. Henning returned to Broadway in 1983 in the full-scale book musical/magic show *Merlin*—with Chita Rivera in support, no less, and Christian Slater, too—but some of the time you can't fool all of the fool people.

BROADWAY SCORECARD
/ PERFS: 1,859 / $: +

RAVE	FAVORABLE	MIXED	UNFAVORABLE	PAN
	2	1	2	1

MAME

"A New Musical," previously entitled *My Best Girl*

music and lyrics by Jerry Herman

book by Jerome Lawrence and Robert E. Lee (with, initially, Joshua Logan)

based on Lawrence and Lee's 1956 play *Auntie Mame,* from the 1955 memoir by Patrick Dennis

directed by Gene Saks (replacing Joshua Logan)

choreographed by Onna White

produced by (Robert) Fryer, (Lawrence) Carr, and (Joseph and Sylvia) Harris

starring Angela Lansbury

with Beatrice Arthur (Saks), Jane Connell, Willard Waterman, Frankie Michaels, Charles Braswell, and Jerry Lanning

opened May 24, 1966   *Winter Garden Theatre*

MARTIN GOTTFRIED, *WOMEN'S WEAR DAILY*

Mame is a camp *Dolly!* (1964)—a slick and shameless copy, song-for-song, dance-for-dance of Jerry Herman's earlier success, moved up from turn-of-the-century to inverted Thirties taste. As such it is a plastic shell concerned with elegance and taste, rather than having those qualities. While it looks perfectly beautiful it is without personality. It is little more than an appreciation of Thirties "sophistication," in the style of an old *New Yorker.* A series of parties, assorted jokes about martinis, a veneer of amateur blasé and the rise and fall of Mame's financial fortunes. Not so much thrown as lobbed in is Mame's nephew Patrick. [The authors], together with various designers, have hung an East Side phony dream show on this thin thread. Flooding the stage with Thirties clothes and bitchy ladies, they have managed to gather their artificial nostalgia to over-adore everything that would amuse the reasonable

Previews May 18-23, Mat. May 21
OPENS TUES. MAY 24
Matinees Wed. and Sat.

FRYER, CARR & HARRIS present

ANGELA LANSBURY
as
MAMIE
a new musical

Book by
JEROME and ROBERT
LAWRENCE E. LEE

Music and Lyrics by
JERRY HERMAN

Based on the novel "Auntie Mame" by PATRICK DENNIS
and the play by LAWRENCE and LEE

with
BEATRICE JANE
ARTHUR CONNELL

WILLARD WATERMAN
and
FRANKIE MICHAELS

Settings Designed by WILLIAM and JEAN ECKART
Costumes Designed by ROBERT MACKINTOSH
Lighting by THARON MUSSER
Musical Direction and Vocal Arrangements by DONALD PIPPIN
Orchestrations by PHILIP J. LANG
Dance Music Arranged by ROGER ADAMS
Assistant Choreographer TOM PANKO
Associate Producer JOHN BOWAB

Dances and Musical Numbers Staged by
ONNA WHITE
Directed by
GENE SAKS
Original Cast Album by Columbia Records

WINTER GARDEN

A generic Auntie Mame toots her bugle. Angela Lansbury became a major star overnight—after 22 years toiling in London, Hollywood (with three Oscar nominations), and New York. (artwork by Berta)

sensibility as being hopelessly old-fashioned and foolish. This, of course, is the essence of camp. There can be no denying that the show is absolutely beautiful. William and Jean Eckart, perhaps the most original and modern designers for the Broadway theatre, give this production a look of sheer glamour, very much like an extremely polished magazine. From start to finish, it looks like glossy, studio color photography. Robert Mackintosh's costumes are in every sense their equal. The fact is that this entire production is geared to looks—to surface—to style. When you try to dig beneath it, that surface resists like plastic. Angela Lansbury's Mame was strong and while the character's sex life is so oddly neuter, she was able to resist the dyke business that was so often implicit in the script. This sometimes became difficult since she was regularly partnered with a mannish, very Tallulah Bankhead character with whom she even sang a "Bosom Buddies" (ho-ho) song that read "I'll always be Alice Toklas/If you'll be Gertrude Stein." Following this pattern, the production was completely without a role that could be reasonably considered "male." The taste of *Mame* is entirely that of the man interested only in female things. Beatrice Arthur was very funny despite the script's inability to make her as brittle as it intended. Jane Connell was still another parody of a female and was supposed to be funny just because she was pregnant (after a while you got the distinct feeling that everybody was in drag).

STANLEY KAUFFMANN, *TIMES*
[Headline: "*Mame* is Back with a Splash"]
It opened last night, replete with lively song and dance, an exceptionally able cast, and a splendidly splashy production. Even the scenery is entertaining. This star vehicle deserves its star, and vice is very much versa. No one can be surprised to learn that Angela Lansbury is an accomplished actress, but not all of us may know that she has an adequate singing voice, can dance trimly, and can combine all these matters into musical *performance*. In short, Lansbury is a singing-dancing actress, not a singer or dancer who also acts. (Somewhat surprisingly, there is even more character color in her singing than in her spoken dialogue.) In this marathon role she has wit, poise, warmth, and a very taking coolth. The visceral test, I suppose, is whether one is jealous of little Patrick growing up with an aunt like that. I was green. It is, fundamentally, one more trip through material that most of us know

very well already; and this is not necessarily a cheery comment on the State of the Theatre or the State of Us. But, whatever those truths may be, the present truth is that *Mame* does its job well with plenty of effective sentiment, laughter and vitality. And with Miss Lansbury.

WALTER KERR, *HERALD TRIBUNE*

Mame isn't a trailblazing musical, any more than Miss Lansbury is a powerhouse personality. But we knew both of these things before we went into the Winter Garden. What is looked for in retracing such familiar material is simply a substantial and professional friendliness, and what we want from Lansbury is her own quality, which is that of the fastest girl in high school who also turned out to be nice. We get it. There is a faintly flyblown delicacy about Lansbury that hints at raffishness while keeping the tea things in order. Frankie Michaels is a child performer who is able to speak *and* sing without being given an extra twenty percent for his tender years, and the moment in which he dashes with his aunt through the home stretch of what probably started out as a tango is one that should be photographed for posterity, since posterity may need a little something to laugh about. The entertainment is further enriched by the vitamin-depleted form of Beatrice Arthur, a girl who looks like a dragon-fly in mourning and who is, as she sees it, Auntie Mame's best friend. Miss Arthur, apparently maddened by her own mascara, is a tragedy queen to set back tragedy a few million light-years, and when she is yodeling a carefully ghastly song about the man in the moon really being a girl for a 1930ish operetta the Shuberts would surely have disowned, the art of no-comment clowning reaches something of a peak. The actress is not deadpan but deadsoul. She is a splendid spook and should have steady work from now on. Which does not exactly bring us to Jerry Herman's music, but here we are, anyway. I long ago swore to myself that I would never call a song or a score derivative without specifying exactly what it was derived from; the term is simply too easy to swing around, like a dead cat. And while in this case I *could* tell you that every time I hummed a certain tune to myself I found it bleeding into "Mack the Knife," just as another bleeds with sudden slipperiness into "Bidin' My Time," I don't really want to describe the tunes that way. For one thing, they're hummable. That's a step in a new direction. And for another, they are not so much directly familiar as atmospherically stock.

NORMAN NADEL, *WORLD JOURNAL*

Whenever I saw *Auntie Mame*—which was about a dozen times—I kept expecting the company to burst into song. They finally did last night. It probably will run longer than *Auntie Mame*, which lasted for 637 performances. Clearly, a hit. Despite an abundance of delights, *Mame* offers very few surprises. In fact, it is one of the least original musicals of the past couple of seasons, and perhaps for that very reason, one of the most entertaining. Everything about it has been tested by the theatre and approved by the public over a number of years, including the story itself. Every dance step and almost every measure of music seems familiar. Even the curtain call is straight out of the book on how to build a musical without chancing anything new. In charm, in poise and certainly in vitality, Angela Lansbury is the match of any previous Mame. One of the loveliest moments in the play is derived more from the set than from anything else. Lansbury and her 10-year-old ward walk up a winding stairway as she is singing "Open a New Window." The stairway separates part way up, to become a platform from which they seat themselves in a window frame suspended as a swing. Exquisite. Composer-lyricist Jerry Herman has prepared an assortment of songs which will please hundreds of thousands, who will be charmed by their ready singability and their essential familiarity. The few of us who had hoped for something less mundane, musically, still have to admit that his score fits the show and its 1920–30s period. I like the dancing which choreographer Onna White has provided because there's a substantial amount of it (as opposed to the sketchy bits in some of the season's musicals), because it is always swift and vigorous, and because her dancers invariably look happy and seem to soar a few inches higher than in any other show. Like the music, however, it is a reworking of familiar elements and, as such, not exciting in a creative sense. The company is good-looking, as well as carefully trained. In this same way, director Gene Saks has kept *Mame* traditional, by using only those ingredients of pace and style which audiences always go for. You always know just what to expect, but the compensation is that almost everything works in *Mame*.

o   o   o

Hey—I saw *Mame*, at thirteen, and I thought it was pretty damn good. (I saw Mr. Herman's *Milk and Honey* [1961] at eight, learning quick and early just how dull and deadly a big Broadway musical could be, thank you very much.) The critics certainly gave *Mame* a hard time, presumably exacting retribution for Herman's success over at *Dolly!* I can certainly understand that, too; but *Mame* worked well on her own. Why hold it to a higher standard than, say, *Skyscraper?* (1965). Enough philosophizing. *Auntie Mame* had barely unpacked her touring trunks when producers Fryer and Carr sent her to Capezio and ordered tap shoes. Morton Da Costa, who followed the Roz Russell funfest with *The Music Man* (1957) and movie versions of both, would have seemed the obvious choice for director. But he and Fryer had in the interim essayed not one but two little horrors so bleak that his name just didn't come up (*Saratoga* [1959] and *Hot Spot* [1963]—you can look 'em up in *Opening Night on Broadway*). Who better than one of the biggest names in theatre, Josh Logan? Funny thing, though, Logan's most recent musicals had been *Mr. President* (1960) and *All American* (1962), and his future held even worse. After signing a contract and getting down to work, Logan was soon sent out to pasture (retaining a highly profitable 1.5-percent slice of the show. When *Mame* finally went on royalty waivers, Logan stubbornly refused to accept cuts). Who's good? the producers asked choreographer Onna White, who'd just received laudatory accolades for her work on *Half a Sixpence* (1965). Why don't you get the guy who took over *Sixpence*, said she. Which they did. It worked out pretty well, with the director helpfully shoehorning his missus—the deadsoul spook maddened by mascara, per Walter K.—into the show for good measure. Original Star Revival Dept.: In the wake of a spate of big-grossing original-star revivals, producer Mitch Leigh—whose Kiley-led 1977 tour of *Man of La Mancha* (1965) cleaned up across the land—tuned the grand up, signed up Angela (at the height of her Broadway fame, following the 1979 *Sweeney Todd*), and sent *Mame* off on what was meant to be a glorious and grand tour. On July 7, 1983, they opened at Philadelphia's Academy of Music to no interest, abysmal business, and managerial panic; on July 13 they canceled the rest of Philadelphia and scheduled Broadway previews on the 19th—allowing no time to advertise or promote the show. They opened, desperately, at the Gershwin on the 24th, and within five weeks the entire enterprise had collapsed and folded, sending the chastened Angela off to TV land—where she became *really* famous.

Tony Awards were won by Angela Lansbury (actress), Frankie Michaels (supporting actor), and Beatrice Arthur (supporting actress).

BROADWAY SCORECARD
/ PERFS: 1,508 / $: +

RAVE	FAVORABLE	MIXED	UNFAVORABLE	PAN
	3	2		1

MAN OF LA MANCHA

"A New Musical Play"

music by Mitch Leigh

lyrics by Joe Darion (replacing W. H. Auden and Chester Kallman)

book by Dale Wasserman

based on his 1959 teleplay *I, Don Quixote*, from the 1615 novel *Don Quixote de la Mancha* by Miguel de Cervantes

directed by Albert Marre

choreographed by Jack Cole

produced by Albert W. Selden and Hal James

starring Richard Kiley, Joan Diener, Irving Jacobson, Ray Middleton, and Robert Rounseville (sixth-billed costar Roberto Iglesias's role eliminated)

with Jon Cypher, Mimi Turque, Eleanore Knapp, and Gino Conforti

opened November 22, 1965   ANTA Washington Square Theatre

JOHN CHAPMAN, *DAILY NEWS*

An exquisite musical play—the finest and most original work in our music theatre since *Fiddler on the Roof* opened. It moves enthrallingly from an imaginative beginning to a heart-wrenching end. I saw it late last June at the Goodspeed Opera house in East Haddam, Conn., just about as it is now and with the same cast. I was impressed by it then, but expressed a lingering doubt that it could tilt with Broadway. That doubt vanished with a puff last evening—and, anyhow, the ANTA Theatre on Washington Square is not Broadway. It is just the right place for a play about a dotty old man who imagines he is a knight-errant of old, and the right place, too, for Howard Bay's simple, evocative set.

WALTER KERR, *HERALD TRIBUNE*

Mr. Marre and Mr. Cole between them have used this playhouse, and its oddities, better than those before them. I wish I did not have to seriously temper my enthusiasm. But just as a director must take responsibility for making proper use of the stage he inherits, so librettist and composer must account in full for the materials they invade. If they cannot do *Don Quixote* altogether—which they cannot—then they are honor-bound to add an ingredient that will make so much shoplifting worthwhile. There isn't much honor, I'm afraid, in reducing the Knight of La Mancha's out-of-kilter idealism to the business of having him exclaim "Ho! A young innocent approaches!" while the closest possible thing to a bellydancer writhes near. There is less honor in pursuing the already out-of-breath jest. When the dancer places Quixote's hand upon her breast instead of her heart, the old warrior remarks that "Such is her innocence she doesn't even know where her heart is." Whereupon Sancho Panza adds, "Or even how many she has." Come, come, now. Cervantes was earthy, but he was not Willie Howard. The billowing "Quest" song is highly serviceable as a finale. There is something essentially vulgar, however, about hearing the inspired madman promise to "reach for an unreachable star, beat an unbeatable foe." Cervantes' rough landscape has been planted with pretty ordinary poesies. The physical production makes everything seem possible; the diminishment of Cervantes puts everything right back in doubt.

GOODSPEED OPERA HOUSE
EAST HADDAM, CONN.

►►1965 SEASON◄◄

3 MUSICAL PLAYS
STARRING

Richard Kiley	Ray Middleton
Luba Malina	Joan Diener
Irwin Corey	Martyn Green
Robert Rounseville	Irving Jacobson

MAN OF LA MANCHA
Opening
June 24 thru July 17

Based on actual incidents in the life of Miguel de Cervantes and from his celebrated novel "Don Quixote", here is a musical which captures the warm and earthy excitement and rhythms of 16th Century Spain.

The author is Dale Wasserman, a well known screen writer whose last broadway play was ONE FLEW OVER THE CUCKOO'S NEST, starring Kirk Douglas.

Mitch Leigh, the composer, leads a double-barrelled musical life as both classical and jazz composer. Joe Darion, the lyricist, is best known for the delightful "Tubby the Tuba" and "Archy and Mehitabel".

Sean O'Casey's
PURPLE DUST
Opening
July 22 thru Aug. 7

This wild Sean O'Casey farce, happily musicalized, takes place in contemporary Ireland. Two misguided Englishmen attempt to set up housekeeping in a disintegrating and famous old Tudor Mansion. The elaborate comic situations involving them and their Irish girl friends develop into one of the merriest musicals ever seen in this country.

Mr. O'Casey wrote the lyrics and Mitch Leigh, the music.

MAN OF LA MANCHA   Aug. 9 thru Aug. 14

CHU CHEM
Opening
Aug. 19 thru Sept. 4

This is undoubtedly the first Zen-Buddhist-Hebrew musical comedy ever written. Imagine Hellzapoppin' combined with Chinese Opera and Yiddish Theater, add a touch of Brecht and Pirandello and the result is clear.

Ted Allen, whose first Broadway credit as an author was OH WHAT A LOVELY WAR, is the creator of this theatrical madness. He has written over 100 radio & TV dramas and is a frequent contributor to the New Yorker.

Lyrics were written by Jim Haines and Jack Wohl both of whom are vice presidents in charge of creative activities at two different well-known New York advertising agencies. Both have extensive television and other professional writing credits.

FOR TICKETS SEE ►

SPECIAL 15% DISCOUNT FOR ALL EMPLOYEES.

Three highly unlikely sounding summer stock tryouts. Which one do *you* think will be a hit?

NORMAN NADEL, *WORLD-TELEGRAM* **&** *SUN*
[Headline: "A Dream of A Musical"]
To reach the unreachable star—what a soaring aspiration for an inde-structible dreamer, and what a glorious summation for a bold and beau-tiful new musical! Who but Miguel de Cervantes' ridiculously noble Don Quixote could pronounce his quest in such ringing phrases—"To dream the impossible dream, to fight the unbeatable foe, to bear with unbearable sorrow, to run where the brave dare not go." Cervantes had begun *Don Quixote* as a satire on romantic literature of his day, about 360 years ago, but he went on to write a durable compendium of human folly as well as a testament to man's unquenchable spirit. It is the last which most brightly illuminates Dale Wasserman's powerful musical play, and sets it in flight toward its own lofty star. . . . Joan Diener is the most commanding sight on the stage. She is emphatically woman, a defiant hellion who sings, out of an unfathomable bitterness, "I was spawned in a ditch." Audiences might be shocked by the scene in which the girl is raped by six mule drivers, but it spares Miss Diener no more than she spares herself. Thus it goes all evening—realism aligned with romanticism, and each sharpened by the other. *Man of La Mancha* mates theatre and music with excitement and invention. In its general aspect, the show is more like Leonard Bernstein's *Candide* [1956] than it is like the conventional musical. Composer Mitch Leigh uses a split orchestra, half on each side of the stage, with arrangements which bring to mind a modern chamber ensemble rather than the usual pit band. The rhythms are essentially Spanish, though the melodies have a kind of contemporary lyricism. The recording of this score should be fasci-nating; the total play, seen and heard, is a prize.

HOWARD TAUBMAN, *TIMES*
[Headline: "Don Quixote, Singing Knight"]
Best of all is Mr. Kiley, who has never given a finer performance. He shuttles back and forth between Cervantes and Don Quixote, and the transformation always is amazingly apt. As Cervantes he is a man of spirit with a quizzical humor and a keen flexible intelligence. Shading into Quixote, he becomes the amiable visionary, childlike in his pre-tensions and oddly, touchingly gallant. His eyes take on a wild, proud, other-worldly look. His posture is preternaturally erect. His folly becomes a kind of humbling wisdom. Watch him as he and Jacobson

sit on their wooden mounts, pulled by actors wearing delicious masks of horses' heads. This is the innocent radiant knight errant ready for any derring-do. Kiley also can sing. . . . One can quibble about other aspects of *Man of La Mancha*. Mitch Leigh and Joe Darion have made every conscientious effort to integrate their songs into the texture of action and character, but their muse, though it aspires, does not always soar in the imaginative vein of Cervantes and Quixote. One could dispense with the added bit where Kiley, with arms around Jacobson and Diener, belts out a chorus in operetta style. One wishes Kiley did not mutter a banal, modern, "Yegh" in an earlier scene. Irving Jacobson is a sympathetic, gentle Sancho, but it is difficult to shake the uneasy feeling that he is a Spaniard with a Jewish accent. One could do without other reminders of show biz here and there that traduce the essential atmosphere. Yet *Man of La Mancha* rates far more plusses than minuses. Whatever concessions they have made to easy popularity, there are charm, gallantry and a delicacy of spirit in this reincarnation of Quixote.

o   o   o

A 1959 teleplay starring Lee J. Cobb, of all people, as the recalcitrant Don might not seem the logical starting place for a Broadway musical—and a smash hit, at that. But logic and art and Broadway do not sit on the same plane, and *La Mancha*—battling the demons and windmills with modesty, innocence, and luck—emerged an impossible, improbable world-beater. In 1963 Albert Selden, an ex-failed-composer-turned-failed-producer with pocketfuls of family money, effected the restoration of the long-defunct Goodspeed Opera House, a former dry-goods emporium that played theatricals upstairs, located near his Connecticut River summer home. After two seasons of miscellaneous revivals, Selden and Albee Marre (of *Kismet* [1953]) hatched an illogical plan: a summer of three new musicals, led by *La Mancha*, in rep. All to be composed by jingle writer Mitch ("Nobody Doesn't Like Sara Lee") Leigh, who had never written a musical, but neither, then, had *I, Don Quixote* author Dale Wasserman (whose only Broadway experience was the failed 1963 adaptation of *One Flew Over the Cuckoo's Nest*, produced by David Merrick and starring Kirk Douglas). And neither had poet W. H. Auden and Chester Kallman, who gave up the lyricist's chair early on in favor of Joe Darion, a small-timer with one full-scale effort—*Shinbone Alley*, the ill-advised 1957 musicalization of *archy and mehitabel*—to his credit. *La Mancha* was to be followed by a musical farce version of Sean O'Casey's *Purple Dust*, and the "Zen Buddhist-Hebrew Musical Comedy, in English" *Chu-Chem*. A cast was assembled to perform all three, the stars of one lending support in the others. Thus the principals of *Purple Dust*—Ray Middleton, leading man of *Annie Get Your Gun* (1946) and *Love Life* (1948), and Robert Rounseville, creator of the title role in *Candide* (1956)—appeared in tiny *La Mancha* roles, while Dick Kiley and director's wife Joan Diener (who'd appeared together in *Kismet*) were barely visible in the O'Casey. Now you know why *La Mancha* had a Yiddish Theatre Sancho Panza—Irving Jacobson was slated to head *Chu-Chem*. (And you should have seen him as a red-bearded, O'Casey postmaster with a Yiddish accent.) After the Goodspeed *La Mancha* showed promise and *Purple Dust* didn't, *Chu-Chem* was yanked in favor of a quick remounting of the first. (The luckless *Chu-Chem* got not one but two future lives, failing dismally both times.) *La Mancha* was booked into the ANTA Washington Square Theatre, an intriguing but out-of-the-way house erected to shelter the Repertory Theatre of Lincoln Center during construction of their Vivian Beaumont home base. Celebrated flamenco dancer Roberto Iglesias, of the *Ballet Español*, was given "also starring" billing in the initial New York ads, but did not make it through rehearsals. Flamenco music first appeared in the early nineteenth century, some 300 years after the adventures of Cervantes's Don, but why quibble? Due to the 1,100-seat capacity and union jurisdictional determinations, this was classified as Broadway; forty blocks from Shubert Alley, perhaps, but only a block and a half from (lower) Broadway. (The show eventually moved uptown to the Martin Beck in March 1968, replacing Selden and James's failed *Hallelujah, Baby!*) This impossibly out-of-the-way site did not hamper *La Mancha*; a commuter transportation strike shortly after the opening even seemed to *help* it. It also helped that the show—the twelfth of fourteen 1965 musicals—was the only decent one of the lot. The next six months brought forth only one additional better-than-terrible offering, the moderately satisfying *Sweet Charity*. But the rousing *La Mancha* would have been a hit in any season; despite some flaws in the fabric of the piece (as pointed out by the gentlemen of the press), it unquestionably worked (as pointed out by the gentlemen of the press). As for the Messrs. Leigh, Marre, Darion,

Selden, and James, fabricators of the impossible *La Mancha*: flop after flop after flop ever since. Talk about battling windmills.

Winner of the New York Drama Critics' Circle Award. In addition to winning the Tony Award for Best Musical, Tonys were won by Mitch Leigh and Joe Darion (score), Albert Marre (director), Richard Kiley (actor), and Howard Bay (scenic designer).

BROADWAY SCORECARD
/ PERFS: 2,328 / $: +

RAVE	FAVORABLE	MIXED	UNFAVORABLE	PAN
3	2	1		

MAN OF LA MANCHA

an "original star" revival of the 1965 musical play

music by Mitch Leigh

lyrics by Joe Darion

book by Dale Wasserman

based on his 1960 teleplay *I, Don Quixote*, from the 1615 novel *Don Quixote de la Mancha* by Miguel de Cervantes

"production and musical staging" by Albert Marre

original choreography by Jack Cole (unbilled)

produced by Eugene V. Wolsk (and Mitch Leigh)

starring Richard Kiley

with Emily Yancy, Tony Martinez, Ian Sullivan, Taylor Reed, Bob Wright, Chev Rodgers, Ted Forlow, Harriet Conrad, and Margret Coleman

opened September 15, 1977   Palace Theatre

MARTIN GOTTFRIED, *POST*

Man of La Mancha last night joined the growing parade of revivals coming into New York and though the musical still isn't anything to get
excited about, its success is understandable. Dale Wasserman's book
captures the heroism and projects a love of Cervantes' masterful *Don
Quixote*. Mitch Leigh's music is unusually tasteful as well as unusually
Spanish for a Broadway accustomed to the show sound. The leading
character is unique and sympathetic. This may not seem enough to have
gotten the show past 2,328 performances and into fourth place on the
all-time musicals list, especially when you think of the ones it's passed.
But the show's basic values and its mixture of idealism and romantic
tragedy evidently have an inexpensive mass appeal. Still, this revival's
greatest asset is Richard Kiley, giving the performance of his career.
Kiley originated the title role, Quixote, Knight of the Woeful
Countenance, but excellent as he was 12 years ago, he was superior last
night. A true actor-singer and good enough at both to have succeeded
at either, Kiley now brings to the role a depth and compassion perhaps
greater than in the script. His voice is still true, rich and powerful. He
is a commanding figure on stage without ever seeming possessive about
it and he is superb. Wasserman's book remains awkward in its details,
even though its spirit has much to do with the show's working. Leigh's
music (set to Joe Darion's weak lyrics) does not improve with repetition,
"The Impossible Dream" least of all. The boleros and *paso dobles* ring
less of Spain than of movie Westerns set in Spanish California, but it is
a musicianly score and the stringless guitar-woodwind-brass orchestrations are stylish. The orchestra is uncomfortably split between the boxes
on either side of the stage (to allow for a thrust platform) and this gives
a stereo effect to live music, putting things the wrong way round.

WALTER KERR, *TIMES*

I have an impossible dream, too. One is that some day, by some
alchemy, I shall come to truly like *Man of La Mancha*. Alas and alack
for high hopes. The 12-week revival that will probably find its loving
audience all over again does, in fact, have points of distinction to cling
to. The first and greatest of these is Richard Kiley's performance (and
how many times has he played the old Don by this time?), a performance richer for the aging, more touching for the ripeness. Never mind
that the Don is a fool; Kiley brushes the fool aside and makes the ide-

alist in his man most winsome. It is the naive faith of the chivalrous wayfarer that moves us, if we are inclined to be moved at all. And Kiley has, this time, a Dulcinea to match his yearnings. Emily Yancy plays the girl who was born in a ditch, and she is a thoroughly vigorous raven-haired wanton. Yet when the text requires her to soften, to ask in wistful bewilderment "What does he want of me?," she, too, is oddly endearing. Problem. Both of these successes tend to underscore what is already false in the entertainment. Librettist and composer have here labored mightily to provide Cervantes with "heart," to turn Miniver Cheevy into the noblest soul in town; irony is sacrificed to sentiment, savage satire to sweetness. Profitless daydreaming is not only given a clean bill of health; it becomes the most exalted of virtues, with the show's best-remembered song (really called "The Quest") huffing and puffing its repetitive way up the scale to drown us all in admiration for a romanticized, thumpingly reactionary, madness. The point, old-hat as it is, is hammered home: when Kiley—now playing Cervantes himself—is asked why poets are so taken with madmen, he replies "I suppose because we have so much in common." The rhetoric runs on like that, straight-faced for the most part, and whatever was once funny about a great comic novel and a great comic figure becomes deathly pale, alarmingly limp. I confess—I tell myself that it is on Cervantes's behalf—I find myself becoming irreverent, and, as I listen once again to a promise to "right the unrightable wrong," I spend my time wondering what an "unrightable wrong" could possibly be, unless it is the one done the original author.

DOUGLAS WATT, *DAILY NEWS*
[Headline: "Dream Again"]
Just as the late Zero Mostel was the definitive Tevye, the vigorous Richard Kiley is the true possessor of the title role in *Man of La Mancha*, which returned last night at the Palace in mostly excellent condition. Kiley, somewhat along the lines of Yul Brynner as the King of Siam, has grown into the role since he created it a dozen years back. He cuts a superb figure as the imprisoned Cervantes, and no one else should ever be permitted to sing the score's musical centerpiece, "The Impossible Dream." He alone can bring this war-horse, a piece so capable of producing shudders, to life. Appearing with Kiley, who is said to have hand-picked his supporting cast from the various companies he

has played with over the years, is the beautifully ripened Emily Yancy, who is both dynamic and touching in the dual role of Aldonza/ Dulcinea. Miss Yancy's contribution is of great help. Howard Bay's moody setting, lighting and costumes, which the latter collaborated on with Patton Campbell, remain perfect examples of theatre design and vital to the enterprise. But the late Jack Cole's name is missing from the program, and though his tense and individual choreography appears to have been followed in most respects, there is a slackness to the dance routines. In particular, the muleteers' dance, the rape scene modestly referred to as "The Abduction," seemed tame, though it was always merely a suggestive diversion. Even though *Man of La Mancha* left us only a half-dozen years or so ago, and has returned since, its holes already appear to grow larger. Dale Wasserman's book is serviceable enough, but Mitch Leigh's score, in spite of affecting moments, was not—never could be—equal to the profundities of *Don Quixote* that inevitably leaped at us even through this commercially distilled version. There are moments, indeed, when the musical Cervantes becomes tri- fling to the point of tedium. Joe Darion's lyrics carry out the pattern for better or worse. Eventually, there is a monotony to the continually lop- ing, flamenco-like rhythms.

•   •   •

In June 1972—less than a year after ending its 2,328-performance orig- inal run—Richard Kiley and *Man of La Mancha* played a four-month return engagement at the Vivian Beaumont and sold the place out. Composer Mitch ("What, you've only seen *Man of La Mancha* once?") Leigh and producer Gene Wolsk (general manager of Leigh's 1976 Yul Brynner debacle, *Home Sweet Homer*) determined to mount a full-scale, cross-country revival. Kiley, whose only post–Quixote musical had been the short-lived *Her First Roman* (1968), readily agreed. Emily Yancy, of the shorter-lived *1600 Pennsylvania Avenue* (1976), was cast as his lady; she'd been a "Matinee Aldonza" late in the original run. Everything was set to go when the Shuberts suddenly pulled their Boston-Philly- Chicago subscription bookings (in favor of *Chicago*; Bob Fosse, coinci- dentally, was their partner on the upcoming *Dancin'* [1978]). Rather than scrub the whole thing, the producers booked whatever houses they could—mostly out-of-the-way, cavernous barns like Chicago's Arie Crown, with room for an unseemly 4,319 patrons instead of the classy, well-located 2,085-seat Shubert. A funny thing happened, though, when *La Mancha* went on sale for its Washington break-in at the National. Ticket sales were phenomenal. Not just by Broadway standards, but by *any* standards. The box office simply could not handle the crush, and the six phone-order lines constantly rang busy. Blanching at the thought of prospective patrons with money waving in the wind being turned away, the producers set up and staffed their own phone rooms in each upcoming city, hooking up as many as *thirty* incoming lines open day and night. (But first they bought out the Nederlanders, who invested when the Shuberts dropped the show.) Before reaching town they would saturate the airwaves with their highly effective testimonial TV ad—closing with a shot from the wings of Kiley reaching the unreachable star as the audience breaks out in cheers—and watch the phone lines light up. Within a few years, credit card phone orders were the major outlet for ticket sales, welcomed by all theatre owners—especially once they learned the words "service charge." Wolsk and Leigh also discovered that those large barns were not so large, after all. The vast Arie Crown's unreachable upper reaches contained endless seats—but Kiley and the heavily aired TV commercial somehow managed to fill 'em! *La Mancha* grossed an astounding $379,168 in the week ending February 5, 1978; Broadway's biggest moneymaker, Liza in *The Act*, sold out with a measly $182,231. (The all-time high legit grosses till then had been for two other original-star-revival tours: Zero as Tevye [October 1976, $301,345] and Carol as Dolly [November 1977, $308,425]—both at the Arie Crown.) The same thing happened at other unconventionally large, booked-in-desperation auditoriums. Competing producers took one look at these grosses and decided that they, too, should follow *La Mancha*'s star. And thus began the era of the mass-marketing of the road, with even small-scale musicals regularly playing to audiences more than double the size of the standard Broadway house. So much for the intimacy of live theatre. Credit Where Credit Is Due Dept.: Choreographer Jack Cole's Estate was offered a modest half a percent royalty. They refused, insisting on more, at which point the producers rescinded the offer and removed Cole's name from the billing. Cole (1914–1974)—who first worked with Marre on *Kismet* (1953)—joined *La Mancha* after the Goodspeed tryout; Marre and Leigh contended that most of the choreography—the dancing horses and such—was pre-Cole work by Goodspeed choreographer Eddie Roll (who remained with the show as dance captain and Muleteer). Cole spent his rehearsal time on two numbers: a "black mass" dance (featuring seminude monks), intended to replace the gypsy scene; and a racy rape for Aldonza and the boys. When the latter was rejected during previews as too violent, Cole stormed out and never returned. No hard feelings, apparently, as the distinctive Cole choreographed and appeared—as the Mongol villain Lord Hoo Hah (no, I'm not making this up)—in the 1966 Marre/Leigh opus *Chu-Chem*, which folded in Philly. The Estate, apparently unaware of the extent of Cole's *La Mancha* contribution, pressed the matter, resulting in public dissemination of the facts and the end of Cole's credit on future productions.

BROADWAY SCORECARD
/ PERFS: 125 / $: +

RAVE	FAVORABLE	MIXED	UNFAVORABLE	PAN
	4	1	1	

MAN ON THE MOON

"A New Musical"

book, music, and lyrics by John Phillips

directed by Paul Morrissey

choreographer unbilled

produced by Andy Warhol in association with Richard Turley

starring Genevieve Waite (Phillips), Monique Van Vooren, and Dennis Doherty (replacing top-billed John Phillips)

with Harlan S. Foss (replacing Dennis Doherty), Eric Lang, and Mark Lawhead

opened January 29, 1975   *Little Theatre*

CLIVE BARNES, *TIMES*

The Andy Warhol Factory of International Art Artifacts has at long last turned its attention to the theatre. It was a musical, appropriately enough about bombs, called *Man on the Moon*. It is the kind of show that can leave a strong man a little numb and a little dumb. The most charitable thing that can be said for this small-scale musical, which opened to the flash of cameras and the rustle of skirts last night, would be that it was silly. After that a little bitterness could conceivably creep in. It has book, music and lyrics by John Phillips, who found fame and fortune with The Mamas and The Papas. The score is in a fairly nostalgic and eclectic vein; perhaps Phillips is hoping to start up a group called the Grandmamas and the Grandpapas. But the music was the best part of the evening. (The best part actually was the half-hour wait before the show started, when all the beautiful people were arriving in well-swept hordes. I wished I had brought my camera.) Warhol's artistic practice—if I have caught his drift aright—is to produce works of art so inept that their ineptitude becomes their value. To some, such a process may sound slightly decadent, but as it did for the man who invented bubble gum and other heroes of our better mousetrap society, it has undoubtedly proved profitable. Warhol gives every impression of believing in himself, and presumably has the bank balance to prove it, should he encounter lingering doubts. Thus for connoisseurs of the truly bad, *Man on the Moon* may be a small milestone. . . . Bring back *Via Galactica* [1972]—at least they had trampolines.

KEITHA MCLEAN, *WOMEN'S WEAR DAILY*

Since the beginnings of time, men have done foolish things for their women, but rarely in the annals of recorded history has such folly been perpetrated in the name of love—for no other rationalization is possible—as *Man on the Moon*, written by John Phillips and starring his wife, Genevieve Waite. Labeled, laughingly one must suppose, a new musical, *Moon* is quite simply excruciatingly bad. Moreover, with the inimitable directorial and production spoons of Paul Morrissey and Andy Warhol in this pot of theatrical gruel, *Moon* incorporates all the finely honed amateurism that marks everything Warhol touches. (Why he doesn't stick to painting or taking Polaroid pictures at parties is a mystery.) Attempting a positive viewpoint, however, I felt the flashing lights around the stage were terrific, as were Ms. Van Vooren's legs. And

I thought the streamer curtain—which I hoped would drop after the third of the 22 songs in four non-intermissioned scenes—did credit to set designer John Moore. When Ms. Waite isn't warbling slightly off-key, she trips around the stage with a vapid inanity surpassed only by her lack of voice and stage presence. If she refuses to stay barefoot and pregnant in the kitchen and needs a career, Phillips would do well to find her a nice little job in the local stenopool.

● ● ●

Well, now, the reviewers certainly seemed out of sorts at Mr. Warhol for rushing in where fools fear to tread. But then, if any stranger with a few spare bucks can rush in and produce a lousy musical, why not Andy Warhol? This item was initially developed by producer Michael (*Hair* [1968]) Butler and director Michael (*Seesaw* [1973]) Bennett, under the title *Space*. So there.

BROADWAY SCORECARD
/ PERFS: 5 / $: –

RAVE	FAVORABLE	MIXED	UNFAVORABLE	PAN
				6

MASS

"A Theatre Piece for Singers, Players and Dancers"

music by Leonard Bernstein

"Texts from the Liturgy of the Catholic Church"

English texts by Stephen Schwartz and Leonard Bernstein

entire production directed by Gordon Davidson; staged by Gordon Davidson and Alvin Ailey

choreographed by Alvin Ailey

produced by The John F. Kennedy Center for the Performing Arts (Roger L. Stevens and Martin Feinstein) and S. Hurok

with Alan Titus (alternating with David Cryer), the Norman Scribner Choir, The Berkshire Boy's Choir, and the Alvin Ailey American Dance Theatre

opened June 28, 1972   *Metropolitan Opera House*

DONALD HENAHAN, *TIMES*

Leonard Bernstein's *Mass* is one of those rare theatrical works that sum up their time and their own place, like it or not, and that is never a simple or useless thing to do. At last night's performance, one point quickly became obvious to one whose only previous exposure to *Mass* had been through the recording and the score: as in his *Kaddish* Symphony, Bernstein has set out to give us a strong dose of himself. He wants us to know him, and ourselves, through his work. The important artists always do that, of course; but they also go on to give us more illumination and substance than *Mass* provides. A great deal of to-do has been made of the eclecticism of *Mass*, but that is no indictment of a musical piece in this time. The question is how well the elements are blended, and to what purpose. Bernstein's score is a minor miracle of skillful mixing, mortising together folksy ballads, blues, rock, Broadway-style song and dance numbers, Lutheran chorales, plain chant and bits of 12-tone music. Orff's *Carmina Burana* [1937] makes what may be a parody appearance, *West Side Story* [1957] comes and goes, and even—for this startled listener at least—hints of *Guys and Dolls* [1950] and other lovably unpretentious shows. In spite of its somewhat dated overall sound, however, the score is not the essential problem with *Mass*. Nothing can really redeem a work whose libretto and texts are so determinedly shallow and yet at the same time so insistent that we take them seriously. Bernstein's *Mass* is unquestionably sincere in every way, but there is about it the earnestness of an interfaith conference at a freshwater university. If resistance to this kind of spiritual pabulum dooms one to be labeled a cynic, so be it. For some people, even in 1972, *Mass* may offer a delicious shiver or two in its simulated blasphemy. The Roman Catholic mass texts jostling with 20th-century Americanese gives the work a texture that unfortunately is not as interesting as it might have been if the modern lyricists had come closer to matching the older ones in any way. This deficiency soon comes to dominate *Mass*, and ultimately to make one lose patience with its theological and philosophical stances. You can't write stale lines such as "I believe in God but does God believe in me?" and expect them to carry conviction.

HARRIET JOHNSON, POST
Leonard Bernstein's *Mass* is a work of vivid contrasts, of dramatic turmoil followed, suddenly, by quiet; then more shouting, then more quiet. *Mass*, named by the composer as "A Theatre Piece for Singers, Players and Dancers," has a cast of more than 150. Its verbal base is the free use of the parts of the Catholic Mass form sung by the choir in the normal church service. It combines these words with folk and rock music, with hymns and instrumental interludes, with two onstage bands, a pit orchestra, plus sweet and bitter words by Stephen Schwartz and Bernstein. There is a drum section that is an orchestra by itself. There are singers and players who walk and talk. They act while they play and sing. The work serves up a unique set of blended materials for dramatic purpose. If nothing else, it certainly is different. No question, the work is a kaleidoscope of sounds and colors; a commentary on the contemporary scene with its conflicts among today's youth; of skepticism at the emptiness of form and ritual opposed to the reality of life minus mys-

tical opiates. In my former view I noted that *Mass* "seemed a little long and vague in its symbolism," and these qualities, ironically (despite some changes to put the action more in focus, according to musical director Maurice Peress) are more apparent than before. The total impact, to me, was less strong than at the world première. At that time there was a crude vitality which brought a like ovation from the audience. Last night the applause was generous but not spontaneously overwhelming and there were even a few mild boos. In the manicuring, and in the toning down of the text to point up the Catholic formalism and dilute the iconoclasm, we are left with a theatre piece which is too naive in its attitudes and with its music coming out as simulated rock and folk minus the rough hurly-burly intensity of the original product. As *Mass* continued, I had the persistent reaction that obvious lines were being repeated far too often. I think the work would have been stronger about half as long.

◦   ◦   ◦

The announcement came in June 1966 that Jacqueline Kennedy had commissioned Leonard Bernstein—no fee accepted—to write a piece to open the John F. Kennedy Center for the Performing Arts. (Jackie had also invited Bernstein to serve as artistic director, a post he turned down after an initial acceptance.) At the time of the assassination, Bernstein had dedicated his just-completed *Kaddish* Symphony to "the beloved memory" of Kennedy, and on a nationwide memorial telecast that weekend Bernstein had conducted Mahler's Second, known as the *Resurrection* Symphony. (He also led the fourth movement ["Adagietto"] from Mahler's Fifth at Robert F. Kennedy's funeral, presumably the only time Mahler has been heard in St. Patrick's.) Thus, one can understand why Bernstein loosely patterned the Kennedy piece after a Catholic Mass, loosely being a not inopportune descriptive. Bernstein was a well-meaning liberal in the best—and worst—sense of the word; his *Mass* was a cornucopia of social and political ideas, some hazily developed, some half-baked, and some obscured by midlife crisis. Bernstein went after religion, war, and the establishment in wildly veering style, perhaps reflecting his own mixed-up view of the world. By the time *Mass*—and the Kennedy Center Opera House—opened on September 8, 1971, the culturally nurturing America of the JFK/LBJ administrations had changed, and Bernstein—a one-time White House regular—was a radical persona non grata. (The President did not attend the dedicatory première of the Kennedy *Mass*, perhaps understandably so as Bernstein was on Nixon's enemies list.) *Mass* was praised by some critics and assailed as vulgar, sacriligious trash by others. Harold Schonberg of the *New York Times*, reporting on the Washington première, called it "a combination of superficiality and pretentiousness, and the greatest mélange of styles since the ladies' magazine recipe for steak fried in peanut butter and marshmallow sauce." The score, though—judged apart from the raw nerves and prejudices of the day— is quite extraordinary. *Mass* ranks high among Bernstein's works, just to the left of *West Side Story*.

BROADWAY SCORECARD
/ PERFS: 22 / $: –

RAVE	FAVORABLE	MIXED	UNFAVORABLE	PAN
	2		2	2

THE ME NOBODY KNOWS

"A New Musical"

music by Gary William Friedman

lyrics by Will Holt

adapted by Robert H. Livingston and Herb Schapiro; "original idea" by Herb Schapiro

based on the 1969 book, edited by Stephen M. Joseph

directed by Robert H. Livingston

choreographed by Patricia Birch

produced by Jeff Britton in association with Sagittarius Productions, Inc. (Edgar M. Bronfman and Henry S. White)

with Northern J. Calloway, Hattie Winston, Beverly Ann Bremers, Irene Cara, Gerri Dean, José Fernandez, Douglas Grant, Melanie Henderson, Kevin Lindsay, Paul Mace, Laura Michaels, and Carl Thoma

opened May 18, 1970   *Orpheum Theatre (Off-Broadway)*
transferred December 18, 1970   *Helen Hayes Theatre*

(Note: the first-night reviewers covered the show at its Orpheum Theatre première)

CLIVE BARNES, *TIMES*
[Headline: "Vivid and Honest"]
I loved it. I loved its understanding and compassion, and I loved its pain and yet also its unsentimental determination for hope. Many musicals have arrived with the tag of being characteristic of New York City attached to them like a gold medal—musicals such as *West Side Story* [1957] or even *Company* [1970]. But *The Me Nobody Knows* is New York, it is the New York nobody wants to remember. Does this sound

depressing? Perhaps, but as I left the audience was cheering, and it was not cheering gloom, but the victory of the human spirit over circumstances. For the slums these kids find themselves in may be squalid, but the kids are beautiful. And the show, assertive and passionate, reflects that beauty. There is no story—rather, it is a picture of a place and a time. Mostly the children talk and sing about being alone and trying to reach not just the world outside but also the world inside. The language is plain and blunt—the music blues-ey and attractive. The direction by Robert H. Livingston, much helped by Patricia Birch's musical staging, is as simple and as effective as the subject matter. It never loses sight of the musical's purpose. Just as in *Hair* [1968], this show is an excursion into a way of life. There is no story, but there are dozens of stories. They have a validity, a feel of truth to them. (They reminded me of those Studs Terkel documentary tape recordings of America, in their frighteningly pertinent inconsequentiality.) And they are given by the cast with just the right unblinking honesty. There are 12 of them—eight black, four white—and I enjoyed them so much that I have no wish to differentiate between them. They acted and sang from their hearts, and it was good. One last word for the media designing of Stan Goldberg. With its very clever projections always assisting Clarke Dunham's lighting, this is not only one of the most meaningful and ultimately joyful shows of the season, it is also technically one of the more advanced. *Hair* at its climax borrows from Hamlet's "What a piece of work is man." It could also stand as a motto for *The Me Nobody Knows*.

WALTER KERR, *TIMES*

Energetic, and in some part enjoyable, is a collage put together of children's school reports, songs developed from some of their phrases, and a band of youngsters (eight black, four white) who are in themselves one and all charming. It's called *The Me Nobody Knows*, and when a girl with an astonishing voice named Gerri Dean is standing like an exposed nerve throbbing out "Dream Babies," or when José Fernandez is thanking someone for paying the least bit of attention to him, the echo of life is firm and strong and evocative. The production is fast, vigorous, clean in its outlines. The evening's difficulty stems from the fact that its materials *are* by schoolchildren who are not necessarily poets. Take a paragraph at random from the collection Stephen M. Joseph has made: "I am not like all the other children. I'm different because I like to hear birds singing but I don't like to hear people shouting. It is not nice to hear people yelling or shouting in the street." Now you feel you would like that child. You wish that child well. But you do not feel that a deeply original voice has spoken. This is, indeed, the world of a 13-year-old plain and true. But two hours of plainness, and some if it is very plain ("men and women they have the power to produce, that's all I have to say"), can wear down the best will in the world. You begin to yearn beyond sincerity, beyond actuality, toward skill—conscious, patterning skill. Maybe the animation of the kids on stage will make it up to you. And, if you do go, watch them when they're in repose. Their faces are most beautiful when they're most solemn.

●   ●   ●

A liberal cry from the ghetto compiled from the poetry and prose of underprivileged schoolchildren—no matter how good—is bound to be a hard sell in the commercial theatre. Fortunately for *The Me Nobody Knows*—which *was* very good, indeed—the main Man from the *Times* loved the show, loved the message, and loved the very notion that a group of (mostly) kids speaking (mostly) honestly could be so (mostly) entertaining. The show was not universally well received—critics who did not appreciate the strongly compassionate point of view found plenty to carp about, including a childlike, semiprofessional aura. But the enthusiasm of Clive Barnes turned *The Me* into a strong Off-Broadway hit—for 208 performances, that is. Then, on November 16, 1970, Actors' Equity staged a thirty-one-day Off-Broadway strike. The word-of-mouth was strong enough to enable *The Me* to pack up and move to 46th Street, where the socially conscious musical—sandwiched between *No, No, Nanette* [1971] next door and *The Rothschilds* [1970] across the street—was able to run an additional eleven months and turn a small profit, thanks to school groups, creative discounting, and low operating costs.

BROADWAY SCORECARD
/ PERFS: 385 / $: +

RAVE	FAVORABLE	MIXED	UNFAVORABLE	PAN
I	I	I	I	2

MERRILY WE ROLL ALONG

"A New Musical Comedy"

music and lyrics by Stephen Sondheim

book by George Furth

based on the 1934 comedy *Merrily We Roll Along* by George S. Kaufman and Moss Hart

directed by Harold Prince

choreographed by Larry Fuller (replacing Ron Field)

produced by Lord (Lew) Grade, Martin Starger, Robert Fryer, and Harold Prince

starring Jim Walton (replacing James Weissenbach), Ann Morrison, and Lonny Price

with Sally Klein, Jason Alexander, and Terry Finn

opened November 16, 1981   Alvin Theatre

CLIVE BARNES, *POST*

The word of mouth on the latest Stephen Sondheim musical, *Merrily We Roll Along*, which opened last night, was so bad that all the words seemed dirty and the mouth was twisted in a permanent sneer. Unquestionably, the show was beset with troubles, but in my opinion it has equally unquestionably triumphed—at least it should as long as people distinguish between what they are actually seeing on stage and what they heard about the show during previews. Probably most composers would have used the time-span to have introduced pastiches of music consonant with the passing years. Sondheim will have none of this. He strictly maintains that rhythmic and acerbic musical profile, so appropriate for the terseness of his dry and wry lyrics, he established in

Company [1970] and *Follies* [1971]. All three works could have been composed by no one else. One difficulty the production did not solve to my entire satisfaction was that of the cast and its aging. From beginning to end, through this entire backward gauntlet race of a Silver Jubilee, the age of the cast scarcely varied. If Prince was to blame for this—and presumably he was—the rest of his work is credit all the way. Aided by the unobtrusively brilliant choreography by Larry Fuller, which always manages to keep out of the way of the actors' feet, Prince keeps the show whirling like confetti in the wind, stopping only for dramatic points and major songs which are punched in with authoritative zest. The style of the show is also much assisted by Eugene Lee's construc- tor set setting, Judith Dolan's costumes (I loved the conceit of sweat- shirts emblazoned with the function of the wearer) and the resourceful lighting by David Hersey. Another work from Sondheim, Prince & Co. Whatever you may have heard about it—go and see it for yourselves. It is far too good a musical to be judged by those twin kangaroo courts of word of mouth and critical consensus. It is the story of success, the complexities of compromise, and life lived amid quicksands. It also has that surging Sondheim sound that is New York set to music.

WALTER KERR, *TIMES*
[Headline: "A Libretto Has To Face the Music"]
I suppose the question most frequently asked around town these days is why Prince and Sondheim should have risked trying to fashion a musi- cal out of *Merrily We Roll Along* when two such able-bodied craftsmen as Kaufman and Hart had such trouble with the material when they did it as a straight play. In effect, Prince and Sondheim were starting out with a known quantity: a weak book. I think they picked it because it was precisely what they wanted to do, precisely what they had been doing for most of their distinguished, if not always rewarding, collabo- ration. *Merrily* offered them the one thing they seem determined to sell: disenchantment. *Company* was a technically fascinating musical devoted to exploring total disenchantment in marriage, climaxed by the hero's now utterly inexplicable decision to marry. *Follies*, heralded by a poster displaying a disastrous crack in the facade of a theatre, examined the death of enchantment in marriage and in the theatre both. Of *Pacific Overtures* [1976], I think we can say that the Japanese were duly

disenchanted with their American guests. And we know about *Sweeney Todd* [1979], with its imposed Brechtian schema, "Man Eats Man." The worm in the apple, the blight on the rose, the fingernail in the tasty meat pie. And here, in *Merrily*, were the worm and the blight and the fingernail ready-made. For here is a man, whatever his talents may be or have been, who has Sold Out. Compromise, the sellout, loss of integrity—these are not so much fighting words to Prince and Sondheim as they are creative words, words that help them choose their materials, words that drive them to work. There is nothing wrong with the choice. It's not our business to tell creative men what to create so long as it's got a whiff of life deep inside it. But the insistence on a single theme, a single attitude, is becoming monotonous. The pair may have been at this particular kind of iconoclastic work for so long that they have begun to take their theme for granted. Taking it for granted, they are neglecting to dramatize it. No need to go back to the sweet continental melancholia of *A Little Night Music* [1973]. Just a need, I suspect, for the frequent collaborators to stop parroting themselves and take fresh stock of their imaginative energies. They are much too innovative to allow themselves to become so predictable.

FRANK RICH, *TIMES*

As we all should probably have learned by now, to be a Stephen Sondheim fan is to have one's heart broken at regular intervals. Usually the heartbreak comes from Sondheim's songs—for his music can tear through us with an emotional force as moving as Gershwin's. And sometimes the pain is compounded by another factor—for some of Sondheim's most powerful work turns up in shows (*Anyone Can Whistle* [1964], *Pacific Overtures*) that fail. Suffice it to say that both kinds of pain are abundant in *Merrily We Roll Along*. Sondheim has given this evening a half-dozen songs that are crushing and beautiful—that soar and linger and hurt. But the show that contains them is a shambles. We keep waiting for some insight into these people, but all we get is fatuous attitudinizing about how ambition, success and money always lead to rack and ruin. George Furth's one-line zingers about showbiz, laced with unearned nastiness, are as facile as those he brought to *The Act* [1977]. He defines the show's principal female character, an alcoholic writer, by giving her labored retreads of the wisecracks he wrote for

Elaine Stritch in his book for *Company*. Meanwhile, the emotional basis of the friendship between the two heroes, a composer and a lyricist—or between them and the heroine—is never established at all. We're just told, repeatedly, that they're lifelong friends. Perhaps the libretto's most unfortunate aspect, however, is its similarity to James Goldman's far fuller one for *Follies*. That 1971 musical also gave us bitter, middle-aged friends, disappointed in love and success, who reunite at a showbiz party, then steadily move back through time until they become the idealistic kids they once were. Forced to contemplate the esthetic gap that separates these two like-minded shows, we see that not only the characters are rolling backward this time out. *Follies* had everything the new version does not—most notably a theatrical metaphor that united all its elements, from its production design and staging and choreography (by Michael Bennett) to its score. [In the penultimate number,] an ironic, idealistic anthem titled "Our Time," Sondheim's searing songwriting voice breaks through to address, as no one else here does, the show's poignant theme of wasted lives. But what's really being wasted here is Sondheim's talent. And that's why we watch *Merrily We Roll Along* with an ever-mounting—and finally upsetting—sense of regret.

DOUGLAS WATT, *DAILY NEWS*
[Headline: "*Merrily We Roll Along* Hits Every Bump on the Road"]
I'm afraid the news this morning is glum. *Merrily We Roll Along*, the new Stephen Sondheim musical, is a dud. Generally speaking (though *Oklahoma!* [1943] is a notable exception to the rule), a weak play is a poor source for a musical, and the triteness that afflicted Kaufman and Hart's ambitious and unwieldy *Merrily We Roll Along* carries over into the musical version. Like the original, George Furth's book moves backward in time over a span of 25 years to show us how success can produce failure, but the story has been updated, the careers altered, and the cast, with a single exception, is made up of youthful unknowns. Sondheim's inspiration is at a remarkably low ebb this time out. The title number ironically rolls along between scenes, sometimes there are faint echoes of *Company*, and it would be unthinkable for Sondheim not to come up with at least one sound ballad, as in "Good Thing Going." But the score is for the most part pallid, and even the unfailing cleverness we have come to expect of his rhyme structure is held in check to erupt at times with such

questionable constructions as "I'll get Leontyne Price to sing / a Medley from *Meistersinger*." But then what on earth could a writer of Sondheim's attainments do with such a book, one in which Furth delivers hotsy-totsy observations on the order of "She's going to hell in a handcart"? The production looks as though it cost all of $28. The players (though, of course, there are costume changes and adornments) mostly wear T-shirts identifying themselves as The Producer, The Secretary, The Lawyer, The Third Mrs. Shepard, and so on. And Eugene Lee's flexible, skeletal stage setting is mainly made up of pipes, ladders, and steps on a revolving central unit. *Merrily We Roll Along* is kid stuff in more than one sense, and a severe letdown for at least one Sondheim admirer.

◦   ◦   ◦

The Prince-Sondheim collaboration, which started in earnest eleven years earlier with *Company*, merrily rolled along until hitting a potholefull of mud. One of the most enervating things about assembling a new musical is that you never do know precisely what you have until you get onstage, in the theatre. When things don't work, panic can set in. On *Merrily*, our friends discovered—to their dismay—that *nothing* worked. But I mean nothing. It is not enough, perhaps, to come up with a generic idea—let's do a show about kids—and then cast about for a vessel to contain it. Prince found said vessel in the old Kaufman and Hart play, which he remembered from his youth (he had read but presumably not seen it, as it opened and closed when he was six). To Sondheim it might have looked like a chance to work out the problems encountered by mentor Oscar Hammerstein in the not-dissimilar *Allegro* (1947), on which the composer-in-training served as teenaged gofer. Whatever their reasons for doing it, the fact remained that the Kaufman and Hart piece was a flawed and not-very-good play notable mostly for its backwards motion, staggeringly innovative in 1934 but merely old hat forty-seven years later. Our friends were, like their leading characters, "Old Friends." *Merrily* begins, chronologically speaking, in 1957—the same year that Sondheim broke through with *West Side Story*, produced by Prince, when young friends on the threshold could indeed stand on a tenement rooftop, gaze into the future, and sing it's "Our Time." *Merrily* is not autobiographical, of course; composer Franklin Shepard sells out his talent and takes the easy way, which is something you could

most assuredly *not* say of Sondheim. Joining the pair were Old Friends
George Furth, who had scripted their groundbreaking *Company*, and
choreographer Ron Field, of Prince's *Cabaret* (1966) and *Zorbá* (1968).
Field's presence was curious. He'd directed all his shows since the hit
Applause (1970); they *had* all failed, though. ("I didn't feel I listened
enough [to Prince] the first time," Field explained.) *Merrily* was the
sort of show you close, with relief, on the road. Except they weren't on
the road, they were in town at *Company's* former habitat, the Alvin.
(Jimmy Nederlander tossed out *Annie* [1977], which he coproduced, to
make way for *Merrily*; the theatre remained hitless and virtually empty
for eighteen months while the orphaned tuner trudged from the Alvin
to the ANTA to the O'Neill to the Uris—all within twelve weeks!) So,
what do you do when panic hits? You throw out the costumes—a big
help, that, with the last minute scramble resulting in those curious, subtitled sweatshirts. During the course of the fifty-two-performance preview period they fired Old Friend Field, who had been bad-mouthing
the show. ("How good could it be?" said he to his former assistant
Michael [*Company*] Bennett. "It's *still* backwards.") Larry Fuller, of *On
the Twentieth Century* (1978) and *Sweeney Todd* (1979)—and Bennett's
one-time roommate—came in to "help." Also canned was the leading
man, a college boy who wandered into Prince's office looking for a
backstage job. He was replaced by the more seasoned Jim Walton (of
Perfectly Frank [1980]); at the same time they corrupted the show's all-
youth cast by adding middle-aged Geoffrey Horne as Franklin Shepard
at forty-three. (In much the same manner and circumstance, they desperately threw four women into the all-male Kabuki-style *Pacific
Overtures* at the last minute. Not that *that* helped any.) The lack of clear
intent was compounded by the bafflingly mundane physical production
of jungle gyms and those sweatshirts, looking as if the creators—unable
to come up with a good idea—settled on whatever came to hand (and
as if they sorely missed Boris Aronson, who died November 16, 1980,
at the age of eighty). Sondheim's score, while not up to some of his
other work, was still way above the caliber of the competition. But the
songs didn't really work in context; even the *context* didn't work in context. Walter Kerr opined that Sondheim and Prince's "insistence on a
single theme, a single attitude, is becoming monotonous," urging that
they "stop parroting themselves and take fresh stock of their imagina-

tive energies." The *Merrily* debacle did, for better or worse, wrench Sondheim and Prince apart. The men who brought us *Company*, *Follies*, *Night Music*, *Pacific Overtures*, and *Sweeney* retained their Old Friendship but haven't worked together since.

BROADWAY SCORECARD
/ PERFS: 16 / $: –

RAVE	FAVORABLE	MIXED	UNFAVORABLE	PAN
			1	5

MINNIE'S BOYS

"A Rollicking New Marx Brothers Musical"

music by Larry Grossman

lyrics by Hal Hackady

book by Arthur Marx and Robert Fisher (replacing Burt Shevelove, who replaced David Steinberg)

based on the lives of the Marx Brothers

"production consultant: Groucho Marx"

directed by Stanley Prager (replacing Lawrence Kornfeld)

choreographed by Marc Breaux (replacing Patricia Birch)

produced by Arthur Whitelaw, Max Brown, and Byron Goldman

starring Shelley Winters

with Arny Freeman, Mort Marshall, Julie Kurnitz, Roland Winters, Lewis J. Stadlen, Daniel Fortus, Irwin Pearl, Alvin Kupperman, Gary Raucher, and Richard B. Shull

opened March 26, 1970   Imperial Theatre

ARTHUR WHITELAW
MAX J. BROWN   BYRON GOLDMAN
present

SHELLEY WINTERS

in

MINNIE'S BOYS

A NEW MUSICAL
(BASED UPON THE LIVES OF THE MARX BROTHERS)

Book by
ARTHUR MARX and ROBERT FISHER

Music by
LARRY GROSSMAN

Lyrics by
HAL HACKADY

Production Consultant
GROUCHO MARX

Settings Designed by
PETER WEXLER

Costumes Designed by
DONALD BROOKS

Lighting Designed by
JULES FISHER

Musical Direction and
Vocal Arrangements by
JOHN BERKMAN

Orchestrations by
RALPH BURNS

Dance Arrangements and
Incidental Music by
MARVIN HAMLISCH

Music Publisher
TOMMY VALANDO
(Metromedia Music, Inc.)

Associate Producer
PETER N. GRAD

Choreography by
PATRICIA BIRCH

Directed by
LAWRENCE KORNFELD

Okay, but which one is Shelley Winters? "I'm the production consultant," said Groucho. "That means they give me some money." Preliminary credits. (artwork by David Byrd/Resta)

CLIVE BARNES, *TIMES*

Minnie's Boys is one of those musicals that positively flirt with success. It has a couple of decent enough numbers and a certain kind of show business vitality, but it lacks a genuine story. The show at its best has you looking back fondly upon the old movies. Padding out the story of down-on-their-luck vaudeville troupers making good is the musical score by Larry Grossman and the lyrics by Hal Hackady. It would probably be unfair to characterize the music as gross and hack, but it certainly never rises to any very considerable heights. Shelley Winters as Minnie Marx looks to be somewhat in search of a part to play. She is clearly an actress who has seen better things and appears determined that the audience shall recognize that fact. Her function is to provide the play with a star name, and in the circumstances it is an ungrateful job. The boys playing the Marx Brothers have all the fun, and the boy playing Groucho, Lewis J. Stadlen, is remarkably good. Whether he has any skills other than playing Groucho Marx I hesitate to say, but as Groucho Marx he reveals a whole bundle of talent. The walk, the talk, the sneer, the leer, everything from the rasp in the throat to the crick in the back, seem perfect. Stadlen also has Marx's sumptuous insolence—his gentle art of the unaimed and therefore unanswerable insult, a manic humor full of surrealistic destruction. The other exceptional performance came from Julie Kurnitz as a landlady [patterned after] Margaret Dumont, that grand and noble lady of high moral principles and bust who was such an integral part of Groucho's comic scene. There was one encounter between Stadlen and Kurnitz that was pure and vintage Marx. Yes, there was a lot to like in the show. But they are small things rather than big things. At the end Groucho himself joined the cast up onstage. He said a few sweet and kind words—including the generous suggestion that Stadlen was more talented than he was himself. In a sense he is probably right but I wonder whether anyone is ever going to impersonate Stadlen, who is only a very fine actor. Mr. Marx himself is a way of life—and it is a way that *Minnie's Boys* can only reflect and hint at.

MARTIN GOTTFRIED, *WOMEN'S WEAR DAILY*

Minnie's Boys stumbled its (their?) way into the Imperial Theatre last night, pinning all hope on the reputation of the Marx Brothers and the idea of *Gypsy* [1959]. The Marx Brothers, in their time a great comedy act, have since become legendary—symbolic of intellectual anarchy to the old, symbolic of political anarchy to the young (and oversymbolized altogether). *Minnie's Boys*, in its decrepit, hollow, unimaginative attempt to borrow some of their life, is a shabby pretender to such show business vitality. Arthur Marx and Robert Fisher have tried to write a musical about Mr. Marx's grandmother and her brood-hen transformation of four sons into the Marx Brothers. They didn't try very hard and succeeded even less. The main character is Minnie, their mother. Minnie doesn't seem especially interested in her husband Sam, and he doesn't seem particularly interesting since the script gives him five or six lines, mostly cues for (I think) jokes. Minnie has a great deal more to say. I know that because Shelley Winters moved her mouth a lot (a lot more than her body). Miss Winters has the presence of a vacuum cleaner, and seems to suck in rather than let out any performing. In fact, I would characterize her performance as being more of a spectator than a participant if it weren't that she seemed as unaware of what everyone else was saying as she was of her own lines. She is a terribly insecure performer—too insecure to star in a musical. *Minnie's Boys* isn't a musical and it isn't a play with songs. It has very little story, no complications or suspense, and less energy. Donald Brooks designed wonderful, funny, period costumes and that's about all that could be appreciated in this horrendous waste of money.

WALTER KERR, *TIMES*

The crazy fools did the hardest thing right. The hardest thing, of course, was to offer us Marx Brothers—any age, any weight—who wouldn't offend our memories, outraging the love that lingers in all loyal hearts. I have gone my long life never seeing an acceptable imitation of any Marx brother. Where *Minnie's Boys* was smart, unbelievably bright really, was in starting them all out in birch-bark canoes, sans wigs, sans mustaches, sans tricks. There must have been a strong temptation to underscore early, to plug for recognition instantly, to borrow their best bits in a hurry in order to get going, to *press*. What they've done, instead, is to let the mannerisms grow casually, almost absentmindedly, even to the point where for quite a while you feel they may have forgotten a few. Thus it's easy to meet Groucho while he's still

leaning against a portal, a couldn't-care-less kid in unaccented spectacles, nose in a book. When he turns toward whatever melee is currently
erupting about him to toss off a one-liner, the one-liner is a baby
Groucho-ism all right, but you don't feel that this mild family icono-
clast imagines there's any money in it yet. He thinks in quick negations,
but they haven't begun to expand into world-destroying sassiness.
Because Lewis J. Stadlen, a performer of intelligence and even instinct,
is so easy for so long about not duplicating Groucho, you are ready for
him at final take-off—a tango with a Margaret Dumont sort of landlady in which he literally leaves the ground, returning to it splayed. The
wig is never put on Harpo until the last two minutes of playing time.
And, somehow, Daniel Fortus is more Harpo without it. Playing an
ordinary kid (who can talk) he only teases us, at first, with an up-and-
down, then right-and-left, then repeat-both, head shake that is utterly
flawless imitation—but only of a detail. The shy, sweet smile crops up
as another detail later, and straight. It isn't until deep in the second act
that he unobtrusively slips his knee into an astonished E. F. Albee's
hand. The whole thing is a sneak attack. You have to put the pieces
together yourself to get the ultimate image, which is exactly what you
are prepared to do—and so thankful to the players for not having tried
to beat you to it.

◦   ◦   ◦

"Nobody fires the producers," commented *Variety* as they essayed the
comings and goings on the week's two musicals, *Minnie's Boys* and *Look
to the Lilies*. The producers in *Minnie's* case were Arthur Whitelaw,
who had two highly successful hits running at the time—the comedy
Butterflies Are Free [1969] and the Off-Broadway revue *You're a Good
Man, Charlie Brown* [1967]—and Max Brown and Byron Goldman,
two of David Merrick's original backers looking to get billing of their
own. (Max and Byron were the largest *Gypsy* [1959] angels, as it happens, with an 18-percent stake between them.) But *Minnie's Boys* was
ill-conceived, with Mama Minnie proving less formidable than
Madam Rose. Shelley Winters wasn't up to Merman or Lansbury,
either. The producers opted to eschew an expensive out-of-town tryout for an extended preview period—sixty-four of them, two months'
worth—making their travails all too visible to potential ticket buyers.

But rather than crying over spilt Borscht, let's hear from Minnie's one surviving Boy: "I'm the production consultant. That means they give me some money. I'm the guy who's supposed to holler if anything stinks; I'm keeping quiet." Asked for his opinion on casting, Groucho commented, "I haven't fished in years." And when faced with caustic early word of mouth, the producers slip-sheeted a "Letter from Groucho" into the *Playbill*: "Imagine tonight you are Philadelphians seeing our show in its try-out period. If it has a few rough spots, we feel you'll be willing to overlook them out of gratitude for not having to live in Philadelphia." One night at Sardi's someone pointed out Bock and Harnick (who were having their own troubles with five sons in two acts). "See those guys? They wrote *The Rothschilds*." Quoth the Groucho, "Did they write back?"

BROADWAY SCORECARD
/ PERFS: 76 / $: −

RAVE	FAVORABLE	MIXED	UNFAVORABLE	PAN
	2	1	2	1

MOLLY

"The New Broadway Musical"

music by Jerry Livingston

lyrics by Leonard Adelson and Mack David

additional music and lyrics by Norman L. Martin (uncredited)

book by Louis Garfinkle and Leonard Adelson (doctored by Murray Schisgal)

based on characters from the radio and TV series *The Goldbergs* (1929–1955) by Gertrude Berg

directed by Alan Arkin (replacing Paul Aaron)

choreographed by Grover Dale (replacing Bert Michaels)

produced by Don Saxon, Don Kaufman, and George Daley in association with Complex IV (Larry Spellman)

starring Kay(e) Ballard

with Swen Swenson, Eli Mintz, Lee Wallace, Daniel Fortus, Lisa Rochelle, Connie Day (replacing Patricia Gosling [Michaels]), and Eddie Phillips

opened November 1, 1973   Alvin Theatre

CLIVE BARNES, *TIMES*

Kay Ballard strode onstage last night to receive a standing ovation. She grinned at the audience with what looked like a mixture of relief and gratitude. She had been Molly in the new musical *Molly*, and not even a White House electronics expert could have worked harder [ref. Nixon's Watergate tapes]. The musical has been based on characters from the radio and TV serial *The Goldbergs*. *Molly* was written (apparently with a little help from some unnamed friends) by Louis Garfinkle and Leonard Adelson. Adelson also helped out on the lyrics, together with Mack David. The music is by Jerry Livingston—once responsible

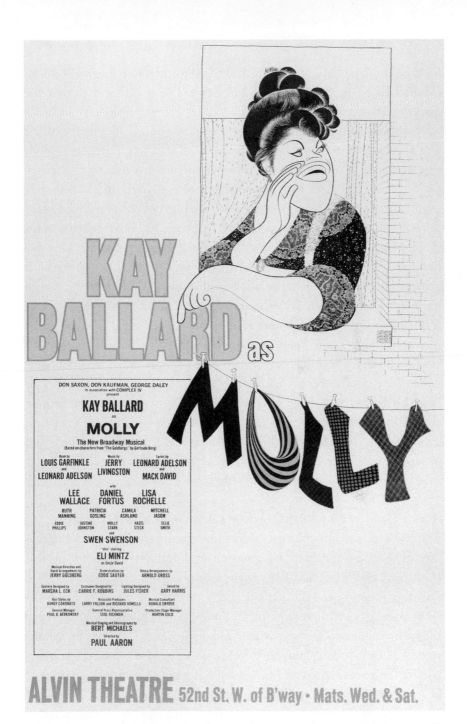

DON SAXON, DON KAUFMAN, GEORGE DALEY
in association with COMPLEX IV
present

KAY BALLARD
as
MOLLY

The New Broadway Musical
(Based on characters from "The Goldbergs" by Gertrude Berg)

Book by   Music by   Lyrics by
LOUIS GARFINKLE   **JERRY**   **LEONARD ADELSON**
and   **LIVINGSTON**   and
LEONARD ADELSON   **MACK DAVID**

with
LEE   DANIEL   LISA
WALLACE   FORTUS   ROCHELLE

RUTH   PATRICIA   CAMILA   MITCHELL
MANNING   GOSLING   ASHLAND   JASON

EDDIE   JUSTINE   MOLLY   HAZEL   ELLIE
PHILLIPS   JOHNSTON   STARK   STECK   SMITH
and
SWEN SWENSON

"also" starring
ELI MINTZ
as Uncle David

Musical Direction and
Vocal Arrangements by   Orchestrations by   Dance Arrangements by
JERRY GOLDBERG   **EDDIE SAUTER**   **ARNOLD GROSS**

Scenery Designed by   Costumes Designed by   Lighting Designed by   Sound by
MARSHA L. ECK   **CARRIE F. ROBBINS**   **JULES FISHER**   **GARY HARRIS**

Hair Styles by   Associate Producers   Musical Consultant
RANDY CORONATO   **LARRY FALLON and RICHARD VONELLA**   **RONALD SNYDER**

General Manager   General Press Representative   Production Stage Manager
PAUL B. BERKOWSKY **SAUL RICHMAN**   **MARTIN GOLD**

Musical Staging and Choreography by
BERT MICHAELS

Directed by
PAUL AARON

KAY BALLARD as **MOLLY**

ALVIN THEATRE 52nd St. W. of B'way · Mats. Wed. & Sat.

"Yoo-hoo, is this a stinker," Kay (a.k.a. Kaye) Ballard seems to be saying. Or, to quote Doug Watt, "*Molly* has the unfortunate look of a warmed-over corpse." Preliminary credits. (artwork by Al Hirschfeld)

for the immortal "Mairzy Doats" and the slightly lesser-known "Bibbidi Bobbidi Boo." So much for the bad news. The good news is that the director Alan Arkin and the choreographer Grover Dale have lashed a talented cast into giving a basically mediocre show a semblance of life and a chance for survival. Of course, it is difficult to put up the essence of a serial in a brief evening, and obviously impossible to capture in depth characters that had presumably been lovingly developed over months and years. This, however, does not prevent the present production's being so thin that its book would perhaps be better called a magazine. Molly's husband, Jake, is a cutter in the garment district. One day he loses his job. Should be move to California where his brother Max grows grapefruits? To say the book is disjointed would make it sound more articulate than it is. What is one to do with a book that unaccountably takes us to a Chinese restaurant on the Grand Concourse, or has its heroine surprisingly exchanging burial plots for remnants of cloth? The music is at its best when it is at its most derivative, but there is one very good song for Molly ["I See a Man," music and lyrics by Norman L. Martin]. I am told that Miss Berg was a quiet performer, and Miss Ballard is loud. But she is also intensely lovable and has a personality as big as a house. All in all, Arkin and the various writers and producers have been blessed with their cast. [They] are really characters in search of a musical that never quite turns up.

MARTIN GOTTFRIED, *WOMEN'S WEAR DAILY*

Molly is a mess—unamusing, untouching, uninteresting and unnecessary. It is utterly without imagination or originality, shabbily professional in a past tense and Broadway businesslike in only the most cynical way. Existing only to exploit the popularity of *The Goldbergs*, the show never grasps the reason for that popularity which, of course, lay in the spirit of Gerrtude Berg, who created the series. Where she understood the beauty and humanity in Jewishness, *Molly* doesn't even feel Jewish. Unless the Goldberg family's problems and solutions are treated in an imaginative, elliptical way, a musical based on them is doomed to be sketchy and episodic, cued for songs and dances. Unfortunately, those attracted to the idea of musicalizing this material are not likely to create imaginative, elliptical theatre structures, because the show is an inherently commercial idea. And such ideas do not appeal to original-theatre people. The production is primitively professional and thoroughly spiritless. Louis Garfinkle and the late Leonard Adelson are credited with a book that Ms. Berg would doubtless have rejected out of hand for an ordinary weekly installment. Jerry Livingston's musical score, hardly reflective of the milieu or the period (the Depression), is merely all-purpose, nondescript, dated but periodless Broadway. Livingston can write a ballad (and did, a lovely one ["In Your Eyes"] sung in a beautiful tenor by Daniel Fortus) but he has not written theatre music, and what he did write may well be too anonymous to be even called music. As for Kay Ballard's Molly, she made the least of an almost impossible job. It is possible for a non-Jewish actor to convincingly play a very Jewish character, but it is as challenging as a white actor convincingly playing a black character or vice versa. Ballard is as believably Jewish as Richard Nixon is, well, believably anything. Eli Mintz is here as he was in the *Goldbergs* series, serving as a brutal reminder of what the original was—something that the producers of the show don't seem to have thought much about. What they did think about, it seems to me, is Jewish customers to drool at *Molly* like Pavlovian dogs.

WALTER KERR, *TIMES*

Ballard is a fine, essentially stylish, performer, make no mistake about that. But it's not style you want here, it's the rock of ages with a soundtrack. What's a sophisticate, a belter of songs, doing dressed up in apron and polka-dots, pretending to parade the Grand Concourse? Surrounded as she is by performers whose Yiddish after-tones flow freely—Eli Mintz from the radio show, looking like a stand-up turtle wearing spectacles—even her accent seems to have no permanent address, no chance of dictating terms to the conquered. Add to this the fact that the librettists haven't bothered to define or even establish the character she is *supposed* to be playing until the 12th scene of 14 and you may begin to grasp the muddle that *Molly* has got itself into. At long last Ballard is given a chance to announce that hereafter she will cease being Miss Fixit, will "give up the business of minding everybody else's business." We react with surprise; it hadn't quite occurred to us that *that* was what she's been up to during all those songs about cemeteries, those out-of-period maxixes in Chinese restaurants (the period is mid-

Depression), those rooftop fandangos celebrating the fact that an otherwise unidentified Irishman [veteran specialty dancer Eddie Phillips]
has at last got a job. The dancing is either irrelevant or undesigned—
even the normally agile Swen Swenson seems to follow a shapeless leap
to the right by a still-in-search leap to the left—and the amount of time
we spend looking at the spinach-and-tomato wallpaper of the Goldberg
living room makes us wonder whether *Molly*, as a piece of material,
offered the stage very many of its freedoms in the first place. . . . Let's
say that we've all lost the battle against body-mikes. But if technology
has won the day, shouldn't it be good technology? I mean, shouldn't
there be an engineer around somewhere? At the Alvin, all of the voices
are pitched to shrill tenor, as though every parakeet in the Bronx had
skipped its cage and were holding congress in the backyard. I really
worried about that boy who wanted to marry an older girl. His voice
seemed to begin somewhere along about high-C, while hers—because
she was taller, I guess—came out a substantial C-plus. If they'd ever
married and had children they'd have given birth to nothing but penny-
whistles.

DOUGLAS WATT, *DAILY NEWS*
The luck of *The Goldbergs* has finally run out. And with songs, yet. Now
you may not have to be Jewish to enjoy *The Goldbergs*, but you've got to
be Gertrude Berg to play Molly, a part as closely associated with the
actress-writer as Amos was to Andy. Kay Ballard, a resourceful comedienne and a talented singer, tries her level best to carry it off, but she
simply can't. Just about all *Molly* has to offer is a fast-stepping, second-
act opener set in a Chinese restaurant on the Grand Concourse. *Molly*
has the unfortunate look of a warmed-over corpse.

◦　　◦　　◦

Composer Jerry Livingston—not to be confused with Jay Livingston, of
Livingston and Evans—coauthored the 1943 hit "Mairzy Doats," making him an eminently suitable choice to score this Bronx-based opus.
Lyricist-librettist Adelson died before *Molly* did; replacement lyricist
Mack David, brother to Hal of *Promises, Promises* (1968), was best
known as the author of "Hello, Dolly!" 'Scuse me, that's "Sunflower,"
which only *sounds* like "Hello, Dolly!" (Mack wrote it back in 1948.)

With such a stellar lineup in the creative department, the producers of *Molly* entrusted their baby to director Paul Aaron, who had been dumped from the 1971 *70, Girls, 70*. After the dismal Boston opening, they brought in Alan Arkin (director of Neil Simon's 1972 hit, *The Sunshine Boys*) and Grover Dale (last seen in Detroit, being nudged off the 1973 *Seesaw*), as well as writer/doctors Murray Schisgal and Norman Martin. So much for salvage. *Molly*'s coproducer Don Saxon had been the driving force, as they say, behind *Jimmy* (1969), and—here's a fascinating tidbit—introduced "Wouldn't You Like to Be on Broadway?" in Kurt Weill's 1947 musical, *Street Scene*. At *Molly*'s tear-swept final performance, Saxon blamed (of course) the critics, vowing to bar them from his future productions because they were "overly vicious." Lucky Number Dept.: Kay(e) Ballard removed the e from her name at the behest of her numerologist. After *Molly* she replaced her e and, presumably, her numerologist.

BROADWAY SCORECARD

/ PERFS: 68 / $: –

RAVE	FAVORABLE	MIXED	UNFAVORABLE	PAN
	1			5

THE MOONY SHAPIRO SONGBOOK

an import of the 1979 British revue *Songbook*

music by Monty Norman

lyrics by Julian More

book by Monty Norman and Julian More

directed by Jonathan Lynn

choreographed by George Faison

produced by Stuart Ostrow in association with T.A.T. Communications Company

with Jeff Goldblum, Judy Kaye, Timothy Jerome, Annie McGreevey, Gary Beach, and the voice of Harold Prince

opened May 3, 1981   *Morosco Theatre*

FRANK RICH, *TIMES*

There's a gem of a funny, spiffy satirical revue in *The Moony Shapiro Songbook*, the forlorn little musical at the Morosco. Monty Norman and Julian More, the show's British authors, are out to mock those proliferating musical anthologies that celebrate the likes of Fats Waller, Stephen Sondheim and Noël Coward. It's a timely premise, and the authors have a clever plan for executing it, too. They've created a fictitious hero who's an amalgam of virtually every songwriter, great and not-so-great, of this century. *The Moony Shapiro Songbook* is a *Side by Side by Shapiro*: five performers take us on a tour of this fellow's anecdote-packed career and sing three dozen of his songs. In the hands of a razor-sharp parodist—Mr. Sondheim, for one—*Songbook* might indeed have made mincemeat out of pop-music history. As it happens, Norman and More practice a toothless and unfocused, if affectionate, brand of satire. They aim too widely at their many targets and hit very few. Worse still, their revue, which was successfully staged in London, has been given a sloppy production on Broadway. Even on those rare occasions when the material clicks, the evening has the scrappy, amateurish air of a collegiate jape. Perhaps *Songbook* would play better if cut and polished to a high gloss. *A Day in Hollywood/A Night in the Ukraine* [1980]—an equally jejune British revue about American show business—has gotten mileage out of its energetic cast, sharp choreography and stylish look. There are no such distractions here. Jonathan Lynn has staged *Songbook* frantically on a drab blue set (abetted by colorless drops and projections). The choreographer, George Faison, squanders his opportunities. Though his routines are announced as parodies of Fred Astaire, Busby Berkeley and such, they're too crude to pass as anything but unusually ragged rehashes of the originals. There can't be satire without a point of view. . . . Two members of the company suggest what might have been—Judy Kaye, a skilled musical-comedy comedienne who sings a pretty ballad at a white piano, and Jeff Goldblum, that delightful, off-center movie actor (*Invasion of the Body Snatchers* [the 1978 remake]), who gamely insists on having fun no matter how badly he's misused. One also must congratulate the producer Harold Prince, who contributes a recorded voiceover cameo appearance to the evening but managed to refrain from producing *The Moony Shapiro Songbook* himself.

DOUGLAS WATT, *DAILY NEWS*
[Headline: "So Take the Songs, For Instance, Please!"]
Moony, to be sure. And loony, too. That's *The Moony Shapiro Songbook*, a monumentally silly mini-musical burlesque. At the risk of sounding sententious, I offer the writers a motto: A lousy song is like a malady. *The Moony Shapiro Songbook* is steadfastly devoted to lousy songs. By the dozen. It is an English musical, which explains a great deal, but not everything. *A Day in Hollywood—A Night in the Ukraine* [1980] came from London also, but was made fit for American consumption by strenuous revamping and magical new staging. The title character is a recently-deceased pop songwriter being honored with performances of his songs. Born Michael Moony of uncertain fatherhood in an Irish backwater, he adopted the other name on emigrating to America and

the Lower East Side to be adopted by a comic Jewish couple (considerably toned down, I'd wager, from their London equivalent). His career is traced (as, say, a Porter or Berlin anthology might) from an "East River Rhapsody" in a 1926 *Follies* to talkies, Broadway book musicals and, with changing times and tastes, to protest songs, rock, and his eventual death at 69 due to electrocution by his synthesizer. The show attempts the impossible task of poking fun at side-by-side-by-songbook musicals by presenting us with a fictitious tunesmith wholly lacking in originality, and whose rise to fame and fortune follows formula movie plots. The end result is neither funny (bar a joke or two) nor musically entertaining. Just vapid. English. The show itself is inane.

○   ○   ○

The final musical entry (to date) in the up-and-down career of producer Stuart Ostrow. Always eschewing the conventional, Ostrow hit two jackpots against five busts (including road folderoos *We Take the Town* [1962]—remember Bob Preston as Pancho Villa?—and the Uhry/Waldman *Swing* [1980]). He had similar luck dramatically, with one success offsetting four quick failures. But let it be said that Ostrow's three hits—*1776* (1969), *Pippin* (1972), and *M. Butterfly* (1988)—were daring, uncompromising, and substantial. As for *Moony Shapiro*, the cheerfully wacky British song-satire *Songbook* seems to have lost a great deal in the translation. Authors Monty Norman and Julian More were the gents responsible for the sparkling English-language adaptation of Marguerite Monnot's *Irma La Douce* (1960), so I'll give them the benefit of the doubt.

BROADWAY SCORECARD				
/ PERFS: 1 / $: –				
RAVE	FAVORABLE	MIXED	UNFAVORABLE	PAN
			2	2

MUSIC IS

"A New Musical"

music by Richard Adler

lyrics by Will Holt

book by George Abbott

based on the 1601 comedy *Twelfth Night* by William Shakespeare

directed by George Abbott

choreographed by Patricia Birch

produced by Richard Adler, Roger Berlind, and Edward R. Downe, Jr.

with Christopher Hewett, David Ben-Zali, David Brummel, Catherine Cox, Joel Higgins, David Holliday, Marc Jordan, Sherry Mathis, William McClary, Paul Michael, Joe Ponazecki, David Sabin, and Laura Waterbury

opened December 20, 1976   St. James Theatre

CLIVE BARNES, *TIMES*

The temptation to say that "*Music Is* is not" should clearly be resisted. But in the circumstances it is difficult to resist, for the show hardly seems one of the more noticeable events of the season. A lot of effort has gone into it—so what else is new? The show has a great deal of taste—some of it good, some of it bad, but most of it sort of decorative. It is somewhat like an elaborate window dressing without goods. What went wrong? Well apart from the music by Richard Adler and the lyrics by Will Holt—two sizable "aparts"—it seems largely a matter of tone. In fairness, George Abbott has done a very clever job of carpentry— indeed his skill at trimming, changing and bending the original narrative while being faithful to the main story is worth studying by any aspirant writers of musical books. However, the framework of a book is not its only concern—there is also the manner of the book. And here

The John F. Kennedy Center for the Performing Arts
presents the

RICHARD   ROGER   EDWARD R.
ADLER   BERLIND   DOWNE, JR.

Production of

MUSIC IS

A New Musical Comedy

Book by   Music by   Lyrics by

GEORGE ABBOTT · RICHARD ADLER · WILL HOLT

(Based on Shakespeare's TWELFTH NIGHT)

Orchestrations by   Musical Director   Dance and Vocal Arrangements by
HERSHY KAY   DON SMITH   WILLIAM COX

Scenery Designed by   Costumes by   Lighting by
ELDON ELDER   LEWIS D. RAMPINO   H. R. POINDEXTER

General Management   Assistant Director   Production Stage Manager
THEATRE NOW, INC.   JUDITH ABBOTT   BOB D. BERNARD

Musical Numbers and Dances Staged by
PATRICIA BIRCH

Directed by
GEORGE ABBOTT

EISENHOWER THEATRE · KENNEDY CENTER
4 WEEKS ONLY! WED. EVG., NOV. 10 THRU SAT. EVG., DEC. 4

TWO SPECIAL PERFS.: SUN., NOV. 14 AT 2 AND 7:30 P.M.
SPECIAL HOLIDAY MAT.: FRI., NOV. 26 AT 2 P.M.

"Like an elaborate window dressing without goods," said Clive Barnes. "The cast suffers from not knowing whether to brush up its Shakespeare or brush down its Abbott." (artwork by Fay Gage)

Abbott understandably falters. Some seasons back we had a rock musical, *Your Own Thing* [1968], which was a modern spoof on *Twelfth Night*, with no pretensions to echo the original. Abbott is tested with a more difficult problem. Sometimes he uses Shakespeare's own words; and for most of the time he is employing a vaguely pseudo-Elizabethan usage. It never quite works. The tone sounds wrong. Perhaps this is where Adler's music drifts adrift. Some of his romantic music is pleasant enough, he has an ear for lyricism, and the catchy numbers are appropriately catchy. Yet somehow the score, while using neither, seems caught between a lute and an electric guitar. Holt's lyrics are just not very bright or clever, but the music as a whole does have the advantages of Hershy Kay's orchestration. However, this music is not the food of love but the bread of commerce. Many of the good aspects of the show arise from the staging—Abbott's direction and Patricia Birch's choreography. Both are nicely melded together and they both have style, [especially] a most imaginative use of trampolines placed behind sofas during the first act finale. This was splendid. The cast suffers from not knowing whether to brush up its Shakespeare or brush down its Abbott. . . . A brave attempt, with some incidental charms. And it is consistently professional. Which is something.

MARTIN GOTTFRIED, POST
[Headline: "*Music Is* Best Forgotten"]
George Abbott is a legendary man of the Broadway theatre, and our musicals in particular would not be where they [are] were it not for him. The fundamentals of book structure, song spotting and traffic management were his invention, many of them. Nevertheless, times and the theatre have changed. At the bedrock of any successful musical are many of the basics developed by Abbott, but shows cannot be staged as they were 40 years ago. Yet, this is what he has done with *Music Is*. Abbott's rule, it has always been, is to only keep material that works. It is a valid rule of the theatre, an inviolable one, but it depends on one's definition of what works. Abbott keeps his script, his company and his stage moving but none of it goes anywhere. The *Twelfth Night* story is played out with no point of view and the show has no spirit other than its own efficiency. It is a busy, talky story that is cued here and there for songs. They start, end, and the production works on. It has an odd

score. Richard Adler has composed songs for it in the traditional Broadway idiom, a few with a rock beat and a handful in the Elizabethan spirit. Those sound a good deal like some songs that Richard Rodgers wrote for last season's *Rex* (which Adler produced), but sounding like Rodgers is hardly the worst that could be said for a song. Adler's music is melodic, and that's nothing to be sneezed at even if the score is not striking, is not of a piece, demonstrates no approach to the show and is hardly innovating. A few of the novelty numbers in the old time show vernacular brought back fond memories of the Broadway style. In general, then, this is a pleasant, innocuous score, tremendously helped by Hershy Kay's stylish orchestrations, which provide it with nice turns of harmony, warm instrumental combinations and rhythmic interest. These orchestrations, unfortunately, could not drown out Will Holt's sappy lyrics. In fact the whole show has no drive. It just pushes ahead. It is but the creaking machinery of very old Broadway.

HOWARD KISSEL, *WOMEN'S WEAR DAILY*

From the way *Music Is* opens—with the cast parading across the stage carrying banners announcing who directed it, who designed the costumes and so forth (like the cover of the original *Candide* album)—you sense the tone director George Abbott wanted to set: breezy, droll and informal (or at least as informal as actors in Elizabethan costume can be). The effect is enhanced by Hershy Kay's orchestrations for the lively opening number—all brass, no strings, a harp and a keyboard; when the brass plays alone, it has the euphoric quality of a circus band. At one point the chorus does a stanza or two on kazoos. For the length of the number, the idea of retelling *Twelfth Night* in this lighthearted style is appealing. There is no lack of inventiveness in the rest of the show. Abbott is grafting his show business expertise onto Shakespeare as he did over a decade ago onto Plautus in *A Funny Thing Happened on the Way to the Forum* [1962]. If this show seems considerably less successful than its predecessor, it is because Shakespeare is considerably more complex than Plautus. He uses some of the same plot devices—identical twins, mistaken identity—but he never leaves his stories mechanical, as Plautus did. Here the characters occasionally open up in Will Holt and Richard Adler's songs—particularly a beautiful ballad,

"Should I Speak of Loving You" and a lovely duet, "Please Be Human." But they never really become characters we care about. However diverting it is, *Music Is* is short on substance, and these days, alas, even in musicals, substance counts.

◦   ◦   ◦

On a visit to the Eastman School of Music at the University of Rochester (NY), Rochester's most distinguished alumnus (Class of 1911) said, "Too bad you haven't the book of a musical to put up for grabs. Let the kids write the music, I'll write the book." So he did, turning to the Bard with whom he'd collaborated (?) some thirty-eight years earlier on a musicalization of *A Comedy of Errors*. His one-time protégé Hal Prince read Mr. Abbott's *Twelfth Night* and opined that it was "too good to waste on amateurs." Abbott's *Pajama Game* (1954)/*Damn Yankees* (1955) collaborator, Richard Adler, was just then producing an Abbott-directed revival of the former hit, and so another new Broadway musical was born. *Music Is*, alas, wasn't *The Boys from Syracuse* (1938); but then, *Music Is* didn't have Dick Rodgers and Larry Hart and George Balanchine. The Last of Mr. Abbott Dept.: While Mr. Abbott had directed (and doctored) numerous plays and musicals since his Pulitzer Prize-winning *Fiorello!* in 1959, the four subsequent Abbott-authored musicals—*Tenderloin* (1960), *Flora, the Red Menace* (1965), *Anya* (1965), and *Music Is*—all failed. Abbott remained somewhat active theatrically until his death in 1995 at the age of 107, but *Music Is* was his final full-scale effort. The last hits came in tandem in 1962, directing both *A Funny Thing Happened on the Way to the Forum* and the long-running comedy hit *Never Too Late*.

BROADWAY SCORECARD

/ PERFS: 8 / $: –

RAVE	FAVORABLE	MIXED	UNFAVORABLE	PAN
	1			5

THE MUSIC MAN

a touring revival of the 1957 musical comedy

book, music, and lyrics by Meredith Willson; "story" by Meredith Willson and Franklin Lacey

based on the 1948 memoir *And There I Stood with My Piccolo* by Meredith Willson

directed and choreographed by Michael Kidd

produced by James M. Nederlander, Raymond Lussa, and Fred Walker

starring Dick Van Dyke

with Meg Bussert, Iggie Wolfington, Carol Arthur, Richard Warren Pugh, Jen Jones, Christian Slater, Jay Stuart, Christina Saffran, and Calvin McRae

opened June 5, 1980   *City Center*

WALTER KERR, *TIMES*

Lanky Dick Van Dyke is taking his turn at playing the con man who persuades the gullible parents of a small Iowa town that their progeny are immensely gifted at playing cornet, fife and trombone. Late in the second act, things are rather catching up with him—especially since it's been discovered that he can't read a note of music—and there's a good bit of hot-footed pursuit going. But it's one of his young charges who finally stops the galloping Van Dyke in his tracks—one of the kids who've come to idolize him. Naturally, the lad is shattered. Voice cracking in elaborate musical-comedy dismay, the boy [Christian Slater] puts the matter to his hero bluntly. "Are you a dirty rotten crook?" he wants to know. Whereupon Van Dyke, acquiring a conscience at last, simply drops to one knee, looks his accuser straight in the eye, and murmurs a penitent, straightforward "Yes." And right then and there we know—if we didn't know earlier—exactly what's been subtly wrong with this *Music Man* from the beginning. Mr. Van Dyke *isn't* a dirty rotten crook.

Dick Van Dyke as con-man Professor Harold Hill. "He's simply—and only—nice," complained Walter Kerr, "and that hurts."

He's not even a natty gentleman crook. He's not a crook at all. He's a nimble and attractive performer, and he's able to bring into play a good bit of the lively *shtik* he's perfected over the years: flights across library tables on tiptoe, reversals in midair that make him resemble a cross-legged dragonfly, exits in march-time on ankles that collapse crunchily with each beat. But he's a straight shooter, honest from the word go, virtue spilling out of every pocket, innocence written all over him where sly graffiti should be. He's simply—and only—nice. And that hurts. Marian's played this time by Meg Bussert, making her Broadway debut. She should be kept in the area indefinitely. She's charming, plausible and, besides that, she sings well. And she has another virtue: she believes in what her lyrics are saying. In fact, the entertainment is musically at its best, by far, when Bussert is at work. But if the most satisfying numbers, the numbers likeliest to stop a show, are all in the hands of the heroine and a neighborly quartet, what crazy kind of *Music Man* have we got? It's not that Van Dyke isn't likable, even good. He just turns out to be good in the wrong sense of the word. He's not a scalawag, and we've got to have one.

HOWARD KISSEL, *WOMEN'S WEAR DAILY*
Older readers may remember a time when Broadway was supposed to set standards for American theatre. In the last few years Broadway has become a dumping ground for uninspired touring shows, of which the latest is *The Music Man*. Meredith Willson's 1957 musical has been revived as a vehicle for Dick Van Dyke, who makes an engaging comic figure with his tall, thin body decked out in a bold black-and-white checked suit. Van Dyke does Kidd's energetic choreography with great agility and aplomb. We are used to seeing dancers with compact bodies, whose limbs are never too far from the control center. Van Dyke is so tall, his body seemingly so unwieldy, that his grace comes as a surprise, which adds to the pleasure. Van Dyke has a natural likableness and charm that compensates somewhat for the lack of zest in his singing and acting. Kidd's production comes alive largely in the dance numbers, which have a precision and energy lacking elsewhere. But the production (conducted with unexpected perfunctoriness by Milton Rosenstock) suffers from the malady of most touring shows, which are intended to be recognizable imitations of the original. And great origi-

nality might lessen product identification in the provinces, where familiarity is the great selling point. I have nothing against revivals of
favorite musicals, but it would be a refreshing change to see one done
with imagination.

o   o   o

You would think that all-American Dick Van Dyke as the all-American
Music Man would be a cinch, if not in New York at least in the all-
American hinterlands. But Van Dyke, who catapulted from *Bye Bye
Birdie* (1960) directly into his eponymous sitcom, was surprisingly
shaky in the role. Several critics pointed out that he was "too nice" to
play the rapscallion Harold Hill, and there might have been other reasons for his peculiarly flat performance. (The actor was on the wagon,
or perhaps off the wagon, and I don't mean the Wells Fargo wagon.) In
any event, the show itself got generally good reviews and the star
received generally decent notices, but audiences along the eight-month
touring route shrugged off this *Music Man*. The show did result in two
notable Broadway debuts, though: Meg Bussert as the sadder-but-wiser
Marian the Librarian, and ten-year-old Christian Slater as her trum-
pet-playing nephew Winthrop Paroo.

BROADWAY SCORECARD
/ PERFS: 21 / $: –

RAVE	FAVORABLE	MIXED	UNFAVORABLE	PAN
3	1		1	1

MUSIC! MUSIC!

"A Cavalcade of American Music with Footnotes by Alan Jay Lerner"

directed by Martin Charnin

choreographed by Tony Stevens

produced by the City Center of Music and Drama (Norman Singer) and Alvin Bojar

starring Gene Nelson (replacing Dan Dailey), Larry Kert, Karen Morrow, Donna McKechnie, and Robert Guillaume

with Will Mackenzie, Gail Nelson (replacing sixth-billed star Jonelle Allen), Ted Pritchard, Arnold Soboloff, and Russ Thacker

opened April 11, 1974   *City Center*

CLIVE BARNES, *TIMES*

Tedium was continually threatening to run riot at the City Center last night. The occasion was a strange anthology called *Music! Music!*. Staged and directed by Martin Charnin, this is described as "a cavalcade of American music with footnotes by Alan Jay Lerner." Mr. Lerner's footnotes needed more choreography. Where they were not trivial they were banal, and I suppose the vice was versa. Mind you no one can go all wrong with 80 years of American popular music to choose from, and some very talented people to perform it. I was merely surprised how close to all wrong the show came. You hear some great songs. But for much of the time, it is just like a record album, or a television special done on the cheap, with hand-me-down choreography and minimal stagings. The orchestra, a good one, is at the back of the stage covered by a scrim, and singers are down front, usually dressed in black and white. The effect is certainly not that of a musical, nor yet that of a revue, but rather of those "salute-programs" that sum up the ABC of show business—awards, benefits and other catastrophes. The numbers chosen were fair enough, and once in a while, too rarely perhaps,

Charnin really exercised his imagination and ours. For example, a staged boxing match between Broadway's two longest-running productions, *Hello, Dolly!* and *Fiddler on the Roof* [both 1964], was witty and imaginative, but also demonstrated the show's major flaw. One heard too little of the major shows, and very often what one heard had been gimmicked. Many of the numbers were presented as run-throughs or auditions, while *The Music Man* [1957], *Camelot* [1960], *Bye Bye Birdie* [1960] and *Gypsy* [1959] were represented by simply a dance solo, ineptly choreographed by Tony Stevens and inadequately danced by Donna McKechnie. It is ironical that the City Center is normally the home of the Joffrey Ballet and the Ailey Dancers. Any of them could dance rings around Miss McKechnie, and Mr. Stevens' choreography has no place on this stage.

MARTIN GOTTFRIED, *WOMEN'S WEAR DAILY*

Music! Music! isn't theatre, and it's unfair to the idea of a "show" to even call it that. Alan Jay Lerner has put together a frankly commercial enterprise that hasn't even the gist of honest life you would find in the most calculated of Broadway ventures. In fact, if this presentation has any interest at all, which is dubious, it makes one wonder whether Lerner ever really felt himself a theatre maker. I know that sounds strange, but more than anything else, *Music! Music!* seems more made by spectators than participants. Just beginning a five-week run at the City Center before taking off on tour, it is subtitled "a cavalcade of American music with footnotes by Alan Jay Lerner." The "cavalcade" part is what gives it the feel of a combined television special and charity benefit. The "American music" part seems to specifically excuse the use of some non-show songs. And the "footnotes" are what give the evening an outsider look, because they are either narration and dialog that make no sense until a song explains the purpose of the introduction, or they are old stories about backer's auditions and songs dropped from shows, trite for show freaks, parochial for general audiences and uninteresting for working people of the musical theatre. Some of our theatre's most prominent composers are omitted—Cole Porter, Irving Berlin, Frank Loesser, Burton Lane and Stephen Sondheim among them—some, I am told, because of contractual difficulties and others out of sheer thoughtlessness. On the other hand, there was somehow squeezed in a song with a lyric by the director, Martin Charnin ["Maman," with music by Edward Thomas, from the 1967 road failure *Mata Hari*], and of course an abundance of Lerner's songs. As for Charnin's direction, as abetted by Lerner's overriding idea and continuity, it keeps everything as smooth and cold as a television program taped without an audience.

WALTER KERR, *TIMES*
[Headline: "Surprise Me (Please!)"]
I am afraid that my reactions to *Music! Music!* were a little peculiar. *Music! Music!* is a limping cavalcade of just about every show-biz standard that ever sold a million copies of something or other, and I came out at the intermission vigorously humming Harold Rome's "Franklin D. Roosevelt Jones" [from *Sing Out the News* (1939)]. Not because it's in the show. Because it isn't. And I couldn't explain why it wasn't. Here they were, these historians onstage, working their way through the Great Depression—making a very good thing of Jay Gorney's very good "Brother, Can You Spare a Dime?"—and trying to find a musical way out of it. The best conceivable way out of it was the heart-lifting energy of "Franklin D. Roosevelt Jones," and they hadn't even thought of it. Struggled through half a dozen less relevant popular tunes instead. It is of course not a reviewer's business to waste time constructing *his* show when he's got an actual show in front of him to attend to. The problem with *Music! Music!* is that it's rather hard to attend to, and invites doodling. One reason for this has already been indicated: if every single number that comes along is exactly the number you've been expecting, you give up hope after a while, having eliminated surprise from your life. It's like going to two successive cocktail parties on two successive evenings to meet the very same people. To make matters worse, whenever a really right performer meets a really right song in the show, the show takes great pains to interrupt, and cruelly abort, the proceedings. Karen Morrow for instance, is a belter *par excellence*; she can also close down, liquidly and lovingly, around a smaller song. O.K., let her start "Bill." Just as you're beginning to become interested in *her* way of doing it, cut off the orchestra to have her ask if the song can't be taken half a step up. Start her in again. Then, as rapture threatens to rear its head once more, begin a rehearsal brouhaha at the rear of the

auditorium—yes, we're re-running the best-known legend in the trade and "Bill" is being cut out of *Oh, Lady! Lady!!* [1918] again—that will keep the melodic line from ever seeing its way home. Same deal on "The Man I Love," though Miss Morrow does get to open up fearsomely on the last three notes, much to the audience's long-delayed delight.

o   o   o

A cavalcade of songs thrown together by Alan Jay Lerner. Thrown together is the operative term, with the once high-flying Lerner reeling after the quick, disappointing demise of the 1973 stage version of *Gigi* and the even quicker, out-of-town foldup of his 1971 *Lolita, My Love*. And things for Lerner would go downhill from here: next stop, *1600 Pennsylvania Avenue* (1976). A highly similar dead-music extravaganza came along the following season, when the virtually defunct Theatre Guild assembled *A Musical Jubilee*, so named because half the cast—Cyril Ritchard, Lillian Gish, Patrice Munsel, John Raitt— seemed about a hundred years old. Both *Music! Music!* and *A Musical Jubilee* were handily eclipsed by a short little guy with thick glasses, no sets, no orchestra, and no star power, just Sammy Cahn and *Words and Music* (1974).

BROADWAY SCORECARD
/ PERFS: 37 / $: —

RAVE	FAVORABLE	MIXED	UNFAVORABLE	PAN
1	1	1		3

MY FAIR LADY

the 20th anniversary revival of the 1956 musical

music by Frederick Loewe

book and lyrics by Alan Jay Lerner

based on the 1914 comedy *Pygmalion* by George Bernard Shaw

directed by Jerry Adler; "based on the original by Moss Hart"

choreographed by Crandall Diehl; "based on the original by Hanya Holm"

produced by Herman Levin

starring Ian Richardson, Christine Andreas, George Rose, and Robert Coote

with Brenda Forbes, Jerrry Lanning, Sylvia O'Brien, John Clarkson, Richard Neilson, Margaretta Warwick, and Eleanor Phelps

opened March 25, 1976   *St. James Theatre*

CLIVE BARNES, *TIMES*

It had to be better and—by and large and by George!—it is. The restoration—revival seems too cold a word for such a sumptuous under-taking—of *My Fair Lady* to Broadway took place last night. It is 20 years since Rex Harrison, Julie Andrews, Stanley Holloway and Robert Coote first danced all night, and now only Mr. Coote, as deliciously bumbling as ever, is left. Where this *Fair Lady* differs from its proto-type and where, in some respects, it may even be superior, is in the per-formances. Heresy? Very likely, and memory does play tricks after 20 years. Yet the new cast—with the cuddly Mr. Coote still intact—does have a very special authority. It stems from Ian Richardson and George Rose, who are both essentially far more serious performers—and better actors—than their illustrious predecessors. Richardson, one of the

finest Shakespearean actors of our time, who happens to have an outstandingly good singing voice, takes command very early on. In his first
number—"Why Can't the English?"—he suddenly replaces Harrison's
bored gravity and genteel exasperation with a genuine flash of anger.
Later, when he sonorously extols "the majesty and grandeur of the
English language," you hear a man in love with his native tongue, a man
of seriousness, a scholar. This is much more Shaw's Higgins than was
Harrison, and Richardson also eschews the patter-song delivery (in
opera it would be called *sprechstimme*) that Harrison made his own, and
sings out in his own voice. As Doolittle, the recalcitrant garbage man
who becomes entrapped in the web of middle-class morality, Rose is
totally without thorns or peers. He explodes across the stage like a
Cockney firecracker, every lewd gesture and lubricious grin, every rich
and twisted syllable not just declaring Bow Bells but ringing them. *My
Fair Lady* has come back as fair, as ladylike and, yes, as welcome, as ever.
She can still dance all night—and does.

MARTIN GOTTFRIED, *POST*
[Headline: "A Few Wrinkles in *My Fair Lady*"]
The musical theatre has changed much in the 20 years since this
beloved show opened. Its devices of structure and production are not
always smooth. We have since seen more integrally conceived musicals,
ones more likely to remain theatre artworks. But *My Fair Lady* will
always manage to entertain and enchant because of those superb elements of song and story. The revival presents some problems that are in
the material. It has some weaknesses in casting and it does not always
look as elegant as it is supposed to. There's no evading this reproduction's overriding nature as a revival. Few musical makers would allow so
many darkened gaps while scenery is being changed. We won't put up
with ballads or brief scenes in front of the curtain. The recreated direction and choreography seem all too much like copying, and Oliver
Smith's sets are sometimes sloppy. The coordination between Theodore
Saidenberg's musical direction and the singing is sometimes spastic
enough to make you wince while his orchestra tries to catch up with
hurrying voices. Yet, this production plainly aspires to be first class. Ian
Richardson, one of England's finest classical actors is, frankly, a disappointment. He pushes too hard as Higgins, as if thinking that the musi-

cal theatre requires excess in performance. Ironically, he isn't strong enough as Higgins—not cruel enough, not intense enough as the cold intellectual who sets out to teach a vulgar girl how to be stylish and winds up falling for her. Christine Andreas is even more disappointing. She has a beautiful voice, so like Julie Andrews' that you might close your eyes and imagine you're hearing the original cast recording. Unfortunately for her, shows should be watched and Miss Andreas is not up to acting the role of Eliza. But this isn't the original, as the production somehow keeps reminding you. Great sections of it, especially the "Ascot Gavotte" and Eliza's unveiling at a grand party, are exemplary musical theatre construction. They will always work wonderfully well. Cecil Beaton's costumes, the elegant ones especially, are breathtaking. Yet *My Fair Lady* is not a musical that will prove classic because its construction as theatre is too often awkward. That is a pity considering the wonderful material, but the craft of musical theatre had gone only so far by 1956.

WALTER KERR, *TIMES*

In a way, Robert Coote was the dare. I don't expect to spend much time on the expansive, expostulating, enchantingly slow-on-the-uptake Mr. Coote this morning, though paragraphs could be written—no, sonnets should be written, he deserves better than prose—on the manly pride he takes in serving as dressmakers dummy for Eliza Doolittle's first fancy-ball gown, or on the resolute manner in which he twitches his mustache in order to stimulate his thinking processes while calling Scotland Yard. But when original producer Herman Levin decided upon a full-scale revival of *My Fair Lady* just 20 years after its first breathtaking opening, and when he decided to recast Mr. Coote in the role he had created to begin with, he was in effect both symbolizing and adding to the risk he knew he was taking: the risk of jogging memory. Everyone was already asking if it wasn't a bit too soon to be renewing our acquaintance with a musical-comedy masterpiece that had run forever in the first place, already wondering if we'd be able to erase the likes of Rex Harrison and Julie Andrews from our heads. And wouldn't putting Coote back in his old place, surrounded by new faces that might seem only substitutes, serve to accent what was different, what was missing, what was lost? Uh uh. All that has happened is that Coote is

20 years funnier, while all that happens to *My Fair Lady* as the actor
finds himself fitting the new company like an old patent-leather shoe is
that it proves 20 years stronger, a show so dazzlingly melodic and visually rich in its first act that it scarcely needs a second—and so emotionally binding in its second that you wonder why you were merely dazzled
by the first. Structurally sound of wind and limb, skipping like springtime and living out its winters on wit, *My Fair Lady* isn't an entertainment that requires certain performers to bring off the Bernard
Shaw–based libretto, the leaping Alan Jay Lerner lyrics, the sweeping
Frederick Loewe score; it's an entertainment that invites any and all
performers to simply lift the lid from its treasure-chest and avail themselves of its glistening baubles. No reason why this shouldn't run as long
as there's justice, and a thirst for lilting bewitchment, in the world.

●   ●   ●

A lesson in revivals. A prime example of what can happen when you are
faithful, careful, and respectful of the material. Of course, you have to
start out with a perfect show, perfectly recast and mounted.
Unfortunately for original producer Herman Levin, the nonstar acting
company proved unable to attract the necessary audiences to bring
commercial success.

A Tony Award was won by George Rose (actor).

BROADWAY SCORECARD
/ PERFS: 377 / $: –

RAVE	FAVORABLE	MIXED	UNFAVORABLE	PAN
4	1	1		

MY FAIR LADY

an "original star" revival of the 1956 musical

music by Frederick Loewe

book and lyrics by Alan Jay Lerner

based on the 1914 comedy *Pygmalion* by George Bernard Shaw

directed by Patrick Garland; "original New York production staged by Moss Hart"

choreographed by Crandall Diehl, "based on the original by Hanya Holm"

produced by Don Gregory and Mike Merrick

starring Rex Harrison

with Nancy Ringham (replacing Cheryl Kennedy), Milo O'Shea, Cathleen Nesbitt, Jack Gwillim, and Nicholas Wyman

opened August 18, 1981   *Uris Theatre*

MEL GUSSOW, *TIMES*

Mr. Harrison is older, but he is still the quintessential Higgins, who, after all, could never be considered youthful. Those who saw the actor in the original engagement on Broadway or in the George Cukor movie may be surprised at one fact. He has become a more commanding musical performer, singing more of his lyrics and with his mellifluous voice finding an even more melodic lilt in the words. It would be difficult, of course, to recapture the excitement of the first Broadway opening, or, in fact, of the closing night some six years later. However, considerable drama was added to the reopening by the last-minute assumption of the title role by the understudy, Nancy Ringham. Because of illness, Cheryl Kennedy, who played Liza Doolittle during the show's pre-Broadway tour, was forced to withdraw from the cast. Ringham, a young American actress, was rushed

Don Gregory
AND
Mike Merrick
PRESENT

Rex
Harrison

Lerner Loewe's

My Fair
Lady

Cheryl
Kennedy

Milo O'Shea
Cathleen Nesbitt
Jack Gwillim
Nicholas Wyman

BOOK AND LYRICS BY
Alan Jay Lerner

MUSIC BY
Frederick Loewe

BASED ON *PYGMALION* BY GEORGE BERNARD SHAW

ORIGINAL NEW YORK PRODUCTION STAGED BY Moss Hart

SCENIC PRODUCTION DESIGN BY   COSTUMES BY   LIGHTING DESIGNED BY
Oliver Smith   Cecil Beaton   Ken Billington

COSTUME SUPERVISION BY   ORCHESTRA CONDUCTED BY
John David Ridge   Robert Kreis

MUSICAL DIRECTOR
Franz Allers

MUSICAL STAGING AND CHOREOGRAPHY BY
Crandall Diehl

BASED ON THE ORIGINAL BY Hanya Holm

DIRECTED BY
Patrick Garland

A DOME/CUTLER-HERMAN PRODUCTION

SEPT. 16-
OCT. 5

S·A·E·N·G·E·R
PERFORMING ARTS CENTER

Is Rex doing *Fair Lady* or *Zorbá*? Neither, it turned out. Preliminary credits. (artwork by "Weller")

in to make her Broadway debut, turning the evening into a Cinderella story within a Cinderella story. She is an appealing leading lady with a strong voice. However, her performance at times seemed strained, missing a measure of the role's charm and buoyancy. Ringham offers a rather mechanical rendition of "Just You Wait," recovers with "The Rain in Spain," but is unable to overwhelm us with her transformation from guttersnipe to duchess. At the same time, her accent wavers from quasi-cockney to indeterminate mid-Atlantic. One imagines that she will improve as she continues to play this challenging role. In addition to the book, music, lyrics and Mr. Harrison, the major asset of the production is Milo O'Shea, who can take his place alongside other ineffable Alfred P. Doolittles, with the added benefit of his barroom saltiness. Quick-stepping into his twin showstoppers, "With a Little Bit of Luck" and "Get Me to the Church on Time," Mr. O'Shea seems marinated in malt.

HOWARD KISSEL, *WOMEN'S WEAR DAILY*

Many of the original components are evident in the Gray Panther revival at the Uris—Oliver Smith and Cecil Beaton's extraordinary designs have been reproduced faithfully (though at the final preview I saw one of the turntables broke down, alas, just before the first act finale); Hart's staging has been recreated, as has Hanya Holm's choreography. Rex Harrison, at 73, has resumed his original role as Prof. Henry Higgins, and Cathleen Nesbitt, at 92 the only actress who could look like his mother rather than his contemporary, has resumed hers. Harrison does not exert himself—we seldom see the fanatical lover of the English language whose passion might have inspired love on the part of his student. Most of Harrison's performance comes from his larynx. . . . *My Fair Lady* is so splendidly constructed that merely seeing this lavish production, and hearing the words and music, are enough to bring pleasure. The audience, after all, is used to summer reruns. They are happy to see something, someone familiar. Not used to "live" theatre, they are content with a faithful reproduction—nowadays no one expects a show actually to be "brought to life."

DON NELSON, *DAILY NEWS*

It could have been a parallel to *42nd Street*. The star of *My Fair Lady* gets sick. A young chorus member is rushed in at the 11th hour. She's brilliant. The audience goes mad. Critics collapse in awe. It could have happened—but didn't. Nancy Ringham replaced Cheryl Kennedy as Eliza Doolittle at Saturday's matinee of the current *My Fair Lady* revival at the Uris. At Monday's preview, she gave a thoroughly professional performance; but it was far from electrifying or even inspiring. One never felt moved to put an elbow into a companions ribs and nod, as if to say: "God, where has she been hiding herself?" But if Ringham at this performance was not the Eliza we dreamed of, neither was Rex Harrison the Henry Higgins of legend. Perhaps he was distracted or piqued by the cast change. Harrison is a very fine, wily actor capable of delicious whimsy yet he acted here as if the role was just another job. Good? Of course. Funny, yes; but we expect more of an actor clearly blessed with so much natural resource. If he wastes it, what's the point? Indeed, I found the chorus members, who gamboled about the stage with joyful aplomb, much more engaging than the principals. . . . Perhaps revivals—a colleague calls them necrophilia—bring with them a certain second-hand aura that forbids one the exhiliration of first-time discovery. *My Fair Lady* is a great musical yet it probably can never satisfy the romantic preconceptions an audience "remembers" from the past. Maybe that is one reason why this performance did not work well.

◦   ◦   ◦

A lesson in revivals. A prime example of what can happen when you are *not* faithful, careful, and respectful of the material. Of course, you *can* earn a fortune with a sloppy star package. (Take, for example, a Ron Field-directed/Robert Goulet-headed *South Pacific*, that unaccountably mopped up big on the road in the late 1980s. Despite the financial windfall, the Rodgers and Hammerstein Estates withheld approval of what would have surely proved an embarrassing New York airing.) In the case of this *My Fair Lady*, Rex's lackadaisical stroll through Wimpole Street did not, surprisingly, do all that well on the road. *Or* in

New York. And the same can be said for a somewhat radically reconfigured, Richard Chamberlain-led stab—and I do mean stab—at the
Lerner and Loewe classic in 1993.

BROADWAY SCORECARD

/ PERFS: 119 / $: –

RAVE	FAVORABLE	MIXED	UNFAVORABLE	PAN
1		1	1	3

LEONARD SILLMAN'S
NEW FACES OF 1968

"The New Edition"

music and lyrics by Ronny Graham, June (Sillman) Carroll, Arthur
Siegel, Clark Gesner, Sam Pottle, David Axelrod, Jerry Powell,
David Shire, Richard Maltby, Jr., Murray Grand, Paul Nassau, Hal
Hackady, Alonzo Levister, Kenny Solms, Gail Parent, Gene P.
Bissell, Carl Friberg, Fred Hellerman, Fran Minkoff, Michael
McWhinney, Michael Cohen, Tony Geiss, and Sidney Shaw

sketches by Ronny Graham, Peter De Vries, William F. Brown,
Kenny Solms, Gail Parent, Jack Sharkey, Robert Klein, and Norman
Kline; continuity and additional dialogue by William F. Brown

"entire production conceived and staged by Leonard Sillman";
directed and choreographed by Frank Wagner

produced by Jack Rollins

with Michael K. Allen, Suzanne Astor, Rod Barry, Gloria
Bleezarde, Marilyn Child, Elaine Giftos, Madeline Kahn, Robert
Klein, Brandon Maggart, Rod Perry, and Leonard Sillman

opened May 2, 1968   *Booth Theatre*

CLIVE BARNES, *TIMES*

The show opens and almost immediately bright voices are informing us: "You've never seen US before—we've never seen YOU before," and suddenly, speaking strictly for myself, I felt we had. This is the beginning of Leonard Sillman's *New Faces of 1968*, and somehow, although the show contains a lot of talent and a few good laughs, it never looks forward. Perhaps the difficulty is that the faces are not new so much as unknown—rather like the show itself. I remember Sillman's *New Faces of 1952* vividly and with affection. I thought it was one of the most dazzling shows I had ever seen in my life. But people should never try to repeat themselves unless they are confident they can top themselves. This new *New Faces* seems like a croaky echo of a once confident voice. The elements of the old show are all there—the cutesy numbers, the cynical numbers, the smart numbers, the production numbers, the sketch numbers, and the monologue numbers. The running gags, the sexy girl who wanders through the show, are running as fast and as furiously as ever. What there isn't is the spirit of a show that could offer "Lucky Pierre," or "The Boston Beguine" or "You Can't Chop Your Momma Up in Massachusetts." For there is no real satirical bite here. No one could possibly be offended—no one, that is, who is not offended by intrinsic mediocrity. The cast is talented—indeed with all of the United States to choose from it would only be remarkable if it were not. I liked particularly Robert Klein, and would have been prepared to have liked him more had he had better material. Madeline Kahn had a strong voice and an incisive personality and was at her best in a Kurt Weill parody, Brandon Maggart enlivened almost everything he was in. But perhaps the real trouble with this *New Faces* is that it almost looks beaten before it starts. Because of the risks involved, a permanent setting is employed representing a living room (a tastelessly furnished living room at that) and Sillman, who acts as his own *compère*, coyly informs us that he is simulating a "backer's audition" in his living room, and we have to use our imagination. Possibly if Sillman and his backers had used a little more imagination, the audience would not have had to use so much.

MARTIN GOTTFRIED, *WOMEN'S WEAR DAILY*

People ask what happened to the revues, remembering *Call Me Mister* [1946] and *Lend an Ear* [1948] and whatever went before them. What happened to them is now onstage at the Booth. *New Faces of 1968* is not a re-hash of old revues because the old revues just weren't this ridiculous. There are some songs that were heard before in other productions and while one would ordinarily be startled by the use of old material, there are too many more startling things in this show to be annoyed by merely that. Swivel-hipped male dancers and songs about "evil" being "live" spelled backwards, and even the producer himself (Leonard Sillman) slipping onstage with a clipboard in hand and a cigaret holder in mouth. So what this *New Faces* really is is an absurd and pathetic, unwitting parody of old-time, show-time on Broadway. Singers with eagle-spread arms and sketches satirizing Miss America contests. Call it low camp if you like and giggle at a girl singer, dressed in a raincoat, singing "rainbows are prisms that spangle my sea." Just to take it easy, assume that it is being done as a backers' audition to cut the production costs—it saves on elaborate scenery and lets you use a small band. But let that pass, along with the plaintive hope that a lot of drumming and amplification would make the arrangements sound big. Now we're into the material and waist deep. We're even forgetting that the opening number is actually the opening number from *New Faces of 1952* and that it was a number that was supposed to (a) parodize opening numbers and (b) be a reading of an opening number. But can we also forget that *New Faces of 1952* starred Ronny Graham and that the star of *1968* (Robert Klein) is almost a double for Graham and is sometimes even doing Graham's material? (Doing it well, it should be added.) There is a very funny girl named Madeline Kahn who sings a very funny song satirizing the Kurt Weill–Bertolt Brecht style ["Das Chicago Song," music by Michael Cohen, lyrics by Tony Geiss]. Her burlesque of Lotte Lenya is wonderful and the lyrics perfectly mock Brecht's unfamiliarity with America ("In old Chicago by the sea") and the clumsiness of his translators ("The thump of the traffic/The roar of the axe"). But these are beauty marks in a sea of acne. The performers are abused, misused, or entirely useless.

●   ●   ●

Leonard Sillman began his career playing the Fred Astaire part, so help us, in a 1926 Deep South bus-and-truck tour of George and Ira Gershwin's *Lady Be Good* (1924). He moved on to producing—shoestring producing, more accurately—and managed to assemble, by hook or by crook, some twenty Broadway shows. Sillman began his *New Faces* in 1934; there were seven editions in all, whenever he was able to scrounge up the money. Only one, the aforementioned *New Faces of 1952*, had much to recommend it. Except, that is, for the new faces that paraded through the series: Henry Fonda, Imogene Coca, Van Johnson, Irwin Corey, Alice Pearce, Ronny Graham, Eartha Kitt, Robert Clary, Alice Ghostley, Paul Lynde, Carol Lawrence, Maggie Smith, Inga Swenson, Tiger Haynes, Virginia Martin, Jane Connell, and Marian Mercer. His haul in this final edition: Robert Klein, Madeline Kahn, and Brandon Maggart. Sillman spent the rest of his days, until his death in 1982, trying to get on—you guessed it—one last *New Faces*.

BROADWAY SCORECARD

/ PERFS: 52 / $: –

RAVE	FAVORABLE	MIXED	UNFAVORABLE	PAN
	1	1	2	2

NO, NO, NANETTE

"The New 1925 Musical," a revised version of the 1925 musical comedy

music by Vincent Youmans (additional music by Charles Gaynor, deleted during the tryout)

lyrics by Irving Caesar and Otto Harbach (additional lyrics by Burt Shevelove, replacing Charles Gaynor)

book by Otto Harbach and Frank Mandel, adapted by Burt Shevelove (replacing Charles Gaynor)

based on the 1919 farce *My Lady Friends* by Emil Nyitray and Frank Mandel

"production supervised by Busby Berkeley"

directed by Burt Shevelove (replacing Busby Berkeley)

choreographed by Donald Saddler (replacing Busby Berkeley; assisted by Ted Cappy, Mary Ann Niles, and Bobby Van)

produced by Pyxidium, Ltd. (Cyma Rubin, replacing the tryout billing "Cyma Rubin and Harry Rigby present")

starring Ruby Keeler, Jack Gilford (replacing Frank McHugh, who replaced Hiram Sherman), Bobby Van, Helen Gallagher, Susan Watson (replacing first-featured Carole Demas), and Patsy Kelly

with Roger Rathburn, Loni Zoe Ackerman, K. C. Townsend, Pat Lysinger, and "The Busby Berkeley Girls"

opened January 19, 1971   46th Street Theatre

CLIVE BARNES, *TIMES*

Nostalgia may prove to be the overriding emotion of the seventies, with remembrance of things past far more comfortable than the realization of things present. For everyone who wishes the world were 50 years younger—and particularly, I suspect, for those who remember it when it *was* 50 years younger—the revival of the 1925 musical *No, No, Nanette* should provide a delightful, carefree evening. It also has a certain amount of taste and imagination. The resuscitation of operettas and musical comedies is a tricky operation, and the producers here have gone about their task with skill. It is described as adapted by Burt Shevelove, who is also the director, and although I do not know the original book, I would take a fair-sized bet that Mr. Shevelove's adaptation has been fairly extensive. What emerges is something like one of the new modish put-ons, such as *Dames at Sea* [1968], but with the original music and lyrics, and, of course, much more of the original spirit. This is far closer to a twenties musical than anything New York has seen since the twenties, but it is seen through a contemporary sensibility. Time-travelers of all ages will revel in the simplicity of Vincent Youman's music. It is music to hum, and particularly music to dance to. Its rhythms suggest their own dancing feet, and the melodies are light, cheerful and exuberant, so that even the blues are not too blue. There are a number of standards and near-standards in the score, and they emerge fresh but with reverberations of the past. They have also been cleverly arranged and orchestrated, so that while they sound familiar they don't sound quite familiar enough to be impertinent. Note also the lyrics by Irving Caesar and Otto Harbach. These are as neat as a playful kitten, and on occasion as daring as a trapeze star. Youmans specialized in short musical phrases, which set his lyricists special technical problems. Those are surmounted with a dexterity that deserves a place in any museum of American musical comedy, and yet live wonderfully today. I doubt whether we will encounter any cleverer or more purely musical lyrics than these all this season. The choreography by Donald Saddler was creatively the most important new element in the show. This choreography dazzled—I had forgotten tap-dancing could be so much fun.

MARTIN GOTTFRIED, *WOMEN'S WEAR DAILY*
No, No, Nanette was the first show this season to come into town with "hit" written all over it, but whoever did the writing must have gone so long without a super-musical that he forgot what the real thing was like. The audience at the 46th Street Theatre had the (still dimly famil-

iar) buzz of grapevine success, all right, and the production obviously
believed it, only it was wishful thinking with a touch of the we-can-
make-it-if-we-try. Not that this glossy revival is unsatisfying. It has
been handsomely mounted, conceived and executed by true professionals, and is rather charming. Somewhere along the way, Burt Shevelove
decided to make this show "nice" and instead of the potentially brilliant
he settled for the vacantly agreeable. As such, it is sometimes amusing,
sometimes not so amusing, very easy to look at and with a couple of
genuinely thrilling production numbers. These were in some way the
responsibility of Busby Berkeley, credited as production supervisor, even
though the musical staging was handled by Donald Saddler. Berkeley,
of course, was *the* choreographer of the massive Hollywood musicals of
the '30s and it is typical of Shevelove to hire him—why satirize
Berkeley? He is his own satirist—as it was typical to cast Ruby Keeler
herself in the show. In its big numbers—monster chorus lines, beach
ball dances on the beach—the show is at its best, and the first of these
especially, with Miss Keeler tap dancing in front of a massive chorus, is
absolutely fantastic. But by and large the staging and the performances
are coy, with more than one too many choruses pouring through the
French windows to start a production number, blithely unconcerned
with an explanation for their entry. Keeler makes it on nostalgia alone
(certainly not on her acting), but she projects a true loveliness and her
big dance is fabulous because of work as well as memory. Jack Gilford,
screwing up his face, overdoes the cuteness as the millionaire and
deserves to be out of that rut. Helen Gallagher alone understood the
Shevelove tone and perhaps that is why he directed her to play for it.
Patsy Kelly virtually stole the show, playing the maid with a firm
knowledge of burlesque comedy.

WALTER KERR, *TIMES*

The secret of *No, No, Nanette* lies in Ruby Keeler's sobriety. Actually,
she isn't the only one who has it, it has spread to infect the earnest,
wide-eyed girls who dance on the tops of beach balls and the straight-
faced, straightlaced boys in plus fours who linger about the grand piano
fingering their well-tempered ukuleles. And Miss Keeler, of course, isn't
onstage *all* of the time. She does only two numbers. (*Only* two, did I
say? I bet they could have donated one to *Ari* and they'd still have a

smash.) [*Ari*, the *Exodus* musical, opened four nights earlier]. . . . As Miss Watson and Mr. Gilford vanish like mice into the wings [after singing the duet portion of "I Want to Be Happy"], five young men stroll in from nowhere, unbidden but dressed to stun. They are wearing sweaters, designed by Raoul Pène du Bois, that resemble a trainload of tigers recently struck by lightning, and when they are joined by a chorus of 20 more the stage seems an explosion of Halloween colors, whorls and zigzags forever, putting psychedelic to shame. The boys' shoes are cleated beneath those diamond-patterned socks, and as the fast-tap begins the stage floor flinches. It is jackhammer time. But it is also Ruby Keeler time, which means something else. Down the staircase once more, her beaver-like mind on her work, comes the dancer, ready to lift, Swanee River-style, her featherweight but fiercely concentrated person from right to left, left to right, across stage in front of the madness. There is no madness in her. She drifts from portal to portal like a paper doll that's been blown from a desk because someone opened a window, easy as eiderdown, attentive as a tot in first grade. Miss Keeler minds what she is doing, her eyes have a faraway look in them that sees some reward in the distance (A merit badge? A pat on the back? A minor place in heaven?) and because she is so dutiful while the men behind her are so demented the effect is just as hilarious as it ought to be but honorable besides. The roars that went up during the opening-night curtain calls—themselves most discreetly managed—were part nostalgia, part astonishment, part pain, part delight. Pain? Yes, a kind of mourning, not for our lost innocence but for our lost pleasure. By insisting on the innocence, and not taking too superior an attitude toward it, *No, No, Nanette* has restored the pleasure. For which, many thanks.

o   o   o

A creaky, old, Prohibition-era musical comedy from Jimmy Walker/Prohibition days? A tap-dancing, sixty-one-year-old grandmother who never *could* act in the first place? A washed-up, has-been movie choreographer who couldn't get arrested? (He could get arrested, actually, and was several times—for drunkenness, second degree murder, etc. But that's another story.) The revival of *No, No, Nanette* sounded rather less than likely and was assembled in hapless, slapdash fashion by an "artsy," never-quite-successful producer—with a reputation for stylish flops bankrolled by middle-aged matron ladies with very rich husbands—and a show business neophyte with a very rich husband. They started with seventy-five-year-old Busby Berkeley, who'd been out of the public eye since a front-page suicide attempt in 1945, and assigned old-time revue writer Charles Gaynor—whose one big hit, *Lend an Ear*, was back in 1948—to adapt the book and replenish the score. Producer Cyma Rubin (nicknamed "The Black Witch" by the cast) bumped Busby from his choreography post early on. She replaced him with Donald Saddler, whose only hit was the 1953 *Wonderful Town*, on which Jerry Robbins rushed to Boston to fix the dances for his four chums Lenny, Betty, Adolph, and Mr. Abbott; Saddler won the Tony. On *Nanette* he was "assisted" by tap expert Ted Cappy, Mary Ann Niles—former wife and dancing partner of Bob Fosse—and costar Bobby Van, an experienced song-and-dance man; Saddler won the Tony. As rehearsals approached it became apparent that Berkeley, sitting in the corner dozing through the casting process, was incapable of directing, so Burt Shevelove (from Rigby's 1967 *Hallelujah, Baby!*) was rushed in. Berkeley remained as a figurehead and served as an effective magnet for publicity, so long as he stayed awake through the interviews. Gaynor's revisions turned out to be unusable, forcing poor *Nanette* into rehearsal scriptless. Shevelove—coauthor of the classic *A Funny Thing Happened on the Way to the Forum* (1962)—got to work on the libretto forthwith; Gaynor's song contributions were cut, gradually, during the tryout. *Nanette* did have a couple of things going for it, though, a couple of magical things. Vincent Youmans's score might have been ancient, but it still displayed infectiously entertaining rhythms and two stunning showstoppers, "I Want to Be Happy" and "Tea for Two." And thanks to the stellar music department—orchestrator Ralph Burns, dance/incidental arranger Luther Henderson, and musical director/vocal arranger Buster Davis—the score sounded spectacularly energetic. (Broadway's two groundbreaking syncopated tunesmiths were born within twenty-four hours of each other: George Gershwin and the slightly younger, vastly underappreciated Vincent Youmans. His first hit show was written with George's elder brother Ira; his second, with young Oscar Hammerstein. But Youmans's personality alienated both, destining him to a succession of second-rank lyricists.) And though '30s tap dancer Ruby Keeler turned out to be not much of a singer or actor or personality, she sure could tap-dance—and audiences went wild when she brushed back that curl falling 'cross her forehead, just like she did in *42nd Street* (1933). *Nanette* was unstoppable from the moment Ruby started tapping at the first tryout performance. It didn't matter if Mrs. Rubin fired leading comic Hiram Sherman *and* his replacement Frank McHugh, a familiar face from the old Keeler films, and even her Nanette, Carole Demas (who went on to create the heroine in *Grease* [1972]). Rubin plotted to move her daughter, featured player Loni Zoe Ackerman, into the title spot; but even if you're the boss you can't *always* have your own way. The Black Witch managed to cap it all off by wiping coproducer Harry Rigby's name off the poster and tossing him out into the cold stage door alley. (Rigby was also "defaced" from *Half a Sixpence* [1965] when he failed to come up with his share of the capitalization, although he eventually sued to get his name reinstated.) Rigby got a $300,000 settlement from Pyxidium, Ltd., a pittance compared to *Nanette*'s earnings but far more than he'd accumulated in his previous twenty years on Broadway. Rubin went on to produce two more nostalgia-laden musicals: a 1978 Donald Saddler/Buster Davis/Raoul Pène du Bois mounting of the Gershwins' *Oh, Kay!*, which shuttered on the road, and the 1975 Buster Davis/Raoul Pène du Bois fiasco *Doctor Jazz*, starring Bobby Van as the good doctor himself. Rigby countered with two old-lady revival megaflops of his own: the 1973 *Irene*, starring Debbie Reynolds (and Patsy Kelly), and the 1974 *Good News*, starring Alice Faye. *No, No,* Harry. *No, No,* Cyma.

Tony Awards were won by Donald Saddler (choreographer), Helen Gallagher (actress), Patsy Kelly (supporting actress), and Raoul Pène du Bois (costume design).

BROADWAY SCORECARD
/ PERFS: 861 / $: +

RAVE	FAVORABLE	MIXED	UNFAVORABLE	PAN
3	2	1		

OH, BROTHER!

"A New Musical Comedy"

music by Michael Valenti

book and lyrics by Donald Driver

based on the 1591 comedy *The Comedy of Errors* by William Shakespeare

"directed and staged" by Donald Driver

produced by Zev Bufman and the Kennedy Center, in association with the Fisher Theatre Foundation, Joan Cullman, and Sidney Shlenker

with Bruce Adler, David-James Carroll, Harry Groener, Judy Kaye, Larry Marshall, Mary Mastrantonio, Joe Morton, Alyson Reed, Richard B. Shull, and Alan Weeks

opened November 10, 1981   ANTA Theatre

CLIVE BARNES, *POST*

Opportunism rarely works in the theatre. It certainly didn't work last night at the ANTA where a bunch of producers—some shows nowadays have more producers than cast members—staged a limply unmusical musical called *Oh, Brother!* Oh, God! The principal cast is most painfully talented—10 lovely people faced with a desert and not even an oasis let alone an oil well in sight. They all pushed and battered along their material like Sisyphus pushing his rock uphill. But there must have been times when it crossed the minds of some of them that there must be some other business than show business, because Donald Driver's direction was unfortunately worthy of his script. Two pluses. There is no intermission, which gets the evening over at a brisk snail's pace, and one good joke. This happens before the curtain rises. The American eagles that flank in golden glory the proscenium arch of the ANTA have been decorated with Arab headdresses and sunglasses. That's *Oh, Brother!*

FRANK RICH, *TIMES*

Oh, Brother! desperately wants to be *A Funny Thing Happened on the Way to the Forum* [1962]. It also wouldn't mind being *The Boys from Syracuse* [1938], the musical version of *Two Gentlemen of Verona* [1971] or maybe even *Milk and Honey* [1961]. In the end—or, for that matter, in the beginning—it has to settle for being a spectacularly silly Las Vegas floor show. But *Oh, Brother!* tries. Oh, brother, does it try. This musical is not without its resources. The cast, though often wasted, is an able one, full of talented, appealing young performers. *Oh, Brother!* also introduces to Broadway a composer, Michael Valenti, from whom we'll want to hear again. Though there's nothing startling about Valenti's music, he writes solid, at times pretty, show tunes. The rest of *Oh, Brother!*—its book lyrics, direction and "staging"—is the work of Donald Driver. With the exception of the lyrics, which are adequate, Driver's contributions encase the show in cement. It is his idea to reset a Plautus-Shakespeare long-lost brothers farce in the contemporary Middle East, and a most misguided idea it is. What's funny about the Middle East today? Not much—unless you want to be completely tasteless. Driver allows himself to be tasteless once—when he drags on Ayatollah Khomeini for burlesque gags—but otherwise he avoids pointed allusions to present-day Middle East headlines like the plague. It's hard to blame him, but why bother to set a show in a region where there's no room, right now, for humor? Thanks to its concept, *Oh, Brother!* is crippled before it even begins. The choreography, which puts great store in the humorous possibilities of belly dancing, is at a college revue level. There isn't much room for it in any case, because the routine unit set, by Michael J. Hotopp and Paul De Pass, limits flat stage space to a downstage strip slightly larger than a beach towel. Judy Kaye, while getting campier each time out, remains a big belter with a sure comic sense. Though she can't quite stop this relentlessly frantic show, perhaps nothing short of a Camp David pact could.

○   ○   ○

Rodgers and Hart and Abbott and Balanchine did just dandy with Shakespeare's *The Comedy of Errors*—under the title *The Boys from Syracuse*—so why shouldn't Donald Driver and Michael Valenti give it a shot? (Answer that one yourself.) Driver had adapted and directed *Twelfth Night* into the 1968 Off-Broadway hit *Your Own Thing* (also for coproducer Zev Bufman). But *Your Own Thing* was an intimate, light-rock spoof of a cartoon on lower Second Avenue in the pre-*Hair* swingin' '60s. By the time Driver got to *Oh, Brother!* things had changed. (Sample song lyric: "Bangle-laden OPEC maiden, your lips exude Arabian crude.")

BROADWAY SCORECARD

/ PERFS: 3 / $: –

RAVE	FAVORABLE	MIXED	UNFAVORABLE	PAN
	1			5

OH! CALCUTTA!

"An Entertainment with Music"

music and lyrics by The Open Window (Robert Dennis, Peter Schickele, and Stanley Walden)

"contributors": Samuel Beckett, Jules Feiffer, Dan Greenburg, John Lennon, Jacques Levy, Leonard Melfi, David Newman and Robert Benton, Sam Shepard, Clovis Trouille, Kenneth Tynan, and Sherman Yellen

devised by Kenneth Tynan

directed by Jacques Levy

choreographed by Margo Sappington

produced by Hillard Elkins in association with Michael White and Gordon Crowe

with Raina Barrett, Mark Dempsey, Katie Drew-Wilkinson, Boni Enten, Bill Macy, Alan Rachins, Leon Russom, Margo Sappington, Nancy Tribush, George Welles, and "The Open Window"

opened June 17, 1969   *Eden Theatre*
transferred February 25, 1971   *Belasco Theatre*

(Note: The first-night reviewers covered the show at its Eden Theatre première)

CLIVE BARNES, *TIMES*

Voyeurs of the city unite, you have nothing to lose but your brains. During *Oh! Calcutta!* a member of the cast—barebacked as it were— announces with a simple but euphoric pride: "Gee, this makes *Hair* [1968] seem like *The Sound of Music* [1959]." On the contrary my friend. I assure you *Oh! Calcutta!* makes *The Sound of Music* seem like *Hair*. There is no more innocent show in town—and certainly none more wit- less—than this silly little diversion, devised by Kenneth Tynan, produced by Hillard Elkins and destined to make the shrewd entrepreneurs the crock of gold that lies there somewhere over the rainbow. Innocent it is, completely. It is curious how anti-erotic public nudity, as opposed to pri- vate nudity, is. There is a clinical lack of mystery to it that, speaking for myself, makes me disconcertingly think pure and beautiful thoughts. Other people of course may have other reactions. For students of form, I should point out that while Margo Sappington (an ex-Joffrey dancer of great promise I always expected to see more of, although hardly as much as this) has devised pleasant choreography, it is not very original. In sum: *Oh! Calcutta!* is likely to disappoint different people in different ways, but disappointment is the order of the night. To be honest, I think I can recommend the show with any vigor only to people who are extra- ordinarily underprivileged either sexually, socially or emotionally. Now is your chance to stand up and be counted.

WALTER KERR, *TIMES*
[Headline: "Not Funny, Just Naked"]
Mr. Tynan's hand is normally an exemplary one—cool, restrained, metic- ulous in motion and suave in repose. When he is using it to write, he is a most admirable critic, an impeccable stylist. When he is using it to select plays for the repertory of the British National Theatre, he is a judicious adviser, idealist and realist at once. Coming to *Oh! Calcutta!*, though, a revue of his own devising designed to play with sex on the stage without robe or reservation, he is suddenly a fevered butterfingers, so agog with a promised glee that he has entirely neglected to notice what is on the pages he has, with a racing heart, handed his director and his so willing actors. Taste, an ear for wit, an eye for form, a heart that insists upon being pleased only in the highlands, have all vanished. The clumsiest, most

labored of jokes are permitted to succeed one another in obsessive monotony. Language no longer matters, structure no longer matters, inspiration no longer matters. Anything will do so long as it meets two requirements: that the actors undress and that they engage in simulated sex play. Lines do not have to be funny nor ideas in any way fresh to pass muster. The people on stage are not engaged in being amusing or pertinent or impertinent or imaginative. They are engaged in being naked. It is an exclusive occupation. The matter is important because it sweeps straight across the board. If Tynan's vision has been blurred in every other way by its absolute focus upon sex, the authors from whom he has drawn material have lost all steadiness as well. They have, in fact, lost character. Samuel Beckett, Jules Feiffer, John Lennon, Leonard Melfi, Sam Shepard and Tynan himself are among the writers credited with sketches. Though the writers are all men whose work we know, whose personalities and stylistic habits are real to us, there is no way at all of distinguishing one from another by the activity or the language on stage. We can make guesses. But there is never any little leap of recognition in the theatre that says, on the spot, that we have found our man. All plod to the same beat and in the plodding all blur. The preoccupation with visual, literal, immediate sex has wiped out not only quality, but also identity.

JERRY TALLMER, *POST*

Mr. Joe Namath was among those present at last night's long-awaited official opening of *Oh! Calcutta!* at the Eden (formerly Phoenix) Theatre, and I hope he got more out of it than I did. But Joe, I should think, swings better than *Oh! Calcutta!* and knows it. In case you've been up in the lunar landing module these past few months, *Oh! Calcutta!* is the evening of "erotic" entertainment "devised" by British critic Kenneth Tynan, with preview tickets having been scalped at $46 a pair (the legit price will presently be $25 a pair). Let's get the good things down first. Yes, there is a great bit of total nudity, and director Jacques Levy must be given credit for (a) selecting good-looking actors and actresses for this, especially in the department of trim, taut, well-developed torsos, and (b) for getting them to be at their unself-conscious ease in all that they have to do. At least they seem completely free and at ease. It's a pleasure to watch them—until the words come out. I have heard better—and many much better—in plain old good burlesque. The audience was perhaps more interesting than the show. On my right there was an old lady, surely almost 90 years of age, peering through her opera glasses, muttering exclamations to herself. The one I caught was, "What's so funny about that?" Agreed.

                       ◦   ◦   ◦

Some wise comedy writer or other—wish I could remember who and pass on credit—once said that if you want to get away with telling a dirty joke it better be twice as funny. *Oh! Calcutta!*, in a word, wasn't. Not funny at all, really. There was certainly an audience for the show, at first among the squares from out of town and later among foreign-language tourists, who couldn't understand the unfunny jokes anyway. But the show was almost breathtakingly mirthless, quite a feat given the subject matter. The most remarkable aspect of the show, perhaps, was its contributors' list. At least some of the men involved (all men, what a surprise) were unquestionably talented; while one is not necessarily amazed by their agreement to participate, one wonders at their inability to come up with anything clever, funny, or even modestly amusing in the process. They were somewhat like naughty schoolboys, allowed (just this once) to say all the dirty words they could come up with in one sitting. Like most naughty schoolboys, they preferred to remain anonymous as to their especial take on naked bodies; however, they allowed their names to be publicized, of course, lest the show end up a hit (which it was) and worth a good chunk of change in royalties (which it was). But you couldn't pick out your favorite writer and identify his contribution by the quality, certainly; we are told that John Lennon wrote the sketch about the Lone Ranger, for what it's worth (which is not much). *Oh! Calcutta!* ran more than three years, transferring midway to the venerable old Belasco. Four years later a revival opened at the mid-Broadway Edison Theatre and ran thirteen years on the backs of Japanese businessmen with a yen. An impressive record, but the show has not enjoyed much of an afterlife in the high school/community theatre circuit, alas.

BROADWAY SCORECARD

/ PERFS: 1,314 / $: +

RAVE	FAVORABLE	MIXED	UNFAVORABLE	PAN

OKLAHOMA!

a revival of the 1943 musical comedy

music by Richard Rodgers

book and lyrics by Oscar Hammerstein 2nd

based on the 1931 folk play *Green Grow the Lilacs* by Lynn Riggs

directed by William Hammerstein

choreographed by Agnes de Mille, re-created by Gemze de Lappe

produced by Zev Bufman and James M. Nederlander in association with Donald C. Carter

starring Laurence Guittard, Christine Andreas, and Mary Wickes

with Martin Vidnovic, Christine Ebersole, Harry Groener, Bruce Adler, and Philip Rash

opened December 13, 1979   Palace Theatre

CLIVE BARNES, *POST*

[Headline: "Still as High as an Elephant's Eye"]

Yes, the corn still stands as high as an elephant's eye, but the lovely thing is that it still isn't corny. A woman is churning butter outside an old farmhouse. A voice is heard singing: "Oh, what a beautiful mornin'!" A cowboy enters—still singing, now even making that rather dubious claim about corn and the elephant, and the Broadway musical stops dead in its tracks, and starts right over again. And still the moment is magic. What music! What sheer good fun! And what wonderfully assertive innocence, what an asseveration of America the proud, America the beautiful, America the unlimited! The thing that strikes everyone about *Oklahoma!* is the score. Virtually every number is a hit. But in a way what was more important, and what made *Oklahoma!* such a landmark in the musical theatre, was its new homogeneity, its specific blend of music, drama and dance, and its new seriousness.

A Hilary Knight-view of the 36-year-old perennial, set against an elephant-eye-high cornstalk. To quote Mr. Hammerstein, "You're doin' fine, *Oklahoma!*" (artwork by Hilary Knight)

Curiously enough when the show was new in 1943 the critics of the time liked it well enough but had little idea of its implications or revolutionary spirit. Stark Young, for example, wrote ". . . reminds us at times of a good college show . . ." and when *Oklahoma!* made it to London, although the reviews were more enthusiastic, the then senior reviewer, James Agate, was still able to sum it up as: "Bouquet, yes; body, no." The new version (I hate the word revival, no one ever talks of a revival of *Rigoletto*) has been directed with a sort of traditional pizzazz by William Hammerstein, the author's son, and choreographer Agnes de Mille has personally supervised the entire show. This is totally appropriate, for de Mille's contribution to the musical's entire fabric was, and is, essential. The curious thing is that the long ballet sequence, that special dream ballet *Laurey Makes Up Her Mind*, is the one part of the musical that seems dated. The rest of the dancing, beautifully melded into the production, is exemplary and was, in its time, trailblazing. So there it is. A show to freshen your heart and make your next morning wonderful. As the old song has it: "You're doing fine Oklahoma!, Oklahoma!, OK!" The most authentic performance comes from Mary Wickes as Aunt Eller. Apart from the fact that she looks remarkably like Miss de Mille herself and has de Mille's style and manner, her pioneer presence and no-nonsense lovability illuminate the whole show.

WALTER KERR, *TIMES*
[Headline: "Free as the Breeze"]
There was a considerable age range in the audience with which I saw the freshly revived *Oklahoma!* at the Palace. As I went up the aisle at intermission, I noticed one and all were beaming. Some were smiling because they remember. The others were smiling because they will. *Oklahoma!* remains the gently enchanting sampler it is because, after hundreds of imitations have come and mostly gone, it is utterly unselfconscious about what it is doing. Rodgers and Hammerstein weren't necessarily determined to change the face of musical comedy forever when they took their curtain up on a woman at a butter-churn listening idly to a strolling cowhand sing a beginning salute to morning with no musical accompaniments at all. They went to work as they did because they were persuaded that this was the way a particular woman,

and a particular cowhand, in a particular piece of wide-open territory *would* behave: lazily, spontaneously, free as the faint breeze that seemed to stir the leafy shadows at the top of the barn, near the window. And besides, it was a beautiful morning. In fact, you can still see—and be charmed by—remnants of the kind of musical that *Oklahoma!* replaced spotted here and there among its didoes. One of the show's most radical innovations, of course, was Agnes de Mille's substitution of ballet's freedoms for the old heel-toe tap routines, done in deadpan precision. Yet, though this is the enterprise in which de Mille sent one trio bobbing and pecking its way across stage as though it were composed of either churchgoers or chickens, while another took straight to the air in exhilarating promise of a new day to come, one of the evening's earliest numbers contains a fast tap—and a tap with a ragtime beat to it, at that. The dance is done by Harry Groener, who plays Will Parker, and it jumps from the floor like so much sudden popcorn, generated by the jolly beat of "Everything's Up to Date in Kansas City." The performer is probably this revival's most unexpected discovery: singing with highly nasal hayseed enthusiasm, letting the shock of hair on his forehead bounce in erratic counterpoint to his swiftly triggered feet, he is both a fine clown and a reasonably authentic bronco buster. . . . The entertainment is now too long, by a good 20 minutes. No one should touch the music, though. All that incredible music.

HOWARD KISSEL, *WOMEN'S WEAR DAILY*

William Hammerstein, son of Oscar, has staged the revival of *Oklahoma!* as if it were as coy and dumb as *Very Good Eddie* [1915]. His father's book has dated considerably, but it has an emotional honesty underneath its corny words. Even the beautiful songs are undercut by the "cute" way they are sung. What should be a thrilling evening is a shockingly amateurish one. Even Agnes de Mille's original choreography is trivialized by what seems an unusually green corps. The dancers have learned the original steps to her landmark dream ballet, but they don't seem to have any idea of the dramatic motivation behind them. Laurence Guittard condescends to the role of Curley, camping up his part, even musically, as if he were embarrassed to be in the show. As Laurey Christine Andreas sings sweetly, but acts without conviction. Together they make such songs as "People Will Say We're in Love" and

"Surrey With the Fringe on Top" lifeless, charmless, sexless. The only two convincing actors in the cast are Harry Groener, an extremely lively Will Parker, and Martin Vidnovic, a compelling Jud. Some of the others could be bettered by high school actors. Jay Blackton conducts the score in the prescribed Rodgers' manner—utterly square, giving the actors little flexibility. The only number that really works is the title song, largely because of the stunning choral arrangement. The sets and costumes are uninspired and cheap looking. In order to work, *Oklahoma!* needed completely fresh interpretations, or, at the very least, a belief in the human values underlying the often dated material. The only belief behind this production is that there is no difference between Broadway standards and those of dinner theatres. At least in the dinner theatres you get fed.

*   *   *

The efficacy of *Oklahoma!* and its old-fashioned, well-made brethren seemed eclipsed by the dawning of the age of Aquarius. A June '69 Richard Rodgers-produced *Oklahoma!* with a cast headed by Bruce Yarnell, Leigh Beery, and Margaret Hamilton looked very quaint indeed. (Rodgers mounted a summer series of musical revivals at the New York State Theatre from 1964 through 1969 under the banner "Music Theatre of Lincoln Center." When their *Oklahoma!* lost money—the first of the shows to do so—Rodgers decided it was time to disband the series.) In January '79 Florida stock producer Zev Bufman threw together a cheap, quick *Oklahoma!* for his Miami Beach/Ft. Lauderdale octogenarian subscribers. Harve Presnell (a forty-six-year-old Curley), Betsy Beard, and Mary Wickes led the cast, with support from Maureen Moore and Lewis J. Stadlen as Annie and Ali Hakim. Surprisingly enough, nonoctogenarians eagerly snapped up all available nonsubscription seats; so Bufman built new sets, upgraded the cast (only Mary Wickes remained), and launched a national tour in May from the Pantages in Los Angeles. With the Palace sitting empty since the closing of *The Grand Tour*, Jimmy Nederlander—who'd been watching the *Oklahoma!* grosses in his road houses—called the R & H oater in off the range, and the "Beautiful Mornin'" was back on Broadway. A hit again, after thirty-seven years. For composer Rodgers—who'd undergone the disappointing *I Remember Mama* that spring and whose previous outings had been the similarly unhappy *Do*

I Hear a Waltz? (1965), *Two by Two* (1970), and *Rex* (1976)—the rejuvenation of *Oklahoma!* was more than welcome. The composer—Broadway's greatest, perhaps?—died two weeks after the opening on December 30, 1979, at the age of seventy-seven.

BROADWAY SCORECARD

/ PERFS: 293 / $: +

RAVE	FAVORABLE	MIXED	UNFAVORABLE	PAN
2	2		1	1

ON A CLEAR DAY YOU CAN SEE FOREVER

"A New Musical," previously entitled *I Picked a Daisy*

music by Burton Lane (replacing Richard Rodgers)

book and lyrics by Alan Jay Lerner

directed by Robert Lewis

choreographed by Herbert Ross

produced by Alan Jay Lerner in association with Rogo Productions (Norman Rosemont/Robert Goulet)

starring Barbara Harris and John Cullum (replacing Louis Jourdan)

with Titos Vandis, William Daniels, Clifford David, Rae Allen, Michael Lewis, Gerry Matthews, and Byron Webster

opened October 17, 1965   Mark Hellinger Theatre

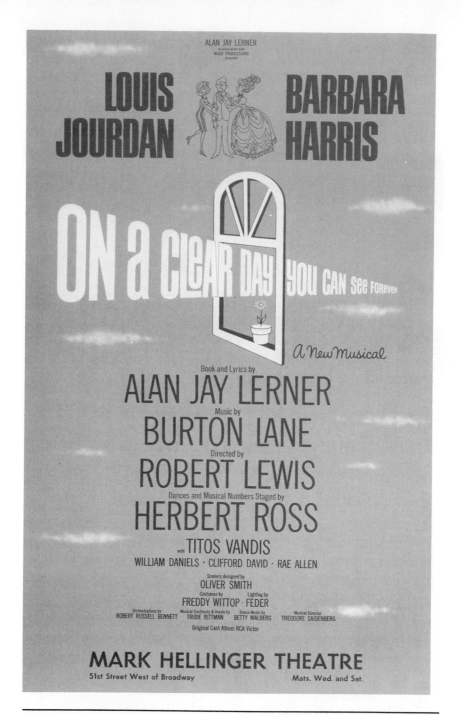

ALAN JAY LERNER
in association with
HOGO PRODUCTIONS
presents

LOUIS JOURDAN

BARBARA HARRIS

ON a CLEAR DAY YOU CAN See FOREVER

A New Musical

Book and Lyrics by
ALAN JAY LERNER
Music by
BURTON LANE
Directed by
ROBERT LEWIS
Dances and Musical Numbers Staged by
HERBERT ROSS

with TITOS VANDIS

WILLIAM DANIELS · CLIFFORD DAVID · RAE ALLEN

Scenery designed by
OLIVER SMITH
Costumes by   Lighting by
FREDDY WITTOP · FEDER

Orchestrations by   Musical Continuity & Vocals by   Dance Music by   Musical Director
ROBERT RUSSELL BENNETT   TRUDE RITTMAN   BETTY WALBERG   THEODORE SAIDENBERG

Original Cast Album RCA Victor

MARK HELLINGER THEATRE
51st Street West of Broadway   Mats. Wed. and Sat.

A foggy *Clear Day*, alas, unable to see its way clear of Alan Jay Lerner's haze. Richard Rodgers and Gower Champion left during the writing, Louis Jourdan shipped out from Boston. Preliminary credits.

WALTER KERR, *HERALD TRIBUNE*

In *On a Clear Day You Can See Forever* flowers grow faster for Barbara Harris, and I don't blame them. She's cute. In *On a Clear Day You Can See Forever* Barbara Harris smokes too much, and I don't blame her. She's in trouble. It's a commonplace in the trade to say that a writer is stuck for a finish, meaning that he hasn't the faintest notion of how to wrap up what he has so confidently, so buoyantly begun. In the new musical, alas, Alan Jay Lerner is stuck for a start. *On a Clear Day* has not only had the nerve to come up with a completely original musical comedy book, it has also had the jauntiness to tackle a pleasantly tricky, and certainly contemporary, subject [extrasensory perception]. Then it quits. Or, rather, dissolves—flashback style—into another musical altogether, one about the passions and perils of reincarnation. In one of her trances Miss Harris's lips turn primrose-prim, her canary-yellow voice drops an octave, and she is heard to mutter a few incoherent things about tumbling onto a cartload of daffodils, while rushing to meet her husband in 1794. Yes, it is eighteenth-century time again, servants in turbans are dancing down the stairs, Hogarthian mothers and fathers are talking dowries between faintly mocking minuets, and Harris was once upon a time named Melinda. The evening has become more than square, it has become *Berkeley Square* [John Balderston's 1929 metaphysical fantasy, which featured Leslie Howard shuttling between the present and 1784]. After that, there is really no rescuing it, not even when choreographer Herbert Ross tosses all of the girls into the air to be turned upside down and hurtled across male shoulders like so many revved-up echoes of—what was it?—*Tom Jones*. In the end the show sighs, gropes for a long way out. But it is hard to end an idea that has never quite been an idea. Two of the masters of our musical theatre, Mr. Lerner and Mr. Lane, have simply started too much from scratch.

JOHN MCCLAIN, *JOURNAL-AMERICAN*

[Headline: "*Clear Day* But Foggy"]

It would be pleasant to say that the result is a charming fantasy, but it seemed to me it is instead a melodious muddle. This is extremely regrettable because there is so much that is charming and decorative and exciting about the show: it has bright sets by Oliver Smith, arresting costumes by Freddy Wittop, some memorable tunes by Burton Lane, and the wonderful services of Barbara Harris and a neophyte, John Cullum, who took over the other leading role when Louis Jourdan backed away from it on the road. There is even the sense that something better, at least less confusing, should have come out of the story. This is a prodigious part for Miss Harris, noted previously for her performance in *Oh, Dad, Poor Dad* [1962], and she displays a very efficient way with a song and an extraordinary sense of comedy. There is something wild and pitiful about her, like Judy Holliday, and when she is being her modern addled self, she can sound a great deal like Geraldine Page. Cullum, who has a fine voice, is entrusted with the show's best song, "On a Clear Day." It is a most ingratiating tune, sure to be heard everywhere, and he delivers it with poise and an excellent sense of timing. However confusing, *Clear Day* is big and bountiful and the popularity of its title song and the performance of Harris are apt to keep it alive for quite a spell.

NORMAN NADEL, *WORLD-TELEGRAM & SUN*

The first musical hit of the season, even if the second act does, for a time, let story and mood slip through its fingers. Generally, on its own highly individual terms, it is a happy wonder and a bewitching, beguiling musical play. Alan Jay Lerner's *Brigadoon* [1947] comes to mind in his new story about a girl endowed with ESP. It is a superbly rich role for a comedienne of the versatility which Barbara Harris possesses. She lilts through it, manufacturing joyous laughter out of such innocent devices as chomping on a cigarette, letting her speaking pitch get out of hand, or falling into a hypnotic sleep as if she'd been clubbed. When she slips into her other self—Melinda, an English girl in the late 18th century—her voice, posture, mood and personality are totally transformed. It is like getting two lovely and individual leading women for the price of one. We can be grateful as well for whatever circumstances catapulted John Cullum into the role of the psychiatrist who works with, and becomes attached to, this baby-faced ESP treasure. His Burtonesque speech is articulate and vibrant. He sings well, if not quite effortlessly, and he emanates strength of character. Even as it stands, *On a Clear Day* is unique and enjoyable. That ESP could mean extra-special pleasure.

HOWARD TAUBMAN, *TIMES*

Although there are several outstandingly genial elements, they do not suffice to turn the new musical into the soaring, satisfying unity it ought to be. The most admirable assets are the songs and the leading lady. The songs have bright, charming lyrics by Lerner and a sheaf of new tunes by Lane that have more melodic grace and inventive distinction than has been heard in years. As for Barbara Harris, who combines something of the brash wistfulness of Judy Holliday and a freshness and vitality of her own, she is a blithe spirit and living doll. Because the story is frail and rickety, the characters, songs and production numbers in *On a Clear Day* do not mesh with the neatness and subtlety Lerner has taught us to expect. The book loses itself in a fog of metaphysics that dares not stray too far from the romantic demands of musicals. What Lerner should have worried about was not another life but a better idea. In any event, it's doubtful that he could have found a more tuneful composer or a more ingratiating leading lady.

o   o   o

It all seemed like a dream: Richard Rodgers, partner of the late Oscar Hammerstein; Alan Jay Lerner, partner of the retired Fritz Loewe; Gower Champion, who had rejuvenated musical comedy with the back-to-back *Bye Bye Birdie* (1960) and *Carnival* (1961); and Barbara Harris, the new about-to-be star who'd stunned the town with her appearance in the Off-Broadway conversation piece *Oh, Dad, Poor Dad, Mama's Hung You in the Closet and I'm Feeling So Sad*. The new musical *I Picked a Daisy*, about an extrasensory perception Daisy who can talk to the flowers and convince them to grow, was announced with much fanfare for a March 1963 opening. Everything was going alone fine except, as coproducer Rodgers noted, "The writing is going a little slower than we thought." When coproducer Lerner skipped one work session too many—jetting to Capri instead, his housekeeper said—Rodgers pulled the plug and that was the end of *Daisy*. Baffled by it all, Rodgers told *Newsweek*: "Larry liked to drink, Oscar never touched the stuff and neither does Alan. But there is one thing common to all three: *not liking to work*." What Rodgers didn't say was that Lerner's inability to concentrate was exacerbated by his addiction to "miracle" injections from Max ("Dr. Feelgood") Jacobsen. Jacobsen had a big society following at the time; Lerner, one of his more prominent patients, became totally dependent. Burton Lane—the immensely talented composer of *Finian's Rainbow* (1947) and collaborator with Lerner on the 1951 Fred Astaire film *Royal Wedding*—was quickly enlisted to fill Rodgers's place at the piano bench. Lane encountered the same problems with Lerner, although as the lesser collaborator (and a nonequal partner), he simply shrugged and waited. Barbara Harris was kept under contract—Lerner knew what he had in this unusually talented, unusual girl—while costar Robert Horton was released (and went into the already-in-rehearsal *110 in the Shade* [1963], causing Hal Holbrook to be fired; Champion also left the stalled project, taking up David Merrick's 1964 musical about that extrasensory *Dolly!*). The Lerner/Lane *Clear Day*, meanwhile, was set for January 1964 rehearsals. The date was put off, though; seems the book and lyrics weren't ready. (At this point the Messrs. Feuer, Martin, and Fosse—the *Little Me* [1962] boys who picked up *Daisy* when Rodgers dropped out—also took their leave.) The underwritten show finally rolled into Boston some eighteen months later, with Robert Lewis (of *Brigadoon*) directing; French actor Louis Jourdan—an international star, courtesy of Lerner's 1958 film *Gigi*—opposite Harris; and Dr. Max, imported from Park Avenue, in constant attendance with his little black bag and magical methedrine injections. Some *Clear Day*. The opening was a bust, and producer/lyricist/librettist Lerner spent days at a time fortified in his hotel room. Lane pressed for and finally effected the replacement of Jourdan; if the show was destined to be a shambles, he figured, at least the score should sound good. John Cullum hailed from *Camelot* (1960), where he started as one of Julie Andrews's singing knights, became Richard Burton's protégé and understudy, and eventually replaced Roddy McDowall as Mordred; in 1964, Burton took him along as Laertes to his legendary Hamlet. So *Clear Day* finally made it to the Hellinger—a musical about a doctor whose treatments give his star patient a miraculous extra sense, written by a star patient being given a miraculous extra sense by his doctor. Only Dr. Max was not in the Louis Jourdan/John Cullum mold, being fat and dumpy. He was eventually dispatched to the Home for Magickal Doctors; the treatments' aftereffects, unfortunately, seemed to plague Lerner for the rest of his not-so-clear days. Looking Back in Retrospect Dept.: In a 1979 discussion of musicals with "original" stories, rather than adaptations, Jimmy (*A Chorus Line*) Kirkwood complimented Lerner: "I remember in the intermission feeling so happy that I didn't know how *On a Clear Day* was going to end." "I didn't either," Lerner responded. "That was the trouble."

BROADWAY SCORECARD

/ PERFS: 280 / $: –

RAVE	FAVORABLE	MIXED	UNFAVORABLE	PAN
	1	2	2	1

ON THE TOWN

a revival of the 1944 musical comedy

music by Leonard Bernstein

book and lyrics by Betty Comden and Adolph Green

based on "an idea" (the 1944 ballet *Fancy Free*) by Jerome Robbins

directed and choreographed by Ron Field

produced by Jerry Schlossberg–Vista Productions

starring Phyllis Newman (Green), Bernadette Peters, and Ron Husmann (replacing 2nd-featured Kurt Peterson)

with Donna McKechnie, Jess Richards, Remak Ramsay (replacing Bill Gerber), Marilyn Cooper, Fran Stevens, Tom Avera, and Zoya Leporska

opened October 31, 1971   Imperial Theatre

CLIVE BARNES, *TIMES*

The Bronx is still up, and the Battery is down—as they still sing—but Leonard Bernstein's 1944 musical *On the Town* is just about in the middle. While some of the glory has doubtless departed, there were moments of brightness if not incandescence. Perhaps—could it be?—that New York has changed. Certainly music has. The musical was inspired by Jerome Robbins's great ballet *Fancy Free*, which also had music by Bernstein. But while the ballet endures, the musical now has only a fitful life. Robbins, it seems, has had the last laugh as well as the first. The book and lyrics by Betty Comden and Adolph Green have ease and a decent few laughs. The music by Bernstein has worn less well, even in the updated orchestrations by Bernstein himself and the splendid Hershy Kay. "New York, New York is a helluva' town" is still a helluva' number, but too many of the nostalgic ballads sound like sub-Puccini filtered through Glenn Miller, and there is a terrifying explosive busy-ness to much of the music. It moves in fits and starts, and often with more fits than starts. Where Field is most successful is in the performances, and the women are markedly better than the men. Best of all is Bernadette Peters as the Bronx-ly nasal taxi driver, who wants to go to her place and has a heart as big as the Stage Door Canteen. Peters sings, acts and dances, in that order, with a saucer-eyed naughtiness and wide-vowelled drawl that is totally enchanting. Phyllis Newman as Claire, the predatory Margaret Mead, also danced and sang with just the right style and gusto. Donna McKechnie made a sweet and talented Ivy Smith. Field has staged the musical numbers with zest and imagination, but, with respect, he is no great shakes as a choreographer. The musical calls for a number of set ballets—these were fashionable in musicals of the day—and Field is no Jerome Robbins. His ideas would have been old-fashioned in 1905, let alone 1944. Like a Late Late Show movie of uncertain vintage, the bloom may be off, the quality of the time evaporated. Yet it may serve to remind people of wartime innocence—when New York was a visitor's paradise and ironically peaceful. And the music—for all its occasional shades of Aaron Copland lyricism—does have a brash and Broadway bounce to it.

MARTIN GOTTFRIED, *WOMEN'S WEAR DAILY*

On the Town is a revival of more than a 1944 musical. It is a revival of 1944 theatre, 1944 audiences. Even the show's opening was a throwback, with star gazers across the street, a crowded lobby of overdressed first nighters, a feeling of gala and a confidence that a hit was about to be born. It is based on *Fancy Free*, and so there is a great deal of dance in it—far more than the ordinary musical—and a great deal of dance music, written and co-orchestrated by the composer. There, however, is one of the problems. Robbins is a seminal figure in our musical theatre and a choreographic genius. In directing and choreographing this revival, Ron Field ran the inevitable risk of comparison and its inevitable result of coming off second best. Though his new dances have manageable, agreeable stretches and even some moments of real interest and delight, he is just not fertile enough to invent enough material for what must be 30 minutes of choreography. However, though comparison is inevitable it is not really fair, and as a separate thing, Field's *On the Town* is generally delightful. If the production is not a continuum of choreography and musical staging, as it should be, it is still nearly always musical and consistent in attitude. Bernstein's score holds up well, reflecting the show business vernacular of the time but still interesting because of its technical depth. Of course, then as now he was under the influence of Stravinsky, Copland and the Weill of *Lady in the Dark* [1941], but it is cozy to notice that he could also borrow from himself (there are patterns here on which he later elaborated in *Wonderful Town* [1957] and *West Side Story* [1957]). He was, as he remains, the most sophisticated composer in American musical theatre history. Perhaps most affecting of all is the Comden and Green book and lyrics, which show them fresh and gleeful in a way that they have seldom been since. Their lyrics are musical and honest, their high spirits contagious. Though it has its lapses, *On the Town* presents an enchanting combination of charm and buoyancy, and Field—one of the few professionals in today's musical theatre—has given it a polished and handsome production.

WALTER KERR, *TIMES*
[Headline: "Pushing the *Town* Around"]
You don't have to go back 28 years to admire *On the Town*. It's not more than 12 since it turned up in a modest off-Broadway production [staged by Joe Layton] and seemed a charmer. At the Imperial, though, they haven't been nice enough to it. The show has, or had, a cool, loose-jointed, rockabye curve of its own, an original way of ambling where it pleased and of being pleased with its way of ambling.

Director-choreographer Ron Field has broken the curve in two unkind ways. He's decided to keep the pressure constant. Apparently fearful that a moment's relaxation with the people will let the air out of the grab-bag, he has got Bernadette Peters pushing from her first appearance as a lady cabdriver whose main objective is to get a male passenger into her apartment as quickly as possible, Phyllis Newman pushing from the time that she pops from beneath a dinosaur's bones to inspect her sample sailor for the day, Donna McKechnie pushing from the moment that she is swung centerstage as the wistful little cooch-dancer who has been chosen Miss Turnstiles for the month. All three work with the supercharge of energy, with such identical vocal thrusts (nearing screeches) and such identical physical attacks (nearing mayhem) that they become, for a time, virtually indistinguishable. They even begin to look alike. And Field has decided, on insubstantial grounds, that *On the Town* is a period piece now, far enough away from us to need dressing-up as pastiche. The strained costuming, not to mention the makeup (yes, we're going to have to mention the makeup), is extremely hard on the girls. Peters, with Dracula lipstick, kewpie-doll powder and a tumbleweed hairdo, comes closer to reminding us of Mae Murray (1925)—she doesn't look period, she looks terrible—while the tailored suit first imposed upon Miss Newman should be sent directly back to the tailor [costumes designed by Ray Aghayan and Bob Mackie, makeup and hair styles by Ted Azar]. Peters, in her Raggedy Ann overalls, rocks the house as she should with her "I Can Cook Too," and when the proper time comes for Newman to growl and grab at her man, she growls and grabs marvelously. But it was her calming down for that placid, philosophical, shining "Oh, well" [in the next-to-closing "Some Other Time"] that made me realize what had been missing earlier, and had left me so detached, from this revival: a kind of kindness, an uninsistent amiability, a sense of young and warm and unworried fun.

o   o   o

The grand success of *Applause* (1970) put Ron Field on top of the heap after twenty-nine years on Broadway. (He started as a seven-year-old figment of Gertie Lawrence's memory in *Lady in the Dark* [1941].) *Cabaret* (1966) and to a lesser extent *Zorbá* (1968), mixed in with a handful of flops (from *Nowhere to Go But Up* [1962] and *Cafe Crown* [1964] to *Sherry!* [1967] and *Golden Rainbow* [1968]), marked him as a choreographer to watch. With the success of *Applause*, which he also directed, Field was primed to join Gower Champion and Bob Fosse. Searching for his sophomore offering, he stumbled upon *On the Town* (by *Applause* librettists Comden and Green). Tackling Jerry Robbins's signature piece, now *there's* a project to prove one's mettle. But Field's mettle proved all too lusterless, his *On the Town* proved all too flat, and he hightailed it to Hollywood. Field's future Broadway visits—*King of Hearts* (1978), patch-up jobs on the *Peter Pan* revival (1979), and *Rags* (1986)—were uninspired, and the career of brilliance promised by *Cabaret* went unfulfilled. A bad production of a good show somehow looks worse than a good production of a bad show. "A 1940s musical and it should have stayed there," opined Kevin Kelly of the Boston *Globe*. "I couldn't wait to get out of the theatre." So they fired two of the sailor leads, which, of course, fixed nothing. More's the pity. Only don't blame the material.

BROADWAY SCORECARD
/ PERFS: 73 / $: —

RAVE	FAVORABLE	MIXED	UNFAVORABLE	PAN
	2	3		1

ON THE TWENTIETH CENTURY

"A New Musical Comedy"

music by Cy Coleman

book and lyrics by Betty Comden and Adolph Green

based on the 1932 farce *20th Century* by Ben Hecht and Charles MacArthur, from the unproduced play *The Napoleon of Broadway* by Bruce Millholand

directed by Harold Prince

choreographed by Larry Fuller

produced by The Producers Circle 2, Inc. (Robert Fryer, Mary Lea Johnson, James Cresson, and Martin Richards) in association with Joseph Harris and Ira Bernstein

starring Madeline Kahn, John Cullum, and Imogene Coca

with George Coe, Dean Dittman, Kevin Kline, Rufus Smith, George Lee Andrews, Tom Batten, Judy Kaye, and Willi Burke

opened February 19, 1978   St. James Theatre

RICHARD EDER, *TIMES*

On the Twentieth Century is Broadway's groundhog. It has come out, and it should stay out, and it is definitely a sign of spring in what had come to seem like a very long winter. It is funny, elegant and totally cheerful. It has rough spots, flat spots and an energy that occasionally ebbs, leaving the cast and the director to regroup their energies for the next assault. But the elegance is there, nevertheless; the kind that allows itself to be unpredictable, playful and even careless. The musical has an exuberance, a bubbly confidence in its own life. This is a big musical, with some extraordinary visual effects that are a wordless extension, both startling and captivating, of the comedy of the performers. But there is a vein of the sensible running through that cuts any tendency to pretentiousness. When anything gets big, it laughs at itself. Cy Coleman's music is invariably used to heighten the spirit of the production. There are grandiloquent and amusing suggestions of everything from Tchaikovsky through Puccini and Friml and up through Kurt Weill. Coleman is witty and inventive, and though much of his energy is spent in serving the comic-theatrical mood of the production, a number of his songs stand beautifully on their own. John Cullum, as Jaffe, is seedy, manic and totally winning. He looks remarkably like John Barrymore, who played the role in the movie, but with more vitality and humor. His first real entrance, when we see him with his face up against the window of the moving train trying to get in, launches a momentum that never stops. Kevin Kline is another very funny performer as Miss Kahn's tame lover. He is all beautiful profile, as insubstantial as a line drawing on tissue paper, and when Kahn makes one of her more ferocious entrances he literally blows around the compartment, finally drifting down to the floor. *Century* has been adjusted, cut and shifted about considerably as it made its way to New York. There is some drifting and choppiness; also some further work to be done. But in general, its assembly of talents has produced something quite delightful [and] brought back what seemed dead or at least endangered: the comedy in musical comedy.

WALTER KERR, *TIMES*
[Headline: "Aboard *20th Century*—Lots of Brio and a Few Bumps"]
When the Messrs. Hecht and MacArthur, together with director George Abbott, first put the clamoring confection together in 1932—and even when John Barrymore and Carole Lombard made a manic film of it several years later—we still had a living tradition of crawl-up-the-wall farce. We also had performers seal-trained to spreadeagle themselves in midair by straddling drawing room seats, Jack-be-nimble adept at getting their profiles caught and crushed in swiftly slammed closet doors. Today, having de-athleticized our farces in a vain search for rationality, we have neither the style in our pockets nor flamboyant performers to shake out of them. And so, with a determined new ringmaster driving not-quite-clowns through old hoops, can they do it?

They can and they can't. . . . Comden and Green have come up with what seems to me a highly intelligent attack on the problem. Don't apply more and more pressure to the dialogue until its seams fly loose. Instead, whenever flamboyance is on the verge of compounding itself, take it—rapidly and candidly—up one-fourth into song. Into clattering narrative song, into clashing character song, into trios, quartets and even sextets that will give the hurry and the scurry of what's going on a legitimate beat. Six people can fling themselves around a crowded compartment more cheerfully and more outrageously if there's a governing rhythm dictating their cross-purpose courses, and the *opera bouffe* effect works handsomely and happily in a second-act free-for-all ["Sign, Lily, Sign"]. You don't get hummable individual songs this way, but you do get speed and elevation. Coleman's resources are up to the rushing demands, and the playful musical mockery (Bizet and Romberg included) pays off in a final, fraudulent, *Tristan*-like death scene as it might have been done by a conniving Nelson Eddy and an insincere Jeanette MacDonald. Possibly the entire evening should have been sung. How do things stand, then? *On the Twentieth Century* is genial, good to look at, fun to listen to whenever the orchestra's giving it the scale and brio its special temper demands. As with most train trips, you grow more relaxed along the way. An imperfect roadbed, but there are those friendly faces across the aisle.

DOUGLAS WATT, *DAILY NEWS*
[Headline: "*20th Century* Limited"]
An uneasy comic operetta. When the book is in command, things go swimmingly. A mustached John Cullum is wonderfully entertaining in an expert and enthusiastic impression of the late John Barrymore's screen portrayal. And Madeline Kahn, sumptuously gowned by costume designer Florence Klotz, is a lovely and spirited Lily. Composer Cy Coleman, in a brave attempt to transcend the obvious temptation to indulge in mere razzle-dazzle, has written a sweeping, extravagant, overly ambitious score that too often works against the brisk, farcical nature of the piece, including the well-fashioned lyrics. The score, to its credit, calls for real singers for a change, and it gets them in abundance, but it lacks any real character of its own, alternating much of the time between early 19th century comic opera mannerisms and early

20th century operetta. Only on a few occasions—a porter's quartet ["Life Is Like a Train"], for one—does Coleman's natural rhythmic bent come into play. Smoke billows from the pit at intervals during the stimulating overture, and as the curtain rises, the trip we are about to begin seems full of promise. But the swift momentum of the great train ride is repeatedly braked by the complexities and the very concept of the score.

•　　•　　•

Musical comedy is like a train, as the authors of *On the Twentieth Century* might say. You get on at the beginning; you get off at the end. Or sometimes at intermission. Designer Robin Wagner's streamlined *Twentieth Century* was sleek, stylized, and imaginatively *un*limited. The baggage onboard, unfortunately, was not. Jazz-pianist Cy Coleman, who had previously written contemporary musicals like *Little Me* (1962) and *Sweet Charity* (1966), provided an impressive *opéra bouffe* score. Impressive, but not necessarily entertaining. And not especially fitting the mid-Depression time period, either, but why quibble? Working with the original play (but not the 1934 screenplay, the rights to which were unavailable), Comden and Green opened things up, added flashbacks, and turned a subsidiary character into a gloriously featured juvenile—gloriously because the role was cast with the up-and-coming Kevin Kline. The combination of Cullum, Kline, and director Prince brought forth some highly welcome, scenery-chewing physical comedy. The featured role of the repentant reformer/nut was rewritten as a woman—the 1932 version was all male except for Lilly and her maid—and upgraded to costar status for Imogene Coca. Comden and Green also saw fit to remove an "l" from the heroine's name. Go figure. Once the show had safely pulled into the St. James, Madeline Kahn began missing performances, ten of the first seventy-four, in fact, citing difficulties with the part's extreme vocal range. (Others cited "personal problems." Rumor had it that half the cast insisted on her replacement, the other half threatening to quit if she were fired.) Kahn suggested she be allowed to play only seven perfs a week, like Liza (*The Act*) Minnelli across the street. Hal Prince suggested understudy Judy Kaye take over the role, which she did on April 25. (Kahn reportedly received a $100,000 settlement of her contract, indicating there's a little more to the story than we're told.) Judy Kaye, at any rate, did very nicely in the role, evidencing no trouble with the extreme vocal range. The producers tried to get a dispensation from the Tony Awards committee to make replacement Kaye eligible, but no dice. (In a similar situation Prince had managed to get Larry Kert a nomination for *Company* [1970] after Dean Jones decamped. But one doesn't expect consistency from the Tony committee.) Kahn was duly nominated, although not likely to get many votes after having walked out of her contract; the seven-perf *Liza* across the street won. None of this really mattered, though; *Twentieth Century* was simply not as good as the train, and it was a very expensive train—stagehand-wise—to keep oiled and polished.

Tony Awards were won by Cy Coleman, Betty Comden, and Adolph Green (score), Betty Comden and Adolph Green (book), John Cullum (actor), Kevin Kline (supporting actor), and Robin Wagner (scenic design).

BROADWAY SCORECARD
/ PERFS: 460 / $: -

RAVE	FAVORABLE	MIXED	UNFAVORABLE	PAN
2	1	1		2

ONWARD VICTORIA

"A New Musical"

music by Keith Herrmann

book and lyrics by Charlotte Anker and Irene Rosenberg

based on events in the life of sufragette Victoria Woodhull (1838–1927)

directed by Julianne Boyd

choreographed by Michael Shawn (replacing Arthur Faria)

produced by John N. Hart Jr., in association with Hugh J. Hubbard and Robert M. Browne

with Jill Eikenberry, Michael Zaslow, Beth Austin (replacing Pamela Blair), Edmond Genest, Ted Thurston, Laura Waterbury, Jim Jansen, and Lenny Wolpe

opened December 14, 1980   Martin Beck Theatre

FRANK RICH, *TIMES*

For most of the way, *Onward Victoria* marches very peaceably to oblivion. This show looks like a dinner theatre's home-grown answer to *Hello, Dolly!* [1964], and it's becalmed almost to a fault. You want a good night's sleep? Pay your money and rest in peace. But late in Act II, a strange event occurs. In a seemingly bland newsboy song called "Read It in the Weekly," the chorus boys suddenly and inexplicably go berserk. The number begins conventionally enough: in the time honored tradition of musical comedy newsboys, those at the Beck are all smiles as they hawk their wares. Yet their dance steps gradually become more and more maniacal until finally these fellows look like demonic puppets being jerked about by some unseen, angry madman. What's going on? It's hard to say for sure, but *Onward Victoria* just may be the first Broadway musical to suffer a nervous breakdown. If so, that's the evening's only distinction. This show casts a pall over the audience from the moment the curtain rises on William Ritman's gray, threadbare set, and the whole enterprise slides effortlessly downhill from there. The book and lyrics battle to a standoff as they attempt to top each other in witlessness. The script is full of hoary double-entendre jokes and sweaty liaisons that are apparently intended to dramatize Victoria's then-pioneering view of female sexuality. Such is the flat, smirky tone of the writing that the heroine comes off as a pioneering vulgarian instead. The songs, inserted willy-nilly, contain some memorable verses: "I'll strip the mask away from your sad masquerade" and "We always crucify our prophets/Keeping our guillotine ready to slice." One of the odder numbers is delivered by the anti-smut crusader Anthony Comstock [Jim Jansen] as he pops in to sing of the joys of banning books. No sooner is "Oedipus Rex" rhymed with "perverted sex" then we get the couplet "I knew it was a shabby drama/When I heard what that king did to his mama." The music that accompanies these sentiments is hard to judge, especially given the tinny miking and crude orchestrations. On a couple of occasions, Keith Herrmann, the composer, does indicate that he may have the talent to create a tune. Julianne Boyd's direction and Michael Shawn's choreography are, respectively, laughable and lame. Almost every scene looks the same—like a static tea party populated by mannekins—and an uncommon number of them end with characters embracing.

DOUGLAS WATT, *DAILY NEWS*
[Headline: "Onward and Downward Marches *Victoria*"]
Onward Victoria loses ground so steadily that after awhile it seems to be going backward. Last night's musical at the Beck, though a handsomely costumed period piece, elevates sluggishness to a form of art. Funny thing is, its heroine is the fire-eating late 19th-century feminist Victoria Woodhull, a figure one would suppose could propel a piece of stagecraft full speed ahead. In this instance, however, our Victoria sets the woman's movement back two-and-a-half hours each performance. To begin with (and I wish we could let the matter drop right here), the writers of the book and lyrics, Charlotte Anker and Irene Rosenberg, have made Mrs. Woodhull so thoroughly uninviting an individual—indeed, such a blamed nuisance—that her laudable stands on the rights of her sex and her farsighted pronouncements are like boomerangs. "Free love, free speech, free thought," proclaim the banners of her sup-

porters, and possibly considering the other available freedoms, several members of Friday's preview audience opted for the freedom of the streets at intermission. The song lyrics are bad enough in themselves, but Keith Herrmann's score, though deftly orchestrated by Michael Gibson, is of absolutely no help. It momentarily clambers out of a prevailing dreariness (accentuated by a fake complexity) only in a moderately enlivening first-act finale ("Unescorted Women") and in a second-act solo ("Everyday I Do a Little Something for the Lord"). Given material lacking both focus and wit, or even the attainment of good solid hack work, the cast, miked to the last capped tooth, is left to flounder. Jill Eikenberry is game enough, heaven knows, and cuts a fine figure of a woman as Victoria, but she looks glum at times as if fully aware that here is a lost cause. It may be said that Julianne Boyd, the over-all director, and Michael Shawn, responsible for the musical staging, have gone about their business with considerable sweep (at times, the ensemble seems to sweep about the stage like a snap-the-whip skate team). With a little more effort, they might happily have swept the stage clean. As things stand, Theoni V. Aldredge's gorgeously opulent period gowns are the show's most notable constituents.

o   o   o

Charlotte Anker and Irene Rosenberg—two Washington, DC, housewives with labor-lawyer husbands—determined to write a Broadway musical, and they sure did. Director Julianne Boyd arranged a reading at the Manhattan Theatre Club, which was followed by three weeks at the Off-Off-Broadway Greenwich Mews Theatre in February 1979 (with Susan Bigelow and Michael Zaslow in the leads). Producer John Hart had a hard time raising money for the Broadway run—is it any wonder?—but he persevered, and Victoria Woodhull ("the thinking man's *Auntie Mame*," per star Jill Eikenberry) came *Onward* to Broadway. One performance and back to the kitchen. Someone Should Write a Musical About . . . Dept.: Producer Albert Selden announced Carol Channing as *Vicky for President* for the spring of 1972. The show—with music by Arthur Schwartz, lyrics by Yip Harburg, and book by Burt Shevelove and Herb Sargent—was slated to be the opening attraction at Selden's Astor Plaza Theatre. *Vicky* never got off the ground, though, and the producer/theatre operator opened with his *Irene* (1973) instead. There'd been talk of naming the house the Merrick—with Merrick's upcoming *Sugar* on tap—but it was decided instead to honor that great man of the theatre, *Irene's* coproducer Jerry Minskoff. (The Uris family named *their* new skyscraper theatre—now the Gershwin—after themselves, so the Minskoff clan did likewise.)

BROADWAY SCORECARD
/ PERFS: | / $: –

RAVE	FAVORABLE	MIXED	UNFAVORABLE	PAN
				6

OVER HERE!

"America's Big Band Musical"

music and lyrics by Richard M. Sherman and Robert B. Sherman

book by Will Holt

directed by Tom Moore

choreographed by Patricia Birch

produced by Kenneth Waissman and Maxine Fox (Waissman)

starring "The Andrews Sisters" (Maxene Andrews and Patty Andrews)

with Janie Sell, Douglass Watson, April Shawhan, MacIntyre Dixon, William Griffis, Bette Henritze, John Driver, Samuel Wright, John Travolta, Jim Weston, Marilu Henner, John Mineo, Ann Reinking, Phyllis Somerville, and Treat Williams

opened March 6, 1974   *Shubert Theatre*

CLIVE BARNES, *TIMES*

Against all promptings of what would normally have been my better judgment, I warmed to the show enormously. As a musical it is preposterously bad, but also preposterously engaging and, in its way, devilishly clever. Douglas W. Schmidt and Carrie F. Robbins have brilliantly evoked the period but by different, complementing methods. Schmidt's scenery suggests, and Robbins's costumes exaggerate—but they work, and work together. Tom Moore's staging flows as rapidly as a virtually bookless musical should, and Patricia Birch does wonders with the musical numbers. Her parody dances on the Misses [Sonja] Henie, [Esther] Williams and [Betty] Grable had real wit and used the show's gimmicked moving walkways with style. So this is it—a shrewdly packaged times past that will appeal most to those who remember when those were times present. Only now and then does a new consciousness break in—when we find Patty Andrews singing a song warning against V.D. (that one would never have made the '44 *Show of Shows*) or a suggestion of black and white inequality in that army of the people. But, fundamentally, it is a band show, finding real fun in the remembrance of past follies. Undeniably, this is a show the pure in mind will have to make allowances for—it is not only corny, it is even intended to be corny—but most will find the allowances well worth making. Incidentally, the show's best part comes after the final curtain. Maxene and Patty come on looking tremendously awful in glitter costumes. Patty says casually: "Do you want to hear some of the old ones?" And you do! And they sing and sing and sing. So, at the end, hold tight!

MARTIN GOTTFRIED, *WOMEN'S WEAR DAILY*

From the people who gave the world *Grease* [1972]—the producer, the director, the choreographer—comes *Over Here!*, a meanwhile-10-years-earlier version for the mass nostalgia market. *Over Here!* opened on the crest of a big-money '40s revival several years, as usual, after the era was trend-set. *American Graffiti* [1973], coming after *Summer of '42* [1971], is one of the year's most successful films and already has spawned a hit television series; Bette Midler sells a million records and concert seats, as do the Pointer Sisters in her wake; so this show's material is overfamiliar to anyone who has been only half-asleep recently. It is also poorly assembled musical theater. It is also unpleasant in its use as objects of The Andrews Sisters, who, as any classy performers, transcend that. But *Over Here!* is not utterly bad. It has a look (designed by Douglas W. Schmidt) quite unlike other shows, capitalizing on clutter and clash to create a mood—Radio City arcs and drops beyond them, covered with the Norman Rockwell style of '40s advertising or newspaper slides. It has a smash opening as the pit band rises on an upstage elevator, the musicians decked out in shawl-collared tuxedos with a cardboard stand in front of each, just the way they used to do at the Capitol and the Paramount and the Strand, and it is kind of thrilling. But . . . there is no theatrical idea behind the show other than nostalgia in music, clothes and jargon. When *Over Here!* gets theatrical at all, it seems only a poor copy of *Follies* [1971]. Moore doesn't seem to know exactly what to do with The Andrews Sisters, since they are unpleasantly cast as living relics and never fit into the company. But the two fine ladies defeat the entire enterprise—class will out—and simply come through as the stars they are, with the unphony presence of the real McCoy. The joke is on the show, not them. They simply underline the hollowness of *Over Here!*—rooted as it is in a condescension toward the past rather than a true, loving memory of it. *Over Here!* may be smirky in its fawning over the '40s, but Patty and Maxene Andrews don't seem to know or care. They were there, they are remembered, they are lovable still. Who will ever love and remember *Over Here?*

DOUGLAS WATT, *DAILY NEWS*

Over Here!, a garish World War II home-front musical, has nothing more on its dizzy mind than the fond and gentle mocking evocation of the largely synthetic entertainment of the period. That's shameless. But thanks to its prevailing good nature and liveliness, it manages to be reasonably diverting. Among other good things, there is Janie Sell's ridiculously funny German spy. Whether making up the third member of the Andrews Sisters trio or doing a hilarious Dietrich imitation, Miss Sell is a joy. Patricia Birch's dance numbers are joyous, too, and the high spot is a fine Lindy display by the stunning Ann Reinking, whose chiseled bad-girl good looks alone should take her far, and John Mineo. They're a dandy team. It beats me how a show about some of the worst aspects of a low period in American entertainment, much of it centered around phony patriotic sentiment, can have anything to recommend it. But *Over Here!*, though certainly no great shakes, has quite a few things in its favor.

◦　◦　◦

The *Grease* group—producers, director, choreographer, and designers—decided to subject the Swing Era to similar treatment, spoofing one of those Andrews Sisters–type B movies of the wartime years. At some point along the way someone got the brilliant idea of inviting the surviving Andrews Sisters *themselves* to play their parodies. Patty and Maxene readily (and expensively) assented, and *Over Here!* was doomed from that very moment. Camp and nostalgia can, of course, be successfully combined (with care). But putting the gals themselves in WAC khakis threw the focus out of kilter. Were the characters lampoons or the real thing? Were you supposed to laugh at 'em or love 'em? Was the show meant to remind the World War II crowd of when they were younger or point up the fact that they—the audience—were fat and dowdy (if still kicking)? And who, exactly, was *Over Here!* aimed at? The oldsters, to see the Andrews Sisters? The youngsters, to catch its glib, hip sensibility? Or just for the tourists? Imagine *Grease* with a pair of sixty-five-year-old ex-rockers playing Danny and Sandy. (Might actually be better, come to think of it.) What *Over Here!* didn't have—and what *Nanette* (1971) and even *Grease* was brimful of—was catchy tunes. Music, yes; *Over Here!* was overloaded with it, but not a tune you'd ever want to caress. The score came from Hollywood's Sherman Brothers, celebrated for their 1964 spoonful-of-sugarful *Mary Poppins*. But celebrated for nothing else, including *Over Here!* (or their stillborn 1995 Tunesical, *Busker Alley*). The whole thing was very frenetic, and that's about it. Although the show *did* give theatregoers the opportunity to pick out a dazzling dancer in saddle shoes, turn to their companion and say, "That girl is going to be a star"—and be proved right. Ann Reinking was back within the year as Joan of Arc, God help her, in the 1975 *Goodtime Charley*.

A Tony Award was won by Janie Sell (supporting actress).

BROADWAY SCORECARD

/ PERFS: 341 / $: –

RAVE	FAVORABLE	MIXED	UNFAVORABLE	PAN
1	4		1	

PACIFIC OVERTURES

"A New Musical"

music and lyrics by Stephen Sondheim

book by John Weidman; additional material by Hugh Wheeler

suggested by U.S. Commodore Matthew Perry's 1853 "visit" to Japan

directed by Harold Prince

choreographed by Patricia Birch

produced by Harold Prince in association with Ruth Mitchell

starring Mako

with Soon-Teck Oh (who received second-star billing during the tryout), Yuki Shimoda, Sab Shimono, Isao Sato, Alvin Ing, Ernest Harada, James Dybas, Mark Hsu Syers, and Patrick Kinser-Lau

opened January 11, 1976   Winter Garden Theatre

CLIVE BARNES, *TIMES*

The translation of a culture—and a translation of a translation at that—this is only the beginning of the beguiling and sometimes bewildering complexities of the new musical *Pacific Overtures*. It is a very serious, almost inordinately ambitious musical, and as such is deserving of equally serious attention. It is the story of what happened when "four black ships" came to "a land of changeless order." It is all about the Westernization of Japan, and, obliquely and finally, why Seiko watches are today the third largest-selling watch in Switzerland. It is about a change of scene, a change of heart—but stylistically it is also about a type of theatre. Somewhere along the line the decision was made to base the performing style very loosely on the Japanese Kabuki theatre—but, of course, it soon becomes much more complicated than that. Sondheim's music is in a style that might be called *Japonaiserie*

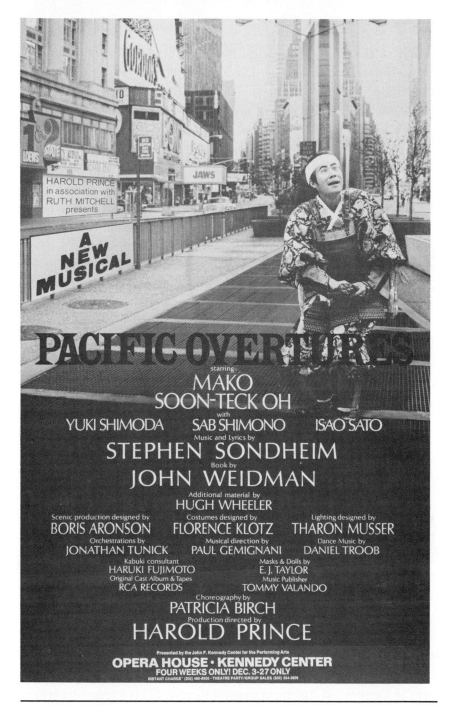

HAROLD PRINCE
in association with
RUTH MITCHELL
presents

A NEW MUSICAL

PACIFIC OVERTURES

starring

MAKO
SOON-TECK OH

with

YUKI SHIMODA   SAB SHIMONO   ISAO SATO

Music and Lyrics by

STEPHEN SONDHEIM

Book by

JOHN WEIDMAN

Additional material by
HUGH WHEELER

Scenic production designed by   Costumes designed by   Lighting designed by
BORIS ARONSON   FLORENCE KLOTZ   THARON MUSSER

Orchestrations by   Musical direction by   Dance Music by
JONATHAN TUNICK   PAUL GEMIGNANI   DANIEL TROOB

Kabuki consultant   Masks & Dolls by
HARUKI FUJIMOTO   E. J. TAYLOR

Original Cast Album & Tapes   Music Publisher
RCA RECORDS   TOMMY VALANDO

Choreography by
PATRICIA BIRCH

Production directed by
HAROLD PRINCE

Presented by the John F. Kennedy Center for the Performing Arts

OPERA HOUSE · KENNEDY CENTER
FOUR WEEKS ONLY! DEC. 3-27 ONLY
INSTANT CHARGE" (202) 466-8500 · THEATRE PARTY/GROUP SALES (202) 254-3626

Soon-Teck Oh seems just a wee bit out of place in Times Square, with *Jaws* playing over his shoulder no less. "*Ittai nani goto da!*" he seems to be saying.

(Leonard Bernstein quite often seems to be trysting with *Madame Butterfly* in the orchestra pit). The lyrics are totally Western and—as is the custom with Sondheim—devilish, wittily and delightfully clever. Musically there is a disparity between Sondheim's operetta-like elegance and ethnic overlay, but even this succeeds with all its carefully applied patina of pastiche—that on demand can embrace Sullivan or Offenbach. Sondheim is the most remarkable man in the Broadway musical today—and here he shows it victoriously. But it could be a pyrrhic victory. The form of the musical itself is perhaps not up to the seriousness of the material and the sensitivity and sensibility with which it is presented. Moreover, Weidman's book, while strikingly original, does not always rest happily within the conceptual format of the show—at times it seems as though we are well and truly in the world of *Suzie Wong* [1959]. One particular aspect of this unusually sophisticated piece of theatre has been the scenic fabrications of Boris Aronson. When Aronson's ships come into port, if you have any visual sense at all, your heart will sing. . . . There are generic and stylistic discrepancies in the musical that are not easily overlooked—but the attempt is so bold and the achievement so fascinating, that its obvious faults demand to be overlooked. It tries to soar—sometimes it only floats, sometimes it actually sinks—but it tries to soar. And the music and lyrics are as pretty and as well-formed as a bonsai tree. *Pacific Overtures* is very, very different.

MARTIN GOTTFRIED, *POST*
[Headline: "A Remarkable Work of Art"]
Risk is the difference between assured mediocrity and possible greatness. By conceiving *Pacific Overtures* as an irony of Japan's Westernization, related through the rituals of Kabuki theatre, Harold Prince was almost begging for a disaster of preciousness, condescension, and who wants to see a Japanese musical anyway? Instead, last night he presented an exquisite, enchanting, touching, intelligent and altogether remarkable work of theatre art. Prince is not merely the most important man in the modern American musical theatre. He is a man who refuses to repeat himself. He will move, almost contrarily, from the chilly brilliance of *Company* [1970] to the utter grandeur of *Follies* [1971]. If there is anything that can be expected of him, it is the unexpected.

Certainly, nobody could have anticipated *Pacific Overtures*. Stephen Sondheim's music, elegantly orchestrated by Jonathan Tunick, is simply formidable—a huge amount of it built into sung sequences so extensive and cubic they rise from and engulf the show. Sondheim didn't pretend to write Oriental music, but instead grasped its texture and, much more importantly, the show's purpose. This is true theatre music, much more melodic than one's hearing suggests, and tremendously varied. The score places him at the very pinnacle of American stage composers and entirely apart from conventional theatre songwriters. His lyrics assume a great responsibility, telling as much of the story as the book. They are not merely impeccable in terms of lyric writing technique, they seem the work of a lover of Japanese poetry and never phony about theatre. I only wish they might have been as open hearted as some of the music. If the production has a lack, it is unavoidable considering its intentions—a cool transparency akin to Oriental airiness and symmetry. This is not an emotional show. If the production includes a mistake, it is an unfortunately tasteless song ["Welcome to Kanagawa"] turning the Orient's high erotic art into a kinky sex comedy song (one of the show's rare "numbers") sung by a madam whose masculinity is emphasized as drag queenliness. The crude number only underlines a sag in the first act. But the production is too fine to be shaken, it recovers to continue through to the end with resumed purity. It is quite an accomplishment.

WALTER KERR, *TIMES*
[Headline: "Neither East Nor West"]
Apparently on the general theory that a Japanese Kabuki play isn't so much interested in telling a story as it is in interrupting the play to tell a dozen other stories, the new Prince-Sondheim musical halts its narrative at will to permit a "Reciter" to recount a tale. The tale is a long one about a father who is departing on a trip and instructs his son, during his absence, to fashion a litter for his now feeble grandmother so that she can be carried into the mountains and there left to die. When the father returns, the son has built two litters. Asked why he has bothered with the second, the son replies that he will keep it for the father until he is approximately as enfeebled as the grandmother, whereupon he will meet the same suitable fate. That is the end of that irony. But I do think the son might have made three litters while he was at it. One

for the show. Normally, Prince and Sondheim know very well what they are about as they turn their restless talents to experimentation—and their restlessness is one of their greatest virtues—but a mishap has occurred here. They do seem firmly knowledgeable, and possessed of a possible idea, as they approach the visual appurtenances of *Pacific Overtures*. But what, really, do they have in mind? When are we seeing through Japanese eyes, when through our own? And what is the drift of what we see and hear, psychologically, socially, personally? We're emotionally baffled—if our emotions continue to function at all—throughout. The manner can be amusing (it can be much more than that in a genuine Kabuki performance, it can be moving in a way that is not even imagined here), but it tends to be most amusing when it is most irrelevant and, as it happens, most Americanized. But no amount of performing, or of incidental charm, can salvage *Pacific Overtures*. The occasion is essentially dull and immobile because we are never properly *placed* in it, drawn neither East nor West, given no specific emotional or cultural bearings. The evening is a Japanese artifact with a stamp on the back of it that says "Made in America." Why tell their story *their* way, when they'd do it better?

DOUGLAS WATT, *DAILY NEWS*
[Headline: "A Pretty Bore"]

> If you lik-a me like I lik-a you,
> Then sing me a nice haiku.

Take away the frills from *Pacific Overtures* and there's not a great deal left to this sluggish musical with an Asian-American cast that came pittipatting into the Winter Garden last evening. Fourth in the series of innovative, and increasingly precious, musicals that composer-lyricist Stephen Sondheim and producer-director Harold Prince have collaborated on, *Pacific Overtures* is as thin and insubstantial as the painted screens used for scenery. Indeed, the frills are everything in a prevailingly dull, semi-documentary entertainment about the corrupting influence of Western civilization on Asian culture. *Pacific Overtures* ends up a message musical, and we end up out in the cold. For, among other things, the dear little isolated empire is, in many ways, a savage society and, worse, a stiflingly mannered one as well, without Gilbert and Sullivan to give it buoyancy [as in *The Mikado*]. Sondheim, whose melodies here generally have a broader line and less thematic or harmonic development than usual, tries a bit of Gilbert and Sullivan, as a matter of fact. Sondheim, Prince and the author of the book, John Weidman, have tossed everything into the sukiyaki pot. There's a *Madame Butterfly*-like suicide, for no clear reason other than to create a picturesque and sobering effect, and every now and then the Reciter, a man who describes the action and from time to time takes part in it, unburdens himself of a haiku, less poetry than fortune-cookie wisdom, as "The bird from the sea, not knowing pine from bamboo, roosts on anything." Overall, if the authors will forgive my further mixing of cultures, *Pacific Overtures* resembles in style an evening-long expansion of that Broadway-Siamese-Stowe divertissement from *The King and I* [1951] called "The Small House of Uncle Thomas." *Pacific Overtures* is, to employ another ethnic term, a mishmash. Or, to paraphrase another of the evening's haikus,

> A blossom falls on Broadway,
> Broadway falls on a blossom;
> All things fall.

◦ ◦ ◦

In their continuing attempt to forge new ground, Harold Prince and Stephen Sondheim came up with another follies. *Pacific Overtures*—with its Kabuki-like storyteller/reciter, exotic musicians twanging away aside the stage, gliding screens "that open wide with scenes of screens like the ones that glide," and traditional ramplike *hanamichi* running through the auditorium—was so overwhelmingly pretentious that the many worthy components were diluted in a sea of chrysanthemum tea. The piece began as a realistic, nonmusical drama by John Weidman (whose father had scripted Prince's *Fiorello!* [1959] and *Tenderloin* [1960]). The play told of Commodore Perry's 1853 visit to Japan, in which Perry—and his warships—convinced the isolated floating kingdom to open its borders to U.S. trade. One thing led to another and the play was transformed into a musical, with Weidman's script Kabukied to pieces. The ancient Japanese theatre-form is an acquired taste—and decidedly not one to be acquired in two and a half hours. (While comparisons are irrelevant, this type of theatrical japonaiserie was handled far more effectively in the 1988 drama *M. Butterfly*.) What was good in *Pacific Overtures*—as in other flawed Prince-Sondheim shows—was the score. The especial challenges of the piece prodded Sondheim to find new ways to communicate drama through song, with stunning results. For example, "Four Black Dragons" described the approach of American warships through the eyes of a fisherman and a thief (who was "rifling through the house of some priests"), with annotations from the omnipresent Reciter. "Someone in a Tree" even more fascinatingly described a central event—the signing of the peace treaty—from three separate vantage points. An old man narrates what happened, while his younger self— he who climbed a tree to view, but not hear, the proceedings— observes what *is* happening. They are supplemented by a warrior hidden beneath the house, who hears—or heard?—but cannot see the event. The encapsulation of time was also undertaken in "A Bowler Hat," a perfectly crafted chronicle that relates more about the Westernization of Japan in four minutes than the rest of *Pacific Overtures* in toto. What Prince and his production puffed and strained to do, Sondheim handily accomplished in understated fashion with a bowler hat, a monocle, and a cutaway tailcoat. If *Pacific Overtures* was an unlikely proposition from the start, the tryout reception made it clear that the show was simply unworkable and a surefire failure (*and* running out of money). The producer, nobly, refrained from folding it in Boston; the score was clearly too important to bury. But, alas, Prince paid the price (the overage coming out of his own pocket) and began to phase himself out of the producing end of Broadway.

Winner of the New York Drama Critics' Circle Award. Tony Awards were won by Boris Aronson (scenic design) and Florence Klotz (costume design).

BROADWAY SCORECARD

/ PERFS: 193 / $: –

RAVE	FAVORABLE	MIXED	UNFAVORABLE	PAN
2	1		1	2

THE PAJAMA GAME

a revival of the 1954 musical comedy

music and lyrics by Richard Adler and Jerry Ross

book by George Abbott and Richard Bissell

based on the 1953 novel *7½ Cents* by Richard Bissell

directed by George Abbott

originally choreographed by Bob Fosse; musical numbers restaged by Zoya Leporska

produced by Richard Adler and Bert Wood in association with Nelson Peltz

starring Barbara McNair, Cab Calloway, and Hal Linden

with Sharron Miller, Willard Waterman, Mary Jo Catlett (replacing Marilyn Nell), Marc Jordan, Chris Calloway, and Tiger Haynes

opened December 9, 1973   Lunt-Fontanne Theatre

CLIVE BARNES, *TIMES*

How classic is a classic musical? It depends a great deal on the musical. *The Pajama Game* was absolutely adored by the paying preview audience I saw it with. My own reaction was more guarded. A remarkable amount of the music has become standard—it is indeed the music and lyrics that remain the best part of the show. Everyone over 40, I suppose, will almost atavistically recall "Hey There," or "Hernando's Hideaway" or "Steam Heat," but this is a show of great and charming numbers. This is the value of the new *Pajama Game*. Pulsing, tough, Broadway music carrying the whole audience with it on the bounce and wit of its melody. This I loved before, and I still love. But times have changed. The book, once so modern (a finale hero who wore pajama bottoms with a finale heroine who wore pajama tops!) has passed, per-

haps not happily, into history, and its social conscience now seems
jejune. The book has worn very badly. The story is not silly enough to
be taken seriously as a musical. It either needs less conviction or, preferably, a great deal more. Mr. Abbott has staged the show as bright as an
old but preserved penny. The "Steam Heat" number, complete with Bob
Fosse's choreography, is a delight, and so are many of the other well-
revered pieces. But much looks mechanical. Barbara McNair sings
vibrantly and looks beautiful, but her acting has the wooden air of a
nightclub singer in search of a torch. Hal Linden is almost as badly miscast. He sings modestly and acts with all of his considerable skill, but
he is not a natural juvenile lead. Cab Calloway makes as many moments
as he can, but even with Calloway the moments are limited. Best I suppose is Sharron Miller as Gladys, who comes over as a tightly packaged
bundle of charm. *The Pajama Game* would not be on my list of the
greatest American musicals—would it be on yours?—yet I can see that
it might evoke memories of a past. I do, however, think it could here
have been better, more imaginatively done. Yet the music still stands.
And the audience I was with obviously enjoyed it.

MARTIN GOTTFRIED, *WOMEN'S WEAR DAILY*
The first good musical of the season. It is not only an incorporably
better-made and more entertaining show than what else has come
along so far, but, though 20 years older, it is fresher and less old-
fashioned. Its basic material is good—a score remarkably consistent for
melody and charm with a book that may be silly but is at least adult
and well-made—and the craftsmanship of its assembly is a nasty
reminder of how far downhill the technique of musical-making has
slid since the Fifties. Frankly, I came to the show with skepticism.
Rock music has struck such terror in the hearts of musical producers
that they don't know what the public wants (the answer: simply a good
show, what ever the kind of music). Broadway economics have only
intensified the problem. As a result, many of today's musicals are cynical packages, hoping to recoup on tour before facing the lions (audiences as well as critics) in New York. This is what *The Pajama Game*
revival appeared to be, especially with its interracial casting that
seemed more a commercial exploitation than a sensible idea. Instead,
the show seems no revival at all and the racial mix has added a depth

to its story—as a matter of fact, this *Pajama Game* makes more sense on racial matters than most of the recent plays that mean to. Yet, the script has been only barely changed to acknowledge the black-white romance (the girl says, "It wouldn't work . . . there's a little thing called racial prejudice," and the guy replies, "You mean you won't go out with us Polacks?") This hardly makes the show's book a major literary or social work, but then the show is only meant as entertainment and that it provides in abundance. There is one song added by Richard Adler to the score he wrote with his late partner, Jerry Ross—a pleasant innocuous ballad that could well have been written in 1954 ["Watch Your Heart," a revised version of "What's Wrong with Me?" from the 1961 *Kwamina*]—but otherwise *The Pajama Game* is as it was, and yet unaged. Remembered with such affection, it is miraculously as fresh as a daisy and just as welcome.

RICHARD WATTS, JR., POST

When *The Pajama Game* was first presented a number of years ago, it was a pleasant, tuneful and successful musical comedy. Now, in the revival which opened last night at the Lunt-Fontanne Theatre, it seems even better; in fact, brilliant. With a splendid cast headed by the beautiful Barbara McNair, the wonderful Cab Calloway and the engaging Hal Linden, a handsome production, and those fine songs, it is a Broadway triumph. Then there is the ingenuity and rapid pace of George Abbott's direction. The evening is filled with the excitement of the staging with its humorous imagination that keeps everything moving along without a moment's faltering. *The Pajama Game* wisely makes no attempt to compromise with the modern vogue of noisy brashness and four-letter language. It is satisfied to be a delightful, melodious entertainment and succeeeds admirably. It is warmhearted fun. I don't see how *The Pajama Game* can fail to be a resounding success.

○   ○   ○

There were a half-dozen undeniably classic musicals in the 1950s (namely *Guys and Dolls*, *The King and I*, *My Fair Lady*, *West Side Story*, *The Music Man*, and *Gypsy*). While obviously not of the same extraspecial caliber, *The Pajama Game* might well be the best of the rest, seventh in a class of 150. *Game* was the epitome of the "Abbott musical": fast, funny, and colorful, with exciting dances from first-time choreographer Bob Fosse. First-time songwriters Richard Adler and Jerry Ross provided the perfect B-level score, with songs like "Hey There," "Hernando's Hideaway," and "Steam Heat." Not Lerner or Loewe or Loesser, certainly, but workable and immensely entertaining. In 1973 the songs and the vintage Fosse dancin' were just as good, but the plotting was old-fashioned—despite the grafting on of an interracial romance—and the physical production looked like remaindered seconds. The show, coproduced by Adler himself, came in for only $300,000—and looked it; *7½ Cents* didn't buy a hell of a lot, certainly not as much as it had back in the "cloth-coat" '50s. (That fall's *Raisin*, with skeletal scenery and pantomimed props, cost $450,000. The same year's stylish *A Little Night Music*—with a cast of eighteen, to *Game*'s thirty-nine—was capitalized at $650,000.) The revival was also ineffectively cast, with a sympathetic but underpowered leading lady and an undisciplined, uncontrollable comic who was frequently falling-down drunk. (One night he stepped down to the apron, midperformance, and started singing "Minnie the Moocher." Hi-dee-hi-dee-hi!) The leading man—following up his Tony-winning performance in *The Rothschilds* (1970)—was considerably stronger; he took a leave of absence to shoot a TV pilot, *Barney Miller*, which kept him employed on the opposite coast for seven seasons. The musical's chintzy production made the material look fadedly worn, and despite a better-than-deserved critical reception the *Game* was soon lost. <u>Backstage Reminiscence Dept.</u>: One night during curtain calls the pass door opened, and Jerry Robbins— who had codirected the original with Abbott—steamed in, a-cursin' and a-mutterin'. He tore onstage, wreaking havoc among the cast, most of whom had never met him and understandably idolized him. (The few who *had* worked for J. R. no longer idolized him, but he seems to have had that effect on people.) The coast was pretty much clear by the time eighty-six-year-old Abbott came skipping through. Five minutes later, the twenty-year-old stage manager crossed upstage in the course of his professional duties and also to find out What They Were Talking About. There, shielded from view by the factory unit, were the two legends of the American Musical Theatre: Jerry Robbins—the Great Man of *West Side Story* (1957) and *Fiddler* (1964)—stood scowling like a naughty, baldpated four-year-old being scolded by his overpowering, overtowering teacher. Not wishing to interrupt them, I just kept to the shadows, listening. Ah, the glamour of the theatre.

BROADWAY SCORECARD
/ PERFS: 65 / $: –

RAVE	FAVORABLE	MIXED	UNFAVORABLE	PAN
3	1		2	

PAL JOEY

a revival of the 1940 musical comedy

music by Richard Rodgers

lyrics by Lorenz Hart

book by John O'Hara (with George Abbott)

based on the 1939 *New Yorker* stories by John O'Hara

directed by Theodore Mann

choreographed by Margo Sappington

produced by Circle in the Square (Theodore Mann and Paul Libin)

starring Joan Copeland (replacing Eleanor Parker), Janie Sell, Joe Sirola, Dixie Carter, and Christopher Chadman (replacing Edward Villella)

with Harold Gary, Boni Enten, Austin Colyer, Adam Petroski, and Ralph Farnworth

opened June 27, 1976   *Circle in the Square Uptown Theatre*

CLIVE BARNES, *TIMES*

With what must have been an almost audible sigh of relief from its producers, that apparently ill-fated revival of *Pal Joey* has finally made it to the Circle in the Square Theatre. It made its official bow yesterday afternoon after many birth pangs and much heartburn. Originally Edward Villella—making his singing and acting debut—was cast as the hoofer and punk's punk, Joey, while Eleanor Parker was to have been Vera, the rich socialite who finds Joey deprived and depraved and decides to befriend his body. On paper the casting sounded a good idea, in practice it apparently worked out disastrously, even despite the loyal ministrations on his behalf by Villella's very own New York City Ballet gurus, George Balanchine and Jerome Robbins. The director, Theodore Mann, finally released Villella and Parker, and decided to go along with their understudies. This was half of a good idea: but the wrong half—Joey, himself, now played by Christopher Chadman, was one of the two strikes against this revival from the beginning. [The second strike is, unfortunately, the theatre itself.] Mann's direction is rather heavy-handed and Margo Sappington's choreography rather weak-legged, [but] the central problem is Mr. Chadman as Joey. He dances indifferently, sings gratingly and acts as if he had had one disastrous acting lesson and decided not to go back. But none of that is his problem. A Joey could conceivably get away with that—but Chadman is charmless. Frank Sinatra in the much bowdlerized and softened movie was probably the archetypal Joey, the kind of disaster that women sell their husbands for. He is a bastard with a heart of lead, but we have to understand the attraction he has for women. Joan Copeland as the bewitched, bothered and bewildered Vera proved a knockout. She was tough, lovely and credible, singing with a husky, whisky smokiness, looking like a well-preserved dream, and effortlessly suggesting that her treats were paved with gold. Super. There were other good performances as well. Joe Sirola and Janie Sell were exuberantly sleazy as the blackmailers, Dixie Carter put zip into "Zip," and Harold Gary was gruffly urbane as a nightclub entrepreneur. But all these swallows never made a summer. At the end of the performance I found myself going out thinking: "Bring Back *Pal Joey*," which is not a proper attitude after instant, if misguided, revivalism.

MARTIN GOTTFRIED, *POST*

[Headline: "*Joey* without a Joey is a *Pal* in Need"]

Withdrawal of the two leading performers strikes a telling blow to any production, especially of *Pal Joey*, whose title role calls for a type in short supply these days: a star male dancer. Like comics they have gone out of fashion. That is our loss, but not as much as the production's. Christopher Chadman plays Joey like the understudy he was and a *Joey* without a Joey is in trouble indeed. And that is but one of this revival's problems. Theodore Mann seems to have directed it by alternating between no choices and mistaken ones, and that would have upset the show even had its cast been ideal. Joan Copeland is excellent as the dallying matron, making the lady likable trouble, singing her songs with strength and heart, though nobody took the trouble to give her any musical staging. As Joey, however, Chadman goes through the show like a chorus boy at an audition for a lead.

*   *   *

Mister Joey Evans is a treacherous heel of a role to pull off, as witness the following follow-up of the original production: "Gene Kelly is no longer in it," noted the drama critic for a major weekly. "Vivienne Segal's still in it and God knows she does all she can, which is a lot. But under the present circumstances, I caution you against going to see *Pal Joey*." What makes this opinion of more than passing interest is that the reviewer in question was none other than the *New Yorker*'s John O'Hara himself (who was, admittedly, disgruntled by his treatment from producer/director/book doctor George Abbott and composer Richard Rodgers). But Joey is an elusive fellow. Gene Kelly created the role, of course; Harold Lang played it successfully in the correspondingly successful 1952 revival; and Lang's understudy—a Chicago hoofer named Fosse—did well by the Chicago hoofer in a 1961 City Center reprise. But otherwise, beware. This ill-fated Circle in the Square version was woefully produced, but then the lavishly produced *Pal Joey* '78, as they called it, was equally woeful despite the presence of Lena Horne and Clifton Davis. (Robert Fryer produced the latter for the Center Theatre Group at the Ahmanson in Los Angeles. Gower Champion—unable to get along with the Lady—ankled the first week and was replaced by

Michael Kidd.) Erstwhile producers continue to try to tackle *Joey*, usually with "fixed" librettos, but the durable chap dodges with a shrug and taps away unvanquished. Although the Hollywooden Frank Sinatra version (1957) almost finished him off.

BROADWAY SCORECARD

/ PERFS: 73 / $: –

RAVE	FAVORABLE	MIXED	UNFAVORABLE	PAN
1	1		2	2

PERFECTLY FRANK

"Frank Loesser Revived," a revue featuring the songs of Frank Loesser (1910–1969)

conceived and written by Kenny Solms (billing removed)

directed by Fritz Holt (replaced by Ron Field)

choreographed by Tony Stevens (with Ron Field)

produced by Gladys Rackmil and Fred Levinson, in association with Emhan, Inc. (Jo Sullivan Loesser)

with Andra Akers, Wayne Cilento, Jill Cook, Don Correia, David Holliday, David Ruprecht, Virginia Sandifur, Debbie Shapiro, Jo Sullivan (Loesser), and Jim Walton

opened November 30, 1980   Helen Hayes Theatre

CLIVE BARNES, *POST*

It would be ridiculous to call him an unsung hero, because happily more than 10 years after his death you can scarcely escape from his music. He wrote standards when people still had standards. But Loesser has perhaps never quite been given his proper place on Broadway's honor rolls.

This is why it is such an enormous pleasure to welcome the new revue *Perfectly Frank*, which is perfectly devoted to Loesser, tunesmith extraordinary. The troubles and transmogrifications of the show have already been much discussed in the public print. Forget them. Apparently it started out as a species of a book musical, in which the composer's widow, Jo Sullivan, and the singer David Holliday put the audience wandering down memory lane reminiscing about the life and times of Frank Loesser. This pseudo-book has been abandoned, although fortunately not the performers, and clearly the loss and the less is more Loesser. For people interested in arcane Broadway gossip—and who reading a column such as this isn't?—the director Fritz Holt and the choreographer Tony Stevens in the sensitive words of Playbill "wish to acknowledge Ron Field and John Calvert [Field's assistant] for their contribution to this production." So who did what, and which, and to whom, is anyone's guess. But the cast seems to have a field day. And frankly, any show that sends me out humming "Once in Love with Amy" must get my unconditional vote. Loesser was a genius. If I were a bell I'd be ringing, hopefully at the Helen Hayes box office.

WALTER KERR, *TIMES*

The irony that most doggedly pursues *Perfectly Frank*, and that all too soon does the musical evening in, is this. The album of 60-plus songs is of course intended as a tribute to the perfectly matched melodies and lyrics that came pouring out of Frank Loesser. Yet in spite of the honor that the production means to confer upon the composer's work, it seems to have very little confidence that the songs can stand on their own—quietly, confidently, free of unnecessary decoration. The curtain has no sooner gone up on a setting that includes a tipsy musical staff looping its giddy way across the cylcorama than the entertainment's 10 singers and dancers are exploding into a bothersome busyness. Feet, hands, shoulders are on the move even before the music is. While the performers are still chatting among themselves, albeit rhythmically, by way of whipping up an introduction to the proceedings, an almighty itch is upon them. Some unlikely dialogue is upon them, too. . . . Given the general treatment of the songs in *Perfectly Frank*—the tendency to overdress them physically for fear we've heard them too often to take them straight one more time—you may imagine the relief that sweeps over the auditorium when a girl named Debbie Shapiro is hauled onto a wartime USO platform, still in her grease monkey's overalls, to part with her mechanic's wrench and stand absolutely still while she sings—simply, clearly, intelligently, affectingly—"I Don't Want to Walk Without You."

FRANK RICH, *TIMES*

Perfectly Frank, the new and long-overdue Loesser revue, contains well over 60 of his songs. As one expects, there's not a clinker in the bunch. Indeed, the musical riches of this evening are so abundant that it's tempting to overlook the shortcomings of the show that contains them. But that, I'm afraid, is not always possible. Though *Perfectly Frank* has other assets besides its song catalogue, it is also pervaded by an aura of tackiness that is antithetical to the Loesser spirit. At the Hayes, one finds Broadway professionalism at both its best and worst on the very same stage. As it happens, the better half of *Perfectly Frank* is the female half. Fritz Holt, the director, has assembled a team of women singer-dancers, both familiar and unfamiliar, who are fully in tune with the Loesser oeuvre. And he may even have discovered a star. The tall, curly-headed Debbie Shapiro has a powerhouse voice and theatrical authority suitable for seemingly all occasions; she's equally at home in the poignant World War II hit "I Don't Want to Walk Without You" and the torchy "The Lady's in Love With You." When she applies her talents to the bluesy "Junk Man" in Act II, Miss Shapiro explodes with a ferocity worthy of *Cat on a Hot Tin Roof.* You had better believe she's on Broadway to stay. It is also a pleasure to remake the acquaintance of Jo Sullivan, Loesser's widow and this revue's unofficial narrator. Miss Sullivan looks as lovely as she did when she appeared in her husband's *The Most Happy Fella* in 1956. It's too bad that the five men of *Perfectly Frank* aren't remotely in the same league. While some of them have big voices or are accomplished showbiz dancers, none of them has much of a personality. Whatever the difference in their ages or in the color of their blow-dried hair, these performers are all interchangeable, blandly cheery chorus boys. What they provide is the impersonally brassy showmanship one associates with Las Vegas floor shows and television variety specials. That wan spirit carries over to other crucial aspects as well. The show's uncredited dialogue, scant as it may be, is mostly vulgar. But if *Perfectly Frank* is a decidedly mixed evening, it nonetheless adds a welcome note to the season. Somehow Broadway always feels more like Broadway when Frank Loesser's songs are being sung.

○   ○   ○

The great Frank Loesser had not fared well since his death in 1969. Actually, his last hurrah had been back in 1961, when the brilliant *How to Succeed in Business Without Really Trying* took the Pulitzer and Tony and Broadway by storm. His final musical, the 1965 costume operetta *Pleasures and Palaces*—about Catherine the Great and John Paul Jones—had gone down in Detroit despite the admiralcy of Bob Fosse. A later project, *Señor Discretion*, went unfinished when Frank succumbed to lung cancer. In 1976 Broadway saw a big revival of Loesser's greatest hit, *Guys and Dolls* (1950); but it was so poorly done, in a Motown adaptation, that the show looked less than an enduring masterpiece. An indifferent Michigan Opera Theatre production of *The Most Happy Fella* visited briefly in 1979, making the piece look dreary, anemic, and terribly old-fashioned (and embarrassing Loesser loyalists). And then came this anthology revue, attempting to honor the songwriter and enhance his memory. But after a successful initial mounting at the intimate Westwood Playhouse in Los Angeles, *Perfectly Frank* seemed to go perfectly awry. The concept was scrapped, and Ron Field—without credit—stepped in to overhaul the piece for New York. (Half the cast was replaced, too, including Kelly [Carole] Bishop and Pamela Myers.) Field and creator Kenny Solms battled through the three-week preview period, with the latter finally yanking his name off the show. (Solms: "This experience hasn't soured me on the theatre. . . . My last Broadway show was *Lorelei* [1974]. Another winner," he added wryly.) But despite all best intentions, *Perfectly Frank* ended up as a group of bright young singers singing a bunch of old songs. (Imagine, Frank Loesser material sounding like "a bunch of old songs!") With time, though, Loesser's work—under the stewardship of his widow, Jo Sullivan—has rebounded to its deserved position. Both *The Most Happy Fella* and *Guys and Dolls* were successfully rehabilitated in 1992; and J. Pierrepont Finch and *How to Succeed* returned to the 46th Street/Richard Rodgers Theatre in 1995, reminding one and all that Frank *is* perfectly unparalleled.

BROADWAY SCORECARD
/ PERFS: 17 / $: –

RAVE	FAVORABLE	MIXED	UNFAVORABLE	PAN
1	2		1	2

PETER PAN
OR THE BOY WHO WOULDN'T GROW UP

a revival of the 1954 musical fantasy

music by Mark (Moose) Charlap; additional music by Jule Styne

lyrics by Carolyn Leigh; additional lyrics by Betty Comden and Adolph Green

book uncredited (doctored by Ron Field)

based on the 1904 play by James M. Barrie

entire production directed and choreographed by Rob Iscove (replaced by Ron Field); original production conceived, directed, and choreographed by Jerome Robbins

produced by Zev Bufman and James M. Nederlander in association with Jack Molthen, Spencer Tandy, and J. Ronald Horowitz

starring Sandy Duncan and George Rose

with Marsha Kramer, Maria Pogee, Beth Fowler, Arnold Soboloff, Alexander Winter, Jonathan Ward, James Cook, Maggy Gorrill, Neva Rae Powers, and Trey Wilson

opened September 6, 1979   Lunt-Fontanne Theatre

WALTER KERR, *TIMES*

[Headline: "Soaring in *Peter Pan*"]

Sandy Duncan has convinced me of one thing, at least. Flying is the only way to go. From the time of her moonburst entrance through the suddenly parted rooftop windows of the Darling nursery right through to her second curtain call—in which she soars rather farther than most performers would care to chance—Miss Duncan is a Peter Pan who is at her most exhilarating when dizzyingly airborne. Isn't every actress who permits herself to be sturdily wired for the part? No. The fact is that I've seen gingerly Peters and determinedly brave Peters and Peters whose false-face grins began to vanish the minute they got anywhere near the too too solid portals. Also seen dandy ones, Mary Martin high among them. But there is something extra about Duncan's invasion of space. Though you can easily glimpse the wire that's keeping her company whenever a follow-spot hits it, it doesn't seem to be doing the heavy work. She's too light for that, and too happy to get going. Instead of the usual little tug that starts a performer off the floor, after which the performer assumes a bent-knee flight position, Duncan seems to make the first move, as though she'd been caught in an updraft. She just lets go of gravity, gracefully and gleefully, and lets the mechanical equipment catch up as best it can. Ditto when she touches down, toes first (no thump), soft as a dust-speck settling into a corner. In between, when she's up there—sometimes pumping her elbows like a miler warming up, mostly making great arcs against the skyline like a seagull gone daft—she's exhilarating. The *Playbill* for the Lunt-Fontanne says "Flying by Foy," whoever Foy may be. But that's nonsense. This flying is by Duncan, and it's the most abandoned I've ever seen. This revival of Barrie's oldest permanent established floating whimsy doesn't run into trouble until it gets its feet on the ground. But there is trouble. *Peter Pan* was never exactly a landmark musical. It was a patch job, hurriedly supplied with seven new songs on the road by Styne, Comden and Green. The entire [second] act seems composed of special material designed to make the most of Miss Martin and Cyril Ritchard. It doesn't serve the new company in the same way. I found myself gradually neutralized, except in midflight.

HOWARD KISSEL, *WOMEN'S WEAR DAILY*

By the time the musical version was created in 1954, the play had become something beyond the mother-fixated story James M. Barrie wrote at the turn of the century. The title role had become the province of Great Ladies of the Theatre, a fact that the musical's creators played with by giving Mary Martin a prima-donna-ish duet with Cyril Ritchard, "Mysterious Lady," a bit of arch theatricality Barrie might not have approved of, but very much in keeping with the star-oriented style of some Fifties musicals. The revival has a completely different kind of Peter Pan. Sandy Duncan, an immensely winning performer, really plays Peter as a little boy—impish, energetic and peevish. She does not mess with the Grand Tradition of alternating between boyishness and arch femininity, so the "Mysterious Lady" number, a focal point of the original production, just seems silly and dumb. Moreover, the direction, still attributed to Rob Iscove, who staged Duncan's nightclub act, but which has, for the last few weeks, been in the hands of Ron Field, weakens the narrative element so much that Duncan's effective characterization doesn't really matter. Also, one of the directors—I assume Field, since he has a predilection for the cute and campy—has given her a bit of business in the first act that betrays the whole spirit of the piece. After tossing fairy dust on the children to enable them to fly, she wipes her hands as if to say, "Feh," a shtik that undercuts what is supposed to be the "moment of truth" of the play—the end of the second act, when, in order to bring Tinker Bell back to life, the audience is supposed to clap to prove they believe in fairies. Of course one seems an awful fuddy-duddy to worry about such matters. *Peter Pan* is such a magical play that it works in spite of any directorial "cleverness." Simply to see a stage full of people flying—and Duncan flies with exhilarating abandon—is exciting. Some time ago Michael Bennett wanted to rethink *Peter Pan* completely—with Peter as a boy really faced with the problem of growing up. Bennett said he gave up the idea because he resolved the issues the play presented to him in analysis. Seeing this enjoyable but not really satisfying revival made me wish he had a less skillful analyst.

DOUGLAS WATT, *DAILY NEWS*
[Headline: "*Peter Pan* Could Really Fly, If . . ."]
Sandy Duncan is a living doll, and George Rose can be an amusing fellow, but it is with limited enthusiasm that I report the opening of a new Broadway season last night at the Lunt-Fontanne with a revival of *Peter Pan*. Duncan is a smashing Peter Pan to behold, and looks, if anything, even younger than she did a decade ago. She flies like a dream, saving her final effect, a swoop right over the heads of the audience, for her ultimate curtain call. She's bright, nifty, and trim as can be, but something of the needed air of exultation is missing from her performance. She sings and cavorts engagingly, but not excitingly except when aloft.

Much the same can be said of Rose, who is giving what is at best a routine performance for him. In fact, in this production, staged by Rob Iscove along the lines originally laid down by Robbins, it is the sumptuous scenery, lighting and special effects, along with the wonderful costumes, which include a splendidly greedy green crocodile and a large white shaggy dog, that almost seem to steal the show. And *Peter Pan* is a show very much in need of stealing. Though some of the songs— "Never Never Land" and "I've Gotta Crow," to cite two of the best— are enjoyable enough, this is hardly a top-notch musical effort, a fact attested to by the realization, 25 years ago, that a second team (Comden-Green-Styne) was needed to bolster the show's musical elements. As for Barrie's play, a sometimes puzzling mixture of childish and adult fantasy (of course, it never was intended solely for children, but mostly for more gullible adults), it shows its age as its none-too-clear plot devices keep shifting gears. At the Wednesday matinee I attended, there were so many children that one realized how few Broadway shows there are for kids and how hungry parents are to find them. I hope the children take it to their hearts, as they surely did the clever laser-beamed Tinker Bell they applauded back to life at the end of Act Two. And they must surely love Sandy Duncan. But the players (there is one noticeably fine pirate) would do well to screw up their courage and believe as strongly in *Peter Pan* as the audience is called upon to express faith in Tinker Bell.

●   ●   ●

The Mary Martin-Jerome Robbins *Peter Pan* was first mounted for Ed Lester's West Coast Civic Light Opera circuit. The show was not very good, but Martin—at the height of her fame—made it unquestionably salvageable. Robbins called in his *On the Town* (1944) pals Comden and Green and his *High Button Shoes* (1947) composer Jule Styne to punch up the score, and punch it up they did. (Styne seems to have been Robbins's favorite music man, also teaming with him for *Bells Are Ringing* [1956], *Gypsy* [1959], and *Funny Girl* [1964].) The new material was of considerably high quality—including "Wendy," "Never Never Land," and the "blimey, slimy" "Captain Hook's Waltz"—and there is no doubt that the team could have come up with a first-class *Peter* all their own (although who in their right minds would want to lose "I've Gotta Crow" or "I'm Flying"?). But the assignment was not to fix *Peter* for posterity, merely to supplement the Charlap-Leigh songs. The show was scheduled for a limited Broadway engagement followed by a live telecast, and who would ever want to mount it again—without Mary, no less—after it had been shown across the nation for free? The result is that this *Peter* comes across somewhat lumpy and half-baked, as typified by the "Mysterious Lady" number. Looking to give the stars a comedy duet, Styne—Mary's vocal coach during her brief-lived early '40s movie career—remembered that she possessed a wild and zany coloratura. Cyril Ritchard himself had a built-in, light-opera style, and Comden and Green had featured fractured operetta parodies in their nightclub days. Why not a zany gypsy-operetta duet featuring Mary's whooping tones? A surefire crowd pleaser for Martin and Ritchard, yes, but nothing to do with *Peter Pan*, and very strange to boot. Here we have a (usually) sexy woman in tights pretending to be a sexless young boy (in tights), pretending to be a sexy woman (in veil) seducing the (usually) effeminate Captain Hook, who is, in fact, Wendy, Michael, and John's stuffy father. The airy J. M. Barrie wove a tangled psychological web in his tale of Peter, but this added bit really takes the (poisoned) green cake. So we're left with an imperfect musical *Peter Pan*, too tasty to discard but somewhat trying in parts. This revival had its origins in a summer-stock tour, which was then expanded into a *real* tour, which was then tuned up for Broadway by Ron Field (who elected to allow the stock director full credit). Sandy Duncan did just fine by *Peter*—more than fine, actually—but still, this Charlap-Leigh-Styne-Comden-Green version made an unsettling brew.

BROADWAY SCORECARD

/ PERFS: 550 / $: +

RAVE	FAVORABLE	MIXED	UNFAVORABLE	PAN
1	2		3	

PICKWICK

an import of the 1963 British "Musical Designed for the Introduction of Diverting Characters and Incidents Attempting No Ingenuity of Plot," previously entitled *Mr. Pickwick*

music by Cyril Ornadel

lyrics by Leslie Bricusse

book by Wolf Mankowitz (doctored by Sidney Michaels); adapted by Keith Waterhouse and Willis Hall (billing removed)

based on the 1837 novel *The Posthumous Papers of the Pickwick Club* by Charles Dickens

directed by Peter Coe

choreographed by Gillian Lynne

produced by David Merrick in association with Bernard Delfont

starring Harry Secombe

with Roy Castle (replacing David Jones), Charlotte Rae, Anton Rodgers, Peter Bull (replacing Brendan Barry), and Julian Orchard

opened October 4, 1965   46th Street Theatre

JOHN CHAPMAN, *DAILY NEWS*

After a year and a half in London and a long spell on the road in the United States, *Pickwick* and Harry Secombe arrived this evening. They have been worth waiting for, and now that they're here they mustn't leave for a year or three. This big, picturesque and captivating show simply overflows with talent—starting, of course, with the daffy genius of Charles Dickens and continuing with every person connected with the David Merrick importation, including Merrick. Sean Kenny's settings are skillfully imagined—and practical, too, because the actors themselves change them while the union stage hands are downstairs

THE *NEW MUSICAL COMEDY*

PICKWICK

Based on Dickens' posthumous papers of the Pickwick Club

Book by **WOLF MANKOWITZ**

Music by **CYRIL ORNADEL**

Lyrics by **LESLIE BRICUSSE**

Setting and Lighting by **SEAN KENNY**

Costumes by	Musical Director	Orchestrations by
PETER RICE	**IAN FRASER**	**ERIC ROGERS**

Choreography by **GILLIAN LYNNE**

Directed by **PETER COE**

FISHER THEATRE DETROIT
Monday, August 9 thru Saturday, September 4
Mon. thru Sat. Eves. at 8:30   Special Perf. Sun., Aug. 15 at 7:30
Mats. Wed. and Sat. at 2:00   (No Mat. Perf. Wed., Aug. 11)
Mon. thru Thurs. Eves. and Sun. Eve. Aug. 15—Orch. $6.50; Mezz. $6.50; Balc. $5.00, 4.30, 3.75, 3.20
Fri. and Sat. Eves.—Orch. $7.00; Mezz. $7.00; Balc. $5.00, 4.30, 3.75, 3.20
Wed. and Sat. Mats.—Orch. $5.00; Mezz. $5.00; Balc. $4.00, 3.50, 2.50   (Tax Included)

"*Pickwick* ran for eighteen months in London," reported Walter Kerr, "and I felt that it was taking up most of the eighteen months last night." (artwork by Nick Nappi)

playing whist or something. It's a veritable plum pudding of a musical—rich and warming and laced with laughter.

WALTER KERR, *HERALD TRIBUNE*

Pickwick ran for eighteen months in London, and while it is too soon
to say how it will do here, I did feel that it was taking up most of the
eighteen months last night. Sluggish is the spirit, tame the temper of
the new show, though not because people aren't busy about their chores.
The Dickensian dancers are busy as badgers, joining hands like good
fellows and sweeping first left and then right, pausing only to let the
girls in gingham bend backwards over their locked arms. What is
Dickensian about that, you may ask? You may well ask. There is nothing particularly Dickensian about that, unless *Blossom Time* [1921] and
Rose Marie [1924] and perhaps *Jumbo* [1935] were derived directly from
Hard Times [Dickens's 1854 novel]. But there they are anyway, sweeping left, sweeping right, leaping four at a time into the unidentified air,
and who would defy them employment? Designer Sean Kenny, who
provided *Oliver!* [1963] with some true mechanical marvels of a sort,
has asked the players to help turn his rotating scaffolding this way and
that in order to transform it, in the blink of an eye, into a rollicking tavern or a debtor's cell or perhaps a full court of law. Clockwise and
counter-clockwise the turntables go, while beams and spindles and
prison-bars rain from the heavenly lumberyard, sleekly, trippingly,
always on time. The only trouble is that all the sets look like scaffolding. But no matter, *Pickwick* would not live, if it did live, by dances
alone, nor could its heart be damaged by being displayed on what often
seem like gallows. A musical version of Dickens' ambling, rambling,
coach-and-fours romp through the joyous world in which honest bumbling is all would have to do just one thing, I think, to plunge it into
motion. It would have to stop long enough to introduce us to the
characters. And that is the one small thing librettist Wolf Mankowitz
hasn't bothered to do. When Sam Weller is trying to revive Mrs.
Bardell after a fainting-fit he tried to do it by what he calls "artifical
desperation." There is artificial desperation in the urgent movement,
the urgent scenery, and the urgent gagging too, when something calmer
and cozier might have been very much nicer.

HOWARD TAUBMAN, *TIMES*

It requires monumentally misdirected gifts to do what *Pickwick* has accomplished. It has squeezed all the fun out of Dickens and has converted his unforgettable, joyous characters into vulgar clichés of the contemporary musical stage. It would not matter if Wolf Mankowitz's book were simply a free and loose adaptation. Dickensians might grumble but could forgive violations of the letter in return for a communication of the spirit. What makes *Pickwick* hard to bear is that the liberties taken with Dickens not only have diluted but also cheapened him. One doesn't object to broad comedy, for Dickens, heaven knows, is wonderfully broad. One is annoyed and repelled by the grafting of the low, tasteless gags and business redolent of modern techniques on the world of 1830. One is disappointed that there is scarcely any humor at all in this musical. Under Peter Coe's direction, Mr. Secombe is allowed to comport himself like a self-indulgent and commonplace musical-comedy comedian. He grimaces and leers, gargles and gurgles, struts complacently, lifts his leg kittenishly and makes a habit of strangulating his high tenor for what is supposed to be droll effect. In the accidental romantic moment with his landlady, this Pickwick carries on like a clown in burlesque. Not to be outdone, Charlotte Rae wraps a leg around a post, tosses feathers from a pillow and chases Pickwick like a famished vixen. The comedy is broad in Dickens but never vulgar like this. Fundamentally, *Pickwick* is cheap, comic-strip Dickens.

• • •

Like Merrick's earlier Dickensian import, *Pickwick* played a highly profitable, extended tryout, but *Pickwick* wasn't *Oliver!* (The episodic *Pickwick Papers* isn't exactly *Oliver Twist*, either.) Merrick determined to "fix" the show in Detroit, as he had with *Hello, Dolly!* (1964), but the tampering seemed to hurt rather than help. The producer finally lost interest and went to Vietnam (with Mary Martin's *Dolly!* company). Having recouped *Pickwick*'s production costs during the tryout, Merrick cut short the Broadway run rather than wait for a deficit to overtake him—which placed *Pickwick* in the hit column, technically. The premature closing resulted in an interesting exchange of lengthy letters, published in *Variety*, between featured actor Peter Bull and the producer. (Responding to Bull's charge that Merrick decided to close without contacting the star, who was out of the show with the mumps at the time, the producer replied: "I didn't speak to Mr. Secombe because as a child I never had the mumps, and I understand it is quite serious in adult males, which might not be of concern to Mr. Bull.") <u>Wisdom from Poor David's Almanack Dept.</u>: "75% of the reviews of my product have been good, which means that the critics were only wrong 25% of the time."

BROADWAY SCORECARD
/ PERFS: 56 / $: +

RAVE	FAVORABLE	MIXED	UNFAVORABLE	PAN
1	1	1	1	2

PIPPIN

"A Musical Comedy"

music and lyrics by Stephen Schwartz

book by Roger O. Hirson

directed and choreographed by Bob Fosse

produced by Stuart Ostrow

starring Eric Berry, Jill Clayburgh, Leland Palmer, Irene Ryan, Ben Vereen, and John Rubinstein

opened October 23, 1972   *Imperial Theatre*

CLIVE BARNES, *TIMES*

An amiable and racy musical, which has three great things to commend it. It is one of the best musical stagings to be seen on Broadway in years, it is most beautifully designed, and it might well do for the actor Ben Vereen what *Cabaret* [1966] did for Joel Grey. It is, I felt, a trite and

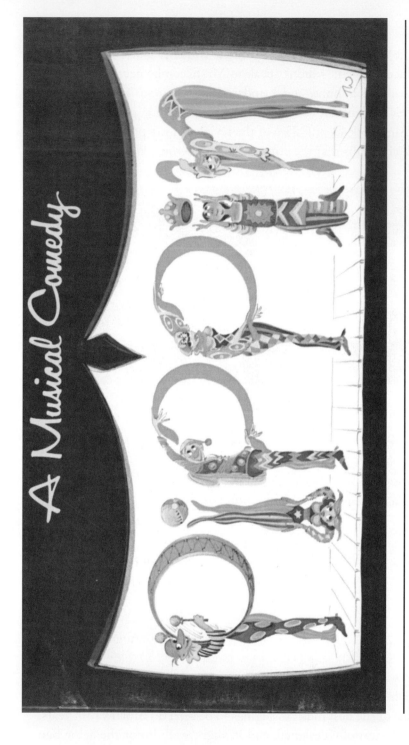

Illuminated manuscript characters out of commedia dell'arte, via Bob Fosse and Tony Walton. (Look at the size of the thighs on the "N" gal.) What would *Pippin* have looked like if Tony had designed costumes as well as sets? (artwork by Tony Walton)

uninteresting story with aspirations to a seriousness it never for one moment fulfills; a commonplace set to rock music. I must say I found most of the music somewhat characterless. It contains a few rock ballads that could prove memorable. What will certainly be memorable is the staging by Bob Fosse. This is fantastic. It takes a painfully ordinary little show and launches it into space. From the first moment until almost the last (for nothing can totally redeem the book's lame duck ending), Fosse never loses his silk and velvet grasp on the show. He works desperately hard to give the tired old idea of a group of clowns some artificial resuscitation—he even makes sense of the superhuman commentator and he gives the show the pace of a roller derby and the finesse of a conjuror. Yet nothing seems strained or exaggerated. Fosse has achieved complete continuity between his staging and his choreography, and his dances themselves have art and imagination. They swing with life. Mind you, he has two master collaborators in Tony Walton and Patricia Zipprodt. Walton's scenery manages an almost impossible combination of Holy Roman Empire and Fifth Avenue chic. He has also provided scenery that will slide, fold, make itself scarce when necessary, and when equally necessary even adaptable. This is exactly suited to Fosse's pell-mell dazzle. Zipprodt has accomplished her task with equal adroitness and elegance—her clowns look Italian and Fellini and her girls look French and naked. It is probably just right for the Holy Roman Empire. It was, I felt, Vereen who really held the show together. Following his demonic performance last season as Judas in *Jesus Christ Superstar*, Vereen here shows all the makings of a superstar himself. His mocking presence and voice, his deft dancing and easy authority, make his performance one of the most impressive aspects of the evening. The book is feeble and the music bland, yet the show runs like a racehorse.

MARTIN GOTTFRIED, *WOMEN'S WEAR DAILY*

Pippin starts out like a house afire with Bob Fosse running the show at peak energy, creativity, confidence and maturity. No musical has been so completely choreographed-directed since *Follies* [1971], every facet timed, meshed and coordinated into a colorful, magical, musical, rhythmic body that moved along for at least 45 minutes until somebody unfortunately asked, great, but what's it all about? Stopping to answer that question, Fosse never really got started again, and before he knew it, a tremendously imaginative entertainment was stopped dead in its tracks by a book writer with no story to tell and a point of view made of solid acne. The show never recovered. In the beginning, the main concern of *Pippin* is being a show. Between its company (a tightly rehearsed and tremendously capable crew) and its magical master of ceremonies—Ben Vereen, who has the talent and the charisma to take center stage and hold it—nothing much more seemed needed. Fosse was making his show a seamless fabric of dance and musical staging. No longer was he bound to the mannerism of tight little trios, their elbows tucked at their sides, doing cute little numbers (all right, one "Steam Heat"). His work was expansive, free and, above all, marvelously original. [But then Pippin kills his father], killing the show for good in the process. Now Fosse abandoned *Pippin* altogether to Roger O. Hirson's book and Stephen Schwartz' music and lyrics. Having pulled his whimsical pageantry up short for some 10 minutes of dialog with virtually no musical sense at all, he never got the ball rolling again. The stage is taken from the spectacular, musical Vereen and given to the lifeless John Rubinstein, who plays *Pippin* as if sitting crosslegged could pass for charm and earnestly carrying a tune could pass for projected singing. So, a tremendous creative burst was stifled, and a lot of good work shot down in midflight. As for individual performances, the show is staged for Rubinstein, Vereen and, especially, the company, but Leland Palmer was in the unfortunate position of doing a long and energetic solo dance obviously choreographed to Gwen Verdon's style. It was a shame, but then, so is *Pippin*.

WALTER KERR, *TIMES*

The kingdom of musical comedy has left the back gate open and the wandering minstrels are all streaming through again. Thus, the new eighth-century musical at the Imperial, awash in jesters' caps, Pulcinella noses, illuminated manuscripts, and a lot of the old soft shoe. The *Chansons de Roland* have been reorchestrated to Swanee rhythms, two-a-day pitter-pat, electric-organ doodles—with a sizable indebtedness to Joan Littlewood's *Oh, What a Lovely War* [1964]—and when the Visigoths are slain in blood "red as sunset, warmer than wine" there is a fine black court fool to dagger-dance the mayhem in spats and silk shirt, his walking-stick carving the air with Ted Lewis *lèse majesté*. It's a lovely way to do a show, whatever one may ultimately wish to say about the material. Any musical with an opening as stunning as the one Bob Fosse has devised for *Pippin* would have a lot of trouble running out of steam for a goodly time thereafter. The curtain rises on a pitch-dark world filled with coiling smoke—and diamond-bright hands. Only hands, riggling fingers in the void, 11 pair of them, shivering a message of welcome and disembodied danger. The hands are Jolson's, Martha Graham's, Alla Nazimova's, the *theatre's*—and you know that unimpeded imagination will be at work tonight. I mentioned earlier that you might find the material of *Pippin* less exhilarating than the method. Bound to be true, I think. The thematic line is, for these days, trite: identity-seekers have been all over the place for quite a while. Nor is the conclusion novel or particularly helpful. Having had his fill of war, sex, and political revolution, Pippin, in effect, turns off, resigning himself to the arms of a strong woman. There's something deflating in that, as though we'd all gone through a lot for a very little. *Pippin* is almost entirely an exercise in style, an opening of the theatre's box of toys without tearing the wrappings, deliberate as dance, disarming as sleight-of-hand. As such, recommended.

DOUGLAS WATT, *DAILY NEWS*
[Headline: "A Splendid Musical, Magnificently Staged & Played"]
Pippin is a musical of enormous style and I hail it. Staged by Bob Fosse within an inch of its life, last night's arrival at the Imperial survives—nay, triumphs—by reason of its grace, humor, imagination and, yes, its very cleverness. Funny, but *Pippin*, in its own beautifully organized fashion, sets out to accomplish pretty much the same thing the dismal and chaotic *Dude* of a couple of weeks ago attempted, succeeding brilliantly where the other failed. For this is yet another story of a young man's search for identity, for a life with meaning. And though it is done tongue-in-cheek, a becoming thread of sincerity informs it throughout, even to the very end with its wisecrack finish. This is all presented in the freest possible manner, as an impromptu entertainment by a performing troupe and with a director (he sometimes demands different readings by the actors) and several asides to the audience. It could all have been unbearably arch but somehow it isn't. There are slack moments but they are rescued by a show that is unusually fluid (in the

best sense of the word) and dynamic and that wears a wonderful smile. Stephen Schwartz' songs are charming. His music rocks, croons, dances and, in general, floats the proceedings most attractively in superb orchestrations by Ralph Burns. His lyrics are equally engaging. There are several showstoppers, perhaps the brightest of them the artless "No Time at All," sung by Irene Ryan (as Pippin's grandma) with the words of the chorus held up, bouncing ball and all, so the audience can join in. John Rubinstein is a throughly engaging Pippin. But it is the remarkable Ben Vereen as the Sportin' Life of a director (here called Leading Player) who ties everything together as he stage manages scenes, interrupts or encourages players and, at the end, sets up a glorious finale only to have it disappointingly fall flat. Fosse, responsible for the entire direction—dances and all—has given us a superlative example of musical staging. The show is animated, sexy and lovely to look at, especially inasmuch as the ensemble boasts several stunning girls. The girls and everybody else have been dressed to the nines by Patricia Zipprodt in the gorgeous display of costumes. Tony Walton's scenery is airy and delightful and Jules Fisher's lighting scheme is the best I've seen in some time. *Pippin* is extraordinary musical theatre.

o   o   o

"We've got magic to do," announced Bob Fosse's alter ego as *Pippin* was enjoined, and that about sums it up. "Mystic, exotic illusions" he promised, and Fosse sure delivered. The director started with material about a teenaged dropout trying to find himself, the sort of protest piece draft-age college boys in the late '60s might propound to convince us war is bad. *Pippin* was, in fact, a college-originated project of Stephen Schwartz, who—with the Off-Broadway *Godspell* (1971) and collaboration on Leonard Bernstein's *Mass* (1972) behind him—was suddenly positioned as the Jerry Herman of the early '70s. (This was to be followed, poor thing, by twenty years of dire obscurity. Accompanied by ongoing royalties from his early works, of course.) The dropout-hero was the son of jolly old Charlemagne, as it happened; at least, they named him after young Pepin and placed him in an anachronistically medieval tapestry. Fosse came up with a dazzling display of pyrotechnics propping up a ninety-pound weakling of a musical comedy. Whether *Pippin* had enough going for it without Fosse is beside the point; the score is tunefully peppy, surely. But Fosse took it over and made it his own, strengthening the entertainment at the expense, perhaps, of the authors' notions. Young Schwartz had already generated a powerful ego, but he was no match for the director-in-chief. Relations strained past breaking, with Fosse ultimately barring Schwartz from rehearsals. The composer was "only twenty-five years old, and some days he's only twelve," said Fosse, who was himself forty-five at the time (some days). If the *Pippin* Fosse formulated—refashioning and rewriting along the way—was a testament to his own especial stage wizardry, and if the "integrity" of the material suffered from the Fosse treatment, it sure worked as theatrical entertainment. *Pippin* was peddled to the public with a well-fashioned TV commercial, which centered *not* on the star or the songs or the spectacle or the production; it featured, simply, a corny old softshoe-for-three in macabre style set to tinkly dance music. This snippet of celluloid turned the moderately well-received *Pippin* into a smash hit, simultaneously bringing the marketing of the Broadway musical into a new era. Less Is More Dept.: Unable to raise the $700,000 capitalization, producer Stuart Ostrow forged ahead with a mere $500,000. Much of the shortfall came out of the scenery budget (which is, understandably, the largest expense item on a Broadway ledger sheet). The cuts forced Fosse and the estimable Tony Walton to redevise their work in a sketchier, more inventive style, which, happily, intensified *Pippin*'s magic. Walton brought along some tricks of his own, including an especially magical skeletal drop that Ben Vereen "pulled" out of the deck (stage floor) like a magician doing a trick with a handkerchief. Nothing up Fosse's sleeve.

Tony Awards were won by Bob Fosse (director and choreographer), Ben Vereen (actor), Tony Walton (scenic designer), and Jules Fisher (lighting designer).

BROADWAY SCORECARD

/ PERFS: 1,944 / $: +

RAVE	FAVORABLE	MIXED	UNFAVORABLE	PAN
3	2		1	

THE PIRATES OF PENZANCE

a new production of the 1879 British comic operetta

music by Arthur Sullivan; adapted by William Elliott

words by William S. Gilbert

directed by Wilford Leach

choreographed by Graciela Daniele

produced by Joseph Papp for the New York Shakespeare Festival

starring Kevin Kline, Estelle Parsons (replacing Patricia Routledge), Linda Ronstadt, George Rose, and Rex Smith

with Tony Azito, Stephen Hanan, Alexandra Korey, and Marcie Shaw

opened January 8, 1981   Uris Theatre

CLIVE BARNES, *POST*

It was a smash in Central Park, and it is even more smashing on Broadway. Joseph Papp's production of *The Pirates of Penzance* opened last night to the sort of standing ovation even Broadway rarely sees. It was a dream opening, with all the stars glittering in the right places and at the right time. When George Rose broke up laughing and had to have the orchestra start one of his encores again it was typically a boost to the general conviviality. There was the unmistakable sense of a Broadway hit taking up residence in style. In a way it is obviously true to the original operetta, but its approach is so radical that it might offend hard-core Savoyard devotees. Without any doubt whatsoever this is Gilbert and Sullivan in a new pop and Broadway guise, and however faithful it may appear it is defiantly different. For me it offered a new awareness for a certain style of operetta that through almost a century of decayed decades I had come to despise. The sheer heady, giddy excitement is perfectly remote from any quasi-operatic version I have seen. And it establishes the validity of an original, now commonly obscured by the scar tissue of antiquity. There is magic here that bubbles like a witch's cauldron. Gilbert's tongue twisting lyrics, underpinned by Sullivan's loyal obbligato, retain an almost unexpected freshness. It is quite simply this special air of freshness that informs the entire production. What they have done—and it is miraculous—is to place, between ourselves and the work, that distance which lends enchantment. William Elliott's arrangements are absolutely delightful—they catch the spirit of Sullivan and bubble with it. Leach has mown down dialogue as if it were corn, which it was, but most importantly, he has imposed on the work a special look. It is part stylization, but even more it represents a crucial conspiracy between the actors and the audience that needs to be aware and sophisticated. He is enormously helped by the choreography of Graciela Daniele. I know most things about dance but I have no idea where this lady stems from. But I guarantee you, she's a talent. . . . Kline is destined to become, if he doesn't go to movies first, the great comic talent of the English-speaking theatre. The man is fantastic—watch his every gesture, his timing, his poise.

WALTER KERR, *TIMES*

The New York Shakespeare Festival's *Pirates of Penzance* is innocence unalloyed and doodling unlimited and I'm sure its very guilelessness of soul will guarantee its continued, galloping success. After all, who among your acquaintances is prepared to resist the radiantly rapacious smile of a buccaneer too tender-hearted to prey upon orphans, who would dare avert his gaze from an ingenue whose blushing sweetness is the purest steel? The innocence. We really need to pause and force ourselves to remember that—long before there was a Kevin Kline to look straight up into the sun to see what time it is, or a Linda Ronstadt to walk into the first two notes of a song as though she were walking over a cliff—a couple of gentle men named William S. Gilbert and Arthur Sullivan were responsible for inventing the delectable naïveté that is so enchanting from square one. Lest we forget—Mr. Gilbert was funny first. As, indeed, was Mr. Sullivan. There. I just wanted to make certain we knew where the nonsense came from, where its bubbles rose and glistened and broke. That done, has Mr. Leach and his insanely energetic crew added a comic resonance—with here and there a whisper, here and there a blast—of their own? Indefatigably. They'll try anything, and succeed at most. Among my favorite successes is a bit in which Kline, having already dueled everyone including the conductor in the pit, means to ram his rapier into its sheath, or perhaps into his belt. He doesn't accomplish his swift, manly, businesslike intention. He drives the point of the rapier into his foot instead. This pins him to a single, if revolving, position for quite a bit of a trio in which he is supposed to be participant. And what I like best is that, two or three minutes after he's managed to unstab himself, he's about to repeat the entire swashbuckling accident when a quick glance—and no doubt a memory of pain—persuades him to jab that sharp point into the floor at a reasonably safe distance from his booted toes. These piratical stances can be treacherous. Kline is a master of stances, trampoline bounces, and dueling the man behind him while fending off the man before. He is probably especially good at missing the spot on which he's planned to land, because missing—on purpose—can be dangerous. Mr. Kline's gleaming teeth looked very dangerous.

FRANK RICH, *TIMES*

Yes, it is every bit as wonderful on Broadway in January as it was in Central Park in July. It may even be more wonderful. The chorus leaps higher, the band plays brighter; the powerhouse stars are now so self-assured that you may think they own the town. Perhaps it seems irrational to be thrown into ecstasy by a century-old Gilbert and Sullivan operetta. After all, *Pirates* isn't about anything except a crew of benign pirates, a bevy of marriageable maidens and a platoon of cowardly bobbies. W. S. Gilbert's Dickensian plot is the quintessence of silly, and his satirical jests limn Victorian manners that mean little to contemporary American audiences. Yet, as Gilbert might say, it really doesn't matter. Once we make the acquaintance of Kevin Kline's Pirate King, George Rose's Major General, and the young lovers played by the rock stars Linda Ronstadt and Rex Smith, we are helplessly transported to an enthralling fantasy land. This show's totally assured tone—funny yet not campy, sweet yet not soupy—is what brings its diverse elements together. By rethinking—but not rewriting—Gilbert and Sullivan's work in the highly charged terms of modern musical comedy, Mr. Papp and company have gained the best of both worlds. Indeed, they have united civilized British wit and American show-biz knowhow in a combustive Broadway musical for the first time since the Messrs. Lerner and Loewe met Shaw halfway in *My Fair Lady* [1956]. Mr. Kline is in a class by himself. He has all the ingredients for conventional leading-man stardom—a big voice, dashing good looks, infinite charm—and yet he's also blessed with the grace and timing of a silent-movie clown. As the Pirate King, he can show off all his gifts. He flies from the stage to the ramp in a single bound; he coddles any woman who isn't nailed down; he engages in sword fights with half the chorus as well as any inanimate objects that cross his path. And then there are those perfect pratfalls: Mr. Kline tumbles from lofty perches only to bounce up in a flash, deadpan and demented, for still more comic punishment. One must wonder how long *Pirates*—or anything—will be able to keep this performer in captivity.

DOUGLAS WATT, *DAILY NEWS*
[Headline: "*Pirates* Sail in with Flying Colors"]
While the cast is fine in depth, a couple of performances stand out above the rest, and one in particular. Younger patrons may think they're going in to catch Linda Ronstadt, the fetching Mabel, and so they will, but they'll come out whistling Kevin Kline. Kline's stupendously athletic Pirate King, a wild mixture of dexterity and bungling, a kind of winged Errol Flynn forever landing in the wrong place, is the show's shooting star. Gilbert, who set the staging pattern for the canon, might have been startled at first, but then, I suspect, overcome with joy. George Rose comes in a very close second with his helmeted, ruddy-complexioned, white-whiskered model of a Major General, very precise and wholly captivating. Ronstadt, gowned in chaste Victorian white and with brunette bangs cascading from beneath a cap, is as pretty in song as in looks, getting off "Poor Wandering One" with all her *fioritura* in place. The rock star even manages to sneak in a couple of growling chest tones in a first-act ensemble number. She still hasn't learned how to read lines, but Mabel hasn't much to say, anyway.

●   ●   ●

The 1975 *Chorus Line* capped a remarkable four-year period in the life of the New York Shakespeare Festival, which saw award-winning transfers of *Two Gentlemen of Verona* (1971), *Sticks and Bones* (1971), *Much Ado About Nothing* (1972), *That Championship Season* (1972), and That Michael Bennett Musical. Alas, this could not go on forever, and anyway, the *Chorus Line* machine took up a considerable amount of the organization's attention (while providing the nonprofit with enough profit to indulge in no-profit experiments, and plenty of 'em). Come the summer of 1980 up in Central Park, spawning place of the Festival's two Shakespearean transfers, Papp turned his attention from the Bard to Gilbert & Sullivan. Rupert D'Oyly Carte—originating producer of the operettas—and his successors had been visiting our fair harbor consistently since 1879. One of their biggest hits actually premièred in Little Old New York, sort of a tryout *way* out-of-town: *The Pirates of Penzance* opened December 31, 1879, at the New Fifth Avenue Theatre (which, logically enough, was not on Fifth Avenue but 28th Street, west of Broadway). The D'Oyly Carte American tours continued regularly into the latter half of the new century, but by 1976 the trouping Savoyards—so named for their home base at London's Savoy Theatre—were tired and dying, as was their audience. The operettas themselves, while technically dazzling, were too arch and silly and old-fashioned for popular consumption. Or so it appeared, when Joe Papp gave director Wilford Leach and musical adapter William Elliott a Shakespeare-in-the-Park slot to give it a go. The rejuvenated, rambunctious, centenarian *Pirates* commandeered Manhattan, sailing downriver (via Columbus Circle) to a rollickingly successful Broadway run. No Prisoners Taken.

Winner of a special citation from the New York Drama Critics' Circle. In addition to winning the Tony Award for Best Revival, Tonys were won by Wilford Leach (director) and Kevin Kline (actor).

BROADWAY SCORECARD
/ PERFS: 787 / $: +

RAVE	FAVORABLE	MIXED	UNFAVORABLE	PAN
5	1			

PLATINUM

"The Musical with a Flip-Side," previously entitled *Sunset*

music by Gary William Friedman

lyrics by Will Holt

book by Will Holt and Bruce Vilanch

based on "an original idea" by Will Holt

directed and choreographed by Joe Layton

produced by Gladys Rackmil, Fritz Holt, and Barry M. Brown

starring Alexis Smith

with Richard Cox, Lisa Mordente, Damita Jo Freeman, Robin Grean, Avery Sommers, Stanley Kamel, and Tony Shultz

opened November 12, 1978   *Mark Hellinger Theatre*

CLIVE BARNES, *POST*

Alexis Smith is a quite extraordinary artist. She is a star of magnitude—she leaves no one in any doubt of that—but a star of unusual contradictions. She has a special quality of gentle steel, of unstressed chutzpah, of opalescent glitter. Last night she opened in *Platinum*, and just for a time there I thought it was going to be a battle royal between Miss Smith and fate. And in a way it was. *Platinum*, which oddly describes itself as "the Musical with a Flip-Side," is partly thrilling and partly terrible, and seems to have no sense of direction. It is an anecdote structured on a skeleton of banal music, but fleshed out with a sweetly razzmatazz staging and some exquisitely conceived performances. The book by Will Holt and Bruce Vilanch, based on an original—it says in the playbill—idea by Holt, could give libraries a bad name. We have lines such as: "For Goodness sake, have respect for a generation other than your own." Right on! Nor is the music anything to cheer for. Gary William Friedman, who composed *The Me Nobody Knows* [1970], has here assembled a pastiche of contemporary pop that could fool no one

"A galaxy of theatrical luminaries have been assembled to combine their efforts in presenting an exciting new concept in stage presentations," said the advertising herald. "The book could give libraries a bad name," said Clive Barnes.

and charm few others. It is not so much bad as so unmemorable that it is to music what Kleenex is to a handkerchief. No fabric. No lace. No substance. Disposable. Joe Layton has taken on this musical, seemingly, as if it were some kind of challenge. And he has met it. Layton swings the show along with zest and expertise, so that you never have, luckily, quite enough time to think.

RICHARD EDER, *TIMES*
Platinum is one less musical about show business. It takes an idea that is limp to the point of formlessness, pours it into an ill-written book, decks it out with inferior rock music, stages it shoddily and performs it with a widespread lack of skill. Bob Mackie's costumes are comically outrageous, and if you can't sing a costume, at least you can laugh at it. There's not a great deal else, and if I mention costumes at the start, it is because it is the kind of show in which Miss Smith's indignant exclamation, "Sables!" when she is complimented on her mink, passes for a laugh, and dramatic shifts are signaled by changing clothes. She is playing a 1940s singing film star trying to make a comeback at a recording studio that specializes in rock singers. At first she refuses to change her style, then she tries to, and finally there is a dialectical synthesis in which it is suggested that each generation has something to learn from the other. After she comes upon [the male lead, a fading rock singer] naked in his Jacuzzi bath—the three woman back-up singers also bathe but they use bathing suits, which seems unfair—a friendship is struck up, and then a love affair. They work together; she takes moaning and writhing lessons from the back-up singers, and finally everything comes together. She teaches the rock singers how to tap dance and they all talk about a new musical style to be called discotap. All is synthesis, harmony, and mush. This attempt to carpenter together the musical generations has very little in it that works. The characters are hasty and unbelievable caricatures; only Miss Smith's weariness is believable and partly because of our own.

WALTER KERR, *TIMES*
[Headline: "All That Glitters Is Alexis Smith"]
I have a feeling that if *Platinum* could just get rid of its book, its songs, its microphones and its almost arrogantly messy setting, it would be light miles ahead. All it would have left is Alexis Smith, which is all it's got anyway, and she could still stand stage center favoring us with the

smile of an Athena about to break into tears, she could still sit on top of a grand piano so that her glistening reflection in its raised lid would make heavenly twins of her, she could still treat her fur coat as though it were the one thing in the world on which she could count absolutely. Funny how much the lady can read into a line that isn't all that strong, that certainly isn't strong enough to give her an applause exit. At one point in the evening's meandering plotting, Smith is storming out of "the newest environmental recording studio in Hollywood." In fact, she has stormed out, ready to call her envisioned career as a recording artist quits forever. In a trice, she's back. "Forget something?" asks one of the snippier backup girls. Smith shakes her head ruefully, swiftly locates the elderly mink she's left behind her and flips it over a stout right arm as she says, very simply, "You can't forget an old friend." Then she goes, having somehow made it sound as though both she and the coat had Character. The fading film goddess—Miss Smith looks the goddess, all right, but the fading is yet to come—has been filling in her time playing *Mame* and *Hello, Dolly!* on the road so regularly that she's apt to get them mixed up in mid-performance. "I *am* the road," she says, with a wickedly wistful look in her eye. . . . Well, it's hard to reach conclusions about a show that keeps shifting the direction of its love-line in practically every scene (one suspects that passages were rewritten out of town without reference to other passages). No problem with the problem-free Miss Smith, of course. Smith can do just about anything and do it with elegance, authority, sunniness and snap. I wish her only one more knack, the knack of picking a show for herself that will match her strength, grace for grace.

HOWARD KISSEL, *WOMEN'S WEAR DAILY*
Several years ago, I attended a rehearsal of the ill-fated *Truckload* (the title told you everything you needed to know) in preparation for an interview with the librettist. As I listened to the chorus plod valiantly through a third-rate rock song of banal lyrics and tiresome, insistent music, I noticed the producer, a charming woman who would later, for reasons having nothing to do with her taste in musicals, be indicted on many counts of fraud, listening carefully. Her response to the musical bilge, uttered in tones of earnest, philosophical detachment, was, "I think the young people will like it." [*Truckload*, a 1975 Adela Holzer–produced rock musical, closed during previews at the Lyceum.]

Similar thinking must have gone into *Platinum*. As the dreary show unfolds, you can fairly hear the "creative" conferences that produced it. Nothing seems to have its own reasons. Everything is there to placate some part of the imagined audience. There are, for example, rock numbers in several of the dominant styles of the last decade, included on the outworn assumption that "the young people" will come to Broadway for ersatz rock when they can get the real thing elsewhere. There is Alexis Smith, there to attract the traditional theatregoers, who are supposed to sit through the deliberately repellent rock stuff for a few pastiche numbers, one a sort of illegitimate grandnephew of a *Follies* [1971] song. There are two black singers engaged in self-caricature, in a benighted attempt to corner the burgeoning black audience. And there is one nude male *derrière* and an arrangement that veers from rock into Jewish to palliate two segments of the traditional Broadway audience. To cap off the appeal to "the young people," the show ends with a slide show retrospective of pop music of the last two decades, including a little eulogy for Janis Joplin. If I were one of "the young people," I would be outraged at this attempt to manipulate my memories. But it has been my experience that shows like this don't work for "the young people." They are taken up by middle-aged swingers from New Jersey, desperate to be "with it." I think *Platinum* will give them what they're looking for.

0   0   0

"The Musical with a Flip Side" indeed. The authors of *The Me Nobody Knows* envisaged an intimate, four-character musical about an over-the-hill movie actress and a "younger" man. During a 1976 staged reading at the Manhattan Theatre Club, the director—James Coco—told the authors that they really *must* expand it into a full-scale musical. And so they did, leading to a première at Buffalo's Studio Arena Theatre in the fall of 1977. Alexis Smith, of *Follies*, and Lisa Mordente, twenty-year-old daughter of Chita Rivera and Tony Mordente, headed the cast. The title was *Sunset* (which gives you a hint as to where Will Holt's "original idea" originally originated); the book was by Louis La Russo II; and the director, according to the program, was one "T. Tune." *Sunset* went *Platinum* for Broadway, with Joe Layton overseeing the production while Bruce Vilanch (a writer for Bette Midler) collaborated with Holt on the new book. *Platinum* flipped out, as it were, losing $1,743,000 (on an intended investment of $1,250,000). On November 7, 1983, with André Ernotte directing a cast headed by Tammy Grimes, the intimate, four-character *Sunset* rose once more (Off-Broadway). But *only* once. Rose-colored, Platinum-rimmed Glasses Dept.: "There are a lot of people who still think *Platinum* was one of the best things ever done on the stage"— producer Gladys Rackmil (Nederlander), while raising money for a subsequent show, in a 1980 interview with the *Times*.

ROADWAY SCORECARD
/ PERFS: 33 / $: –

RAVE	FAVORABLE	MIXED	UNFAVORABLE	PAN
I		I		4

PORGY AND BESS

an operatic restoration of the 1935 folk opera

music by George Gershwin

lyrics by DuBose Heyward and Ira Gershwin

libretto by DuBose Heyward

based on the 1927 drama *Porgy* by Dorothy and DuBose Heyward, from the 1926 novel by DuBose Heyward

directed by Jack O'Brien

choreographed by Mabel Robinson

produced by Sherwin M. Goldman and Houston Grand Opera

starring Donnie Ray Albert, Clamma Dale, Wilma Snakesnider, Abraham Lind-Oquendo, Esther Hinds, Delores Ivory-Davis, Robert Mosley, Irene Oliver, Carol Brice, and Larry Marshall

opened September 25, 1976   Uris Theatre

CLIVE BARNES, *TIMES*

The best musical on Broadway tonight is not a musical. It is an opera. It is *Porgy and Bess*. This production was a revelation. In most previous productions, Gershwin's wishes for recitative have been disregarded. The opera has been given with spoken dialogue, as if it were a Broadway musical. But Gershwin wanted a grand opera in a folk style, and this is what his present producer, Sherwin M. Goldman, envisaged. I had never taken *Porgy and Bess* all that seriously as an opera. I loved some of the music—you would have to be stone-tone-deaf not to—but the musical pretensions of Gershwin have always disturbed me. But seeing the opera in this finally authentic version, it struck me as a masterpiece. It reminded me strongly, in every way, of the operas of Janácek. The dramatic material is oddly similar, but, more important, the orchestral and vocal texture seems remarkably the same. Both Gershwin and Janácek are here using their own folk material, and making extraordinarily similar sounds. Before this landmark production one would never have guessed this. The casting has been impeccable, and the entire production has an air—can I be elitest?—of class that is regrettably rare on Broadway. What is so beautiful about *Porgy and Bess* is really its original concept score. It can be taken very seriously as by far the best of all North American operas, and as one of the very few endurable operas written in the English language, ever. Ever. The company is first rate. These are operatic roles and are not to be sung every night, as if they were friendly vocal exercises. In this spirit there are, for example, three Porgys and three Besses. The present cast proved a pure delight. Their voices floated up in the style of Verdi, yet the acting was pure Negro Ensemble Company. Probably this, and a musical revelation of what Gershwin really meant, is what the opera needed. For yes, it is an opera. But if you have ever worried about going to an opera, think of it as a musical. Either way, *Porgy and Bess* is one of the best shows in town. Just listen to the music while it's hot. What other white man has captured blues and spirituals in this way? The answer is redundant.

WALTER KERR, *TIMES*

[Headline: "Gershwin, True to Himself"]

The jokes are legion about George Gershwin's egocentricity—he was an egocentric, of course, of the most generous sort, being perfectly willing to play his tunes for anybody, any place, any time—but the joke, in the end, is on us, on music, on opera, on the world he took by the tail and snapped to his bidding. For it is his very arrogance, supreme confidence, relentless self-assertion that leave us with an actual opera today. Most people didn't want to call *Porgy and Bess* an opera when it was written—pretentious of the musical-comedy man, wasn't it, to try to elbow his way into the company of the immortals?— and the houses regularly devoted to *Traviata* wouldn't touch it. The Theatre Guild summoned up sufficient nerve to mount it as a sort-of opera, with much of the recitative (which means much of the actual music and, in fact, the entire musical ambience) cut. But it did get *Porgy and Bess* on, in a production so opulent that it had to lose money even at capacity, and I'd be betraying my youth if I didn't still stand at attention before the memory of Rouben Mamoulian's staging, above all the empty courtyard of Catfish Row with an empty rocking chair slightly to left of center—a rocking chair that, after the sultry lift and fall of "Summertime" had grown insistent enough in the pit, began to rock back and forth all by itself. The production now at the Uris has at last unabashedly put the piece on the stage approximately as its composer envisioned it. It's opera, all right, and it's opera because Gershwin was stubborn, cocky, unintimidated. I think that it survives (or emerges) with its independent character intact precisely because Gershwin did not get down on his knees before the notion of "opera" but stood on his own two feet and, if he felt like it, tapped them. Gershwin took on stature with *Porgy and Bess* not because it is an opera but because it is *his* opera; he saw to that, and he was right. Now that we hear all he wrote, the characters themselves take on a stature— a size and a splendor—we have never seen before. The music that has been so long missing lifts them up; they stand astride it like giants, long-suffering but secure now, conscious of power, eager to share a sound that is whole.

DOUGLAS WATT, *DAILY NEWS*
[Headline: "A Grand Native Opera Heard at its Grandest"]
The whole truth at last. Forty-one years after its Broadway première, and with several revivals in between, we finally have the complete *Porgy and Bess*. And what a grand opera it is! Of course, we've known that all

along. But now, with the recitatives and whole chunks of the score restored (the trimming began during the original Boston tryout), the George Gershwin masterpiece stands revealed as grander than ever, and it is being given its full due in an enthralling production. *Porgy and Bess* is not just a great American opera; it is the single great American opera. It has its flaws; there is some commonplace writing; but its power is such that even scaled-down versions can make a remarkable impression, and taken as a whole the effect is tremendous. The fact that so many of the set pieces are essentially enrichments and extensions of the American popular song idiom of the day is not only a completely natural and cheering outgrowth of the musical-comedy world in which Gershwin had long been a master; it is also precisely in keeping with the idiom, American folk opera. And in addition to the excellent lyrics by DuBose Heyward and Ira Gershwin, the Heyward book itself is foolproof, as near-perfect as the libretto for *Carmen* [1875] (which also lacked recitatives to begin with, you'll recall). Besides the natural-sounding sung dialogue (only the few white characters lack music), the restorations include Gershwin's original opening, in which honky-tonk piano and glimpses of Catfish Row nightlife precede "Summertime"; much choral music, including the familiarly omitted "Oh, Doctor Jesus" sextet at the start of the Storm Scene; and other items. With all the score's delights, if I were forced to choose one particular scene above the rest it would inevitably be the Wake Scene in Serena's room with, at its core, the stunning "My Man's Gone Now," possibly the most profoundly moving piece of music Gershwin ever set down. What a night! What an opera! What a Gershwin!

○   ○   ○

As everybody is well aware, the folk opera *Porgy and Bess* was a failure when it first trod the boards in 1935. This is usually ascribed to the extensive use of operatic recitative and/or excessive out-of-town trimming. What is ignored is that *most* mid-Depression musicals failed—even some of the "hits" lost money. *Porgy* was outsized and relatively expensive, with a large cast, a large orchestra, and understandably not-so-popular subject matter. The piece became a hit when it was revived—with dialogue replacing recitative—in 1942. But was it the different version? Or a combination of the posthumous lionization of the composer, the increasing familiarity of the music, the "popular price" ticket scale, and the wartime theatrical boom? At any event, by its tenth anniversary *Porgy and Bess* was a well-known classic. The 1953 Broadway revival—following a triumphant European tour—was an even bigger success, leading to engagements throughout the world throughout the decade. (This also led to a star-filled 1959 motion picture adaptation that the surviving authors frowned upon.) *Porgy* lay low during the racially sensitive '60s but returned triumphantly with this full-scale "opera house" version, which opened on the eve of what would have been George Gershwin's seventy-eighth birthday. The composer died on July 11, 1937, at the age of thirty-eight. The residuary value of *Porgy and Bess*, at the time of his death, was appraised at $250.

A Tony Award was won for Best Revival (the first year this award was given).

BROADWAY SCORECARD
/ PERFS: 122 / $: +

RAVE	FAVORABLE	MIXED	UNFAVORABLE	PAN
6				

POUSSE-CAFÉ

"A New Musical," previously entitled *Sugar City* and *Red Petticoats*

music by Duke Ellington

lyrics by Marshall Barer and Fred Tobias

book by Jerome Weidman (with billing for coauthor Melvin Isaacson removed; replacing Don Appell)

based on the 1930 screenplay *Der Blaue Engel* (*The Blue Angel*) by Carl Zuckmayer, Karl Vollmöller and Robert Liebmann, from the 1905 novel *Professor Unrat* by Heinrich Mann

directed by José Quintero (replacing Richard Altman)

choreographed by Valerie Bettis (replacing Marvin Gordon, who retained "Musical Numbers and Dances Staged by" credit)

produced by Guy de la Passardière

starring Theodore Bikel (replacing Walter Slezak) and Lilo (de la Passardière)

with Gary Krawford, Richard Tone, Travis Hudson (replacing Beatrice Kay), Al Nesor, and Coley Worth

opened March 18, 1966   46th Street Theatre

STANLEY KAUFFMANN, *TIMES*

What's new, *Pousse-Café*? [ref: Bacharach and David's 1965 song hit "What's New, Pussycat?"] Answer: nothing good. The musical of that name, which opened last night, is dismal. Jerome Weidman has caricatured the characters, scuttled the drama and provided dialogue that would disgrace a dub, let alone an experienced author. Duke Ellington has provided a tuneless score. Marshall Barer and Fred Tobias have collaborated on lyrics that would be discredit enough to one author. The program says that the dances were staged by Marvin Gordon and that the choreography is by Valerie Bettis. This distinction—whatever it

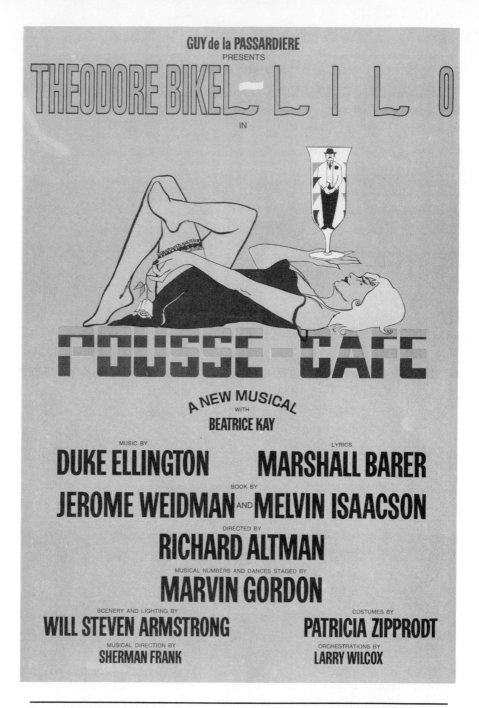

GUY de la PASSARDIERE
PRESENTS

THEODORE BIKEL — LILO
IN

POUSSE-CAFÉ

A NEW MUSICAL
WITH
BEATRICE KAY

MUSIC BY
DUKE ELLINGTON

LYRICS
MARSHALL BARER

BOOK BY
JEROME WEIDMAN AND **MELVIN ISAACSON**

DIRECTED BY
RICHARD ALTMAN

MUSICAL NUMBERS AND DANCES STAGED BY
MARVIN GORDON

SCENERY AND LIGHTING BY
WILL STEVEN ARMSTRONG

COSTUMES BY
PATRICIA ZIPPRODT

MUSICAL DIRECTION BY
SHERMAN FRANK

ORCHESTRATIONS BY
LARRY WILCOX

Poor Theodore Bikel looks trapped, and not in a bottle. "A drawn-out torture of embarrassment," wrote Norman Nadel, while Walter Kerr reported that "*The Blue Angel* emerges a black-and-blue angel instead." Preliminary credits.

means—is the only one that the dancing contains. José Quintero has directed in a commonplace, cut-and-dried manner that will further discourage those who once held hopes for him. Theodore Bikel, as the professor, gives a performance that begins at the mediocre and declines to the maudlin. A young man named Gary Krawford, as the student who gets in trouble, sounds as if two invisible hands were clutching his throat. The fatal *femme* is played by Lilo, a lady who lacks enough sexuality, self-amusement and complicated hardness to make the role interesting. *The Blue Angel* would probably make a good musical. But the present attempt is so close to total disaster that we may as well give it the benefit of the doubt: call it total.

WALTER KERR, *HERALD TRIBUNE*
Actually, the people who have put *Pousse-Café* together haven't put *Pousse-Café* together. They have left it splattered and sprawling over most of two continents, and it may take years to tidy up the debris. The new "play with music" has been transplanted to New Orleans and provided with a Duke Ellington score. But hanging right up there on the schoolmaster's wall, in very plain view, is a spiked German helmet, for the schoolmaster is still a graduate of Old Heidelberg where he once crossed swords with the Crown Prince. (No scar to show for it, sorry to say). The trollop-*chanteuse* for whom the aging schoolmaster falls is Lilo, whose voice is as French as the gravel on the hills of Montmartre. All of the cadets who attend the military school at which the schoolmaster teaches are clean-cut, well-drilled, ardently whoring young American gentlemen, and the music is "Mood Indigo" chopped up in little pieces and flung to the winds that blew the 1920s away. Over all of this hovers the ineradicable images of Emil Jannings and Marlene Dietrich, so that we have the uncanny sensation of watching dubbed ectoplasm relayed by Telstar, and *The Blue Angel* emerges a black-and-blue angel instead. All of the bits and pieces that go to make a musical are here not on speaking terms. Will Steven Armstrong's somber settings look as though they were still stacked in the truck that brought them, the girls who wrap themselves around sailors seem rather coarse for prostitutes, and when I looked to see who didn't do the dances I discovered that Marvin Gordon was responsible for keeping the boys and girls in dark and distant corners of the stage except for the one time

they line up and kick. Virtually everything is irrelevant, I think for a reason. The show doesn't need its music, it doesn't need its pretense at dances, doesn't need its busy turntables, because the story tells itself without them and tells it in just about twenty minutes. The show is really over once the prim professor has spent a night in the forbidden hay. No, I am wrong about that. As things stand, the show was really over on the day they released the film.

NORMAN NADEL, *WORLD-TELEGRAM & SUN*
[Headline: "A Disastrous New Musical"]
A drawn-out torture of embarrassment. It can be painful to watch grown men and women appear so foolish on stage. Because they are working for a living, and probably need the money, they cannot walk out. The audience suffers for them and with them, even when we are also suffering because of them. Most of you lucky civilians never get to see anything this bad, simply because a play or musical of this caliber is quick to close. So you come to me, and to other critics, asking doubtfully if it really was so terrible, and if so, how could it have come all the way to Broadway? The answers are, respectively, yes and I don't know. I watched it not in anger or irritation but in pity and dismay. What went wrong? Everything. Even the orchestrations [by Larry Wilcox] are trite, and the music certainly is far from the best Duke Ellington ever composed. Still, nothing about *Pousse-Café* is quite as appalling as the lyrics by Marshall Barer and Fred Tobias. And poor, poor Bikel. He is enough of an actor—a good one, in fact—to approach the role honestly. Actually, the role, as written and directed, is impossible; maybe it's unfair to put any of the blame on Bikel.

○   ○   ○

The Marquis de la Passardière wanted to give his wife—the gal who "Loved Paris" in Cole Porter's 1953 *Can-Can*—a splashy return to Broadway, and the New Orleans-based *Pousse-Café* was certainly sloggy. The Marquis, whose title was conferred on an ancestor by Louis XI in 1470, assembled an admirably third-rate group around the Duke: librettist Don Appell of *Milk and Honey* (1961); lyricist Marshall Barer of *Once Upon a Mattress* (1959); director Richard Altman, assistant to J. R. on *Fiddler* (1964); and choreographer Marvin Gordon of the Off-

Broadway folk musical *Cindy* (1964). All experienced, I guess you could say, and de la Passardière got what he paid for. José Quintero and Jerome Weidman joined the show Valentine's Day in Detroit, with the latter entirely rewriting the book "in one, gruelling 48-hour hotel-room session" per Quintero. "I have never, never—for good or for bad or whatever—seen a thing like that done." For good or for bad or whatever? Anyway, *Pousse-Café* marked novelist-turned-librettist Weidman's departure from the Rialto, for his Pulitzer-winning *Fiorello!* (1959) was followed by four consecutive failures, including the 1964 *Faust*-ian Philadelphian folderoo *Cool Off!* (Son John followed in his father's footsteps with *Pacific Overtures* [1976], the 1987 revision of *Anything Goes*, *Assassins* [1991], and *Big* [1996].)

BROADWAY SCORECARD				
/ PERFS: 3 / $: –				
RAVE	FAVORABLE	MIXED	UNFAVORABLE	PAN
				6

PROMISES, PROMISES

"A New Musical"

music by Burt Bacharach

lyrics by Hal David

book by Neil Simon

based on the 1960 screenplay *The Apartment* by Billy Wilder and I. A. L. Diamond

directed by Robert Moore (replacing Bob Fosse)

choreographed by Michael Bennett (replacing Bob Fosse)

produced by David Merrick

starring Jerry Orbach, Jill O'Hara, and Edward Winter

with A. Larry Haines, Paul Reed, Dick O'Neill, Norman Shelly, Vince O'Brien, Marian Mercer, Millie Slavin, Adrienne Angel, Donna McKechnie, and Baayork Lee

opened December 1, 1968   Shubert Theatre

CLIVE BARNES, *TIMES*

Yes, of course, yes! *Promises, Promises* came to the Shubert Theatre last night and fulfilled them all without a single breach. In fact it proved to be one of those shows that do not so much open as start to take root, the kind of show where you feel more in the mood to send it a congratulatory telegram than write a review. Neil Simon has produced one of the wittiest books a musical has possessed in years, the Burt Bacharach music excitingly reflects today rather than the day before yesterday, and the performances, especially from Jerry Orbach as the put-upon and morally diffident hero, contrive to combine zip with charm. Also it is a "new musical" that does, for once, seem entitled to call itself "new." To an extent the new element is to be found in the book, for although ancestors can be found for the story in *How to Succeed in Business* [1961] and *How Now, Dow Jones* [1967] the intimacy

Five provocatively dressed chorines frolic on—what is that, a large, long key? The artwork was changed in Boston to a somewhat less provocative red-haired lady with black-stockinged legs thrown high above her head. (artwork by Flavin)

of the piece is fresh. Even more, there is the beat of the music; this is the first musical where you go out feeling rhythms rather than humming tunes. The cast was virtually perfect. Mr. Orbach has the kind of wrists that look as though they are about to lose their hands, and the kind of neck that seems to be on nodding acquaintanceship with his head. He makes gangle into a verb, because that is just what he does. He gangles. He also sings most effectively, dances most occasionally, and acts with an engaging and perfectly controlled sense of desperation. Jill O'Hara, sweet, tender and most innocently beddable, looks enchanting and sings like a slightly misty lark. Of the rest I enjoyed Paul Reed, Norman Shelly, Vince O'Brien and Dick O'Neill as a quartet of tired businessmen hoping to get themselves tireder, and two beautifully judged character performances from A. Larry Haines as a doctor in a more than usually general practice, and Marian Mercer as a tiny-voiced hustler with a heart as big as a saloon. I liked finally the girl, Donna McKechnie, who led the dance number at the end of the first act ["Turkey Lurkey Time"] with the power and drive of a steam hammer in heat.

JOHN CHAPMAN, *DAILY NEWS*
[Headline: "*Promises, Promises* is more like *Promiscuity, Promiscuity*"]

MARTIN GOTTFRIED, *WOMEN'S WEAR DAILY*
If its music had been written by your ordinary hack, *Promises, Promises* would be a perfectly entertaining musical—even a little more than that—though as a matter of fact, it is put together in a style that ordinarily prompts the usual Broadway brass. But the musical that opened last night has a score by Burt Bacharach and that has turned it into something very special. There are songs and more songs and more songs, one better then the other—tricky rhythm songs, funny songs (not just funny lyrics but funny *music*), fresh harmony songs, lovely little guitar songs. One coming after the other and it is the first music I've heard on Broadway since I don't know when. (I've heard songs, I haven't heard music.) Between the Bacharach score, with its neat, tricky lyrics by Hal David, and the more than good enough Neil Simon book, with its regular spurts of giddy comedy, *Promises, Promises* is easily the most satisfying and successful musical in a very long time. . . . I hope

Bacharach some day has the chance to really write music, not just in the song form, and has a theatre person pushing him beyond his sound. He is capable of all kinds of things. But this score is swell enough, and a real breakthrough for Broadway. Not only has orchestrator Jonathan Tunick been faithful to Bacharach rather than the show-tune cliché, but the whole archaic system of show-biz has been shattered by the use of an amplified orchestra and electric instruments (organ, bass fiddle, guitar). Loud-speakers run up the sides of the theatre, right to the second balcony, and an honest-to-God recording engineer is in the house [system design by Phil Ramone]. There is a four-girl group, yet, in the orchestra pit. Now all of this isn't working up to full potential, but it can and it will. For the moment, Bacharach has proved that modern sound can be put live in a theatre—not just his class rock but the qualities made possible by modern electronics.

WALTER KERR, *TIMES*
[Headline: "All Fun and No Fuss"]
God takes care of babies, drunks and good directors. If I speak of the stage direction of *Promises, Promises* first, it's not because Robert Moore has done his job any better than everybody else at the Shubert has done his. The new David Merrick musical is afloat with good jobs, filled to the Plimsoll-line with good jobs, practically ready to capsize with good jobs. The thing about Mr. Moore, whose only previous directorial credit was the considerable one of *Boys in the Band*, is that he has understood exactly what everybody else's good job consisted of, and then made exact use of it. Never too much use, never too little, always exact use. That's why the evening, even if it is a smash, seems so perfect. Moore has noticed, for instance, how legitimately Neil Simon has developed the evening's libretto, living dangerously all the while. It would have been quite easy for Simon to go wrong; for one thing, he was working from a film script which had been brilliant to begin with. Just enough loving improvement might have wrecked it. And so Simon, his intuitions in excellent working order, has come in gently, and from under. There are no lines marked as Killers, no yocks built to black out on. The book is, if anything, on the shy side, cautious, grinning, hoping to be friends, candid, fond of kidding, nice. Ironically, Simon may have written his very straightest comedy material for a musical, that normally

broad and brassy form. Moore has then seen to it that the musical elements behaved themselves responsibly, too. *Promises, Promises* is all of a piece, all intimate, all emotional, all bright and chatty and fun and no fuss. The score clatters along like office typewriter keys, telling you something swiftly, noncommittally, efficiently, making a certain percussive music of its own. It's part new sound, part old, rock for over-30's, with a parakeet insistence, a fingers drumming-the-desk impatience, a soft white wail coming up under an edgy beat. (Listen carefully to a duet, with guitar, called "I'll Never Fall in Love Again" and you will know what the phrase Having the Best of Both Worlds means.) Composer Burt Bacharach and lyricist Hal David have, at least temporarily, solved the problem of what to do about music in an age moving too fast for melody but missing it.

RICHARD WATTS, JR., POST

Promises, Promises lives up to all of them. The new musical comedy has a witty and sparkling book by Neil Simon, a brilliant modernistic score by Burt Bacharach, bright lyrics by Hal David, and a superb performance by Jerry Orbach in the vital leading role. Add to all of this a generally expert and imaginative production directed by Robert Moore, and you have what is certain to be Broadway's latest and deserved smash hit. Simon has brought his rare talent for humorous writing to bear on the book and has created several richly entertaining characters. The doctor next door, shrewdly played by A. Larry Haines, who is firmly convinced that his neighbor is up to sex skullduggery, is at once very funny and thoroughly real. And the evening includes one of the most unusual figures known to the stage or actuality, a drunkenly amorous young woman who is not only hilarious but charming. Marian Mercer plays her delightfully. The score is a remarkable one. Being vague on such matters, I am not sure whether its beat is in the most up-to-the-moment rhythm, but it suggests it without going to extremes. I kept admiring the songs and yet found myself wishing the composer would give us at least one that was romantically tuneful. And then, as if he had been listening to my prayer, he suddenly came through with a wonderful ballad, "I'll Never Fall in Love Again," that was just what I had been hoping he would provide. Robin Wagner's settings are ingenious and effective, and Michael Bennett's choreography captures the proper spirit. Everything connected with *Promises, Promises* has turned out right and the result is a musical comedy of exceptional quality.

●   ●   ●

Having collaborated on *Little Me* (1962) and *Sweet Charity* (1966), director/choreographer Bob Fosse and librettist Neil Simon turned to Broadway's most successful producer with their next project. David Merrick, who hadn't enjoyed a blockbuster since *Hello, Dolly!* opened in 1964, leapt at the opportunity and quickly obtained the rights to film-maker Billy Wilder's dark comedy *The Apartment*. Simon went to work on the adaptation, but a snag developed six months before rehearsals began when Fosse—immersed in filming *Charity*—withdrew from the project. Simon proceeded nevertheless, and in a felicitous moment selected pop songwriters Burt Bacharach and Hal David as collabora-tors. The authors forged ahead, with no director in sight. Gower Champion wasn't in the running, not with the *Happy Time* (1968) fiasco still fresh in the memory. Merrick offered the show to Hal Prince, who was preparing his own *Zorbá* (1968). (Merrick had asked Prince to direct *Dolly!* on the strength of *She Loves Me* [1963]. "You'll fire me," Prince responded. "I can see it now in the *New York Times*. You're hiring me so you can fire me.") Merrick finally settled on Robert Moore, who had appeared in Merrick's 1965 comedy hit *Cactus Flower* before turning director (in April 1968) with the Off-Broadway hit *The Boys in the Band*. Michael Bennett, who doctored the dances on Merrick's just-shuttered big business musical *How Now, Dow Jones*, completed the team as choreographer. This mostly untried group came up with a smashingly funny show, just right for its time. Not a great musical, perhaps; the score, while bright, peppy, and contemporary, is more repetitive than memorable, and ultimately too perky. At the time, though, the mere presence of pop music in the theatre was startlingly refreshing. The methods used by Bacharach and orchestrator Jonathan Tunick to bring "recording studio sound" into the theatre—electronic instruments, carefully calibrated miking, and vocalizing backup voices ("pit singers") for sweetening—made vast and immediate changes in the Broadway music department. If these innovations merely served to enhance the rhythms of *Promises*, they were used to far-reaching effect in Tunick's next show, *Company* (1970). Most important, *Promises*—

written by Neil Simon at the height of his hilarity—was excruciatingly funny, and buoyed by the expert comedy performance of Jerry Orbach (and supporting comics A. Larry Haines and Marian Mercer). The overall ebullience of *Promises* came not only from Simon's joke book but from three little-known craftsmen who—alone and together—proceeded to revolutionize the look and sound of musical theatre: Michael Bennett, Jonathan Tunick, and Robin Wagner. <u>Equal Opportunity Dept.</u>: When musical director Arthur Rubinstein left during the Boston tryout, Merrick corralled dance arranger Harold Wheeler and tossed him into the pit, making *Promises* the first "white" show with a nonwhite conductor. The showman had broken color-blind lines before, visibly so in 1957 when he forced the stagehands' local to accept black stagehands for *Jamaica*. (A longtime associate commented, nostalgically, that Merrick was an equal-opportunity bastard: "He'd screw you no matter *what* color you were.") Merrick, in fact, had an integrated staff on his very first show, pulling Charles Blackwell out of the dance ensemble and making him stage manager. Blackwell became Merrick's top musical man, serving such shows as *Jamaica*, *Breakfast at Tiffany's* (1966), *Promises*, and *Sugar* (1972). Over the course of a forty-year career, the multitalented Blackwell was also a producer (*Ain't Supposed to Die a Natural Death* [1971]), a director (*The Poison Tree* [1976]), a librettist (*The Tap Dance Kid* [1983]), and an all-around favorite along Broadway.

Tony Awards were won by Jerry Orbach (actor) and Marian Mercer (supporting actress).

BROADWAY SCORECARD
/ PERFS: 1,281 / $: +

RAVE	FAVORABLE	MIXED	UNFAVORABLE	PAN
5	1			

PURLIE

"A New Musical Comedy"

music by Gary Geld

lyrics by Peter Udell

book by Ossie Davis, Peter Udell, and Philip Rose

based on the 1961 satire *Purlie Victorious* by Ossie Davis

directed by Philip Rose

choreographed by Louis Johnson

produced by Philip Rose

starring Cleavon Little, Melba Moore, and John Heffernan

with Sherman Hemsley, Novella Nelson, C. David Colson, Helen Martin, and Linda Hopkins

opened March 15, 1970   Broadway Theatre

CLIVE BARNES, *TIMES*

[Headline: "*Purlie* Is a Victor Again"]

Purlie is victorious, or as near to victorious as it takes. The music is only adequate, the show could be cut, but the book is so strong, the performance so magnificent, that this musical should have you calling out "Hallelujah!" *Purlie*, which is surely destined to make stars out of Melba Moore and Cleavon Little, is based on the Ossie Davis play of life way down on the old plantation, *Purlie Victorious*. How Purlie gets his church and wins Lutiebelle for his wife is a fairly thin story, but it works well as the framework for a musical. From the opening number—a smashing crash of gospel singing and great jazz dancing, which is a Prologue describing the none-too-unhappy funeral of Ol' Cap'n—right to the end, the musical blends a fine mixture of humor and passion. This is by far the most successful and richest of all black musicals, chiefly I think for the depth of the characterizations and the salty wit

"*Purlie* is Victorious!" New fangled preacher man exults while his Lutiebelle looks on. (artwork by Mozelle)

of the dialogue. Gary Geld's music and Peter Udell's lyrics are admirable enough in a good-naturedly fervent way, but they never raise the roof or even inflame the spirit. Yet again they are a decent cut above the average Broadway musical score—superior, you might say, without being brilliant. Philip Rose's staging is a good deal less impressive than the choreography by Louis Johnson, which, particularly in the Prologue, pounds away at steam heat. And then the performances—and these I think would carry an even lesser show. Melba Moore, looking as if butter wouldn't melt in her mouth, with a voice that goes from a giggle to a growl in one second, made the kind of Broadway debut people talk about years afterward. Moore has an irresistibly knowing innocence, the timing of a superb comedian and the God-given ability to walk straight into an audience's heart and hang around there. Cleavon Little's Purlie is a strutting, gutsy guy—part fake, part con man, yet with his soul in the right place, and he belted into [his Broadway debut] with a punchy enthusiasm. His voice was pleasant, his acting and presence both splendid, and he handled the gospel-speaking with a virtuoso verve. I enjoyed the show, and so it seems did the first-night audience at the Broadway. I hope now that Broadway opens its pearly gates for *Purlie*.

MARTIN GOTTFRIED, *WOMEN'S WEAR DAILY*
And we're still going to have to wait for the big black musical—the one that catapults all the muscle and anger and music and spirit and mood of modern black men into the theatre—the one written and composed and directed by black men (and not the *Porgy and Bess* [1935])—the one that finally gets it all out, and out of everybody's system. For now, it's going to be a long time sitting through the tries. *Purlie* tried last night. It has absolutely fabulous numbers opening each act. It has a whole lot of black music (some soul, some gospel, some talking blues, even something pretty close to Top-40 rhythm and blues). It has Cleavon Little playing the title role—playing it with such power and confidence that instead of being afraid of Melba Moore, who could have pulled the show out from under the feet of a lesser man, he welcomed her as a stimulating partner. Gary Geld's music is the old Broadway show-tune brass almost as often as it is black. With but a momentary exception at the very beginning, there is no dancing. And

the book is a disaster in trivia. It is indicative of the whole show's attitude toward black people, which is kind of patronizing and not very different from, well, from *Porgy and Bess*. The whole tenant farm situation, including the owner himself (played by a bewildered John Heffernan), is handled as if everything is a whole lot of fun and that things between the blacks and the owner, for all the bigotry, are very affectionate at heart. You would think such an attitude impossible these days, especially since Ossie Davis is an intelligent black man living in a time of serious change. But there it is and that's how disastrously white America has tied its black people up in conditioned thought. . . . Miss Moore was simply sensational. Her singing reminds you now and again of Pearl Bailey, Dionne Warwick or Aretha Franklin, but she is an individualist, a thrills and chills lady. She can also act and be funny so I think there's nothing much that can stop her. Novella Nelson could have been right up there with her, playing (I think) Purlie's sister; she is a great singer but they didn't give her much material. Then again, there wasn't much material for anyone.

WALTER KERR, *TIMES*
[Headline: "What Happened to the Fun?"]
They don't laugh when Purlie pulls out the bullwhip [in the final, climactic confrontation], and that's what's happened to *Purlie Victorious*. If Ol' Cap'n Cotchipee, ranting rapscallion and tender-hearted bigot that he is, is funny, and if Purlie, a man of mighty words but mousier deeds, is funny, then the notion of a confrontation that could end in Purlie's coming away nonchalantly with that ultimate symbol of power in his fist should be funny, too. Everything's been upended, deliciously. I can't swear for certain now, but I'm sure people must have squealed with delight nine years ago. Today it just seems sober fact. You see, in the nine years we've been talking about, all the wild, preposterous, unlikely but necessary dreams that Purlie dreamed when he was half out of his head with talk have simply become down-the-street realities. Purlie dreamed "not of fatback, but of fight back." But he doesn't have to dream it now. The fighting has long since started. And so the element of fantasy in *Purlie Victorious* collapses. Once it was glorious caricature, with clichéd Negroes and clichéd white masters blown up to such proportions that it was just a matter of time to see which cliché

would burst first, a battle between Uncle Toms who didn't mean it and a Cotchipee dumb enough to think they did. Perhaps the diminution, and the shift from satire to less interesting direct statement, can best be seen not in Purlie—who can no longer come into clear focus and dominate as he once did, despite Cleavon Little's energetic performance—but Lutiebelle, the choir lass. When Ruby Dee played her, she could have been Topsy. Topsy kidded, Topsy borrowed from the white man and thrown back at him, Topsy pretending to be Topsy but on the inside sassing away. As Melba Moore plays her—and Miss Moore is an enchanting creature—she's straight through and through, pigeon-toed stance notwithstanding. As she slips from a rocker to detonate the liquid syllables of "I Got Love," or as she joins the placidly powerful Novella Nelson in "He Can Do It," she is making plain pronouncements with passionate urgency, winning us but no longer winking at us. The comic deviousness which made the earlier portrait so sly has vanished. It's all drier now, turned from fun into fact. Its earlier and special distinction as an eruption of the high lunatic imagination, its spit-in-the-eye zaniness have gone. Social gain, comic loss.

•   •   •

Purlie was vibrant, joyous, and refreshing. Though not without some flaws—including a painfully long songless stretch in the first act and a highly questionable white-man's-idea-of-a-protest-song growled by grunting cotton pickers in the second—*Purlie* was rather more jubilant than less. It was also the first of the modern-day black musicals, written with at least the partial participation of black writers (unlike earlier pro-integration efforts like *No Strings* [1962], *Golden Boy* [1964], and *Hallelujah, Baby!* [1967]). Ossie Davis penned *Purlie Victorious*, his deft farce-satire on race relations, as a vehicle for himself and wife Ruby Dee. Phil Rose, producer of the 1959 *Raisin in the Sun* (which featured Dee), mounted the Davis play in 1961 to a decent but not overwhelming response. For the musical version Rose enlisted pop songwriters Gary Geld and Peter Udell, with the book from Davis (with Udell and Rose) and direction by the producer himself. If *Purlie* turned out slightly uneven, it might well be because none of the four had ever written (or directed) a musical. Rose, as a producer, had a reputation for discovering acting talent (Diana Sands, Alan Alda, Godfrey Cambridge, Al Pacino).

Purlie was enhanced by a spellbinding performance from Cleavon Little and a virtual explosion of song from Melba Moore, with notably strong support from Novella Nelson and Sherman Hemsley. But *Purlie* had a problem: it was a theatrical also-ran, a small-fry production with no important names attached. Coming from an independent and poorly connected producer, *Purlie* had to struggle for financing and settle for the out-of-the-way Broadway Theatre. It surprised everyone on its opening but remained a poor relation. Nine months into its run *Purlie* had its house yanked out from under it by *Fiddler on the Roof* (1964), which had come to take advantage of the Broadway's extra-large capacity for the final, heavily discounted year and a half of its record-breaking run. *Fiddler* had left the Majestic to make way for a surefire hit from the producer of *My Fair Lady* (1956). *Purlie* was offered the Winter Garden—but only for thirteen weeks, as it was skedded for a surefire hit from the producer of *Fiddler*. The new Majestic tenant immediately fizzled. Could *Purlie* move down to 44th Street? Nope, they had a better offer, a surefire hit from the director of *Dolly!* So *Purlie* was relegated to the bottom-of-the-barrel ANTA Theatre (now the freshly appointed Virginia). *Purlie* outran all three surefires combined: *Lovely Ladies, Kind Gentlemen, Follies,* and the Angela Lansbury vehicle *Prettybelle,* which never made it out of Boston. The coveted Majestic, in fact, stood empty from January '71 till April '72, when *Sugar* came along. Moving costs being what they are, *Purlie's* three-stop, two-block Broadway tour doused the show in an ineradicable pit of red ink. "*Purlie* is victorious," said Clive Barnes and all the quote ads; the playing field, alas, was slightly uneven.

Tony Awards were won by Cleavon Little (actor) and Melba Moore (supporting actress).

BROADWAY SCORECARD

/ PERFS: 689 / $: −

RAVE	FAVORABLE	MIXED	UNFAVORABLE	PAN
2	1		2	1

RAINBOW JONES

"A New Musical," previously entitled *R. J.*

book, music, and lyrics by Jill Williams

directed by Gene Persson

choreographed by Sammy Bayes

produced by Rubykate, Inc. (Gene and Ruby Persson) in association with Phil Gillin and Gene Bambic

with Ruby Persson, Peter Kastner, Daniel Keyes, Peggy Hagen Lamprey, Gil Robbins, Andy Rohrer, Stephanie Silver, and Kay St. Germain

opened February 13, 1974   Music Box Theatre

CLIVE BARNES, *TIMES*

A new coy and simpering little musical, the kind of show that gives people proclaiming the death of Broadway something to point to. It has book, music and lyrics by Jill Williams. They are very even in quality. The book is as bad as the music, the music as bad as the lyrics, and the lyrics are as bad as either. Miss Williams apparently started her musical career writing advertising jingles. After listening to *Rainbow Jones*, I'm not a bit surprised. The saddest question that can be asked of a show is: Why? So, Why? Why? Why?

MARTIN GOTTFRIED, *WOMEN'S WEAR DAILY*

How long ago was it—12 years?—*The Fantasticks* [1960] originated the charming little off-Broadway musical? We've had to deal with its coy imitators ever since. Coy is bad enough in a little house, but when moved to Broadway—the Music Box in the case of *Rainbow Jones*—it becomes embarrassing, an aunt in pigtails. Gene Persson, who had a huge success producing one of these imitations—*You're a Good Man, Charlie Brown* [1967]—has now tried his hand at directing one. His name isn't listed as producer on the program credits nor is the "Ruby" in the name of the listed producer, "Rubykate Productions," identified as either the leading lady, Ruby Persson, or Persson's relative. But the whole business smacks of nepotism and vanity, which are as good for the theatre as coy musicals in Broadway houses. Jill Williams is responsible for the book, lyrics and music. Her lyrics sound like a collection of *Fantasticks* cast albums. ("Did you ever see a butterfly weak in the knees?") Her music is so quiet and shy it becomes innocuous, beginning as bravely as possible, under the circumstances, with a mild rock beat and then falling inevitably back on that intimate, trite off-Broadway sound so well known for its use of the triangle. It becomes as invisible as the [imaginary] animals, as well as the show. So invisible, in fact, that I disappeared myself at intermission.

DOUGLAS WATT, *DAILY NEWS*

Whenever theatre people, as they often do, get that dopey look and start imagining how nice it would be to wrap your troubles in dreams, beware. The latest such idiocy opened last night at the Music Box. I don't think there's much you need to be told about this show, which has a curious way of turning up in one form or another at least once every seasason and of going by such titles as *Shelter* [1973], *Park* [1970] and *Celebration* [1969], to name but a few past mistakes. Gene Persson has both produced and staged it, and Ruby Persson, who I'm told is Mrs. Persson, plays the title role. There are seven other performers, but I'd rather not mention them, because I don't really ever want to see any of them again. As for Miss Williams, she should, for the common good, henceforth be denied access either to a typewriter or a musical instrument of any kind. Pity the poor Music Box. There was a day when prospective tenants fought for the use of this lovely playhouse. Now it must suffer fools.

o   o   o

A vanity production, in vain. From the coproducer of the 1967 Off-Broadway hit *You're a Good Man, Charlie Brown*. Starring his wife, and written by—who knows? His mother? A cousin? The butcher's wife? No, actually, the wife of Hollywood songwriter Joel Hirschhorn, who himself would bring us *Copperfield* (1981). Ms. Williams herself was "a well-known songwriter," per *Playbill*, who wrote jingles for the Ford Motor Company.

BROADWAY SCORECARD

/ PERFS: | / $: −

RAVE	FAVORABLE	MIXED	UNFAVORABLE	PAN
			1	5

RAISIN

"The New Musical"

music by Judd Woldin

lyrics by Robert Brittan

book by Robert Nemiroff and Charlotte Zaltzberg

based on the 1959 drama *A Raisin in the Sun* by Lorraine Hansberry (Nemiroff)

directed and choreographed by Donald McKayle

produced by Robert Nemiroff

starring Virginia Capers, Joe Morton, and Ernestine Jackson

with Robert Jackson, Deborah (Debbie) Allen (replacing Shezwae Powell), Helen Martin, Ralph Carter, Loretta Abbott, Walter P. Brown, Herb Downer, Al Perryman, Ted Ross, and Richard Sanders

opened October 18, 1973   46th Street Theatre

CLIVE BARNES, *TIMES*

Raisin warms the heart and touches the soul. It retains all of Miss Hansberry's finest dramatic encounters, with the dialogue as cutting and as honest as ever, intact. But the shaping of the piece is slightly firmer and better. The play has an oddly period flavor now. Today it is not the color of the piece that overwhelms one but its tremendous story, and its touching picture of a family fighting for life. This is a family that could be almost anywhere at any time. You only need oppression to bring out the tragedy and heroism in people. When *Raisin* was first given by the Arena Stage in Washington this spring I was most enthusiastic about Donald McKayle's fluent and simple staging and the toughly personal performances of the cast. Yet I was a shade dubious about its Broadway production. Well, they have pulled it off. McKayle has opened up his staging to its advantage. The dance numbers rank among the best in years. Like Jerome Robbins, McKayle comes to the musical theatre as a ranking choreographer, but also like Robbins his skill with actors must now be unquestioned. The performances blaze—not just one, or two, but every single one of them. As the Mama, Virginia Capers, a vast and loving Gibraltar of a woman, was tremendous in just about every sense you can use the word. But her almost overpowering matriarch was matched by the rest. Joe Morton sang with passion and had just the right mixture of foolishness, ambition and decency; Ernestine Jackson was beautiful, womanly and appealing as the wife; and Deborah Allen proved spirited and witty as the kid sister. Finally, there is that mighty little atom of a child star, Ralph Carter, who gives cuteness a new dimension of decency, and might well be the kind of child actor W. C. Fields could grow to love. The chorus was outstanding and the dancing had an energy and grace rarely seen on Broadway these days. *Raisin* is one of those unusual musicals that should not only delight people who love musicals, but might also well delight people who don't. It is a show with a heartbeat very much of its own.

MARTIN GOTTFRIED, *WOMEN'S WEAR DAILY*

Raisin is a skimpy musical. I don't mean just physically skimpy, though it certainly is that. It is a skimpy reduction of Lorraine Hansberry's play. It has been skimpily musicalized. There is a skimpy connection between the songs, the dances and the story, and each of those contributions is skimpy in itself. Everything is in outline, none of its elements connect and the show proceeds with nothing to hold interest, to excite or even, really, to watch. *Raisin* is simply, in show business terms, a "property"—

an attempt to capitalize on the familiar title of a successful play, and still another ugly attempt by Robert Nemiroff (the producer and co-author) to profiteer on the talent of his late ex-wife, Ms. Hansberry. Nemiroff and Charlotte Zaltzberg have not adapted it for the musical stage in any sense of understanding the difference between a play and a musical's book. They have simply snipped away at the script to leave the room and time for songs and dances. Moreover, instead of helping to musicalize what they didn't do, Donald McKayle—the choreographer/director—ignored it. The story stops and a song is sung. The story continues, stops and a dance is danced. There is virtually no musical staging, in fact the singers seldom move when they are singing, and the dances are alike and irrelevant. Just as the show is strictly divided between story, song and dance, the stage itself is separated into a story half and a dance half. When Hansberry's tale is outlined, it all happens on stage left. When McKayle's dances are danced, they all happen on stage right. This is absurd. Doubtless, composer Woldin and lyricist Brittan were sincere in their motives, but Woldin has not even managed to write a black score. His score is essentially white jazz, and his attempts at African styling are embarrassingly like movie scores. The [ensemble] has nothing to do with anything and shows up only when it is time for the noisy, trite, spineless, indistinguishable dances. The Robert U. Taylor set looks like the scaffolding it is, seems to have nothing to do with anything and, together with the few shabby abstract sticks of furniture, gives the show a bare-boned look ironically consistent with its bare-boned nature.

WALTER KERR, *TIMES*
[Headline: "*Raisin* Is Sweet, Could Be Sweeter"]
The strength of *Raisin* lies in the keen intelligence and restless invention of a musical underscoring that has simply invaded Lorraine Hansberry's once tightly knit, four-walled, close-quartered play, plucking the walls away, spilling the action onto the streets with a jittery downflight of strings, mocking and matching realistic speech with frog-throated sass from the heavy-breathing bass viols. The weakness of *Raisin* lies in the ultimate monotony of its melodic line, sometimes making you wish that a song were over so that the family infighting could get going again. The naturalistic compression of the earlier play

has been wiped away, handsomely, right off the bat with a stage that resembles a jungle-gym of escape stairwells, hot light from the right, a cool green from the left. Rubbery bodies skip across space, a dervish in a brightly flowered vest [Al Perryman] jackknifes his knees high in the air as a ghetto morning begins. Al Cohn and Robert Freedman have done the orchestrations, and done them brilliantly. If a pretty young wife, Ernestine Jackson, orders her ambitious young husband, Joe Morton, to eat his eggs, the weary admonition is seconded by a mock-scolding echo from the orchestra: not too literally, just double-edged enough to say how many mornings this tone has fallen on a rebellious man's ears, and all the while there is a metallic rustle skittering about among the chords to say that kitchen utensils are at work. Donald McKayle snatches at every opportunity to propel the evening from its musical set-pieces into open drama. There is an extraordinary transition [that opens Act II]. We've been listening to a massed gospel call ["He Come Down This Morning"], its participants holding firmly in place. Then fragments of the group seem to fly away at the edges, separately and centrifugally, as though a heart had exploded; the effect is both dizzying and controlled. Into the center of the dispersal, as though into the eye of a hurricane, steps the remarkable Ralph Carter, professional from the tips of his sneakers to the green cap on his young head. As the pit yields sounds that might have come from some demented cathedral organist, Master Carter throws one palm to the winds, curls up the other hand as though he might catch lightning in it, and whips his legs to a frenzy that still has an interior shape to it. Master Carter is a most serious performer: at his most abandoned, his letting go is ruled by style.

●　　●　　●

Robert Nemiroff coproduced ex-wife Lorraine Hansberry's second play, *The Sign in Sidney Brustein's Window* (1964), shortly before her death (from cancer, on January 12, 1965, at the age of thirty-four). As executor of her estate—the couple met on a picket line at New York University in 1952—he kept her words and works on stage with the successful Off-Broadway revue *To Be Young, Gifted and Black* (1969), her unfinished and underdeveloped drama *Les Blancs* (1970), and a five-performance 1972 revision of *Sidney Brustein*—all of which Nemiroff himself adapted. He watched with interest as producer Phil Rose—who introduced Hansberry to Broadway in 1959 with *A Raisin in the Sun*—launched the 1970 musical version of *his* post–*Raisin* offering, the 1961 black satire *Purlie Victorious*. Why not do the same with *Raisin in the Sun*? (*Purlie*, play and musical, was written by Ossie Davis, who costarred in the play version with his wife, Ruby Dee—who had played Sidney Poitier's wife in *Raisin in the Sun*. And Rose, as original producer of the Hansberry play, had an ongoing share in its subsidiary rights including any musicalization. So there were firm familial ties between *Purlie* and *Raisin*.) Nemiroff, needless to say, cut himself in on the *Raisin* adaptation, collaborating with his secretary, Charlotte Zaltzberg. Zaltzberg—sister-in-law of Joe (*Fiddler on the Roof*) Stein—was herself in the final stages of cancer by the time *Raisin* went into production; she died shortly after the Broadway opening. Donald McKayle was a respected choreographer, with the 1962 jazz ballet *District Storyville* prominent among his credits; his Broadway work, though—*Golden Boy* (1964), *A Time for Singing* (1966), *I'm Solomon* (1968)—had been less than overwhelming. He turned in an intriguing and inventive job of staging, though he was unable to get the writers to integrate their materials satisfactorily. The songs came from Judd Woldin—pit-piano player for Pearl Bailey's 1967 *Dolly!* company—and lyricist Bob Brittan, who had been developing a *Raisin* score since 1966 (without the rights) as a class project in Lehman Engel's BMI Workshop. The results were strong on rhythm but weak on melody, serving the choreography better than the book; while *Raisin* contained some dozen songs, the music seemed mostly dance arrangements and underscoring. And the libretto, not surprisingly, was strongest in the uninterrupted, undiluted sections of Hansberry. So you got less a well-made musical than a (good) play interrupted by (not-so-good) songs, well performed and inventively staged. The show got off to a fast start and upbeat business, but producetorial procrastination and some misguided decisions took their toll, and *Raisin* withered deeply into the red. (In a highly unusual situation Nemiroff warned his limited partners—i.e., investors—that the government might go directly after them; they had early on received a 33% return on their investment, which was now needed to cover back taxes and other liens against Nemiroff and the *Raisin* Company.) Literary Note: George C. Wolfe wasn't, to my knowledge, anywhere near the original Broadway production, but his playlet *The Last Mama-on-the-Couch Play*, in *The Colored*

Museum (1986), perfectly captured the atmosphere 'round *Raisin*—and its bigger-than-life Mama on the Couch, Virginia Capers. <u>Chip Off the Old Auction Block Dept.</u>: In the spring of '74 Bob Nemiroff sold little Ralphie Carter to Norman Lear, for the sitcom *Good Times*, for $75,000. Gone are the days.

In addition to winning the Tony Award for Best Musical, a Tony was won by Virginia Capers (actress).

BROADWAY SCORECARD
/ PERFS: 847 / $: –

RAVE	FAVORABLE	MIXED	UNFAVORABLE	PAN
1	3	1		1

RED, WHITE AND MADDOX

"A Thing with Music"

by Don Tucker (music and lyrics) and Jay Broad (book)

based on events in the life of Lester G. Maddox (1915–)

directed by Jay Broad and Don Tucker

produced by Theatre Atlanta, presented by Edward Padula

with Jay Garner

opened January 26, 1969   *Cort Theatre*

CLIVE BARNES, *TIMES*

Political satire on Broadway is as rare as a flamingo in Central Park, or as a palm tree growing in Brooklyn. It is exotic, outrageous, and deserves to be treated with loving care. *Red, White and Maddox* is

Everybody's a critic. Satire closes on Saturday night, as George S. Kaufman used to say. Phooey.

Georgia's satirical comment upon Georgia's favorite son, Gov. Lester G. Maddox. The musical originated in Atlanta, where the dismemberment of Mr. Maddox is possibly of considerable local interest. Governor Maddox is, however, more of a national joke than a national figure. A satire about George C. Wallace—even now—might have been more to a national, and therefore a New York, point. It does, however, say something—and with pride—about the workings of American democracy that this slashing, scathing, excoriating attack on Maddox should have been permitted in Atlanta. My one regret is that the company, Theatre Atlanta, should have been evicted from its theatre almost immediately afterward. It was doubtless a sad coincidence. Time and time again [the authors] hit a bull's-eye. Broadway has not, I think, ever seen its like. The musical's basic difficulty is that you cannot legitimately make fun of a laughingstock. A satire on President Nixon or Hubert H. Humphrey could have people bleeding in the aisles. The first part traces the history of Maddox the chicken king, making, in his tiny restaurant, the world safe for segregation. Could this little man, purveyor of fried chicken and even deeper-fried idiocies, ever be Governor of Georgia? It is Maddox's conquest of Georgia—together with the attacks on the city of Atlanta and its newspapers—that provides the most impressive part of the play. Jay Garner's performance as Lester Maddox is as fantastically funny as it is tellingly accurate. Garner carries the musical like a bland, bespectacled Colossus. He has acquired the same water-wing ears as Governor Maddox, that strange habit of somehow attaching the tongue to the lower lip and, of course, the flat nasal delivery that makes everything sound like a peculiarly derelict telephone director. Yet, even more, Garner has gotten to the heart of Governor Maddox and the world he stands for. This is the joy of the performance. When it looks at the immediate past and equally immediate present, it cuts deep. When it suggests an impossible nightmare, it does, of course, go too far. Yet despite failings, believe me, *Red, White and Maddox* is fun in the first place and significant in the second. Who needs a third place?

MARTIN GOTTFRIED, *WOMEN'S WEAR DAILY*
Red, White and Maddox was both pertinent and impertinent mocking Governor Maddox in his home state, and it was a great deal of fun there. But Broadway is a longer way from Atlanta than a two-hour

765 RED, WHITE AND MADDOX

flight. The silliness and (worse) ignorance of Mr. Maddox is pretty remote and his idiosyncrasies are neither familiar nor interesting. So while this political lampoon tries to be about America rather than just Georgia, too much time is concentrated on regional jokes and points. Imported just about intact with the Theatre Atlanta company that originated it, the show moved into the Cort Theatre last night. Though, in fact, it is at a New York address, it is still in Atlanta. *Red, White and Maddox* is a cartoon documentary by Jay Broad (book) and Don Tucker (music), tracing the rise of Lester Garfield Maddox from restaurant owner to Governor of Georgia. Broadly played by Jay Garner as a petulant, mindless, dangerous but not unlikable child, Maddox is shown as a nitwit who is elected mostly because he is more fun than the other candidates. The second half of the show is given over to pure fantasy, Maddox being elected president and starting the war that ends the world. The point is that America is Maddox country and that the Governor is an absurd cartoon of something very real and very powerful. This is true in many ways, I think, but Mr. Broad's book has not found a fresh way to say it. The Maddox inclination to violence is analogized to the Kennedy and King assassinations, and America-Maddox is saddled with the traits of materialism, militarism and religious hypocrisy. Hardly novel criticisms. Nor does *Red, White and Maddox* make any attempt to state them originally (and it incredibly ignores today's revolutionary movements). The photographic slides are no fresher and it isn't fun to find that slums, riots, starving children and the murdered faces of good men have become cliché. We have been overexposed by the commercially sensitive. As resident theatres go, Theatre Atlanta is middling in technique but unusually perky because of Mr. Broad's convictions and temperament as artistic director. *Red, White and Maddox* is just the kind of thing any such company should be doing. It is obviously relevant and serious to the community. A transfer to New York misunderstands the point of such a production.

●   ●   ●

Satire, as George S. Kaufman used to say, closes Saturday night. *Red, White and Maddox* lasted but five Saturdays, but it was nevertheless a memorable evening. Lester G. Maddox, strange to tell, actually did exist. A lisping, baldpated segregationist famous for standing outside his Atlanta fried chicken restaurant swinging axes at blacks who tried to enter, the outspoken Maddox babbled his way into the governorship of Georgia. (This was back in olden days gone by, when reactionary buffoons could still be elected down South.) Theatre Atlanta, the original producer of *Red, White and Maddox*, was evicted from its home base—but Atlanta's loss, in character man Jay Garner, became Broadway's gain: he's been sparking a chain of musicals ever since (including *Goodtime Charley* [1975], *The Best Little Whorehouse in Texas* [1978], *La Cage aux Folles* [1983], and the 1995 revival of *Hello, Dolly!*). *Red, White and Maddox* was flawed, certainly; it didn't have much to recommend it in the music department (aside from an exceedingly catchy theme song called "Jubilee Joe"); and it went awry in its *Dr. Strangelove*-like second act. Still, the image of an incoherently blathering Jay Garner—swinging out past the proscenium on a giant swing, dropping bombs of doomsday to end the world, looking like a mad combination of Frank Perdue and Tweetie Pie—remains unforgettable.

BROADWAY SCORECARD

/ PERFS: 41 / $: –

RAVE	FAVORABLE	MIXED	UNFAVORABLE	PAN
3		1		2

REGGAE

"A Musical Revelation"

music and lyrics by Ras Karbi, Michael Kamen, Kendrew Lascelles, Max Romeo, Randy Bishop, Jackie Mitto, and Stafford Harrison

book by Melvin Van Peebles, Kendrew Lascelles, and Stafford Harrison

based on a story by Kendrew Lascelles

"concept and production by Michael Butler"

directed by Glenda Dickerson; "additional direction" by Gui Andrisano

choreographed by Mike Malone

produced by Michael Butler and Eric Nezhad with David Cogan

starring Philip Michael Thomas, Sheryl Lee Ralph, and Calvin Lockhart

with Obba Babatunde, Ras Karbi, Fran Salisbury, and Charles Wisnet

opened March 27, 1980   Biltmore Theatre

CLIVE BARNES, POST

One nice thing about going to the theatre every night is that you live and learn. Last night *Reggae* opened, and it certainly taught me a great deal I did not know about Reggae music, Jamaica where it comes from, and the neo-Christian religious sect of the Rastafarians, who believe in the divinity of the late Haile Selassie, Lion of Judah and former Emperor of Ethiopia. In fact, I think I learned rather more than I wanted to know. *Reggae* has been produced by Michael Butler, the Broadway producer of *Hair* (1968), and there are certain similarities betwen the two musicals. Both concentrated on a style of music, both possessed very simple, almost vestigial stories, and both offered tourist trips to unfamiliar subcultures. The American hippie has here been replaced by the Jamaican Rasta. Both smoked a lot of grass—here called ganja. *Reggae* is doubtlessly more seriously intended than it will be taken. However, it is too murky, too diffuse, too poorly amplified, and far too uneven to be normally acceptable Broadway entertainment.

MEL GUSSOW, *TIMES*

The show is subtitled "a musical celebration," but more accurately could be labeled a musical confusion. There is talent to spare on stage at the Biltmore Theatre, but the evening is clotted with characters and plot. Three people are credited with the book, seven with the music and lyrics and two with the direction. The evening appears as if it were put together by a committee and there seem to be leftovers from earlier versions of the show. For example, there is one white actor on stage, who has featured billing but does as little as a member of the chorus. He looks like a lost tourist. The head rude boy (Obba Babatunde) tries devilishly hard to be mean, but ends up by seeming more like Toshiro Mifune [ref. Akira Kurosawa] playing the Cowardly Lion [ref. Bert Lahr].

•   •   •

Michael Butler's follow-up to *Hair*—a Rastafarian love-rock musical, if you will—was long in gestation and short in duration. *Hair* had a strong director in Tom O'Horgan, an industrious and disciplined composer in Galt MacDermot, and author/stars—Rado and Ragni—who were marvels of organization compared to the *Reggae* assemblage. *Reggae* had been in the hands of Leon Gluckman, the South African director/author known for his 1962 international hit *Wait a Minim*. (*Reggae* coauthor Kendrew Lascelles, who also contributed the original story, was *Wait a Minim*'s leading comic and choreographer.) But Gluckman died in 1978, and the show clearly ended up in too many hands. Despite its dreadlocks, *Reggae* was less of *Hair* and more of *Heathen!* (1972).

BROADWAY SCORECARD

/ PERFS: 21 / $: –

RAVE	FAVORABLE	MIXED	UNFAVORABLE	PAN
				6

REX

"The New Richard Rodgers Musical"

music by Richard Rodgers

lyrics by Sheldon Harnick

book by Sherman Yellen (replacing Jerome Lawrence and Robert E. Lee)

based on events in the life of Henry VIII of England (1491–1547)

directed by Edwin Sherin (replaced by Harold Prince, unbilled)

choreographed by Dania Krupska

produced by Richard Adler in association with Roger Berlind and Edward R. Downe Jr.

starring Nicol Williamson and Penny Fuller

with Tom Aldredge, Barbara Andres, Glenn Close, Martha Danielle, Ed Evanko, Merwin Goldsmith, William Griffis, Michael John, Keith Koppmeier, Stephen D. Newman, and April Shawhan

opened April 25, 1976   *Lunt-Fontanne Theatre*

CLIVE BARNES, *TIMES*

One of the most interminable musicals in years. Richard Rodgers is a great man who has done the American musical theatre some service. But even Othello went wrong. Mr. Rodgers's new musical *Rex*, which opened, or at least began, last night, has almost everything not going for it. The succession of wives perpetrated by Henry VIII of England in his search for domestic bliss, sexual satisfaction and a male heir to his throne may make an old-time virtuoso show-off film piece for a Charles Laughton, or even one of those historical soap operas that British television so dotes on, but it is not much as the basis for a musi-cal. We don't even get to see—or even hear about—a decent beheading. What kind of music do you write for a musical about Henry VIII?

RICHARD ADLER
in association with
ROGER BERLIND & EDWARD R. DOWNE, JR.
presents

NICOL WILLIAMSON

The New Richard Rodgers Musical

REX

REX

Music by
RICHARD RODGERS

Lyrics by
SHELDON HARNICK

Book by
SHERMAN YELLEN

Also Starring
PENNY FULLER

Scenery and Costumes by
JOHN CONKLIN

Lighting by
JENNIFER TIPTON

Original Broadway Cast Album recorded by
RCA RECORDS & TAPES

General Management
THEATRE NOW, INC.

Choreography by
DANIA KRUPSKA

Directed by
EDWIN SHERIN

Presented by the John F. Kennedy Center for the Performing Arts.

OPERA HOUSE · KENNEDY CENTER · MAR. 3-20 ONLY

"The royalty, romance and intrigue of the court of King Henry VIII is brought vividly and melodically to life" promised the herald. *Rex* delivered little romance, no royalties, and plenty of (backstage) intrigue. Note the empty void where Henry's face should be. (artwork by Gilbert Lesser)

Airy-fairy madrigals, lute-songs jazzed up for a Broadway orchestra, a sort of mixture of Benjamin Britten and Irving Berlin? Probably not, but that is exactly what Rodgers appears to have done, with the somewhat sad result that we appear to be hearing an anthology of songs from *Camelot* [1960] that were ditched on the road. The atmosphere of the piece is not one bit helped by the staging, which looks opulently tacky. Edwin Sherin is nominally discredited with the slow direction, although it appears that other hands have been called in to give advice (if such a term of manual intellectualism may be allowed), and it all has the air of a not quite royal pageant. The choreography by Dania Krupska seems to be chiefly middle-aged lads doing morris dancing— far less competently than do the children from Britain's Royal Ballet School. Oddly enough, the show's principal and often radiant virtue also turns out to be slightly self-destructive. It is Nicol Williamson, whose performance is so beautiful, real, passionate and alive that he walks through the musical like a Gulliver through toytown. It would be difficult to admire or pity Williamson more. His eyes command an audience, and his voice is so unobtrusively musical that its hard brilliance is lost in the softer cadences of melody. But melody—there's the rub. For while Williamson has a very good singing voice, when he sings his voice loses his character. It is most remarkable; suddenly the genius leaves him and he becomes just another singer. *Rex* seems more of an abdication ceremony than a musical celebration.

MARTIN GOTTFRIED, *POST*

Rodgers has provided his finest score since *No Strings* [1962]. Here, once more, were lilting, surprising melodies, singing out with no apologies to current musical theatre sophistication, nor any need for them. The first act of the new musical is more than bearable. Though it is short on energy and behaves as if it had never heard of laughter, it plays with efficiency and is handsome to look at indeed. That and the truly lovely songs seemed a fair enough shake. Unfortunately, however, even that proved too much for it to sustain. Sherman Yellen's book, which was pretty much being carried by the songs and the settings anyhow, finally caved in, the minimal energy dissipating entirely, and the second act played as if it couldn't wait to get itself over with. *Rex* isn't a disaster but, as a musical, it is a bad idea with half a salvage job. The scenes are played out as if they were drama, which they aren't, and as if they make sense, which they don't. Performances under such conditions are almost out of the question. The formidable acting technique and stage power of Nicol Williamson are wasted. Such writing and play construction just aren't on his level and with no character to play he is a power in search of a purpose. He ambles through the role as it it were beneath him. Which it is, but that isn't excuse enough. Even with a final deathbed scene looking suspiciously like *The King and I* [1951], Williamson can make no tragedy of the story, because none has been set up but also because he isn't putting much into it. Sheldon Harnick's lyrics are a deliberate attempt to write in the Hammerstein style, simply and straightforwardly. Sometimes it works very nicely ("You'll see in time/You'll know in time/You'll change in time/And grow in time—If you put your faith and trust in time"). Sometimes it doesn't ("I love you just as you are/I must love you from afar"). Another problem Harnick had is that this Hammerstein kind of disregard for period just can't go anymore. A composer like Rodgers can get away with writing his own style of music in disregard of period because music is so abstract and he has melody to go with, but a lyricist can't disregard a historical setting today, as Hammerstein used to.

WALTER KERR, *TIMES*

Once upon a time there was a form called musical comedy, but some sort of wicked witch came along and took the comedy out of it, leaving sobersided narratives and thoughtfully motivated tunes—often good tunes—to do all of the evening's work. Now they're trying to take the music away, too, after which we can wear hair shirts and do penance for the sin of having, for so many carefree years, enjoyed ourselves. Look at what they're doing to Richard Rodgers. Not that they can stop the man from writing melody altogether. In *Rex*, which details with leaden persistence the efforts of Henry VIII of England to beget himself a male heir (it takes him one act and four wives, if I counted aright, leaving him with nobody to seduce, marry or behead in Act Two), there are at least two sweet songs that seem to have escaped the show's textbook blight ["No Song More Pleasing" and "Elizabeth"]. But the rest of the time? The rest of the time librettist Sherman Yellen, lyricist Sheldon Harnick, and everyone else who has any say about such things are loading Rodgers down with expository work, asking him to fashion into chorded structures all of the information that ought to have been incorporated into the book or sent back, its dust intact, to the British Museum. Thus if we need to know (and we certainly don't) all about Henry's lineage, childhood, siblings and unexpected succession to the throne, Williamson is given what might be called a document in dotted eighth-notes ("What Now?"), ending with the entirely relevant plaint, "Why? Why? Why?" Why, indeed, must the composer be asked to account, in long listings that cannot escape sounding like rambling recitative, for Henry's political, theological and even astrological beliefs? And so *Rex*, for all its visual splendor and its one eruption into conventional but welcome dance (jugglers with oranges and flaming torches, feet flicking in a lively morris-jig) ["Christmas in Hampton Court"], no longer seems a "musical," let alone a musical comedy. It's a history trot for a high school exam, crammed with factual background too familiar to be of fresh interest or so arcane it'll be forgotten by the morrow.

o　　o　　o

While coproducing the shoestring 1973 revival of his 1954 *Pajama Game*, songwriter Richard Adler determined to become a big-time producer and launched two simultaneous projects. One was a musical version of *Twelfth Night*, with book and libretto by *Pajama Game* author/director George Abbott (produced in December 1976 as *Music Is*); the other was a full-scale Henry VIII musical. Adler learned that the seventy-four-year-old Richard Rodgers was looking to come back after a stroke, and thus *Rex* was born. The most prominent name on the list of available lyricists was Sheldon Harnick, who had been silent since the dissolution of his partnership with Jerry Bock over *The Rothschilds* in 1970. The project was announced in April '74 with Jerome Lawrence and Robert E. Lee (of *Mame* [1966] and *Dear World* [1969]) as librettists, but by the following winter they'd been displaced by Sherman Yellen—whose only musical credit, *The Rothschilds*, was not much of a credit. As director, Adler lined up the up-and-coming Michael Bennett. After codirecting the 1971 *Follies* with Hal Prince, Bennett had staged the 1971 comedy hit *Twigs* and performed an admirable if unsuccessful salvage job on *Seesaw* (1973) in Detroit. But Adler balked when Bennett demanded the princely sum of 10 percent of the net profits. "Who does he think he is?" asked the neophyte. "I don't need Michael Bennett." So he got Ed Sherin, whose only musical experience had been . . . *Seesaw* in Detroit. (Instead of *Rex*, Bennett went directly on to *A Chorus Line* [1975]). Adler then jetted to London in search of a star, a *really* big legend-of-a-star. But Britain's legends—Burton, O'Toole, Finney, and even Rex—weren't interested in *Rex*, so Adler settled on the fiery but lower-echelon Nicol Williamson. With a tired-and-ailing Rodgers, a misplaced Harnick (whose warm-and-clever style was out of tune in the sixteenth century), a weak librettist, a wrong-headed director, and an ill-favored star, it was perhaps inevitable that the entertainment, which premièred in Wilmington, was star-crossed. Word on *Rex*'s dire condition began to spread—quick and far—after the show moved to the Kennedy Center Opera House. Nicol himself sent forth this cheery missive in Liz Smith's syndicated column: "I feel as though I'm dying. Every single moment is like being taken away in an ambulance." Not exactly conducive to building advance sales for the upcoming Boston and Broadway engagements. "Look," said producer Adler in an interesting bit of spin control, "this show has a cough, it hasn't got cancer." Or how's this? "If I got angry at every bad notice, I'd end up in Bellevue." Librettist Yellen also took exception to the reviews: "The words don't just fly out of Nicol Williamson's mouth because he's had a vision. Nicol could hardly have been brilliant, which is what the critics called him, if I hadn't put those words in his mouth." Songs came, songs went—including the title song. "Nicol was up there bellowing: "'Rex! Rex!,'" said Harnick. "It sounded like he was calling his dog." Anne Boleyn's beheading was cut, too; it was "a downer," said Sherin. The star continued to be his charming, mercurial self. "He should work with dead writers in the future, like Shakespeare," said Yellen. "It's misery for the people who have to work with him." "You don't know if he's going to be nice to you or punch you in the mouth," said one cast member in Boston. Sherin was having problems of his own: "I was under fire in Korea and that was simple compared to this." Producer Adler responded by bringing in Hal Prince as a friend at court. "I've followed Hal's career with great interest and admiration ever since he was a baby-faced kid working on his first show for George Abbott," said Adler, who in fact was *himself* a baby-faced kid when

Prince hired *him* to write *The Pajama Game*. Sherin admitted that Hal would be "very helpful. But as long as my name is on the program, it's going to be my show." (You'd think Sherin would've wanted to get his name *off* the program.) So they all knocked their heads together to fix *Rex*, but *Rex* resisted. While waiting for the advance sale to run out, Nicol—who refused to do publicity—managed to get a fistful of clippings when he did, indeed, punch chorister Jim Litten in the mouth one night during curtain calls. (Litten whispered to a fellow actor, "That's a wrap," which the hypersensitive star heard as "crap.") But that was the only excitement *Rex* created. Prince, meanwhile, knocked Williamson off the short list for the male lead opposite Liz Taylor in the 1978 filmization of *A Little Night Music* (1973), commenting that he'd "rather go back to being George Abbott's assistant" than have anything further to do with Nicol. Announced Shows That Never Happened Dept.: Rodgers and Harnick and Prince had been linked several years earlier on a stillborn *Arsenic and Old Lace*, with book by Mike Stewart and starring Mary and Ethel, for the spring of '73. But you can't always believe everything you read in the papers.

BROADWAY SCORECARD

/ PERFS: 49 / $: −

RAVE	FAVORABLE	MIXED	UNFAVORABLE	PAN
			1	5

THE ROAR OF THE GREASEPAINT— THE SMELL OF THE CROWD

"The New Leslie Bricusse–Anthony Newley Musical," a revised import of their 1964 British musical

book, music, and lyrics by Leslie Bricusse and Anthony Newley

directed by Anthony Newley

choreographed by Gillian Lynne

produced by David Merrick in association with Bernard Delfont

starring Anthony Newley and Cyril Ritchard

with Sally Smith, Gilbert Price, and Joyce Jillson

opened May 16, 1965   *Shubert Theatre*

WALTER KERR, *HERALD TRIBUNE*

If he keeps at it, Anthony Newley is going to wind up producing a Tin Pan Alley version of *Pilgrim's Progress* performed by the Little Lost Boys from *Peter Pan*. What am I saying? He's done it. One of these characters is called Cocky and he could be mistaken, by a really bright kindergartener, for The Common Man. Another character is simply named Sir and if you worked good and hard at it you could probably identify him with The Upper Classes. Now Sir dictates the rules of the game, and Cocky hops about the board, mostly backward, doing Sir's bidding until his limbs and your patience are about to give out, at which point he revolts. Before he revolts, and while he is still sniveling, fifteen fly-by-night urchins left over from *Oliver Twist* (just to give you some

"Third-rate commerce masquerading as art," per Walter Kerr. Tony Newley and Cyril Ritchard in "a Tin Pan Alley version of *Pilgrim's Progress* performed by the Little Lost Boys from *Peter Pan*." (artwork by Kenerson)

clue to their identity they are called Urchins in the program) splatter themselves stage left and stage right, climb a Chinese sort of gatepost referred to as The Ladder of Success, and weave about under the moon like so many mermaids while the orchestra makes sounds you haven't heard since Metro-Goldwyn-Mayer stopped filming underwater ballets. I wish to say here that I have nothing against Anthony Newley as a performer except that he isn't a performer at all. I certainly have nothing against Cyril Ritchard, who is a professional to his high-handed finger tips. But I do most seriously have something against the sort of thing that is going on at the Shubert, and I wish to say what it is. *The Roar of the Greasepaint—The Smell of the Crowd* is third-rate commerce masquerading as art. Everything that works in *The Roar of the Greasepaint* is old-hat. What hurts is the facade of freshness, greasepaint smeared on the wrong face.

NORMAN NADEL, *WORLD-TELEGRAM* **&** *SUN*

A triumph of showmanship over material. It reaffirms the power of personality in the musical theatre. Put the right man on stage and you can't lose. The right *men*, in the case of the musical entertainment that opened last night. They are Anthony Newley and Cyril Ritchard, either of whom could provide a scintillating evening just quoting *McGuffey's Third Reader*. *McGuffey* happens to be one of the few sources untapped by Newley and Leslie Bricusse in preparing this successor to their *Stop the World—I Want to Get Off* [1962]. The authors have borrowed from Wagner's *Tristan und Isolde* [1865], *My Fair Lady* [1956], Shakespeare, Mendelssohn, Gershwin, Tchaikovsky, Charlie Chaplin, music hall, burlesque, vaudeville, religion, also from earlier Bricusse and Newley. Whether the material is borrowed or new, simple or sophisticated it is dispensed with joyous *élan*. There is so much exuberance in this show, especially among its chorus of small female urchins, that you'd feel like a traitor if you didn't enjoy yourself. This show needs Newley to lift its ordinary material out of the ordinary, by a shrug, an eyebrow dismissal, the resonant intoning of a patent platitude, or a good, base grovel, as only Newley can grovel. In all situations, his sense of showmanship is an asset; without it, this musical would not measure large—with it, it at least looks bigger.

HOWARD TAUBMAN, *TIMES*

Anthony Newley and Leslie Bricusse have a penchant for Big
Themes. Their hearts generally are in the right place. In *The Roar of
the Greasepaint—The Smell of the Crowd*, they are firmly on the side of
the underdog, the little man, the exploited of this planet. But my, oh
my are they pretentious and corny! . . . Gilbert Price, as the Negro,
gives the second half its biggest shot in the arm. Price, of course, cannot help it if the authors use his appearance on the stage to comment
on the racial question in their tritest, well-meaning way. Allowed to
sing, this engaging young performer turns "Feeling Good" into an
incantation of defiance and jubilation. Despite the amplification, his
velvety bass tones are reminiscent of the young Paul Robeson's voice.
Newley himself tries very hard to be Chaplinesque; his success should
alarm him, for Cocky emerges as imitation. The sad fact is that nearly
everything *Greasepaint* touches is either belittled by the obviousness
of the treatment or cheapened by the vulgarity of the humor. In a time
when the stage is hungry for Brave, New Voices, one hates to discourage anyone who tackles Big Themes, especially one so immense
as Playing the Game. But, unhappily, the name of *Greasepaint's* game
is Banality.

RICHARD WATTS, JR., *POST*

With its enchanting score and unusual freshness of imagination, *The
Roar of the Greasepaint—The Smell of the Crowd* justifies the remarkable
advance interest it seems to have aroused everywhere. The new musical
faces certain problems from its ambitious and unconventional libretto,
but even its oddities in this respect add to its quality of provocative fascination. It has sometimes been complained in recent years that audiences go out of the new musical shows humming the songs from an old
one, but there is no likelihood of that here. In the fashion of the score
the same authors composed for *Stop the World*, the numbers in *Roar of
the Greasepaint* are not only delightful on first hearing but grow in
appeal with familiarity, and the evening is filled with melodies that
become increasingly haunting. In some curious way, the Newley-
Bricusse libretto made me think of what might have happened if the
collaborators had decided to make a musical comedy out of the episode

of Lucky, the slave, and Pozzo, the tyrannical taskmaster, in *Waiting for Godot* [1953]. But don't let this scare you. *The Roar of the Greasepaint* is a musical of interesting originality.

●   ●   ●

When the 1964 British production of *Greaspaint* (with Norman Wisdom as Cocky) rolled over and died during its tryout, everyone assumed it was terminal. Everyone but Merrick, who had made a mint on his $75,000 *Stop the World* investment and knew that he could sell coauthor Newley in just about anything—even an allegorical *Everyman*. The showman exercised his rights; arranged a lengthy, guaranteed-profit pre-Broadway tour as he had for *Oliver!* (1963); gave a push to "Who Can I Turn To?" (already a hit, thanks to Tony Bennett's recording); and collected the dollars. So what if nobody liked it?

BROADWAY SCORECARD
/ PERFS: 232 / $: +

RAVE	FAVORABLE	MIXED	UNFAVORABLE	PAN
1	1	1	1	2

THE ROBBER BRIDEGROOM

"A New Musical"

music by Robert Waldman

book and lyrics by Alfred Uhry

based on the 1942 novella by Eudora Welty

directed by Gerald Freedman

choreographed by Donald Saddler

produced by John Houseman, Margot Harley, and Michael B. Kapon by arrangement with The Acting Company

starring Barry Bostwick, Rhonda Coullet, and Barbara Lang

with Lawrence John Moss, Stephen Vinovich, B. J. Hardin, Mary (Gordon) Murray, Trip Plymale, Ernie Sabella, Jana Schnieder, and Dennis Warning

opened October 9, 1976   *Ethel Barrymore Theatre*

CLIVE BARNES, *TIMES*

One of the surprise Off-Broadway hits of last season has now arrived on Broadway. It is a bright and lively musical, a sort of country and western fairy tale called *The Robber Bridegroom.* The musical has already had an eventful career. It began life last year in Stuart Ostrow's Musical Theater Lab. John Houseman saw this "work in progress," liked it, and decided to present it with his own troupe, the Acting Company at the Saratoga Festival. This was so successful that it was brought briefly to New York at the Harkness Theatre last October, and now, in a slightly different and a new Broadway production, it has come to town. This is the way more and more Broadway musicals are being generated these days, often with a comparatively humble start in the institutional theatre. In this fashion reasonable experiments can be taken without the costs being prohibitive. Not that *The Robber Bridegroom* is unduly experimental, for its charms are fundamentally rustic and hillbilly, but it does have an unusual story, and its entire staging and concept, an ingenious mixture of square-dance and folk play, are given like an immensely invigorating charade in some Mississippi barnyard. And everyone is helped by a most enjoyable and boisterous cast. Most praise must be lavished upon Barry Bostwick as the eponymous hero who finally gets his girl. And this praise is not just for his performance—which is exemplary enough—but also for simple gallantry. A few days ago Bostwick fell 12 feet to the stage and broke his elbow; he is now performing with his arm in a sling. The odd thing is that Bostwick's performance is so authoritative, his movements so compelling and his presence so impressive, that you simply do not notice the arm in the sling—and when you do it merely looks like an eye-patch in a shirt advertisement. The rest of the cast is also good. Rhonda Coullet makes an attractive heroine (is she the first heroine, apart from the *Hair* [1968] tribe, to go naked, albeit tactfully naked, in a Broadway musical?). *The Robber Bridegroom* is an unpretentious show but extremely stylish. Also, despite the presence of a little bareness and a certain bawdiness in the language, it should prove a show suitable for children, which is always nice to have around.

MARTIN GOTTFRIED, POST
[Headline: "*Kinky Fun* with the *Bridegroom*"]
After having first shown up as part of the Acting Company's repertory last year, *The Robber Bridegroom* resurfaced Saturday night at the Biltmore. Though the company has been changed, and some music added, the production is virtually the same. And if a certain zip is gone, it is still the original, unusual and surprising musical that was so refreshing a season ago. There are so many explorations yet to be developed in musical theatre. This is but one example, a turning away from tired formulas of overall design, book construction, musical styles and general tone. Alfred Uhry has written the story with quirky humor and in that lies much of the show's charm. *The Robber Bridegroom* is entirely tongue in cheek, presenting oddball humor with the innocence and stylized spareness of American primitive painting. Now 90 intermissionless minutes of tongue in cheek can get on one's nerves and it is Uhry's accomplishment that they don't, but not only his. Robert

Waldman has written a truly ingenious score, somehow managing to be country and theatrical, melodic and interesting, catchy but not obvious. There is a cross-breeding here that ranges from Stravinsky and Copland to the mood but not the banality of country music. Waldman has orchestrated it for a small string group with simple ingenuity, a spareness that applies the lucidity of chamber music to the coziness of a country band. Here is the combination of theatrical instinct and musicianly technique that has always invigorated our musical stage and Waldman is surely capable of applying it to any kind of show. He is a real discovery. *The Robber Bridegroom* is not quite as appealing as it can be and it is sometimes slow. But it is still a charming and fresh entertainment, an example of how different musicals can be.

CHRISTOPHER SHARP, *WOMEN'S WEAR DAILY*

The new production would seem to have all the ingredients for a better show. The lead role is played by Barry Bostwick, who has a little of that old fashioned Hollywood heroism in his presence—something that has been so hard to find these days that writers are almost forced to create scripts for anti-heroes. He is supported by two fine actresses in this show, Barbara Lang and Rhonda Coullet. Five new musical numbers have been introduced, and Donald Saddler is doing the choreography. But in spite of all these positive ingredients, there just doesn't seem to be as much fun in this show as there was in the Acting Company's. Fun is not something that can be bought by big Broadway backers. Perhaps the big difference in *The Robber Bridegroom* of this year over last year's is in the attitude of the performers. Last year it seemed as if the actors were enjoying every minute that they were on stage. This year's production has been hampered by an accident that fractured Bostwick's arm and confusion about opening the play with or without Bostwick. As it is, Bostwick plays his role with his arm in a sling without any trouble. In fact, he has the easy confidence of someone who will go far in his business. The company as a whole fails him. There is something too slick and professional about all the goosing and the joking in the evening. Last year it looked improvisational; this year it is too obviously schemed, with the result that it looks jaded. About midway through this show, the momentum starts to build, and the last half of the evening is considerably more entertaining than the first. The music in this work is somewhat effective in providing ambience, but by itself (i.e., if you close your eyes) it sounds a little like the cries of an upset Country Western stomach.

o   o   o

You've got bad shows that fail, deservedly; bad shows that succeed, luckily; and good shows that succeed, naturally. But there's a fourth, sad category: good shows that unhappily fail. *The Robber Bridegroom* was tuneful, unconventional, and delightfully refreshing. No, it wasn't perfect, but how many shows are? Songwriters Robert Waldman and Alfred Uhry, whose only Broadway credit (?) was the ill-conceived *East of Eden* musical *Here's Where I Belong* (1968), provided an inventive, colorful, and entertaining score. Even Gerald Freedman, whose other musicals—*The Gay Life* (1961), *A Time for Singing* (1966), *The Grand Tour* (1979)—suffered from a weak directorial hand, did a marvelously atmospheric job on this backwoods fairy tale. The only problem was nobody wanted to see it. The saddest possible Broadway fate, perhaps, is to do admirable work that audiences just won't bother with. As the wise and wonderful Oscar Hammerstein, a man who underwent his share of failure, once said, "The number of people who won't go to shows they don't want to see is unlimited." Developed at Stuart Ostrow's Musical Theatre Lab, *The Robber Bridegroom* was initially produced as part of the Acting Company's '75–'76 touring season. It began a limited engagement of fifteen performances on October 7, 1975, at the Harkness Theatre on (upper) Broadway; the cast of Juilliard graduates was led by unknowns Kevin Kline and Patti LuPone. Unaccountably, Waldman and Uhry haven't returned to Broadway since. Their only subsequently produced effort—Stuart Ostrow's *Swing*—swung itself out in its 1980 Washington tryout. Uhry rebounded, though, with a little ninety-minute three-character charmer called *Driving Miss Daisy* (1987).

A Tony Award was won by Barry Bostwick (actor).

BROADWAY SCORECARD
/ PERFS: 145 / $: -

RAVE	FAVORABLE	MIXED	UNFAVORABLE	PAN
	5		1	

ROCKABYE HAMLET

"A Musical," previously entitled *Kronberg: 1582*

book, music, and lyrics by Cliff Jones

based on the 1602 tragedy *Hamlet* by William Shakespeare (uncredited)

directed and choreographed by Gower Champion

co-choreographed by Tony Stevens

produced by Lester Osterman Productions and Joseph Kipness, in association with Martin Richards, Victor D'Arc, and Marilyn Strauss

starring Larry Marshall and Alan Weeks

with Beverly D'Angelo, Leata Galloway, Randal Wilson, Kim Milford, Meat Loaf, Irving Lee, Christopher Chadman, and Winston DeWitt Hemsley

opened February 17, 1976   Minskoff Theatre

CLIVE BARNES, *TIMES*

Rockabye Hamlet is a pungent mixture of the flashy and the vulgar—not all the flashiness is bad, but precious little of the vulgarity is good. Why, in heaven's name, *Hamlet*? Has not that gentle ghost suffered enough—and what are these people to Hamlet, or Hamlet to these people? This rock version is quite disturbingly banal—empty, vacuous and a little conceited. Cliff Jones has written the music and the lyrics and indeed has done the entire thing except put it on the stage. That has been achieved by Gower Champion. Interestingly, understandably and illuminatingly, Champion's name is in a larger typeface on the program than Jones's. There is a very good reason for that. Somehow, Jones blows *Rockabye Hamlet* with the very first number. The setting (a nice job by Kert F. Lundell) is interesting—it looks like a modified rock concert hall, with batteries of lights, instruments, microphones, rostrums, the whole paraphernalia of all those screaming nights of rock—and into

"An experience as limitless as your imagination!" reads the unattributed quote atop the window card. Guess it depends on the limits of your imagination. (artwork by Doug Johnson)

this comes Hamlet [Larry Marshall]. He is dressed mod, but semi-traditional. He is good looking, and carries a microphone as if he knows what to do with it. He starts his first song—the voice rises into a plaintive wail, and the melody is sort of Muzak-rock, not the real thing but a middle-aged apology for the real thing. Hamlet sings: "I have a question if you have an answer: Why did he have to die?" Right there I had a question, too. I also had an answer. Jones is a second-rate musician with a third-rate mind. His lyrics throughout the long-short evening were deplorable. They started at a low and never got up—they ranged from soft-core rock, to country and western (although I was not quite sure of which country!) and even an attempt at a smudgy blues. Champion has done a most remarkable job in his choreography and staging. His choreography is not entirely to my taste—he seems to be a graduate of the flailing arms and semaphore school of choreography— but his use of dramatic movement is flawless. There are some lovely directorial touches to this musical, including one of the best deaths for Claudius I have ever seen in any production, a most innovative use of a central ramp, and a total production sense that made hand-held microphones (normally an anathema to drama) part of the conceptual staging. It was really a beautiful staging—inappropriate but beautiful.

MARTIN GOTTFRIED, *POST*
[Headline: "*Hamlet* Hits Rock Bottom"]
A musical version of *Hamlet* was always a show business joke. Unfortunately, the joke opened last night at the Minskoff Theatre. Nor is *Rockabye Hamlet* merely a musical. It is a rock musical. A rock opera. It is perfectly and impeccably awful. Did anyone connected with this show wonder what *Hamlet* has to do with rock music? Did anyone have a reason for making a rock opera of it? The problem with lesser rock musicians, as with most mediocre artists, is that their pretentions are directly proportionate to their incompetence. The worse they are, the bigger the subjects they choose. What should have made some difference with *Rockabye Hamlet* was that it was being staged by Gower Champion, a master showman. Champion knows a great deal about the musical theatre but he evidently has no feeling for rock music. His dances go no further than variations on the frug and the monkey, which are only five or ten years late. These are regularly interspersed with

Broadway show dances. None of them are any good. The rest of the production is spent with a ramp that seems to have obsessed Champion, going up and down throughout, like a drawbridge to disaster. There is no way to adequately describe the foolishness and waste of such a show. It is obviously done with a dependence on Champion, but he is not dependable if he thinks he can put anything on stage and make it work through production. Here is proof, if it was ever needed, that there is no such thing as the bad show made to look good through "Broadway slickness." Some material just has to be there. Maybe *Home, Sweet Homer* [which opened and closed six weeks earlier] wasn't that bad after all.

HOWARD KISSEL, *WOMEN'S WEAR DAILY*
[Headline: "Something's Rotten in New York"]
Cliff Jones's *Rockabye Hamlet* might just as well have been titled *Hamlet Goes to Las Vegas,* for the things that impress one about the production directed—alas, by Gower Champion—are effects with lights, with neon, with stage gimmickry of the sort one associates with Las Vegas girlie shows. "I loved the ramp," someone behind me remarked on the way out. The ramp was indeed one of the high points—for most of the show it led like a gangplank or the drawbridge over a moat from a stage door at the back of the stage down to the major playing area down front. Occasionally there were lights on it. During the funeral of Ophelia, in which the corpse is borne in a Lucite coffin, suddenly the ramp rose, blue lights glowing on its underbelly and, from underneath, the chorus danced forward. The moment drew applause, as did an earlier one in which the leader of the troupe of traveling players was lowered onto the stage in an enormous circle with lights on its rim—precisely the sort of entrance for a Las Vegas featured singer, not quite as appropriate for someone singing "Something's Rotten in Denmark." [Lighting design by Jules Fisher.] Nothing about the material has any honesty or genuineness. The major interactions between characters come when they hand one another microphones. Microphones often steal the show—Ophelia's mad scene is almost stolen from her by a mike rising from the floor in front of her (this is the first time I have ever seen an actor "downstaged"); one's attention is diverted from the Hamlet–Laertes duel by one's fascination with an enormous boom mike being maneuvered over the duelers. The omnipresence, indeed the

symbolic importance, of the microphone is pointed up by the fact that in this version Ophelia does not die by drowning—she strangles herself with a microphonic cord. It would be nice to say Gower Champion had somehow redeemed all this with the sort of inventive stagecraft that made *Mack & Mabel* [1974] fun to watch despite the material. But apart from the occasional effect of turning on the neon or raising the ramp, none of the movement on stage has any more character than Cliff Jones's adolescent music and words. *Rockabye Hamlet* works neither as a send-up of the idea of a rock *Hamlet* nor as a genuine rock *Hamlet*.

DOUGLAS WATT, *DAILY NEWS*
[Headline: "*Rockabye Hamlet* Gaudy, Lifeless"]
To watch *Rockabye Hamlet*, a gaudy and anachronistic exercise in musical kitsch that flopped about the stage of the Minskoff last night like a dying swordfish, is to marvel at the heights of folly attainable along Broadway. Kert F. Lundell's open stage setting looks like an electrical appliances warehouse. Row upon row of spotlights clog the ceiling area, with the rest of the space, occupied by platforms for the musicians and their electrified instruments and consoles, pipe scaffolding, and, center, a sort of *Hello, Hamlet!* ramp down which the actors approach us and that can also be raised like a drawbridge. Colored light tubing is used extensively to create a garish effect. It is one of the ugliest stage settings I have ever seen. *Rockabye Hamlet* is like a last gasp of an era that we thought we had left behind a long time ago. And in common with other art forms (in this case, rock) that have reached the end of their usefulness, it is afflicted with gigantism, a disease that first evidenced itself deceptively in the rock world a decade ago with the Beatles' vastly admired *Sergeant Pepper* album [1967]. But that's another story. And who needs another story after *Rockabye Hamlet*?

                    ◦   ◦   ◦

Toronto musician/TV-music director Cliff Jones's radio-rock *Hamlet* was first aired by the Canadian Broadcasting Corporation in December 1973. The broadcast's success led to full stage productions the following two summers at the Charlottetown Festival on Prince Edward Island, Canada. It was there that Charlottetown's favorite daughter— Colleen Dewhurst—saw *Kronberg: 1582*, liked it, called producer

Lester Osterman (who had presented her in the highly successful 1973 revival of *A Moon for the Misbegotten*), and told him to bring it to Broadway. So, unfortunately and with great difficulty, he did. "*Rockabye Hamlet* is told in sights and sounds, rather than words," said the press release. Well, okay. The producers—reportedly at the suggestion of Clive Barnes, of all people—placed their rock-musical baby in the hands of Gower ("I'm the only one beside the producers who is over thirty") Champion, who was in his post–*Mack & Mabel* tailspin and apparently willing to try *anything*. The results were as essayed above. A month after the Broadway opening—and three weeks after the closing—the CBC did an eight-hour broadcast chronicling the rise and (especially) the fall of their homegrown *Hamlet*. Bardic Adaptation Dept.: Back in the days when brevity was the soul of wit, Howard Dietz and Arthur Schwartz once disposed of an entire Shakespearean tragedy in sixteen bluesy measures, to wit: "[R:] I'm not the kind of a boy for a girl like you/You are a Capulet, I'm a Montague/ [J:] To show you my devotion, I'm gonna drink a potion/[Both:] For I'm not the kind of a boy (girl) for a girl (boy) like you."

BROADWAY SCORECARD
/ PERFS: 8 / $: –

RAVE	FAVORABLE	MIXED	UNFAVORABLE	PAN
				6

THE ROCKY HORROR SHOW

an import of the 1973 British musical spoof

book, music, and lyrics by Richard O'Brien

directed by Jim Sharman

"The Michael White Production," presented by Lou Adler

starring Tim Curry

with Graham Jarvis, Jamie Donnelly, Boni Enten, Abigale Haness, Meat Loaf, Kim Milford, Bill Miller, and Ritz (Richard) O'Brien

opened March 10, 1975   *Belasco Theatre*

CLIVE BARNES, *TIMES*

The Rocky Horror Show is a kind of mixture between a horror and science-fiction movie, a rock show and a transvestite display. So you see there should be something for everyone to like. Or dislike if it comes to that. In London the show started in the attic of the Royal Court Theatre, and landed up in a seedy movie house ripe and ready for demolition. Serendipity played a large part in the show's charm—it was unexpected, unpretentious, and the cinema itself, from the peeling walls to the grubby seats, provided it with a perfect ambiance. Something of this ambiance has been conscientiously attempted at the Belasco, and a brave pretense is maintained that we are in a cinema in the initial throes of demolition. But we know we are not—we know that we are sitting in a comfortable cabaret theatre, with obliging girls serving drinks, and the atmosphere is totally different and far grander. The show stopped on the way in Los Angeles, and this was almost certainly a mistake. It is smarter now, but nothing like so crazy or, if one were in a mildly tolerant mood, so endearing. It now looks flashy, expensive and overstaged. The cast is better, the lights are brighter, the noise is more loudly amplified. But jokes—sick jokes, silly jokes, or even dirty jokes— are rarely improved by shouting them down a megaphone. More is often less. The idea of Frankenstein as a bisexual transvestite, with a baritone voice, fish-net tights and black lipstick, was also perversely attractive. The performances were camp and dreadful, but the style provided the enjoyment. Now the style is partly lacking. Tim Curry, of the London cast, plays the dire transexual villain from Transylvania, Frank 'N' Furter. Curry can be very funny, flashing his eyes like headlamps, tossing his curls roguishly and talking in a voice of sugared bile. He can also sing, and puts over his numbers with the venomous zest of a David Bowie. The rest of the cast are fair enough. They sing better than did their London counterparts. They probably even act better. Yet why did not someone understand—before the Los Angeles paint job—that the entire point of *The Rocky Horror Show* in London was that it was tacky? Tacky, tacky, tacky! They should have found a filthy old cinema in the East Village and just thrown it on there.

MARTIN GOTTFRIED, POST

England's reputation for sexual prudishness has always had its perverse reverse. Weird happenings on the moors and all that. Yet, even British sexual deviation seems naive. It is as if, with the Empire lost, the country retreated into childishness. *The Rocky Horror Show* seems to really think it is sexually daring with its transvestite doings, and refreshingly campy, asking "whatever happened to Fay Wray?" The show might be fun for the hair-spray hip. When done in London a couple of years ago, it was skimpily produced in an old movie house, an amateurish imitation of what was already passé off-off Broadway. For last night's opening, the orchestra floor of the Belasco Theatre was ripped out and replaced with nightclub tables. The reasons for that are beyond me since this show never claims to be happening in a cabaret and there is no worse way to see anything. Drinks being served throughout don't help. The show has been redesigned to the teeth by Brian Thomson, with flashy and fabulous sets that include a bulb-lit runway; neon lighting; lots of steaming dry ice; neon bolts of lightning; and rear screen projections. For much of the time, these physical values support a production concept that looks like modernized German Expressionism and is very impressive. This momentarily disguises things. . . . The fact is that Charles Ludlam's Ridiculous Theatrical Company beautifully camped horror movies with its *Bluebeard* [1970]. The fact is that glitter rock is over. The fact is that [the 1974 films] *Young Frankenstein* and *Andy Warhol's Frankenstein*, not new themselves, are all over town. The fact is that *The Rocky Horror Show* is simpleminded, however beautifully it has been produced.

JAMES SPINA, *WOMEN'S WEAR DAILY*
Previous British and West Coast praise should guarantee undeserved success for the Broadway production of *The Rocky Horror Show* at the revamped Belasco Theatre. A conceptual mishmash of parodied '50s music, situation horror-comedy borrowed from the *Addams Family* [1964–1966] and dated transvestite ordeals, the show is tacky, boring and highly forgettable. Oh yeah, so why has it been so successful elsewhere? As evidenced by *Hair* [1968], *Superstar* [1971], and numerous other rock-theatre unions, critics wheeling huge charter buses of group-rate audiences deem rock to be the needed new blood of Theatre. Rock is an approved forbidden fruit, the required final course for those theatre majors already well-graded in transvestitism, bisexuality and gore. There are no stars. Head pretender Tim Curry is only mildly irritating in his sweaty drive to blend the mannerisms of Mick Jagger, Alice Cooper and Fay Wray gone ghoul. Most of my wandering attention went to Boni Enten in the role of a greaser street-vamp. Keep your eyes on her and you're lucky enough to miss Kim Milford, the ultimate example of a counterculture hip-hack. He has the stage presence of a muscle-toned eraser and a time-consuming wont for exhibitionist calisthenics. The night would be better spent listening to a New York Dolls album while watching reruns of *The Munsters* [also 1964–1966].

o   o   o

This strange little satire began its eventful life on June 19, 1973, at the Royal Court's "Theatre Upstairs," moving November 3 to the King's Road. Despite its somewhat surprising Broadway failure, *The Rocky Horror Picture Show*—which opened later in 1975—became a major midnight monster movie. So there. (Oddest of all was to find Frank 'N' Furter himself returning to Broadway, triumphantly, in 1980 in the title role of *Amadeus*). Although the Belasco's brief cabaretization was long since undone, the poor old playhouse has never been quite the same since the Shuberts allowed *Rocky* to tear out those lower boxes.

BROADWAY SCORECARD
/ PERFS: 45 / $: −

RAVE	FAVORABLE	MIXED	UNFAVORABLE	PAN
				6

THE ROTHSCHILDS

"A Musical Legend"

music by Jerry Bock

lyrics by Sheldon Harnick

book by Sherman Yellen (doctored by William Gibson and Joseph Stein)

based on the 1962 biography by Frederic Morton

directed by Michael Kidd (replacing Derek Goldby)

choreographed by Michael Kidd (replacing Eliot Feld, who replaced Grover Dale)

produced by Hillard Elkins, presented by Lester Osterman

starring Paul Hecht, Leila Martin (replacing Joan Hackett), Keene Curtis, Jill Clayburgh, and Hal Linden

with Leo Leyden, Chris Sarandon, Timothy Jerome, David Garfield, and Allan Gruet

opened October 19, 1970   Lunt-Fontanne Theatre

CLIVE BARNES, *TIMES*

Take a good Jewish family like the Rothschilds, throw in music by Jerry Bock, lyrics by Sheldon Harnick and a literate and engrossing book (by Sherman Yellen) and you should have a hit. And I think *The Rothschilds* will give a lot of pleasure to a lot of people. It has geniality rather than incandescence, there are show-stopping performances rather than show-stopping numbers, and the structure of the show lacks that simple sweep of action more often than not a prerequisite of a hit musical. Yet it is interesting, in parts very witty, has a certain moral force and, best of all, it has style. Bock's music makes a neat nod in the direction of the 18th century, but blends period pastiche with a gentler, more cultivated version of those Jewish folk melodies that were so successful in *Fiddler on the Roof* [1964]. The fiddle has become a violin, but it still sounds pretty sweet. The lyrics also have style and a lot of gusto, even if the gusto is more 18th century in spirit than the style, which is rightly pure Broadway. Yellen's book has to face the difficulty of making a gripping story about bankers who don't even have the grace to go broke once in a while. History dealt Yellen a difficult hand of cards, and he had to play them the best he could. In many ways the current show that *The Rothschilds* most resembles is not, unexpectedly, *Fiddler* but *1776* [1969]. It has the same underlying seriousness, the same stress upon character and the same widespread opportunities for its cast to act. And the cast in *The Rothschilds* is a delight. Hal Linden's Mayer Rothschild is one of the best musical performances now on Broadway. It has depth, power and humor, and Linden can sing as well as he can act. Keene Curtis, in a virtuoso display, played four roles, from William of Hesse to Metternich, and each one was so different that you would not have been all that surprised if one of his characters had met one of his other characters right there on stage. *The Rothschilds* is a good and solid start to the musical season. Wonder of wonder I think it might even make money. But the Rothschilds always have.

MARTIN GOTTFRIED, *WOMEN'S WEAR DAILY*

[Headline: "*The Rothschilds* . . . Morass of Vulgarity"]

Put bluntly, *The Rothschilds* is a musical about Jews and money. Either would be an excellent subject for any kind of theatre, and of course the depth of Jewishness was the basis for *Fiddler on the Roof.* The idea of money, which is a troublesome and emotional problem for everybody, will someday be the subject of an important piece of theatre. But *The Rothschilds* does not explore these subjects—it is about them—and it is about them in the most superficial sense: Jews as just "Jews" and money as just "money." This lead-footed and overstuffed musical, oldest of old fashioned, only represents the vulgarity of money and the vulgarization of Jewishness. It also represents the vulgarization of the musical theatre. The irony is that the authors of *The Rothschilds* had already made their move away from old styles into the new. For Jerry Bock and Sheldon Harnick, *The Rothschilds* is a depressing step backward. Prompted by Jerome Robbins, this team had taken the total musical a great step toward consummation with *Fiddler*. Their work on *The Apple Tree* [1966], though hardly as successful, showed them still exploring this territory. With *The Rothschilds* they have gone all the way back to the operetta, the patchwork musical, the shorthand story sprinkled with songs, dances and production numbers. It is ludicrously expensive, naive and misled. Michael Kidd, ultimately given credit for directing and choreographing the whole thing, didn't do much of either. Not only is there no coordination between dance and drama, there isn't even a connection. There is nothing musical about the dramatic sequences and nothing dramatic about the musical ones. Bock's music is occasionally classical and occasionally "Jewish" (when that, very reminiscent of *Fiddler*), usually settling for the plain and anonymous show tune. In an effort to write long-lined music rather than just songs (an effort I appreciate), he lost the melodic sense which has always been his greatest gift. The production itself is a hymn to desperation and uncoordination. The stage is alternately overpopulated and empty, either filled with dancers for a princely hall or forlorn with Rothschild and his five sons trying to work up a little Broadway sentiment. Private scenes between Rothschild and his wife are played in a set so small and far away it might well represent the Shubert Alley brain that conceived all of this.

WALTER KERR, *TIMES*
[Headline: "Dollars Just Don't Sing"]
It is probable that *The Rothschilds* has succeeded in becoming exactly what it meant to be: an unhappy musical comedy. Do your eyebrows lift? What else was to be got out of an account, very lightly dusted by powdered wigs and twirled parasols, of a Jewish family that fought its

way up out of the ghetto, servile bow by servile bow, until it had amassed enough money to help finance the Napoleonic wars and to extract promises [of freedom] that would never be kept? Joy unconfined, or even temporary satisfaction? And that is the truth of the matter. But is it a truth with much music in it? . . . [Midway through the first act] Michael Kidd, styling everything handsomely, comes up with his most fetching coup. (Perhaps it was indicated by his librettist; but he manages it extremely well.) The ghetto is regularly visited by marauders, folk from the town who are only too happy to smash windows, shatter counters, knock down what little the Jews beyond the barbed-wire fences have succeeded in putting up. During one such raid, the children wipe the shelves clean as though a selective windstorm had dropped by to help them and then, their few treasures hidden, disappear into a cellar. In sudden darkness the rioters attack, disperse. When the invasion is over and the stage lights have risen to survey the damage, the cellar door opens and the family emerges. The sons are all grown. In one swift shaft of staging, more than a necessary transition in time has been achieved; the transition has also told us that the raids never did stop, that growing up was a matter of learning to live daily with irrational danger for company. *The Rothschilds* is, given its intentions, intelligently put together. But in the second act we are confronted, head-on, with those intentions, and the results are, ultimately, and no doubt inevitably, bleak. We have moved away from what is attractively personal in the first act to what is irremediably sterile and cold: cash on the line. High finance can, of course, have its own fascination (this may be one of the few instances in recorded history where a musical comedy hints, halfway through, that its source material may be a great deal more lively than its onstage counterpart), but that fascination is not precisely a lyrical one. Bonds don't dance, dollars don't sing.

⁕   ⁕   ⁕

A classy new musical from the man who brought you *Oh! Calcutta!* (1969), which is not to say that one show had anything to do with the other. But *The Rothschilds* was assembled as a moneymaking venture by a wheeling-dealing entrepreneur, rather than a creative producer. The lack of a strong, guiding hand resulted in a wandering and meandering saga. (During the tryout they replaced the under-title slogan "A Musical Legend" with the less disputable "A Musical.") A Broadway musical about a personable, crafty, ghetto-dwelling Jewish peddler with five children was workable, perhaps, when Hilly Elkins optioned Frederic Morton's best-selling chronicle. But that was back in 1963, when the producer—a street kid from Brooklyn turned talent agent—was struggling with another out-of-the-ghetto tale, Clifford Odets's *Golden Boy* (which flopped in 1964 despite the presence of Sammy Davis). By the time *The Rothschilds* lumbered in after the turn of the decade, things had changed politically, socially, and artistically. There was also the matter of that *other* musical about a Jewish papa with five kids. Elkins first hired British writer Wolf Mankowitz to prepare a libretto, which was submitted to the post–*Fiddler* Bock and Harnick, who understandably turned it down. Mankowitz left the project and was followed by Sidney Michaels, who was similarily cashiered. Elkins then discovered one Sherman Yellen, a TV writer with no stage experience (but two unproduced playscripts that impressed the discerning producer). British director Derek Goldby, who'd just created a stir with *Rosencrantz and Guildenstern Are Dead* [1967] but himself had no musical theatre experience, next joined the project. Bock and Harnick, approached once more following their disappointing *The Apple Tree*, reluctantly agreed to sign up, and *The Rothschilds* was under way in earnest. Elkins, meanwhile, was busy assembling his *Oh! Calcutta!*, which gives you some idea of the producer's discriminating taste. Librettist Yellen contributed the "Delicious Indignities" sketch, which gives you some idea of *his* discriminating taste. (Bock and Harnick no doubt turned down Elkins's offer to join Samuel Beckett, Jules Feiffer, John Lennon, Sam Shepard, Ken Tynan, and Yellen with their clothes off. They did, though, join Goldby in doctoring the ailing *Her First Roman* [1968].) On the dance front, Grover Dale—who attracted notice with his work on the one-performance *Billy* (1969)—was choreographer-designate through the planning stages, with Eliot Feld taking over during auditions. Unable to get a talented newcomer to work dirt cheap, though, Elkins figured he might as well get some insurance and hired Michael Kidd. Not a bad idea to have an experienced veteran on board capable of replacing the director, right? Just in case?? Elkins also took on theatre operator Lester Osterman as a producing partner to help raise the not-so-easy money. (One bystander reports that the pair spent more energy working out their billing—"Lester Osterman presents the Hillard Elkins production of *The Rothschilds*"—than on the show itself.) *The Rothschilds* went to Detroit, where it became apparent that the story—about ghetto-bound papa Mayer trying to earn some respect, on the one hand, while his sons earn interest and a controlling hand over European finance on the other—suffered from gaping structural problems. Favorable reaction to Hal Linden's performance convinced the creators to keep Mayer alive well into the second act, long past his actual death, so the boys wrote him an effective theme song— "In My Own Lifetime"—to sing amid the financial maneuvering. Didn't help the show any, but earned Hal a Tony Award. Goldby, meanwhile, was fired in Detroit and replaced by the aforementioned Michael Kidd. This move caused the breakup of the especially well-matched songwriting pair, who brought us *Fiorello!* (1959), *She Loves Me* (1963), and *Fiddler*; Bock appears to have been surprised and wounded when Harnick, without consultation, sided against the director and approved the axe. Harnick has been only marginally active on Broadway since, while Bock has remained completely unheard along the Rialto for more than twenty-five years, except for revivals of *Fiddler* and the cherished *She Loves Me*, that is.

Tony Awards were won by Hal Linden (actor) and Keene Curtis (supporting actor).

BROADWAY SCORECARD

/ PERFS: 505 / $: −

RAVE	FAVORABLE	MIXED	UNFAVORABLE	PAN
1	1	2	2	

SARAVÁ

"The New *Hot* Musical"

music by Mitch Leigh

book and lyrics by N. Richard Nash

based on the 1966 Brazilian novel *Doña Flor and Her Two Husbands* by Jorge Amado

directed and choreographed by Rick Atwell

"The Mitch Leigh Production," produced by Eugene V. Wolsk

starring Tovah Feldshuh

with P. J. Benjamin, Michael Ingram, Betty Walker (replacing Grace Keagy), Carol Jean Lewis, and Randy Graff

opened February 23, 1979   Mark Hellinger Theatre

CLIVE BARNES, *POST*

[Headline: "*Saravá* Sneaks into Town"]

To review or not to review—that was the question. So let us get the ethical question out of the way first, particularly as it is more interesting than the show that prompted it. *Saravá* is a Mitch Leigh musical, Leigh being better known as the composer of *Man of La Mancha* [1965]. It seems that Leigh and his producer Eugene V. Wolsk had an impossible dream. It appears that they wanted to get their musical into New York with as little attention from the critics as possible. The show started out of town, encountered difficulties, moved into New York ahead of schedule, and embarked upon a lengthy but not unprecedented series of previews, accompanied by a blitz of TV advertising spots, which was unprecedented. Twice, or was it three times?, the management postponed its opening. The last two proposed openings were planned for Friday evenings, so, presumably, the reviews would find themselves tucked away in the relatively harmless obscurity of a Saturday newspaper. Eventually the critics of New York's three major daily newspapers decided—after consultation and a vote of two-to-one, myself being the losing minority—to say, like gangbusters in a game of hide and seek: "Ready or Not, We Are Coming In." We sent out messengers to buy regular seats (it was doubtless salutary for the three of us to find out how much regular seats cost these days), arranged between ourselves an arbitrary release date and prepared our Olympian judgments. Having now seen *Saravá*, had I been its producer, I think I would have used machine guns to have kept critics out, or at least employed program ladies well-versed in karate. *Saravá* might have gotten better in the next weeks—they had, for example, put new material in during the last week—but I doubt it. The show is just as good as that jingling TV commercial that so ubiquitously advertises it. What it shows, they certainly have got. It suggests an honestly trashy show with an honestly trashy commercial. The musical is cheap (in everything but its cost) and vulgar. . . . Mitch Leigh's music finds him in a Latin-American mood, slightly to the West of Xavier Cugat.

DOUGLAS WATT, *DAILY NEWS*
[Headline: "*Saravá* Has Ghost of a Chance to Succeed"]
When a ghost and the carnival spirit he embodies are of livelier interest in a musical than the living, that show has a problem. It's called *Saravá*, after a salutation in Brazilian dialect that seems to be equally serviceable for hello or goodbye, and it has been offering previews at top prices for the past month or so at the Hellinger, where it is now scheduled, after a couple of postponements, to "open" on Feb. 23, just before it must vacate the theatre [making way for the Russell Baker–Cy Coleman musical *Home Again, Home Again*, which ultimately closed prior to Broadway], allegedly to reopen several days later as an interim booking at another house [the Broadway, where it transferred]. Although *Saravá* is reportedly still undergoing certain refinements, it clearly resembled a finished product last Friday night. But neither N. Richard Nash's book and lyrics nor Mitch Leigh's music seemed more than hack work. While Leigh's score resounds with Latin rhythms, sometimes jogging along interminably, the simple and catchy title samba, which is used repeatedly throughout the show and as a sort of *leitmotif* for the ghost, is just about the sole musical asset the show possesses. At other junctures, we hear what sounds like portentous leftovers from Leigh's *Man of La Mancha*. As for Nash's lyrics, they are on the same commonplace level as his book.

The show is visually stunning. Santo Loquasto has designed a basic setting of fairy-tale proportions, somewhat in the style of Beni Montresor, and with colorful costumes to match. There are hanging and trailing vine-like pieces, long stairways that recede and reappear, small unit sets that glide smoothly into view, and a high platform at the rear on which the orchestra, sometimes visible but mostly screened, is perched. In all respects, the production itself seems polished. But it is like a shine on an ill-made pair of boots. As it bounces along from casino to bedroom, from funeral and wedding services to bedroom, and ultimately, to no place at all, *Saravá* is without inner energy.

o   o   o

Producers Leigh and Wolsk had successfully mass-marketed the 1977 revival of *Man of La Mancha* across the country by copiously plugging the TV commercial, opening up their own phone-sale lines, et cetera. The question with *Saravá* was not whether they could *produce* a good show, but whether they could *sell* it. And they provided themselves with a massive marketing budget to that end. When *Saravá* postponed its opening—originally announced for January 30, then February 9—to February 23, the Messrs. Barnes, Eder, and Watt paid their money, stormed in, and reviewed the February 12 performance of the show-in-(not-much)-progress. ("Richard Eder is an unreasonable - - - -, and I hope he jumps off the roof of the Times Building," railed Mr. Wolsk.) *Saravá* went on to play thirty-seven previews in all before finally "opening." The producers discovered that while a vigorous TV campaign—featuring the animated logo, with dancing legs—can indeed sell an impressive number of tickets, the quality of the product itself does, ultimately, make a difference. At least on Broadway. (And for what it's worth Richard Eder was terminated by the *Times* in June.)

BROADWAY SCORECARD
/ PERFS: 140 / $: –

RAVE	FAVORABLE	MIXED	UNFAVORABLE	PAN
			2	4

SEESAW

"A New Musical"

music by Cy Coleman

lyrics by Dorothy Fields

book by Michael Bennett (with Neil Simon, replacing Michael Stewart)

based on the 1958 comedy *Two for the Seesaw* by William Gibson

directed by Michael Bennett (replacing Edwin Sherin)

choreographed by Michael Bennett (with "associate choreographers" Bob Avian and Tommy Tune; replacing Grover Dale, who remained as co-choreographer)

produced by Joseph Kipness and Lawrence Kasha, James Nederlander, George M. Steinbrenner III, and Lorin E. Price

starring Michele Lee (replacing Lainie Kazan) and Ken Howard

with Tommy Tune (replacing Bill Starr), Cecelia Norfleet (replacing Joshie Jo Armstead), Giancarlo Esposito, LaMonté Peterson (DesFontaines), Baayork Lee, and Anita Morris (Dale)

opened March 18, 1973   Uris Theatre

CLIVE BARNES, *TIMES*

Seesaw certainly has its ups and downs. Yet it has three fine performances to call its own, a bland yet efficient slickness and a certain New York brashness to it. It is the second, or maybe third, best musical of the season so far [after *A Little Night Music* and *Pippin*], which isn't really saying too much. It has a constructed air to it, and it is quite obviously built rather than inspired. The music by Cy Coleman is tuneful but not especially memorable. The score is not, perhaps, at the level of either *Little Me* [1962] or *Sweet Charity* [1966], but it has pulse and invention. There is a very right and proper show-business feel here, but the big number is missed. The music never quite takes off to the skies. Much the same is true of Dorothy Fields's lyrics, which are deft and apt

SEESAW·SEESAW·SEESAW·SEESAW·SEESAW·SEESAW·SEESAW·SEESAW·SEESAW·SEESAW·SEESAW·SEESAW·SEESAW·SEESAW

JOSEPH KIPNESS and LAWRENCE KASHA
JAMES NEDERLANDER and GEORGE M. STEINBRENNER III
present

LAINIE KAZAN   KEN HOWARD

in

SEESAW

A NEW MUSICAL

Book by MICHAEL STEWART
Music by CY COLEMAN
Lyrics by DOROTHY FIELDS

Based on the play "Two For The Seesaw" by William Gibson

with

JOSHIE JO ARMSTEAD   BILL STARR
RICHARD RYDER   CHRISTINE WILZAK

Scenic Design by   Costumes Designed by   Lighting by
ROBIN WAGNER   ANN ROTH   JULES FISHER

Musical Director
and Vocal Arrangements by   Orchestrations by   Dance Music Arranged by   Hairstyles by
DON PIPPIN   LARRY FALLON   HUGH FORRESTER   ERNEST ADLER

Associate Producer LORIN PRICE

Choreography by
GROVER DALE

Entire Production Directed by
EDWIN SHERIN

FISHER THEATRE
DETROIT
TUES., JANUARY 16 thru SAT., FEBRUARY 10
Mon. thru Sat. Evenings at 8:30   -:-   Matinees Wed. and Sat. at 2:00
Two Perfs. Sun. Jan. 28 at 2:00 & 7:00 — No Perfs. Mon. Eve. Jan. 22 & Wed. Mat. Jan. 24

SEESAW·SEESAW·SEESAW·SEESAW·SEESAW·SEESAW·SEESAW·SEESAW·SEESAW·SEESAW·SEESAW·SEESAW·SEESAW·SEESAW

An off-balanced *Two for the Seesaw*. The director, choreographer, librettist, dance arranger, and all the actors 'cept Ken Howard were replaced before *Seesaw* finally tottered to town. Maybe they should just have fired the producers? Preliminary credits. (artwork by Stubis)

enough, but seem to have more dexterity than lyricism. Michael Bennett has directed and choreographed (there are two associate choreographers and one co-choreographer listed, so it seems Bennett had a little help from his friends) with great resource and energy. And the dance numbers in particular come over with an assertive charm. Michele Lee as the Bronx waif, with shining eyes and a slightly husky voice, proved a delicious mixture of both the tough and vulnerable. She seemed perfectly credible and zany, with a show-biz passion that was absolutely exultant. Ken Howard as the slightly square, slightly hip Nebraskan lawyer, acted with a kind of out-of-town suavity, and sang and danced with zest. The best dance opportunites actually went to Tommy Tune, who was playing a choreographer, who was gay, bright and charming, and in love, in his fashion, with the girl. Tune, who is 6 feet 6 inches of chiefly leg, is a lithe, eccentric dancer and a natural performer. He stopped the show with his big number, a flamboyant affair, with high steps, balloons, confetti and spangles. And it was also a pleasure to renew acquaintance with the huge voice and easy personality of young Giancarlo Esposito [from the 1972 revival of *Lost in the Stars*], who despite his tender years is getting to be a Broadway character. *Seesaw* is probably not top-drawer Broadway musical material. You may not come out walking on air, but at least you will come out walking.

MARTIN GOTTFRIED, *WOMEN'S WEAR DAILY*

Seesaw gives its money's worth of entertainment, and that's more than I can say for most of the musicals I've seen over the last five years. Its story seems all continuity—as if the only parts cut to leave room for songs and dances were the funny parts, the interesting parts and the exciting parts. And who ever heard of a musical whose first-act finale is a bleeding ulcer attack for the heroine? But Michael Bennett has created an armful of colorful, expansive, cheerful dance numbers and given the production a professional look our musical theatre has almost forgotten; and Cy Coleman has written a score of honest-to-goodness songs that are sung by honest-to-goodness singers. Together, they have fashioned a musical that will give anyone the feeling he has seen a good show, the kind of Broadway theatre that cannot be duplicated on a movie or television screen. It is this experience, this feeling that pushes *Seesaw* beyond the obvious failure of its intentions, its patchwork construction and its practically raging inconsistency. All of this has to be to

Bennett's credit, having taken over a show that originated with an absurd idea. Not only is the story irrelevant to the secondary characters and company, but also it is far too intimate, low-keyed and unmusical in its tone and setting. The only way to make a musical out of *Two for the Seesaw* was to make a musical despite it. And that is exactly what Bennett did. He created the flimsiest excuses for dance numbers (a visit to a nightclub ["Ride Out the Storm"] being the silliest example, but there are others to challenge it). Although he has worked with Hal Prince on two landmark musicals (*Follies* [1971] and *Company* [1970]), he obviously hasn't yet developed Prince's staging imagination for conceiving the shape, look and style of an entire production. Bennett's way of dealing with the dull, heavy, show-killing story was the way of a choreographer rather than a director, throwing in one dance number after another. He wound up with dances that were external rather than inherent, but he did make a show. In fact, it is the professionalism of *Seesaw* that is its strength. The show isn't great, but it works.

WALTER KERR, *TIMES*
[Headline: "*Seesaw*—A Love of a Show"]
In what may be the nuttiest—and maybe just plain funniest—number I have ever seen in a musical ["It's Not Where You Start"], dancer Tommy Tune of *Seesaw* uses his supple heron's legs to summon on stage a chorus in blue top hats and a vast mantle of balloons, spins them about stage in a crack-the-whip exuberance that makes them seem lighter than their lighter-than-air clothing, climbs a staircase made of balloons beneath a chandelier made of balloons, and, in his irrepressible idiocy, keeps calling for ever bigger and bigger finishes. The finishes finally get so big that the floor seems knee-deep in confetti, whereupon Mr. Tune is handed a broom from the wings and ordered to clean the whole thing up. He is still very happy as he sweeps that last litter, and the last lone dancer, away. *Seesaw*, as it happens, doesn't need big finishes. It's a love of a show that knows just when to keep pressure low and when to open up. Michele Lee plays Gittel Mosca with a hip that swings so far left she'd have to break if she were breakable, all ratchety rough edges when her tart tongue is going and not a trace of a spine when a tall man is kissing her. She *says* she would break if the man who is bending her double were the least bit taller, but you know she wouldn't. When the man, who has barely met her, suggests they might try it lying down, she flaps her hap-

less hands as though they might flyaway like starlings and merely wonders aloud, "Whatever happened to leading up?" Ken Howard, who begins to look so much like John Lindsay that when he finishes this run he'll have to run for something else, is perfectly well able to meet the song-and-dance demands made on him. Director Michael Bennett has placed his stresses sensitively (except for those left-field dances in Act One), designer Robin Wagner's rising and falling panels nicely frame the amber-and-green beehive that stands in for New York, and the supporting company is just dandy. The *show* is just dandy, wonderfully satisfying simply as fun and then again as honest eavesdropping on two troubled but thoroughly engaging people.

o   o   o

When the director, librettist, star, and half the cast all decamp in Detroit, there is usually some high-powered producing going on. In this case you had a restaurateur-producer who managed to plug his fish house (Joe's Pier 52) in the opening number. But that opening number was an abrasive, ugly thing with a bunch of street hookers hassling a gentle tourist from Nebraska—the sort of setting any restaurateur in his right mind would have sued to keep his name *out* of. The artful two-character *Two for the Seesaw* was turned into *Fifty-four for the Seesaw*, and not surprisingly the dang thing tottered out of balance. Ed Sherin, of the award-winning 1968 play *The Great White Hope*, proved to be a misguided choice as director. When the Detroit première was a shambles, Joseph Kipness opted not to just fold the costly enterprise (which, as it turned out, would've *saved* him half a million); instead, he brought in Michael Bennett—codirector of *Follies*—and gave him the opportunity to delve into all aspects of the production. And delve he did. If he couldn't fix *Seesaw*, he certainly decked it out. Most visible of the departures was Lainie Kazan. Recriminations flew back and forth in the press; seems that the star had promised to shed forty pounds before the out-of-town opening, which she sure didn't, although that was only one of the problems with her performance. The authors were so anxious to see Kazan depart—she played the part "as if she were Elizabeth Barrett Browning, just about to die," per Stewart—that they agreed to have her $3,000-a-week run-of-the-play salary deducted from their royalties. (That was the plan, anyway, but *Seesaw* never did pay much in the way of royalties.) Stewart, meanwhile, balked when Bennett started rewriting the libretto.

("Everybody must be replaced in this business someday," Stewart said while trying out his *next* musical-in-trouble, the 1974 *Mack & Mabel*, "but if I'm fool enough to get myself in that position again, I promise you I won't go out with any dignity.") The final version remained mostly Stewart's, with sections—Jerry's phone calls and the Japanese restaurant scene—from Neil Simon and assorted bits and pieces from everyone else. Neither Stewart nor Simon nor accomplished librettist Dorothy Fields wanted credit, so Bennett put his name on the libretto and received a Tony nomination in the process. He split the dance chores among original choreographer Grover Dale and two assistants he imported, Bob Avian and Tommy Tune. The latter not only staged "Chapter 54, Number 1909 (The Late Great State of New York)" and "It's Not Where You Start," he ended up dancing them himself. But the 6-foot, 6-inch Tommy Tune with balloons and ribbons—and his memorable pas de deux with 4-foot, 10-inch Baayork Lee—was not enough to balance the rest of *Seesaw*. One fortunate aspect of the show was the reunion of Bennett and set designer Robin Wagner. The pair had done some marvelous "choreographed" set changes in 1968 in *Promises, Promises*; in *Seesaw* they began experimenting with the use of scenic motion as a key conceptual element. This was especially effective in the title number, with its chorus of cityfolk weaving among a stageful of scenic screens that flew up and down—just like a playground seesaw. At any rate, the battered and bloody musical comedy finally made it to Broadway, complete with a closing notice posted on opening night. The reviews were kindly, in face of the show's well-publicized woes, and business was given a boost shortly after the opening when Mayor John Lindsay—a Ken Howard look-alike—made a (well-publicized) cameo appearance. But the interesting elements of *Seesaw* were far outweighed by the weaknesses, and the $750,000 show staggered on to a hefty-for-the-time loss of $1,275,000.

Tony Awards were won by Michael Bennett (choreographer) and Tommy Tune (supporting actor).

BROADWAY SCORECARD

/ PERFS: 296 / $: –

RAVE	FAVORABLE	MIXED	UNFAVORABLE	PAN
1	3	2		

THE SELLING OF THE PRESIDENT

"An Electronic Vaudeville!"

music by Bob James

lyrics by Jack O'Brien

book by Jack O'Brien and Stuart Hample (doctored by Kenny Solms and Gail Parent)

based on the 1969 book by Joe McGinniss

director unbilled (Jack O'Brien, replacing Robert H. Livingston)

choreographed by Ethel Martin (replacing Talley Beatty)

produced by John Flaxman in association with Harold Hastings and Franklin Roberts

starring Pat Hingle

with Karen Morrow, Barbara Barrie, Johnny Olson, Robert Darnell, John Glover, and Robert Fitzsimmons (replacing Howard St. John)

opened March 22, 1972   Shubert Theatre

CLIVE BARNES, *TIMES*

The Selling of the President has an absolutely great idea for a musical. Someone should have written book, lyrics and music for it. A few years ago a very bright young journalist wrote a book about the marketing of Richard M. Nixon during his successful 1968 campaign to become the 37th President of the United States of America. The journalist was Joe McGinniss, and he entitled his book *The Selling of the President*. This musical is based on that title—not based on the book, but based on the title. It purports to describe the campaign in—note this—1976 of a fictional Senator Mason and his efforts to become the 39th President. So it seems that the authors know the result of that year's Presidential elec-

Broadway's first and only musical in which the three top-billed players had nonsinging roles. The termites were fun, though. Preliminary credits.

tion. They know less about musicals. Or at least they have some diffi-culty in putting their knowledge into practice. The music is by Bob James and is so unmemorable that you have forgotten it before you have even heard it, the lyrics are by Jack O'Brien, and the book, which could grace few libraries, is by O'Brien and Stuart Hample. The director left in Philadelphia, I am told. There is no doubt in my mind that a satiri-cal show about the ever-increasing role of the media in politics could have been hilarious. And timely. McGinniss's own book was wry, funny and sad. And it found a tone that this musical never even looks like dis-covering. The cast struggles gallantly enough with the material—rather like butterflies in a spider's web. Pat Hingle as the Presidential candi-date bustles with good humor, befuddled rhetoric and bland assurance. But the character is written as more of a Vice President than a President—that is when the character is written at all. I understand that the show cost half a million dollars to stage. Do you know there are still some states where you can enter a primary for only that, and really have some fun with your money?

MARTIN GOTTFRIED, *WOMEN'S WEAR DAILY*

The overture is the only part of *The Selling of the President* that resem-bles musical theatre. The rest of the new show alternates between being a nuisance and a shambles. For some reason, having no doubt to do with relevance and a best-selling title, the producers have tried to make musical theatre of the Joe McGinniss book that documented the tele-vision sales techniques used in President Nixon's 1968 campaign. They have not adapted it in the sense of transforming it into something musical, nor even in the sense of demonstrating the very real, inane and offensive use that modern politics makes of advertising techniques. The idea of the show is to have [the candidate] conduct his campaign in a television studio, making musical commercials. This is not only a min-imally creative idea but is totally false—song and dance commercials just aren't used in political campaigns. Also, as often as commercials have been satirized in movies and theatre, they have never come close to being like the real thing. In fact, the only commercial in *The Selling of the President* that looks like a real commercial *is* a real commercial for the company of one of the show's investors. That would represent the crudest kind of amateurism were it not challenged for the title by the

rest of the show. Every single musical number in the first act is a commercial. Not one of them is relevant to the story or characters of the
show, in fact, incredibly, not one of them is even *sung* by one of the
characters. Despite the proved musical talents of two of the lead actors
(Karen Morrow and Barbara Barrie), all songs have been assigned to
chorus members. Moreover, Pat Hingle is asked to play a candidate
who, we are told, is totally boring. Bob James' music is not music
(despite the efforts of Jonathan Tunick at disguise through orchestration). It is never even as good as the music in the commercials it is
claiming to mock. Jack O'Brien's lyrics are technically competent, but
there is nothing to be said for the book he wrote with Stuart Hample—
a book that has no story to call dull, no jokes to call unfunny, no dialogue that ever need have been spoken. I found the prospect of returning for the second act unbearable. I find the degradation of our
once-proud musical theatre by such primitives insufferable.

RICHARD WATTS, JR., POST
[Headline: "How to Elect a President?"]
A national election can be pretty dull, and to this extent *The Selling of
the President* lives up to reality. The musical comedy which crept unexpectedly into the Shubert Theatre last night is an attempt to be satirical without offense to anyone on the subject of an imaginary campaign.
While it is not painful, it has the bad luck to be completely uninspired,
lacking in anything faintly approaching stimulation. It struck me as
typical of the show's lack of expert use of its possibilities that Karen
Morrow, one of the best song-belters this side of Ethel Merman, isn't
given a number.

●   ●   ●

Joe McGinnis's dissection of the '68 Nixon campaign served as the title,
if little else, of this awkward entertainment. Not that anyone especially
wanted to hear Pat Hingle sing, but casting Barbara Barrie and especially Karen Morrow in nonsinging roles in a musical was somewhat
perplexing. *The Selling of the President* started with an April 1971 tryout
at San Francisco's A.C.T., under the hand of director Ellis Rabb (of the
floundering A.P.A. Repertory Company). He assigned the songwriting
chores to Jack O'Brien, an assistant director for the A.P.A., and Bob
James; the pair had written incidental music and lyrics for the A.P.A.'s

1968 production of *Pantagleize*. *The Selling* continued without Rabb, but as troubles multiplied, O'Brien was drafted to step in as co-librettist and—when Robert (*The Me Nobody Knows* [1970]) Livingston ankled in Philadelphia—director as well. O'Brien went on to become an award-winning director himself, but *The Selling of the President* was not the sort of showcase on which overnight success is staked. Producer John Flaxman was Hal Prince's partner in Media Productions and producer of Prince's first film, the 1970 Angela Lansbury/Hugh Wheeler *Something for Everyone*, which explains the presence of musical director/associate producer Hal Hastings and orchestrator Jonathan Tunick. While the show was produced out of the Prince office, Prince himself knew enough to stay away. (Flaxman also claimed credit [?] for the genesis of the 1968 *Maggie Flynn*.) Typically, the show stirred up more attention offstage than on. Included in the satirical proceedings—about a presidential campaign centered on modern-day television techniques—was an animated commercial for a pest control company. It was actually quite amusing: assorted animals approached Noah's Ark, two by two, with a last moment dash up the gangplank by a pair of termites. Very Nixonian, eh? The problem, though, was that this was actually a *real* commercial. Terminix, a nationwide exterminator, had invested $50,000—of $500,000—in the show. (Flaxman also arranged a $50,000 chunk from Stax Records, a Memphis-based "soul" label flush from its best-selling soundtrack from the 1971 movie *Shaft*. The *Selling* cast album was never pressed, alas.) The termites undermined the integrity of the work, assailed McGinniss and Hample in a lawsuit. "The play has mixed notices and it's being revised," complained McGinniss. "The only part they refuse to touch is the commercials." The courts allowed the show to temporarily proceed with termites intact, and *The Selling of the President* was a memory before they could be, well, exterminated. Integrity or no, the termites were the liveliest component of the evening.

BROADWAY SCORECARD
/ PERFS: 5 / $: –

RAVE	FAVORABLE	MIXED	UNFAVORABLE	PAN
				6

1776

"A New Musical"

music and lyrics by Sherman Edwards

book by Peter Stone

based on a conception by Sherman Edwards, suggested by events surrounding the signing of the Declaration of Independence on July 4, 1776

directed by Peter H. Hunt

choreographed by Onna White (replacing Rhoda Levine)

produced by Stuart Ostrow

starring William Daniels, Paul Hecht, Clifford David, Roy Poole, and Howard Da Silva

with David Ford, Ken Howard, Virginia Vestoff, Ronald Holgate, Betty Buckley (replacing Pamela Burrell), Bruce MacKay, Jonathan Moore, Ralston Hill, Robert Gaus, Emory Bass, William Duell, and Scott Jarvis

opened March 16, 1969   46th Street Theatre

CLIVE BARNES, *TIMES*

On the face of it, few historic incidents seem more unlikely to spawn a Broadway musical than that solemn moment in the history of mankind, the signing of the Declaration of Independence. Yet *1776* most handsomely demonstrated that people who merely go "on the face of it" are occasionally outrageously wrong. *1776* is a most striking, most gripping musical. I recommend it without reservation. It makes even an Englishman's heart beat a little faster. This is a musical with style, humanity, wit and passion. The characterizations are most unusually full for a musical, and even though the outcome of the story is never in very serious doubt, *1776* is consistently exciting and entertaining, for Mr. Stone's book is literate, urbane and, on occasion, very amusing. For the

1776
A New Musical Comedy

Yes, a musical comedy about the signing of the Declaration of Independence! "1776" is an original based on nothing less than one of the most significant events in the history of these United States of America. It tells it how it was. And how it was is so apropos to how it is.

In "1776," John Adams, Thomas Jefferson, Benjamin Franklin and the members of the Second Continental Congress are portrayed as the very real and fallible people they were. Composer-lyricist Sherman Edwards and librettist Peter Stone have not approached their subject matter with scholastic reverence, but rather with a theatrical vitality, as in fact was practiced by the representatives of the thirteen colonies. "1776" is not a pageant. It is an honest revelation of what went on behind the scenes during the amazing days of our Revolution. The birth of our nation contains the elements of human farce, not to mention the usual human stupidities. But in spite of everything, and perhaps because of everything, there came forth the most masterful expression of the American mind.

"1776" is not necessarily designed for flag-waving. It is mostly funny and mostly musical and is designed to entertain theater audiences. But if you feel like standing up once again for your country . . . we'll understand.

"If you feel like standing up once again for your country . . . we'll understand," wrote the copywriter. How to sell a musical about the signing of the Declaration of Independence? Not easy—until the critics and word of mouth made *1776* the sleeper hit of the late '60s. (artwork by Fay Gage)

music it would have been easy for Mr. Edwards to have produced a pastiche of Revolutionary tunes, but this he has studiously avoided. There is admittedly a flavor here, but the music is absolutely modern in its sound, and it is apt, convincing and enjoyable. The authors have, bravely perhaps although in the event it seems perfectly natural, omitted any chorus, so that absolutely everyone in the cast has a significant part to play. This offers a great challenge to the actors and to the people responsible for the staging. William Daniels has given many persuasive performances in the past, but nothing, I think, can have been so effective as his John Adams here. This is a beautiful mixture of pride, ambition, an almost priggish sense of justice and yet—the saving grace in the character—an ironic self-awareness. Stone and Edwards provided Daniels with the character to play, but Daniels plays it to the hilt. Also, notably, he still remains perfectly in character when he sings. The other star performance is provided by Howard Da Silva as Ben Franklin. Da Silva has a voice as sweet as molasses and as mellow as rum, and his humor and good nature are a constant delight. But enough. I cannot mention all 26 of the actors, and yet utter fairness would demand no less. The musical will, I suspect, prove to be the sleeper of the season. Who knows, it might even run until the celebration of the bicentenary in 1976. I rather hope so. Certainly you don't have to be a historian to love *1776*.

JOHN CHAPMAN, *DAILY NEWS*
[Headline: "It's Funny, Moving and Artistic"]
A magnificently staged and stunningly original musical. It is far, far off the Broadway path and far away in time. Its simple title is *1776*. It is warm with a life of its own; it is funny, it is moving. It plays without intermission, because an intermission would break its spell. It is an artistic creation such as we do not often find in our theatre. Often, as I sat enchanted in my seat, it reminded me of Gilbert and Sullivan in its amused regard of human frailties; again, in its music, it struck me as a new opera. All the performances are good, and in particular I bring to mind a brash and breezy impersonation of Richard Henry Lee—one of the Lees of Virginia, of course—by Ronald Holgate. And Ken Howard is stubborn and stalwart as Thomas Jefferson. The songs and lyrics are remarkably original. Some of them are big and heroic, others are light and deft. One of the light ones which particularly took my fancy was

"He Plays the Violin," an affectionate tribute to Jefferson sung and danced by Betty Buckley, Da Silva, and Daniels. See *1776* right away, before Broadway kills it.

MARTIN GOTTFRIED, *WOMEN'S WEAR DAILY*

What Broadway needed was a patriotic musical, right? I don't think so. *1776* has thrown in two lines (maybe three) about "commitment," as if they referred the show to the current revolutionary movements, but the new musical has as much to do with present rebellion as a watermelon to a race riot. *1776* is pure patriotic documentary, right down to the Liberty Bell ringing at the finale, and its only surprise is no American flag with every program. It's really kind of difficult to believe that Peter Stone actually set out to write a musical about the decision of the Continental Congress to declare America independent. Yet there it is, complete with a calendar ticking off (I believe the expression is) the days until the Fourth of July. Nor is that the only peculiar thing about this show. It begins with at least 10 solid minutes of music—music that seems written, if you can imagine, for an operetta by Mozart, complete with recitative and harpsichord. Need I say, this is soon enough abandoned for show-time patriotism, but then again, music is almost abandoned entirely. There are endless stretches without any songs at all, and not a single dance (well, a suggested minuet and that's it). Then suddenly, there is a burst of long and rather involved song. It is rather a strange production, even aside from the fact that it has no intermission at all, stretching its two hours and twenty minutes from the endless to the eternal. Peter Hunt's staging left everything to be desired, and then some. His big ending is to leave the signers of the Declaration in a tableau exactly like the famous painting, but since they were more or less glued to those spots all night, it was hardly a feat. Anyhow, I wouldn't have believed I would ever see such a tableau in any theatre. Mr. Hunt is inclined to running jokes (a soldier clonking cross-stage, or repeated remarks by the same character) and that tactic more or less sums up his finesse. The individual performances were examples of professionals on their own—Howard Da Silva (Franklin), William Daniels (Adams). They earned all the praise such professionalism deserves. That's more than I can say for their vehicle—a wooden replica of souvenir-shop patriotism.

WALTER KERR, *TIMES*

1776 is, quite properly, the most independent new musical in years, and if you've got any character of your own you'll probably go to see it instantly, just to keep its independence company. Look at what it's up to. It really is about the American Revolution, seriously, playfully, plainly, preposterously. Wigs and all. In addition to having no title, it has no stars, not what the ticket agencies would call stars, anyway. And in addition to having no title and no stars, it hasn't got a chorus line. In fact, it hasn't even got an intermission. And it's just dandy. Just dandy precisely because it has a mind of its own. It will not do things anybody else's way, even if everybody else has always been right, and for a while you naturally think it's going to be just too young and green and naive—rather like the country that's being hatched between songs—for the sophisticated commerce of Broadway. Isn't it going to fall into pageantry, or patriotism, or something absolutely awful? How, pray, do you get a musical, rather than a Channel 13 television show, out of [the subject]? By going about your business without compromise, apology, self-consciousness, piety or fear, I guess. For instance, *1776* isn't the least bit afraid to be clear about the whole technical matter of rounding up the necessary number of delegates to get the Declaration passed. It assumes that the process is interesting, it is willing to rip through an entire scene without a musical number to interrupt the political needle-work, and it is so successful in its assumption that you find yourself grasping without effort the relative positions of all 13 colonies, a triumph you probably weren't able to manage when you took American History in high school. The show makes you feel smarter than you used to be, which is a gracious thing for librettist Peter Stone to have arranged, and smarter without having had to slave for it. Mr. Stone's book has the outline and energy of a hockey game: he's convinced you it's fun to keep score. Book and music do what they want to do, not what musical-comedy custom dictates, and they do it confidently and so well that you grin and go along quietly. An original, strangely determined, immensely pleasing evening.

*   *   *

How about a musical about the signing of the Declaration of Independence? Thus mused Sherman Edwards, a history teacher turned pop songwriter ("Wonderful, Wonderful") from Morristown, New Jersey, where G. Washington headquartered during the cold, cold winter of 1776–1777. Edwards toiled ten long years on this not-so-hot proposition, but then it had taken Broadway neophyte Meredith Willson nearly as long to land his 1957 *Music Man*. (Edwards, Willson, and producer Stuart Ostrow all shared a not-so-common denominator: mentor Frank Loesser.) Strange things happen along the rialto, though, and *1776* finally swept into town—with a measly $60,000 box office advance on a full half-million-dollar cost. Columbia Records, which had fronted the entire capitalization of Ostrow's *We Take the Town* [1962] and *The Apple Tree* [1966], understandably—but unwisely—cut their investment down to only 20 percent. Oh, well. Edgar M. Bronfman, of Seagram's, astutely anted up $250,000. 1600 Pennsylvania Avenue Dept.: On G. Washington's birthday in 1970— his 238th—*1776*'s cast played a special performance commemorating the event in the East Room of the White House. Presidential aide William Safire requested that they cut some material, namely the pacifistic dirge "Momma Look Sharp" and the righteously Right "Cool, Cool Considerate Men." Nope, said Ostrow, take the whole show or nothing. He also insisted that the cast approve the command appearance (this being mid-Vietnam). After the show the President pointed out that original tenant Abigail Adams had used the East Room to do the laundry. "You can hang your wash in here anytime," jested Mr. Nixon.

Winner of the New York Drama Critics' Circle Award. In addition to winning the Tony Award for Best Musical, Tonys were won by Peter Hunt (director) and Ron Holgate (supporting actor). William Daniels—a shoo-in for the latter award—refused his supporting actor nomination, arguing that his first-star billing entitled him to a nomination for the leading actor Tony (which went to Jerry Orbach for *Promises, Promises*).

BROADWAY SCORECARD

/ PERFS: 1,217 / $: +

RAVE	FAVORABLE	MIXED	UNFAVORABLE	PAN
5				1

70, GIRLS, 70

"A New Musical"

music by John Kander

lyrics by Fred Ebb

book by Fred Ebb and Norman L. Martin (replacing Joe Masteroff); "adaptation by Joe Masteroff"

based on the 1958 British comedy *Breath of Spring* by Peter Coke

"entire production supervised by Stanley Prager"

directed by Paul Aaron (replaced by Stanley Prager, who replaced original director/choreographer Ron Field)

choreographed by Onna White

produced by Arthur Whitelaw

starring Mildred Natwick, Hans Conried (replacing David Burns, who replaced Eddie Foy), and Lillian Roth

with Gil Lamb, Lillian Hayman, Lucie Lancaster, Goldye Shaw, Dorothea Freitag, Joey Faye, Henrietta Jacobson, Coley Worth, and Tommy Breslin

opened April 15, 1971   *Broadhurst Theatre*

MARTIN GOTTFRIED, *WOMEN'S WEAR DAILY*

I have never been able to walk out on Broadway musicals because something in my nice-Jewish-boy background told me that respect must be paid when the financial investment is so great. We are supposed to be embarrassed by such instincts, and I duly am, admitting them only now that *70, Girls, 70* had the negative power to overcome the near overwhelming strength of my conditioning. In its technical quality, *70, Girls, 70* is hardly unprofessional, but as a whole (should I say as a half?)

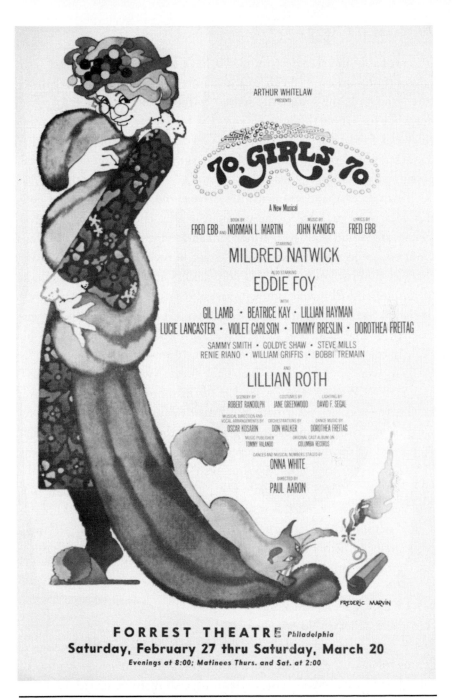

ARTHUR WHITELAW
PRESENTS

70, GIRLS, 70

A New Musical

BOOK BY
FRED EBB AND NORMAN L. MARTIN

MUSIC BY
JOHN KANDER

LYRICS BY
FRED EBB

STARRING

MILDRED NATWICK

ALSO STARRING

EDDIE FOY

WITH

GIL LAMB · BEATRICE KAY · LILLIAN HAYMAN
LUCIE LANCASTER · VIOLET CARLSON · TOMMY BRESLIN · DOROTHEA FREITAG

SAMMY SMITH · GOLDYE SHAW · STEVE MILLS
RENIE RIANO · WILLIAM GRIFFIS · BOBBI TREMAIN

AND

LILLIAN ROTH

SCENERY BY
ROBERT RANDOLPH

COSTUMES BY
JANE GREENWOOD

LIGHTING BY
DAVID F. SEGAL

MUSICAL DIRECTION AND
VOCAL ARRANGEMENTS BY
OSCAR KOSARIN

ORCHESTRATIONS BY
DON WALKER

DANCE MUSIC BY
DOROTHEA FREITAG

MUSIC PUBLISHER
TOMMY VALANDO

ORIGINAL CAST ALBUM ON
COLUMBIA RECORDS

DANCES AND MUSICAL NUMBERS STAGED BY

ONNA WHITE

DIRECTED BY

PAUL AARON

FREDERIC MARVIN

FORREST THEATRE Philadelphia
Saturday, February 27 thru Saturday, March 20
Evenings at 8:00; Matinees Thurs. and Sat. at 2:00

Little old lady in slippers and fur plays with dynamite, guess what happens. Six of the "Old Folks" and the director were gone by the time *70, Girls* limped into the Broadhurst. Preliminary credits. (artwork by Frederic Marvin)

it is probably the sloppiest musical I have ever seen. Its creators have concentrated on every detail of the standard Broadway musical structure—the look, the sound, the sense—without once (seeming to) wonder what the whole thing was about. Evidently, the only reason for this story was to cast the production with 70-year-olds to explore the (rather condescending) theme that people that age can be energetic and vital, presumably thrilling us with that spectacle. Aside from treating these people in its cast, and implicitly all 70-year-olds, as some kind of pets, this idea only guaranteed the production of a chorus of semi-professionals and some leads who either looked a stage-version of 190 (Hans Conried) or just looked as if they didn't know what they were doing there in the first place (Mildred Natwick). The pity is that the talents of Kander and Ebb were not just wasted on such nonsense—they were degraded. Kander might have tried harder, even within this trashy vernacular, but he evidently didn't have the inclination. Ebb had all his beats in the right places, but not his heart. It must have been curious for them to work with directors like Paul Aaron (who started the show) and Stanley Prager (who finished it off in more ways than one) after having spent their career with the likes of Harold Prince and Gower Champion. Most composers and lyricists think only as far as their scores and let the directors do the conceiving. *Zorbá* [1968] and *Cabaret* [1966], whether they worked or not, were aiming for something worthwhile. Now, at least, they know the humiliation of being a part of a mindless Broadway musical machine. Be kind to Miss Natwick. She is a good actress with a fine quality, put in the position here of playing a cross between Deborah Kerr and Molly Picon. It is the only kindness the degrading production deserves.

WALTER KERR, *TIMES*
[Headline: "Please, No *80, Girls, 80*"]
Someone connected with *70, Girls, 70* has an almost mathematical genius for taking risks that are certain to fail. Let me go over a few of them just in case anyone else is planning a show to be called *80, Girls, 80*. (It was once a novel and then a British film called *Make Mine Mink* and then about six other things, if the program credits are to be believed, before two good tunesmiths, John Kander and Fred Ebb, thought of adding tunes to it without thinking how.) The very form that the show takes is, I think, a misunderstanding. Approximately half

of the numbers are sung inside the storyline—Lillian Roth, her dimples still leaping to life every time she parts her lips in song, caroling away while she keeps store detectives at bay—and the other half are deliberately out-of-frame, disconnected. These laughs are straight vaudeville turns, done mainly and marvelously by anatomy-snapping Lillian Hayman, who has more anatomy to snap than most people, with some first-rate assistance from Henrietta Jacobson and Tommy Breslin; they are simply listed as taking place on the stage of the Broadhurst Theatre, which is where we are. This halved format, I suspect, is derived from the splendid use to which Kander-Ebb songs were put in *Cabaret*. There, a good half of the musical eruptions were simply flash-acts in a nightclub floor show, standing on their own without direct connections to the narrative. But, in *Cabaret*, they served a clear and consistent purpose. Here there is no link, subtle or otherwise. The old-folk aren't one-time performers as, say, at least some of them are in *Follies* [1971]. And nothing they do depends upon a showbiz ambiance, with Miss Hayman belting out "Broadway My Street" or a rainfall of banjos dropping from the skies so that the whole Senior Citizen gang can strum away mightily. The effect is merely schizoid, not a cunning trick of style. The songs are independently attractive, the Don Walker orchestrations are astonishingly fresh, the performers are personable, and the determination to do things the wrong way 'round is a lot like that of the animal-trainer who spent years teaching a camel the extraordinary feat of walking backwards. He never could get his act into a circus because nobody out front knew that camels don't walk backwards.

DOUGLAS WATT, *DAILY NEWS*
About as enlivening an affair as a New Year's Eve party thrown by the members of a St. Petersburg shuffleboard club. For that's exactly what this musical is up to, trying to reassure us that old age can be fun, by golly. The message was so encouraging that it had me squirming in my seat. (The pit musicians all wear colored jerseys, by the way.)

•   •   •

Old folks sitting around a retirement home plotting to pilfer fur coats. Not an especially likely follow-up for the authors of *Cabaret*, what? *70, Girls, 70*, actually, *was* quite like the two-track *Cabaret*, with performers singing in character and out of character (and out of lack of character, in some places). The action and framework were split in two, as in the earlier piece; in place of Joel Grey and his Kit Kat Klub turns we had a mismatched odd couple—the great Lillian Hayman and little old Jewish lady Goldye Shaw—doing corny vaudeville routines while the plot characters were offstage changing costumes and gulping oxygen. (*Variety*'s out-of-town correspondent referred to the company as Medicare Minstrels.) It seems ludicrous to compare *70, Girls* to *Cabaret* or to Kander and Ebb's subsequent "Musical Vaudeville" *Chicago* (1975); but somehow or other this geriatric romp was more sympathetic, more charming, and more playfully likable than its two stylish betters. Even with its fraying weak spots and threadbare holes. The idea had been to musicalize the 1960 British film farce *Make Mine Mink*. The rights were unavailable, though, so the authors proceeded with the rights to the underlying play (leaving improvements made for the screenplay off limits). *Cabaret* librettist Joe Masteroff left the project early on, with his name remaining on the "adaptation"; director/choreographer Ron Field, of *Cabaret* and *Zorbá*, also dropped out before rehearsals. The next director, Paul Aaron (from the 1969 Off-Broadway rock musical *Salvation*), was fired in Philadelphia. He was replaced by Stanley Prager, who had similarly stepped in—to similar effect—on producer Arthur Whitelaw's previous *Minnie's Boys* (1970). Medicare Minstrel Dept.: The Philadelphia tryout was cut short during the Saturday matinee on March 12 when the much-loved funnyman Davey Burns—*Dolly!*'s gruff Vandergelder, Pseudolus's licentious master in *A Funny Thing* (1962), Mayor Shinn of *The Music Man* (1957)—keeled over in the wings of the Forrest after singing and dancing and doing what was described as "an hysterical xylophone act without touching the keys" to the song "Go Visit Your Grandmother." And what better way for a greasepaint-in-the-blood trouper to go?

BROADWAY SCORECARD

/ PERFS: 36 / $: –

RAVE	FAVORABLE	MIXED	UNFAVORABLE	PAN
	2	1		3

SHELTER

"A Musical"

music by Nancy Ford

book and lyrics by Gretchen Cryer

directed by Austin Pendleton

choreographed by Sammy Bayes

produced by Richard Fields and Peter Flood

starring Marcia Rodd, Terry Kiser, Susan Browning, and Joanna Merlin

with Tony Wells, Philip Kraus, Charles Collins, and Britt Swanson

opened February 6, 1973   John Golden Theatre

MARTIN GOTTFRIED, *WOMEN'S WEAR DAILY*

If there hasn't been much good theatre to anticipate lately, *Shelter* was one show I had really been looking forward to—the Broadway debut of Gretchen Cryer and Nancy Ford, who had written the extremely clever and unusual *Last Sweet Days of Isaac* [1970, Off-Broadway] a few seasons back. But the musical at the Golden Theatre is two steps backward for the writing team, a beginner's off-Broadway show rather than proven talent given more money to work with. Although *Shelter* again deals with television and computers, where *Isaac* was modern in a very MacLuhan way, the new show is linear and ultra-conventional for all its doodads and gizmos. Moreover and worse, it is an unmusical musical and an undramatic play. . . . Nearly all the remaining time in the play involves the writer's best friend (almost too trite, coy and foolish to describe), a computer named Arthur who performs tricks for his master's comfort, company and assistance, a sort of visual-audio seduction aid. Arthur projects slides on a cyclorama and two screens, all of them in the gross, Kodachrome style of picture postcards (sunrises, rural summer and winterscapes, night skies, etc.). These were designed by the very talented Tony Walton. I hope satirically. (If so, the satire wasn't obvious enough, and if not, God help him.) Arthur also sings songs, a good deal louder than the principals and in a nondescript voice. Since there is much earnest talk throughout the play about reality, this plastic, singing commercial voice (Tony Wells) could possibly have been meant to be inhuman too, but I think that is a generous allowance. Musically, *Shelter* is, well, unmusical. Nancy Ford's songs have neither harmonic lines nor melodic ones, which is something of a handicap when it comes to composing. They are almost all haphazardly inserted at arbitrary points in the script. Between their similarity (they are nearly all in the Peter, Paul and Mary vernacular), the relatively small number of them, and the seemingly endless drone of undeveloping plot, they don't seem part of the show at all.

DOUGLAS WATT, *DAILY NEWS*
[Headline: "A Whimsy with Music"]
I don't expect you to believe any of this, but the hero of *Shelter*, an unnerving bit of musical whimsy that came to the Golden last night, is a happily married fellow who lives apart from his wife and their seven adopted children of as many races. He lives in a set—kitchen, bedroom and bath—in a television studio. And he is regularly visited by a young woman named Wednesday November. I mean every word, though I'm beginning to feel queasy. . . . When Miss November, clutching a stringless (more whimsy) guitar, confessed, "I only know two chords," I realized she was speaking for the composer. Believe it or not, though, it is Wednesday November, a cleaning woman who also sleeps with Michael, who invests the evening with its single bit of charm. She is given just as stupid things to say as any of the others are, but ah! she is played by Susan Browning, who possesses an enchantment all her own, unfettered by witless books and inane songs. Miss Browning, who is adorable, dwells in a strange, fanciful world undreamed of by such pedestrian fantasists as the Misses Cryer and Ford. I seem to recall that *The Last Sweet Days of Isaac* took place in an elevator. There's an elevator in *Shelter*, too, and the ladies [in the cast] use it to depart, one by one. I wish I'd thought of it first.

◦   ◦   ◦

Finally: a Broadway musical written entirely by women! Cause for celebration, it seemed, although it turned out to be a reduced-scale *Celebration* (1969). Women writers, clearly, are as talented and capable as men, but for some reason very few have displayed the desire or had the opportunity to enter musical theatre (with an emphasis on the opportunity). Back during World War I, Anne Caldwell (1867–1936) had become one of the more steadily successful musical theatre writers of her time, writing seven shows for star Fred Stone and eight to tunes by Jerome Kern. Dorothy Donnelly (1880–1928) collaborated with Sigmund Romberg on long-running operettas *Blossom Time* (1921) and *The Student Prince* (1924). Dorothy Fields (1904–1974) came along in the late 1920s—a top-rate writer who happened to be a woman, rather than a woman who could write—and remained in the upper echelon until her death. By the time Betty Comden (1915–) reached Broadway in 1944, gender didn't really matter. At least in the word department, that is; all of the above were lyricist/librettists. Broadway's first exceptional female composer, which is to say a good composer who happened not to be a man, was Kay Swift (1905–1995). Swift gained instant acclaim as the stock market tumbled, with two brilliant revue songs—"Can't We Be Friends?" and "Can This Be Love"—and the hit show *Fine and Dandy* (1930), whose title song has long since been commandeered by magicians (to the point that nobody can hum more than four bars). Swift then left lyricist/husband Paul James—in real life banker James P. Warburg—and cut short her career to become muse to George Gershwin. And we didn't hear from another female composer until Mary Rodgers (1931–) wrote the refreshing *Once Upon a Mattress* in 1959. The 1963 Judy Holliday megaflop *Hot Spot* sent Rodgers running for cover, though. The dexterous but underexposed Carolyn Leigh (1926–1983) wrote lyrics for four musicals, including *Peter Pan* (1954) and *Little Me* (1962). There were several other women songwriters over the years, fringe players like Alma Sanders (of Carlo and Sanders), June Sillman Carroll of her brother Leonard's *New Faces* series, Anne Croswell of *Tovarich* (1963), and Marian Grudeff of *Baker Street* (1965)—but that was it. So it was big news when Off-Broadway's Gretchen Cryer and Nancy Ford stormed 45th Street with the first Broadway musical written exclusively by women (other than some prewar vanity productions). And it was extremely disappointing to find their *Shelter* just another negligible trifle. Cryer—whose then-husband, David, leading man of *Come Summer* (1969) and *Ari* (1971), was also thwarted in his Broadway bid—and Ford never returned to Broadway, although they enjoyed a long-running downtown hit with *I'm Getting My Act Together and Taking It on the Road* (1978). <u>Off the Record Dept.</u>: Many musicals had preopening record deals—hence plugs for nonexistent cast albums on the billing pages of many a flop. *Shelter* was an unusual case in that Columbia Records actually recorded the show but never released it. The only other unreleased major-label original cast album that comes to mind is the Saul Chaplin/Betty Comden/Adolph Green *Bonanza Bound!* (1948), recorded by RCA during the musical's aborted, nine-performance Philadelphia tryout. The Gold Rush farce featured lyricist/librettist Green as Leonardo da Vinci (not the Italian da Vinci, the *other* one) and Green's then-wife, Allyn McLerie, as unlikely lovers. Both recordings have surfaced on bootleg tapes; *Bonanza* is, needless to say, far more interesting than the hapless *Shelter*.

BROADWAY SCORECARD
/ PERFS: 31 / $: —

RAVE	FAVORABLE	MIXED	UNFAVORABLE	PAN
	1		3	2

SHENANDOAH

"The New Musical," previously entitled *Shenandoah, The Only Home I Know*

music by Gary Geld

lyrics by Peter Udell

book by James Lee Barrett, with Peter Udell and Philip Rose

based on the 1965 screenplay by James Lee Barrett

directed by Philip Rose

choreographed by Robert Tucker

produced by Philip Rose and Gloria and Louis K. Sher

starring John Cullum

with Donna Theodore, Penelope Milford, Joel Higgins, Ted Agress, Gordon Halliday, Chip Ford, and Joseph Shapiro

opened January 7, 1975   Alvin Theatre

CLIVE BARNES, *TIMES*

The traditional American musical, full of high principles and strong ballads, simple truths and simpler sentiments, seems to have passed out of favor in recent seasons. Well, *Shenandoah* is an attempt to bring it back into style. In some respects it succeeds, such as the fine cast, with the superlative acting and singing of John Cullum in the leading role, and in other respects it is less fortunate. But the aspirations are brave and the results, despite a distressing sentimentality, remain lusty. *Shenandoah* was originally tried out last summer at the Goodspeed Opera House in East Haddam, Conn., where it won golden opinions. The overall look of the show is poor—it seems as though it came all too hotfoot from Connecticut, without really stopping on the way in to get gussied up for Broadway. This was a mistake. John Cullum has had many Broadway chances, including the starring role in *On a Clear Day*

You Can See Forever [1965], but no role has extended him so well and to such splendid advantage. He is an actor-singer of the quality of Richard Kiley, and *Shenandoah* shows it all. He can even make partially convincing some maudlin conversations with the grave of his wife, and the warmth, tone and characterization of his voice are exemplary. *Shenandoah* will please most those who like musicals a little serious and a trifle old-fashioned. But it is nice to have a show around that not only dares to be tuneful but is even willing to throw in a morsel of moral uplift along with the country-style jokes. So even if some people may find the sweetness of that Southern molasses somewhat cloying (it even has a wet-eye ending), a lot of people will have a good time. It is a very likable musical.

MARTIN GOTTFRIED, POST

Shenandoah is as corny as Kansas and Iowa and *Oklahoma!* [1943] would wish it had never invented fake farmland musicals if it saw the one that opened last night. With all its homespun wisdom and sentimental Americana, *Shenandoah* should be sold at Disneyland souvenir shops. As musical theatre it is contemporary enough to be recorded at 78 rpm. The show is based on the 1965 James Stewart movie of the same name—one I don't remember, though it had to have had a better second act. The book is told in sketches of dialogue, patched together for a shorthand story. These episodes are separated by ballads, comic numbers and many songs of sterling courage. Such construction is so strictly according to the old Rodgers and Hammerstein formula you can almost see the director, onstage, with a mixed-up instruction manual in his hand. Even still, I don't see why he bothered with the second act since there was more energy spent on raising and lowering the curtain than on what happened between. The show has a theme that says war is bad. It also has very little choreography. When it does dance everyone hooks a thumb into a waistband or slaps a knee and whoops and hollers and does farmy things. Almost everything is played to the audience and aside from looking chintzy, the show appears like a pop-up kiddie picture book only less active. I would like to think that *Shenandoah* was a cynical attempt to commercialize Americana. Condescension isn't much, but it's better than delivering this nonsense seriously and amateurishly. Heaven help them, I think the show's makers were sincere.

WALTER KERR, *TIMES*

[Headline: "*Shenandoah* Finds Beauty in Old Truths"]

Why am I so deeply moved by *Shenandoah*, a musical that strikes me as singularly beautiful in its spareness? Surely each of its Civil War folk gestures is a gesture we have seen made before, fifty or a hundred times to boot. Clichés, the lot of them. But clichés are not born. They are made. No familiar situation, no swiftly recognizable speech pattern, was old hat to begin with. It was once—on some odd day, out of some sudden impulse—a fresh, blunt perception of the way things were, a *seeing* that might later be sewn into a farmhouse sampler but that was just now simple, direct, revealing. It was foursquare before it was square. It must also have had some sort of recognizable truth about it or it would not have been repeated so endlessly. I confess that when I first saw *Shenandoah* at the Goodspeed Opera House last summer I felt embarrassed by, among other things, the so-conventional friendship between a Tom Sawyerish white boy and a Topsy-and-Eva-ish young slave. But *Shenandoah* had fooled me, had been making subliminal claims on my emotions; I wound up, quite startled, in tears. For what James Lee Barrett, Gary Geld and Peter Udell have done is to seize upon the most commonplace of *Saturday Evening Post* covers, strip it of both the prettification and the mockery we've progressively applied to it, and offer it as the original bare bones of legend—lean, unapologetic, glistening in just that degree of stylization that makes it seem a reflection on water. The show is going to have a try at recovering the dawn of all we know so well, and it is going to do it on firmly booted feet, with open throat, plain as plain can be. Whatever its occasional faults (narrative, mainly), it is all of a piece; it belongs to itself. Innocence, in the theatre, is hard to come by, harder to believe in. It is also a quality difficult to tap in ourselves; few of us possess much, worn as we are. Put worn materials and worn eyes together and *Shenandoah* may elude you. Seeing it, don't *think* too soon. Let it make the first move; it knows where it's going and just possibly where it's come from.

HOWARD KISSEL, *WOMEN'S WEAR DAILY*

Shenandoah seems altogether like a high-school pageant. The earnest artlessness of it is rather a novelty for Broadway, where it is likely to be taken as a sign of innocence and purity rather than simply lack of craft. Granted that the book does almost nothing in the way of developing either character or situation, it is hard to fault the performers for having a historical pageant stiffness. The men do knee-slapping dances and strike poses of hearty camaraderie—as if American males of the 1860s were all jocks in the chorus of the varsity show. The opening number has the men of the chorus divided equally into Yanks and Rebs, who do maneuvers with rifles and ultimately point them at the audience, an amateurish gesture that inevitably recalls the big production number in Mel Brooks's *The Producers* [the 1968 film] and is, alas, all too characteristic of choreographer Robert Tucker's pre–Agnes de Mille style. John Cullum as the father brings a strong stage presence and a rich, dramatic voice to basically insipid material. It is sad to think how few opportunities Broadway has made for genuine talent like Cullum's in the last few years, but *Shenandoah* is not really a return to traditional Broadway musical styles, just a weak imitation.

*   *   *

When people speak of the old-fashioned, Rodgers and Hammerstein-type musical, they rarely stop to point out that, in the first place, the stories were interesting and well told, and in the second place, the songs—which were the only reason for musical theatre in the first place—were typically wonderful. An "old-fashioned musical" with poor book and middling songs, history tells us, is just as bad as a contemporary musical with poor book and middling songs. Worse, even. *Shenandoah* was a pacifist musical so baldly vapid that antiwar protesters—most of whom wouldn't be caught dead at a traditional musical in 1975 anyway—could only roll their eyes in disbelief at the clunky corn. Unable to raise the necessary funds for Broadway, Phil Rose arranged a tryout at the Goodspeed Opera House, which had launched *Man of La Mancha* nine summers earlier. The leading role (created by James Stewart in the film) was written for Robert Ryan, who died in 1973. Jack Palance was cast next, but he wasn't going to work for summer stock money. Thus, John Cullum, who had starred the previous summer in Goodspeed's well-received production of John Philip Sousa's *El Capitan* (1896), was tapped for the role. The tryout—under the mellifluous title *Shenandoah, The Only Home I Know*—fortuitously received two book-those-theatre-parties raves from Walter Kerr in the *New York Times* and Kevin Kelly in the *Boston Globe*. Which directly translated into the $500,000 capitalization and a booking at the Alvin, preceded by a shakedown in Boston. (If the truth be known, the major chunk of financing came from a sweet, sun-tanned gentleman from Phoenix under indictment for transporting and distributing pornographic films—*School Girls* was the title cited—who figured *Shenandoah* would buy him some points with the Feds. So much for family values.) Cullum, with Kerr and Kelly firmly in his corner, stayed in place and proved to be the sturdy rock on which *Shenandoah* was built. The critical reception to the show itself was mixed to unfavorable; the only critics who really loved the post–Goodspeed production were, you guessed it, Kerr and Kelly. The show managed to get by thanks to Cullum's performance, modest running costs, and a lack of other product for audiences in search of an old-fashioned musical. It also profited from an innovative television campaign. Instead of filming one of those expensively glossy Madison Avenue spots in favor at the time (following the example set by the 1971 *Pippin*), *Shenandoah* prepared four different commercials—shot outdoors on economical videotape—and targeted each to a specific audience. Thus, the soap opera ladies got Cullum sitting on a porch crooning "Papa's Gonna Make it Alright" to an infant who didn't appear in the show (baby courtesy of adwoman Nancy Coyne). The more rugged audiences got the strong-voiced Cullum striding through the marshes of Pound Ridge, New York, intoning "this land don't belong to Virginia." The Broadway run was cut short when the show was bumped from the Alvin into the more expensive Hellinger to make way for its stepsister from Goodspeed, the one about the little red-headed orphan and her sandy-colored dog. *Shenandoah* managed to turn a modest profit, though. (I'm pleased to report that my 1995 profit distribution check was for a walloping 63¢!) A revival, for some unfathomable reason, trudged into the Virginia on August 8, 1989, for thirty-one soapy perfs.

Tony Awards were won by James Lee Barrett, Peter Udell, and Philip Rose (book), and John Cullum (actor).

BROADWAY SCORECARD

/ PERFS: 1,050 / $: +

RAVE	FAVORABLE	MIXED	UNFAVORABLE	PAN
1	1	1		3

SHERRY!

"An Intoxicating Musical," previously entitled *Dinner with Sherry*

music by Laurence Rosenthal

book and lyrics by James Lipton

based on the 1939 comedy *The Man Who Came to Dinner* by George S. Kaufman and Moss Hart

"staging and direction supervised by Joe Layton" (replacing director Morton Da Costa and choreographer Ronald Field)

produced by Lee Guber, Frank Ford, and Shelly Gross

starring Clive Revill (replacing George Sanders), Dolores Gray, and Elizabeth Allen

with Jon Cypher, Byron Webster, Janet Fox, Eddie Lawrence, Cliff Hall, Paula Trueman, Donald Burr, and Mary Loane

opened March 28, 1967   Alvin Theatre

MARTIN GOTTFRIED, *WOMEN'S WEAR DAILY*

Like *The Man Who Came to Dinner, Sherry!* moved into the Alvin Theatre last night and simply refused to move. Or do anything else, for that matter. The trouble is, it is perfectly awful. The humor is seldom amusing for three reasons: in the first place, it is a terribly dated kind of comedy. Secondly, the remarks themselves are not especially sharp ("You reform school fugitive"). Third, they—as well as Algonquin Circle sophistication and the production's whole Thirties milieu—have grown into camp. Now you can have it only one way, either playing for nostalgia, hoping the wit still works, or camping it. Some of *Sherry!* is played straight while other parts are preciously mocked. Mr. Lipton enjoys a deep swim in Thirties dances and turned out a very funny mock-Fred Astaire scene, but Lipton was still being very straightforward. This could never possibly work, especially with Dolores Gray pouring everything on for the benefit of the boys in the balcony. Now I

LEE GUBER   FRANK FORD   SHELLY GROSS
present

GEORGE SANDERS

DOLORES GRAY   ELIZABETH ALLEN

in

SHERRY!

a new musical comedy

Entire Production Directed By
MORTON DA COSTA

Monday thru Thursday at 8:30: $7.95, 6.75, 6.00, 5.50, 4.50, 3.00.
Friday & Saturday at 8:30: $8.95, 8.00, 7.00, 6.00, 5.00, 4.00, 3.00.
Wednesday Matinees at 2:30: $5.50, 5.00, 4.50, 3.50, 2.50, 2.00.
Saturday Matinees at 2:30: $6.50, 6.00, 5.50, 4.50, 3.00.

SHUBERT THEATRE 250 SOUTH BROAD STREET PE 5-4768

George Sanders cracks a mean whip as *Sherry!*'s wheelchair runs out of control. The show lamely staggered to town with neither Sanders, director "Tec" Da Costa, nor choreographer Ron Field in attendance. Preliminary credits. (artwork by Jack Davis)

honestly do not know whether Miss Gray is aware of her special, camp appeal, but in her ultra-brassy, female-parody performance; in the ridiculous costumes [designed by Robert Mackintosh] stretched for her almost-matronly figure; in the tap dance (that's right) routine that Layton designed for her; and finally in her singing of an unabashedly "Dolly"-like title song, she was playing not for the sake of a theatre production and its purposes but for a special taste, homosexual group. It is small time. Layton directed with no interest in musical staging (there was nothing to be done but let them sing, unfortunately, those songs). What emerged from this aimless, disorganized, shadow of a machine was an aimless, disorganized shadow of a dated comedy with aimless, disorganized songs and dances tacked onto it and with no sense of musical theatre.

WALTER KERR, *TIMES*

Inasmuch as *Sherry!* is a newly minted musical comedy version of *The Man Who Came to Dinner*, it is quite naturally full of old jokes and new jokes. The trouble with the old jokes is that you remember them. The trouble with the new jokes is that no one ever will. All that pluck, grit, determination, near-atomic energy and plain hard work can do for a light entertainment has been done for the exhumation. There's bounce and brass coming straight up through the floorboards, rather as though the boiler had let go in the basement, whenever Dolores Gray stops fussing with her furs (of all colors, including ginger) long enough to let a low note stir in her throat, creep stealthily upward and then embrace the balcony in a house-sweeping bleat. She does it practically the minute she's on. Having taken approximately two steps into the room, and having paused long enough to get rid of the hussar's cap she is insecurely balancing on the top of her runaway crop of blond curls, she glides into the title song, which quickly turns into a fast rattle of racy 1930's gossip. The gossip isn't much, the 1930's having decided to move on a while back. But the velvet in the voice shows not the least sign of wear or tear, and the performer stops the show right there in its Guy Lombardo–Edgar Guest–Major Bowes tracks. . . . Why must every line be delivered with a fresh charge of dynamite, as though it ought to—and *had* to— rock the back walls? The old lines, the celebrated and in consequence now dated lines, won't take that kind of treatment. The walls won't buckle at "I may vomit" or "you sex-ridden hag" any more. When you deal with good old plays, you've got to be kind to them. They tire. [The jokes are] pushed and prodded beyond their innate strength, and when the whole company gets 'round to the first-act finale, it's as though every gag man in the West had been hurled into service. But most of the evening in the Alvin is an exercise in subtraction. The farce solidity of the old play is thinned out by wandering about, searching for songs and scenery. And the perspiration points a finger at the holes, old and new.

NORMAN NADEL, *WORLD JOURNAL TRIBUNE*

Scarred and seasoned by their forays into the provinces, Guber, Ford, and Gross [operators of a chain of suburban tent theatres] have become too tough to quit. Only a short time ago, their new musical *Sherry!* had fallen upon evil days in its out-of-town tryouts, and the word was not good. If they despaired, they kept it to themselves, meanwhile making changes in the show—some pretty drastic, such as replacing the star. Their perseverance has paid off, as has their trust in the 28-year-old comedy hit, *The Man Who Came to Dinner*, which has aged into a mellow *Sherry!* It hardly could be called a major musical, and there are moments when it creaks, but it is generously entertaining much of the time, and zestfully performed. Instead of a conventional overture, there's a Pathé newsreel to fill the audience in on Sheridan Whiteside, who is shown advising President Roosevelt on the wording of a speech about ". . . nothing to fear but fear itself," and playing furious badminton with Shirley Temple. Best thing all evening is a satire on a Fred Astaire–Ginger Rogers musical, with the lead roles danced with amazing accuracy by Revill and Leslie Franzos.

RICHARD WATTS, JR., *POST*

Sherry! appeared to be in frequent combat with the celebrated play upon which it was based. Most of what laurels were won went to the original play, which was sharply and wittily amusing. When *Sherry!* stops going in for song and dance and confines itself to the dialogue of *The Man Who Came to Dinner*, it retains much of its old zest, comic spirit and malicious fun. There is a slight suggestion of softening of time.

Sheridan Whiteside may be insulting to everyone else, but he is carefully courteous to the Negro servants.

○   ○   ○

You know you've got trouble when you open out of town and the local scribe—Kevin Kelly of the *Boston Globe*, in this case—tells the world your show is "so awful it makes *Holly Golightly* [1966] look like a nostalgic work of art, and I'm not kidding." (Boston's last big tryout was perhaps the disaster of the decade. Producer David Merrick called in a new director, a new librettist—Edward Albee, no less—and changed the title to *Breakfast at Tiffany's*, ultimately pulling the plug during Broadway previews.) *Sherry*'s director, choreographer, and leading man George Sanders all decamped en route, the latter ascribing his departure to "the illness of his wife," Benita Hume (Ronald Colman's widow). Movie-star villain Sanders never did make it to Broadway, having walked out of his two previous signed-and-announced stints as replacement for Robert Morley in *Edward, My Son* (1948) and Ray Middleton—who replaced Ezio Pinza—in *South Pacific* (1949). Clive Revill, who starred in the Broadway imports of *Irma La Douce* (1960) and *Oliver!* (1963), slipped into Sanders's wheelchair, but there wasn't much he could do but keep out of the wake of Dolores Gray. Oh, and a word about those snappy catchphrases folks sometimes dream up. The producers of *Sherry!* quickly jettisoned "An Intoxicating Musical" after critic Kelly advised that, if you go, "you fortify yourself with several neat shots."

BROADWAY SCORECARD
/ PERFS: 72 / $: −

RAVE	FAVORABLE	MIXED	UNFAVORABLE	PAN
1	2			1

SIDE BY SIDE BY SONDHEIM

"A Musical Entertainment," an import of the 1976 British anthology revue

music and lyrics by Stephen Sondheim

additional music by Leonard Bernstein, Mary Rodgers, Richard Rodgers, and Jule Styne

directed by Ned Sherrin

produced by Harold Prince in association with Ruth Mitchell, by arrangement with The Incomes Company Ltd.

with Millicent Martin, Julie N. McKenzie, David Kernan, and Ned Sherrin

opened April 18, 1977   *Music Box Theatre*

CLIVE BARNES, *TIMES*

[Headline: "*Side by Side by Sondheim* is a Dream"]

The British have a proverb about coals to Newcastle. As Newcastle has coals in plenty, this is generally regarded as a somewhat futile effort. Something of the same pessimism could have been turned upon *Side by Side by Sondheim*, which most gorgeously opened last night and is a kind of Broadway musical imported to Broadway from London. How wrong such pessimism would have been—for here is a tiny, many-faceted gem that lights up Broadway. As a musical this is a revue, and as a revue this is a recital—but what a recital! It is Stephen Sondheim revealed as Stephen Sondheim has never been revealed before. It is—and please don't be frightened—Stephen Sondheim as a composer of *lieder*. Very cheerful *lieder*—but, well face it, *lieder*. The show was the brainchild of David Kernan, who is also one of the performers, and the idea struck him while he was playing in the [1975] London production of *A Little Night Music* [1973]. The concert was a potpourri of Sondheim songs given by three singers, two pianists and a friendly commentator, to explain, more or less, what was going on. Of course, it must be remembered that many of these songs were new to London—not every Sondheim musical has played there—whereas in New York, with a few exceptions, they are well known in their usually well-remembered context. Yet, oddly enough, away from their shows, they have taken on a new sheen. Another aspect of this show that should be brought to your attention is its essential Englishness. It is a London view of Sondheim, and, by inference, a London view of New York. Remember how Europe has traditionally regarded New York and the United States—think merely of Brecht, Weill and Kafka. There was an affection of wonderment there, and these same qualities come through in the present show. The show will eventually get an American cast—naturally enough—but I suggest it might prove rather different. The saucer-eyed glint of love and cynicism might just evaporate. This is a dream of a show. To me it is the essential Sondheim. It places him—more confidently perhaps than any of the individual musicals—as the master lyricist of American popular music, and one of the two or three most interesting theatre composers around. This show is happy, funny, witty and so compassionate. It makes you feel good. Turn cartwheels to the box office for this British celebration of a rare American.

MARTIN GOTTFRIED, *POST*
[Headline: "Foggy Sondheim by British Cast"]
It's difficult to see the sense in an all–Stephen Sondheim revue being done in a Broadway theatre by an all-British cast, and it was even more difficult after seeing *Side by Side by Sondheim.* Sondheim is, of course, the most important composer and lyricist working in the American musical theatre today. By "important" I mean that his contributions have gone beyond the creation of fine songs. He has added to the very structure of our musical theatre, developing approaches and techniques that have expanded its possibilities. In the process he has helped to make several landmark musicals and all of this is in addition to truly brilliant musical scores. But true as that is, he has still written but six shows as a composer-lyricist and three as just a lyricist. That is not enough to establish him as a legendary figure as I'm sure he would be the first to insist. The show isn't awful, mind you. The trouble is that the performance itself is insensitive to both the musicianship and theatricality of Sondheim's that have made him so important. There simply is no vitality to the production, no imagination in its concept. The three singers sing and the nar-

rator off at the side narrates. At the very end, vertical rows of lightbulbs put on a spectacular show but by then it's too late. Most of the songs are done in imitation of original cast album performances. When they stray toward original interpretation, they turn bland. Ned Sherrin's narration is, unfortunately, more noticeable. When he isn't being smarmy or topical in an undergraduate way, Sherrin is simply sycophantic. His background stories are trivial, familiar, and obsequious. For him Sondheim is not only the greatest composer and lyricist of our time, but also our major "musical dramatist," whatever that means. These superlatives make no sense. There are many other marvelous contemporary composers and lyricists. Besides, Sherrin's supercilious manner and campy attitude turn the whole performance slantwise. Playing to the boys in the balcony, he regularly colors the show lavender blue and all too unfortunately, the three singers go along with it. The performers are adequate, though each has one terrific number—"Broadway Baby" for Julie N. McKenzie, "I Never Do Anything Twice" for Millicent Martin and David Kernan must have had something besides a poor pitch, a white suit with satin trim and black shoes. Not enough for a show.

WALTER KERR, *TIMES*

I needn't tell you that Stephen Sondheim is, both musically and lyricly, the most sophisticated composer now working for the Broadway theatre. I needn't even tell you that he is somewhat indifferent to, perhaps skeptical of, a "rememberable" melodic line and that his real interest is in a song's interior architecture, in the superb mathematical balances that make it functional—for the show, for the orchestra, for second and third and fourth hearings. He can, of course, combine the two, and when the voluptuous, red-headed and in other ways magnetic Millicent Martin arrives at "Send in the Clowns," we are well aware that words rich enough and mysterious enough to stand alone as a poem have found their precise mates in a handful of notes. Martin is admirable elsewhere (everywhere, I might say), wriggling a straw hat, wrapping a feather boa about her, above all in the explosive dramatic affect with which she concludes "I'm Still Here." Martin demonstrates to a fair-thee-well the Sondheim gift for theatrical dynamics, and let prettiness go hang. She also suggests, to me at least, that songs carefully tooled to a given moment in a give show don't go for much when the show proper isn't working. "I'm Still Here" is from *Follies* [1971] but I didn't remember it from *Follies* because, I realize, I didn't hear it in *Follies*. I've heard it now. I had reservations about the evening. Quite a few of the numbers seem somewhat homeless out of context. They're also badly bunched at times. And I see no point in stressing the Sondheim reluctance to write tunes melodic enough to become "standards" by being snide about DeSylva, Brown and Henderson. *Conferencier* Sherrin makes the comment—which almost sounds like an apology for the man whose work he is there to celebrate—and I found Sherrin, who seems to have a bad case of the jollies, arch and tedious throughout. His little jokes had best be left at home, I fear. More importantly, I hope that Sondheim is going to be allowed to remain a composer and not a cult. Opening nights are given to wild acclaim; but wilder acclaim I've never heard. "Recognition" applause began with the first bar or two of almost everything introduced, including a tune that had been quickly dropped from a show during its Boston run and never heard in a theatre again. Music is all that is wanted, not madness.

∘　∘　∘

While Sondheim fans had been rapidly accumulating since (at least) *Company* opened in 1970, the traditional theatregoing audience was decidedly not interested. They'd sat and suffered through *Follies*, enraged in their high-priced charity benefit seats; they'd sat and suffered through *Pacific Overtures* (1976), baffled, in their high-priced charity benefit seats; and if they didn't mind *Company* and sort of enjoyed *Night Music* (1973), it certainly wasn't thanks to the music. Sondheim concocted clever lyrics, sure, but he couldn't write a tune like Jerry Herman. So it was a surprise to see an evening of Sondheim songs—just Sondheim songs—come to Broadway. Who would buy tickets, after his core audience ran out? Didn't they remember the severe apathy that met the award-winning, short-running *Pacific Overtures*? Had Hal Prince lost his mind? What happened, of course, is that all those people who found Sondheim's work unaccessible in grand trappings were now able to sit back undistractedly and just *listen* to the songs. And what do you know? Many of them realized—sitting in the Music Box, the house that Irving Berlin built so he could "Say It with Music"—that Sondheim *was* Broadway's most important composer. While he didn't turn overnight into Mr. Mainstream, and while his music became even more complex and uncompromising (next stop,

Sweeney Todd [1979]), you never again had to explain to theatregoers who this Sondheim fellow was and why his work—whether you liked it or not—was critical to the future of musical theatre. And for that we can thank the unlikely little *Side by Side by Sondheim*.

BROADWAY SCORECARD

/ PERFS: 384 / $ +

RAVE	FAVORABLE	MIXED	UNFAVORABLE	PAN
3	1		1	1

1600 PENNSYLVANIA AVENUE

"A Musical About the Problems of Housekeeping"

music by Leonard Bernstein

book and lyrics by Alan Jay Lerner

"entire production co-directed, staged, and choreographed" by Gilbert Moses and George Faison (replacing director Frank Corsaro and choreographer Donald McKayle)

produced by Roger L. Stevens and Robert Whitehead ("produced in association with The Coca-Cola Company" billing removed during tryout)

starring Ken Howard, Patricia Routledge, and Gilbert Price

with Emily Yancy, Reid Shelton, Edwin Steffe, John Witham, Ralph Farnworth, Hector Jaime Mercado, Carl Hall, Howard Ross, David E. Thomas, and Guy Costley

opened May 4, 1976   *Mark Hellinger Theatre*

CLIVE BARNES, *TIMES*

What is one to say about the new Alan Jay Lerner and Leonard Bernstein musical *1600 Pennsylvania Avenue?* Bring back *Rex!* [The Richard Rodgers musical opened the preceding week.] Possibly? The show is subtitled "A Musical About the Problems of Housekeeping." One would idly have imagined that housekeeping was among the least of the musical's problems, for the book, the lyrics and even the music enjoyed infinitely higher priority. It is a musical actually about a building—one hopes it will not start a trend. It is done in the most tedious and simplistic way imaginable. From George Washington to Teddy Roosevelt, a lot of history flows along the Potomac. How is one to give it thematic coherence? Lerner, who has clearly spent too much time watching the television series *Upstairs, Downstairs* [aired locally 1974–77], decided to take a theme of race relations—with the whites upstairs in the ballrooms of history, and the blacks downstairs in the kitchens of the past. It works most terribly. The show's racial conscience bleeds like a seeping but superficial wound throughout. Someone, some time, obviously envisaged the musical as a minstrel show and, although this depressing device had, by the first night, been largely abandoned, odd vestiges of it remained. The scenery is described as "supervised" by Kert Lundell—and probably cost a great deal more than it looks. Because it looks cheap. The costumes (about which the same could be said) have needed two "supervisors," Whitney Blausen and Dona Granata. Who were all these people supervising? Slaves, perhaps? The "entire production" has been "co-directed, staged and choreographed" by Gilbert Moses and George Faison, and the results are as lively as could be hoped for. Personally I saw too much of the stagehands in the wings from where I was sitting. I realize that stagehands are usually paid more than actors, but actors are generally better to look at.

MARTIN GOTTFRIED, *POST*

1600 Pennsylvania Avenue had no business opening last night. It is a largely marvelous Leonard Bernstein score that drags Alan Jay Lerner's book and lyrics behind it like an unwanted relative. What this leaves on stage, in the name of theatre, is an absence of plot populated by anonymous characters, lumbering along without organization or attitude. The new musical begins with a superb Bernstein overture, one in the class of

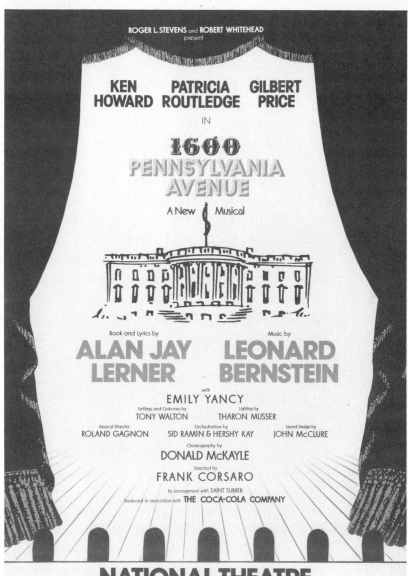

ROGER L. STEVENS and ROBERT WHITEHEAD
present

KEN   PATRICIA   GILBERT
HOWARD   ROUTLEDGE   PRICE

IN

1600
PENNSYLVANIA
AVENUE

A New Musical

Book and Lyrics by   Music by
ALAN JAY   LEONARD
LERNER   BERNSTEIN

with
EMILY YANCY

Settings and Costumes by   Lighting by
TONY WALTON   THARON MUSSER

Musical Director   Orchestrations by   Sound Design by
ROLAND GAGNON   SID RAMIN & HERSHY KAY   JOHN McCLURE

Choreography by
DONALD McKAYLE

Directed by
FRANK CORSARO

By arrangement with SAINT SUBBER
Produced in association with THE COCA-COLA COMPANY

NATIONAL THEATRE
1321 E. St., N.W., Wash., D.C.
5 WEEKS ONLY! MAR. 17 through APR. 17

The director and choreographer were both fired from this "Bicentennial bore" in Philadelphia. Designer Tony Walton and the Coca-Cola Company both demanded their billing be removed; Tony got to keep his fee, but Coke lost more than a million Bicentennial bucks. Preliminary credits.

his *Candide* and surely destined to join it as a concert staple. Bernstein's score hardly stops there. *1600* is filled with music and that is its strength as well as its problem. This is rich, performable music, sometimes irresistibly catchy ("The President Jefferson Sunday Luncheon Party March") and sometimes stirring ("Take Care of This House"). It has been orchestrated to the hilt by Sid Ramin and Hershy Kay. It is melodic, ambitious music, filled with challenging harmonies, set to surprising rhythms and written to expansive lengths. But it dominates the show. On the one hand, nothing else is its match; but on the other, it leaves room for nothing else. Either everything in *1600 Pennsylvania Avenue* went out the window for the sake of the score or nothing was there to resist its domination. Whatever, the show emerges as a staged concert piece. There is a series of minstrel numbers at the end, and they suggest that *1600* once had historical criticism on its mind. But this, like almost all of the show, is now incomprehensible. Frankly, of all the patched-up musicals that have limped into New York, this is the most pitifully pieced together one I have ever seen. The direction is not energetic enough to be called lethargic. The choreography, mostly trite but occasionally promising, is sloppily performed. These are jointly credited to Gilbert Moses and George Faison, but it doesn't seem as if the show is theirs to blame, or theirs at all. It is a bum idea that has arrived in confusion. Though its music is generally superb and frequently tremendous, it has drowned out any sense of theatre. It is an embarrassment.

HOWARD KISSEL, *WOMEN'S WEAR DAILY*

100 years of American history seen as a series of collegiate skits. Lerner's book, which does parallel glimpses of the presidents who occupy the White House and the backstairs blacks who keep it going, is equally offensive to both. The presidents are the objects of Lerner's sometimes pedantic, invariable sophomoric ridicule: the blacks are the recipients of his condescending affection. The book is stilted—most of the dialogue sounds as if it had been rejected from a '30s Hollywood "biography." The lyrics are too clever by half, full of polysyllabic rhymes and cute conceits that might seem outrageous in a college show, but are not witty enough to be taken seriously from an adult. When the lyrics aim for eloquence, they are embarrassing ("You could drive a team of horses through my soul/Where the holy light of freedom burned a hole," the blacks sing at

one point). An overall incoherence about the conception is reflected in the scenery and costume design—the designers don't even want to take credit: costumes and sets are listed in the program as "supervised' rather than "designed." The direction and choreography similarly put nothing in focus—one is always conscious of the vastness of the Mark Hellinger stage and the ineffectualness of what happens on it. The intent may indeed be allegorical, but the impression is of amateurism. The cast performs valiantly, with an enthusiasm that must require awesome effort, and the orchestra plays Sid Ramin and Hershy Kay's rich arrangements beautifully, but there is no getting around the fact that *1600 Pennsylvania Avenue* is a colossal embarrassment.

DOUGLAS WATT, *DAILY NEWS*

On the evidence of *1600 Pennsylvania Avenue,* both the show and American history would have been more fun if our Presidents had been women. Certainly the liveliest sally of the evening, an evening which whisks us through a 100-year tour of the White House, is provided by Patricia Routledge who, as Rutherford B. Hayes is taking the oath of office, plays both a fluttery Lucy Hayes and a caustic Julia Grant in a Leonard Bernstein–Alan Jay Lerner number called "Duet for One." That's fun. And a brief scene in which a cussing Andrew Johnson tries to comfort his ailing wife and talk political turkey to a hostile black servant, while at the same time the Senate is voting on impeachment, quickens our interest. But aside from these moments and one beautiful, soaring hymn, "Take Care of This House," the evening is slack and as unsure of itself as a primary hopeful in January. How could it have been otherwise? Though *1600 Pennsylvania Avenue,* which is coyly subtitled "a musical about the problems of housekeeping," is the creation of two of our most-distinguished professionals, the very conception is more suitable to a school pageant than a Broadway musical. Ken Howard, wearing a variety of wigs, whiskers and costumes, plays Ken Howard posing as Washington and then seven or eight Presidents. Miss Routledge, mostly relegated to the background, plays the first ladies. And Gilbert Price and Emily Yancy play a black couple, the principal White House servants, through the years. There's also a chorus of about 26 playing politicians, Britishers, members of the White House staff, etc. Where on earth did they think they could go with such a concept?

No time to establish personalities and hardly time to change clothes. *1600 Pennsylvania Avenue* is, finally, an impossible enterprise, just one more Bicentennial burden.

o   o   o

Talk about "the problems of housekeeping." Lerner started work on his patriotic (?) musical in 1972, back during the Watergate hearings. Bernstein, who had just been under attack for his 1971 *Mass* (in honor of John F. Kennedy) and was on Richard Nixon's little list, seemed the perfect collaborator for the project. Bernstein and Lerner had been schoolmates, vaguely, at Harvard (class of '39 and '40, respectively); they collaborated, in fact, on two songs for a 1957 Carnegie Hall concert by the Harvard Glee Club. They were also both longtime friends of JFK, '41: Bernstein was a White House regular, of course ("Bernstein on the Bechstein," as Sondheim might say), while Lerner was the "Camelot" poet with long links to First Sister Jean Smith. Lerner mentioned the project to boyhood friend John Paul Austin, who got the Coca-Cola company—of which he was chairman of the board—to cough up $900,000 with which to back it. Good publicity for the Bicentennial year, you see. So you had the author of *My Fair Lady* (1956), you had the composer of *West Side Story* (1957), and you had an intriguingly patriotic theme and unlimited coffers. Everything but a script. Lerner, whose working speed was notoriously slow, never did seem to finish *1600*, while Bernstein wrote music by the yard (some of which was, not surprisingly, truly exceptional). But there was nobody to push Lerner and nobody to edit Bernstein. Saint-Subber—fresh from the 1973 stage musicalization of *Gigi*—was producer until, after a couple of years of wrangling, he threw up his hands in horror. (Besides, he said, "I loathed it.") In came Roger Stevens, chairman of the Kennedy Center and longtime Bernstein backer (the Jean Arthur/Boris Karloff *Peter Pan* [1950], *West Side Story, Mass*). Despite—or perhaps because of—the luminosity of the authors, it was impossible to attract a top director or stars. Frank Corsaro, with drama credits and opera credits but *no* Broadway musicals came in to direct, with Donny McKayle of *Raisin* (1973) as choreographer. Everything proceeded smoothly (?) until the Philadelphia opening, when the show clocked in at an astounding three hours and forty-five minutes. "Stupefying, crashingly

dull," said the *Bulletin*, while *Variety* dubbed it "a Bicentennial bore."
This is not the sort of thing that generated good word of mouth. "You
think the minorities are oppressed?" asked William B. Collins in the
Inquirer. "Consider the plight of the audience. So have a Coke, anyway,"
he jested. (Coca-Cola removed their name from the credits forthwith,
but they couldn't remove their dollars, which ultimately topped 1.2 million.) Corsaro and McKayle were bounced, replaced by Gilbert Moses
and George Faison of *The Wiz* (1975), and the racial ambiguity of the
show became even *more* muddled and incoherent. The show, in performance, became so disjointed that scenic/costume designer Tony Walton
hightailed it out of town, resulting in the "design supervisor" credits so
amusing to the critics. "Only two titans could have a failure like this,"
said Jerry Robbins, who knew enough to stay far away from this project
of his old pal Lenny. So have a Coke, anyway. Small-Print-in-the-
Back-of-the-Program Dept.: Patrons who carefully perused their
Philadelphia *Playbill* might well have noted in the credit section—you
know, where they list the friendly folk who provide free merchandise in
exchange for a plug—that the legend "Ginger Ale courtesy of Canada
Dry Corp" had been printed over with a heavy black box, which, of
course, served not to obscure the unfortunate slip but to accentuate it.
So have a Coke, anyway.

BROADWAY SCORECARD

/ PERFS: 7 / $: –

RAVE	FAVORABLE	MIXED	UNFAVORABLE	PAN
				6

SKYSCRAPER

"The New Musical Comedy"

music by James Van Heusen

lyrics by Sammy Cahn

book by Peter Stone

based on the 1945 comedy *Dream Girl* by Elmer Rice

directed by Cy Feuer

choreographed by Michael Kidd

produced by Cy Feuer and Ernest H. Martin

starring Julie Harris, Peter L. Marshall, and Charles Nelson Reilly (replacing Victor Spinetti)

with Nancy Cushman, Dick O'Neill, Donald Burr, Rex Everhart, and Lesley Stewart

opened November 13, 1965   Lunt-Fontanne Theatre

WALTER KERR, *HERALD TRIBUNE*

Twenty more previews and I'll bet they'd have got it right. Even as it stands, for all intents and purposes and for your uncles and your aunts, *Skyscraper* is a reasonably entertaining show. No, I'm probably wrong about the extra previews. The new musical was probably never going to be more than a reasonably entertaining show because it is split straight down the middle. Exactly one half has to do with the fact that Julie Harris daydreams; the other half has to do with the fact that the same Miss Harris—the Julie Harris who has never appeared in a musical before and may never again but who need not apologize for being penny-bright in this one—owns a troublesome building. The two halves of the story line never meet. Because the two isolated feet on which the show tries to walk are really strangers to one another, moving in parallel lines in approximately the same direction at approximately the same rate of speed, they produce an optical illusion: they

"A JOYOUS, BOISTEROUS, BRASH, FAST-MOVING MUSICAL" TAUBMAN —N.Y. TIMES

FEUER and MARTIN present

JULIE HARRIS in

SKYSCRAPER

The New Musical Comedy

co-starring

PETER L. MARSHALL   CHARLES NELSON REILLY

Lyrics by SAMMY CAHN   Music by JAMES VAN HEUSEN

Book by PETER STONE

with

NANCY CUSHMAN   DICK O'NEILL
DONALD BURR   REX EVERHART   LESLEY STEWART

Settings & Lighting by ROBERT RANDOLPH   Costumes Designed by THEONI V. ALDREDGE

Based on "DREAM GIRL" by Elmer Rice
Original Cast Album on CAPITOL RECORDS

Musical Director JOHN LESKO   Orchestrations by FRED WERNER   Dance Music Arranged by MARVIN LAIRD

Directed by CY FEUER

Dances and Musical Numbers Staged by MICHAEL KIDD

LUNT FONTANNE THEATRE   46 ST. W. OF B'WAY
MATS. WED. & SAT

What's a nice dreamgirl like Julie Harris doing in a place like this? Columnist Dorothy Kilgallen reported that the turkey served at the Four Seasons "is far more enjoyable than that dished up at the Lunt-Fontanne."

often seem to be standing still. But against this fairly elementary diffi-culty must be set a certain naively shining energy. A great deal of this flows, of course, from the star, from whom Con Edison could take lessons. Miss Harris never seems presumptuous but she always seems confident, perhaps most so when the male dancers are skipping her sky-ward. She doesn't seem to worry about singing because she knows she can act, and what are lyrics for but to be meant? You may not always hear music, but you hear meanings when she's around.

JOHN MCCLAIN, *JOURNAL-AMERICAN*

It has been in town doing previews for so long that it has been labeled old hat, and not very good hat at that. It opened officially last night and I thought they had done a wonderful job of pulling it into shape. I don't think they succeeded in making it a big memorable smash in the *How to Succeed* [Feuer and Martin's 1961 hit] tradition, but they do give you a fast-paced, highly professional first act; they give you a couple of great tunes; and certainly some of the most exciting choreography seen here-abouts this season. The story seems to wear thin in the last act, so does the pace. They stumble over the transition from dream to reality, and finally one ceases to care which is which. It is puzzling to think why Julie Harris tackled this one, since she is not a musical comedy person, but she is incapable of being less than lovable, as everyone will agree, and she seems to be having a fine time appearing frequently in an abbreviated nightgown.

NORMAN NADEL, *WORLD-TELEGRAM & SUN*

A love affair with New York. Director Cy Feuer has captured the per-sonality of this city, and that hasn't happened much on the musical stage since *On the Town* [1944]. Robert Randolph has designed a steelwork setting, with the grandeur of New York visible behind it, that would be exhilarating to look at even if nothing were happening on stage. Not everything about *Skyscraper* succeeds this handsomely, though its over-all effect is stimulating and pleasant. The only fault I find with Julie Harris is that she's a nonsinger. (I am one of the few remaining natives who likes to hear musicians in musicals.) The fault is tolerable, however, in that she is such a good actress, and such an enthusiastic worker, that she gets the idea of a song across, if not all its lyric grace.

HOWARD TAUBMAN, *TIMES*

Georgina Allerton has been transformed from the sentimental *Dream Girl* to the joyous, boisterous, hard-hitting orbit of *Skyscraper*. The alteration hasn't hurt Georgina a bit. Her daydreams two decades ago were rather sticky. In the new musical, they have become broadly comic cartoons of romance, among the funniest moments in a brash, fast-moving musical. A few imperfections keep *Skyscraper* from being a tower of a musical. It punches too hard; some of its jokes are strained. Not all the songs have wit and melodic grace equal to their opportunities. And to accommodate a lively production number the architecture of the piece is allowed to become conventional. It is as if the musical feared to relax and be charming. . . . Charles Nelson Reilly, who is becoming a splendidly sure-footed comedian, is the most consistent source of merriment. As a fluttery chap who once got a one-night run out of an off-Broadway show, he now wants to create a film festival. In response to Georgina's daydreams, Reilly materializes as an English lieutenant, a Southern gentleman, an F.B.I. agent and a toreador. For each phantom he has the right comic accent; in each guise he woos the eager Georgina with droll ardor.

o   o   o

Producers Feuer and Martin—undisputed champs through 1961, with six hits including *Guys and Dolls* (1950) and *How to Succeed*—suffered a terminal reversal thereafter and descended into the musical comedy abyss. (This happened just about the time that Feuer started directing the shows himself. Hmmm. . . .) If the disjointed *Skyscraper* seemed like two misjointed shows, that might be because they took two musicals in development—one about gentrification and the other about Elmer Rice's *Dream Girl*—and kind of melded them together. Kind of. After a troublesome tryout, which saw the departure of costar Victor Spinetti (a Tony-winner for the 1964 *Oh, What a Lovely War*), *Skyscraper* lumbered onto 46th Street. As the preview period extended, high-priced high-society benefitgoers found themselves viewing an unfinished show very much in progress—although progress might not be precisely the correct term. Hearst columnist Dorothy Kilgallen, who liked to throw her weight around, exercised her prerogative and on October 22 wrote, "I wish someone would pass a law making it ille-

gal for a columnist to see a Broadway show before its official premiere." She went on prematurely to lay the show out—cold. The performance was followed by a glamorous supper party at the Four
Seasons, she noted, "where the turkey served is far more enjoyable than
that dished up at the Lunt-Fontanne." (Kilgallen's husband, Richard
Kollmar, curiously enough, was a Broadway juvenile [*Knickerbocker
Holiday* (1938), *Too Many Girls* (1939)] turned producer [*Plain and
Fancy* (1955), *The Body Beautiful* (1958)]). This unmannerly intrusion
caused a bit of an uproar, with the condemned columnist noting that
nobody complained when she wrote that an incoming show was a surefire hit and people had better order their tickets now. The gentlemen
of the press agreed en masse to honor *Skyscraper*'s official opening date,
and the brouhaha seemed to have paid off: the critics were far more
lenient than usual, giving the show a better reception than the material seems to warrant. (Better reviews, mystifyingly, than *Mame* received
later that season!) The public didn't buy it, though, and *Skyscraper* was
unable to scrape by. Perhaps it's just as well that Kilgallen didn't wait
for the official opening—she died on November 8, under mysterious
circumstances. Turkey poisoning, perhaps?

BROADWAY SCORECARD
/ PERFS: 241 / $: –

RAVE	FAVORABLE	MIXED	UNFAVORABLE	PAN
1	3	2		

SO LONG, 174TH STREET

"A New Musical Comedy"

music and lyrics by Stan Daniels

book by Joseph Stein

based on Joseph Stein's 1963 comedy *Enter Laughing*, from Carl Reiner's 1958 autobiographical novel

directed by Burt Shevelove

choreographed by Alan Johnson

produced by Frederick Brisson in association with The Harkness Organization and Wyatt Dickerson

starring Robert Morse

with George S. Irving, Mitchell Jason, Loni Ackerman, Robert Barry, Sydney Blake, Lee Goodman, Barbara Lang (replacing Marian Winters), Lawrence John Moss, and Gene Varrone

opened April 27, 1976   Harkness Theatre

CLIVE BARNES, *TIMES*

If you ever wondered what happened to the old-fashioned musicals of yesteryear, you can find out at the Harkness Theatre, where a musical called *So Long, 174th Street* opened last night. One resists the temptation to say "So long!" and leave it at that, but only narrowly. It is always a puzzle when a show like *So Long, 174th Street* thuds into town. Why? The people involved are talented enough. Frederick Brisson is a talented producer, the show is based on a respectable comedy by Joseph Stein called *Enter Laughing*, which ran for a year on Broadway in 1963, and was based on a novel by that very funny man, Carl Reiner. The show has been directed by Burt Shevelove, who is brilliant, and it stars

Great artwork, yes, but the 45-year-old Bobby Morse of *So Long, 174th Street* looked like this fellow's grandfather. Preliminary credits. (artwork by Tom Morrow)

Robert Morse and George S. Irving, who are two of the joys of our musical theatre. Stein—who had what one might call a certain success with *Fiddler on the Roof* (1964)—wrote his own book. So what went wrong? How did *Enter Laughing* end up leaving us yawning? . . . Then there was the music and lyrics by Stan Daniels. Daniels is a producer of the *Mary Tyler Moore Show* on television, and he should stay where he is well off. Morse was wide-eyed and adorable, singing and even dancing his heart out, running around in concentric circles like a harassed juggler trying to make everything somehow work. Irving, avuncular and superior, also did his most considerable best. But when the music and lyrics do not work for a musical, the musical does not work. People should listen before putting money where their ears are.

MARTIN GOTTFRIED, *POST*

In opening *So Long, 174th Street* last night, the Harkness Theatre, previously used for ballet and off-Broadway, made a bid to become a big-time Broadway house and it won. The show is a traditional theatrical disaster, is such stage misery that it is the week's best argument for euthanasia. The new musical is taken from *Enter Laughing* which, in turn, was based on Carl Reiner's book remembering his youthful entry into show business. Joseph Stein's play wasn't anything special, but it was made wonderful by Alan Arkin's hysterically funny playing of the leading role and a by-no-means-incidental supporting performance of Michael J. Pollard. Stein has now adapted the play in the obsolete, shorthand style of the traditional musical, snipping every scene and then aborting it to make room for one irrelevant song or dance after another. It is, consequently, the shell of what was once mediocre. Replacing Arkin is Robert Morse, who is not only an ultimately un-Jewish middle-aged adolescent but who has managed to even outmug himself. Pollard's kinky sidekick is now being played by Lawrence John Moss, winning this year's award for the most invisible performance in the most invisible role. And things go downhill from there. The score, both music and lyrics by Stan Daniels, could pass for a parody of Broadway past, one bland, stereotyped number after another. These are so perfectly complemented by Alan Johnson's trite dances that the Milliken people could well forgo the trouble of putting their annual industrial show together and just pick up this one, lock, stock and schlock. Frankly, this is junk from top to bottom. Morse is embarrassing, not funny as a clown, not believable as a boy, not even convincing in reading the simplest of lines. George Irving, on the other hand, is merely embarrassed. I am frankly at a loss to understand how a director with the style, skill and class of Burt Shevelove could have become involved with such a hopelessly unmusical project, so amateurishly endowed. His work, I regret to say, is as mechanical and as industrial-show as his material. The Harkness has been inaugurated.

WALTER KERR, *TIMES*

What really hurts about *So Long, 174th Street* is watching Robert Morse, that faun-like combination of Tom Sawyer and *Mad* Magazine's Alfred E. Neuman, exhaust his whole repertory of amiable tricks before your eyes. He does everything that's been so funny before, listening hard with all his teeth (both of them), raveling his head shyly until it comes to rest on his or somebody's shoulder, shifting his voice from a woodland growl to a Minnie Mouse squeak, stabilizing his tilting form on a tilting planet by dropping his hands into his pockets as anchors. And it's as though an overtrained seal had been given no props to work with, no beach-balls, no circus-drums, nothing. Behind an irresistibly sheepish smile there's got to be something to play, to sing, to join. Here he gets Stan Daniels' lyrics that kill themselves off in their very titles: if the song is called "Undressing Girls with My Eyes," what else do you do with it? Undress girls, to be sure, but that's now dwindling aftermath, obvious statement. Only George S. Irving, as a fantasy butler answering the Hollywood telephone for this would-be star (Morse is trying to escape 174th Street and a career in pharmacy to become an actor) is able to make something of a number, perhaps because *his* is in tango rhythm and Irving has good tango fingers to snap with. Otherwise we spend the evening listening to "It's so nice being with you/Being with you/Being with you/I wish it would never end," and before long we've developed a slightly different desire.

⚬   ⚬   ⚬

Like a child star whose voice has changed, poor Bobby Morse's career was in turmoil. In the years following the 1961 *How to Succeed in Business Without Really Trying* his unique but flamboyant talent made it difficult for him to succeed despite myriad opportunities on big screen and small. A second musical finally came along for him to throw himself into, but his brilliant comic performance couldn't make *Sugar* (1972) anything more than a mediocre musical showcasing a brilliant comic performance. This left Morse *really* stranded. Desperate times call for desperate measures, and desperate is as good a term as any to apply to *So Long, 174th Street*. Morse was long blessed (or in some ways cursed?) by his baby-faced looks; he established himself, in fact, playing the sixteen-year-old juvenile in *Take Me Along* (1959) at the age of twenty-eight. But here in 1976 was Morse again playing a teenager, at forty-five, and the baby face had long since started to slip. But a job was a job, at least for two weeks plus previews. After another thirteen lean and hungry years, someone had the ridiculous idea of making Morse over for a one-man show about Truman Capote, which turned his career around and put him back on top, where he always belonged.

BROADWAY SCORECARD

/ PERFS: 16 / $: –

RAVE	FAVORABLE	MIXED	UNFAVORABLE	PAN
1				5

SOMETHING'S AFOOT

a musical spoof

book, music, and lyrics by James McDonald, David Vos, and Robert Gerlach

additional music by Ed Linderman

suggested, presumably, by the 1940 detective novel *Ten Little Indians* by Agatha Christie (uncredited)

directed and choreographed by Tony Tanner

produced by Emanuel Azenberg, Dasha Epstein, and John Mason Kirby

starring Tessie O'Shea

with Gary Beach, Willard Beckham, Gary Gage, Barbara Heuman, Marc Jordan, Jack Schmidt, Liz Sheridan, Neva Small, and Sel Vitella

opened May 27, 1976   Lyceum Theatre

CLIVE BARNES, *TIMES*

The ending, the authors say in their program note, they do not wish disclosed. Understandably. They have a certain difficulty with the beginning as well. And, if anyone is counting, the middle is something of a muddle. Yet, I saw the show at its final preview with a typical rather than first-night audience. First-night audiences one tries to dismiss like a minor attack of cholera, yet audience-audiences, live people in paid-for seats, do have an interest. And this audience adored the show. It was a little misguided perhaps, because the music is terrible, the lyrics clumsy and the point of the production, which has been directed by Tony Tanner, is camp taken to lengths that are almost as distasteful as they are ridiculous. Subtlety does not seem to be a word in Mr. Tanner's lexicon, and he has instructed his cast, a rather raw cast, accordingly. I notice I have forgotten the book, music and lyrics by James McDonald, David Vos and Robert Gerlach—and this is because I have. They were all three somewhat forgettable. So far as the music is concerned, it is the sort that might give "unmemorable" a good name. The murders were innocuous and the performances were frantic and the music should have been left somewhere else. This is the kind of musical that might be rewarding after a good dinner in the hot summer at the Goodspeed Opera House in East Haddam, Connecticut, which indeed is where it started.

WALTER KERR, *TIMES*

Now let's just lay down a few rules around here: (1) If you're doing a musical that is also supposed to be a "whodunit," it's best not to kill off the entire chorus. It thins out the sound. *Something's Afoot*, in which British music-hall entertainer Tessie O'Shea's white teeth and spread talons seem more ferocious than the electrical storms that rage outside (especially when Miss O'Shea, wearing a straw hat, is also to be seen busily plucking a banjo), ignores this simple principle to its peril. Obviously indebted to Agatha Christie's *Ten Little Indians*, in which the cast of characters does indeed diminish one by one, the enterprise starts out with a hale and hearty, and fairly rousing, houseful of baritones and wild sopranos, then steadily reduces its octets to quartets, its quartets to duets, its duets to—well, that would be telling too much. (2) There is no such thing as a musical that is also supposed to be a "whodunit." People have been trying this sort of thing ever since Earl Carroll's *Murder at the Vanities* (1933) and it's never worked. Reason: the music totally relaxes the suspense, and the suspense makes the music seem intrusive. *Something's Afoot*, of course, is supposed to be a parody of the mystery musical, with a sleekly pomaded Hairbreadth Harry type [Gary Beach] hissing "Alone at last!" as an excuse to go into a solo dance on the fireplace mantel-top and a seductress who looks like Fanny Brice out of Theda Bara [Liz Sheridan] draping herself all over the balcony railing with a stay-thither stogie in her mouth. The whole thing does bring up another rule: (3) You can't parody what didn't exist in the first place. (4) If someone on the premises is totally without taste or judgment, get someone with taste and judgment to lock him in a closet until after the production's opened. Or maybe he could be killed first. I'm thinking of the kind of creative chap who imagines that dunking a servant's face into a chamberpot is hilarious for starters, or the sort of lyricist who lovingly works in a song about a small boat ("I've got a teeny little dinghy") for all the *double entendres* it's not worth. By this time you may have gathered that with *Something's Afoot* something's amiss.

◦   ◦   ◦

Question: What did the Goodspeed Opera House send to Broadway amidst their 1975 hits *Shenandoah* and *Very Good Eddie* and their 1977 blockbuster *Annie*? Answer: you're looking at it. *Something's Afoot* was roundly trounced and quickly dispatched, but—and it's a big but—the show could just as easily have been a massive hit. It was, simply put, a silly little amateurish spoof. Like *Dames at Sea* (1968). Like *Grease* (1972). Like, some years later, *Nunsense* (1985) and *Forever Plaid* (1990). Just the sort of show that can take off with or without the critics, spawn multiple companies, and make everybody *very* rich. Didn't work, though, not in this case. But close and surely worth the (low-cost) gamble.

BROADWAY SCORECARD
/ PERFS: 61 / $: –

RAVE	FAVORABLE	MIXED	UNFAVORABLE	PAN
	2		1	3

SOON

"A Rock Opera"

music by Joseph Martinez Kookoolis and Scott Fagan

lyrics by Scott Fagan

book uncredited (Robert Greenwald, Joseph Martinez Kookoolis, and Scott Fagan); "adaptation" by Martin Duberman

based on an original story by Joseph Martinez Kookoolis and Scott Fagan

director uncredited (Robert Greenwald); "additional staging" by Gerald Freedman

choreographed by Fred Benjamin

produced by Bruce W. Stark and Sagittarius Productions, Inc. (Edgar M. Bronfman and Henry S. White)

with Peter Allen (replacing Scott Fagan), Barry Bostwick, Pendleton Brown, Nell Carter, Leata Galloway, Richard Gere, Marta Heflin, Michael Jason, and Marion Ramsey

opened January 12, 1971   Ritz Theatre

CLIVE BARNES, *TIMES*

One of the difficulties encountered by Kookoolis and Fagan is that they are writing a commercial musical (they presumably wish for it to be a success) about the horrors of music commercialism. A strongly satiric approach might have helped here, but it is lacking. So much of the music is as feeble and as cheap as the writers say it is. The cast is uniformly good. I particularly liked Marta Heflin and Barry Bostwick as the romantic lovers, but all the others had zest and honestly projected, pop voices. They also all had distinctive personalities. Unfortunately, I fear they needed them.

MARTIN GOTTFRIED, *WOMEN'S WEAR DAILY*

It is so self-contemptuous that the director has removed his name from the program. This doesn't mean that no one can be blamed—it only means that he can't be named. The book is a disaster. Martin Duberman is credited with the adaptation, but it is an adaptation from what? Duberman is a superb playwright but he obviously knows little about the pop music industry or the language of today's kids. The company, when it is singing, is nice to listen to and dull to watch. When it is acting, it is embarrassing. And boring. And, finally, saddening.

DOUGLAS WATT, *DAILY NEWS*

Soon, a rock show that opened last night, sets the youth movement back just under two hours. It's too bad, too, because there was a valid enough basic idea to begin with. But something happened to it, it went all soft and misty-eyed and phony and collapsed on the way to the theatre. The songs, especially the music, aren't at all bad and they have been effectively scored, though I question the wisdom of ending the first half in a crowded theatre by having the cast exhort the audience by singing: "This house is gonna burn down! This house is on fire!" at the top of its lungs. Among the singers in the sizable cast I admired most the gospel-trained voice of Nell Carter, the nicely throaty and bluesy voice of Leata Galloway, and the sweet one of heroine Marta Heflin. The leading man, Barry Bostwick, was lost in a totally unconvincing role.

o   o   o

Soon reclaimed the Ritz as a legitimate house, having wallowed as a radio and TV studio since 1939. (It continued to wallow in second-rate legitimacy until 1990, when it underwent a classy renovation and was redubbed the Walter Kerr.) The rock quartet central to *Soon* included Barry Bostwick, Richard Gere, and Liza Minnelli's estranged husband, Peter Allen, who replaced coauthor Fagan when the show shuttered midway through previews for massive revisions. The ladies of the ensemble, listed in the program as "Groupies," included the remarkable voices of Nell Carter, Leata Galloway, and

Marion Ramsey. Louis S. Louis provided the vocal arrangements and led the orchestra, which *Playbill* listed as "Pit-Shit."

BROADWAY SCORECARD
/ PERFS: 3 / $: —

RAVE	FAVORABLE	MIXED	UNFAVORABLE	PAN
	1	2	1	2

DUKE ELLINGTON'S SOPHISTICATED LADIES

"Based on the Music of Duke Ellington" (1899–1974)

concept by Donald McKayle (book material by Donald McKayle and revisions by Samm-Art Williams cut during tryout)

directed by Michael Smuin (replacing Donald McKayle)

"musical staging and choreography" by Donald McKayle and Michael Smuin; "co-choreography and tap choreography" by Henry LeTang

produced by Roger S. Berlind, Manheim Fox, Sondra Gilman, Burton L. Litwin, and Louise Westergaard, in association with Belwin Mills Publishing Corp. and NorZar Productions (Jacques Nordman and Sidney Lazard)

starring Gregory Hines, Judith Jamison, Phyllis Hyman, and P. J. Benjamin

with Terri Klausner, Hinton Battle, Gregg Burge, Mercedes Ellington, and Priscilla Baskerville

opened March 1, 1981   *Lunt–Fontanne Theatre*

CLIVE BARNES, *POST*

[Headline: "Lively *Ladies* Far From *Sophisticated*"]

One of the most lavish musical non-musicals that Broadway has ever seen. In fairness, it is simply a handsomely tarted-up band-show, full of Ellington music, dancing and talent. Yet the total is less than the sum of its parts. The idea for an Ellington musical came to Donald McKayle, who devised this present concept. McKayle was dropped in Washington, exiting about the same time as former President Jimmy Carter, although some of his choreography and staging obviously remain in the present version. Whether there was any kind of book to the show, or at least vestigial dramatic linking, in the Washington version I have no idea. The Broadway show, which has bad teething problems and still bears the teeth marks to prove it, has been staged by classicist Michael Smuin, codirector of the San Francisco Ballet. With a huge band on stage, framed by the most elegant setting by Tony Walton—which features illuminated staircases in the Hollywood tradition and neon signs in the motel mode—and a large cast, dressed to the nines by Willa Kim, the show is undeniably sumptuous. The Ellington music, under the direction of the composer's son, Mercer Ellington, makes up a formidable compendium. But the actual sound, and this could be nothing but the fertile imagination of my memory, seems more like homogenized Broadway anonymous than the authentic sound of the old Ellington band [orchestrations by Al Cohn]. However the show certainly moves along, with one zingy dance number succeeding the next. This is fundamentally a dance marathon, but the type of jazz and cabaret style dancing being offered is a touch too predictable. It is like a seven-course dinner, with each course consisting of lemon meringue pie. Smuin obviously knows this style. Although a classic choreographer, his veins are pumped full of showbiz. He paid dues as a Broadway gypsy, and for two years worked with his wife in a cabaret act. Despite Smuin's skill and consummate expertise—the tap numbers, by the way, were choreographed by Henry LeTang—the show misses the sublime simplicity of Fats Waller's *Ain't Misbehavin'* [1978] which presumably inspired it. Smuin's dynamo runs at full throttle throughout the evening, but gives little time for grace or subtlety. A cast of many talents, music steeped with nostalgia, relentlessly crackerjack dancing and a setting full of nightclub chic—

but not exactly a Broadway musical. And, despite the title, not perhaps for the sophisticated.

WALTER KERR, *TIMES*

A sleekly fashioned, dynamically paced, irresistibly friendly medley of some 35 songs written in part or entirely by the masterly Duke Ellington. We've been having a great many of these musical albums of late. This is one in which the performers, remarkable as they are, consistently honor their composer. Duke Ellington sounds very, very good. The spotlight is never entirely off him. If I had to chose someone I thought deserved first billing, I guess I'd have to do the radical thing and select the man who actually gets first billing, Gregory Hines. The fact is that Hines is a quadruple-threat man. He is extremely funny as he whips onto the stage riding an inflated yellow taxi composed of four fellows in checkerboard sleeves, waving a mighty cigar as he lives it up in a doodle called "I'm Just a Lucky So-And-So." If you want to know how well he *sings* when uninterrupted by motorized props and sinuous people, listen to him do "Don't Get Around Much Anymore" or the even simpler "Something to Live For." As for his dancing, you'll have seen him work in *Eubie* [1978] and—with his brother and father—in clubs before that. But with *Sophisticated Ladies* it's different. The big night has come. Having already worked softly and swiftly and up and down stairs that begin to glow as he passes, he comes to a second-act solo spot that simply and plainly says "Now." And now he makes it: the spotlight that covers him is his for keeps. The fierce cross-legged tap, the backward glides done in a forward rhythm, the long sweeps that end in a stammer of toes, the crazy skips that aren't skips at all because both feet are off the ground, the sudden silence we weren't expecting that becomes the perfect ending for the dizzying patter he's painted on space—these all add up. Searching for a summary, I scribbled "incredible" on my notepaper and threw up my hands. Let us be clear about Hines. He is a genuine, top-rank original, right up there with the greats of our time.

FRANK RICH, *TIMES*

In the course of his extraordinary career, Duke Ellington did just about everything with jazz that any mortal could be expected to do. Yet, strangely enough, there was one goal that eluded this giant of American music right up to his death in 1974: he never had a hit Broadway show to call his own. Well, it sure looks as if he has one now. *Sophisticated Ladies* is an Ellington celebration that just won't quit until it has won over the audience with dynamic showmanship. It's not a perfect entertainment but it rides so high on affection, skill and, of course, stunning music that the lapses don't begin to spoil the fun. What's more, this is the only Broadway revue of recent vintage that operates on a truly grand scale. There's a lavishness in this show's physical production (right up to the last spangle on the last top hat) and in its depth of performing talent that actually squares with current Broadway ticket prices. Ellington, who had an extravagant style to go with his genius, would undoubtedly be pleased. Indeed, there are times in this evening when he might be beside himself. That certainly seems the only fitting response to the show's star, the esteemed Gregory Hines. It's no secret that Hines may be the best tap dancer of our day, but he's never had a chance to show himself to quite the advantage that he does here. But don't think that *Sophisticated Ladies* is a one-man show. The towering, charismatic Judith Jamison, on furlough from Alvin Ailey, is a commanding work of art just when she's standing still. Too much of the time, perhaps, she does just stand there—as if the show's creators were too intimidated to figure out what to do with her. But Miss Jamison sings well when asked; more important, she gives the evening a presence that no one else can provide. Beaming and sassy, wearing one spectacular Willa Kim costume after another, she becomes a mesmerizing incarnation of 1920's Cotton Club glamour. By the time she descends a staircase, a vision in white, to Hines's rendition of "Sophisticated Lady," she'll take your breath away. Miss Kim's costumes are so profuse and brightly hued that they transform the cast into an everchanging satin rainbow. That's just how it should be when you've got Duke Ellington to back up your rainbow with pure musical gold.

DOUGLAS WATT, *DAILY NEWS*
The Duke would have been pleased, I think. Although *Sophisticated Ladies*, a sleek song-and-dance show that opened last night, touches but lightly on the genius of the late Edward Kennedy Ellington, whose music has coursed through the century like a lively, twisting stream, it

has flash and class and, above all, some of the elegance that was always his. I loved it madly. While fast stepping, lusty singing and the irresistible drive of a 20-piece onstage band led by Mercer Ellington dominate the evening, the peak of artistry is reached with "Solitude." Coming midway in the first half, the brass sections sliding away on either side to leave the rhythm sextet in the middle, it offers the stunning Judith Jamison in a lovely dance solo as, high in the rear, the crystal-clear soprano of Priscilla Baskerville floats the Eddie DeLange lyric. . . . Yes, I'm sure the Duke would have loved this show. But then, that was him up there, anyway, wasn't it? Him all over.

○ ○ ○

Sophisticated Ladies featured the sophisticated stylings of Duke Ellington, a fine cast sparked by emerging star Gregory Hines, a lush physical production, and the fightingest bunch of producers since Cyma Rubin stripped Harry Rigby of his billing on the opening night of *No, No, Nanette* (1971). Donny McKayle's conception, as they say, was a parade of Ellingtonia with brief lead-ins (written by McKayle). The show wasn't quite ready when the curtain went up on the Philadelphia opening; in addition to the usual problems, much of the neon—an integral part of the scenic design—arrived at the theatre broken in shipping. The resulting delays robbed the company of the onstage rehearsal time critical to pacing a revue, especially one with plenty of dance on a complicated set. And the firm hand necessary to take charge was lacking, the enterprise being blessed with *too* many hands. (Lead producer Roger Berlind was, indeed, a professional; his partners, though, while inexperienced theatrically, were very good at shouting.) Awful reviews. The decision was made to bring in Samm-Art Williams—whose 1980 three-character play, *Home,* had just ended an eight-month Broadway run—to revise the show for its Washington stand. Williams wrote a succession of monologues for Gregory Hines to deliver, sort of an Ellington surrogate describing the progression of the music. The new, revamped, and totally reformatted show wasn't ready when the curtain went up on the Washington opening. Awful reviews. Heated, as they say, discussions followed, and the producetorial committee fired Hines. ("Everybody was offering suggestions," the star later explained. "I gave mine loudly, in not too nice a way.") Only thing is, there was no show without Hines: understudy Gregg Burge knew the Philadelphia version, but he hadn't learned the "new" show that had been so roughly pasted together. With no option, the producers sheepishly called Hines, who'd already checked out of his hotel. That day's matinee was canceled while Washington was scoured for the recalcitrant tapper. Meanwhile, back at the theatre, they spent the afternoon getting Burge ready for that night's performance, removing the improvements (and Samm-Art Williams's material), and restoring the Philadelphia show. The rehearsal was run by the stage manager and dance captain, but the cast refused to work with McKayle, blaming him for the firing of Hines—who arrived back at the theatre at twilight, having been tracked down at a restaurant where he was lunching before leaving town. The show—the Philadelphia version—went on with Hines, who was then in a position to have his suggestions heard. Michael Smuin, of the San Francisco Ballet, was imported, as was legendary tap specialist Henry LeTang. McKayle was sent packing, although a fair amount of his choreography was retained; Samm-Art Williams had already left, with his briefly heard Ellington monologues. *Sophisticated Ladies* built itself into a surprise hit. But not an easy one.

Tony Awards were won by Hinton Battle (supporting actor) and Willa Kim (costume design).

BROADWAY SCORECARD

/ PERFS: 765 / +

RAVE	FAVORABLE	MIXED	UNFAVORABLE	PAN
3	2		1	

STOP THE WORLD—I WANT TO GET OFF

a revised version of the 1961 British "New-Style Musical"

book, music, and lyrics by Leslie Bricusse and Anthony Newley

directed by Mel Shapiro

choreographed by Billy Wilson

produced by Hillard Elkins, presented by James and Joseph Nederlander in association with City Center for Music and Drama, Inc.

starring Sammy Davis and Marian Mercer

opened August 3, 1978   *New York State Theatre*

CLIVE BARNES, *POST*

[Headline: "Sammy Davis' *World* is out of Orbit"]

On July 20, 1961, *Stop the World* opened in London where I was then working. Writing for the *Daily Express*, I appeared to be the only critic in town, apart from the public, who really liked it. Newley sent me a cheerful but plaintive note of thanks saying: "I only hope you're right." I was right, and I kept the letter because I thought some theatre collection would want it some day. The show opened on Broadway the following October and did great business for more than a year, first starring Newley himself, and later giving a big break to Joel Grey. *Stop the World* was from the first a strange musical. It was the story of Littlechap, from birth to death, his struggles, affairs, success, failures and indomitability. Everyman. Or something like that. It was first set by that great designer the late Sean Kenny in a circus ring, and it made freely acknowledged use of the mime techniques of Marcel Marceau. It was witty, and if not subtle, at least brashly intriguing. This new production is simply brash. It is a sort of disaster on wheels that overplays everything that was bad

"Stop the Show and Let Sammy Get Off," pleaded Doug Watt, noting that the star's startlingly slight figure "oddly suggests a child suffering from malnutrition."

in the original, and neglects everything that was good. The director Mel Shapiro, who could have known better, should probably do time for it, and possibly will. The choreographer Billy Wilson was given the task of making a vulgarity into an art—as well as linking passages between non-sense—and, no skin off his nose, failed. The sets and costumes by Santo Loquasto—the most indeterminate designing genius of the American stage—were a disastrous pinball extravaganza. From then on it was almost all downhill. The improvements, the changes, the updatings and the frantic explanations that have overtaken this production since the original do not help. This is a musical that would have been far better kept in the archives, except for one oddity: Davis. This is a vulgar production of a show that should not have been reproduced. Sammy Davis is marvelous but should either have sung the songs so brilliantly in concert, or been given a new musical.

MEL GUSSOW, *TIMES*

Sammy Davis drove an updated, Americanized, occasionally down-home version of *Stop the World* into the New York State Theatre last night. The star was operating at the very top of his form. He is a large talent—as a singer, dancer, actor and mimic—who can light up any stage. However, *Stop the World*, despite the star and the renovation, remains what it was when it first opened on Broadway in 1962—a pretentious, sentimental act of self-piety about a little man, named Littlechap, pushing his way to the top against surmountable obstacles. The uncredited adaptors—one assumes the work was done by the original authors in concert with the director, Mel Shapiro—would have to change much more to make this show work. Yet, in its original version, *Stop the World* ran 556 performances on Broadway and became popular in many countries. Call it universality or banality. The secret of the show's popularity is, of course, the score, or rather part of the score. There are three powerhouse, anthem-like numbers, "Gonna Build a Mountain," "Once in a Lifetime" and "What Kind of Fool Am I?" These have become inspirational standards. Nobody, not even Newley himself, who created the role of Littlechap, can sing those songs as beautifully as Davis does. *Stop the World* reminds us of his potent, emotion-filled voice, which has in these songs a cantor-like purity. I found Davis much more effective in the role than Newley was as an actor as well as a singer. He brings a certain humility to Littlechap's pomposity. As thin as a bone, he is almost a Chaplinesque tramp, then as he enters prosperity he begins to revel in his new role. The pantomime that was Newley's own hallmark in the show has been eliminated. But on several occasions Davis gets to demonstrate his comic sense and his gift for mimicry. Singing "Mumbo Jumbo," he campaigns for office as an all-purpose candidate. First, he puts on sunshades and swaggers as a street black. Then he breaks into a hip-wriggling Hispanic rhythm. Finally he dons a Tevye hat and a Yiddish accent and charms the Hadassah. Davis is very funny—but Las Vegas cannot be far away.

DOUGLAS WATT, *DAILY NEWS*
[Headline: "Stop the Show and Let Sammy Get Off"]
If you go, and I'm not necessarily advising you to do so, try to get a seat well toward the rear, as I did for the second half. From there, Santo Loquasto's garish unit setting which somewhat resembles a multicolored candy box that has started to melt, takes on a soft look under Pat Collins' moody lighting. And since the whole show is so thoroughly miked (and apparently recorded in spots) that you sometimes gain the uneasy impression that the two stars (Marian Mercer is the other) are lounging some place in Hollywood while look-alikes mouth their words, you can hear everything just as clearly, and less deafeningly, from a distance. Davis—a startlingly slight figure with a small paunch, so that he oddly suggests a child suffering from malnutrition—plays Littlechap, the role created by Anthony Newley. Wearing dark, unpressed, velvety slacks and a shiny, dark, loose-fitting T-shirt throughout, Davis is less arch than his predecessor but still subject to the demands of an intolerably cute show, as well as an almost utterly senseless and lifeless one. The show has been changed a lot in book as well as appearance. Updated, if the word can apply to such a work. There's some disco dancing (though not enough, just as there's not enough of Davis dancing, since Littlechap mostly slouches flat-footedly about), references to jogging and other matters of either no great interest or else unheard of in 1962. And there are slick new band arrangements [by Billy Byers and Joseph Lipman]. Mainly, the revival is a showcase for the versatile and winning Davis, a chance to sing a lot of generally commonplace songs and play the clown. But he is lost in it,

and you wish he were out there in a decent suit, strolling with a hand mike, backed up by a few other singers, and, of course, doing "What Kind of Fool Am I?" and a batch of other songs neither Newley or Bricusse had anything to do with. And no book. Not even this negligible a one.

o   o   o

By 1978 Sammy Davis had undergone a roller coaster of a career, reflective of the tumultuous societal changes of the past thirty years. The singer rose to the top of his profession in the segregated days of the 1950s, participated in the breakthroughs of the integrated 1960s, and—like many other super-celebrities of the time—succumbed to the excesses of the 1970s. (Davis made two earlier Broadway visits, as the amazingly talented but modest *Mr. Wonderful* in 1956 and the self-assured, very much in control *Golden Boy* in 1964.) By 1978 Sammy Davis was indeed "an empty shell," as the lyric says; the image presented by Doug Watt—a startlingly slight figure with a small paunch, suggesting a child suffering from malnutrition—is rather haunting. Producer Hilly (*Golden Boy*) Elkins paid Sammy $60,000 a week, anticipating enormous box office demand. Not for very many weeks, though. Another touring revival of *Stop the World*, starring Anthony Newley himself, seemed similarly out of date in 1986 and quickly fizzled.

BROADWAY SCORECARD

/ PERFS: 29 / $: −

RAVE	FAVORABLE	MIXED	UNFAVORABLE	PAN
	1		1	4

SUGAR

"A New Musical Comedy," previously entitled *Fanfare, One of the Girls, All for Sugar,* and *Doing It for Sugar*

music by Jule Styne (replacing Jerry Herman)

lyrics by Bob Merrill (replacing Jerry Herman)

book by Peter Stone (replacing George Axelrod, who replaced Michael Stewart; doctored by Neil Simon)

based on the 1959 screenplay *Some Like It Hot* by Billy Wilder and I. A. L. Diamond, from the 1935 German screenplay *Fanfaren Der Liebe* (*Fanfares of Love*) by Robert Thoeren

directed and choreographed by Gower Champion (with additional choreography by Donald Saddler and Steve Condos)

produced by David Merrick

starring Robert Morse, Tony Roberts, and Cyril Ritchard

with Elaine Joyce, Sheila Smith, Steve Condos (replacing Johnny Desmond), and Alan Kass

opened April 9, 1972   Majestic Theatre

CLIVE BARNES, *TIMES*

Well, it finally happened. After many previews, postponements and assorted pandemonia, *Sugar* officially opened last night. Rarely in show-business history has so much been done by so many for so little. This Jule Styne, Bob Merrill and Peter Stone musical has been taken from the Billy Wilder film, *Some Like It Hot.* It should have been left right there. It doesn't work as a musical, and I imagine it wouldn't even have worked had it had better music, lyrics and book than the largely lamentable material that the cast bravely displayed last night. The performances may just about provide a reason to see *Sugar,* and if you go expecting the worst you certainly won't be disappointed. Robert Morse is absolutely brilliant, and Cyril Ritchard, Tony Roberts and Elaine Joyce are not far behind. Gower Champion has staged the show with demonic energy and verve, and the whole show is in perfect shape. For what it is, it could not have been done better. There is, however, a dearth of jokes, a shortage of wit and a scarcity of verbal humor that is almost remarkable. Jule Styne is a very talented composer, but here the score scarcely leaves the ground. The lyrics by Bob Merrill sound oddly graceless and uninteresting. Almost everything has been done for the show short of closing it out of town—and if it had closed out of town New York would have been the poorer for not having the very positive treat of seeing Robert Morse playing Robert Morse in drag. From the moment when Mr. Morse, slightly simpering in full makeup and frumpy dress, replies to Mr. Roberts's question as to why he calls himself Daphne by saying with simple dignity: "I *see* myself as Daphne," it is obvious that Morse is going to be all right even if the show sinks under him. While never offering a female impersonation—he is always clearly a man—his acting shows a sharp insight into feminine psychology, and his girlish delight at becoming betrothed is funny and also moving. For my money any evening spent with the slyly irrepressible Robert Morse can be recommended at its own level, but honesty compels me to admit that I didn't pay for my seat.

MARTIN GOTTFRIED, *WOMEN'S WEAR DAILY*

There is something to be said for sitting in a big house like the Majestic Theatre and listening to a Jule Styne overture. It makes things seem as if it were still possible to glow in the exuberance of a brash, brassy and ultraprofessional Broadway musical. And, indeed, it did seem possible during the overture for *Sugar*—in fact, the melodies, the lilt, the bounce and the excitement of a Styne Broadway score were there as they had not been since his *Funny Girl* [1964]. The promise was to prove illusory, and Broadway's present crisis of confidence quickly made *Sugar* a show without heart or reason. The show is like a dream technical rehearsal where all the light cues, all the set changes, all the music and all the supporting devices function impeccably. Only there is nothing else. It is hard to believe Champion is responsible for this. He is a director/choreographer who plots every step in his shows—yet what he wound up with was a listless, humorless and dreary book credited to

Peter Stone; a handful of isolated dance numbers that, while impeccably performed, were not connected to a show idea; a score that included
some of Styne's best work in years, as well as some wasteful fillers; and
a typical set of lyrics by Bob Merrill—with typically clumsy rhymes,
awkward prosody and inane content. The company can hardly be
faulted for not rising above the material, and its work was as mechanically professional as the machinery itself. Robert Morse did transcend
that emptiness to give a genuinely comic performance, managing burlesque and pathos with the drive that was so utterly lacking around him.
Tony Roberts as the other fleeing musician, looked a little too much like
Carol Burnett for comfort and had little to do other than singing the
score's best song ["Doin' It for Sugar"]. And while everyone looked
spiffy in Alvin Colt's costumes, upon Robin Wagner's clean, cartoon
sets, they might well have been driven by little machines. For this is a
show that had no reason to be done other than to work and so, predictably enough, it didn't.

WALTER KERR, *TIMES*

Morse is playing—or dandling, or dallying with, or dancing around—
the original Jack Lemmon role of the musician who, with his buddy, is
on the run from a killing he's witnessed, mobsters at his heels. Even
before he's got into drag and joined that all-girl orchestra as the best
way of having fun while hiding out, he's funny. His hands, for instance,
seem to be at the mercy of a puppeteer's strings, and if they never do
achieve any objective they grope for but fall haplessly limp between here
and there, it is probably because the puppeteer drinks. Morse is always
working against headwinds, bouncing hither and yon, but he has a
secret formula for survival. Go with the wind. Morse rolls with the
action, breaking into smiles that display the two front teeth he got for
Christmas, executing in the course of it all two of the nicest stage curves
I've seen in seasons: once, pinched, he keeps on moving but in a circle
that brings him right back to the pincher, meanwhile, speculatively
weighing the heavy musical instruments [string bass and sax] he carries
in his hands; at the end when a gangster called Spats spots him in a
chorus line (top hat, net stockings) he executes a *curved* double take, not
a neck-snapper. (He doesn't dare snap that neck; heaven knows what
would happen.) It's an interesting improvement, and should be incor-

porated into textbooks on Technique for Actors. Morse (I seem to be repeating myself) is also just dandy while perched in an upper berth with the Sugar of the occasion, a winning blonde curiosity named Elaine Joyce, arranging himself in postures that will bring him what Horace wanted out of the arts, pleasure and profit. But it is here that we become aware of how much he is doing, how much he *has* to do, entirely on his own to make the scene work. If he weren't so malleable, he simply couldn't bring it off, because librettist Stone has gone strangely tongue-tied (I am not sure he has added anything to the original screenplay, and he has subtracted quite a bit) and even director Gower Champion hasn't helped him.

DOUGLAS WATT, *DAILY NEWS*

Sugar, a chase musical based on *Some Like It Hot*, spends two hours trying to catch up to the movie. It never does. It just winds up breathless. From the early scene, in which two unemployed male musicians become involved in a Chicago gang massacre in the winter of 1931, until the last, in which one of them is on the verge of marrying a millionaire in Florida, *Sugar* desperately attempts to capture everything on the stage that the camera caught so easily. Along the way there are songs with bouncy music by Jule Styne and pedestrian lyrics by Bob Merrill, who likes to rhyme words like "laundry" and "quandary." And a couple of lively dances by Gower Champion, who staged the whole thing. And Robert Morse. Thank heavens for Morse. The stocky comedian, wearing a blonde wig that makes him look a bit like a cherubic Mr. Hyde and all sorts of other finery, is splendid as "Daphne," the bass player in an all-girl band who becomes the apple of a millionaire's eye. *Sugar* is a musical of such unswerving mediocrity that it is sometimes hard to keep one's mind on it. At such moments, I found myself almost convinced that I was watching the immensely entertaining Morse in a revival of *Charley's Aunt* [1892], or even *Where's Charley?* [1948]. But it was merely *Sugar*.

●   ●   ●

With the smashing success of *Promises, Promises* (1968), Neil Simon's breezy adaptation of Billy Wilder's expert adult comedy *The Apartment*, it seemed only logical for David Merrick to turn to Wilder's even funnier *Some Like It Hot*. That's when the trouble started. Having tied up the rights to the original German screenplay—about two unemployed musicians in search of jobs who dress up in a variety of disguises, including women's clothes, gypsy costumes, and blackface—Merrick found himself unable, initially, to clear Wilder and Diamond's American adaptation. (Fryer, Carr, and Harris—sires of the 1966 twin hits *Mame* and *Charity*—dropped their earlier option on *Fanfaren* due to the Wilder problem.) Merrick put Mike Stewart on the project nonetheless, and his *Dolly!* (1964) librettist came up with *One of the Girls*. Stewart moved the action from 1930s Germany—*Cabaret* [1966] territory—to May 1945, with two back-from-overseas G.I.s joining Dixie Trotter's All-Girl Orchestra to flee black-marketeer mafioso Antonio "Gumdrops" DeLuca. When the *Hot* rights holders finally acquiesced, Merrick determined to start again with Wilder's Chicago/gangland *dramatis personae*. Stewart and songwriter Jerry Herman (who had started writing the score) were apprehensive of being compared to the nigh-perfect film and pressed to stick with the Swing era version. Merrick prevailed, and when his original authors wouldn't budge, he called in Jule Styne and Bob Merrill. Each had written three Merrick musicals, including the former's *Gypsy* (1959) and the latter's *Carnival* (1961). Merrill also penned *Breakfast at Tiffany's* (1966), the biggest flop of the 1960s. It was Merrick who first paired the two for *Funny Girl*, although he himself decamped prior to production. The new libretto was assigned to George Axelrod, author of the hit 1952 comedy *The Seven Year Itch* and the 1955 Styne-produced *Will Success Spoil Rock Hunter?* But Axelrod had been successless since *Success*. He was axed from *Sugar* shortly before rehearsals began, with Peter Stone—coming off *Two by Two* (1970)—as replacement. Rounding out the package was Gower, with Merrick and Champion calling an uneasy truce to their *Happy Time* (1968) clashes. Champion, Styne, and Merrill were just then wrapping up Alex Cohen's Angela Lansbury-starrer *Prettybelle* (1971), the biggest flop of the 1970s. This was *not* a good sign. Champion's relations with the *Sugar* producer and authors grew so frosty that he banned them from rehearsals. (He actually had red and green lights installed outside the rehearsal rooms. When Gower was working, the red light was on, meaning *keep out*.) The Washington tryout was, not surprisingly, troubled. From the outset only one thing worked: Bobby Morse's inspired performance as Daphne, the gal with the big bass fiddle. The first major change came when they lopped off the Spats of Johnny Desmond, the band singer who starred in Styne's 1958 *Say, Darling* and replaced Sydney Chaplin in *Funny Girl*. It was immediately evident that the menacing gangster, played by George Raft in the film, was negligible onstage. Without the constant threat, what were our hero(ine)s running from? Desmond was gone the first week, and someone—perhaps Jule Styne of Chicago, who in the Roaring Twenties had been Al Capone's favorite bandleader—came up with the idea of transforming the gangsters into machine gun-rapid, rat-tat-tat tap dancers. In came tap expert Steve Condos—a *Say, Darling* alumnus, like Desmond and Morse—and *Sugar* had a new Spats. Washington also saw Merrick making the most drastic, expensive change possible: he threw out the entire set and legendary scenic/lighting designer Jo (*Gypsy*) Mielziner as well. Robin (*Promises*) Wagner quickly redrafted the show, and the scene shop worked round-the-expensive-clock until the original set could be replaced. *Sugar* also underwent visits from just about every tinkerer Merrick could find. Most of the visitors left little mark, as the authors vehemently defended against interlopers. Some of Neil Simon's material for the opening scenes apparently made it into the show, which might explain why the opening scenes were better and funnier than the rest. None of the proffered songs were included, however. (Merrill brought "Elegance" and "Motherhood March" to *Dolly!* in Detroit, but none of Jerry Herman's pieces of *Sugar/One of the Girls* were used. At least two *Mack & Mabel* [1974] songs seem to have originated here, namely "Hundreds of Girls" and "Big Time.") Gower, however, allowed Condos to provide the gangster tap sequences and Donald Saddler to stage two numbers, "Hey, Why Not!" and "Beautiful Through and Through." The Broadway opening was pushed back from February 29 to March 14 to April 9, as the scrambling Merrick added Philadelphia and Boston bookings while the work progressed. (Why not? They were cleaning up at the box office, despite bad reviews.) *Sugar* finally made it into the Majestic, which had sat empty since *Prettybelle* canceled its March 15, 1971, opening. The most remarkable thing about *Sugar*, perhaps, was that Merrick managed to get a profitable run out of it—due solely to a tightly stacked, presold schedule of theatre parties and, most especially, the glorious performance of Bobby Morse. <u>Gower on Gower's Limitations Dept.</u>: "I use dance to embellish, extend or enlarge upon a existing emotion. None of it could really stand alone. Fosse's can. Robbins is a genius."

BROADWAY SCORECARD

/ PERFS: 505 / $: +

RAVE	FAVORABLE	MIXED	UNFAVORABLE	PAN
1		1	2	2

SUGAR BABIES

"The Burlesque Musical"

music by Jimmy McHugh

lyrics by Dorothy Fields and Al Dubin

additional music and lyrics by Arthur Malvin; "Sugar Baby Bounce" by Jay Livingston and Ray Evans

conceived by Ralph G. Allen and Harry Rigby

sketches by Ralph G. Allen, "based on traditional material"

"staged and choreographed" by Ernest Flatt (who was also given "entire production supervised by" billing); "sketches directed" by Rudy Tronto

produced by Terry Allen Kramer and Harry Rigby in association with Columbia Pictures

starring Mickey Rooney and Ann Miller

with Sid Stone, Ann Jillian, Jack Fletcher, Bob Williams, Peter Leeds, Jimmy Mathews, Scot Stewart, and Tom Boyd

opened October 8, 1979   Mark Hellinger Theatre

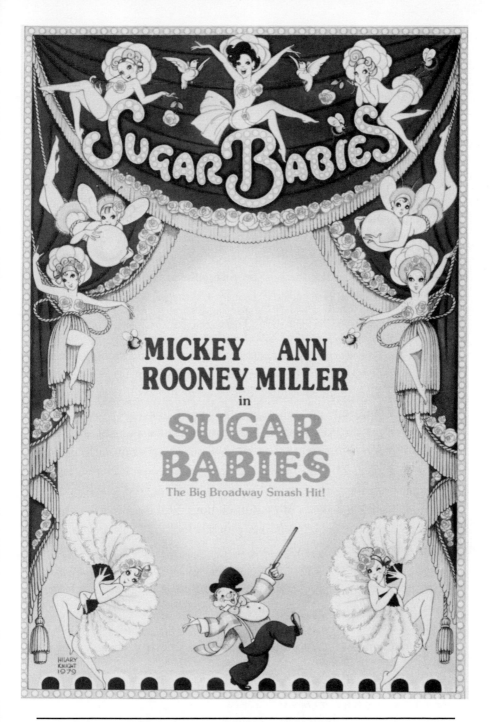

A fanciful depiction of Ann Miller sits atop the proscenium while Mickey (?) traipses center stage. (artwork by Hilary Knight)

CLIVE BARNES, *POST*

Whatever it was that killed burlesque is not all that evident in *Sugar Babies*. With Mickey Rooney, the mighty atom, at his tumultuous best, and Ann Miller tip-tapping her way into second-stardom it should prove a sizable Broadway hit, especially as the ideal musical for people who don't really want to go see a musical. Let me tell you a story. Years ago in London I saw a horrendous musical version of *Gone With the Wind* [1972; the 1973 American tryout closed on the road], which was graced with a very fine horse in the second act. At the end the producer [Harold Fielding], his eyes gleaming with Broadway glitter, rushed up and said: "Clive, Clive, what did you think of the show?" I replied: "When a horse is giving the best performance of the evening, you're in trouble." Unabashed, he cried: "Does that mean you didn't like it?" There was much in *Sugar Babies* I liked but I admit that apart from the indefatigable, inextinguishable, lovable and perfectly inimitable Rooney, the dog was giving the best performance of the evening. Ernest Flatt has staged and choreographed the show—except for the sketches left in the stylish hands of Rudy Tronto—with all the gloss of wet paint, but not perhaps quite enough of the tackiness. The show, with its lavish Raoul Pène du Bois scenery and costumes, seems aimed at imitating the *Ziegfeld Follies* rather than the humbler reaches of burlesque. In this respect I rather prefer the sleazier, more ribald downtown burlesque resuscitation called *Big Bad Burlesque* [1979, at the off-Broadway Orpheum], which strikes a more human note. Still the Broadway belles are pretty and plentiful, Ann Miller pluckily looking like a frozen clone of her former self is spirited, and there are some neat old burlesque comics. Rooney delivers with manic grace. He sings, he dances, he plays the piano, he plays the fool, and he is the glorious epitome of the clown. With his lopsided grin, his geriatrically boyish air, his warmth, total naturalness, Rooney is something to experience. For all the synthetic goo poured on by the producers, Rooney is the true icing on *Sugar Babies*. A top banana if ever we had one.

WALTER KERR, *TIMES*

The occasion is essentially a Rooney occasion (it seems to me extremely unlikely that anyone would have shaken the mothballs out of 60-year-old burlesque routines and done them, throttle open and all flags flying, without him), and the indefatigable Rooney is exactly as energetic and exactly as talented as he was when, at the age of 3 or 4, he rammed a cigar into his mouth, raked a derby over his brow, and made a star of himself. Which is very, very energetic and even more talented. The star is at his funniest, to my way of thinking, in drag, stalking the stage with a top-heavy waddle that suggests a bisected camel, batting the great false eyelashes that reach to a monstrous coiffeur (looks like a mound of congealed tapioca flecked with dead orange peel), and coming closer to us to let us see that his lip is quivering mightily as he dwells on his (her) misspent life: "Oh friends," he quavers, "it isn't easy for a girl to live along the river." I broke up right there, though I can't say where it'll all catch up with you. And he is at his *best*, to my way of thinking, when he joins Miss Miller in an easygoing session at the grand piano. Here, after sprinkling his fingers over the keys for a bit, he drops from his emphatic show-voice to the huskier intimacy with which he once did "Manhattan" (who did it better?), this time for "I Can't Give You Anything but Love." After that, they go lively again for the shared high kicks of "Sunny Side of the Street." (Miller kicks higher than he does.) You will gather I liked Rooney. Liked Miller, too, in stunning shape at whatever age she must be, ready to leap from a baggage cart, whip off gloves and overskirt, and tap as though there'd been no yesterday. She's still possessed of a voice as penetrating as a noon whistle, and she can hold onto the note for the word "blue" until the only thing that's bluer is her eye-shadow. Strides through sketches, split-skirt put to good advantage, with a hammer-and-tongs authority, too. Directors Ernest Flatt and Rudy Tronto work company and material as through arthritis had never been invented. And I had a grand time, thank you.

DOUGLAS WATT, *DAILY NEWS*
[Headline: "Rooney and Miller Headline Weak Burlesque Show"]
Ann Miller, every shiny black hair in place, is svelte and can still shake a shapely leg and do a mean tap routine, and Mickey Rooney, her co-star in last night's *Sugar Babies*, is a round, gray-haired, baggy-pants bundle of energy, but burlesque is dead, dead, dead, and it is the misfortune of *Sugar Babies* that it insists of showing us why. Although there are pretty girls to spare in lavish, amusing, mildly revealing and altogether striking costumes by Raoul Pène du Bois, the show is built

mainly around several classic burlesque comedy routines adapted by Ralph G. Allen. They are no longer funny, if they ever were, or perhaps Allen or Rooney and his fellow comics, or the sketch director Rudy Tronto have missed a beat here and there or muffed a blackout line. The broad *double-entendres* fall flat. Or perhaps the difficulty is that whereas, visually, *Sugar Babies* (the title refers to the line of girls) belongs on Broadway, in most other respects it reeks of 14th St. Everybody grins, smiles, struts and walks happy, but it's mostly in vain. Try as they will, *Sugar Babies*, like that springer spaniel [in the dog act], refuses to budge most of the time. It ends up with a full-dress patriotic finale, "You Can't Blame Your Uncle Sammy." Some art forms are deservedly forgotten.

◦   ◦   ◦

Who would have thought that Broadway was ready for an old-fashioned burlesque revue featuring two faded old movie stars? Harry Rigby, that's who. Starting with a bunch of moldy sketches compiled by college professor Ralph Allen and the not overly distinguished song catalog of Jimmy McHugh, Rigby—whose 1970s revisicals of pre–Depression musical comedies had revivified Ruby Keeler, Patsy Kelly, Debbie Reynolds, and Alice Faye—keenly tossed Mickey Rooney and Ann Miller into the mix and out came a hit. *Sugar Babies* pretty much illustrated why burlesque was dead and gone, but there's no accounting for taste, and those unpredictable audiences decided to embrace Mickey and Ann and the whole candy-corny lot. (Old-fashioned, nonadventurous theatregoers were starved for something inoffensive to counteract the concurrent *Sweeney Todd, The Best Little Whorehouse in Texas*, and *Evita*—not to mention *Ballroom, Platinum*, and *King of Hearts*.) And so *Sugar Babies* wowed 'em, running three years. Credit the Mickey/Ann chemistry; the first national company, which headlined two *real* musical comedy stars—Ms. Channing and Mr. Morse—unaccountably fizzled after only eleven weeks on the road.

BROADWAY SCORECARD
/ PERFS: 1,208 / $: +

RAVE	FAVORABLE	MIXED	UNFAVORABLE	PAN
2		1	1	2

SWEENEY TODD
THE DEMON BARBER OF FLEET STREET

"A Musical Thriller"

music and lyrics by Stephen Sondheim

book by Hugh Wheeler

based on the 1973 British play *Sweeney Todd* by Christopher Bond, adapted from the 1847 British melodrama *The String of Pearls, or the Fiend of Fleet Street* by George Dibdin Pitt, from the 1846 serial novel *The String of Pearls, A Romance* by Thomas Peckett Prest, from the 1825 *Tell-Tale Magazine* article "A Terrible Story of the Rue de la Harpe," from an earlier account in the French *Archives of the Police* by Joseph Fouché

directed by Harold Prince

choreographed by Larry Fuller

produced by Richard Barr, Charles Woodward, Robert Fryer, Mary Lea Johnson, and Martin Richards, in association with Dean and Judy Manos (and Marc Howard)

starring Angela Lansbury and Len Cariou

with Victor Garber, Ken Jennings, Merle Louise, Edmund Lyndeck, Sarah Rice, Joaquín Romaguera, and Jack Eric Williams

opened March 1, 1979   Uris Theatre

CLIVE BARNES, *POST*

[Headline: "A Bloody Good Musical"]

It was certainly different and arguably terrific. It was not your ordinary little Broadway musical—not by any means. It was *Sweeney Todd*, it opened last night and I thought it was simply great. Unusual, yes. Not only does it have the first heroine to be incinerated since Joan of Arc, but the show ends with as many dead bodies as *Hamlet*, and during its course many of the gentlemen of the chorus are eaten in the shape of meat pies. It also looks as though the whole musical is taking place in a boiler factory. *Sweeney Todd* is indeed different. Although Stephen Sondheim describes the work as "a musical thriller," it seems to me that he has finally created what he has been aiming for in most of his later works, a genuine folk-opera. This is sensationally entertaining theatre, for all but the oversqueamish. It is far more serious than any other version of *Sweeney Todd*, with a good socialist motive. This murderer of the people makes the distinction between "who gets eaten and who gets to eat," and what could be more Brechtian than that? Because of the Brechtian nature of the piece, and its staging, to say nothing of the declamatory ballad which opens and closes the show that is reminiscent of Kurt Weill, the show will almost certainly be compared with *The Threepenny Opera* [1928]. Yet Sondheim's score—the most distinguished to grace Broadway in years—owes more to Mahler, Alban Berg, and Benjamin Britten than Weill. The score is, of course, popularly intended, nothing highbrow, gorgeous lyricism, some extraordinarily atmospheric orchestrations by Jonathan Tunick, and lyrics as deft as only Sondheim can make them. The performances are great—individually. But there is one flaw. Angela Lansbury as Mrs. Lovett and Len Cariou as Sweeney are playing in different styles. Lansbury is magnificent as a comic cockney, Cariou is equally magnificent as the doom-haunted killer. But the styles of magnificence are quite different and this (it runs through the fabric of the show) makes it less of a crafted piece of integral theatre and more a vehicle for Miss Lansbury. The first night audience could not have cared less. The company is a good one. If you have any interest in the musical theatre you must see *Sweeney Todd*. It is not just next month's cocktail party conversation—it will be talked about for years.

RICHARD EDER, *TIMES*

The musical and dramatic achievements of Stephen Sondheim's black and bloody *Sweeney Todd* are so numerous and so clamorous that they trample and jam each other in that invisible but finite doorway that connects a stage and its audience, doing themselves some harm in the process. That is a serious reservation, and I will get back to it. But it is necessary to give the dimensions of the event. There is more of artistic energy, creative personality and plain excitement in *Sweeney Todd* than in a dozen average musicals. Sondheim has composed an endlessly inventive, highly expressive score that works indivisibly from his brilliant and abrasive lyrics. It is a powerful, coruscating instrument, this muscular partnership of words and music. Prince has staged the unfolding story in a series of scenes, contrasting with each other, but sharing the central tone of comedy laid over grimness. Prince's effects are always powerful, and sometimes excessively so. The throat cuttings, for example, repeated half a dozen times, are simply too bloody. They are used on us like beatings. There is very little in *Sweeney Todd* that is not, in one way or other, a display of extraordinary talent. What keeps all its brilliance from coming together as a major work of art is a kind of confusion of purpose. For one thing, Sondheim and Prince's artistic force makes the Grand Guignol subject matter work excessively well. That is, what needs a certain disbelief to be tolerable—we have to be able to laugh at the crudity of the characters and their actions—is given too much artistic power. The music, beautiful as it is, succeeds, in a sense, in making an intensity that is unacceptable. Furthermore, the effort to fuse this Grand Guignol with a Brechtian style of sardonic social commentary doesn't work. There is, in fact, no serious social message in *Sweeney*; and at the end, when the cast lines up on the stage and points to us, singing that there are Sweeneys all about, the point is unproven. These are defects, vital ones; but they are the failures of an extraordinary, fascinating, and often ravishingly lovely effort.

WALTER KERR, *TIMES*
[Headline: "Is *Sweeney* on Target?"]
I am afraid that what *Sweeney Todd* most wants to be is impressive. It succeeds in that. From the time that we enter the Uris we are all but overwhelmed by the vast industrial warehouse, complete with moving cranes, descending catwalks, and an organist hunched over his keyboard beneath rippling Victorian pipes, that is going to serve as everything from love-nest to slaughterhouse before the determined evening is done. When the corrugated back wall finally rises to give us a warehouse-and-river view, the effect is breathtaking. The spectacle does not so much let in light as invite despair. Yet with so much to occupy our eyes and ears, and so much to respect, there is an uncomfortable void in

the evening, to my mind a most serious one. The story, as told, leaves us puzzled as to why its creators went to so much trouble to tell it. We are forced to ask ourselves: what is this musical about? Efforts are made to provide just such a base. At the evening's outset, we hear that "There's a hole in the world like a great black pit/And the vermin of the world inhabit it." We also hear that the name of the hole is London, though that doesn't begin to take us toward mass murder. [Later, Sweeney describes the sound of "Man devouring man."] That does sound like the beginnings of a Brechtian parable, all right. But the analogy doesn't work: we haven't really been watching others behave in this fashion, haven't concerned ourselves with a social structure erected upon it. If anything, the hint seems pretentious here. We are without a perspective from which to view the mayhem, then, and can only sit back and admire the earnestness and the efficiency with which [everyone has] worked. The turntables spin, bodies are popped into an oven, we quite believe a filthy hag when she speaks of the stench and the strange fire in the sky over London. We are plainly in the hands of intelligent and talented people possessed of a complex, macabre, assiduously offbeat vision. Unhappily, that vision remains a private and personal one. We haven't been lured into sharing it.

DOUGLAS WATT, *DAILY NEWS*

Sweeney Todd is a staggering theatre spectacle and more fun than a graveyard on the night of the annual skeleton's ball. Subtitled *The Demon Barber of Fleet Street*, this "musical thriller" finds Sondheim, director Harold Prince, stars Angela Lansbury and Len Cariou, and practically everyone connected with this wonderful enterprise operating at the top of their form. The story, which has its origins in a 18th Century French legend that became a favorite—in various versions, often with songs—of Victorian and later English audiences delighting in bloodcurdling melodramas, is quite simply about a 19th Century London barber who slits the throats of stray customers and turns the corpses over to a female accomplice in the shop below his, a woman who grinds up the remains and bakes them into meat pies. Well, that's better than making gingerbread cakes out of children, now, isn't it? Since the show is largely sung, the evening belongs mainly to Sondheim, whose fine score has been so brilliantly orchestrated by Jonathan Tunick. Although there is no shortage of beguilingly romantic strains, and although he relies heavily on recitative in place of spoken dialogue, this is Sondheim's most playful score. "The Ballad of Sweeney Todd," which opens and closes the show and turns up at intervals throughout like a silent-movie scare theme, will follow you down the street afterward with such lines as "he killed for love and he loved to kill," while comic pieces like the Lansbury-Cariou duet, "Try the Priest," and her "By the Sea" and "The Worst Pies in London" are pure fun. And one of the most tender and lyrical of all the songs, "Pretty Women," is caressingly sung by Cariou, the "demon barber," as he is preparing a judge's throat for the slitting. Lansbury is an endless delight as the gaudily splendid Mrs. Lovett. She is the grandest, funniest, most bewitching witch of a fairy-tale fright you're ever likely to encounter. And Cariou, hair parted in the middle and with visage of deathly pallor, is a magnificently obsessed Todd. So joy to the world, dear children! *Sweeney Todd* is here to enrich your nightmares. A triumphant occasion, indeed.

o   o   o

Stephen Sondheim caught Christopher Bond's adaptation of the bloody old British thriller during rehearsals for the 1973 London production of *Gypsy* (1959)—which starred local gal Angela Lansbury, as it happens—and thus began this grand Grand Guignol musical thriller. Producer Richard Barr—whose esoteric offerings included most of Edward Albee's work, notably *Who's Afraid of Virginia Woolf?* (1962), Mart Crowley's *The Boys in the Band* (1968), and the ill-fated 1971 musicalization of Truman Capote's *The Grass Harp*—already controlled the rights, so Sondheim signed up for his first non-Prince-produced show since *Company* (1970). Prince, who had taken a Japanese bath on *Pacific Overtures* (1976), was no doubt glad to direct *Sweeney* without having to worry about financing what was obviously going to be a risky venture. (As his mentor George Abbott once noted, in his typically terse manner, "The personal problems in producing a show are not as pleasant as directing one.") Unable to raise the show's ballooning production costs on their own, Barr and partner Charles Woodward joined forces with Bobby Fryer, Mary Lea Johnson, and Marty Richards, Prince's producers on the 1978 *On the Twentieth Century*—another big-budget, over-budget monster musical that drowned in red ink. The five producers needed another three associate producers and some 271 investors to amass *Sweeney*'s $1.3 million production cost. (Prince and Ruth Mitchell had been the only names above the title on the previous Sondheim-Prince shows, but escalating costs began to take their toll. Within a few years any "angel" contributing enough money could get his or her name on the poster, although few did any actual producing.) Sondheim's score was chock-full of music, like an overstuffed Victorian sofa or a succulent meat pie, for that matter. Comparisons are senseless when talking Sondheim, but *Sweeney* sits high atop his work and therefore all musical theatre of its time; *Sweeney* is easily the finest score of the 1970s. Sondheim created some remarkable sequences, such as the astounding fifteen minutes that end the first act: the lovely romantic ballad "Pretty Women," during which our hero prepares to slice the villain's throat; followed by the unparalleled "Epiphany," in which our hero chillingly crosses over into revenge-fueled insanity; and capped with the devilishly delicious "A Little Priest," set to a cannibalistically crunchy waltz in which Sondheim saucily serves up "shepherd's pie peppered with actual shepherd." He follows up with a bravura second-act opener, in which the chorus enthuses over those savory, sweet meat pies ("Things like being careful with your coriander," offers Mrs. Lovett, "that's what makes the gravy grander"), while a grander executioner's chair is delivered and put to immediate use by the demon barber ("Bless my eyes—fresh supplies!" exclaims the demented bakeress). And these are but random threads of Sondheim's tapestry. Sure, you can pick out a few flaws along the way. Like why doesn't Todd use that friendly razor early on, when he first has it poised above Judge Turpin's gullet? (Because then there'd be no second act, that's why—and no meat pies, either.) The show was overproduced, certainly, with an overwhelming set—actually a dismantled hangarlike foundry from Rhode Island— and what seemed like acres of open space. This worked against the effectiveness of the piece on the one hand, and the economic feasibility on the other, fating the venture to financial failure. *Sweeney* has worked better in other productions—Declan Donnellan's 1993 National Theatre production, just across the bridge from Fleet Street, springs to mind—but one must remember that despite the excesses of the Broadway production, *Sweeney Todd* would not exist as the work of art that it is but for the original editorial guidance and direction of Hal Prince.

Winner of the New York Drama Critics' Circle Award. In addition to winning the Tony Award for Best Musical, Tonys were won by Stephen Sondheim (score), Hugh Wheeler (book), Harold Prince (director), Angela Lansbury (actress), Len Cariou (actor), Eugene Lee (scenic design), and Franne Lee (costume design).

BROADWAY SCORECARD
/ PERFS: 558 / $: –

RAVE	FAVORABLE	MIXED	UNFAVORABLE	PAN
3	2		1	

SWEET CHARITY

"A New Musical Comedy," previously entitled *The Small World of Charity*

music by Cy Coleman

lyrics by Dorothy Fields

book by Neil Simon (replacing Bert Lewis [Bob Fosse])

based on the 1957 screenplay *Le Notti di Cabiria* (*Nights of Cabiria*) by Federico Fellini, Tullio Pinelli, and Ennio Flaiano

directed and choreographed by Bob Fosse

produced by (Robert) Fryer, (Lawrence) Carr, and (Joseph and Sylvia) Harris

starring Gwen Verdon

with John McMartin, Helen Gallagher, Thelma Oliver, James Luisi, Arnold Soboloff, Ruth Buzzi, Sharon Ritchie, John Wheeler, and Barbara Sharma

opened January 29, 1966   Palace Theatre

FRYER, CARR *and* HARRIS
present

GWEN VERDON

as

Sweet Charity

A New Musical Comedy

with
JOHN McMARTIN
and
HELEN GALLAGHER

Music by
CY COLEMAN
Lyrics by
DOROTHY FIELDS
Book by
BERT LEWIS
Based upon an original screenplay by
FEDERICO FELLINI
Scenery and Lighting by
ROBERT RANDOLPH
Costumes Designed by
IRENE SHARAFF
Musical Direction & Dance Music Arranged by
FRED WERNER
Orchestrations by
RALPH BURNS
Production Manager
ROBERT LINDEN
Associate Producer
JOHN BOWAB

Staged and Choreographed by
BOB FOSSE

Original Cast Album by COLUMBIA RECORDS

SHUBERT THEATRE
PHILADELPHIA
Mon. Dec. 6 thru Sat. Dec. 18
Opening Night at 7:30   Other Eves. at 8:30   Thurs. and Sat. Mats. at 2:00
A Theatre Guild-American Theatre Society Subscription Play

"Charlie" is the name on Charity's tattoo. "Bert Lewis" is the name on Charity's libretto, although he—Fosse—allowed the credit to be removed when part-time helper "Doc" Simon joined the show for the tryout. Preliminary credits. (photograph by Friedman-Abeles)

STANLEY KAUFFMANN, *TIMES*

It is Bob Fosse's evening at the Palace. The show's chief attractions are the staging and the dances by Fosse, which have style and theatrical vitality. The same cannot be said for the book or score. The book has been supplied by Neil Simon without the air—or even the wise-cracks—that have previously marked his comedies. Possibly Simon is hampered by working on someone else's ideas. In any event, the result is a series of pattern scenes, generally with pattern characters filling in the shape of the scene with pattern dialogue. The chief trouble with the show is that it is so patently designed from Moment One to be a heart tugger. Gwen Verdon, in the name role, appears in silhouette and dances forward as title "credits" are lowered from the flies. The signs read: "The Story of a Girl Who Wanted to be Loved." It is a typographical error: this is the story of a show that wants to be loved. *Charity* tugs and tugs and tugs at our hearts, and the exercise builds up some pretty stiff resistance. Fosse's staging of numbers is often superb. "Big Spender," in which the hostesses line up at a railing that has arisen just behind the footlights, is a splendid mobile frieze of floozies. "Rich Man's Frug" and "Rhythm of Life," the "religious" beatnik number with a sharp vocal arrangement, are electric uses of jazz. Cy Coleman here joins the company of the many current show composers who supply appropriate rhythms but no tunes that can be remembered. There is not even a tune that one would *want* to remember. Dorothy Fields's lyrics are no more than serviceable. Irene Sharaff's costumes, as we have come to expect from her, are much more than serviceable—vivid yet not overstated cartoons. But *Sweet Charity* grows tedious between its brightest numbers, despite Fosse's work and Verdon's professionalism, because it so heavily emphasizes the adjective in its title. The good-hearted dumb broad is one of the oldest of stage clichés. No one connected with this show persuades us that she is anything more than a mechanism with which they hope to "get" the audience. Despite all the heat and skill applied, the mechanism remains mechanical.

WALTER KERR, *HERALD TRIBUNE*

There are at least six things that will interest you in *Sweet Charity*—the dances, the scenery, the songs, Gwen Verdon, Gwen Verdon, Gwen

Verdon. On the other hand, you're apt to come away feeling a bit wistful, because the show has tried very hard for one quality it doesn't get: wistfulness. Ironically, the event is trapped by its virtues. Bob Fosse, directing the dances and everything else, has made the dances and everything else breeze by, whiz by, strut by, and fly by like a galaxy of comets on the loose. But the [fast-paced production] is too much for the tenderness everyone wants. Neil Simon's libretto has skimped sorely and unexpectedly on the comedy, apparently because bittersweet is to be the mood of the hour. Dance-hall girls don't wind up married; they get pushed into rivers by the men they love. The little chick we like is a waif, after all, a lost innocent. We are meant to feel for her, not soar with her. The inside is downbeat, rueful, a sigh at heart. But *Sweet Charity* won't work out that way. The emotional line of the show is dry and plain, a kind of wasteland. And I think it is precisely because so much of the entertainment has been paced for holiday, driven by polished brass, pushed and pushed until both the dancers and the dialogue are breathless, that the barrenness appears. No gentle time has been allowed for it. . . . Miss Verdon's first appearance is stunning: designer Robert Randolph simply, slowly opens a tilted diamond out of sheer blackness to let us see the gamine poised with her hand on her knee and her head angled as though to bless them. Thereafter the lady moves toward us, with a winking black bow in her burning bush of orange hair, to let her hips fight it out between their clockwise and counterclockwise inclinations.

JOHN McCLAIN, *JOURNAL-AMERICAN*

The word was all around that *Sweet Charity* was a hit and after catching it I can only add that it is a big fat one. It was a glittering affair in the resplendently refurbished Palace, and there was that wonderful electricity which crackles through an audience at a successful première. Gwen Verdon is the pert and lissome redhead who dominates the piece and she has never been in better form. She is backed up by a rousing and persuasive score by Cy Coleman and Dorothy Fields, an ingratiating book by Neil Simon, and the best choreography by Bob Fosse that I have seen since I can't remember when. The entire evening—music, sets, costumes, lights, orchestration [by Ralph Burns] and dancing—is the kind of thing we do better than anybody else in the world and this is an extremely exciting example of it. *Sweet Charity* is quite simply an atomic smash.

NORMAN NADEL, *WORLD JOURNAL TRIBUNE*
Sweet Charity will be enjoyed more for what it contains than for what it is. That is to say, it isn't an artistically integrated creation such as *Fiddler on the Roof* [1964], *Man of La Mancha* [1965] or, ideally, *West Side Story* [1957], in which the show as a whole enfolds you. Yet there are production numbers and individual personalities as theatrically exciting as anything that's hit town in years. These lavish goodies include Gwen Verdon, Helen Gallagher, an absolutely triumphant dance scene in a discothèque, several songs—each staged buoyantly— which are a combination of tinsel and sentiment, and a sustained level of humor both carefree and sophisticated. What director-choreographer Bob Fosse has done is to detail the hilarious and sometimes poignant adventures of Charity essentially in the crystal-clear language of the dance, individual and ensemble. The truth is that the red-headed, ball-bearing-jointed Verdon is always dancing, even when she's walking. Dialogue becomes a mere accessory for Verdon, even though she speaks it well enough. She can say more with the casual pivoting of a knee than Webster ever catalogued. Miss Gallagher, I note, understudies Miss Verdon, and I'll bet she can do it beautifully. . . . Most of the songs are attractively old-fashioned in lyric design and rhythms, and enlivened with an ingenious variety of structural and harmonic touches—the suggestion of a Bach fugue in "Rhythm of Life," for example. Leaving the theatre, I found myself humming "Waiting for the Robert E. Lee." Several of the songs have that kind of a beat— wonderful for a dancing show.

○   ○   ○

Casting for a vehicle with which to bring his wife (and mother of his child) back to Broadway for her first show since the 1959 *Redhead*, Bob Fosse settled on Fellini's foreign-language Oscar winner *Nights of Cabiria*. (Runners-up: *Chicago*, which in 1975 would become a big deal of a musical, and Mario Monicelli's film *Big Deal on Madonna Street*, which in 1987 would become a Big Mess. *The Small World of Charity* was to have been one of two one-act musicals, with the companion piece to have been provided by Elaine May.) Fosse himself had undergone a few bumpy years, with severe disappointments on his post–*Redhead* director/choreographer gigs: *The Conquering Hero* (1961), from which he was konked, and Frank Loesser's costume operetta *Pleasures and Palaces* (1965), which died in Detroit. Fosse called *Little Me* (1962) composer Cy Coleman for *Charity*, ditching Coleman's "difficult" lyricist, Carolyn Leigh, in favor of Dorothy Fields (of the Fosse/Verdon/Fryer *Redhead*). *Charity*'s book was developed by "Bert Lewis"—Robert Louis Fosse, get it?—with advice and aid from *Little Me* librettist Neil Simon. When Fosse wisely realized that what was best for the show was best for him, he assigned Simon to full authorship. *Charity* ultimately emerged lustrous but somewhat uneven and heartless; Verdon's performance and Fosse's staging, though, were more than sufficient to carry the show to moderate success. Producer Fryer and his partners didn't much mind the lack of "smash" status; they had a second lady—*Mame*—tuning the grand up for a May opening.

A Tony Award was won by Bob Fosse (choreographer).

BROADWAY SCORECARD
/ PERFS: 608 / $: +

RAVE	FAVORABLE	MIXED	UNFAVORABLE	PAN
2	3		1	

THEY'RE PLAYING OUR SONG

"A New Musical Comedy"

music by Marvin Hamlisch

lyrics by Carole Bayer Sager

book by Neil Simon

directed by Robert Moore

choreographed by Patricia Birch

produced by Emanuel Azenberg

starring Robert Klein and Lucie Arnaz

with Helen Castillo, Celia Celnik Matthau, Wayne Mattson, Andy Roth, Debbie Shapiro, and Greg Zadikov

opened February 11, 1979   Imperial Theatre

CLIVE BARNES, *POST*

Happiness is a warm ticket and the new Neil Simon musical *They're Playing Our Song*. It is fun and it is funny, full of blithe good humor, hilarious jokes, and witty pointed characterizations that are credible and lovable. Oh, I almost forgot it also has music. In fact it is a musical about a composer and lyricist, based, it is widely publicized, on the real-life characters and lifestyle of the real-life composer and lyricist, Marvin Hamlisch and Carole Bayer Sager. The concept of the musical is absolutely beguiling. Aspiring lyricist meets successful composer—object, collaboration. She is enchanting, crazy and talented, not necessarily in that order. They start a meaningful relationship, but meanings and relationship are all somewhat blurred. So here we are up and running, and Simon has gotten himself another odd couple even odder than his first. Professionally the partnership works, and soon people are certainly playing their songs. But things on the love front are running less smooth. If they had not been there would scarcely have been a story. Simon is at his most sprightly and acidly comic. He is one of those droll poets that New York City spawns once in a while—a singer whose tune is beautifully consonant with the tone of his time. The show is not flawless. It is perhaps a little long, and while one can see the purpose of having each of the protagonists equipped with three alter egos who can come on to do the occasional song and dance number, the device becomes somewhat tiresome. . . . Then there were the two stars themselves. They are irreplaceable for one thing, and immeasurably pleasing for another. The manic Klein, his eyes shining out at the world like dangerous, dark buttons of intelligence, his shambles of a marionette body, is the nervously anguished epitome of smart showbiz success, New York-style. Yet, and this is the neat trick, likeable rather than brash. His calculatedly natural performance is perfectly matched by Arnaz' bemusedly moralistic songwriter, full of angst, guilt and defensive insecurity. Complex people these two, but the song they are playing will sound familiar. Simon, a rich but underrated playwright by everyone except the public and bank managers, is so often written about as if he were a soulless joke machine. Yet perhaps his most distinguishing quality is warmth—certainly here is a show to heat up Broadway's currently cold climate.

RICHARD EDER, *TIMES*

Neil Simon's book for *They're Playing Our Song* is suspended from four standing jokes. It is about the emotional difficulties two songwriters find in loving each other, and it is very heavy. Pretty soon the standing jokes begin to buckle and before long they have collapsed altogether. *They're Playing Our Song* has some important things in its favor. Marvin Hamlisch's score, though not quite up to his *Chorus Line* [1975], is intelligent and often exhilarating. Lucie Arnaz, as the lyricist, plays a charming drip and goes a considerable distance with the charm before the drip floods it out. *Song* is more a play with songs than a musical in any classic or even unconventional sense; and it is one of Simon's weakest. [The leads] meet cute, which is a Simon specialty and one he is good at. While voicing a hero-worshiping admiration for Klein's music, Arnaz manages to deflate him amusingly enough by suggesting extensive rewrites. But they go on to love cute, work cute, quarrel cute, separate cute and make up cute. They are even named cute: he is Vernon Gersch and she is Sonia Walsk. As for the four standing jokes, they vary in quality. The nicest is the notion that Sonia buys all her clothes from stage productions that are closing. She enters dressed in something from *The Cherry Orchard*, goes out dancing in a *Pippin* costume and works at the studio in a polka-dot number from *Of Human Bondage* as staged in Dallas. This is fine; but Simon brings the joke back nine or ten times. Other, feebler conceits appear over and over again. One is Vernon's use of a tape recorder to voice his deepest feelings; another, the periodic eruption of three male and three female performers to portray the fragmented personalities of the two protagonists. The fourth is the interruption of critical scenes between Sonia and Vernon by telephone calls from Leon, a hapless former lover of hers. Leon never appears but he gets himself so thoroughly discussed that by the third call he has established himself as a prodigy among off-stage bores. In general, though, its humor is second-rate Simon. There is a decided kinship with Simon's *Chapter Two* [1977]. Once again, the theme is whether an older man can open himself to the love of a younger woman; only *Chapter Two*'s jokes were quite good and Chapter Three's are much thinner.

WALTER KERR, *TIMES*

One of the nicest moments in *They're Playing Our Song* (one of the few nicest moments, I'm sorry to say) turns up while our hero Robert Klein is all trundled up in a hospital bed. One leg is in a cast because he's attempted to cross a Los Angeles street while the light said "Walk." (No, I don't think that's quite funny enough; it's the sort of joke you make with one hand tied behind your back, or perhaps one foot in a cast). Anyway, Lucie Arnaz brings him a tiny red piano. And, after she's gone, Klein is moved to tinkle out an incomplete tune called "Fill in the Words." That's to say, he completes melody and lyric but leaves just four or five notes wide open on that miniature instrument in his lap, the purpose of the gap being to let everyone say "I love you" in his own inadequate way. He's eventually joined during the finger-exercise by his three "voices," who are simply apparitions he talks to when he's drumming up inspiration for his work. The trio is playfully decked out in short white hospital gowns, each of the pranksters has his own little red piano, and the doodlers onstage now leap into a very cheerful, very childlike, hop, skip and dance that somehow manages to sound like a Christmas-morning concerto. A jolly spot, and, in its simplicity and plunked-out giddiness, it displays Marvin Hamlish at his most irrepressible. Unfortunately, the number also serves to remind us of what librettist Neil Simon has been doing during the preceding 11 scenes. He's been filling in the words. It's as though someone had come to him with a nonexistent plot, two agreeably efficient principals (just two), and seven or eight baggage-cars full of tricky, tinseled scenery and politely asked him to give the principals something, anything, to say. Which he has done, loyally, doggedly, and without the helpful inspiration of any "voices" of his own. Simon, so often described as a manufacturer of one- and two-line gags, has never been that. He's always needed a situation to suggest what the laugh's going to be about, needed a character idio- syncracy to prod him into phrasing responses that will explode. As if proof were required, here he has neither. Result: the characteristic Simon ebullience, the compulsive crackle, disappears; the gags chug uphill.

DOUGLAS WATT, *DAILY NEWS*
Though Simon has Vernon make a rather snide remark at the start about hating songs that rhyme such things as "Massachusetts" and "two sets" (a gratuitous slap at Lorenz Hart), I myself wince at pieces rhyming "together" with "clever," as Sager does here.

o   o   o

Neil Simon turned to Marvin (*Chorus Line*) Hamlisch for a proposed musicalization of his 1970 comedy-drama *The Gingerbread Lady*. That idea didn't pan out, but the playwright—observing the composer and his then-girlfriend, lyricist Carole Bayer Sager (of the 1970 *Georgy*)— came up with a sketch of an idea about a neurotic songwriting couple. This became a sketchy, gimmicky musical with a negligible score pro- vided by the prototypes themselves. *They're Playing Our Song* was a severe letdown compared to Simon's previous musicals, *Little Me* (1962), *Sweet Charity* (1966), and *Promises, Promises* (1968). It was nev- ertheless the funniest musical of the year—against the likes of *Ballroom*, *King of Hearts*, and *Sweeney Todd*—and buoyed by Simon's jokes, the only song-and-dancer of the season to turn a profit. And a huge profit it was, too, thanks to big business in large-size theatres (in New York, on the road, and abroad) and minimal running costs (with a cast of two low-salaried principals and six chorus). If Hamlisch got by with substandard work his second time out, his three subsequent musicals have all been bona fide disasters: the biomusical *Jean Seberg* (1983, lyrics by Christopher Adler), produced in London by the National Theatre; the beauty contest satire *Smile* (1986, lyrics by Howard Ashman); and the ill-fated *Goodbye Girl* (1993, lyrics by David Zippel), from Neil Simon's motion picture of the same name. One *Chorus Line*, certainly, goes a long way.

BROADWAY SCORECARD
/ PERFS: 1,082 / $: +

RAVE	FAVORABLE	MIXED	UNFAVORABLE	PAN
1	3			2

THREEPENNY OPERA

a third American translation of the 1928 musical *Die Dreigroschenoper* (*The Threepenny Opera*)

music by Kurt Weill

book and lyrics by Bertolt Brecht; new translation by Ralph Manheim and John Willett

based on the 1728 opera *The Beggar's Opera* by John Gay

directed by Richard Foreman

produced by the New York Shakespeare Festival, presented by Joseph Papp

with C. K. Alexander, Blair Brown, Ellen Greene, Raul Julia, Caroline Kava, David Sabin, and Elizabeth Wilson

opened May 1, 1976   *Vivian Beaumont Theatre*

MARTIN GOTTFRIED, *POST*

The New York Shakespeare Festival is taking great pains to explain to audiences that its new production of *Threepenny Opera* is more faithful to the letter and spirit of the original than the immensely popular revival of the Fifties was. A detailed specification is enclosed with every program. The motivation behind this is plain: to forestall disappointment. There is a better way to do that, however. By presenting a production that is effective, and that is something the Festival hasn't done. Aside from its translation, the production isn't nearly as close to the Brecht-Weill intentions as it thinks it is. Blitzstein made it considerably sweeter and more conventional than Brecht and Weill had meant. The Manheim-Willett translation corrects all of that. It seems to be translation at its most successful, grasping Brecht's poetic vulgarity, even his conscious misplacing of words to music. The program notes point this out accurately and clearly. What they do not mention, however, is that Foreman's version is no more like the Berliner Ensemble's in look, manner or effect than the off-Broadway one was. And it is considerably less effective. Foreman's production is based on a visual look and a style of movement. The visual look is cold, sleek and surreal, seeking the displacement of our sense of perception through a series of horizontal strings at various heights and depths. The style of movement is a slipping step, something like eccentric dancing. This step is repeatedly demonstrated by a character I do not believe is in the original script, an assistant to Mr. Peachum, played with startling flair by Tony Azito. It is apparent that Azito is the subject of Foreman's greatest attention and satisfaction. Consequently, good as he is, Azito exemplifies the director's misplaced interests. For *Threepenny Opera* is not about surreal appearances and eccentric movement. Like it or not, and nobody in America seems to, it is about the evils of capital in theme, and about German cabaret theatre in music. Its style, of course, is Brecht's own—a whole-theatre, reducing romance, suffering, justice and injustice to caricature and marionette show. But Foreman has not grasped it. This new *Threepenny Opera* has mistakenly placed too much faith on Brecht's theorizing—he didn't place as much faith in it himself. It goes off in other directions anyhow. And as a result it ends up nowhere.

WALTER KERR, *TIMES*

[Headline: "Moralizing is a Bore, but Good Music Helps"]

I wish that *Threepenny Opera* had been an opera so that we might have listened to music the night long without interference from that interminably moralizing libretto. Needless to say, the unforgotten and unforgettable Kurt Weill score is there to haunt the Beaumont with its sweet deathlike fragrance, pitting solemn organ chords against the gamiest of lyrics, using a sudden rush of banjo to insult the insincerities on stage, keeping a cabaret concertina at hand to accent the smokiness of melodies that seem as faintly scarred as Macheath's neck in the half-dark. The abandonment of the familiar Marc Blitzstein and the substitution of a deliberately coarser, more accurate translation do not make that much difference to the sounds we once again revel in. Weill was always the true wit of the occasion, setting his acridly liquid tunes against the grossness of the whores, thieves and other statesmen who hustled through a worm-eaten world, and both melody and mockery survive as a perfectly matched pair. But that's it. The now-longer libretto that is served by the imagery and saved by the score remains a laboriously didactic, one-dimensional business. Instead of permitting a scoundrel to say one thing while we slyly infer another, it's all laid out for us. No criminal says he is virtuous, which is where the joke and an ironic truth both lie; corruption merely advertises itself freely, and where's the satirical edge to that? *The Beggar's Opera*, ancestor of the Brecht-Weill vision, kept up a constant pretense of gentility, indeed of a pastoral innocence, while the worst sort of skullduggery went on; that gave the work its comedy and its murderous bite. I must assume that when Brecht wrote for a decadent Berlin, he was able to strike sparks with parallels between the gross misbehavior on stage and the "respectable" Germany clinging to power. Here, in spite of our own very recent experience of thorough-going corruption, we are out of touch, staring soberly at a museum piece, acknowledging the obvious in what the libretto has to say but aware that it is obvious, never devious, never delightfully, maliciously curved. Thus the evening is more nearly a work of scholarship than an entertainment. It's not boring; more likely it'll leave you slack—except for the satisfaction your eye may take in Foreman's firm grotesqueries and the certainty that any moment now Mr. Weill will be heard from again.

DOUGLAS WATT, *DAILY NEWS*

A fantastic and sensationally theatrical production. It is a rebirth, rather than a revival, of a blazing 20th-century masterpiece, grafted onto an 18th-century one, a collaboration that, though almost 50 years old, seems as immediate as tomorrow's headlines. Be warned, it will mesmerize, thrill, blind and perhaps blister you. And underlying its bitter cynicism lies a pity that makes it, finally, a work of feverish beauty. A new translation by Ralph Manheim and John Willett is subtler and allegedly more faithful to the Brecht original than is the Marc Blitzstein one, though at the same time it is often more difficult to sing. The Blitzstein adaptation was, of course, of tremendous importance in establishing *The Threepenny Opera* in this country during its six-year run off-Broadway during the '50s. But the new treatment is more compelling. With Kurt Weill's brilliantly poisonous score, which can lift you right out of your seat in number after number, the total effect is devastating. Raul Julia is a tall, mustached, monocled and elegant Mack the Knife given to walking with head slightly forward and feet carefully lifted and set down like the hooves of a horse in dressage steps. The most electrifying performance comes from Ellen Greene as the whore Jenny, who turns her lover Macheath in for a few shillings. Her account of the bitter aria "Pirate Jenny" is enthralling, and the tango "Ballad of Immoral Earnings" will dissolve you as presented by Greene, Julia and the small band (off to one side) under the excellent direction of Stanley Silverman.

◦   ◦   ◦

Kurt Weill and Bertolt Brecht's *Die Dreigroschenoper* achieved international success when it premièred at Berlin's Theatre am Schiffbauerdamm on August 31, 1928. It was immortalized in a series of contemporary recordings and G. W. Pabst's 1931 motion picture version (disputed by the authors but a classic nevetherless). Stateside acceptance was another matter. *The Threepenny Opera* opened at Broadway's fabled Empire Theatre on April 13, 1933. The adaptation, by Gifford Cochran (a coproducer) and Jerrold Krimsky (brother of the other producer), was presumably indifferent; neither author was able to make the trip over—Weill was taking refuge in Paris, having fled the Nazis on March 21—so the production went unsupervised. In any event, it caused hardly a stir and closed after only twelve performances. Composer/lyricist Marc Blitzstein knew and loved the piece from his days as a composition student in Berlin. Following the demise of his 1949 *Regina* he called Weill, whose *Lost in the Stars* (which opened the day before *Regina*) was also faltering. Blitzstein had written a translation of "Pirate Jenny"; sing it (over the phone), said Weill. Blitzstein did, and Weill saw a way to revive *Threepenny*'s fortunes and his own. But the composer soon died of a heart attack. Blitzstein went ahead, with his version premièring on June 14, 1952, at an arts festival at Brandeis College (Waltham, Massachusetts). The adaptor narrated, his protégé Leonard Bernstein conducted, and Weill's widow, Lotte Lenya, sang. This led to an Off-Broadway limited engagement, opening on March 10, 1954, for ten weeks, with Lenya recreating her 1928 role. Popular acclaim resulted in a 1955 remounting, and the production ultimately racking up an astounding 2,706 performances. (Broadway's long-run musical champ at the time was *Oklahoma!* [1943], with 2,248.) The success of the Blitzstein version, in New York and around the country, established the previously obscure *Threepenny* as a classic, launched a revival of interest in the works of Weill, and made "Mack the Knife" Weill's biggest hit song. The Blitzstein adaptation made its only Broadway appearance with a 1966 Swedish puppet version from the Stockholm Marionette Theatre, imported to the Billy Rose for thirteen performances. Ten years later came the New York Shakespeare Festival, with a new translation by Ralph Manheim and John Willett, who restored the "political and sexual thrust" of the German original, Blitzstein's version being "quite clearly at odds with the dramatist's purpose and dramatic sensibilities." So said Joe Papp, anyway. The new version was outspoken in ways the '50s version could not be, given Brecht's notoriety (he was a featured guest of the House Un-American Activities Committee). For all its sanitization, though, Blitzstein's adaptation serves the score far better. Blitzstein was not a literary academic; he was a composer, a man of the theatre, a colleague (and competitor) of Weill, and—most important—an accomplished lyricist who could complement Weill's music. The foundation of *Threepenny Opera*'s modern-day reputation is "Mack the Knife." Not just the song lyric, but the song title itself. And these are Blitzstein's words. Yes, Brecht called his character Mackie Messer, and *messer* is indeed the German word for knife, but it was Blitzstein who came up with the streetwise sobriquet that gives old Mack a bigger-than-life infamy (like Jack the Ripper or Billy the Kid). And that was not an obvious translation; one imagines that Blitzstein dug into Weill's hurdy-gurdy melody, selected the last three notes of the A section as his title phrase, and experimented until he came up with those three little words. (I don't reckon Louis Armstrong or Frank or Ella or anyone would have otherwise recorded the "*Moritat*.") People keep coming along with new productions with "more authentic" translations—there was a fourth Broadway version in 1989 starring Sting for sixty-five showings—but they always seem to call their boy "Mack the Knife." Which is not Brecht, but Blitzstein. (Papp's translators spelled it "Mac the Knife," as if that made a difference.) Borrowing Blitzstein's chillingly apt word picture is pardonable perhaps, but borrowing it while denigrating Blitzstein's work borders on gravedigging. The Off-Broadway version "is indelibly imprinted in my mind and I assume the minds of many who have bought tickets to our new production," said Papp on a program note—entitled "The Real *Threepenny Opera*"—slip-sheeted into the opening night *Playbill*. "Even though I am producing a new translation of this work, the old Blitzstein lyrics refuse to leave my head." Which leaves us just where? "Oh, the shark has pretty teeth, dear, and he shows them pearly white. . . ."

BROADWAY SCORECARD

/ PERFS: 307 / $. : +

RAVE	FAVORABLE	MIXED	UNFAVORABLE	PAN
2	1	2		1

TIMBUKTU!

"A Musical Fable based on *Kismet*"

music and lyrics by Robert Wright and George Forrest "from themes by Alexander Borodin [1833–1887] and African folk music"

book by Luther Davis

based on the 1953 libretto *Kismet* by Charles Lederer and Luther Davis, from the 1911 play by Edward Knoblock

"directed, choreographed, and costumed" by Geoffrey Holder

produced by Luther Davis

starring Eartha Kitt, Melba Moore, and Gilbert Price

with Ira Hawkins (replacing first-billed William Marshall), Miguel Godreau, George Bell, Bruce Hubbard, Eleanor McCoy, and Daniel Barton

opened March 1, 1978   *Mark Hellinger Theatre*

CLIVE BARNES, *POST*

Do you remember *Kismet*? The show opened right at the end of 1953, during a newspaper strike. Some unkind people say it was the newspaper strike that made it. The critics never got to it until it was up and away. It played 583 performances—a sizable run for those days—but the critics, when they finally emerged from their hibernating strike, had scarely a kind word to say for it. It used Borodin music adapted, mildly shamefully, by Robert Wright and George Forrest, who had earlier done the same painless and expenseless surgery on Grieg for *Song of Norway* [1944]. They were experts in the graveyards of helpless genius. *Timbuktu!* is an Afro-styled retread of *Kismet*. After nearly a quarter of a century the collaborators have discovered that there is also a black audience out there—so *Kismet* has moved, as a program note tactfully puts it, to somewhere "black, opulent and remote." What can I tell you?

What do you think *they* were selling? No, that's not supposed to be Eartha Kitt. Preliminary credits. (artwork by Joe Eula)

It is a lot better than the more sensitive among you might feel. But, for that matter, it is a great deal worse than the more optimistic among you might have hoped. It has a great visual production, a stupid book, a travesty of a score, one peculiarly great performance—from Eartha Kitt, who is here both the good Eartha and the bad Eartha all in one frozen time capsule—and a dazzling conception, direction, choreography and costuming by Geoffrey Holder. The man is a wiz. The music has been hyped up with, they say, African folk music. It does sound different, and there are undeniably African tribal sounds at the back of the steppes. Let me admit that I am prejudiced about this kind of musical. I don't think you can steal music from the graves of dead composers—at least not with authority. And authority is what this score so miserably lacks. It was cheap to start with, and has gotten cheaper over the last quarter century and its original collaborators' attempt to blacken its face and give it one last natural tap dance. Holder has done a lovely job. The musical floats with its costumes, and Holder's entire extravagant concept is slow-spinning yet entrancing. Holder's view of the musical as some black never-never land of the soul is precisely on key. But also Holder's choreographic concept of a musical as a masque—a dance concept prancing through the landscape of an impossible fairytale—proves equally brilliant.

WALTER KERR, *TIMES*

You've got to fight your way through an awful mess of feathers to get anywhere near the attractive people who, from time to time, sing the musical's songs. *Timbuktu!*, as if you didn't know, is an all-black variation on the earlier bauble-bangle-and-bead show called *Kismet*, and it's still got the melodies borrowed from Borodin to keep itself warm: "Stranger in Paradise," "And This Is My Beloved," and, of course, the B, B, and B thing ["Baubles, Bangles and Beads"]. The difficulty at the Mark Hellinger is to get at them. Not because they're inadequately sung (some are most beautifully sung, when the mikes aren't screeching back at the soloists) but because director/choreographer/costumer Geoffrey Holder seems to have taken his third obligation much more seriously than his first two. Whatever clothes may do for a man, they don't make a show, and *Timbuktu!* keeps turning into a mighty fuss of cockatoo headpieces, egrets' wings, towering platform shoes, tasseled parasols, flying tricolor streamers, West African masks and spinning maypoles, while the principals struggle to emerge from the fashion parade. The trouble is doubled by the fact that nobody in the background will stand still, or cease rotating their tattered tall umbrellas, so that we can fix our attention on a number, or perhaps the plot. (I'm not truly concerned about the plot, which is unfollowable in any case, but about the talented players who might please us up front if only the extras would either freeze now and again or get out of there altogether.) The extras, you understand, aren't doing anything significant or remotely helpful, they're just waving colors around as they aimlessly wander this way and that. Holder's interest in the looks of the show keeps even the skilled Melba Moore, who certainly knows how to phrase a song, from asserting her powers as persuasively as she ought. Gilbert Price survives very nicely because—as the disguised prince who falls in love with a beggar's daughter—he has nothing to do but sing. So far as I was concerned, he could have sung all night. But *Timbuktu!* keeps you waiting for a long, dull time before a familiar melody lifts your spirits temporarily.

HOWARD KISSEL, *WOMEN'S WEAR DAILY*

A lethargic, lustreless version of *Kismet.* Apart from changing the setting from North Africa to the River Niger, the current production has reduced both book and score to rubble, in conception as well as execution. Everything about the production is disastrous. Melba Moore, who struck me as such a powerful singer a few years ago in a cabaret stint at the Waldorf, does some of the ugliest singing I have ever heard. Gilbert Price sings with greater skill, but his voice generally sounds strained. Eartha Kitt has very little to sing and a lot of lame comedy material, which she delivers like a female impersonator "doing" Eartha Kitt. As bad as most of the singing is, it sounds even worse because the sound system constantly crackles, the way your record player does when you need a new needle. (I am commenting only on the singing because, as far as I could see, there was no acting.) The one moment that has any class is a dance by two birds of paradise [Miguel Godreau and Eleanor McCoy], whose costumes have some wit to them and whose movements have the elegance of birds of high plumage. The rest of the choreography lacks style. It is always a sign of desperation when a director has his dancers trundle through the audience. Holder does it at the end of the first act. Since the dancers are all in white it might be interpreted as, in effect, waving the flag of surrender. I would have been willing to call a truce and forego the second act. Alas, duty kept me in my seat another hour. It seemed infinitely longer.

DOUGLAS WATT, *DAILY NEWS*
[Headline: "Melba Toasted, Show Is Not"]
Allah be merciful; look down with forbearance on the toiling throng in *Timbuktu!*, last night's soggy rehash of the quarter-century-old *Kismet*, itself a mostly humdrum musical enlivened only by the presence of Alfred Drake as the dashing thief of Baghdad. And Allah be kind; give that vibrant little chick Melba Moore a classy new musical comedy and let her shine forevermore, or what passes for such in Broadway's sands of time. For she, sweet and saucy, is the one bright light in this confusion of vivid colors and borrowed Borodin melodies. Geoffrey Holder, who has staged the entire piece, dances and all, with more sweep and boldness than distinction, and, with emphasis on his characteristic West Indian vein, also has costumed the show. And here he has really let himself go, practically smothering the show with more yards of material of every color and description than it would take to drape an oil sheik's fleet of Bentleys. In the final palace scene, the riot of colors is reduced to gold, in which practically everybody is swathed from head to toe. In sharp contrast, there is also a great deal of near nudity, with the male ensemble—looking extremely silly with their oiled, glistening bodies sporting bejeweled G-strings and other doodads—oddly more exposed than the females. *Timbuktu!* is a gaudy bore, with a pearl named Melba bobbing about in it.

o   o   o

The Wiz [1975] had been a stylish new look at *The Wonderful Wizard of Oz*, specifically conceived for an all-black cast. *Timbuktu!* was but a warmed-over rehash of *Kismet*, turned black simply for the sake of tapping the new audience that had flocked to *The Wiz*. Producer/librettist Luther Davis was the driving force behind this new version, with Geoffrey Holder serving as stage magician as he had on the *Oz* musical. *Kismet* was not an especially well-written musical, although some-what stronger and more entertaining than the original reviews indi-cated. But the cornerstone of *Kismet*'s success in 1953, and again in the 1965 Music Theatre of Lincoln Center revival, was the bravura per-formance of Alfred Drake as the mastermind poet-beggar at the story's center. William Marshall wasn't very effective in the role during the tryout; his replacement, Ira Hawkins, was considerably better but unable to dominate the proceedings, leaving *Timbuktu!* a pale *Kismet* indeed. (Drake, in '53, also had Doretta Morrow, Joan Diener, and Richard Kiley in support, giving the show four strong-voiced person-alities.) What *Timbuktu!* did have was Eartha Kitt and a bunch of near-naked musclemen prancing about—not enough for most audi-ences. ("*Timbuktu*-tu-much," reported *Variety*'s out-of-town corre-spondent.)

BROADWAY SCORECARD

/ PERFS: 221 / $: –

RAVE	FAVORABLE	MIXED	UNFAVORABLE	PAN
		1		5

A TIME FOR SINGING

"A New Musical"

music by John Morris

book and lyrics by Gerald Freedman and John Morris

based on the 1940 novel *How Green Was My Valley* by Richard Llewellyn

directed by Gerald Freedman

choreographed by Donald McKayle (doctored by Gower Champion)

produced by Alexander H. Cohen in association with Joseph Wishy

starring Ivor Emmanuel, Tessie O'Shea, Shani Wallis, and Laurence Naismith

with Frank Griso, Elizabeth Hubbard, Gene Rupert, and George Hearn

opened May 21, 1966   *Broadway Theatre*

STANLEY KAUFFMANN, *TIMES*

I enjoyed the first 10 minutes of *A Time for Singing* very much. I thought I was about to see a good sentimental musical. I was wrong. The book is faultily built and, despite its length, only skims emotion. The lyrics and the music are generally insipid. What is left that is valuable is damaged by two of the leading performers and is notably helped by none. It begins promisingly. No overture—just male Welsh voices joining in song far behind a scrim. Mr. Griffith [Ivor Emmanuel] steps forward to induct us into the play, and there is a good short scene deep in the coal pits—with a work song and some fierce brief dancing (the only moment when choreographer Donald McKayle gets a real chance

ALEXANDER H. COHEN
presents

a Time for Singing

Book and Lyrics by **Gerald Freedman** and **John Morris**

Music by **John Morris**

Based on the novel "How Green Was My Valley" by Richard Llewellyn

IVOR EMMANUEL · TESSIE O'SHEA
SHANI WALLIS
LAURENCE NAISMITH

Production Designed by **Ming Cho Lee** Lighting by **Jean Rosenthal** Costumes Designed by **Theoni V. Aldredge**

Musical Direction by **Jay Blackton** Orchestrations by **Don Walker**

Production Associate **Hildy Parks** Produced in Association with **Joseph Wishy**

Original Cast Album Recorded by Warner Bros. Records

Choreography by **Donald McKayle**

Directed by **Gerald Freedman**

AIR CONDITIONED
BROADWAY THEATRE
B'way at 53 St., N. Y. C. 247-7992

Advance word from the Boston tryout—emblazoned across the back of the herald—proclaimed *Time for Singing* "the finest musical show I have ever seen." This was not the *Globe* or the *Post*, unfortunately, but one Terry Carter of WBZ-TV. So much for advance word from Boston.

to show his quality). We then go to the surface and the superficial. As we move along, every scene, every incident is wrenched out of reality and pared into a Show Number: the happy mealtime number, the wedding number, the roistering men's number, and so on. Each of these moments could conceivably have been heightened by good music and fresh treatment, but here they are drained and die-stamped into stale theatricalities. Tessie O'Shea, the matriarch, is not only an experienced vaudevillian, she is a shameless one. She inflicts on the role of the sturdy Welsh mother all the transparent tricks of the music hall. Shani Wallis sings well but did not win at least one viewer with her arrant winsomeness. The key role of little Huw is played by 12-year-old Frank Griso, very appealing in looks but with few signs of talent. Some of the time he cannot even be understood. Too bad. This promised to be an enjoyable show. But none of the performances is compelling, and some injure the reality that this show needs. (Not all musicals need it.) And the score does little to enrich a script that dilutes the emotions of *How Green Was My Valley*. The effect is almost as if a different Welsh antecedent had taken over. At the Broadway Theatre the corn is green.

WALTER KERR, *HERALD TRIBUNE*

A Time for Singing spends too much of its time singing. Just as a scene threatens to become verbally interesting, they go walloping off into a bleat that neither satisfies the scene nor justifies itself independently. The entertainment has too much drama to be a good musical and too much music to be a good drama. There are several lessons to be learned from it. One is that musicals ought not to be taken from fat books—from books containing years and years of remembered narrative complexity. Another current truism is that no amount of professional tightening out of town will make up for a missing link in the emotional structure of an entertainment. *A Time for Singing* has no lapses of pace or obvious moments of woolgathering. Everything is neatly in place, and as hot on the heels of whatever preceded it, as a conscientious director would wish. The show looked "frozen," as the trade says when people have stopped experimenting and decided instead to make the existing material taut. But it lacks that one little moment near the opening when we might pause and see who the characters are and what they mean to one another. Everything is both pressed and compressed. A word should be said, I think, about Shani Wallis's pressing. Wallis plays the unlucky girl who never gets her minister, and midway through the first act she is required to express her fierce yearning in a song called "When He Looks at Me." As performed, the yearning is certainly fierce. Miss Wallis, obviously determined to bring the house down by compounding the more energetic qualities of Nellie Forbush and Eliza Doolittle, skips, swings, kicks, thrashes, and in general lays waste to the Broadway stage until she has at last collapsed flat on her back, with all her white petticoats showing, in a state of total, and hopefully adorable, exhaustion. Director Gerald Freedman must bear some of the responsibility. But by the time the girl has popped a kettle onto her head and virtually driven holes through the scenery, we feel rather more like the *Michelangelo* having come through an ocean storm than like ebullient folk tripping the light fantastic. Miss Wallis does produce the effect she intends, which is enormous, automatic applause. But she does it by twisting the arms of the audience.

NORMAN NADEL, *WORLD JOURNAL*

A Time for Singing isn't a really bad musical; it contains one very good voice [Emmanuel], two or three bright personalities and several mildly entertaining scenes. But it still must be written off as a bitter disappointment simply because it falls so far below what it could have—and should have—been. Where the musical should have emphasized the individuality of the story and its people [as in the "unique, individual and authentic" novel], it has, instead, erased all the distinguishing characteristics and made them ordinary. This overlay of banality was imposed on the story and lyrics by Gerald Freedman and John Morris. As composer, Morris has written second-class Broadway musical stuff—the expected nostalgia song, romance, comedy, rebellion and so forth. Musically, he has managed to place Llewellyn's vigorous tale somewhere between Brooklyn and the Ozarks.

◦   ◦   ◦

Producer Alexander H. Cohen moved from *Baker Street* (1965) up north to Wales for this jolly song-and-dancer. The former had Queen Victoria's Golden Jubilee and the Bil Baird puppets; the latter had plenty of time for singing and a mining collapse—complete with dead principals—to climax the rollicking second act. *Baker Street* was shepherded by director Hal Prince and the ghosts of Bock and Harnick, all of whom might have been able to make Llewellyn's *Valley* sing. With Cohen at the helm, both shows displayed great creative showmanship on the advertising pages, if nowhere else. "I'm not one of those producers who think a flop, like a disease, should never be mentioned," commented the huckstering Alex, who is indeed mentioned frequently in these pages.

BROADWAY SCORECARD
/ PERFS: 41 / $: —

RAVE	FAVORABLE	MIXED	UNFAVORABLE	PAN
			1	5

TINTYPES

"The New Musical"

music and lyrics traditional, arranged by Mel Marvin

conceived by Mary Kyte, with Mel Marvin and Gary Pearle

directed by Gary Pearle

choreographed by Mary Kyte

The American National Theatre and Academy Production, produced by Richmond Crinkley, Royal Pardon Productions, Ivan Bloch, Larry J. Silva, and Eve Skina, in association with Joan F. Tobin

with Carolyn Mignini, Lynne Thigpen, Trey Wilson, Mary Catherine Wright, and Jerry Zaks

opened October 23, 1980   *John Golden Theatre*

CLIVE BARNES, *POST*

A most winsomely agreeable cabaret-style musical. It is a cunningly contrived nosegay to impossible times impossibly past—the nostalgic never-never land of cultural memory. And it is a winner. What really makes the show adorable is its cast, and the opportunities it has been given. It has been handcrafted. The outstanding performer is Jerry Zaks, who combines total involvement with a nuclear radiance and a show-biz pizzazz. Just to hear him at the beginning, singing "Yankee Doodle Dandy" in a precisely articulated Russian-Jewish accent, is alone worth the price of the experience. See *Tintypes*—it will take you back to a world you never knew but have always wistfully wondered about.

WALTER KERR, *TIMES*

I'd like to mention one aspect of the entertainment about which there can be no question. Her name is Lynne Thigpen, and I don't even have to tell you to keep an eye on her because you'll find it impossible not to. She's a winner even when she isn't doing much, perhaps no more than standing over Anna Held's bathtub and blowing soap bubbles out of a children's pipe. There's a moment when I expected her to do one thing and she did quite another, abruptly, soberly, stunningly. Miss Thigpen is the only black performer in the company of five and she adopts a very funny, faintly sour, highly skeptical expression as she listens to her white colleagues doing their own four-part version of "Shortnin' Bread." Just why they should be appropriating a traditional—and traditionally black—tune is a good question in itself, and what I imagined she'd do is retaliate by taking over a "white" tune and showing them how it should be sung. A bit of upmanship was quite in order. But the lady did, and does nothing of the sort. Instead, from far left field, she simply glides into an old Bert Williams number called "Nobody" and makes a magically melancholy, bitterly powerful thing of it. Now, I wasn't lucky enough ever to hear Bert Williams, but I have some vague memory of hearing either a phonograph record or an early impersonator making a wonderfully idiosyncratic doodle of it—and the doodle was composed of grumbling hesitations and very carefully timed laughs. Laughter is probably what it was written for. Thigpen doesn't make a complete U-turn of it, doesn't ask for anything like tears. But just behind the pulsing beat there's a hint of tears suppressed, of regret brushed aside, of anger postponed until another day. The notes themselves aren't doing the work: Thigpen's vocal cords, combined with her musical intelligence, are arriving at a curious, full-throttled and yet vigorously restrained, combination of sorrow and exultation. It's like heartache done to a cakewalk. And it's as satisfying as it is surprising. The performer also has fun—a more transparent kind of fun—as she appears beneath a pancake hat topped by a blazing orange feather to tilt one way while her hat tilts another to the strains of that blaring plaint, "Bill Bailey, won't you please come home?" She's just dandy.

DOUGLAS WATT, *DAILY NEWS*

It's dainty-quainty time again now that *Tintypes*, the turn-of-the-century musical potpourri seen off-off-Broadway last spring, has come to Broadway. Glowingly patriotic, despite occasional barbs aimed at the seats of power; impeccably produced and staged; and, furthermore, all smiles—it should have found in me an ardent admirer. Instead, I found myself more often than not wincing at its cuteness as I watched it slip mincingly by. There are telling moments, several of them in pantomime, as the show's young Jewish immigrant (performed in cap and muffler and baggy pants by Jerry Zaks, with references to Chaplin, George M. Cohan, Cagney *playing* Cohan, and others) encounters the wide assortment of characters played by the rest.

◦   ◦   ◦

Tintypes, a "nice" (in the negative sense) cavalcade of old-time songs, began life at Washington's Arena Stage. An Off-Off-Broadway production, under the auspices of ANTA, opened on April 17, 1980, at the Theatre of St. Peter's Church. After 137 performances it closed down to prepare for the move to the big time. *Tintypes* looked awfully tiny in a Broadway house—even the small Golden—and stirred up not much of a fuss. It remains notable, mostly, for the presence of *Grease*-graduate/director-to-be Jerry Zaks.

BROADWAY SCORECARD

/ PERFS: 93 / $: −

RAVE	FAVORABLE	MIXED	UNFAVORABLE	PAN
4		1	1	

SCOTT JOPLIN'S
TREEMONISHA

the premiere production of the 1908 ragtime opera

music and lyrics by Scott Joplin (1868–1917); music supervision by Gunther Schuller

directed by Frank Corsaro

choreographed by Louis Johnson

produced by the Houston Grand Opera Association, presented by Adela Holzer, James Nederlander, and Victor Lurie

starring Carmen Balthrop, Betty Allen, Curtis Rayam, and Willard White

with Edward Pierson, Ben Harney, Cora Johnson, Kenneth Hicks, Dorceal Duckens, Dwight Ransom, Raymond Bazemore, and the Louis Johnson Dance Theatre

opened October 21, 1975   *Uris Theatre*

DONAL HENAHAN, *TIMES*

The time is the legendary past—1866, to be precise—in the legendary State of Arkansas, where, in the words of Scott Joplin's preface to his opera *Treemonisha*, the recently freed blacks live "in dense ignorance, with no one to guide them." As often happens in legends, and sometimes in real life as well, a great and good young leader comes forward. Her name (for this is a women's liberation legend, not only a parable of black history) is Treemonisha, who believes that education (and no doubt neighborhood control) is her people's salvation. But you must know all this by now, for the Joplin opera that opened last night has been coming our way for quite a while. Frank Corsaro has staged this production, which was imported from the Houston Grand Opera Association, with a sophisticated naïveté that closely matches the Joplin

music and the libretto in particular. The score is a disarming mixture of
19th-century music hall and operetta idioms, although it was completed in 1911. It takes a delicate hand these days to handle a work that
has cotton pickers, conjurers, plantations, and even rabbits' feet. But
Joplin meant every word and every note, and in the end it would be a
hard-hearted audience that, in 1975, would not respond to *Treemonisha*
as the legend it has already become. . . . Miss Balthrop is, of course, the
centerpiece, a shorthaired Joan of Arkansas whom any community
would be wise to follow. It was always obvious that she has a spendid
voice (she won this year's Metropolitan Opera auditions), though some
of her highest notes went off pitch this time. But vocal comment is
hardly to the point, since the show was amplified, not unobtrusively.
Sometimes one heard stray snatches of chorus chatter much more
clearly than the words of leading singers. One hears that the theatre was
carpeted specifically for *Treemonisha*, in hopes of ironing out imbal-
ances between voices and orchestra. It didn't work. The producers
reported yesterday that the run at the Uris was sold out and that
Treemonisha would move to the Palace. After waiting 64 years to make
his Broadway debut, the ragtime king deserves an extended run.

MARTIN GOTTFRIED, *POST*
[Headline: "*Treemonisha* Fails As Good Opera or Theatre"]
As everyone must know by now, *Treemonisha* is the opera that Scott
Joplin wrote in 1907 and then just about killed himself trying vainly to
get it done. During the recent Joplin rage, it was inevitable that somebody would fully stage the opera at last. It was brought into the Uris last
night, demonstrating why Joplin had such problems with it. *Treemonisha*
really isn't very good opera, very good theatre or very good Joplin. The
opera is based on Joplin's early life and is a cry for education as the only
way out of black suppression, according to Vera Brodsky Lawrence
[Joplin musicologist and *Treemonisha*'s "artistic consultant"]. This interpretation notwithstanding, as an opera it must stand on its music and
theatricality and it does not work, on the latter grounds particularly. The
libretto is so boring, and Joplin seemed so uninterested in writing it—so
unprepared to do that ably—that the first act is sheer slumber until its
rousing finale ("Aunt Dinah Has Blowed de Horn"). The second act just
about forgets the story to settle for a concert. Knowing so little about the

musical theatre, he paid no attention to the needs for variety in tempo and style. But when it came time for something special to end the short (90-minute) work, he could pull out "A Real Slow Drag," which is so beautiful and so fresh it might justify an evening of almost anything. Here is music that ranks with anything he wrote. *Treemonisha* should have begun there. As for the production itself, it is more static than could be imagined for anything set to music, let alone Joplin's. Considering Joplin's newfound popularity, the opera is certainly a curiosity but the production represents an awfully big expense to satisfy a curiosity, particularly when the payoff is so slim.

WALTER KERR, *TIMES*

The deliberate creation of folk materials by sophisticates for sophisticates is one of the riskiest tasks literature—in the theatre or out of it—can undertake. Legend, folk fantasy, is the kind of thing that seems never to have been born but to have been plucked in passing from a bush or overheard as a tune drifting downwind; to force it into existence, to cultivate its qualities knowingly, is to rob it of its spontaneity and chance producing a folk-fake. Mr. Joplin was surely flirting with a possible folk-fake when he strove, in *Treemonisha*, to adapt the native imagery of backwoods Arkansas—conjur men ruling recently freed plantation blacks through superstition, a savior-heroine who would lead them to literacy found as a babe beneath a tree—to the musical structures of Sir Arthur Sullivan, if not of Puccini. He was of course a thoroughly educated, as well as melodically inspired, musician; but "education" in 1910 or thereabouts still meant learning about violins from Vienna, about recitative from Italy, about counterpoint, perhaps, from Great Britain. All of which was alien to his inspiration, which came from the pain and the lift and the liquid trill of his people. The clash ought to have been head-on. It's not. So far from sensing a profound clash of material and method in *Treemonisha*, you're apt to find the blend strangely soothing, simple and sweet as a cradlesong. Joplin was no born dramatist and was never going to write *Carmen* [1875]. *Treemonisha* isn't going into the permanent major repertory, we shan't see it often, our curiosity about it is due to the rediscovery of his great rags. But the fact that we'll not be seeing it often is the very best reason for seeing it now. If it isn't everything its composer wished it to be, neither is it fake: an honest man stretched himself to his limits in contrary ways, did his honest best to reconcile the contraries, and went on writing unaffected melody—there's no posture in it, and much pride—all the while.

◦   ◦   ◦

Scott Joplin, the King of Ragtime, was long forgotten until 1973, when the motion picture *The Sting* brought his rags back into prominence. The renewed interest in this lost American innovator resulted in the reconstruction of his unproduced *Treemonisha*, which the Houston Grand Opera decided to give a full-scale mounting. A worthy experiment, certainly not to be faulted. The piece itself turned out to be more of a curiousity than an entertainment, interesting nonetheless (but once only, please). While sections of ragtime break through, Joplin seemed constricted by the confines of European grand opera; *Treemonisha* was written in 1908, back when Puccini was still turning 'em out. (*Madama Butterfly* premièred in 1904, *Turandot* in 1926). Joplin spent the rest of his life vainly trying to get *Treemonisha* produced. After bankrolling a futile backer's audition in 1915, he was committed to a mental hospital, where he died in 1917.

BROADWAY SCORECARD / PERFS: 64 / $: –				
RAVE	FAVORABLE	MIXED	UNFAVORABLE	PAN
	4	1		1

TRICKS

"A New Musical Comedy"

music by Jerry Blatt

lyrics by Lonnie Burstein

book by Jon Jory

based on the 1671 farce *Les Fourbièrres de Scapin* by Molière

directed by Jon Jory

choreographed by Donald Saddler (replacing John Sharpe)

produced by Herman Levin

with René Auberjonois, Walter Bobbie, John Handy, June Helmers, Ernestine Jackson, Mitchell Jason, Carolyn Mignini, Joe Morton, Christopher Murney, Jo Ann Ogawa, Shezwae Powell, Lani Sundsten, and Tom Toner

opened January 8, 1973   Alvin Theatre

CLIVE BARNES, *TIMES*

There was a great deal of vivacity at the Alvin Theatre last night, but rather less life. *Tricks* is unassuming and sprightly, without a great deal of substance but a certain cheerful boisterousness. Its main attraction is the presence of René Auberjonois, graduating for the first time to full Broadway stardom. Jon Jory is one of those directors who will do anything for a laugh. And does. Sight gags abound—for there is a lot more of Olsen and Johnson around here than Molière. Jory never gives either his cast or his audience time to take breath. One particularly happy aspect of the show is Oliver Smith's permanent setting and Miles White's tastefully gaudy costumes. The decor, a versatile structure all in bright toy-town yellow and orange not only serves as a background for the actors, but also as a platform to house the orchestra and the vocal quartet, described in the program as "The Commedia." These four, three women and a man, sing quiet rock while all hell breaks out down beneath. With all the disguises, deceptions, trapdoors, slides, screens, slapsticks (yes, literal slapsticks), straw hats, canes, soft-shoe shuffles, gypsy dances, and other assorted mayhem, there is scarcely time for a dull moment. Yet the restless activity insufficiently disciplined by a clearly perceived style does here and there get tiring. The great exception is Mr. Auberjonois. Auberjonois works like a dog all through the show, but is still perky enough to be wagging his tail at the end. As Scapin he is called upon to do everything except actually fly. He sings, dances, mimes, acts, poses, and accomplishes it all with a manic energy and the sweetest of styles. Auberjonois is giving one of the most engaging and brilliant performances currently to be found in the Broadway musical theatre. *Tricks* is probably too tricksy in its theatrical chicanery, yet not stylized enough in its style.

DOUGLAS WATT, *DAILY NEWS*

The only trick of any consequence is that of taking all the fun out of Molière. Before our very eyes and ears, the poor fellow is knocked about and drained dry of humor. A jest intended for actors has been entrusted to clowns or actors portraying clowns, which is even worse. Anything for a laugh, but the laughs don't come. This noisy and compulsively energetic musical is mainly a sorry trick. When Scapin appears, in the gangling person of René Auberjonois, we all too readily realize that it is going to be a difficult evening. Wearing a clown face, and with his hair sticking out at all angles, he prances into the dialogue and never stops prancing, tumbling, rolling on the floor, grimacing and using slapstick and other devices to emphasize every last joke Jory has left in the script. We know, from past experience, how able Auberjonois is as both actor and comedian, but all we learn about him here is that he is exceedingly agile.

◦   ◦   ◦

Producer Herman (*My Fair Lady* [1956]) Levin found this intimate musical at the Actors' Theatre of Louisville and decided to dress it up for Broadway. He went so far as to reunite two of the great names in postwar theatrical design, Oliver Smith (sets) and the retired Miles White (costumes); the pair's joint credits included Levin's own 1949

Gentlemen Prefer Blondes. If the physical production was bright and first class, the material wasn't, and René Auberjonois—who arrived bearing his Tony Award from *Coco* (1969)—couldn't pull off *Tricks*. (British actor Jim Dale could, and did, when he came to town the following season with *Scapino*, his own adaptation of the Molière.) *Tricks's* score was neither Broadway nor country nor rock nor good. The onstage singing quartet, though, included Joe Morton, Ernestine Jackson, and Shezwae Powell—all of whom went directly into leading roles in *Raisin* (1973). Author's Note Dept.: Opening night I got to meet the fabled Max (*The Band Wagon* [1931]) Gordon, who once produced a show so bad that he tried to kill himself by jumping from the upper lobby of the Forrest Theatre in Philadelphia. I also learned firsthand the wisdom of asking a casual acquaintance how he liked the show when you're standing in Sardi's with the opening night party in progress at your table and the casual acquaintance, who happens to be the Gentleman from the *Times*, says, "Here, let me have it back when you're done" and in full view hands you an onionskin of his less-than-salutary notice.

BROADWAY SCORECARD
/ PERFS: 8 / $: –

RAVE	FAVORABLE	MIXED	UNFAVORABLE	PAN
			2	4

TWO BY TWO

"A New Musical"

music by Richard Rodgers

lyrics by Martin Charnin

book by Peter Stone

based on the 1954 comedy *The Flowering Peach* by Clifford Odets

"conceived and directed" by Joe Layton

produced by Richard Rodgers

starring Danny Kaye

with Harry Goz, Joan Copeland, Madeline Kahn, Michael Karm, Walter Willison, Tricia O'Neil, and Marilyn Cooper

opened November 10, 1970   Imperial Theatre

CLIVE BARNES, *TIMES*

Danny Kaye is a great and a good man, and last night he returned to the Broadway stage after an absence of nearly 30 years. You had better go and see him now, because at this rate he won't be back until 1999. And even though he then might possibly be in a better play, is it really worth the wait? Kaye is so warm and lovable an entertainer that for me, at least, he can do no wrong. It need take no unduly critical mind to note the flaws in the musical itself, *Two by Two*, which stars Noah and all 40 days and nights of his rain. There is too much rain, but then there is also a great deal of Kaye as compensation. The musical has been based upon *The Flowering Peach*, and right there was the producer's first mistake. This retelling of the Genesis story of Noah in the merrily anachronistic terms of a family from the Borscht Belt could never have been much of a play. The next mistake was to get Peter Stone to write the book for it. This is almost as cutely sentimental as the original Odets, and if anything more prolix. The show seems so long that at times you feel it ought to be called *Three by Three*. However, having

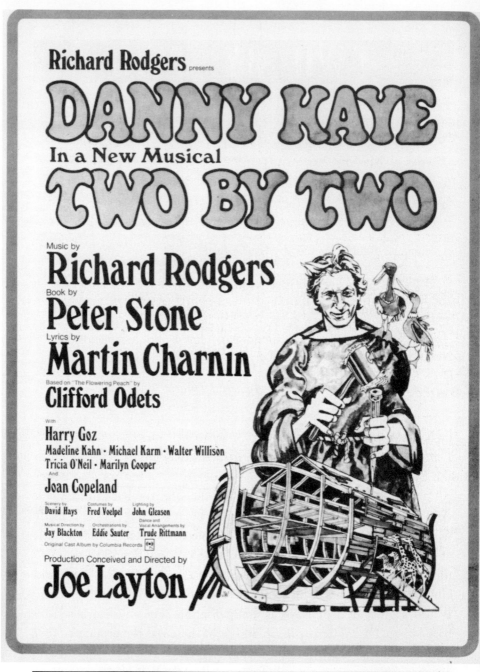

Richard Rodgers presents

DANNY KAYE
In a New Musical
TWO BY TWO

Music by
Richard Rodgers
Book by
Peter Stone
Lyrics by
Martin Charnin
Based on "The Flowering Peach" by
Clifford Odets

With
Harry Goz
Madeline Kahn · Michael Karm · Walter Willison
Tricia O'Neil · Marilyn Cooper
And
Joan Copeland

Scenery by   Costumes by   Lighting by
David Hays   Fred Voelpel   John Gleason

Musical Direction by   Orchestrations by   Dance and Vocal Arrangements by
Jay Blackton   Eddie Sauter   Trude Rittmann

Original Cast Album by Columbia Records

Production Conceived and Directed by
Joe Layton

Mr. Kaye builds his own vehicle. "This thing's sure gonna leak," says the duck on Danny's shoulder. (artwork by "J.W.")

made those two mistakes, the producer then did a very smart thing. He hired himself to write the music, and since he happens to be Richard Rodgers, writing his 38th Broadway musical, this was highly suitable. Rodgers has delivered some very good numbers; he can still write a ballad better than anyone around. Of course, the trouble is the story. Who really wants to hear about Noah? Who hasn't heard already? We had even guessed he was Jewish; we just didn't know he was half-brother to Sholem Aleichem's Tevye. Finally, I was distressed to find that Odets's original use of the word "Manure!" has been replaced with something more modish and shorter by two letters. This is the second time a major family musical has used a four-letter word [following Katharine Hepburn's use of same in *Coco* (1969)]. While it may be fashionable, in the view of many perfectly ordinary people it removes the musical from the realm of family entertainment. Let us keep obscenity for legitimate plays, or musicals with an exclusively adult appeal. But for Danny Kaye—it is only a matter of taste but surely no!

MARTIN GOTTFRIED, *WOMEN'S WEAR DAILY*

Richard Rodgers hasn't had his heart in a show since Oscar Hammerstein died 10 years ago. Since then, his composing has been lifeless, sporadic and strictly business, none of which was very good for music or the man. *Two by Two* is typical of his corporate work of this period. I never saw Odets' play, but it's hard to believe that, like Peter Stone's book, it was merely a paraphrase of the Old Testament. What I suspect—and I suspect it because Menasha Skulnik was Odets' Noah—is that *The Flowering Peach* looked for humor in the congruity of a Biblical story told with the accents, values and culture of urban Jewishness. *Two by Two* has virtually no Jewishness to it. In fact, Rodgers has always avoided Jewishness in his shows. Whenever the tone arises in *Two by Two*, it is promply swept under the carpet. Without such a motif, or any other to replace it, *Two by Two* becomes a plain retelling of Noah's story, which is kind of incredible coming in a professional Broadway production. They even have God speaking in thunderclaps and kettledrums. Noah tells his sons to build an ark, the rains come, the rains end and they go off. Needless to say, the story's major elements can't be shown on stage—the ark itself or the 40 day's worth of rain. I'm talking so much about the story because there is an awful lot of it considering that this is supposed to be a musical. In fact, there isn't any music at all for the first 15 minutes and, in a sense, there isn't any during the rest of the evening either. There isn't much musical about *Two by Two.* Joe Layton has directed it with very little movement and no dancing at all, but even more unmusical than that, there is no rhythm to the show—no musicality in the feel of it. And getting down to specifics, Rodgers' score is so unmemorable it's a wonder the pit musicians didn't forget the tunes between looking at the sheet music and turning to their instruments. *Two by Two* is merely, in the jargon of the entertainment business, "product."

WALTER KERR, *TIMES*

Tricia O'Neil, as the darkly handsome neglected wife of son Ham, composes herself sadly, all alone at stage left, to sing of her marriage. The song is called "Something Doesn't Happen," it penetrates the atmosphere like an arrow halving the sky, it gives body and scale to all the bickering that's been going on. We're going to be able to stand more marital wrangling after this; the melody shores the show up by giving its problems emotional validity; the clean, long rhythmic line will happily drive it on. Listen, once more, to what happens when Japheth, Noah's youngest and most rebellious son [Walter Willison], finally dares to speak—which is to say sing—of his secret love for this girl. He is poised above her on the farmyard framework that is being rapidly dismantled to make an ark. He has kept his silence long enough. He begins at a hush. The first notes of "I Do Not Know a Day I Did Not Love You" press forward as softly as leaves falling in a forest, falling irregularly, now this one, then that, up a note, down, questioning, yearning, moving tentatively but inevitably toward open statement. By the time the full phrase does open, we are already enchanted with the song; it is one of the very best, surely, that Rodgers has ever written. . . . Mr. Kaye is a presence, he is Golden Boy moved into a different Odets play. He is part energy, part astonishment with the pleasure of being alive, part sobriety. The energy erupts with his antelope leap down a gangplank, immediately after God has made him younger with a thunderbolt. Arriving at center stage like an acrobat safely down from the highwire, he is a mocking but deeply satisfied combination of Superman, Sir Galahad and slightly seedy ballet master. And yet he is not out to slaughter us with his unleashed vitality. He wants to keep it on tap, like a hum in the near distance, but always in reserve. He wants us to know it's there in order to give credence to his seriousness, to the tenderness with which he can slyly approach Esther, to the authority he means to exercise in a battle over the ship's rudder. Like Rodgers, Kaye uses his power to point the play in a direction, not to stop it with clowning or counterpoint.

∘   ∘   ∘

Two by Two originated with lyricist Martin Charnin, Mary Rodgers's collaborator on the tepid 1963 Judy Holliday vehicle *Hot Spot* (which was not much of a recommendation). Poppa's prior lyricist had been another friend of Mary's—a better friend of Mary's—named Sondheim. Richard Rodgers enlisted librettist Peter Stone, with whom he'd written a 1967 television adaptation of *Androcles and the Lion* (also not much of a recommendation, although Stone had in the interim penned *1776* [1969]). Danny Kaye signed on to make his first Broadway appearance since being swept to Hollywood on the strength of Cole Porter's 1941 *Let's Face It*. The Rodgers-Kaye tandem made *Two by Two* a theatre party lady's dream. ("Two by Two by Two"—the most-likely-to-succeed song in the 1965 *Do I Hear a Waltz?*—was cut in Boston. "Two by Two" served as the title song for Rodgers's next musical, while Sondheim's next—initially announced as *Threes*—featured a song called "Side by Side by Side." Totally different songs, all with the same message.) *The Flowering Peach*, a philosophical comedy dealing with old man Noah and his menagerie, was not your typical source material, and *Two by Two* was not to be your typical musical. "I want this to be a huge success or the bomb of all time," commented the star just prior to opening. "I did not want to return to Broadway in an *Applause* [1970], which Betty Bacall is marvelous in, but it's commercial theatre. I don't want to have to say to myself, Christ, I gotta go to the goddam theatre again tonight." OK, Mr. K. The mirthless *Two by Two* opened mirthlessly, with aforesaid advance sale for ballast, and continued uneventfully until February 5, when Kaye slipped on a prop and tore a ligament in his leg. Mass refunds caused receipts to plummet as the star missed thirteen performances. At which point he returned in plaster cast, running down the other actors in his wheelchair, goosing the girls with his crutch, and transforming *Two by Two* into, well, commercial theatre. "Since I hurt my leg and was forcibly immobilized," Kaye philosophized, "we have been forced to change it into an entertainment. People now like it better than they did before." "I have no objection," chimed in producer Rodgers, in public at least. "The people seem to like the show as it is, and tickets are being sold"—enough to enable the enterprise to show a modest profit. Kaye's condition eventually healed, but not the show. "I'm glad you're here," he would tell the audience, "but I'm glad the authors aren't." (Seven years later *Two by Two*'s Madeline Kahn—now a star herself, of the upcoming *On the Twentieth Century* [1978]—vociferously vetoed Kaye for the role of Oscar Jaffe.)

BROADWAY SCORECARD

/ PERFS: 343 / $: +

RAVE	FAVORABLE	MIXED	UNFAVORABLE	PAN
1	1	2	1	1

TWO GENTLEMEN OF VERONA

"A Grand New Musical"

music by Galt MacDermot

lyrics by John Guare

book by John Guare and Mel Shapiro

based on the 1592 comedy by William Shakespeare

directed by Mel Shapiro

choreographed by Jean Erdman (replaced by Dennis Nahat); "additional musical staging" by Dennis Nahat (who was billed as choreographer for post–Broadway tour)

produced by the New York Shakespeare Festival (Joseph Papp, producer)

starring Jonelle Allen, Diana Davila (replacing Carla Pinza), Clifton Davis, and Raul Julia

with Norman Matlock, Alix Elias, Frank O'Brien, José Perez, Frederic Warriner, Alvin Lum, and John Bottoms (replacing Jerry Stiller)

opened December 1, 1971   St. James Theatre

CLIVE BARNES, *TIMES*

Love is in bloom and back in style. *Two Gentlemen of Verona* opened last night at the St. James Theatre. It has music by Galt MacDermot—who gave you *Hair* [1968]—lyrics by John Guare—who gave you *House of Blue Leaves* [1971]—a book more or less by William Shakespeare— who gave you *Hamlet*—and is produced by Joseph Papp and the New York Shakespeare Festival, who have already given it in the park. It is a lovely fun show that joyously survives its transplanting. But what began

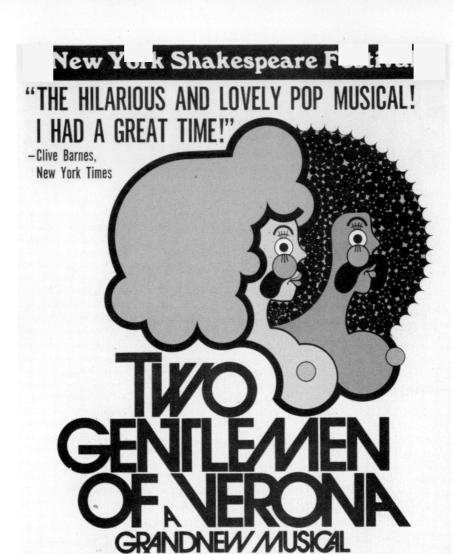

Mod Shakespeare, circa 1971. Those are strategically placed teardrops; the two ladies are lonely for their gents. (artwork by Peter Whorf)

for New York as a summer tryst has now successfully become a winter affair, and should go on for a long, long time. It is a little different now perhaps, but I assure you, no less sweet. The musical has a strangely New York feel to it—in the music, a mixture of rock, lyricism and Caribbean patter, in Guare's spare, at times even abrasive lyrics, in the story itself of small-town kids and big town love. It also has a very New York sense of irreverence. It is graffito written across a classic play, but the graffito has an insolent sense of style, and the classic play can still be clearly glimpsed underneath. Galt MacDermot's music is more subtly shaded and more variegated than his score for *Hair*. He uses guitars, mandolins, marimbas, as well as more conventional strings and trumpets, and some of the numbers are beautiful, and many more are perkily funny. Mr. Guare's lyrics have a brusque toughness that is admirable, and his rhymes are occasionally as acerbic and as rugged as his sentiments. The show is also a special triumph for the director, Mel Shapiro, and the set designer, Ming Cho Lee, who has given scaffolding a new chic. Shapiro keeps the whole musical going as if it were a merry-go-round that had got slightly drunk wherever it is that merry-go-rounds go when they need to celebrate. What I really love about *Two Gentlemen* is its simplicity. Beneath all the multi-colored gimmicks and extravagances there are real people living and loving, and this I find very moving. I had a great time. I only wish that it had been three or four gentlemen instead of only two.

MARTIN GOTTFRIED, *WOMEN'S WEAR DAILY*

Crazy and wonderful. Though something has been lost in the [transfer], it remains playful and bright and very grand fun. A conservatism has cost the show some of its original abandon, and some revisions have been made in the wrong places. Even still it is an alternative to the formula Broadway musical, and that is desperately needed. There is more to musical theatre than overtures, production numbers and changes of scenery. Here is a show with the size of physique and spirit to fill a big stage (and house) while doing it a fresh way. It has energy, wit and originality. The book by John Guare and Mel Shapiro is an anarchic adaptation of Shakespeare's perfectly awful comedy. It starts out fairly close to the original, but as the story proceeds, more and more of Guare's upside-down humor creeps into the Shakespeare, finally elbowing it aside for a lunacy so Elizabethan in its classicism that the evening remains very true to the original in both spirit and style even though it is shamelessly anachronistic and colloquial. One of the central humors in the Guare-Shapiro version was the racial polyglot of the production. Valentine and Sylvia were black and her father, the Duke of Milan, was a big, bad, black daddy; Proteus and Julia were both Puerto Rican; Launce, the manservant, was Jewish, and Eglamour, Sylvia's fiance, was Chinese. This was not just a matter of casting—the lines were spoken in dialect and the contrast between the accents and the story-characters-language was wildly funny. A combination of cast changes and altered directorial emphases by Shapiro has stifled a lot of this good humor. Most of the original company remains, and all of them have gotten better—Jonelle Allen even more charismatic as Sylvia (and still deservedly starring in the show); Clifton Davis acting classically and singing soulfully as Valentine; and Raul Julia, most of all, still funnier as Proteus, a swell clown as well as a superb actor. He can do more with a pair of steel-rimmed glasses than most actors can do with four years of acting lessons. Shapiro's direction, though not tyrannical enough to keep the big company under precise control, keeps the show's energy and spirits high, and these are prime assets. Guare's lyrics remain a marvelous combination of technical devil-may-carelessness and inspired inanity. It really is delightful.

WALTER KERR, *TIMES*
[Headline: "Simply Carefree, Simply Wonderful"]
On the night I saw it [in the park] Mayor Lindsay was present, and when the jumping-jack boys and girls of Verona ripped into a finale composed of soaring Frisbees, furiously flipped ping-pong paddles and showers of shredded flowers, the contagion out front grew so intense that Mr. Lindsay found himself propelled stageward. Hurdling the few tiers of seats that separated him from the gyrating, elbow-jogging revelers, he managed to make it to the stage, safe and grinning, where he proceeded to keep pace with the rest and the best of them. He was luminous, memorable. He was even on beat. Although he has not been retained for the present company, nearly everyone else has, which means we can now have June in January. Lyricist Guare has perfectly insinuated himself into the small rift that exists between Shakespeare's sensibility and our own. Shakespeare was often a cynic, always a realist. His plots are not paeans to constancy. We merely phrase our double-dealings a bit differently, while going about the same double-dealings.

Guare is impertinent but alway probable; you feel Shakespeare would grasp his way of putting it, and not mind the rock or Latin-American beats. As a result it is easy for the entertainment to move either way—into now or into iambic pentameter. After Shakespeare's, Guare's contribution to the festivities may be the greatest. The evening is inventive but not too inventive. It knows when to use Shakespeare, when to put him on the telephone, when to doodle freely and musically on themes that might just as well belong to both of us. It's an improvisation with no malice in it; it has a kink of its own, a certain mirth of mind. . . . Guare has also put the ground under the manic feet of one Jonelle Allen, a performer who was working off-off-Broadway just last spring and is now likely to wipe out the very floor of the St. James if they don't carry her off—which they have to do—sooner and sooner each night. Miss Allen quivers even when she is standing absolutely still; let one foot go and nothing is safe. She finishes her first number ["Love Me"], in a deceptively prim white gown with yellow trim, with her back to us, shoulders still tingling, head in electrified profile.

DOUGLAS WATT, *DAILY NEWS*

As we all knew it would when it showered its delights on Central Park audiences this summer, the musical *Two Gentlemen of Verona* has come to Broadway. And now joy is rampant on the stage of the St. James, where it opened last night in a tighter presentation. It is even more beguiling than before. This is a fast and loose and smiling treatment of Shakespeare's sunny comedy about love's vagaries. The play bounces this way and that in the adaptation, peppered with the slang of today, and the sudden shifts, which bothered me before, now seem perfectly natural. The evening is mainly, though, a procession of charming songs and dances with music by Galt MacDermot in a wide variety of pop styles set to cheerfully nutty lyrics by John Guare. It is again Jonelle Allen who stops the show cold with her first appearance. A bundle of sensuous joy all by herself, she lights up the stage immediately, dancing and singing with a controlled ferocity that is beautiful to behold. But striking as she is, Allen's performance is nicely matched by the other leads. Clifton Davis is an extremely winning Valentine, an energetic dancer and a splendid singer. And cast opposite the black pair in Spanish-American characterizations of Proteus and Julia are Raul Julia and Diana Davila. The former is marvelously sly and the tiny but perfectly formed Davila, whose mouth is apparently too small to accommodate most words so that she has to first chew them and then spit them out in odd-shaped pieces, is endearingly funny. Who says you can't do Shakespeare on Broadway? Joseph Papp and his New York Shakespeare Festival have found the loveliest way possible.

*   *   *

Joseph Papp's free Shakespeare in the Park had periodically gone in for lighter fare, and they hit the jackpot with their musical comedy overhaul of Shakespeare's *Two Gentlemen of Verona*. Composer Galt MacDermot returned to the Festival, for whom he had written the original production of *Hair*. He was joined by John Guare and Mel Shapiro, author and director of the absurdly wonderful 1971 Off-Broadway hit *The House of Blue Leaves*. New York had already enjoyed contemporary-pop musical Shakespeare with the long-running 1968 Off-Broadway hit *Your Own Thing* (from *Twelfth Night*), but *Two Gents* was no small-scale, chamber-rock affair, and it happily rollicked its way down to 44th Street. The adaptation was very much of its time, which is to say that we've never seen a revival and it's just as well. But it was quite the delight in 1971. Some readers may blanch on noting that the show took the Best Musical Tony over Hal Prince's *Follies*. The latter, while certainly more memorable, was memorably and certainly flawed (except in the music department, that is. Sondheim's score easily wins out). But onstage, in 1971, *Two Gents* was clearly the more enjoyable and satisfying show. As a result of which it was also handily profitable and—rather surprisingly—one of the few musicals to receive unanimous raves (as tabulated in this book). No mean feat, especially considering the cusswords liberally sprinkled about.

Winner of the New York Drama Critics' Circle Award. In addition to winning the Tony Award for Best Musical, a Tony was won by John Guare and Mel Shapiro (book).

BROADWAY SCORECARD

/ PERFS: 613 / $: +

RAVE	FAVORABLE	MIXED	UNFAVORABLE	PAN
6				

THE UTTER GLORY OF MORRISSEY HALL

"A New Musical"

music and lyrics by Clark Gesner

book by Clark Gesner and Nagle Jackson

directed by Nagle Jackson

choreographed by Buddy Schwab (replacing Arthur Faria)

produced by Arthur Whitelaw, Albert W. Selden, and H. Ridgely Bullock in association with Marc Howard

starring Celeste Holm (replacing Patricia Falkenhain, who replaced Eileen Heckart)

with Taina Elg, Patricia Falkenhain, Laurie Franks, Marilyn Caskey, Willard Beckham, Karen Gibson, John Wardwell, and Robert Lanchester

opened May 13, 1979   *Mark Hellinger Theatre*

CLIVE BARNES, *POST*

In my innocence I used to imagine it was only the English who couldn't write English musicals—now a couple of Americans, Clark Gesner and Nagle Jackson, have practically convinced me that Americans cannot write English musicals either. The occasion, if such it could be called, was the opening last night of a peculiarly tedious musical called *The Utter Glory of Morrissey Hall.* What was good in this musical can be summed up in two words: Celeste Holm—who was celestial even if not at home. What was bad can be summed up in eight words—book, lyrics, music, direction, choreography, setting and costumes. I hope I haven't left out anything. Gesner and Jackson have decided to improvise [rather than making an accredited adaptation of Ronald Searle's cartoon series, filmed in 1954 as *Belles of St. Trinian's*]. And improvise

ARTHUR   ALBERT W.   H. RIDGELY
WHITELAW   SELDEN   BULLOCK
In Association with MARC HOWARD
Present

CELESTE HOLM

in

The Utter Glory of
MORRISSEY HALL

A New Musical

Book By

CLARK & NAGLE
GESNER   JACKSON

Music & Lyrics By

CLARK
GESNER

With

PATRICIA   LAURIE   MARILYN
FALKENHAIN   FRANKS   CASKEY

and

TAINA ELG

Sets & Lighting Designed By   Costumes Designed By   Musical Director
HOWARD BAY   DAVID GRADEN   JOHN LESKO

Orchestrations   Dance Music Arranged By
JAY BLACKTON & RUSSELL WARNER   ALLEN COHEN

Associate Producer SANDY STERN

Musical Numbers and Dances Staged by

BUDDY SCHWAB

Directed by

NAGLE JACKSON

Originally produced by The McCarter
Theatre Co., Princeton, N.J.

**A SPARKLING NEW MUSICAL BY THE AUTHOR OF
"YOU'RE A GOOD MAN, CHARLIE BROWN" AND THE
PRODUCERS OF "MAN OF LA MANCHA" AND
"BUTTERFLIES ARE FREE"!**

PREVIEWS BEGIN THURS. EVG., MAY 3rd • OPENS SUN. EVG., MAY 13th at 6:45 P.M.

Tuesday thru Friday Evenings at 8 PM and Saturday Matinees at 2 PM & Sunday Matinees at 3 PM: Orchestra & Mezzanine $20.00; Balcony $18.00, 16.00, 14.00. Saturday Evenings at 8 PM: Orchestra & Mezzanine $22.50; Balcony $20.00, 18.00, 16.00. Wednesday Matinees at 2 PM: Orchestra & Mezzanine $18.50; Balcony $16.00, 14.00, 12.00. Please enclose a self-addressed, stamped envelope along with check or money order made payable to MARK HELLINGER THEATRE. Please list alternate dates.

CHARGE YOUR SEATS BY PHONE WITH ANY MAJOR CREDIT CARD!
CALL CHARGIT: (212) 239-7177
TICKETRON: (212) 977-9020

FOR GROUP SALES CALL: (212) 796-3074
or Toll Free (800) 223-8052 outside New York State.

MARK HELLINGER THEATRE
B'way & 51st St. New York, N.Y. 10019 (212) 757-7064

"What was bad can be summed up in eight words—book, lyrics, music, direction, choreography, setting and costumes," reported Clive Barnes. "I hope I haven't left out anything." (artwork by Hendersen)

they do—but it is all rather like improvising a steam engine out of a Lego set in a sinking canoe. Things happen that are possessed of an almost glorious lack of interest. The lyrics humble along like scrambled, mumbled fortune cookies, and the music sounds as though it has been largely adapted from the English hymnal, with some obscure tea-dance music lavishly thrown in to make the numbers up. There are no characters—even Miss Holm, as utterly glorious as she is, has to go it alone with precious little help from Morrissey Hall, and the rest of the people are all the kind of stereotypes that make stereotypes stereotyped. The first part of the evening is concerned with such anecdotes as a schoolboy being imported in a steamer trunk, and the school being shown a pornographic film by mistake. (There were times there when I fancied I might have preferred the porno movie to the show—it might conceivably have shown more invention.) The performances were terrible, but I do not blame the performers, for there was nothing they could do but scream for help and the director, Nagle himself, was presumably deaf. Enough is enough. I frankly doubt whether Broadway is yet ready for a bad musical about a whimsically cartooned English girl's school.

RICHARD EDER, *TIMES*
The overture is conducted by John Lesko as if he were Miss Potts, leader of the Morrissey Hall Concert Orchestra. Paper airplanes soar about him, balloons rise and collapse, a kettle drum falls over while Mr. Lesko, wearing earrings, a wig of white curls and a sensible dress keeps on conducting.

o   o   o

Here was a simply awful show that had no place on Broadway—or anywhere else. A November '77 tryout at the McCarter Theatre in Princeton, with Eileen Heckart walking out days before the opening, demonstrated that the show was hopeless; hopeful producers, nonetheless, went to great trouble to get the show to its Broadway burial. Who are these producers who seem to thrive on flop shows? *Utter Glory* had two veterans. Arthur Whitelaw's presence is understandable, as he'd made a mint with Clark Gesner's *You're a Good Man, Charlie Brown*, which began a four-year Off-Broadway run in 1967 (and made an unsuccessful thirty-one-performance Broadway visit in 1971).

Whitelaw's first Broadway show was also an enormous moneymaker, the 1969 *Butterflies Are Free* (starring—guess who—Eileen Heckart), but he followed it in quick succession with expensive failures *Minnie's Boys* (1970) and *70, Girls, 70* (1971). *Utter Glory* was his third and final Broadway musical, with a handful of undistinguished plays along the way. Coproducer Albert Selden's career is even more interesting. He started out as a composer, working with fellow Yale man Burt Shevelove. Their revue *Small Wonder* had a modest run in 1948. (Burt, hesitant at being billed as both director and lyricist, used the nom de plume Billings Brown for the songs.) This was followed by a big out-of-town flop, the 1951 Nancy Walker-starrer *Month of Sundays*, which caused Shevelove to set down his rhyming dictionary for good. Selden rebounded in 1955, writing music and lyrics *and* producing an even bigger out-of-town flop, *The Amazing Adele* (scripted by Anita Loos, with Adele played by the amazing—if unknown—Tammy Grimes.) This one caused Selden to put down *his* author's pencil. His sporadic producing career continued, with *The Body Beautiful* (1958, Bock and Harnick's first collaboration), *The Girls Against the Boys* (1959), *Hallelujah, Baby!* (1967), *Come Summer* (1969), Mitch Leigh's closed-out-of-town *Halloween* (1972), *Irene* (1973), *The Utter Glory of Morrissey Hall*, and *Comin' Uptown* (1979). All flops, with assorted nonmusical flops as well. We left one out, though, purposely so. *Man of La Mancha* (1965) more than paid for Selden's losses on the rest of 'em, one would hope—though one doubts Selden would've been able to finance the last five without *La Mancha*'s success. With that one exception, Selden's career was a total bust, illustrating why the role of the Broadway producer is so often the province of the independently wealthy. Not successful overall, certainly, but how many producers would kill for just one *La Mancha*? Or a *Charlie Brown*, even?

BROADWAY SCORECARD

/ PERFS: | / $: –

RAVE	FAVORABLE	MIXED	UNFAVORABLE	PAN
			1	5

VERY GOOD EDDIE

a reconstruction of the 1915 "Princess Theatre Show"

music by Jerome Kern

lyrics mostly by Schuyler Greene

book by Guy Bolton

based on the 1911 farce *Over Night* by Phillip Bartholomae

directed by Bill Gile

choreographed by Dan Siretta

produced by the Goodspeed Opera House (Michael P. Price), presented by David Merrick, Max Brown, and Byron Goldman

with David Christmas, Joel Craig, Spring Fairbank, James Harder (replacing Eddie Phillips), Travis Hudson, Charles Repole, Virginia Seidel, Cynthia Wells, and Nicholas Wyman

opened December 21, 1975   Booth Theatre

CLIVE BARNES, *TIMES*

An absolutely enchanting old musical by Jerome Kern and Guy Bolton has just tiptoed through the tulips to Broadway. It is called *Very Good Eddie*, it has come to Broadway almost 60 years to the day since its debut, it turned up at the Booth Theater on Sunday, and to call it "very good" could well be the last understatement of a fading but overstating year. It is a delight. It takes off. It flies. And it lands in a territory of innocence that we all think we ought to remember. But never do. This present production—complete in cast, settings, costumes and attitudes—started its life this summer at the Goodspeed Opera House in East Haddam, Conn. People saw it and liked it, and it survived the summer and is now happily going to brighten our winter of discontent. When I first saw it in Connecticut a couple of months back, I really loved it, but thought it was probably not for Broadway. Its measures were perhaps too sweet and delicate, and yet its comic dimensions a shade too broad. I was totally wrong. It moved into the Booth like a millionaire taking up a lease. The audience clearly liked it here as much as I had loved it in East Haddam, and it should be around for a while. It would be easy to label *Very Good Eddie* as one of those shows of the nostalgic genre of *Nanette* [1971] or "No, No, *Irene* [1973]." But this is something a little different. It is a perfectly straight, unemphasized revival of an old musical from a very interesting period in the history of our musical theatre. What a fantastic composer Kern was! In fact, this musical contains not one of his standards—only two years earlier he had written his first great ballad, "They Didn't Believe Me," and all the rest were in the future—but the musical texture of the score, its sheer sense of fun and liveliness, its attentiveness to the story, its variations of pace and mood, are pure delight. Call it David Merrick's Christmas present to New York.

WALTER KERR, *TIMES*

[Headline: "Can a 1915 Musical Sound Fresh? Yes"]

I began enjoying *Very Good Eddie* during the overture, and do you know why? Didn't recognize a single tune in it. Now that is undoubtedly remiss of me, because even if this early Jerome Kern score (1915) has never been among his most celebrated I certainly ought to have heard hummed, and never forgotten, as enchantingly plaintive a duet as "Babes in the Wood." However, remissness has its good side. Not having heard the numbers, and the numbers having been written by Jerome Kern, I was overwhelmed by their freshness, as though dawn had come calling and only the first birds were up yet. If a melody is a melody, it doesn't matter whether it's new or old, whether you've heard it or not. It's still honey, and it pleaseth the ear. Once the curtain is up, the songs remain unfamiliar and fresh. In trimming and amplifying to make an ancient entertainment entirely seaworthy again, the current producers have in fact gone beyond the original score, adding a quartet here and an ensemble glide there from other Kern sources. But they've obeyed what I take to be the basic rule: they haven't stolen anything that obviously belongs to another show, that is swiftly associated with a quite different entertainment. Whenever this sort of thievery is attempted, as it was in recent revivals of *Irene* and *Good News* [1974], it immediately destroys the property, and the pleasure of the property, at hand. We are not seeing *Irene* or *Good News* any more, we're having a random and ultimately indigestible smorgasbord crammed down our throats. *Very Good Eddie* has been discriminating in its borrowings, incorporating not only what seems to belong to the same musical

year (things were changing rapidly in those days, what with Berlin sneak-
ily turning rag into foxtrot) but lyrical pleasantries that come from the
same limbo of lost tunes that the show's own score does. The program
note at the Booth, detailing the history of Mr. Kern's early and resoundingly successful venture, concludes thusly, "It is the hope of the producers
that with *Very Good Eddie* the Booth Theater will become the home of a
series of melodic, intimate and charming musical shows." If the honorable, nearly straightfaced, piquantly happy standard of *Very Good Eddie*
can be kept up, we should all hope so, too.

HOWARD KISSEL, *WOMEN'S WEAR DAILY*

If there were no notation on the program to tell you Jerome Kern wrote
the score for *Very Good Eddie*, you might imagine it had been composed by
Sandy Wilson as an exercise in preparation for *The Boy Friend* [1954].
Nothing about the music suggests the haunting, romantic quality of Kern
at his best. When it was first produced in 1915, *Eddie* may indeed have
stood in marked contrast to the operettas that dominated Broadway; it
may indeed have set the pattern for musicals like *No, No, Nanette* and *Good
News* , but its groundbreaking qualities are no longer apparent, and being
revived after the others makes it seem like just "another one" rather than
the original. In its time *Eddie* was also celebrated as one of the first of a
series of intimate musicals. Today "intimate" still means small cast but also
implies music with character, with personal qualities, inventiveness and
emotional authenticity—what more perfect example could there be.
However intimate it seemed in its day, *Eddie* now strikes us as merely
inane. A lyric like "Each morning, if you'll show me how/I will milk
Clarisse the cow" is dreary even if it was written, as this was, by P. G.
Wodehouse. A line like "Poor, precious Percy pining in Poughkeepsie" is
off-putting even if it comes from Guy Bolton. *Very Good Eddie* has evidently been an enormous success at the Goodspeed Opera House in East
Haddam, Conn., where this production (as well as *Shenandoah* [1975])
originated. This has much to do with an audience's expectations, which are
quite different in East Haddam than they are on Broadway (in the old
days when it cost less to go to theatre off-Broadway audience expectations
were different there too). But now to pay Broadway prices for a musical
that is intimate in a way that implies not emotional depth or rapport but
rather modest production values can satisfy only the most innocent tastes.
The tedium of *Eddie* is attributable solely to the material, not to the tal-

ented cast, the clean direction or the fine sets and costumes. The dances and an extended scene of farcial door opening and shutting are well chore-ographed, the singing all round is good, but ultimately nothing really counterbalances the deadly coyness of the material.

o o o

Broadway hadn't heard from Connecticut's Goodspeed Opera House since its third season, when *Man of La Mancha* transferred triumphantly in the fall of 1965. Things up in East Haddam weren't quiet, though. Michael P. Price became executive director in 1968, instituting a policy of two vintage revivals and one new work each summer. Nineteen-seventy-four's new musical *Shenandoah* came to Broadway on January 7, 1975, and the year closed with this transfer of Goodspeed's 1975 summer show. *Very Good Eddie* was the second of the Princess shows, so-called because they were written for and produced at the 299-seat Princess Theatre. The small stage size and seating capacity necessitated a new type of musical, forced to make due with less in the way of cast, scenery, and musicians. Composer Jerome Kern, librettist Guy Bolton, and lyricist-librettist P. G. Wodehouse (who joined the team just after *Eddie* opened) used these constraints as positives, coming up with stimulating, funny, and relatively intelligent "musical comedies." Although the Princess series lasted only four years, it was especially influential to teenaged members of the next generation (including, notably, Rodgers, Hart, and the brothers Gershwin). Goodspeed's fourth and fifth transfers, the musical spoof *Something's Afoot* and the negligible *Going Up* (from 1917), were quick 1976 flops, but the house on the Connecticut River made up for it—and how!—with their 1977 transfer, *Annie.* Seven other revivals have tranferred to date, though only one—the 1992 two-piano reconception of Frank Loesser's *The Most Happy Fella*—was especially well served. Goodspeed is, like the Princess Theatre was, an intimate house with severe physical limitations—which is perhaps why *Very Good Eddie* remains the most successful of their revivals.

BROADWAY SCORECARD
/ PERFS: 288 / $: +

RAVE	FAVORABLE	MIXED	UNFAVORABLE	PAN
4	1			1

VIA GALACTICA

"A Musical of the Future," previously entitled *Up!*

music by Galt MacDermot

lyrics by Christopher Gore

book by Christopher Gore and Judith Ross (story by Gore, musical dialogue by Ross)

"entire production conceived and directed" by Peter Hall

produced by George W. George and Barnard S. Strauss in association with Nat Shapiro

starring Raul Julia and Keene Curtis

with Virginia Vestoff, Damon Evans, Louise Heath, Irene Cara, and Ralph Carter

opened November 28, 1972   Uris Theatre

CLIVE BARNES, *TIMES*

Well, there is always the theatre. The new Uris Theatre is absolutely splendid. It has space and grandeur. It holds 1,800 persons, and from the inside—it has no outside, for it is tucked away in a basement—it looks like one of those modern German opera houses. It probably would be suitable for both opera and ballet. It had its official opening last night with a musical called *Via Galactica*. It is a space-age musical, they say. But at times there appeared to be more inner vacuum than outer space. The attempt was a worthy one to produce a new kind of musical. It was to be more operatic than before, with no spoken dialogue. The idea is sensible. So what went wrong? Not Galt MacDermot's music. This is perhaps not such a melodious or inventive score as he provided earlier in the season for *Dude*, which was very good indeed, but it does have the bounce and radiance that are MacDermot trademarks. Also, the mechanical, space-age look of the musical is appealing and imaginative. I think the basic trouble with the evening is the banality of the book, which has no interest and no point of contact with the audience. It is a

"The most wondrous musical of our times." For 7 performances, anyway.

difficult show to care for. The well-publicized use of trampolines, to suggest weightlessness, suggests nothing more than people pointlessly bouncing up and down on trampolines. The mechanical space garbage cart (looking not at all futuristic, incidentally) is all too clearly chained to the stage, and the attacking space ship from earth looks like a displaced lighting fitting. By splitting the stage up into segments with his trampolines, director Peter Hall not only puts two clashingly different movement patterns on stage at once, he also makes the stage difficult to work on. The trampolines should have gone, but with the trampolines would also have gone the show's one small claim to innovation. Hall, then, seems to have outsmarted himself, but the scenery and costumes by John Bury are mostly brilliant. The look of the show is very classy; it has whirling stars and shimmering asteroids. The space ships themselves are altogether less effective, but that was presumably inevitable.

MARTIN GOTTFRIED, *WOMEN'S WEAR DAILY*
The huge, plush Uris Theatre has opened with the Theatre Hall of Fame in its lobby and a bomb on stage. But *Via Galactica* is a strange kind of bomb, a plastic one, perhaps in keeping with the supermotel decor of the house and the futurism of its setting. Watching this new musical is like watching a show at Disneyland, as if there were a pane of glass between you and a performance by disembodied mechanical dolls. Maybe this is partly because the acoustics and sheer size of the Uris make the stage activity remote and dwarfed. But there are no excuses for what is a lumbering, incomprehensible, unmusical and absolute disaster. To begin with, the program includes a summary of the story, hardly a good sign when a show is in English, though I sometimes wondered. Summary notwithstanding, the show is unfollowable. *Via Galactica* is an opera in the most primitive sense, that is, virtually everything is sung (in the most primitive sense). There are even attempts at recitative and on occasion there are reminders of Rossini, though most of Galt MacDermot's music ranges from near to utter drek. This was depressing coming from MacDermot, a talented but erratic and self-indulgent composer. Between a company of dispirited, disorganized actors and a series of giant props, the next more ludicrous than the last, Peter Hall belied his considerable reputation as a director of opera and drama (formerly head of the Royal Shakespeare Company and now director of England's National Theatre). Hall seized upon the

idea of using trampolines to simulate weightlessness, and set six of them into the stage floor. Unfortunately this did not leave much room for the actors to walk, dance or just stand. Finally, there were lyrics by Gore ("I believe in butterflies, rainbows and balloons") that seemed as uninterested in the music as the music was in them. MacDermot is a composer who apparently does not care about lyrics, which is somewhat of a drawback when writing for the theatre. "Finally," is the glad word about *Via Galactica* because, while you know it must end sometime, you have to wonder whether you'll make it there yourself.

WALTER KERR, *TIMES*
[Headline: "When It Rained Tapioca"]
Via Galactica was a musical about the future that had none. It was doggerel opera, nursery-rhyme opera, cracker-barrel opera, and by the time you had listened to several hundred short, flat constructions like "Bring him back/And then we pack" or "Why delay?/Take your hat off, try my way" or "Earth is on its way here/We can't stay here," you were terribly relieved to get at least one that didn't rhyme ("I don't want to be no oyster/I don't like those clammy bars"). I would call the text childish but children are clearer. I have not yet mentioned the oddest thing about *Via Galactica*, and I am astonished that the distinguished British director Peter Hall did not notice it before he put foot to stage (or to trampoline, as it happened). Everything that was meant to make *Via Galactica* move immobilized it. Irene Cara, a singing narrator, descended from the high vault of the new playhouse on a fixed trapeze, explaining the plot to us while suspended in mid-air. But she was frozen there. A giant crane moved the clamshell trash-ship slowly about the vast stage, portal to portal. But the people inside it were as good as strapped to their seats, unable to do anything but relay us those foursquare lyrics. Keene Curtis was of course totally confined to his box—the box itself could go back and forth, up and down, if that's action—and even the six trampolines that pitted the stage floor proved inhibiting. People could bounce up and down in place, which became rather monotonous after a while, or they could leap from one springboard to another, which was only a little less monotonous. But we were effectively denied choreography: dance depends upon having and seeing a floor from which bodies can depart under their own power. The evening was, in consequence, entirely, quite staggeringly, static. As for the scenery, it was almost entirely composed

of little white dots like the ones they sprinkle on those candies called nonpareils, with the result that we spent the evening staring at what seemed a steady rainfall of tapioca.

•   •   •

The immense financial success of *Hair* (1968), followed by the award-winning (if less spectacularly lucrative) *Two Gentlemen of Verona* (1971), translated into not one but two sky's-the-limit rock musicals by composer Galt MacDermot. The one-two punch of *Dude* and *Via Galactica*, dropping $1,800,000 within seven weeks, not only ended MacDermot's Broadway presence; it tolled the death knell for rock musicals themselves (noted with appreciation). While *Hair* and *Dude* had been ragtag offerings, reflecting the sartorial splendor of librettist Gerry Ragni, *Via Galactica* was lavished with top-notch theatricality. Director Peter Hall of the National Theatre was imported, along with super set designer John Bury, to create a space-age extravaganza. And create they did, with devices including a spacecraft trash-mobile suspended on a cherry picker; a disembodied star-in-a-box, with Keene Curtis playing a bald, body-less head (poor thing lost all his organs 'cept his brain, it seems); a stage floor containing six trampolines to simulate antigravity, although in practice whatever went up always came down with a thud; and a curtain consisting of 375,000 Ping-Pong balls. Yes, I said 375,000 Ping-Pong balls, which were supposed to lend a supragalactical texture to the multimedia projections. Talk about the Black Hole. As for composer MacDermot, he did return to Broadway in 1984—via the Shakespeare Festival—with a quick-flop musicalization of William Saroyan's *The Human Comedy*, of all things. Thirteen performances and out. Etymological Note: *Via Galactica*'s original title was, indeed, *Up!*; they were booked at the new Uris. While looking at preliminary advertising copy, the producers realized that their teaser ads said, in effect, "Up Uris." They shamefacedly changed the title, although the first one was, perhaps, more fitting.

BROADWAY SCORECARD

/ PERFS: 7 / $: –

RAVE	FAVORABLE	MIXED	UNFAVORABLE	PAN
			1	5

WALKING HAPPY

"The New Musical," previously entitled *The Bespoke Lover*

music by James Van Heusen

lyrics by Sammy Cahn

book by Roger O. Hirson and Ketti Frings (Hirson replaced Frings, who retained billing)

based on the 1915 comedy *Hobson's Choice* by Harold Brighouse

directed by Cy Feuer

choreographed by Danny Daniels

produced by Cy Feuer and Ernest Martin by arrangement with Lester Linsk

starring Norman Wisdom, Louise Troy, and George Rose

with Ed Bakey, Gordon Dilworth, and Emma Trekman

opened November 26, 1966   Lunt-Fontanne Theatre

JOHN CHAPMAN, *DAILY NEWS*

You'll be sitting happy during every moment of *Walking Happy*, the ebullient new musical comedy. It is a joyous performance—and now that Norman Wisdom has been brought over from England we should adopt him and never let him go. This is a completely professional work, and it rejoices in good taste as well as high spirits. The title, though, might be *Dancing Happy*, for it reaches several peaks of enjoyment during several novel and captivating dance numbers staged by Danny Daniels. The dances begin with an exciting men's clog, continue with a wild romp for everybody on barrel-tops and are climaxed by a fine "Walking Happy" number.

MARTIN GOTTFRIED, *WOMEN'S WEAR DAILY*

Considering that so little happens in it, it really is a wonder that *Walking Happy* occupies time. The musical is remarkably without any identity at all—a collection of vague (and pointless) chraracters in a vague (and pointless) story singing vague (and pointless) songs in a pointless (and vague) production. Robert Randolph's scenery is the only interesting thing going for it. And that is interesting only because it is so terribly complicated, revolving, opening, closing and revolving some more. It is overdone, distracting scenery created according to a Fifties Broadway formula and in that sense matches the structure of this show. James Van Heusen composed a score that was pleasantly understated for Broadway (thanks, in great measure, to Larry Wilcox's nice woodwinded orchestrations), but unfortunately carried through that understatement to the point of being innocuous, same-sounding, and manufactured for obsolete juke boxes. It is pop-music in a style not only outmoded but never even related to theatre needs in the first place.

WALTER KERR, *HERALD TRIBUNE*

Norman Wisdom is a jack-in-the-box absolute, a forlorn Punch on a spring, and when an overloaded barrow he's tugging suddenly tilts backward and lifts him high in the air—turning him into a dervish clinging to the handlebars for dear life—you're not the least bit surprised. It is his fate to be caught by the scruff of the neck and shaken out regularly, like a well-used duster, and each time he's pounced upon our pleasure grows greater. Danny Daniels [the choreographer] has had the further good sense to notice, and make use of, Wisdom's angular, knockabout, rag-doll shape. If the performer's knees knock together, for instance, all the rest of him does, too, leaving his elbows suspended in a most mysterious void, and an image of that sort can be parlayed—come dance time—into broken-necked struts, stiff-legged leaps, and a seven-league stride that George Cohan might have envied. Actually, Wisdom looks rather more like Fred Astaire crossed with Stan Laurel, but he is, it must be said, his own man, a zany original with ruffled hair, ruffled eyes, and an altogether irresistible appeal. All in all? *Walking Happy* is an easygoing, unpretentious, minor-league musical given its one genuine flash of distinction by Wisdom's gift for being indelibly present no matter what he is doing—leaning cross-legged against the proscenium, catching his foot in a cantankerous stool, stealing backward in a crouch from the striped night shirt he is expected to wear once he's married.

He is Harlequin come to life among the British lower classes, and it was nice getting to know him on Saturday night.

NORMAN NADEL, *WORLD-TELEGRAM & SUN*
Hobson's Choice is a lovely play, though you'd scarcely suspect it from *Walking Happy*, which stumbled onto the stage of the Lunt-Fontanne Theatre Saturday night. The English classic about the imperious Lancashire boot merchant, his determined eldest daughter and the timid little shoemaker she marries has been reduced to an utterly commonplace musical. It is burdened with the season's worst lyrics and partly redeemed only through one shining performance [Wisdom], one that is better than adequate [Louise Troy], a few exhilirating dance numbers and some ingeniously designed scenery. The scenes that work are those in which writers Roger O. Hirson and Ketti Frings have tampered least with the original play. Even so, they probably are less guilty of damage than composer James Van Heusen, lyricist Sammy Cahn and director Cy Feuer. These are all talented people, and it's hard to understand how they could have turned out a product so stiflingly prosaic, but they certainly have done so. Generally, the lyrics are of a type discarded 25 years ago, with, as one example, "adorable" rhymed with "Sodom and Gomorrah-ble."

○   ○   ○

David Lean's delectable 1953 filmization of *Hobson's Choice* (with Charles Laughton, Brenda de Banzie, and John Mills) indicated strong musical comedy potential. For musical comedy you'd want to play up the romance, naturally; and who better for the not-so-young shop mistress who makes a man out of the guttersnipe cobbler than Mary Martin? *Walking Happy* was thus signed and sealed, one of two simultaneous Feuer and Martin/Cahn and Van Heusen star vehicles. Julie Harris and *Skyscraper* made it—or, rather, didn't make it—first, with *Hobson* taking a little longer to cobble together. Then Mary Martin took a hike, leaving them leading lady-less. No problem, just change the focus to lowly Will Mossup and place an authentic British music-hall low comedian in the role. Norman Wisdom was unknown hereabouts, but he had played the Ray Bolger role in the 1958 West End edition of Feuer and Martin's Loesser musical *Where's Charley?* (1948). He also created the role of Cocky—subsequently played by Anthony Newley on Broadway—in *The Roar of the Greasepaint—The Smell of the Crowd*, which closed during its pre-London tryout in 1964. Mary's role went to Louise Troy, who had nearly held her own against Bea Lillie and Tammy Grimes in the 1964 *High Spirits*, while classical actor George Rose—known stateside for his role of the Common Man in the 1961 *A Man for All Seasons*—unexpectedly entered the world of musical comedy (and stayed). As things turned out, the unknown Wisdom did very well for himself on Broadway and was almost able to carry the flat-footed *Walking Happy*. But only almost.

BROADWAY SCORECARD

/ PERFS: 161 / $: −

RAVE	FAVORABLE	MIXED	UNFAVORABLE	PAN
1	1	2		2

WEST SIDE STORY

a revival of the 1957 musical

music by Leonard Bernstein

lyrics by Stephen Sondheim

book by Arthur Laurents

"based on a Jerome Robbins conception," suggested by the 1595 tragedy *Romeo and Juliet* by William Shakespeare (unbilled)

"entire production directed and choreographed by Jerome Robbins"

book co-directed by Gerald Freedman

co-choreographed by Peter Gennaro; choreography reproduced with the assistance of Tom Abbott and Lee Becker Theodore

produced by Gladys Rackmil, the John F. Kennedy Center, and James M. Nederlander, in association with Zev Bufman; Ruth Mitchell, executive producer

starring Josie De Guzman, Ken Marshall, and Debbie Allen

with Hector Jaime Mercado, James J. Mellon, Sammy Smith, Ray Contreras, Jake Turner, and Arch Johnson

opened February 14, 1980   Minskoff Theatre

WALTER KERR, *TIMES*

By some odd metamorphosis, *West Side Story* seems to have grown younger, more innocent, more endearing over the years. Perhaps that's a strange thing to say about a musical that prided itself on its toughness, its back-alley know-how, its open hatreds expressed in defiant dance, its flashing knives and probing police-car lights ominously searching out bodies beneath a bridge. If the celebrated musical invasion of street-gang territory seems less dynamic this time around, it is also—in one of those fair-play turnabouts—rather more winning. Perhaps the relative lightness, almost a softness, of the revival stems partly from the fact that we are looking at the dancers differently. When we first saw them,

The air is humming.
Something great is coming!
Live on stage!

WEST SIDE STORY

Arthur Laurents
THE BOOK

Leonard Bernstein
THE MUSIC

Stephen Sondheim
THE LYRICS

Jerome Robbins
THE DIRECTOR

GLADYS RACKMIL, THE JOHN F. KENNEDY CENTER, and JAMES M. NEDERLANDER
in association with ZEV Buffman

EXECUTIVE PRODUCER: RUTH MITCHELL

present

WEST SIDE STORY

Based on a Jerome Robbins Conception

Book by

ARTHUR LAURENTS

Music by

LEONARD BERNSTEIN

Lyrics by

STEPHEN SONDHEIM

Book Directed by

GERALD FREEDMAN and JEROME ROBBINS

ENTIRE PRODUCTION DIRECTED AND CHOREOGRAPHED BY JEROME ROBBINS

Scenery Designed by   Costumes Designed by   Lighting Designed by
OLIVER SMITH   IRENE SHARAFF   JEAN ROSENTHAL

Co-Choreographer   Musical Direction   Choreography reproduced with the assistance of
PETER GENNARO   JOHN DEMAIN   TOM ABBOTT, LEE THEODORE
DONALD JENNINGS

Orchestrations by
LEONARD BERNSTEIN with SID RAMIN
and
IRWIN KOSTAL

"Live on stage!" They had to tell us? Everyone looks 22 years older; this *West Side Story* production came across slightly embalmed.

roughly 23 years ago, we were stunned by the malevolent drive that could be got into controlled footwork as Puerto Rican Sharks and "white" Jets advanced upon one another, inch by inch, leap by leap. We watched shoulders brush as these teen-age rivals strode challengingly through disputed terrain, and we saw in the cat's cradle of criss-crossing bodies, choreographed hate, threat, contempt and the final kill. The new look in movement was mesmerizing. But we know all about that now, which means that we may be freer to watch the dance as dance. Watching it, we're surprised to see how much silence, restraint, sheer elevation has gone into it. I should mention at this point that some aspects of *West Side Story* have always bothered me. Whenever the story line begins to press its Shakespearean parallels too hard—the "balcony" scene played on a fire escape, the falsely relayed news that Maria-Juliet is dead—the borrowings seem pat and synthetic. Worse, they rob us of emotions we ought to feel. Mr. Laurents's street jargon, with its "buddy boys" and its "daddy-o's" and its injunction to "walk tall," is never as authentic as the switchblades that come whipping out of dirty pockets. And—though we've got to remember here how unreliable memory is— I was surprised to find so little real dance in the first act's climactic "Rumble." It's a fine dramatic fight, vigorously staged; but I'd always thought it a more extensively choreographed one. I've run over these points because you may find some of them troubling, too. That done, let me assure you that most of what's on view at the Minskoff is colorful, edgy with energy, exciting in its dance confrontations—and worth checking out for that curious new tone it's uncovered.

HOWARD KISSEL, *WOMEN'S WEAR DAILY*

The revival of *West Side Story* is useful largely as a documentation of how our musical theatre has disintegrated in 20-odd years. You are aware of the decline from the instant the overture starts. Leonard Bernstein's abrasive, brilliant music, which hit you in the gut when it was played in a real theatre with a real orchestra pit, sounds like Muzak in the Minskoff, where the orchestra is buried practically under the stage and the sound comes out of speakers less impressive than those you probably have at home. As soon as the curtain goes up you see Jerome Robbins' difficult, exhilarating dance in which the Jets and Sharks threaten one another and protect their pathetic, slummy turfs. Here the young dancers do the steps with precision, with energy, even with enthusiasm. All that is lacking are menace and guts. These are good dancers doing their work well, not street toughs brimming over with tension, aggression or violence. And so it goes. Bernstein's songs are not badly sung. But they do not soar. Robbins's dances are not badly done, but they do not have the urgency of a banner headline, which they did 20 years ago. Arthur Laurents's book has dated less than I expected—some of the language seems a little quaint (did street gangs ever say anything as literary as "Womb to tomb . . . Sperm to worm?"), but the book's core, the idea that the gulf between kids and adults is wider than that between Jets and Sharks, still seems strong. But for these actors, all this seems as much ancient history as *Oklahoma!* [1943]—perhaps more so, since they have a well-scrubbed likableness to them that suggests *Oklahoma!* might be less remote. But it is not just the kids. The show does not look like vintage Broadway. This then is a routine revival, which is a disappointment, since *West Side Story* is not a routine show.

DOUGLAS WATT, *DAILY NEWS*
[Headline: "*West Side Story* Now Quaint"]
Leonard Bernstein's score is as striking as ever, Stephen Sondheim's lyrics remain fleet, and Jerome Robbins's trailblazing direction retains much of its former spell. Yet an air of quaintness has begun to overtake *West Side Story*, which returned to us last night at the Minskoff in a production not quite up to the mark and with a certain loss of intimacy in this barn of a theatre. It is still a remarkable creation, this conception of director-choreographer Jerome Robbins, who is taking time out from the world of pure dance for his first Broadway effort, albeit a recreation, since *Fiddler on the Roof* [1964]. But it is the very cleverness of this singing, acting, balletic adaptation of the story of *Romeo and Juliet* to West Side Manhattan in the late 1950s and gang rivalry between Puerto Rican youths and the sons of older settlers that occasionally works against it. There are times when Robbins seems, and perhaps justifiably so, to be straining to tell the whole story in dance terms. And there are other times when the more conventional Broadway musical idiom takes charge. Musically and balletically, the work reaches its apotheosis with "Somewhere," the dream sequence falling into precisely the right place near the start of the second half. On the other hand, the

idealized, balletic finish of the evening is weak. I also always have found the love duet "Tonight" more elegiac than passionate for all its prettiness, just as the meetings of the lovers are, despite the bedroom scene, diminished by the air of holiness and lack of human warmth attaching to them. But the flashing rhythms of "America" and the blunt clowning of "Gee, Officer Krupke" burst through the poetic fabric with refreshing vigor. It is all the more difficult to voice these reservations inasmuch as the score, tellingly orchestrated by the composer (with the assistance of Sid Ramin and Irwin Kostal), is so superior to the Broadway standard, both in its direct statements and underscoring. It still has the power and versatility to astonish. Arthur Laurents' book, while still serviceable, reveals more and more weak spots. *West Side Story* remains a vivid, precedent-shattering Broadway musical, flawed but essential theatregoing for those approaching it for the first time.

o   o   o

West Side Story unquestionably rests high among Broadway's Most Perfect Musical list. Here we had the original creators come together to assemble the definitive production. No money problems, this time; no anxieties as to how the innovative combination of ballet and theatre would be received; no question as to whether Bernstein's turbulent, roiling rhythms would be too esoteric for popular acceptance and the Hit Parade. Faced with heartily welcoming audiences and unalloyed adulation, this *West Side* unaccountably fell flat. Despite everything the show had going for it, despite the actual presence of the Great Robbins himself (instead of the usual assistants dispatched to re-create his work), the great *West Side Story* was simply dull. No spark—that's what was lacking. But don't blame the material.

BROADWAY SCORECARD
/ PERFS: 333 / $: –

RAVE	FAVORABLE	MIXED	UNFAVORABLE	PAN
1	1	3		1

WHERE'S CHARLEY?

a revival of the 1948 musical comedy

music and lyrics by Frank Loesser

book by George Abbott

based on the 1892 farce *Charley's Aunt* by Brandon Thomas

directed by Theodore Mann

choreographed by Margo Sappington

produced by Circle in the Square, Inc. (Theodore Mann and Paul Libin)

starring Raul Julia

with Tom Aldredge, Louis Beachner, Taina Elg, Jerry Lanning, Carol Jo Lugenbeal, Marcia McClain, and Peter Walker

opened December 19, 1974   Circle in the Square Uptown Theatre

CLIVE BARNES, *TIMES*

There is nothing quite so dated as a dated musical, unless it is an old election promise or an obsolete calendar. More than a quarter of a century ago George Abbott and Frank Loesser fabricated a musical out of the English classic farce *Charley's Aunt* and called it *Where's Charley?* The project in the first place was just about as sensible and as sensitive as if Noël Coward had tried to make a musical out of Damon Runyon's *Guys and Dolls*. However, helped out by the gangling presence of Ray Bolger, it gave Loesser his first Broadway hit. Last night it was a little difficult to see why. Just as Bolger may be presumed to have been the raison d'être of the the original production, so, one imagines, Raul Julia is the raison d'être of this revival. Julia is not the first person one might think of to replace Bolger. He is, however, an extraordinarily accomplished actor with the most winning way with him. He has that nowadays uncommon stage commodity that can be called allure, or even glamour. Shy, ingratiating, at times he seems to have slipped into the theatre by accident, but once there he proves himself a star. *Where's Charley?* is certainly not badly done—with Julia's performance being a distinct blessing—the only question is whether it was worth doing.

MARTIN GOTTFRIED, *POST*

For *Where's Charley?* to survive a disastrous casting of the title role is proof enough that it is a classic American musical. The revival that opened last night is sure to be a good show for the holidays. That it is a good production isn't quite so easy to prove. Even discounting the absurdity of putting Raul Julia in the role of Charley, the company is uneven. Theodore Mann's direction is obvious and spiritless. Margo Sappington's choreography is uneven, sometimes silly but sometimes delightful. Yet, the musical qualities are wonderful. As for Julia, what is there to say? An extremely gifted actor, he has no excuse for retaining his Puerto Rican accent and it sounds positively ridiculous coming from the lips of an English undergraduate. In the midst of "Once in Love with Amy," Julia virtually steps out of character and pokes fun at himself but this simply violates the reality of the show. Also during that number, Sappington tried to capitalize on his dancing inadequacy by turning his movements into a joke. Not only is this a basic staging mistake—the audience is asked to laugh with the actor at the expense of his character—but it is foolishly motivated. The motivation is the memory of Ray Bolger in the role and the impossibility of matching his performance. But if a great many people remember Bolger, and I doubt it, dancing badly makes the memory and comparison stronger. There's just no getting around it: the show is a vehicle for whoever plays Charley and Julia shouldn't have been cast in it. The supporting players are mostly on the level of summer tent productions. George Abbott's book makes hash of Thomas' well-constructed original, riding along the old Broadway rail of what "works," even if it is a line that destroys plot or character sense. Yet, it does work. The production isn't a mess. It is merely mediocre. But the show has class.

WALTER KERR, *TIMES*

Revivals are never a waste of time. You always learn something. Certainly I didn't realize, when I first saw *Where's Charley?*, precisely how delicate—how deliberately delicate—Mr. Loesser's gentlemanly score was. If you listen to the tunes again you'll realize that Loesser knew what he was doing in the first place and that what he was doing was creating a chamber musical for a mezzotint world, paying a kind of constant compliment to springtime. We just didn't quite hear it the first time for the simple reason that in those days—about 26 years ago—we expected musicals to come down upon our heads with a cymbal-proud thump. Now, listening with ears that don't demand thunderclaps by the dozen, we can hear Loesser's filigreed intentions more clearly. Raul Julia is the new Charley, an impeccable choice. Impeccable because he doesn't press, has no need to. Julia is a deceptive fellow, born abashed but secretly dangerous. He may have the most ingratiating leer since Chico Marx, a leer that proclaims itself when he is smiling most modestly. His sloe-eyes lurk wantonly beneath very chaste lids, he seems to be erasing himself from the landscape when he is really preparing to spring, he can stand still and play straight while insulting everyone in sight, including the girl of his dreams. He is ready with a fast curve when his authors require one, literally spinning saucers through the air to those who care for tea, adopting the rocking gait of a seasick ostrich when he is decked out in black skirts and borrowed ringlets. Essentially, though, he is a man who bides his time, content to hold his straw hat in his hand until he can hit someone with it, and so, when it comes to "Once in Love with Amy," he is prepared for the best. He does no more than undulate his eyebrows rhythmically while the first notes are being struck. In time, he is more active than that: spinning around a bandstand center pole like a soon-to-topple top, diving over garden swings and pools into the arms of waiting saviors. But he has come to his eruptions slyly, which is how Loesser's score is meant to work.

○   ○   ○

Frank Loesser's first Broadway score is playfully contrived, sprightfully tuneful, and marvelously crafted. His remarkable emergence was unexpected; the well-known, firmly established Hollywood lyricist had only recently started writing his own tunes. In hindsight, anyone familiar with *Guys and Dolls* (1950), *The Most Happy Fella* (1956), *Greenwillow* (1960), or *How to Succeed* (1962) would naturally *expect* the score of *Where's Charley?* to be out of the ordinary. The original production ran 792 performances, longer than concurrent hits *Finian's Rainbow* (1947), *Brigadoon* (1947), *Gentlemen Prefer Blondes* (1949), and *Call Me*

Madam (1950). *Charley* has nevertheless been relegated to musical comedy limbo; the causes include the lack of an original Broadway cast album (due to a recording industry strike) and the indelible personal stamp Ray Bolger put on the material. If *Where's Charley?* is still workable—and it might well be—you're not going to be able to tell from a cheaply produced, poorly directed, musically miserly thrust-stage production such as that lavished on it by Circle in the Square. But *Charley* and his cheroot-chomping aunt from Brazil ("where the nuts come from") might just surprise us all one of these days.

BROADWAY SCORECARD

/ PERFS: 78 / $: –

RAVE	FAVORABLE	MIXED	UNFAVORABLE	PAN
	3		1	2

WILD AND WONDERFUL

"A Big City Fable"

music and lyrics by Bob Goodman

book by Phil Phillips

based on "an original work" by Bob Brotherton and Bob Miller

directed by Burry Fredrik

choreographed by Ronn Forella

produced by Rick Hobard in association with Raymonde Weil

starring Laura McDuffie (replacing Julie Budd), Walter Willison, Robert Burr, Ted Thurston, and Larry Small

opened December 7, 1971   Lyceum Theatre

RICK HOBARD PRESENTS
in association with RAYMONDE WEIL

WILD AND WONDERFUL
A NEW MUSICAL

STARRING

WALTER   LAURA
WILLISON   McDUFFIE

ROBERT BURR

LARRY SMALL
AND
TED THURSTON

Music and Lyrics	Book	From an original work by	
BOB GOODMAN	PHIL PHILLIPS	BOB BROTHERTON & MILLER	BOB

Setting	Costumes	Lighting
STEPHEN HENDRICKSON	FRANK THOMPSON	NEIL PETER JAMPOLIS

Musical Direction; Vocal Arrangements
Dance Music Composed & Arranged by
THOM JANUSZ

Orchestrations
by
LUTHER HENDERSON

Associate Producer:
JOHN C. O'REGAN

Dances and Musical Numbers staged by
RONN FORELLA

Directed by
BURRY FREDRIK

LYCEUM THEATRE
45th Street East of Broadway
Mats. Wed & Sat.

"Wet, windy and wretched," said Clive Barnes. "Tame and terrible," opined Doug Watt. "A musical like this makes critics wonder whether they should ask their publishers for hazardous duty pay." (artwork by Kenerson)

CLIVE BARNES, *TIMES*

Wet, windy and wretched. The music was bad, the lyrics were bad, the book was worse than bad, the choreography unsupportable, the costumes proved singularly hideous and spectacularly unflattering to every woman in the cast and, in the context, the settings seemed gratefully close to what we think of as professional [set design by Stephen Hendrickson]. A musical like this makes critics wonder whether they should ask their publishers for hazardous duty pay or, failing that, a precise statement of where they stand with Blue Cross and Blue Shield. The role of the heroine—who had to carry the most stupid of cumulative gags about late, late show movies—was played with more charm than it deserved by Laura McDuffie, and Walter Willison threw in everything but his kitchen sink, range and refrigerator in an effort to make the hero viable. Even Mr. Willison failed, and Mr. Willison is unusually talented.

DOUGLAS WATT, *DAILY NEWS*

[Headline: "A Pathetic Musical"]
Tame and terrible.

*   *   *

A second musical—following the unlamented *Frank Merriwell*—presented under that year's "Broadway Limited Gross Contract" for productions scaled to gross less than $25,000 per week, although there was little danger of *Wild and Wonderful* grossing *anything*. This intimate musical was slated to mark the Broadway debut of seventeen-year-old singing star Julie Budd, a funny girl from the same neighborhood—and with the same nose—as you know who. Budd dropped out shortly before the first preview, but even that other funny girl from Brooklyn couldn't have helped *Wild and Wonderful*. Though the latter sure would've sold a lot of tickets, especially at a five-dollar top.

BROADWAY SCORECARD

/ PERFS: 1 / $: –

RAVE	FAVORABLE	MIXED	UNFAVORABLE	PAN
			1	5

THE WIZ

"The New Musical Version of *The Wonderful Wizard of Oz*"

music and lyrics by Charlie Smalls

book by William F. Brown

based on the 1900 novel *The Wonderful Wizard of Oz* by L. Frank Baum

directed by Geoffrey Holder (replacing Gilbert Moses)

choreographed by George Faison

produced by Ken Harper

starring Tiger Haynes, Ted Ross, Hinton Battle (replacing Stu Gilliam), and Stephanie Mills

with Clarice Taylor, Mabel King, Andre De Shields, Tasha Thomas, and Dee Dee Bridgewater

opened January 5, 1975   *Majestic Theatre*

CLIVE BARNES, *TIMES*

Criticism is not objective. This does not mean that a critic cannot see qualities in a work that does not evoke much personal response in himself. A case in point is *The Wiz*. It has obvious vitality and a very evident and gorgeous sense of style. I found myself unmoved for too much of the evening, but I was respectfully unmoved, not insultingly unmoved. There is a high and mighty difference. *The Wiz* is intended as a new kind of fantasy, colorful, mysterious, opulent and fanciful. It was also obviously meant to be a fantasy for today—very modern, a dream dreamed by a space-age child. The concept is very good in theory, but the practice is not made perfect. Mr. Smalls' music—vastly overamplified by the way—sounded all too insistent and oddly familiar. It had plenty of verve but it lacked individuality. It is the over-all style of *The Wiz* that gives it its overriding impact. It has all been very carefully conceived and shaped. Not only is Smalls' music all of a piece but the visual aspect of the production—with handsomely, stylized settings by Tom H. John and vibrantly colored and wackily imaginative costumes by Geoffrey Holder—offers a fresh and startling profile. This is first-rate and highly innovative. Unfortunately, the total result is a little cold. This is not helped by a somewhat charmless book by William F. Brown. When so much is individually good it is difficult to justify a personal sense of disappointment. The stylistic unity of the show, which may prove very exciting to many Broadway theatregoers, is, of course, familiar to me from years of going to the ballet and the opera, so its originality is diluted. There are many things to enjoy in *The Wiz*, but, with apologies, this critic noticed them without actually enjoying them.

MARTIN GOTTFRIED, *POST*

Considering all the foolish things inherent in the very idea of a new, musical, all-black *Wizard of Oz*, it would have been amazing if anything about it worked at all. Imagine, then, that up until the moments before the first act curtain, the show is practically fabulous. Instead of sitting smugly unsurprised at a disaster, we're left with deep disappointment that the second act fell apart. *The Wiz* is half of something when it might have been something and a half. What was foolish about the idea? To begin with, an all-black anything never had any business anywhere. (How about an all-Jewish *Oklahoma*? Or *My Fair Lady* cast with short Irishmen?) It reminds you of *Carmen Jones* [1943] and *The Hot Mikado* [1939]—a minstrel show with black skin instead of burnt cork. Let white audiences watch the darkies sing and dance. And then there is the classic movie to contend with, and its classic songs. . . . It is great fun and circusy and driving right up toward that intermission when, of all things, the curtain comes down on book rather than music. That didn't have the look of knowledge. Neither did what was going on before, but that had been working—on sheer energy as it turned out. Sooner or later, if you really don't know what you're doing, your machine is going to fall apart and that's what happened to *The Wiz*. Too bad. It was great fun while it lasted.

WALTER KERR, *TIMES*

[Headline: "*The Wiz* Misses"]

The unfailingly appealing Clarice Taylor plays one of the witches in the all-black version of *The Wizard of Oz* and it is she who gives Dorothy the pair of silver slippers that will see her safely through anything provided she never, never parts with them. Once Dorothy has gone through virtually everything—including an assault by flying monkeys and a timely rescue by the Mice Squad—she wants to know just what it was about those slippers that made them so helpful. Witch Taylor compresses her rubbery face into a mashed-up grin and gives her an honest answer. "Oh, I could have told you the secret of the slippers right off," she cackles, "but it just didn't seem good theatre." A candid creature, Miss Taylor, and sassy about the kind of work she's employed in. I wish that everyone else connected with *The Wiz* had taken equal time to consider what constitutes good theater. It's not just a matter of working in, now and again, some remarkable octave-jumps in the songs, some dynamic full-stage dancing. *The Wiz* has both of these, though as often as not it seems spur-of-the-moment stuff. What good theatre's got to do, if it's going to arrive safe and smiling at 10 o'clock, is make up its mind what it is, and then stick with the head-or-tails choice. Are we all for innocence tonight, with Toto the dog leaping into Dorothy's loving arms on command and the rusty Tin Man showing his deep gratitude for being properly oiled by easing into a lightly rhythmic tap? Or do we know better than that, pockets loaded with jokes meant to make the whole thing mod? The narrative clings to its naïveté, staking a claim on charm. The libretto does nothing of the sort. It opts for smart, pallidly. The contemporary overlay, alas, is feeble at every turn. The broken-backed snappers succeed in knocking off the naïveté without providing a comic spine to replace it. The show wanders about in search of a dateline, not to mention a decent laugh. Everything is *done* confidently, mind you; it just doesn't have firm ground beneath it to say, where it's come from: Kansas, Harlem, M-G-M, or a kiddies' matinee. Somebody forgot to say, "We'll do *The Wizard* this way, this time."

HOWARD KISSEL, *WOMEN'S WEAR DAILY*

"It's the song that makes a fellow want to get right up, no matter where he is, and begin whistling and dancing all over the place, that makes a hit these days," Eubie Blake told a reporter in 1921. "The mushy, sobby, sentimental love songs of 20 or more years ago would not be at all popular today." Blake's comments seem just as appropriate to explain why it was a good idea to do a "soul" version of *The Wizard of Oz*. Soul is an idiom so far removed from the style of the Harold Arlen–E. Y. Harburg movie score [1939] that comparisons become unthinkable. Moreover, one of the chief virtues of soul music is the omnipresent beat, which is a constant invitation to dance—and the stage of the Majestic is wonderfully alive with movement. Every one of the familiar characters in this version of L. Frank Baum's perenially fresh fantasy has his own way of moving—Hinton Battle as the Scarecrow slides around the stage as if he had no joints to speak of; Tiger Haynes, as a tinman made from scraps of garbage pails and beer cans, tap dances; Ted Ross, as the cowardly lion, with a fur-dappled lion suit and a mammoth blond Afro, struts to beat the band; the tornado that flies Dorothy from her native Kansas to Oz is, of course, a dancing tornado, a chorus in black with upturned umbrellas and tortured dance steps; even the yellow brick road is a foursome, with oversized yellow shoes constantly in motion. Part of what makes *The Wiz* so entertaining is that the physical production is dazzling. Tom John has designed imaginative settings that flow with the action and provide interesting spaces for the dancing. Geoffrey Holder, in addition to his directorial duties, has designed some delicious costumes. Though there are occasional lapses in invention and the second act seems less well-placed than the first, Holder keeps the show moving well. What really gives *The Wiz* drive is George Faison's excellent choreography. I must confess that I fell in love with Stephanie Mills, who plays Dorothy, from the moment she stepped on stage. Her eyes are filled with wonder and sometimes seem brimming with tears, and her voice is just sensational. When she moves into her upper register it's quite enough to send you over the rainbow.

o   o   o

A music-business man named Ken Harper (who'd never been on Broadway) had the audacious idea of taking *The Wonderful Wizard of Oz* and turning it into a Broadway musical. Not the Harold Arlen/Yip Harburg version made famous by Judy Garland at M-G-M. No, throw out all that stuff, "Over the Rainbow" and "If I Only Had a Brain" and the rest, and start from scratch with a score by Charlie Smalls (who'd barely been on Broadway) and book by William F. Brown (who'd barely been on Broadway). Twentieth Century-Fox saw fit to bankroll the show at $650,000 and poured in a substantial amount more as the enterprise underwent various struggles down on the not-so-ease-y road. When the tryout met with a bad reception, bad business, and bad word of mouth, director Gilbert Moses was axed, and Geoffrey Holder—already onboard as costume designer—danced into the director's chair. When the Broadway opening met with a bad reception, bad business, and *good* word of mouth, the deep-pocketed Fox spent the requisite funds to cover losses, mount a TV campaign, and plug "Ease on Down the Road" into a hit single. All of which translated into a new, enthusiastic audience—many of whom had never before been to a Broadway show—and *The Wiz* soon worked its way into an SRO hit. Having earned millions from its investment, Fox was clever enough to sell off the movie rights. The 1978 film version was a bust, and a 1984 Broadway return—with Stephanie Mills recreating her original role—folded after only thirteen repeats.

In addition to winning the Tony Award for Best Musical, Tonys were won by Charlie Smalls (score), Geoffrey Holder (director), George Faison (choreographer), Ted Ross (supporting actor), Dee Dee Bridgewater (supporting actress), and Geoffrey Holder (costume design).

BROADWAY SCORECARD

/ PERFS: 1,666 / $: +

RAVE	FAVORABLE	MIXED	UNFAVORABLE	PAN
1	1	2	2	

WOMAN OF THE YEAR

"A New Musical Comedy"

music by John Kander

lyrics by Fred Ebb

book by Peter Stone

based on the 1942 screenplay *Woman of the Year* by Ring Lardner Jr. and Michael Kanin

directed by Robert Moore (doctored by Tommy Tune)

choreographed by Tony Charmoli

produced by Lawrence Kasha, David S. Landay, James M. Nederlander, Warner Theatre Productions/Claire Nichtern, Carole J. Shorenstein, and Stewart F. Lane

starring Lauren Bacall and Harry Guardino

with Roderick Cook, Eivind Harum, Grace Keagy, Daren Kelly, Rex Hays, Gerry Vichi, Marilyn Cooper, Rex Everhart, and Jamie Ross

opened March 29, 1981   *Palace Theatre*

WALTER KERR, *TIMES*

In Act Two there's a fine little to-do between Miss Bacall and two decisive cleaning ladies as each of them assiduously takes a mop to the stage floor, the cleaning ladies doing a spot of what I still consider Duncan Sisters yodeling while the star assures the world that "I Wrote the Book." And we're only coming to the topper, which occurs when the lonely Bacall hies herself to a cabin in the woods, there to acquire a few pointers from the only happily married woman she knows. The only happily married woman she knows (skip the plot complications) looks rather like a badger in distress, a nightmare compounded of hair curlers and ventilated slippers. She is played and sung by an unforgettable creature named Marilyn Cooper, and by the time Miss Cooper and The Lady Bacall have hoisted themselves onto tallish kitchen stools and compared their respective virtues and inadequacies, it's all over, the show's in the bag, Kander and Ebb have followed their musical premise to its frumpy, thundering conclusion. Nothing remains to be done but for Mr. Guardino to douse Miss Bacall with a full pitcher of water so that she has to take her curtain call in a bathrobe, drying her hair. Tricks again, but this time you're happy. And do you know one thing that's helped? Bacall's obvious delight in the hilarity Cooper is producing as the two of them do that career vs. homebody number called "The Grass Is Greener." The star actually looks happiest when someone else is lifting the 11 o'clock spot. Unheard of. And yet, come to think of it, that kind of plain common sense is one of the things that goes into the making of a star, too.

HOWARD KISSEL, *WOMEN'S WEAR DAILY*

Woman of the Year seems less like a piece of theatre than a product, the result not of artistic decisions but of test marketing. Peter Stone's book is an update of the 1942 Katharine Hepburn–Spencer Tracy movie, the international columnist now a TV personality, the easygoing sports columnist now a cartoonist, the wit of Ring Lardner's screenplay replaced by a humor carefully determined by a demographic survey of the Broadway audience—jokes for the Hadassah theatre parties ("*Zei gesunt*, Zubin"); jokes for the expense account crowd (references to Pearl's); and tired off-colored humor for the tourists ("What a dumb piece," the cartoonist says of an editorial. "Who are you calling a dumb piece?" the heroine asks). The score by John Kander and Fred Ebb is a step backward even from *The Act* [1977]. The lyrics and music seem to assume the audience could not deal with more than a few words at a time (one song consists almost entirely of "I was right—She was right"). or with a melody more than four notes long (some of the songs seem positively monotonic). Much of the score has the coyness and simplemindedness of Early Jerry Herman. As usual, Kander and Ebb are best at pastiche, and the most enjoyable number is a parody of a Forties novelty song, "It Isn't Working," which comes complete with a big band orchestration [by Michael Gibson]. The show's one undeniable asset is Lauren Bacall, though even the treatment of a big star has become a matter of clichés rather than imagination. The big dance number ["One of the Boys"]—in which she allows herself to be tossed about like a beanbag, an impressive feat—sounds like a parody of "One" in *A Chorus Line* [1975], which was a parody of all the songs in which chorus boys sing the praises of the star. The point of much of this is to show what a "good sport" she is. Bacall manages to rise above the material, even to surmount her own complicity in the campy proceedings, largely because of the good-natured brazenness that is a key part of her image. As her leading man, Harry Guardino is something of an enigma—not as handsome as he once was, not very charming. His major virtue seems to be that his gravelly voice blends so smoothly with hers.

FRANK RICH, *TIMES*

"I wrote the book on class," sings Lauren Bacall in her new musical, *Woman of the Year*, and you had better believe it. This star's elegance is no charade, no mere matter of beautiful looks and gorgeous gowns. Her class begins where real class must—in her spirit—and only then makes its way to her angular physique, her big, sensuous eyes and that snapdragon of a voice. Even when her leading man, Harry Guardino, dumps a pot of water over her head, she remains not only mesmerizing, but also completely fresh. As hard and well as Bacall works in *Woman of the Year*, she never lets us see any sweat. That's why this actress is a natural musical-comedy star. By making life and art look as easy and elegant as a perfect song, Bacall embodies the very spirit of the carefree American musical. She also, as a result, makes extraordinary demands on her theatrical collaborators. When we see Bacall on stage, we want the entertainment that contains her to come together as simply and delightfully as her performance. If it doesn't, we're going to notice the esthetic gap between the star and her vehicle very fast. *Woman of the Year* is an amiable show that suffers from such a gap. It boasts other assets besides Bacall—most crucially a tuneful score by John Kander—but it often huffs and puffs to achieve effects that its leading lady can pull off with a flick of her regal head. And, even then, it doesn't always deliver. While this show never drops below a certain, hard-nosed level of Broadway professionalism, neither does it rise to a steadily exciting pitch. Its creators are most fortunate to have a star who crackles whether they light a fire under her or not, but the people who concocted this musical know what their show is really about. Bacall is on hand virtually the whole time, and she's vibrant whether no-nonsense or tipsy, domineering or moony, dry or wet. If *Woman of the Year* is tired around the edges, it is always smart enough to keep its live wire center stage.

DOUGLAS WATT, *DAILY NEWS*
[Headline: "A Tepid Tribute to the *Woman of the Year*"]
A big, splashy musical comedy. It begins with a sleek, beaming Lauren Bacall encased in a skin-tight, gold-beaded evening sheath, bathing in the audience's welcoming applause while behind a scrim she is being hailed as "Woman of the Year" at an award ceremony. It's a hard act to follow. Impossible, in fact. Not that the evening is a total loss. But perversely, the scrappy love story keeps letting us down, with the subsidiary characters picking us up in between times. *Woman of the Year* rarely catches fire.

o   o   o

Bacall did just fine filling Hepburn's shoes as the *Woman of the Year*, but the authors neglected to provide her a bigger-than-life foil to spar against. Kate without Cary Grant, Humphrey Bogart, or Spencer Tracy could be overpowering and antiromantic; Hepburn had Tracy in the *Woman of the Year* film, but Bacall was left on her own. Yes, there was a leading man to provide an onstage clinch as the curtain fell (and an offstage clinch as well), but there was only room for one star on stage. Remove Petruchio from *Taming of the Shrew* and you're left with—well, an unkissable Kate. Bacall-by-herself had provided more than enough star power for *Applause* (1970), but then Bette Davis had similarly dominated *All About Eve*. The only foil the authors of *Woman of the Year* gave their star was Marilyn Cooper, in a single, showstopping ten o'clock song that woke everyone up. Not enough at $35 a ticket. Ring Lardner Jr. and Michael Kanin's tip-top Oscar-winning screenplay was unaccountably stripped bare for the Broadway stage and replaced by a Betty Bacall showcase, with meager results. The 1942 original concerned an intrepid reporteress and a gruff sportswriter, while the "modernized" 1981 edition called for an intrepid morning talk-show hostess and a gruff syndicated cartoonist. (Bacall's character was up-to-the-minute contemporary, munching jelly beans at the Reagan White House but also boasting that she "had tea with Gertrude and Alice." Gertrude died thirty-five years before Ron and Nancy took residency, so just what year was this dame woman of, anyway?) Despite kindly reviews and a quartet of Tony Awards, Bacall and company were unable to counteract audience apathy and outsized costs; capitalized at $2 million, the show came in at an astounding $2.7 million with a whoppingly high royalty package (21.25% of the gross *plus* 10% to Bacall and, of course, the theatre rental of 6%). Business picked up when Raquel Welch, of all people, stepped in as the *Woman of the* Second *Year*, but the shot in the arm was shortlived. Debbie Reynolds—of the similarly royalty-logged, high-grossing flop *Irene* (1973)—followed as mop-up, with the show embarrassingly folding on her after only two weeks. Producer Larry (*Applause*) Kasha announced that *Woman of the Year* was closing due to "a series of problems with the weather and train strikes." It Happened in Boston Dept.: Two chorus boys were lazing in the lobby of the Ritz-Carlton one afternoon during the tryout. In swept Tommy Tune, wrapped head-to-hoof in glamorous black mink—full-length takes on a new meaning when you're talking Tommy Tune—and followed by a bellhop laden with five Louis Vuitton suitcases. "Uh-oh," said one male dancer to the other, "we're being fixed!" Tune took one look at the show, told the producers to "leave it as it is," and hightailed it out of Beantown—with an already agreed-upon consultation fee of 25,000 bucks plus 1 percent of the gross! Not bad for a night's work, but not good for the show's budget, but *very* good for Tune's budget.

Tony Awards were won by John Kander and Fred Ebb (score), Peter Stone (book), Lauren Bacall (actress), and Marilyn Cooper (supporting actress).

BROADWAY SCORECARD

/ PERFS: 770 / $: –

RAVE	FAVORABLE	MIXED	UNFAVORABLE	PAN
2	2			2

WORDS AND MUSIC

a musical revue, featuring lyrics coauthored by Sammy Cahn (1915–1993)

directed by Jerry Adler

produced by Alexander H. Cohen in association with Harvey Granat

starring Sammy Cahn

with Kelly Garrett, Jon Peck, Shirley Lemmon, and Richard Leonard

opened April 16, 1974   *John Golden Theatre*

CLIVE BARNES, *TIMES*

Why are such shows as *Words and Music* simple and enchanting, and other shows complex and morose? *Words and Music* opened last night. I adored it, and so did Sammy Cahn. He wrote the words and his friends wrote the music. Most of the songs are lasting hits, and if he ever gets bored he can sit in his dressing room and figure out his royalties. For Mr. Cahn was born with a golden typewriter in his mouth. It has by now given him a tight smile but Fort Knox ulcers. This is a lovely, fun show. Cahn pretends to be a lyricist and certainly he has labored in those vineyards, both in Hollywood and on Broadway. But don't be fooled. Inside every songwriter there is a performer trying to get either in or out. No songwriter has ever written a song he did not think he was going to sing. In this humane and civilized show, Cahn very modestly, and with ineffable charm, demonstrates his two claims to fame. The first is interesting. He is undeniably one of the most successful, memorable and happy lyric writers of the last 40 years. His second claim is even more interesting. He is probably the best bad singer in the world. Cahn produces sounds that are a travesty of the inner workings of his voice. As a singer he has so much style that if God had made him Frank Sinatra, then the world would have seen something. Mr. Cahn sings with heart—and somehow, although he may sound like an attractive frog, you forget Sinatra, Crosby and all those mass-produced imitations, and listen to Sammy. There is more than this. Cahn is not just the best bad singer in town, he is a great humorist, dry, self-deprecating and lovable in an entirely unvulnerable fashion. (The guy is as vulnerable as a tank at the Charge of the Light Brigade, which come to think of it is the way he sings.)

MARTIN GOTTFRIED, *WOMEN'S WEAR DAILY*

I came to *Words and Music* a skeptic and I left a convert. I really thought producer Alexander H. Cohen had his nerve and not his brains, taking one of the songwriter lectures that had been a two-performance success at the 92nd St. "Y" and putting it into Broadway's John Golden Theatre. As it turns out, Cohen's brain was as steady as his nerve, and business should be too. *Words and Music* is a warm, funny, utterly congenial evening with Sammy Cahn, the lyricist for an unbelievable number of hit songs—a performer who maintains a disarming amateurism while being thoroughly professional—and the perfect present for anyone who likes the show-business story behind the wonderful old song. Somehow, impossibly, Cahn's evening never becomes an and-then-I-wrote one, and it is because he is so unphonily modest and self-effacing. He doesn't take his lyrics terribly seriously and he seems entirely without competitiveness toward other lyricists. Much of this is due to the confidence of success, but a lot of it, too, is because his lyrics aren't that great. Cahn is no Gilbert or Hart or Porter or Sondheim, and he seems to know it—seems almost to be surprised that he lasted as a songwriter at all; as if he got away with something. He almost never talks about lyric-writing technique, rhymes and patterns and prosody, or about content. How could he? His lyrics are not clever. They are invariably June-moon songs or zippy songs or gimmick songs. Of them, only one—"The Second Time Around"—sounds as if he really wanted to say something. And yet, there are great lyric-writing lessons to be learned from his work, which invariably builds a song on a clear, succinct thought, stated in a colloquial, conversational way ("I'll walk alone, because to tell you the truth I'll be lonely," "I fall in love too easily, I fall in love too fast"). And for all the lyrics he admits are silly ("Three Coins in the Fountain," "Give Me Five Minutes More"), he is capable of writing a set as technically fascinating as "My Kind of Town (Chicago Is)."

DOUGLAS WATT, *DAILY NEWS*
Sammy Cahn is selling some songs at the Golden. They're his own—the lyrics, anyway—and the show, a simple affair, is called *Words and Music*. I think you'll buy it. Sammy Cahn could sell you the Brooklyn Bridge if it had a tune to go with it. A short, bald, owlish-looking gent of 60, Cahn swells with the firm conviction that he knows more about putting across a song than Sinatra, Crosby, Lanza or any of the other people he's written for. All he lacks is a voice. So, to sort of embellish his easy conversational style, deft footwork and unparalleled chutzpah (that's probably one of the very few words he's never rhymed, though I'm sure he could), he's brought along three singers. But the evening—and it's a full one—is Cahn's as he traces his career in short and amusing anecdotes leading into such songs as "It's Magic," "All the Way," "I've Heard That Song Before," "Papa, Won't You Dance With Me," "I Should Care" and dozens more. The best demonstrator in the business, he loves every one of them. It doesn't matter that none of the songs can touch the Gershwins or Porter or Rodgers and Hart. They're unfailingly pleasant and skillfully turned, and the main thing is that they're presented so disarmingly.

•   •   •

The Broadway minefields are slagged with the shards of Hollywood songwriters hoping to show that they, too, could make it on the Boulevard of Broken Dreams. Only two proved adept, really, and Sammy Cahn wasn't one of 'em. (Close, though perhaps too close for comfort: one was Cahn's longtime collaborator Jule Styne and the other was the man Cahn replaced as Styne's lyricist, Frank Loesser.) *High Button Shoes* (1947) was a hit, thanks to star Phil Silvers and choreographer Jerome Robbins, and despite lackluster lyrics; *Glad to See Ya!* (1944), *Two's Company* (1952), *Skyscraper* (1965), *Walking Happy* (1966), and *Look to the Lilies* (1970) all slid down the tin pan hopper, and deservedly so. (We can only imagine that the unproduced *Bojangles* [1979], to tunes by Charles Strouse, would have landed on the wrong side of the ledger, too.) Cahn never earned much respect on Broadway, but he was good-natured enough—and realistic enough—to accept his limitations and be content with the talents he possessed. Thus it was that the no-longer-active wordsmith could walk out on stage, talk the Words, sing the Music, and generally charm his way through four months on Broadway. With all those tuneful tunes and entertaining stories, the prolific Cahn—in a small dose—proved hard to resist.

BROADWAY SCORECARD
/ PERFS: 127 / $: +

RAVE	FAVORABLE	MIXED	UNFAVORABLE	PAN
6				

WORKING

"A New Musical"

music and lyrics by Craig Carnelia, Micki Grant, Mary Rodgers (music)/Susan Birkenhead (lyrics), Stephen Schwartz, and James Taylor

adapted by Stephen Schwartz (with Nina Faso)

based on the 1974 oral history *Working: People Talk About What They Do All Day and How They Feel About What They Do* by Studs Terkel

directed by Stephen Schwartz

choreographed by Onna White (replacing Graciela Daniele)

produced by Stephen R. Friedman and Irwin Meyer in association with Joseph Harris

with Susan Bigelow (replacing D'Jamin Bartlett), Rex Everhart, Arny Freeman, Bob Gunton, David Patrick Kelly, Bobo Lewis, Patti LuPone, Joe Mantegna, Lenora Nemetz, and Lynne Thigpen

opened May 14, 1978　　　　*46th Street Theatre*

CLIVE BARNES, *POST*

Ambivalence here we come! Think of the *Reader's Digest*. Think of that feature in it—unmemorable, unlikely, but not unamusing and, oddly enough, not untruthful—called something like "The Most Unforgettable Person I Have Ever Met." The idea is to find the eccentric heart of normality and to equate it with godliness. This is what *Working* is fundamentally about. It is about the sheer fascination of being an ordinary person. You may be a fireman, you may be a whore, you may be a truck driver, but whatever it is, you have a job to do, a story to tell, and a life worth memorializing. Studs Terkel has written a number of successful books of living history. I have read bits of his books, but realize now, not at length. But the bits I read were better than last night's show. The message is that people talking about their jobs are interesting. Absolutely. And some people will find such stories very comforting. But more people—especially the people who go to the theatre—might find them a trifle banal. Basic honesty and banality are the two qualities of this show, which has been adapted and directed by Stephen Schwartz. He wrote the score for *Godspell* [1971], *Pippin* [1972], and *The Magic Show* [1974]. In his *Playbill* biography he omits this past, and merely points out that the "non-theatre jobs he has held include parking lot attendant, silent movie accompanist, camp counselor and grounds maintenance man." Well, modesty never got anyone anywhere. Schwartz' staging seems to be chiefly based on a theatrical form of roller skates. His sliding stage [designed by David Mitchell] can move in virtually any direction and frequently does. He has also contributed quite a lot of the music and lyrics. It is, however, a very, very talky musical. It is a personal reminiscence interrupted by the occasional feeble song. All over the world people want to be heard. But this fact is a cliché. Truthfulness is only interesting when it reveals a difference. When it offers an already suspected similarity it is nothing but a statistic. *Working* is fundamentally an attempt to make statistics into musical drama. I honestly cannot imagine that lengthy, if distinctively recognizable, conversations to the bland sound of muzak, will ever add up to a truly stimulating evening in the theatre. There were some moments of truth. But there were also moments of desperation, trying to transform platitudes into experience.

RICHARD EDER, *TIMES*

In the few moments when the voices of Studs Terkel's working Americans rise from perceptive self-description to dramatic self-revelation, the musical *Working* comes excitingly alive. There are many other moments, less exciting, when a touching anecdote or a bit of wry humor or clowning, put over by a devoted and absolutely first-rate cast, produces some considerable pleasure. But by and large, Stephen Schwartz's idea of making a musical out of Terkel's chronicle of men and women talking about their work is out of focus. Despite the talents involved, the show lacks a workable form and combines elements that don't agree. The fundamental problem is that Terkel's book is a record whose value comes from setting down the words in which a wide selection of Americans think of themselves. The housewife in *Working* talks about a tedious routine with a note of smiling defiance; the call girl with a hint of tearful defiance. As written these are not really clichés; most of all because they have the drama of real people straining to define what part of life it is that they are ill with. Furthermore, Terkel finds a detail or two, a turn of phrase, a whimsical jump out of the ordinary, that marks his people. On paper but not on stage. On stage, in the context of a series of musical skits, these real narrations inevitably become dramatic fictions. They are usually too frail; and they are overburdened. Terkel's waitress has an odd and appealing leap of imagination when she talks about her work; she thinks of herself as an actress, she says, or a gypsy. But Lenora Nemetz must turn all this into song and dance. The flash of fantasy becomes a stage cliché because all we see is a bounding, effusive waitress doing a gypsy number with a tray. Nemetz is magnificently pale and tired and awkward, but the problem is with the whole conception. Which brings us to the songs. There is one stunning number by James Taylor, "Millwork," with words by Graciela Daniele and Matt Landers. But in general the songs are musically uninteresting and what is worse, trite and sentimental in their lyrics. The contrast in Craig Carnelia's "Just a Housewife" and in the deadly "Father and Sons" by Schwartz, between their inflated and banal words and Terkel's living record, is devastating.

WALTER KERR, *TIMES*

Working, with its playfully agile company clambering all over the block letters that spell out the show's title, announces at once that it means to add exuberance to the reflections, many of them downbeat, of its clock-driven people. (Clocks abound, dropping in from the heavens in various sizes, though not always telling the precisely right time.) And, in its excursions into music, it sometimes succeeds in lifting what is melancholy and forlorn into gratifying lyric energy. Susan Bigelow, for instance, is given the exceedingly familiar complaint that "all I am is just a housewife," but she is able to take Craig Carnelia's melodic line and pump it to the brim with belief; ardor and some delicate vocal shading combine to bring the number off. At other times, though, the strain of trying to produce dance elaboration and show-stopping climaxes out of verbal imagery as obvious and flat as "We truckers, we compare ourselves to sailors, we sail out on to the highways" pretty much blows the evening. A waitress works hard and slinkily to build to an applause finish, but all she's got to go on is the information that "Everybody has to eat, everybody has hunger," while a dancer weakly attempts to persuade us that he is taking a moment off to skate about on a street pond created by an open hydrant. The moments of invention are necessarily small in a humdrum world; the very presence of rhyme calls attention to the absence of anything remotely resembling poetry, even folk poetry. In doing his interviews, Terkel isn't necessarily trying to trap poetry. He's trying to trap personality, and in print he often does. But here the material has been truncated, whittling away personality, at the same time that what's left is being musically magnified. It's the plainness that's being blown up, but that only makes it all the plainer. I suppose you could say that first there is life, then there is life listened to (Terkel's preserve), and then there is life dramatized. The last is what's missing in *Working*, as might have been expected; the bits and pieces seem to resist full staging, refuse to rise to their respective "toppers," because they've had no theatre in their blood to begin with. Amiability, yes. Honesty, no doubt. A need for exposure beneath a proscenium arch and all those lights, no.

◦   ◦   ◦

Riding high on the success of *Annie* (1977), producers Stephen Friedman and Irwin Meyer not only booked the 46th Street for their new musical—they bought it as well. They also bought Stephen Schwartz's reputation as Broadway's golden boy. After all, didn't *Godspell* and *Pippin* and *The Magic Show* run forever? Yes, indeed, they did; but Schwartz's trouble-laden fourth effort, *The Baker's Wife* (1976), never made it to town. His fifth work, *Working*, initially worked out at Chicago's Goodman Theatre, where it needed work. The overproduced Broadway version opened cold in New York, with previews of the unpolished work-in-progress facing increasingly hostile audiences. Novice director Schwartz was totally in charge and totally out of control; the turmoil at the 46th Street was messy and well publicized, which only served to accentuate the negative. *Working* opened to jeers, and the previously golden Schwartz hightailed it out of town. He's made but one local appearance since, in 1986, with the similarly strife-ridden *Rags* (to music by Charles Strouse). *Children of Eden*, his Old Testament epic, was an expensive West End fiasco in 1991. Schwartz finally emerged from almost twenty years of darkness with his lyrics for Disney's 1995 animated feature, *Pocahontas*. Things didn't work out so well for producers Friedman and Meyer either: after three flops in ten months (including Cy Coleman's 1979 road-fold *Home Again, Home Again*), they landed in the hoosegow for a coal mining tax-shelter fraud. Their biggest victim was one E. Presley, a deceased former pop singer, who dropped $510,000.

BROADWAY SCORECARD
/ PERFS: 25 / $: –

RAVE	FAVORABLE	MIXED	UNFAVORABLE	PAN
			3	3

THE YEARLING

"A Musical"

music by Michael Leonard

lyrics by Herbert Martin

book by Herbert Martin and Lore Noto

based on the 1938 Pulitzer Prize-winning novel by Marjorie Kinnan Rawlings

directed by Lloyd Richards (replaced by Herbert Ross)

choreographed by Ralph Beaumont (replaced by Vernon Lusby)

produced by Lore Noto

starring David Wayne, Dolores Wilson, Carmen Matthews, and Carmen Alvarez

with Steve Sanders, Peter Falzone, Robert Goss, Allan Louw, David Hartman, and Gordon B. Clarke

opened December 10, 1965   Alvin Theatre

WALTER KERR, *HERALD TRIBUNE*

The musical version of *The Yearling* is such a decent disaster that some effort should be made to learn from it. Perhaps two rules can be laid down against adding future entertainments to the catalogue of Lost Causes. The first: narratives of unrelieved misery, no matter how earnest their intentions or poignant their themes, probably require the vocal openness of opera if they are to be musicalized at all. The slighter, lighter forms of popular melody, trimmed to a thirty-two-bar neatness and to swiftly recognizable refrains, seem only like so many roller skates trying to carry burdens appropriate to Mack Trucks. The emotion that all of this [tragedy] should generate simply cannot be absorbed or released by a dozen or so tinkly Christmas-tree tunes, not even when the lyrics are straining ardently to say that "I'm in need of her, she's been

LORE NOTO
presents
DAVID WAYNE
in
THE YEARLING
A MUSICAL
Based on the novel by
MARJORIE KINNAN RAWLINGS

also starring
DOLORES WILSON **CARMEN MATHEWS**
Introducing
STEVE SANDERS as "JODY"
with
ROBERT GOSS **ALLAN LOUW** **GORDON B. CLARKE**
and **JOE E. MARKS**

Book by
HERBERT MARTIN and **LORE NOTO**
Lyrics by   Music by
HERBERT MARTIN **MICHAEL LEONARD**

Sets and Costumes Designed by   Lighting Designed by
ED WITTSTEIN **JULES FISHER**
Vocal Arrangements & Music Direction by   Orchestrations by
JULIAN STEIN **HERSHY KAY**
Original Cast Album Recorded by   Score Published by
MERCURY RECORDS **EDWIN H. MORRIS & COMPANY**
Associate Producer
MICHAEL BALISTRERI

Directed by
LLOYD RICHARDS

SHUBERT THEATRE
250 SO. BROAD ST., PHILA.
TUES. NOV. 9
thru
SAT. NOV. 27

"The year's most eagerly awaited new Broadway musical with the stars of the year and the songs of the year"—per the advertising herald—got lost in the swamp. Preliminary credits. (artwork by Harvey Schmidt)

a strength to me." A second point: narratives which depend for their direct effectiveness on objects or events which must, in the nature of things, be concealed from our onstage view are born crippled. We are not going to see rattlesnakes biting, deer leaping eight-foot fences, bears being tracked in faraway woods. Yet every vital moment in *The Yearling*, everything that would make the issue graphic and the recorded pain personal, depends upon just such eavesdropping. The problem should be obvious, long before librettists plunge in; but it has not stayed the authors from attempting to embroil us in crises that must be echoes. The result is an atmosphere that seems evasion. We can hear of hard times, we can understand; but we cannot be present when the excitement erupts or despair clamps down. In the end we seem to be passing the theatre, casually along the sidewalk, overhearing some activity inside but kept from it by glass doors. The show seems absentminded because the naturally perilous world the people live in is not there.

NORMAN NADEL, *WORLD-TELEGRAM & SUN*

Can *The Yearling* be made into a musical? I'm afraid that the question is still unanswered. Only here and there does it capture the gentle harmony of innocence and intuitive knowledge that sets the book apart from all others. I don't know if much will be accomplished by cataloguing its attractions and faults, except to show how *The Yearling* might have come close to what it should have been. The problem is more than cast changes and details of staging could correct. There is a prevailing lack of inspiration, first in the script, second in the direction by Lloyd Richards and Herbert Ross (both of whom had left the show prior to last night's opening), and third in the overall production. When Jody and Fodder-Wing sing "Some Day I'm Gonna Fly," you hope that the show is about to. The boys do wind up on the roof, but *The Yearling* never gets off the ground.

HOWARD TAUBMAN, *TIMES*

The po' white folks in *The Yearling* could use an antipoverty program, and so could the musical. *The Yearling* is desperately undernourished. It lacks a spine for its book, a pulse for its songs and vitamins for its production. The only thing it has in suberabundance is corn, which is not particularly nutritious for a stage work. The book by Herbert Martin and Lore Noto drips with the clichés of backwoods musicals. Everything about it is soggy and droopy. *The Yearling* has a dog, a rabbit and a fawn among its dramatis personae, and you would think that the animals would be tough competition for the human performers. For a moment at the first-act curtain the fawn, held by Jody, quivers with eagerness. This is about the only valid communication *The Yearling* has to offer.

·   ·   ·

Following an impressive Broadway debut in 1959 with Lorraine Hansberry's *A Raisin in the Sun*, director Lloyd Richards was hired for—nothing much. His experience with *Raisin*'s fine actors (Sidney Poitier, Claudia McNeil, Ruby Dee, Diana Sands) made him the logical (?) choice to helm the 1964 Buddy Hackett laff-fest *I Had a Ball*, from which he was rolled early on. This in turn made him the ideal person for the swamp-'n'-hurricane *Yearling*, right? Amazing the way these things work. You can't blame Richards, of course; these were, presumably, the only Broadway jobs offered him. (And would this fine director have ever gotten back to town if it weren't for the August Wilson plays, starting in 1984?) With *The Yearling* in terminal trouble, Richards was again sent out to pasture while medic Herb (*Kelly* [1965]) Ross was rushed to the scene. ("If Herb is such a great show doctor," wifie Nora Kaye once asked, "why do all the patients die?") *The Yearling*'s producer was Lore Noto, whose unconventional *The Fantasticks* (1960) was then in its unprecedented sixth year Off-Broadway. Noto was determined to crack the Main Stem with his unprecedentedly unconventional musical tragedy; he cracked it, all right, after which he licked his wounds and limped back down to Sullivan Street (where he remained happily ever after). *The Yearling* attracted a modicum of attention thanks to Barbra Streisand, an acquaintance of rehearsal-pianist-turned-composer Michael Leonard; she recorded "I'm All Smiles" on her best-selling *People* album (released a year before *The Yearling* opened). She also recorded three other songs from the score, making *The Yearling* an anomaly in a day when *On a Clear Day* or *Do I Hear a Waltz?* (both 1965) were lucky to get one or two pop "covers" before coming to town. This activity didn't, in the end, help sell any *Yearling* tickets, but it did facilitate a cast album deal and a $100,000 investment from Mercury

Records (which, needless to say, never recorded the show). *The Yearling* was given another shot twenty years later, with a summer production at Atlanta's Theatre of the Stars (directed by Lucia Victor, starring John Cullum and D'Jamin Bartlett). Same material, same problems, same results.

BROADWAY SCORECARD

/ PERFS: 3 / $: —

RAVE	FAVORABLE	MIXED	UNFAVORABLE	PAN
		1		5

ZORBÁ

"A Musical"

music by John Kander

lyrics by Fred Ebb

book by Joseph Stein

based on the 1946 novel *Vois Kai Politeia Tou Alexi Zorbá* (*Zorbá, the Greek*) by Nikos Kazantzakis

directed by Harold Prince

choreographed by Ronald Field

produced by Harold Prince in association with Ruth Mitchell

starring Herschel Bernardi and Maria Karnilova

with John Cunningham, Carmen Alvarez, and Lorraine Serabian

opened November 17, 1968   Imperial Theatre

Looks like a nice, cheery, chipper dance musical, right? But this sure-fire smash follow-up to *Cabaret* and *Fiddler* was hoist on its own pretensions. (artwork by Tom Morrow)

CLIVE BARNES, *TIMES*

Apart from the aberrant yet delightful *Hair* [1968], *Zorbá* is the best musical to be seen on Broadway since *Fiddler on the Roof* [1964] and *Man of La Mancha* [1965]. Of course, this does not mean too much. Hal Prince is one of the very few creative producers on Broadway—a man who can put his own imprint on a show, and that imprint is planted all over *Zorbá* like a sterling silver mark. From beginning to end this is a musical with exquisite style and finesse. Prince calculates his effects like a Mozart, whereas most of his competitors tend more toward, say, Meyerbeer. Prince possibly makes the most commanding attempt yet at a truly serious musical. He is trying to demonstrate, admittedly with only uncertain success, that the musical can be a reflection of life. Indeed, life and its meaning is the essential theme of *Zorbá*. The idea of having a kind of Greek chorus—led by a black-garbed girl supported by a couple of Bouzouki musicians—is perhaps a variable advantage, at times apposite in its commentary. Yet the concept of playing the entire action within the framework of a café works very well, giving the piece a shape it would otherwise have lacked. Prince is clearly a disciple of Jerome Robbins—if disciple is not too crude a word, for it is meant flatteringly—and from Robbins, Prince has learned the principle of the musical as a *gesamtumskwerk*, the Wagnerian ideal of theatrical unity where every part plays its role in the whole. The entire production seems to have a signature of its own, as if it were the work of one man. Sadly, however, Prince has made one major miscalculation. He saw the film of Kazantzakis's novel, and presumably as a result, he has permitted Herschel Bernardi, his star, not to play Zorbá but to play Anthony Quinn playing Zorbá. The result is far from disaster, but it remains a pity. Bernardi is marvelous. He acts, sings, dances with just the assertiveness the role demands. I cannot imagine anyone playing Mr. Quinn better—other than Mr. Quinn. But Prince is to be blamed for not demanding more. It is here I think Prince, and indeed the show, has gone wrong. For all the brouhaha preceding it, it is not a great classic American musical. But it will still serve admirably until the next one comes along.

JOHN CHAPMAN, *DAILY NEWS*

Zorbá is magnificent—a great work of musical theatre. My advice to a reader is to hurry to the Imperial and get the tickets he wants if it takes all day. The tale of *Zorbá the Greek* is not unfamiliar. First it was a best-selling novel by Nikos Kazantzakis. Then it was a movie. Now it is what it really should be—a throbbing, zestful, absorbing musical play which has been given everything. It has two star-spangled, throat-catching performances by Herschel Bernardi as Zorbá and Maria Karnilova as his fading lady love—and a dozen or more which are equally fitting. There are three men who seem to keep *Zorbá* under control at every moment. First there is Bernardi, whose lusty playing of the title role is irresistible. Then there is Joseph Stein, who has written a taut libretto. And there is producer Prince, who has directed the production with flawless taste. *Zorbá* makes an unforgettable evening.

MARTIN GOTTFRIED, *WOMEN'S WEAR DAILY*

Harold Prince is one of the few theatre people who sense just how far the musical has come and where it can go. Like them, he is now confronting the crucial problem of modern musicals—the battle of the book: how to replace the idea of a story (or find a new way to tell it). Prince and a couple of other people know all about blending dance with music and song. The question is, how to tie it all together and Prince's new show, *Zorbá*, gives no answer. Moreover, it doesn't manage to camouflage the problem with a sheer wholeness of conception, as in some of the other shows he has produced. Conception is the big word here—it is what is coming to replace the idea of a "book"—but the concept of *Zorbá* has not been completely thought out and as a result it is a mixed-up musical whose parts are not consistent with its idea. It is a show of great interest from a theoretical point of view, but of vague vitality as theatre. But what was that concept? [The quasi-Greek chorus] was doubtless Prince's basic image of the show—an image in which he delighted and I can't blame him—but it is impossible to tell just what he meant it to be and like his vision for *Cabaret* [1966], it splits the show between the story and the conception. The problem is that Prince was inspired by Jerome Robbins [but] Prince is no Robbins. The actual playing out of *Zorbá* is curiously heartless, as if the show never got out of the theory stage. The *Fiddler on the Roof* influence is embarassingly obvious. Kander composes to suit a show's location and period, as a good theatre composer should (and few do), but his music is too mental. Don Walker's orchestrations were among the finest I've ever heard in a Broadway theatre. As for Ebb's lyrics, they were not up to his usual standards (which are high) simply, I hope, because he had trouble grasping the production sense. That was clearly the problem with Boris Aronson's handsome, artful but oddly moodless sets. Herschel Bernardi's performance in the title part was, frankly, terrible. His dancing, crucial to the role, had the relaxed freedom of Lyndon Johnson at the Electric Circus. As Mr. Prince undoubtedly learned, it isn't so easy to make ouzo from schnapps.

WALTER KERR, *TIMES*

I must say that I admire Harold Prince's no compromise assault on materials that insist on dancing before death, dancing after death, but always dancing in the immediate company of death. You may have noticed that the billboards themselves, the signs gaunt over the marquee, are ruthlessly monochromatic, blacks and deep rusts. Much of the evening suggests that Bertolt Brecht has been tamed and made useful on the musical stage; the technique talks to the audience at will, and the players are all members of a café audience, smoke curling from their cigarettes as they look at life (so reliably related to death) from the outside. But if we are going to have so much candor and so little color, we must have something else as well. We now want a dimension and a richness onstage, a sense of the fullness of life while it is still busy dancing, that will return to us in people what has been taken from the palette. *Zorbá* reaches for, and misses, just this solidity. Zorbá himself is with us too soon in the play, all put together out of contrary characteristics; he isn't slowly and endearingly born to us. We never get a chance to ask, "Who was that?" as he goes by, interested on our own. He comes on to be interesting, making that his specific task for tonight. The silent love story between the student and the widow is much too much a matter of silence, helpful Furies notwithstanding. The young man, well enough spoken and sung by John Cunningham, is no one we know at all. It seems odd demanding that a musical lure us into such complexity. But it is the musical itself that makes the demand, having forsworn all other pleasures. And *Zorbá* is an entertainment to be taken somewhat seriously, even to be respected: not only for the severity and inventiveness of the mounting but for the vagrant charm Miss Karnilova is able to uncover in a tinkly music-hall tune or the soberly melodic tambourine thrashings John Kander and Fred Ebb have arranged to accompany the constant promise of violence. *Zorbá* takes itself seriously. But it is thin where it dare not be—in the cement that should hold clashing moods together and make them one, in the soil that should give difficult people a sturdy toe hold. Call it honestly ambitious and emotionally bleak.

* * *

Beware of Greeks bearing scripts. Herschel Bernardi wasn't Greek, of course, but then neither was Anthony Quinn. Bernardi—Tevye number three—enlisted *Fiddler* librettist Joe Stein to adapt Nikos Kazantzakis's novel, and the pair ran the project over to *Fiddler* producer Hal Prince. Who duly drafted his *Cabaret* songwriters and choreographer, his *Fiddler/Cabaret* set and costume designers, and Bernardi's own Golde, the Robbins-ballerina-turned-comic-actress Maria Karnilova. Everybody was primed for a smashing *Fiddler* follow-up—including audiences, who provided a two-million-dollar advance. Only trouble was, the show was ponderously leaden and just plain dull. *Zorbá* begins with the refrain "Life is what you do while you're waiting to die." After around forty minutes it felt like *Zorbá*'s what you do while you're waiting. . . .

A Tony Award was won by Boris Aronson (scenic designer).

BROADWAY SCORECARD
/ PERFS: 305 / $: –

RAVE	FAVORABLE	MIXED	UNFAVORABLE	PAN
2		2	2	

THE ZULU AND THE ZAYDA

"A Play With Music"

music and lyrics by Harold Rome

play by Howard Da Silva and Felix Leon

based on the 1959 short story *The Zulu and the Zeide* by Dan Jacobson

directed by Dore Schary

produced by Theodore Mann and Dore Schary

starring Menasha Skulnik and Ossie Davis

with Louis Gossett, Joe Silver, Sarah Cunningham, John Pleshette, and Philip Vandervort

opened November 10, 1965   Cort Theatre

WALTER KERR, *HERALD TRIBUNE*

Menasha Skulnik is such a nice fellow that it is extremely difficult to imagine anyone wanting to be mean to him, a fact which also makes it difficult to wrap much of a plot about him. Howard Da Silva and Felix Leon have given it a brave try in *The Zulu and the Zayda*, borrowing various South African racial indignities from a story by Dan Jacobson, but by the time their evening's work is done love has conquered all, including the possibility of any very stimulating drama. Mr. Skulnik is a many splendored thing as he circles his new companion [Louis Gossett] rather as though he had just come upon Michelangelo's David and were about to get a crick in his neck. Craning upward at the decorative bone the Zulu sports in his ear, and even seeming to crane in order to examine the powder-horn at his belt (Skulnik himself is roughly five feet minus, and clearly was designed to walk under tables), the actor sighs out his awe in a rich nasal symphony. Slipping into Yiddish only a fraction of a second before the Zulu does (there is a slight surplus of this sort of thing, by the way, enough to make the non-Yiddish-speaking audience jealous about missing the jokes), Skulnik is quickly a one-man United Nations, and internationally indispensable. Louis Gossett, padding about after him on sandals made of discarded automobile tires, makes an excellent companion, particularly when he has just been informed that he is really a king descended from Solomon's time. The evening is now and again pleasantly relieved of its padded-foot pace by snatches of song—a gourd-rattling beat set against longer Yiddish strains—provided by Harold Rome, though a curious thing happens here. Whenever Ossie Davis, as the servant-narrator who arranges the Zulu's arrival, ambles across stage to relax into song, the music is instantly form-fitting, snug, conversational, flavorsome. Whenever anyone else comes upon a number, it seems a number. A psychological beat asserts itself that says "musical comedy," which is not precisely what the entertainment means to be. Mr. Skulnik is winsome, the atmosphere is winning. But the evening always goes where you know it's going, placidly.

HOWARD TAUBMAN, *TIMES*

When Menasha Skulnik and Louis Gossett sing a cheerful song, "It's Good to Be Alive," and accompany it with a dance step that might celebrate a Jewish wedding, *The Zulu and Zayda* is in its element. For this new play has its soft heart in the sentimental land of musical comedy. Its story tells of the tender relationship between a zayda, the Yiddish word for grandpa, and his young Zulu servant. When *The Zulu and the Zayda* makes itself completely at home in the world of the musical theatre, it has engaging interludes. At such moments even its sentimentality, represented by Skulnik's singing of a rueful song lamenting the way things are under the oppressive laws of South Africa's apartheid ["Rivers of Tears"], can be tolerated. But as a play *The Zulu and the Zayda*, despite its goodwill, cannot be taken seriously. It makes its point about the kinship of a white old man and young Zulu with an unabashed resort to all the trite devices of comedy and emotion. In its alleged dramatic sections it is corn unlimited. Harold Rome's songs bubble along for the most part in the best of musical-comedy spirits.

His two native numbers may not be exactly African, but the one he has written for a group of Negroes to sing at a party in their segregated location drives forward with brisk, rhythmic lift ["Like the Breeze Blows"]. Like any good production number, it stops the show. Then to top it, he provides Skulnik with a vivacious response, a song explaining what his favorite Yiddish word of approval, "Oisgetzaichnet," means (translation: out of this world). Skulnik does this one like the ideal turn it is for him, punching out a chorus and then doing a dainty step, lining out another chorus and inviting his African friends into a joyous circle, just as if it were at a Jewish wedding. Although *The Zulu and the Zayda* is aware of the bitter brew South Africa keeps stirring for its blacks and for anyone who dissents from its policies, it has chosen to frame its awareness in a sugary fantasy. When it uses music for its purpose, it can be disarming. When it seeks to be dramatic, it makes one wish one knew the Zulu word to go with the Yiddish descriptive *schmaltz*.

◦   ◦   ◦

Underemployed just-out-of-Yale architect Harold Rome started his theatrical career late in the Depression, writing songs of social significance for the 1937 revue *Pins and Needles* (which broke the musical long-run mark with an astounding 1,108 performances; the longest-running musical had been the Gershwins' 1931 Pulitzer-winner *Of Thee I Sing*, with 441). Rome switched to propaganda material during his Army service, culminating in the mustering-out revue hit *Call Me Mister* (1946). He revealed a heretofore unexpected romantic strain with *Fanny* (1954) and put everything together in 1962 with his finely crafted *I Can Get It for You Wholesale*. So why not a South African/Yiddish score? Rome was an expert on native music of both stripes, it turned out, and the understated *Zulu* is actually quite entrancing when taken on its own terms. It was tied to a hopeless interracial soap opera plot, though, causing songs and show to disappear quickly. The mid-'60s being an especially dry era for writers of traditional musicals, *The Zulu and the Zayda* turned out to be Rome's last Broadway show. His final effort opened out of town, *way* out of town, in Tokyo. *Scarlett*—yes, *that* Scarlett—was initially produced in 1970 in Japan, in Japanese, directed and choreographed (in Japanese?) by Joe Layton. A London production, under the title *Gone with the Wind*, played at the Drury Lane in 1972; the American edition, starring Lesley Ann Warren and Pernell Roberts as Vivien and Clark, opened August 28, 1973, at the Dorothy Chandler Pavillion in Los Angeles but never made it back East—not even to Atlanta. And that was it for the underappreciated Rome, who died on October 26, 1993, at the age of eighty-five.

BROADWAY SCORECARD
/ PERFS: 179 / $: −

RAVE	FAVORABLE	MIXED	UNFAVORABLE	PAN
	2	4		

CURTAIN CALLS

GLOSSARY OF BROADWAY MUSICALS THAT NEVER OPENED ON BROADWAY

You have shows that got bad reviews, ran out their advance, and closed; shows that got bad reviews, ran out the week, and closed; and shows that got bad reviews and just plain closed. But then there were shows that gave up the ghost before the ghost walked, which is to say they closed out of town or—in a few advanced cases—closed during previews in New York. (It is almost impossible to close out of town if you don't go out of town.) These musicals did not face the Broadway opening night critics, which makes them fall outside the range of this book. But—and it's an important but—many were interconnected with shows represented in this book. Therefore, we herewith offer brief information about some thirty productions the reader may find of interest. The date and place of the initial out-of-town opening is given, followed by the final performance date (and place, if different). Due to the ignominious anonymity of these shows, a disproportionately large amount of illustrative material has been included.

ALICE

"A New Musical"

music and lyrics by Micki Grant

"conceived, written and directed" by Vinnette Carroll

based on *Alice's Adventures in Wonderland* (1865) and *Through the Looking-Glass* (1872) by Lewis Carroll (no relation)

choreographed by Talley Beatty

produced by Mike Nichols and Lewis Allen in association with Urban Arts Corps (Vinnette Carroll) and Anita MacShane

starring Debbie Allen, Alice Ghostley, Paula Kelly, Jane White, and Hamilton Camp

with Jeffrey Anderson-Gunter, Alberta Bradford, Cleavant Derricks (Carroll), Clinton Derricks-Carroll, Douglas Houston, and Thomas Pinnock

opened May 31, 1978   *Forrest Theatre, Philadelphia*
closed June 11, 1978

Mike Nichols, of *Annie* (1977) fame, decided to try it again with an eye on *The Wiz* (1975). No dice. Following *Truckload* (1975) and *Alice*, Debbie Allen—a veteran of *Purlie* (1970) and *Raisin* (1973)—started developing her offstage talents and soon found herself a choreographic niche. Afterlife: *But Never Jam Today*, with a different score but Vinnette Carroll, Talley Beatty, and Cleavant Derricks in attendance, made it to Broadway's Longacre on July 31, 1979, for a scant seven performances.

Poor Debbie Allen. Talk about a pain in the neck . . .

BACK COUNTRY

a musical

music by Stanley Walden

book and lyrics by Jacques Levy

based on the 1907 Irish comedy *The Playboy of the Western World* by John Millington Synge

directed by Jacques Levy

choreographed by Margo Sappington

produced by Eugene V. Wolsk in association with Harvey Granat

with Ken Marshall, Suzanne Lederer, Harry Groener, Stuart Germain, Barbara Andres, and Rex Everhart

opened August 15, 1978   *Cohoes Musical Hall, Cohoes, NY*
closed September 23, 1978   *Wilbur Theatre, Boston*

The folks from *Oh! Calcutta!* (1969) tried their hand at *Playboy* and got synged.

THE BAKER'S WIFE

"A New Musical"

music and lyrics by Stephen Schwartz

book by Joseph Stein

based onthe 1938 screenplay *La Femme du Boulanger* by Marcel Pagnol and Jean Giono

directed by John Berry (replacing Joseph Hardy)

choreographed by Robert Tucker (replacing Dan Siretta)

produced by David Merrick

starring Paul Sorvino (replacing Topol)

with Patti LuPone (replacing Carole Demas), Kurt Peterson, Keene Curtis, David Rounds, Timothy Jerome, Portia Nelson, Gordon Connell, Pierre Epstein, Teri Ralston, and Charles Rule (replacing Benjamin Rayson)

opened May 11, 1976   Dorothy Chandler Pavilion, Los Angeles
closed November 13, 1976   Kennedy Center Opera House, Washington
[announced opening: November 21, 1976, Martin Beck Theatre]

The big new musical from the producer of *Dolly!* (1964)—the author of *Fiddler* (1964)—the composer of *Pippin* (1972)! No Gower or Jerry or Bob in sight, though, and what a mess. Merrick not only fired director, choreographer, and two stars, he even chucked the orchestrations, bringing in the great Don Walker midway through the tryout. But the problems were in the adaptation. Afterlife: Trevor Nunn mounted an "improved" version in London on October 27, 1989, which also proved to be half-baked. Almost-life: Feuer and Martin had plotted their own musicalization as a 1952 follow-up to *Guys and Dolls* (1950), with Loesser, Burrows, and Lahr in the recipe; they were thwarted when original author Jean Giono withheld his portion of the rights. (Loesser

WORLD PREMIERE ENGAGEMENT

TOPOL

the international star in his
first American stage appearance
in

THE BAKER'S WIFE

A New Musical

A new production for
Broadway's 1976-77
Season — based on the
classic French play and
film, "La Femme du
Boulanger"—
a captivating story
transformed into
a very musical romantic
comedy by the author
of "Fiddler on the Roof"
and the lyricist-composer
of "Godspell" and
"Pippin."

SAN FRANCISCO

Civic Light Opera

ASSOCIATION

SECOND EVENT • 39TH ANNUAL SEASON

DAVID MERRICK
presents
TOPOL
in
THE BAKER'S WIFE
Book by
JOSEPH STEIN
Based on the play and film "La Femme du Boulanger" by
MARCEL PAGNOL and JEAN GIONO
Music and Lyrics by
STEPHEN SCHWARTZ
with
PATTI LuPONE   KURT PETERSON
DAVID ROUNDS   TIMOTHY JEROME   PORTIA NELSON
DARLENE CONLEY   GORDON CONNELL
TARA LEIGH   JEAN McLAUGHLIN   PIERRE EPSTEIN
TERI RALSTON   BENJAMIN RAYSON   CYNTHIA PARVA
TONY SHULTZ
and
KEENE CURTIS
Settings Designed by   Costumes Designed by   Lighting Designed by
JO MIELZINER   THEONI V. ALDREDGE   JENNIFER TIPTON
Musical Direction by   Dance Arrangements by   Orchestrations by
DON JENNINGS   DANIEL TROOB   THOMAS PIERSON
Directed by
JOSEPH HARDY

CURRAN THEATRE

JUNE 29 thru AUGUST 14
Box Office Opens June 14

ORDER HERE (Give at least 2 dates on which you can attend.)

	Date	Mat. or Eve.	Section	No. of Tickets	Price	Total Amount
1st						
2nd						

☐ BankAmericard ☐ Master Charge   Exp. Date

Make check payable or indicate charge and mail to:
Civic Light Opera, 445 Geary St., San Francisco 94102
Please enclose self-addressed stamped envelope.
Add 25¢ for handling charge.

Name
_____
(please print)

Street _____ Day Phone _____

City _____ Zip _____

SECTION	EVENINGS 8:30 p.m.		MATINEES 2:30 p.m.	
	*Mon., Tues., Wed. & Thurs.	Fri. & Sat.	**1st Thurs. and 6 subsequent Wed.'s	Saturday
ORCHESTRA & LOGE	$12.75	$13.75	$9.75	$10.75
1st BALCONY — 1st 6 ROWS	11.50	12.50	8.00	9.00
1st BALCONY — NEXT 6 ROWS	9.75	11.25	6.75	7.75
2nd BALCONY — 1st 6 ROWS	5.50	6.75	4.75	5.50
2nd BALCONY — NEXT 6 ROWS	4.25	5.50	3.75	4.75

*Dark Mon., July 5. **The first midweek mat. is on Thurs. instead of on Wed. Thereafter, midweek mats. are on Weds. Crossed-out prices indicate seats unavailable.

TICKET & GROUP SALES INFO. (415) 673-4400

Star, director, and orchestrator were all gone by the time *The Baker's Wife* fell, like a soufflé, in Washington. The original choreographer and one leading lady had already been fired when this early herald was printed. Preliminary credits.

turned his attention to what he called *Project Three*, similarly dealing with a middle-aged, undereducated hero of peasant stock whose underaged wife runs off with the resident tenor. His long-in-preparation masterwork finally opened in 1956 under the title *The Most Happy Fella*.)

BRAINCHILD

"A Musical in the Mind"

music by Michel Legrand

lyrics by Hal David

"written and directed" by Maxine Klein

produced by Adela Holzer

with Tovah Feldshuh, Nancy Ann Denning, Dorian Harewood, Louise Hoven, Gene Lindsey, Barbara Niles, and Marilyn Pasekoff

opened March 25, 1974   *Forrest Theatre, Philadelphia*
closed April 6, 1974

Adela (*Dude*) Holzer's *Brainchild*. Enough said? (A Musical in the Mind???)

BREAKFAST AT TIFFANY'S

"A New Musical Comedy," alternatively entitled *Holly Golightly*

music and lyrics by Bob Merrill

"adapted" by Edward Albee (replacing Abe Burrows, who replaced Nunnally Johnson)

based on the 1958 novella *Breakfast at Tiffany's* by Truman Capote

directed by Joseph Anthony (replacing Abe Burrows, who replaced Joshua Logan)

choreographed by Michael Kidd

produced by David Merrick

starring Mary Tyler Moore and Richard Chamberlain

with Art Lund, Sally Kellerman, Larry Kert (replacing Mitchell Gregg), James Olson, Paul Michael, Martin Wolfson, Charles Welch, Brooks Morton, and Paula Bauersmith

opened October 15, 1966   *Forrest Theatre, Philadelphia*
closed December 14, 1966   *Majestic Theatre, New York*
[announced opening: December 26, 1966]

"Rather than subject the drama critics and the theatre-going public—who invested one million dollars in advance ticket sales—to an excruciatingly boring evening, I have decided to close the show. Since the idea of adapting *Breakfast at Tiffany's* to the musical stage was mine in the first place, the closing is entirely my fault and should not be attributed to the three top writers who had a go at it." Thus said the producer, whose program bio for his next musical read: "Mr. Merrick is best known as the distinguished producer of the musical *Breakfast at Tiffany's*."

CHU CHEM

"A Zen Buddhist–Hebrew Musical Comedy, in English"

music by Mitch Leigh

lyrics by Jim Haines and Jack Wohl

"conceived and written" by Ted Allan

directed by Albert Marre

choreographed by Jack Cole

produced by Cheryl Crawford and Mitch Leigh

starring Menasha Skulnik, James Shigeta, and Jack Cole

with Henrietta Jacobson (replacing top-billed Molly Picon), Marcia Rodd, Robert Ito, Yuki Shimoda, Virginia Wing, Buzz Miller, J. C. McCord, and Khigh Dhiegh

opened November 15, 1966   New Locust Theatre, Philadelphia
closed November 19, 1966
[announced booking: George Abbott Theatre]

Ernie Schier of the *Evening Bulletin*, dubbed it *The King and Oy*, and I'm not going to try to top that. <u>Afterlife:</u> Having followed *Man of La Mancha* (1965) with seven—count 'em—consecutive flops, Mitch Leigh finally brought *Chu Chem* to Broadway's Ritz Theatre (now the Walter Kerr) on March 17, 1989. Surprisingly enough, it failed.

GENE KELLY'S
CLOWNAROUND

"A Funny Kind of Musical for the Entire Family," previously entitled *Clown Alley*

music by Moose Charlap

"conceived, written and lyrics" by Alvin Cooperman

directed by Gene Kelly

choreographed by Howard Jeffrey (replacing Danny Daniels)

produced by Theatre Now, Inc. (Edward H. Davis and William Court Cohen) in association with Harry Lashinsky and Franklin Roberts

starring Ruth Buzzi "and a cast of 70"

with Dennis Allen, the Burgesses, Carillo Bros., Miss Damorra, Zamperla Family and Atos Troupe, and Chrys Holt

opened April 27, 1972　　*Oakland Coliseum, Oakland, CA*
closed May 6, 1972　　*Cow Palace, San Francisco*

A hybrid musical comedy/circus aimed at the lucrative family market (Campbell's Soup put up $130,000 of the $650,000). The big draw, supposedly, was the (offstage) presence of Gene Kelly, who had been absent from the theatre since directing the 1958 *Flower Drum Song*. Also along to provide marquee lure (?) was Ruth Buzzi, from TV's *Laugh-In*. The ingenious Irish scenic designer Sean Kenny—best known stateside for *Oliver!* (1963)—came up with a 134-foot-long, 50-foot-wide, 12-level, 22-ton "clown machine" complete with elevators, turntables, high-wire rigging, and so on. This self-contained stage fit in seven vans for travel, and could be erected in no time flat (in theory). The neophyte producers went ahead without enough time, know-how, or money to get the clown machine up and running, and *Clownaround*

"A funny kind of musical for the entire family," which even Gene Kelly's presence couldn't save. Window cards for touring shows regularly left blank space to insert local theatre information and dates. *Clownaround* ran aground after its second of 26 scheduled stops. (artwork by Tim Lewis)

ran aground after their second of twenty-six scheduled stops. They did leave behind an original cast album (RCA LSP-4741), which is hard to find and even harder to listen to.

COMEDY

"A Musical Commedia"

music and lyrics by Hugo Peretti & Luigi Creatore and George David Weiss

book by Lawrence Carra

based on the 1622 commedia dell'arte sketch *The Great Magician* by Basillio Locatelli

directed by Lawrence Carra

choreographed by Stephen Reinhardt

produced by Edgar Lansbury, Stuart Duncan, and Joseph Beruh

with George Lee Andrews, Joseph Bova, Suellen Estey, Merwin Goldsmith, George S. Irving, Marc Jordan, Bill McCutcheon, Marty Morris, Joseph R. Sicari, and John Witham

opened November 6, 1972   Colonial Theatre, Boston
closed November 18, 1972
[announced opening: November 28, 1972, Martin Beck Theatre]

The producers of *Godspell* (1971) put the *Maggie Flynn* (1968) tunesmiths on this "musical commedia," which laid an Italianate egg. Afterlife: Stuart Duncan presented the revised *Smile, Smile, Smile*, with Hugo & Luigi and George Weiss providing book as well as score, on April 4, 1974, at the Off-Broadway Eastside Playhouse for a scant seven performances.

MEREDITH WILLSON'S
1491

"A Romantic Speculation"

music and lyrics by Meredith Willson

book by Meredith Willson and Richard Morris, "with collaboration by Ira Barmak"

based on an idea by Ed Ainsworth, suggested by events in the lives of Cristoforo Colombo (1451–1506) and Isabella I of Spain (1451–1504)

directed by Richard Morris

choreographed by Danny Daniels

produced by Edwin Lester, for the Civic Light Opera

starring John Cullum, Jean Fenn, and Chita Rivera

with Gino Conforti, Steve Brice Gordon, Joseph Nell, and Kathryn Hays

opened September 2, 1969   *Dorothy Chandler Pavilion, Los Angeles*

closed December 13, 1969   *Curran Theatre, San Francisco*

"An expensive voyage to nowhere," said Dan Sullivan in the *Los Angeles Times*. *Music Man* (1957) Meredith Willson's second musical, about that *Unsinkable Molly Brown* (1960), was a moderate hit; his third, *Here's Love* (1963), floundered on the road and failed on Broadway. His final opus just floundered.

MARGARET MITCHELL'S GONE WITH THE WIND

"The Epic Musical"

music and lyrics by Harold Rome

book by Horton Foote

based on the 1936 novel by Margaret Mitchell

directed and choreographed by Joe Layton

produced by Harold Fielding

starring Lesley Ann Warren and Pernell Roberts

with Terence Monk, Udana Power, Robert Nichols, Ann Hodges, Theresa Merritt, and Cheryl Robinson

opened August 28, 1973	*Dorothy Chandler Pavilion, Los Angeles*
closed November 24, 1973	*Curran Theatre, San Francisco*
[announced opening: April 7, 1974]	

Having transformed Margaret Mitchell's epic novel into a two-part, nine-hour 1966 stage extravaganza, Kazuo Kikuta and the Toho company commissioned composer Harold Rome (of the 1954 *Fanny*) and director/choreographer Joe Layton to musicalize the thing. In Japanese. (Rome had been the late David Selznick's idea; they briefly toyed with a musical *Gone with the Wind* back in 1959.) *Scarlett*, as it was called, opened on January 2, 1970, and was immensely successful—the locals saw something of themselves in this story of the vanquished American Confederacy, perhaps—and it was preordained that the piece would be exported for worldwide consumption. British showman Harold

Fielding mounted the retitled *Gone with the Wind*—now in English, thank you—on May 3, 1972, at London's Drury Lane with June Ritchie and our very own Harve Presnell (of *The Unsinkable Molly Brown* [1960]) in the leads, to somewhat less success and 397 performances. The American reception was even more forbidding, and *Gone with the Wind* was soon just plain gone. It's a long march from Tokyo to Tara, and a soggy one to boot.

HALLOWEEN

"A New Musical"

music by Mitch Leigh

book and lyrics by Sidney Michaels

based on his unproduced play *Saltpeter in the Rhubarb*

directed by Albert Marre

choreographed by Bert Michaels

produced by Albert W. Selden and Jerome Minskoff

starring David Wayne, Dick Shawn, and Margot Moser

with Luis de Jesus, Richard Godouse, Tommy Madden, Jerry Maren, Yvonne Moray, Felix Silla, Emory Souza, "and introducing Billy Barty"

opened September 20, 1972   Bucks County Playhouse,
*   New Hope, PA*

closed October 1, 1972
[announced opening: October 30, 1972, Martin Beck Theatre]

Crazy doings in the insane asylum, from the composer, director, and producer of *La Mancha* (1965). Complete with midgets. Don't ask.

HELLZAPOPPIN' '67

"The World's Funniest Musical"

music and lyrics by Marian Grudeff and Raymond Jessel

sketches uncredited (by Mark Richards, replacing Goodman Ace, Bill Angelos, and Buzz Kohan)

"based on a format" (the 1938 revue *Hellzapoppin'!*) by Ole Olsen and Chic Johnson

directed by Jerry Adler

choreographed by Buddy Schwab

produced and assembled by Alexander H. Cohen

starring Soupy Sales

with Johnny Melfi, Betty Madigan (replacing Gretta Thyssen), Luba Lisa, Claiborne Cary, Jackie Alloway, Brandon Maggart, Jack Fletcher, Ted Thurston, Suzanne Clemm, and Will B. Able and Graziella

opened July 1, 1967   Garden of Stars, Expo '67, Montreal closed September 16, 1967

"Please do not reveal the ending to your friends" implored the playbill. In his never-ending quest to out-Merrick Merrick, Alexander H. Cohen latched onto the zanily lowbrow 1938 revue *Hellzapoppin'!*—the title, anyway—signed up pie-in-the-face TV comedian Soupy Sales to headline, and set his *Baker Street* (1965) songwriters to the task. Cohen's *Hellzapoppin' '67* opened at Montreal's Expo '67 and never made it south of the border. (Was Soupy well known in Quebec? Perhaps Cohen should have opted for that beloved-by-the-French clown Jerry Lewis.) <u>Afterlife</u>: Read on, if you must.

HELLZAPOPPIN

"A Musical Circus"

music by Jule Styne, Hank Beebe, and Cy Coleman

lyrics by Carolyn Leigh and Bill Heyer

book by Abe Burrows, Bill Heyer, and Hank Beebe (doctored by Joseph Stein)

"based on a format" (the 1938 revue *Hellzapoppin'!*) by Ole Olsen and Chic Johnson

directed by Jerry Adler (replacing Abe Burrows)

choreographed by Donald Saddler (doctored by Tommy Tune)

produced by Alexander H. Cohen in association with Maggie and Jerome Minskoff

starring Jerry Lewis and Lynn Redgrave

with Herb Edelman, Joey Faye, Brandon Maggart, Jill Choder, Robert Fitch, Tom Batten, Mace Barrett, Justine Johnston, Bob Harvey, The Volantes, Bob Williams and Louie, and Leonardo

opened November 22, 1976   Mechanic Theatre, Baltimore

Sugar Babies (1979) without the sugar or Mickey Rooney. *Hellzafloppin*, they called it. Whatever became of Soupy Sales, anyway?

HOME AGAIN, HOME AGAIN

"A New Musical Comedy," previously entitled *Home Again*

music by Cy Coleman

lyrics by Barbara Fried

book by Russell Baker

directed by Gene Saks

choreographed by Onna White

produced by Irwin Meyer and Stephen R. Friedman, in association with Kenneth D. Laub and Warner Plays, Inc.

starring Dick Shawn, Ronny Cox, Lisa Kirk, and Mike Kellin

with Teri Ralston, Anita Morris, Rex Everhart, Jeannine Taylor, Robert Polenz, Mordecai Lawner, Tim Waldrip, and William Morrison

opened March 12, 1979   *American Shakespeare Theatre, Stratford, CT*
closed April 14, 1979   *Royal Alexandra Theatre, Toronto*
[announced opening: April 26, 1979, Mark Hellinger Theatre]

Columnist Russell Baker essayed this turgid chronicle of one man's search for the meaning of life. As Thomas Wolfe used to say, "You can't go home again, home again."

HOT SEPTEMBER

"A New Musical"

music by Kenneth Jacobson

lyrics by Rhoda Roberts

book by Paul Osborn (with Joshua Logan)

based on the 1953 Pulitzer Prize–winning drama *Picnic* by William Inge

directed by Joshua Logan

"dances staged by Danny Daniels; musical numbers staged by Joshua Logan and Danny Daniels"

produced by Leland Hayward and David Merrick

with Sean Garrison, Sheila Sullivan (replacing Kathryn Hays), Betty Lester (replacing Patricia Roe), Lovelady Powell, Eddie Bracken, Lee Lawson, John Stewart, and Paula Trueman

opened September 14, 1965   Shubert Theatre, Boston
closed October 9, 1965
[announced opening: October 20, 1965, Alvin Theatre]

Josh Logan, who played a key role in molding Bill Inge's *Picnic* for stage (1953) and screen (1956), came up moldy in September 1965 in not-so-hot Boston. The background is more interesting than the show itself: Inge's grant of rights to Hayward was contested by Fryer, Carr, and Harris, who had a previous interest in the project. The litigation was determined in favor of Inge, freeing Hayward to proceed. He handily arranged for the full $500,000 backing from Columbia Pictures and NBC, at which point Merrick exercised *his* option—left over from *Gypsy* (1959)—to invite himself, free of any financial responsibility, into any Hayward production of his choice. All for naught.

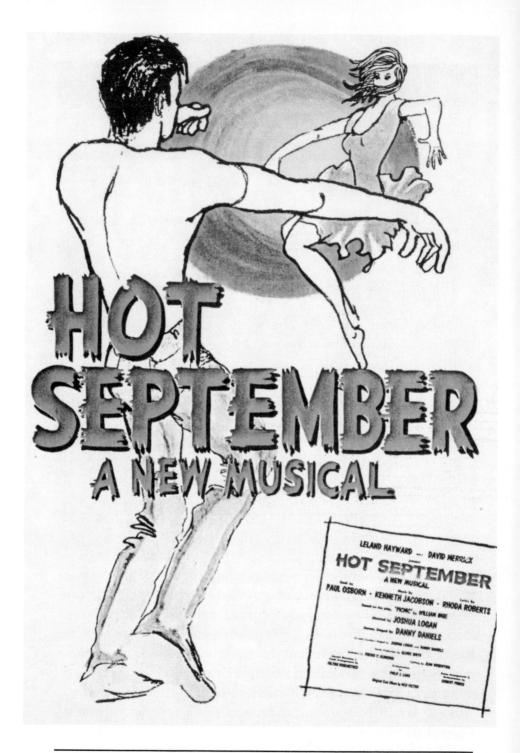

A soggy Labor Day *Picnic*, in not-so-*Hot September*. (artwork by Kenerson)

LOLITA, MY LOVE

"A Musical Play"

music by John Barry

book and lyrics by Alan Jay Lerner

based on the 1955 novel *Lolita* by Vladimir Nabokov

directed by Noel Willman (replacing Tito Capobianco)

choreographed by Dan Siretta (replacing Danny Daniels, who replaced Jack Cole)

produced by Norman Twain

starring John Neville, Dorothy Loudon, and Leonard Frey

with Denise Nickerson (replacing Annette Ferra)

opened February 16, 1971   Shubert Theatre, Philadelphia
closed March 27, 1971   Shubert Theatre, Boston
[announced opening: March 30, 1970, Mark Hellinger Theatre]

Nabokov's tantalyzing teen temptress proved treacherously tamper-proof. "Going, Going, Gone" went the opening number in Alan Lerner's *Lolita*, and the mess of a musical soon followed suit.

NORMAN TWAIN
presents

JOHN NEVILLE

in

A Musical Play

Lolita, My Love

Book and Lyrics by
ALAN JAY LERNER

Music by
JOHN BARRY

Based on the novel, "Lolita" by
VLADIMIR NABOKOV

also starring

DOROTHY LOUDON   LEONARD FREY

with
ANNETTE FERRA

Settings by
MING CHO LEE

Costumes by
JOSE VARONA

Lighting designed by
JULES FISHER

Musical direction
and choral arrangements by
HERBERT GROSSMAN

Orchestrations
by
EDDIE SAUTER

Dance arrangements
by
JOHN MORRIS

Associate producer
STONE WIDNEY

Production associate
LARRY COLEMAN

Original cast album
COLUMBIA RECORDS

Choreography by
DANNY DANIELS

Directed by
TITO CAPOBIANCO

OPENS FEBRUARY 16 thru MARCH 20
Preview Feb. 15 • MAIL ORDERS FILLED

SHUBERT THEATRE
250 South Broad St., Philadelphia, Pa., 19102

No wonder poor Annette Ferra looks fuzzily glum. Bounced after two weeks in Philadelphia, washed up at 15. Preliminary credits.

LOVE MATCH

"The New Sparkling Musical," previously titled *The Loving Couple*

music by David Shire

lyrics by Richard Maltby Jr.

book by Christian Hamilton

suggested by events in the life of Queen Victoria (1819–1901) and Prince Albert (1819–1861)

directed by Elliot Martin

choreographed by Danny Daniels

produced by Center Theatre Group by arrangement with Elliot Martin and Ivor David Balding Associates, Ltd.

starring Patricia Routledge "as the teenage Queen Victoria"

with Michael Allinson, Hal Linden, Laurence Guittard (replacing Max von Sydow), Patricia Ripley, Bill Hinnant, Rex Robbins, and Ronald Drake

opened November 3, 1968   Palace West Theatre, Phoenix, AZ
closed January 4, 1969   Ahmanson Theatre, Los Angeles
[announced opening: February 1969]

Americans did not seem all too keen for good old Queen Victoria—that rollicking gal—and her Albert. Maltby and Shire's offering promised to mark their Broadway debut, but the pair didn't get a main-stem hearing until 1983 when *Baby* bounced in (and out). Adams and Strouse also essayed a Victorian musical comedy, with libretto by Jay Presson Allen, which likewise never made it to town; *I and Albert* (a.k.a. *H. R. H.*) did receive a November 6, 1972, West End mounting. London audiences were not amused, for 120 performances.

MATA HARI

"A New Musical," previously entitled *Facade*

music by Edward Thomas

lyrics by Martin Charnin

book by Jerome Coopersmith

suggested by events in the life of Margaretha Geertruida Zelle (1876–1917)

directed by Vincente Minnelli

choreographed by Jack Cole

produced by David Merrick

starring Marisa Mell and Pernell Roberts

with Jake Holmes, Martha Schlamme, W. B. Brydon, Mark Dempsey, George Marcy, Nadine Lewis, Blythe Danner, and Dominic Chianese

opened November 18, 1967   National Theatre, Washington, DC
closed December 9, 1967
[announced opening: January 13, 1968, Alvin Theatre]

The bullet-riddled corpse of poor old Mata reached up at the final curtain of the Washington première to scratch her nose. Well, it got a laugh. Producer Merrick, who'd made quite a fanfare of the demise of the previous year's *Breakfast at Tiffany's*, let Mata die unheralded. "Let's send out for coffee," someone suggested amidst the chaos of a post–preview postmortem. "I'll go," offered Minnelli eagerly. Afterlife: Mata Hari breathed again when she appeared Off-Broadway at the Theatre de Lys on December 11, 1968—retitled *Ballad for a Firing Squad*, produced by the composer and directed by the lyricist—for a scant seven performances. And *Mata* returned yet again Off-Off-Broadway in 1996. Same show, same director, same results.

DAVID MERRICK PRODUCTIONS
246 WEST 44TH STREET
NEW YORK, N. Y. 10036
LO 3-7520

JACK SCHLISSEL   SAMUEL LIFF
GENERAL MANAGER   PRODUCTION SUPERVISOR

C O M P A N Y   N O T I C E

THIS IS TO ADVISE ALL MEMBERS OF THE COMPANY, I.E.

CAST, CREW, STAGE HANDS, MUSICIANS, WARDROBE, ETC.,

THAT "MATA HARI" WILL CLOSE AFTER THE EVENING PERFORMANCE

ON SATURDAY, DECEMBER 9, 1967.

THANK YOU FOR YOUR WORK WITH THE COMPANY.

JACK SCHLISSEL
GENERAL MANAGER

Here's a piece of history, an actual, authentic, original closing notice.
They cheered when this one was posted on the callboard.

MISS MOFFAT

"A New Musical"

music by Albert Hague

lyrics by Emlyn Williams

book by Emlyn Williams and Joshua Logan

based on the 1938 drama *The Corn Is Green* by Emlyn Williams

directed by Joshua Logan

choreographed by Donald Saddler

produced by Eugene V. Wolsk, Joshua Logan, and Slade Brown

starring Bette Davis

with Dorian Harewood, Dody Goodman, David Sabin, Marion Ramsey, Nell Carter, Lee Goodman, Avon Long, Anne Francine, and Gil Robbins

opened October 7, 1974   *Shubert Theatre, Philadelphia*
closed October 17, 1974

Josh Logan's Nellie Forbush—the redoubtable Mary Martin—opted out of this R&H musical without R&H, so the director/coauthor/coproducer of the long-ago hit *South Pacific* (1949) naturally turned to . . . Bette Davis?? The most remarkable thing about this misguided *Moffat* was that the producers managed to pay back their investors—thanks to the insurance man—when the star wrenched her back and needed bed rest. (What she needed was a new score and book and director, for beginners.)

WORLD PREMIERE!

2 WEEKS ONLY
MON., SEPT. 9 thru SAT., SEPT. 21

Eugene V. Wolsk and Joshua Logan
present

BETTE DAVIS
AS
MISS MOFFAT

A new musical

based on 'The Corn is Green' by EMLYN WILLIAMS

Book by
EMLYN WILLIAMS & JOSHUA LOGAN

Music by
ALBERT HAGUE

Lyrics by
EMLYN WILLIAMS

with

DODY
GOODMAN

DAVID
SABIN

MARION
RAMSEY

NELL
CARTER

LEE
GOODMAN

AVON
LONG

ANNE
FRANCINE

GIL
ROBBINS

and

DORIAN HAREWOOD

Scenery and Lighting by
JO MIELZINER

Costumes by
ROBERT MACKINTOSH

Musical Direction by
JAY BLACKTON

Orchestrations by
ROBERT M. FREEDMAN

Musical Numbers Staged by
DONALD SADDLER

Directed by
JOSHUA LOGAN

MECHANIC THEATRE
Charles Center, Baltimore, Md.

Evenings Mon. thru Thurs. at 8 PM, Fri. & Sat. at 8:30 PM, Wed. & Sat. Mat. at 2 PM
Prices: Mon. thru Thurs. Eves. Orch. & Mezz. $9.50; Balc. $7.50, $5.00 — Fri. & Sat.
Eves. Orch. & Mezz. $10.50; Balc. $8.50, $5.50 — Wed. & Sat. Matinees; Orch. &
Mezz. $8.50; Balc. $6.50, $4.50

PHONE RESERVATIONS ACCEPTED! CALL NOW 685-2624

Bette Davis sat on the wall, B. D. had a great fall. They couldn't put
Miss Moffat together again, but they collected on the insurance. (artwork
by Michaele Vollbrach)

A MOTHER'S KISSES

"A New Musical Comedy"

music by Richard Adler

lyrics by Richard Adler (replacing Bob Merrill)

book by Bruce Jay Friedman (replacing Jerome Chodorov)

based on the 1964 novel by Bruce Jay Friedman

directed by Gene Saks

choreographed by Onna White

produced by Lester Osterman Productions (Lester Osterman, Richard Horner, and Lawrence Kasha) in association with Frederic S. and Barbara Mates

with Beatrice Arthur (Saks), Bill Callaway, Carl Ballantine, Rudy Bond, Alan North, Ned Wertimer, Renee Roy, Kate Wilkinson, Ruth Jaroslow, Daniel Goldman, and Arthur Anderson

opened September 23, 1968   Shubert Theatre, New Haven
closed October 19, 1968   Mechanic Theatre, Baltimore
[announced opening: October 29, 1968, 46th Street Theatre]

The award-winning composer/lyricist of *The Pajama Game* (1954) and *Damn Yankees* (1955) returned to Broadway—well almost—with *A Mother's Kisses*. "Richard Adler played the score for me," reported David Merrick. "I told him to start a new project the next hour. I told him not to wait till the next day."

LESTER OSTERMAN PRODUCTIONS
(LESTER OSTERMAN · RICHARD HORNER · LAWRENCE KASHA)
IN ASSOCIATION WITH FREDERIC S. AND BARBARA MATES PRESENTS

A MOTHER'S KISSES

A NEW MUSICAL COMEDY

BOOK BY
BRUCE JAY FRIEDMAN

MUSIC & LYRICS BY
RICHARD ADLER

WITH

BEATRICE ARTHUR

CARL BALLANTINE

BERNADETTE PETERS   MARTIN WOLFSON   RUDY BOND   ALAN NORTH
NED WERTIMER   RENEE ROY   KATE WILKINSON
RUTH JAROSLOW   DANIEL GOLDMAN   ARTHUR ANDERSON

AND **BILL CALLAWAY**

ASSOCIATE PRODUCER ORIN LEHMAN

SETTINGS BY WILLIAM & JEAN ECKART   COSTUMES BY ALVIN COLT   LIGHTING BY THARON MUSSER
MUSICAL DIRECTION & VOCAL ARRANGEMENTS COLIN ROMOFF   ORCHESTRATIONS BY JACK ANDREWS   DANCE MUSIC BY ROGER ADAMS

DANCES & MUSICAL NUMBERS STAGED BY
ONNA WHITE

DIRECTED BY
GENE SAKS

Galster

46th ST. THEATRE
46th ST. W. of B'way   Mats. Wed. & Sat.

Lots of billing on this one, including fourth-listed Bernadette Peters—
who disappeared during rehearsals but quickly turned up in *Dames at
Sea*. Preliminary credits. (artwork by Galster)

NEFERTITI

"A Musical Romance"

music by David Spangler

book and lyrics by Christopher Gore (book doctored by Joe Masteroff)

based on events in the life of Egyptian Queen Nefertiti (circa 1372–1350 B.C.)

directed by Jack O'Brien

choreographed by Daniel Lewis

produced by Sherwin M. Goldman

starring Andrea Marcovicci, Robert LuPone, Michael Nouri, Marilyn Cooper, Benjamin Rayson, Michael V. Smart, and Jane White

opened September 20, 1977   Blackstone Theatre, Chicago
closed October 22, 1977

Having come a cropper with his space-age fantasy *Via Galactica* (1972), Christopher Gore set back the calendar 3,300 years with a trumped-up triangle of old Egypt. This from Sherwin Goldman, Jack O'Brien, and musical director John DeMain, whose prior collaboration on the 1976 revival of *Porgy and Bess* proved far more memorable (except for those who happened to be in Chicago that month and cherish hapless, helpless disasters).

OH, KAY!

a revival of the 1926 musical comedy

music by George Gershwin

lyrics by Ira Gershwin

book by Thomas Meehan

based on the original libretto by Guy Bolton and P. G. Wodehouse

directed and choreographed by Donald Saddler

produced by Cyma Rubin

starring Jack Weston

with Jane Summerhays, Jim Weston (replacing David-James Carroll), Gene Castle, Marie Cheatham, Eddie Lawrence (replacing David Cromwell), Alexandra Korey, Thomas Ruisinger, Reno Roop, Joe Palmieri, and Janet and Louise Arters

opened July 20, 1978   *Royal Alexandra Theatre, Toronto*
closed September 23, 1978   *Kennedy Center Opera House, Washington, DC*

Having reaped a huge profit from her 1971 revival of Vincent Youmans's 1925 *No, No, Nanette*, the 1926 *Oh, Kay!*—with an even more dazzling score, from the Gershwins—must have seemed a sure thing to Cyma Rubin. But there are no sure things, not in this business, and *Oh, Kay!*—without Gertie Lawrence and Victor Moore, or the *Nanette* revival's Burt Shevelove and Harry Rigby—fell flat. Afterlife: Having reaped a small profit from his 1976 transfer of the Goodspeed Opera House revival of Jerome Kern's 1915 *Very Good Eddie*, David Merrick decided to pick up Goodspeed's all-black version of *Oh, Kay!* The showman's penultimate production opened November 2, 1990, at the Richard Rodgers (46th Street) Theatre for a scant seventy-seven performances. Three months after closing, Merrick reopened the show with new leads across the street at the Lunt on April. Sixteen previews and out.

ONE NIGHT STAND

a musical

music by Jule Styne

book and lyrics by Herb Gardner

directed by John Dexter

choreographed by Peter Gennaro

produced by Joseph Kipness, Lester Osterman, Joan Cullman, James M. Nederlander, and Alfred Taubman

starring Jack Weston and Charles Kimbrough

with Catherine Cox, Brandon Maggart, Kate Mostel, Charles Levin, William Morrison, Christopher Balcom, Terri Treas, and Paul Binotto

previewed October 20, 1980   Nederlander Theatre, New York
closed October 25, 1980

"Gardner and Dexter could not agree on one thing, and there was nothing the producers could do about it," said cryin' Joe Kipness of *Seesaw* (1973) fame. Composer Styne returned to the mainstem but once more, with the 1993 *The Red Shoes* (or *Jule's Last Jam*).

PLEASURES AND PALACES

"A New Musical Comedy," previously entitled *Ex-Lover*

music and lyrics by Frank Loesser

book by Frank Loesser and Sam Spewack

based on the 1961 comedy *Once There Was a Russian* by Sam Spewack

directed and choreographed by Bob Fosse

produced by Allen B. Whitehead in association with Frank Productions, Inc. (Frank Loesser)

starring Jack Cassidy (replacing Alfred Marks), Phyllis Newman, Hy Hazell, and John McMartin

with Leon Janney, Mort Marshall, Eric Brotherson, Sammy Smith, Woody Romoff, John Anania, Barbara Sharma, and Michael Quinn

opened March 11, 1965   *Fisher Theatre, Detroit*
closed April 10, 1965
[announced opening: May 10, 1965, Lunt-Fontanne Theatre]

Catherine the Great, Potemkin, and John Paul Jones? The underlying play by Sam Spewack—who with his wife had scripted the great *Kiss Me Kate* (1948)—lasted only one performance (despite Walter Matthau as Potemkin). A longer run than the musical, anyhow. And this, unhappily, was the last of the great Loesser.

PRETTYBELLE

"A New Musical"

music by Jule Styne

book and lyrics by Bob Merrill

based on the 1970 novel *Prettybelle, a Lively Tale of Rape and Resurrection* by Jean Arnold

directed and choreographed by Gower Champion

produced by Alexander H. Cohen

starring Angela Lansbury

with Jon Cypher, Mark Dawson, Peter Lombard, Charlotte Rae, William Larsen, Bert Michaels, Michael Jason, Joe Morton, and Igors Gavon

opened February 1, 1971   Shubert Theatre, Boston
closed March 6, 1971
[announced opening: March 15, 1971, Majestic Theatre]

Gower and Jule hit rock bottom with this outlandishly unconventional musical. Alexander H. Cohen—who'd busted with *Dear World* (1969), despite Angela's bravura performance—did the same despite the same; this time he didn't even bother bringing his mess into town. Not so pretty, Belle.

An idealized Angela Lansbury lifts up her skirt in this deadly "lively tale of rape and resurrection." *Dear World* redux, without the Sewerman. (artwork by Frederic Marvin)

THE PRINCE OF GRAND STREET

"A New Musical"

book, music, and lyrics by Bob Merrill

directed by Gene Saks

choreographed by Lee Theodore

produced by Robert Whitehead, Roger L. Stevens, and the Shubert Organization

starring Robert Preston

with Neva Small, Werner Klemperer, Sam Levene, David Margulies, Bernice Massi, Sammy Smith, Alan Manson, Addison Powell, Alexander Orfaly, Richard Muenz, and Walter Charles

opened March 7, 1978   *Forrest Theatre, Philadelphia*
closed April 15, 1978   *Shubert Theatre, Boston*
[announced opening: May 11, 1978, Palace Theatre]

Bob Preston as the prince of the Yiddish Theatre? Press's post–*Music Man* (1957) musical, *We Take the Town* (1962), was similarly ill-conceived; Pancho Villa he played in that one, with a droopy mustache. Bob ("How Much Is that Doggie in the Window?") Merrill appears not once but thrice in this glossary, with three enormous, star-laden advance sale blockbusters, the others being *Breakfast at Tiffany's* (1966) and *Prettybelle* (1971). The ones that actually made it to town—*Henry, Sweet Henry* (1967) and *Sugar* (1972)—were no great shakes, either.

RACHAEL LILY ROSENBLOOM—AND DON'T YOU *EVER* FORGET IT!

"A New Musical"

music and lyrics by Paul Jabara (additional lyrics by David Debin and Paul Issa)

book by Paul Jabara and Tom Eyen

directed by Tom Eyen

choreographed by Tony Stevens (replaced by Grover Dale, who received equal-size billing for "choreographic supervision")

produced by Robert Stigwood and Ahmet Ertegun

starring Ellen Greene, Anita Morris (Dale), Marion Ramsey, and Paul Jabara

previewed November 26, 1973   *Broadhurst Theatre, New York*

closed December 1, 1973

Paul Jabara, a cutup from *Hair* (1968) and the British edition of *Superstar* (1971), wrote songs and script and starred in this one-week nightmare. Who'd he think he was—Gerry Ragni?

A SONG FOR CYRANO

"A New Musical Romance"

music and lyrics by Robert Craig Wright and George Forrest

book by J. Vincent Smith (José Vincente Ferrer)

based on the 1897 French drama *Cyrano de Bergerac* by Edmond Rostand

directed by José Ferrer

choreographed by Rich Rann

produced by José Ferrer

starring José Ferrer

with Willi Burke, Don McKay, Edmund Lyndeck, Keith Kaldenberg, Marshall Borden, Helon Blount, and Adam Petroski

opened June 18, 1973	*Westport Country Playhouse,*
	Westport, CT
closed September 16, 1973	*Pocono Playhouse,*
	Mountainhome, PA

With Chris Plummer simultaneously hamming it up on Broadway (and winning a Tony Award in the process), Joe Ferrer—the *real* Cyrano—hit the strawhat trail with this soggy operetta from olde-timers Wright and Forrest (of *The Song of Norway* [1944]). Ferrer directed himself in the title role, writing the book as well; the program informed us that librettist J. Vincent Smith "became involved in the theatre because of his lifelong acquaintance with José Ferrer." *Song for Cyrano* wasn't any worse than the Plummer version or the 1993 *Cyrano: The Musical*; they were all pretty deadly.

SPOTLIGHT

"A New Musical"

music by Jerry Bresler

lyrics by Lyn Duddy

book by Richard Seff (replacing Leonard Starr)

based on a story by Leonard Starr (i.e., the plot of the discarded libretto)

directed by David Black

choreographed by Tony Stevens

produced by Sheldon R. Lubliner (and David Black)

starring Gene Barry

with Lenora Nemetz, D'Jamin Bartlett, Polly Rowles, Marc Jordan, and David-James Carroll

opened January 11, 1978   *National Theatre, Washington, DC*
closed January 14, 1978
[announced booking: Palace Theatre]

"Gene Barry dances like an arthritic pugilist," wrote one local scribe. And he *did*. Lyricist Lyn Duddy switched on the TV during the opening night party just in time to hear himself dubbed "the appropriately-named Lyn Duddy." Egoists take heed.

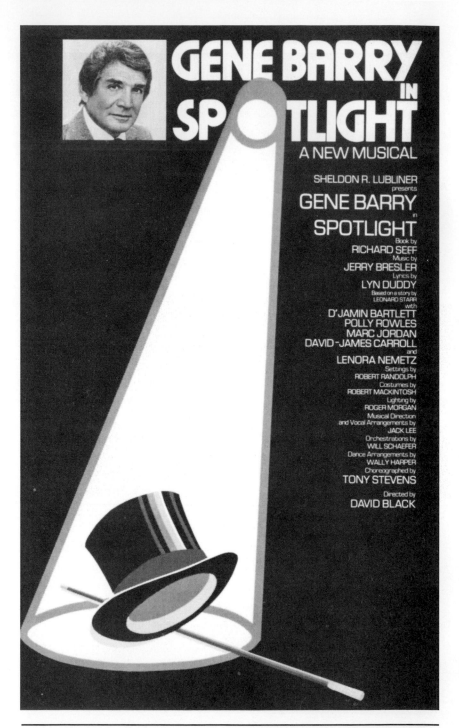

"Gene Barry dances like an arthritic pugilist," they said. And he did.
(artwork by Joel Mitnick)

SWING

"A New Musical"

music by Robert Waldman

lyrics by Alfred Uhry

book by Conn Fleming

directed by Stuart Ostrow

choreographed by Kenneth Rinker

produced by Stuart Ostrow in association with Edgar M. Bronfman

with Raymond Baker, Paul Binotto, Paul Bogaev, Jerry Colker, Janet Eilber, Robert LuPone, Pat Lysinger, Adam Redfield, Debbie Shapiro, and Mary Catherine Wright

opened February 25, 1980   *Playhouse Theatre, Wilmington, DE*
closed March 30, 1980   *Kennedy Center Opera House,*
                              Washington, DC

Folks at the Kennedy Center still cringe when you bring up this clinker from the on-again, off-again showshop of Stuart Ostrow. When his shows were good, they were very, very good, like *1776* (1969) and *M. Butterfly* (1988). However. . . .

TRUCKLOAD

"The Musical"

music by Louis St. Louis

lyrics by Wes Harris

book by Hugh Wheeler

conceived by Patricia Birch and Louis St. Louis

directed and choreographed by Patricia Birch

produced by Adela Holzer, The Shubert Organization, and Dick Clark

with Deborah (Debbie) Allen, Cheryl Barnes, Donny Burks, José Fernandez, Ilene Graff, Sherry Mathis, Kelly Ward, "and featuring Louis St. Louis and the All Night Drivers"

previewed September 6, 1975   Lyceum Theatre, New York
closed September 11, 1975
[announced opening: September 23, 1975]

Pat Birch and Louis St. Louis, choreographer and musical director/ arranger of *Grease* (1972), dreamed this one up. Birch called in designers Doug Schmidt and Carrie Robbins from *Grease* and librettist Hugh Wheeler from *Night Music* (1973) and *Candide* (1974). "Depending on how you look at it," explained Wheeler, "the show has either no plot or twelve plots." *Truckload* of *what*, you well may ask.

W. C.

"(A New Musical)"

music and lyrics by Al Carmines

book by Milton Sperling and Sam Locke

based on the 1949 biography *W. C. Fields, His Follies and Fortunes* by Robert Lewis Taylor

directed by Richard Altman

choreographed by Bob Herget

produced by David Black (with Lee Guber and Shelly Gross)

starring Mickey Rooney and Bernadette Peters

with Virginia Martin, Gary Oakes, Rudy Tronto, Jack Bittman, David Vaughan, Sam Stoneburner, and Martin J. Cassidy

opened June 15, 1971	*Painters Mill Music Fair, Owing Mills, MD*
closed July 25, 1971	*Westbury Music Fair, Westbury, NY*

The Reverend Al Carmines was the king of esoteric Off-Broadway composers, with an uneven bunch of unconventional musicals to his credit—including the first-rate and very worthy *Promenade* (which opened the theatre of the same name in 1969). This didn't make him the likeliest candidate, perhaps, for a musical about old Bill Fields. The diminutive Mickey Rooney wasn't the likeliest candidate to essay the comic juggler, either, but he'd been washed up for so long that he was game for anything. (The previous summer he'd appeared on the citronella circuit in producer Black's 1968 bio-tuner *George M!*). If Rooney's first shot at a new Broadway musical failed, he made it—and made it big—in 1979 with *Sugar Babies*. Bernadette Peters also made it to Broadway, and how, with *Mack & Mabel* (1974).

BROADWAY SCORECARD SUMMARY

Rating shows by their critical reception does not reflect their true quality, any more than ranking them by the number of performances would. One must keep in mind that the scorecards reflect only the opinions of those critics tabulated, major critics but only six in number, and that the totals give each critic equal weight, while in actuality a rave from the *Daily News* does not necessarily counteract a devastating pan from the *New York Times*. The Scorecard Summary does lead to some interesting observations, though. And while we're at it, it seems relevant to compare the 1965–1981 shows with similarly classified titles from the so-called Golden Era of 1943 through 1964, covered in *Opening Night on Broadway*.

Only six productions received unanimous raves across the board:

A Chorus Line
Two Gentlemen of Verona

[revues]
Lena Horne: The Lady and Her Music
Words and Music

[revivals]
Hello, Dolly! (Pearl Bailey)
Porgy and Bess

The first named is no surprise, while the second might raise a few eyebrows. Both were transfers from Joe Papp's Shakespeare Festival, which is to say that they were developed in a nontraditional manner, tried out *in* New York, opened triumphantly, and moved uptown (or downtown). The other four were not newly created musicals but personality revues or revivals. Looking back at the Golden Era, we see a full seven new musicals in the unanimous rave category—and the list does not include *Dolly!* or *Fiddler* or *Oklahoma!* Read 'em and weep:

Brigadoon
Guys and Dolls
How to Succeed in Business Without Really Trying
The Music Man
My Fair Lady
South Pacific
Wonderful Town

[revue]
An Evening with Beatrice Lillie

The following received five raves (out of six reviews), and thus belong more or less at the top of the class:

Promises, Promises
1776

[revue]
Ain't Misbehavin'

[revivals]
Candide
Fiddler on the Roof (Herschel Bernardi)
A Funny Thing Happened on the Way to the Forum
The Pirates of Penzance

Pearl Bailey's replacement cast of *Dolly!*, the revised version of *Candide*, and the revivals of *Fiddler* and *Forum* all received better reviews than on their original visits. The Golden Era's list (not including revivals), for comparison's sake:

The Boy Friend
Bye Bye Birdie
Carmen Jones
Carousel
Gentlemen Prefer Blondes
Kiss Me, Kate
The Pajama Game

Another six shows were a further notch below, with a still-impressive four raves:

Annie
42nd Street

   [revivals]
Gypsy
Lost in the Stars
My Fair Lady (Ian Richardson)
Very Good Eddie

The perceptive reader will note, ruefully, that only six of the 1965–1981 offerings listed so far (with four or more raves) were brand new Broadway musicals—and one of them, *42nd Street*, used recycled songs. This is measured against *thirty* in the Golden Era. Depressing, eh? Before moving on, let us point out that all of the new 1965–1981 musicals and revues were financially successful, though some of the revivals failed despite critical encomiums (namely *Candide*, *Forum*, *Lost in the Stars*, and *My Fair Lady*).

There were another twelve musicals that received, on average, a better-than-favorable rating. We converted the scorecards to complicated mathematical tables for the sake of classification, but let's just look at the results:

Applause
Barnum
The Best Little Whorehouse in Texas
Company

Hair
I Do! I Do!
Man of La Mancha
Pippin
Sweeney Todd

[revues]
A Day in Hollywood—A Night in the Ukraine
Sophisticated Ladies

[revivals]
Fiddler on the Roof (Zero Mostel)
No, No, Nanette

Not a bad group, and all hits—financially speaking—except the overproduced *Sweeney Todd* (which received only one poor review, unfortunately in the *Times*). This better-than-favorable rating seems to mark the dividing line, though, in terms of financial success; numerous shows made money with worse reviews but it didn't work both ways. We might pause to note that of the 206 productions covered in this book, only 18—7 new, 4 revues, 7 revivals—received unanimously good reviews (which is to say all raves and favorables, no mixed or worse). The Golden Era, you won't be surprised to learn, had 38 (of 275): 7 revues, 4 revivals, and—here's the critical figure—*27 new musicals with unanimously good reviews.*

Another 7 shows managed to average a favorable rating, but this in itself was not enough to ensure success. All except *Cabaret, Charity,* and *Bubbling* lost money:

The Apple Tree
Cabaret
Follies
Sweet Charity

[revues]
Bubbling Brown Sugar
Eubie!

[revival]
Brigadoon

Follies, again, was favorably received by everyone except the Messrs. Barnes and Kerr of the *Times*. From here on we need only enumerate the hits; there's little need to list failed shows with poor reviews. (Except those scraping the bottom of the barrel, of course, which are in some ways instructive and retain a ghoulish charm.) The reception of the following financially profitable shows fell somewhere between mixed and favorable. All were flawed, perhaps, but there was usually at least one element that more than made up for the weaknesses. (Two of 'em, *A Little Night Music* and *Mame*, seem ludicrously out of place down here—to me at least.):

Half a Sixpence
I Love My Wife
Joseph and the Amazing Technicolor Dreamcoat
A Little Night Music
Mame
They're Playing Our Song
The Wiz

[revues]
Dancin'
Side by Side by Sondheim

[revivals]
The King and I
Man of La Mancha
Oklahoma!
Peter Pan

Another four hits were evenly mixed, split right down the middle. The first two were controversial modernistic musicals, with flaws; the others were crassly commercial attempts, artless in the worst sense of the word:

Chicago
Dreamgirls
The Magic Show
Two by Two

This evenly mixed category also includes two intriguing failures, stunningly conceptualized musicals gone stultifyingly awry:

Ballroom
Pacific Overtures

Then there were the hits with critical receptions that fell somewhere between mixed and unfavorable. The great American theatregoing public bought tickets nevertheless, and presumably enjoyed themselves:

[just below mixed]

Grease
Jesus Christ Superstar
Sugar Babies

[closer to unfavorable]

Godspell
Pickwick
The Roar of the Greasepaint

[marginally above unfavorable, in descending order]

Shenandoah
Evita
Sugar

And then we hit rock bottom. A frightening 67 of the 206 shows were greeted with receptions on the far side of unfavorable. Twenty-five of these garnered five pans, while a full 20 genuine, authentic, professional Broadway musicals received six no-holds-barred, string-'em-up-from-the-nearest-lamppost blasts. What makes this especially disheartening is that these titles represent the work of not only your typical Broadway hack but also the likes of George Abbott, Michael Bennett, Leonard Bernstein, Abe Burrows, Ron Field, Sheldon Harnick, Jerry Herman, Michael Kidd, Joe Layton, Alan Jay Lerner, Hal Prince, Richard Rodgers, Stephen Sondheim, Michael Stewart, and Charles Strouse. Many of them twice, and poor Gower Champion three times. (Cy Coleman, Bob Fosse, Frank Loesser, Jule Styne, and others are absent only because their qualifying shows closed before the Broadway critics could get their hands on them.) The Golden Era had its share of potboilers, but there were only a handful of titles—Loesser's *Greenwillow*, Weill and Ira Gershwin's *The Firebrand of Florence*, Dietz and Schwartz's *Jennie*, and Berlin's *Mr. President*—from top talents. As with the hats-in-the-air rave garnerers at the head of this summary, there's no question about quality here. The dishonor roll:

[with 5 pans]

Ambassador
Ari
Billy
A Broadway Musical
Coco
Good News
Goodtime Charley
Her First Roman
Here's Where I Belong
I Remember Mama
La Strada
Mack & Mabel
Merrily We Roll Along
Molly
Music Is
Oh, Brother!
Rainbow Jones
Rex
So Long, 174th Street
Timbuktu!
A Time for Singing
The Utter Glory of Morrissey Hall
Via Galactica
Wild and Wonderful
The Yearling

[with 6-out-of-6 pans]

Bring Back Birdie
Doctor Jazz
Dude
Frank Merriwell

Got Tu Go Disco
Hair (revival)
Heathen!
Home Sweet Homer
Hurry, Harry
Jimmy
Kelly
Man on the Moon
Oh! Calcutta!
Onward Victoria
Pousse-Café
Reggae
Rockabye Hamlet
The Rocky Horror Show
The Selling of the President
1600 Pennsylvania Avenue

The hit with the poorest reviews, not surprisingly, was *Oh! Calcutta!* A close second (from the bottom) was the barely profitable *Coco*, which shows what you can do with Katharine Hepburn in a basic black dress.

CHRONOLOGICAL LISTING OF PRODUCTIONS

The productions discussed in this book are listed below, by order of date of official Broadway opening. This provides an at-a-glance look at what was playing on the night that such-and-such came to town—and what was to come next. (Brackets indicate contemporary musicals that closed without facing the Broadway critics, which are included in the Glossary of Broadway Musicals That Never Opened on Broadway. In these cases, the date of the final performance is given.) The title is followed by the official number of performances and an indication of the show's profitability (or lack of same).

	1965		
February 6	*Kelly*	1	-
February 16	*Baker Street*	313	-
March 18	*Do I Hear a Waltz?*	220	-
[April 10	*Pleasures and Palaces*]	0	-
April 25	*Half a Sixpence*	512	+
May 11	*Flora, the Red Menace*	87	-
May 16	*The Roar of the Greasepaint*	232	+
October 4	*Pickwick*	56	+
[October 9	*Hot September*]	0	-
October 10	*Drat! The Cat!*	8	-
October 17	*On a Clear Day You Can See Forever*	280	-

November 10	*The Zulu and the Zayda*	179	-
November 13	*Skyscraper*	241	-
November 22	*Man of La Mancha*	2,328	+
November 29	*Anya*	16	-
December 10	*The Yearling*	3	-

1966

January 29	*Sweet Charity*	608	+
March 18	*Pousse-Café*	3	-
March 29	*"It's a Bird, It's a Plane,*		
	It's Superman"	129	-
May 15	*A Time for Singing*	41	-
May 24	*Mame*	1,508	+
October 18	*The Apple Tree*	463	-
[November 19	*Chu Chem*]	0	-
November 20	*Cabaret*	1,166	+
November 26	*Walking Happy*	161	-
December 5	*I Do! I Do!*	561	+
[December 14	*Breakfast at Tiffany's*]	0	-
December 15	*A Joyful Noise*	12	-

1967

March 28	*Sherry!*	72	-
April 11	*Illya Darling*	320	-
April 26	*Hallelujah, Baby!*	293	-
[September 16	*Hellzapoppin' '67* (Soupy Sales)]	0	-
October 23	*Henry, Sweet Henry*	80	-
November 12	*Hello, Dolly!* (Pearl Bailey)	2,844	+
December 7	*How Now, Dow Jones*	221	-
[December 9	*Mata Hari*]	0	-
December 28	*How to Be a Jewish Mother*	21	-

1968

| January 18 | *The Happy Time* | 286 | - |
| January 27 | *Darling of the Day* | 32 | - |

February 4	*Golden Rainbow*	385	-
March 3	*Here's Where I Belong*	1	-
April 4	*The Education of H*Y*M*A*N K*A*P*L*A*N*	28	-
April 10	*George M!*	427	-
April 23	*I'm Solomon*	7	-
April 29	*Hair*	1,742	+
May 2	*New Faces of 1968*	52	-
[October 19	*A Mother's Kisses*]	0	-
October 20	*Her First Roman*	17	-
October 23	*Maggie Flynn*	82	-
November 17	*Zorbá*	305	-
December 1	*Promises, Promises*	1,281	+

1969

January 2	*The Fig Leaves Are Falling*	4	-
[January 4	*Love Match*]	0	-
January 22	*Celebration*	110	-
January 26	*Red, White and Maddox*	41	-
February 3	*Canterbury Tales*	121	-
February 6	*Dear World*	132	-
March 16	*1776*	1,217	+
March 18	*Come Summer*	7	-
March 22	*Billy*	1	-
June 17	*Oh! Calcutta!*	1,314	+
October 23	*Jimmy*	84	-
December 2	*Buck White*	7	-
[December 13	*1491*]	0	-
December 14	*La Strada*	1	-
December 18	*Coco*	332	+

1970

February 14	*Gantry*	1	-
February 26	*Georgy*	4	-
March 15	*Purlie*	689	-
March 26	*Minnie's Boys*	76	-
March 29	*Look to the Lilies*	25	-
March 30	*Applause*	896	+

April 8	*Cry for Us All*	9	-
April 14	*The Boy Friend*	111	-
April 26	*Company*	706	+
October 19	*The Rothschilds*	505	-
November 10	*Two by Two*	343	+
December 18	*The Me Nobody Knows*	385	+
December 28	*Lovely Ladies, Kind Gentlemen*	19	-

1971

January 12	*Soon*	3	-
January 15	*Ari*	19	-
January 19	*No, No, Nanette!*	861	+
[March 6	*Prettybelle*]	0	-
[March 27	*Lolita, My Love*]	0	-
April 4	*Follies*	522	-
April 15	*70, Girls, 70*	36	-
April 24	*Frank Merriwell*	1	-
[July 25	*W. C.*]	0	-
October 12	*Jesus Christ Superstar*	711	+
October 31	*On the Town*	73	-
November 2	*The Grass Harp*	7	-
December 1	*Two Gentlemen of Verona*	613	+
December 7	*Wild and Wonderful*	1	-

1972

February 14	*Grease*	3,388	+
March 22	*The Selling of the President*	5	-
March 30	*A Funny Thing Happened on the Way to the Forum*	156	-
April 9	*Sugar*	505	+
April 18	*Lost in the Stars*	39	-
[May 6	*Clownaround*]	0	-
May 21	*Heathen!*	1	-
June 28	*Mass*	22	-
[October 1	*Halloween*]	0	-
October 9	*Dude*	16	-
October 12	*Hurry, Harry*	2	-

October 23	*Pippin*	1,944	+
[November 18	*Comedy*]	0	-
November 19	*Ambassador*	9	-
November 28	*Via Galactica*	7	-

1973

January 8	*Tricks*	8	-
February 6	*Shelter*	31	-
February 25	*A Little Night Music*	601	+
March 13	*Irene*	594	-
March 18	*Seesaw*	296	-
May 13	*Cyrano*	49	-
September 5	*The Desert Song*	15	-
[September 16	*A Song for Cyrano*]	0	-
October 18	*Raisin*	847	-
November 1	*Molly*	68	-
November 13	*Gigi*	103	-
[November 24	*Gone with the Wind*]	0	-
[December 1	*Rachael Lily Rosenbloom*]	0	-
December 9	*The Pajama Game*	65	-

1974

January 27	*Lorelei*	320	-
February 13	*Rainbow Jones*	1	-
March 6	*Over Here!*	341	-
March 10	*Candide*	740	-
[April 6	*Brainchild*]	0	-
April 11	*Music! Music!*	37	-
April 16	*Words and Music*	127	+
May 28	*The Magic Show*	1,859	+
September 23	*Gypsy* (revival)	120	+
October 6	*Mack & Mabel*	65	-
[October 17	*Miss Moffat*]	0	-
December 19	*Where's Charley?*	78	-
December 23	*Good News*	16	-

1975

January 5	The Wiz	1,666	+
January 7	Shenandoah	1,050	+
January 29	Man on the Moon	5	-
March 3	Goodtime Charley	104	-
March 9	The Lieutenant	9	-
March 10	The Rocky Horror Show	45	-
March 19	Doctor Jazz	5	-
June 3	Chicago	923	+
[September 11	Truckload]	0	-
October 19	A Chorus Line	6,137	+
October 21	Treemonisha	64	-
[November 13	Back Country]	0	-
December 21	Very Good Eddie	288	+

1976

January 4	Home Sweet Homer	1	-
January 11	Pacific Overtures	193	-
February 17	Rockabye Hamlet	8	-
March 2	Bubbling Brown Sugar	766	+
March 25	My Fair Lady (20th anniversary)	377	-
April 25	Rex	49	-
April 27	So Long, 174th Street	16	-
May 1	The Threepenny Opera	307	+
May 4	1600 Pennsylvania Avenue	7	-
May 27	Something's Afoot	61	-
June 22	Godspell	527	+
June 27	Pal Joey	73	-
July 21	Guys and Dolls	239	-
September 25	Porgy and Bess	122	+
October 9	The Robber Bridegroom	145	-
[November 13	The Baker's Wife]	0	-
December 20	Music Is	8	-
December 28	Fiddler on the Roof (Zero Mostel)	167	+

1977

[January 22	Hellzapoppin (Jerry Lewis)]	0	-
April 17	I Love My Wife	872	+
April 18	Side by Side by Sondheim	384	+
April 21	Annie	2,377	+

May 2	*The King and I* (revival)	719	+
May 7	*Happy End*	75	-
September 15	*Man of La Mancha* (revival)	125	+
October 5	*Hair* (revival)	43	-
[October 22	*Nefertiti*]	0	-
October 29	*The Act*	233	-

1978

[January 14	*Spotlight*]	0	-
February 19	*On the Twentieth Century*	460	-
March 1	*Timbuktu!*	221	-
March 27	*Dancin'*	1,774	+
[April 15	*The Prince of Grand Street*]	0	-
April 17	*The Best Little Whorehouse*	1,584	+
May 8	*Ain't Misbehavin'*	1,604	+
May 10	*Angel*	5	-
May 14	*Working*	25	-
[June 11	*Alice*]	0	-
August 3	*Stop the World*	29	-
September 20	*Eubie!*	439	-
[September 23	*Oh, Kay!*]	0	-
October 22	*King of Hearts*	48	-
November 12	*Platinum*	33	-
December 14	*Ballroom*	116	-
December 21	*A Broadway Musical*	1	-

1979

January 11	*The Grand Tour*	61	-
February 11	*They're Playing Our Song*	1,082	+
February 23	*Saravá*	140	-
March 1	*Sweeney Todd*	558	-
April 8	*Carmelina*	17	-
[April 14	*Home Again, Home Again*]	0	-
May 13	*The Utter Glory of Morrissey Hall*	1	-
May 31	*I Remember Mama*	108	-
June 25	*Got Tu Go Disco*	8	-
September 6	*Peter Pan*	550	+
September 25	*Evita*	1,566	+
October 8	*Sugar Babies*	1,208	+
December 13	*Oklahoma!*	293	+
December 20	*Comin' Uptown*	45	-

1980

February 14	*West Side Story*	333	-
March 27	*Reggae*	21	-
[March 30	*Swing*]	0	-
April 27	*Happy New Year*	17	-
April 30	*Barnum*	854	+
May 1	*A Day in Hollywood*	588	+
June 5	*The Music Man*	21	-
July 8	*Camelot* (Richard Burton)	56	+
August 25	*42nd Street*	3,486	+
September 14	*Charlie and Algernon*	17	-
October 16	*Brigadoon*	134	-
October 23	*Tintypes*	93	-
[October 25	*One Night Stand*]	0	-
November 30	*Perfectly Frank*	17	-
December 14	*Onward Victoria*	1	-

1981

January 8	*The Pirates of Penzance*	787	+
March 1	*Sophisticated Ladies*	765	+
March 5	*Bring Back Birdie*	4	-
March 29	*Woman of the Year*	770	-
April 16	*Copperfield*	13	-
April 30	*Can-Can*	5	-
May 3	*The Moony Shapiro Songbook*	1	-
May 12	*Lena Horne*	333	+
July 9	*Fiddler on the Roof* (Hershel Bernardi)	53	+
August 18	*My Fair Lady* (Rex Harrison)	119	-
November 10	*Oh, Brother!*	3	-
November 15	*Camelot* (Richard Harris)	48	+
November 16	*Merrily We Roll Along*	16	-
November 17	*The First*	37	-
November 18	*Joseph and the Amazing Technicolor Dreamcoat*	757	+
December 20	*Dreamgirls*	1,522	+

NOTABLE CAREERS IN THE MUSICAL THEATRE

This section will help the reader follow the careers of specific writers, directors, choreographers, producers, and designers. Forty notable musical theatre folk have been selected. In some cases they did not officially receive credit. In others, they might have been associated in an unlikely capacity (e.g., someone we know as a choreographer appearing as a dancer). For details, see the show entry. There are, of course, many passing references to these people in discussions of shows with which they weren't associated. These citations are noted in the general index.

GEORGE ABBOTT   *director; librettist*
Born: *June 25, 1887, Forrestville, NY*
Died: *January 31, 1995, Miami Beach, FL*

Veteran actor George Abbott became a playwright/director in 1926— at the advanced age of 39—with the hit melodrama *Broadway*. He began producing his own plays in 1932, entering the musical field with five Rodgers and Hart tuners including *On Your Toes* (1936, introducing George Balanchine to Broadway), *The Boys from Syracuse* (1938), and *Pal Joey* (1940). Other notable musicals included *On the Town* (1944, introducing Bernstein, Comden, Green, and Robbins), *High Button Shoes* (1947, introducing Styne), *Where's Charley?* (1948, introducing Loesser), *Call Me Madam* (1950), *Wonderful Town* (1953), *The*

Pajama Game (1954, introducing Adler, Ross, Fosse, and producer Prince), *Damn Yankees* (1955), *Once Upon a Mattress* (1959), *Fiorello!* (1959), *A Funny Thing Happened on the Way to the Forum* (1962, introducing Sondheim-as-composer), and *Fade Out—Fade In* (1964), not to mention dozens and dozens of plays.

Flora, the Red Menace	May 11, 1965
Anya	November 29, 1965
How Now, Dow Jones	December 7, 1967
The Education of H*Y*M*A*N K*A*P*L*A*N	April 4, 1968
The Fig Leaves Are Falling	January 2, 1969
The Pajama Game (revival)	December 9, 1973
Where's Charley? (revival)	December 19, 1974
Pal Joey (revival)	June 27, 1976
Music Is	December 20, 1976

Abbott ended his Broadway directing career with the 1982 revival of *On Your Toes* and a revival of *Broadway*, which opened on the eve of his 100th birthday (and closed when G. A. was 100 years and 2 days old).

THEONI V. ALDREDGE   *costume designer*
Born: *August 22, 1932, Salonika, Greece*

Aldredge made her Broadway debut in 1959 providing Geraldine Page's costumes for Tennessee Williams's *Sweet Bird of Youth.* Early musicals included the 1959 *The Nervous Set* (which featured husband Tom Aldredge), *I Can Get It for You Wholesale* (1962), *Mr. President* (1962), and *Anyone Can Whistle* (1964). Long-running nonmusicals included *Mary, Mary* (1961), *Who's Afraid of Virginia Woolf* (1962), *Any Wednesday* (1964), and *Luv* (1964).

[*Hot September*	October 9, 1965]
Skyscraper	November 13, 1965
A Time for Singing	May 15, 1966
Illya Darling	April 11, 1967
Billy	March 22, 1969
Two Gentlemen of Verona	December 1, 1971

Music! Music!	April 11, 1974
A Chorus Line	October 19, 1975
The Threepenny Opera (revival)	May 1, 1976
[*The Baker's Wife*	November 13, 1976]
Annie	April 21, 1977
Ballroom	December 14, 1978
The Grand Tour	January 11, 1979
I Remember Mama	May 31, 1979
Barnum	April 30, 1980
42nd Street	August 25, 1980
Onward Victoria	December 14, 1980
Woman of the Year	March 29, 1981
Dreamgirls	December 20, 1981

Subsequent musicals include *La Cage aux Folles* (1983), *Merlin* (1983), *Teddy and Alice* (1987), *Chess* (1988), the 1989 revival of *Gypsy*, the 1990 revival of *Oh, Kay!*, *Annie 2* (1990), *Nick and Nora* (1991), *The Secret Garden* (1991), and *Annie Warbucks* (1993).

BORIS ARONSON   *scenic designer*
Born: *October 15, 1900, Kiev, Russia*
Died: *November 16, 1980, Nyack, NY*

Aronson started his New York career in 1924 designing for the Yiddish theatre. His first Broadway opportunity came in 1932 with Russian-born composer Vernon ("April in Paris") Duke's revue *Walk a Little Faster*. Aronson designed many plays, including *Three Men on a Horse* (1935), *Awake and Sing* (1935), *I Am a Camera* (1951), *Bus Stop* (1955), and *The Diary of Anne Frank* (1955). His musical outings were curiously limited, though, to three additional Duke musicals (*Cabin in the Sky* [1940], *Sadie Thompson* [1944], and *Sweet Bye and Bye* [1946]); two Alan Jay Lerner flops (*What's Up* [1943] and *Love Life* [1948]); and the Merrick-Comden-Styne-Green *Do Re Mi* (1960). All this changed in 1964, when Harold Prince tapped him for *Fiddler on the Roof*.

Cabaret	November 20, 1966
Zorbá	November 17, 1968

Company	April 26, 1970
Follies	April 4, 1971
A Little Night Music	February 25, 1973
Pacific Overtures	January 11, 1976
Fiddler on the Roof (revival—Zero Mostel)	December 28, 1976
Fiddler on the Roof (revival—Herschel Bernardi)	July 9, 1981

MICHAEL BENNETT   *director; choreographer; producer*
Born: *April 8, 1943, Buffalo, NY*
Died: *July 2, 1987, Tucson, AZ*

Following a stint as Baby John in a touring *West Side Story*, Bennett danced on Broadway in *Subways Are for Sleeping* (1961), *Here's Love* (1963), and *Bajour* (1964). He also served as choreographer Ron Field's assistant on *Nowhere to Go But Up* (1962).

A Joyful Noise	December 15, 1966
Henry, Sweet Henry	October 23, 1967
How Now, Dow Jones	December 7, 1967
Promises, Promises	December 1, 1968
Coco	December 18, 1969
Company	April 26, 1970
Follies	April 4, 1971
Seesaw	March 18, 1973
A Chorus Line	October 19, 1975
Ballroom	December 14, 1978
Dreamgirls	December 20, 1981

Bennett canceled his final project, *Scandal* (1983), after several developmental workshops. A touring revival of *Dreamgirls* returned to Broadway in 1987, opening four days before Bennett's death.

LEONARD BERNSTEIN   *composer*
Born: *August 25, 1918, Lawrence, MA*
Died: *October 14, 1990, New York, NY*

Bernstein catapulted to front-page prominence on November 14, 1943, when due to a last-minute illness—and the lack of a more "suitable" replacement—the lowly assistant conductor triumphantly led a concert of the New York Philharmonic. In 1944 Ballet Theatre mounted his ballet *Fancy Free* (choreographed by Jerome Robbins, designed by Oliver Smith)—which the three 25-year-olds transformed into that year's musical hit *On the Town* (which Smith also produced). Maestro Bernstein's infrequent theatre visits included *Wonderful Town* (1953), *Trouble in Tahiti* (presented on Broadway in 1955), *Candide* (1956), and *West Side Story* (1957).

On the Town (revival)	October 31, 1971
Mass	June 28, 1972
Candide (revision)	March 10, 1974
1600 Pennsylvania Avenue	May 4, 1976
West Side Story (revival)	February 14, 1980

JERRY BOCK   *composer*
Born: *November 23, 1928, New Haven, CT*

Bock began his career with the Jule Styne-produced Sammy Davis vehicle *Mr. Wonderful* (1956). He first collaborated with lyricist Sheldon Harnick on *The Body Beautiful* (1958), which was followed by four Harold Prince-produced musicals: *Fiorello!* (1959), *Tenderloin* (1960), *She Loves Me* (1963), and *Fiddler on the Roof* (1964).

Baker Street	February 16, 1965
The Apple Tree	October 18, 1966
Her First Roman	October 20, 1968
The Rothschilds	October 19, 1970
Fiddler on the Roof (revival—Zero Mostel)	December 28, 1976
Fiddler on the Roof (revival—Herschel Bernardi)	July 9, 1981

GOWER CHAMPION   *director; choreographer*
Born: *June 22, 1920, Geneva, IL*
Died: *August 25, 1980, New York, NY*

Champion came to Broadway when his supper-club dance act "Gower and Jeanne" (with Jeanne Tyler) was included in the 1939 revue *The*

Streets of Paris. "Gower Champion Seaman 1C" made his choreographic debut with the Vernon Duke/Howard Dietz Coast Guard recruiting show *Tars and Spars* (1944). After the war he choreographed *Small Wonder* (1948), *Lend an Ear* (1948), *Make a Wish* (1951), and the revue *Three for Tonight* (1955), which he also directed and starred in. The "Champion Era" began in 1960 when he directed and choreographed *Bye Bye Birdie*, which was followed by Merrick musicals *Carnival* (1961) and *Hello, Dolly!* (1964).

A Time for Singing	May 15, 1966
I Do! I Do!	December 5, 1966
Hello, Dolly! (Pearl Bailey company)	November 12, 1967
The Happy Time	January 18, 1968
[*Prettybelle*	March 6, 1971]
Sugar	April 9, 1972
Irene	March 13, 1973
Mack & Mabel	October 6, 1974
Rockabye Hamlet	February 17, 1976
The Act	October 29, 1977
A Broadway Musical	December 21, 1978
42nd Street	August 25, 1980

ALEXANDER H. COHEN   *producer*
Born: *July 24, 1920, New York, NY*

Cohen came to Broadway in 1941 as associate producer of the long-running melodrama *Angel Street*. His early musicals were failures, namely *Of "V" We Sing* (1942), *Bright Lights of 1944* (1943), *Make a Wish* (1951), *Courtin' Time* (1951), and *Rugantino* (1964). Cohen began producing a series of "specialty" revues in 1959, including the highly successful 1962 import *Beyond the Fringe* (1962).

Baker Street	February 16, 1965
A Time for Singing	May 15, 1966
[*Hellzapoppin' '67* (Soupy Sales)	September 16, 1967]
Dear World	February 6, 1969
[*Prettybelle*	March 6, 1971]
Words and Music	April 16, 1974

[*Hellzapoppin* (Jerry Lewis)   January 22, 1977]
I Remember Mama   May 31, 1979
A Day in Hollywood–A Night in the Ukraine May 1, 1980

Cohen returned to the musical field in 1994—for nine mirthless per-formances—with the misnamed *Comedy Tonight.*

CY COLEMAN   *composer*
Born: *June 14, 1929, Bronx, NY*

Jazz-pianist Coleman was first heard on Broadway with an interpola-tion in *John Murray Anderson's Almanac* (1953) and instrumental music for the drama *Compulsion* (1957). His first two Broadway scores, writ-ten with lyricist Carolyn Leigh, were the unsuccessful *Wildcat* (1960) and *Little Me* (1962).

Sweet Charity   January 29, 1966
Seesaw   March 18, 1973
[*Hellzapoppin* (Jerry Lewis)   January 22, 1977]
I Love My Wife   April 17, 1977
On the Twentieth Century   February 19, 1978
[*Home Again, Home Again*   April 14, 1979]
Barnum   April 30, 1980

Coleman's up-and-down career resumed almost a decade later with the dismal *Welcome to the Club* (1989), the fine *City of Angels* (1989), and the not-so-fine *Will Rogers Follies* (1991).

BETTY COMDEN & ADOLPH GREEN   *lyricists; librettists*
(Comden) Born: *May 3, 1915, New York, NY*
(Green) Born: *December 2, 1915, New York, NY*

Comden and Green came to Broadway—in league with newcomers Leonard Bernstein (Green's ex-roommate) and Jerome Robbins—with *On the Town* (1944). This was followed by such musicals as *Billion Dollar Baby* (1945), *Two on the Aisle* (1951), *Wonderful Town* (1953), *Peter Pan* (1954), *Bells Are Ringing* (1956), *Do Re Mi* (1960), *Subways Are for Sleeping* (1961), and *Fade Out—Fade In* (1964).

Hallelujah, Baby!	April 26, 1967
Applause	March 30, 1970
On the Town (revival)	October 31, 1971
Lorelei	January 27, 1974
On the Twentieth Century	February 19, 1978
Peter Pan (revival)	September 6, 1979

Comden and Green continued their long partnership with three additional unsuccessful musicals, *A Doll's Life* (1982), *Singin' in the Rain* (1985), and *The Will Rogers Follies* (1991).

RON FIELD   *director; choreographer*
Born: *1934, Queens, NY*
Died: *February 6, 1989, New York, NY*

Field began his career as a child actor in the original production of *Lady in the Dark* (1941). He danced in such musicals as *Gentlemen Prefer Blondes* (1949), *Carnival in Flanders* (1953), *Kismet* (1953), and *The Boy Friend* (1954) before choreographing the 1962 Off-Broadway revival of *Anything Goes*. This led to his first Broadway choreographic jobs, on *Nowhere to Go But Up* (1962) and *Cafe Crown* (1964).

Cabaret	November 20, 1966
Sherry!	March 28, 1967
Golden Rainbow	February 4, 1968
Zorbá	November 17, 1968
Applause	March 30, 1970
On the Town (revival)	October 31, 1971
King of Hearts	October 22, 1978
Peter Pan (revival)	September 6, 1979
Perfectly Frank	November 30, 1980
Merrily We Roll Along	November 16, 1981

Field's final Broadway credits came on the 1986 *Rags* (as replacement choreographer) and the 1987 revival of *Cabaret*.

JULES FISHER   *lighting designer; producer*
Born: *November 12, 1937, Norristown, PA*

Fisher made his New York debut with an Off-Broadway production of *All the King's Men* (1959). Other Off-Broadway shows included the musicals *All in Love* (1961), *Riverwind* (1962), and *Best Foot Forward* (1963). Fisher made his Broadway debut with *An Evening with Maurice Chevalier* (1963), which was followed in 1964 by *Anyone Can Whistle*, *High Spirits*, and the Pulitzer Prize-winning drama *The Subject Was Roses*.

Do I Hear a Waltz?	March 18, 1965
Half a Sixpence	April 25, 1965
Pickwick	October 4, 1965
The Yearling	December 10, 1965
[*Hellzapoppin' '67* (Soupy Sales)	September 16, 1967]
Here's Where I Belong	March 3, 1968
Hair	April 29, 1968
[*Love Match*	January 4, 1969]
Canterbury Tales	February 3, 1969
Gantry	February 14, 1970
Minnie's Boys	March 26, 1970
Soon	January 12, 1971
No, No, Nanette!	January 19, 1971
[*Lolita, My Love*	March 27, 1971]
Jesus Christ Superstar	October 12, 1971
Pippin	October 23, 1972
Seesaw	March 18, 1973
Molly	November 1, 1973
[*Rachael Lily Rosenbloom*	December 1, 1973]
Man on the Moon	January 29, 1975
Chicago	June 3, 1975
Rockabye Hamlet	February 17, 1976
Hair (revival)	October 5, 1977
Dancin'	March 27, 1978

Fisher coproduced as well as designed *Dancin'*, the drama *Lenny* (1971), *Rock 'N' Roll! The First 5,000 Years* (1982), *The Rink* (1984), *Big Deal* (1986), and *Dangerous Games* (1991). Other Fisher-designed musicals include *La Cage aux Folles* (1983), *Song and Dance* (1985), *Rags* (1986), *Legs Diamond* (1988), *Grand Hotel* (1990), *The Will Rogers Follies*

(1991), *Nick and Nora* (1991), *Jelly's Last Jam* (1992), *Victor/Victoria* (1995), and *Bring in 'Da Noise, Bring in 'Da Funk*, (1996).

BOB FOSSE   *director; choreographer*
Born: *June 23, 1927, Chicago, IL*
Died: *September 23, 1987, Washington, DC*

Fosse appeared in national tours of *Call Me Mister* (1946) and *Make Mine Manhattan* (1948) before dancing on Broadway in *Dance Me a Song* (1950). He made his choreographic debut in 1954 with *The Pajama Game*, which was followed by *Damn Yankees* (1955) and *New Girl in Town* (1957); all three were directed by Abbott and coproduced by Prince. Fosse made his director/choreographer debut with *Redhead* (1959), which starred soon-to-be-wife, Gwen Verdon, in her third of five Fosse shows. Following the 1961 musical *The Conquering Hero* (from which he was fired), Fosse choreographed Frank Loesser's *How to Succeed in Business Without Really Trying* (1961) and served as chore-ographer/codirector of *Little Me* (1962).

[*Pleasures and Palaces*	April 10, 1965]
Sweet Charity	January 29, 1966
Pippin	October 23, 1972
The Pajama Game (revival)	December 9, 1973
Goodtime Charley	March 3, 1975
Chicago	June 3, 1975
Dancin'	March 27, 1978

Fosse staged a revival of *Sweet Charity* in 1986, which was followed by his final musical, the ill-conceived *Big Deal* (1987).

ROBERT FRYER   *producer*
Born: *November 18, 1920, Washington, DC*

Fryer began his career as George Abbott's associate producer on *A Tree Grows in Brooklyn* (1951). He followed this with the hit *Wonderful Town* (1953) and the nonhit *By the Beautiful Sea* (1954). *Shangri-La* (1956), *Saratoga* (1959), and *Hot Spot* (1963) were massive failures, alleviated by the hit comedy *Auntie Mame* (1956) and the Verdon-Fosse mystery musical *Redhead* (1959).

Sweet Charity	January 29, 1966
Mame	May 24, 1966
Chicago	June 3, 1975
On the Twentieth Century	February 19, 1978
Sweeney Todd	March 1, 1979
Merrily We Roll Along	November 16, 1981

Fryer's final musical was Hal Prince's *A Doll's Life* (1982). He ended his Broadway career with three Michael Frayn plays, the hit *Noises Off* (1983) and the unsuccessful *Benefactors* (1985) and *Wild Honey* (1986).

SHELDON HARNICK   *lyricist*
Born: *December 27, 1924, Chicago, IL*

Harnick began his career interpolating lyrics—and music as well—to the 1952 revues *New Faces of 1952* and *Two's Company*. He first collaborated with composer Jerry Bock in 1958 on *The Body Beautiful*, which was followed by four Harold Prince-produced musicals: *Fiorello!* (1959), *Tenderloin* (1960), *She Loves Me* (1963), and *Fiddler on the Roof* (1964).

Baker Street	February 16, 1965
The Apple Tree	October 18, 1966
Her First Roman	October 20, 1968
The Rothschilds	October 19, 1970
Rex	April 25, 1976
Fiddler on the Roof (revival—Zero Mostel)	December 28, 1976
Fiddler on the Roof (revival—Herschel Bernardi)	July 9, 1981

Two collaborations with Michel Legrand—*The Umbrellas of Cherbourg* (1979) and *A Christmas Carol* (1981)—and *Wonderful Life* (music by Joe Raposo) were performed regionally but never made it to Broadway. Harnick returned in 1993, contributing additional lyrics to the Netherlandish behemoth *Cyrano: The Musical*.

JERRY HERMAN   *composer; lyricist*
Born: *July 10, 1933, New York, NY*

Herman made his Broadway debut with an interpolation in the 1960 revue *From A to Z*. His first full score was for the unsuccessful *Milk and Honey* (1961), but his next effort—the Merrick/Champion *Hello, Dolly!* (1964)—firmly established him as a top tunesmith.

Mame	May 24, 1966
Hello, Dolly! (Pearl Bailey company)	November 12, 1967
Dear World	February 6, 1969
Mack & Mabel	October 6, 1974
The Grand Tour	January 11, 1979
A Day in Hollywood—A Night in the Ukraine	May 1, 1980

Herman ended a long personal drought in 1983 with *La Cage aux Folles*—seventeen long years after his previous hit, *Mame*. *Jerry's Girls* was a short-lived 1985 anthology revue of his work, and 1995 saw a revised but unsuccessful *Mack & Mabel* on the West End.

JOHN KANDER and FRED EBB   *composer/lyricist*
(Kander) Born: *March 18, 1927, Kansas City, MO*
(Ebb) Born: *April 8, 1932, New York, NY*

After serving as dance music arranger of *Gypsy* (1959) and *Irma La Douce* (1960), Kander made his debut—along with novice director Hal Prince—on *A Family Affair* (1962). Ebb reached Broadway in 1960 as a contributor to the revue *From A to Z* (in company with Jerry Herman and Woody Allen, as it happens).

Flora, the Red Menace	May 11, 1965
Cabaret	November 20, 1966
The Happy Time	January 18, 1968
Zorbá	November 17, 1968
70, Girls, 70	April 15, 1971
Chicago	June 3, 1975
The Act	October 29, 1977
Woman of the Year	March 29, 1981

Subsequent Kander and Ebb musicals include *The Rink* (1984), *And the World Goes Round* (1991), and *Kiss of the Spider Woman* (1993), all of which proved unsuccessful.

MICHAEL KIDD   *director; choreographer*
Born: *August 12, 1919, Brooklyn, NY*

Kidd—who danced one of the leads in the 1944 première of the Leonard Bernstein-Jerome Robbins ballet *Fancy Free*—made a dazzling choreographic debut in 1947 with *Finian's Rainbow*. Subsequent musicals included *Love Life* (1948), *Guys and Dolls* (1950), and *Can-Can* (1953). He directed as well as choreographed *Li'l Abner* (1956), *Destry Rides Again* (1959), *Wildcat* (1960), *Subways Are for Sleeping* (1961), *Here's Love* (1963, choreographer only), and *Ben Franklin in Paris* (1964).

Skyscraper	November 13, 1965
[*Breakfast at Tiffany's*	December 14, 1966]
The Rothschilds	October 19, 1970
Cyrano	May 13, 1973
Good News	December 23, 1974
The Music Man (revival)	June 5, 1980

Kidd briefly returned from retirement in 1993 to take over the faltering *The Goodbye Girl*. All of his post–*Li'l Abner* shows, strangely enough, were failures.

PHILIP J. LANG   *orchestrator*
Born: *April 17, 1911, New York, NY*
Died: *February 22, 1986, Branford, CT*

Lang made a somewhat inauspicious Broadway debut when Irving Berlin replaced him with Russell Bennett during the New Haven tryout of *Annie Get Your Gun* (1946). George Abbott rescued him, using Lang on his *Barefoot Boy with Cheek* (1947), *High Button Shoes* (1947), and *Where's Charley?* (1948). These were followed by numerous shows including *Make a Wish* (1951), *Fanny* (1954), *My Fair Lady* (1956), *Li'l Abner* (1956), *New Girl in Town* (1957), *Jamaica* (1957), *Goldilocks* (1958), *Whoop-Up* (1958), *Redhead* (1959), *Destry Rides Again* (1959),

Take Me Along (1959), *Saratoga* (1959), *Camelot* (1960), *Carnival* (1961), *Subways are for Sleeping* (1961), Irving Berlin's *Mr. President* (1962), *Tovarich* (1963), *Jennie* (1963), *Hello, Dolly!* (1964), *Ben Franklin in Paris* (1964), and *I Had a Ball* (1964).

[*Pleasures and Palaces*	April 10, 1965]
The Roar of the Greasepaint	May 16, 1965
[*Hot September*	October 9, 1965]
Mame	May 24, 1966
I Do! I Do!	December 5, 1966
Sherry!	March 28, 1967
Hello, Dolly! (Pearl Bailey company)	November 12, 1967
How Now, Dow Jones	December 7, 1967
Maggie Flynn	October 23, 1968
Dear World	February 6, 1969
Applause	March 30, 1970
Lovely Ladies, Kind Gentlemen	December 28, 1970
Ari	January 15, 1971
Sugar	April 9, 1972
Ambassador	November 19, 1972
Cyrano	May 13, 1973
Lorelei	January 27, 1974
Mack & Mabel	October 6, 1974
Good News	December 23, 1974
My Fair Lady (revival—25th Anniversary)	March 25, 1976
Annie	April 21, 1977
The Grand Tour	January 11, 1979
Carmelina	April 8, 1979
I Remember Mama	May 31, 1979
Camelot (revival—Richard Burton)	July 8, 1980
42nd Street	August 25, 1980
Charlie and Algernon	September 14, 1980
[*One Night Stand*	October 25, 1980]
Can-Can (revival)	April 30, 1981
My Fair Lady (revival—Rex Harrison)	August 18, 1981
Camelot (revival—Richard Harris)	November 15, 1981

JOE LAYTON   *director; choreographer*
Born: *May 3, 1931, Brooklyn, NY*
Died: *May 5, 1995, Key West, FL*

Layton began his Broadway career in 1947 as a replacement dancer in Richard Rodgers's *Oklahoma!* He also danced in such musicals as *High Button Shoes* (1948), *Miss Liberty* (1949), and *Wonderful Town* (1953). His choreography for an acclaimed 1959 Off-Broadway revival of *On the Town* earned him the dance assignment on Mary Rodgers's *Once Upon a Mattress*, which was followed by Richard Rodgers's *The Sound of Music* (1959), *Greenwillow* (1960), *Tenderloin* (1960), and *Sail Away* (1961). He graduated to director/choreographer with his innovative work on Richard Rodgers's *No Strings* (1962), after which he turned to Noël Coward's *The Girl Who Came to Supper* (1963).

Drat! The Cat!	October 10, 1965
Sherry!	March 28, 1967
George M!	April 10, 1968
Dear World	February 6, 1969
Two By Two	November 10, 1970
[*Gone with the Wind*	November 24, 1973]
Lorelei	January 27, 1974
I Love My Wife	April 17, 1977
Platinum	November 12, 1978
Barnum	April 30, 1980
Bring Back Birdie	March 5, 1981

Layton's subsequent shows were all unsuccessful: the multimedia *Rock 'N' Roll! The First 5,000 Years* (1982); the 1983 touring version of *Woman of the Year* (starring Lauren Bacall); *Harrigan 'N Hart* (1985); *Pieces of Eight*, a 1985 Jule Styne musicalization of *Treasure Island*, which closed after a regional theatre tryout; and the 1988 London extravaganza *Ziegfeld*.

ALAN JAY LERNER   *lyricist; librettist*
Born: *August 31, 1918, New York, NY*
Died: *June 14, 1986, New York, NY*

Lerner made his Broadway debut writing lyrics to Frederick Loewe's music for *What's Up* (1943) and *The Day Before Spring* (1945), which were followed by their first hit, *Brigadoon* (1947). After writing *Love Life* (1948) with Kurt Weill, he rejoined Loewe for *Paint Your Wagon* (1951), *My Fair Lady* (1956), and *Camelot* (1960).

On a Clear Day You Can See Forever	October 17, 1965
Coco	December 18, 1969
[*Lolita, My Love*	March 27, 1971]
Gigi	November 13, 1973
Music! Music!	April 11, 1974
My Fair Lady (revival—25th Anniversary)	March 25, 1976
1600 Pennsylvania Avenue	May 4, 1976
Carmelina	April 8, 1979
Camelot (revival—Richard Burton)	July 8, 1980
Brigadoon (revival)	October 16, 1980
My Fair Lady (revival—Rex Harrison)	August 18, 1981
Camelot (revival—Richard Harris)	November 15, 1981

Lerner's final musical, written with composer Charles Strouse, was the one-performance *Dance a Little Closer* (1983).

DAVID MERRICK   *producer*
Born: *November 27, 1911, St. Louis, MO*

After a fifteen-year Broadway apprenticeship, former lawyer Merrick produced his first musical, *Fanny* (1954). He quickly became Broadway's most active and successful showman, with such musicals as *Jamaica* (1957), *Destry Rides Again* (1959), *Gypsy* (1959), *Take Me Along* (1959), *Irma La Douce* (1960), *Do Re Mi* (1960), *Carnival* (1961), *I Can Get It for You Wholesale* (1962), *Stop the World—I Want to Get Off* (1962), *Oliver!* (1963), *110 in the Shade* (1963), and *Hello, Dolly!* (1964), not to mention a packet of nonmusical hits.

The Roar of the Greasepaint	May 16, 1965
Pickwick	October 4, 1965
[*Hot September*	October 9, 1965]

I Do! I Do!	December 5, 1966
[*Breakfast at Tiffany's*	December 14, 1966]
Hello, Dolly! (Pearl Bailey company)	November 12, 1967
How Now, Dow Jones	December 7, 1967
[*Mata Hari*	December 9, 1967]
The Happy Time	January 18, 1968
Promises, Promises	December 1, 1968
Sugar	April 9, 1972
Mack & Mabel	October 6, 1974
Very Good Eddie	December 21, 1975
[*The Baker's Wife*	November 13, 1976]
42nd Street	August 25, 1980

Merrick returned to Broadway with two final musicals, an ill-fated 1990 revival of the Gershwin musical *Oh, Kay!* and an ill-advised stage version of Rodgers and Hammerstein's *State Fair* (1996).

THARON MUSSER   *lighting designer*
Born: *January 8, 1925, Roanoke, VA*

Musser made her Broadway debut with Eugene O'Neill's posthumous *Long Day's Journey into Night* (1956). Early musicals included *Shinbone Alley* (1957), *Once Upon a Mattress* (1959), *Nowhere to Go But Up* (1962), *Here's Love* (1963), and *Golden Boy* (1964).

Kelly	February 6, 1965
Flora, the Red Menace	May 11, 1965
Mame	May 24, 1966
Hallelujah, Baby!	April 26, 1967
[*A Mother's Kisses*	October 19, 1968]
Maggie Flynn	October 23, 1968
The Fig Leaves Are Falling	January 2, 1969
Applause	March 30, 1970
The Boy Friend (revival)	April 14, 1970
Follies	April 4, 1971
On the Town (revival)	October 31, 1971
A Little Night Music	February 25, 1973
Good News (revival)	December 23, 1974

The Wiz	January 5, 1975
A Chorus Line	October 19, 1975
Pacific Overtures	January 11, 1976
The Act	October 29, 1977
Ballroom	December 14, 1978
They're Playing Our Song	February 11, 1979
42nd Street	August 25, 1980
Dreamgirls	December 20, 1981

Subsequent musicals include *Merlin* (1983), *Jerry's Girls* (1985), *Teddy and Alice* (1987), *Welcome to the Club* (1989), *The Secret Garden* (1991), and *The Goodbye Girl* (1993).

STUART OSTROW   *producer*
Born: *February 8, 1932, New York, NY*

Loesser-protegé Ostrow began his career on the staff of Frank Loegger's Frank Music. His first production, the 1962 *We Take the Town* (with Robert Preston as Pancho Villa, score by Matt Dubey and Harold Karr of the 1956 *Happy Hunting*), failed pre–Broadway; his second, Meredith Willson's *Here's Love* (1963), failed on Broadway (with Ostrow himself replacing Norman Jewison as director.

The Apple Tree	October 18, 1966
1776	March 16, 1969
Pippin	October 23, 1972
Chicago	June 3, 1975
[*Swing*	March 30, 1980]
The Moony Shapiro Songbook	May 3, 1981

The drama *Stages*, which Ostrow wrote as well as produced, had a one-performance run in 1978. Ostrow's subsequent productions included three unconventional plays: *M. Butterfly* (1988) was a substantial and deserved hit; *La Bête* (1991) was a three-week failure; and *Face Value* (1993) closed during previews.

HAROLD S. (HAL) PRINCE   *producer; director*
Born: *January 30, 1928, New York, NY*

After several years of tutelage under the wing of George Abbott, "H. Smith Prince"—as he was initially billed—joined fellow Abbott stage manager Robert H. Griffith to produce *The Pajama Game* (1954), *Damn Yankees* (1955), *New Girl in Town* (1957), *West Side Story* (1957), *Fiorello!* (1959), and *Tenderloin* (1960). Following Griffith's death, he directed *A Family Affair* (1962) and produced *A Funny Thing Happened on the Way to the Forum* (1962), *She Loves Me* (1963), and *Fiddler on the Roof* (1964).

Baker Street	February 16, 1965
Flora, the Red Menace	May 11, 1965
"It's a Bird, It's a Plane, It's Superman"	March 9, 1966
Cabaret	November 20, 1966
Zorbá	November 17, 1968
Company	April 26, 1970
Follies	April 4, 1971
A Little Night Music	February 25, 1973
Candide (revision)	March 10, 1974
Pacific Overtures	January 11, 1976
Rex	April 25, 1976
Side by Side by Sondheim	April 18, 1977
On the Twentieth Century	February 19, 1978
Sweeney Todd	March 1, 1979
Evita	September 25, 1979
The Moony Shapiro Songbook	May 3, 1981
Merrily We Roll Along	November 16, 1981

Prince continued his mid-career series of failures with *A Doll's Life* (1982), *Grind* (1985), and *Roza* (1987). Things turned around in 1988 with his biggest hit, *Phantom of the Opera*, which was followed by *Kiss of the Spider Woman* (1993) and the 1994 revival of *Show Boat*.

RICHARD RODGERS   *composer; producer*
Born: *June 28, 1902, New York, NY*
Died: *December 30, 1979, New York, NY*

Rodgers and lyricist/partner Lorenz Hart first came to Broadway with an interpolation in the 1919 revue *A Lonely Romeo*. After six years of struggle, success finally arrived in 1925 with *The Garrick Gaieties* (and the song hit "Manhattan"). Rodgers was to remain active along Broadway for a full 60 years. Early musicals included *The Girl Friend* (1926), *A Connecticut Yankee* (1927), *On Your Toes* (1936), *Babes in Arms* (1937), *The Boys from Syracuse* (1938), and *Pal Joey* (1940). Rodgers joined with Oscar Hammerstein II in 1943 for *Oklahoma!*, which the new team followed up with such works as *Carousel* (1945), *South Pacific* (1949), *The King and I* (1951), *Flower Drum Song* (1958), and *The Sound of Music* (1959). Following Hammerstein's death in 1960, Rodgers wrote his own lyrics for *No Strings* (1962) while casting about—unsuccessfully, as it turned out—for a third productive collaboration.

Do I Hear a Waltz?	March 18, 1965
On a Clear Day You Can See Forever	October 17, 1965
Two by Two	November 10, 1970
Rex	April 25, 1976
Pal Joey (revival)	June 27, 1976
The King and I (revival)	May 2, 1977
I Remember Mama	May 31, 1979
Oklahoma! (revival)	December 13, 1979

OLIVER SMITH   *scenic designer*
Born: *February 13, 1918, Wawpawn, WI*
Died: *January 23, 1994, Brooklyn Heights, NY*

Smith made his Broadway debut in 1942 with *Rosalinda*. Having designed Ballet Theatre's *Fancy Free* (1944), he joined Leonard Bernstein and Jerome Robbins to transform it into that year's *On the Town* (which he also produced). The designer quickly revolutionized the look of the Broadway musical and became a choreographer's favorite; he simultaneously maintained strong ties with the dance world, serving as codirector of (American) Ballet Theatre. Smith's many musicals included Robbins's *Billion Dollar Baby* (1945), de Mille's *Brigadoon* (1947), Robbins's *High Button Shoes* (1948), de Mille's *Gentlemen Prefer Blondes* (1949), de Mille's *Paint Your Wagon* (1951), *My Fair Lady* (1956), Bernstein's *Candide* (1956), Robbins and Bernstein's *West Side Story* (1957), *The Sound of Music* (1959), *Camelot*

(1960), de Mille's *110 in the Shade* (1963), and Champion's *Hello Dolly!* (1964).

Kelly	February 6, 1965
Baker Street	February 16, 1965
[*Hot September*	October 9, 1965]
On a Clear Day You Can See Forever	October 17, 1965
I Do! I Do!	December 5, 1966
[*Breakfast at Tiffany's*	December 14, 1966]
Illya Darling	April 11, 1967
Hello Dolly! (Pearl Bailey Company)	November 12, 1967
Darling of the Day	January 27, 1968
Dear World	February 6, 1969
Come Summer	March 18, 1969
Jimmy	October 23, 1969
Lovely Ladies, Kind Gentlemen	December 28, 1970
[*Prettybelle*	March 6, 1971]
Lost in the Stars	April 18, 1972
Mass	June 28, 1972
Tricks	January 8, 1973
Gigi	November 13, 1973
My Fair Lady (revival—25th Anniversary)	March 25, 1976
Carmelina	April 8, 1979
West Side Story (revival)	February 14, 1980
My Fair Lady (revival—Rex Harrison)	August 18, 1981

Smith's final Broadway assignment was the 1982 play *84 Charing Cross Road*.

STEPHEN SONDHEIM   *composer; lyricist*
Born: *March 22, 1930, New York, NY*

Sondheim came to Broadway in 1956, with incidental music for N. Richard Nash's drama *The Girls of Summer*. He served as lyricist for the legendary Robbins musicals *West Side Story* (1957) and *Gypsy* (1959), and then wrote music and lyrics for *A Funny Thing Happened on the Way to the Forum* (1962) and *Anyone Can Whistle* (1964).

Do I Hear a Waltz	March 18, 1965
Illya Darling	April 11, 1967
Company	April 26, 1970
Follies	April 4, 1971
A Funny Thing Happened . . . (revival)	March 30, 1972
A Little Night Music	February 25, 1973
Candide (revision)	March 10, 1974
Gypsy (revival)	September 23, 1974
Pacific Overtures	January 11, 1976
Side by Side Sondheim	April 18, 1977
Sweeney Todd	March 1, 1979
West Side Story (revival)	February 14, 1980
Merrily We Roll Along	November 16, 1981

Following the final Sondheim/Prince collaboration, the composer continued his career with *Sunday in the Park with George* (1984), *Into the Woods* (1987), *Assassins* (1991, Off-Broadway), the anthology revue *Putting It Together* (1993), *Passion* (1994), in collaboration with George Furth, the nonmusical mystery *Getting Away with Murder* (1996), and the 1996 revival of *A Funny Thing*.

JOSEPH STEIN   *librettist*
Born: *May 30, 1912, New York, NY*

Stein made his Broadway bow with *Plain and Fancy* (1955), which was followed by *Mr. Wonderful* (1955) and the initial Bock/Harnick musical *The Body Beautiful* (1958). Other early works include *Juno* (1959), *Take Me Along* (1959), the nonmusical dramatization of Carl Reiner's *Enter Laughing* (1963), and *Fiddler on the Roof* (1964).

Zorbá	November 17, 1968
Irene	March 13, 1973
Doctor Jazz	March 19, 1975
So Long, 174th Street	April 27, 1976
[*The Baker's Wife*	November 13, 1976]
Fiddler on the Roof (revival—Zero Mostel)	December 28, 1976
[*Hellzapoppin* (Jerry Lewis)	January 22, 1977]
King of Hearts	October 22, 1978

Carmelina	April 8, 1979
Fiddler on the Roof (revival—Herschel Bernardi)	July 9, 1981

Stein collaborated with Stephen Schwartz on two massive failures: *The Baker's Wife* (1976), which closed out of town, and *Rags* (1986), which *didn't* close out of town but just as well might have.

MICHAEL STEWART	*librettist; lyricist*
Born:	*August 1, 1929, New York, NY*
Died:	*September 20, 1987, New York, NY*

Stewart made his Broadway debut in 1949 with the revue *Alive and Kicking* and was principal author/lyricist of the 1951 revue *Razzle Dazzle*. He provided sketches for several revues of the 1950s, and revised Lillian Hellman's libretto for the 1959 London production of *Candide*. Stewart reappeared on Broadway with three consecutive Gower Champion-staged hits, *Bye Bye Birdie* (1960), *Carnival* (1961), and *Hello, Dolly!* (1964).

Hello Dolly! (Pearl Bailey company)	November 12, 1967
George M!	April 10, 1968
Sugar	April 9, 1972
Seesaw	March 18, 1973
Mack & Mabel	October 6, 1974
I Love My Wife	April 17, 1977
The Grand Tour	January 11, 1979
Barnum	April 30, 1980
Bring Back Birdie	March 5, 1981

Stewart's final musicals were *Elizabeth and Essex* (1984, Off-Broadway); *Harrigan 'N Hart* (1985), which moved from the Goodspeed Opera House to Broadway for a five-performance run; and *Pieces of Eight*, a 1985 Jule Styne musicalization of *Treasure Island*, which played a regional theatre tryout.

CHARLES STROUSE	*composer*
Born:	*June 7, 1928, New York, NY*

Strouse burst upon the Broadway scene in 1956, for two performances, with incidental music for *Sixth Finger in a Five Finger Glove* (which was instantly proclaimed one of the worst plays of the decade). He cooled his heels writing revue songs with Lee Adams until hitting it big with the sleeper hit *Bye Bye Birdie* (1960). His next efforts, though—the Ray Bolger vehicle *All American* (1962) and the Sammy Davis vehicle *Golden Boy* (1964)—were unsuccessful.

"It's a Bird, It's a Plane, It's Superman"	March 29, 1966
Applause	March 30, 1970
Annie	April 21, 1977
A Broadway Musical	December 21, 1978
Charlie and Algernon	September 14, 1980
Bring Back Birdie	March 5, 1981

Strouse followed his three post–*Annie* flops with six more, namely *Dance a Little Closer* (1983), *Mayor* (1985), *Rags* (1986), *Annie 2: Miss Hannigan's Revenge* (1990), *Nick and Nora* (1991), and *Annie Warbucks* (1993).

JULE STYNE   *composer*
Born: *December 31, 1905, London, England*
Died: *September 20, 1994, New York, NY*

Following a prosperous career as a Hollywood tunesmith, Styne came to Broadway in 1947 with *High Button Shoes* and stayed to compose such musicals as *Gentlemen Prefer Blondes* (1949), *Two on the Aisle* (1951), *Peter Pan* (1954), *Bells Are Ringing* (1956), *Gypsy* (1959), *Do Re Mi* (1960), *Subways Are for Sleeping* (1961), *Funny Girl* (1964), and *Fade Out—Fade In* (1964).

Hallelujah, Baby!	April 26, 1967
Darling of the Day	January 27, 1968
Look to the Lillies	March 29, 1970
[Prettybelle	March 6, 1971]
Sugar	April 9, 1972
Lorelei	January 27, 1974
Gypsy (revival)	September 27, 1974

[*Hellzapoppin* (Jerry Lewis)	January 22, 1977
Peter Pan (revival)	September 6, 1979
[*One Night Stand*	October 25, 1980]

Pieces of Eight—a 1985 musicalization of *Treasure Island*—closed after a regional tryout. Styne reappeared on Broadway in 1993 shortly before his death with one last effort, the ill-cobbled *The Red Shoes*.

TOMMY TUNE	*director; choreographer; actor*
Born:	*February 28, 1939, Wichita Falls, TX*

Baker Street	February 16, 1965
A Joyful Noise	December 15, 1966
How Now, Dow Jones	December 7, 1967
Seesaw	March 18, 1973
[*Hellzapoppin* (Jerry Lewis)	January 22, 1977]
The Best Little Whorehouse in Texas	April 17, 1978
A Day in Hollywood—A Night in the Ukraine	May 1, 1980
Woman of the Year	March 29, 1981

Tune graduated to the top rank of Broadway director/choreographers with *Nine* (1982). Subsequent productions include *My One and Only* (1983); *Grand Hotel: The Musical* (1989), *The Best Little Whorehouse Goes Public* (1994), the 1994 revival of *Grease*, and *Busker Alley* (1995), which closed out of town when leading man Tune buskered his foot.

JONATHAN TUNICK	*orchestrator*
Born:	*April 19, 1938, New York, NY*

Tunick began his Broadway career assisting orchestrator Robert (*How to Succeed*) Ginzler during the early 1960s, although his only official early musical theatre credits were for the 1960 revue *From A to Z* and *All in Love*, the niftily orchestrated 1961 Off-Broadway musicalization of *The Rivals*.

Here's Where I Belong	March 3, 1968
Promises, Promises	December 1, 1968
Company	April 26, 1970
Follies	April 4, 1971

The Grass Harp	November 2, 1971
The Selling of the President	March 22, 1972
A Little Night Music	February 25, 1973
Goodtime Charlie	March 3, 1975
A Chorus Line	October 19, 1975
Pacific Overtures	January 11, 1976
Ballroom	December 14, 1978
Merrily We Roll Along	November 16, 1981

Tunick turned to composing for movies and television in the 1980s, with Broadway visits limited to *Nine* (1982), *Baby* (1983), *Into the Woods* (1987), *Nick and Nora* (1991), *Passion* (1994), and the 1996 revival of *A Funny Thing*.

ROBIN WAGNER   *scenic designer*
Born: *August 31, 1933, San Francisco, CA*

Wagner came to Broadway from the Arena Stage in Washington, where he attracted notice with his work on *The Great White Hope* (which didn't arrive in New York until October 1968). He made his Broadway debut in 1967 with the short-lived drama *The Trial of Lee Harvey Oswald*.

Hair	April 29, 1968
Promises, Promises	December 1, 1968
[*Love Match*	January 4, 1969]
Gantry	February 14, 1970
Jesus Christ Superstar	October 12, 1971
Sugar	April 9, 1972
Seesaw	March 18, 1973
[*Rachael Lily Rosenbloom*	December 1, 1973]
Mack & Mabel	October 6, 1974
A Chorus Line	October 19, 1975
Hair (revival)	October 5, 1977
On the Twentieth Century	February 19, 1978
Ballroom	December 20, 1979
Comin' Uptown	December 20, 1979

[*Swing*	March 30, 1980]
42nd Street	August 25, 1980
[*One Night Stand*	October 25, 1980]
Dreamgirls	December 20, 1981

Subsequent Wagnerian musicals include *Merlin* (1983), *Song and Dance* (1985), *Chess* (1988), *City of Angels* (1989), *Crazy for You* (1992), *Jelly's Last Jam* (1992), *Putting It Together* (1993), *Victor/Victoria* (1995), and *Big* (1996).

DON WALKER   *orchestrator*
Born: *October 28, 1907, Lambertville, NJ*
Died: *September 12, 1989, Trenton, NJ*

Walker's overwhelming portfolio of musicals includes *By Jupiter* (1942), *Beat the Band* (1942), the 1943 revival of *A Connecticut Yankee*, *Up in Central Park* (1945), *Carousel* (1945), *Finian's Rainbow* (1947), *Look Ma, I'm Dancin'* (1948), *Gentlemen Prefer Blondes* (1948), *Miss Liberty* (1949), *Call Me Madam* (1950), the 1952 revivals of *Pal Joey* and *Of Thee I Sing*, *Wish You Were Here* (1952), *Wonderful Town* (1953), *Me and Juliet* (1953), *The Pajama Game* (1954), *Silk Stockings* (1955), *Damn Yankees* (1955), *The Most Happy Fella* (1956), *The Music Man* (1957), *Greenwillow* (1960), *The Unsinkable Molly Brown* (1960), *The Gay Life* (1961), *She Loves Me* (1963), *Here's Love* (1963), *What Makes Sammy Run?* (1964), *Anyone Can Whistle* (1964), and *Fiddler on the Roof* (1964).

Baker Street	February 16, 1965
Anya	November 29, 1965
A Time for Singing	May 15, 1966
Cabaret	November 20, 1966
[*Hellzapoppin' '67* (Soupy Sales)	September 16, 1967
The Happy Time	January 18, 1968
Her First Roman	October 20, 1968
The Rothschilds	October 19, 1970
70, Girls, 70	April 15, 1971
The Pajama Game (revival)	December 9, 1973
Shenandoah	January 7, 1975

The Baker's Wife	November 13, 1976
Fiddler on the Roof (revival—Zero Mostel)	December 9, 1973
Angel	May 10, 1978
The Music Man (revival)	June 5, 1980
Fiddler on the Roof (revival—Herschel Bernardi)	July 9, 1981

Walker's final show was the 1982 *The Little Prince and the Aviator*, which closed during previews.

TONY WALTON   *scenic designer*
Born: *October 24, 1934, Walton-on-Thames, Surrey, England*

Walton made his West End design debut with Sandy Wilson's *Valmouth* (1958), which he also designed Off-Broadway (1960). He made his Broadway debut with the 1961 comedy *Once There Was a Russian*, entering the musical field with *A Funny Thing Happened on the Way to the Forum* (1962) and *Golden Boy* (1964). He also designed costumes for all of the above, as well as *The Apple Tree*.

The Apple Tree	October 18, 1966
Pippin	October 23, 1972
Shelter	February 6, 1973
Chicago	June 3, 1975
1600 Pennsylvania Avenue	May 4, 1976
The Act	October 29, 1977
A Day in Hollywood—A Night in the Ukraine	May 1, 1980
Sophisticated Ladies	March 1, 1981
Woman of the Year	March 29, 1981

Subsequent work includes *Grand Hotel: The Musical* (1989), *The Will Rogers Follies* (1991), *A Christmas Carol* (1994), and *Busker Alley* (1995). Walton has also designed Broadway revivals of *Little Me* (1982), *She Loves Me* (1993), *Anything Goes* (1987), *Guys and Dolls* (1992), *Company* (1995), and *A Funny Thing* (1996).

PATRICIA ZIPPRODT   *costume designer*
Born: *February 24, 1925, Evanston, IL*

Zipprodt made her Broadway debut in 1957 with two plays in ten days, Graham Greene's *The Potting Shed* and Gore Vidal's *Visit to a Small Planet*. Her first two Broadway musicals were Hal Prince's *She Loves Me* (1963) and *Fiddler on the Roof* (1964).

Anya	November 29, 1965
Pousse-Café	March 18, 1966
Cabaret	November 20, 1966
Zorbá	November 17, 1968
1776	March 16, 1969
Georgy	February 26, 1970
Pippin	October 23, 1972
Mack & Mabel	October 6, 1974
Chicago	June 3, 1975
Fiddler on the Roof (revival—Zero Mostel)	December 28, 1976
King of Hearts	October 22, 1978
[*Swing*	March 20, 1980]
[*One Night Stand*	October 25, 1980
Fiddler on the Roof (revival Herschel Bernardi)	July 9, 1981

Subsequent musicals include the 1986 revival of *Sweet Charity*, *Big Deal* (1986), *Into the Woods* (1987), the 1987 revival of *Cabaret*, and *Shogun: The Musical* (1990).

THE CRITICS

This section offers brief biographical data on the major critics of the era. All newspapers referred to were based in New York unless otherwise indicated.

CLIVE BARNES   *Times*, 1967–1977
                                       Post, 1978–present
Born: *May 13, 1927, London, England*

Barnes joined the *Times* as dance critic in 1965, coming over from the same position at the London *Times*. He moved into the drama chair—which had been in flux since the retirement of Brooks Atkinson in 1960—in 1967. Barnes left the *Times* in 1978 for the *Post*, where he remains.

JOHN CHAPMAN   *Daily News*, 1943–1971
Born: *June 25, 1900, Denver, CO*
Died: *January 19, 1972, Westport, CT*

Chapman joined the *Daily News* in 1920 as a police reporter, becoming drama editor in 1929. He replaced Burns Mantle as first-string critic in 1943, and remained on the aisle until his retirement in 1971.

RICHARD EDER   *Times*, 1977–1978
Born: *August 16, 1932, Washington, DC*

A twenty-year *Times* man, Eder came in from the Washington bureau in 1976 to become assistant film critic. He was quickly moved over to replace Clive Barnes in the fall of 1977, and lasted but one stormy season.

MARTIN GOTTFRIED *Women's Wear Daily*, 1963–1971
Post, 1971–1977
Born: *October 9, 1933, New York, NY*

Gottfried moved to *Women's Wear Daily* from the *Village Voice* in 1963. He took over as first-string critic at the *Post* on Richard Watts's retirement in 1971, and remained there until being bumped by Clive Barnes (moving over from the *Times*).

STANLEY KAUFFMANN *Times*, 1966
Born: *April 24, 1916, New York, NY*

Kauffmann took over Howard Taubman's chair at the *Times* in January 1966. His tenure was so problematic—and the attacks from producer David Merrick so vitriolic—that he was ousted within half a season.

WALTER KERR *Herald Tribune*, 1951–1966
Times, 1966–1983
Born: *July 8, 1913, Evanston, IL*
Died: *October 9, 1996, Dobbs Ferry, NY*

The dean of modern-day drama critics, Kerr also worked—from time to time—as a Broadway director, playwright, author, librettist, and lyricist. He was swooped up by the *Times* when the *Herald Tribune* ceased publication in 1966. Wishing to get away from the then-prevailing post–performance deadline, he moved over to the Sunday *Times* in 1967 to give "second opinions" of the previous week's openings. Kerr occasionally filled in as first-stringer during the unsteady years between the reigns of Clive Barnes and Frank Rich.

HOWARD KISSEL *Women's Wear Daily*, 1974–1986
Daily News 1986–present

Kissel replaced Martin Gottfried at *Women's Wear Daily* when the latter left for the *Post* in 1974. He remained at *WWD* until 1986, when he moved over to fill Doug Watt's chair at the *Daily News*.

JOHN MCCLAIN   *Journal-American*, 1951–1966
Born: *August 7, 1904, Marion, OH*
Died: *May 3, 1967, London, England*

McClain—formerly of the *Sun*—took over the drama chair at the *Journal-American* in 1951. When the *Journal* merged with the *World-Telegram* and the *Trib* in 1966, McClain moved over to become travel editor of the brief-lived *World Journal Tribune*.

NORMAN NADEL   *World-Telegram & Sun*, 1961–1966
                        World Journal Tribune, 1966–1967
Born: *June 19, 1915, Newark, NJ*

A drama critic for the *Columbus* (Ohio) *Citizen* (and trombonist in the Columbus Symphony), Nadel came to the *World-Telegram* in 1961 and remained when the paper merged—briefly, as it turned out—with the similarly faltering *Journal-American* and *Herald Tribune*.

FRANK RICH   *Times*, 1980–1993
Born: *June 2, 1949, Washington, DC*

Rich came to the *Times* in 1980, having served as film critic for *New Times* (1973–1975), the *New York Post* (1975–1977), and *Time* magazine (1977–1979). In 1993 he withdrew from the drama section and moved to the *Times*'s op-ed page as a columnist.

HOWARD TAUBMAN   *Times*, 1960–1965
Born: *July 4, 1907, New York, NY*
Died: *January 8, 1996, Sarasota, FL*

The long-time *Times* music critic replaced the legendary Brooks Atkinson when he retired in 1960. Taubman moved on to become the paper's critic-at-large in 1965.

DOUGLAS WATT   *Daily News*, 1971–1986
Born: *January 20, 1914, New York, NY*

Watt joined the *News* as a copyboy in 1936, becoming a drama reporter in 1940. He served as second-string critic until he replaced the ailing John Chapman in 1971. After leaving the first-string chair in 1986, he remained at the *News* giving second opinions through 1992.

RICHARD WATTS JR.   *Post*, 1946–1974
Born: *January 12, 1898, Parkersburg, WV*
Died: *January 2, 1981, New York, NY*

The former drama critic of the *Herald Tribune*, Watts returned from World War II in 1946 and took over the first-string post at the *Post*. Having begun at the *Trib* in 1924—initially as (silent) movie critic, with occasional theatre assignments—Watts covered Broadway openings for almost fifty years.

BIBLIOGRAPHY

Abbott, George. *Mister Abbott*. New York: Random House, 1963.

Bloom, Ken. *American Song*. New York: Facts on File, 1985.

Blum, Daniel, editor. *Theatre World*. Vols. 1–4. New York: Daniel C. Blum, Theatre World, 1945–1948

———. Vols. 5–13. New York: Greenberg, 1949–1957.

———. Vols. 14–20. Philadelphia: Chilton, 1958–1964.

Bosworth, Patricia. "'Dude,' An $800,000 Disaster; Where Did They Go Wrong?" *New York Times*, 22 October 1972.

Brien, Alan. "The Making of a Musical." London: *The Sunday Telegraph*, 26 March 1967.

Bronner, Edwin J. *The Encyclopedia of the American Theatre, 1900–1975*. San Diego: Barnes, 1980.

Burton, Humphrey. *Leonard Bernstein*. Boston: Faber & Faber, 1994.

Chase, Chris. "No, No, 'Irene.'" *New York Magazine* (March 12, 1973).

Crawford, Cheryl. *One Naked Individual*. Indianapolis: Bobbs-Merrill, 1977.

Davis, Christopher. *The Producer*. New York: Harper & Row, 1972.

Drew, David. *Kurt Weill: A Handbook*. Berkeley: University of California Press, 1987.

Dunn, Don. *The Making of "No, No, Nanette."* Secaucus, NJ: Citadel, 1972.

Engel, Lehman. *This Bright Day*. New York: Macmillan, 1974.

Gordon, Eric A. *Marc the Music: The Life and Work of Marc Blitzstein.* New York: St. Martin's, 1989.

Gaver, Jack. *Season In Season Out, 1965–1966.* New York: Hawthorne, 1966.

Goldman, William. *The Season: A Candid Look at Broadway.* New York: Harcourt, Brace, 1969.

Gordon, Joanne. *Art Isn't Easy.* New York: Da Capo, 1992.

Gottfried, Martin. *All His Jazz: The Life and Death of Bob Fosse.* New York: Bantam, 1990.

Green, Stanley. *Encyclopedia of the Musical Theatre.* New York: Dodd, Mead, 1976.

———. *The World of Musical Comedy.* 4th ed. San Diego: Barnes, 1980.

Grubb, Kevin Boyd. *Razzle Dazzle: The Life and Work of Bob Fosse.* New York: St. Martin's, 1989.

Guernsey, Otis L., Jr., ed. *The Best Plays.* Vols. 1964–1965 through 1982–1983. New York: Dodd, Mead, 1965–1983.

———. *Broadway Song & Story: Playwrights/Lyricists/Composers Discuss Their Hits.* New York: Dodd, Mead, 1985.

Halliwell, Leslie. *Halliwell's Film Guide.* 4th ed. New York: Scribner's, 1983.

Hirsch, Foster. *Harold Prince and the American Musical Theatre.* Cambridge: Cambridge University Press, 1989.

Kanfer, Stefan. *A Journal of the Plague Years.* New York: Atheneum, 1973.

Kelly, Kevin. *One Singular Sensation: The Michael Bennett Story.* New York: Doubleday, 1990.

Lapham, Lewis H. "Has Anybody Here Seen 'Kelly'?" *Saturday Evening Post* (April 24, 1965).

Leonard, William Torbert. *Broadway Bound.* Metuchen, NJ: Scarecrow, 1983.

Lerner, Alan Jay. *The Street Where I Live.* New York: Norton, 1978.

Mandlebaum, Ken. *"A Chorus Line" and the Musicals of Michael Bennett.* New York: St. Martin's, 1991.

———. *Not Since "Carrie."* New York: St. Martin's, 1991.

Marlowe, Joan, and Betty Blake, eds. *"New York Theatre Critics' Reviews.* Vols. 26–42. New York: Critics' Theatre Reviews, 1965–1981.

Martin, Mary. *My Heart Belongs.* New York: Morrow, 1976.

McNeil, Alex. *Total Television.* 2d ed. New York: Penguin, 1984.

Parker, John, et al., eds. *Who's Who in the Theatre.* 1st through 16th eds. London: Pitman, 1912–1977.

Prince, Hal. *Contradictions: Notes on Twenty-Six Years in the Theatre.* New York: Dodd, Mead, 1974.

Rigdon, Walter, ed. *Biographical Encyclopedia and Who's Who of the American Theatre.* New York: Heineman, 1966.

Rivers, Caryl. "Hal Prince's Rx for 'Rex.'" *New York Times,* 25 April 1976.

Rodgers, Richard. *Musical Stages.* New York: Random House, 1975.

Sanders, Ronald. *The Days Grow Short: The Life and Music of Kurt Weill.* New York: Holt, Rinehart, 1980.

Shapiro, Doris. *We Danced All Night: My Life behind the Scenes with Alan Jay Lerner.* New York: Morrow, 1990.

Silvers, Phil, with Robert Saffron. *This Laugh Is on Me: The Phil Silvers Story.* Engelwood Cliffs, NJ: Prentice-Hall, 1973.

Stevenson, Isabelle. *The Tony Award: A Complete Listing with a History of the American Theatre Wing.* Portsmouth, NH: Heinemann, 1994.

Suskin, Steven. *Opening Night on Broadway: A Critical Quotebook of the Golden Era of the Musical Theatre.* New York: Schirmer, 1990.

———. *Show Tunes, 1905–1991: The Songs, Show and Careers of Broadway's Major Composers.* 2d ed. Rev. and exp. New York: Limelight, 1992.

Taylor, Theodore. *Jule: The Story of Composer Jule Styne.* New York: Random House, 1979.

Tyler, Ralph. "The Doctoring of 'Mama'—Is She Now Fit for Broadway?" *New York Times,* 27 May 1979.

Willis, John, ed. *Theatre World.* Vols. 21–46. New York: Crown, 1965–1991.

———. Vols. 47 and 48. New York: Applause, 1992, 1994.

Zadan, Craig. *Sondheim & Co..* 2d ed. New York: Harper & Row, 1989.

INDEX

Promises, Promises, Reggae, Rex, The Roar of the Greasepaint, The Robber Bridegroom, Rockabye Hamlet, The Rocky Horror Show, Saravá, The Selling of the President, Shenandoah, Sherry!, Side by Side by Sondheim, 1600 Pennsylvania Avenue, So Long, 174th Street, Sophisticated Ladies, Stop the World—I Want to Get Off, Sugar Babies, Sweeney Todd, They're Playing Our Song, The Threepenny Opera, Timbuktu!, Tintypes, Treemonisha, The Utter Glory of Morrissey Hall, Where's Charley?, The Wiz, and Working

The Act, Ain't Misbehavin', Ambassador, Angel, Annie, Applause, The Apple Tree, Ari, Baker Street, Ballroom, Barnum, The Best Little Whorehouse in Texas, Billy, The Boy Friend, Brigadoon, Bring Back Birdie, A Broadway Musical, Bubbling Brown Sugar, Buck White, Cabaret, Camelot (1980), *Camelot* (1981), *Can-Can, A Chorus Line, Coco, Come Summer, Comin' Uptown, Company, Copperfield, Cry for Us All, Cyrano, Dancin', Darling of the Day, A Day in Hollywood, Dear World, The Desert Song, Doctor Jazz, Dreamgirls, Dude, The Education of H*Y*M*A*N K*A*P*L*A*N, Eubie!, Evita, Fiddler on the Roof* (1976), *Fiddler on the Roof* (1981), *The Fig Leaves Are Falling, The First, Flora, the Red Menace, Follies, 42nd Street, Frank Merriwell, A Funny Thing Happened on the Way to the Forum, Gantry, George M!, Georgy, Gigi, Godspell, Golden Rainbow, Good News, Goodtime Charley, Got Tu Go Disco, The Grand Tour, The Grass Harp, Grease, Guys and Dolls, Gypsy, Hair* (1968), *Hair* (1977), *Half a Sixpence, Hallelujah, Baby!, Happy End, Happy New Year, The Happy Time, Heathen!, Hello, Dolly!* (1967), *Henry, Sweet Henry, Her First Roman, Here's Where I Belong, Home Sweet Homer, How Now, Dow Jones, How to Be a Jewish Mother, Hurry, Harry, I Do! I Do!, I Love My Wife, I Remember Mama, I'm Solomon, Illya Darling, Irene, "It's Superman," Jesus Christ Superstar, Jimmy, A Joyful Noise, Kelly, The King and I, King of Hearts, La Strada, Lena Horne: The Lady and Her Music, The Lieutenant, A Little Night Music, Look to the Lilies, Lorelei, Lost in the Stars, Lovely Ladies, Kind Gentlemen, Mack & Mabel, Maggie Flynn, The Magic Show, Mame, Man of La Mancha* (1965), *Man of La Mancha* (1977), *Man on the Moon, Mass, The Me Nobody Knows, Merrily We Roll Along, Minnie's Boys, Molly, The Moony Shapiro Songbook, Music! Music!, Music Is, The Music Man, My Fair Lady* (1976), *My Fair Lady* (1981), *No, No, Nanette, Oh, Brother!, Oh! Calcutta!, Oklahoma!, On a Clear Day, On the Town, On the Twentieth Century, Onward Victoria, Over Here!, Pacific Overtures, The Pajama Game, Pal Joey, Perfectly Frank, Peter Pan, Pickwick, Pippin, The Pirates of Penzance, Platinum, Porgy and Bess, Pousse-Café, Promises, Promises, Purlie, Rainbow Jones, Raisin, Red, White and Maddox, Reggae, Rex, The Roar of the Greasepaint, The Robber Bridegroom, Rockabye Hamlet, The Rocky Horror Show, The Rothschilds, Seesaw, The Selling of the President, 1776, 70, Girls, 70,*

Shenendoah, Sherry!, Side by Side by Sondheim, 1600 Pennsylvania Avenue, Skyscraper, So Long, 174th Street, Something's Afoot, Soon, Sophisticated Ladies, Stop the World—I Want to Get Off, Sugar, Sugar Babies, Sweeney Todd, Sweet Charity, They're Playing Our Song, The Threepenny Opera, Timbuktu!, A Time for Singing, Tintypes, Treemonisha, Tricks, Two by Two, Two Gentlemen of Verona, The Utter Glory of Morrissey Hall, Very Good Eddie, Via Galactica, Walking Happy, West Side Story, Where's Charley?, Wild and Wonderful, The Wiz, Woman of the Year, Words and Music, Working, The Yearling, Zorbá, and *The Zula and the Zayda.*

Excerpts from the following reviews from *Women's Wear Daily.* Reprinted with permission:

The Act, Ambassador, Angel, Applause, The Apple Tree, Ari, Barnum, Best Little Whorehouse in Texas, Billy, The Boy Friend, Brigadoon, A Broadway Musical, Buck White, Cabaret, Camelot (1981), *Can-Can, Candide, Canterbury Tales, Celebration, Charlie and Algernon, Coco, Come Summer, Company, Cry for Us All, Cyrano, Darling of the Day, Dear World, The Desert Song, Dude, The Education of H*Y*M*A*N K*A*P*L*A*N, Eubie!, Evita, The Fig Leaves Are Falling, Follies, 42nd Street, A Funny Thing Happened on the Way to the Forum, Gantry, George M!, Georgy, Gigi, Golden Rainbow, Goodtime Charley, The Grand Tour, The Grass Harp, Grease, Guys and Dolls, Gypsy, Hair* (1977), *Hallelujah, Baby!, The Happy Time, Henry, Sweet Henry, Her First Roman, Here's Where I Belong, How Now, Dow Jones, How to Be a Jewish Mother, Hurry, Harry, I Do! I Do!, I'm Solomon, Illya Darling, Irene, Jesus Christ Superstar, Joseph and the Amazing Technicolor Dreamcoat, A Joyful Noise, King of Hearts, La Strada, A Little Night Music, Look to the Lilies, Lorelei, Lost in the Stars, Lovely Ladies, Kind Gentlemen, Maggie Flynn, The Magic Show, Mame, Man on the Moon, Minnie's Boys, Molly, Music! Music!, Music Is, The Music Man, My Fair Lady* (1981), *New Faces of 1968, No, No, Nanette, Oklahoma!, On the Town, Over Here!, The Pajama Game, Peter Pan, Pippin, Platinum, Promises, Promises, Purlie, Rainbow Jones, Raisin, Red, White and Maddox, The Robber Bridegroom, Rockabye Hamlet, The Rocky Horror Show, The Rothschilds, Seesaw, The Selling of the President, 1776, 70, Girls, 70, Shelter, Shenendoah, Sherry!, 1600 Pennsylvania Avenue, Soon, Sugar, Timbuktu!, Two by Two, Two Gentlemen of Verona, Very Good Eddie, Via Galactica, Walking Happy, West Side Story, The Wiz, Woman of the Year, Words and Music,* and *Zorbá.*

The author thanks the following people for graciously providing illustrative material reproduced in this book.

Theodore S. Chapin: *Follies.*

Goodspeed Opera House Library of the Musical Theatre: *Man of La Mancha.*

Paul Gruber: *La Strada.*

Richard Kidwell: *The Baker's Wife, Camelot, Coco, Darling of the Day, The Education of H*Y*M*A*N K*A*P*L*A*N, How Now, Dow Jones, How to Be a Jewish Mother, Lena Horne: The Lady and Her Music, Lolita, My Love, Lovely Ladies, Kind Gentlemen, Mack & Mabel, Mata Hari, Miss Moffat, My Fair Lady, Sherry!, Sweet Charity,* and *A Time for Singing.*

Paul Newman: *Cabaret, Cry for Us All, Do I Hear a Waltz?, The Fig Leaves Are Falling, Hallelujah, Baby!, Hot September, Pousse-Café,* and *Prettybelle.*

Bill Rosenfield: *Gantry.*

Max A. Woodward: *The Act, Anya, Applause, Billy, Buck White, Chicago, Clownaround, Come Summer, Dear World, Doctor Jazz, Dude, Flora, the Red Menace, A Funny Thing Happened on the Way to the Forum, Georgy, Heathen!, Henry, Sweet Henry, Here's Where I Belong, Home Sweet Homer, I'm Solomon, Illya Darling, A Joyful Noise, King of Hearts, Look to the Lilies, Maggie Flynn, Minnie's Boys, Molly, A Mother's Kisses, The Music Man, On a Clear Day You Can See Forever, Pacific Overtures, Pippin, Red, White and Maddox, Rockabye Hamlet, Seesaw, The Selling of the President, 1600 Pennsylvania Avenue, Skyscraper, So Long, 174th Street, Stop the World—I Want to Get Off, Sugar Babies, Timbuktu!, Two by Two, Wild and Wonderful,* and *Zorbá.*

Max Woodward/Richard Kidwell: *Ambassador, Ari, Barnum, Carmelina, Dancin', A Day in Hollywood—A Night in the Ukraine, 42nd Street, Good News, Gypsy, Half a Sixpence, Lorelei, Music Is, Oklahoma!, Platinum, Rex, 1776, 70, Girls, 70, Two Gentlemen of Verona, The Utter Glory of Morrissey Hall, Via Galactica, West Side Story,* and *The Yearling.*